Antique Trader®

ANTIQUES&

COLLECTIBLES

2009 PRICE GUIDE

Edited by **Kyle Husfloen**

©2008 by Krause Publications

Published by

An Imprint of F+W Publications

700 East State Street • Iola, WI 54990-0001
715-445-2214 • 888-457-2873
www.krausebooks.com

Our toll-free number to place an order or obtain
a free catalog is (800) 258-0929.

ISSN 1536-2884

ISBN-13: 978-0-89689-649-9
ISBN-10: 0-89689-649-8

Designed by Wendy Wendt
Edited by Kyle Husfloen

Printed in the United States of America

ANOTHER YEAR AND ANOTHER BIG ANNIVERSARY!

The *Antique Trader Antiques & Collectibles Price Guide 2009* is pretty special, not that all our annual price guides aren't. However, this volume represents the silver anniversary of the introduction of the *Antique Trader* price guide. For the first time, in late 1984, we released a single large volume covering the full gamut of the antiques and collectibles marketplace. We're all very proud to reach this benchmark and look forward to continuing to provide you with the best price guide for the collecting community.

You may notice that the *Antique Trader Antiques & Collectibles Price Guide* is coming to you a bit earlier this year. We decided to move our deadline ahead a few months in order to get all this information out to you earlier and to make sure you have copies ready to give as Christmas and holiday presents! It has been a bit of a challenge for me to get everything that I wanted into this volume, but I think you'll find it another comprehensive and detailed pricing reference. There's a huge volume of data out there, but I strive to cover as many categories as possible. Even in a book of over 1,000 pages I can't fit everything in. If your favorite collectible doesn't show up here, you're likely to find it in one of our recent past editions or waiting in the wings to appear next year.

It's always a great pleasure to complete this guide and get it into the hands of collectors, dealers, auctioneers, and students of antiques. I've always been proud that our price guide provides some of the most detailed listings of any similar guide. This helps make it not just a guide but a learning tool, too. This year we include nearly 9,500 price listings illustrated by over 5,500 full-color photos! Since it's always been said that "a photo is worth a thousand words," that blows the amount of information we provide off the scale!

In talking with readers of this guide, I'm also happy to report that they tell me the *Antique Trader Antiques & Collectibles Price Guide* is also one of the easiest to use. The format established over a quarter century ago seems to still work well. All of our categories are arranged alphabetically by name. Since there are so many separate categories within the fields of ceramics, glass and furniture, you will find these sections arranged together, again with each topic arranged alphabetically. Also, to aid you in your search, we've provided a detailed and cross-referenced index at the conclusion of our listings.

Of course, it takes a lot of teamwork to produce a book of this size and scope, and I couldn't have done it without the assistance of numerous special contributors, as well as various auction houses. You'll find a complete listing of all these folks at the conclusion of our price listings. In addition to recognizing the huge volume of listings they provide, I must acknowledge the wonderful color images they provide. In our new "digital" age we like to work with high-resolution digital images whenever possible. I'm especially appreciative of the hard work it can take to shoot and copy such photos in full color. I must also take a moment to thank my friend and part-time assistant, Torsten (Tor) Kerr, for his many hours of work in preparing photos and listings for this edition, as well as Wendy Wendt, the talented book designer at Krause Publications, who brings this vast amount of material together in one handsome and easy-to-use book.

Because the world of collecting is continually changing and evolving, I follow new collecting trends and add interesting new categories that have developed a dedicated following among collectors. In this 2009 edition I'm adding two new sections in our general listings: souvenir novelties and, under "Records," the unusual Vogue Picture Records. In the ceramics section I'm including for the first time Hadley Pottery, a popular range of wares produced in Louisville, Kentucky, and in the glass section I'm including Lenox crystal and Mats Jonasson crystal.

We always do our best to provide you with detailed and accurate listings with lots of proofreading going on throughout the production process. With the very specialized vocabulary in the antiques and collectibles world, you can imagine what a challenge that can be. Hundreds of names and terms we use constantly will never show up under "Spell Check." It is also important for you to keep in mind that this reference should be used only as a guide to values. There are many factors that impact what a particular piece may sell for, including regional interest, condition, rarity, and market appeal.

The majority of the prices included in this volume reflect a retail selling value in a specific location or at a special sale. Of course it's fun if you come across an item you own listed and illustrated here, but please keep in mind you might or might not be able to obtain a similar price. Another common problem is deciding whether you have an item "just like the one in the book" or featured on a TV program such as "Antiques Roadshow." It quite often takes additional research or the services of a professional appraiser to verify what you own and its likely replacement value in your area. Our detailed descriptions should help you get started and, with luck, you may turn up a real treasure.

For 25 years we've been here to help identify your treasures and educate you, and we hope to be around for another 25 years. By then there will be a whole new generation of collectors searching for rare antiques and collectibles of the late 20th and early 21st centuries. Good luck and happy hunting!

Kyle Husfloen, Editor

Please note: *Although our descriptions, prices and illustrations have been double-checked to ensure accuracy, neither the editor, publisher nor contributors can assume responsibility for any losses that might be incurred as a result of consulting this guide, or of typographical or other errors.*

A PROSPECTIVE FOR OUR 25TH SILVER ANNIVERSARY EDITION

Kyle Husfloen, Editor

There's nothing like another landmark anniversary to remind us how we've aged and how much the world has changed in recent decades. I think of the 1980s as "just yesterday," while realizing that many younger collectors were just growing up during those years! As the world around us has changed and evolved, so has the world of collecting, and this is reflected quite well in the format and contents of our annual price guides.

It was in 1984 that the then-editor of the *Antique Trader Price Guide*, Katherine Murphy, first planned and produced our single-volume annual edition. Previously we had produced a series of bimonthly magazine-style price guides that, during the span of the year, provided comprehensive coverage of the collecting world. In 1984 it was decided to combine the contents of these issues into a large, single volume. For a number of years, the bimonthly price guides continued to be produced and then compiled into the annual format. That practice ended a number of years ago, and now I have to compile categories anew for each edition.

The *Antique Trader Antiques & Collectibles Price Guide* has also seen a number of design changes. The earliest editions were only about 900 pages (compared to over 1,000 pages now), there were fewer photographs and they were all in black and white (now in full color). The system of price compilation has also evolved over the decades. Initially the editor relied heavily on prices drawn from advertisements in *Antique Trader Weekly, Depression Glass Daze,* and other trade publications, many of which have now faded away. Many dealers and collectors, especially from the Midwest region, also provided listings and photographs with not as much material drawn from auction houses and experts from a much broader geographic range. Today we are able to provide a wider and more detailed overview of collecting around the United States and the world.

I also find it interesting to compare the variety of categories that we ran in 1984 to what we publish today. Many of the categories have remained the same but many have been expanded. Some that appeared in that first edition haven't been repeated in recent years. A few of these include collector plates, stretch glass, hand collectibles, Kellogg prints, Lehn ware and stirrup cups. If some of these are your favorites, I apologize. However, the available market information on them is scarce. They tend to have a limited market presence, so we've moved ahead and added numerous other topics that better reflect current collecting trends.

Some larger collecting fields, such as pattern glass and carnival glass, still have a core of collectors but perhaps not the broader market appeal they once had. Also reflecting a trend in the current antiques and collectibles market, I hear over and over that the "best" will still sell well, however, mid- and lower-range examples tend to be slow movers. This seems to be true across the board. It does make sense because, as I've often stated, it's much better to purchase one top-notch piece than a half-dozen more common examples. A quality item is more likely to hold its market value and appreciate more over the years. To give you some additional insights into how the market has changed since 1984, I have pulled together some direct comparisons for items listed in the first edition and our current 2009 edition. As you will see, some categories have seen remarkable market value increases while some have shown less dramatic gains:

Whiting & Davis:

Enameled mesh purse with a geometric Art Deco design:	1984 - **$55**	2009 - **$200-250**

Flow Blue China:

Argyle pattern (Grindley) 10" plate:	1984 - **$37**	2009 - **$95**
Lonsdale pattern (Ridgways) covered vegetable:	1984 - **$165**	2009 - **$250**
Scinde pattern (Alcock, ca. 1840) 14" large platter:	1984 - **$225**	2009 - **$450**

Roseville Pottery:

Baneda pattern 8" vase:	1984 - **$135**	2009 - **$1,150**
Jonquil pattern 8" high basket:	1984 - **$115-$135**	2009 - **$500**
Panel (Rosecraft) pattern, 11" vase with nudes:	1984 - **$245**	2009 - **$460**

Carnival Glass:

Acorn Burrs pattern purple 7 pc. berry set:	1984 - **$358**	2009 - **$525**
Beaded Cable pattern green rose bowl:	1984 - **$60**	2009 - **$200**
Grape & Cable pattern marigold hatpin holder:	1984 - **$140**	2009 - **$450**
Holly pattern 9"-10" blue plate:	1984 - **$80-155**	2009 - **$260**

Coca Cola:

1927 long calendar with pretty lady:	1984 - **$225**	2009 - **$2,310**

Grueby Pottery:

7 1/2"-7 3/4" vase with squatty bulbous lower body and tall neck, molded wide leaves alternating with slender flower buds, dark matte green glaze:	1984 - **$413**	2009 - **$1,610**

Tiffany Lamps:

"Acorn" pattern table lamp, 16" diameter shade, urn-form base:	1984 - **$5,900**	2009 - **$14,950**
"Nasturium" pattern table lamp, 23" diameter shade, bronze base:	1984 - **$22,000**	2009 - **$186,700**

Bitters Bottles:

- Drakes (ST) 1860 – Plantation X Bitters, cabin-shaped with four logs, yellow:	1984 - **$240**	2009 - **$448**
- Herb (H.P.) Wild Cherry Bitters, cabin-shaped, amber:	1984 - **$95**	2009 - **$784**

Marbles:

Sulphide with Dog seated:	1984 - **$60**	2009 - **$110**

I think the information above gives you a general idea of how some popular categories have fared during the past quarter century. As I mentioned, many different "hot" categories have been included, reflecting current interests, such as mid-20th-century design (furniture, glassware, ceramics, lighting).

Jewelry of all types is also a strong seller, just as it was back in the 1980s and as it likely will continue to be. (Let's hope not too many great pieces are scrapped during the recent jump in gold prices. Remember when the Hunt brothers tried to corner the silver market back in the 1980s? That surge didn't last too long.)

One of the biggest challenges in the collecting world today is an aging collector base. Because of this, many "old standards" avidly sought 25 to 50 years ago are today seeing values level off and demand soften. Everyone in the trade is trying to figure out how to attract younger collectors—those born in the 1970s, 1980s and later. Although some of these young adults are developing a taste for true antiques, many others either have no understanding or appreciation of treasures pre-dating the "ancient" 1960s or are collecting things from their childhood (think of Star Wars, the Smurfs and Pee Wee Herman). Makes you wonder what youngsters today will search out in the future—memorabilia for Hannah Montana, Harry Potter and American Idol?

Of course, one of the biggest changes in the buying and selling of objects since 1984 is the growth of the Internet. Now nearly anyone anywhere in the world has the opportunity to shop or bid online. The huge scope of items now available online has increased demand for some antiques and collectibles and lowered demand in other areas. This method of marketing may well continue for years to come, but I recently have been hearing stirrings of discontent among collectors and dealers. They may have had some problems with an online transaction or may have come to realize how much they miss the one-on-one personal interaction with a live person and the chance to see and handle a treasure before they lay down hard-earned cash for it.

I've been asked over and over again during the past 36 years of my career, "What is the next hot collectible?" If I had the answer to that one, I would be rich and retired by now. It's the fun of learning about new collecting interests, working to expand the pool of eager collectors, and searching out treasures that keep us all going. It's the real spice in the bubbling stew that is our world of collecting. *Bon appetit!*

ON THE COVER:

Lower left: Limoges porcelain 23 1/2" h. vase with "blown-out" figures of a cherub and a lady, hand-painted roses, mark of Charles Field Haviland, **$7,000; center bottom:** McKee Glass "Rock Crystal" pattern compote in amber, 8 3/4" d., 7" h., **$55; center top:** antique butterfly-shaped pin composed of turquoise and diamonds, France, late 19th c., 1" l., **$940; right:** Federal-style banjo clock in gilt gesso and mahogany, figural gold eagle finial above the dial, reverse-painted glass panels in the throat & round base, panel in throat lettered "L. Curtis, Concord," the bottom panel titled "Commerce," early 20th c., 44 1/2" h., **$11,750.**

A ADVERTISING ITEMS

Thousands of objects made in various materials, some intended as gifts with purchases, others used for display or given away for publicity, are now being collected. Also see various other categories and Antique Trader Advertising Price Guide.

Fine 1904 DuPont Powder Calendar

Calendar, 1904, "DuPont Powder Co.," long rectangular color-lithographed paper w/a large scene of various men & hunting dogs on a railroad train platform, titled "The first day of the open season," advertising & partial calendar pad below, small damages, 15 1/2 x 28 1/4" (ILLUS.)........ **$3,220**

1940s Winston Cigarettes Ashtray

Ashtray, "Winston Cigarettes - Taste Good," stamped metal, wording around rim, image of cigarette pack in the bottom, 1940s, 3 1/2" d. (ILLUS.)...................... **$3**

Framed 1901 Ceresota Flour Calendar

Calendar, 1901, "Ceresota Flour," color-printed cardboard, a large scene of the Ceresota boy cutting a large loaf of bread, the small calendar in the lower right corner, original top & bottom metal strips, small water mark in top right edge, matted & framed, 12 3/4 x 17" (ILLUS.) **$345**

Rare 1905 DuPont Powder Co. Calendar

Calendar, 1905, "DuPont Powder Co.," long rectangular color-lithographed paper w/a large scene of a hunting dog retrieving a duck w/advertising & complete calendar pad in red, white & black, tear about halfway across the top, some wrinkles & creases, 15 x 29" (ILLUS.) **$4,025**

Charming 1905 George Miller Calendar

Calendar, 1905, "George Miller, Coal & Ice Dealer," color-printed die-cut paper, a scene of a young Victorian boy & girl reading a wooden signpost w/advertising, tiny calendar pad at the bottom, matted & framed, 8 1/2 x 14 1/2" (ILLUS.) **$575**

1893 Hires' Rootbeer Calendar Top

Drip-O-Lator Premium Cookie Cutter

Cookie cutter, "Drip-O-Lator - The Better Drip Coffee maker," stamped tin, product give-away, 1930s-40s, 2 1/2" w. (ILLUS.) **$4**

1935 Firestone Tires Calendar

Calendar, 1935, "Firestone Tires," color-lithographed paper w/a dramatic design of a large tire at the top above the small full calendar, labeled for the Rome Tire and Battery Service, Rome, New York, original metal hanging strip, 20 3/4 x 42" (ILLUS.).. **$288**

Calendar top, 1893, "Hires' Rootbeer - Calendar 1893," lithographed in color w/two cute children w/a cat, 7" sq. (ILLUS., top next column)................................. **$230**

Bear Brand Hosiery Figural Display

Counter display, "Bear Brand Hosiery Wears," papier-mâché figural, modeled as the Three Bears out walking, on plinth base w/wording in red, spots of wear on base, early 20th c., 18 1/2" h. (ILLUS.) ... **$1,035**

A

Early Chalkware Buster Brown Shoes Display

Counter display, "Buster Brown Shoes," figural chalkware figure of Buster Brown dressed in red w/his dog Tiger, a small sign in front, all on a round base, several chips & paint loss to base, shoe sign & Buster's leg, early 20th c., 16 1/2" h. (ILLUS.) **$460**

Unusual Early Crawford Cigars Display

Counter display, "Crawford Cigars," wooden upright tapering tower w/flat top w/center tube, the black ground printed on front in yellow "Smoke The Crawford 5¢ Cigar," red wording down sides, designed to have smoke pumped through tube in back to a pipe that sat on the top, few chips, late 19th - early 20th c., 12 x 20 1/2", 28" h. (ILLUS.) **$805**

Scarce Early Edison Mazda Display

Counter display, "Edison Mazda Lamps," lithographed tin, designed as an upright flattened light bulb in dark yellow centered by the Edison Mazda logo designed by Maxfield Parrish, on a rectangular platform base w/sloping sides printed in dark yellow w/"There's a Right Edison Mazda Lamp For every Fixture," the edges mounted w/twelve bulb sockets, each w/an individual on-off switch, a few fine scratches, back panel w/some color loss one socket w/old break, original cord frayed, ca. 1920s, 15 3/4 x 23 1/2" (ILLUS.) **$2,300**

Unusual Quoddy Moccasins Display

Counter display, "Quoddy Moccasins," figural composition model of a seated Native American warrior holding a wooden pole flying a pale blue wooden banner w/yellow wording, some weathering, early 20th c., 20 x 20", 29" h. (ILLUS.) **$1,000-1,500**

A

Rare Whitman's Chocolate Counter Display

Counter display, "Whitman's Chocolates," color-printed paper on wood featuring the angular figure of a running messenger boy dressed in blue & carrying a large Whitman's Sampler box under one arm, on a red plinth case w/white wording, ca. 1920s, some corner wear, 18 3/4" h. (ILLUS.) **$2,645**

The "Fairy" Diamond Dyes Cabinet

Counter display cabinet, "Diamond Dyes," the "Fairy" model, oak upright form w/the door inset w/a color-lithographed panel centered by a vignette of a fairy surrounded by vignettes of people using the product, good condition, some interior compartments loose or missing, late 19th - early 20th c., 23 1/2 x 30 1/2" (ILLUS.)
.... **$1,840**

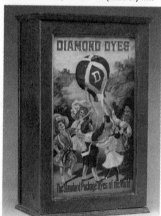

The "Balloon" Diamond Dyes Cabinet

Counter display cabinet, "Diamond Dyes," the "Balloon" model, oak upright form w/the door inset w/a color-lithographed panel w/a vignette of children dancing around a small hot air balloon tied down w/ribbons, some spots of color loss, water damage on cardboard rear door insert, cabinet missing most vertical dividers, late 19th - early 20th c., 15 1/2 x 24 1/2" (ILLUS.)............................. **$460**

The "Governess" Diamond Dyes Cabinet

Counter display cabinet, "Diamond Dyes," the "Governess" model, oak upright form w/the door inset w/a color-lithographed panel w/a scene of a governess playing w/children in a grassy yard, panel w/few spots of paint loss, cabinet stripped, missing some horizontal & most vertical interior dividers, late 19th - early 20th c., 22 3/4 x 29 3/4" (ILLUS.)............................. **$805**

A

Early Amos & Andy Pepsodent Displays

Counter displays, "Pepsodent Tooth-paste," color-printed die-cut cardboard, two tall narrow cut-out figures, one of Amos & the other of Andy of Amos & Andy team, one w/language box reading "Oh! Sho-Sho - Pepsodent! - Check an' Double Check," the other reads "Um! Um! - Ain't dis sumpin!," fair condition w/some paper loss, staining creases & edge tears, copyrighted in 1930, 21 x 54" & 22 x 61", the pair (ILLUS.) **$460**

Boardman's Rye Whiskey Counter Display

Country display, "Boardman's Rye Whis-key," chalkware, an upright round disk molded in low-relief w/an early airplane w/the company name & a vapor trail reading "Above All," on a narrow rect-angular plinth base molded w/the com-pany name, ca. 1930s, few small nicks (ILLUS.) **$250-500**

Tokens from "Shell Gasoline" Game Set

Game tokens, "Shell Gasoline," from "Shell's Famous Facts and Faces Game," stamped metal token, each print-ed w/the name & portrait of a famous American, 1970, each (ILLUS. of Tho-mas Edison & John Paul Jones) **$8**

Esso Gasoline Advertising Key Chain

Key chain, "Esso Gasoline," round stamped metal, cast on the front w/the Esso tiger head & "Esso - Put A Tiger in Your Tank," the back stamped "Drop in any mailbox if lost - Happy Motoring Key Club...Postage Guaranteed," 1960s, 1 1/4" d. (ILLUS.) **$20**

Scarce Early Moxie Poster

Poster, "Drink Moxie," lithographed paper in red, blue & white, features the Moxie Boy holding a bottle w/a wooden crate in the foreground, early 20th c., several fold lines, small edge tears, one small water stain, 27 x 41" (ILLUS.) **$1,150**

A

1897 Winchester Shotguns Poster

Poster, "Winchester Shotguns and Shells," long rectangular paper printed at the top w/a scene of a Model 1897 pump shotgun above a picture of a man standing leaning on the shotgun, advertising down the sides & across the bottom, very dark & faded, water damage on edges, several small scrapes & tack holes, 14 1/4 x 22 3/4" (ILLUS.) **$1,898**

Columbia Biscuit Co. Large Tin

Product container, "Columbia Biscuit Co. & Family Goods," lithographed tin, deep rectangular container w/hinged flat cover, bright orange background printed in blue & white w/advertising on the lid & front highlighted by a round vignette showing Miss Columbia, late 19th - early 20th c., slight fading, cover lid needs reattachment, 8 x 10 1/4", 7" h. (ILLUS.) **$300**

Product container, "Elephant Java Coffee," printed tin, rectangular 3 lb. tin w/hinged flat lid, the pinkish tan ground printed in black w/detailed black advertising & a scene of an elephant, a steam locomotive on the end panels, American Can Co., late 19th - early 20th c., moderate wear & some fading, 5 1/2 x 7 3/4", 5 1/4" h. (ILLUS., top next column) **$403**

Three-Pound Elephant Java Coffee Tin

Unusual Victorian Baking Soda Barrel

Product container, "J. Monroe Taylor's Gold Medal Soda & Saleratus," cylindrical cardboard barrel w/fitted flat wood top & wood bottom, in orange w/a color-printed label showing Victorian figures in an interior, late 19th c., some paper loss, splatter, wood chips & scuffs, 14" d., 19 1/2" h. (ILLUS.) **$316**

Lucky Curve Cut Plug Tobacco Tin

Product container, "Lucky Curve Cut Plug Tobacco," printed tin, rectangular one-pound size w/pry-off lid, decorated in orange w/yellow wording & a central figure of an early baseball pitcher, few areas of crazing, scattered scuffs & blemishes, early 20th c., 4 1/2 x 7", 4 1/4" h. (ILLUS.) **$230**

A

Waldorf Java Roasted Coffee Store Bin

Store bin, "Waldorf Java Roasted Coffee," color-printed tin, upright rectangular form w/curved top top lift lid w/knob in red, front printed in white, black & red w/a red ground & one panel in color showing a pretty Victorian lady & a lower color panel showing an exotic landscape, late 19th c., moderate wear, 12 1/2 x 20 1/4", 21" h. (ILLUS.) **$460**

Unusual Lowney's Cocoa String Holder

String holder, "Lowney's Cocoa," store-type, color-printed tin, hanging upright rectangular w/a dark brown ground w/red lettering & a color image of a package at the top above an arched opening holding a large spindle of string, some areas of pitting & paint loss, tin die-cut cup replaced, late 19th c., 14 1/2 x 25 1/2" (ILLUS.)........................ **$1,553**

Early Moxie Wall Thermometer

Thermometer, "Moxie," wall-type, color-lithographed tin, vertical rectangular shape w/rounded corners, printed w/a row of red, turquoise blue & green sections, the upper section featuring a Moxie bottle & "Drink Moxie - Take home a case tonight" in white in a black dot, the center section printed "Drink Moxie - Good at any Temperature," lower section features Moxie Boy logo, early 20th c., scattered scuffs & minor dents at bottom, 9 3/4 x 25 1/2" (ILLUS.)........................... **$1,020**

Rare Moxie Horsemobile Tin Toy

Toy, "Moxie," color-lithographed tin Moxie Horsemobile, rare version w/blue auto fitted w/a man riding the cut-out of a white horse, patented in 1917, few soft bends, scattered paint chips, 6 1/2 x 8 1/2" (ILLUS.)........................... **$1,495**

Rare Five-Part Winchester Rifles Window Display

Window display, "Winchester Rifles," five-panel color-printed cardboard, center three panels form an outdoor scene of boys from the Winchester Junior Rifle Corps practicing at a firing range, end panels w/large crossed rifles & company logo w/advertising, dated 1923, w/original shipping envelope & display instructions, each section 18 1/4 x 40" (ILLUS.) **$4,313**

ART DECO

Interest in Art Deco, a name given an art movement stemming from the Paris International Exhibition of 1925, continues to grow today. This style flowered in the 1930s and actually continued into the 1940s. A mood of flippancy is found in its varied characteristics - zigzag lines resembling the lightning bolt, sometimes steps, often the use of sharply contrasting colors such as black and white and others. Look for prices for the best examples of Art Deco design to continue to rise. Also see JEWELRY, MODERN.

around the crestrail & down the sloped arms, deep cushion seat, deep upholstered apron on a thin birch band, raised on tapering fluted legs w/scrolled tops & ending in small knob feet, attributed to Maurice Defrene, France, ca. 1925, 34 1/4" h. (ILLUS.) **$7,800**

Unusual Art Deco Lamp with Fish

Lamp, table-type, nickel-plate & milk glass, the long narrow rectangular base mounted at each end w/a stylized fish w/a very tall curled fin, centered by a socket fitted w/a tall cylindrical milk glass shade fitted w/a metal cap, some minor scratches, re-wired, 12" l., 8 1/2" h. (ILLUS.).................. **$104**

Fine French Art Deco Upholstered Chair

Armchair, upholstered birch, the upholstered barrel-back w/a thin band of birch

Rare Art Deco Nickel-plate Table Lamp

A **Lamp,** table-type, nickel-plate, the round foot w/a central shaft mounted w/graduated open flat bar rectangles that swivel, stamped "Desny - Paris - Made in France - Déposé," ca. 1930, 12 3/8" h. (ILLUS., previous page) **$28,800**

Very Rare E. Brandt Art Deco Table

Table, silvered wrought iron & marble, the thick round black & white marble top fitted into a narrow iron frame w/a pierced leaf design raised on four flat iron legs w/a band of shell-like devices & ending in curled feet mounted on another round slab of black & white marble raised on thin iron feet, designed by Edgar Brandt, marked, France, ca. 1925, 28 1/2" d., 30 1/2" h. (ILLUS.) **$62,400**

Extremely Rare Lacroix Art Deco Lamps

Lamps, table-type, nickel-plate, a round foot & central shaft mounted w/graduated spaced flat disks, designed by Boris Lacroix, one stamped "Boris Lacroix," France, ca. 1930, 14 1/4" h., pr. (ILLUS.) **$60,000**

Fine Teague-Designed Art Deco Radio

Radio, table model, a large flat disk of blue mirrored glass decorated in the lower half w/three narrow horizontal chrome bands intersecting the round speaker panel centered by the dial, supported on black feet, designed by Waler D. Teague, manufactured by the Sparton Corp. of Michigan, ca. 1934, 14 7/8" d. (ILLUS.).... **$5,400**

Rare & Unique Art Deco Glass Vase

Vase, acid-etched & cut clear glass, the heavy slightly tapering cylindrical form cut w/two thick spiral bands down the sides against an acid-etched ground, designed by Aristide Colotte, acid-etched mark "Colotte Nancy Piece Unique," ca. 1925, 5 1/2" d., 10 1/4" h. (ILLUS.) **$15,600**

One of a Pair of Rare Brandt Wall Sconces

Wall sconces, patented wrought iron & glass, the iron mount w/a tiered & fluted base supporting a pair of tall flat curled arms w/a pierced leafy vine design, each fitted w/an electric socket mounted w/a trumpet-form flute & loop-etched pale yellow Daum Nancy shade, designed by Edgar Brandt, marked, France, ca. 1925, 14 1/2" w., 20 3/4" h., pr. (ILLUS. of one) **$42,000**

ART NOUVEAU

Art Nouveau's primary thrust was between 1890 and 1905, but commercial Art Nouveau productions continued until about World War I. This style was a rebellion against historic tradition in art. Using natural forms as inspiration, it is primarily characterized by undulating or wavelike lines and whiplashes. Many objects were made in materials ranging from glass to metals. Figural pieces with seductive maidens with long, flowing hair are especially popular in this style. Interest in Art Nouveau remains high, with the best pieces by well known designers bringing strong prices. Also see JEWELRY, ANTIQUE.

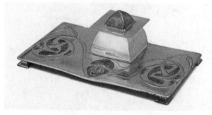

Fine Art Nouveau Inkwell by A. Knox

Inkwell, enameled sterling silver, the thin rectangular base on tiny feet decorated w/swirled & looping devices highlighted by dark blue enamel, the square inkwell at the center back w/a hinged square cover centered by a malachite button, opening to a glass well, designed by Archibald Knox, retailed by Liberty & Co., England, ca. 1904, 8 3/4" w. (ILLUS.)..... **$9,828**

Rare Bronze Loie Fuller Table Lamp

Lamp, gilt-bronze, figural, designed as the dancer Loie Fuller wearing a swirling gown & cape, foundry mark of Siot Decauville, designed by Raoul Larche, France, ca. 1900, 18" h. (ILLUS.) **$15,600**

Art Nouveau Bronze Figural Lamp

Lamp, table, gilt-bronze, figural, the figure of the dancer Loie Fuller posed w/her arms raised over her head amid her swirling gown, from a model by Francois-Raoul Larche, Siot-Decauville Foundry, Paris, France, ca. 1900, 13" h. (ILLUS.) **$8,365**

A

Art Nouveau Vitrine by Louis Majorelle

Vitrine cabinet, marquetry & fruitwood the
high back w/a flat molded crestrail above
a veneered panel above a tall slender
central cabinet w/a long glazed door w/a
fine lower panel of marquetry w/a leaf vine
design, three small curved open shelves
down each sides, narrow vine-carved
apron continuing into simple cabriole legs,
Louis Majorelle, France, ca. 1900,
15 1/4 x 31 1/4", 68 5/8" h. (ILLUS.)......... **$6,000**

AUDUBON PRINTS

*John James Audubon, American orni-
thologist and artist, is considered the finest
nature artist in history. In about 1820 he
conceived the idea of publishing a full color
book portraying every known species of
American bird in its natural habitat. He
spent years in the wilderness capturing
their beauty in vivid color only to have
great difficulty finding a publisher. In 1826
he visited England, received immediate
acclaim, and selected Robert Havell as his
engraver. "Birds of America," when completed, consisted of four volumes of 435
individual plates, double-elephant folio
size, a combination of aquatint, etching
and line engraving. W.H. Lizars of Edin-
burgh engraved the first ten plates of this
four-volume series. These were later
retouched by Havell, who produced the
complete set between 1827 and early 1839.
In the 1840s, another definitive work,
"Viviparous Quadrupeds of North America," containing 150 plates, was published
in America. Prices for Audubon's original
double-elephant folio size prints are very
high and beyond the means of the average
collector. Subsequent editions of "Birds of
America," especially the chromolithographs*

*done by Julius Bien in New York (1859-60)
and the smaller octavo (7 x 10 1/2") edition
of prints done by J.T. Bowen of Philadelphia in the 1840s, are those that are most
frequently offered for sale.*

*Anyone interested in Audubon prints
needs to be aware that many photographi-
cally produced copies of the prints have
been issued during this century for use on
calendars or as decorative accessories, so it
is best to check with a print expert before
spending a large sum on an Audubon pur-
ported to be from an early edition.*

American Sparrow Hawk Print

American Sparrow Hawk - Plate CXLII -
hand-colored etching, engraving & aquatint by Robert Havell, Jr., London, 1827-
38, full margins, pale foxing, mat & time
staining, minor rim damages, framed,
print 20 3/4 x 25 15/16" (ILLUS.)............. **$5,760**

Audubon Great horned-Owl Print

A

Great horned-Owl - Plate LXI, hand-colored etching, engraving & aquatint w/touches of gum arabic by Robert Havell, Jr., London, 1827-38, framed, trimmed to platemark, minor soiling, very small edge tears & splits, 24 15/16 x 37 1/2" (ILLUS., previous page)
.... **$12,000**

Great Marbled Godwit Audubon Print

Great Marbled Godwit - Plate CCXXXVIII - hand-colored etching, engraving & aquatint by Robert Havell, Jr., London, 1823-38, wide margins folded over, small area of surface staining, pale mat staining, creasing & tears, framed, print 13 1/2 x 21 1/8" (ILLUS.)......................... **$2,880**

Rare Ivory-billed Woodpecker Print

Ivory-billed Woodpecker - Plate 66, hand-colored etching, engraving & aquatint by Robert Havell, London, 1827-38, framed, trimmed to platemark, minor soiling, skillfully repaired edge tears & losses, 25 1/4 x 38" (ILLUS.)............................. **$39,600**

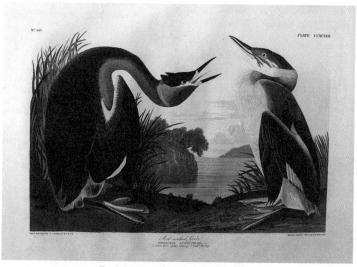

Red-necked Grebe Audubon Print

Red-necked Grebe - Plate CCXCVIII - hand-colored etching, engraving & aquatint by Robert Havell, Jr., London, 1827-38, sight 16 1/2 x 22 1/4" (ILLUS.) **$2,185**

AUTOMOBILES

1998 Audi A6 Quattro Station Wagon

Audi, 1998 A6 2.8 Quattro wagon, black w/grey leather interior, alloy wheels, roof rack, rear spoiler & sliding sun roof, 21,253 miles (ILLUS.) **$10,350**

1999 Mercedes-Benz Coupe

Mercedes-Benz, 1999, Model CLK320 Coupe, black body w/neutral interior, odometer reads 3,341 miles, six-cylinder automatic, good condition (ILLUS.)....... **$28,200**

AUTOMOTIVE COLLECTIBLES

Also see Antique Trader Advertising Price Guide.

Rare 1907 Pennsylvania License Plate

License plate, 1907 Pennsylvania, porcelain, rectangular w/wording & numbers in white on a dark orange background, a few edge chips, 6 1/2 x 8" (ILLUS.)............ **$345**

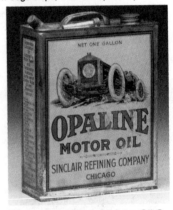

Scarce Early Opaline Motor Oil Can

Oil can, "Opaline Motor Oil - Sinclair Refining Company - Chicago," one-gallon can w/top handle, screw-on cap & short spout w/cap, printed paper labels, the front on w/a large race car above the wording in dark green & black, some light surface scuffing, early 20th c., 8" w., 11" h. (ILLUS.)................................ **$920**

Early Mobiloil Gargoyle Service Sign

Sign, "Authorized Service - Genuine Gargoyle - Mobiloil," porcelain, single-side

A

Unusual Early Auto Service Sign

rectangle w/top center tab, white ground w/red gargoyle logo & printing in dark blue, black & red, overall edge chipping, Vacuum Oil Company, early 20th c., 22 1/2 x 30" (ILLUS.)................................. **$259**

1930s Auto Service Sign

Sign, "Official Service - Blue List - AOAA," porcelain, double-sided oval w/dark blue border w/white lettering, yellow center w/shield in dark blue & white, missing top grommets, tiny edge chips, ca. 1930s, 14 1/2 x 20" (ILLUS.)................................. **$403**

Sign, "United Motors - Service," porcelain, double-sided oval w/an orange background w/an early auto in the center & wording in dark blue & white, some chips to the field & top mounting holes, some surface discoloration, early 20th c., 28 1/2 x 48" (ILLUS., top of page).............. **$780**

AVIATION COLLECTIBLES

Recently much interest has been shown in collecting items associated with the early days of the "flying machine." In addition to relics, flying adjuncts and literature relating to the early days of flight, collectors also seek out items that picture the more renowned early pilots, some of whom became folk-heroes in their own lifetimes, as well as the early planes themselves.

Charles Lindberg Book Ends

Book ends, bronzed cast metal, arched flat-back style w/a cast bust portrait of Charles Lindberg above the Spirit of St. Louis & an eagle, late 1920s, 6 x 6", pr. (ILLUS.)...................................... **$173**

Antique Airplanes Coloring Book

Coloring book, "Antique Airplanes Coloring Book," by Peter F. Copeland, Dover Publishing Co., 1975, 8 1/4 x 11" (ILLUS.)......... **$15**

A

Figural Spirit of St. Louis Glass Decanter

Decanter, figural blown glass "Spirit of St. Louis," cobalt blue glass body w/attached metal nose propeller, wheels, body rings to hold the wings & tail assembly spigot w/handle, 75% of original gold trim, name of plane across the nose, missing the six shot glasses that fit into the wings, ca. 1927, 13" l. (ILLUS., top of page) **$392**

Scarce WWI Air Service Poster

Poster, "Join The Air Service and Serve in France - Do It Now," World War I recruiting poster printed in color w/a bold design of a period biplane above two figures in uniform, minor flaws, professionally matted & framed, 24 1/2 x 36" (ILLUS.) **$805**

Toy, "The Spirit of St. Louis," pressed steel model of the Lindbergh plane w/construction similar to an Erector set, w/original orange & cream box illustrating the plane & original instruction sheet, Metalcraft, ca. 1927, 11 1/2" wingspan (ILLUS., top next column) **$115**

Metalcraft Spirit of St. Louis Airplane Kit

BANKS

Mechanical

Cabin Bank with Red & Green Walls

Cabin - 33 - cabin w/man standing in doorway, red & green cabin walls, pivoting man kicks coin through roof, J. & E. Stevens, PL 93 (ILLUS.) **$633**

B

Always Did 'Spise a Mule Bank

(I) Always Did 'Spise a Mule - 4 - boy on bench facing mule, orange base, by J. E. Stevens Co., paint wear, coin trap missing, 10" w., PL 250 (ILLUS.)....................... **$489**

Rare Liberty Mechanical Bank

Liberty Bank - white metal figure of Lady Liberty holding her torch fitted w/a small light bulb, mounted on a rectangular leatherette-covered wooden base w/name tag on the front also reads "Patent Applied For. Directions Use Pennies or Dimes Only. Press Coin Down to the Left," deposited coin lights up bulb, slide open bottom, early 20th c., some chipping to leatherette, 4 3/4" w., 8" h., PL 294 (ILLUS.) **$2,875**

Chief Big Moon Mechanical Bank

Chief Big Moon - 42 - Indian seated in front of teepee holding fish w/flipping frog and pond, J. & E. Stevens, 1899, red-painted base version, frog & lever detached, PL 108 (ILLUS.)... **$2,300**

Mammy & Child Mechanical Bank

Mammy & Child - 155 - mammy feeding child laying across lap, multicolored, Kyser & Rex, 1884, spoon missing, overall paint wear, coin trap missing, PL 318 (ILLUS.) **$2,280**

Still

Colorful Tin World Globe Still Bank

Globe - tin world globe printed in color, on a round metal base, slot in top for coins, Ohio Art Company, ca. 1950, 4 1/2" h. (ILLUS.).. **$45**

B

Stevens Roof "Bank" Building Bank

Building - Roof "Bank" - 1122 - cast iron, domed mansard roof, the front w/"Bank" in a small arched panel above the large arched door w/fan light flanked by arched windows, gilt highlights, J. & E. Stevens Co., 1887, 3 1 /4 x 3 3/4 x 5 1/4" h., W. 366 (ILLUS.).. **$316**

BARBERIANA

A wide variety of antiques related to the tonsorial arts have been highly collectible for many years, especially 19th- and early-20th-century shaving mugs and barber bottles and, more recently, razors. We are now combining these closely related categories under one heading for easier reference. A selection of other varied pieces relating to barbering will also be found below.

Barber Bottles

Decorated Amber Barber Bottle

Amber, bulbous body tapering to a tall lady's leg neck w/rolled lip, pontil scar, optic coinspot design, enameled in orange & white w/thin arches of tiny dots over arches of stylized flower heads, late 19th - early 20th c., 8" h. (ILLUS.)..................... **$101**

Amethyst Bottle with Art Nouveau Florals

Amethyst, footed bulbous body w/a sharply angled shoulder tapering to a tall slender ringed neck, vertical optic ribbing, pontil scar, an Art Nouveau design of stylized flowers & leaves in yellow & gold enamel, late 19th - early 20th c., 7 3/4" h. (ILLUS.) .. **$420**

Amethyst Bottle with Grist Mill Scene

Amethyst, ovoid body tapering to a lady's leg neck w/rolled lip, pontil scar, the side enameled in white w/a scene of a grist mill below "Bay Rum," late 19th - early 20th c., 7 5/8" h. (ILLUS.) **$420**

ted flowers, late 19th - early 20th c., 8 7/8" h. (ILLUS.) **$134**

Blue Opalescent Coral Barber Bottle

Blue opalescent, Coral patt., bulbous body tapering to a slender neck w/rolled lip, polished pontil, late 19th - early 20th c., 6 7/8" h. (ILLUS.) **$246**

Blue Bottle with Profile Portrait

Cobalt blue, ovoid body tapering to a tall lady's leg neck w/rolled lip, pontil scar, enameled in white w/the bust profile portrait of a woman framed by floral sprigs above leaf sprigs tied w/a bowl, late 19th - early 20th c., 8 1/4" h. (ILLUS.)............... **$308**

Cobalt Barber Bottle with Dotted Flowers

Cobalt blue, cylindrical body tapering to a cylindrical neck w/tooled lip, vertical optic ribbing, enameled in yellow, orange & white w/a middle band of stylized dot flower heads above clusters of small dot-

Cranberry Opalescent Fern Barber Bottle

Cranberry opalescent, Fern patt., bulbous lobed body tapering to a tall slender neck w/a rolled lip, light interior stain, late 19th - early 20th c., 6 7/8" h. (ILLUS.)............... **$146**

B

Facing Pair of Mary Gregory Barber Bottles

Mary Gregory, bulbous body tapering to a tall lady's leg neck, cobalt blue w/a white enameled figure of a girl or a boy playing tennis, ca. 1900, 8 1/4" h., facing pr. (ILLUS.)... **$420**

Mary Gregory Bottle with Girl in Garden

Mary Gregory, bulbous body w/a vertical optic ribbed design tapering to a tall waisted neck, pontil scar, green w/a white enameled figure of a girl walking in a garden, ca. 1900, 8" h. (ILLUS.) **$269**

Mary Gregory Bottle with Boy in Garden

Mary Gregory, bulbous body w/a vertical optic ribbed design tapering to a tall waisted neck, pontil scar, cobalt blue w/a white enameled figure of a boy standing in a garden, ca. 1900, 7 5/8" h. (ILLUS.).... **$246**

Mary Gregory Bottle with Girl on Rock

Mary Gregory, footed bulbous body tapering to a ringed lady's leg neck, amethyst w/a white enameled figure of a girl seated on rock work in a garden, ca. 1900, 7 5/8" h. (ILLUS.) **$190**

Barber Bottle with Cherub Scene

Milk glass, tapering cylindrical body w/a tall slender neck w/sheared & ground lip, enameled w/a floral & green leaf wreath enclosing a scene of cherubs around a dove in a cage, late 19th - early 20th c., 7 3/4" h. (ILLUS.) **$280**

Milk Glass Hair Tonic Bottle with Bird

Milk glass, tapering smooth cylindrical body w/a tall slender neck w/metal cap, enameled w/a scene of a bird perched on a branch above grass & below "Hair Tonic," mark of the Koken Company of St. Louis on the bottom, late 19th - early 20th c., 9 1/8" h. (ILLUS.)......................... **$308**

B

Bell-shaped Blue Decorated Barber Bottle

Turquoise blue, tapering bell-form vertical optic ribbed body w/a tall cylindrical neck w/tooled mouth, pontil scar, enameled in red, yellow & white w/a cluster of stylized daisy-like flowers, late 19th - early 20th c., 7 3/4" h. (ILLUS.) **$308**

Decorative Venetian-style Barber Bottle

B

Venetian-style, cylindrical body tapering to a very tall slender neck w/sheared & polished lip, overall swirled latticino white stripes alternating w/gold aventurine stripes, early 20th c., 9 7/8" h. (ILLUS., previous page) **$213**

White Opalescent Coral Pattern Bottle

White opalescent, Coral patt., squared body tapering to a slender neck w/rolled lip, polished pontil, late 19th - early 20th c., 8 3/8" h. (ILLUS.) **$235**

Green Banded Art Nouveau Barber Bottle

Yellowish green, footed bulbous body tapering to a tall slender double-bulbed neck w/tooled mouth, pontil scar, vertical optic ribbing, decorated w/gold, white & blue w/a banded design suspending stylized Art Nouveau flowers, late 19th - early 20th c., 7 3/4" h. (ILLUS.) **$420**

Green Barber Bottle with Portrait

Yellowish green, ovoid body tapering to a lady's leg neck w/rolled lip, pontil scar, the side enameled in white w/a bust portrait of a lady w/long flowing hair above "Vegederma," some wear, late 19th - early 20th c., 7 3/4" h. (ILLUS.) **$168**

Mugs

Fraternal Order

Improved Order of Redmen Mug

Improved Order of Redmen, decorated in color w/the Indian head emblem of the order & the shield logo of a lodge, name in gold above, French-made blank, 3 5/8" h. (ILLUS.) **$420**

B

Detailed Odd Fellows Shaving Mug

Independent Order of Odd Fellows, decorated in color w/various emblems of the order including a tent, skull & Bible, name in gold at the sides, manufacturing glaze crack in upper part of handle, 3 1/2" h. (ILLUS.) **$100**

Order of United American Mechanics Mug

Order of United American Mechanics, emblem in color above gold leafy wreath, name in gold at the top, Austrian-made blank, 3 5/8"h. (ILLUS.) **$67**

General

Odd Fellows & Order of Redmen Mug

Independent Order of Odd Fellows & Improved Order of Redmen, gold & color logos of each order at the top above the name, French-made blank, small chip on top of base rim, 3 5/8" h. (ILLUS.) **$235**

Shaving Mug with Portrait of Woman

Bust profile portrait of a pretty woman, color portrait on a black oval w/a gold border, arched name in gold above, trimmed w/gold leafy scrolls, 3 1/2" h. (ILLUS.) **$115**

Knights of Pythias & Foresters of America Mug

Knights of Pythias & Order of Foresters of America, emblems of both orders in color around the sides below the name in gold & trimmed w/gold leafy branches, large clusters of roses on each side, 3 7/8" h. (ILLUS.) **$258**

Unusual Figural Owl Head Shaving Mug

Character mug, figural, modeled as a detailed owl head w/colorful decoration & applied amber glass eyes, w/the original figural owl shaving brush, eyes may be replaced, 4" h. (ILLUS.) **$392**

B

Shaving Mug with Sportsman Scene

Sportsman scene, a large color scene of a hunter aiming his rifle, his dog below, name in gold at top, 3 5/8" h. (ILLUS.) **$123**

Occupational

Mug with Detailed Scene of a Baker

Baker, large detailed scene of a baker placing loaves of bread in an oven, name in gold above, 3 5/8" h. (ILLUS.) **$364**

Rare Baseball Player Shaving Mug

Baseball player, color scene of a batter & catcher at home plate, name in gold below, 4" h. (ILLUS.) **$2,016**

Unusual Bicycle Racer's Shaving Mug

Bicycle racer, color scene of a man riding a bicycle, name in gold above, flower sprigs at the sides, French-made blank, 3 7/8" h. (ILLUS.) **$952**

Shaving Mug with Blacksmithing Scene

Blacksmith, color scene of two blacksmiths working at an anvil, name in gold above, colorful flower sprigs at the sides, base marked "T & V Limoges France," 4" h. (ILLUS.) **$504**

Butcher's Shaving Mug with Detailed Scene

Butcher, decorated w/a large color scene of a butcher standing & chopping cuts of meat, name in gold above, 3 1/2" h. (ILLUS.) **$672**

Milk Wagon Driver Shaving Mug

Milk wagon driver, color scene of a black-topped wagon drawn by a brown horse, name in gold above, stamped on base w/mark of the blank maker, 3 7/8" h. (ILLUS.) **$532**

Railroad Engineer Shaving Mug

Railroad engineer, decorated in color w/a large steam locomotive, name in gold above, French-made blank, 3 5/8" h. (ILLUS.) **$336**

Railroadman's Mug with Red Caboose

Railroadman, decorated w/a large red caboose below the name in gold, colorful floral sprigs at the sides, base marked "T & V Limoges France - SCH," 3 5/8" h. (ILLUS.) **$420**

Undertaker's Mug with Detailed Scene

Undertaker, color scene of an undertaker driving a horse-drawn hearse, name worn off above, worn word "Undertaker" at bottom in gold, French-made blank, 3 5/8" h. (ILLUS.) **$1,120**

Watchmaker's Occupational Mug

Watchmaker, decorated w/a large gold pocket watch flanked by leafy scrolls, name of owner replaces numbers on dial, 3 5/8" h. (ILLUS.) **$360**

Patriotic

"The Union forever" Patriotic Mug

"The Union forever," slogan printed in gold on a white middle band flanked by a red & blue band, possibly made for a Civil War veteran, 3 1/4" h. (ILLUS.) **$115**

General Items

Nice Antique Shaving Mug Rack

Mug rack, upright rectangular wood construction w/20 open compartments for mugs, a hinged glazed door (missing glass) at the bottom center, original brown stain & hardware, late 19th - early 20th c., 39 1/2" w., 26 1/2" h. (ILLUS.)....... **$224**

Vintage Porcelain Barber Shop Sign

Shop sign, porcelain, long half-round design w/alternating chevron-shaped red, white & blue bars, printed in red at the top "Look Better" & at the base "Feel Better," a chip & a few tiny nicks, 1930s-40s, 8" w., 48" h. (ILLUS.).................................. **$275**

Towel steamer, copper, wide cylindrical design w/a flat hinged top opening to a metal screen, ring loop rim handles, a brass spigot w/a wooden handle at the front base, late 19th - early 20th c., 11" d., 13 1/2" h. (ILLUS., top next column) **$308**

Unusual Early Copper Towel Steamer

BASEBALL MEMORABILIA

Baseball was reputedly invented by Abner Doubleday as he laid out a diamond-shaped field with four bases at Cooperstown, New York. A popular game from its inception, by 1869 it was able to support its first all-professional team, the Cincinnati Red Stockings. The National League was organized in 1876, and though the American League was first formed in 1900, it was not officially recognized until 1903. Today, the "national pastime" has millions of fans, and collecting baseball memorabilia has become a major hobby with enthusiastic collectors seeking out items associated with players such as Babe Ruth, Lou Gehrig, and others who became legends in their own lifetimes. Although baseball cards, issued as advertising premiums for bubble gum and other products, seem to dominate the field, there are numerous other items available.

B

1950 Jackie Robinson Mock-up Calendar

Calendar, 1950 mock-up design w/a large color picture of Jackie Robinson at the top above the date pads, probably a salesman's sample, near mint, 7 x 14" (ILLUS.)...................................... **$144**

Rare "Ruth's Home Run" Candy Wrapper

Candy bar wrapper, "Ruth's Home Run," printed in red, white & blue w/photo of Ruth in an oval, early 1920s, short-lived brand, excellent condition, 6 x 7 1/2" (ILLUS.) **$1,624**

Jackie Robinson Metal Charm

Charm, cast metal bust portrait of Jackie Robinson w/his facsimile signature along

the bottom edge, on a small chain, late 1940s, near mint (ILLUS.)......................... **$127**

Early "Cleveland Indians" Cigarette Case

Cigarette case, "Cleveland Indians," light gauge steel in red w/printed team logo & name in white, 1930s, near mint (ILLUS.) **$86**

Dodgers Baseball Comic Book

Comic book, "The All-Star Story of the Dodgers," color portraits of various star players, Stadium Comics, 1979 (ILLUS.) **$20-50**

Hartland Stan Musial Figure Box

Figure of Stan Musial, plastic, Hartland, in original color-printed cardboard box w/"Major League Baseball Stars," figure near mint, box w/wear & some damage, 1950s (ILLUS.)... **$438**

B

1937 Chicago World Series Program

Program, 1937 Chicago Cubs World Series, Game 4, Art Deco cover graphics in black, yellow, red & white, scored, couple of cover creases (ILLUS.) **$382**

BASKETS

The American Indians were the first basket weavers on this continent and, of necessity, the early Colonial settlers and their descendants pursued this artistic handicraft to provide essential containers for berries, eggs and endless other items to be carried or stored. Rye straw, split willow and reeds are but a few of the wide variety of materials used. Nantucket baskets, plainly and sturdily constructed, along with those made by specialized groups, would seem to draw the greatest attention to this area of collecting.

Fine 60-Rib Buttocks Basket

"Buttocks" basket, woven splint, 60-rib construction, wide wrapped rim, bentwood handle, 12 1/4" l., 5" h. plus handle (ILLUS.) **$891**

Large Deep Buttocks Basket

"Buttocks" basket, woven splint, 32-rib construction, wide wrapped rim, bentwood handle, copper ribets w/embossed stars, 16 1/2" l., 8 3/4" h. plus handle (ILLUS.) **$460**

Rare Punched Leather Key Basket

Key basket, polychrome-decorated leather, oval, an arched center handle terminating in punched hearts, bands of punched leaf bands & geometric designs around the sides, Richmond, Virginia area, 19th c., 6 1/4 x 7 1/2", 6 3/4" h. (ILLUS.).................................. **$12,000**

Early Nantucket Basket

Nantucket basket, woven splint, round w/wrapped rim & carved swing handle secured w/brass tacks, probably late 19th - early 20th c., losses to rim lashing, 8 7/8" d., 8 1/4" h. (ILLUS.) **$1,528**

Very Rare Decorated American 19th Century Basket

Woven & Decorated Eastern Indian Basket

Storage, cov., woven splint, deep round shape w/square bottom & fitted cover, decorated w/salmon, blue & yellow painted horizontal splints, the cover decorated w/salmon-colored lobed flowers outlined in black dots Eastern Woodland Indian, 19th c., minor breaks & losses, 20" d., 14 1/2" h. (ILLUS.) **$823**

Utility, woven splint, deep rectangular sides w/arched intersecting overhead bentwood handles, finished w/alternating splint ribes over the rim, narrowed to a point & tucked into a weaver, the exterior ribs painted creamy white w/black & iron-red painted bands, handles painted black, 19th c., 9 3/4 x 11 1/4", 9 1/2" h. (ILLUS., top of page)............................. **$6,463**

BIG LITTLE BOOKS

The original "Big Little Books" and "Better Little Books" small format series were started in the mid-1930s by Whitman Publishing Co., Racine, Wisconsin, and covered a variety of subjects from adventure stories to tales based on comic strip characters and movie and radio stars. The publisher originally assigned each book a serial number. Most prices are now in the $30 to $60 range, with scarce examples bringing more.

Buck Rogers 25th Century A.D.

Buck Rogers, 25th Century A.D., No. 742, 1933, cover & binding wear (ILLUS.) **$100-150**

B

Flash Gordon - Fiery Desert of Mongo

Flash Gordon, Fiery Desert of Mongo, No.
1447, 1948, cover & binding damage &
wear (ILLUS.) **$55**

Men of the Mounted Big Little Book

Houdini's Magic Big Little Book

Houdini's Magic - Easy for Everyone,
give-away, 1927, damaged binding,
4 1/2 x 5 1/4" (ILLUS.)............................. **$40-50**
**Men of the Mounted - Adventures of the
Canadian Royal Mounted,** 1934 Coco-
malt giveaway, good condition (ILLUS.,
top next column).. **$65**

Moon Mullins & The Plushbottom Twins

**Moon Mullins and The Plushbottom
Twins,** No. 1134, 1935, very good condi-
tion (ILLUS.)... **$60**
Tom Mix, Terror Trail, No. 762, 1934, The
Big Little Book series (binding damaged
& taped) **$30-40**

BIRDCAGES

Brass Birdcage on Tall Stand

Brass, domed footed wire cage suspended in a large brass ring supported on a tall decorative brass & iron stand w/a pierced rectangular base, overall 66" h. (ILLUS.) ... **$259**

Rare Large Early American Birdcage

Wood & wire, architectural design w/a rectangular wooden base & tall wire sides divided into three compartments w/the large center one flanked by smaller ones, each section topped by a wire domed fitted w/a turned wood finial, fitted w/hanging perch drops, original finish, American walnut & mahogany, ca. 1800-1810, 16 x 36", 43" h. (ILLUS.) **$2,875**

BLACK AMERICANA

Over the past decade or so, this field of collecting has rapidly grown. Today almost anything that relates to Black culture or illustrates Black Americana is considered a

desirable collectible. Although many representations of African-Americans, especially on 19th- and early-20th-century advertising pieces and housewares, were cruel stereotypes, even these are collected as poignant reminders of how far American society has come since the dawning of the Civil Rights movement, and how far we still have to go. Other pieces related to this category will be found from time to time in such categories as Advertising Items, Banks, Character Collectibles, Kitchenwares, Signs and Signboards, Toys and several others. For a complete overview of this subject see Antique Trader Black Americana Price Guide, 2nd Edition.

B

Rare Early Sambo Cap Gun

Cap gun, "Sambo," cast-iron, floral-embossed gun w/two black men on top, when trigger pulled one flips head over heels ganging into the other man's head to explode cap, 95% original japanning, main spring broken, early 20th c., 6" l. (ILLUS.)... **$3,163**

Rare Mechanized Store Display Figure

Countertop store display figure, clockwork mechanism, a standing caricature

B

Colorful Minstrel Show Poster with Dancers

of a black soldier w/an oversized head, large smile w/a cigarette (missing) protruding from his mouth, side-glancing eyes, holding his rifle in front of him, torn cloth military hat & soiled cloth uniform, on a rectangular black base, mechanism in head activates his eyes, missing finger on one hand, used as a trade stimulator, ca. 1920s, 22" h. (ILLUS.).... **$2,990**

Minstrel show poster, "Arthur Hockwald Presents - Struttin' Sam - 50 People," colorful lithographed rectangular design w/three vignettes of black dancing, one scene w/a country dance, the other two w/elegantly dressed dancers, professional restoration along creases & tears, early 20th c., 28 1/2 x 41 1/2" (ILLUS., top of page)... **$1,265**

Early Advertising Match Holder

Match holder, advertising-type, die-cut cardboard, the top w/the cut-out figure of a grinning black man wearing an old red coat & torn white & blue-striped pants, a white panel below w/red advertising for Green's August Flower German Syrup, a cardboard match pocket at the bottom center, late 19th c., 4 1/2" w., 8" h. (ILLUS.)............................ **$230**

Hilson's Minstrels Poster

Minstrel show poster, "Hilson's Famous Minstrels," colorful lithograph, rectangular design w/large bust portrait of a minstrel in black face, early 20th c., 19 x 27" (ILLUS.)... **$115**

Sign, "Cooks Beer," colorful lithographed scene at a Southern plantation w/a black butler racing past a black cook & carrying a tray of beer to serve to his boss on the front porch, small red & white logo in lower left corner, framed, some light surface pitting, original brass chain hanger, ca. 1930s, 13 x 21" (ILLUS., top next page) **$288**

B

Cooks Beer Sign with Black Butler & Cook

Paul Jones Whiskey Sign with Black Stereotypes

Scarce Early Gunthermann Black Woman

Sign, "Paul Jones & Co. Whiskey," colorful self-framed lithographed tin scene in a roadway w/a black Mammy standing on the left holding a slice or watermelon & an elderly black gentleman standing on the right holding a bottle of whiskey, a kneeling young man in the center, titled "The Temptation of St. Anthony," scalloped rectangular frame w/advertising in narrow white bands at the top & bottom borders, touch-up on border w/lettering probably redone, early 20th c., 13 1/2 x 19 1/2" (ILLUS.) **$575**

Toy, clockwork mechanism, painted metal figure of a black woman wearing a bonnet, missing a parasol, Gunthermann, Germany, overall paint loss, late 19th - early 20th c., 7 1/4" h. (ILLUS., top next column) **$633**

Toy, crank-type, "The Five Jolly Darkies Way down in Old Virginie" & "The Old Plantation," color-lithographed paper on wood, rectangular box-form w/side crank handle, turning crank makes color-printed figures of blacks dance, two black musicians outside a cabin at the bottom front, by Reed Co., Massachusetts, late 19th - early 20th c., 6 1/2" w., 9" h. (ILLUS., bottom next column) **$403**

Scarce Early Five Jolly Darkies Toy

Rare Marx Spic and Span Windup Tin Toy

Strauss Windup Tin Rollo-Chair Toy

Toy, windup tin, "Rollo-Chair - Riding On The Boardwalk," open-fronted wheeled chair pushed by a uniformed black man, Ferdinand Strauss, ca. 1920s-30s, some paint flaking, 7 3/4" l., 5 1/2" h. (ILLUS.) **$1,035**

Toy, windup tin "Spic and Span - The Hams What Am," two black men in colorful outfits, one seated on a drum & playing a drum, the other standing & dancing, on a rectangular platform base w/colorful graphis, w/original colorful box, Louis Marx, ca. 1930s, Span missing violin, Spic w/replaced drum sticks, 10" h. (ILLUS., top of page) **$2,640**

BOTTLES
Bitters

(Numbers with some listings below refer to those used in Carlyn Ring's For Bitters Only.*)*

Balsdons Golden Bitters Bottle

Balsdons - Golden Bitters - 1856 N.Y., triangular w/applied mouth & smooth base, yellowish amber, short horizontal hairlines at one corner, ca. 1860-70, 9 7/8" h. (ILLUS.) **$1,232**

B

Labeled Big Bill Best Bitters Bottle

Big Bill Best Bitters, tapering square w/paneled sides, tooled lip, smooth base, 99% original colorful paper labels, original contents, amber, ca. 1900-1910, 12 1/8" h. (ILLUS.) **$616**

Medium Amber Brown's Indian Bitters

Brown's Celebrated Indian Herb Bitters - Patented 1867, figural Indian Queen, rolled lip, smooth base, medium amber, tiny potstone in cheek w/cooling crack, tiny flake on base, 12 1/4" h. (ILLUS.) **$560**

Boerhaves Holland Bitters Bottle

Boerhaves Holland Bitters - B. Page Jr & Co - Pittsburgh, PA, rectangular w/paneled sides, tall neck w/applied double collar mouth, smooth base, bluish aqua, 7 7/8" h. (ILLUS.) **$179**

Dr. Caldwell's Great Tonic Herb Bitters

Caldwell's (Dr.) - [between] The Great Tonic - Herb Bitters, triangular w/tall slender tapering neck w/applied sloping double collar mouth, smooth base, yellowish amber, ca. 1860-70, 12 1/8" h. (ILLUS.)... **$336**

B

Purple Drake's 1860 Plantation Bitters

Drake's (S T) - 1860 - Plantation - X - Bitters - Patented - 1862, cabin-shaped, six-log, applied mouth, smooth base, dark purple amethyst, tiny open bubble on lip, 10" h. D-105 (ILLUS.) **$960**

Yellowish Amber Drake's Bitters

Drake's (S T) - 1860 - Plantation - X - Bitters - Patented - 1862, cabin-shaped, four-log, applied sloping collar mouth, ca. 1862-70, yellowish amber, 10" h., D-110 (ILLUS.).. **$448**

Drake's 1860 Plantation Bitters in Puce

Drake's (S T) - 1860 - Plantation - X - Bitters - Patented - 1862, cabin-shaped, six-log, applied mouth, smooth base, copper puce, 10" h. D-105 (ILLUS.)........... **$258**

Figural Fish Bitters Bottle

Fish (The) Bitters - W.H. Ware - Patented 1866, figural fish, smooth base, applied mouth, ca. 1866-75, amber, shallow chip on lip from shearing, 11 1/4" h. (ILLUS.).... **$202**

B

Labeled Herb Wild Cherry Bitters Bottle

Herb (H.P.) Wild Cherry Bitters, Reading, Pa., cabin-shaped, square w/cherry tree motif & roped corners, tooled mouth, smooth base, 85% paper label reading "H.P. Herb Wild Cherry Bark Bitters," medium amber, 10" h. (ILLUS.) **$784**

Labeled Herkules Bitter Bottle

Herkules Bitter - AC (monogram) - 1 Quart, ball-shaped, tooled mouth w/ring, smooth base, two flattened side panels, 97% original paper body & shoulder labels, deep emerald green, 1890-1900, 7 1/2" h. (ILLUS.) **$2,016**

Smaller Herb Wild Cherry Bitters Bottle

Herb (H.P.) Wild Cherry Bitters, Reading, Pa., cabin-shaped, square w/cherry tree motif & roped corners, tooled mouth, smooth base, amber, 9" h. (ILLUS.).......... **$784**

Labeled King Solomon's Bitters Bottle

King Solomon's Bitters - Seattle Wash. (down sides), rectangular w/tooled mouth w/part of original neck foil, smooth base, 90% original colorful paper front label & 70% rear label, amber, ca. 1890-1900, 8 3/8" h. (ILLUS.) **$504**

B

Aqua Moffat Phoenix Bitters Bottle

Moffat (Jno.) - Phoenix Bitters - New York - Price 1$, rectangular w/wide beveled corners, applied mouth, open pontil, aqua, ca. 1840-60, 5 1/2" h. (ILLUS.) **$134**

Morning (Star) Bitters in Rare Color

Morning (design of star) Bitters - Inceptum 5869 - Patented - 5869, triangular slender form w/slanted ridges on neck, applied sloping mouth, red iron pontil, ca. 1869-75, chocolate amber, 11 7/8" h. (ILLUS.) **$476**

Rare Moffat Phoenix Bitters Bottle

Moffat (Jno.) - Phoenix Bitters - New York - Price 1$, rectangular w/wide beveled corners, outward rolled lip, open pontil, medium to deep amber, nicely whittled, ca. 1840-60, 5 1/2" h. (ILLUS.)
.... **$2,800**

Old Homestead Wild Cherry Bitters

Old - Homestead - Wild Cherry - Bitters - Patent, cabin-shaped, scalloped shingles on four-sided roof, applied sloping collar mouth, amber, ca. 1865-75, 9 3/4" h. (ILLUS.) **$392**

B

Amber Sazerac Bitters with Contents

Sazerac Armotic Bitters (on base) - monogram in ring on shoulder, cylindrical w/tall lady's leg neck & applied rim ring, smooth base, original cork in mouth, most of original contents, ca. 1870s, yellowish amber, 10 1/4" h. (ILLUS.) **$728**

H.H. Warner Tippecanoe Bitters Bottle

Tippecanoe (birch bark & canoe design), H.H. Warner & Co., cylindrical, "Patent Nov. 20. 83 - Rochester - N.Y." on smooth base, applied disc mouth, ca. 1880-95, yellowish amber, 9" h. (ILLUS.) .. **$168**

Sharp's Mountain Herb Bitters Bottle

Sharp's Mountain Herb Bitters, square w/paneled sides, applied sloping collar mouth, smooth base, ca. 1870-80, medium amber, 9 3/4" h. (ILLUS.) **$420**

Rare Dr. Wise's Olive Bitters Bottle

Wise's (Dr.) Olive Bitters Cincinnati, O., footed waisted cylindrical w/tapering neck & tooled lip, smooth base, ca. 1890-1910, clear w/strong amethystine tint, 10 1/2" h. (ILLUS.) **$2,240**

B

Figurals

Atlas & Globe Figural Bottle

Atlas holding globe, clear globe rotates between upraised arms of kneeling metal Atlas, ground lip, original metal screw cap, probably American, ca. 1890-1915, 4 1/8" h. (ILLUS.) **$190**

Boy on Chamber Pot Figural Bottle

Boy sitting on chamber pot, clear, molded on front of plinth base "Tommy Dodd," tooled mouth, smooth base marked "C.F. Knapp Phila.," ca. 1890-1910, 4 5/8" h. (ILLUS.).. **$190**

James Garfield Bust Figural Bottle

Bust of James Garfield, clear glass, ground lip, original wooden base w/original gold paint, 95% original label for "The Garfield Cologne," ca. 1880-84, 7 1/4" h. (ILLUS.).. **$364**

Figural Cat Head Bottle

Cat head, clear, tooled mouth, smooth base, fine detail, ca. 1890-1910, 3 3/8" h. (ILLUS.).. **$157**

Egyptian Pharoah Figural Bottle

Egyptian Pharaoh, clear, rolled lip, pontil-scarred base, embossed "281 MA" on back of base, tiny chip off top edge of lip, probably French, ca. 1880-1910, 6 1/8" h. (ILLUS.) **$157**

Early Figural Ham Bottle

Ham, amber, ground lip, original screw-on cap, ca. 1890-1910, 6" h. (ILLUS.).............. **$78**

Figural Globe Bottle with Original Box

Globe on metal stand, clear rotating globe on original stand w/original cap marked "Our Country," small label on side reads "Pat. Applied For," ground mouth, w/original box showing globe & labeled "The Earth - Filled with Choice Perfume - Wm. H. Brown & Co. - Perfumers - Baltimore, MD ...U.S.A.," ca. 1885-1910, 4 1/4" h. (ILLUS.).. **$258**

French Joan of Arc Figural Bottle

Joan of Arc, standing woman wearing armor, embossed "Jeanne d'Arc - Bon Bons - John Tavernier," milk glass w/original brown paint, glass stopper head w/original black, red & cream colored paint, original label reads "Quartiers de Citron," "Deposé" on smooth base, France, late 19th - early 20th c., 13 3/4" h. (ILLUS.) **$364**

B

Figural Spaniard Bottle

Spaniard, bluish aqua w/75% original gold
paint, standing figure of a man in costume, tooled mouth, smooth base, some
light interior stain, ca. 1890-1915, 9" h.
(ILLUS.)... **$96**

Torso of Woman Figural Bottle

Torso of woman, clear, ground lip, smooth
base, original metal screw-on cap, 85%
original faded paper label reading "Santa

Clara Cologne," ca. 1890-1910, 6 1/2" h.
(ILLUS.)... **$96**

Rare Yellow Kid Figural Bottle

Yellow Kid, milk glass body & original clear
frosted glass head, back embossed "Say -
Ain't I Hot Stuff," early comic strip
character, ca. 1895-98, 5 1/4" h. (ILLUS.)... **$1,120**

Flasks

*Flasks are listed according to the num-
bers provided in* American Bottles & Flasks
and Their Ancestry *by Helen McKearin and
Kenneth M. Wilson.*

Washington - American Eagle Flask

GI-2 - Washington bust below "General Washington" - American Eagle w/shield w/seven bars on breast, head turned to right, edges w/horizontal beading w/vertical medial rib, sheared lip, open pontil, greenish aqua, pt. (ILLUS., previous page) **$784**

GI-16 - Washington bust below "General Washington" - American eagle w/shield w/seven bars on breast, head turned to right, vertically ribbed edges, sheared mouth, pontil scar, aqua, pt. (ILLUS.) **$258**

GI-11 Washington - Eagle Flask

GI-11 - Washington bust below branches - American eagle w/head turned right & body curving, sunrays above eagle's head & 13 small stars, horizontal beading w/vertical medial rib, deep bluish aqua, shallow chip on top edge of lip, pt. (ILLUS.) **$616**

Scarce Washington - Taylor Clear Flask

GI-17 - Washington bust facing left w/long queue below "Washington" - Taylor bust facing left below "Baltimore Glass Works," sheared & tooled lip, open pontil, vertically ribbed sides, clear w/light pinkish amethyst tone, ca. 1835, light overall inside stain, pt. (ILLUS.)........................... **$1,344**

GI-16 Washington Bust & Eagle Flask

Washington - Baltimore Monument Flask

GI-20 - Washington bust facing left w/"Fells" above & "Point" below - Monument without statue above "Balto.," sheared & tooled lip, open pontil, vertical medial rib, clear w/light to medium pink amethyst, pt. (ILLUS., previous page) **$840**

full-rigged ship sailing to right, applied sloping collared mouth, pontil scar, vertically ribbed edges, pebbly, golden yellowish amber, pt. (ILLUS.) **$5,320**

Rare Washington - American Eagle Flask

GI-26 - Washington bust - American Eagle w/shield w/eight vertical & two horizontal bars on breast, head turned to right, sheared mouth, open pontil, clear w/light amethystine tint, qt. (ILLUS.).................. **$1,344**

Very Rare Washington - Ship Flask

GI-28 - Washington bust below "Albany Glass Works," "Albany NY" below bust - full-rigged ship sailing to right, applied sloping collared mouth, pontil scar, vertically ribbed edges, medium sapphire blue, pt. (ILLUS.).................................. **$12,320**

Rare Washington Bust - Ship Flask

GI-28 - Washington bust below "Albany Glass Works," "Albany NY" below bust -

Olive Amber Washington - Jackson Flask

GI-34 - "Washington" above bust - "Jackson" above bust, sheared lip, open pontil, vertically ribbed edges w/heavy medial rib, yellowish olive amber, small chip on medial rib at base, 1/2 pt. ILLUS.) **$235**

B

Olive Amber Lafayette - Clinton Flask

GI-80 - "Lafayette" above bust & "T. S." & bar below - "De Witt Clinton" above bust & "Coventry C-T" below, corrugated edges, tooled mouth, pontil, yellowish olive amber, bubbly, pt. (ILLUS.) **$1,232**

Very Rare "Jeny" Lind Calabash Flask

GI-104 - "Jeny. Lind" (sic) above bust - view of glasshouse, calabash, vertically ribbed edges, rounded collar, pontil scar, deep teal blue, milky interior stain, qt. (ILLUS.) **$6,160**

Scarce Clear Franklin - Dyott Flask

GI-94 - Franklin bust below "Benjamin Franklin - Where Liberty Dwells There Is My Country" - Dyott bust below "T.W. Dyott, M.D. - Kensington Glass Works Philadelphia," ribbed edges, sheared lip, pontil, clear w/greyish tint, pt. (ILLUS.) **$1,456**

Byron - Scott Olive Amber Flask

GI-114 - Classical draped bust of Byron facing left - Classical draped bust of Scott facing right, vertically ribbed edges, sheared & tooled lip, open pontil, yellowish olive amber, crude & bubbly, 1/2 pt. (ILLUS.)... **$392**

B

Aqua Columbia - Eagle Flask

GI-117 - Bust of Columbia with Liberty cap w/"Kensington" inscribed below - American eagle w/"Union Co." inscribed below, single broad vertical rib, sheared & tooled lip, pontil, lip slightly polished, aqua (ILLUS.) **$476**

Rare Clear Eagle - Cornucopia Flask

GII-11 - American eagle facing left w/eleven stars above, standing on oval frame w/inner band of eighteen pearls - Cornucopia with Produce, horizontally beaded edges w/vertical medial rib, inward rolled lip, open pontil, clear, 1/2 pt. (ILLUS.) **$2,016**

Green Eagle - Sheaf & Implements Flask

GII-10 - American eagle w/"W. Ihmsen's" above & "Glass" below in oval frame - Sheaf of Rye w/"Agriculture" above & farm implements below, vertically ribbed edges, sheared lip, open pontil, pale green, shallow chip on lip, light outside stain, pt. (ILLUS.) **$952**

Very Rare Sapphire Blue Eagle Flask

GII-24 - American eagle facing left w/ribbon above head w/random ribbing, two arched rows of four-point stars at top, arrows & olive branch in talons above bottom oval frame enclosing an elongated eight-point star - large conventionalized floral medallion above an oval frame enclosing an elongated eight-point star, horizontally corrugated edges, sheared mouth, pontil scar, sapphire blue, shallow small chip on lip, pt. (ILLUS.)............ **$3,080**

Eagle - Cornucopia Yellow Olive Flask

GII-73 - American eagle w/head turned right
& standing on rocks - Cornucopia w/pro-
duce & X to the left, vertically ribbed edges, sheared neck, open pontil, medium
yellowish olive, pt. (ILLUS.)........................ **$134**

Scarce Eagle - Eagle Blue Flask

GII-91 - American eagle facing left above
large oval frame obverse & reverse, applied rim band, smooth base, medium cobalt blue, several shallow chips on edge
of lip, qt. (ILLUS.) **$784**

Double American Eagle Stoddard Flask

GII-82 - American eagle above oval with no
inscription - reverse the same except
oval w/inscription in small letters "Stoddard - NH," faint periods after the "N" &
"H," narrow vertical edge rib, sheared
mouth, pontil scar, yellowish amber, pt.
(ILLUS.).. **$202**

Rare Double American Eagle Blue Flask

GII-93 - American eagle in smaller size
w/shield below banner & above oval obverse & reverse, smooth edges, applied
ringed mouth, red iron pontil, medium cobalt blue, some interior stain, pt. (ILLUS.)
.... **$4,200**

B

Bluish Green Cornucopia - Urn Flask

GIII-4 - Cornucopia w/produce - Urn w/produce, vertically ribbed edges, pontil scarred base, sheared & tooled lip, medium bluish green, pt. (ILLUS.) **$728**

Masonic Arch - Eagle Bluish Green Flask

GIV-1 - Masonic emblems - American eagle w/ribbon reading "E Pluribus Unum" above & "I-P" (old-fashioned J) below in oval frame, sheared & tooled lip, open pontil, medium bluish green, pt. (ILLUS.)... **$672**

Variation of Cornucopia - Urn Flask

GIII-18 - Cornucopia w/Produce & curled to right - urn with Produce, vertically ribbed edges, sheared & tooled mouth, pontil, medium bluish green, pt. (ILLUS.) **$784**

Clear Variation of Masonic Arch - Eagle Flask

GIV-11 - Masonic emblems - American eagle w/ribbon reading "E Pluribus Unum" above oval panel enclosing an eight-point star, vertically ribbed sides, sheared & tooled lip, pontil scar, very crude & pebbly, clear, pt. (ILLUS.).......... **$1,568**

B

Scarce Masonic Arch - Eagle Green Flask

GIV-4 - Masonic emblems - American eagle w/ribbon reading "E Pluribus Unum" above oval panel enclosing "J.K.B.," vertically ribbed sides, sheared & tooled lip, pontil scar, some minor inside stain, brilliant yellowish green, pt. (ILLUS.) **$2,688**

Olive Amber Masonic Arch - Eagle Flask

GIV-17 - Masonic Arch, pillars & pavement w/Masonic emblems - American eagle w/oval frame enclosing "Keene" below, edges smooth w/single vertical rib, sheared & tooled lip, pontil scar, olive amber, pt. (ILLUS.) **$392**

Clear Green Masonic Arch - Eagle Flask

GIV-14 - Masonic Arch, pillars & pavement w/Masonic emblems inside the arch - American eagle above oval frame w/elongated eight-pointed star, plain rim, vertically ribbed sides, pontil scarred base, sheared & tooled lip, small flake on one side of medial rib, bold impression, clear green, 1/2 pt. (ILLUS.) **$784**

Forest Green Masonic Arch - Eagle Flask

GIV-24 - Masonic Arch, pillars & pavement w/Masonic emblems - American eagle grasping large balls in talons & without shield on breast, plain oval frame below, smooth edges w/single medial rib, sheared & tooled lip, pontil, forest green, bubble on arch side near base w/short crack, 1/2 pt. (ILLUS.) **$560**

B

Aqua Masonic Arch - Sailing Frigate Flask

GIV-34 - Masonic Arch w/"Farmer's Arms" &
   sheaf of rye & farm implements within arch
   & "Kensington Glass Works Philadelphia"
   around edge - Sailing frigate above "Franklin" w/"Free Trade and Sailors Rights"
   around the edge, sheared & tooled mouth,
   pontil scar, aqua, pt. (ILLUS.) **$448**

Greenish Aqua Masonic Arch - Ship Flask

GIV-36 - Masonic arch w/"Farmer's Arms" &
   sheaf of rye & farm implements missing
   the sickle within arch - Sailing frigate

above "Franklin," sheared & tooled lip,
open pontil, greenish aqua, pinhead flake
on lip, pt. (ILLUS.) **$960**

Chartreuse Success to Railroad Flask

GV-5 - "Success to the Railroad" around
   embossed horse pulling cart - similar reverse, vertically ribbed edges, sheared &
   tooled lip, pontil scar, chartreuse green,
   crude & bubbly, pt. (ILLUS.)........................ **$560**

Horse & Cart - Eagle Crude Flask

GV-9 - Horse pulling loaded cart & no inscription - Large American Eagle with

shield lengthwise, no stars, sheared & tooled lip, pontil scar, olive green, crude & bubbly, pt. (ILLUS.) **$224**

Baltimore Monument - Corn Aqua Flask

GVI-4 - "Baltimore" below monument - "Corn For The World" in semicircle above ear of corn, smooth edges, applied mouth, smooth base, aqua, qt. (ILLUS.) **$213**

Yellow Amber Baltimore - Corn Flask

GVI-4 - "Baltimore" below monument - "Corn For The World" in semicircle above ear of corn, smooth edges, applied lip band, smooth base, golden yellow amber, qt. (ILLUS.) **$2,016**

Clear Green GVIII-1 Sunburst Flask

GVIII-1 - Sunburst w/twenty-four triangular sectioned rays w/two concentric rings in the center obverse & reverse, sheared lip, pontil scar, clear green, pt. (ILLUS.) **$1,344**

Sunburst Variation Flask in Clear Green

GVIII-2 - Sunburst w/twenty-four triangular sectioned rays obverse & reverse, sheared mouth, pontil scar, clear green, pt. (ILLUS.) **$960**

B

Clear Sunburst Flask GVIII-26

GVIII-26 - Sunburst w/sixteen rays obverse & reverse, ray converging to a definite point at center & covering entire side of flask, horizontally corrugated edges, inward rolled lip, open pontil, clear, pt. (ILLUS.).................................... **$960**

Scarce Yellowish Amber Scroll Flask

GIX-1 - Scroll w/two six-point stars obverse & reverse, long neck w/sheared lip, open pontil, deep yellowish amber, shallow small chip on edge of lip, some light inside stain, qt. (ILLUS.) **$1,344**

Teal Blue Sunburst Flask GVIII-29

GVIII-29 - Sunburst in small sunken oval w/twelve rays obverse & reverse, panel w/band of tiny ornaments around inner edge, sides around panels w/narrow spaced vertical ribbing, sheared & tooled lip, pontil scar, deep teal blue, 3/4 pt. (ILLUS.) **$672**

Teal Green Scroll Flask GIX-2

GIX-2 - Scroll w/large inverted heart-shaped frame formed by medial & inferior scrolls & containing a large six-point star w/a similar star above frame, sheared & tooled lip, open pontil, medium teal bluish green, tiny potstone in neck, qt. (ILLUS.) **$1,064**

B

Scroll Flask in Unusual Color

GIX-2 - Scroll w/large inverted heart-shaped frame formed by medial & inferior scrolls & containing a large six-point star w/a similar star above frame, sheared & tooled lip, open pontil, moonstone w/pink tint, some faint interior stain, qt. (ILLUS.) **$1,456**

Rare Cobalt Blue Scroll Flask GIX-11

GIX-11 - Scroll w/six-point stars, a small one in upper space & medium sized one in lower space obverse & reverse, vertical medial rib, sheared & tooled lip, pontil scar, cobalt blue, pt. (ILLUS.) **$2,690**

Rare Cobalt Blue Scroll Flask Variation

GIX-2c - Scroll w/large inverted heart-shaped frame formed by medial & inferior scrolls & containing a small six-point star w/a similar star above frame, sheared lip, open pontil, medium cobalt blue, qt. (ILLUS.) **$2,800**

Yellowish Green Scroll Flask GIX-20

GIX-20 - Scroll with large oval ornament at top above central eight-point star, a large six-petal flower at bottom center obverse & reverse, sheared & tooled mouth, pontil scar, medium yellowish green, pt. (ILLUS.).................................. **$1,064**

B

Rare Bluish Green Scroll Flask GIX-36

GIX-36 - Scroll w/medium-sized eight-point star above a medium-sized pearl over a large fleur-de-lis obverse & reverse, vertical medial rib on edge, sheared & tooled lip, pontil scar, medium bluish green, 1/2 pt. (ILLUS.)... **$2,460**

Corseted Scroll Flask GIX-44

GIX-44 - Scroll, corset-waist style, large frame formed by ribs, scrolled at top & looped at bottom, parallel inner frame terminating at top in long oval finial & containing a large pearl & large pearl below each curved line at bottom, two large pearls below scrolls at top of frame, long oval ornament within each loop at bottom of frame - scrolled at top & bottom containing large fleur-de-lis w/two large pearls at sides below top scrolls, crescent-shaped ornament connecting scrolls at center bottom, vertical medial rib, sheared lip, pontil scar, bluish aqua, pt. (ILLUS.).. **$728**

Stag & Willow Tree Aqua Flask

GX-1 - Stag standing above "Good Game" - Weeping willow tree, vertically ribbed edges, sheared & tooled lip, pontil scar, aqua, shallow small flake on edge of lip, pt. (ILLUS.)... **$392**

Cannon - Capt. Bragg Greenish Aqua Flask

GX-4 - Cannon framed by "Genl Taylor Never Surrenders" - Grapevine frame around "A Little More Grape Capt Bragg," vertically ribbed sides, sheared & tooled mouth, pontil scar, greenish aqua, tiny flake on tip of medial rib at base, pt. (ILLUS., previous page) **$616**

Variation of Sailboat - Sunburst Flask

GX-9 - Sailboat (sloop) w/pennant (no waves) - Eight-point star (no ornaments), smooth sides, sheared & tooled lip, pontil scar, medium green, shallow flake on edge of lip, 1/2 pt. (ILLUS.) **$960**

Yellowish Green Summer - Winter Flask

GX-15 - "Summer" over tree in circle - "Winter" over tree in circle, applied double collar mouth, smooth base, yellowish green, some light milky inside stain, pt. (ILLUS.) .. **$672**

Scarce Green Summer Tree Flask

GX-17 - Summer tree in oval panel obverse & reverse, sheared lip, pontil scar, medium emerald green, pt. (ILLUS.) **$1,568**

Spring Tree - Summer Tree Green Flask

GX-18 - Spring Tree (leaves & buds) - Summer Tree, smooth edges, applied "top hat" mouth, pontil scar, light bluish green, very pebbly, qt. (ILLUS.) **$420**

B

Scarce Variation of Prospector - Eagle Flask

GXI-30 - "For Pike's Peak" in large letters above tall prospector w/narrow head & wearing peaked cap w/knapsack on shoulder & walking w/a cane above an oval - American eagle w/shield & banner above large oblong panel, applied ringed mouth, smooth base, yellowish olive, two thin chips on lip, qt. (ILLUS.) **$1,792**

Rare Variation of Prospector - Eagle Flask

GXI-32 - "For Pike's Peak" in large letters above tall prospector w/narrow head & wearing peaked cap w/knapsack on shoulder & walking w/a cane above an oval - American eagle w/shield & banner

above large oblong panel, applied ringed mouth, smooth base, yellowish amber, thin flake on lip, 1/2 pt. (ILLUS.) **$3,080**

Scarce Clasped Hands - Waterford Flask

GXII-2 - Shield with Clasped Hands above seven wide bars & a blank oval, below an arch of 13 stars & "Waterford" in small letters, laurels branches flank the shield - American eagle spreadwinged atop a shield & holding a long plain banner in its beak, a large empty oval peaked in the center top & bottom below, applied mouth, smooth base, light bluish green w/heavy striations, tiny flake on edge of base, qt. (ILLUS.) **$2,240**

Rare Union-Clasped Hands - Eagle Flask

GXII-21 - Shield with Clasped Hands above five groups of three vertical bars & a blank oval, below an arch of 13 stars & "Union" in small letters, laurels branches flank the shield - American eagle spread-winged atop a shield & holding a long banner w/"A & Co." in its beak, a large empty oval peaked in the center top & bottom below, applied ringed lip, smooth base, medium sapphire blue, shallow flake on lip, pt. (ILLUS.)............................ **$4,200**

mouth, smooth base, olive amber, 1/2 pt. (ILLUS.).. **$190**

Variation of Sheaf of Grain - Tree Flask

GXIII-47 - Sheaf of Grain (slender) above crossed rake & pitchfork - Tree w/bark & foliage, a bird at the top, calabash, vertically ribbed, applied double collar mouth, open pontil, medium bluish green, qt. (ILLUS.).................................... **$952**

Amber Horseman - Hound Flask

GXIII-16 - Horseman in full-dress uniform on high-stepping steed riding to right, saber held erect - Large hound walking right, applied collar mouth, smooth base, yellowish amber, very faint inside haze qt. (ILLUS.)... **$476**

Westford - Sheaf of Grain Amber Flask

GXIII-37 - Sheaf of Grain on crossed rack & pitchfork - "Westford Glass Co., Westford, Conn.," applied double collar

Green Anchor - Phoenix Flask

GXIII-53 - Anchor w/fork-ended pennants inscribed "Baltimore" & "Glass Works" on obverse - Phoenix rising from flames on rectangular panel inscribed "Resurgam" on reverse, applied mouth, smooth base, yellowish green, faint bruise on lip, pt. (ILLUS.) **$952**

B

Anchor - Log Cabin Amber Flask

GXIII-58 - Anchor w/fork-ended pennants inscribed "Spring Garden" & "Glass Works" - three-quarter view of log cabin, smooth edges, applied double collar mouth, smooth base, orangish amber, heavily whittled, pt. (ILLUS.)................................ **$1,792**

Amber "Patent" Flask with Paper Label

GXV-16 - "Patent" arched below shoulder - plain reverse, applied double collar mouth, smooth base, original paper label reading "Cognac Brandy, George L. Forbush, Pharmacist, Petersboro, New Hampshire," yellowish amber, pt. (ILLUS.) **$115**

Chestnut, 24 vertical ribs, blown in German half-post method, tooled mouth, pontil, medium cobalt blue, 7 1/2" h. (ILLUS., top next column)................................ **$616**

Cobalt Vertical-Ribbed Chestnut Flask

25-Rib Amber Chestnut Flask

Chestnut, 25 vertical ribs, open pontil, tooled lip, tobacco amber, Zanesville, Ohio, early 19th c., 6 3/4" h. (ILLUS.) **$336**

Free-Blown Olive Chestnut Flask

Chestnut, free-blown w/outward rolled lip, open pontil, light yellowish olive, 5 5/8" h. (ILLUS.)... **$784**

Inks

Unusual Lobed Green Teakettle Well

**Teakettle-type fountain inkwell w/neck
extending up at angle from base,** deep
grass green, tapering lobed sides
w/molded bumps around the bottom, flat
top, ground & polished lip, smooth base,
rare form, possibly European, ca. 1875-
95, 1 7/8" h. (ILLUS.) **$960**

Early Greenish Aqua Pitkin Flask

Pitkin, thirty broken ribs swirled to the right,
light greenish aqua, sheared & tooled lip,
open pontil, Pitkin Glassworks,
Connecticut, ca. 1790-1810, 5 3/8" h.
(ILLUS.)... **$952**

Unusual Figural Teakettle Well

**Teakettle-type fountain inkwell w/neck
extending up at angle from base,** figural porcelain, a standing figure of an Oriental man in tan wearing a blue robe beside the hexagonal well h.p. w/cobalt
blue & orange flowers & leaves & blue
trim, gold trim, probably Europe, ca.
1875-1900, 4" h. (ILLUS.) **$616**

Early Olive Green Pitkin Flask

Pitkin, thirty-six broken ribs swirled to the
right, medium yellowish olive green,
sheared & tooled lip, open pontil, Pitkin
Glassworks, Connecticut, ca. 1790-
1810, 5 3/4" h. (ILLUS.) **$1,064**

B

B

Pinkish Amethyst Teakettle Well

Teakettle-type fountain inkwell w/neck extending up at angle from base, medium pinkish amethyst, octagonal tapering ribbed panels, ground lip, smooth base, original brass neck ring, ca. 1875-95, 2" h. (ILLUS.) **$364**

Rare Opaque Blue Teakettle Well

Teakettle-type fountain inkwell w/neck extending up at angle from base, opaque powder blue, pear-shaped lobed form w/a long petal in each lobe, polished lip, smooth base, American, ca. 1875-95, rare, 2 7/8" h. (ILLUS.) **$476**

Porcelain Teakettle Inkwell

Teakettle-type fountain inkwell w/neck extending up at angle from base, porcelain, white w/h.p. floral decoration on the sides, gold trim, two pen rest grooves on top, Europe, ca. 1875-95 (ILLUS.) **$168**
Teakettle-type fountain inkwell w/neck extending up at angle from base, powder blue opaque w/satin finish, ribbed melon-form body, ground lip w/original brass neck band & hinged cap, smooth base, attributed to the Boston & Sandwich Glass Co., ca. 1875-85, 2 3/4" h. (ILLUS., top next column) **$476**

Powder Blue Teakettle-type Inkwell

Master Size Harrison's Columbian Ink

Twelve-sided w/central neck, bluish aqua, master-size, applied mouth, open pontil, molded up the sides "Harrison's Columbian Ink," some inside residue, ca. 1840-60, 7 1/2" h. (ILLUS.) **$213**

Medicines

Allen Concentrated Electric Paste Bottle

Allen (E.C.) Concentrated Electric Paste - or Arabian Pain Extractor - Lancaster, PA, square w/flattened shoulder, inward rolled lip, open pontil, light bluish green, ca. 1840-60, 3" h. (ILLUS., previous page) **$476**

dian Tonic, Infallible Cure for Ague & Fever, G.W. House, Nashville, Tenn.," hand-written name at bottom of label, aqua, 5 3/4" h. (ILLUS. of front & back) **$960**

John Bull Extract of Sarsaparilla Bottle

Bull (John) Extract of Sarsaparilla - Louisville, KY, rectangular w/paneled sides, applied mouth, iron pontil, deep bluish aqua, 9" h. (ILLUS.) **$476**

Scarce Dr. Davis's Depurative Bottle

Davis's (Dr.) - Depurative, square w/beveled corners, applied sloping collar mouth, iron pontil, ca. 1845-55, medium bluish green, 9 7/8" h. (ILLUS.)............... **$2,460**

Front & Back of Clemen's Indian Tonic

Clemen's Indian Tonic - Prepared by Geo. W. House (w/standing Indian), oval w/tall neck w/wide rolled lip, open pontil scar, ca. 1840-60, reverse w/99% original paper label reading "Clemen's In-

Flagg's Good Samaritan's Relief Bottle

Flagg's Good Samaritan's Immediate Relief - Cincinnati, O, slender five-sides w/outward rolled lip, open pontil, ca. 1840-60, 3 3/4" h. (ILLUS.) **$392**

B

Hampton's V. Tincture Amber Bottle

**Hampton's V. Tincture - Mortimer & Mow-
bray Balto.,** round w/rounded shoulder,
applied mouth, open pontil, yellowish
amber w/hint of olive, small chip off side
of lip (ILLUS.) **$448**

Johnson's Pure Herb Tonic Bottle

**Johnson's (W.M.) Pure Herb Tonic Sure
Cure For All Malarial Diseases,** square
w/narrow beveled corners, tooled mouth,
smooth base, deep amber, ca. 1890-
1900, 8 3/4" h. (ILLUS.) **$146**

C.F. Haskell New York Aqua Bottle

**Haskell (C.F.) (below) New York - Coloris
Capilli Restitutor,** oval w/rounded
shoulder, applied mouth, open pontil,
aqua, some outside dullness, ca. 1840-
60, 7 1/2" h. (ILLUS.) **$123**

Keeley's Double Chloride of Gold Bottle

**Keeley's (Dr. L.E.) Double Chloride of
Gold Cure For Drunkenness - A Tested and Infallible Remedy Discovered
by Dr. L.E. Keeley Dwight, Ills. - K.C.C.,**
rectangular w/sloping shoulders, tooled
mouth w/pour spout, smooth base, some
very light interior stains, ca. 1885-1900,
5 1/2" h. (ILLUS.) **$134**

B

Masury's Sarsaparilla Cathartic Bottle

Masury's Sarsaparilla Cathartic, rectangular w/beveled corners & paneled sides, applied double collar mouth, smooth base, bluish aqua, ca. 1855-70, curde & pebbly, 9" h. (ILLUS.) **$224**

McLane's (Doctor) - American Worm Specific, slender cylinder w/rolled lip, pontil, bluish aqua, ca. 1840-60, 3 3/4" h. **$56**

Labeled Dr. Meeker's Casca Rilla Tonic

Meeker's (Dr.) Casca Rilla Tonic (on paper label) octagonal w/applied double collar mouth, pontil scar, olive green, 99% of label reading "Meeker's Casca

Rilla Tonic - Meeker Medicine Co., Established 1854, Chicago, Ill.," ca. 1855-60, 5 7/8" h. (ILLUS.) **$560**

G.W. Merchant Variant Bottle

Merchant (G.W.) - From the Laboratory of - Chemist - Lockport, N.Y., rectangular w/paneled side, applied slopping collared mouth, smooth base, deep emerald green, Lockport Glass Works, Lockport, New York, 1860-75, 5 3/4" h. (ILLUS.) **$308**

G.W. Merchant Lockport Green Bottle

Merchant (G.W.) - Lockport, N.Y., rectangular w/tall neck & applied sloping mouth, pontil scar, deep Lockport green, ca. 1840-60, 5 1/8" h. (ILLUS.) **$308**

Rare Morse's Celebrated Syrup Bottle

Morse's Celebrated Syrup - Prov. R.I., oval w/applied sloping collared mouth, pontil, medium emerald green, two pin-head flakes on base, ca. 1845-60, 9 3/8" h. (ILLUS.) **$2,464**

B

Radium Radia Bottle & Original Box

Radium Radia (on paper label), oval, 100% original labels, box & literature, label reads "Trade Mark - Radium Radia For External Application Only - Radium Radia Co., Los Angeles, Cal. 13 W. 26th St., N. Y. City - Price $1.00," clear, ca. 1895-1905, 5 3/8" h. (ILLUS.) **$125**

Sparks Perfect Health in Deep Amber

Sparks Perfect Health (below Trade Mark) - bust of man - for Kidney & Liver Diseases, Camden, N.J., rectangular w/cabin-type roof shoulder & beveled corners, tooled mouth, smooth base, ca. 1880-95, root beer amber, 9 1/2" h. (ILLUS.) **$392**

Sparks Perfect Health Bottle

Sparks Perfect Health (below Trade Mark) - bust of man - for Kidney & Liver Diseases, Camden, N.J., rectangular w/beveled corners, tooled mouth, smooth base, ca. 1880-95, medium amber, area of outside stain on shoulder, 9 1/2" h. (ILLUS.) **$308**

Ice Blue Vaughn's Mixture Bottle

Vaughn's (Dr. G.C.) - Vegetable Lithontriptic Mixture - Buffalo, square w/arched paneled sides, applied sloping collared mouth, smooth base, ice blue, ca. 1855-70, 8 1/8" h. (ILLUS.).......... **$728**

Mineral Waters, Sodas & Sarsaparillas

Scarce Alburgh A Springs Bottle

Alburgh - A - Springs, VT, cylindrical w/applied sloping double collar mouth, smooth base, yellowish amber, two shallow flakes on lip & collar, some milky interior stain, ca. 1865-75, qt. (ILLUS.) **$960**

Brown Chemist Soda Water Bottle

Brown (J.T.) Chemist - Boston - Double Soda Water, ten-pin shape w/rough textured smooth rounded base, applied mouth, deep bluish green, light interior stain, ca. 1855-75, 8 1/8" h. (ILLUS.) **$532**

Early Vicksburg Hutchinson Bottle

Biedenharn Candy Co. - Vicksburg, Miss. (below) Registered, Hutchinson-type, cylindrical w/short tooled mouth, "B.C.C." on smooth base, aqua, cleaned, ca. 1890-1900, 7 1/4" h. (ILLUS.) **$364**

Scarce Clarke's Mineral Waters Bottle

Clarke's (William) Mineral Waters - Providence, R.I., torpedo-shaped w/applied mouth & original wire closure, smooth base, aqua, ca. 1870-80, 8 1/2" h. (ILLUS.)
.... **$616**

B

B

Scarce Middletown Healing Spring Bottle

Hathorn Spring Mineral Water Bottle

Hathorn Spring - Saratoga N.Y., cylindrical w/applied double collar mouth, smooth base, medium gold yellowish amber, ca. 1865-75, 9 3/8" h. (ILLUS.) **$45**

McKeon - Washington, D.C. Bottle

McKeon - Washington, D.C., ten-pin form w/applied top, smooth base, yellowish green, ca. 1855-65, repaired lip chip, overall wear, 8 1/2" h. (ILLUS.) **$728**

Middletown Healing Spring - A.W. Gray & Son - Middletown, Vt., cylindrical w/tall neck & applied sloping double collar mouth, smooth base, deep emerald green, ca. 1865-75, qt. (ILLUS., top next column) **$960**

Variation of Middletown Spring Bottle

Middletown Mineral Spring Co. - Nature's Remedy - Middletown, Vt., cylindrical w/tall neck & applied sloping double collar mouth, smooth base, emerald green, ca. 1865-75, qt. (ILLUS.) **$280**

B

Rare Early Cobalt Root Beer Bottle

Owen (C.B.) - Root Beer - Cincinnati, twelve-sided w/tapering shoulder to applied mouth, iron pontil, bright cobalt blue, ca. 1845-60, lightly cleaned, 8 7/8" h. (ILLUS.) **$1,456**

Pablo & Co. New Orleans Soda Bottle

Pablo & Co. - 334 & 336 - Royal Street NO, cylindrical w/tapering shoulder & tall neck w/applied blob mouth, iron pontil, bright yellowish green, ca. 1845-60, lightly cleaned, 7 1/2" h. (ILLUS.) **$1,068**
Pineapple (embossed pineapple) Cordial - Dr. B. Bates - Bottle Never Sold, slender club-form w/round bottom & applied mouth, aqua, cleaned, ca. 1860-80, 9 1/4" h. (ILLUS., top next column) **$392**
Rushton & Aspinwall - New York, ten-pin shaped soda water w/rounded bottom, outward rolled lip, greenish aqua, lightly cleaned, postone w/moon in neck, ca. 1830-40, 7 1/2" h. (ILLUS., bottom next column) **$1,904**

Pineapple Cordial Bottle

Rare Rushton & Aspinwall Bottle

B

Saratoga Spring Mineral Water Bottle

Saratoga (design of star) Spring (backwards S), cylindrical w/applied sloping double collar mouth, smooth base, dark chocolate amber, ca. 1865-75, tiny flake of inside of lip, qt. (ILLUS.) **$157**

Large Turner's Sarsaparilla Bottle

Turner's Sarsaparilla - Buffalo, N.Y., oval w/applied sloping mouth & smooth base, greenish aqua, ca. 1855-65, largest sarsaparilla bottle blown, minor spots of inside haze, 12 1/4" h. (ILLUS.) **$1,064**

Star Spring Co. Mineral Water Bottle

Star Spring Co. (design of star) Saratoga, N.Y., cylindrical w/applied sloping double collar mouth, smooth base, medium yellowish amber, ca. 1865-75, pt. (ILLUS.)..... **$110**

Washington Spring Mineral Water Bottle

Washington Spring - Saratoga - N.Y., cylindrical w/rounded shoulder, applied sloping double collar mouth, medium emerald green, ca. 1865-80, pt. (ILLUS.) **$246**

B

Pickle Bottles & Jars

Cathedral Pickle Bottle Variation

Bluish aqua, four-sided cathedral-type w/Gothic windows w/a cross at the top, applied mouth, smooth base, bluish aqua, ca. 1860-70, 11 3/8" h. (ILLUS.) **$280**

Bluish Green Four-Sided Cathedral Pickle

Medium bluish green, four-sided cathedral-type w/Gothic windows, rolled lip, smooth base, ca. 1860-70, medium bluish green, 11" h. (ILLUS.)........................... **$728**

Poisons

Large Whittled Cathedral Pickle Bottle

Deep bluish aqua, four-sided cathedral-type w/Gothic windows w/a trefoil at the top, rolled lip, smooth base, deep bluish aqua, heavily whittled, ca. 1860-70, 13 1/8" h. (ILLUS.) **$190**

Rare Aqua Poison Bottle

Aqua w/greenish tint, rectangular w/wide flattened shoulders, tooled mouth, smooth base, embossed "Poison" on each side, ca. 1890-1910, 5 5/8" h. (ILLUS.) **$1,064**

B

Two Views of Very Rare Blue Poison

Cobalt blue, coffin-shaped w/tooled mouth & smooth base, pointed hobnails on three sides, fourth side w/skull & crossed bones over "DP Co.," back w/99% original faded paper label w/skull & crossed bones over "Poison," also hand-written notation "R, 3 cents a piece," ca. 1890-1910, 5" h. (ILLUS. of two views) **$7,840**

Whiskey & Other Spirits

Early Yellowish Olive Case Gin Bottle

Case gin, tall slender square tapering shape w/outward rolled lip, open pontil, ca. 1770-1800, medium yellowish olive, 10 3/8" h. (ILLUS.) **$213**

Blue London Royal Imperial Gin Bottle

Gin, "London - Royal - Imperial Gin," square w/beveled corners, applied sloping collar mouth, smooth base, cobalt blue, American, ca. 1870-80, lightly cleaned, 10" h. (ILLUS.) **$728**

Early English Double-Magnum Bottle

Spirits, free-blown bulbous onion-form, tall tapering neck w/applied string lip, open pontil, England, 1700-10, olive amber, milky inside stain, double-magnum size, 9" d., 9 5/8" h. (ILLUS.) **$2,800**

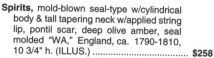

Spirits, mold-blown seal-type w/cylindrical body & tall tapering neck w/applied string lip, pontil scar, deep olive amber, seal molded "WA," England, ca. 1790-1810, 10 3/4" h. (ILLUS.) **$258**

B

Early Zanesville Mold-Blown Bottle

Spirits, mold-blown, globular, twenty-four ribs swirled to the right, tall neck w/outward rolled lip, pontil scar, Zanesville, Ohio, ca. 1825-35, medium amber, shallow surface bottle, 7 1/2" h. (ILLUS.) **$616**

English Seal Bottle Marked "HHC"

Spirits, mold-blown seal-type w/cylindrical body & tall tapering neck w/applied string lip, pontil scar, dark olive amber, seal molded "HHC," England, ca. 1790-1810, 10 3/4" h. (ILLUS.) **$420**

Whiskey, "Beiser & Fisher - N.Y.," figural pig, applied double collar mouth, smooth base, medium amber, ca. 1865-75, chip on side of snout, cooling fissure on collar, 9 1/2" l. (ILLUS., bottom of page).............. **$420**

English Seal Bottle in Olive Amber

Pig-shaped Beiser & Fisher Bottle

B

Barrel-shaped Bininger Bourbon Bottle

Whiskey, "Bininger (A.M.) & Co - 338 Broadway N.Y. - Distilled in 1848 - Old Kentucky - 1849 Reserve Bourbon," ringed barrel shape w/applied mouth, open pontil, amber, ca. 1865-75, 8 1/8" h. (ILLUS.) **$392**

Topaz Bininger No. 375 Broadway Bottle

Whiskey, "Bininger (A.M.) & Co. No. 375 Broadway N.Y.," square w/beveled corners, applied sloping collar mouth, smooth base, medium topaz, crude & bubbly, ca. 1865-75, 9 3/4" h. (ILLUS.)...... **$784**

Rarer Bininger Whiskey Bottle

Whiskey, "Bininger (A.M.) & Co. - Heidelberg - Branntwein," square w/beveled corners, applied sloping collar mouth, smooth base, olive green, bubbly, ca. 1865-75, 9 5/8" h. (ILLUS.) **$1,064**

Puce Bininger No. 375 Broadway Bottle

Whiskey, "Bininger (A.M.) & Co. No. 375 Broadway N.Y.," square w/beveled corners, applied sloping collar mouth, smooth base, strawberry puce, ca. 1865-75, 9 3/4" h. (ILLUS.) **$1,232**

B

Green Bininger No. 375 Broadway Bottle

Whiskey, "Bininger (A.M.) & Co. No. 375 Broadway N.Y.," square w/beveled corners, applied sloping collar mouth, smooth base, moss green, ca. 1865-75, 9 5/8" h. (ILLUS.) **$1,456**

Rare Barrel-shaped Nelson's Old Bourbon

Whiskey, "Nelson's (I.) Old Bourbon Maysville, KY," barrel-shaped w/applied mouth & smooth base, yellowish olive amber, ca. 1860-70, shallow flake on edge of lip, 7 3/8" h. (ILLUS.) **$4,408**

J.F.T. & Co. Handled Whiskey

Whiskey, "J.F.T. & Co. - Philad." embossed in circular seal on the shoulder, mold-blown pear shape w/twenty-six vertical ribs, applied double collared mouth & applied handle w/fancy rigaree at base, pontil scar, medium golden amber, American, 1840-60, 7 1/8" h. (ILLUS.) **$840**

Perrine's Apple Ginger Bottle

Whiskey, "Perrine's - Apple - Ginger - Phila" on roof, "Perrine's (design of apple) Ginger," cabin-shaped w/ropetwist corners, tooled mouth, smooth base, yellowish amber, ca. 1880-90, 10" h. (ILLUS.) **$308**

BOXES

Early Painted Bible Box

Bible box, painted & decorated pine, square nail construction, rectangular w/a hinged flat cover, molded apron raised on ogee bracket feet, original black paint w/yellow & bittersweet sponging, attributed to Pennsylvania, some edge damage w/touch up, late 18th - early 19th c., 13 1/2 x 17", 10 1/2" h. (ILLUS.) **$1,553**

Nicely Painted Early Bride's Box

Bride's box, painted bentwood, oval w/fitted cover & laced seams, original light blue background h.p. on the top w/a floral spray w/a songbird, stylized tulips & leaves around the sides, Europe, 19th c., some edge damage & splits, 10 1/2 x 17 1/2", 7 3/4" h. (ILLUS.) **$1,093**

Early Bride's Box with Figures on Cover

Bride's box, painted bentwood, oval w/fitted cover & laced seams, original dark ivory ground w/blue flowers & a blue cover decorated w/a woman in colonial dress & a man in a tall hat dressed as a traveler, edge of cover w/German script, some wear & edge damage, split in cover, 12 x 18", 8" h. (ILLUS.) **$575**

Nicely Decorated Early Candle Box

Candle box, painted & decorated pine, long rectangular shape w/inset slide cover, original h.p. decoration w/a brown ground w/traces of orange graining & bold vining foliage w/a starflower & melon in yellow & green, missing interior dividers, square nails attach base, minor wear, repaired split on lid edge, 19th c., 6 1/2 x 12 3/8", 4 3/8" h. (ILLUS.) **$3,450**

Painted Storage Box Attributed to Soap Hollow

B

Rare Early Painted Dome-Topped Box

Storage box, cov., low rectangular shape w/hinged cover w/applied edge moldings, pine w/original dark red paint, gold-stenciled decorations on the front, sides & cover including hearts, arrows & starflowers, lined w/block-printed wallpaper in green & grey on ivory, attributed to Soap Hollow, some areas of touch up, wear & minor damage including reset hinges, 19th c., 9 1/2 x 14 1/2", 5" h. (ILLUS., bottom previous page) **$259**

Storage box, cov., rectangular w/low domed hinged cover, pine w/original red over mustard yellow vinegar grained decoration, incised & inlaid diamond-shaped ivory keyhole escutcheon, 19th c., minor wear, 5 1/4 x 8 3/4", 4 1/2" h. (ILLUS., top of page) **$3,330**

Rare Early Painted Pine Storage Box

Storage box, painted pine, rectangular w/domed cover w/iron hinges & latch, painted light blue ground w/red, green & yellow fruit or love apples, leaf & flower swag borders, possibly Ohio or Pennsylvania, early 19th c., paint wear, age cracks, 14 x 26", 11 3/8" h. (ILLUS.) **$7,638**

BREWERIANA

Beer is still popular in this country, but the number of breweries has greatly diminished. More than 1,900 breweries were in operation in the 1870s, but we find fewer than 40 major breweries supply the

demands of the country a century later, although microbreweries have recently sprung up across the country.

Advertising items used to promote various breweries, especially those issued prior to Prohibition, now attract an ever growing number of collectors. The breweriana items listed are a sampling of the many items available. Also see Antique Trader Advertising Price Guide.

Iroquois Beer Advertising Clock

Clock, advertising-type, "Iroquois Beer - Ale," round double-bubble electric wall clock w/a gold background printed in color w/a large Indian Chief profile bust above wording in red & white, a gold border band printed w/white Arabic numerals at 12 - 3 - 6 & 9, red handles & a white sweep seconds hand, ca. 1950s, missing one rear bulb cover, 15" d. (ILLUS.) **$920**

Mug, advertising-type, barrel-shaped, salt-glazed stoneware w/incised blue-trimmed double bands above & below a wide center band impressed & blue-trimmed w/"Rochester Brew. Co.," a bottom band further impressed "Rochester, NY," ca. 1900, 5" h. (ILLUS. right with other advertising brewery mug, next page) **$176**

B

Two Early Brewery Advertising Mugs

Mug, advertising-type, Bristol-glazed stone-ware, footed cylindrical form w/incised dark blue accent lines around the base & top, impressed & blue-trimmed wide center band w/"Iroquois Trademark Brewing Co. - Buffalo, NY" w/a profile bust logo of an Indian chief, faint small hairline on one side, ca. 1900, 5" h. (ILLUS. left with other advertising mug) **$77**

CANDLESTICKS & CANDLEHOLDERS

Also see Antique Trader Books Lamps & Lighting Price Guide.

Early Turned Brass Candlestick

Candlestick, brass, a domed ringed base w/knopped stem below a wide mid-drip pan & a knob- and ring-turned socket, early, 9" h. (ILLUS.) **$316**

Candlestick, brass, a square flat rimmed base below the ringed knob standard & cylindrical socket, probably 18th c., 5 1/4" sq., 5 1/4" h. (ILLUS., top next column) **$288**

Early Square-based Brass Candlestick

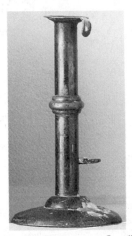

Early English Hog scraper Candlestick

Candlestick, iron & brass, hog scraper-type, domed round foot & tall slender stem w/a brass center band, low flared rim, push-up w/tab handle marked "Shaw's Birm.," England, 19th c., 7 1/8" h. (ILLUS.) **$431**

Open Spiral Brass Candlesticks

Candlesticks, brass, round domed & ringed base below the open spiraling-stem & tall cylindrical socket, 19th c., 12" h., pr. (ILLUS., previous page) **$230**

One of a Pair of Early Candlesticks

Candlesticks, brass, seamed construction w/a paneled & domed base & tall ringed stem w/a knob handle on the push-up, probably 18th c., 7" h., pr. (ILLUS. of one).. **$776**

Fine Silver Plate Candlestick from Pair

Candlesticks, silver plate, round domed base w/four paw feet below serpentine griffins, the standard w/a base ring below the tall waisted section decorated w/further scrolls, the trumpet-form socket w/scrolled ribs, second half 19th c., 14" h. pr. (ILLUS. of one) **$575**

Pair of French Silvered Brass Candlesticks

Candlesticks, silvered brass, round disc foot below ring- and baluster-turned stem w/tulip-form candle socket, overall engraved leaf designs, France, Charles X era, ca. 1820, 10" h., pr. (ILLUS.) **$3,220**

Early Three-Piece Brass Girandole Set

Girandole set, figural one-stick candlesticks & figural center three-light candelabra; each on a rectangular white marble base, the single sticks w/a figural standard of a Native American below a slender stem supporting a ring suspending triangular prisms around the socket, the central piece w/a figure of Daniel Boone seated by a Native American, matching stem issuing two arms flanking the taller center stem, by Cornelius & Co., Philadelphia, minor prism flakes, mid-19th c., 18" h., the set (ILLUS.)............................. **$633**

C

CANES & WALKING STICKS

C

Folk Art Cane with Heads & Snakes

Carved & painted walking stick, folk art style, wooden shaft w/original nubs of various branches along the side w/thorns carved in relief, two snakes intertwined down the shaft, carved heads near top of shaft fitted w/glass eyes (one missing) & red split tongues, shaft sprinkled w/red & black painted dots, painted black handle w/tip fitted w/a piece of hardwood, original untouched surface, 35" l. (ILLUS.) **$230**

Fine Gold-headed & Inlaid Walking Stick

Gold-headed & inlaid fruitwood walking stick, the paneled gold top w/raised initials "P.B.X." encrusted w/small mine-cut diamonds & rubies, the collar consists of panels of mother-of-pearl, wooden shaft inlaid w/a scrolled vine of delicate ma-

hogany leaves & flowers, the tip mounted w/a gold collar & a solid brass tip, 39" l. (ILLUS.) **$1,323**

Gold-Headed Presentation Walking Stick

Gold-headed walking stick, head w/lavish relief répoussé & engraved sprays of flowers & leaves, top w/engraved presentation dated 1891, ebony shaft, w/silk-lined case w/worn label of C.D. Thompson, London, 35" l. (ILLUS.) **$4,025**

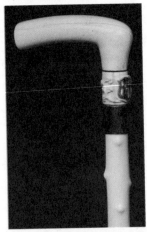

Ivory Cane Presented to Maximillian I

Ivory cane, a simple 90-degree ivory handle w/a deep relief-carved collar w/mounted gold initials, a gold collar & ivory shaft carved to mimic a tree branch, tip mounted w/a dark silver ferrule, relief-carved ivory ring at top w/ivory scrolled ferns & mounted initials "RSB," gift to Emperor Maximillian I of Mexico from diplomats of French Indo-China, passed down through his family, w/velour-lined case, mid-19th c., 36" l. (ILLUS.) **$9,200**

CANS & CONTAINERS

See ADVERTISING ITEMS

Black Hawk Coffee & Spice Store Bin

Coffee, "Black Hawk Coffee and Spice Co. Roasters," painted tin store bin, worn blue background w/gold lettering, ca. 1900, 20" h. (ILLUS.) **$82**

Unusual Tasty-Food Coffee Tin Train Set

Coffee, "Tasty-Food Limited - Limited Brand 100% Pure High Grade Coffee - Roasted and Packed by Tasty Food Products Co., Brownwood, Texas," four horizontal cylindrical metal containers made to resemble a train engine & three cars, each in a different color of red, blue, green & orange & labeled "Tasty-Food Limited," each on a metal base w/small red metal wheels, aimed at children & also labeled "You will like Coffee too," locomotive w/additional letters "T.F.P.C. 103," first half 20th c., minor flaws, each piece 12" l., 7" h., the set (ILLUS.)........................ **$258**

Honey, "Pure Honey - Van's Honey Farms, Hebron, Indiana," cylindrical 10 lb. bucket w/pry-off lid & wire bail handle, gold lettering & clover design against a pale orange & yellow ground, minor flaws, early 20th c., 7 1/2" h. (ILLUS., top next column) **$146**

Van's Honey Farms Pure Honey Bucket

Louisiana Perique Tobacco Tin

Tobacco, "Allen & Ginter's Genuine Louisiana Perique - Grown in St. James Parish, Louisiana," painted tin shallow rectangular tin in black w/gold lettering, hinged kudm writing on all four sides, ca. 1900, 2 1/2 x 3 7/8", 1 1/2" h. (ILLUS.) **$134**

CAROUSEL FIGURES

The ever-popular amusement park merry-go-round or carousel has ancient antecedents but evolved into its most colorful and complex form in the decades from 1880 to 1930. In America a number of pioneering firms, begun by men such as Gustav Dentzel, Charles Looff and Allan Herschell, produced these wonderful rides with beautifully hand-carved animals, the horse being the most popular. Some of the noted carvers included M.C. Illusions, Charles Carmel, Solomon Stein and Harry Goldstein.

Today many of the grand old carousels are gone and remaining ones are often broken up and the animals sold separately as collectors search for choice examples. A fine reference to this field is Painted Ponies, American Carousel Art, *by William Mannas, Peggy Shank and Marianne Stevens (Zon International Publishing Company, Millwood, New York, 1986).*

C

Early Prancing Carousel Horse

Horse, prancer, off-white body w/gray dappled highlights, glass eyes, pastel floral-decorated oval pendant trappings, carved horseshoes, black horsehair tail, includes original iron factory rocking stand, old surface, late 19th - early 20th c., 50" l., 47 1/2" h. (ILLUS.) **$9,400**

Brightly Painted Carousel Horse

Horse, galloping pose w/head raised, nicely carved saddle w/eagle back, glass jewels on the harness, white body w/black mane & black real hair tail, brightly painted, attributed to Herschel-Spellman, on a custom wood stand, some paint chipping & cracks, 54" l., 40" h. (ILLUS.) **$1,320**

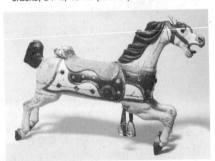

Parker Jumper Carousel Horse

Horse, jumper, carved wood w/glass eyes & jewels on the saddle, leather & metal stirrups, carved dog head on the cantle of the saddle, worn white body w/black tail & mane, saddle in worn yellow, red & blue, some edge damage & loose seams, attributed to Charles Wallace Parker, early 20th c., 58" l., 40 1/2" h. (ILLUS.)... **$1,208**

Rearing Carousel Horse on Rockers

Horse, rearing stance, carved wood w/polychrome repaint & glass eyes, white body w/black mane, worn w/loose seams & sections, missing tail, mounted on later rockers, attributed to Frederick Heyn, German, 58" l., 52" h. (ILLUS.) **$1,265**

C

Child-sized Crouching Pig Animal

Pig, carved wood child-sized crouching animal resembling the cartoon character Porky Pig wearing a blue sweater, several layers of paint, early 20th c., 28" l., 19" h. (ILLUS.) **$978**

CASTORS & CASTOR SETS

Castor bottles were made to hold condiments for table use. Some were produced in sets of several bottles housed in silver plated frames. The word also is sometimes spelled "Caster."

Victorian Pattern Glass Castor Set

Castor set, four-bottle, pressed glass, Heavy Paneled Fine Cut patt., the squared glass base fitted w/two shakers, a cruet w/stopper & mustard jar w/lid, centered by an upright squared metal loop handle, canary yellow, ca. 1880s, polished under platform, overall 8 7/8" h., the set (ILLUS.) **$523**

Fine Lobed Cranberry Glass Pickle Caster

Pickle castor, cranberry mold-blown glass melon-lobed insert w/plain lobes decorated w/enameled flowers alternating w/lobes embossed w/tall feathered scrolls, in an ornate silver plate frame w/a high arched handle & tongs, ca. 1900, 10 1/2" h. (ILLUS.) **$499**

CERAMICS

Abingdon

From about 1934 until 1950, Abingdon Pottery Company, Abingdon, Illinois, manufactured decorative pottery, mainly cookie jars, flowerpots and vases. Decorated with various glazes, these items are becoming popular with collectors who are especially attracted to Abingdon's novelty cookie jars. Also see Antique Trader Pottery & Porcelain - Ceramics Price Guide, 6th Edition

Abingdon Mark

Abingdon Round Ashtray

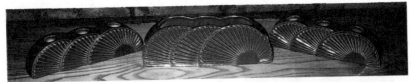

Sunburst Candleholders & Window Box

Ashtray, round, turquoise, No. 555, 1941-46, 8" d. (ILLUS., previous page) $25
Book ends/planters, model of dolphin, No. 444D, blue glaze, 5 3/4" h., pr. $80
Candleholder, double, No. 479, Scroll patt., 4 1/2" h. $15

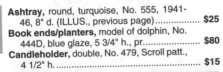

Bamboo Candleholders & Console Plate

Candleholders, Bamboo patt., No. 716, pr. (ILLUS. left & right w/console plate)............. $50
Candleholders, Sunburst, in the form of three ribbed connected semicircles, rose, No. 447, 1938, 8" l., pr. (ILLUS. right & left w/window box, top of page).................... $80
Console bowl, No. 532, Scroll patt., 14 1/2" l. $20
Console plate, Bamboo patt., No. 715, 10 1/2" d. (ILLUS. w/candleholders, above) $125
Cookie jar, Baby, No. 561, 11" h. $750-1,000
Cookie jar, Clock, No. 563, 9" h...................... $130
Cookie jar, Floral/Plaid, No. 697, 8 1/2" h. $150-250
Cookie jar, Humpty Dumpty, No. 663, 10 1/2" h. $275
Cookie jar, Miss Muffet, No. 662D, 11" h....... $275
Cookie jar, Mother Goose, No. 695D, 1950, 12" h. (ILLUS., top next column) $425
Cookie jar, Pineapple, No. 664, 1949-50, 10 1/2" h. (ILLUS., bottom next column) $200
Cookie jar, Pumpkin, No. 674D, 8" h. $550
Cookie jar, Windmill, No. 678, 10 1/2" h. $500

Mother Goose Cookie Jar

Pineapple Cookie Jar

Abingdon Lamp Base

Lamp base, No. 254, draped shaft, 13" h.
(ILLUS.) **$200**
Model of heron, No. 574, tan glaze,
5 1/4" h. **$68**
Model of peacock, No. 416, turquoise
glaze, 7" h. **$96**
Model of penguin, white, 3" h. **$50**
Planter, model of a puppy, No. 652D,
6 3/4" l. **$75**
String holder, Chinese head, No. 702,
5 1/2" h. **$500**
Vase, 5" h., No. B1, whatnot type **$100**
Vase, 5" h., white floral decoration on blue
ground, small handles, No. 567D, 1942-
46, No. 570D (ILLUS. right w/window
box, top of page 92) **$40**
Vase, 5 1/2" h., No. 142, Classic line **$40**
Vase, 7" h., No. 171, Classic line **$40**

Abingdon Delta Vase

Vase, 8" h., Delta, handles, ribbed base,
rose, No. 108, 1938-39 (ILLUS.) **$40**

Abingdon Gamma Vase

Vase, 8" h., Gamma, short bulbous base
connected to tall slightly flaring lobed
neck by applied side handles, turquoise,
No. 107, 1938-39 (ILLUS.) **$40**

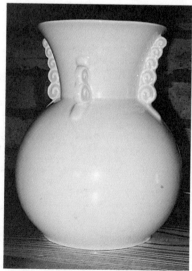

Abingdon Scroll Vase

Vase, 8" h., Scroll, bulbous body, neck
w/four handles tapers out at top, green,
No. 417, 1937-38 (ILLUS.) **$125**

C

Abingdon Window Box & Vase

Window box, oblong, scalloped rim, white floral decoration on blue ground, No. 570D, 1942-46, 10" l. (ILLUS. left w/vase No. 567D, top of page) **$35**

Window box, Sunburst, in the form of three connected ribbed semicircles, rose, No. 448, 1938-39, 9" l. (ILLUS. center w/Sunburst candleholders, top of page 90)............ **$85**

American Painted Porcelain

Jewelry

Brooch, oval, decorated w/forget-me-nots on a pale yellow center w/pale blue border, gold-plated bezel, signed "A. Jibbing," ca. 1900-20, 1 3/8 x 1 1/2" **$75**

Brooch, round, decorated w/a conventional-style trillium w/raised paste & burnished gold pistils & burnished gold background, brass-plated bezel, ca. 1910-15, 1 9/16" d. **$55**

Brooch/pendant, heart shape, decorated w/daisies on a light shading to dark blue ground, gold-plated bezel, ca. 1900-20, 1 13/16 x 2".. **$55**

Brooches, oval, decorated w/forget-me-nots on a pale pink & blue ground w/white enamel highlights on petal edges, burnished gold rims, gold-plated bezels, gold wear, ca. 1900-20, 13/16 x 1", pr. **$75**

Handy pin, crescent-shaped, decorated w/pink & ruby roses & green leaves on an ivory ground, w/white enamel highlights & one burnished gold tip, gold-plated bezel, ca. 1890-1915, 2 3/16" w..................... **$45**

Hatpin, circular head, decorated w/a conventional geometric design in raised paste dots & scrolls, covered w/burnished gold, turquoise enamel jewels, cobalt blue flat enamel, gold-plated bezel, ca. 1905-20, 1" d., 6 3/8" shaft **$110**

Hatpin, circular head, decorated w/pink roses & greenery on a pale blue & yellow ground, burnished gold border, gold-plated bezel, ca. 1890-1920, some gold wear, 1" d., 7 3/4" shaft.................... **$125**

Hatpin Head with Ruby Roses

Hatpin, circular head, decorated w/ruby roses & green leaves, embellished w/burnished gold scrolls, gold-plated bezel, head 1 3/8" d., shaft 7 3/4" l. (ILLUS. of head) **$125**

Unusual Portrait Shirtwaist Button

Shirtwaist button, round w/shank, decorated w/the bust portrait of a young blonde-haired girl, wearing a pale blue dress, against a shaded yellow to black ground, 1 3/8" d. (ILLUS.)............................... **$90**

Shirtwaist buttons, heart-shaped, decorated w/pink roses, raised paste scrolled border covered w/burnished gold, ca. 1890-1910, 1 1/8 x 1 3/16", pr........................ **$85**

C

Shirtwaist Buttons with Pinwheels

Shirtwaist buttons, round, each decorated w/a geometric pinwheel design in light blue, black & gold trimmed w/burnished gold dots & a center turquoise "jewel," on a burnished gold ground, two 1" d., three 7/8" d., the set (ILLUS., top of page) **$125**

Shirtwaist set: oval cuff links & three round buttons w/shanks; decorated w/clusters of violets on pale yellow ground, burnished gold rim, gold-plated bezel on cuff links, ca. 1900-15, cuff links 3/4 x 1 1/4", buttons 1 1/4" d., the set **$175**

Various Amphora-Teplitz Factory Marks

Amphora - Teplitz

In the late 19th and early 20th centuries numerous potteries operated in the vicinity of Teplitz in the Bohemian region of what was Austria but is now the Czech Republic. They included Amphora, RStK, Stellmacher, Ernst Wahliss, Paul Dachsel, Imperial and lesser-known potteries such as Johanne Maresh, Julius Dressler, Bernard Bloch and Heliosine.

The number of collectors in this category is growing while availability of pieces is shrinking. Prices for better, rarer pieces, including those with restoration, are continuing to appreciate.

The price ranges presented here are retail. They presume mint or near mint condition or, in the case of very rare damaged pieces, proper restoration. They reflect such variables as rarity, design, quality of glaze, size and the intangible "in-vogue factor." They are the prices that knowledgeable sellers will charge and knowledgeable collectors will pay.

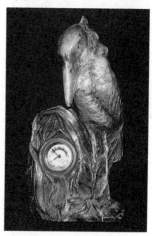

Fantasy Stork Clock

Clock, table model, a fantasy stork, similar to Martin Bros. birds, stands next to a clock dial framed by Art Nouveau-style leaves, fine detailing, soft brownish tan glaze, rare, raised rectangle w/factory logo & "AK-Turn," impressed "319," 13" h. (ILLUS.) **$7,500-8,000**

C

Amphora Jeweled Compote

Compote, open, 11" d., 9" h., the round footed w/colored jeweled trim supporting a pair of curved legs centered by a tree trunk leg holding the wide shallow bowl w/round flower heads inset w/jewels around the exterior, mottled mauve, rose & green ground, signed "Made in Czechoslovakia - Amphora," early 20th c. (ILLUS.) **$1,320**

Amphora Teplitz Ewer

Ewer, an Art Nouveau design w/extraordinary detail combining a reticulated handle suggesting Paul Dachsel & varied circles on the body suggesting Gustav Klimt, a reticulated top, many "jewels" of different colors & sizes randomly located over the body suggesting a spectrum of stars in the Milky Way, unusual gold bud spout, high-glazed blue garlands randomly draped about the body, heavy gold trim on the upper part of the handle, top & spout, a subdued gold trim extends down the handle to & around the bottom where there is an abstract tree design, very difficult to produce, rare, impressed "Amphora" in a circle & "40 -537," 14" h. (ILLUS.).. **$9,500-10,000**

Figure group, a small fine scenic figural group w/a rooster & hen perched side by side overlooking a pond, a small gold frog climbing into the pond, gives a barnyard feeling, soft muted shades of tan w/highlights of gold, a realistic theme & valuable because of the small size, impressed "Amphora" in an oval & illegible numbers, 6 1/2" w., 7 3/4" h. **$1,250-1,300**

Extremely Rare Amphora Maiden Figure

Figure of an Art Nouveau maiden, the standing maiden emerging from the sea w/her arms extended & resting on two large aquatic plant leaves, at her feet the head of another maiden w/her hair flowing, decorated in blues & gold, mark of E. Stellmucher, impressed "Amphora 775/2," firing crack running from bottom up, 19 1/2" h. (ILLUS.) **$9,315**

Unique Figural Humidor

Humidor, cov., figural, a fantasy piece featuring a large globe representing the world being shot from a tiny cannon & caught by a jester lying on his back, the jester reputedly represents a prime minister of the time, a hat at the top of the globe forms the handles, soft muted grey Amphora glaze, rare, impressed "Amphora" in an oval & "4216," 14" w., 9" h. (ILLUS.)... **$7,500-8,500**

Amphora Russian Folk Art Teapot

Teapot, cov., Russian Folk Art Series, tall ovoid form w/flared foot & flat rim, arched C-form handle from rim to shoulder, short angled shoulder spout w/an arched brace to the rim, decorated on center front w/a large stylized bust portrait of a Russian cleric w/black beard & brown & blue hat, the portrait enclosed by a ring of blue stars & blue dots w/other bands of dots & teardrops about the top & base, all against a tan ground, the reverse w/a design of multiple triangles enclosed w/a ring of stars, impressed "Austria - Amphora" in ovals & "11892,47 - G" plus a crown, ca. 1907-08, 8 1/4" h. (ILLUS.) **$295**

Fine Amphora Portrait Vase

Vase, 5 3/8" h., gourd-form w/a wide squatty bulbous lower body tapering to a slender neck w/bulbed top, decorated w/a large portrait of an Art Nouveau maiden in shades of gold, white & blue w/a mot-

tled green ground, impressed Amphora mark (ILLUS.) **$1,840**

Vase, 5 3/4" h., figural, elegantly executed Paul Dachsel creation w/a greenish cast & numerous vertical ribs extending up from the base, four intertwined gold-bodied dragonflies form a reticulated top, immediately below a series of smaller dragonflies encircle the vase, two multilayered handles within handles complete the design, stamped over glaze w/intertwined "PD - Turn - Teplitz," impressed "104" **$3,500-4,000**

Double-gourd Amphora Vase with Rabbits

Vase, 6 3/8" h., double-gourd form w/a wide squatty bulbous lower body in green decorated w/molded light green leaves & a pair of rabbits in mottled blue & tan, slip-marked "Amphora - Austria - Turn" w/partial Amphora label, few minor glaze nicks, one leaf mended (ILLUS.) **$920**

Unusual Amphora Double-handled Vase

Vase, 6 3/8" h., footed wide squatty body tapering sharply to a slender neck w/a cupped rim, double-arched handles loop handles from rim to shoulder, dec-

C

orated w/dark rose on the neck, handles & body band all accented w/stylized roses & flower sprigs, tan ground w/scattered small gold blossoms, Riessner & Kessel, Amphora, Austria marks & numbers 8978 & 44, minor grinding chips on base (ILLUS., previous page)... **$345**

Fine Figural Vase with Maiden

Vase, 7" h., figural, demure, elegant wonderfully detailed young woman seated & reaching down to retrieve a flower, against an upright flowering vine-covered wall, mixed iridescent colors of blue, magenta, silver, purple & gold all w/a bronze-like finish, a top-of-the-line creation of Ernst Wahliss, marked "EW - Turn - Vienna - Made in Austria" & an incised "I" & 4838/8/360/7 (ILLUS.).. **$3,000-3,500**

Vase, 7 1/2" h., a playful expression of Amphora w/a pink snake draped around the body of the bulbous vase & extending to the top where its delicate tongue protrudes, a subtle leaf design extends around the bottom, the pink color of the snake distinguishes this piece from more drab versions, impressed in ovals "Amphora" & "Austria," & "4114 - 52"... **$2,500-3,000**

Vase, 7 3/4" h., round bulbous shape, decorated w/a profile of a young girl w/long flowing brownish hair full of numerous multicolored high-glazed flowers w/gold touches, all surrounded by a brownish tan forest scene, finely executed, impressed "Amphora - 663," overglaze red mark "RStK - Turn - Teplitz - Made in Austria".. **$2,500-3,000**

Vase, 8 1/2" h., organic vegetal form w/a sharply tapering conical body w/small open loop handles around the base continuing to form panels up the sides, the widely rolled & turned-down rim w/four drippy handles tapering to the side of the neck, mark of Riessner, Stellmacher & Kessel, ca. 1905, overall crazing, faint line in one of the short base handles (ILLUS., top next column) **$1,265**

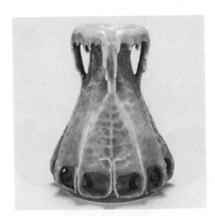

Vegetal-shaped Amphora Vase

Vase, 8 3/4" h., four-paneled high-shouldered squared form w/a front-faced Mucha-style Art Nouveau princess portrait, elaborate gold enameling against a landscape decorated w/blue & purple trees w/gold highlights above a base decorated w/Paul Dachsel-style abstract red flowers in a green base, impressed "Amphora" in oval & "579-40," red "RStK Austria" overglaze mark, artist mark "Fr" in gold overglaze............................... **$4,000-4,500**

Teplitz Vase Decorated with Forest Scene

Vase, 9" h., bulbous ovoid body w/a small ringed gold neck w/widely flaring molded rim, the body decorated w/a continuous landscape w/tall leafy trees in the foreground & a forest beyond, in shades of blue, yellow & green, marked "Turn-Teplitz-Bohemia - R St K - Made in Austria - 523," minor gold wear (ILLUS.).......... **$345**

C

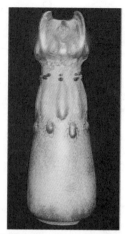

Tall Amphora Vase with Insects

Vase, 14 3/4" h., tall gently tapering ovoid body w/a swelled top, decorated w/eight three-dimensional iridescent indigo blue insects of varying sizes crawling up the side toward a series of leaves adorned w/berries, above the berries is a four-handled 3" h. heavily gilded top, the rest of the body in iridescent light blue w/gold highlights, rare, impressed "Amphora" & "Austria" in ovals, a crown & 3987/58 (ILLUS.) **$9,000-9,500**

Flower-decorated Art Nouveau Vase

Vase, 15" h., bulbous squatty base tapering to a slender neck w/fanned rim, unique Art Nouveau design w/an open flower blossom tinged in gold at the top, two curved vine handles extend from the neck to the base, the base relief-molded w/detailed leaves, found in numerous color variations & glazes, the most magnificent being a bronze glaze, value depends on the glaze w/bronze being the rarest, impressed "Amphora" & "Austria" in oval, a crown & 3852/42 (ILLUS.)............................ **$4,500-5,500**

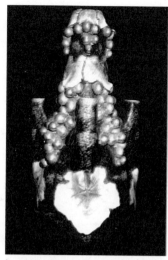

Amphora Vase with Golden Grapes

Vase, 15 1/2" h., cascades of golden grapes stream down on all sides between four funnel necks, the central funnel projecting skyward, this funnel design suggests Paul Dachsel, especially desirable because the piece is viewable from any angle, metallic purplish glaze w/metallic gold highlights containing numerous little gold circles, marked "Amphora" & "Austria" in ovals, a crown & "3680" (ILLUS.)
.... **$4,000-4,500**

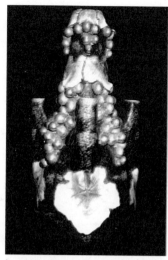

Rare Jeweled Amphora Vase

Vase, 16" h., bulbous ovoid body tapering to a slender flaring lobed reticulated neck, outswept loop handles at the lower sides, shimmering burnished gold ground w/red touches, adorned randomly w/twenty large variously colored 'jewels,' one handle in red, the other in gold, overall molded vertical ribbing, rare form, impressed "Amphora" in an oval, crown, old "RStK" mark & "3349" (ILLUS.)............. **$15,000-18,000**

Austrian

Numerous potteries in Austria produced good-quality ceramic wares over many years. Some factories were established by American entrepreneurs, particularly in the Carlsbad area, and other factories made china under special brand names for American importers. Marks on various pieces are indicated in many listings.

C

Austrian Marks

Austrian Porcelain Fancy Teapot

Teapot, cov., ruffle-footed ribbed baluster-form body w/a domed cover & ring finial, serpentine spout & ornate C-scroll handle, gold trim, Imperial Crown China, Vienna, Austria, ca. 1890s (ILLUS.) **$45**

Ornate Austrian Porcelain & Metal Urn

Urn, an elongated inverted pear-shaped body h.p. w/a large oblong reserve showing a standing lady wearing a blue gown standing in a landscape & reaching down to a cherub, the maroon & light blue background, raised on a square gilt-metal plinth foot & slender colorfully enameled pedestal & fitted w/a slender trumpet-shaped colorfully enameled metal neck w/gilt-metal gadrooned leaf band, artist-signed, 9 1/2" h. (ILLUS.) **$403**

Ornate Flower-decorated Austrian Vase

Vase, cov., 25" h., tall ovoid urn-form body raised on a gold-trimmed molded scrolling foot, pierced long scroll-molded handles w/gold trim, the high domed cover w/a high gold flame-form finial & h.p. w/flower sprigs, the body h.p. w/large bouquets of colorful flowers, illegible impressed mark, late 19th c., some minor professional repair & chips (ILLUS.) ... **$400-800**

Bauer

The Bauer Pottery was moved to Los Angeles, California, from Paducah, Kentucky, in 1909 in the hope that the climate would prove beneficial to the principal organizer, John Andrew Bauer, who suffered from severe asthma. Flowerpots made of California adobe clay were the first production at the new location, but soon they were able to resume production of stoneware crocks and jugs, the mainstay of the Kentucky operation. In the early 1930s, Bauer's colorfully glazed earthen dinnerwares, especially the popular Ring-Ware pattern, became an immediate success. Sometimes confused with its imitator, Fiesta Ware (first registered by Homer Laughlin in 1937), Bauer pottery is collectible in its own right and is especially popular with West Coast collectors. Bauer Pottery ceased operation in 1962.

Bauer Mark

Batter bowl, Ring-Ware patt., green, 1 qt..... **$125**
Bowl, berry, 5 1/2" d., Ring-Ware patt., yellow.. **$25**
Bowl, 13" d., Cal-Art line, green...................... **$35**
Cake plate, Monterey patt., yellow................ **$185**
Casserole, cov., individual, Ring-Ware patt., cobalt blue, 5 1/2" d. **$300**
Casserole, cov., individual, Ring-Ware patt., orange/red, 5 1/2" d. **$200**
Coffee carafe, cov., Ring-Ware patt., copper handle, orange/red............................. **$150**
Cookie jar, cov., Monterey Moderne patt., chartreuse **$100**

Monterey Midget Creamer

Creamer, midget, Monterey patt., orange/red (ILLUS.)....................................... **$20**
Creamer & cov. sugar bowl, Ring-Ware patt., orange, pr... **$75**
Flowerpot, Speckleware, flesh pink, 8 1/4" d., 6 1/2" h.. **$40**
Gravy boat, Ring-Ware patt., burgundy......... **$145**
Mixing bowl, nesting-type, Ring-Ware patt., No. 18, chartreuse............................... **$75**

Bauer Oil Jar

Oil jar, No. 100, orange, 16" h. (ILLUS.) **$1,000**
Oil jars, No. 100, white, 12" h., pr. **$3,000**

Pitcher, Ring-Ware patt., orange, 1 qt. **$85**
Pitcher, cov., jug-type, ice water, Monterey patt., turquoise **$325**
Plate, 9" d., Ring-Ware patt., grey.................. **$65**
Plate, 10 1/2" d., dinner, Ring-Ware patt., cobalt or delph blue, each.......................... **$95**
Plate, chop, 12" d., Ring-Ware patt., white **$230**
Plate, chop, Monterey Moderne patt., yellow **$45**
Punch bowl, Ring-Ware patt., three-footed, jade green, 14" d. **$550**
Salt & pepper shakers, beehive-shaped, Ring-Ware patt., orange/red, pr. **$60**
Sugar shaker, Ring-Ware patt., jade green... **$350**
Teapot, cov., Ring-Ware patt., burgundy, 2-cup size... **$325**
Vase, 8" h., Hi-Fire line, deep trumpet-shaped form w/widely flaring sides fluted on the exterior, yellow **$90**

Matt Carlton Line Vase

Vase, 8" h., ovoid base w/widely flared rim, twist shoulder handles, orange, Matt Carlton Artware line (ILLUS.)......................... **$650**
Vase, 13" h., ovoid base w/widely flared rim, twist shoulder handles, jade green, Matt Carlton Artware line **$1,200**

Bennington

Bennington wares, which ranged from stoneware to parian and porcelain, were made in Bennington, Vermont, primarily in two potteries, one in which Captain John Norton and his descendants were principals, and the other in which Christopher Webber Fenton (also once associated with the Nortons) was a principal. Various marks are found on the wares made in the two major potteries, including J. & E. Norton, E. & L. P. Norton, L. Norton & Co., Norton & Fenton, Edward Norton, Lyman Fenton & Co., Fenton's Works, United States Pottery Co., U.S.P. and others.

The popular pottery with the mottled brown on yellowware glaze was also produced in Bennington, but wares should be referred to as "Rockingham" or "Bennington-type" unless they can be specifically attributed to a Bennington, Vermont factory.

C

C

Round Waisted Bennington Cuspidor

Cuspidor, short round waisted shape w/side hole, Flint Enamel glaze, Type A impress mark on base, mid-19th c., 8" d., 3 3/4" h. (ILLUS.) **$144**

Bennington Rockingham Toby Pitcher

Toby pitcher, figural seated Mr. Toby, dark brown mottled Rockingham glaze, unmarked, 6" h. (ILLUS.) **$259**

Berlin (KPM)

The mark KPM was used at Meissen from 1724 to 1725, and was later adopted by the Royal Factory, Konigliche Porzellan Manufaktur, in Berlin. At various periods it has been incorporated with the Brandenburg scepter, the Prussian eagle or the crowned globe. The same letters were also adopted by other factories in Germany in the late 19th and early 20th centuries. With the end of the German monarchy in 1918, the name of the firm was changed to Staatliche Porzellan Manufaktur and though production was halted during World War II, the factory was rebuilt and is still in business. The exquisite paintings on porcelain were produced at the close of the 19th century and are eagerly sought by collectors today.

Plaque, oval, decorated w/a bust portrait of a lovely young woman w/a red flower in her long flowing brown hair, a deep yellow off-the-shoulder shawl, in an ornately molded oval gilt-plaster frame, KPM mark on the back, late 19th c., plaque 8 1/2 x 10 1/2", overall 15 x 18" (ILLUS., top next column) **$11,155**

Plaque, oval, titled "Meditation," bust-length portrait of a brunette beauty w/a red flower in her hair, diaphonous white & pale blue drapery around her shoulders, artist-signed, impressed monogram & sceptre marks, late 19th - early 20th c., unframed, 6 5/8 x 8 7/8" (ILLUS., middle next column) **$7,800**

Rare KPM Oval Portrait Plaque

Berlin Plaque of Young Beauty

Plaque of Pretty Young Girl

Plaque, rectangular, three-quarter length portrait of a young girl seated in a woodland setting winding thread for her em-

broidery, impressed monogram & sceptre mark, late 19th - early 20th c., in giltwood frame, 8 3/4 x 10 3/4" (ILLUS.)
.... **$7,200**

Plaque with Women and Child

Plaque, rectangular, titled "Bonheur Maternal," depicting an interior scene w/two young women rocking a child in a hammock accented in gold, impressed monogram & sceptre mark, early 20th c., in giltwood frame, 7 1/2 x 10" (ILLUS.)............ **$6,000**

Rare Plaque of Woodland Beauty

Plaque, rectangular, titled "Fruhling," a bust-length portrait of a dark haired beauty w/white blossoms in her hair in a wooden background of blossoming trees, wearing diaphanous white draped gown, artist-signed, impressed monogram & sceptre mark, late 19th - early 20th c., in giltwood frame, 10 1/4 x 12 3/8" (ILLUS.)
.... **$12,000**

Part of a Set of Vegetable-decorated Salad Plates

Plates, salad, 8 1/2" d., each finely painted at the top w/a still-life of vegetables, herbs & grains, titled in German on the back, the lobed rim trimmed in gold, blue sceptre & iron-red orb marks, late 19th c., set of 12 (ILLUS. of part)... **$60,000**

Blue Ridge Dinnerwares

The small town of Erwin, Tennessee, was the home of the Southern Potteries, Inc., originally founded by E.J. Owen in 1917 and first called the Clinchfield Pottery.

In the early 1920s Charles W. Foreman purchased the plant and revolutionized the company's output, developing the popular line of handpainted wares sold as "Blue Ridge" dinnerwares. Freehand painted by women from the surrounding hills, these colorful dishes in many patterns continued in production until the plant's closing in 1957.

Blue Ridge Dinnerwares Mark

Ashtray, advertising for Clinchfield Railroad $75
Ashtray, regular type, Staccato patt. $15
Bowl, 6" d., cereal, Candlewick shape, Quaker Apple patt. $10
Bowl, 10" d., salad-type, Candlewick shape, Mount Vernon patt...................... $30
Cake lifter, Berry Delicious patt. $35
Cake plate, handled, Yellow Nocturne patt. $50
Cake plate, round, Candlewick shape, Bleeding Heart patt., 11 1/2" d. $30
Casserole, cov., Colonial shape, Ridge Daisy patt. $45
Cigarette box, cov., Ridge Rose patt. $100
Coaster/butter pat, Mariner patt. $100
Creamer, demitasse size, Astor shape, Forget-Me-Not patt. $45
Creamer, regular size, Candlewick shape, Mountain Ivy patt. $15
Cup & saucer, jumbo size, Colonial shape, Red Apple patt., cup 3 3/4" h., the set $100
Cup & saucer, regular size, Colonial shape, Rock Rose patt. $15
Egg cup, double, Brittany patt......................... $100
Feeding dish, child's, Flower Children patt. .. $150
Pie baker, round, Triplet patt., 10" d. $30
Pitcher, 4 1/2" h., Alice shape, Romance patt. $65
Pitcher, 5 1/2" h., Chick shape, Flora patt. $100
Pitcher, 5 3/4" h., Helen shape, Sea Mist patt. $100
Pitcher, 6 3/4" h., Sculptured Fruit shape, decorated w/blue grapes........................... $100
Pitcher, 6 3/4" h., Sculptured Fruit shape, decorated w/yellow grapes......................... $75
Pitcher, 8 1/8" h., Betsy shape, Anniversary Song patt.................................... $250
Pitcher, 8 1/4" h., Rebecca shape, Whig Rose patt.................................... $150

Plate, child's, Flower Children patt. $100
Plate, 7" d., round, dessert-type, Colonial shape, Orchard Glory patt........................... $10
Plate, 7" w., square, Apple Trio patt. $25
Plate, 8" d., round salad-type, Colonial shape, Tiger Lily patt...................... $15
Plate, 9" d., round, dinner-type, Candlewick shape, Bluebell Bouquet patt. $15
Plate, 10" d., round, dinner-type, Colonial shape, Christmas Tree patt.................. $85
Plate, 10" d., round, dinner-type, Skyline shape, Christmas Doorway patt.................. $90
Platter, 12" d., Colonial shape, Berryville patt. $30
Platter, 13" d., Candlewick shape, Blue Moon patt. $30
Salad fork, Fruit Fantasy patt. $50
Salt & pepper shakers, Barrel shape, Paper Roses patt., pr. $75
Salt & pepper shakers, Bud Top patt., one w/yellow bud top, other w/pink bud top, pr. $75
Salt & pepper shakers, Range shape, Mardi Gras patt., pr. $30
Salt & pepper shakers, Tall China shape, Chintz patt., pr.. $100
Snack set: plate w/cup well & matching cup; Colonial shape, Garden Lane patt., 8" d., the set....................................... $30
Snack tray, Martha shape, Garden Lane patt. $100
Soup bowl, tab-handled, Colonial shape, Mickey patt., 7" d.. $15
Sugar bowl, open, demitasse size, Astor shape, Forget-Me-Not patt., 1 7/8" h........... $45
Sugar bowl, pedestal base, Chintz patt.......... $75
Teapot, cov., demitasse size, Astor shape, Hollyberry patt., 6 1/2" h............................ $350
Tidbit tray, two-tier, Colonial shape, Northstar Cherry patt. $45
Tray, demitasse size, Candlewick patt., Rosebuds patt... $90
Vase, 5 1/4" h., Bud shape, Helen patt. $150
Vase, 8" h., Handled shape, Stephanie patt. $105
Vegetable bowl, oval, Candlewick shape, Brunswick patt., 9" l..................................... $20

Blue & White Pottery

Embossed Peacock Baking Dish

Baking dish, embossed Peacock patt., round w/heavy egg-and-dart-molded rim over gently curved sides, Brush-McCoy Pottery Co., 9" d. (ILLUS.) $800

Rose Decal Brush Vase, Soap Dish, Shaving Mug and Hot Water Pitcher

Embossed Greek Key Bowl

Bowl, 6" to 12" d., embossed Greek Key patt., Red Wing Pottery Co., depending on size (ILLUS. of one).............. **$100-170**

Brush vase, Rose decal, ovoid body w/forked flaring rim, Western Stoneware, 5 1/2" h. (ILLUS. second from left with Rose decal soap dish, shaving mug & hot water pitcher, top of page) **$175**

Red Wing Daisy Pattern Butter Crock

Butter crock, cov., embossed Daisy patt., Red Wing Pottery Co., found in three sizes, 3 1/2" h. (ILLUS.)................................. **$395**

Butter crock, cov., stenciled Dutch Scene patt., Brush-McCoy Pottery Co., 6 3/4" d., 5" h. **$325**

Canister, cov., embossed Willow (Basketweave & Morning Glory) patt., "Crackers" (short), Brush-McCoy Pottery Co. (ILLUS. left with tall canister, top next page)... **$550**

Canister, cov., embossed Willow (Basketweave & Morning Glory) patt., "Crackers" (tall), Brush-McCoy Pottery Co., average 6 1/2 to 7" h. (ILLUS. right with short canister, top next page) **$1,000**

Two Stenciled Vines Canisters

Canister, cov., stenciled Vines patt., "Oat Meal," A.E. Hull Pottery Co., 7 1/4" h. (ILLUS. left with smaller Rice canister) **$400**

Canister, cov., stenciled Vines patt., "Rice", A.E. Hull Pottery Co., 5 1/2 to 6" h. (ILLUS. right with larger Oat Meal canister) **$250**

Small & Large Embossed Willow Crackers Canisters

Embossed Flying Bird Casserole & Cover

Casserole, cov., embossed Flying Bird patt., A.E. Hull Pottery Co., 9 1/2" d. (ILLUS.)........................... **$600**

Willow Chamber Pot & Slop Jar

Chamber pot, cov., embossed Willow (Basketweave & Morning Glory) patt., Brush-McCoy Pottery Co., 9 1/2" d., 8" h. (ILLUS. right with Willow slop jar)..... **$325**

Hot water pitcher, 7" h., Rose decal, bulbous lobed body w/wide flaring rim, loop handle, Western Stoneware (ILLUS. far right with Rose decal brush vase, soap dish & shaving mug, top of page 103) **$200**

Pitcher, 5" h., stenciled Conifer Tree patt., printed advertising on the reverse, Brush-McCoy Pottery Co. **$350**

7 1/2" Embossed Dainty Fruit Pitcher

Pitcher, 7 1/2" h., embossed Dainty Fruit patt., A.E. Hull Pottery Co. (ILLUS.)........... **$650**

Stenciled Acorn 8" Pitcher

Pitcher, 8" h., stenciled Acorn patt., Brush-McCoy Pottery Co. (ILLUS.)...................... **$300**

Pitcher, 9" h., 6 1/2" d., embossed Cosmos or Wild Rose patt., w/overall blue sponging, Nelson McCoy Sanitary Stoneware Co... **$750**

9" Embossed Cosmos Pitcher

Pitcher, 9" h., 6 1/2" d., embossed Cosmos or Wild Rose patt., w/advertising, Nelson McCoy Sanitary Stoneware Co. (ILLUS.) **$2,500**

8" Stenciled Wildflower Waisted Pitcher

Pitcher, 8" h., stenciled Wildflower patt., tall waisted body w/long spout, five stencils per side, Brush-McCoy Pottery Co., also found in 8 1/2" h. size (ILLUS.) **$800**

C

C

Stenciled Nautilus Salt Crock & Vase

Salt crock w/wooden lid, hanging-type, stenciled Nautilus patt., printed Gothic script "Salt," A.E. Hull Pottery Co., 6" d., 4 1/4" h. (ILLUS. right with bulbous vase, top of page) **$225**

Shaving mug, Rose decal, bulbous lobed body w/loop handle, Western Stoneware, 3 3/4" h. (ILLUS. second from right with Rose decal brush vase, soap dish & hot water pitcher, top of page 103) **$150**

Embossed Daisy on Snowflake Salt Box

Salt box, cov., embossed Daisy on Snowflake patt., unknown maker, 6" d., 4" h. (ILLUS.) **$250**

Embossed Raspberry Salt Box

Salt box, cov., embossed Raspberry patt., Brush-McCoy Pottery Co., 6" d., 4" h. (ILLUS.) **$175**

Rare Diffused Blue Scuttle Shaving Mug

Shaving mug, scuttle-style, Diffused Blue, 6" h. (ILLUS.) **$1,250**

Slop jar, cov., embossed Willow (Basketweave & Morning Glory) patt., Brush-McCoy Pottery Co., 9 1/2" d., 12 1/2" h. (ILLUS. left with chamber pot, bottom of page 104) **$350**

Soap dish, cover & drainer, Rose decal, squatty bulbous form w/domed cover & loop handle, Western Stoneware, 5 1/4" d., 2" h. (ILLUS. far left with Rose decal brush vase, shaving mug and hot water pitcher, top of page 103) **$350**

Vase, 6" h., stenciled Nautilus patt., bulbous form, A.E. Hull Pottery Co. (ILLUS. left with Nautilus salt crock, top of page) **$325**

C

Very Rare Wildflower Water Cooler

Water cooler, cov., stenciled Wildflower patt., domed cover w/button knob atop a tall cylindrical section above the wider cylindrical base section w/a "3" in a circle above the metal spigot, 3 gal. (ILLUS.)... **$4,500**

Barrel-shaped Blue Banded Water Cooler

Water cooler, cover & metal spigot, barrel-shaped, decorated w/narrow blue bands & printed "5" above the spigot, Robinson Clay Products - Robinson Ransbottom Pottery, 5 gal. (ILLUS.) **$350**

Brayton Laguna Pottery

In the 1940s California saw an influx of pottery companies; however, it was Durlin Brayton who earlier, about 1927, began his enterprise. During these previous years Brayton created an assortment of products along with many beautiful glazes, honing his skills before other artists arrived. He married his second wife, an artist, Ellen Webster Grieve, in 1936 and together they became very successful. Durlin Brayton's talent caught the eye of Walt Disney, who bestowed on him the honor of being the first pottery licensed to create ceramic copies of some of Disney's most famous characters. Brayton did this from 1938 until 1940. Ellen Grieve Brayton died in 1948 and Durlin Brayton followed shortly after in 1951. The pottery continued to operate until 1968.

Brayton collectors need to familiarize themselves with the marks, lines and glazes produced by this firm. There are as many as a dozen marks, however, not all Brayton is marked. Hand-turned pieces were the first used and many were marked with Durlin Brayton's handwriting with "Brayton Laguna" or "Brayton Tile." These items have become scarce. Assorted lines include: African-American figures, animals, Art Deco designs, Blackamoors, Calasia (a design of circles and feathers), Children's Series, Circus Series, Disney Characters, Gay Nineties, Hillbilly Shotgun Wedding, kitchen items, sculptures, tiles, Webtonware and the Wedding Series, plus a few others.

Bowl, 10" d., 2" h., Calasia line, feather design in bottom, scalloped rim w/raised circles on inner rim, pale green........................ **$90**

Box, cov., round, white base w/red strawberries, one white flower & green leaves on cover, marked "Copyright 1943 by Brayton Laguna Pottery," 5 1/2" d., 5" h. **$30**

Box, cov., trinket-type, pale blue w/darker blue flowers on the cover & base, marked "Brayton Laguna," 4 x 5", 2" h. **$35**

Bust of woman, chin down w/head slightly turned, white or black crackle glaze, incised "Brayton's Laguna, Beach, Calif. F-1P," 13 1/4" l., 12" h. **$700**

Candleholders, figural Blackamoor, pr......... **$250**

Cigarette box, cov., black flecked glossy red, stamp mark "Brayton Calif. U.S.A.," 3 1/4 x 5", 2" h... **$63**

Rare Brayton Laguna Mammy Cookie Jar

C

Cookie jar, cov., figural black Mammy, bright blue dress, white apron w/yellow, black, green & blue trim, red bandana on head, yellow earrings, rare early version, stamped "Brayton Calif. U.S.A.," 12 5/8" h. (ILLUS., previous page) **$850**

Cookie jar, cov., model of a chicken, brilliant glazes of blue, red, green & yellow, hard to find, 10" h. **$750**

Cookie jar, figure of Swedish Maid (Christina), produced 1941, incised mark, 11" h. .. **$610**

Brayton Calico Kitten Creamer

Creamer, figural, model of a seated calico kitten w/a white body decorated w/pink, mauve & blue flowers & brown stitching, blue ribbon around neck, glossy glaze, ink-stamped "Copyright 1942 by Brayton Laguna Pottery," 6 1/2" h. (ILLUS.) **$65**

Creamer & sugar, individual, eggplant, unglazed bottom, created by Durlin Brayton, incised mark "Brayton Laguna Pottery," pr. **$270**

Creamer & sugar bowl, figural, in the form of a sprinkler can & wheelbarrow, w/floral pale pinks & blues on a white ground, 3" h., pr. .... **$**

Creamer & sugar bowl, round, eggplant glaze, created by Durlin Brayton, incised mark on unglazed bottom "Brayton Laguna Pottery," 2 1/2" h., pr. **$85**

Provincial Line Cup with Tea Bag Holder

Cup w/tea bag holder, Provincial line, brown bisque stain w/white & yellow flowers & green leaves outside, gloss yellow inside, marked "Brayton Laguna Calif. K-31," 1 3/4" h. (ILLUS.) **$26**

Figure, baby on all fours **$110**

Figure, Blackamoor, kneeling & holding open cornucopia, heavily jeweled w/gold trim, 10" h. **$260**

Figure, Blackamoor, walking & carrying a bowl in his hands, glossy gold earrings, white bowl & shoes, burgundy scarf, shirt & pantaloons, 8 1/4" h. **$249**

Figure, Children's Series, "Ellen," girl standing w/pigtails & a hat tied at neck, arms bent & palms forward, one leg slightly twisted, 7 1/4" h. **$98**

Figure, Children's Series, "Jon," boy standing & carrying a basket in one hand, rooster in other, 8 1/4" h. **$126**

Figure, sailor boy holding a gun **$336**

Figure, woman wearing a blue dress & bonnet & holding a book **$140**

African-American Boy & Girl

Figure group, African-American boy & girl, boy holding basket of flowers in each hand, black shoes, yellow socks, barefoot girl, created by L.A. Dowd, early 1940s, paper label, 4 1/4" base, boy 7" h., girl 5 1/2" h. (ILLUS.) **$540**

Figure group, an abstract sculpture of a man & a cat, black glaze, ca. 1957, 21" h. .. **$835**

Figure group, an African-American boy & girl on a single base, boy holding a basket of flowers in each hand, created by L.A. Dowd, ca. 1942, paper label, scarce, base 4 1/4" d., girl 5 1/2" h., boy 7" h. **$850**

Figure group, "One Year Later," mother seated on left w/green dress holding baby in white dress, man standing w/striped trousers, black hair, mustache, jacket & shoes, stamp mark, 4" l., 8 1/4" h. **$199**

Figure group, "Seashore Honeymoon," a woman & man w/man wearing a red & white-striped top & red swimming trunks, the woman w/a pale blue swim-dress, white hat w/blue polka dots, "Laguna Beach Calif. 1895" printed in black around a life preserver on the back, part of the "Wedding Series," stamped mark "copyright 1943 by Brayton Laguna Pottery," 9" h. **$250**

Model of cat, "Kiki," seated on oval base, tail wraps around to hide back legs and paws, socks on front paws, hat perched on head & tied at front, eyes closed, colorful sweater, assorted colors of pink, blue, black & white, marked on unglazed bottom, "Brayton Laguna" above a line & "Kiki" below the line, 6" l. base, 9 1/4" h. **$150**

Model of cat, seated on oval base, socks on front paws w/left paw over right paw, head turned to left looking back, blue eyes open, hat perched on head between ears, bluebird on front of hat, colorful colors of blue, pink, white & black, unglazed, bottom w/no marks, 6 1/4" l. base, 9" h...... **$145**

Model of duck, standing w/head down, Provincial line, brown overall stain w/glossy yellow bill, 6 1/2" h. **$64**

Model of fox, seated, No. H-57 ...... **$150**

Model of purple cow, original sticker **$130**

Brayton-Laguna White Squirrel

Model of squirrel, crouched w/tail behind & curving slightly upward on end, head & ears up, nondescript face, White Crackle glaze, incised mark, "Brayton's Laguna Calif. T-15," 12 3/4" l, 6" h. (ILLUS.)........... **$145**

Models of monkeys, a male & female, white crackle glaze w/brown stained faces, unmarked, not easy to find, 13" h., pr. **$575**

Pair of Brayton Laguna Quails

Models of quails, brown w/black speckles on white breasts, black & white feather details on wings, incised mark "Brayton's Laguna Beach," 9" & 11" h., pr. (ILLUS.) ... **$165**

Mug, w/pretzel-shaped handle, raised pretzel shapes on gold, stamp mark "Brayton Calif. U.S.A.," 5" h. **$34**

Salt & pepper shakers, figural peasant couple, Provincial patt., pr. **$73**

Tile, chartreuse & yellow bird, turquoise, yellow & white flowers, black background incised mark, "Laguna Pottery," 7 x 7" **$495**

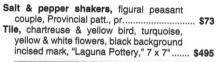

Rare Mexican Theme Brayton Tile

Tile, square, decorated in bold colors w/a Mexican woman followed by two children & a dog w/a palm tree & cactus in the background, incised mark "Brayton Tile," 7" sq. (ILLUS.)................. **$700**

Vase, 5 1/2" h., round foot flaring to a scalloped rim, created by Durlin Brayton in the early period, turquoise glaze rising to a deeper turquoise, incised mark "Brayton Laguna Pottery," 7" sq. **$450**

Vase, 7 1/4" h., 7" w., 7" l., pillow shape w/feather design on each side & raised circles on recessed short base, fern green............. **$93**

Sea Horse Vase

Vase, 8 1/2" h., model of a sea horse, white body w/pink, yellow & turquoise accents, stamp mark underglaze "Brayton Calif. U.S.A." (ILLUS.)...................... **$312**

Vase, 9" h., figure of a gypsy woman's head, beads around her neck, ca. 1939, incised mark "Brayton Laguna Pottery"...... **$300**

Vase, 9" h., round foot w/raised circles, Calasia patt., slightly bulbous body w/feathered design, flaring gently at rim, light blue w/lighter blue inside, Model No. A-7.. **$95**

Brayton Figural Man Wall Pocket

Wall pocket, figure of a standing man w/his arms above his head, wearing a long white robe w/pink socks, belt & hat, Webton Ware mark, hard to find, 13" h. (ILLUS.).. **$175**

Webton Ware Wall Pocket Bowl

Wall pocket, model of a bowl w/shaped rim, two holes for hanging, Webton Ware mark on unglazed back, 2 3/4" w., 4 1/4" h. (ILLUS.) **$125**

Caliente Pottery

In 1979 the pottery world lost a man who used his talents to create satin matte glazes and blended colors. Virgil Haldeman's career got its start after he graduated from the University of Illinois in 1923. In 1927 he moved to Southern California and it was there that he and his partner opened the Haldeman Tile Manufacturing Company in Los Angeles. The business was sold just a few years later and Haldeman went to work for the Catalina Clay Products Company on Catalina Island. When Virgil quit his job as ceramics engineer and plant superintendent three years later he opened the Haldeman Pottery in Burbank, California.

In the early years, the word "Caliente" was used as a line name to designate flower frogs, figurines and flower bowls. Collectors now use the Caliente name almost exclusively to indicate all products made at the Haldeman pottery.

At best, items were randomly marked and some simply bear a deeply impressed "Made in California" mark. However, in 1987 Wilbur Held wrote a privately printed book titled Collectable Caliente Pottery, which aided tremendously in identifying Caliente products by a numbering system that the Haldeman Company used. According to Held, molded pieces usually are numbered in the 100s; handmade pieces, 200s; mostly animals and fowl, 300s; dancing girls, 400s; continuation of handmade pieces, 500-549; and molded pieces with roses added, 550 and above. Stickers were also used and many are still firmly attached to the items.

Caliente Marks

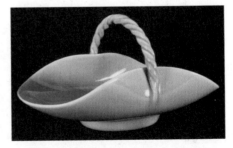

Rope-handled Green Caliente Basket

Basket, round, footed rim w/rope handle, green, Model No. 222, incised "Handmade Calif.," 7" l. (ILLUS.) **$48**

Bowl, 8" d., 2 1/2" h., green, rolled edge, Model No. 14-1, early ware (ILLUS. right w/handled vases, bottom next page) **$154**

Candy dish, figural, swan w/head bent at neck serving as handle, pink inside, white outside, Model No. 64, 9" l., 6" h. **$82**

Ewer, w/handles, yellow gloss ground w/applied two white roses & three yellow leaves in relief, incised mark "554 U.S.A.," 5 1/2" h. **$48**

Caliente Dancing Girl in Bloomers

Figure of dancing girl in bloomers, a scarf in each hand draping to the floor, head bent & slightly tilted, face features indistinct, left hand resting on waist, Model No. 406, very hard to find, 6 1/2" h. (ILLUS.) **$170**

Floater, flat & shallow dish to float flowers, oval w/two overlapping rim cuts w/candle rings in two rose petals & four inward rim bends, script-incised mark, Model No. 509, 16" l. **$68**

Floater, pink inside, white outside, Model No. 205 14" l. **$41**

Caliente Rooster & Hen

Model of a hen, standing on round base, unusual hand-decorated, brown body w/darker brown highlights, green & white base incised "336" & "USA," 3 1/2" h. (ILLUS. left w/rooster) **$83**

Model of a rooster, seated on round base, unusual hand-decorated brown body w/darker brown highlights, green & white base, incised "306" & "USA," 3 3/4" h. (ILLUS. right w/hen) **$83**

Planter, model of a Dutch shoe w/one rose & leaves, green glaze w/pink, unmarked, Model No. 555, 5" l., 2 1/2" h. **$41**

Vase, 3 3/4" h., one handle, yellow, Model No. 37 (ILLUS. second from left w/handled vases & bowl, bottom of page) **$42**

Vase, 7" h., footed w/ring at shoulder & two handles at top, orange, Model No. 9 (ILLUS. left w/handled vases & bowl, bottom of page) **$195**

Vase, 9" h., two small handles at top, green early ware, Model No. 1-1 (ILLUS. second from right w/handled vases & bowl, bottom of page) **$230**

Wall pocket, three plumes w/bow near bottom, satin matte white glaze, incised mark, Model No. 6, 6 1/2" h. **$89**

Caliente Handled Vases & Bowl

Cambridge Art Pottery

The Cambridge Art Pottery was incorporated in Cambridge, Ohio, in 1900 and began production of artwares in early 1901. Its earliest lines, Terrhea and Oakwood, were slip-decorated glossy-glazed wares similar to the products of other Ohio potteries of that era.

In 1902 it began production of an earthenware cooking ware line called Guernsey that featured a dark brown exterior and porcelain white lining. This eventually became its leading seller, and in 1909 the name of the firm was changed to The Guernsey Earthenware Company to reflect this fact. In 1907 the company introduced a matte green-glazed art line it called Otoe, but all production of its art pottery lines ceased in 1908. The company eventually became part of The Atlas Globe China Company, which closed in 1933.

Cambridge Oakwood Line Vase

Vase, 7 3/4" h., Oakwood line, simple baluster-form body tapering to a small flaring neck, overall drippy black, brown & yellow glaze, marked on base "Oakwood - 200," bruise at rim, stilt pull on base (ILLUS.)......... **$81**

Canton

This ware has been decorated for nearly two centuries in factories near Canton, China. Intended for export sale, much of it was originally inexpensive blue-and-white hand-decorated ware. Late-18th- and early-19th-century pieces are superior to later ones and fetch higher prices.

Cambridge Oakwood Line Cruet

Cruet, Oakwood line, footed bulbous body tapering to a tall cylindrical neck w/wide spout, small looped shoulder handle, streaky mottled tan & green to dark brown & brick red glossy glaze, impressed on the bottom "Oakwood 34," 5 1/4" h. (ILLUS.) **$70**

Canton Bowl with Cut Corners

Bowl, 10 1/2" w., 4 3/4" h., squared w/cut corners, simple island landscape in the center bottom, 19th c. (ILLUS.)................. **$881**

C

Scarce Canton Candlesticks

Candlesticks, slender tapering cylindrical form w/flattened socket rim, 19th c., rim chip, 7 1/2" h., pr. (ILLUS.)..................... **$2,233**

Charger, wide round shape w/dished rim, large round central landscape, small edge fleck, 19th c., 14 3/4" d. **$403**

Punch bowl, narrow footring below deep rounded sides, early 19th c., 13 1/4" d., 5 1/2" h. (ILLUS., top next column) **$3,055**

Fine Early Canton China Punch Bowl

Canton Tureen, Cover & Undertray

Tureen, cover & undertray, oblong w/beveled corners, molded boar's head handles on base & molded stem handle on the cover, 19th c., overall 12 5/8" l., 9" h., the set (ILLUS.)...................................... **$1,998**

Warming platter, oval w/flanged rim, small tab handle at one end & filling hole at other end, 19th c., 15 3/4" l., 2 1/2" h. (ILLUS., bottom of page).......................... **$441**

Unusual Canton China Warming Platter

Catalina Island Pottery

The Clay Products Division of the Santa Catalina Island Co. produced a variety of wares during its brief ten-year operation. The brainchild of chewing-gum magnate William Wrigley Jr., owner of Catalina Island at the time, and business associate D.M. Retton, the plant was established at Pebbly Beach, near Avalon, in 1927. Its twofold goal was to provide year-round work for the island's residents and to produce building material for Wrigley's ongoing development of a major tourist attraction at Avalon. Early production consisted of bricks and roof and patio tiles. Later, art pottery, including vases, flower bowls, lamps and home accessories, were made from a local brown-based clay; in about 1930, tablewares were introduced. These early wares carried vivid glazes but had a tendency to chip easily, and a white-bodied, more chip-resistant clay imported from the mainland was used after 1932. The costs associated with importing clay eventually caused the Catalina pottery to be sold to Gladding, McBean & Co. in 1937. Gladding McBean continued to use the Catalina name and molds for are ware and dinnerware for products manufactured on the mainland until 1942. After 1942, some of the molds were sold to and used by Weil of California. Gladding, McBean items usually have an ink stamped mark and can be distinguished from Island ware by the glaze and clay as well.

CATALINA MADE IN U.S.A. POTTERY   CATALINA ISLAND   CATALINA C 801 POTTERY

Catalina Island Pottery Marks

Ashtray, figural fish, decorated, Model No. 551, Toyon red glaze, 6 1/2" .... **$550+**
Ashtray, figural goat, 4" w. .... **$550+**
Book ends, figural monk, pearly white glaze, 4 x 5", pr. .... **$1,200+**
Bowl, flower-type, fluted, 10 x 15", 2" h. **$125**
Bowl, 9 1/2 x 14", flared sides, white glaze.... **$150**
Candleholder, low, Model No. 380 .... **$125**
Carafe, cov., handled, Toyon red glaze **$145**
Casserole, cov., rope edge.......................... **$265**
Charger, Mexican scene, 11 1/2" d............ **$1,200**
Charger, rolled edge, Toyon red glaze, 14 1/2" d.. **$225**
Coffee server, cov. **$250**
Console bowl, fluted.................................. **$225+**
Creamer, 6" h... **$250**
Cup & saucer, rope edge **$75**

Flask, model of a cactus, Descanso green, 6 1/4" h.. **$600+**
Flower frog, model of a stork, 7" h. **$550**
Indian bowl, rare **$650**
Model of clamshell, pearly white glaze........ **$600**
Oil jar, No. 351, Toyon red glaze, 18" h..... **$1,200**
Planter, model of a cat, cactus planter, Cat-Lina **$475**
Plate, 8 1/2" d., salad, rope edge **$55**
Plate, chop, 11" d., Descanso green glaze **$95**
Plate, chop, 12 1/2" d., Toyon red glaze **$145**
Plate, 14" d., submarine garden decoration **$1,250**

Clover-shaped Relish Tray

Relish tray, handled, clover-shaped, sea foam glaze (ILLUS.) **$1,300**
Salt & pepper shakers, gourd-shaped, pr. ... **$125**
Salt & pepper shakers, model of tulip, blue glaze, pr. **$125**
Sugar bowl, cov., rope edge **$85**
Tile, Spanish design, 6 x 6" sq. .... **$295+**

Tortilla Warmer

Tortilla warmer, cov., Monterey brown glaze (ILLUS.) **$750**
Vase, 5" h., handled, Model No. 612, Mandarin yellow glaze **$225**
Vase, bud, 5" h., Model No. 300, Descanso green glaze **$170**
Vase, 6" h., ribbed body, blue glaze.............. **$175**
Vase, 7 3/4" h., Model No. 627, blue glaze **$225**
Vase, 10" h., fluted **$225**
Wall pocket, basketweave design, 9" l. **$450**

Ceramic Arts Studio of Madison

During its 15 years of operation, Ceramic Arts Studio of Madison, Wisconsin, was one of the nation's most prolific producers of figurines, shakers, and other decorative ceramics. The Studio began in 1940 as the joint venture of potter

Lawrence Rabbitt and entrepreneur Reuben Sand. Early products included hand-thrown bowls, pots, and vases, exploring the potential of Wisconsin clay. However, the arrival of Betty Harrington in 1941 took CAS in a new direction, leading to the type of work it is best known for. Under Mrs. Harrington's artistic leadership, the focus was changed to the production of finely sculpted decorative figurines. Among the many subjects covered were adults in varied costumes and poses, charming depictions of children, fantasy and theatrical figures, and animals. The inventory soon expanded to include figural wall plaques, head vases, salt-and-pepper shakers, self-sitters, and "snuggle pairs".

Metal display accessories complementing the ceramics were produced by another Reuben Sand firm, Jon-San Creations, under the direction of Zona Liberace (stepmother of the famed pianist). Mrs. Liberace also served as the studio's decorating director.

During World War II, Ceramic Arts Studio flourished, since the import of decorative items from overseas was suspended. In its prime during the late 1940s, CAS produced over 500,000 pieces annually, and employed nearly 100 workers.

As primary designer, the talented Betty Harrington is credited with creating the vast majority of the 800-plus designs in the Studio inventory—a remarkable achievement for a self-taught artist. The only other CAS designer of note was Ulle Cohen ("Rebus"), who contributed a series of modernistic animal figurines in the early 1950s.

The popularity of Ceramic Arts Studio pieces eventually resulted in many imitations of lesser quality. After World War II, lower-priced imports began to flood the market, forcing the studio to close its doors in 1955. An attempt to continue the enterprise in Japan, using some of the Madison master molds as well as new designs, did not prove successful. An additional number of molds and copyrights were sold to Mahana Imports, which released a series of figures based on the CAS originals. Both the Ceramic Arts Studio-Japan and Mahana pieces utilized a clay both whiter and more lightweight than that of Madison pieces. Additionally, their markings differ from the "Ceramic Arts Studio, Madison Wis." logo, which appears in black on the base of many Studio pieces. However, not all authentic Studio pieces were marked (particularly in pairs); a more reliable indicator of authenticity is the "decorator tick mark". This series of colored dots, which appears at the drain hole on the bottom of every Ceramic Arts Studio piece, served as an in-house identifier for the decorator who worked on a specific piece. The tick mark is a sure sign that a figurine is the work of the studio.

Ceramic Arts Studio is one of the few figural ceramics firms of the 1940s and '50s that operated successfully outside of the West Coast. Today, CAS pieces remain in high demand, thanks to their skillful design and decoration, warm use of color,

distinctively glossy glaze, and highly imaginative and exquisitely realized themes.

Many pieces in the Ceramic Arts Studio inventory were released both as figurines and as salt-and-pepper shakers. For items not specifically noted as shakers in this listing, add 50 percent to the shaker price estimate.

Complete reference information on the studio can be found in Ceramic Arts Studio: The Legacy of Betty Harrington by Donald-Brian Johnson, Timothy J. Holthaus, and James E. Petzold (Schiffer Publishing Ltd., 2003). The official Ceramic Arts Studio collectors group, "CAS Collectors", publishes a quarterly newsletter, hosts an annual convention, and can be contacted at www.cascollectors.com. The studio also has an official historical site, www.ceramicartsstudio.org. Photos for this category are by John Petzold.

C

Ceramic Arts Studio Marks

Rare Adonis & Aphrodite Figures

Adonis & Aphrodite, 7" h. & 9" h., pr. (ILLUS.) **$500-700**
Arched Window with Cross metal accessory, 14" h. **$100-120**
Blackamoor salt & pepper shakers, an "S" on one, a "P" on the other, 4 3/4" h., pr. **$140-160**
Bonnie head vase, 7" h. **$125-150**

C

Chinese Boy & Girl & Wee Chinese Boy & Girl

Boy & Puppy & Girl & Kitten Shelf-Sitters

Dutch Love Boy & Dutch Love Girl

Boy with Puppy & Girl with Kitten, shelf-
sitters, 4 1/4" h., pr. (ILLUS.)............... **$150-200**
Chinese Boy & Girl, 4 1/4" h. & 4" h., pr.
(ILLUS. far left & far right with Wee Chi-
nese Boy & Girl, top of page)................. **$30-40**
Deer plaque, stylized, 5 1/2" l. **$1,000-1,200**

Dutch Love Boy & Dutch Love Girl, 5" h.,
pr. (ILLUS.) **$120-140**
Fish up on tails, A & B., 4" h., pr............... **$40-70**
Fox & Goose, 3 1/4" h., 2 1/4" h., pr. (ILLUS.,
bottom of page)................................. **$300-350**
Goosey Gander plaque, 4 1/2" h. **$140-160**

Fox & Goose Ceramic Arts Figures

Ceramic Arts Hippo Ashtray

Hippo ashtray, 3 1/2" h. (ILLUS.) **$100-120**
Horsehead server, miniature, 2 1/2" l........ **$60-70**
Isaac, 10" h... **$70-100**
Kitten Scratching (A), 2" h............................. **$50-60**
Kitten Sleeping (A), 2" h. **$50-60**
Kitten Washing (A), 2" h. **$50-60**
Lotus wall plaque, 8 1/2" h. **$200-225**

Ceramic Arts M'amselle Figure

M'amselle, kneeling girl, all-white, 7" h.
(ILLUS.) **$250-350**
Manchu wall plaque, 8 1/2" h................. **$200-225**
Modern Collie, reclining, 4 1/2" l............ **$400-500**
Rebekah, 10" h.. **$70-100**
Salome, 14" h. (ILLUS., top next column)
.... **$1,800-2,000**
Swan Lake Man & Swan Lake Woman,
7" h., pr. (ILLUS., middle next column)
.... **$1,800-1,900**
Swan teapot, miniature, 3" h........................ **$60-75**
The Four Seasons, Autumn Andy, 5" h.
(ILLUS. far right with three other figures,
bottom of page) **$160-190**

Very Rare Ceramic Arts Salome Figure

Swan Lake Man & Swan Lake Woman

The Four Seasons, Spring Sue, 5" h.
(ILLUS. second from left with three other
figures, bottom of page) **$140-170**
The Four Seasons, Summer Sally, 3 1/2" h.
(ILLUS. second from right with three other
figures, bottom of page)...................... **$100-130**
The Four Seasons, Winter Willie, 4" h.
(ILLUS. far left with three other figures,
bottom of page) **$90-120**
Wee Chinese Boy & Girl, 3" h., pr. (ILLUS.
center with Chinese Boy & Chinese Girl,
top of page 116)...................................... **$30-40**

The Four Seasons Ceramic Arts Figures

Cleminson Clay

Betty Cleminson, a hobbyist, began working in her Monterey Park, California garage in 1941. She called the business Cleminson Clay. However, the business proved so successful that two years later Betty was forced to make several key decisions: She moved to El Monte, California and built a large factory; hired over fifty employees including many artists; and changed the name to "The California Cleminson." Later, another major decision was made to encourage her husband, George, to join the company. He had taught school but was also proficient at handling the financial affairs. He also oversaw the construction of the new building. At one point during the later years, the Cleminsons had about 150 employees. Due to the competition from imports, Betty, like so many American potters, was forced to close her operation in 1963. She died on September 30, 1996 at the age of 86.

The Cleminsons created a variety of giftwares including butter dishes, canisters, cookie jars, salt and pepper shakers and string holders. An assortment of hand painted plates, wall plaques and other items with novelty sayings were a big hit with collectors. Distlefink was a highly successful dinnerware line when it was introduced. However, today the light brown ground is not nearly as popular as the white ground. Galagray was a small line consisting of mostly trays, serving dishes and flowerpots with a country theme.

The incised, stylized "BC" mark signifies Betty Cleminson. It was the first mark used. Another mark was a facsimile of a plate with a ribbon at the top and the words "The California" over "Cleminson" with the initials "bc" in the center, along with a boy and girl, one on each side of the plate. The words "hand painted" appear below the plate. This mark is the most familiar to collectors and can be found with our without the boy and girl. - Susan Cox

Left: Most commonly found stamped mark with or without boy & girl on the sides.

Right: Early Betty Cleminson incised mark with her initials. Sometimes confused with the copyright symbol.

Ashtray, round w/six cigarette rest, three feet, decorated w/abstract designs, 1950s, 8 1/4" d., 3 3/4" h. **$50**

Bank, figural hanging-type, modeled as a stocking in red & white stripes, coin slot in top, mark w/boy & girl outside circle & Cleminson inside, 8 1/2" h. **$25**

Grouping of Cleminson Distlefink Pieces

Butter dish, cov., figural, model of a Distlefink sitting on an oblong base, bird's head turned toward back, brown glossy glaze w/dark brown & rust accents, 7 1/2" l., 5 3/4" h. (ILLUS. bottom right with other Distlefink pieces)... **$65**

*Cleminson Cheese Keeper, Cookie Jar
& Salt Box*

Cleminson Clay Laundry Sprinkler

Cheese keeper, cov., figural, the cover modeled as a round pudgy woman w/a wide domed skirt, in dark & light green, dark brown, black & white glossy glaze, on a green round dish base, 6 1/2" h. (ILLUS. bottom right with cookie jar & salt box) **$160**

Cleanser shaker, figure of woman standing, yellow hair, brown scarf, white & brown apron over yellow dress, blue accents, very common, 6 1/2" h....................... **$40**

Cookie jar, cov., cylindrical w/peaked cover w/knob handle, the sides in white h.p. w/red cherries, green leaves & brown branches encircling "Cookies," 9" h. (ILLUS. bottom left with cheese keeper and salt box) **$75**

Cookie jar, cov., heart-shaped cover w/two lovebirds forming handle, yellow ground w/white center, w/wording "The Way To A Man's Heart" in blue, black & pink, California Cleminsons in circle & copyright symbol mark, 9 1/4" h. **$255**

Cotton ball holder, figural, a baby's head w/one tooth, pale pink ground, brown eyes, blue collar bow, hard to find, 4" h. **$95**

Egg cup, face on boy on front, "For A Good Egg" on reverse, 3 3/4" h. **$60**

Egg timer, Humpty-Dumpty head, yellow hat w/blue band, blue nose, yellow bow tie w/blue dots, black smile & eyes looking upward, glass w/sand attached to his back, marked w/a circle w/California Cleminson inside, scarce, 3 1/2" h. **$90**

Gravy boat, Distlefink patt., white ground w/green, purple, blue & black decorations, 10 1/2" l. **$28**

Laundry sprinkler, figural, Oriental man, hat forms metal top, stamped mark, 9" h. (ILLUS., top next column) **$106**

Match holder, white ground w/a yellow bird on a branch w/blue flowers below, flowers on both sides w/blue & yellow trim, marked w/boy & girl, 6 1/2" h. **$125**

Mug with Head of Man & Woman

Mug, cylindrical w/loop handle, colored heads of a mustached brown-haired man & blonde-haired lady along with the wording "Now Is The Hour," 4 1/2" h. (ILLUS.) **$30**

Juvenile Mug

C

Bathtub-shaped Cleminson Planter

Mug, juvenile, round knobs on sides, scene of Native American boy & his dog playing on front, stamped mark, 4 1/4" h. (ILLUS., previous page) **$69**

Pitcher, 10 1/2" h., figural, model of a Distlefink, beak forms spout, tail is handle, white body w/brown & green accents (ILLUS. bottom left with other Distlefink pieces, bottom of page 118) **$63**

Pitcher, 6 1/2" h., Galagray line, handle rises above the rim, country theme w/a boy & girl in red & grey **$45**

Planter, figural, modeled as an old-fashioned claw-foot bathtub, white interior & claw feet, exterior in light blue w/h.p. pink roses & green leaves, 7" l., 3 1/4" h. (ILLUS., top of page) **$40**

Plate, 6 1/2" d., pale blue ground w/a white & black silhouette scene of a woman sitting at a spinning wheel, two holes for hanging **$43**

Cleminson Plate with Woman Singing

Plate, 7 1/4" d., blue rim w/pink stylized flowers, center w/h.p. profile bust of a lady singing, mark w/Cleminson in circle & boy & girl outside circle (ILLUS.) **$28**

Fluted Plate with Flowers & Butterflies

Plate, 7" d., fluted body & scalloped rim, decorated w/flowers & butterflies on a blue shaded top white ground, two holes for hanging, stamped mark (ILLUS.) **$38**

Cleminson Clay Ring Holder

Ring holder, figural, model of a dog w/tail straight up to hold jewelry, white body w/tan & dark brown accents, marked w/copyright symbol & plate w/a boy & girl on either side, 3" l., 2 3/4" h. (ILLUS.).......... **$49**

Wall pocket, figural, model of a teapot w/bail handle w/black ceramic center w/painted flowers, black cover & cobalt blue glazed body body w/a beige heart-shaped center, printed in the center "A Kitchen Bright & A Singing Kettle Make a Home The Place You Want To Settle," 8 1/4" h.. **$30**

Wall pocket, model of a frying pan w/design on bottom, "Them that works hard eats hearty," hole in handle for hanging, ink stamp mark, 11 3/8" l. including handle **$54**

Wall pocket, slightly flared top & bottom w/top showing "Let's pay off the Mortgage" & bottom showing a house & trees, gloss rose, 7" h. **$47**

Cowan

R. Guy Cowan opened his first pottery studio in 1912 in Lakewood, Ohio. The pottery operated almost continuously, with the exception of a break during the First World War, at various locations in the Cleveland area until it was forced to close in 1931 due to financial difficulties.

Many of this century's finest artists began with Cowan and its associate, the Cleveland School of Art. This fine art pottery, particularly the designer pieces, are highly sought after by collectors.

Many people are unaware that it was due to R. Guy Cowan's perseverance and tireless work that art pottery is today considered an art form and found in many art museums.

Cowan Marks

C

Cowan Bowl with Abstract Decoration

Bowl, 7 1/2" d., 4" h., wide cylindrical body w/flaring rim, hand-applied abstract decoration in black on a white to pale green ground, impressed mark, crazing (ILLUS.)....................................... **$345**

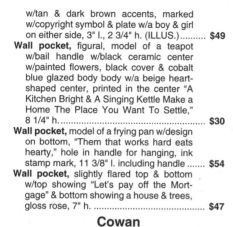

Long Oval Cowan Bowl with Molded Seahorses

Bowl, 16 1/4" l., 4 1/2" h., footed long slender oval shape w/fluted sides, molded down each end w/a seahorse, ivory exterior, blue interior, impressed mark, crazing (ILLUS.) **$81**

C

Tall Slender Green Cowan Vase

Vase, 13 7/8" h., tall slender swelled cylindrical melon-ribbed body w/a narrow shoulder & tall trumpet-form neck, teal green glossy glaze, impressed mark, crazing (ILLUS.) **$345**

deLee Art

Delores and Lee Mitchell, owners of deLee Art based in Los Angeles, California, seem to have quite accidentally enveloped themselves and their products in obscurity. While the Mitchells seemed to do everything possible to make deLee a household name, little is known about this company except that the products created are popular with collectors today. Almost all pieces are marked in some fashion. The Mitchells even gave names to their figurines, animals and so forth. Stickers with a silver background and black lettering have been found, often with the proper names of many items. Perhaps realizing that the stickers might be destroyed, the same pieces can be identified with an underglaze mark with the name deLee Art and might also include the name of the figurine and the date it was produced. Adding to this you can also find a deLee Art sticker. However, collectors do find deLee pieces void of any permanent mark and if the deLee sticker has been destroyed, there is no mark to indicate the maker. Knowing the products made by the Mitchells along with glazes helps immensely in identifying their unmarked products.

Today their skunk line is probably the least desirable among collectors. This could be because so many, in varied positions, were created. Two exceptions are the boy skunk figurine with blue hat and the matching girl skunk with her large, wide-brimmed blue hat. These skunks were produced in the late 1940s. Many deLee pieces bear a 1935 or 1938 mark and some have been found marked with a 1944 date so researchers have

speculated that deLee was in business from the early to mid-1930s through the 1940s.

de Lee Art
© 1938

delee Art

deLee Art Marks

Bank, "Money Bunny," figural rabbit, ears up, pink w/blue purse w/flower on purse, silver w/black lettering sticker, "deLee" sticker & incised underglaze "deLee," 9" h. **$140**
Figure of African American boy, "8 Ball," incised mark "deLee Art © 40 USA - A Walter Lantz Creation," 4 1/2" h. **$180**
Figure of boy, lying on his stomach, head up, arms folded under his chest, 2 3/4" l. **$100**
Figures of Latino dancers, black & white w/gold accents, incised "deLee Art, U.S.A.," 11 1/2" & 12 1/2" h., pr. **$335**

Bunny Hug Figure of Bunny

Model of bunny, "Bunny Hug" on sticker, ears up, white ground w/tan on ears, colorful small flowers on top of head & chest, marked "deLee," 6" h. (ILLUS.) **$48**
Model of elephant, seated on back legs, trunk up, head bent to right touching shoulder, white ground w/small pink & blue flowers w/green leaves, 4 3/4" h. **$76**
Models of lambs, "Tom & Jerry," "Tom" has blue bell, "Jerry" has blue flower, no marks, 4" h., pr. (ILLUS., top next page).... **$105**

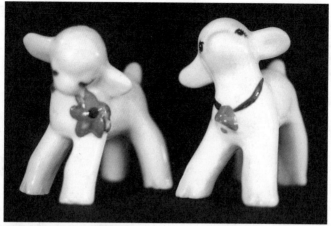

deLee Art "Jerry & Tom" Lambs

C

Figural deLee Girl Planter

"Mr. Skunk" Figural Planter

Planter, figural, girl dressed in white w/blue polka-dots, brown piping at edge of apron & collar of dress, large blue bow at waist in back, eyes closed w/brown eyelashes, holds up apron to form small planter in front, incised underglaze mark "deLee Art, 1938, Irene," 6" h. (ILLUS.) **$69**

Planter, "Mr. Skunk" on sticker, model of skunk w/black body & white upright tail, pink mouth & nose, white eyes & hair, blue derby hat, tiny planter is formed where tail meets back, marked "deLee Art 1940 ©," 6" h. (ILLUS., top next column) **$56**

Planter, "Sahara Sue," model of a camel seated w/front hoofs crossed, head up & slightly tilted to right, pale pink gloss w/caramel glaze highlights on hoofs, mouth & ears, flowers between neck, open hump forms small planter, 5 1/2" h. .. **$146**

Wall pocket, "Mr. Stinkie," model of a skunk, gloss black w/white, colorful flowers at left shoulder, small opening near stomach for matches, marked "deLee Art," 7 1/4" h. **$44**

Delft

In the early 17th century Italian potters settled in Holland and began producing tin-glazed earthenwares, often decorated with pseudo-Oriental designs based on Chinese porcelain wares. The city of Delft became the center of this pottery production and several firms produced the wares throughout the 17th and early 18th century. A majority of the pieces featured blue on white designs, but polychrome wares were also made. The Dutch Delftwares were also shipped to England, where eventually the English copied them at potteries in such cities as Bristol, Lambeth and Liverpool. Although still produced today, Delft peaked in popularity by the mid-18th century.

C

Lobed English Delft Bowl

Bowl, 8 5/8" d., 2" h., scalloped rim on low lobed body, h.p. w/blue stylized flowers on a powder blue ground, England, mid-18th c., minor rim chips & glaze wear (ILLUS.) **$470**

Large Dutch Delft Floral Charger

Charger, round shallow dished form w/a narrow flanged rim, the center w/a large rounded panel-sided reserve h.p. w/leafy scrolls around a round center w/a stylized leafy blossom, the border band decorated w/small oval reserves decorated w/scrolls & squiggles, a blue initial or X under the bottom, various glaze & rim chips, Holland, 18th c., 13 3/4" d. (ILLUS.) **$460**

Plate, 8 3/4" d., shallow dished form w/a wide flanged rim, the center h.p. in dark blue w/a large urn filled w/fruit & fanned & feathery leaves & flowers, the border h.p. in dark blue w/wide half-leaves alternating w/squiggle bands, Holland, 18th c., tight hairline from rim nearly to center, small rim chip (ILLUS., top next column) ... **$230**

Plate, 12 3/8" d., round, h.p. in dark blue w/the Peacock patt. in the center & round the flanged rim, Netherlands, first half 18th c. (minor rim chips)............................. **$558**

Urn-decorated Dutch Delft Plate

Large Scenic Delft Tile

Tile, rectangular, decorated in blue & white w/a seaside scene w/women standing on the shore & sailing ships heading out to sea, after a painting by Hendrik Willem Mesdag, marked w/Delft & other painted & impressed marks, late 19th - early 20th c., 7 7/8 x 10" (ILLUS.)............. **$500**

Doulton & Royal Doulton

Animals & Birds

Bird, Bullfinch, blue & pale blue feathers, red breast, HN 2551, 1941-46, 5 1/2" h. **$80**

Dog, Airedale Terrier, K 5, 1931-55, 1 1/4 x 2 1/4" **$275**

Dog, Bulldog, HN 1044, brown & white, 1931-68, 3 1/4" h.. **$250**

Standing Bulldog HN 1074 Figurine

Dog, Bulldog, HN 1074, standing, white & brown, 1932-85, 3 1/4" (ILLUS.) **$195**

Dog, Cocker Spaniel, Ch. "Lucky Star of Ware," black coat w/grey markings, HN 1021, 1931-68, 3 1/2" h............................ **$195**

Golden Brown Cocker Spaniel

Dog, Cocker Spaniel, golden w/dark brown patches, HN 1187, 1937-69, 5" (ILLUS.) ... **$125**

Collie in Dark & Light Brown, HN 1059

Dog, Collie, dark & light brown coat, white chest, shoulders & feet, HN 1059, 1931-85, 3 1/2" (ILLUS.) **$195**

Dog, Dalmatian, "Goworth Victor," white w/black spots, black ears, HN 1114, 1937-68, 4 1/4".. **$375**

Dog, Fox Terrier, K 8, seated, white w/brown & black patches, 1931-77, 2 1/2".. **$90**

Doulton Seated Foxhound No. K7

Dog, Foxhound, K 7, seated, white w/brown & black patches, 1931-77, 2 1/2" (ILLUS.).. **$110**

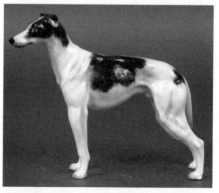

Greyhound in White with Brown Patches

Dog, Greyhound, white w/dark brown patches, HN 1077, 1932-55, 4 1/2" (ILLUS.) **$575**

Dog, Irish Setter, Ch. "Pat O'Moy," reddish brown, HN 1054, 1931-60, 7 1/2" h............ **$725**

C

Susan, DB 70, white, blue & yellow, 1988-93 .... **$125**

Bunnykins Sweetheart

Sweetheart, DB 174, white & blue, pink heart, 1997, limited edition of 2,500 (ILLUS.) **$205**
Tally Ho!, DB 12, burgundy, yellow, blue, white & green, 1973-88 .... **$105**
Touchdown, DB 29B (Boston College), maroon & gold, 1985, limited edition of 50 ... **$2,000**
Touchdown, DB 99 (Notre Dame), green & yellow, 1990, limited edition of 200 .... **$625**
Tyrolean Dancer, DB 246, black & white, 2001 .... **$60**
Will Scarlet, DB 264, green & orange, 2002 .... **$60**
Wizard, DB 168, brown rabbit, purple robes & hat, 1997, limited edition of 2,000 .... **$400**

Burslem Wares

Early Doulton Advertising Ashtray

Ashtray, earthenware, advertising-type, low squared white shape w/rounded cor-ners w/notches for cigarettes, the rounded sides printed w/advertising for De Reszke Cigarettes, Burslem, ca. 1925, 5 1/2" w. (ILLUS.) **$250**
Bowl, 8 7/8" d., 3 3/4" h., wide shallow rounded form, interior w/transfer-printed polychrome fox hunt scenes, green vintage border w/gilt trim, early 20th c. **$125**

Vellum Centerpiece with Dragon Handle

Centerpiece, Vellum Ware, low oblong floral-decorated dish w/crimped & ruffled sides curving up at one end to form a high curved handle molded w/a figural gold dragon, designed by Charles Noke, ca. 1895 (ILLUS.) **$2,000**

Colorful Bewick Birds Cracker Jar

Cracker jar, cov., Bewick Birds Series, barrel-shaped w/a low molded rim & inset cover, the sides decorated w/a design of Bewick birds perched in a leafy branch, done in the print & tint technique in shades of brown, blue, yellow, rose red, green & pale blue, Burslem, ca. 1905 (ILLUS.) **$500**

Tinworth Tribute "Tug of War" Figural

Figure group, earthenware, limited edition tribute to George Tinworth, the oval brown base inscribed "The Tug of War," a green grassy mound w/three dark blue frogs pulling against three brown mice, Model No. LW2, one of 150, designed by Martyn Alcock, Burslem, 2005, 5 1/2" l. (ILLUS.).. **$600**

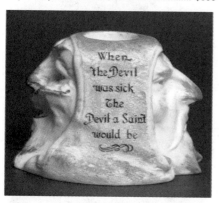

Bone China Mephistopheles Match Holder

Match holder, bone china, figural, an upright oblong shape molded on one side w/the smiling face of Mephistopheles & on the other side w/his frowning face, the sides in blue inscribed w/a motto, designed by Charles Noke, Burslem, ca. 1900 (ILLUS.).. **$1,000**

Ruby Lustre Pitcher in de Morgan Style

Pitcher, Ruby Lustre, wide bulbous body tapering to a short cylindrical wide neck w/spout, simple loop handle, h.p. design of stylized dragons in the style of William de Morgan, ca. 1890 (ILLUS.)................ **$1,500**
Plate, 9 1/8" d., Peony patt., dark blue floral center w/rectangular panels around the border, trimmed w/reddish rust & beige, ca. 1900 .... **$65**

Small Footed Doulton Salt Dip

Salt dip, small gilded ball feet supporting the squatty bulbous dish decorated w/flowers on a pale blue ground, gilt rim band, w/a salt spoon, ca. 1900 (ILLUS.).... **$400**

Two Views of the Norman & Saxon Royal Doulton Teapot

Teapot, cov., figural Norman and Saxon model, designed by Anthony Cartlidge, limited edition of 1,500, introduced in 2003 (ILLUS. of both sides)... **$300**

C

Cobalt Blue Vase with Floral Bouquet

Vase, bone china, tall pedestal foot supporting the slightly tapering cylindrical body w/a flared & ruffled rim, gold loop handles at the lower body, h.p. white reserve w/a colorful floral bouquet within a raised gilt border, the cobalt blue background further trimmed w/ornate gold, ca. 1910 (ILLUS.) **$600**

Vase, cov., Vellum exhibition-type, round foot & ringed pedestal in gold supporting the wide bulbous body w/a small cylindrical gold neck w/flaring rim & a low domed cover w/knob finial, decorated in the Spanish style w/colorful florals, ca. 1895 (ILLUS.) **$1,000**

Rembrandt Ware Dante Portrait Vase

Vase, Rembrandt Ware, squatty wide bulbous body tapering to a small rolled mouth, a central round reserve decorated w/a bust portrait of Dante against a shaded brown ground, titled "Dante Alligheri," ca. 1895 (ILLUS.) **$1,100**

Doulton Vellum Exhibition Vase

Doulton Vellum Vase with Ornate Handles

Vase, Vellum Ware, flared foot supporting the wide squatty lower body tapering sharply to a very slender stick neck w/flared rim, ornate gold lacy openwork handles from the lower neck to the edge of the shoulders, decorated w/Spanish style florals, ca. 1895 (ILLUS.) **$1,200**

Tall China Vase with Classical Maiden

Vase, 12 1/4" h., bone china, small pedestal foot supporting the tall slender ovoid body w/an low angled shoulder centering a small trumpet neck, ornate gold shoulder handles, the body h.p. w/the figure of a pretty classical maiden against a pale blue ground, designed by Leslie Johnson, ca. 1900 (ILLUS.) **$3,000**

Fine Doulton Vase with Pastoral Scene

Vase, 18 1/2" h., bulbous tulip-shaped body on a fluted pedestal base, the sides of the body finely h.p. w/a continuous pastoral & wooded landscape, high flar-

ing & fluted mouth w/a ruffled rim matches the base & molded to resemble folds of cloth w/gilt-trimmed dark green panels alternating w/gilt-trimmed pale green panels, attributed to Arthur Eaton, ca. 1880 (ILLUS.) **$4,560**

Vellum Vases with Molded Designs

Vases, Vellum Ware, buff-colored, a scalloped foot below the wide bell-shaped body molded w/a decoration of a frog & a mouse, a slender ringed neck w/cupped rim, small loop shoulder handles, pr. (ILLUS.) **$1,000**

Figural Bell Whisky Pottery Decanter

Whiskey decanter w/stopper, figural bell, shaded dark to light brown, advertising Bells Whisky (sic), 1955, 10 1/2" h. (ILLUS.) **$150**

Character Jugs
Mr. Quaker, large, D 6738, 7 1/2" h. **$650**

C

Night Watchman

Night Watchman, large, D 6569, 7" h.
(ILLUS.) **$130**
North American Indian, small, D 6614,
4 1/4" h. **$45**
Old Charley, tiny, D 6144, 1 1/4" h. **$75**
Old Salt, miniature, D 6557, 2 1/2" h................. **$50**

Paddy

Paddy, large, D 5753, 6" h. (ILLUS.).............. **$120**
Parson Brown "A", small, D 5529,
3 1/4" h. **$63**
Pearly Queen, small, D 6843, 3 1/2" h............. **$60**
Pied Piper, large, D 6403, 7" h. **$75**
Poacher (The), small, D 6464, 4" h................... **$45**
Porthos, large, D 440, 7 1/4" h. **$90**
Red Queen (The), large, D 6777, 7 1/4" h. **$125**

Rip Van Winkle

Rip Van Winkle, large, D 6438, 6 1/2" h.
(ILLUS.).. **$115**
Robin Hood, 1st version, miniature, D
6252, 2 1/4" h.. **$50**
Robin Hood, large, D 6205, 6 1/4" h. **$125**
Robinson Crusoe, small, D 6539, 4" h. **$60**
Sairey Gamp, miniature, D 6045, 2 1/8" h. **$40**

Sam Weller

Sam Weller, large, D 6064, 6 1/2" h. (ILLUS.)..... **$80**
Sancho Panza, large, D 6456, 6 1/2" h. **$85**
Sancho Panza, small, D 6461, 3 1/4" h. **$60**
Santa Claus, reindeer handle, large, D
6675, 7 1/4" h.. **$265**
Scaramouche, small, D 6561, 3 1/4" h.......... **$525**
Sir Francis Drake, large, D 6805, 7" h. **$105**
Sleuth (The), miniature, D 6639, 2 3/4" h. **$65**
Snooker Player (The), small, D 6879, 4" h. **$55**

Figurines

Adele, HN 2480, flowered white dress,
1987-92.. **$175**
Affection, HN 2236, purple, 1962-94............. **$115**
Ajax, HN 2908, red, green & gold, 1980, lim-
ited edition of 950...................................... **$475**
Amy, HN 3316, blue & rose, Figure of the
Year series, 1991 .... **$950**
An Old King, HN 2134, purple, red, green &
brown, 1954-92 .... **$450**
April, HN 2708, white dress w/flowers,
Flower of the Month series, 1987............... **$225**
Artful Dodger, M 55, black & brown, Dick-
ens Miniatures Series, 1932-83 .... **$75**

The Auctioneer

Auctioneer (The), HN 2988, black, grey & brown, 1986, R.D.I.C.C. Series (ILLUS., previous page) **$195**

August, HN 3165, white & blue dress w/poppies, Flower of the Month Series, 1987 .... **$275**

Autumn Breezes, HN 2147, black & white, 1955-71 .... **$350**

Ballad Seller, HN 2266, pink, 1968-73 .... **$250**

Beat You To It, HN 2871, pink, gold & blue, 1980-87 .... **$475**

Bedtime

Bedtime, HN 1978, white w/black base, 1945-97 (ILLUS.) **$80**

Belle, HN 2340, green dress, 1968-88 .... **$70**

Biddy, HN 1513, red dress, blue shawl, 1932-51 .... **$180**

Blithe Morning, HN 2021, mauve & pink dress, 1949-71 .... **$295**

Bonnie Lassie, HN 1626, red dress, 1934-53 .... **$575**

Boy from Williamsburg, HN 2183, blue & pink, 1969-83 .... **$215**

Bridget, HN 2070, green, brown & lavender, 1951-73... **$280**

Broken Lance (The), HN 2041, blue, red & yellow, 1949-75 .... **$450**

Bunny's Bedtime, HN 3370, pale blue, pink ribbon, 1991, RDICC Series, limited edition of 9,500 .... **$175**

Buttercup, HN 2309, green dress w/yellow sleeves, 1964-97 .... **$185**

Captain Cuttle, M 77, yellow & black, 1939-82 .... **$65**

Catherine, HN 3044, white, 1985-96 .... **$75**

Catherine of Aragon, HN 3233, green, blue & white dress, 1990, limited edition of 9,500 .... **$695**

Charlotte

Charlotte, HN 3813, brown figure, ivory dress, 1996-97 (ILLUS.)............................. **$225**

Chloe, HN 1765, blue, 1936-50 .... **$450**

Christmas Time, HN 2110, red w/white frills, 1953-67 .... **$545**

Claribel, HN 1951, red dress, 1940-49 .... **$400**

Clown (The), HN 2890, gold & grey, 1979-88 .... **$425**

Cup O' Tea, HN 2322, dark blue & grey, 1964-83.. **$175**

Dainty May, M 67, pink skirt, blue over-dress, 1935-49 .... **$625**

Easter Day, HN 1976, white dress, blue flowers, 1945-51 .... **$650**

Eventide, HN 2814, blue, white, red, yellow & green, 1977-91 .... **$275**

Fair Maiden, HN 2211, green dress, yellow sleeves, 1967-94...................................... **$80**

Farmer's Wife, HN 2069, red, green & brown, 1951-55...................................... **$250**

Friar Tuck, HN 2143, brown, 1954-65 .... **$595**

Frodo, HN 2912, black & white, Middle Earth Series, 1980-84 .... **$175**

Golfer, HN 2992, blue, white & pale brown, 1988-91 .... **$275**

Good King Wenceslas, HN 2118, brown & purple, 1953-76 .... **$275**

Goody Two Shoes, M 80, blue skirt, red overdress, 1939-49 .... **$115**

Grand Manner, HN 2723, lavender-yellow, 1975-81.. **$245**

Gypsy Dance, HN 2230, lavender dress, 1959-71... **$275**

Happy Anniversary, HN 3097, style one, purple & white, 1987-93 .... **$205**

C

Harmony

Polly Peachum, HN 550, red dress, 1922-
49 .... **$750**
Premiere, HN 2343, hand holds cloak,
green dress, 1969-79 .... **$195**

Pride & Joy

Harmony, HN 2824, grey dress, 1978-84
(ILLUS.) **$225**
Hazel, HN 1797, orange & green dress,
1936-49 .... **$550**
Hilary, HN 2335, blue dress, 1967-81 .... **$195**
Honey, HN 1909, pink, 1939-49 .... **$525**
Hornpipe (The), HN 2161, blue jacket, blue
& white striped trousers, 1955-62 .... **$750**
Ibrahim, HN 2095, brown & yellow, 1952-55
.... **$625**
Invitation, HN 2170, pink, 1956-75 .... **$215**
Isadora, HN 2938, lavender, 1986-92 .... **$350**
Jack, HN 2060, green, white & black, 1950-
71 .... **$175**
Janet, HN 1537, red dress, 1932-95 .... **$125**
Janice, HN 2022, green dress, 1949-55 .... **$715**
Joker (The), HN 2252, white, 1990-92 .... **$250**
Judith, HN 2278, yellow, 1986-89 .... **$225**
Karen, HN 1994, red dress, 1947-55 .... **$450**
Kate, HN 2789, white dress, 1978-87 .... **$150**
Katrina, HN 2327, red, 1967-69 .... **$275**
Lady April, HN 1958, red dress, 1940-49 ...... **$425**
Mayor (The), HN 2280, red & white, 1963-
71 .... **$275**
Omar Khayyam, HN 2247, brown, 1965-83 .. **$195**
Parisian, HN 2445, blue & grey, matte
glaze,1972-75 .... **$150**
Penny, HN 2338, green & white dress,
1968-95 .... **$75**
Pensive, HN 3109, white w/yellow flowers
on skirt, 1986-88 .... **$175**
Pied Piper (The), HN 2102, brown cloak,
grey hat & boots, 1953-76 .... **$275**
Polka (The), HN 2156, pale pink dress,
1955-69 .... **$295**

Pride & Joy, HN 2945, brown, gold & green,
RDICC, 1984 (ILLUS.) **$275**
Priscilla, M 24, red, 1932-45 .... **$600**
Queen Elizabeth I, HN 3099, red & gold,
1987, Queens of the Realm Series, limit-
ed edition of 5,000 .... **$650**
Rebecca, HN 2805, pale blue & lavender,
1980-96 .... **$450**
Regal Lady, HN 2709, turquoise & cream,
1975-83 .... **$195**

Rosemary

Rosemary, HN 3698, mauve & yellow, 1995-97 (ILLUS., previous page) **$315**

Sairey Gamp, HN 2100, white dress, green cape, 1952-67 .... **$475**

Sam Weller, M 48, yellow & brown, 1932-81 .... **$65**

Samwise, HN 2925, black & brown, Middle Earth Series, 1982-84 .... **$725**

Sandra, HN 2275, gold, 1969-97 .... **$225**

Sharon, HN 3047, white, 1984-95.................... **$90**

Shore Leave, HN 2254, 1965-79 .... **$295**

Simone, HN 2378, green dress, 1971-81 ...... **$135**

Soiree, HN 2312, white dress, green over-skirt, 1967-84 .... **$175**

Spring, HN 2085, 1952-59 .... **$395**

Summer's Day, HN 2181, 1957-62 .... **$275**

Teatime, HN 2255, 1972-95.......................... **$250**

This Little Pig, HN 1793, red robe, 1936-95 .... **$85**

Uriah Heep, HN 554, black jacket & trousers, 1923-39 .... **$525**

Writing, HN 3049, flowered yellow dress, 1986, limited edition of 750, Gentle Arts Series **$1,150**

Flambé Glazes

Animals & Birds

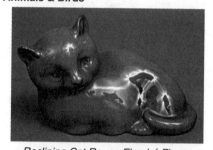

Reclining Cat Rouge Flambé Figure

Cat, reclining curled up w/head slightly raised to the side, Rouge Flambé glaze, Model 70, ca. 1920, 3 1/2" h. (ILLUS.).... **$1,600**

Flambé Alsatian on Pin Tray Rim

Dog, Alsatian seated on the rim of an oval alabaster pin tray, Rougle Flambé glaze, Model 497A, ca. 1930, 5" h. (ILLUS.) **$1,600**

Rouge Flambé Pekinese

Dog, Pekinese, Rouge Flambé, Model 544, ca. 1927, 2 1/2" h. (ILLUS.)............. **$1,500**

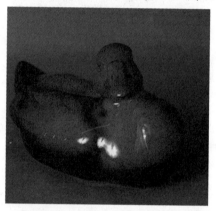

Rouge Flambé Duck Preening Figure

Duck, preening pose, Model 4, Rouge Flambé glaze, ca. 1912, 1 1/2" h. (ILLUS.) **$600**

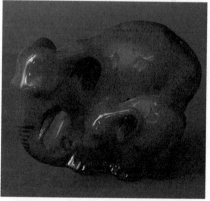

Elephant & Young in Rouge Flambé

Elephant & young, Rouge Flambé glaze, HN3548, designed by Eric Griffiths, 1990-96, 3 1/4" h. (ILLUS.) **$400**

C

C

Miscellaneous Pieces

Rouge Flambé Floral Band Bowl

Bowl, Rouge Flambé, round shallow shape w/inner bands of stylized flowers in black on a red ground, black border band, ca. 1930 (ILLUS.).. **$3,000**

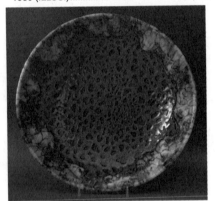

Doulton Wenzhou Flambé Bowl

Bowl, Wenzhou model, round shallow shape, Flambé glaze w/red speckles on black in the center w/a streaky border band in white, red & black, Model BA 13, limited edition of 250, 2000, 15" d. (ILLUS.) **$1,000**

Sung Ware Bowl with Rabbit Band

Bowl, 9" d., Sung Ware glaze, black ground w/a red border band decorated w/rabbits & meandering berry vines, ca. 1930 (ILLUS.) **$3,000**

Sung Ware Inscribed Deer Charger

Charger, Sung Ware glaze, deep round center w/a wide flat flanged rim, the center decorated w/a large stylized stag & vines, the rim inscribed in black "Many a Race is Lost Ere Ever a Step is Taken," ca. 1925 (ILLUS.)...................... **$6,000**

Flambé Canton Ginger Jar

Ginger jar, cov., Canton model, bulbous ovoid body w/small domed cover, Flambé glaze, Model BA 102, limited edition of 250, 1999, 7" h. (ILLUS.) **$800**

Veined Sung Ware Small Vase

Vase, 5 1/2" h., Veined Sung Ware glaze, cylindrical body flared at the base & rim (ILLUS.)... **$1,000**

Vase, 9 1/4" h., Rouge Flambé Veined, footed spherical body tapering to a stick neck, frothy blue texture on lower body, stamped logo, Shape No. 1618.................. **$500**

Rouge Flambé Veined Doulton Vase

Vase, 10 3/4" h., Rouge Flambé Veined, ovoid body tapering to a tiny trumpet neck, Shape No. 1619 (ILLUS.) **$748**

Large Veined Sung Ware Vase

Vase, 11 3/4" h., Veined Sung Ware glaze, bulbous body tapering to a tall trumpet neck, bold streaked dark blue & red glaze, ca. 1955 (ILLUS.) **$2,500**

Rouge Flambé Veined Tall Vase

Vase, 13 1/8" h., Rouge Flambé Veined, slender swelled cylindrical body tapering to a slender stick neck, Shape No. 1617 (ILLUS.).. **$345**

Tall Rouge Flambé Veined Doulton Vase

Vase, 13 1/2" h., Rouge Flambé Veined, slender swelled cylindrical body tapering to a slender stick neck, Shape No. 1617 (ILLUS.).. **$345**

C

C

Pair of Doulton Flambé Vases

Vases, 6 1/4" h., footed ovoid body tapering sharply to a slender neck w/flared rim, red, gold & black flambé glaze, stamped mark, pr. (ILLUS.)...................................... **$288**

Kingsware Tony Weller Portrait Flask

Sung Ware Flying Peacock Vases

Vases, 11" h., Sung Ware glaze, tall gently swelled cylindrical body w/a low flared mouth, decorated w/colorful flying peacock against a swirled red, black & yellow ground, ca. 1985, pr. (ILLUS.)................. **$4,000**

Kingsware

Flask, footed tall ovoid body tapering to a small neck & spout, small shoulder loop handle, ball stopper, molded portrait of Tony Weller from Dickens, made for Dewars Whiskey, 8" h. (ILLUS., top next column) **$1,000**

Kingsware Chadband Portrait Flask

Flask, simple ovoid body tapering to a small neck & rim spout, D-form shoulder handle, silver stopper, molded portrait of Chadband, inspired by a character in Bleak House by Dickens, 8" h. (ILLUS.) . **$1,800**

Kingsware Huntsman Loving Cup

Loving cup, cylindrical form w/flared rim & long pointed loop handles, molded bust portrait of the Huntsman, 1907, 7" h. (ILLUS.) **$1,000**

Kingsware Mephisto Match Holder

Match holder, wide low squatty bulbous shape tapering to a small silver rim band, molded Mephisto scene w/half-length portrait of the devil. ca. 1902 (ILLUS.) **$850**

Kingsware Quince Design Pitcher

Pitcher, jug-type, Quince design, flared foot & swelled cylindrical body w/a flaring rim w/spout, long D-form handle, molded w/a half-length portrait of a man smoking a long pipe, ca. 1905 (ILLUS.) **$1,000**

Lambeth Art Wares

Miniature Simple Stoneware Bottle

Bottle, stoneware, miniature, simple cylindrical body w/angled shoulder to the bulbed neck, mottled brown glaze, ca. 1920 (ILLUS.).. **$150**

Small Slip-Decorated Doulton Bowl

Bowl, 4 1/4" d., stoneware, widely flaring rounded sides, brown base band below the white-glazed sides decorated in raised slip w/wave-like scroll designs, blue interior, ca. 1920 (ILLUS.) **$300**

C

C

Early Doulton Stoneware Candlesticks

Candlesticks, stoneware, funnel-shaped base tapering w/a flaring drip pan centered by a tall cylindrical shaft w/looped base handles, decorated w/incised designs trimmed in blue & brown, ca. 1872, 11" h., pr. (ILLUS.) **$2,000**

Doulton Egg Cup with Raised Dots

Egg cup, stoneware, a ringed pedestal base in brown & dark blue, the dark blue cup molded overall w/small graduated raised dots, silver rim band, late 19th c. (ILLUS.).. **$400**

1930s Doulton Stoneware Cracker Jar

Cracker jar, cov., gently tapering cylindrical shape in lightly mottled brown trimmed w/brown ring bands, squared overhead caned bail handle, ca. 1935 (ILLUS.)......... **$200**

Carrara Ware Ewers with Children

Ewers, Carrara Ware, tall ovoid body tapering to a cylindrical divided neck w/a tall vertical spout & high arched shoulder handle, cream ground, the body decorated overall w/large bluish green swirling leafy floral vines centered by oval medallions painted in color w/charming scenes of Victorian children, designed by Ada Dennis, Arthur Pearce & Josephine Durtnall, ca. 1890, 12" h., pr. (ILLUS.) .... **Rare**

C

Doulton Stoneware Banded Ice Bucket

Ice bucket, stoneware, wide slightly tapering cylindrical form, molded w/two narrow body bands decorated w/small diamonds, the two wide body bands incised w/ornate leafy scrolls in light & dark green & cobalt blue, ca. 1880 (ILLUS.)...... **$800**

Ornately Decorated Stoneware Isobath

Isobath, stoneware, a round domed foot supporting a wide cylindrical cup-shaped body w/a side cup spout & a conical cover w/knob finial, brown w/blue band rim, the body & cover decorated w/ornate large cream-colored floral & scrolling leaf panels, made for Thos. de la Rue, ca. 1893, 6" h. (ILLUS.) **$500**

Stoneware Brown-headed Baby Inkwell

Inkwell, stoneware, figural, figure of a chubby standing baby wearing a long apron & dress w/ruffled shoulders, the dress in streaky green & tan, the ruffles in blue & the head in dark brown, designed by Leslie Harradine, ca. 1910, 3 1/2" h. (ILLUS.).................................. **$1,200**

Stoneware Jardiniere with Swimming Fish

Jardiniere, stoneware, squatty bulbous shaped w/a wide, low cylindrical neck, molded in high-relief w/stylized long fish in green & brown swimming through large scrolling brown, grey & tan waves, designed by Mark Marshall, ca. 1900, 9" h. (ILLUS.) **$2,000**

C

Doulton Pepper Shaker with Swag Band

Pepper shaker, stoneware, footed waisted
cylindrical body in streaky bluish green
below the brown domed top, molded
around the top of the neck w/a leafy swag
band, ca. 1912, 4" h. (ILLUS.)................... **$500**

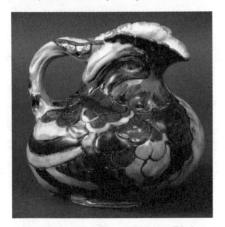

Unique Doulton Figural Chicken Pitcher

Pitcher, stoneware, jug-form, figural, modeled as a squatty bulbous chicken w/the
head forming the spout, boldly glazed in
browns, black & white, designed by Mark
Marshall, ca. 1895 (ILLUS.) .... **Rare**

Tall Tankard Pitcher by G. Tinworth

Pitcher, stoneware, tankard-style, flared
base ring below the tall cylindrical body
w/a neck ring & short neck w/rim spout,
C-form handle, the main body applied &
incised w/a stylized scrolling blue &
green foliate design, designed by George
Tinworth, ca. 1880 (ILLUS.)................... **$1,500**

Doulton Stoneware Soccer Players Pitcher

Pitcher, 6" h., jug-style, stoneware, footed
cylindrical body swelled at the bottom &
flaring at the rim w/a small rim spout, long
C-form handle, mottled brown ground applied around the bottom w/a blue leaf
band & around the rim w/a thin blossom
band, the main body applied w/a repeating design of applied light blue socker
players in action, attributed to Harry Bar-
nard, 1883 (ILLUS.) **$600**

Doulton-Lambeth Dragon Design Teapot

C

Miniature Silicon Tankard with Silver Rim

Doulton Marqueterie Ware Teapot

Tankard, miniature, Silicon Ware, footed ovoid black body w/a C-form handle tapering to the silver rim band, the sides molded to resemble stitched leather panels, ca. 1890 (ILLUS.) **$200**

Teapot, cov., Marqueterie Ware, spherical body w/ribs around the lower half, short angled spout, squared handle, small domed cover, Doulton & Rix patent, ca. 1890 (ILLUS., top next column) **$2,000**

Teapot, cov., stoneware, spherical body molded in relief w/a serpentine dragon design, Doulton-Lambeth, ca. 1895 (ILLUS., top of page) **$1,000**

Tobacco jar, cov., stoneware, figural Mr. Toby, bulbous cylindrical shape w/molded flaring rim, polychrome decoration, inscribed "The best is not too good," designed by Harry Simeon, ca. 1925, 4 1/2" h. (ILLUS., bottom next column) ... **$2,000**

Stoneware Mr. Toby Tobacco Jar

C

Ovoid Stoneware Vase with Blue Flowers

Vase, stoneware, ovoid tapering to a short trumpet neck, mottled brown ground, a base ring applied w/a band of vertical blue leaves, the body decorated overall w/large stylized blue flowers, designed by George Hugo Tabor, ca. 1885 (ILLUS.) **$1,000**

Miniature Bottle Vase with Blue Blossoms

Vase, 3 1/2" h., stoneware, miniature, bottle-shaped w/a flared base & ringed tapering neck, the neck & shoulder in dark brown, the tan body applied around the shoulder w/blue blossoms, ca. 1900 (ILLUS.)............. **$150**

Miniature Stoneware Vase with Ribbing

Vase, 2 3/4" h., miniature, stoneware, foot-ed sharply tapering conical body w/a tiny cylindrical neck, the buff lower body molded w/ribbing, dark brown-glazed neck, ca. 1905 (ILLUS.) **$150**

Doulton Pate-sur-Pate Vase with Otter

Vase, 6" h., stoneware, small foot below a large bulbous ovoid body tapering to a wide short rolled neck, wide body band in shades of blue decorated in pate-sur-pate w/an otter, brown rim & base bands, designed by W. Edward Dunn, 1883, 6" h. (ILLUS.) **$1,200**

C

1920s Bird-decorated Stoneware Vase

Vase, 9" h., stoneware, waisted cylindrical shape, the lower body w/a streaky blue & brown glaze, the upper body tube-line decorated w/a wide white band featuring a large brown & white bird perched on a brown brown w/green leaves, designed by Harry Simeon, ca. 1925 (ILLUS.) **$1,300**

Moon Flask Vase with Wild Roses

Vase, 14" h., faience, moon flask-shaped, the flattened round sides in shaded dark green h.p. w/a large cluster of white wild roses w/greenish yellow leaves all issuing from a small brick red circle, raised on pointed flaring brick red feet, ca. 1880 (ILLUS.).. **$1,500**

Vase, 16" h., stoneware, footed very slender ovoid body tapering to a flaring rim, Art Nouveau style, the base band w/blue & brown spearpoints below a large band of tube-lined round flowerheads in grey & blue against a speckled blue ground & w/green spearpoints issuing from the top of each flower, designed by Eliza Simmance, ca. 1905 (ILLUS., top next column) **$2,000**

Slender Tall Art Nouveau Floral Vase

Tall Hannah Barlow Livestock Vase

Vase, 18 1/4" h., stoneware, very tall baluster-form body w/a tall trumpet neck, the wide body band incised w/a scene of cattle & horses & flanked by bands of pointed brown & blue scrolls & blossoms, mottled glossy dark green & blue ground, decorated by Hannah Barlow w/flowers probably by Florence Roberts, signed (ILLUS.).. **$1,955**

C

Hannah Barlow Vase with Cattle

Vase, 18 1/2" h., stoneware, very tall baluster-form body w/a tall trumpet neck, the wide body band incised w/a scene of cattle & flanked by bands of pointed brown & blue scrolls & blossoms, mottled glossy dark green & blue ground, decorated by Hannah Barlow w/flowers probably by Florence Roberts, signed (ILLUS.)........ **$1,955**

Pair of Vases with Bold Scroll Medallions

Vases, stoneware, footed ovoid body w/a short widely flaring trumpet neck, dark cobalt blue ground, the sides decorated w/arched & looping thin tan white-beaded bands forming panels enclosing large tan ornate leafy scroll medallions, designed by Eliza Simmance, ca. 1885, pr. (ILLUS.).................................... **$1,200**

Lovely Chiné Faience Sunflower Vases

Vases, 12 1/4" h., Chiné Faience Ware, large urn-shaped body w/a pedestal base & upright scroll shoulder handles, the base & wide neck in pale blue bands w/striped decorations, the body w/a textured tan ground h.p. w/large yellow & white sunflowers w/green leafy stems, ca. 1901, pr. (ILLUS.) **$2,000**

Series Wares

Charger, Shakespeare Plays Series, scene from "A Midsummer Night's Dream," 12 5/8" d.. **$65**

Pitcher, 9 1/4" h., Shakespeare Characters Series, standing portrait of Sir John Falstaff, tall waisted cylindrical form w/high arched spout, printed around the bottom border "A Tapster is a Good Trade," early 20th c. **$150**

Plate, 10 1/2" d., Shakespeare Characters Series, blue transfer w/center portrait of Shakespeare, border w/twelve characters from his plays.. **$75**

Rare Royal Doulton Gnomes Series Teapot

Teapot, cov., Gnomes Series, color scene of strange gnomes amid mushrooms, introduced in 1927 (ILLUS.)...................... **$2,000**

Old Mother Hubbard Teapot from Nursery Rhymes Series

Teapot, cov., Nursery Rhymes Series, scene of Old Mother Hubbard, designed by William Savage Cooper, introduced in 1903 (ILLUS.)... **$650**

A Royal Doulton Teapot from the Shakespeare Series

Teapot, cov., Shakespeare Character Series, color scene of a young woman standing alone in a landscape, introduced in 1912 (ILLUS.) **$600**

Sir Roger de Coverley Series Teapot

Teapot, cov., Sir Roger de Coverley Series, scene of Sir Roger riding a white horse, introduced in 1911 (ILLUS.) **$600**

Vase, 9" h., Welsh Ladies Series, Welsh Ladies decoration... **$225**

Blue Children - Babes in Wood Series

Girl & Boy at Tree Blue Children Plaque

Plaque, oval, scene of a girl & boy peeping into a tree hole, ca. 1900 (ILLUS.) **$1,500**

Girls & Umbrella Blue Children Plaque

Plaque, oval, scene of two girls sheltering under an umbrella, ca. 1900 (ILLUS.)..... **$1,500**

C

C

Woman in Snowstorm Blue Children Vase

Vase, square upright flaring sides tapering near the top to a flat squared mouth, small angular shoulder handles, scene of a woman w/a muff in a snowstorm, ca. 1910 (ILLUS.)... **$800**

Girls Under Umbrella Blue Children Vase

Vase, 4 3/4" h., footed wide waisted cylindrical body w/a short cylindrical neck, decorated w/a scene of two girls sheltering under an umbrella, ca. 1905 (ILLUS.) **$500**

Vase, 16 1/2" h., flat-bottomed ovoid lower body tapering to a tall slender trumpet neck, scene of three girls watching Tinkerbell, ca. 1900 (ILLUS., top next column) **$1,200**

Tall Blue Girls & Tinkerbell Vase

Coaching Days Series
  This series was first introduced in 1905 and produced until 1945. Then production resumed in 1948 and continued until 1967. Each piece features one of several early English coaching scenes in color based on the artwork of Victor Venner.

Coaching Days Footed, Lobed Bowl

Bowl, round domed foot supporting the widely flaring melon-lobed bowl w/a wide flat mouth, a scene of horses trudging through snow pulling a loaded coach (ILLUS.) **$850**

C

Coaching Days Series Cracker Jar

Cracker jar w/silver plate rim, cover & bail handle, deeply waisted cylindrical body, scene of a stopped coach w/a man in a grey coat standing beside it (ILLUS.) **$600**

Coaching Days Series Oatmeal Bowl

Coaching Days Rocket Shape Pitcher

Stopped Coach & Man Square Dish

Dish, square w/low flaring sides & rounded corners, scene of a stopped coach w/a man wearing a grey coat standing nearby (ILLUS.) **$100-200**

Oatmeal bowl, rounded shape w/scalloped rim, scene of a stopped coach w/a man in a grey coat standing nearby (ILLUS., top next column) **$300**

Pitcher, Rocket shape, cylindrical w/a flaring base & long angular handle, scene of people waving goodbye to a departing coach (ILLUS., middle next column) **$350**

Plate with Stopped Coach Scene

Plate, round w/flanged rim, scene of a stopped coach w/a man walking beside it (ILLUS.) **$200**

C

Variation of Boarding Passengers Plate

Plate, round w/flanged rim, scene of a stopped coach w/three men boarding & groom holding nervous lead horse, red tree leaf & green tree to the right color variation (ILLUS.) **$200**

Coaching Days Herrick Shape Teapot

Teapot, cov., Herrick shape, footed pear-shaped body, decorated w/a rear view of a coach being followed by three walking men (ILLUS.)... **$450**

Coaching Days Moon Flask Vase

Vase, moon-flask shape w/low blocked feet, flattened horizontal oval body w/a low curved top neck, scene of horses trudging through snow pulling a passenger-filled coach (ILLUS.)................................... **$600**

Wash bowl & pitcher set, Royal Mail set, early English coaching scenes around the sides of each, four in polychrome, early 20th c., bowl 11 7/8" d., pitcher 7 3/8" h., pr.. **$225**

Dickens Ware Series

Dickens Ware Deep Mr. Pickwick Bowl

Bowl, small foot & deep cylindrical sides, color scene of Mr. Pickwick, Charles Noke, 1931 (ILLUS.) **$300**

Tony Weller Dickens Ware Charger

Charger, round, color scene of Tony Weller, early 20th c., 13 1/2" d. (ILLUS.)......... **$200-300**

Dickens Ware Captain Cuttle Oval Dish

Dish, oval, Leeds shape, low flaring & lightly ruffled sides, color scene of Captain Cuttle, Charles Noke, 1931 (ILLUS.) **$450**

Old Peggotty Dickens Ware Pitcher

Pitcher, jug-type, rectangular upright shape, molded in relief w/a scene of Old Peggotty, brown branch handle, No.D6292, Charles Noke, 1949 (ILLUS.) **$600**

Dickens Ware Tony Weller Pitcher

Pitcher, tankard-type, tall slender tapering cylindrical body w/a rim spout & pointed angled green handle, color scene of Tony Weller, Charles Noke, 1912 (ILLUS.)......... **$500**

C

Round Dickens Ware Trotty Veck Plate

Plate, round, color scene of Trotty Veck, Charles Noke, 1931 (ILLUS.).................... **$200**

1931 Dickens Ware Bill Sykes Plate

Plate, round w/flanged rim, color scene of Bill Sykes, Charles Noke, 1931 (ILLUS.) ... **$200**

1912 Dickens Ware Mr. Micawber Plate

Plate, round w/flanged rim, color scene of Mr. Micawber, Charles Noke, pale colors variation, 1912 (ILLUS.) **$200-250**

C

Dickens Ware Alfred Jingle Vase

Vase, waisted cylindrical shape w/long loop handles, color scene of Alfred Jingle, Charles Noke, 1912 (ILLUS.) **$350**

Head Rack Plates
Plate, 10" d., rack-type, Old Jarvey **$75**
Plate, 10 1/2" d., rack-type, The Mayor **$75**
Plate, 10 1/2" d., rack-type, The Squire **$75**

Barlow Family Doulton Wares

Hannah Barlow Beaker with Child & Sheep

Beaker (tall tumbler), stoneware, slightly tapering cylindrical body, the wide center band incised w/a scene of a child w/sheep, decorated by Hannah Barlow, ca. 1880, 5 1/2" h. (ILLUS.) **$750**

Foliate-decorated Florence Barlow Bowl

Bowl, 5 1/4" h.., stoneware, footed squatty bulbous shaped w/a wide flat rim, the banded sides carved w/foliate decoration, decorated by Florence Barlow, ca. 1875 (ILLUS.) **$500**

Barlow-Simmance Horses Cache Pot

Cache pot, stoneware, bulbous ovoid form w/a wide, short cylindrical neck, the sides incised w/panels of horses framed by bold cobalt blue scrolling legs, tan neck, decorated by Hannah Barlow & Eliza Simmance, ca. 1885 (ILLUS.) **$2,000**

Hannah Barlow Ewer with Goats & Child

Ewer, stoneware, footed bulbous ovoid body w/a tapering shoulder to the cylindrical neck w/flaring rim w/pinched spout & high arched handle, the wide body band incised w/a scene of goats & a child, decorated by Hannah Barlow, 1881, 11" h. (ILLUS.) **$2,400**

Pair of Hannah Barlow Horses Ewers

Ewers, stoneware, footed ovoid body tapering to a tall cylindrical neck w/pinched rim
spout & high arched C-scroll handle, the
body incised w/a scene of horses below
a foliate shoulder band, decorated by
Hannah Barlow, ca. 1905, pr. (ILLUS.) ... **$3,000**

Hannah Barlow Fox Hunting Scene Jug

Jug, stoneware, footed ovoid body tapering
to a cylindrical slightly flaring neck
w/pinched rim spout, strap handle, incised w/a large scene of a huntsman, his
horse & a fox, decorated by Hannah
Barlow, ca. 1880 (ILLUS.) **$2,000**

Early Hannah Barlow Tankard Pitcher

Pitcher, stoneware, tankard-style, tall gently tapering sides w/a molded base & rim
bands & small rim spout, the sides incised w/a continuous scene of cattle on a
tan ground, decorated by Hannah
Barlow, ca. 1875 (ILLUS.) **$2,500**

C

Stoneware Salt Shaker by Hannah Barlow

Salt shaker w/silver domed lid, stoneware, footed baluster-form body, dark
blue & brown spearpoint base & neck
bands, the wide body band incised w/a
scene of deer in dark blue, decorated by
Hannah Barlow, ca. 1875 (ILLUS.) **$500**

Hannah Barlow Tyg with Donkeys

Tyg, stoneware, wide cylindrical body w/a
silver rim band & long flattened loop handles, incised w/a continuous scene of
donkeys, decorated by Hannah
Barlow, ca. 1880, 6 3/4" h. (ILLUS.)........ **$2,500**

Hannah Barlow Sheep Scene Vase

C

Vase, stoneware, footed ovoid body tapering to a trumpet neck, the wide body band incised w/a scene of sheep, decorative base & neck bands, decorated by Hannah Barlow, ca. 1880 (ILLUS., previous page) **$1,800**

Pair Hannah Barlow Sheep Panel Vases

Vases, 7 1/4" h., stoneware, footed ovoid body tapering to a trumpet neck, the lower body & shoulders decorated w/dark blue paneled sides, the neck in mottled dark brown, the main body decorated w/large round reserves incised w/scenes of sheep & framed by cobalt blue leaf sprigs, decorated by Hannah Barlow, ca. 1885, pr. (ILLUS.).................................... **$3,500**

Pair of Florence Barlow Bird Vases

Vases, 12 3/4" h., stoneware, footed wide baluster-form body w/a wide trumpet neck, the main body decorated w/a continuous pate-sur-pate design of birds, decorated by Florence Barlow, ca. 1885 (ILLUS.).. **$2,500**

Tinworth Doulton Pieces

Beaker, stoneware, funnel foot tapering to a gently flaring cylindrical bowl w/a silver rim band, the foot incised w/blue, green & brown lappet leaves below the wide dark blue central band flanked by white dotted bands & decorated w/continuous light blue scroll bands w/leaves & molded florettes, the dark brown rim band incised w/a band of vertical green leaves, ca. 1880 (ILLUS., top next column) **$800**

Tinworth Stoneware Banded Beaker

Tall Ornate Tinworth Ewer

Ewer, stoneware, footed tall ovoid body w/a tall gently flaring neck w/rim spout & large C-form handle, the base band incised w/vertical pale blue lappets alternating w/beaded bands on a dark blue ground below a white beaded band, the wide brown central band incised w/a continuous scrolling band of pale green leaves & applied blue florettes, an upper thin white beaded band below the round shoulder incised w/alternating dark green spearpoints & pale blue petals, the brown neck applied w/blue florettes, ca. 1880 (ILLUS.) **$3,000**

C

Merry Musicians Bell Ringer Figure

Figure, stoneware, young man wearing a hat & seated on a tall pedestal playing hand bells, part of the Merry Musicians series, brown glaze, ca. 1895, 5" h. (ILLUS.)....... **$2,500**

Rare Tinworth Mouse "Playgoers" Menu Holder

Menu holder, stoneware, figural, a group of mice seated around a puppet show, titled "Playgoers," in shades of pale blue & brown, 1886, 5 1/4" h. (ILLUS.)............... **$6,500**

Figural Mouse Musicians Menu Holder

Menu holder, stoneware, figural, two white mouse musicians on a brown & blue molded round base, titled "Harp and Concertina," ca. 1884, 4" h. (ILLUS.) **$3,000**

Fine Pair of Tinworth Religious Terra Cotta Panels

Panels, terra cotta, tall rectangular forms w/religious scenes, one depicting "Christ on the Cross," the other "Descent from the Cross," 1902, 14" h., framed, pr. (ILLUS.) **$5,000**

Tinworth Chinè Ware Vase with Putti

Vase, Chinè Ware, a thin foot below the very wide disk-form lower body tapering to cylindrical sides w/the wide flat mouth flanked by the white figures of putti w/a white leafy swag draped between them, the dark blue ground w/brown decoration (ILLUS.)... **$2,500**

Ornately Decorated Tinworth Vase

Vase, stoneware, large ovoid body w/a wide short cylindrical neck, applied & incised overall w/ornate scrolling & leaf designs in dark blue, brick re, brown & blue, ca. 1880 (ILLUS.)... **$3,500**

Florence Ceramics

Some of the finest figurines and artwares were produced between 1940 and 1962 by the Florence Ceramics Company of Pasadena, California. Florence Ward began working with ceramics following the death of her son, Jack, in 1939.

Mrs. Ward had not worked with clay before her involvement with classes at the Pasadena Hobby School. After study and firsthand experience, she began production in her garage, using a kiln located outside the garage to conform with city regulations. The years 1942-44 were considered her "garage" period.

In 1944 Florence Ceramics moved to a small plant in Pasadena, employing fifty-four employees and receiving orders of $250,000 per year. In 1948 it was again necessary to move to a larger facility in the area with the most up-to-date equipment. The number of employees increased to more than 100. Within five years Florence Ceramics was considered one of the finest producers of semi-porcelain figurines and artwares.

Florence created a wide range of items including figurines, lamps, picture frames, planters and models of animals and birds. It was her extensive line of women in beautiful gowns and gentlemen in fine clothes that gave her the most pleasure and was the foundation of her business. Two of her most popular lines of figurines were inspired by the famous 1860 Godey's Ladies' Book and by famous artists from the Old Master group. In the mid-1950s two bird lines were produced for several years. One of the bird lines was designed by Don Winton and the other was a line of contemporary sculpted bird and animal figures designed by the well-known sculptor Betty Davenport Ford.

There were several unsuccessful contemporary artware lines produced for a short time. The Driftwave line consisted of modern freeform bowls and accessories. The Floraline is a rococo line with overglazed decoration. The Gourmet Pottery, a division of Florence Ceramics Company, produced accessory serving pieces under the name of Scandia and Sierra.

Florence products were manufactured in the traditional porcelain process with a second firing at a higher temperature after the glaze had been applied. Many pieces had overglaze paint decoration and clay ruffles, roses and lace dipped in slip prior to the third firing.

Florence Marks

Figures
"**Amber,**" brown hair, pink ruffled long dress & large bonnet, right arm bent & holding a pink parasol at right shoulder,

left arm extended w/fingers touching her dress, articulated fingers, 9 1/4" h....... **$425-475**

Florence "Angel," Downcast Eyes

"**Angel,**" downcast eyes, yellow hair, arms bent across upper body, part of angel's wings showing, white robe w/gold trimmed rope sash, cuffs & collar, gold & brown ribbon sticker, 7" h. (ILLUS.) **$50-75**

"**Annabel,**" Godey lady, standing w/right arm bent & carrying a basket of flowers, left arm in outward position, long full jacket w/gold trim, large hat, articulated fingers, 8 " h... **$400-450**

"**Ballet,**" 7" h. **$225-250**

Rare Birthday Girl Figure

"Birthday Girl," standing w/her arms bent & hands close together, wearing a long flaring aqua gown, 9 3/4" h. (ILLUS., previous page).. **$750-825**
"Bride," porcelain veil, 8 1/2" h........ **$1,000-1,250**
"Butch," boy w/hands in pockets, 5" h. .. **$100-125**
"Camille," woman standing & wearing white dress trimmed in gold, shawl over both arms made entirely of hand-dipped lace, brown hair, white triangular hat w/applied pink rose, ribbon tied to right side of neck, two hands, 8 1/2" h. **$300-50**
"Caroline," brocade fabric dress, 15" h. **$3,500-4,500**
"Charles," man standing & wearing 18th c. attire w/a long cape, 8" h..................... **$150-175**
"Charmaine," woman holding a parasol, wearing ruffled long dress, large hat w/flowers, w/articulated hands, 8 1/2" h **$250-350**

"The Christening" Figure Group

"Christening (The)," woman w/dress trimmed in lace at neck, sleeves & front of dress holding an infant in a long white christening dress, articulated fingers, 10" h. (ILLUS.) **$2,000-2,500**
"Clarissa," woman in full-sleeved jacket & long swirled & pleated skirt, bonnet & holding a muff in right hand, left hand on her shoulder, articulated hand, 7 3/4" h. **$175-200**
"Colleen," woman standing w/head slightly turned to left, right hand behind back & left arm to the front w/articulated hand, long wind-blown dress w/white collar, bonnet w/ribbon tied under chin, 8" h.. **$150-200**
"Darleen," standing w/head tilted, brown hair w/curls & roses at neck, long dress w/white underskirt, white lace trim on bodice & extending to bottom of dress, right arm bent & holding an open parasol at right shoulder, left arm at waist, articulated fingers, 8 1/4" h. (ILLUS., top next column) **$600-650**

Florence Figure of "Darleen"

"Denise," off-the-shoulder white dress w/gold trim extending down the dress front, violet overskirt, brown hair w/roses, both arms bent at waist w/right hand holding a closed fan, articulated fingers, 10" h... **$500-650**
"Edward," man in late Victorian costume sitting in an armchair, holding his bowler hat on one knee, 7" h. **$200-250**

Rare Variation of "Elizabeth"

"Elizabeth," woman in 18th c. costume w/a wide flaring aqua gown w/half-sleeves & a lace-trimmed bodice, long curls down her neck, seated on a white settee, rare white settee variation, 7" w., 8 1/4" h. (ILLUS.) **$1,200-1,400**

C

"Melanie," Godey lady, wearing a close-fitting bonnet & long-sleeved long coat over a wide dress, arms at her sides, 7 1/2" h. **$100-125**

"Our Lady of Grace," Madonna figure wearing long cloak w/gathered arms over long gown, on rounded domed base, 10 3/4" h............................... **$175-200**

"Peter," man standing wearing Victorian frock coat over lacy cravat, one leg to side & leaning on a scroll pedestal w/a hand holding his top hat, 9 1/4" h....... **$225-250**

"Reggie," boy standing wearing Victorian outfit, Eton jacket & vest & long pants, scrolls at the side bottom, 7" h. **$225-250**

"Sally," woman wearing Victorian outfit, high rounded bonnet tied w/bow, simple ruffled collar & long-sleeved coat over wide swirled & ruffled gown, both hands at sides, 6 3/4" h. **$125-150**

"Story Hour," seated mother & girl, woman reading book held in left hand, wearing rose dress w/lace at neck, roses in her hair, & girl w/blonde hair w/right arm on bench, wearing ruffled lace short-sleeved white dress w/blue & pink trim, no little boy, 8" l., 6 3/4" h. **$800-850**

"Tess," woman standing wearing long dress w/lace ruffle at neckline, large picture hat, arms away w/one hand holding edge of skirt up over shoe, 7 1/4" h. **$250-300**

"Victor," man w/head tilted wearing a Victorian outfit, holding top hat in right hand, frock coat over long pants, swirling long cape, 9 1/4" h. **$175-225**

"Wynkin," boy toddler wearing long blue pajamas & holding a Teddy bear, 5 1/2" h................................ **$150-200**

Other Items

Bust, "American Lady," heavy lace trim, 7 3/4" h................................ **$350-400**

Bust, "Modern Girl," 9 1/2" h. **$100-125**

Flower holder, "Beth," woman standing in a dirndl-style dress & holding up one corner of her long apron, holder at the back, 7 1/2" h................................ **$50-75**

Flower holder, "Chinese Child/Girl," bamboo-form holder at side, 7" h. **$100-125**

Flower holder, "Molly," standing girl wearing long gown w/short ruffled sleeves at shoulder, standing beside a large cylinder vase embossed w/leafy boughs, 6 1/2" h................................ **$35-40**

Head vase, "Fern," girl wearing long lightly ruffled hat & dress w/small ruffled collar & wide ruffles at the shoulders, 7" h. **$125-150**

TV lamp, "Dear Ruth," 9" h.................. **$800-1,000**

Flow Blue

Flow Blue ironstone and semi-porcelain was manufactured mainly in England during the second half of the 19th century. The early ironstone was produced by many of the well known English potters and was either transfer-printed or hand-painted (brush stroke). The bulk of the ware was exported to the United States or Canada.

The "flow" or running quality of the cobalt blue designs was the result of introducing certain chemicals into the kiln during the final firing. Some patterns are so "flown" that it is difficult to ascertain the design. The transfers were of several types: Asian, Scenic, Marble or Floral.

The earliest Flow Blue ironstone patterns were produced during the period between about 1840 and 1860. After the Civil War Flow Blue went out of style for some years but was again manufactured and exported to the United States beginning about the 1880s and continuing through the turn of the century. These later Flow Blue designs are on a semi-porcelain body rather than heavier ironstone and the designs are mainly florals. Also see Antique Trader Pottery & Porcelain Ceramics Price Guide, *5th Edition.*

AMOY (Davenport, ca. 1844)

Large 16" Amoy Platter

Platter, 16" l. (ILLUS.) **$450**

ARABESQUE (T.J. and J. Mayer, ca. 1845)

Creamer **$325**

Creamer, Classic Gothic style, 6" h. **$325**

Plate, 7 1/2" d.. **$65**

Soup plate w/flanged rim, 10" d................... **$175**

Sugar bowl, cov., Classic Gothic style **$350**

Teapot, cov., Classic Gothic style................. **$800**

ARCADIA (Arthur J. Wilkinson, ca. 1907)

Tea cup & saucer, cup, 3 1/4" d., 2 1/4" h., saucer, 5 1/2" d. **$75**

ARGYLE (Myott, Son & Co., ca. 1898)

Teapot, cov., 6" h. **$300**

ARGYLE (W.H. Grindley & Co., ca. 1896)

Butter, cover & drainer.................................. **$300**

Butter dish, cover & drainer **$350**

Butter pat, 3 1/2" d. **$60**

Cup & saucer, handled................................... **$95**

Demitasse cup & saucer, cup 3" d. x 3 1/2" h., saucer 4 1/2" d............... **$165**

Gravy boat **$195**

Ladle, sauce... **$700**

Oyster bowl, 6" d. x 3" h.............................. **$195**

Pitcher, 1 1/2 pt. **$425**

Pitcher, 1 pt. **$375**

Plate, 7" d. $55
Plate, 8" d. $60
Plate, 9" d. $75
Plate, 10" d. $95
Platter, 14" l. $275

Argyle Platter

Platter, 16" l. (ILLUS.) $350
Platter, 18" l. $450
Sauce dish $50
Sauce tureen, cover & undertray, 3 pcs. $495
Soup plate w/flanged rim, 9" d. $90
Vegetable bowl, open, medium $185
Vegetable bowl, open, small $165

ARVISTA (Wiltshaw & Robinson, 1906)

Arvista Flow Blue Salad Set

Salad set: master bowl w/brass rim & matching fork & spoon w/brass fittings, pr. (ILLUS.) $450

ASTER & GRAPESHOT (Joseph Clementson, ca. 1840) - Brush-stroke
Pitcher, 11" h. (ILLUS., top next column) $550

ASTRAL (W.H. Grindley & Co., ca. 1891)
Cake plate, w/tab handles, 9 x 9 1/2" $150
Compote, w/pedestal, 9 1/2" d., 4 1/2" h. $175
Egg cup, 3 3/4" h. $125

Platter, 16" l. $250

Aster & Grapeshot 11" Pitcher

BIRDS AND BLOOM (George Jones & Sons, ca. 1885)

Birds and Bloom Cache Pot

Cache pot, 7" h. (ILLUS.) $325

BLUE BELL (William Ridgway & Co., ca. 1834-1854)
Dessert tray, leaf shape, one open handle, impressed "Opaque Granite China," 12" l. $350
Vegetable dish, cov., 10 1/4 x 12", 6" h. $350

BLUE DIAMOND (Wheeling and La Belle Potteries, American, ca. 1896)
Charger, 13" d. $350
Creamer & cov. sugar, creamer 4" h., sugar 4 1/2" h., pr. $425

C

Blue Diamond Iced Beverage Jug

Lemonade/iced beverage jug, cov., pewter lid, 9" h. (ILLUS.)........................ **$850**

CHEN-SI (John Meir, ca. 1835)

Chen-Si Primary Shape Creamer

Creamer, Primary shape, 5" h. (ILLUS.) **$350**

Chen-Si Flow Blue Teapot by Meir

Teapot, cov., Eight Sided Primary Belted body shape (ILLUS.) **$650**

CHUSAN (J. Clementson, ca. 1840)
Creamer, 6" h.. **$250**
Plate, 7 1/2" d.. **$75**
Plate, 9 1/2" d.. **$95**
Platter, 13" l. **$300**
Platter, 14" l. **$350**

Clementson Chusan Pattern Flow Blue Teapot

Teapot, cov., Long Hexagon body shape (ILLUS.).. **$650**
Vegetable bowl, open, 8" l. **$200**

CHUSAN (Podmore, Walker & Co., ca. 1834-1859)
Vegetable dish, cov...................................... **$450**

CLOVER (W.H. Grindley & Co., ca. 1910)
Platter, 16" l. **$250**

COBURG (John Edwards, ca. 1860)
Cup & saucer, handleless **$150**
Plate, 8 1/2" d... **$85**
Plate, 10 1/2" d.. **$125**
Platter, 16" **$300**
Teapot, cov. **$650**
Vegetable bowl, open, 10" l. **$250**

CONWAY (New Wharf Pottery & Co., ca. 1891)

Conway Pattern Butter Dish

Butter dish, cov. (ILLUS.)............................. **$650**

Conway Pattern 8 1/2" Pitcher

Pitcher, 8 1/2" h. (ILLUS.)............................. **$650**

Conway (Wood & Son, ca. 1895)

Wood & Son Conway Cup & Saucer

Cup & saucer the set (ILLUS.) **$95**

COREA (Wedgwood & Co., ca. 1900)
Meat well platter & cover, 8 1/2 x 11 1/2"
   w/cover (ILLUS., bottom of page) **$450**

COUNTESS (W.H. Grindley & Co., ca. 1891)
Creamer, 4 1/2" h.. **$125**
Sugar, cov., 5" h.. **$150**
Teapot, cov., 6 1/2" h. **$375**

CRUMLIN (Myott, Son & Co., ca. 1900)
Creamer, 4 1/2" h.. **$125**
Pitcher, 8" h. **$275**
Plate, 10" d., w/scalloped rim **$85**

CYPRUS (Wm. Davenport, ca. 1850)
Platter, 16" l. **$350**

DAINTY (John Maddock & Son, ca. 1896)
Platter, 12" l. **$150**

DEVON (Alfred Meakin, ca. 1907)
Dinner service: thirteen 9 3/4" d. dinner
   plates, twelve 7 1/2" d. soup plates,
   twelve bread & butter plates, eleven dessert plates, twelve dessert bowls, seven-
   teen saucers-underplates, eight coffee
   cups & four saucers, eight teacups & four
   saucers, one gravy boat, open sugar
   bowl, creamer, 8 1/2" d. vegetable dish,
   small oval relish dish, two open oval vegetable dishes, one two-handled cov. vegetable tureen, oval chop platter & matching 16" l. roasted meats platter & cov.
   butter dish, the set (ILLUS., top next
   page).. **$3,220**

DOROTHY (Johnson Bros., ca. 1900)
Bone dish **$40**
Butter pat, 3 1/2" d. **$35**
Pitcher, 6 1/2" h. **$125**
Plate, 8" d.. **$40**
Plate, 9" d.. **$50**
Vegetable bowl, cov. **$150**

DUDLEY (Ford & Sons, ca. 1890)
Platter, 16" l. **$275**

DUNDEE (Ridgways, ca. 1910)
Bone dish **$45**

C

Corea Meat Well Platter

C

Meakin Devon Pattern Flow Blue Dinner Service

FLENSBURG (James Edwards, ca. 1865)

Edwards Flensburg Pattern Pitcher

Pitcher, 6 1/2" h. (ILLUS.) **$350**

Flowers (maker unknown, ca. 1898)

Rare Flowers Child's Pitcher & Bowl Set

Pitcher & bowl set, child's, the set (ILLUS.)
.... **$2,500**

GIRONDE (W.H. Grindley & Co., ca. 1891)

Gironde Pattern Soup Bowl

Soup bowl, 9" w. (ILLUS.) **$65**

KREMLIN (Samuel Alcock & Co., ca. 1843)

Kremlin Pattern Flow Blue Mug

Mug (ILLUS.) **$350**

Kremling (See Kremlin)

LONSDALE (Ford & Sons, ca. 1898)
Plate, 10 1/2" d. **$95**

LONSDALE (Ridgways, ca. 1910)
Demitasse cup & saucer, 2 1/2" h. **$125**

Manhattan Pattern Cup & Saucer

C

Lonsdale Platter by Ridgways

Platter, 14 x 17" (ILLUS.) **$350**
Vegetable dish, cov., 12" l., 6" h. **$250**

LUCERNE (New Wharf Pottery & Co., ca. 1891)
Bowl, 9" d. **$90**
Cup & saucer **$65**
Plate, 9" d. **$55**
Vegetable bowl, cov. **$150**
Vegetable dish, cov. **$140**

LUGANO (Ridgways, ca. 1890)
Creamer, 4 1/2" h. **$195**
Gravy boat **$150**

LUNÉVILLE BLUE (Keller & Guerin, French, ca. 1891)
Tom & Jerry punch bowl, footed, 16" d. **$1,400**

MADRAS (Doulton & Co., ca. 1900)
Plate, 6 1/2" d. **$45**
Soup plate, flanged rim, 8 1/2" d. **$75**
Tea set: teapot, cov. sugar & creamer; the
set **$750**
Vegetable bowl, cov. **$250**

MALTESE (Cotton & Barlow, ca. 1850)
Platter, 14" l. **$350**

MANDARIN (John Maddock, ca. 1850)
Pitcher, 6" h. **$225**

MANHATTAN (Henry Alcock & Co., ca. 1900)
Cup & saucer, the set (ILLUS., top next col-
umn) **$65**

MANHATTAN (Johnson Bros., ca. 1895)
Creamer **$185**
Sugar, cov. **$185**
Wash basin **$150**

MARBLE (Warwick China Co., American, ca. 1893)
Ferner, 8" d. **$275**
Syrup pitcher, 6" h. **$325**

MARECHAL NEIL (W.H. Grindley & Co., ca. 1895)
Oyster bowl, 5 1/2" d., 3" h. **$175**
Plate, 10" d. **$75**
Platter, 14" l. **$200**

Marechal Neil Flow Blue Teapot

Teapot, cov., deeply waisted & lobed un-
named body shape (ILLUS.) **$450**
Vegetable dish, cov. **$250**
Vegetable dish, individual size, 5 1/2" **$90**

MARIE (W. H. Grindley & Co., ca. 1891)

Marie Pattern Soup Tureen

Soup tureen, cov., round, 13" d. (ILLUS., previous page) $350

MARQUIS, The (Also See Marquis II) (W. H. Grindley & Co., ca. 1906)

Tea Cup & Saucer in The Marquis Pattern

Tea cup & saucer (ILLUS.).............................. $65

MATLOCK (F. Winkle & Co., ca. 1890)

Matlock Covered Vegetable Dish

Vegetable dish, cov., 7 x 11 1/2", 5 1/2" h. (ILLUS.)... $150

MELBOURNE (W.H. Grindley & Co., ca. 1891)

Melbourne Demitasse Cup & Saucer

Demitasse cup & saucer, the set (ILLUS.) $110

NON PAREIL (Burgess & Leigh - Middleport Potteries, ca. 1891)

Non Pareil Pattern Covered Vegetable

Vegetable dish, cov., oval (ILLUS.)............... $325

OSBORNE (Ridgways, ca. 1905)

Osborne Flow Blue Vegetable Dish

Vegetable dish, cov., oval (ILLUS.)............... $195

Osborne (unknown maker, late 19th c.)

Rare Persian Pattern Cheese Dome

Cheese dome & underplate, 13" h., the set (ILLUS.).. $3,500

RELIEF-MOLDED JUGS (makers unknown, mid-19th c.)

Molded Foresters' Arms Jug

Foresters' Arms patt. (ILLUS.) **$450**

Flow Blue Molded Pears Pattern Jug

Pears patt., 7 1/2" h. (ILLUS.)........................ **$275**
Tulip patt., 7" h. **$250**
Tulip patt., 8" h. **$250**

Two Birds with Chicks in Nest Jug

Two Birds with Chicks in Nest patt., 6 1/2" h. (ILLUS.) **$350**

SCINDE (J. & G. Alcock, ca. 1840)

Scinde Pattern 14" l. Platter

Platter, 14" l. (ILLUS.) **$450**

SHELL (Wood & Challinor, ca. 1840; E. Challinor, ca. 1860)

Shell Flow Blue Pattern 16" Platter

C

Adams Tonquin Pattern Mitten-shaped Relish Dish

Platter, 16" l. (ILLUS., bottom previous page) **$450**

TONQUIN (Wm. Adams & Son, ca. 1845)
Relish dish, mitten-shaped (ILLUS., top of page) **$225**

TROY (Charles Meigh, ca. 1840)

Very Rare Troy Soup Tureen Set

Soup tureen, cover, ladle & undertray, the set (ILLUS.) **$3,750**

WAGON WHEEL (unknown maker, brush-stroke, ca. 1860)

Early Flow Blue Wagon Wheel Mug
Mug (ILLUS.) **$125**

WALDORF (New Wharf Pottery & Co., ca. 1892)

Waldorf Pattern 10" d. Plate
Plate, 10" d. (ILLUS.) **$95**

Franciscan Ware

A product of Gladding, McBean & Company of Glendale and Los Angeles, California, Franciscan Ware was one of a number of lines produced by that firm over its long history. Introduced in 1934 as a pottery dinnerware, Franciscan Ware was produced in many patterns including "Desert Rose," introduced in 1941 and reportedly the most popular dinnerware pattern ever made in this country. Beginning in 1942 some vitrified china patterns were also produced under the Franciscan name.

After a merger in 1963 the company name was changed to Interpace Corporation and in 1979 Josiah Wedgwood & Sons purchased the Gladding, McBean & Co. plant from Interpace. American production ceased in 1984.

Franciscan Mark

Ashtray, Apple patt., 4 3/4" sq. $150
Ashtray, Desert Rose patt., square $125
Ashtray, individual, Apple patt., apple-shaped, 4" w., 4 1/2" l. $28
Ashtray, individual, Desert Rose patt., 3 1/2" d.. $22
Ashtray, individual, Wildflower patt., Mariposa Lily shape, 3 1/2" d............................ $95
Baking dish, Apple patt., 1 qt. $275
Baking dish, October patt., 1 qt. $100
Baking dish, Apple patt., 1 1/2 qt. $350
Baking dish, Desert Rose patt., 9 x 14", 2 1/4" h., 1 1/12 qt. $225
Bell, Desert Rose patt., Danbury Mint, 4 1/4" h.. $65
Bell, Cafe Royal patt., 3 3/4" d., 6" h. $65
Bowl, fruit, 4 1/2" d., California Poppy patt....... $33
Bowl, fruit, 5 1/4" d., Desert Rose patt. $12
Bowl, fruit, 5 1/2" d., Wildflower patt. $95
Bowl, soup, footed, 5 1/2" d., Desert Rose patt. $32
Bowl, cereal or soup, 6" d., Apple patt., ca. 1940 .... $16
Bowl, cereal or soup, 6" d., Ivy patt.................. $25
Bowl, cereal or soup, 6" d., Wildflower patt.... $125
Bowl, cereal, 7" d., October patt. $18
Bowl, salad, 10" d., Desert Rose patt. $95
Bowl, salad, 11" d., Daisy patt. $45
Bowl, fruit, Arden patt................................. $12
Box, cov., Desert Rose patt., egg-shaped, 1 1/2 x 4 3/4" .... $350+
Butter dish, cov., California Poppy patt......... $175
Butter dish, cov., Ivy patt............................... $75
Butter dish, cov., Twilight Rose patt. $125
Candleholders, Desert Rose patt., pr............. $75
Casserole, cov., Apple patt., in metal holder $1,500
Casserole, cov., Desert Rose patt., 1 1/2 qt., 4 3/4" h. $95
Casserole, cov., Wildflower patt., 1 1/2 qt. $850
Cigarette box, cov., Apple patt., 3 1/2 x 4 1/2, 2" h. $140
Coaster, Apple patt., 3 3/4" d. $53
Coffee server, El Patio tableware, turquoise glossy glaze.................................... $40

Westwood Coffee & Tea Service

Coffee & tea service: cov. coffeepot, cov. teapot, round serving plate, creamer & cov. sugar; Fine China, Westwood patt., the set (ILLUS.) $165
Coffeepot, cov., Apple patt., ... $100
Coffeepot, cov., Ivy patt., green rim band, 7 1/2" h.. $235

Compote, open, Apple patt., 8" d., 4" h. $75
Compote, open, Meadow Rose patt., 8" d., 4" h.. $85
Cookie jar, cov., Desert Rose patt................ $200
Creamer, Bountiful patt. $35
Creamer, Desert Rose patt., 4 1/4" h.............. $28
Creamer, October patt. $24
Creamer & cov. sugar bowl, Apple patt., pr. $55
Creamer & cov. sugar bowl, El Patio tableware, Mexican blue glossy glaze, pr. $35
Creamer & cov. sugar bowl, individual, Apple patt., pr.. $53
Creamer & cov. sugar bowl, Meadow Rose patt., pr. $45
Creamer & open sugar bowl, individual, El Patio Nuevo patt., orange, pr. $50
Cup & saucer, Apple patt., jumbo size $78
Cup & saucer, California Poppy patt. $35
Cup & saucer, demitasse, Apple patt. $55
Cup & saucer, demitasse, El Patio tableware, Mexican blue glossy glaze $20
Cup & saucer, Desert Rose patt., jumbo size... $60
Cup & saucer, Ivy patt. $22
Cup & saucer, Starburst patt. $16
Cup & saucer, tea, Desert Rose patt. $5
Dinner service: 6 each dinner plates, soup plates, berry bowls, cups & saucers, 3 salad plates, one each open sugar bowl, creamer, oval platter & vegetable bowl; Coronado patt., matte coral, the set.......... $135
Egg cup, Apple patt., double $32
Egg cup, Meadow Rose patt., 2 3/4 d., 3 3/4" h. $36
Ginger jar, cov., Desert Rose patt. $295
Goblet, Meadow Rose patt., 6 1/2" h. $85
Gravy boat, Arden patt. $65
Gravy boat, California Poppy patt. $95
Gravy boat, Tiempo patt., lime green $20
Gravy boat w/attached undertray, Apple patt... $42
Gravy boat w/attached undertray, Ivy patt. $62
Jam jar, cov., Apple patt., redesigned style ... $275
Microwave dish, oblong, Desert Rose patt., 1 1/2 qt.. $275
Mixing bowl, Apple patt., 7 1/2" d. $95
Mixing bowl, Desert Rose patt., 6" d.............. $75
Mixing bowl, Desert Rose patt., 9" d $125
Mixing bowl set, Desert Rose patt., 3 pcs. ... $350
Mug, Apple patt., 7 oz. $28
Mug, Desert Rose patt., 10 oz. $125
Mug, Desert Rose patt., 7 oz. $18
Napkin ring, Desert Rose patt........................ $45
Pepper mill, Starburst patt............................. $165
Pickle/relish boat, Desert Rose patt., interior decoration, 4 1/2 x 11"......................... $350
Pitcher, 4" h., Desert Rose patt. $395
Pitcher, milk, 6 1/4" h., Apple patt., 1 qt.......... $90
Pitcher, milk, 8 1/2" h., Daisy patt.................. $50
Pitcher, water, 8 3/4" h., Desert Rose patt., 2 1/2 qt.. $95
Pitcher w/ice lip, El Patio tableware, turquoise glossy glaze, 2 1/2 qt....................... $85
Plate, dinner, Arden patt. $15
Plate, luncheon, 9 1/2" d., Coronado Table Ware, coral satin glaze $10
Plate, salad, Arden patt. $8

C

Various El Patio Plates & Tumblers

Plate, bread & butter, 6 1/4" d., Ivy patt........... **$10**
Plate, bread & butter, 6 1/2" d., Desert Rose patt. **$6**
Plate, bread & butter, 6 1/2" d., El Patio, apple green (ILLUS. w/various El Patio plates & tumblers, top of page) **$6**
Plate, bread & butter, 6 1/2" d., Wildflower patt. **$45**
Plate, coupe dessert, 7 1/2" d., Apple patt. **$65**
Plate, coupe dessert, 7 1/2" d., Desert Rose patt. **$65**
Plate, dessert, 7 1/2" d., El Patio, Mexican blue (ILLUS. w/various El Patio plates & tumblers, top of page) **$12**
Plate, snack, 8" sq., Apple patt..................... **$145**
Plate, side salad, 4 1/2 x 8", Apple patt., crescent-shaped.. **$38**
Plate, side salad, 4 1/2 x 8", Ivy patt., crescent-shaped **$49**
Plate, salad, 8 1/2" d., Apple patt. **$16**
Plate, salad, 8 1/2" d., El Patio, bright yellow (ILLUS. w/various El Patio plates & tumblers, top of page) **$14**
Plate, salad, 8 1/2" d., Ivy patt...................... **$28**
Plate, salad, 8 1/2" d., October patt.................. **$16**
Plate, salad, 8 1/2" d., Wildflower patt............. **$95**
Plate, child's, 7 1/4 x 9", divided, Apple patt. .. **$145**
Plate, luncheon, 8 1/2" d., El Patio, coral satin (ILLUS. w/various El Patio plates & tumblers, top of page) **$14**
Plate, luncheon, 9 1/2" d., Coronado Table Ware, glossy coral glaze **$10**
Plate, luncheon, 9 1/2" d., Coronado Table Ware, matt ivory glaze (ILLUS., top next column) **$8**
Plate, luncheon, 9 1/2" d., Wildflower patt...... **$125**
Plate, small dinner, 9 1/2" d., El Patio, maroon (ILLUS. w/various El Patio plates & tumblers, top of page) **$14**
Plate, coupe, party w/cup well, 10 1/2" d., Desert Rose patt. **$160**
Plate, dinner, 10 1/2" d., California Poppy patt. **$32**

Coronado Table Ware Luncheon Plate

Plate, dinner, 10 1/2" d., Meadow Rose patt. **$26**
Plate, dinner, 10 1/2" d., Picnic patt. **$10**
Plate, large dinner, 10 1/2" d., grey (ILLUS. w/various El Patio plates & tumblers, top of page).. **$26**
Plate, coupe, steak, 11" l., Desert Rose patt. **$125**
Plate, grill, 11" d., Apple patt. **$95**
Plate, chop, 11 1/2" d., Desert Rose patt. **$52**
Plate, chop, 12" d., California Poppy patt....... **$125**
Plate, chop, 14" d., Apple patt......................... **$95**
Plate, chop, 14" d., Ivy patt. **$155**
Plate, chop, 14" d., Willow tableware (1937-40).. **$145**
Plate, T.V. w/cup well, 8 1/4 x 14", Starburst patt. **$75**
Platter, 11" l., oval, Arden patt. **$45**
Platter, 8 1/2 x 12" oval, Cafe Royal patt. **$32**
Platter, 12 3/4" l., Desert Rose patt. **$38**
Platter, 14" l., Apple patt. **$55**
Platter, 14" l., Meadow Rose patt. **$36**

Platter, 14" l. oval, Wildflower patt. $425
Platter, 19" l., oval, Apple patt....................... $225
Platter, 19" l., turkey-size, Desert Rose
   patt., ... $225
Relish dish, three-part, Apple patt.,
   11 3/4" l $70
Relish/pickle dish, Wildflower patt., interior
   design, 4 1/4 x 12" oval $245
Salt & pepper shakers, Apple patt.,
   6 1/4" h., pr. $95
Salt & pepper shakers, California Poppy
   patt., 2 3/4" h., pr...................................... $55
Salt & pepper shakers, figural rose bud,
   Desert Rose patt., pr. $22
Salt & pepper shakers, Meadow Rose
   patt., 6 1/4" h., pr...................................... $35
Salt & pepper shakers, Strawberry Time
   patt., 3" h., pr.. $45
Salt shaker & pepper mill, Desert Rose
   patt., 6" h., pr. $225
Serving bowl, Desert Rose patt., aka Long
   & Narrow, 7 3/4 x 15 1/2", 2 1/4 " h. $350
Sherbet, Coronado Table Ware, ivory matte
   glaze.. $12
Sherbet, Ivy patt., footed, 4" d., 2 1/2" h. $32
Soup bowl, rimmed, Desert Rose patt............. $35
Soup plate w/flanged rim, Arden patt. $15
Soup tureen, cov., Desert Rose patt. $525
Sugar bowl, cov., Bountiful patt....................... $45
Sugar bowl, cov., Desert Rose patt................. $38
Sugar bowl, cov., October patt........................ $25
Sugar bowl, open, individual size, Desert
   Rose patt.. $75
Syrup pitcher, Desert Rose patt., 1 pt.,
   6 1/2" h... $85
Tea tile, Apple patt., 6" sq. $45
Teapot, cov., Arden patt................................... $95
Teapot, cov., individual size, Desert Rose
   patt., 6 1/4" h. $295
Tidbit tray, two-tier, center handle, Ivy patt. .. $145
Tile, Desert Rose patt., 6" sq........................... $45
Trivet, Apple patt., 6" d.................................. $245
Tumbler, Apple patt., 10 oz., 5 1/4" h. $38
Tumbler, California Poppy patt., water, 10
   oz., 5 1/4" h. $125
Tumbler, Desert Rose patt., juice, 6 oz.,
   3 1/4" h... $35
Tumbler, El Patio tableware, apple green
   (ILLUS. w/various El Patio plates & tum-
   blers, top previous page)............................. $28
Tumbler, El Patio tableware, flame orange
   (ILLUS. w/various El Patio plates & tum-
   blers, top previous page)............................. $28
Tumbler, El Patio tableware, glacial blue
   glossy glaze (ILLUS. w/various El Patio
   plates & tumblers, top previous page)......... $28
Tumbler, El Patio tableware, golden glow
   (ILLUS. w/various El Patio plates & tum-
   blers, top previous page)............................. $28
Tumbler, Ivy patt., 10 oz., 5" h. $55
Tumbler, Wildflower patt., water, 10 oz.,
   5 1/2" h. $250
Tureen, cov., footed, Apple patt., 8 3/4" d.,
   5 3/4" h. $450
Vase, bud, 6" h., Meadow Rose patt. $65
Vegetable bowl, divided, Desert Rose patt.,
   7 x 10 3/4" $55
Vegetable bowl, open, oval, Arden patt.,
   large $45

Vegetable bowl, open, oval, Desert Rose
   patt., 9" l.. $35
Vegetable bowl, open, round, Apple patt.,
   8 1/4" d... $45
Vegetable bowl, open, round, California
   Poppy patt., 9" d...................................... $125
Vegetable bowl, open, round, Ivy patt.,
   7 1/4" d... $45
Vegetable bowl, open, round, Wildflower
   patt., 9" d. $225

Frankoma

John Frank started his pottery company in 1933 in Norman, Oklahoma. However, when he moved the business to Sapula, Oklahoma, in 1938 he felt he was home. Still, Mr. Frank could not know the horrendous storms and trials that would follow him.

Just after his move, on November 11, 1938, a fire destroyed the entire operation, which included the pot and leopard mark he had created in 1935. Then, in 1942, the war effort needed men and materials so Frankoma could not survive. However, in 1943, John and Grace Lee Frank bought the plant as junk salvage and began again. The time in Norman had produced some of the finest art ware that John would ever create and most of the items were marked either "Frank Potteries," "Frank Pottery," or to a lesser degree, the "pot and leopard" mark. Today these marks are avidly and enthusiastically sought by collectors.

Another elusive mark wanted by collectors shows "Firsts Kiln Sapula 6-7-38." The mark was used for one day only and denotes the first firing in Sapulpa. It has been estimated that perhaps 50 to 75 pieces were fired on that day.

The clay Frankoma used is helpful to collectors in determining when an item was made. Creamy beige clay know as "Ada" clay was in use until 1953. Then a red brick shale was found in Sapulpa and used until about 1985 when, by the addition of an additive, the clay became a reddish pink. Rutile glazes were used early in Frankoma's history. Glazes with rutile have caused more confusion among collectors than any other glazes. For example, a Prairie Green piece shows a lot of green and it also has some brown' the same is true for the Desert Gold glaze; the piece shows a sandy-beige glaze with some amount of brown. Generally speaking, Prairie Green, Desert Gold, White Sand and Woodland Moss will be the most puzzling to collectors. In 1970 the government closed the rutile mines in America, and Frankoma had to buy rutile from Australia. It was not the same and the results were different. Values are higher for the glazes with rutile. Also, the pre-Australian Woodland Moss glaze is more desirable than that created after 1970.

In 1973 John Frank died and his daughter, Joniece Frank, who was a ceramic designer at the pottery, became president of the company. In 1983 another fire destroyed everything Frankoma had worked so hard to create. They rebuilt but in 1990, after the IRS shut the doors for nonpayment, Joniece, true to the Frank legacy, filed for Chapter 11 (instead of bankruptcy) so she could reopen and continue the work she loved. In 1991 Richard Bernstein purchased the pottery and the name was changed to Frankoma Industries.

The company sold again in 2006. The new buyers are concentrating mostly on dinnerware, none of which is like the old Frankoma. They have a "Collectors Series," "Souvenir & State Items," and "Heartwarming Trivets." None of these is anything like what Frankoma originally created. The company is doing some Frankoma miniatures such as a dolphin on a wave, a fish, a wolf, a bear, etc. These, too, do not resemble Frankoma miniatures. All their glazes are new.

Frankoma Mark

Ashtray, oval shape w/a cocker spaniel sleeping on the top of one side, Prairie Green, 1942-49 .... **$195**

Frankoma Creative Ceramics Award

Award, Creative Ceramics, originally made for the San Antonio, Texas State Fair, a prize trophy given at art shows for the most original pottery items, Desert Gold medallion w/a person's profile & "Frankoma Pottery Award - Creative Ceramics" around the rim, Prairie Green vase, marked "Frankoma USA" & a piece of red unfired clay, late 1950s - early 1960s, 7" h. (ILLUS.) **$150**

Baker, cov., Wagon Wheel patt., Model No. 94w, Prairie Green, 3 qt. **$75**

Bell, Joniece Frank wedding commemorative, 1-11-62, White Sand, unmarked, 1 3/4" h. **$67**

Bolo tie holder, in the shape of an arrowhead, original strap, White Sand **$65**

Book ends, Bucking Bronco, Model No. 423, Prairie Green glaze, 5 1/2" h., pr. (ILLUS., bottom of page) **$560**

Book ends, model of a seahorse, Model No. 426, Prairie Green, 1934-38, 5" h., pr. **$2,000**

Book ends, seated figure, Ivory glaze, Model No. 425, pot & leopard mark, 1934-38, 5 3/4" h., pr. **$1,400**

Bottle-vase, V-1, small black foot w/Prairie Green body, limited edition of 4,000, 1969, 15" h. **$145**

Bottle-vase, V-7, limited edition, 3,500 created, Desert Gold glaze, body w/coffee glazed stopper & base, signed by Joniece Frank, 13" h. **$120**

Unusual Frankoma Tiki God Bowl

Frankoma Bucking Bronco Book Ends

Bowl, 6 1/4" d., 3 1/2" h., deep round shape w/three full-figure Tiki gods around the sides, incised "Club Trade Winds, Tulsa, Okla. 6," Prairie Green, Sapulpa clay, early 1960s (ILLUS., previous page).......... **$195**

Bowl, 11" l., divided, Lazybones patt., Brown Satin glaze, Model No. 4qd.............. **$25**

Brooch, four-leaf clover-shape, Desert Gold glaze, w/original card, 1 1/4" h. **$52**

Special Order Frankoma Carafe

Carafe & cover, footed bulbous body tapering to a short cylindrical neck, domed cover w/rounded tab handle, made from the No. 93 pitcher mold created in 1940 & discontinued in 1964, made for an organization, below the five-point colored star is the name "Ted Witt," reverse incised w/a sailboat on water & the dates 1946-47, Turquoise glaze, marked "Frankoma," 6 1/2" h. (ILLUS.) **$90**

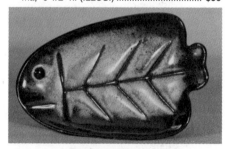

Frankoma Fish Tray

Christmas card, figural fish tray, Woodland Moss glaze, marked, "1960 the Franks, Frankoma Christmas Frankoma," 4" l. (ILLUS.)... **$95**

Christmas card, in the form of a creamer, Lazybones dinnerware patt., blue glaze, Ada clay, incised "Xmas - The Franks - 1953," 3" l., 2 1/4" h. (ILLUS., top next column) **$95**

Christmas card, in the form of a creamer, Model No. 560, incised into Ada clay "Xmas - The Franks - 1948," Prairie Green glaze, rare, 2 1/4" h. **$125**

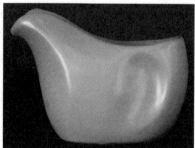

1953 Frank Family Christmas Card

Christmas card tray, cork bark treatment, front marked "The Franks - Christmas 1958," the reverse marked "Frankoma," Desert Gold, 3 3/4" l., 1 1/4" h. **$80**

Christmas plate, marked "God's Chosen Family," 1987, White Sand, 8 1/2" d. **$30**

Christmas plate, marked "Good Will Toward Men," 1965, first edition, White Sand, 8 1/2" d. **$250**

Dealer sign, plain wood frame w/milky white Plexiglas, two pencil-thin green borders, one inside the other & a tan artist's palette-type shape inside the green borders, marked "Frankoma Pottery Sold Here!," scarce, 12" sq. **$155**

Earrings, clip-on type, rectangular, Mayan-Aztec patt., pink, pr. **$30**

Figure group, a group of deer, Model No. 109, Bronze Green, pot & leopard mark, 9" l., 8 1/4" h... **$2,500**

Figure of farmer boy, wearing dark blue overalls, light blue short-sleeved shirt, black scarf tied around neck, yellow hair & ivory wide-brim hat w/only brim showing from front, black shoes, bisque arms, hands, face & neck, marked "Frankoma 702," 6 3/4" h.. **$150**

Frankoma Indian Chief Figure

Figure of Indian Chief, No. 142, Desert Gold glaze, Ada clay, 7" h. (ILLUS.) **$190**

C

C

Frankoma Pottery Show Advertising Sign

Sign, advertising "Pottery Show - Calif. 1987," Prairie Green, 9" l. (ILLUS., top of page) **$115**

John Frank Tournament Stein

Stein, footed, advertising-type, for John Frank Memorial Charity Gold Tournament, Blue, 150 created, 1973 (ILLUS.)....... **$30**

Trivet, decorated w/an eagle sitting on a branch, the large wings filling most of the trivet, Model No. 2tr, Desert Gold, 1966-67, 6" sq. **$69**

Tumbler, juice, Plainsman patt., Model No. 51c, Autumn Yellow glaze, 6 oz. **$15**

Miniature Frankoma Spherical Vase

Vase, 2 3/4" h., miniature, spherical ringed shape, Desert Gold, Ada clay, marked "Frankoma 500" (ILLUS.) **$190**

Vase, 4" h., small foot rising to a flat, narrow body w/tab handle on each side, Ivory glaze, marked "Frankoma" **$120**

Vase, 4" h., small foot rising to a flat, narrow body w/tab handle on each side, Ivory glaze, pot & leopard mark **$225**

Frankoma Stovepipe Vase

Vase, 8 3/4" h., stovepipe, Prairie Green w/silver overlay, 1940s, marked "Frankoma" (ILLUS.) **$645**

Wall masks, bust of Oriental man, No. 134 & Oriental woman, No. 133, Jade Green glaze, pot & leopard mark, Ada clay, man 5 1/2" h., woman 4 3/4" h., pr.................... **$610**

Frankoma Peter Pan Head Wall Pocket

Wall plaque, figural, modeled as the head of Peter Pan, designed by Joseph Taylor, made 1936-38 & 1972-75, Ada clay, Prairie Green, 6" h. (ILLUS.) **$148**

Wall plaque, miniature, African-American head, black glossy glaze, ca. 1940, very rare, 3 1/4" h. **$185**

Wall vase, figural, model of a Billiken, Ada clay, incised on the bottom "Tulsa Court - No. 47 R.O.J.," Praire Green, ca. 1951-55, 7" h. **$145**

Fulper Pottery

The Fulper Pottery was founded in Flemington, New Jersey, in 1805 and operated until 1935, although operations were curtailed in 1929 when its main plant was destroyed by fire. The name was changed in 1929 to Stangl Pottery, which continued in operation until July of 1978, when Pfaltzgraff, a division of Susquehanna Broadcasting Company of York, Pennsylvania, purchased the assets of the Stangl Pottery, including the name.

Fulper Marks

Fulper Galleon Book Ends

Book ends, modeled as a galleon under sail on scrolling waves, thick rectangular base, cafe au lait glaze, oval racetrack mark, 6 1/2" h., pr. (ILLUS.) **$288**

Bowl, 10 3/4" d., 2 1/2" h., low wide flat-bottomed form w/incurved sides, Chinese Blue Flambé glaze, impressed vertical mark, typical burst glaze bubbles, small grinding chips, some crystalline effect (ILLUS., top next column) **$184**

Wide & Low Fulper Flambé Bowl

C

Fulper Box with Colorful Cover

Box, cov., wide rounded black base w/a wide overhanging cover sharply pointed in the center & decorated overall w/colorful flowers & leaves, vertical Fulper mark & monogram of Martin Stangl, 7" d., 4" h. (ILLUS.).. **$345**

Fine Fulper Drippy Glazed Lamp Base

Lamp base, footed tall ovoid body w/a molded mouth, crystalline Mirrored Black glaze dripped over cream on vertical ribbing, cast hole in bottom, unmarked, 13 3/8" h. (ILLUS.) **$546**

C

Fulper Lamp Base with Flambé Glaze

Lamp base, 7" h., wide bulbous ovoid body w/the wide shoulder centered by a short flaring neck, Ivory Flambé glaze over a mustard yellow matte glaze, cast hole in the bottom, unmarked (ILLUS.).................. **$403**

Figural Fulper Powder Box

Powder box, cov., figural, a cylindrical base & a low domed cover centered by the half-length figure of a woman, impressed vertical race track mark & impressed Martin Stangl monogram, ca. 1920s, 7 1/4" h. (ILLUS.) **$345**

Vase, 4 1/2" h., footed wide squatty rounded body w/an angled shoulder to the short, wide cylindrical neck, deep Chinese Blue Flambé glaze w/patches of small blue crystals, vertical racetrack inkstamp mark (ILLUS., top next column)....... **$138**

Squatty Chinese Blue Flambé Vase

Fulper Spherical Vase with Marbleized Glaze

Vase, 6 3/8" h., bulbous nearly spherical body tapering to small squared handles flanking the small mouth, swirled & marbleized dark blue & purple glazes, vertical inkstamp mark (ILLUS.)........................ **$374**

Footed Squatty Fulper Vase

Vase, 7" h., footed squatty bulbous body tapering to a widely flaring neck, dark blue flambé glaze accented w/brown & green, raised oval racetrack mark, small chip off foot (ILLUS.).. **$403**

C

Green & Yellow Fulper Phoenix Wall Pocket

Wall pocket, figural, model of a long-tailed phoenix in greens, yellow, black & grey, vertical inkstamp mark, Shape 375, small glaze nick on tail feather, 9 1/2" h. (ILLUS.) **$259**

Colorful Fulper Phoenix Wall Pocket

Wall pocket, figural, model of a long-tailed phoenix in yellow, red, blue & black, vertical inkstamp mark, Shape 369, 9" h. (ILLUS.) **$219**

Gallé Pottery

Fine pottery was made by Emile Gallé, the multitalented French designer and artisan who is also famous for his glass and furniture. The pottery is relatively scarce.

Gallé Pottery Mark

Unusual Gallé Fish-handled Basket

Basket, the flaring body composed of ribbed feather-like panels resting on large knobs w/tiny ball feet, the high arched handle formed by two facing fish w/their tails curving up to the top, glazed in steaky glazes in shades of red, green, orange & blue, accent w/overall gold spatter, signed "Emile Gallé - Nancy Déposé," professionally repaired handle, ca. 1890, 8 1/2" h. (ILLUS.)........ **$1,410**

Ewer, a squatty bulbous body centered by a tall slender stick neck, a long flat handle from near the top of the neck to the shoulder, a crimson glazed decorated w/gold-trimmed dark blackish green foliage & a praying mantis, white blossoms around the neck, accented w/gold spatter, signed in black enamel w/the Cross of Lorraine & "E & G dépose - E. Gallé Nancy," ca. 1890, 9 3/4" h. **$1,880**

Unusual Gallé Decorated Pitcher

C

Pitcher, 7 1/2" h., footed squatty bulbous body tapering to a cylindrical section & widely flaring cupped rim, applied strap handle, the upper half w/a thick drippy light blue glaze w/gold trim above a mottled brown lower half, enameled w/a large flying insect above long leaved plant, stamped in the glaze "Emile Galle Nancy Déposé" & the E & G monogram, short hairline in bottom, ca. 1890 (ILLUS., previous page) **$3,760**

Bulbous Pinched Floral-decorated Vase

Vase, 7 1/2" h., a footed bulbous lower body w/deeply pinched-in sides, tapering to a wide cylindrical upper body, glazed in mottled shades of dark mustard brown & black, enameled w/naturalistic flowers & two polychrome butterflies, small low curved side handles trimmed in blue, stamped w/the Cross of Lorraine & "Emilé Gallé - Nancy Déposé" (ILLUS.) **$2,350**

Gaudy Welsh

This is a name for wares made in England for the American market about 1830 to 1860, with some examples dating much later. Decorated with Imari-style flower patterns, often highlighted with copper lustre, it should not be confused with Gaudy Dutch wares, the colors of which differ somewhat.

Cups & saucers, handleless, paneled rim, Urn patt., pink, orange, green cobalt blue & lustre trim, 19th c., set of 6 (some minor staining).. **$715**
Plates, 8 1/2" d., paneled rim, Urn patt., pink, orange, green cobalt blue & lustre trim, 19th c., set of 6 (three w/light staining) **$715**

Geisha Girl Wares

Geisha Girl Porcelain features scenes of Japanese women in colorful kimonos along with the flora and architecture of turn-of-the-century Japan. Although bearing an Oriental motif, the wares were produced for Western use in dinnerware and household accessory forms favored during the late 1800s through the early 1940s. There was minimal production during the Occupied Japan period. Less ornate wares were distributed through gift shops and catalogs during the 1960s-70s; some of these are believed to have been manufactured in Hong Kong. Beware overly ornate items with fake Nippon marks that are in current production today, imported from China. More than a hundred porcelain manufacturers and decorating houses were involved with production of these wares during their heyday.

Prices cited here are for excellent to mint condition items. Enamel wear, flaking, hairlines or missing parts all serve to lower the value of an item. Prices in your area may vary.

More than 275 Geisha Girl Porcelain patterns and pattern variations have been catalogued; others are still coming to light.

The most common patterns include:

Bamboo Tree

Battledore

Child Reaching for Butterfly

Fan series

Garden Bench series

Geisha in Sampan series

Meeting series

Parasol series

Pointing series

The rarest patterns include:

... And They're Off

Bellflower

Bicycle Race

Capricious

Elegance in Motion

Fishing series

Foreign Garden

In Flight

Steamboat

The most popular patterns include:

Boat Festival

Butterfly Dancers

By Land and By Sea

Cloud series

Courtesan Processional

Dragonboat

Small Sounds of Summer

So Big

Temple A

A complete listing of patterns and their descriptions can be found in The Collector's Encyclopedia of Geisha Girl Porcelain. *Additional patterns discovered since publication of the book are documented in* The Geisha Girl Porcelain Newsletter.

References: Litts, E., Collector's Encyclopedia of Geisha Girl Porcelain, *Collector Books, 1988;* Geisha Girl Porcelain Newsletter, *P.O. Box 3394, Morris Plains, NJ 07950.*

Geisha Parasol F Chocolate Pot

Chocolate pot, cov., Parasol F patt., cobalt blue border w/gold lacing, unusual spout, 8 1/2" h. (ILLUS.) **$125**

Cup & saucer, bouillon w/lid, Pointing D patt., black border, signed in Japanese "Tashiro" **$45**

Two Geisha Girl Fan A Sauce Dishes

Sauce dish, Fan A patt., refined, detailed & unusual underglaze blue, signed in Japanese, 2 5/8" d., 1" h. (ILLUS. of two) **$30**

Geisha Parasol B Pattern Tea Caddy

Tea caddy, cov., Parasol B patt., cobalt blue, scalloped border w/gold, missing interior lid, 4" h. (ILLUS.) **$28**

Gonder

Lawton Gonder founded Gonder Ceramic Arts in Zanesville, Ohio, in 1941 and it continued in operation until 1957.

The firm produced a higher priced and better quality of commercial art potteries than many firms of the time and employed Jamie Matchet and Chester Kirk, both of whom were outstanding ceramic designers. Several special glazes were developed during the company's history and Gonder even duplicated some museum pieces of Chinese ceramic. In 1955 the firm converted to the production of tile due to increased foreign competition. By 1957 its years of finest production were over.

Increase price ranges as indicated for the following glaze colors: red flambé - 50 percent, antique gold crackle - 70 percent, turquoise Chinese crackle - 40 per cent, white Chinese crackle - 30 per cent.

Gonder E-1
GONDER
U.S.A.

Gonder Pottery Mark

Ashtray, boomerang shape, Mold No. 223, 6 1/4 x 10 1/2" l. **$15-35**

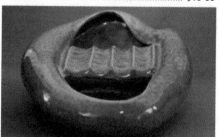

Center Rest Cigar Ashtray

Ashtray, Center Rest Cigar, marked "Gonder Original 219" in script, Red Flambé glaze, 2 1/4 x 7 1/2" (ILLUS., previous page) **$50-75**

Ashtray, round, pie crust rim, Mold No. 807, 9" d. **$10-30**

Ashtray, "S" Swirl, Mold No. 626, 6 1/2 x 9 1/8" l. **$20-30**

Ashtray, Sovereign Fluted Round, Mold No. 808, 2 3/4" d. **$20-30**

Ashtray, square, Mold No. 1800A, 10 11/16" sq. **$60-75**

Ashtray, square, Mold No. 805, 9 1/4" w. **$20-40**

Base, for Chinese Imperial dragon handle vase No. 535, footed, 4 5/8 x 5 13/16", 2 1/16" h. **$55-80**

Basket, Mold No. L-19, 9 x 13" **$30-45**

Beverage set: 8" h. pitcher & six 5" h. mugs; LaGonda patt., Mold No. 917 & 909, the set **$50-75**

Book ends, in the form of horses, Mold No. 211, 10" h., pr. **$125-150**

Bowl, 5 11/16" d., 1 3/8" h., w/small leaves, Mold No. B-17 .... **$30-50**

Bowl, 8" d., 2 3/8" h., Mold No. 715 .... **$10-20**

Candleholder, fluted, Mold No. 314, 414, E-14, 4 5/8" w., 1 7/8" h. **$5-10**

Candleholder, Mold No. 520/C, Freeform, 4 1/4" w. x 5 1/2" l., 1 13/16" h. **$20-35**

Candleholders, Mold No. 521/C, Shell, 6 1/4" l., 3 3/4" h., pr. **$25-35**

Casserole, cov., handled lid, La Gonda, Mold No. 953, 5 1/4 x 8 1/4", 4" h. **$15-25**

Cigarette box, cov., Mold. No. 806, 3 1/2 x 4 3/8", 2 5/8" h. **$80-95**

Console bowl, Mold No. 520, 8 7/8" w. x 11 1/4" l, 2 5/8" h. **$50-75**

Console bowl, crescent moon shape, Mold J-55, 5 x 12" **$30-45**

Console bowl, seashell design, Mold No. 505, 7 1/4 x 17 1/2" **$75-90**

Console set: 16" l. bowl & pr. of candle-holders; "Banana Boat" bowl, Mold Nos. 565 & 567, the set **$100-130**

Cookie jar, cov., Pirate, Mold No. 951, 10 1/2" or 12" h. **$900-1,200**

Cookie jar, cov., Sheriff, Mold No. 950, green glaze, 12" h. **$800-1,000**

Cornucopia-vase, ribbed, Mold No. 360, 7" h. **$20-35**

Cornucopia-vase, held by figural hand, oval base, Mold No. 675, 7 1/2 x 8" **$75-100**

Cornucopia-vase, square base, Mold No. H-14, 9" h. **$15-25**

Cornucopia-vase, on flat square base, Mold No. J-66, 10" l. **$20-35**

Creamer, La Gonda, Mold No. 907, 7" w., 4" h. **$20-30**

Dish, oak leaf design, Mold No. 591, 13" l. **$30-50**

Ewer, fluted, Mold No. E-60, brown w/yellow mottling, 6" h. (ILLUS., top next column) **$5-15**

Ewer, w/stopper, carafe-shaped, gunmetal glaze, Mold No. 994, 8" (ILLUS., second next column)............................... **$35-50**

Ewer, Mold No. J-25, 8 x 11" **$50-75**

Gonder Mold No. E-60 Fluted Ewer

Carafe-shaped Ewer

Figure of bearded Oriental man, Mold No. 775, 8 5/8" h. **$50-60**

Figure of coolie, kneeling & bending for-ward, Mold No. 547, 5" h. **$15-30**

Figure of Oriental male, Mold No. 773, 11" h. **$40-60**

Figure of Oriental woman, holding ginger jar, Mold No. 573, 4 7/8" h. **$40-60**

Figure of turbaned woman w/baskets, Mold No. 762, 14 1/2" h. **$125-150**

Ginger jar, cov., square, 10" h. **$100-150**

Lamp, bullet-shaped, Mold No. 2228, 11" h. **$75-100**

Lamp, ewer form, Mold No. 4046, 11" h. **$35-55**

Lamp, Geometric Planes, Mold No. 4037, 9" w., 10" h. **$60-80**

Lamp, Mold No. 522, Scarla Sunfish, 10" l., 9" h. **$150-175**

Lamp, cookie jar shape, Mold No. P-24, 8 1/2" h. **$20-40**

Lamp, model of two horse heads, 12" h. **$40-50**

Tankard, shell, Mold No. 400, very hard to find, 9 1/2" h. **$150-175**
Teapot, cov., rectangular, La Gonda patt., Mold No. 396, 6 1/4" h. **$50-75**
Teapot, cov., Mold No. P-31, 6 1/2" h. **$15-25**
Tray, rectangular, flat, Mold No. 700 .... **$20-35**
TV lamp, model of Chanticleer rooster, hard to find, 9 1/2 x 14" **$75-100**
Vase, 5" h., cylindrical, Mold No. 710 .... **$10-20**
Vase, 5 3/4" h., square pillow form, Mold No. 705.. **$10-20**
Vase, 6" h., footed, bulbous lobed base w/flaring square top, Mold E-71 .... **$20-35**
Vase, 6 1/16" h., "Z"-handled ewer, Mold No. 365, E-65, E-365 .... **$15-25**
Vase, 6 1/4" h., applied leaf, Mold No. E368 .... **$20-25**

Gonder Butterfly-shaped Vase

Vase, 6 3/8" h., 8 1/2" w., Ribbed Fan, butterfly-like shape, marked "Gonder H-82 USA" in script, Antique Gold Crackle glaze (ILLUS.) **$40-60**
Vase, 6 1/2" h., hourglass shape w/large applied leaf, Mold E-70 .... **$15-25**
Vase, 6 1/2" h., ribbed, swirl design, Mold No. 381.. **$20-35**
Vase, 6 1/2" h., urn shape w/leaf design, single handle, Mold No. H-80................. **$20-30**
Vase, 4 1/2 x 7", ovoid body w/flared top, shoulder handles, Mold E-1 .... **$5-15**
Vase, 4 1/2 x 7 1/2", footed, model of single flower, Mold No. E-3.............................. **$10-20**
Vase, 7 x 7 1/2", model of seashell w/two dolphins at base, Mold No. 558............. **$75-100**
Vase, 6 x 8", model of starfish, Mold No. H-79 .... **$15-25**
Vase, 8" h., flaring form w/relief-molded swans at base, Mold No. H-47 .... **$20-30**
Vase, 8" h., raised circular ewer, Mold No. 410 .... **$25-40**
Vase, 8 5/16" h., butterfly w/flowers, Mold No. H-88.. **$50-75**
Vase, 8 3/8" h., medium cylindrical, Mold No. 711 .... **$15-75**
Vase, 7 x 8 1/2", flaring body w/one angled handle at rim, the other at base, Mold No. H-56 .... **$15-30**
Vase, 8 1/2" h., bottle form, Mold No. 1211 .... **$50-75**
Vase, 8 1/2" h., rectangular, decorated w/relief-molded crane, Mold No. H-76..... **$30-40**

Vase, 8 1/2" h., tapering pillow form, Mold No. 702 .... **$35-50**
Vase, 8 5/8" h., flat multi-leaf design, Mold No. 478, H-78.................................... **$30-45**
Vase, 6 x 9", basketweave design w/flared top, Mold H-36 .... **$40-50**
Vase, 9 1/8" h., 4 x 6 3/16", tapering cylindrical form w/relief-molded pea pod decoration, Mold No. 487 H-87 .... **$30-40**
Vase, 9" h., footed, square double bulb form, Mold No. 607 & H-607 .... **$125-150**
Vase, 9" h., lyre shape, Mold No. J-57 .... **$65-85**
Vase, 9" h., tieback drape design, Mold No. 605 & H-605 .... **$40-65**
Vase, 9 1/4" h., footed leaf form w/open circle in center, Mold No. H-603 .... **$35-50**
Vase, 9 1/2" h., model of fawn head, Mold No. 518 .... **$50-75**
Vase, 9 5/8" h., Chinese w/uneven handles, Mold No. 720...................................... **$75-100**
Vase, 10" h., Art Deco freeform design, Mold No. 636... **$80-100**
Vase, 10" h., model of Trojan horse head, Mold No. 540....................................... **$75-100**
Vase, 7 x 10", conical w/relief-molded leaves at base, Mold J-64 .... **$40-50**
Vase, 9 x 10", model of angel fish on waves, Mold No. 522.................................... **$100-125**
Vase, 10 1/4" h., flared flower, Mold No. 876 .... **$150-175**

Gonder Pegasus Vase

Vase, 10 1/2" h., 9 3/4" w., Pegasus, marked "Gonder 526," French Lilac glaze, very hard to find (ILLUS.) **$225-250**
Vase, 10 3/4" h., round leaf-in-leaf, Mold No. J-59 .... **$60-80**
Vase, 11" h., flat form, model of swan, Mold No. 530 .... **$100-125**
Vase, 8 x 11", figural leaf design, Mold No. 504 .... **$25-35**
Vase, 11 1/2" h., fan shape, relief-molded shell decoration, Mold No. J-60 .... **$40-55**
Vase, 8 x 11 1/2", leaf swirl design, Mold No. 596 .... **$50-75**
Vase, 11 3/4" h., swallow design, Mold K-25, very hard to find **$150-200**
Vase, 12" h., swirl design w/two openings, Mold No. 862............................... **$75-125**

C

Vase, 12 1/2" h., Mold No. M-4, very hard to
find **$125-150**
Vase, 9 3/4" h., uneven double swirl cornu-
copia, Mold No. H-48 .... **$50-60**

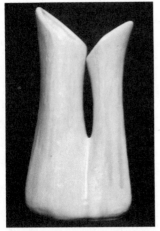

Double Cylindrical Form Vase

Vase, 6 1/2 x 13", double, tall slender cylin-
drical forms joined at triangular-form
base, slanted rim, mottled green glaze,
Mold No. 868 (ILLUS.) **$150-200**
Vase, 15 3/4" h., leaves & twigs design,
Mold No. 599, hard to find **$100-150**

Grueby

*Some fine art pottery was produced by the
Grueby Faience and Tile Company, established in
Boston in 1891. Choice pieces were created with
molded designs on a semi-porcelain body. The
ware is marked and often bears the initials of the
decorators. The pottery closed in 1907.*

GRUEBY

Grueby Pottery Mark

Bowl, 7 1/2" d., 1 1/4" h., wide flattened
form w/low incurved sides, bluish green
glossy glaze **$161**

Grueby Blue Scarab Paperweight

Paperweight, model of a scarab beetle,
oval, matte blue glaze, impressed circular mark, some small glaze chips at base,
3 7/8" l. (ILLUS.) **$196**

Grueby Scarab with Oatmeal Glaze

Paperweight, model of a scarab beetle,
oval, matte oatmeal glaze, impressed
circular mark, glaze peppering, 3 7/8" l.
(ILLUS.) **$345**

Grueby Matte Blue Vase

Vase, 6 3/4" h., footed simple ovoid body tapering to a flat mouth, textured matte blue
glaze, impressed Grueby mark (ILLUS.) **$690**

Grueby Vase with Molded Florals

Vase, 7 3/4" h., squatty bulbous base w/an angled shoulder to the tall gently flaring neck, tooled floral designs, dark matte green glaze, impressed tulip mark (ILLUS., previous page) **$1,610**

Grueby Vase with Typical Green Glaze

Vase, 9 1/2" h., footed squatty bulbous lower body tapering to a wide cylindrical neck w/a molded rim, dark green matte glaze (ILLUS.) **$1,265**

Tall Grueby Matte Green Vase

Vase, 12 1/2" h., swelled cylindrical body tapering to a short flared neck, matte green glaze w/a number of pinhead burst bubbles, area of thin glaze on side (ILLUS.)

.... **$1,265**

Hadley Pottery

Mary Alice Hale was born in Terre Haute, Indiana in 1911. Her father owned Vigo American clay Company and she spent many childhood hours marking clay figures. In 1930 she married George Hadley and the couple moved briefly to New York City. In 1936 Hadley accepted a teaching job and the couple permanently relocated to Louisville, Kentucky. While Mr. Hadley taught, Mary spent her days painting watercolors and oils.

During the summer months the couple enjoyed boating on the Ohio River. Unable to find dishes she liked for the boat, Mary Hadley created her own beautiful yet functional pieces. Friends raved about her creations and she was soon overwhelmed with requests for her unique dishes.

In 1940 Mary Hadley turned all her talents to making pottery. The business grew so fast that in 1994 the couple purchased an 1840s building, a former factory and wool mill. Mr. Hadley left his teaching career to design pottery making equipment, tend kilns and handle business affairs while his wife created patterns, hired artists and was the firm's salesperson. Mary Alice Hadley continued working until her death from cancer in 1965. Mr. Hadley sold the company in 1979.

Still located in the Butchertown neighborhood of Louisville, the building and pottery making process has changed little over the years. Eighteen patterns, including eight developed by Mary Hadley, continue to be made in a variety of dinnerware and ornamental pieces featuring their distinctive handpainted blue on grey color. Her Country design is the most popular. Visitors can shop for seconds at the showroom, admire her original artwork and take a free factory tour.

Although most pieces illustrated here are of fairly recent production, some of the designs are classics, such as the Bouquet and Farm patterns. Newer patterns include Frog, Turtle, Lighthouse, Palm Tree, Lob Cabin and Fishing, among others.

Hadley Pottery Bunny Rabbit Cereal Bowl

Bowl, cereal, Bunny Rabbit patt. (ILLUS.) **$10**

C

Hadley Turtle Pattern Soup Bowl

Bowl, soup, Turtle patt. (ILLUS.)..................... **$10**

Hadley Happy Father's Day Coaster

Coaster, "Happy Father's Day" patt. (ILLUS.) **$9**

Hadley Rearing Stallion Cachepot

Cachepot, tapering cylindrical form, Rearing Stallion patt. (ILLUS.) **$15**

Hadley Rearing Stallion Flaring Mug

Mug, flaring rim, Rearing Stallion patt. (ILLUS.)... **$13**

Merry Christmas Pattern Coaster

Coaster, "A Very Merry Christmas" patt. (ILLUS.) **$8**

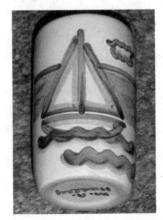

Hadley Sailboat Pattern Pencil Cup

Pencil cup, cylindrical, Sailboat patt. (ILLUS.) **$10**

Hadley Pottery Large Duck Planter

Planter, figural duck, large size (ILLUS., top of page) **$35**

Hadley Fishing on the Bank Dinner Plate

Plate, dinner, Fishing on the Bank patt. (ILLUS.) **$10-18**

Hadley Turtle Pattern Dinner Plate

Plate, dinner, Turtle patt. (ILLUS.).............. **$10-15**

Hadley Pottery Farm Cow Trivet

Trivet, Farm Cow patt. (ILLUS.) **$15**

Harker Pottery

Harker Pottery was in business for more than 100 years (1840-1972) in the East Liverpool area of eastern Ohio. One of the oldest potteries in Ohio, it advertised itself as one of the oldest in America. The pottery produced numerous lines that are favorites of collectors.

Some of their most popular lines were intended for oven to table use and were marked with BAKERITE, COLUMBIA BAKERITE, HOTOVEN, OVEN-WARE, Bungalow Ware, Cameo Ware, White Rose Carv-Kraft (for Montgomery Ward) and Harkerware Stone China/Stone Ware brand names.

Harker also made Reproduction Rockingham, Royal Gadroon, Pate sur Pate, Windsong, and many souvenir items and a line designed by Russel Wright that have gained popularity with collectors.

Like many pottery manufacturers, Harker reused popular decal patterns on several ware shapes. Harker was marketed under more than 200 backstamps in its history.

C

Group of Three Early Harker ABC Plates

Children's Ware

Plate, ABC, color-printed center scene of Sunbonnet Sue titled "I Love You," 6 1/8" d. (ILLUS. center with two other ABC plates, top of page) **$50-75**

Plate, ABC, color-printed center scene titled "Baby Bunting & Bunch while crossing a log were stared at boldly by an ugly green frog," 6 1/8" d. (ILLUS. left with two other ABC plates, top of page) **$50-75**

Plate, ABC, color-printed center scene titled "Dolly's Sail," shows two girls, a dog, doll & toy sailboat, 6" d. (ILLUS. right with two other ABC plates, top of page) **$50-75**

Decaled Ware

Countryside (Thatched Roof English Cottage)

Countryside Pattern Plates & Teapot

Plate, 8" sq. (ILLUS. first of three behind teapot) **$10-15**

Plate, 8 7/8" sq. (ILLUS. second of three behind teapot) **$15-20**

Plate, 9 3/4" sq. (ILLUS. third of three behind teapot) **$25-30**

Teapot, cov., Bump Handle style, 8 3/4" l., 5 1/2" h. (ILLUS. front with three plates) **$90-110**

Crayon Apple (pink & orange with green leaves & a few black leaves, black trim)

Cake plate, Concentric Rings shape, 10 7/8" d. **$18-25**

Casserole, cov., vent hole in cover, 8 1/2" w. **$25-35**

Custard, G.C. shape (General Clay with vertical ribs), 2" h. **$5-8**

Lard/drippings jar, cov., Skyscraper shape, 4 1/2" h. **$20-25**

Plate, 10" d. **$25-35**

Stack dish, cov., paneled shape, 6 7/8" w., 2 7/8" h. **$25-35**

Utility plate, Virginia shape, tab handles, 12 1/8" w. **$20-25**

English Ivy

Ashtray, Modern Age shape, 4 7/8" d. **$25-35**

Bowl & cover with lifesaver finial, 6" d., 5 3/4" h. **$40-45**

Creamer, Gem shape, 3" h. **$8-12**

Creamer & cover with lifesaver finial, Modern Age shape, 5" h. **$25-30**

Creamer with flat lid, Ohio shape, 3 3/4" h. **$30-40**

Fork, Modern Age shape, w/splayed tines for holding spaghetti, 8 3/4" l. **$25-30**

Lifter, Modern Age shape, narrow blade, 8 1/2" l. **$18-25**

Shortening knife/spoon, Modern Age shape, 8 5/8" l. **$20-25**

Spoon, Modern Age shape, 8 1/2" l. **$18-24**

Sugar bowl, open, Gem shape, 3" h. **$8-12**

English Ivy (red poinsettia with grey leaves)

Bowl set, three-piece, 4", 5" & 6" w., the set **$30-40**

Harker Ivy Pattern Pieces

Bowl with flat cover, 5 1/8" w., 3 3/4" h.,
Modern Age shape.................................. **$20-30**
Casserole, cov., 7 1/2" w., 4 1/2" h........... **$18-25**
Spoon, 8 5/8" l... **$15-20**

Honeymoon Cottage (red roof on yellow cottage, multi-colored flowers along narrowing sidewalk leading to cottage, red trim)
Bean pot, 2 1/2" h. **$10-12**
Dish, cov., paneled shape, 6 1/2" w., 4 1/2" h... **$20-25**
Egg cup, 4 1/8" h. **$15-20**
Pie baker, either 8 3/4" or 9 3/4" d., each ... **$20-30**
Salt & pepper shakers, Skyscraper shape, 4 1/2" h., each.. **$15-20**
Trivet (tea tile), 6 3/8" w. **$35-40**

Ivy Pattern
Grease jar, cov., D'Ware shape (ILLUS. left with other Ivy pieces, top of page) **$20-30**
Pie baker (ILLUS. second from right with other Ivy pattern pieces, top of page)...... **$12-20**
Pitcher, jug-type, round (ILLUS. right with other Ivy pieces, top of page)........................ **$4**
Plate, 10" d., dinner, plain round (ILLUS. second from left other Ivy pieces, top of page).. **$5-10**
Spoon, serving (ILLUS. center with other Ivy pieces, top of page)........................... **$15-20**

Jewel Weed (large red & blue flowers with large yellow centers)
Bean pot, 2 1/2" h. **$5-8**

Bowl, oval, 8 3/8" or 9 1/2" l., each **$15-20**
Canister, cov., 6 3/8" w., 5 1/2" h................ **$35-40**
Casserole, cov., Sun-Glow (lobed) shape, 7 7/8" w. **$45-60**
Cookie jar, cov., 6 3/8" w., 8 1/2" h............. **$60-75**
Custard, 3 3/8" w., 2" h. **$5-8**
Jug, cov., 7 3/4" h., straight-sided w/flat cover **$45-60**
Pie baker, large decals, 9 1/8" d. **$15-20**
Pie baker, small decals, 9 1/4" d................. **$20-25**
Plate, 8 3/4" sq. **$10-15**
Stack dish set, cov., three-piece, 6 1/2" w., 6 1/2" h., the set..................................... **$40-50**

Lisa (large single flower in either red, blue or burgundy with different color side flowers)
Bowl, 8 1/8" d., tab handles, red, blue or burgundy **$12-15**
Jug, Gargoyle Handle, yellow glaze w/blue flowers, 4 1/2" h. **$25-35**
Jug, Gargoyle Handle, burgundy, 6 1/2" h. **$35-50**
Jug, Gargoyle Handle, red or blue, 6 1/2" h. **$20-25**
Jug, Gargoyle Handle, yellow glaze w/blue flowers, 7 3/4" h. **$45-55**

Mallow Pattern
Coffeepot, cov., GC shape **$45-65**
Creamer, cov., paneled Ohio jug shape (ILLUS. top right with other Mallow pieces, bottom of page)........................ **$35-45**

Harker Mallow Pattern Pieces

Custard cup (ILLUS. top left with other Mallow pieces, bottom previous page)............ **$8-12**
Mixing bowl, 9" d. (ILLUS. bottom right with other Mallow pattern pieces, bottom previous page)... **$25-30**
Mixing bowl, 9" d., w/rim spout (ILLUS. bottom left other Mallow pattern pieces, bottom previous page) **$25-35**

Older White Ware (1879 to 1930)

Three Old Harker Shape Jugs

Jug, Harker shape, decorated w/Dutch children scene w/blue trim, 9" h. (ILLUS. center with two other Harker shape jugs) **$90-110**
Jug, Harker shape, h.p. yellow & burgundy pansies, 9" h. (ILLUS. right with two other Harker shape jugs).............................. **$90-110**
Jug, Harker shape, transfer-printed red, pink, yellow & white old roses, 9 1/4" h.

(ILLUS. left with two other Harker shape jugs) **$60-75**

Republic Ice Water Pitcher & Mug

Jug, Republic shape, heavy wire bail handle & ice retainer spout, Winter scene in brown & white, name printed in gold on front "G.A. Doren, M.D.," 9 7/8" h. (ILLUS. back with matching shaving mug) **$225-275**
Shaving mug, Iolanthe shape, Winter scene in brown & white, 3 5/8" h. (ILLUS. front with handled Republic jug)............ **$90-110**
Teapot, cov., Savoy shape, Bird of Paradise patt. w/pink & blue flowers, black trim, 7 7/8" w. (ILLUS. left with two other Savoy teapots, bottom of page) **$50-70**
Teapot, cov., Savoy shape, blue blush w/large white & small blue flowers, 7 7/8" w. (ILLUS. center with two other Savoy teapots, bottom of page) **$70-80**

Three Harker Savoy Shape Teapots

Group of Four Harker Rolling Pins

Teapot, cov., Savoy shape, blue & red Oriental flowers, 7 7/8" w. (ILLUS. right with two other Savoy teapots, bottom previous page) **$50-70**

Moss Rose Vegetable Dish & Undertray

Underplate, square, Elodie (Gargoyle) shape, hand-colored Moss Rose patt., 8 x 9 1/2" (ILLUS. back with Moss Rose vegetable dish)...................................... **$15-25**
Vegetable dish, cov., Elodie (Gargoyle) shape, hand-colored Moss Rose patt., 5 1/4 x 11 5/8" (ILLUS. front with Moss Rose underplate).................................... **$35-50**

Papyrus (two red flowers on green stems plus black leaves, platinum trim)
Bowl, rectangular, 9" l. **$20-30**
Creamer, Gem shape, 3 1/8" h. **$12-15**
Jug, Gargoyle Handle, 4 3/4" h. **$30-35**
Jug, Gargoyle Handle, 7 3/4" h. **$40-50**
Sugar bowl, Gem shape, 3 1/8" h.............. **$12-15**

Rolling Pins - 14 1/2" l.
Anti-Q patt. (ILLUS. top with three other rolling pins, top of page)...................... **$90-125**
Blue Roses patt., (ILLUS. bottom with three other rolling pins, top of page) **$90-125**

Godey (Colonial Couple) (ILLUS. second from bottom with three other rolling pins, top of page)... **$90-125**
Pink Cyclamen (ILLUS. second from top with three other rolling pins, top of page) **$90-125**

Gadroon and Royal Gadroon
This shape, with its distinctive scalloped edge, was extremely popular and was produced in several glaze colors, with the classic Chesterton grey and Corinthian green (which commands slightly higher prices) presenting an especially elegant table setting. Pate sur pate, though frequently used, is only one of several marks found on this ware. The Royal Gadroon shape was also decorated with numerous colorful decals, including Bridal Rose, Shadow Rose, Royal Rose, Wild Rose, Currier & Ives, Godey, Game Birds, Morning Glories, Violets and White Thistle (silk-screened on yellow and pink glazed ware).

Gadroon
Bowl, cereal/soup, lug handles (ILLUS. middle right with Chesterton collection, top next page) **$3-5**
Cake set: 10" lug-handled cake plate, six dessert plates & lifter; 8 pcs. **$25-35**
Creamer (ILLUS. front right with Chesterton collection, top next page) **$4-8**
Cup & saucer (ILLUS. middle left with Chesterton collection, top next page) **$7-10**
Gravy boat (ILLUS. middle row, center with Chesterton collection, top next page) **$5-8**
Plate, 7" sq., salad (ILLUS. rear right with Chesterton collection, top next page) **$3-5**
Plate, 9" d., dinner (ILLUS. left rear with Chesterton collection, top next page) **$4-6**
Platter, 13" l., oval...................................... **$10-12**
Spoon, serving... **$8-12**
Sugar bowl, cov. (ILLUS. front left with Chesterton collection, top next page) **$5-8**
Vegetable dish, cover w/lug handles **$10-15**

Harker Chesterton Collection

Reproduction Rockingham

Harker Reproduction Rockingham was made in the early 1960s. This line included hound-handled pitchers (the only pieces actually made in the mid-19th century), hound-handled mugs, Jolly Roger jugs*, Daniel Boone jugs*, ashtrays, Armed Forces logo plates and ashtrays, soap dishes, candleholders (for hound-handled mugs), tobacco leaf candy dish / ashtrays, Rebecca at the Well teapots, tidbit trays, Give Us This Day Our Daily Bread plates, octagonal trivets, a 7 1/2" h. bald eagle figure, 6" l. skillet spoon holders (unmarked), Jolly Roger pipes (extremely rare), and even a rolling pin (only one found to date). Colors included brown, gold (honey brown), and bottle green, and light creamy brown trivets and soap dishes have also turned up. Because some pieces have a date of "1840" and are not marked as reproductions, some confusion has resulted, but modern pieces should not confuse anyone familiar with mid-19th century wares and their glazes.

*(Harker called them "jugs" but they were really mugs.)

Ashtray (candy dish), model of a leaf, brown **$12-18**
Ashtray (candy dish), model of a leaf, honey brown or bottle green, each **$20-30**
Bread tray, bottle green **$30-40**
Bread tray, honey brown (gold) **$20-25**
Jug (mug), figural Daniel Boone head, bottle green **$30-40**
Jug (mug), figural Daniel Boone head, brown **$18-24**
Jug (mug), figural Daniel Boone head, honey brown... **$18-24**
Jug (mug), figural Jolly Roger head, bottle green **$25-35**
Jug (mug), figural Jolly Roger head, honey brown **$20-30**
Mug, figural hound handle, bottle green **$25-35**
Mug, figural hound handle, honey brown **$20-30**
Pitcher, jug-type w/figural hound handle, bottle green **$65-80**
Pitcher, jug-type w/figural hound handle, honey brown... **$50-60**

Plate, relief-molded American eagle (Great Seal of the U.S.), honey brown or bottle green, each **$18-24**

Harris Strong Designs

Harris Strong (1920-2006) is so identified with the decorative tiles produced by his company during the 1950s and 1960s that even unsigned tiles of that era are often attributed to him although the style may be markedly different.

Born in Wisconsin, Strong studied ceramics and chemical engineerings at North Carolina State University. In 1947, after working for Kelby Originals, a Brooklyn pottery, Strong and co-worker Robert Krasner founded Potters of Wall Street. Their new firm specialized in ceramic lamps, ashtrays and other decorative pieces, including tiles.

The tiles for which Strong became famous were actually a secondary focus of his, created primarily to test glazes. However, their novelty, whether used as individual accent pieces or grouped together to form a tile "painting," caught on with the public. Buoyed by this success Strong opened his own firm in the Bronx in the early 1950s.

Strong's tile scenes, framed or mounted on burnished wood backings, proved popular with architects, interior decorators and consumers seeking contemporary wall art at affordable prices. Themes included portraits, abstracts and exotic locales as well as medieval and other period depictions. Strong's tile plaques are noted for their vibrant color combinations, the three-dimensionality of the figures and scenes, and an attention to detail. Color and form are filtered through the precise parameters of ceramic tile as well as through Strong's own visual sense that encompasses both the primitive and the contemporary.

The sheer size of many Harris Strong plaques made them especially well suited to corporate, hotel and restaurant decor where they made arresting focal points in the interior. In essence, Strong created the early 1950s market for tile-based decorative wall hangings, adapting his designs for nearly every location: ship's lounges, office building facades, elevator interiors and even bowling alleys. One particularly challenging commissioin was the massive "Cathedral Wall" divider created for New York's Waldorf-Astoria Hotel which spanned the entire interior of the hotel's Marco Polo Club.

Attribution of Harris works has often been haphazard since paper labels were used on the back of his plaques rather than a permanent signature. In the absence of a label, one reliable indicator of a Strong plaque is the heart-shaped hooks used for hanging.

Harris G. Strong, Inc. relocated to Maine in 1970 and eventually phased out tile production, focusing instead on paintings, collages and other types of wall decor. For the company's 40th anniversary in 1992 a series of commemorative tiles were produced. The company ceased all production in 1999.

In looking back on his career, Mr. Strong noted, "Nobody ever handled tiles the way we did because we regarded them as a piece of pottery; a lot of us worked together to achieve our goal. What I provided, I hope, was the continuing thread that went through all the years — of quality, workmanship and good design. If I did that, then that's enough."

Advisor for this category, Donald-Brian Johnson, is an author and lecturer specializing in Mid-Twentieth century design. Photos are by his frequent collaborator, Leslie Pina.

Bowl, dark brown rim, light brown body, early, 6" d. **$50-75**
Clock, three robed figures, on walnut, 30" w., 16" h. **$325-350**

Harris Strong Dish with Musicians

Dish, triangular, #B-75, stylized female musicians, 9 1/2" l. (ILLUS.)..................... **$175-200**
Lamp, table model, decorated w/an incised abstract design on black, 23 3/4" h. **$175-200**
Mirror, wall-type, diamond-shaped, centered in four tiles, wooden frame, 12 1/2" sq. **$75-100**

Plate, 10" l., No. B-76A, ram decoration **$175-200**
Tile, decorated w/a single reindeer, framed, 11 1/2" sq.. **$150-175**
Tile, decorated w/autumn trees, framed, 10 3/4" sq. **$150-175**

A Sheep & Ram Tile by Harris Strong

Tile, design of a ram figure in dark blue on a light blue ground, framed, 11" sq. (ILLUS. right with sheep tile) **$150-175**
Tile, design of a sheep figure in dark blue on a light blue ground, framed, 11" sq. (ILLUS. left with ram tile)................... **$150-175**
Tile, design of multicolored swimming fish on a white ground, framed, 10 3/4" sq. **$150-175**
Tile, "Impressionist Series," decoration of two strolling women w/parasols, single tile on walnut background, 10 1/2" sq. **$175-200**
Tile, multicolored leaves on a white ground, framed, 10 3/4" sq............................... **$150-175**

Nightscape Scene on Harris Strong Tile

Tile, nightscape scene w/black background, framed, 10 3/4" sq. (ILLUS.) **$150-175**

Harris Strong Tile with Swimming Frogs

Tile, No. E-32, stylized design of swimming frogs, framed, 10 3/4" sq. (ILLUS.) **$150-175**

C

Harris Strong Tile with Swimming Fish

Tile, No. E-78, two stylized fish, framed, 10 3/4" sq. (ILLUS.).............................. **$150-175**

Tile assembly, abstract flames design, mounted on walnut, composed of three tiles, 6 x 29".. **$175-200**

Tile assembly, decorated w/a Siamese cat, composed of four tiles, framed, 25" l., 7" h... **$225-250**

Harris Strong Seashells Tile Assembly

Tile assembly, decorated w/a variety of seashells, composed of eight tiles, on a beige linen backing, framed, 20 x 32" (ILLUS.) **$200-225**

Tile assembly, decorated w/vegetables, composed of six tiles, framed, 17 1/2 x 23 1/4" **$100-125**

Tile assembly, depiction of three medieval musicians, composed of twelve tiles, framed, 24 1/2 x 30 1/4" **$600-700**

Tile assembly, design of a medieval queen, mounted on walnut, 9 1/2 x 41 1/4" **$400-500**

Tile assembly, design of fishermen w/nets, composed of twelve tiles, framed, 18 1/4 x 60 1/4" **$1,000-1,200**

Tile assembly, design of penguins, composed of four tiles, each tile 6" sq. **$75-100**

Tile on oiled walnut, six individual tiles w/designs representing ancient Egyptian temple art, 4 x 16" **$700-800**

Tile picture, rectangular, No. 141, a landscape w/sailboats in a bay & mountains beyond, composed of six tiles, framed, 15 1/4" w., 21 1/2" h. (ILLUS., top next column) **$300-400**

Tiles, puffins depicted on two 6 x 6" tiles **$50-75**

Tray, No. B-78 B, decorated w/a reclining woman, 17" l. **$200-225**

Tile Assembly with Landscape Design

Haviland

Haviland porcelain was originated by Americans in Limoges, France, shortly before the mid-19th century and continues in production. Some Haviland was made by Theodore Haviland in the United States during the last World War. Numerous other factories also made china in Limoges. Also see LIMOGES.

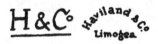

Haviland Marks

Baker, oblong open bowl shape, unglazed bottom, Schleiger 33, Blank 19 .... **$85**

Beaner, open, oval, Schleiger 876, 3 1/2 x 5"... **$45**

Bone dish, Schleiger 72, decorated w/roses & green flowers.............................. **$30**

Bouillon cup & saucer, Drop Rose patt., Schleiger 55C, pale pink **$125**

Bouillon cups & saucers, No. 72 patt., Blank No. 22, ten sets **$550**

Bowl, 9 1/2" d., soup, cobalt & gold w/floral center, Theodore Haviland...................... **$125**

Bowl, 8 3/8 x 10 3/8", 3 1/2" h., Christmas Rose patt., Blank No. 418 .... **$425**

Butter dish, cov., No. 133 patt. **$145**

Butter pat, Schleiger 271A, decorated w/blue flowers & pink roses, 3" **$25**

Cake plate, handled, 87C patt., Blank No. 2, 10 1/2" d.. **$125**

Cake plate, handled, No. 72 patt., Blank No. 22... **$175**

Candleholders, Swirl patt., decorated w/dainty roses, pr...................................... **$135**

Haviland Albany Pattern Chocolate Set

Celery tray, Schleiger 150, Harrison Rose, decorated w/small pink roses, 12" l. **$125**

Celery tray, Blank No. 305, titled "Her Majesty," 13" l. **$145**

Cheese dish w/underplate, CFH/GDM, straight sides, high dome w/flat top, small hole in top near handle, decorated w/blue flowers & gold trim...................................... **$250**

Chocolate pot, Autumn Leaf patt., 9" h. **$325**

Chocolate set: cov. pot & eight cups & saucers; decorated w/pink & blue flowers w/green stems, Blank No. 1, the set **$650**

Chocolate set: tall tapering pot & six tall cups & saucers; Albany patt., white w/narrow floral rim bands & gold trim, late 19th - early 20th c., the set (ILLUS., top of page) **$450-650**

Coffee set: cov. coffeepot, creamer, sugar bowl & twelve cups & saucers; Ranson blank No. 1, the set **$950**

Coffeepot, cov., Old Wedding Ring patt., white w/gold trim, Old H & Co **$225**

Coffeepot, cov., Schleiger 98, Cloverleaf, 9" h... **$450**

Comport, divided, shell-shaped, white w/green trim, full-bodied red lobster at center, non-factory decor of red, green & black.. **$450**

Comport, round, English, shaped like regular pedestal comport without pedestal, Schleiger 56 variation, decorated w/lavender flowers, 9" d. **$125**

Cracker jar, cov., floral decoration, cobalt, gold & blue bells, 1900 & decorator's marks **$550**

Cream soup w/underplate, Schleiger 31, Ranson blank, decorated w/pink roses, 5" d. bowl, 2 pcs. **$55**

Creamer, Moss Rose patt., gold trim, 5 1/2" h.. **$50**

Creamer & open sugar, Ranson blank, Drop Rose patt., w/very ornate gold trim, pr.. **$695**

Creamer & sugar bowl, Montméry patt., ca. 1953, pr. **$125**

Cup & saucer, demitasse, Arcadia, bird patt. **$45**

Cup & saucer, breakfast, Moss Rose patt. w/gold trim... **$55**

Cup & saucer, demitasse, Papillon Butterfly patt., floral by Pallandre **$75**

Cup & saucer, Moss Rose patt., "Haviland & Co. - Limoges - France"........................... **$45**

Cuspidor, Moss Rose patt., smooth blank, 8" d., 3 1/4" h. **$450**

Dessert set: 9 x 15" oblong tray w/twelve 7" square matching plates; centers decorated w/Meadow Visitors patt. & bordered in rich cobalt blue w/gold trim, commissioned for Mrs. Wm. A. Wilson, 13 pcs. ... **$2,000**

Haviland Dinnerware in Blank No. 5

Dinner service: service for eight w/five-piece place settings & additional bowls, pitcher, gravy boat & other pieces; mostly Blank No. 5 w/delicate pink floral decoration, late 19th - early 20th c., 54 pcs. (ILLUS. of part) **$1,000-1,200**

Haviland Dinner Service in the Albany Pattern

Dinner service: twelve 8-piece place settings w/additional open & cov. vegetable dishes & oval platter; Albany patt., white w/narrow floral rim bands & gold trim, late 19th - early 20th c., the set (ILLUS.) .. **$800-1,000**

C

Pitcher, 9 1/2" h., No. 279 patt., Blank No. 643 .... $225
Plate, dinner, No. 72 .... $40
Plate, dinner, Rosalinde patt. $32
Plate, ice cream, 5" l., leaf-shaped w/handle, cobalt & gold $125
Plate, bread & butter, 6 1/2" d., Schleiger 340, decorated w/pink roses & blue scrolls $28
Plate, 8 1/2" d., cobalt & gold Pallandre patt. $175

Plate with Draped Pink Roses

Plate, luncheon, 8 1/2" d., smooth edge, design on border of draped pink roses, Schleiger 152, Theodore Haviland (ILLUS.) $28
Plate, 9 1/2" d., scalloped edge, cobalt & gold w/floral center $225
Plate, dinner, 9 1/2" d., Dammouse antique rose w/gold medallion & flowers $180
Plate, dinner, 9 1/2" d., Schleiger 19, Silver Anniversary $35
Plate, 9 3/4" d., portrait of woman in forest scene, artist-signed, Blank No. 116 .... $125
Plate, 10 1/2" d., service, Blank 20, white w/gold trim $45
Plate, chop, 12" d., Schleiger 233, The Norma, decorated w/small pink & yellow flowers $125
Platter, 16" l., rectangular, Marseilles, Schleiger 9 .... $125

Platter, 14 x 20", Ranson blank No. 1 .... $275
Punch bowl, Baltimore Rose patt. $2,000
Ramekins & underplates, Ranson Blank No. 1, set of 12 .... $540
Salad plate, bean-shaped, variation of Schleiger 1190, decorated w/orange flowers & gold trim, 4 1/2 x 9" $95
Salt, Schleiger 31, decorated w/pink roses & gold trim, 2 x 1" $65
Sauce tureen w/attached undertray, cov., oval, Schleiger 619, green design w/gold trim, Theodore Haviland $145
Serving bowl, Schleiger 235B, 12" d., 2" h. $195

Multifloral Serving Dish

Serving dish, quatrefoil form, Multifloral patt., Old H & Co, 9" sq., 2" h. (ILLUS.) $125
Serving dish, scalloped rectangular form w/a scalloped foot ring below the flaring side w/low open side handles, decorated w/pale yellowish green to dark green poppies & pale pink shadows, gold trim, variation of Schleiger No. 665, Haviland & Co. mark, 8 x 10" (ILLUS., bottom of page) $225
Serving plate, blue & burgundy Art Deco decoration, black ground, "Haviland & Co. - Limoges - France," 10 1/2" d. $95
Sipper dishes, Meadow Visitors patt., smooth blank, 4 3/4" d., set of 8 .... $176
Sorbet, footed, w/gold embossed trim, Schleiger 276 .... $65
Soup plate w/flanged rim, No. 761 .... $35

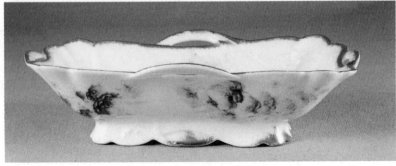

Haviland Serving Dish with Poppies

C

Squatty Haviland Porcelain Teapot

Soup tureen, round, Ranson blank, Schleiger 29M, decorated w/tiny blue flowers.. **$350**

Tea caddy, cov., Ranson blank...................... **$325**

Tea set: small cov. teapot, creamer & sugar bowl, six cups & saucers; No. 19 patt., 15 pcs.. **$700**

Tea & toast tray & cup, No. 482 patt., Blank No. 208, pr. **$275**

Butterfly-handled Cup and Saucer

Teacup & saucer, cup w/tapering cylindrical bowl & figural butterfly handle, h.p. grey band design on rim & border, Haviland & Co. (ILLUS.) **$125**

Teapot, cov., Henri II blank w/gold & silver decoration **$275**

Teapot, cov., wide squatty bulbous tapering sides w/a flat rim, low domed cover w/arched finial, upright serpentine spout & C-scroll handle, white w/gold trim & thin yellow leaf tip bands around the rim & cover, double Haviland mark, ca. 1900 (ILLUS., top of page).................................. **$75**

Vegetable dish, cov., Marseille patt., Blank No. 9, 9 1/2" l. **$145**

Wash pitcher, Moss Rose patt. w/gold trim, smooth blank, 12" h. **$350**

Historical & Commemorative Wares

Numerous potteries, especially in England and the United States, made various porcelain and earthenware pieces to commemorate people, places and events. Scarce English historical wares with American views command highest prices. Objects are listed here alphabetically by title of the view.

Most pieces listed here will date between about 1820 and 1850. The maker's name is noted at the end of the entry.

Very Rare Arms of North Carolina Serving Dish

Regent Street, London Dark Blue Staffordshire Fruit Basket

Arms of North Carolina serving dish,
flowers & vines border, spoked wheels
equidistant around border, oval
w/flanged rim, dark blue, minor edge
wear, Mayer, 9 3/4 x 12 3/4", 2 3/4" h.
(ILLUS., bottom previous page) **$5,115**

Castle Howard Staffordshire Teapot

Castle Howard, Scotland teapot, cov., fruit
& floral borders, dark blue, J. Hall &
Sons, 6 1/4" h. (ILLUS.) **$382**
Regent Street, London fruit basket, oval
w/reticulated sides & loop end handles,
dark blue, William Adams & Sons,
11 1/4" d., 4 3/8" h. (ILLUS., top of page) .. **$529**

Hull

*In 1905 Addis E. Hull purchased the Acme
Pottery Company in Crooksville, Ohio. In 1917
the A.E. Hull Pottery Company began to make a
line of art pottery for florists and gift shops. The
company also made novelties, kitchenware and
stoneware.*

*Hull's Little Red Riding Hood kitchenware
was manufactured between 1943 and 1957 and is
a favorite of collectors, as are the beautiful matte
glaze vases it produced.*

*In 1950 the factory was destroyed by a flood
and fire, but by 1952 it was back in production.
Hull added its newer glossy glazed pottery plus
pieces sold in flower shops under the names Regal*

*and Floraline. Hull's brown dinnerware lines
achieved great popularity and were the main
lines being produced prior to the plant's closing in
1986.*

*References on Hull Pottery include: Hull, The
Heavenly Pottery, 7th Edition, 2001 and Hull,
The Heavenly Pottery Shirt Pocket Price Guide,
4th Edition, 1999, by Joan Hull. Also The Din-
nerwares Lines by Barbara Loveless Click-Burke
(Collector Books 1993) and Robert's Ultimate
Encyclopedia of Hull Pottery by Brenda Roberts
(Walsworth Publishing Co., 1992). -- Joan Hull,
Advisor.*

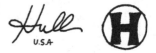

Hull Marks

Basket, Tokay patt., round "moon" form,
No. 11, 10 1/2" h. **$125**
Basket, Ebb Tide patt., model of a large
shell w/long fish handle, No. E-11,
16 1/2" l. **$300**
Bowl, 10 1/2" d., lobed fruit-style, Butterfly
patt., No. B16 .... **$150**
Canister, cov., Little Red Riding Hood patt.,
"Sugar," "Coffee," or "Salt," each **$750**

Sun Glow Pattern Casserole

Casserole, cov., Sun Glow patt., No. 51-7 1/2", 7 1/2" d. (ILLUS., previous page) $50

Cornucopia-vase, Woodland patt., Post 1950, No. W2-5 1/2", 5 1/2" h. $85

Cornucopia-vase, Water Lily Matte patt., L-7, 6 1/2" h. $95

Cornucopia-vase, double, Magnolia Matte patt., No. 6, 12" h. $165

Cornucopia-vase, Parchment & Pine patt., No. S-6, 12" $100

Dish, leaf-shaped, Capri patt., No. C63, 14" l. $85

Ewer, Wildflower Matte patt., No. W-11, 8 1/2" h. $145

Ewer, Capri patt., molded pine cone on the side, No. C87, 12" h. $100

Ewer, Wild Flower Number Series, No. 55, 13 1/2" h. $1,200

Ewer, Ebb Tide patt., No. E-10, figural fish handle, 14" h. $250

Jardiniere, Dogwood patt., No. 514, 4" h. $110

Jardiniere, Woodland Gloss patt., No. W7-5 1/2", 5 1/2" h. $65

Jardiniere, Woodland Matte patt., No. W7-5 1/2", 5 1/2" h. $140

Jardiniere, Water Lily Matte patt., No. L-24, 8 1/2" h. $350

Jardiniere, Iris (Narcissus) patt., No. 413, 9" h. $350

Mug, Serenade patt., No. S22, 8 oz., 5 1/2" h. $55

Pitcher, 11 1/2" h., Dogwood (Wild Rose) patt., No. 5106 .... $350

Planter, model of swan, Capri patt., No. C23, 8 1/2" h. $35

Spice jar, cov. Little Red Riding Hood patt. $850

Tea set: cov. teapot No. 16, creamer No. 17 & cov. sugar No. 18; Tokay patt., the set $250

Tea set: cov. teapot No. 16, creamer No. 17 & cov. sugar No. 18; Tuscany patt., the set $250

Tea set: cov. teapot No. L-18, 6" h., cov. sugar bowl No. L-20 5" h. & creamer L-19 5" h.; Water Lily Matte patt., 3 pcs. $375

Tea set: cov. teapot No. T14 8" h., creamer No. T15 & cov. sugar bowl No. T16; Blossom Flite patt., the set $200

Vase, 4" h., Tulip patt., No. 100-33 .... $95

Vase, 4 3/4" h., Poppy patt., No. 605 .... $175

Vase, 5" h., Rosella patt., No. R-2 .... $35

Vase, 5 1/2" h., Wild Flower Number Series patt., No. 52 .... $155

Vase, 6" h., Orchid patt., No. 303 .... $145

Vase, 6" h., Thistle patt., No. 52 .... $150

Vase, 6" h., Thistle patt., No. 54 .... $150

Vase, 6 1/2" h., Bow-Knot patt., No. B6-6 1/2" $215

Vase, 6 1/2" h., Wildflower Matte patt., No. W-4 .... $80

Vase, 6 1/2" h., Woodland Gloss patt., No. W4 .... $45

Vase, 8" h., Tulip patt., No. 100-33 .... $225

Vase, 8 1/2" h., Iris (Narcissus) patt., No. 404-8 1/2" $150

Open Rose Hand & Fan Vase

Vase, 8 1/2" h., Open Rose (Camellia) patt., No. 126, hand & fan design (ILLUS.) $325

Vase, 8 1/2" h., Wild Flower Number Series, No. 67 .... $325

Vase, 10" h., Calla Lily (Jack-in-the-Pulpit) patt., No. 510-33 .... $145

Vase, 10" h., Orchid patt., No. 307 .... $325

Vase, 10" h., Tulip patt., No. 100-33 .... $350

Vase, 10 1/2" h., Butterfly patt., No. B14-10 1/2" $100

Vase, 10 1/2" h., Serenade, No. S11 .... $95

Vase, 10 1/2" h., Wild Flower Number Series patt., No. 77 .... $350

Vase, 10 1/2" h., Wildflower Matte patt., No. W-15 .... $175

Vase, 12" h., Open Rose (Camellia) patt., No. 124 .... $400

Vase, 12 1/2" h., Magnolia Matte patt., No. 17-12 1/2", wing-form handles $300

Wall pocket, Bow-Knot patt., model of a bulbous pitcher, B-26-6" $265

Wall pocket, Sun Glow patt., model of an iron, No. 83, 6" h. $65

Wall pocket, Rosella patt., No. R-10, 6 1/2" h. $85

Wall pocket, Woodland Matte patt., conch shell shape, No. W13-7 12", 7 1/2" l. $195

Wall pocket, Woodland patt., Post 1950, conch shell shape, No. W13-7 12", 7 1/2" l. $145

Wall pocket, Poppy patt., cornucopia-shaped w/asymmetrical handles, No. 609, 9" l. $450

Window box, Parchment & Pine patt., No. S-5, 10 1/2" l. $95

Window box, Woodland Gloss patt., No. W19-10 1/2", 10 1/2" l. $95

Hull Early Utility & Artware: Stoneware & Semi-Porcelain

Jardiniere, stepped & ringed tapering cylindrical form w/molded florette bands, drippy dark & light green glaze, No. 536, 8" h. .. $100

Vase, 7" h., flat-bottomed bulbous body tapering to a wide flared neck, green neck band above a tan body, matte glaze, No. 40, 7" h. **$95**

Imari

This is a multicolor ware that originated in Japan, was copied by the Chinese, and imitated by English and European potteries. It was decorated in overglaze enamel and underglaze-blue. Made in Hizen Province and Arita, much of it was exported through the port of Imari in Japan. Imari often has brocade patterns.

Colorful Imari Brush Pot

Brush pot, simple wide cylindrical form, a blue striped base band below the main body h.p. w/bright red & dark blue stylized blossoms, an upper rim band w/undulated blue band w/deep red half-round panels, inside spider crack does not show through, 19th c., 4" d., 6" h. (ILLUS.) **$201**

Gilt-Bronze Mounted Imari Jardiniere

Jardiniere, large bulbous ovoid pot w/short flaring rim, mounted on a gilt-bronze base w/four animal head & paw feet & a pierced leaf tip gilt-bronze rim band joined to the base by ornate scrolling handles, late 19th c., 22" d., 16 1/2" h. (ILLUS.).. **$2,750**

Ironstone

The first successful ironstone was patented in 1813 by C.J. Mason in England. The body contains iron slag incorporated with the clay. Other potters imitated Mason's ware, and today much hard, thick ware is lumped under the term ironstone. Earlier it was called by various names, including graniteware. Both plain white and decorated wares were made throughout the 19th century. Tea Leaf Lustre ironstone was made by several firms.

General

Baker, Prairie Flowers shape, all-white, Powell & Bishop, 8" l. **$60**
Bread plate, "Give Us This Day Our Daily Bread" all-white, John Moses, Trenton, New Jersey, 13" l. **$125-150**
Cake plate, Cherry Scroll shape, all-white, T. & R. Boote, 11 1/2" d. **$75-85**

Atlantic Shape Ironstone Chamber Pot

Chamber pot, cov., Atlantic shape, all-white, T. & R. Boote (ILLUS.).............. **$125-150**
Chestnut bowl, Pierced Scroll shape, elaborate pedestaled bowl & tray w/cut openwork design, all-white, John Alcock, ca. 1840s **$550-600**

President Shape All-White Oval Compote

Compote, open, oval, President shape, all-white, John Edwards (ILLUS.) **$350-400**
Compote, open, Classic Gothic shape, all-white, Red Cliff copy, ca. 1960s, 10" d. **$65**
Cup & saucer, child's, handleless cup, Ceres shape, all-white, Elsmore & Forster, the set **$50-75**

East Liverpool Ironstone Soap Slab

Soap slab, rectangular w/molded scroll edges, all-white, marked "ELO" [East Liverpool, Ohio] (ILLUS., top of page) **$20-30**

Soup plate, flanged rim, Columbia shape, all-white, J. Meir & Son., ca. 1855, 9 1/4" d. **$50**

Gothic Octagon 3-Piece Soup Tureen

Soup tureen, cover & undertray, Gothic Octagon shape, all-white, Wedgwood & Co., 3 pcs. (ILLUS.).................................. **$900**

Soup tureen, cover, undertray & ladle, Blackberry shape, all-white, Red Cliff copy, ca. 1960s, the set **$125-150**

Sugar bowl, cov., Cable & Bar shape, all-white, Dale & Davis, Trenton, New Jersey, ca. 1870..................................... **$30-40**

Sugar bowl, cov., Four Square Wheat shape, all-white, unmarked (ILLUS., top next column)... **$80**

Sugar bowl, cov., Lily of the Valley with Thumbprint shape, all-white, Jacob Furnival.. **$110-125**

Syllabub cup, Hyacinth shape, all-white, Wedgwood & Co., ca. 1865 (ILLUS., last in next column)... **$45**

Four Square Wheat Sugar Bowl

Hyacinth Shape Syllabub Cup

C

Teapot, cov., child's, Primary Gothic shape,
all-white, Wooliscroft, 4" h. **$200**

Full Paneled Gothic Ironstone Teapot

Teapot, cov., Full Paneled Gothic shape,
all-white, John Alcock, ca. 1850 (ILLUS.)
.... **$275-300**
Toothbrush box, cov., Chinese shape, fluted panels w/split pod finial, all-white, T. &
R. Boote **$125-150**

Sydenham Shape Vegetable Tureen

Vegetable tureen, cov., Sydenham shape,
all-white, T. & R. Boote, 1853 (ILLUS.)
.... **$190-240**

Tea Leaf Ironstone

Tea Leaf Brocade Butter Dish

Butter dish, cover & insert. Brocade patt.,
Alfred Meakin, flanks inside base, chip on
insert (ILLUS.) **$110**

Meakin Butter Dish

Butter dish, cover & insert, Chelsea patt.,
Alfred Meakin, the set (minor flaws)
(ILLUS.) **$60**
Butter dish, cover & insert, Chelsea
shape, H. Burgess, 3 pcs. **$200**

Tea Leaf Micratex Cake Plate

Cake plate, Empress patt., Micratex by
Adams, ca. 1960s (ILLUS.) **$160**
Cake plate, Favorite shape, Grindley, minor
glaze wear **$190**

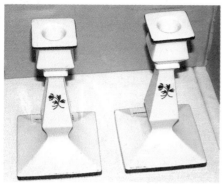

Red Cliff Tea Leaf Candlesticks

Candlesticks, square, Red Cliff, ca. 1970, pr. (ILLUS.)... **$360**
Chamber pot, cov., Cable shape, Anthony Shaw **$175**
Chamber pot, cov., Peerless/Feather shape, J. Edwards................................... **$300**

Mayer King Charles Open Chamber Pot

Chamber pot, open, King Charles patt., Mayer (ILLUS.)... **$100**

Corn Woodland Pattern Coffeepot

Coffeepot, cov., Woodland patt., W. & E. Corn, minor flaws (ILLUS.)........................... **$60**

Compote, open, square w/rounded corners, pedestal base, H. Burgess **$185**
Creamer, Blanket Stitch shape, gold Tea Leaf, Alcock **$170**
Creamer, Chinese shape, Anthony Shaw...... **$410**
Creamer, Favorite shape, Grindley............... **$310**

Maidenhair Fern Tea Leaf Creamer

Creamer, Maidenhair Fern patt., T. Wilkinson (ILLUS.)... **$150**
Creamer & cov. sugar bowl, child's, slant-sided shape, Mellor Taylor, pr. **$100**
Egg cup, T. Mayer **$110**
Gravy boat, Bullet shape, small size, Anthony Shaw **$130**
Gravy boat, Cable shape, T. Furnival............. **$70**
Gravy boat & underplate, Simple Square shape, J. Wedgwood, 2 pcs...................... **$160**

Empress Micratex Gravy Boat & Tray

Gravy boat with attached undertray, Empress patt., Micratex by Adams, ca. 1960 (ILLUS.).. **$80**
Ladle, sauce tureen-size, Anthony Shaw....... **$400**
Ladle, sauce tureen-size, some crazing (ILLUS., top next page) **$200**
Mustache cup & saucer, Edge Malkin, professional rim repair **$500**
Pitcher, water, Cable shape, Anthony Shaw, rare **$1,200**

C

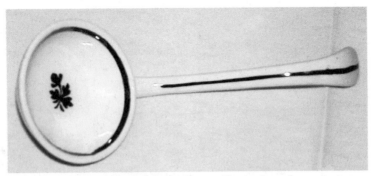

Tea Leaf Sauce Tureen Size Ladle

Fleur-de-Lis Chain Tea Leaf Platter

Pitcher, water-size, Chinese shape, minor discoloration, Anthony Shaw **$150**

Pitcher, 8" h., Blanket Stitch shape, Alcock .. **$140**

Pitcher, 8" h., Square Ridged shape, Wedgwood **$50**

Platter, oval, Fleur-de-Lis Chain patt., Wedgwood & Co., large (ILLUS., second from top of page).. **$50**

Platter, 18" l., Square Ridged II shape, Mellor, Taylor, mild discoloration **$50**

Punch bowl, Cable shape, Anthony Shaw **$400**

Relish dish, Cable shape, oval, under rim flake, Anthony Shaw **$40**

Relish dish, mitten-shaped, Lily of the Valley shape, slight discoloration, Anthony Shaw **$200**

Salt & pepper shakers, Empress patt., Micratex by Adams, ca. 1960s, pr. (ILLUS., next column)... **$130**

Adams Empress Salt & Pepper Shakers

C

Edge Malkin Tea Leaf Vegetable Dish

Ginger Jar Pattern Tea Leaf Sugar Bowl

Teapot, cov., Ginger Jar patt., unmarked,
repeat to spout (ILLUS.) **$60**
Teapot, cov., Scroll shape, Alfred Meakin...... **$160**
Toothbrush vase, cylindrical w/molded
handles near pedestal base, drain holes,
no underplate, possibly by Shaw **$850**
Vegetable dish, cov., Brocade shape, Alfred   Meakin,   moderate   crazing,
6 1/4 x 9 1/2" **$60**

Shaw Bullet Tea Leaf Vegetable Dish

Vegetable dish, cov., Bullet patt., A. Shaw,
minor flaws (ILLUS.).................................... **$65**
Vegetable dish, cov., Cable patt., Anthony
Shaw, 11" l. **$120**
Vegetable dish, cov., oval, Edge Malkin
(ILLUS., top of page) **$325**

Wash bowl & pitcher set, Cable shape,
Anthony Shaw, the set **$225**

Chrysanthemum Wash Bowl & Pitcher

Wash bowl & pitcher set, Chrysanthemum
patt., H. Burgess, the set (ILLUS.) **$575**
Wash pitcher, Square Ridged shape, J.
Wedgwood **$95**

Tea Leaf Variants
Cake plate, Prairie Flower shape, lustre
band trim, slight discoloration, Powell &
Bishop **$275**

Grape Octagon Lustre Band Chamber Pot

C

Chamber pot, cov., Grape Octagon shape, lustre band trim, E. Walley, minor flaws (ILLUS., previous page) $150

Chamber pot, cov., Pre-Tea Leaf patt., Niagara shape, E. Walley $1,050

Pinwheel Grape Octagon Coffeepot

Coffeepot, cov., Pinwheel patt., Grape Octagon shape, E. Walley, slight crazing on cover (ILLUS.) $230

Coffeepot, cov., Wheat in Meadow shape, lustre band trim, Powell & Bishop $325

Creamer, Teaberry patt., Crystal shape, minor flaws, Clementson................................. $190

Creamer, Wrapped Sydenham shape, lustre bands & pinstripes, Edward Walley $260

Cup & saucer, handleless, Pre-Tea Leaf patt., Niagara shape, E. Walley $90

Gravy boat, Scallops patt., Sydenham shape, E. Walley $250

Mug, Gothic shape, paneled sides, lustre band, Livesley & Powell $100

Laurel Wreath Lustre-trimmed Pitcher

Pitcher, 7 3/4" h., Laurel Wreath patt., lustre trim, Elsmore & Forster, minor flaws (ILLUS.).. $325

Posset cup, Tobacco Leaf patt., Tulip shape, Elsmore & Forster $325

Sauce tureen, cov., Gothic Cameo shape, lustre band trim, Edward Walley $250

Sauce tureen, cover, undertray & ladle, Moss Rose patt., H. Burgess, the set $375

Soap dish, cover & insert, Lily of the Valley shape, lustre band trim, chip inside lip, Anthony Shaw, the set $205

Sugar bowl, cov., Morning Glory patt., Richelieu shape, unmarked slight glaze wear $80

Sugar bowl, cov., Quartered Rose shape, copper lustre bands & cobalt blue plumes, minor flaws, J. Furnival $180

Syrup pitcher w/hinged metal lid, Moss Rose patt., George Scott $325

Teapot, cov., Moss Rose patt. $100

Teapot, cov., Quartered Rose shape, copper lustre bands & cobalt blue plumes, possibly J. Furnival $225

Teaberry - Ring O' Hearts Teapot

Teapot, cov., Teaberry patt., Ring O' Hearts shape, J. Furnival (ILLUS.) $650

Toothbrush box, cov., Lily of the Valley shape, lustre band trim, flake on finial, Anthony Shaw... $250

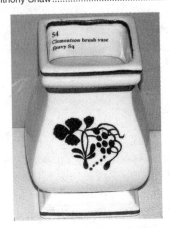

Rare Teaberry Heavy Square Toothbrush Vase

C

Reverse Teaberry Portland Vegetable Dish

Toothbrush vase, Teaberry patt., Heavy Square shape, Clementson Bros., slight flaws (ILLUS., previous page) **$1,350**

Vegetable dish, cov., Quartered Rose shape, copper lustre bands & trim & cobalt blue plumes, slight flaws **$250**

Vegetable dish, cov., Reverse Teaberry patt., Portland shape, Elsmore & Forster (ILLUS., top of page) **$380**

Waste bowl, Gothic shape, Chelsea Grape patt., minor flaws **$35**

Lenox

The Ceramic Art Company was established at Trenton, New Jersey, in 1889 by Jonathan Coxon and Walter Scott Lenox. In addition to true porcelain, it also made a Belleek-type ware. Renamed Lenox Company in 1906, it is still in operation today.

Lenox China Mark

Game plates, 9" d., ivory ground, h.p. in the center w/a vignette w/a different game bird perched or in flight, narrow gilt border band, artist-signed, green printed marks, ca. 1925, set of 12 (ILLUS. flanking the equestrian fox hunt plate, bottom of page) **$5,040**

Plate, 10 1/2" d., the center painted w/a detailed scene of three mounted fox hunters in a woodland landscape, wide gold acid-etched border band of scrollwork & a thin double blue line rim bands, artist-signed, printed green marks, ca. 1925 (ILLUS. center front with Lenox game plates, bottom of page) **$1,800**

Set of Game Plates and Foxhunt Scene Plate

Beautiful Pheasant-decorated Lenox Plates

Plates, 10 1/2" d., each finely h.p. w/a different species of pheasant in their natural habitat, wide gold rim band w/a rinceau scroll within seeded bands, green printed marks, artist-signed, ca. 125, set of 12 (ILLUS. of part, top of page)................... **$4,560**

Fine Decorated Lenox Service Plates

Service plates, round w/slightly scalloped rim, an ivory center decorated in the middle w/a small flower-filled urn within a floral ring, the wide border decorated w/pale blue panels centered by floral urns & separated by narrow floral bars, base marked "Made Expressley for Ovington Bros. New York - 1445/A.326," 10 1/2" d., set of 10 (ILLUS.)................... **$1,200**

Tea set: 6" h. cov. teapot, 3 3/4" h. cov. sugar bowl & 4" h. creamer; each of bulbous ovoid form wrapped around the body w/slender scrolls & starburst designs in sterling silver, each w/the green laurel leaf mark, the set (ILLUS., top next column) **$288**

Lenox Silver-Overlaid Tea Set

Limoges

Limoges is the generic name for hard paste porcelain that was produced in one of the Limoges factories in the Limoges region of France during the 19th and 20th centuries. There are more than 400 different factory identification marks, the Haviland factory marks being some of the most familiar. Dinnerware was commonly decorated by the transfer method and then exported to the United States.

Decorative pieces were hand painted by a factory artist or were imported to the United States as blank pieces of porcelain. At the turn of the 20th century, thousands of undecorated Limoges blanks poured into the United States, where any of the more than 25,000 American porcelain painters decorated them. Today hand-painted decorative pieces are considered fine art. Limoges is not to be confused with American Limoges. (The series on collecting Limoges by Debby DeBay, Living With Limoges, Antique Limoges at Home and Collecting Limoges Boxes to Vases and Antique Trader Limoges Price Guide 2007 are excellent reference books.)

C

Limoges Large Rose-Decorated Basket

Rare Limoges Ashtray-Matchbox Holder

Ashtray-matchbox holder, squared dished base w/a cigarette indentation at each corner, a vertical holder for a matchbox in the center, h.p. w/violets on a cream ground, underglaze Tresseman & Vogt Mark 7, rare (ILLUS.)...................... **$350**

Basket, long rectangular form w/deeply scalloped sides, gold border band & arched flower-molded gold handle across the center, the interior h.p. at one end w/large red roses & green leaves on a dark green shaded to pale yellow ground, artist-signed "Segur," underglaze green factory mark of Jean Pouyat, 5 x 9" (ILLUS., top of page)........................ **$550**

Gold-trimmed Limoges Basket

Basket, round w/flattened & scalloped gold rim & arched center gold handle, the interior h.p. w/pink & red roses & green leaves on a pink to blue ground, artist-signed "Pierre," underglaze Limoges, France Mark 2 & overglaze Blakeman & Henderson decorating mark, 6" d., 2 1/2" h. (ILLUS.) **$350**

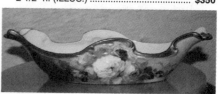

Long Scalloped Limoges Bonbon Dish

Bonbon dish, long oval shaped w/deeply scalloped & scrolled sides, h.p. w/colorful flowers & leaves on a shaded green & yellow ground, artist-signed "Duval," underglaze green factory mark of Jean Pouyat, Mark 5, 5 x 9" (ILLUS.) **$550**

White Poodle Limoges Box from 1970s

Box, cov., figural, a standing white poodle w/a pink ribbon on one ear, on an oval box base w/metal hinge & bands, marked "Peint Main - Limoges France - DE," ca. 1970 (ILLUS.).. **$300**

C

Fine Haviland, Limoges Fish Platter

Limoges Porcelain Coffee Set

Coffee set: 9 1/2" h. cov. coffeepot, creamer, cov. sugar & five cups & saucers;
each of tapering cylindrical form in pale
blue shaded to white, trimmed w/gold
bands, mark of Londé Limoges, the set
(ILLUS. of part)... **$150**

Haviland Lobed Cracker Jar with Pink Roses

Cracker jar, cov., footed oval low lobed
form w/gold loop end handles, four-lobed
domed cover w/gold-trimmed lobed knob
finial, amateur-painted & signed w/large
pink roses & green leaves, underglaze
factory green mark for Haviland, France,
Mark I, ca. 1894-1931 (ILLUS.).................. **$550**
Fish platter, oval w/a scalloped rim, h.p.
w/a large game fish framed by white water lilies & leafage, underglaze factory
mark in green for Haviland, France, Mark
I, ca. 1894-1931, 13 x 19" (ILLUS., top of
page)... **$1,800**
Fruit bowl, oblong boat-shaped w/high in-
ward-scrolled gold end handles, raised
on four gold feet, the exterior h.p. w/pur-
ple grapes & green leaves, heavy gold
border band, amateur artist-signed, underglaze factory mark for Elite - L -
France, ca. 1900, 8 x 12 1/2" (ILLUS., at
bottom of page)... **$550**

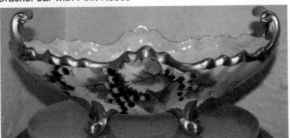

Boat-shaped Fruit Bowl Decorated with Grapes

C

Limoges Tankard Pitcher with Grapes

Limoges Painting of Couple in Garden

Painting on porcelain, rectangular, scene of a romantic couple in 18th c. attire in a garden, he kissing her hand, by an unknown artist, new ornate gold framed, underglaze factory green for for Tresseman & Vogt, early 20th c., one of a pair, 11 x 14", each (ILLUS. of one) **$1,500**

Rose-decorated Limoges Planter

Planter, round w/upright waisted sides & a slightly scalloped rim, raised on four gold scroll feet, decorated w/large deep red & pink roses & green leaves on a dark ground, underglaze green Tresseman & Vogt Mark 7, 8" d., 5 1/2" h. (ILLUS.) **$850**

Limoges Painting of 18th Century Couple

Painting on porcelain, rectangular, scene of a romantic couple in 18th c. attire in a garden, he wearing a blue jacket, she wearing a pink & yellow gown, by an unknown artist, new ornate gold frame, underglaze factory green for for Tresseman & Vogt, early 20th c., one of a pair, 11 x 14", each (ILLUS. of one) **$1,500**

Pitcher, 14 1/2" h., tankard-type, tall cylindrical form w/a scalloped rim & arched spout, long dragon-form handle, h.p. w/green grapes on a shaded rust to pale yellow & blue ground, Thomas importer mark, Jean Pouyat, Limoges - J.P.L. (ILLUS., top next column) **$518**

Fine Limoges Pate-Sur-Pate Plaque

Plaque, pate-sur-pate, rectangular, dark blue ground finely decorated w/h.p. & hand-tooled white slip w/a scene of a scantily clad maiden in a flower-filled glen attended by birds in flight, one perched on her extended hand, impressed monogram & Grand Feu, Limoges mark, artist-signed, ca. 1900, 6 1/2 x 9 1/2" (ILLUS.) **$4,800**

C

Pretty Limoges Sauceboat & Undertray

Sauceboat & undertray, footed boat-shaped vessel w/scroll-molded rim & wide arched spout, ornate looped gold handle, h.p. w/white roses on a shaded pink, blue & green ground, matching decor on undertray, underglaze Elite factory Mark 5, 5" l., 6" h., 2 pcs. (ILLUS.)............. **$275**

Six-cup Limoges Teapot From Set

Tea set: six-cup cov. footed spherical teapot w/a low scalloped rim, domed cover w/loop finial, serpentine spout & C-scroll handle, h.p. w/lovely shaded red & pink roses & green leaves, gold trim, matching four-cup teapot, cov. sugar, creamer, cups & saucers & an 18" l. double-handled tray, France, late 19th c., the set (ILLUS. of six-cup teapot) **$1,400-2,000**

Tall Teapot from Three-Piece Set

Tea set: tall cov. teapot, cov. sugar & creamer; teapot w/wide rounded bottom

& tall tapering sides, each piece in white w/heavy gold trim on spout, handles, rims & finials, green factory mark "France P.M. deM - Limoges," decorator mark of "Coronet France - Borgfeldt," ca. 1908-14, the set (ILLUS. of teapot) **$350**

Tressemann & Vogt Limoges Teapot

Teapot, cov., bulbous tapering ovoid body w/long serpentine spout, high C-form handle & low domed cover w/loop finial, white w/simple trim, mark of Tressemann & Vogt, Limoges, ca. 1900 (ILLUS.) **$200**

Ornately Decorated Limoges Teapot

Teapot, cov., bulbous tapering ribbed body w/wide domed cover w/fancy loop finial, gold serpentine spout & C-scroll handle, star mark of the Coiffe factory & Flambeau China mark of decorating firm, also a Haviland & Co. mark, France, early 20th c. (ILLUS.).. **$100**

Pretty Tressemann & Vogt Teapot

Teapot, cov., squatty bulbous footed body w/domed cover w/double-loop gold finial, serpentine spout, gold C-form handle, h.p. w/swags of roses, factory mark of Tressemann & Vogt, Limoges, France, ca. 1892-1907, 4" h. (ILLUS.) **$400**

Guerin Gold & White Limoges Teapot

Teapot, cov., wide flat bottom w/tapering cylindrical sides & flat rim, slightly domed cover w/pointed disk finial, angled handle, serpentine spout, white w/gold bands & scrollwork around the neck & a gold finial, spout & handle, marks of Wm. Guerin & Co., Limoges, France, ca. 1891-1932 (ILLUS.)...................................... **$150**

Squatty Limoges Vase with Roses

Vase, 6" h., 9" d., wide low squatty compressed body centered by a short flaring neck, h.p. w/large pink & white roses & green leaves on a blue ground, underglaze Tresseman & Vogt Mark 7 (ILLUS.) .. **$850**

Large Rose-Decorated Limoges Vase

Vase, 12" h., simple ovoid body w/small gold-trimmed mouth, h.p. up the sides w/large red roses & green leaves on a mottled background, signed by an amateur artist, underglaze green GDA (Gerard, Dufraisseix & Abbot) Mark 7 (ILLUS.) **$1,500**

Very Rare "Blown-Out" Limoges Vase

Vase, 23 1/2" h., tall slender baluster shape w/"blown-out" figures of a cherub & a lady on the sides & further h.p. colorful roses, underglaze green marked "CFH/GDM - France" (Charles F. Haviland), very rare blank, ca. 1891-1900 (ILLUS.) **$7,000**

Fine Pair of Limoges Vases

Vases, 15 1/2" h., in the Louis XVI taste, a round pedestal foot on four paw feet supporting a baluster-form body w/a flaring neck, figural Grecian helmet handles at the shoulder, deep gold ground w/one side decorated w/a square reserve enclosing a dockside scene w/figures & a sailing vessel, each reverse decorated w/colorful military trophies, ca. 1900, pr. (ILLUS.).. **$1,610**

Longwy

This faience factory was established in 1798 in the town of Longwy, France and is noted for its enameled pottery, which resembles cloisonné. Utilitarian wares were the first production here, but by the 1870s an Oriental-style art pottery that imitated cloisonné was created through the use of heavy enamels in relief. By 1912, a modern Art Deco style became part of Longwy's production; these wares, together with the Oriental-style pieces, have made this art pottery popular with collectors today. As interest in Art Deco has soared in recent years, values of Longwy's modern-style wares have risen sharply.

Longwy Mark

Fine Pair of Longwy Chinoiserie Vases

Vases, 9" h., swelled cylindrical form w/a cylindrical neck & flaring rim, colorful chinoiserie decoration enameled in the famile rose palette on a crackled white ground w/a phoenix amid flowering plants issuing from rockwork, the neck w/a stylized flower band below the rim decorated w/turquoise blue gadroons, impressed mark, ca. 1885, pr. (ILLUS.) **$1,920**

Doughnut-shaped Longwy Wine Flask

Wine flask, footed, doughnut-shaped w/open center, tapering to a cylindrical neck w/a pointed rim spout, arched turquoise blue ropetwist handle, decorated w/ornate exotic birds & flowers in bright shades of pink, blue, green, purple, yellow & brown, stamped on base "Longwy - 1115 - 16 - D486," 6 1/2" w., 11 1/2" h. (ILLUS.) **$259**

Lotus Ware - Knowles, Taylor & Knowles (KT&K)

Knowles, Taylor & Knowles made Lotus Ware (bone china) for a very short time. Reference books differ on the starting date but it ranges between 1889 and 1892. There is agreement that production of the ware ceased sometime in 1896. KT&K tried to make Lotus Ware again in 1904 but it proved too costly and was soon abandoned. Many pieces of this ware were hand-painted and hand-decorated. Lotus rivaled some of the finest European decorated bone china in quality and refinement of decoration and artwork. KT&K employed skilled artists, whose work is highly prized to this day by knowledgeable collectors. All photos Courtesy of Nancy Wetzel, East Liverpool, Ohio.

Creamer, Davenport design, yellow & orange blush w/h.p. pink flowers, 2 5/8" h. **$70-80**

C

Valenciennces Creamer & Two Shell-shaped Trays

Creamer, Valenciennes design w/fishnet trim, green blush & h.p. multi-colored pansies, 3" h. (ILLUS. center with two shell-shaped trays, top of page)......... **$175-250**

Lotus Ware Ewer & Vase

Ewer, Tiberian design, white body w/applied Celadon green flowers & leaves, 6 7/8" h. (ILLUS. left with Parmian vase) **$900-1,200**
Jar, cov., Luxor design, white body w/filigreed sides & cover, h.p. pink & white flowers, 7" h. (ILLUS. left with Orleans rose jar, bottom of page)................. **$900-1,000**
Nappy (round bowl), white body w/scalloped rim, 5 1/4" w., 2 1/2" h. **$40-60**
Rose jar, cov., Orleans design, white body w/extensive filigree on body & cover, hand-decorated w/red, blue & gold accents, 7 1/8" h. (ILLUS. right with Luxor jar, bottom of page)....................... **$1,200-1,500**
Saucer, Lotus design, surface embossing w/pink & cream blush, 5 7/8" w. **$25-40**
Sugar bowl, cov., Davenport design, yellow & orange blush w/h.p. pink flowers, 4" h. **$75-90**
Tray, shell-shaped, yellow blush w/h.p. blackberries, 5 1/8" w. (ILLUS. left with creamer & other shell-shaped tray, top of page)... **$175-250**
Tray, shell-shaped, yellow blush w/h.p. gooseberries, 5 1/8" w. (ILLUS. right with creamer & other shell-shaped tray, top of page)... **$175-250**
Vase, 8" h., Tuscan design, white body w/filigree ribbing around bottom, beaded rim & beaded star design around mid-vase & ball feet **$400-700**
Vase, 8 3/4" h., Lily design, white body w/applied stems & leaves **$500-760**
Vase, 9 1/2" h., 5 1/4" w., Celadon green body w/applied white flowers & leaves (ILLUS. right with Tiberian ewer, left column)... **$900-1,200**

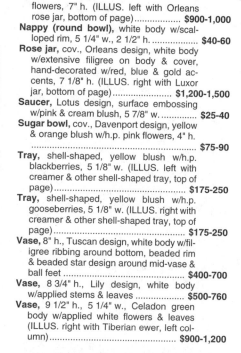

Luxor Jar and Orleans Rose Jar

C

Etruscan Shell & Seaweed Dessert Service

Majolica

Majolica, a tin-enameled glazed pottery, has been produced for centuries. It originally took its name from the island of Majorca, a source of figurine (potter's clay). Subsequently it was widely produced in England, Europe and the United States. Etruscan majolica, now avidly sought, was made by Griffen, Smith & Hill, Phoenixville, Pa., in the last quarter of the 19th century. Most majolica advertised today is 19th or 20th century. Once scorned by most collectors, interest in this colorful ware so popular during the Victorian era has now revived and prices have risen dramatically in the past few years. Also SEE OYSTER PLATES

Etruscan

Dessert service: a footed compote, two creamers, a waste bowl, three shell-shaped dishes in two designs, three cake plates & six dessert plates; Shell & Seaweed patt., ca. 1880, compote 9 1/4" d., the set (ILLUS., top of page) **$1,320**

General

Elephant-shaped Majolica Box

Box, cov., figural, modeled as a walking elephant w/a mahout seated at his neck, a scroll-molded & blanketed howdah forms the cover, possibly Sarreguemines, France, ca. 1880, 11" h. (ILLUS.) **$1,560**

Unusual Majolica Elephant Centerpiece

Centerpiece, figural, modeled as a walking elephant wearing a pink-trimmed pale blue & deep red blanket & supporting a large tall shell-shaped howdah, England, ca. 1870, 15 1/2" h. (ILLUS.)..... **$4,200**

Ornate Sarreguemines Centerpiece

Centerpiece, the large wide flaring oval bowl molded & pierced w/an entwined guilloche band suspending floral garlands above stiff leaftips, supported on figural adorsed mermaids linked by cornucopias & leafy scrolls, the base raised on four scroll feet, Sarreguemines, France, ca. 1880, 23" d. (ILLUS.) **$6,000**

Majolica Jardiniere & Undertray

Jardiniere & undertray, tapering square form molded on each side w/lily-of-the-valley & white bellflowers against a cobalt blue ground, matching blue understray, by George Jones, England, ca. 1860, 8 3/4" h. (ILLUS.) **$1,320**

Butterfly Plate & Stork in Rushes Wall Plaque

Plate, 9 1/2" w., Butterfly patt., a large rounded green leaf molded in relief w/a large spread-winged butterfly, some surface wear, Minton (ILLUS. front with French Stork in Rushes wall plaque) **$605**

Wedgwood Ocean Crate Sardine Box

Sardine box, cov., square shape, the square flat domed cover molded to resemble a dark blue crate tied w/a yellow rope & w/brown bands, floating on the ocean wave-molded matching base, Wedgwood, professional repair to corner of tray (ILLUS.)... **$1,540**

C

Minton Sardine Box

Sardine box, cov., squared domed cover molded in relief w/grey sardines on green leaves on a cobalt blue ground, the cobalt blue box attached to the cobalt blue undertray w/green leaf band border, Minton, date code for 1884 (ILLUS.)....... **$1,980**

Minton Mussel Shell-shaped Tureen

Seafood tureen, cov., modeled as a large mussel shell in grey w/a coral & seaweed handle, raised on green seaweed feet, Minton, 8 1/2" l. (ILLUS.)........................... **$990**

George Jones Triple Shell Server

Server, designed as three pink shell dishes centered by a high looped green & brown dolphin handle & raised on a green shell base, George Jones, professional repair to one shell, 15" w. (ILLUS.) **$1,320**

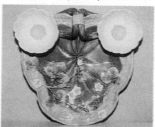

Decorative G. Jones Strawberry Server

Strawberry server, modeled as a large green & blue lily pad style base molded w/vining strawberry blossoms, one edge attached w/two white & yellow lily blossoms forming dishes raised on a twig handle, George Jones, professional repair to one lily flower (ILLUS.) **$1,760**

Monkey on Coconut Figural Teapot

Teapot, cov., Monkey & Coconut patt., modeled as a large cobalt blue coconut w/green leaves & a dark grey figure of a monkey seated at the top end above the brown branch handle, brown branch spout, small cover w/figural pink bud & green leaves, J. Roth, England, late 19th c., 10" l., 7 1/4" h. (ILLUS.) **$3,696**

Tall Flower-encrusted Majolica Vase

Vase, 34 1/4" h., footed slender ovoid body tapering to a very slender tall neck, decorated overall in the Barbotine style w/a large & tall green stem w/pink marguerite daisies & hanging floral garlands, attributed to Capo-di-Monte, Italy, ca. 1900 (ILLUS.) **$1,920**

Wall plaque, pierced to hang, oval w/wide deep molded border w/cattails on a yellow round, the center molded w/a scene of a stork standing in water among reeds, France, late 19th c., 13 1/2" l. (ILLUS. back with Minton Butterfly plate, previous page) **$385**

Martin Brothers

Martinware, the term used for this pottery, dates from 1873 and is the product of the Martin brothers—Robert, Wallace, Edwin, Walter and Charles—often considered the first British studio potters. From first to final stages, their hand-thrown pottery was completely the work of the team. The early wares may be simple and conventional, but the Martin brothers built up their reputation by producing ornately engraved, incised or carved designs as well as rather bizarre figural wares. The amusing face-jugs are considered some of their finest work. After 1910, the work of the pottery declined and can be considered finished by 1915, though some attempts were made to fire pottery as late as the 1920s.

R.W. Martin & Brothers
London & Southall

Martin Brothers Mark

Martin Bros. Flattened Face Jug

Face jug, large flattened round sides molded w/a detailed smiling face w/wavy hair at the top forming a pair of scroll handles flanking the short neck w/flared rim, dark reddish brown glaze, incised "9-1891 - R.W. Martin Bros. - London & Southall," 8 3/4" h. (ILLUS.) **$5,400**

Dark Brown & Blue Martin Face Jug

Face jug, spherical form w/a tri-lobed short neck & long applied handle, a well-detailed smiling face w/a dark reddish brown glaze below the blue neck, the back w/a scrolling design in shades of dark blue & white, incised "11-1901 - Martin Bros. - London & Southall," 7 7/8" h. (ILLUS., previous page) **$4,200**

Very Rare Martin Bros. Tall Bird Jar

Jar, cov., figural, modeled as a large bird w/big talons, the head w/a long thick beak forms the cover, mottled brown & blue glaze, incised "Martin Bros . 10-1895 - London & Southall," 17 1/2" h. (ILLUS.) **$66,000**

Very Rare Martin Bros. Creature Jar

Jar, cov., figural, modeled as a seated cat-like creature w/huminoid facial features, mottled dark brown & tan glaze, incised "R.W. Martin & Bros. - London & Southall - 11-1884," & paper label reading "R.W.

Martin & Bros. - Art Potters - Sixteen Brownlow St. - High Holborn," 1884, 9 5/8" h. (ILLUS.) **$20,400**

Very Rare Large Martin Bros. Bird Jar

Jar, cov., modeled as a large grotesque bird w/a very thick pointed beak & arched eyebrows, mottled light brown & dark blue glaze, "Martin & Bros. 2 -1898 - London & Southall," also a painted mark, on a wooden base, 14 1/2" h. (ILLUS.) **$36,000**

Martin Bros. Bird Jar with Ridged Brow

Jar, cov., modeled as a large grotesque bird w/its wings pulled back, long brown pointed beak & wide ridged brow, mottled dark blue & brown glaze, "R.W. Martin & Bros. - London & Southall -...1890," also a painted mark, on a wooden base, 11" h. (ILLUS.).. **$31,200**

C

McCoy

Collectors are now seeking the art wares of two McCoy potteries. One was founded in Roseville, Ohio, in the late 19th century as the J.W. McCoy Pottery, subsequently becoming Brush-McCoy Pottery Co., later Brush Pottery. The other was also founded in Roseville in 1910 as Nelson McCoy Sanitary Stoneware Co., later becoming Nelson McCoy Pottery. In 1967 the pottery was sold to D.T. Chase of the Mount Clemens Pottery Co., who sold his interest to the Lancaster Colony Corp. in 1974. The pottery shop closed in 1985. Cookie jars are especially collectible today.

A helpful reference book is The Collector's Encyclopedia of McCoy Pottery, by the Huxfords (Collector Books), and McCoy Cookie Jars From the First to the Latest, by Harold Nichols (Nichols Publishing, 1987).

McCoy Mark

Astronaut Cookie Jar

Christmas Tree Cookie Jar

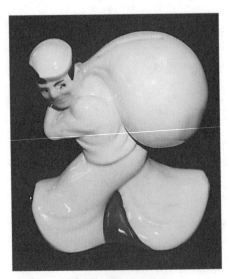

McCoy Seaman's Bank

Bank, figural seaman w/sack over shoulder, white, blue & black, 5 3/4" h. (ILLUS.) .... **$$115-130**

Book ends, decorated w/swallows, ca. 1956, 5 1/2 x 6" **$200-250**

Cookie jar, Astronaut, 1963, good gold trim (ILLUS., top next column) **$500-800**

Cookie jar, Christmas Tree, ca. 1959 (ILLUS., middle next column) .... **$1,000+**

Cookie jar, Hobby Horse, ca. 1948......... **$100-150**

Koala Bear Cookie Jar

Cookie jar, Koala Bear, ca. 1983 (ILLUS., previous page) **$125-150**
Cookie jar, Teepee, 1956-59 .... **$403**
Figurine, head of witch, ca. early 1940s, 3" h. **$400-600**
Iced tea server, El Rancho Bar-B-Que line, ca. 1960, 11 1/2" h. **$250-300**
Jardiniere, Loy-Nel-Art line, wide bulbous shape w/a wide molded flat rim, painted w/large orange tulips & green leaves on a shaded dark brown ground, unmarked, ca. 1905, 6 1/2" h. **$173**

McCoy Quilted Pattern Jardiniere

Jardiniere, Quilted patt., glossy glaze, deep aqua, marked, 1954, 10 1/2" d., 7 1/2" h. (ILLUS.) **$144**
Jardiniere, fish decoration, ca. 1958, 7 1/2" h. **$350-400**

Leaves & Berries Jardiniere & Pedestal

Jardiniere & pedestal base, Leaves & Berries design, ca. 1930s, overall 21" h., 2 pcs. (ILLUS.) **$250-350**
Model of cat, ca. 1940s, 3" h. **$300-400**
Oil jar, bulbous ovoid body w/slightly flaring rim, angled shoulder handles, red sponged glaze, 18" h. **$300-400**
Pitcher, embossed w/parading ducks, ca. 1930s, 4 pt. **$90-125**
Pitcher, 10" h., Butterfly line **$150-225**

Rare Madonna Planter

Planter, figural, Madonna, white, ca. 1960s, rare, 6" h. (ILLUS.) **$200-250**
Planter, model of Cope monkey head, 5 1/2" h. **$100-200**

Rare Fish Planter

Planter, model of fish, green, ca. 1955, 7 x 12" (ILLUS.) **$1,000-1,200**
Planter, model of pomegranate, ca. 1953, 5 x 6 1/2" **$125-150**
Planter, model of snowman, ca. 1940s, 4 x 6" **$70-90**
Planter, model of "stretch" dachshund, 8 1/4" l. **$150-175**
Planting dish, rectangular, front w/five relief-molded Scottie dog heads, white, brown & green, ca. 1949, 8" l. **$50-60**
Platter, 14" l., Butterfly line, ca. 1940s **$250-600**

C

Spoon rest, Butterfly line, ca. 1953, 4 x 7 1/2" **$90-125**

McCoy Pottery Shaded Brown Teapot

Teapot, cov., spherical body w/molded rings around the bottom, short spout, squared handle, low domed cover w/pointed loop finial, shaded brown glaze, ca. 1948 (ILLUS.) **$25**

McCoy Strawberry Country Teapot

Teapot, cov., Strawberry Country patt., heavy cylindrical white body w/short spout & C-form handle, printed w/a cluster of strawberries, blossoms & leaves, flat green cover w/knob finial, 1970s (ILLUS.) **$25**

McCoy Fireplace TV Lamp

TV lamp, model of fireplace, ca. 1950s, 6 x 9" (ILLUS.) **$75-100**

Vase, 6" h., footed, heart-shape w/embossed roses, ca. 1940s **$60-80**

Vase, 8" h., footed bulbous base w/trumpet-form neck & scrolled handles, embossed peacock decoration, ca. 1948 .... **$40-60**

McCoy Magnolia Vase

Vase, 8 1/4" h., figural magnolia, pink, white, brown & green, ca. 1953 (ILLUS.) **$250-300**

Vase, 8 1/2" h., figural wide lily-form, white, brown & green, ca. 1956 .... **$100-125**

Vase, 14" h., Antique Curio line, ca. 1962 .... **$75-100**

McCoy Clown Wall Pocket

Wall pocket, figural, clown, white w/red & black trim, ca. 1940s, 8" l. (ILLUS.)..... **$100-150**

Wall pocket, model of apple, ca. early
1950s, 6 x 7" **$200-225**
Wall pocket, model of bird bath, late 1940s,
5 x 6 1/2" **$90-110**

Meissen

*The secret of true hard paste porcelain, known
long before to the Chinese, was "discovered" accidentally in Meissen, Germany by J.F. Bottger, an
alchemist working with E.W. Tschirnhausen. The
first European true porcelain was made in the
Meissen Porcelain Works, organized about 1709.
Meissen marks have been widely copied by other
factories. Some pieces listed here are recent.*

Meissen Mark

Pretty Meissen Pate-Sur-Pate Box

Box, cov., pate-sur-pate, low squatty rounded shape w/gilt-metal hinged fittings, the
cover decorated w/a central roundel of a
putto tossing flowers on a peach ground,
within a band of alternating dark & light
blue lappets enriched w/pate-sur-pate
flowers & foliage trimmed w/gold, all on a
pale celadon ground w/further flowers,
the interior decorated w/a flower spray,
blue Crossed Swords mark, late 19th -
early 20th c., 6 1/4" d. (ILLUS.).............. **$4,800**

Meissen Satyr & Putti Figure Group

Figure group, a large seated satyr on a car-
peted mound taking grapes from a putto
on his left shoulder, another putto pulling
his vine, a third playing his pipes & the
last tying on a sandel, a goat climbs up
the side to eat vegetables from the satyr's lap, on a gilt-trimmed round scrolled
base, blue Crossed Swords mark, late
19th - early 20th c., 14 1/2" h. (ILLUS.)
.... **$2,880**

Two Beautiful Late Victorian Meissen Figure Groups

Figure group, titled "Amor in Noten," the round platform base edged w/a gilt repeating ring design, modeled
w/a seated classical woman in a chair beside a young maiden seated on a stool, a naughty Cupid having
his wings clipped by the woman, finely decorated in color, blue Crossed Swords mark, late 19th c.,
13 1/2" d. (ILLUS. left with other figure group) **$9,560**

Oval Meissen Plaque Decorated with Venus & Putti

Figure group, titled "Amors Fesselung," the round platform base edged w/a gilt repeating ring design, modeled w/a seated classical woman in a chair beside a young maiden seated on a stool, the woman untethering Cupid, the maiden feeding billing doves, a wreath, bow & quiver at their feet, finely decorated in color, blue Crossed Swords mark, late 19th c., 13 1/2" d. (ILLUS. right with other figure group, bottom previous page) **$10,755**

Plaque, oval w/molded gilt scroll border band, the center finely painted in the manner of Boucher w/Venus attended by two nymphs & two putti resting in clouds, stringing garlands of flowers, a basket at their right & two further putti above, blue Crossed Swords mark, late 19th c., 21" l. (ILLUS., top of page) **$10,200**

Lovely Meissen Plate with Center Scene

Plate, 9" d., a small h.p. round central scene in color showing a half-nude Classical male holding a wreath above the head of a half-nude woman, a narrow reticulated outer border band enclosing a wide cobalt blue ground ornately decorated w/delicate gold, blue Crossed-Swords mark, titled "Le Printemps - Watteau," ca. 1900 (ILLUS.) **$1,691**

Plate, 9 1/2" d., titled "Hope," the center painted w/a half-length portrait of a bru-nette beauty leaning on an anchor within a gold border, wide green border band decorated w/trailing gilt grapevine, blue Crossed Swords mark, mid-19th c. (ILLUS., top next column) **$1,320**

Meissen Plate with Portrait of Hope

One of a Pair of Meissen Potpourri Vases

Potpourri vases, cov., a triangular gilt-trimmed base supporting three angular gilt-trimmed legs enclosing a green garland & supporting the bulbous ovoid body w/rounded pierced shoulder supporting the domed cover w/a green wreath finial, figural female head handles, each decorated w/a rectangular polychrome reserve featuring equestrian hunting scene & bordered by gilt scrolls, blue Crossed Swords marks & incised numbers, 19th c., 9 3/8" h., pr. (ILLUS. of one) **$8,365**

Serving dish, figural, a long scroll-mounted gilt-trimmed base mounted at one end of a deep pointed oval floral-decorated dish, the reclining figure of a scantially-clad young woman reaching along the back edge of the dish, some restorations, late 18th c., blue Crossed Swords mark, 7" l. **$764**

Elaborate Floral-decorated Meissen Vase

C

Small Meissen Vase with Putti Scenes

Vase, 6 1/8" h., in the Neo-rococo taste, a square foot below the fluted socle supporting a squatty bulbous body tapering to a short, wide neck w/heavy gilt scrolls around the rim, the front of the body decorated w/a scene after Boucher showing a sleeping putto being tickled by another w/a stalk of wheat, the reverse w/a scene of putti drawing, both within flower-encrusted borders, socle & base trimmed in gold, blue Crossed Swords mark, late 19th - early 20th c. (ILLUS.) **$1,020**

Vase, cov., 29 1/2" h., ringed pedestal base below the wide inverted pear-shaped body w/a domed cover topped by a tall finial composed of applied colorful flowers, the body painted w/small vignette of figures in a garden near ruins, the reverse decorated w/a reserve of flowers, all surrounded by large applied flower blossoms & fruits scrolling around the sides & forming vine handles, the lower pedestal base mounted w/the figure of a small nymph holding a basket of flowers, a putto above on the opposite side, blue Crossed Swords mark, late 19th c. (ILLUS., top next column) **$15,600**

Ornate Meissen Allegorical Vases

Vases, 13 1/4" h., in the neo-Rococo taste, one w/an ornate pedestal base applied w/a leafy tree w/fruit & a fish, the other w/the pedestal base decorated w/icicles, each w/a bulbous inverted pear-shaped body molded w/scrolls & applied decorations, each w/an applied figure seated on the shoulder, one w/a putto representing Summer & the other w/a putto representing Winter, each h.p. w/a small reserve featuring lovers in 18th c. attire, the Summer vase w/a tall slender neck w/ruffled rim & applied summer motifs, the Winter vase w/a matching neck issuing large orange flames, blue Crossed Swords mark, late 19th c., pr. (ILLUS.) **$8,365**

C

Two Mettlach Rustic Houses Plaques

Mettlach Cavaliers & Water Pump Plaques

Mettlach

Ceramics with the name Mettlach were pro-duced by Villeroy & Boch and other potteries in the Mettlach area of Germany. Villeroy and Boch's finest years of production are thought to be from about 1890 to 1910. Also see STEINS.

Mettlach Mark

Plaque, No. 1044-1066, PUG decoration of a rustic water pump, some gold wear, art-ist-signed, 17" d. (ILLUS. right with plaque No. 1044-1143, top of page) **$362**

Plaque, No. 1044-1105, painted under glaze (PUG) decoration of a German farmhouse w/a young couple & animals in the foreground, titled on the back, mi-nor gold wear, 17" d. (ILLUS. left with plaque No. 1044-1407B, top of page) **$460**

Plaque, No. 1044-1143, PUG color scene of a group of drunken cavaliers, artist-signed, minor gold wear, 17" d. (ILLUS. left with plaque No. 1044-1066, second from top of page)..................................... **$581**

Plaque, No. 1044-1407B, PUG decoration of a chalet-like house on a hillside, 17" d. (ILLUS. right with plaque No. 1044-1105, second from top of page) **$460**

Plaque, No. 2041, etched color scene of a gentleman & lady in fox hunting gear on horseback jumping a fence, artist-signed, minor gold wear, 15" d. (ILLUS. right with Cameo plaque No. 2443, bottom of page) .. **$374**

A Cameo and an Etched Mettlach Plaque

Plaque, No. 2443, Cameo-type, a white relief scene of classical women on a green
ground, artist-signed, 18" d. (ILLUS. left
with etched plaque No. 2041, bottom pre-
vious page).. **$513**

Mettlach Vase with Nightingales

Vase, 7 1/2" h., wide ovoid body tapering to
a short flaring neck, applied w/two nightingales perched on pine boughs w/a gold
moon beyond, on a dark green ground,
marked, No. 1514 (ILLUS.) **$288**

Minton

*The Minton factory in England was estab-
lished by Thomas Minton in 1793. The factory
made earthenware, especially the blue-printed
variety, and Thomas Minton is sometimes credited with the invention of the blue "Willow" pattern. For a time majolica and tiles were also
important parts of production, but bone china
soon became the principal ware. Mintons, Ltd.,*
*continues in operation today. Also see OYSTER
PLATES.*

Minton Marks

Bottle coolers, pate-sur-pate, four gilt-
trimmed scroll feet support the squared
upright container in ivory white w/ornate
gold trim, four pilasters & leafy scroll handles alternate w/chocolate brown reserve
decorated w/a white slip pair of putti bordered in gilt, reverse w/reserve decorated w/a putto eating a peach or listening to
a shell, gently flared rim band w/pierced
repeating loop sections, gilt crowned
globe mark & impressed marks, retailer
mark for Goode & Co., London, date
cypher for 1883, 8" h., pr. (ILLUS., bot-
tom of page) **$71,700**

Rare Minton Pate-Sur-Pate Cachepot

Extraordinary Pair of Minton Pate-sur-Pate Bottle Coolers

Minton Dessert Service & Covered Vases

Cachepot, pate-sur-pate, low round foot & deep cylindrical sides w/a flat rim, molded small scroll handles, peacock blue ground, the sides centered by large round reserves w/a chocolate brown field finely painted & hand-tooled in white slip on one side w/a putto symbolizing Ceramic Art, depicting seated on a stool painting a small standing putto, the other side w/another reserve decorated w/a Berainesque urn suspending foliage & flaming torches, both within a scrolling gold border w/gilt trim on the handles & a dotted gold band around the rim, signed by Alboin Birks, cypher date for 1909, 7" h. (ILLUS., previous page) **$19,200**

Fine Mintons Figural Centerpiece

Centerpiece, allegorical figure-style, the top center mounted w/a tall white molded figure of a classical woman representing Science holding a small globe & caliper, on a turquoise cylindrical ringed pedestal trimmed w/ gilt guillouche bands, centered in a wide concave base w/the rolled rim mounted w/four large raised panels con-

tinuing to form strap feet, each in white w/a wide gold border enclosing a delicate trellis design, the turquoise rolled rim also banded in gold, impressed marks, after a model by T. N. Maclean, date cypher for 1876, 20 1/2" h. (ILLUS.) **$4,560**

Dessert service: two footed open compotes & nine 10" d. plates; each piece w/a turquoise pierced trellis border flanked by banded gilt ribbons, the center enriched w/ "jeweled" egg-and-dart band, printed crowned globe mark & mark of retailer T. Goode & Co., London & the prince of Wales feather Paris Exhibition of 1878 mark, ca. 1878, the set (ILLUS. back with covered vases, top of page).... **$1,800**

Fish & game plates, round, six naturalistically h.p. w/various game birds & six h.p. w/various fish, each scene above a large gilt cell-pattern cartouche, the gilt border acid-etched w/fruiting grapevine, each marked w/painted marks & name of the retailer, Tiffany & Co., date letter for 1902, 8 7/8" d., set of 12 (ILLUS., top next page) **$5,040**

Minton Majolica Figural Garden Seat

Fine Set of Minton Fish and Game Plates

Garden seat, majolica, figural, modeled as a blackamoor boy seated on a corded & tasseled tufted cushion, wearing a lion pelt, yellow-trimmed green jacket & pale blue tunic, tied at the waist w/a striped sash, above matching boots, supporting a second similar cushion on his inclined head & neck, impressed mark, dated 1883, 19 1/4" h. (ILLUS., previous page)
.... **$16,800**

Plaque, majolica, oval, molded in high-relief w/the head & torso of a Renaissance cavalier holding a torch, within a berried laurel wreath border, bold coloring, unmarked, ca. 1860, 18 1/2" h. (ILLUS., top next column).................................. **$10,200**

Plaque, rectangular, pate-sur-pate, the dark green ground finely painted & hand-tooled in white slip w/six diaphanously draped maidens brewing love potions, one maiden kneels pouring a basket filled w/hearts into the mix while others prod putti w/three-tined forks, a garland above suspends cooking implements & produce, signed by Louis Solon & dated 1879, in a white-washed wooden frame,

8 1/2 x 15 3/4" (ILLUS., bottom of page)
.... **$38,400**

Rare Minton Figural Majolican Plaque

Exquisite Minton Pate-Sur-Pate Rectangular Plaque

C

C

Fine Pair of Minton Pate-sur-Pate Vases

Vases, 7 1/2" h., pate-sur-pate, tapering cylindrical body w/a short shoulder & narrow dotted gold mouth band, the peacock blue ground finely painted & hand-tooled in white slip w/paired mythic arches & putti symbolizing Love & War, the reverse w/corresponding ribbon-tied trophies, signed by Alboin Birks, ca. 1900, pr. (ILLUS.).. **$18,000**

Vases, cov., 12 1/4" h., designed after Sevres "Vases de Cote Deparis," a square foot & slender tapering pedestal supporting the classical urn-form body w/a tapering neck w/flanked by leaf-cast loop handles, small domed cover w/pine cone finial, the decoration inspired by the service made for Catherine the Great, each w/a turquoise ground, the pedestal base & neck w/gold fluting, each h.p. on the side en grisaille w/small round portrait medallions above long ribbon-tied floral garlands, impressed marks & date cypher for 1889, pr. (ILLUS. front with dessert service, page 222)..................... **$4,800**

Mocha

Mocha decoration is found on basically utilitarian creamware or yellowware articles and is achieved by a simple chemical reaction. A color pigment of brown, blue, green or black is given an acid nature by infusion of tobacco or hops. When this acid nature colorant is applied in blobs to an alkaline ground color, it reacts by spreading in feathery seaweed designs. This type of decoration is usually accompanied by horizontal bands of light color slip. Produced in numerous Staffordshire potteries from the late 18th until the late 19th centuries, its name is derived from the similar markings found on mocha quartz. In addition to the seaweed decoration, mocha wares are also seen with Earthworm and Cat's Eye patterns or a marbleized effect.

Nice Mocha Yellowware Jar

Jar, cov., cylindrical w/molded base band, fitted flat cover w/low button knob, yellowware w/white band around body & cover decorated w/dark green seaweed design, some wear & chip on bottom, 19th c., 7" d., 5" h. (ILLUS.) **$546**

Rare Early Earthworm Mocha Shaker

Pepper pot, footed baluster-form body w/domed top, decorated w/slat blue & burnt orange bands w/the wide middle orange band w/a dotted earthworm design in blue, white & black, 4 1/4" h. (ILLUS.) **$2,530**

Moorcroft

William Moorcroft became a designer for James Macintyre & Co. in 1897 and was put in charge of the art pottery production there. Moorcroft developed a number of popular designs, including Florian Ware, while with Macintyre and continued with that firm until 1913, when it discontinued the production of art pottery.

After leaving Macintyre in 1913, Moorcroft set up his own pottery in Burslem, where he contin-

ued producing the art wares he had designed ear-lier, introducing new patterns as well. After William's death in 1945, the pottery was operated by his son, Walter.

MOORCROFT

Moorcroft Marks

Early Moorcroft Tudor Rose Pattern Vase

Vase, 9 3/4" h., footed spherical body tapering to a swelled neck & bulbed top, Tudor Rose patt. in purple, dark blue & green on a pale green ground, made for Liberty & Company & so marked, ca. 1904 (ILLUS.) **$1,035**

Newcomb College

This pottery was established in the art department of Newcomb College, New Orleans, Louisiana, in 1897. Each piece was hand-thrown and bore the potter's mark & decorator's monogram on the base. It was always a studio business and never operated as a factory. Its pieces are, therefore, scarce, with the early wares being eagerly sought. The pottery closed in 1940.

Moorcroft Pansy Pattern Vase

Vase, 6 5/8" h., Pansy patt., bulbous ovoid body tapering to a cylindrical neck, marked, light crazing (ILLUS.) **$316**

Newcomb College Pottery Mark

Newcomb College Bowl with Floral Band

Bowl, 5" d., 2 1/2" h., footed wide squatty bulbous body tapering to a wide flat mouth, molded around the rim w/a band of pink blossoms & green leaves against a blue ground, Newcomb logo, date code & marks of decorator Anna Frances Simpson & potter Joseph Meyer, 1925, tiny chip on base (ILLUS.) **$1,265**

Moorcroft Anemone Pattern Vase

Vase, 6 7/8" h., Anemone patt., footed ovoid body w/a short flared neck, large red & blue & purple flowers around the upper half of the body, marked (ILLUS.) **$288**

Vase, 7 1/8" h., Clematis patt., footed bulbous body tapering to a cylindrical neck, red flambé glaze, marked, light crazing **$575**

C

Newcomb Mug with Glossy Glaze

Mug, tapering cylindrical form w/a C-form handle, decorated around the sides w/tall stems w/leaves & white & yellow blossoms around the top, dark blue base band & handle, marked w/Newcomb insignia, monogram of decorator Sarah Henderson & initials of potter Joseph Meyer, glossy glaze, 1902, crazing, 4 1/4" h. (ILLUS.) **$1,380**

Small Bulbous Newcomb College Pitcher

Pitcher, 2 1/2" h., squatty bulbous body w/a pinched spout & applied angled handle, decorated w/a repeated design of pale green swirled S-shaped devices on a blue ground, marks of decorator Aurelia Arbo & pottery Joseph Meyer, date code for 1931, tiny bit of roughness at base (ILLUS.) **$460**

Pitcher, 5" h., Espanol style, cylindrical body flaring at the top w/a pinched spout & applied C-form handle, a wide band of stylized pickets in shades of pale green dark blue & pink around the top, dark blue ground, marked w/shape number 207 (ILLUS., top next column) **$805**

Vase, 3 5/8" h., wide bulbous ovoid shape tapering to a wide flat rim, molded w/a repeating pattern of wide swirled panels alternating pale green & medium blue, Newcomb College logo, shape number & date code for 1931, impressed mark of potter Josephy Meyer (ILLUS., middle next column) **$805**

Newcomb College Espanol Style Pitcher

Bulbous Newcomb Vase by J. Meyer

Spanish Moss & Trees Newcomb Vase

Vase, 6" h., swelled cylindrical body tapering to a flat rim, Moon & Spanish Moss decoration in shades of dark blue, pale blue & yellow, unknown artist, potted by Joseph Meyer, date code & shape number on the bottom, 1930 (ILLUS., previous page) **$3,680**

Ovoid Newcomb Moon & Moss Vase

Vase, 8 1/4" h., bulbous ovoid form tapering toward the base & rim, Moon & Spanish Moss decoration in shades of dark blue, pale blue & yellow, decorated by Anna Frances Simpson, potted by Joseph Meyer, date code & shape number on the bottom, 1919, small grinding mark on base (ILLUS.) **$4,435**

Nice Newcomb Moon & Moss Vase

Vase, 8 1/4" h., 3 3/4" d., simple swelled cylindrical form, Moon & Spanish Moss

decoration in shades of dark blue, pale blue & yellow, decorated by Anna Frances Simpson, various marks on the bottom, 1919 (ILLUS.)............................ **$6,325**

Rare New College Pottery Vase

Vase, 10" h., 9" d., bulbous baluster-form body w/a wide short flat neck, glazed in moss green & splattered gunmetal, decorated by Elizabeth Rogers & signed on the base, ca. 1900, rare (ILLUS.)............ **$3,450**

Niloak Pottery

This pottery was made in Benton, Arkansas, and featured hand-thrown varicolored swirled clay decoration in objects of classic forms. Designated Mission Ware, this line is the most desirable of Niloak's production, which began early in this century. Less expensive to produce, the cast Hywood Line, finished with either high gloss or semi-matte glazes, was introduced during the Depression of the 1930s. The pottery ceased operation about 1946.

NILOAK

Niloak Pottery Mark

Niloak Mission Ware Jardiniere

C

Jardiniere, Mission Ware, wide slightly swelled cylindrical form, swirled brown, blue & tan clays, stamped mark, 7" d., 7" h. (ILLUS., previous page) **$411**

Niloak Ovoid Mission Ware Vase

Vase, 6" h., Mission Ware, simple ovoid body tapering to a widely flaring flattened neck, swirled clays in red, taupe, brown tan & blue, impressed mark (ILLUS.) **$138**

Tall Niloak Mission Ware Vase

Vase, 10" h., 5" d., Mission Ware, footed w/bulbous lower body w/sharp shoulder tapering to a tall cylindrical neck, swirled dark teal & brown clays, minute inside rim flecks, stamped mark (ILLUS.) **$294**

Nippon

"Nippon" is a term used to describe a wide range of porcelain wares produced in Japan from the late 19th century until about 1921. It was in 1891 that the United States implemented the McKinley Tariff Act, which required that all wares exported to the United States carry a marking indicating their country of origin. The Japanese chose to use "Nippon," their name for Japan. In 1921 the import laws were revised and the words "Made in" had to be added to the markings. Japan was also required to replace the "Nippon" with the English name "Japan" on all wares sent to the United States.

Many Japanese factories produced Nippon porcelain, much of it hand-painted with ornate floral or landscape decoration and heavy gold decoration, applied beading and slip-trailed designs referred to as "moriage." We indicate the specific marking used on a piece, when known, at the end of each listing. Be aware that a number of Nippon markings have been reproduced and used on new porcelain wares.

Important reference books on Nippon include: The Collector's Encyclopedia of Nippon Porcelain, Series One through Three, by Joan F. Van Patten (Collector Books, Paducah, Kentucky) and The Wonderful World of Nippon Porcelain, 1891-1921 by Kathy Wojciechowski (Schiffer Publishing, Ltd., Atglen, Pennsylvania).

Nut set: 7 1/2" d. master bowl & five 3" d. individual dishes; each rounded w/notched corners, the master bowl w/small rim handles, the interior h.p. w/a sheep in the meadow scene w/a large tree & farmhouse on the left side, border band in pale yellow trimmed w/gold vining scrolls, individual dishes w/match borders & white interiors, green "M" in Wreath mark, the set (ILLUS. bottom row, right, with five Nippon vases, top next page) **$127**

Vase, 6" h., cylindrical waisted shape w/long floral-embossed pale green handles down the sides, green band around neck, the body h.p. w/an autumn landscape w/leafless trees in the foreground & a lane in the distance, blue "M" in Wreath mark (ILLUS. bottom row, second from left with Nippon nut set, top next page) **$518**

Vase, 7 1/2" h., bulbous ovoid body tapering to a shaped neck, four small Moriage-decorated loop handles around the shoulder, body w/h.p. large pink flowers on green & gold leafy stems, trimmed w/white Moriage unmarked (ILLUS. second from right with three other Nippon vases, middle next page) **$230**

Vase, 7 1/2" h., ovoid body tapering to a show neck w/flaring rim flanked by high square loop handles, h.p. landscape scene w/tall trees in foreground & woods & a cottage in the background, green "M" in Wreath mark (ILLUS. far right with three other Nippon vases, middle next page) **$173**

Nippon Nut Set & Five Vases

Row of Nice Nippon Vases

Vase, 7 1/2" h., ovoid pillow-shape w/short scalloped neck flanked by loop handle, h.p. farmstead in the snow scene, Moriage bands around the shoulder, neck & foot, green "M" in Wreath mark (ILLUS. far left with three other Nippon vases, middle of page).. **$1,380**

Vase, 8" h., footed hexagonal body w/angled shoulder flanked by upright gold curved handles, the body h.p. w/a continuous landscape scene w/a fence & trees in the foreground & a windmill in the distance, blue "M" in Wreath mark (ILLUS. bottom row, far left with Nippon nut set, top of page)... **$460**

Vase, 8 3/4" h., footed ovoid body w/a wide shoulder to the short trumpet-form neck flanked by high C-scroll handles, body decorated w/a fine lakeside landscape w/birch trees in the foreground w/swans & a cottage in the background, glossy glaze, green "M" in Wreath mark (ILLUS. second from left with three other Nippon vases, middle of page)................................. **$518**

Vase, 9" h., squatty bulbous base tapering to a cylindrical body w/a flared neck, h.p. w/a continuous landscape w/a path & flowering tree in the foreground & a cottage & sea in the distance, green "M" in Wreath mark (ILLUS. top row, far right with Nippon nut set, top of page) **$230**

Vase, 9 1/2" h., slender ovoid body tapering to a small mouth flanked by pointed loop gold handles, h.p. w/a landscape w/purple wisteria blossoms in the foreground & a path & trees in the distance, green "M" in Wreath mark (ILLUS. top row, second from right with Nippon nut set, top of page).. **$345**

Vase, 10 1/4" h., footed ovoid body tapering to a trumpet neck, gold molded C-scroll handles on the shoulder, the body h.p. w/a continuous landscape w/a meadow w/cows in the foreground & a lake & mountains in the distance, gold foot, gold vining bands around the neck & shoulder, green "M" in Wreath mark (ILLUS. top row, far left with Nippon nut set, top of page)... **$805**

Noritake

Noritake china, still in production in Japan, has been exported in large quantities to this country since early in the last century. Although the Noritake Company first registered in 1904, it did not use "Noritake" as part of its backstamp until 1918. Interest in Noritake has escalated as collectors now seek out pieces made between the "Nippon" era and World War II (1921-41). The Azalea pattern is also popular with collectors.

C

Noritake Mark

Ashtray, center Queen of Clubs decoration, 4" w. **$38**
Ashtray, figural polar bear, blue ground, 4 1/4" d., 2 1/2" h. **$250**

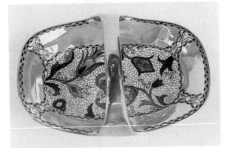

Noritake Basket with Flowers

Basket, oblong w/center handle, gold lustre ground, interior w/center stylized floral decoration & geometric design in each corner & around rim, 7 3/4" l., 3" h. (ILLUS.) **$85**
Basket-vase, 7 1/2" h. **$115**
Bonbon, raised gold decoration, 6 1/4" w. **$25**

Art Deco Bowl

Bowl, 6 1/2" d., 2" h., fluted sides of alternating light & dark grey panels w/pointed rims, center w/Art Deco floral decoration (ILLUS.)... **$160**
Bowl, 7" w., square w/incurved sides, three-footed, interior w/relief-molded filbert nuts in brown trimmed w/h.p. autumn leaves... **$85**
Bowl, soup, Azalea patt. **$30**
Butter dish, cover & drain insert, Azalea patt., 3 pcs. **$80**

Noritake Oriental Scene Cake Plate

Cake plate, rectangular, open-handled, turquoise border w/oval center Oriental scene on black ground, 10" l. (ILLUS.) **$140**
Cake set: 14 x 6 1/4" oblong tray w/pierced handles & six 6 1/2" d. serving plates; white w/pale green & gold floral border, 7 pcs. **$90**
Candy dish, octagonal, Tree in Meadow patt. **$60**
Celery set: celery tray & 6 individual salt dips, decal & h.p. florals & butterflies decoration, 7 pcs. **$90**

Cigarette Jar in Art Deco Style

Cigarette jar, cov., bell-shaped cover w/bird finial, Art Deco-style silhouetted scenic decoration of woman in chair & man standing, both holding cigarettes, 4 3/4" h., 3 1/2" d. (ILLUS.) **$575**

Powder box, cov., figural, an Art Deco-style female figure on a chair in colors of orange, black, green, white & brown w/a lustre finish, 1930s, 4 1/4 x 5", 7" h. **$6,800**

Noritake Disc-form Powder Puff Box

Powder puff box, cov., disc-form, stylized floral decoration in red, blue, white & black on a white iridized ground w/blue lustre border, 4" d. (ILLUS.) **$160**

Ring holder, model of a hand **$40**

Salt & pepper shakers, Tree in Meadow patt., pr. **$20**

Shaving mug, landscape scene w/tree, birds & moon decoration **$70**

Noritake Double Spoon Holder

Spoon holder, double tray-form, oblong shape w/gold angular center handle, orange lustre interior, exterior decorated w/flowers & butterfly on black ground, 6 1/2" l., 2 1/2" h. (ILLUS.) **$90**

Sugar shaker, lavender & gold decoration, blue lustre trim.. **$40**

Syrup jug, Azalea patt. **$70**

Crinoline Lady Noritake Teapot

Teapot, cov., Crinoline Lady patt., bulbous slightly tapering body w/C-form handle & long serpentine spout, domed cover w/knob finial, Victorian lady in a garden

against a blue background, Noritake mark "38.016 DS," 5 1/2" l., 3 3/4" h. (ILLUS.) **$175**

Noritake Teapot with Stylized Flowers

Teapot, cov., footed bulbous ovoid body w/angled green shoulder & domed cover w/oval loop finial, C-scroll handle & long serpentine spout, large stylized blossoms on a slender leafy tree, in shades of blue, purple, green & brown, Noritake mark "27.1 DS," 8 1/4" l., 5 3/4" h. (ILLUS.) **$45**

Rare Noritake Lady & Bird Teapot

Teapot, cov., Lady & Bird in Garden patt., tall footed urn-form body w/long serpentine spout, tall arched black-trimmed blue handle, domed cover w/black urn-shaped finial, dark blue background w/an Art Deco-style scene of a crinolined lady holding a bird in one hand w/a birdcage in front of her, in shades of yellow, green, black, white, light blue & orange, Noritake mark "27.1 DS," 6 3/4" l., 6 1/4" h. (ILLUS.)................................... **$645**

Tray, pierced handles, decal & h.p. fruit border, lustre center, 11" w. **$80**

Long Floral-decorated Noritake Tray

Tray, rectangular, pierced end handles, floral decoration on white ground, green edge trim w/brown trim on handles, 17 1/2" l. (ILLUS.)... **$90**

C

C

Unusual Noritake Butterfly Vase

Vase, 8" h., footed ovoid body w/squared rim handles, butterfly decoration on shaded & streaked blue & orange ground (ILLUS.)... **$250**

Vase, 8 1/4" h., Indian motif & lustre decoration **$140**

Vase, 8 1/2" h., bulbous body, Tree in Meadow patt.. **$90**

Vegetable dish, cov., round, Azalea patt......... **$75**

Scenic Noritake Wall Plaque

Wall plaque, pierced to hang, silhouetted Art Deco-style scene of woman in gown w/full ruffled skirt, sitting on couch & holding mirror, white lustre ground, 8 3/4" d. (ILLUS.)... **$840**

Wall pocket, double, conical two-part form w/arched backplate, decorated w/an exotic blue & yellow bird among branches of red & blue stylized blossoms against a cream ground, purple lustre rim band, 8" l. **$165**

Wall pocket, trumpet-form, wide upper band decorated w/an autumn sunset scene, lavender lustre rim band & base, 8 1/4" l. **$90**

Waste bowl, Azalea patt. **$55**

North Dakota School of Mines

All pottery produced at the University of North Dakota School of Mines was made from North Dakota clay. In 1910, the University hired Margaret Kelly Cable to teach pottery making, and she remained at the school until her retirement. Julia Mattson and Margaret Pachl also served as instructors between 1923 and 1970. Designs and glazes varied through the years, ranging from Art Nouveau to modern styles. Pieces were marked "University of North Dakota - Grand Forks, N.D. - Made at School of Mines, N.D." within a circle and also signed by the students until 1963. Since that time, the pieces bear only the students' signatures. Items signed "Huck" are by the artist Flora Huckfield and were made between 1923 and 1949.

North Dakota School of Mines Mark

Pasque Flowers Bowl-Vase by M. Cable

Bowl-vase, wide squatty bottom tapering sharply to a flat mouth, decorated w/a wide band of stylized flowers in lavender, dark blue & pale green against a white ground, UND inkstamp & incised "Pasque Flowers - M. Cable 154," 3 3/8" h. (ILLUS.)... **$575**

Scarce North Dakota Lamp Base

Lamp base, round domed foot below the tall cylindrical body w/a molded rim fitted w/a cap, body & base marked w/ink stamp logo, bottom of vase marked "T-538 - 20," incised initials of Freida Hammers under the cap, h.p. w/large dark blue flowers on a dark shaded to light blue ground, flat chip on bottom of base, ca. 1926, overall 11" h. (ILLUS., previous page)............... **$1,610**

University of North Dakota Paperweight

Paperweight, round flattened form, molded w/the seal of the University of North Dakota, overall dark blue glaze, back marked w/blue UND inkstamp logo & name of M. Cable, ca. 1930, 3 5/8" d. (ILLUS.) **$81**

Covered Wagon Design on Paperweight

Paperweight-dish, round dished form w/an incised center design of oxen pulling a covered wagon, medium brown glaze, blue inkstamp UND logo & incised initials of student finisher (ILLUS.) **$173**

Vase, 4 7/8" h., rounded tapering cylindrical form, decorated w/stylized floral trees in dark blue & green accented w/blue & green bands all on a cream ground, inkstamped UND logo & incised "Huck 226," Flora Huckfield (ILLUS., top next column) **$374**

Banded Floral Vase by Flora Huckfield

Spherical Vase with Abstract Animals

Vase, 6" h., squatty nearly spherical body w/a closed rim, decorated around the top w/a band of abstract animals in dark & light blue on a bluish white ground, decorated by June Marks, dated 1949 (ILLUS.) **$863**

Ringed Vase by the Cable Sisters

C

Vase, 8 1/8" h., gently swelled cylindrical form w/a narrow shoulder & short rolled neck, molded ring design down the sides glazed in shades of brown & green, UND inkstamp logo & incised "M. Cable - 1934 - 1118 - Huckfield-," Margaret Cable & Flora Cable Huckfield, 1934, very faint crazing (ILLUS., previous page)................. **$345**

Old Ivory

Old Ivory china was produced in Silesia, Germany, in the late 1800s and takes its name from the soft white background coloring. A wide range of table pieces was made with the various patterns, usually identified by a number rather than a name.

The following prices are averages for Old Ivory at this time. Rare patterns will command higher prices, and there is some variance in prices geographically. These prices are also based on the item being perfect. Cups are measured across the top opening.

Basket, No. 200, Deco blank **$250**
Berry bowl, No. 33, Empire blank, 10" d. **$100**
Berry set, No. 16, Clairon blank, 7 pc........... **$150**

Very Rare No. 27 Bouillon Cup & Saucer

Bouillon cup & saucer, No. 27, Alice blank, very rare (ILLUS.)...................................... **$400**
Bowl, 10" d., No. 5, Elysee blank.................. **$400**
Bowl, 6 1/2" d., No. 84, Empire blank **$65**
Bowl, 5 1/2" d., No. 28, Empire blank **$40**
Bun tray, No. U2, Deco blank, 10" l. **$475**
Butter pat, No. 16, Clairon blank, 3 3/4" d. **$115**
Cake plate, No. 21, Clairon blank, 10" d. **$250**
Cake set, No. 16 or No. 84, Clairon blank, 7 pcs.. **$200**
Celery dish, No. 99, Empire blank, rare, 11 1/4" l. **$400**
Charger, No. 14, Clairon blank, very rare, 13" d. **$950**
Charger, No. 5, Elysee blank, rare, 13" d. (ILLUS., top next column) **$850**
Chocolate set, No. 15, Clairon blank, pot 9 1/2" h., 7 pcs. **$850**
Coffeepot, cov., No. 84, Deco Variant blank, 9" h. **$1,500**

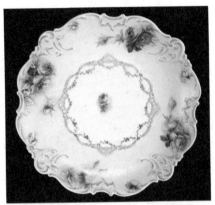

Rare No. 5 Elysee Blank Charger

Rare No. 84 Alice Blank Comport

Comport, open, No. 84, Alice blank, rare (ILLUS.).. **$975**
Cracker jar, cov., No. 200, Deco blank, 5" h... **$475**

No. 204 Deco Blank Cracker Jar

Cracker jar, cov., No. 204, Deco blank, 5" h. (ILLUS.) **$800**
Creamer & cov. sugar bowl, No. 16, Clairon blank, service size, very rare, pr.... **$700**
Cup & saucer, demitasse-size, No. 22, Clairon blank, 2 1/2" h................................. **$300**

C

No. 53 Demitasse Cup & Saucer Set

Cup & saucer, demitasse-size, No. 53, Empire blank, 2 1/2" h. (ILLUS.) **$350**
Demitasse pot, cov., No. 119, Clairon blank, very rare, 7 1/2" h. **$2,000**
Demitasse pot, cov., No. 33, Empire blank, 7 1/2" h. **$500**
Dresser tray, No. 7, Clairon blank, 11 1/2" l. .. **$145**
Horseradish dish, clear glaze, Mignon blank, 3" l. **$150**
Jam jar, cov., No. 200, Deco blank, 4 1/2" h. **$400**
Mustache cup & saucer, No. U22, Eglantine blank, 4" h. **$450**

No. 123 Alice Blank Mustard Pot

Mustard pot, cov., No. 123, Alice blank, 3 3/4" h. (ILLUS.) **$375**
Pickle dish, No. 10, Clairon blank, 6 1/2" l. **$85**
Pitcher, 8" h., water, No. 7, Acanthus blank **$1,300**
Pitcher, 8" h., water, No. 73, Acanthus blank (ILLUS., top next column) **$2,000**
Plate, 6 1/2" d., No. 16 or No. 84, Clairon blank **$25**
Plate, 8 1/2" d., No. 82, Empire blank **$100**
Plate, 7 1/2" d., No. 75, Empire blank **$45**
Shaving mug, No. 22, Clairon blank, 3 1/4" h. **$2,000**

Rare No. 73 Acanthus Blank Pitcher

Small Old Ivory Louis XVI Teapot

Teapot, cov., Louis XVI blank, footed ovoid body, applied cut-out C-scroll handle, serpentine spout, tapering shoulder w/scalloped ruffled beaded rim, domed lid w/finial, decorated on body & lid w/delicate lavender flowers & vining green leaves, silver line decoration on spout, handle, foot & finial, clear glaze, Hermann Ohme, Germany, 5 1/2" h. (ILLUS.) **$100-125**

Old Ivory Melon-shaped Teapot

Teapot, cov., melon-lobed bulbous body on short quatrefoil foot, short flaring neck, domed lobed lid w/finial in the shape of a melon/gourd stem, C-form handle, serpentine spout, the body & lid decorated w/delicate blue & yellow floral designs, the spout & rim w/gold line decoration, Hermann Ohme, Germany, 7 1/2" h. (ILLUS.) **$250**

Owens

Owens pottery was the product of the J.B. Owens Pottery Company, which operated in Ohio from 1890 to 1929. In 1891 it located in Zanesville and produced art pottery from 1896, introducing "Utopian" wares as its first art pottery. The company switched to tile after 1907. Efforts to rebuild after the factory burned in 1928 failed, and the company closed in 1929.

C

Owens Pottery Mark

Owens Utopian Humidor with Cigar

Humidor, cov., Utopian line, footed bulbous tapering body w/a wide fitted cover w/mushroom knob, h.p. brown cigar & matches on a dark brown to dark green ground, unmarked, some small chips to cover interior, some surface scratches, 7 1/8" h. (ILLUS.) **$288**

Owens Cyrano Line Jardiniere

Jardiniere, Cyrano line, footed waisted cylindrical body, lacy squeezebag applied filigree band around the middle & bead-

ing at rim, glossy mottled dark brown & pale yellow ground, white & brown band, unmarked, small piece of filigree missing, glaze crazing, 7 1/2" h. (ILLUS.) **$230**

Blue Speckled Owens Cyrano Jardiniere

Jardiniere, Cyrano line, footed waisted cylindrical body, lacy squeezebag applied filigree band around the middle & beading at rim, glossy streaky & speckled blue ground, light green & blue band, unmarked, 8 1/8" h. (ILLUS.) **$288**

Owens Etched Delft Line Jardiniere

Jardiniere, Delft line, bulbous ovoid body w/a low wide flaring rim, "Old Holland" scene w/an etched design of a Dutch mother & daughter looking out to see, in blue, white & brown, unmarked, 8 x 9 1/2" (ILLUS.)..................................... **$374**

Fine Owens Henri Deux Jardiniere

Jardiniere, Henri Deux line, four-sided gently arched foot trimmed in gold support the wide gently waisted cylindrical body w/a gently swelled & scalloped rim, etched design of a seated Art Nouveau maiden in a landscape in black, dark brown & dark blue, gilt trim around bottom, unmarked, 7 1/2" h. (ILLUS., previous page) **$460**

Owens Moss Aztec Umbrella Stand

Umbrella stand, 21 5/8" h., Moss Aztec line, tall cylindrical form w/flared rim, molded "Springtime" landscape design w/semi-nude maidens, Shape No. 530 (ILLUS.)..................................... **$575**

Owens Utopian Tapering Vase

Vase, 8 5/8" h., Utopian line, flaring foot below cylindrical sides flaring up to a bulbous upper body tapering to a small flaring neck, h.p w/vining white morning glories on a dark brown shaded to greenish yellow ground, bit of loose glaze (ILLUS.)... **$173**

C

Rare Tall Owens Opalesce Vase

Vase, 13" h., Opalesce line, flared foot & gently flaring cylindrical body w/a rounded shoulder to the short rolled neck, gold iridescent ground h.p w/Art Nouveau style vining deep red blossoms & dark green leaves hanging from the rim (ILLUS.)... **$978**

Tall Slender Owens Art Vellum Vase

Vase, 13 1/4" h., Art Vellum line, very slender baluster-form body w/a tiny mouth, decorated w/shaded purple grape clus-ter w/mottled greenish blue leaves & brown vine, on a shaded dark blue to cream to dark blue ground, Owens torch mark & Shape No. 1046, two glaze nicks (ILLUS.) **$690**

Tall Slender Owens Utopian Vase

Vase, 15" h., Utopian line, very tall slender slightly waisted cylindrical body tapering to a tiny cylindrical neck, h.p. thistle & leaves on a shaded dark brown to green ground, artist-signed, impressed mark, Shape No. 1067, some slight scratches (ILLUS.).. **$288**

Oyster Plates

These special plates were very stylish during the second half of the 19th century. Used to serve fresh oysters on the half-shell, they are most often found made of porcelain or majolica, although other materials were sometimes used. In recent years fine individual pieces and sets have become extremely sought after.

Glass, five-well, wide crescent shape w/central sauce indentation, molded pineapple in each well, Lalique, France, 20th c., 8" w. (ILLUS. second row, cen-ter, with other silver plate & glass oyster plates, next page)..................................... **$220**

Glass, six-well, shell-shaped wells around a center sauce well, clear w/beaded border band, early 20th c., 9 1/2" d. (ILLUS. bot-tom row, center, with other silver plate & glass oyster plates, next page) **$28**

Glass, six-well, shell-shaped wells around a center sauce well, opaque, Portieux, France, early 20th c., 8 3/4" d. **$55**

Glass, six-well, shell-shaped wells around center sauce well, clear, Cambridge Glass Co., w/original paper label, early

20th c., 10 1/4" d. (ILLUS. bottom row, right, with other silver plate & glass wells, next page).. **$28**

Glass, six-well, shell-shaped wells spiraling around a round sauce well, Portieux, France, early 20th c., 8 3/4" d. (ILLUS. bottom row, left, with other silver plate & glass oyster plates, next page) **$28**

French 12-Well Majolica Oyster Plate

Majolica, 12-well, hexagonal, the shaded dark grey to light grey shell-shaped wells against a green ground, center handle, France, 19th c., 12 1/2" w. (ILLUS.)........... **$440**

Five Well Oyster Plate with Pink Wells

Majolica, five-well, crescent-shaped, pink wells on a dark brown ground w/a green coral sprig at the center top, 19th c., 10" w. (ILLUS.)...................................... **$1,100**

Very Rare Fish & Shell Minton Plate

Majolica, five-well, dark blue shell-shaped wells alternating w/green & yellow fish, all on a brown ground, Minton, 10 1/2" d. (ILLUS.)... **$6,050**

C

Fine Set of German Porcelain Oyster Plates

Unusual Russian Oyster Plate

Majolica, six-well, unusual stylized maple leaf shape w/fanned & pointed wells & fleur-de-lis shaped handle, glazed in blue, blue & dark yellow, Russian Imperial Eagle mark, 7 x 9" (ILLUS.).................... **$825**

Porcelain, six-well, shell-shaped wells alternating pale pink & yellow & pale blue, pink central sauce compartment, brown ground, Germany, late 19th c., 9" d., set of 12 (ILLUS., top of page)..................... **$1,610**

Silver plate, eight-well, round wells centered by a sauce compartment, Reed & Barton, late 19th - early 20th c., 12 1/2" d. (ILLUS. top row, left, with other silver plate & glass oyster plates, top next column) **$193**

Silver plate, six-well, shell-shaped wells & center sauce compartment, from the Palace Hotel, Denver, Colorado, late 19th - early 20th c., 11" d. (ILLUS. top row, right, with other silver plate & glass oyster plates, top next column) **$358**

Silver plate, three-well, round w/upright center dolphin-shaped handle, Canterbury Silver Plate, early 20th c., 9" d. (ILLUS. top row, center, with other silver plate & glass oyster plates, top next column) **$110**

Grouping of Silver Plate & Glass Plates

Silver plate cast metal, six-well, baking dish w/shell-shaped wells w/hinged covers & round center sauce compartment, shell-shaped handle, marked "Property - Cape Cod Products Co. No. 204," 20th c., 7 1/2" w. (ILLUS. second row, right, with other silver plate & glass oyster plates, above) **$220**

Silver plate cast metal, six-well, shell-shaped wells & central sauce indentation, 8" d. (ILLUS. second row, left, with other silver plate & glass oyster plates, above) **$110**

Paris & Old Paris

China known by the generic name of "Paris" and "Old Paris" was made by several Parisian factories from the 18th through the 19th century; some of it is marked and some is not. Much of it was handsomely decorated.

C

Fine Old Paris Reticulated Compote

Compote, open, 9 x 12 1/2", 8 1/4" h., large oval deep flaring reticulated bowl trimmed in gold & h.p. w/narrow floral reserves about the base, raised on a gilt-trimmed pedestal w/a square foot, early 19th c. (ILLUS.) **$2,645**

Paris Porcelain Models of Parrots

Models of parrots, flatback-style, in the Meissen style, each naturally modeled w/brightly colorfed plumage, one w/its crown raised, each perched on tree stumps applied w/flowers, leaves & berries, inverted blue crossed swords mark & mark of Achille & Block, late 19th - early 20th c., 13 1/2" & 13 3/4" h., pr. (ILLUS.) **$2,000-3,000**

Old Paris Pots de Creme Service

Pots de creme service: 12 cov. cups & a two-tier stand; each cup w/a footed bulbous ovoid body w/a wide mouth & domed cover w/ovoid pointed finial, each w/a cream-colored upper half & white lower half h.p. w/a floral bouquet, the round pedestal-based stand w/matching h.p. decoration, some chipping, early 19th c., stand 12" d., 12" h., the set (ILLUS.)...................................... **$3,220**

Vases, 7 1/8" h., in the Japonisme taste, round low pedestal foot supporting the ovoid body tapering to a wide molded mouth, platinum-ground, the gilt rims finely enriched in black, brightly enameled w/exotic song birds perched on blooming cacti among berried briar & foliage, ca. 1880, pr. (ILLUS., bottom of page)...................................... **$3,120**

Fine Pair of Platinum-Ground Vases

Unusual Figural Old Paris Veilleuse

Veilleuse (night-light/drink warmer), figural, in the form of an elegant lady in 18th c. costume holding her small spaniel on a dark red pillow, finely detailed h.p. costume, head & shoulders form the top, in the manner of Jacob Petit, possibly depicting Marie Antoinette, mid-19th c., 5" w., 12" h. (ILLUS.) **$863**

Paul Revere Pottery

This pottery was established in Boston, Massachusetts, in 1906, by a group of philanthropists seeking to establish better conditions for underprivileged young girls of the area. Edith Brown served as supervisor of the small "Saturday Evening Girls Club" pottery operation, which was moved, in 1912, to a house close to the Old North Church where Paul Revere's signal lanterns had been placed. The wares were mostly hand decorated in mineral colors, and both sgraffito and molded decorations were employed. Although it became popular, it was never a profitable operation and always depended on financial contributions to operate. After the death of Edith Brown in 1932, the pottery foundered and finally closed in 1942.

C

Paul Revere Marks

Paul Revere Bowl with Scarabs

Bowl, 4 1/4" d., bulbous ovoid body w/a wide flat mouth, decorated around the top w/a yellow band accented by flying scarabs in light green, streaky pale blue glaze, marked "S.E.G. - 05-1-14," crazing, 1914 (ILLUS.) **$1,093**

Set of 12 Paul Revere - Saturday Evening Girls Luncheon Plates

C

Paul Revere - Saturday Evening Girls Tea Set

Plates, 8 1/2" d., luncheon, creamy white w/a dark blue border band decorated w/stylized white lotus blossoms, Saturday Evening Girls mark & dated 1910, set of 12 (ILLUS., bottom previous page) **$2,645**

Tea set: cov. bulbous 4 3/4" h. teapot, 4 1/4" h. cylindrical creamer, 4" h. cylindrical cov. sugar bowl & 5 1/4" w. square tea tile; each decorated w/a dark blue glaze w/a border band of stylized white lotus blossoms, all marked w/the Saturday Evening Girls mark & dated 1910, teapot cover cracked, glued chip on inner rim of teapot, the set (ILLUS., top of page) **$1,955**

Peters & Reed

In 1897 John D. Peters and Adam Reed formed a partnership to produce flowerpots in Zanesville, Ohio. Formally incorporated as Peters and Reed in 1901, this type of production was the mainstay until after 1907, when they gradually expanded into the art pottery field. Frank Ferrell, a former designer at the Weller Pottery, developed the "Moss Aztec" line while associated with Peters and Reed, and other art lines followed. Although unmarked, attribution is not difficult once familiar with the various lines. In 1921, Peters and Reed became Zane Pottery, which continued in production until 1941.

Peters & Reed Mark

Vase, 5 7/8" h., Shadowware line, flaring foot tapering to tall slender cylindrical body, swirled blue & yellow over a dark blue ground, unmarked (ILLUS., top next column) **$127**

Vase, 6 3/4" h., Shadowware line, baluster-form body w/a short flared neck, streaky dripping dark blues & pale green over a tan background, unmarked, few tiny underglaze inclusions (ILLUS., bottom next column) **$150**

Small Peters & Reed Shadowware Vase

Peters & Reed Shadowware Vase

C

Peters & Reed Mottled Landsun Vase

Vase, 7 5/8" h., Landsun Ware, footed gently swelled cylindrical body w/a flaring molded rim, mottled matt green & dark blue on a tan ground, unmarked (ILLUS.) **$259**

Shadowware Vase with Unusual Shape

Vase, 8 7/8" h., Shadowware line, cylindrical body below a squatty compressed top w/a wide flat mouth, streaky & drippy dark blue & brown over a tan ground, impressed mark, crazing (ILLUS.) **$230**

Shadowware Vase with Swirled Design

Vase, 8 5/8" h., Shadowware line, simple ovoid body w/a low flaring neck, mottled & swirled blue & olive green on a dark blue ground, unmarked (ILLUS.)............... **$374**

Cylindrical Peters & Reed Shadowware Vase

Vase, 8 7/8" h., Shadowware line, cylindrical body w/a molded rim, streaky dripping dark blues & browns over a tan ground, faintly marked w/Zane Pottery logo, crazing (ILLUS.).. **$259**

Pierce (Howard) Porcelains

Born in Chicago, Illinois in 1912, Howard Pierce was destined to become one of the most talented ceramic wildlife creators of his time. He attended the Chicago Art Institute and in 1935 he decided to move to Claremont, California. For about three years Mr. Pierce worked for William Manker. In 1941, he married Ellen Voorhees who was a resident of National City, California. For a few years they lived in Claremont where Howard built their small home and art studio. In 1968, they moved to Joshia, California.

In the beginning, Howard created miniature animal figures, some of which he made in a very short time he discovered he was allergic to this material so only few a were made. They are high on collectors' lists today.

Howard Pierce was prolific in his output. He was also curious and experimented with a number of different mediums: Wedgwood Jasperware-type body; porcelain bisque animals and plants that he put near or in open areas of vases; Mt. St. Helens ash which is probably the most scarce of any products made by Howard; a lava treatment which he described as "...bubbling up from the bottom...," gold leaf, which is hard to find; a gold treatment that he did for Sears and not being happy with it he stopped production as soon as possible; a "tipping" process that is clearly shown in such pieces as the droopy-eared dogs and the ermine.

Near the end of 1992, due to health problems, Howard and Ellen Pierce destroyed all the molds they had created over the years. Still, Mr. Pierce needed to create. So he purchased a smaller kiln and began creating miniature versions of past porcelain wares. He also added a few new items as there seemed to be no way for him to block his creative processes. These smaller pieces were simply stamped "Pierce." Today, many collectors search only for the pieces marked "Pierce," which has created a demand, causing the values to rise quickly. Howard Pierce passed away in February 1994.

Howard Pierce Round Bowl

Bowl, 7" d., 4 1/4" h., small round black base flaring gently to a larger rim, sky blue inside, incised "Pierce 1990" & H52 (ILLUS.).. **$75**

Bowl, 7 1/4" d., 4 1/4" h., fluted body flaring to a fluted rim, Manker influence, pale & deep blue w/black accents, incised mark, "Pierce 1983" in script.............................. **$205**

Bowl, 7 1/4" d., 4 1/4" h., fluted body flaring to a fluted rim, William Manker influence, pale & deep blue w/black accents, incised "Pierce" & 1983 in script................... **$125**

Figure group, boy standing w/head bent & left arm extended to feed dog seated at his left side, nondescript mottled brown glaze, marked "Howard Pierce," 5" h. **$140**

HOWARD Hp
PIERCE

Pierce　Howard Pierce
(Claremont, Calif)

Pierce (Howard) Marks

Bank, model of a turtle, speckled glossy glaze in teal w/black accents, stamped "Howard Pierce," hard to find, 7 3/4" l. **$275**

Pierce Owls in a Tree Figure Group

Figure group, two owls in a tree, perched on branches, three open branches for small flowers, dull dark brown tree, light & dark brown owls, larger, unusual size for Pierce owls in tree, stamp mark "Howard Pierce," tree, 6" w., 13" h., large owl, 6" h., small owl, 3 1/2" h. (ILLUS., previous page) **$265**

Figure of an angel, standing, applied wings outward, grey glaze, marked "Howard Pierce," hard to find, 11 3/4" h. **$270**

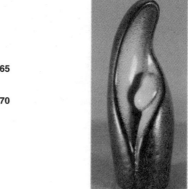

Howard Pierce Madonna & Child

Figures of Hawaiian boy & girl, overall black bodies w/green mottled pants on boy, green mottled grass skirt on girl, both w/hands in Hula dance position, 1950s, boy, 7" h., girl, 6 3/4" h., pr. **$230**

Jug, bulbous body w/small pouring spout & small finger hold, brown mottled rough-textured glaze, stamp mark "Howard Pierce," 5 3/4' h. **$130**

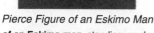

Pierce Figure of an Eskimo Man

Figure of an Eskimo man, standing, crude facial features, arms indistinct against body, brown "tipping" face & feet over white body, Model No. 206P, ca. 1953, 7" h. (ILLUS.) **$150**

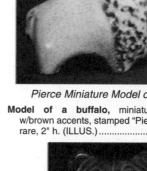

Pierce Miniature Model of a Buffalo

Model of a buffalo, miniature, grey w/brown accents, stamped "Pierce," very rare, 2" h. (ILLUS.) **$450**

Howard Pierce Figure of Girl

Figure of girl holding bird, purple high glaze, "Howard Pierce" stamp, 7" h. (ILLUS.) **$140**

Figure of Madonna & Child, stylized modernistic design, brown texture w/white accents, stamped "Howard Pierce," 7 3/4" h. (ILLUS., top next column) **$135**

Pierce Model of a Bulldog

C

C

Howard Pierce Model of a Dachshund

Model of a bulldog, seated, large & dark brown glaze, base w/raised letters "USMC," stamped "Howard Pierce," 5" h. (ILLUS., previous page) **$325**

Model of a circus horse, leaping position w/head down & tail straight, middle of body attached to a small, round center base, light blue w/cobalt blue accents, 7 1/2" l., 6 1/2" h. **$250**

Model of a dachshund, elongated thin body w/brown matte glaze, stamped "Howard Pierce," 10" l. (ILLUS., top of page) **$155**

Pierce Model of a Roadrunner

Model of a roadrunner, standing on a rock, cement, brown & white glaze, incised "Pierce" on edge of base & hand-signed "Pierce" on bottom, 8 1/4" h. (ILLUS.)........ **$295**

Howard Pierce Stylized Giraffe

Model of a giraffe, stylized animal on a long narrow rectangular base, bluish green glaze, mid-1950s, in mold mark "Howard Pierce Claremont Ca." & copyright symbol w/Model No. 25P, 9 3/4" h. (ILLUS.) **$350**

Model of a horse, standing, black lower body & below the eyes to the mouth, grey on the remaining body, stamped "Howard Pierce Porcelain," 9" l., 8 1/2" h. .. **$300**

Model of a horse, wind-blown mane, matte black glaze w/speckled mane & tail, stamped "Howard Pierce," 10" l., 8" h. **$175**

Model of a rabbit, cement, pale green, rare, 11" l., 5 1/2" h. **$790**

Model of a rabbit, extra long ears, black glossy glaze w/grey accents, incised "Howard Pierce 102P," overall 10 3/4" h. **$175**

Howard Pierce Model of a Skunk

Model of a skunk, rough textured black matte glaze w/white on tail & around top of body, stamped "Howard Pierce," 5 1/4" h. (ILLUS.) **$200**

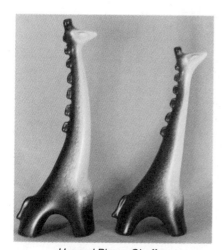

Howard Pierce Giraffes

Models of giraffes, brown & white, 1950s, 9" h., 10" h., pr. (ILLUS.) **$242**
Models of monkeys, grey, pr. **$177**

Set of Howard Pierce Quails

Models of quails, miniatures, caramel brown textured glaze, stamped "Pierce," small 1 3/4" h., medium 2" h., large 4" h., the set (ILLUS.) **$100**
Mug, seven male nudes around the outside, light & dark brown, incised "HP," scarce, 3 1/4" d., 3 3/4" h. **$150**
Pencil holder, designed w/a roadrunner running on one side & a standing w/tail up on other side, light & dark brown glaze, incised "HP," 3" d., 3 3/4" h. **$100**

C

Howard Pierce Ostrich Pin

Pin, figure of ostrich, pewter, incised "Howard Pierce," 2 3/4" h. (ILLUS.) **$256**
Pin, model of a Scottie dog, copper, incised "Howard Pierce" & "HP16" in ink, 1 1/2" d., 1 3/4" h. **$225**
Planter, footed oblong form w/upright sides, pale green matte ground, molded in relief w/a long dark green leaf & matte white flower, incised "Howard Pierce Claremont, Calif.," 10 1/4" l., 5 1/4" h. (ILLUS., bottom of page) **$135**

Howard Pierce Planter with Large Leaf & Flower

Howard Pierce Face Vase

Vase, 6 1/2" h., white w/brown faces in relief, very few produced, "Howard Pierce"
stamp (ILLUS.) **$245**
Vase, 7" h., model of an owl, dark & light
brown, stamped "Howard Pierce Porce-
lain" **$85**
Vase, 7 3/4" h., lime green w/white fish &
coral silhouette, incised underglaze
"Howard Pierce, Claremont, Calif., P-
400" (number does not denote experi-
mental piece).. **$155**

Large Pierce Wall Plaque with Songbirds

Wall plaque, rectangular, molded in relief
w/nine songbirds, pale green ground
w/darker green birds, unmarked, 8" w.,
13" h. (ILLUS.) **$710**
Whistle, snake crawling, w/body forming an
"M" shape, brown w/white glaze, 3 1/4" l.,
2 3/4" h. **$202**

Quimper

*This French earthenware pottery has been
made in France since the end of the 17th century
and is still in production today. Because the colorful decoration on this ware, predominantly of
Breton peasant figures, is all hand-painted and
each piece is unique, it has become increasingly
popular with collectors in recent years. Most
pieces offered today date from about the mid-19th
century to the present. Modern potteries continue
to operate today, with contemporary examples
available in gift shops.*

The standard reference in this field is Quimper
Pottery A French Folk Art Faience *by Sandra V.
Bondhus (privately printed, 1981).*

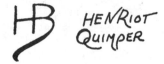

Quimper Marks

Bank, figural, model of a pig, decorated on
the side w/a seated man w/a pipe in his
mouth, bold red daisy on the reverse,
HenRiot Quimper mark, 4" h. **$100**
Candlesticks, each decorated w/a peasant
couple & flowers, stamped mark "HB
Henriot Quimper f. 130 d 318," 5 3/4" h.,
pr.. **$175**
Egg cup, Modern Movement style decorat-
ed w/a kneeling lady holding a basket on
her back, HenRiot Quimper & C. Maillard
mark, 2 1/2" h.. **$150**

Tall Quimper Ewer with Musicians

Ewer, tall classical form w/pedestal base,
tall ovoid ovoid & slender cylindrical neck
w/high arched spout continuing into the
high arched handle, Decor riche patt. featuring a pair of musicians on the front & a
bouquet of Breton wild flowers on the
back, HB Quimper France mark, 18" h.
(ILLUS.).. **$375**

Figure of a lady, standing holding a folded umbrella w/"MARIK" written on the base, Modern Movement colors, marked "HenRiot Quimper France 597," 3 1/2" h. **$85**

Inkwell, round, on an attached scalloped dish, decorated w/a seated peasant lady holding a flower, complete w/cover & insert, HR Quimper mark, 3 3/4" h. **$150**

Knife rest, figural, modeled as a man stretched out on his stomach, Modern Movement colors, HenRiot Quimper & C. Maillard mark, 4" l. **$100**

Knife rest, triangular, decorated on one side w/a peasant lady, flowers on the reverse, marked "HenRiot Quimper France 492," 3 3/4" l. **$30**

Quimper Modern Movement Lamp Base

Lamp base, figural, modeled as a standing peasant lady holding a basket on her shoulder, a blue pond in front of her & figural ducks & hens flanking her feet, Modern Movement style, by artist C. Maillard, HenRiot Quimper & CM mark, 9 1/2" h. (ILLUS.) **$375**

Menu card holder, figural, modeled as a bagpipe, decorated w/a peasant lady & flowers, HenRiot Quimper mark, 3 1/2" h. **$200**

Pitcher, 7" h., decorated w/a traditional peasant man & flowers, signed on the side near the handle "HenRiot Quimper France 70" **$55**

Double-spouted Odetta Pitcher

Pitcher, 8" h., 9" l., gresware, Odetta style double-spouted squatty bulbous body w/high arched handle joining the spouts, in brown, charcoal & white, linear & triangular designs, marked "HB Quimper Odetta 64.1086" (ILLUS.) **$450**

Planter, figural, model of a swan, a trefoil cartouche on the breast encloses a seated man playing the flute, marked "HenRiot Quimper France 89," 4" h. **$100**

Planter, rectangular w/beveled corners, loop end handles, raised on small tab feet, Demi-fantasie patt. w/a couple seated in a field w/latticework at the corners, the reverse w/blue forget-me-nots & a stylized rose, one handle professionally repaired, HR Quimper mark, 5 x 11" (ILLUS., bottom of page) **$225**

Plate, doll's, 2 1/4" d., Modern Movement geometric design, marked "HenRiot Quimper France 83" mark **$35**

Plate, 9" d., dinner, decorated w/a traditional peasant man holding a walking stick, Sujet ordinaire patt., yellow & blue concentric banded border, HenRiot Quimper France mark **$45**

Quimper Rectangular Planter in the Demi-fantasie Pattern

C

Quimper Oval Platter with Naive Peasant Couple

Quimper Decor Riche Dinner Plate

Snuff bottle, heart-shaped, decorated w/a peasant man on one side, a pansy on the reverse, pale blue spongework outer edge, HB Quimper mark, 3" h. **$250**

Quimper Decor Riche Fan-shaped Vase

Vase, 5" h., 8" l., fan-shaped, Decor riche patt., HB Quimper mark (ILLUS.) **$350**

Rare Quimper Pique Fleurs Vase

Plate, 9 1/2" d., dinner, scalloped rim w/pinking shears edges, Decor riche patt. w/peasant couple & Crest of Brittany at the top, blue scrolling acanthus leaf border, marked "HenRiot Quimper 142" in dark blue (ILLUS.) **$350**

Plate, 9 1/2" d., "faience populaire," decorated w/a large flower & concentric border bands in yellow & blue, mid-19th c., unsigned... **$200**

Plate, 10 1/4" w., dinner, cut-corners, Soleil yellow pattern w/modern stamped mark **$35**

Platter, 8 x 12" oval, yellow ground w/a traditional peasant lady, twisted rope blue sponged handles, HenRiot Quimper France mark **$175**

Platter, 9 1/2 x 13" oval, naive detailed peasant couple decoration, signed only "HB," 19th c. (ILLUS., top of page)............. **$325**

Salt dip, figural, modeled as a pair of wooden shoes w/a ring handle, decorated on one shoe w/a peasant lady, a flower sprig on the other shoe, marked "HenRiot Quimper France 596," 4" l. **$35**

Vase, 8" h., 9" l., pique-fleurs style, Modern Movement style, figural, a kneeling

peasant lady lifting a large round basket-form holder, top pierced w/holes for
flowers, HenRiot Quimper & C. Maillard
mark (ILLUS.) **$750**

Quimper Cone-shaped Wall Pockets

Wall pockets, cone-shaped, decorated in
the Demi-fantasie patt., marked "HenRiot
Quimper France 8," 10 3/4" l., pr. (ILLUS.) .. **$200**

R.S. Prussia & Related Wares

*Ornately decorated china marked "R.S. Prus-
sia" and "R.S. Germany" continues to grow in
popularity. According to the Third Series of Mary
Frank Gaston's* Encyclopedia of R.S.
Prussia *(Collector Books, Paducah, Kentucky), these
marks were used by the Reinhold Schlegelmilch
porcelain factories located in Suhl in the Germanic regions known as "Prussia" prior to World
War I, and in Tillowitz, Silesia, which became
part of Poland after World War II. Other marks
sought by collectors include "R.S. Suhl," "R.S."
steeple or church marks, and "R.S. Poland."*

*The Suhl factory was founded by Reinhold
Schlegelmilch in 1869 and closed in 1917. The
Tillowitz factory was established in 1895 by
Erhard Schlegelmilch, Reinhold's son. This china
customarily bears the phrase "R.S. Germany" and
"R.S. Tillowitz." The Tillowitz factory closed in
1945, but it was reopened for a few years under
Polish administration.*

*Prices are high and collectors should beware of
the forgeries that sometimes find their way onto
the market. Mold names and numbers are taken
from Mary Frank Gaston's books on R.S. Prussia.*

*The "Prussia" and "R.S. Suhl" marks have
been reproduced, so buy with care. Later copies of
these marks are well done, but quality of porcelain
is inferior to the production in the 1890-1920 era.*

*Collectors are also interested in the porcelain
products made by the Erdmann Schlegelmilch
factory. This factory was founded by three brothers in Suhl in 1861. They named the factory in
honor of their father, Erdmann Schlegelmilch. A
variety of marks incorporating the "E.S." initials
were used. The factory closed circa 1935. The*

*Erdmann Schlegelmilch factory was an earlier
and entirely separate business from the Reinhold
Schlegelmilch factory. The two were not related to
each other.*

R.S. Prussia & Related Marks

R.S. Germany

Berry set: 9" master bowl & six matching
5 1/2" sauce dishes, Iris mold, decorated
w/large red roses, 7 pcs. **$600-900**
Bowl, 10" d., decorated w/wild roses, rasp-
berries & blueberries, glossy glaze **$350-400**
Bowl, large, Lettuce mold, floral decoration.
lustre finish **$325-375**

R.S. Germany Cake Plate

Cake plate, double-pierced small gold side
handles, decorated w/a scene of a maid-
en near a cottage at the edge of a dark
forest, 10" d. (ILLUS.) **$300-325**
Creamer, Mold 640, decorated w/roses,
gold trim on ruffled rim & ornate handle
.... **$40-60**
Cup & saucer, demitasse, ornate handle,
eight-footed **$80-125**
Mustard jar, cov., calla lily decoration **$100-150**
Plate, 7 1/4" d., poppy decoration **$40-60**
Salad set, 10 1/2" d. lettuce bowl & six 8" d.
matching plates, Mold 12, Iris decoration
on pearl lustre finish, 7 pcs. **$350-450**
Tray, handled, decorated w/large white &
green poppies, 15 1/4" l. **$300-350**

C

Ribbon & Jewel Melon Eaters Berry Set

R.S. Prussia

Bell, tall trumpet-form ruffled body w/twig handle, decorated w/small purple flowers & green leaves on white ground, unmarked, 3 1/2" l. **$325-375**

Berry set: master bowl & six sauce dishes; five-lobed, floral relief rim w/forget-me-nots & water lilies decoration, artist-signed, 7 pcs. **$400-450**

Berry set: master bowl & six sauce dishes; Ribbon & Jewel mold (Mold 18) w/Melon Eaters decoration, 7 pcs. (ILLUS., top of page) **$3,000-4,000**

Bowl, 9 3/4" d., Iris variant mold, rosette center & pale green floral decoration .. **$200-400**

Bowl, 10" d., Mold 202, gold beaded rim, double swans center scene in shades of beige & white, unmarked..................... **$200-225**

Bowl, 10 1/4" d., center decoration of pink roses w/pearlized finish, border in shades of lavender & blue w/satin finish, lavish gold trim (unlisted mold)............ **$300-500**

Bowl, 10 1/2" d., Countess Potocka portrait decoration, heavy gold trim **$1,800-2,200**

Bowl, 10 1/2" d., decorated w/scene of Dice Throwers, red trim **$1,200-1,800**

Bowl, 10 1/2" d., Iris mold, poppy decoration **$400-500**

Bowl, 10 1/2" d., Point & Clover mold (Mold 82), decorated w/pink roses & green leaves w/shadow flowers & a Tiffany finish.. **$250-400**

Bowl, 11" d., 3" h., Sunflower mold, satin finish... **$350-550**

Bowl, 11" d., Mold 22, four large jewels, satin finish **$300-400**

Bowl, 11" d., 3" h., Fishscale mold, decorated w/white lilies on purple & orange lustre ground, artist-signed **$400-450**

Bowl, 15" d., Icicle mold (Mold 7), Snow Bird decoration, scenic reserves around the rim, very rare **$15,000-18,000**

Butter dish, cover & insert, Mold 51, floral decoration, unmarked **$200-400**

Floral Decorated Cake Plate

Cake plate, open handled, decorated w/pink & white flowers, green leaves, pink & yellow ground, gold trim, 9 3/4" d. (ILLUS.)... **$250-350**

Cake plate, open-handled, Fleur-de-Lis mold, Spring Season portrait, 9 3/4" d. **$1,400-1,800**

Cake plate, open-handled, Mold 155, hanging basket decoration, 10" d............... **$300-400**

Cake plate, open-handled, Mold 259, decorated w/pink & yellow roses, pearl button finish, 10" d. **$300-400**

Cake plate, open-handled, Fleur-de-Lis mold, decorated w/a castle scene in rust, gold, lavender & yellow, 10 1/4" d. **$1,000-1,350**

Cake plate, open-handled, Medallion mold, center Flora portrait, Tiffany finish w/four cupid medallions, unmarked, 10 1/2" d. **$900-1,000**

Cake plate, Iris mold, yellow poppy decoration, 11" d. **$300-400**

C

Lebrun-decorated Chocolate Set

Cake plate, open-handled, Carnation mold (Mold 28), dark pink roses against teal & green w/gold trim, 11" d. **$600-800**

Cake plate, open-handled, modified Fleur-de-Lis mold, floral decoration, beaded, satin finish, artist-signed, 11" d. **$300-400**

Cake plate, Hidden Image mold, light blue highlights, 11 1/2" d. **$450-500**

Cake plate, open handles, Mold 256, satin ground decorated w/flowers in blue, pink & white w/gold trim, 11 1/2" d. **$300-400**

Cake plate, open-handled, Mold 330, decorated w/snapdragons on pastel ground, artist-signed, 11 1/2" d. **$300-400**

Cake plate, open-handled, Mold 343, Winter figural portrait in keyhole medallion, cobalt blue inner border, gold outer border, 12 1/2" d. **$3,000-3,500**

Cake plate, Bow-tie mold, pink & gold **$500-600**

Cake plate, open-handled, Carnation mold, decorated w/multicolored roses **$400-600**

Celery dish, Carnation mold, carnations & pink roses decoration on white shaded to peach ground, iridescent Tiffany finish, 9" l. **$400-600**

Celery dish, Hidden Image mold, colored hair, 5 x 12" **$400-450**

Celery dish, Mold 25, oblong, pearlized finish w/Surreal Dogwood blossoms w/gold trim, 6 x 12 1/4" **$250-350**

Celery tray, Mold 254, decorated w/green & pink roses, lavish gold tracery, artist-signed, 12" l. **$250-350**

Celery tray, Ribbon & Jewel mold (Mold 18), pink roses & white snowball blossoms within a wide cobalt blue border w/gilt trim, 12" l. **$600-800**

Celery tray, Mold 255, decorated w/Surreal Dogwood decoration, pearlized lustre finish, artist-signed, 12 1/4" l. **$350-400**

Celery tray, open-handled, decorated w/soft pink & white flower center w/lily-of-the-valley, embossed edge of ferns & pastel colors w/gold highlights, 12 1/2" l. **$200-250**

Centerpiece bowl, Carnation mold, decorated w/pink & yellow roses, 15 1/2" d. **$3,500-4,500**

Chocolate cup & saucer, decorated w/castle scene **$150-250**

Chocolate pot, cov., Carnation mold (Mold 526), pink background & pink roses w/gold-trimmed leaves & blossoms & ornate gold handle, 12" h. **$1,200-1,600**

Chocolate pot, cov., Icicle mold (Mold 641), rosebush decoration, 10" h. **$400-500**

Chocolate pot, cov., Hidden Image mold, image on both sides, light green, 9 3/4" h. **$1,000-1,100**

Chocolate pot, cov., peacock & pine trees decoration **$650-750**

Chocolate pot, cov., Swag & Tassel mold, decorated w/scene of sheepherder & swallows **$900-1,000**

Chocolate set: cov. pot & four cups & saucers; sunflower decoration, the set .. **$800-1,200**

Chocolate set: 10" h. cov. chocolate pot & four cups & saucers; Mold 729, pansy decoration w/gold trim, the set **$900-975**

Chocolate set: 10" h. cov. chocolate pot & four cups & saucers; Ribbon and Jewel mold, scene of Dice Throwers decoration on pot & single Melon Eater scene on cups, the set **$4,500-6,000**

Chocolate set: tankard-style cov. pot & six cups & saucers; Mold 510, laurel chain decoration, the set **$1,000-1,300**

Chocolate set: 10" h. cov. chocolate pot & six cups & saucers; Mold 517, Madame Lebrun portrait decoration, the set (ILLUS., top of page) **$7,500-8,200**

Coffeepot, cov., Mold 517, raised floral designs as part of border, unmarked **$250-300**

Cracker jar, cov., Mold 540a, beige satin ground w/floral decoration in orchid, yellow & gold, 9 1/2" w. handle to handle, overall 5 1/2" h. **$300-350**

Cracker jar, cov., Mold 634, molded feet, surreal dogwood blossoms decoration on pearlized lustre finish, 8" d., 6 1/2" h. **$250-300**

C

Carnation - Summer Season Pitcher

Pitcher, tankard, 12 1/2" h., Carnation mold
(Mold 526), Summer Season decoration,
pink border trim (ILLUS.).............. **$7,000-8,000**
Pitcher, tankard, 13" h., Carnation mold
(Mold 526), decorated w/clusters of dark
pink & creamy white roses w/a shaded
dark green ground & pale green molded
blossoms (ILLUS., bottom next column)
.... **$1,000-1,200**
Pitcher, cider, 7" h., iris decoration w/green
& gold background **$250-300**
Pitcher, tankard, 10" h., Mold 584, decorated w/hanging basket of pink & white
roses **$700-750**
Pitcher, tankard, 12" h., Mold 538, decorat-
ed w/Melon Eaters scene (ILLUS. left,
bottom of page)............................ **$3,500-4,000**
Pitcher, tankard, 13" h., decorated w/scene
of Old Man in Mountain & swans on lake

(ILLUS. right w/other tankard pitcher,
bottom of page)............................ **$4,000-4,500**
Pitcher, tankard, 13 1/2" h., Carnation
Mold, pink poppy decoration, green
ground... **$1,400-1,800**
Plaque, decorated w/scene of woman
w/dog, 9 1/4 x 13" **$2,000-2,500**
Plate, 7 1/2" d., Carnation mold, decorated
w/pink roses, lavender ground, satin fin-
ish **$400-500**
Plate, 8 1/2" d., Gibson Girl portrait decora-
tion, maroon bonnet......................... **$800-1,200**
Plate, 8 1/2" d., Mold 263, pink & white
roses decoration **$175-200**
Plate, 8 3/4" d., Mold 278, center decoration
of pink poppies on white ground, green
border... **$175-200**

Carnation Mold Pitcher with Roses

R.S. Prussia Tankard Pitchers

Mold 91 Rose-decorated Plate

Plate, 8 3/4" d., Mold 91, yellow roses decoration on pink ground, shiny yellow border (ILLUS.) **$200-300**

Plate, 9 3/4" d., Icicle mold, swan decoration **$800-900**

Plate, 11" d., Point & Clover mold, Melon Eaters decoration **$900-1,100**

Plate, dessert, Mold 506, branches of pink roses & green leaves against a shaded bluish green to white ground w/shadow flowers & satin finish **$100-125**

Relish dish, Iris mold (Mold 25), oval w/scalloped sides & end loop handles, Spring Season portrait surrounded by dark border w/iris, 4 1/2 x 9 1/2" . **$1,500-1,800**

Relish dish, scene of masted ship, 4 1/2 x 9 1/2" **$250-300**

Relish dish, Mold 82, decorated w/forget-me-nots & multicolored carnations, six jeweled domes **$125-175**

Spooner/vase, Mold 502, three-handled, decorated w/delicate roses & gold trim, unsigned, 4 1/4" h. **$75-100**

Syrup pitcher & underplate, Mold 507, white & pink roses on a shaded brown to pale yellow ground, 2 pcs. **$200-250**

Tea set: cov. teapot, creamer & cov. sugar bowl; floral decoration, the set **$300-350**

Tea set: cov. teapot, creamer & cov. sugar bowl; pedestal base, scene of Colonial children, 3 pcs. **$600-700**

Toothpick holder, ribbed hexagonal shape w/two handles, decorated w/colorful roses **$265-300**

Toothpick holder, three-handled, decorated w/white daisies on blue ground, gold handles & trim on top **$150-175**

Tray, pierced handles, Mold 82, decorated w/full blossom red & pink roses, gold Royal Vienna mark, 8 x 11 1/8" **$250-300**

Vase, 4" h., salesman's sample, handled, Mold 914, decorated w/large lilies & green foliage, raised beading around shoulder, gold handles, shaded green ground, artist-signed **$150-250**

Vase, 5 1/2" h., cottage & mill scene decoration, cobalt trim **$600-900**

Vase, 6 1/4" h., decorated w/brown & cream shadow flowers **$100-200**

Vase, 8" h., cylindrical body w/incurved angled shoulder handles, decorated w/parrots on white satin ground, unmarked **$2,200-2,600**

Vase, 8" h., ovoid body w/wide shoulder tapering to cylindrical neck w/flared rim, decorated w/scene of black swans (ILLUS. left, bottom of page) **$1,200-1,500**

Vase, 10" h., ovoid body decorated w/scene of two tigers, pastel satin finish (ILLUS. right, bottom of page) **$5,500-7,000**

C

R.S. Prussia Vases with Animals

R.S. Suhl Coffee Set with Romantic Scenes

Other Marks

Bowl, 10" d., Cabbage mold w/center rose decoration (R.S. Tillowitz) **$250-300**

Chocolate pot, cov., Art Nouveau decoration, glossy finish (R.S. Tillowitz - Silesia) **$55**

Coffee set: 6 5/8" l., 3 1/4" d., cov. ovoid coffeepot & two cups & saucers; each piece decorated w/a color oval reserve w/a different romantic scene within a thin gilt border & a deep burgundy panel against a creamy white ground trimmed w/gilt scrolls, a wide red & narrow dark green border band on each, saucers 2 3/4" d., cups 2 1/4" h., blue beehive & R.S. Suhl marks, the set (ILLUS., top of page) **$500-800**

Match holder, hanging-type on attached backplate decorated w/a scene of a man w/mug of beer & pipe (E.S. Prov. Saxe) **$175-200**

Plate, 7 3/4" d., Sunflower mold, rose pink & yellow roses w/Tiffany finish (Wheelock Prussia) **$125-150**

Plate, 10 1/2" d., lovely center portrait of Madame DuBarry, four cameos in different poses on a deep burgundy lustre border band (E.W. Prov. Saxe) **$500-600**

Server, center-handled, decorated w/orange, white & pink poppies on a shaded bluish grey ground, w/a narrow gilt border band, 8 1/2" d., 3 3/4" h., E. Schlegelmilch - Thuringia (ILLUS.) **$100-150**

Tray, rectangular, open-handled, bright colored bird decoration, 5 x 14" (R.S. Tillowitz) **$75-100**

Melon Eaters Vase

Vase, 6 3/8" h., 3" d., wide, ovoid, shouldered body tapering to slender, flaring cylindrical neck, Melon Eaters decoration surrounded by gold border w/reverse decorated w/heart-shaped area w/dainty pink roses on pastel ground, two-thirds of vase covered in purplish lustre w/fine gold leaves & flowers overall, neck in off white w/fine gold floral decoration, artist-signed in gold, Red Crown "Viersa" mark, Suhl or Tillowitz (ILLUS.) **$400-500**

Vase, 7 1/2" h., wide, squatty, bulbous base tapering sharply to a tall, slender, cylindrical neck w/an upturned four-lobed rim, long slender gold handles from rim to

E. Schlegelmilch Handled Server

C

shoulder, decorated w/a center reserve of a standing Art Nouveau maiden w/her hands behind her head & a peacock behind her framed by delicate gold scrolls & beading & floral bouquets, all on a pearl lustre ground (Prov. Saxe - E.W. Germany) **$375-425**

Vase, 9 1/4" h., gently tapering cylindrical body w/a wide, cupped, scalloped gilt rim, pierced gold serpentine handles from rim to center of sides, decorated around the body w/large blossoms in purple, pink, yellow & green on a shaded brownish green ground (Prove. Saxe)................ **$125-150**

Vase, 10" h., gold Rococo handles, scene of sleeping maiden w/cherub decoration (E.S. Royal Saxe).............................. **$350-400**

Vase, 13 1/2" h., twisted gold handles, portrait of "Goddess of Fire," iridescent burgundy & opalescent colors w/lavish gold trim (Prov. Saxe, E.S. Germany)......... **$650-700**

Redware

Red earthenware pottery was made in the American colonies from the late 1600s. Bowls, crocks and all types of utilitarian wares were turned out in great abundance to supplement the pewter and handmade treenware. The ready availability of the clay, the same used in making bricks and roof tiles, accounted for the vast production. The lead-glazed redware retained its reddish color, although a variety of colors could be obtained by adding various metals to the glaze. Interesting effects occurred accidentally through unsuspected impurities in the clay or uneven temperatures in the firing kiln, which sometimes resulted in streaks or mottled splotches.

Redware pottery was seldom marked by the maker.

Early Redward Fish Food Mold

Rare Early Basket-form Redware Jar

Large Old Redware Bowl

Bowl, 14 1/2" d., 4" h., flat-bottom w/widely flaring angled side, orange ground w/streaking dark brown decoration, probably New England, first half 19th c. (ILLUS.) **$345**

Food mold, modeled as a jumping fish w/detailed scales & fins on the interior, brown-daubed glaze, edge chips, 19th c., 10" l. (ILLUS., top next column) **$173**

Jar, basket-shaped, ovoid body w/thick molded rim & applied arched handle, running daubs of manganese glaze, glaze flakes, missing cover, attributed to Pennsylvania, 19th c., 7 1/2" h. (ILLUS., middle next column).................................... **$2,530**

Rare Green-glazed Redware Jar

Jar, bulbous ovoid body tapering to a rolled neck, light green glaze overall on exterior, 19th c., some minor rim roughness, 7" d., 9" h. (ILLUS.) **$1,495**

Early New England Redware Jar

Jar, bulbous ovoid body tapering to a short neck, lead-glazed w/olive green streaked w/manganese & yellowish orange halos, glaze losses, rim chip, New England, late 18th - early 19th c., 9 1/2" h. (ILLUS.) **$1,998**

Jar, bulbous ovoid body tapering to a wide flat mouth, eared handles, green glaze w/orange lines resembling surface cracks, 19th c., two small rim chips, some glaze roughness, 5 1/2" d., 6 1/2" h. **$173**

Old Redware Covered Jar

Jar, cov., cylindrical w/tapering shoulder to a cupped mouth w/an inset cover, incised

lines around rim & shoulder, lead glaze w/brown splotches, glass loss around rim, probably Connecticut, ca. 1830-60, 11" h. (ILLUS.) **$353**

Early Eastern U.S. Redware Jug

Jug, bulbous ovoid body tapering to a small mouth, applied reeded strap shoulder handle, incised lines around the shoulder, splotches of transparent olive green glaze on neck & shoulder, early United State, early 19th c., chips, glaze wear, 10 3/4" h. (ILLUS.) **$881**

Fine Redware Jug with Green Glaze

Jug, bulbous ovoid body w/a small neck & applied strap handle, light green glaze w/orange highlights, 19th c., 5" d., 6 1/4" h. (ILLUS.) **$1,265**

Footed Redware Pot

C

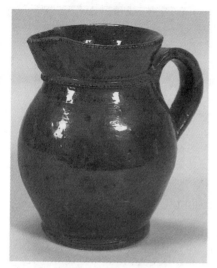

Early New England Redware Pitcher

Pitcher, 7 3/8" h., ovoid body tapering to a coggled neck band & flaring neck w/pinched spout & coggled rim, applied reeded strap handle, lead-glazed w/brown mottling, probably New England, early 19th c. (ILLUS.) **$499**

Very Rare Redware Covered Pitcher

Pitcher, cov., 8 1/2" h., 7" d., tapering ovoid body w/short flaring rim w/pinch spout, applied strap handle, inset cover w/knob finial, green slip glaze streaked w/dark brown, wavy incised line at the neck, cover w/light brown glaze w/splotchy green & yellow, 19th c. (ILLUS.) **$4,313**

Pot, footed bulbous ovoid body w/a wide flat molded rim, orange glaze w/small red dots outside & inside, unglazed rim, small rim chip & tight hairline, 19th c., 6 1/2" d., 5 1/4" h. (ILLUS., top next column) **$173**

Rookwood

Considered America's foremost art pottery, the Rookwood Pottery Company was established in Cincinnati, Ohio, in 1880 by Mrs. Maria Nichols Longworth Storer. To accurately record its development, each piece carried the Rookwood insignia or mark, was dated, and, if individually decorated, was usually signed by the artist. The pottery remained in Cincinnati until 1959, when it was sold to Herschede Hall Clock Company and moved to Starkville, Mississippi, where it continued in operation until 1967.

A private company is now producing a limited variety of pieces using original Rookwood molds.

Rookwood Mark

Rookwood Silver-Overlaid Sea Green Mug

Mug, gently tapering cylindrical form, shaded green ground decorated w/pale green clover leaves & red blossoms, silver-overlay flower embossed rim band continuing to form the long handle, Sea Green glaze, silver marked by Gorham, Sally E. Coyne, 1905, 5" d., 5 1/2" h. (ILLUS.) **$978**

Early Crab-decorated Rookwood Pitcher

Pitcher, 8 1/4" h., 6 3/4" d., bulbous ovoid body w/a tall cylindrical neck & applied arched handle, in the Japanese style, h.p. w/large brown & red crabs on a speckled sea foam green ground, Albert R. Alentien, 1884 (ILLUS.) **$2,300**

Exceptional Shirayamadani Iris Glaze vase

Vase, 7 3/4" h., gently tapering cylindrical form w/a short flared rim, Iris glass, decorated w/a continuous forest scene w/tall thin leafy trees & bushes against a blue shaded to pale pink sky, Shape No. 1658 E, Kataro Shirayamadani, 1911 (ILLUS.) **$16,675**

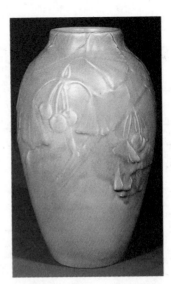

Rare Rookwood Carved Mat Vase

Vase, 10 1/2" h., 6 1/2" d., Carved Mat glaze, simple ovoid body modeled w/branches of ginkgo leaves & berries in relief under a green & yellow mat glaze, Kataro Shirayamadani, 1905 (ILLUS.).. **$11,500**

Rare Rookwood Silver-Overlay Vase

Vase, 13 1/4" h., 10 1/2" d., bulbous ovoid body tapering to a short flaring neck, Standard Glaze, shaded dark to light brown ground decorated w/large orange mums & green leaves, decorated w/ornate leafy scroll silver-overlay marked by Gorham, Matthew A. Daly, 1893 (ILLUS.) **$14,950**

Rare Tall Rookwood Vase with Birds

Vase, 15 1/2" h., 6" d., footed tall slender ovoid body w/a cylindrical neck, Standard Glaze, painted & lightly molded w/a panoramic view of two grey birds flying above crashing deep green vases on a shaded brown ground, Kataro Shirayamadani, 1898 (ILLUS.) **$12,650**

Rosenthal

The Rosenthal porcelain manufactory has been in operation since 1880, when it was established by P. Rosenthal in Selb, Bavaria. Tablewares and figure groups are among its specialties.

Rosenthal Marks

1960s Modernist Rosenthal Vase

Vase, 9 7/8" h., cylindrical, all white molded w/a stylized leaf design, marked

"Rosenthal Germany - Cuno Fischer - Studio Linie," ca. 1963 (ILLUS.) **$115**

Rosenthal 1930s Silver-Overlay Vase

Vase, cov., 12 1/4" h., temple jar form w/tapering ovoid body w/short cylindrical neck supporting a domed flanged cover w/a knob finial, black ground decorated w/a silver overlay design of a large bird of Paradise flying over an intricate flower highlighted in orange & white, marked, ca. 1936 (ILLUS.) **$575**

Roseville

Roseville Pottery Company operated in Zanesville, Ohio, from 1898 to 1954, having been in business for six years prior to that in Muskingum County, Ohio. Art wares similar to those of Owens and Weller Potteries were produced. Items listed here are by patterns or lines.

Roseville Mark

Apple Blossom (1948)
White apple blossoms in relief on blue, green or pink ground; brown tree branch handles.

Blue Apple Blossom Hanging Basket

Basket, hanging-type, bulbous form tapering to a pointed base, narrow shoulder & wide flat neck flanked by tiny branch handles, blue ground, No. 361-5", 8" (ILLUS.) **$173**

C

Grouping of Various Roseville Basket, Book Ends, Jardinieres, Teapot & Vases

Basket, footed, long narrow oval body w/arched sides & arched low overhead branch handle, green ground, No. 310-10", 11 1/2" l., 10" h. (ILLUS. third row, far left, with other Roseville basket, book ends, jardinieres, teapot & vases, top of page) **$242**

Roseville Apple Blossom Console Bowl

Console bowl, long boat-shaped form w/branch end handles, pink ground, No. 331-12", 12" l. (ILLUS.) **$75-150**

Pink Apple Blossom Trumpet-form Vase

Vase, 10" h., wide flaring foot w/base twig handles, trumpet-form body, pink ground, some crazing, No. 388-10" (ILLUS.)............ **$138**

Baneda (1933)
Band of embossed pods, blossoms and leaves on green or raspberry pink ground.

Small Roseville Baneda Vase

Vase, 4" h., footed bulbous body w/incurved flat rim, flat shoulder handles, green ground, No. 587-4" (ILLUS.) **$403**

Small Squatty Roseville Baneda Vase

C

Vase, 4" h., footed, wide squatty bulbous base tapering sharply to small molded mouth, tiny rim handles, green ground, No. 603-4" (ILLUS., previous page) **$518**

Slender Ovoid Roseville Baneda Vase

Squatty 6" Roseville Baneda Vase

Footed Globular Roseville Baneda Vase

Vase, 6" h., footed slender ovoid body w/a wide cylindrical mouth flanked by small C-scroll handles, green ground, No. 588-6" (ILLUS.) **$518**

Vase, 6" h., footed squatty bulbous body tapering sharply to a small neck flanked by C-scroll handles, green ground, No. 605-6" (ILLUS., top next column) **$690**

Vase, 7" h., footed wide cylindrical body w/wide collared rim, small loop handles from shoulder to rim, green ground, pea-sized repaired base chip, No. 610-7" **$518**

Vase, 8" h., footed, globular w/low flat neck & shoulder handles, green ground, No. 595-8" (ILLUS., bottom next column) **$1,150**

Bleeding Heart (1938)

Pink blossoms and green leaves on shaded blue, green or pink ground.

Bleeding Heart Vase with Large Grouping of Other Roseville Vases

Vase, 8" h., footed w/wide squatty lower body w/a wide shoulder tapering to a tall trumpet-form neck w/flaring paneled rim, angular handles from lower neck to shoulder, blue ground, minor professional repair to rim tip, No. 969-8" (ILLUS. third row, second from left, with large grouping of Roseville vases & bowls, bottom previous page) **$150**

C

Bushberry (1948)
Berries and leaves on blue, green or russet bark-textured ground; brown or green branch handles.

Console set: footed ovoid basket No. 369-6 1/2" w/angled rim & high pointed branch handle & pair of No. 153-6" cornucopias, the set (ILLUS. front row, center, with Roseville Apple Blossom basket & other book ends, jardineres, teapot & vases, bottom previous page) **$345**
Vase, 6" h., footed cylindrical body w/asymmetrical branch handles near rim, russet ground, No. 29-6" (ILLUS. third row, second from left, with Apple Blossom basket & other book ends, jardinieres, teapot & vases, top of page 262) **$138**
Vase, 7" h., footed ovoid body w/closed rim flanked by long pointed handles, russet ground, No. 31-7" (ILLUS. third row, far left, with grouping of Bleed Heart Roseville vases & other vases & bowls, bottom previous page) **$207**

Carnelian I (1915-27)
Matte smooth glaze with a combination of two colors or two shades of the same color with the darker dripping over the lighter tone. Generally in colors of blue, pink and green.

Carnelian I Flaring Flower Holder

Flower holder, wide tapering foot supporting a wide flattened half-round container w/a row of small round openings along the top rim, drippy dark blue over pale blue, ink stamp mark, No. 50-4", 6 1/2" w., 4 1/8" h. (ILLUS.).......................... **$81**
Flower holder, widely flaring oval foot tapering sharply to a short ringed stem below the wide flat-sided fanned upper container supported by delicate scrolled side legs & pierced across the top w/a row of flower holes, dark blue dripping over tan, blue stamped mark, No. 63-5 1/2", 5 1/2" h. (ILLUS., top next column) **$81**

Blue & Tan Carnelian I Flower Holder

Carnelian I Green Fan-shaped Vase

Vase, 8" h., fan-shaped, base handles, drippy dark over light green No. 354-8" (ILLUS.) **$92**

Squatty Bulbous Carnelian I Vase

Vase, 5" h., squatty bulbous form w/a wide short flared neck flanked by upright oval loop handles, dark drippy green over turquoise blue, No. 357-5" (ILLUS.) **$100-125**

Squatty Bulbous Blue Carnelian I Vase

Vase, 5" h., squatty bulbous form w/a wide short flared neck flanked by upright oval loop handles, dark drippy blue over turquoise blue, No. 357-5" (ILLUS.) **$100-150**

Green Double-gourd Carnelian I Vase

Vase, 7" h., double gourd-form w/wide neck & flaring rim, ornate pointed & scrolled handles from mid-section of base to below rim, dark drippy moss green over pale green, ink stamp mark, No. 310-7" (ILLUS.)... **$125-150**

Carnelian I Green to Tan Vase

Vase, 7 " h., footed wide flaring ovoid body w/a wide angled shoulder to the low flat mouth flanked by low S-scroll shoulder

handles, drippy dark bluish green above tan, stamped mark & partial paper label, No. 331-7" (ILLUS.)................................... **$115**

Carnelian II (1915-31)

Intermingled colors, some with a drip effect, giving a textured surface appearance. Colors similar to Carnelian I.

Double-gourd Carnelian II Vase

Vase, 7" h., double-gourd form graduated body w/a swelled neck w/a widely flaring rim, angular downswept handles from the neck to the shoulder, greenish blue over dark blue mottled drip glaze, No. 310-7" (ILLUS.)... **$200-300**

Carnelian II Ovoid Handled Vase

Vase, 7" h., footed ovoid body tapering to a short cylindrical neck flanked by angled scroll handles, overall mottled dark & light greenish blue, No. 311-7" (ILLUS.) **$175-250**

Vase, 7" h., footed widely flaring lower body w/a wide angled shoulder to a small rolled neck flanked by low S-scroll shoulder handles, mottled & drippy dark green glaze over a dark rose pink mottled ground, No. 331-7" (ILLUS., next page) **$250-300**

C

Carnelian II Green & Dark Pink Vase

Carnelian II Vase with Fine Glaze

Vase, 7" h., footed widely flaring lower body w/a wide angled shoulder to a small rolled neck flanked by low S-scroll shoulder handles, mottled drippy light blue over mauve glaze, No. 331-7", minor grinding chips on base (ILLUS.)................. **$546**

Carnelian II Swelled Cylindrical Vase

Vase, 7 1/2" h., footed gently swelled cylindrical body w/a short wide flared neck, dark green mottled & drippy glaze over mottled dark pink, No. 308-7" (ILLUS.) **$316**

Squatty Bulbous Carnelian II Vase

Vase, 8" h., footed wide squatty bulbous body w/a short cylindrical neck flanked by angled handles, mottled rose ground w/olive green to mulberry drip glaze, No. 335-8", repaired handle chip (ILLUS.)........ **$230**

Carnelian II Swelled Cylindrical Vase

Vase, 8 1/4" h., footed gently swelled cylindrical body w/a narrow shoulder to the short, wide cylindrical neck, dark drippy mottled lavender over mottled dark pink, No. 316-8" (ILLUS.)............................. **$350-400**

Mottled Blue Carnelian II Vase

Vase, 10" h., compressed globular base w/trumpet form neck, ornate angled handles from base to midsection, mottled blue glaze, No. 323-10" (ILLUS.) **$250-300**

C

Cherry Blossom (1933)

Sprigs of cherry blossoms, green leaves and twigs with pink fence against a combed blue-green ground or creamy ivory fence against a terra cotta ground shading to dark brown.

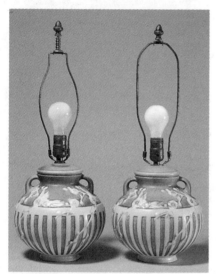

Pair of Blue-Green Cherry Blossom Lamps

Lamps, footed spherical vase body w/a short neck flanked by small loop handles, a low domed cap at the top for wiring, blue-green ground, No. 625-8", 9" h., pr. (ILLUS.) **$1,840**

Clematis (1944)

Clematis blossoms and heart-shaped green leaves against a vertically textured ground, white blossoms on blue, rose-pink blossoms on green and ivory blossoms on golden brown.

Book ends, open book-shaped w/blossom in center, green ground, minor glaze flake on one blossom point, No. 14, pr. (ILLUS. front row, far left, with Roseville Apple Blossom basket & other book ends, jardineres, teapot & vases, top of page 262) **$150**

Ewer, footed squatty bulbous lower body tapering sharply to a tall forked neck w/a very tall arched spout, long pointed handle from rim to shoulder, shaded pale green ground w/white flowers, No. 17-10", 10 1/2" h. (ILLUS. back row, second from right, with Roseville Bleeding Heart vases & other vases & bowls, bottom of page 263) **$305**

Ewer, footed tall ovoid body tapering to a split rim w/a tall duck-bill spout & long pointed handle, body crazed, blue ground, No. 18-15", 15" h. (ILLUS., top next column) **$173**

Tall Roseville Clematis Ewer

Cosmos (1940)

Embossed blossoms against a wavy horizontal ridged band on a textured ground, ivory band with yellow and orchid blossoms on blue, blue band with white, and orchid blossoms on green or tan.

Short Tapering Bulbous Cosmos Vase

Vase, 4" h., footed bulbous sharply tapering body w/a fluted cylindrical neck flanked by long arched handles to mid-body, tan ground, glazed-over chip on rim, No. 944-4" (ILLUS.) **$81**

C

Early Embossed Pitchers (pre-1916)
High-gloss utility line of pitchers with various embossed scenes.

Early Roseville Tulip Pitcher

Tulip, blue blossom, green leaves & stem on a cream shaded to brown ground, 7 1/2" h. (ILLUS.) **$127**

Foxglove (1940s)
Sprays of pink and white blossoms embossed against a shaded dark blue, green or pink matte-finish ground.

Vase, 8" h., footed cylindrical body, angled handles from lower base to rim, green ground, No. 48-8" (ILLUS. second row, far right, with Roseville Bleeding Heart vase & other vases & bowls, top of page 262) **$184**

Blue Fuchsia Pattern Floor Vase

Vase, 18" h., floor-type, two-handled, footed baluster-form w/narrow flared rim, blue ground, No. 56-18" (ILLUS.) **$690**

Fuchsia (1939)
Coral pink fuchsia blossoms and green leaves against a background of blue shading to yellow, green shading to terra cotta, or terra cotta shading to gold.

Jardiniere, footed spherical body w/short wide neck flanked by small angled

handles, blue ground, No. 645-3", 3" h. (ILLUS., top next column) **$115**

Small Spherical Fuchsia Jardiniere

Futura (1928)
Varied line with shapes ranging from Art Deco geometrics to futuristic. Matte glaze is typical although an occasional piece may be high gloss.

Roseville Future 6" Jardiniere

Jardiniere, squared handles rising from wide sloping shoulders to wide flat molded rim, sharply canted sides, terra cotta ground w/green & orange florals, No. 616-6", 6" h. (ILLUS.) **$288**

Pink Rectangular Roseville Futura Vase

Vase, 4" h., 6 1/2" l., called the "Two-Pole Pink Budvase," rectangular w/pointed ends & upright rim above tapering sides flanked by end stick handles to the flaring paneled foot, pink ground, pinhead piece of clay on base, No. 85-4" (ILLUS.) **$259**

C

Blue & Apricot Futura Vase

Vase, 6" h., 3 1/2" d., cylindrical body swelling to wider bands at the top & base, long pierced angled handles down the sides, apricot w/blue bands & handles, light crazing, No. 381-6" (ILLUS.) **$259**

Green & Apricot Futura Vase

Vase, 6" h., 3 1/2" d., cylindrical body swelling to wider bands at the top & base, long pierced angled handles down the sides, apricot w/green bands & handles, No. 381-6" (ILLUS.) **$403**

Vase, 7" h., spherical top w/large pointed dark blue & green leaves curving up the sides, resting on a gently sloped rectangular foot, shaded blue & green blue ground, No. 387-7" (ILLUS., top next column) **$750-1,000**

Spherical Futura Footed Vase

Roseville Futura Ball Bottle Vase

Vase, 8" h., known as "The Ball Bottle" vase, bottle-shaped w/stepped back bands, grey-blue & pink, No. 384-8" (ILLUS.) **$403**

Futura Pink Twist 8" Vase

Vase, 8" h., known as the "Pink Twist" vase, square, slightly tapering body twisting toward the rim, pink ground, No. 425-8" (ILLUS.) **$500**

C

Roseville Futura Emerald Urn Vase

Vase, 9" h., "Emerald Urn," angular handles rising from bulbous base to rim, sharply stepped neck shaded dark to light green high gloss glaze, No. 389-9", some uneven places in the glaze, unmarked (ILLUS.) **$374**

Bulbous 9" Futura Vase

Vase, 9" h., footed bulbous base w/canted sides to wide sloping shoulder w/tapering stepped cylindrical neck, angled handles from shoulder to neck, green ribbed leaf design on shaded tan to brown ground, No. 409-9" (ILLUS.)................................... **$758**

Vase, 12" h., nicknamed the "Four Ball Vase," square foot supporting four spherical half-balls below the gently flaring square body w/spearpoints at each corner, tan & green glaze, two glaze nicks professionally repaired, No. 393-12" (ILLUS., top next column)............ **$620-920**

Wall pocket, sharply tapering sides to pointed base, wide flat mouth flanked by angular rim handles, geometric design in blue, yellow, green & lavender on brown ground, black Roseville sticker, No. 1261-8", 6" w., 8 1/4" h. (ILLUS., middle next column)....................................... **$300-400**

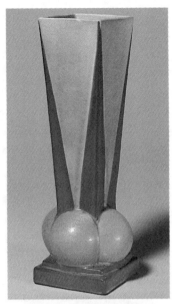

Futura "Four Ball" Vase

Colorful Futura Wall Pocket

Gardenia (1940s)
Large white gardenia blossoms and green leaves over a textured impressed band on a shaded green, grey or tan ground.

Ewer, footed tall slender ovoid body w/a very slender neck & tall upright split rim w/wide spout, handle from lower neck to shoulder, grey ground, No. 618-15", 15" h. (ILLUS. back row, second from left, with Roseville Bleeding Heart vase & other vases & bowls, bottom of page 263) **$431**

Imperial II (1924)

Varied line with no common characteristics. Many of the pieces are heavily glazed with colors that run and blend.

Deep Roseville Imperial II Bowl

Bowl, 7" d., 4 5/8" h., footed wide & deep form w/gently rounded sides, repeating design of double bars w/rounded tops, tan & brown glaze, tight line from rim, spider cracks in base, No. 202-6" (ILLUS.) **$670**

Large Roseville Imperial II Bowl

Bowl, 9" d., 5" h., wide cylindrical form w/a ringed body below a border band of repeating stylized rounded leaves, streaky brown, pale green & pink glaze, No. 206-8", small nick inside rim (ILLUS.) **$978**

Large Oval Imperial II Bowl

Bowl, 8 x 12 1/2", 5" h., oval, footed deep widely flaring sides w/bands around the lower body, streaky blue & ochre crystalline glaze, No. 207-8 x 12" (ILLUS.)........... **$403**

Rare Imperial II Trumpet-form Vase

Vase, 5 3/4" h., wide trumpet-form body, dark maroon dripping over a pale bluish green ground, No. 470-5 1/2", crazing, small rim chip (ILLUS.)........................... **$1,725**

Iris (1938)

White or yellow blossoms and green leaves on rose blending with green, light blue deepening to a darker blue or tan shading to green or brown.

Tan Iris Pattern Rose Bowl

Rose bowl, tan ground, footed squatty bulbous body tapering to a flat mouth flanked by angular shoulder handles, No. 357-4", 4" h. (ILLUS.)................................ **$104**

Ixia (1930s)

Embossed spray of tiny bell-shaped flowers and slender leaves, white blossoms on pink ground, lavender blossoms on green or yellow ground.

Console bowl, oval base band on oval body w/molded tab end handles & arched & notched rim, pink ground, No. 330-9", 9" l. (ILLUS. second row, far left, with Roseville Bleeding Heart vase & other vases & bowls, bottom of page 263)......... **$150**

Jonquil (1931)

White jonquil blossoms and green leaves in relief against textured tan ground, green lining.

C

C

Jonquil Basket with Tall Pointed Handle

Basket w/tall pointed overhead handle, bulbous body, No. 324-8", 8" h. (ILLUS.) ... **$500**

Small Roseville Jonquil Vase

Vase, 3" h., wide, low, squatty, tapering, cylindrical body w/wide flat mouth, inverted D-form loop handles from rim to edge of base, No. 523-3" (ILLUS.) **$173**

Jonquil Vase No. 526-6 1/2"

Vase, 6 1/2" h., bulbous base w/wide, slightly tapering sides to a wide flat mouth, curved handles from rim to mid-section, glaze separation on exterior base, dark spider crack on interior, light crazing, No. 526-6 1/2" (ILLUS.) **$230**

Slender Jonquil Bud Vase

Vase, bud, 7" h., swelled base & a tall slender tapering body w/a widely flaring trumpet mouth, low arched handles from edge of base to part way up the sides, small rough spot at base, crazing, No. 102-7" (ILLUS.) ... **$230**

Jonquil Vase with Turned-down Handles

Vase, 8" h., ovoid body tapering to short cylindrical neck, turned-down shoulder handles, No. 529-8" (ILLUS.) **$345**

Luffa (1934)
Relief-molded ivy leaves and blossoms on shaded brown or green wavy horizontal ridges.

Roseville Luffa 6" Jardiniere

Jardiniere, large squatty bulbous body w/a wide flat rim flanked by tiny squared shoulder handles, brown ground, No. 631-6", 6" (ILLUS.) **$138**

Luffa Lamp with Jardiniere Base

Lamp, spherical body w/a wide flat mouth flanked by small squared handles, attached copper foot & cap w/electric fitting, green ground, jardiniere conversion, No. 631-7", overall 12" h. (ILLUS.) **$288**

Magnolia (1943)
Large white blossoms with rose centers and black stems in relief against a blue, green or tan textured ground.

Basket, footed large snail-shaped body w/a long asymmetrical overhead handle, green ground, minor glaze skip, flakes on base, No. 386-12", 12" h. (ILLUS. second row, second from right, with Roseville Bleeding Heart vase & other vases & bowls, bottom of page 263) **$230**
Vase, 8" h., footed bulbous ovoid body tapering to a flat mouth flanked by long pointed handles down the sides, tan ground, No. 91-8" **$138**
Vase, 8" h., footed bulbous ovoid body tapering to a flat mouth, pointed angled shoulder handles, green ground, No. 92-8" (ILLUS. top row, far left, with Roseville Apple Blossom baskets & other baskets, book ends, jardiniere, teapot & vases, top of page 262) **$150**

Matt Green (before 1916)
Matte green glaze on smoking set, jardinieres, fern dishes, hanging baskets, planters, some smooth with no pattern, some embossed with leaves or children's faces spaced evenly around the top.

Matt Green Gate-form Double Bud Vase

Vase, double bud, 5" h., 8" w., fluted columns joined by a gate, No. 7, small glaze skp on one foot (ILLUS.) **$81**

Ming Tree (1949)
High gloss glaze in mint green, turquoise, or white is decorated with Ming branch; handles are formed from gnarled branches.

Green Ming Tree Cylindrical Vase

Vase, 6" h., cylindrical w/asymmetrical branch handles at top, green ground, No. 581-6" (ILLUS.) **$58**

Montacello (1931)
White stylized trumpet flowers with black accents on a terra cotta band, light terra cotta mottled in blue, or light green mottled and blended with blue backgrounds.

Montacello Trumpet-form Vase

Vase, 10" h., footed trumpet-form w/base handles, blue ground, minor glaze flaws, No. 565-10" (ILLUS.) **$500-550**

C

Vase, 10" h., footed trumpet-form w/base handles, terra cotta ground, No. 565-10"
.... **$1,760**

Mostique (1915)
Indian designs of stylized flowers and arrowhead leaves, slip decorated on bisque, glazed interiors. Occasional bowl glazed on outside as well.

Cylindrical Mostique Vase with Leaves

Cylindrical Mostique Vase with Swelled Rim

Vase, 9 3/4" h., cylindrical w/squatty swelled mouth, blue & grey ground, No. 21-10" (ILLUS.) **$345**

Vase, 10" h., cylindrical w/wide closed mouth, dark green incised rings around the base & light green matching rings around the top, decorated w/a dark green square enclosing a square white blossom & suspending a pale green sprig of

incised leaves, light tan ground, N0. 15-10" (ILLUS.) **$345**

Orian (1935)
Characterized by handles formed on blade-like leaves with suggestion of berries at base of handle, high-gloss glaze; blue or tan with darker drip glaze forming delicate band around rim, deep rose exterior & turquoise blue interior or in plain yellow with no over drip.

Console bowl, 8 x 12", square pedestal foot below the very long oval bowl w/fluted ends, deep rose exterior, turquoise blue interior, gold foil sticker, tiny rim & base chips, corner of base cracked, No. 275-12 x 8" (ILLUS., bottom of page)
.... **$70-100**

Orian Deep Rose Console Bowl

Orian Cylindrical Handled Rose Vase

Vase, 6" h., flared foot below a cylindrical body w/a spherical top & short cylindrical neck, long & low loop handles down the sides, glossy deep rose w/turquoise lining, slight crazing, No. 733-6" (ILLUS.)...... **$207**

Panel (Rosecraft Panel 1920)

Background colors are dark green or dark brown; decorations embossed within the recessed panels are of natural or stylized floral arrangements or female nudes.

Rare Rosecraft Panel Green Lamp Base

Lamp base, ovoid body on low foot, collared neck w/small squared handles, female nudes, green ground, No. X1, 10" h. (ILLUS.) **$1,840**

Bulbous Rosecraft Panel Vase

Vase, 8" h., wide bulbous body w/a round shoulder to the molded neck, decorated w/vines, leaves & fruit in orange on brown ground, No. 293-8" (ILLUS.)........... **$546**

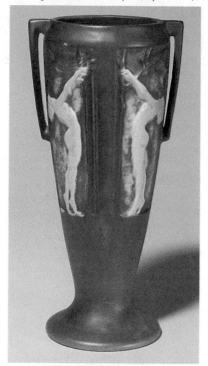

Tall Dark Green Rosecraft Panel Vase

Vase, 11" h., footed conical form w/long low angular handles from rim down sides, nude in panel, dark green ground, professional restoration to one handle, some glaze bubbling, No. 298-11" (ILLUS.) **$460**

Peony (1942)

Floral arrangement of white or dark yellow blossoms with green leaves on textured, shaded backgrounds in yellow with mixed green and brown, pink with blue, and solid green.

Teapot, cov., pink shading to green ground, No. 3 (ILLUS. third row, far right, with Roseville Bleeding Heart basket & other baskets, book ends, jardinieres & vases, bottom of page 263) **$207**

Persian (1916)

Creamware decorated by means of pouncing technique, in bright colors. Water lily and pad most common motif, although a variety of others were also used.

Colorful Small Persian Jardiniere

Jardiniere, small foot below wide rounded bottom & cylindrical sides w/a shoulder band below the wide molded mouth, vining repeated stylized lotus blossom design in yellow, tan, marron & grey w/pale green accent bands, No. 557, 5" h. (ILLUS.) **$150**

Pine Cone (1935 & 1953)

Realistic embossed brown pine cones and green pine needles on shaded blue, brown or green ground. (Pink is extremely rare.)

Blue Pine Cone Hanging Basket

Basket, hanging-type, squatty bulbous body tapering slightly toward the base, w/a short wide cylindrical neck flanked by tiny branch hanging handles, blue ground, one hanging hole w/pinhead nick, No. 352-5", 7" d., 5 1/2" h. (ILLUS.) **$250-350**

Green Pine Cone Basket

Basket, w/overhead branch handle, asymmetrical fanned & pleated body, green ground, No. 408-6", 6 1/2" h. (ILLUS.) **$230**

Book ends, open book-form w/pine sprig from top to base, green ground, minor touch-up on one corner, No. 1, pr. (ILLUS. bottom row, far left, with Roseville Bleeding Heart vase & other vases & bowls, bottom of page 263) **$316**

Small Brown Pine Cone Bowl

Bowl, 6" l., 2 3/4" h., oval boat-shape w/banded sides & angled twig handle at one end, brown ground, No. 455-6" (ILLUS.) **$259**

Bowl, 9" l., 4" h., footed oval low body w/fanned sections at each end & small twig end handles, green ground, No. 279-9" (ILLUS. bottom row, second from left, with Roseville Bleeding Heart vase & other vases & bowls, bottom of page 263) **$259**

Pine Cone Wide Round Bowl

Bowl, 11" d., 4 1/4" h., flat bottom & rounded sides w/wide flat mouth, small twig handles at rim, green ground, No. 276-9", small silver foil sticker (ILLUS.) **$104**

C

Small Green Pine Cone Candleholer

Candleholder, flat disc base supporting candle nozzle in the form of a pine cone flanked by needles on one side & branch handle on the other, green ground, partial gold foil label, No. 112-3", 3" h. (ILLUS.) ... **$115**

Brown Pine Cone Candleholders

Candleholders, flat disc base supporting candle nozzle in the form of a pine cone flanked by needles on one side & branch handle on the other, brown ground, No. 112-3", 3" h., pr. (ILLUS.)........................... **$230**

Tall Brown Roseville Pine Cone Ewer

Ewer, footed tall swelled cylindrical body w/narrow shoulder to short neck & high arched spout, long branch handle down from the shoulder, brown ground, No. 851-15", 15" h. (ILLUS.)............................ **$805**

Very Small Blue Pine Cone Jardiniere

Jardiniere, spherical w/two twig handles, blue ground, No. 632-3", 3" h. (ILLUS.) **$230**

Small Blue Pine Cone Jardiniere

Jardiniere, footed wide squatty bulbous body w/a wide flat mouth, small asymmetrical twig handles, blue ground, No. 632-4", 4" h. (ILLUS.)................................ **$316**

Large Bulbous Pine Cone Jardiniere

Jardiniere, footed bulbous spherical body w/a low wide mouth flanked by small twig handles, green ground, No. 403-10", 10" h. (ILLUS.) **$288**
Jardinieres, footed wide squatty bulbous body w/a wide flat mouth, small asymmetrical twig handles, brown ground, one w/foot flake & minor repair, No. 632-4", 4" h., pr. (ILLUS. third row, second from right, with Roseville Apple Blossom basket & other baskets, book ends, jardinere, teapot & vases, top of page 262)...... **$184**

C

Spherical Green Pine Cone Vase

Vase, 6" h., 6 1/2" d., footed spherical body w/closed rim, small branch handle at one side of rim, green ground, soft mold, No. 261-6" (ILLUS.) **$173**

Vase, 6" h., footed bulbous base w/wide cylindrical neck, handles from shoulder to midsection of neck, green ground, No. 839-6" (ILLUS. third row, third from right, with Roseville Apple Blossom basket & other baskets, book ends, jardinieres, teapot & vases, top of page 262) **$184**

Brown Pine Cone Waisted Shape Vase

Vase, 7" h., footed waisted cylindrical body tapering to slightly flaring rim, asymmetrical twig handles, brown ground, minor glaze inclusions, No. 840-7" (ILLUS.) **$219**

Vase, 7" h., footed waisted cylindrical body w/small asymmetrical twig handles, brown ground, No. 841-7" (ILLUS., top next column)... **$259**

Vase, 7" h., footed gently flaring cylindrical body w/a flaring wide rim flanked by large angular branch handles, blue ground, No. 907-7" (ILLUS., middle next column)
.... **$316**

Brown Pine Cone Vase

Handled Cylindrical Blue Pine Cone Vase

Handled Pine Cone Bud Vase

Vase, 7 1/4" h., bud-type, round foot & slender tall ovoid body w/twig handle down one side, green ground, small base chips professionally repaired, No. 841-7" (ILLUS.)... **$104**

C

Footed Cylindrical Pine Cone Vase

Vase, 7 1/2" h., footed wide cylinder w/flat rim & small asymmetrical twig handles, silver foil label, minor glaze inconsistencies, brown ground, No. 704-7" (ILLUS.) ... **$288**

Brown Footed Ovoid Pine Cone Vase

Vase, 8" h., footed ovoid body w/flat shoulder to short flaring neck, angular twig handles on shoulder, brown ground, small kiln kiss, No. 844-8" (ILLUS.) **$374**

Vase, 8" h., footed wide pillow-shape w/two notches in wide arched rim, small twig handles, brown ground, No. 845-8" (ILLUS. top row, far right, with Roseville Bleeding Heart vase & other vases & bowls, bottom of page 263) **$460**

Vase, 8" h., footed wide pillow-shape w/two notches in wide arched rim, small twig handles, blue ground, No. 845-8" (ILLUS., top next column) **$500**

Vase, 8 1/2" h., pillow-type, wide flattened bulbous body w/asymmetrical branch handles, brown ground, gold foil label, No. 114-8" (ILLUS., middle next column) **$633**

Vase, 8 1/2" h., horn-shaped w/fanned & pleated rim, pine needles & cone-form handle from base of oval foot to mid-section, brown ground, No. 490-8" (ILLUS., bottom next column) **$316**

Blue Pine Cone Pillow-shaped Vase

Brown Pine Cone Pillow-type Vase

Brown Pine Cone Horn-shaped Vase

Vase, 10 1/2" h., flaring foot beneath an expanding conical body flanked by long handles from base to mid-section in the form of pine needles & pine cone, green ground, original paper sticker, minute rim bruise, No. 747-10" (ILLUS. top row, third from left, with Roseville Bleeding Heart vase & other vases & bowls, bottom of page 263) **$288**

Blue Pine Cone 10 1/2" Vase

Vase, 10 1/2" h., flaring foot beneath an expanding conical body flanked by long handles from base to mid-section in the form of pine needles & pine cone, blue ground, No. 747-10" (ILLUS.) **$660**

Green Pine Cone Wall Shelf

Wall shelf, long pointed shelf supported by a pine sprig, green ground, No. 1-5 x 8", 8 1/4" h. (ILLUS.) **$518**

Poppy (1930s)
Shaded backgrounds of blue or pink with decoration of poppy flower and green leaves.

Vase, 6" h., footed ovoid body w/a short cylindrical neck flanked by C-scroll handles, pink ground, No. 867-6" (ILLUS. second row, second from left with other Roseville vases & bowls, bottom of page 263) **$173**

Primrose (1932)
Cluster of single blossoms on tall stems, low pad-like leaves; backgrounds are blue, tan, or pink.

Rose bowl, footed spherical body w/closed rim flanked by small pointed handles, pink ground, No. 284-4", 4" d. (ILLUS.

front row, second from right, with Roseville Bleeding Heart vase & other vases & bowls, bottom of page 263) **$104**

Vase, 6 1/2" h., gently flaring cylindrical body tapering to a short neck, long angular side handles, pink ground, No. 760-6" (ILLUS. third row, second from right, with Roseville Bleeding Heart vase & other vases & bowls, bottom of page 263) **$104**

Blue Primrose Pattern Vase

Vase, 6 1/2" h., gently flaring cylindrical body tapering to a short neck, long angular side handles, blue ground, No. 760-6" (ILLUS.) **$138**

Rozane (1900)
Dark blended backgrounds; slip decorated underglaze artware.

Tall Bulbous Rozane Ewer with Iris

Ewer, bulbous ovoid body tapering sharply to a tall slender cylindrical neck w/a tricorner rim, long C-scroll handle from rim to shoulder, shaded dark brown to green ground decorated w/a large brown & yellow iris, initialed by the artist, glaze bruise on handle, crazing, No. 905, 10 3/4" h. (ILLUS.).. **$207**

Rozane Royal Dark Mug with Plums

Mug, Royal Dark, slightly tapering cylindrical sides w/fancy C-scroll handle, dark brown ground decorated w/plums hanging from leafy branches, artist-signed by Hester Pillsbury, crazing, No. 886 (ILLUS.) **$115**

Roseville Rozane Paperweight with Pansies

Paperweight, rectangular w/rounded corners, dark brown & green ground decorated w/dark brown & yellow pansies, artist-signed by Grace Neff, some light scratching, crazing, 3 3/4 x 4", 2 1/2" h. (ILLUS.).. **$150**

Fine Rozane Vase with Lion Portrait

Vase, 9" h., 11" w., Royal Dark, pillow-type, squatty flattened body w/scroll shoulder handles continuing to form a band under the base, tapering to a flaring crimped rim, decorated w/a head portrait of a lion by artist Claude Leffler, some tiny base chips, crazing, No. 882 (ILLUS.) **$1,150**

Rozane Vase with Portrait of Spaniel

Vase, 12 3/4" h., swelled cylindrical body w/a short flaring neck, dark brown ground decorated w/the head of a brown & white spaniel, artwork by Mae Timberlake, overglazed chip on rim, two chips & hairline at base, crazing, No. 812 (ILLUS.) **$500**

Fine Rozane Vase with Roses

Vase, 20 3/4" h., tall ovoid body tapering to a short trumpet neck, h.p. w/yellow & peach roses & green leaves on a shaded greenish yellow to dark brown ground, artist-signed, crazing (ILLUS.) **$2,990**

C

C

Silhouette (1950)

Recessed area silhouettes nature study or female nudes. Colors are rose, orange, turquoise, tan and white with turquoise.

Vase, 9" h., double, base w/canted sides supporting two square vases w/sloping rims, joined by a stylized branch-form center post, florals, orange shading to green ground, No. 757-9" (ILLUS. second row, far left, with Roseville Apple Blossom basket & other baskets, book ends, jardinieres, teapot & vases, top of page 262) **$288**

Snowberry (1946)

Brown branch with small white berries and green leaves embossed over spider-web design in various background colors (blue, green and rose).

Book ends, open book-shaped, shaded blue ground, one w/some professional repair, 1BE, 5 1/4" h., pr. (ILLUS. front row, far right, with Roseville Apple Blossom basket & other baskets, book ends, jardineres, teapot & vases, top of page 262) **$150**

Squatty Rose Snowberry Candleholders

Candleholders, squatty w/angular handles at shoulder, shaded rose ground, No. 1CS1-2", 2" h., pr. (ILLUS.) **$69**

Roseville Snowberry Rose Console Set

Console set: 12" l. long low oval bowl w/gently arched sides & upright ends w/small pointed end handles & pair of No. 1CS1- 2" candleholders; shaded rose ground, No. 1BL2-12, 3 pcs. (ILLUS.) **$161**

Console set: 12" l. long low oval bowl w/gently arched sides & upright ends w/small pointed end handles & pair of No. 1CS1- 2" candleholders; shaded blue ground, No. 1BL2-12, 3 pcs. (ILLUS. of bowl, bottom row, far right, with Roseville Bleeding Heart vase & other vases & bowls, bottom of page 263) **$259**

Snowberry Green 4" Jardiniere

Jardiniere, two-handled, shaded green ground, No. 1J-4", 4" h. (ILLUS.) **$58**

Tall Rose Snowberry Vase

Vase, 12 1/2" h., conical base tapering to a tall, fanned body w/a flaring stepped rim, pointed handles at the lower body, shaded rose ground, No. 1V2-12" (ILLUS.) **$150**

Thorn Apple (1930s)

White trumpet flower with leaves reverses to thorny pod with leaves. Colors are shaded blue, brown and pink.

Pink Thorn Apple 6" Vase

Vase, 6" h., footed bulbous ovoid body w/wide cylindrical neck, small angular shoulder handles, shaded pink ground, No. 811-6" (ILLUS., previous page) **$115**

Tourmaline (1933)

Although the semi-gloss medium blue, highlighted around the rim with lighter high gloss and gold effect seems to be accepted as the standard Tourmaline glaze, the catalogue definitely shows this and two other types as well. One is a mottled overall turquoise, the other a mottled salmon that appears to be lined in the high gloss but with no overrun to the outside.

Mottled Blue Ovoid Tourmaline Vase

Turquoise Tourmaline Candlesticks

Candlesticks, flared ribbed base, flaring nozzle, mottled turquoise ground, No. 1089-4 1/2", 4 1/2" h., pr. (ILLUS.) **$100-150**

Tourmaline Bulbous Vase

Tourmaline Tan Speckled Vase

Vase, 6" h., ovoid body tapering to a cylindrical neck flanked by loop handles to the shoulder, tan ground speckled w/dark reddish brown, No. 679-6" (ILLUS.) **$81**

Vase, 6" h., ovoid body tapering to a cylindrical neck flanked by loop handles to the shoulder, mottled dark blue glaze, No. 679-6" (ILLUS., top next column) **$138**

Vase, 7" h., simple bulbous ovoid body tapering to a small flat mouth, streaky blue below cream & amber dripping from the rim, small glazed-over chip on base, No. 472-7" (ILLUS., middle next column) **$138**

Tourmaline Square Mottled Blue Vase

C

Vase, 7 1/2" h., square, tapering slightly towards base, embossed design around rim, mottled blue over tannish grey glaze, foil label on base, No. 612-7" (ILLUS., previous page) **$184**

Twisted Hexagonal Tourmaline Vase

Vase, 8" h., tall hexagonal twisted paneled shape, medium streaky blue w/ivory & amethyst drips from the rim, No. A-425-8" (ILLUS.) **$230**

Tourmaline Blue Waisted Vase

Vase, 8" h., ringed foot below the waisted cylindrical body w/a band of rings near the rim, mottled white to dark blue matte glaze, No. 613-8" (ILLUS.) **$115**

Vase, 8 1/4" h., flattened loop base handles flanking the footed bulbous lower body tapering to a tall trumpet neck, streaky medium blue w/creamy tan drips from the rim, No. A-332-8" (ILLUS., top next column) **$127**

Streaky Blue Tourmaline Vase

White Rose (1940s)
White roses and green leaves against a vertically combed ground of blended blue, brown shading to green, or pink shading to green.

White Rose Blended Blue Console Bowl

Console bowl, long low oval form w/small loop end handles, blended blue ground, No. 391-10", 10" l. (ILLUS.) **$127**

Console bowl, long low oval form w/small loop end handles, brown shading to green ground, No. 391-10", 10" l. **$100-125**

Console bowl, footed oblong paneled body w/large pointed end handles, blended blue ground, No. 393-12", 16 1/2" l. (ILLUS. second row, center, with Roseville Apple Blossom basket & other baskets, book ends, jardineres, teapot & vases, top of page 262) **$150**

Vase, 8 1/2" h., small footring below a squatty, bulbous base & tall, wide, cylindrical body w/notched flat rim, long loop handles from rim to edge of base, blended blue ground, No. 985-8" (ILLUS. top row, center, with Roseville Apple Blossom basket & other baskets, book ends, jardineres, teapot & vases, top of page 262) **$207**

Pair of Pink to Green White Rose Vases

Vases, 6" h., cylindrical w/short collared neck, angular handles at shoulder, pink shading to green ground, No. 979-6", pr. (ILLUS.).. **$207**

Wincraft (1948)

Revived shapes from older lines such as Pine Cone, Bushberry, Cremona, Primrose and others. Vases with animal motifs, contemporary shapes in high gloss of blue, tan, lime and green.

Brown Wincraft Console Set

Console set: No. 268-12" rectangular bowl w/narrow tab end handles & pair of No. 252 candleholders; brown ground, the set (ILLUS.) **$161**

Asymmetrical Blue Wincraft Vase

Vase, 6" h., asymmetrical fan shape, pine cones & needles in relief on shaded blue ground, crazing, No. 272-6" (ILLUS.) **$81**
Vase, 8" h., flowing lily form w/asymmetrical side handles, tulip & foliage in relief on glossy brown ground, No. 282-8" (ILLUS., top next column)........................... **$69**

Wincraft Lily-form Brown Vase

Zephyr Lily (1946)

Tall lilies and slender leaves adorn swirl-textured backgrounds of Bermuda Blue, Evergreen and Sienna Tan.

Zephyr Lily Terra Cotta Flowerpot

Flowerpot, terra cotta ground, water deposits in bottom, no undertray, No. 672-5", 5" h. (ILLUS.) **$81**

Royal Bayreuth

Good china in numerous patterns and designs has been made at the Royal Bayreuth factory in Tettau, Germany since 1794. Listings below are by the company's lines, plus miscellaneous pieces. Interest in this china remains at a peak and prices continue to rise. Pieces listed carry the company's blue mark except where noted otherwise.

Among the important reference books in this field are Royal Bayreuth - A Collectors' Guide *and*

Royal Bayreuth - A Collectors' Guide - Book II *by Mary McCaslin (see Special Contributors list).*

Royal Bayreuth Mark

Corinthian

Cake plate, classical figures on black ground, 10" d................................ $100-175

Creamer & cov. sugar bowl, classical figures on black ground, pr. $100-125

Corinthian Pitcher

Pitcher, tankard, 6 7/8" h., 3 3/4" d., orange inside top, classical figures on black satin ground, gold bands w/black & white geometric design around neck & base (ILLUS.) $175-200

Planter, classical figures on red ground $120-140

Devil & Cards

Ashtray $175-200

Ashtray w/match holder $275-300

Creamer, figural red devil, 4 1/2" h.......... $400-650

Mug, 4 3/4" h. $450-600

Salt dip, master size $300-400

Stamp box, cov., 3 1/2" l........................ $700-900

Sugar bowl, open, short $400-550

Mother-of-Pearl

Ashtray, Spiky Shell patt........................... $60-75

Bowl, 5 1/2" d., grape cluster mold, pearlized white finish................................... $100-125

Bowl, 10" oval, handled, figural poppy mold, apricot satin finish $500-600

Compote, open, 4 1/2" d., 4 1/2" h., reticulated bowl & base, decorated w/delicate roses, pearlized finish $100-150

Creamer, grape cluster mold, pearlized white, 3 3/4" h. $125-175

Creamer & cov. sugar bowl, grape cluster mold, pearlized yellow, colorful foliage, pr.. $250-350

Cup & saucer, demitasse, Oyster & Pearl mold $200-350

Hatpin holder, white pearlized finish $125-175

Mustard jar, cov., Spiky Shell patt., white pearlized finish, 3 1/2" h...................... $125-225

Nappy, handled, figural poppy mold, pearlized satin finish $150-200

Sugar bowl, cov., footed, figural Spiky Shell patt., pearlized finish, 3 1/2" h............ $200-250

Toothpick holder, Spiky Shell patt., pearlized finish $125-175

Rose Tapestry

Basket, rope handle, base & outer rim, three color roses, 4 1/4" w., 4" h. $200-300

Basket, three-color roses, 4 3/4 x 5 1/4" $300-400

Bell, gold loop handle, three-color roses, 3 1/4" h.. $300-400

Bowl, 10 1/2" d., shell- & scroll-molded rim, three-color roses $800-1,000

Box, cov., two-color roses, 1 1/2 x 2 1/2" $150-175

Box, w/domed cover, three-color roses, 4 1/2" d., 2 3/4" h. $350-400

Cake plate, three-color roses, freeform fancy rim w/gold beading, 9 1/2" w. $350-400

Candy dish, three-color roses, 8" oval ... $200-300

Chocolate pot, cov., apricot, white, pink & yellow roses, leaf finial, gold trim, 8 1/2" h....................................... $1,400-1,800

Clock, table-model, three-color roses, upright rectangular case w/a flaring base & domed top $800-1,000

Creamer, ovoid body w/flared base & long pinched spout, three-color roses, 3 1/2" h.. $150-200

Creamer, corset-shaped, three-color roses, 3 3/4" h.. $150-250

Creamer, pinched spout, two-color roses $200-350

Creamer & cov. sugar bowl, pink & white roses, pr. $500-600

Dessert set: large cake plate & six matching small serving plates; three-color roses, 7 pcs.. $800-1,000

Dish, handled, clover-shaped, decorated w/yellow roses, 5" w. $150-200

Flowerpot & underplate, three-color roses, 3 x 4", 2 pcs. $250-300

Hatpin holder, small red roses at top & base, large yellow roses on body, reticulated base, gold trim, 4 1/2" h. $450-500

Match holder, hanging-type, three-color roses $400-450

Model of a shoe, decorated w/pink roses & original shoe lace $400-500

Nappy, tri-lobed leaf shape, decorated w/orange roses, 4 1/2" l. $100-150

Pitcher, 5 3/4" h., waisted shape, C-scroll handle angled at bottom, three-color roses **$300-400**
Plate, 6" d. **$150-200**
Plate, 7" d., three-color roses **$200-250**
Powder box, cov., footed, three-color roses, 4" d., 2 1/2" h. **$300-400**
Relish dish, open-handled, three-color roses, 4 x 8" **$300-350**
Salt dip, ruffled rim, 3" d. **$150-250**
Salt shaker, pink roses **$200-250**
Tray, rectangular, with short rim, three-color roses, 11 1/2 x 8" **$450-600**
Vase, 4 1/2" h., ovoid body decorated w/clusters of small red roses at top & base, large yellow roses in center, short neck flaring slightly at rim **$200-250**
Vase, 6 1/2" h., decorated w/roses & shadow ferns **$350-450**
Wall pocket, three-color roses, 5 x 9" **$1,000-1,200**

Sunbonnet Babies

Ashtray, babies cleaning **$200-250**
Candlestick, babies washing, 5" d., 1 3/4" h. **$250-300**
Creamer, babies ironing, 3" h. **$250-300**
Creamer & open sugar bowl, boat-shaped, babies fishing on sugar, babies cleaning on creamer, pr. **$400-500**
Cup & saucer, babies washing **$200-250**
Tea set, child's **$750-900**

Tomato Items

Tomato bowls, 5 3/4" d., set of 4 .... **$100-150**
Tomato creamer, cov., small **$50-75**

Tomato Creamer & Sugar Bowl

Tomato creamer & cov. sugar bowl, creamer 3" d., 3" h., sugar bowl 3 1/2" d., 4" h., pr. (ILLUS.) **$75-100**
Tomato plate, 4 1/4" d., ring-handled, figural lettuce leaf **$20-35**
Tomato plate, 7" d., ring-handled, figural lettuce leaf w/molded yellow flowers **$30-45**
Tomato tea set: cov. teapot, creamer & cov. sugar bowl; 3 pcs. **$250-350**

Miscellaneous

Ashtray, figural elk **$200-250**
Ashtray, figural shell, 4 1/2 x 4 1/2" **$50-75**
Ashtray, scenic decoration of Dutch woman w/basket, 5 1/2" d. **$50-75**
Ashtray, stork decoration, artist-signed, 4 1/2" l. **$75-100**
Basket, miniature, scene w/cows, unmarked **$50-75**

Basket, "tapestry," footed, bulbous body w/a ruffled rim & ornate gold-trimmed overhead handle, portrait of woman w/horse, 5" h. **$500-600**
Basket, w/reticulated handles, decorated w/white roses, 7 3/4" l., 3 1/2" h. **$100-150**
Bell, nursery rhyme decoration w/Little Bo Peep **$300-400**
Bell, scene of musicians, men playing a cello & mandolin **$250-300**
Bell, peacock decoration, 2 1/2" d., 3" h. **$300-350**

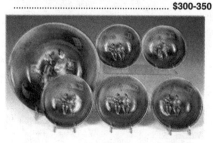

Royal Bayreuth Musicians Berry Set

Berry set: 9 3/4" d. bowl & five 5" d. sauce dishes; Peasant Musicians decoration, 6 pcs. (ILLUS.) **$350-450**
Berry set: 9 1/2" d. bowl & six 5" d. sauce dishes; portrait decoration, 7 pcs. **$650-750**
Bowl, 9 1/2" l., 3 3/4" h., raised enameled white roses & foliage on creamy ivory ground, flared, gently ruffled rim, four gold-trimmed reticulated reserves, four short gold feet **$250-350**
Bowl, 6 7/8" d., 2 1/2" h., footed, shallow slightly scalloped sides, Cavalier Musicians decoration, gold trim on feet **$75-150**
Bowl, 9 1/2" d., figural poppy **$135**
Bowl, 10" d., decorated w/pink roses **$125-150**
Bowl, 10 1/2" d., floral decoration, blown-out mold **$250-300**
Box, cov., shell-shaped, nursery rhyme scene, Little Boy Blue decoration **$200-225**

Royal Bayreuth Box with Arab Scene

Box, cov., square, desert scene decoration on cover, Arabs w/camels on background colors of pink & brown, unmarked, 2 x 2 1/2", 1 3/4" h. (ILLUS.) **$50-75**
Box, cov., scene of woman on horse, woman & man w/rake watching, 4 1/4" d., 2 1/4" h. **$150-200**

C

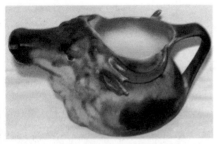

Water Buffalo Creamer

Creamer, figural water buffalo, black & white (ILLUS.) **$125-200**
Creamer, figural water buffalo, souvenir of Portland, Oregon................................. **$150-250**
Creamer, flow blue, Babes in Woods decoration **$200-250**
Creamer, left-handled, scene of two girls under umbrella, 3 1/2" h. **$300-400**
Creamer, miniature, "tapestry" scene of girl & horse.. **$200-250**
Creamer, pasture scene w/cows & trees, 3 1/4" h. **$50-100**
Creamer, pinched spout, "tapestry," goats decoration, 4" h. **$300-350**
Creamer, scene of girl w/basket, salmon color **$500-700**
Creamer & cov. sugar bowl, figural apple, pr. **$250-350**
Creamer & cov. sugar bowl, figural grape cluster, purple, pr. **$150-250**
Creamer & cov. sugar bowl, figural pansy, lavender, pr. **$300-400**
Creamer & cov. sugar bowl, figural poppy, pr. **$300-350**
Creamer & cov. sugar bowl, figural rooster, pr. **$300-350**
Creamer & cov. sugar bowl, figural strawberry, unmarked, pr. **$400-450**
Creamer & open sugar bowl, each decorated w/a mountain landscape w/a boy & donkey, 3" h., pr. **$200-350**
Creamer & open sugar bowl, figural strawberry, unmarked, pr. **$400-600**
Cup & saucer, figural rose...................... **$150-200**
Cup & saucer, scene of man w/turkeys.... **$75-125**
Cup & saucer, demitasse, Castle scene decoration, artist-signed...................... **$110-150**
Cup & saucer, demitasse, figural orange **$100-150**
Dish, leaf-shaped, "tapestry," scenic Lady & Prince decoration **$100-150**
Dresser tray, rectangular w/rounded corners, scene of boy & three donkeys in landscape, 8 x 11" (ILLUS., top next column) **$150-250**
Dresser tray, decorated w/hunting scene **$200-250**
Ewer, scene of hunter w/dog, 4 1/2" h..... **$150-200**
Ewer, cobalt blue, Babes in Woods decoration, 6" h. **$500-650**
Gravy boat w/attached liner, decorated w/multicolored floral sprays, gadrooned border, gold trim, cream ground.............. **$50-75**

Boy & Donkeys Dresser Tray

Hair receiver, cov., "tapestry," scene of farmer w/turkeys **$200-300**

Royal Bayreuth "Tapestry" Hair Receiver

Hair receiver, cov., "tapestry," small gold scroll feet & low squatty rounded body w/a fitted low cover w/a small ruffled center opening, decorated w/a scene of swans on a lake, 4" d. (ILLUS.).......... **$200-300**
Hair receiver, cov., decorated w/a scene of a Dutch boy & girl, 3 1/4" h. **$100-150**

Penguin Hatpin Holder

Hatpin holder, model of a penguin, in red, white & grey, signed (ILLUS.) **$600-800**
Hatpin holder, hexagonal shape, decorated w/pink & white roses, green leaves & gold trim on rim, satin finish **$300-350**
Humidor, cov., figural gorilla, black **$1,750**
Humidor, cov., purple & lavender floral decoration **$325**

C

Royal Bayreuth Vase, Shoe & Sprinkling Can

Match holder, hanging-type, figural shell
.... $250-350
Match holder, hanging-type, scene of Arab
on horseback....................................... $250-350
Match holder, hanging-type, stork decoration on yellow ground $300-350

Pin tray, triangular, "tapestry" portrait decoration of woman wearing large purple
plumed hat, 5 x 5 x 5" $200-250
Pincushion, figural elk head.................. $300-350
Pipe holder, figural bassett hound, black
.... $350-500

Royal Bayreuth Match Striker

Match holder w/striker, bulbous shape,
decorated water scene w/brown "Shadow Trees" & boats on orange & gold
ground, unmarked, 3 1/4" d., 2 1/2" h.
(ILLUS.)... $100-150
Model of a man's high top slipper $300-350
Model of woman's shoe, old fashioned
high-button shoe in silver tapestry de-
sign, 5" l., 3 1/2" h. (ILLUS. center w/tap-
estry vase with lady & sprinkling can, top
of page) $2,000-2,500
Mug, figural clown $400-500
Mug, candle lady decoration, 5" h. $250-350
Mustard jar, cov., figural lobster $150-250
Mustard jar, cov., figural shell................ $100-160
Mustard jar, cov., figural pansy, 3 1/4" h.
.... $300-600
Mustard jar, cover & spoon, figural poppy,
red, green spoon, 3 pcs. $200-300
Nappy, handled, figural poppy $100-150
Nut set: large pedestal-based open com-
pote & six matching servers; each deco-
rated w/a colorful pastoral scene w/ani-
mals, 7 pcs. $400-450
Pin dish, decorated w/Arab scene $75-100

Royal Bayreuth Water Pitcher

Pitcher, water, bulbous body w/scene of
fisherman standing in boat against wooded backdrop, flaring neck & spout, ap-
plied handle (ILLUS.) $400-500

Royal Bayreuth Tapestry Water Pitcher

Pitcher, water, jug-type body w/applied
handle, set-in spout, portrait "tapestry"
decoration of 18th c. lady in plumed hat
(ILLUS.)... $750-900

C

Pitcher, milk, 5 1/4" h., figural elk............ **$200-300**
Pitcher, milk, 5 1/2" h., figural lamplighter,
green... **$350-450**
Pitcher, water, tankard, 9 1/2" h., h.p. pas-
toral cow scene **$200-300**

Royal Bayreuth Figural Apple Pitcher

Pitcher, water, 6" h., figural apple (ILLUS.)
.... **$500-700**
Pitcher, water, 6" h., figural pelican **$500-700**
Pitcher, water, 6" h., figural Santa Claus,
red... **$6,000-8,000**
Pitcher, water, 6 1/2" h., figural strawberry
.... **$800-1,000**
Pitcher, water, 6 3/4" h., figural lobster... **$350-450**
Pitcher, water, 7" h., figural duck **$800-1,000**

Royal Bayreuth Elk Water Pitcher

Pitcher, water, 7" h., figural elk (ILLUS.)
.... **$500-700**
Pitcher, water, 7" h., figural seal **$3,600-4,000**
Pitcher, water, 7 1/4" h., pinched spout,
scenic decoration of cows in pasture
.... **$250-300**
Pitcher, water, 7 3/4" h., 6" d., figural lob-
ster, red shaded to orange w/green han-
dle **$400-550**
Pitcher, sheep scene **$125-175**
Plaque, decorated w/scene of Arab on
horse, 9 1/2" d.................................... **$100-150**

Plate, 5 1/4" d., leaf-shaped, decorated
w/small yellow flowers on green ground,
green curved handle **$25-50**
Plate, 6" d., handled, figural leaf & flower . **$60-100**
Plate, 7 1/2" d., nursery rhyme scene w/Lit-
tle Bo Peep **$100-150**
Plate, 8" d., decorated w/pink & yellow flow-
ers, gold rim, pink ground, blue mark...... **$50-75**
Plate, 8" d., scene of man hunting **$75-150**
Plate, 8 1/2" d., scene of man fishing........ **$75-150**
Plate, 8 1/2" d., scene of man hunting **$75-150**
Plate, 9" d., candle girl decoration.......... **$125-185**
Plate, 9" d., Cavalier Musicians scene.... **$225-275**
Plate, 9" d., figural ear of corn................ **$450-500**
Plate, 9" d., scene of man smoking pipe . **$150-200**
Plate, 9 1/2" d., scroll-molded rim, "tapes-
try," toasting Cavalier scene **$700-825**
Playing card box, cov., decorated w/a sail-
ing ship scene **$150-250**
Powder box, cov., round, "tapestry," scenic
Lady & Prince decoration.................... **$150-200**
Relish   dish,   figural   cucumber,
5 1/4 x 12 1/2"..................................... **$100-250**
Salt & pepper shakers, figural conch shell,
unmarked, pr... **$75-125**
Salt & pepper shakers, figural poppy, red,
pr... **$250-400**
Salt shaker, figural elk **$135**
Sprinkling can, miniature size, "tapestry,"
decoration of woman & pony, 2 3/4" h.
(ILLUS. right w/tapestry vase with lady &
shoe, top of page 289) **$500-700**
Stamp box, cov., "tapestry," Cottage by
Water Fall scene **$150-250**
String holder, hanging-type, figural rooster
head **$350-550**
Sugar bowl, cov., Brittany Girl decoration
.... **$50-125**
Sugar bowl, cov., figural lemon **$100-150**
Sugar bowl, cov., figural poppy, red....... **$150-250**
Sugar bowl, cov., figural shell w/lobster
handle **$125-225**
Tea set: child's, cov. teapot, cov. sugar,
creamer, two plates, & two cups & sau-
cers; ovoid bodies, each piece decorat-
ed w/a scene of children playing, the set
(ILLUS., top next page) **$700-800**
Tea strainer, figural red poppy, 5 3/4" l. . **$200-300**
Teapot, cov., child's, boy & donkey decora-
tion, green, unmarked, 4" h................ **$150-250**
Teapot, cov., figural orange, 6 1/2" h. **$350-450**
Toothpick holder, Bird of Paradise decora-
tion **$200-250**
Toothpick holder, figural bell ringer,
3 1/2" h.. **$200-250**
Toothpick holder, figural Murex Shell.......... **$175**
Toothpick holder, man hunting turkeys
scene **$150-250**
Toothpick holder, round, one side handle,
decorated w/scene of man tending tur-
keys.. **$200-300**
Toothpick holder, "tapestry," scene of
woman w/pony & trees, 2 2/5" h. **$400-550**
Toothpick holder, three-handled, floral
decoration, 2 1/4" h............................ **$150-225**
Toothpick holder, three-handled, harvest
scene decoration................................. **$150-200**

Royal Bayreuth Child's Tea Set

Toothpick holder, three-handled, hunt scene decoration, 3" h. **$200-275**
Toothpick holder, three-handled, scene of horse & wagon **$125-200**
Toothpick holder, three-handled, three feet, nursery rhyme decoration w/Little Boy Blue... **$200-250**
Toothpick holder, two-handled, four-footed, scene of horsemen, unmarked........ **$75-150**
Tray, club-shaped, scene of hunter w/dog **$100-175**

Tray with Girl & Geese Scene

Tray, decorated w/scene of girl w/geese, molded rim w/gold trim, 9 x 12 1/4" (ILLUS.)... **$350-500**
Tray, "tapestry," scene of train on bridge over raging river, 7 3/4 x 11" **$600-800**
Vase, 2 3/4" h., conical body on three tab feet, tapering to a short flaring neck, small knob handles at shoulders, decorated w/a scene of cows...................... **$100-150**
Vase, 3" h., scene of children w/St. Bernard dog **$50-125**
Vase, 3" h., 3 1/2" d., spherical body w/two flaring spouts at the top centered by a small loop handle, Cavalier Musicians decoration (ILLUS., top next column).... **$50-125**
Vase, 3 1/2" h., spherical shape w/small gold rim opening, w/scenic "tapestry" decoration of woman in garden (ILLUS. left w/shoe & sprinkling can, top of page 289).. **$500-650**
Vase, 3 5/8" h., footed conical body tapering to a swelled neck flanked by four loop handles, decorated w/hunting scene, man & woman on horses, unmarked **$50-100**

Miniature Royal Bayreuth Spouted Vase

Vase, 4" h., two-handled, decorated w/long-tailed Bird of Paradise......................... **$250-375**
Vase, 4 1/2" h., sailing scene decoration **$100-150**
Vase, 4 1/2" h., "tapestry," courting couple decoration **$450-550**
Vase, bud, 4 1/2" h., two handles, Babes in Wood scene, cobalt blue & white........ **$200-325**
Vase, 4 3/4" h., handled, Babes in Woods decoration, girl holding doll **$450-550**
Vase, bud, 4 3/4" h., "tapestry," rounded body w/a thin tall neck, Lady & Prince scenic decoration **$100-150**
Vase, 5" h., "tapestry," bulbous ovoid body tapering to a short slender flaring neck, "Castle by the Lake" landscape scene **$250-350**
Vase, 5" h., "tapestry," bulbous ovoid body tapering to a short slender flaring neck, cottage by a waterfall landscape......... **$250-300**
Vase, 5" h., "tapestry," decoration of cockfight against scenic ground **$150-200**
Vase, 5 1/4" h., ovoid body w/short cylindrical neck, medallion portrait framed w/gold band in incised leaf design w/enamel trim...................................... **$200-250**
Vase, 5 1/2" h., decorated w/brown & white bust portrait of woman on dark green ground, artist-signed **$400-475**
Vase, 5 1/2" h., teardrop-shaped, colorful floral decoration **$125**
Vase, 6" h., "tapestry," decorated w/a scene of an elk & three hounds in a river **$400-475**

C

Vase, 7" h., decorated w/Arab scene **$100-150**
Vase, 7" h., decorated w/portrait of a woman **$200-350**
Vase, 7 3/4" h., mercury & floral finish, ca. 1919, artist-signed & signed "Kgl. Priv. Tettau" **$200-275**
Vase, 8" h., bulbous body on short quatrefoil foot, side C-scroll handles w/decorative ends, short reticulated neck w/flaring rim, decorated w/waterfall scene **$200-300**
Vase, 8" h., decorated w/scene of hunter & dogs **$150-250**
Vase, 9" h., tall, slender, waisted, cylindrical body w/a gently scalloped flaring rim, three long green scroll & bead loop handles down the sides, the top body w/a band decorated w/a toasting Cavaliers scene in color on one side & "Ye Old Bell" scene on the other, the lower body all in dark green, ca. 1902 .... **$200-325**

Ornate Handled Vase with Peacock

Vase, 9 1/2" h., peacock decoration, openwork on neck & at base, ornate scroll handles, lavish gold trim (ILLUS.) **$600-725**
Vase, double-bud, ovoid body w/two angled short flaring necks joined by a small handle, scene of Dutch children **$100-150**
Vases, 2 1/2" h., decorated w/sunset scene of a ship, pr. **$100-150**

Small Royal Bayreuth Vases

Vases, 3 1/8" h., 2 5/8" d., squatty bulbous lower body below the tall tapering sides ending in a ringed neck & flanked by loop handles, one w/scene of Dutch boy & girl playing w/brown dog & the other w/scene of Dutch boy & girl playing w/white & brown dog, green mark, pr. (ILLUS.) **$50-150**
Wall pocket, figural grape cluster, yellow **$250-300**
Wall pocket, figural red poppy, 9 1/2" l... **$600-700**

Royal Vienna

The second factory in Europe to make hard paste porcelain was established in Vienna in 1719 by Claud Innocentius de Paquier. The factory underwent various changes of administration through the years and finally closed in 1865. Since then, however, the porcelain has been reproduced by various factories in Austria and Germany, many of which have also reproduced the early beehive mark. Early pieces, naturally, bring far higher prices than the later ones or the reproductions.

Royal Vienna Mark

Vienna Style Charger with Romantic Scene

Charger, round, h.p. w/a romantic mythological scene of a pretty maiden seated on a garden bench beside a fountain & playfully scolding Cupid who has broken his bow, an orb at her feet, artist-signed, within a pink velvet & giltwood frame, early 20th c., 11" d. (ILLUS.) **$2,400**

Vienna Vase with Allegorical Love Scene

Vase, 10" h., tapering cylindrical body w/an angled shoulder to the small flaring neck, iridescent lavender ground w/a tall oval reserve decorated w/an allegorical scene of Love, a winged Cupid arranging roses in the dark hair of a standing classical young woman in a garden setting, the sides & shoulder ornately decorated w/delicate beaded gold trellis & leafy scroll designs, blue Beehive mark, artist-signed, titled on the bottom, late 19th - early 20th c. (ILLUS.) **$2,640**

Vienna Vase with Classical Figure

Vase, 15" h., small domed foot & tall ovoid body tapering to a tall trumpet neck, iridescent amethyst ground decorated on one side w/a large oval reserve h.p. w/a scene of a classical maiden seated in a wooded landscape, a book in her lap, gold border trimmed w/raised gilt bouquets & C-scrolls, the back w/an oval re-

serve of white 'jeweled' radiating foliate design among trellis & leaves within gilt rims, blue Beehive mark, artist-signed, late 19th - early 20th c. (ILLUS.) **$2,880**

Large Royal Vienna Portrait Vase

Vase, 22" h., a low cylindrical base attached to a short ringed pedestal supporting the wide bulbous urn-form body w/a short rolled neck flanked by bold leafy scroll handles from the rim to the side of the body, burgundy ground w/the body centered w/a large reserve h.p. w/a shoulder-length portrait of an auburn haired beauty within a raised gilt floral border, edged by trellis & foliate scrolls, the back in gilt w/a trellis arabesque design, the base h.p. w/gold rectangular panels flanked by gold leafy scrolls, delicate gold lacy bands around the shoulder & neck, blue Beehive mark, artist-signed, ca. 1880 (ILLUS.)... **$8,400**

Napoleon & Josephine Vienna Vases

Vases, 7 5/8" h., tall slightly tapering squared body w/a rounded shoulder & short cylindrical neck w/rolled rim, short gold scroll handles from rim to shoul-

C

der, ruby ground, each centered by an oval reserve h.p. w/a color bust portrait of Napoleon or Josephine, each within a raised gold border below a trellis & diaper cartouche, the back decorated w/an octagonal turquoise 'jeweled' panel of scrolling leaves above ribbon-tied floral garlands, red Beehive mark, early 20th c., pr. (ILLUS.) **$3,360**

Vases, cov., 13 3/4" h., a stepped molded high square plinth base attached to a slender tapering pedestal supporting a flaring urn-form body w/an angled shoulder & short flaring neck flanked by angular long gold handles, a tapering pointed cover w/pointed gold finial, ruby & gold ground, the body h.p. w/a continuous scene of youths drinking, eating, playing cards & singing reserved on a richly gilt-seeded ground, ornate leaf & scroll decoration on the lower body, neck, cover & plinth base, gilt & blue border bands, blue Beehive mark, titled in German under the base, late 19th c., pr. **$5,040**

One of Two Very Ornate Vienna Vases

Vases, cov., 45" h., the high octagonal base w/a flaring foot supporting a large bulbous ovoid body on a ringed pedestal, the tapering neck flanked by ornate arched & looping gold dragon handles, the domed cover w/two figures, a man & a woman dressed as Classical warriors, the main body of each painted on each side w/colorful scenes of Achilles, Diana, Hector or Thetis, the body & base in deep maroon trimmed w/elaborate gilt scrolls & leaf designs & bands of white & gold bands, the pedestal base decorated w/four panels showing Classical scenes in color alternating of maroon panels w/elaborate gilt scrolling, late 19th c., blue shield marks, one handle possibly reattached, the other w/minor professional repairs, pr. (ILLUS. of one)............... **$43,475**

Royal Worcester

This porcelain has been made by the Royal Worcester Porcelain Co. at Worcester, England, from 1862 to the present. Royal Worcester is distinguished from wares made at Worcester between 1751 and 1862, which are referred to only as Worcester by collectors.

Royal Worcester Marks

Pierced Royal Worcester Charger

Charger, round, in the Persian taste, ivory ground, the center pierced w/a quatrefoil panel decorated in three-tone gold w/scrolling vines & enameled flower blossoms in coral, white & turquoise, a matching pierced border band, puce printed crowned mark, date cypher for 1880, 11 1/4" d. (ILLUS.) **$1,200**

Set of 12 Demitasse Cups & Saucers

C

Set of Castle Scene Royal Worcester Plates

Demitasse cups & saucers, cobalt blue ground, each printed & enriched around the rim w/a flowering rinceau vine above a stepped geometric gilt band, the interiors & wells decorated in gilt, puce printed monogram mark, date cyphers for 1903, original box, set of 12 (ILLUS., previous page) **$1,800**

Lovely Figure of the Goddess Diana

Figure of Diana, titled "The Bather Surprised," the standing semi-draped goddess w/three-tone metallic robe resting on a tree stump, raised on a canted rectangular gold base, gilt crowned monogram mark, date cypher for 1919, 23 1/8" h. (ILLUS.) **$1,920**

Plates, 10 1/2" d., each h.p. with a detailed landscape w/a castle in the distance, shaped gold rim band, puce printed crowned monogram mark, date cypher for 1930, set of 12 (ILLUS., top of page) **$5,400**

Royal Worcester Commemorative Plates

Plates, 10 5/8" d., commemorative, yellow ground ornately decorated w/delicate gilt scrollwork issuing flaming torches, the center h.p. in color w/a tight floral bouquet, the back w/a presentation inscription dated 1927, gilt printed crowned marks, set of 12 (ILLUS.) **$2,400**

Lovely Decorated Royal Worcester Plates

C

Plates, 10 5/8" d., ruby & ivory ground, the wide border decorated w/ornate gilt scrollwork issuing flaming torches, the further ornate gold on the ivory band surrounding the central reserve of a tight bouquet of colorful flowers, puce printed crowned monogram mark, date cypher for 1909 (ILLUS., previous page) **$1,440**

Rare Reticulated Royal Worcester Vase

Vase, 4 3/8" h., a small lobed & flaring gilt-trimmed foot below the spherical reticulated yellow ground body w/a creamy shoulder decorated w/delicate gilt scrolls & four small gilt lug handles, a short flaring ringed & reticulated neck, attributed to George Owen, puce printed crowned monogram mark, ca. 1891 (ILLUS.)........ **$9,600**

Grainger's Worcester Pate-Sur-Pate Vase

Vase, 8 1/2" h., pate-sur-pate, footed tapering ovoid body w/a wide cupped rim, double loop vine handles down the neck, blue ground finely h.p. in white slip & hand-tooled w/a blossoming branch of cinquefoil blossoms & leaves, the back w/an insect in flight, Royal China Works mark of Grainger's Worcester, date letter for 1893 (ILLUS.).................................... **$2,400**

Scarce Royal Worcester Sabrina Ware Vase

Vase, 9 3/4" h., Sabrina Ware, tall ovoid body w/a short flared neck, decorated in dark blue & white w/a landscape w/white cranes wading in a marsh w/large trees in the distance, marked "Royal Worcester England - Sabrina Ware - 2472" (ILLUS.) .. **$805**

Elaborate Persian Style Tall Vase

Vase, cov., 21 3/4" h., in the Persian taste, ivory ground, a square foot w/angled corners supports the bell-form stem & tall ovoid body tapering to a ringed cylindrical neck w/flaring rim topped by a domed & pierced cover w/a pierced ball-form finial, the front & back of the body w/quatrefoil panels h.p. w/large chrysanthemums in shades red & green trimmed in gold, joined at the sides by rosettes & acanthus leaf panels among delicate elaborate leafy scrolls, the lower body & socle base w/conforming beaded strapwork lappets, iron-red crowned monogram mark, mark of retailer Davis Collamore & Co., New York City, ca. 1880 (ILLUS.) ... **$4,800**

Rozart Letter Holders

C

Rozart Pottery

George and Rose Rydings were aspiring Kansas City, Missouri potters who, in the late 1960s, began to produce a line of fine underglaze pottery. An inheritance of vintage American-made artware gave the Rydings inspiration to re-create old ceramic masters' techniques. Some design influence also came from Fred Radford, grandson of well-known Ohio artist Albert Radford (ca. 1890s-1904). Experimenting with Radford's formula for Jasperware and sharing ideas with Fred about glazing techniques and ceramic chemistry led the Rydings to a look reminiscent of the ware made by turn-of-the-century American art pottery masters such as Weller and Rookwood. The result of their work became Rozart, the name of the Rydings' pottery.

Many lines have been created since Rozart's beginning. Twainware, Sylvan, Cameoware, Rozart Royal, Rusticware, Deko, Krakatoa, Koma and Sateen are a few. It is rare to find a piece of Rozart that is not marked in some way. The earliest mark is "Rozart" at the top of a circle with "Handmade" in the center and "K.C.M.O." (Kansas City, Missouri) at the bottom. Other marks followed over the years, including a seal that was used extensively. Along with artist initials, collectors will find a date code (either two digits representing the year or a month separated by a slash followed by a two-digit year). George signs his pieces "GMR," "GR," or "RG" (with a backwards "R"). Working on Twainware, Jasperware and Cameoware in the early years, George has many wheel-thrown pieces to his credit. Rose, who is very knowledgeable about Native Americans, does scenics and portraits. Her mark is either "RR" or "Rydings." Four of the seven Rydings children have worked in the pottery as well. Anne Rydings White (mark is "Anne" or "AR" or "ARW") designed and executed many original pieces in addition to her work on the original Twainware line. Susan Rydings Ubert (mark is "S" over "R") has specialized in Sylvan pieces and is an accomplished sculptor and mold maker. Susan's daughter Maureen does female figures in the Art Deco style. Becky (mark is "B" over "R"), now a commercial artist, designed lines such as Fleamarket, Nature's Jewels, and Animals. Cindy Rydings Cushing (mark is "C" over "R" or "CRC") developed the very popular Kittypots line. Mark Rydings is the Rozart mold maker. The Rozart Pottery is still active today. Pottery enthusiasts are taking notice of the family history, high quality and reminiscent beauty of Rozart. Its affordability may soon cease as Rozart's popularity and recognition are on the rise.

Letter holders, rectangular, w/various designs painted on front, limited edition, 4 1/2" h., 6 1/2" l., each (ILLUS. of three, top of page) **$75**

Rozart Duck

Model of duck, on base (ILLUS.) **$82**

Rozart Advertising Mug

Mug, advertising Gatsby Days Excelsior Springs, Missouri, May 1998, w/picture of woman in old-fashioned picture hat on front, 3 1/2" h. (ILLUS., previous page)........ **$56**

C

Rozart Pottery Dealer Sign

Sign, for Rozart Pottery dealer, "Rozart Pottery" in script, w/base, Copperverde glaze, 5 1/2" l. (ILLUS.) **$125**

Rozart Floral-decorated Teapot

Teapot, cov., two-cup size, hi-glaze, shaded grey ground h.p. w/large white & pink blossoms & dark green leaves, late 1960s+ (ILLUS.).. **$175**

Rozart Kittypot Vase

Vase, 4 1/2" h., Kittypot, black & white cat on front, Cindy Cushing (ILLUS.) **$88**

Rozart Indian Portrait Vase

Vase, 14 1/2" h., w/Indian portrait on front, Becky White (ILLUS.)................................ **$290**

Russel Wright Designs

The innovative dinnerware designed by Russel Wright and produced by various companies beginning in the late 1930s was an immediate success with a society that was turning to a more casual and informal lifestyle. His designs, with their flowing lines and unconventional shapes, were produced in many different colors, which allowed a hostess to arrange creative tables.

Although not antique, these designs, which we list here by line and manufacturer, are highly collectible. In addition to dinnerwares, Wright was also known as a trendsetter in the design of furniture, glassware, lamps, fabric and a multitude of other household goods.

Russel Wright Marks

American Modern (Steubenville Pottery Co.)

Baker, glacier blue, small................................. **$55**
Bowl, child's, black chutney **$100**
Bowl, fruit, lug handle, cedar green **$30**

Group of American Modern Pieces

Bowl, fruit, lug handle, chartreuse (ILLUS. left) $20
Bowl, salad, cedar green $100
Bowl, soup, lug handle, bean brown $35
Butter dish, cov., white................................. $365
Carafe, granite grey (no stopper) $200
Carafe w/stopper, bean brown....................... $500
Coaster, granite grey $20
Coffee cup cover, black chutney.................. $175
Coffeepot, cov., after dinner, chartreuse $120
Coffeepot, cov., after dinner, coral $120
Coffeepot, cov., black chutney $250
Coffeepot, cov., cedar green $275
Creamer, cedar green $30
Cup & saucer, coffee, cantaloupe $40
Cup & saucer, demitasse, cantaloupe............ $60
Cup & saucer, demitasse, chartreuse $30
Gravy boat, chartreuse $20
Gravy liner/pickle dish, white $45
Hostess plate & cup, cedar green, pr. $90
Ice box jar, cov., black chutney $225
Ice box jar, cov., coral.................................. $225
Mug (tumbler), black chutney.......................... $90
Pitcher, cov., water, cedar green .... $400+
Pitcher, cov., water, white........................... $500+
Pitcher, water, 12" h., seafoam blue............. $125
Plate, salad, 8" d., seafoam blue..................... $18
Plate, salad, 8" d., white................................. $25

Plate, dinner, 10" d., cantaloupe $40
Plate, chop, 13" sq., chartreuse $30
Plate, chop, 13" sq., seafoam blue.................. $50
Plate, child's, coral $60
Platter, 13 3/4" l., oblong, granite grey............. $30
Ramekin, cov., individual, granite grey $170
Relish dish, divided, raffia handle, coral $175
Relish rosette, granite grey........................... $200
Salad fork & spoon, white, pr. $300
Sauceboat, bean brown................................... $75
Shaker, single, chartreuse $8
Stack server, cov., cedar green (ILLUS. back, with fruit bowl, previous column) $300
Sugar bowl, cov., granite grey......................... $20
Teapot, cov., seafoam blue $135
Tumbler, child's, granite grey $125
Vegetable bowl, cov., cedar green, 12" l........ $75
Vegetable dish, open, divided, cedar green (ILLUS. right front, with fruit bowl, previous column) $130
Vegetable dish, open, oval, cantaloupe, 10" l. $75

Casual China (Iroquois China Co.)

Bowl, 5" d., cereal, ripe apricot $15
Bowl, 5 3/4" d., fruit, oyster grey $20
Butter dish, cov., brick red, 1/4 lb. .... $1,000+
Butter dish, cov., white, 1/2 lb. $150
Carafe, oyster grey...................................... $900+
Casserole, deep tureen, lemon yellow $250
Coffeepot, cov., nutmeg brown $140
Coffeepot, cov., oyster grey (ILLUS. right with creamer and pitcher, bottom of page)... $225
Coffeepot, cov., sugar white.......................... $200
Coffeepot, cov., after dinner, lemon yellow ... $125
Cover for 4 qt. casserole, oyster grey........... $45
Cover for vegetable bowl, open/divided, ice blue... $35
Cover for water pitcher, ripe apricot $60
Creamer, family-style, oyster grey (ILLUS. left w/coffeepot & pitcher, bottom of page)... $55
Creamer, family-style, pink sherbet $40

Casual Creamer, Pitcher & Coffeepot

C

Rare Mustard Gold Creamer & Sugar

Three Casual China Original Mugs

Creamer & cov. sugar bowl, redesigned, mustard gold (color produced only one year), the set (ILLUS., top of page)............ **$100**

Cup & saucer, coffee, redesigned, lemon yellow **$25**

Cup & saucer, demitasse, sugar white.......... **$225**

Gravy, redesigned w/cover which becomes stand, ripe apricot..................... **$185**

Gravy bowl, 5 1/4", 12 oz. **$40**

Gravy stand, oyster grey **$70**

Gravy w/attached stand, avocado yellow..... **$100**

Gumbo soup bowl, charcoal, 21 oz............. **$50**

Gumbo soup bowl, ice blue, 21 oz. **$40**

Hostess set: plate w/well & matching cup; sugar white, 2 pcs. **$90**

Mug, original design, ice blue (ILLUS. center with two other mugs, second from the top of page)... **$60-85**

Mug, original design, pink sherbet (ILLUS. left with two other mugs, second from the top of page)... **$60-85**

Mug, original design, ripe apricot (ILLUS. right with two other mugs, second from the top of page)... **$60-85**

Mug, restyled, aqua...................................... **$225**

Mug, restyled, ice blue **$100**

Pepper mill, lemon yellow........................... **$300+**

Pitcher, cov., ice blue, 1 1/2 qt....................... **$150**

Pitcher, nutmeg brown.................................. **$200**

Pitcher, redesigned, ripe apricot (ILLUS. center with creamer & coffeepot, bottom of page 299).. **$200**

Plate, bread & butter, 6 1/2" d., lettuce green.. **$10**

Plate, luncheon, 9 1/2" d., pink sherbet........... **$17**

Platter, 10 1/4" oval, individual, lettuce green.. **$50**

Platter, 12 3/4" oval, brick red........................ **$90**

Salt & pepper shakers, stacking-type, ice blue, pr. **$25**

Sugar, redesigned, aqua.............................. **$150**

Sugar, redesigned, brick red........................ **$225+**

Sugar, stacking-type, pink sherbet.................. **$15**

Tumbler, iced tea, Pinch patt., seafoam blue, Imperial Glass Co., 14 oz. **$50**

Tumbler, water, Pinch patt., ruby red, Imperial Glass Co., 11 oz............................... **$125+**

Vegetable dish, open, cantaloupe, 10" d. **$85**

Vegetable dish, open or divided (casserole), 10", sugar white **$60**

Iroquois Casual Cookware

Casserole, 3 qt. .... **$225+**

Dutch oven .... **$500+**

Fry pan, cov. .... **$500+**

Sauce pan, cov. .... **$500+**

Serving tray, electric, 12 3/4 x 17 1/2" ..... **$2,000+**

Knowles Esquire Line (Edwin M. Knowles China Co.)

Knowles Esquire Grass Pattern Pitcher

Pitcher, water, Grass patt., pink, unusual (ILLUS.) .... **$225+**

Residential Pattern (Plastic tablewares by Northern)

Plastic Residential Pattern Tumblers

Tumbler, red or blue, each (ILLUS. of two) **$50**

Sterling Line (Sterling China Co.)

Sterling China Gray Creamer

Creamer, gray (ILLUS.) **$50**

Sarreguemines

This factory was established in Lorraine, France, about 1770. Subsequently Wedgwood-type pieces were produced as was Mocha ware. In the 19th century, the factory turned to pottery and stoneware.

Sarreguemines Mark

C

Unusual Sarreguemines Bud Vase

Vase, 6 1/8" h., double bud style, in the form of a sideways "C" w/two flared mouths, resting on four tab feet, the sides decorated w/green panels w/fruiting branches outlined in pale green or blue, applied beading at the interior top sides, impressed "Sarreguemines 1391 S 486," firing line in one rim (ILLUS.) **$316**

Large Sarreguemines Wall Plaque

Wall plaque, round, titled "Printemps" (Spring), border features blue band w/six birds perched on flowering boughs, central profile bust portrait of a young woman w/daisies in her hair representing Spring, impressed "Sarreguemines 3 09 228 10 1744 682 - Made in Germany," made during era of German control of Lorraine, 15" d. (ILLUS.) **$345**

Sascha Brastoff

An endlessly inventive mind, a flair for dramatic illustration and unerring promotional skills made Sascha Brastoff (1918-1993) one of the best known ceramics designers of the 1950s and '60s. Brastoff's varied projects embraced everything from the practical, such as candelabra and cigarette boxes, to purely art objects such as wall plaques and decorative obelisks as well as lines of china and earthen dinnerwares. Every item carried his signature and was brought to the public's attention through intense promotional efforts by the artist. His name recognition was so widespread that, even after ill health forced his retirement in the early 1960s, the Brastoff company continued to successfully turn out pieces in his style for ten more years. (Items with a full "Sascha Brastoff" signature were decorated by Brastoff himself; those with only a "Sascha B." signature or the Brastoff name and a 'rooster stamp' were products of the decorating staff.

Born Sanuel Brostofsky, Brastoff trained briefly at Cleveland's Western Reserve School of Art, then moved to New York. Following military service during World War II, his flair for theatrical design found an outlet at 20th Century Fox where he designed costumes for, among others, Carmen Miranda. His ongoing ceramic work attracted the attention of philanthropist/investor Winthrop Rockefeller, who became Brastoff's patron, an association that lasted throughout the artist's career.

The 35,000-foot Brastoff studio in Los Angeles, which opened in 1953, became a mecca for tourists and movie stars. An endless array of ceramic products was on view, from ashtrays and lamps to enameled wares and sculptures done in such fanciful designs as "Star Steed" and "Rooftops." Brastoff supervised all design, turning out over 400 new items yearly.

The "designer extraordinaire," as his firm's publicity called him, worked in a variety of media. Included in his output were freeform metal sculptures, mosaic wall masks, terra cotta figurines, fabric and even a line of "hologram jewelry." Popular with the movie community, Brastoff's designs eventually found their way into films; his "Illusion" sculpture can be seen in the movie "Forbidden Planet."

Although Sascha Brastoff's mercurial creative interests led him in many directions, one element remains constant in his work: the presentation is always highly theatrical and laced with whimsy. A signature element was the use of unusual color combinations, sometimes metallic or with metallic accents. As his enduring popularity indicates, Bratoff had a keen ability to make the extraordinary commercially and artistically appealing.

Advisor for this category, Donald-Brian Johnson, is an author and lecturer specializing in mid-twentieth century design.

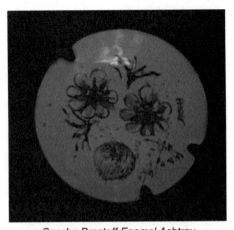

Sascha Brastoff Enamel Ashtray

Ashtray, enamel, floral design on white, 5 1/2" d. (ILLUS.) **$30**

Sascha Brastoff Fish-shaped Ashtray

Ashtray, fish-shaped, multicolored glaze, 6 1/4" d. (ILLUS.) **$75-100**

Ashtray, "Rooftops" patt., reverse inscribed w/invitation to 1953 Brastoff studio opening, 6 1/2" sq. **$250-275**

Ashtray, Western scene w/covered wagon, rare promotional piece, 14" w. **$225**

Bowl, banana shape, Mosaic design outside, solid color inside (ILLUS., top next page).. **$65-75**

Bowl, 8" d., footed, abstract design **$52**

Bowl, 13" d., footed, decorated w/grapes & leaves on a black background (ILLUS., next page) **$200-225**

Sascha Brastoff Mosaic Bowl

Brastoff Grape-decorated Bowl

Box, cov., rectangular, "Rooftops" patt., No. 021, 5 x 8" (ILLUS.)................................. **$50-75**
Candleholder, resin, green or blue, 6" h., each **$67**
Candleholder, resin, red w/molded grapes & leaves, 10" h. (ILLUS. right with yellow resin candleholder) **$50-75**

Yellow & Red Resin Brastoff Candleholders

Candleholder, resin, yellow w/incised diamond design, 6" h. (ILLUS. left with red resin candleholder) **$25-50**
Candleholders, "Star Steed" patt., 7 3/4" h., pr.. **$50-75**
Cigarette box, cov., "Star Steed" decoration **$125**
Cigarette lighter, gold base w/blue floral top, 4 1/2" h.. **$25-50**
Coffeepot, cov., "Surf Ballet" patt., 10 1/2" h.. **$50-75**
Compote, polar bear decoration, No. 085 .... **$92**
Decanter, "Star Steed" patt., 13" h." h. **$25-50**
Dish, decorated w/a housefly in gold, white & pink on a black background, 5 1/2 x 7" **$50-75**
Dish, horse decoration on green ground, 6 1/2" sq. **$60**

Brastoff Box in Rooftops Pattern

C

Sascha Brastoff Pipe

Pipe, sinuous shape, abstract design w/gold accents, 4" l. (ILLUS.) **$84**
Pitcher, 10 1/2" h., decorated w/a poodle **$150-175**

Sascha Brastoff Fish Plate

Plate, 6 1/2" d., fish shape & design (ILLUS.) .. **$125**

Sascha Brastoff Plate with House Design

Plate, 8" d., w/house & tree design (ILLUS.) **$50-75**
Plate, 9" d., Merbaby patt. **$205**

Brown & White S. Brastoff Plate

Plate, 9 1/2" d., wide brown rim w/abstract design, white center, full signature (ILLUS.) **$350-375**
Plate, 11 1/2" d., decorated w/a reclining nude **$175-200**

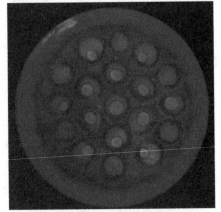

Sascha Brastoff Enamel Plate

Plate, 11 1/2" d., enamel, orange & gold abstract design, factory hanger on back (ILLUS.) **$100**

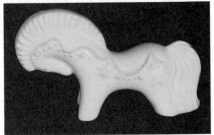

Sascha Brastoff Horse Salt Shaker

Salt shaker, model of a horse, white, produced in 1947-1948, 5 1/4" l., 3 1/4" h. (ILLUS.).. **$125-150**

Sculpture, abstract, in magnesium, 14 1/2" h. **$250-275**

Jeweled Leaf Teacup & Saucer

Teacup & saucer, "Jeweled Leaf" patt., on black background, saucer 5" d., the set (ILLUS.).. **$20-30**
Vase, 5" h., Provincial Rooster patt., No. F20.. **$540**
Vase, 17" h., bottle-shaped, "Jeweled Leaf" patt. on a grey ground **$25-50**
Wall pocket, Rooftops patt., No. 031, 20" h. **$300-350**

Schoop (Hedi) Art Creations

Hedi Schoop (1906-1966) was one of the most popular (and most imitated) California ceramic artists of the 1940s and '50s. Born in Switzerland, Schoop spent her early years studying sculpture, fashion design and acting. With her husband, famed movie composer, Frederick Hollander, she fled Nazi Germany in the early 1930s, settling in Hollywood, where his career flourished.

In her new environment, Schoop amused herself by creating plaster dolls, which she then painted and dressed in fashions of the day. A successful showing of the dolls at a Los Angeles department store prompted her to adapt these ideas to a more permanent medium: ceramics. Early slip-cast figures sold well from Schoop's small workshop, and a larger, North Hollywood facility, "Hedi Schoop Art Creations," opened in 1940.

Schoop designed and modeled most of the figurines released by her company, and many came equipped for secondary uses — from flower holders and wall pockets to candlesticks and soap dishes. She was perhaps the most commercially successful California ceramics designer of the postwar period, and certainly the most ubiquitous. If a Schoop figure proved popular with consumers, an entire line of accompanying decor objects, such as planters, bowls, ashtrays and candy dishes, would be built around it. At its busiest in the late 1940s, the studio produced over 30,000 giftware items per year and employed over fifty workers.

Hedi Schoop figurines are largely representational and achieve their visual impart through overall shape and size rather than through minute detailing. The figures are often caught in motion - arms extended, skirts aflutter, heads bowed - but that motion is fluid and unhurried. Rough and incised textures combine with smooth ones; colorful glossy glazes contrast with bisque.

Her subjects — ethnic dancers, musicians, peasant boys and girls — are captured at a specific moment in time. A figurine by Hedi Schoop is a captivating still photo.

The broadly drawn features, soft colors, and rippling garments of Schoop's oversize figurines and planters unfortunately made them easy to copy. During the height of her career, similar designs were turned out by a variety of other California ceramics firms, usually run by former Schoop employees. The most persistent was one-time Schoop decorator Katherine Schueftan. As "Kim Ward," her imitations resulted in a 1942 court injunction prohibiting "Kim" from copying the Schoop line. Schueftan complied until 1945, when she resurfaced with a new name, "Kaye of Hollywood," but similar Schoop-like figures. No further court action is reported.

Due to look-alike stylings by the numerous Schoop competitors, signature identification is an important means of object verification. While some pieces carried paper labels, most featured stamped or incised signatures, often with the additional words "Hollywood, Cal." or "California."

The Schoop factory was destroyed by fire in 1958. After collaborating for a time with The California Cleminsons, popular creators of decorative kitchenwares, Schoop retired from ceramic design, focusing instead on painting — but her glamorous legacy lives on.

Advisor for this category is Donald-Brian Johnson, an author and lecturer specializing in mid-twentieth century design. Photos are by his frequent collaborator, Leslie Piña.

Hedi Schoop Bird-shaped Ashtray

Ashtray, model of a bird, 7 1/2" l., 5 1/4" h. (ILLUS.).. **$50-75**
Ashtrays, butterfly-shaped, white w/gold decoration, 5 1/2" w., pr. **$25-50**
Candleholder, figural, a mermaid holding a single candle socket in each hand above her head, rare, ca. 1950, 13 1/2" h. **$695**
Candleholder, figure of dancing girl kneeling, 10" h. **$75-100**
Candleholders, pink swirl pattern, 5 1/4" d., 5" h., pr.. **$25-50**

Young Chinese Musicians Console Set

Console set: "Young China Musicians,"
Chinese boy & Chinese girl w/rectangular planter; planter 11" l., girl 10 1/4" h.,
boy 10 3/4" h., the set (ILLUS., previous
page) **$300-350**
Dish, experimental, kidney-shaped, etched
lines on black through yellow glaze..... **$150-175**
Figure, Madonna & Child, 7" h. ...." **$175-200**

Hedi Schoop Chinese Woman Figure

Figure of Chinese woman, standing on a
round black base, white floor-length skirt,
black, white & green blouse w/long
sleeves flaring at wrists, a white flower in
black hair above each ear, right fingers
bent to hold a pot w/black cloth handle &
in same colors as blouse, right leg bent at
knee, woman 9" h., pot 2 1/2" h., 2 pcs.
(ILLUS.) **$215**
Figure of girl, "Debutante," standing &
holding handmade flowers in both arms,
rough textured finish, ca. 1943, 12 1/2" h.
.... **$260**
Figure of girl, standing on cobalt blue-
glazed round base, legs slightly apart,
arms stretched out to sides, hands folded
to hold jump rope, rough textured black
hair w/pigtails out to sides & held in place
w/cobalt blue glossy ties, light blue long
sleeved shirt, cobalt blue overblouse
w/straps, rough textured cobalt blue
short skirt & socks, inkstamp on unglazed
bottom, "Hedi Schoop Hollywood, Cal.,"
8 1/2" h. **$240**
Figure of woman, standing on one foot &
holding large basket above her head
w/both hands, dressed in yellow top & full
yellow skirt w/blue & green stripes, on
yellow oval base, incised overglaze "Hedi
Schoop Design, California U.S.A.," 14" h.
(ILLUS., top next column) **$395**

Schoop Figure of Woman with Basket

Hedi Schoop Lantern Girls Figures

Figures, "Lantern Girls," squatting Chinese
girls each holding a stick suspending a
lantern, accompanying figures for the
"Young China Musicians" console set, in
red, 8 1/2" h., each (ILLUS.) **$100-125**
Figures, models of poodles, 12 1/4" h., pr.
.... **$425-450**

Oriental Couple with Baskets Figures

Figures, Oriental couple each holding a
basket, black & gold shirts & white
pants, woman 11 1/2" h., man
12 1/2" h., pr. (ILLUS.) **$275-300**

Vase, model of a tulip, pink, 10 1/2" h. **$25-50**

Vase, 9" h. at highest point, 4 1/2" h., at lowest point, 9" l., seashell-form, footed oval base, fluted edge rising from the low end to the higher end, dark green base w/dark green & gold fading to light green, rim trimmed in gold, transparent textured glossy glaze, marked w/a silver label w/red block letters, "Hedi Schoop Hollywood, Calif." on two lines **$110**

Sèvres & Sèvres-Style

Some of the most desirable porcelain ever produced was made at the Sèvres factory, originally established at Vincennes, France, and transferred, through permission of Madame de Pompadour, to Sèvres as the Royal Manufactory about the middle of the 18th century. King Louis XV took sole responsibility for the works in 1759, when production of hard paste wares began. Between 1850 and 1900, many biscuit and soft-paste pieces were made again. Fine early pieces are scarce and high-priced. Many of those available today are late productions. The various Sèvres marks have been copied, and pieces listed as "Sèvres-Style" are similar to actual Sèvres wares but not necessarily from that factory. Three of the many Sèvres marks are illustrated here.

Sèvres marks

Fine Sèvres Figure of Catherine the Great

Figure of Catherine II of Russia, bisque, the empress shown seated on a rocky ledge in formal dress, her left hand resting on a crowned orb, her right hand holding a scepter, a branch of laurel, symbolizing her artistic talents, growing up the rock at her left, impressed uppercase lozenge mark & name of artist, dated 1898, 17 3/8" h. (ILLUS.) **$19,200**

C

Sèvres Bisque Figure of Cupid

Figure of Cupid, the winged bisque figure seated on a rock holding his right index finger to his lips, his left hand on the quiver of arrows, raised on a bleu nouveau cylindrical stand w/four projecting buttress feet, titled & trimmed in gold, impressed company mark, after the model by Etienne-Maurice Falconet, date cyphers for 1889-1890, 12 1/2" h. (ILLUS.) **$1,920**

Rare Reticulated Sèvres Cup & Saucer

C

Teacup & saucer, handleless cup w/a raised foot, double-walled w/the exterior pierced w/two tiers of quatrefoils within ogival arches, the interior painted w/gilt lines radiating from a central lozenge, a stylized chrysanthemum on each line, the gilt lines extending to issue from scrolls between each lappet of the border of flowers within red-edged ogival lappets, matching saucer w/a matching pierced border band, from a dejeuner chinois set, blue printed Louis Philippe decorating cypher, artist-signed, 1836, the set (ILLUS., previous page) **$6,600**

Vase, 6 1/8" h., pate-sur-pate, footed bulbous body tapering to a tall slightly flaring cylindrical neck, the mauve ground decorated w/layers of colored paste & centered by a round reserve w/the portrait head of an early Grecian hero suspended from crossed branches within a gilt surround further enclosed within wreaths & flowering vine, the far side undecorated, the mouth delicately gilt w/beading & pendants, the foot w/a cell design band, printed "RF" monogram marks, artist-signed, 1886-92 (ILLUS.)................................. **$6,000**

Unusual Sévres Ear of Corn Vase

Vase, 5 3/4" h., Art Nouveau style, "pate nouvelle" type, naturalistically molded as an ear of corn w/two green husk leaves forming loop handles, textured yellow corn kernels showing between the leaves, black-stencilled triangle mark for 1903 (ILLUS.) **$3,840**

Extremely Rare Large Sévres Vase

Vase, 27 3/4" h., "Vase Cordelier 3e Grandeur," the round flaring pedestal base supports the large swelling ovoid body tapering to a widely flaring neck, the neck decorated w/entwined gilt ribbons, the body finely h.p. front & back w/rich ribbon-tied garlands of flowers including lilacs, peonies, daffodils, stock, sweet William & others, flanked by applied ormolu figural Bacchic satyr-mask handles suspending pendant bouquets & boughs of berried vine, the base decorated in gold linked stylized flowerheads above stiff leaftips, iron-red Republique Francais mark, date 1849 (ILLUS.)..................................... **$54,000**

Fine Sèvres Pate-Sur-Pate Vase

Fine Sèvres-Style Covered Vases

Vases, cov., Sèvres-style, each of baluster-form, turquoise blue ground, the domed cover, neck & socle w/gilt trailing vine decoration, each w/a large squared reserve on the front w/portraits of Emperor Napoleon I or Empress Josephine after works by David, framed within a gilt beaded cartouche w/leafy scrolls & Napoleonic symbols, cover, stem & squared foot of each w/a gilt crowned eagle, spurious Sèvres marks, late 19th c., 16 1/8" h., pr. (ILLUS.)......... **$4,541**

Shelley China

Members of the Shelley family were in the pottery business in England as early as the 18th century. In 1872 Joseph Shelley formed a partnership with James Wileman of Wileman & Co., who operated the Foley China Works. The Wileman & Co. name was used for the firm for the next fifty years,

and between 1890 and 1910 the words "The Foley" appeared above conjoined "WC" initials.

Beginning in 1910 the Shelley family name in a shield appeared on wares, although the firm's official name was still Wileman & Co. The company's name was finally changed to Shelley in 1925 and then Shelley China Ltd. after 1965. The firm changed hands in the 1960s and became part of the Doulton Group in 1971.

At first only average quality earthenwares were produced, but in the late 1890s new shapes and better quality decorations were used.

Bone china was introduced at Shelley before World War I, and these fine dinnerwares became very popular in the United States and are increasingly popular today with collectors. Thin "eggshell china" teawares, miniatures and souvenir items were widely marketed during the 1920s and 1930s and are sought-after today.

Shelley
CHINA
ENGLAND

Shelley Mark

Undecorated Dainty Shape Teapot

Teapot, cov., Dainty Shape, undecorated, ca. 1912-25, overall 7 1/8" l., 4" h. (ILLUS.)
.... **$100-150**

Dainty Shape Teapot with Pink Roses Pattern No. 7447

C

Teapot, cov., Dainty Shape, Wileman &
Co., patt. No. 7447, introduced in 1896,
designed by William Morris, shape continued in production until factory closing
in 1966 (ILLUS., bottom previous page)
.... **$300-350**

*Dainty Shape Teapot with Floral Pattern
No. 9056*

Teapot, cov., Dainty Shape, Wileman &
Co., patt. No. 9056, 1896-1966, 5 1/2" h.
(ILLUS.)... **$300-600**

*Empire Shape Spano Lustra Teapot
by Wileman*

Teapot, cov., Empire Shape, Spano Lustra
patt., Wileman & Co., 1893-1912, 5" h.
(ILLUS.)... **$300-600**

*Shelley Blue Duchess Teapot in
Gainsborough Shape*

Teapot, cov., Gainsborough Shape, Blue
Duchess patt. No. 13403, Elegant style,
from the Best Ware group, 1943 (ILLUS.)
.... **$100-200**

*Wileman Gainsborough Teapot with
Delicate Florals*

Teapot, cov., Gainsborough Shape, Wileman & Co., unnumbered floral patt., intro-
duced in 1900 (ILLUS.) **$300-600**

Shelley Bluebell Wood Teapot

Teapot, cov., Globe Shape, Bluebell Wood
patt. No. 12108, Scenic style, from the
Best Ware group, 1932 (ILLUS.)......... **$100-200**

Green Daisy Teapot in Henley Shape

Teapot, cov., Henley Shape, Chintz Green
Daisy patt. No. 13450, from the Best
Ware group, 1943 (ILLUS.)................. **$200-300**

Fine Wileman Shell Shape Teapot

Teapot, cov., Shell Shape, Wileman & Co., patt. No. 5137, introduced in 1891 (ILLUS.) **$500-600**

Slipware

This term refers to ceramics, primarily redware, decorated by the application of slip (semi-liquid paste made of clay). Such wares were made for decades in England and Germany and elsewhere on the Continent, and in the Pennsylvania Dutch country and elsewhere in the United States. Today, contemporary copies of early Slipware items are featured in numerous decorator magazines and offered for sale in gift catalogs.

Slipware Bowl with Lines & Initials

Bowl, 11 1/4" d., 3 1/2" h., deep flat flaring sides w/a smooth rim, decorated around the interior rim w/a thin wavy line & a swagged line in yellow slip, initial "M" in the bottom, 19th c. (ILLUS.) **$480**

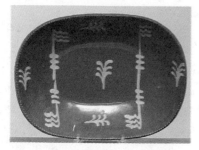

Fine Early Slipware Loaf Dish

Loaf dish, oval dished form decorated w/two long lines trimmed w/dashes &

wavy short banners at each end, scattered stylized leaf sprigs, all in yellow slip on the reddish ground, coggled rim, minor edge flaws, 19th c., 11 3/4 x 16", 3" h. (ILLUS.) **$1,093**

Slipware Loaf Dish with Diamond Lattice

Loaf dish, rectangular w/rounded corners & a coggled rim, overall wavy diamond lattice decoration in yellow slip, edge flakes, possibly late, 10 1/2 x 13" (ILLUS.) **$144**
Pie plate, round w/coggled rim, a group of three elongated S-scrolls w/feathered ends in the center, edge flakes, 9" d. (ILLUS. top with 8" pie plate, below) **$173**

Two Yellow Slipware Pie Plates

Pie plate, round w/coggled rim, a long band across the center composed of four triple-line sections, a side band at each side w/three short wavy lines at each end, 19th c., 8" d. (ILLUS. bottom with 9" pie plate) **$345**

Early Pie Plate with Bar & Scroll Designs

Pie plate, round w/coggled rim, a long yellow slip bar across the center w/forked ends, four slip S-scroll devices w/crossbars, some wear, minor edge flakes, 19th c., 10 1/4" d. (ILLUS.) **$259**

Spatterware

This ceramic ware takes its name from the "spattered" decoration, in various colors, generally used to trim pieces handpainted with rustic center designs of flowers, birds, houses, etc. Popular in the early 19th century, most was imported from England.

Related wares, called "stick spatter," had freehand designs applied with pieces of cut sponge attached to sticks, hence the name. Examples date from the 19th and early 20th century and were produced in England, Europe and America.

Some early spatter-decorated wares were marked by the manufacturers, but not many. Twentieth century reproductions are also sometimes marked, including those produced by Boleslaw Cybis.

Bowl, Leeds-type, 7 1/4" d., 3 1/2" h., Peafowl patt. in five colors w/spatter trees around the border, two rim hairline, flakes on table rim **$1,840**

Creamer, paneled shaped, molded shell under fan, Rainbow patt. w/dark blue & deep red stripes, stains, hairline & minor flakes, 4 5/8" h. **$345**

Creamer, Rainbow patt. w/red & blue stripes, stains, hairlines, minor rim flakes, 3 1/2" h. **$488**

Cup, handleless, miniature, elongated Schoolhouse patt. in red, yellow & blue, blue spatter border, rim hairline w/stain **$488**

Cup, handleless, miniature, Rainbow patt. in green & deep plum, 1 5/8" h. **$400-800**

Cup & saucer, handleless, Acorn patt. in yellow & green, red spatter border, light stains, the set **$1,725**

Cup & saucer, handleless, Four Petal Flower patt. in blue & red, red spatter background, cup w/minor roughness, the set (bottom row, second from right, with large grouping of spatter pieces, bottom of page) **$288**

Cup & saucer, handleless, Thistle patt. in red & green, rainbow spatter borders in red & mustard yellow, saucer w/filled-in flake, the set **$1,150**

Cups & saucers, handleless, Peafowl patt. in blue, yellow & red, green spatter ground, one cup w/ flake, one saucer w/flake & hairline, set of 2 (ILLUS. top row, far left & right, with large grouping of spatter pieces, bottom of page) **$575**

Plate, 8" d., Peafowl patt. in blue, yellow & red, green spatter border **$518**

Plate, 8" d., Peafowl patt. in red, yellow & green, blue spatter ground, impressed mark "Pearl Stone Ware - PW & Co." (ILLUS. bottom row, far right, with large grouping of spatter pieces, bottom of page) **$173**

Plate, 8 1/4" d., Thistle patt. in red & green, wide blue spatter border, faintly molded feather-edge, spider crack **$172**

Plate, 8 3/8" d., Schoolhouse patt. in red, green spatter tree.................................... **$2,645**

Plate, 8 1/2" d., Peafowl patt. in blue, yellow & green, paneled red spatter border, faint wear **$200**

Plate, 9 1/2" d., Schoolhouse patt. in red, green & black, red spatter border, repaired rim flakes (ILLUS. bottom row, far left, with large group of various spatter pieces, bottom of page) **$489**

Plate, 9 5/8" d., Pomegranate patt. in red, green, blue & yellow, blue spatter border **$288**

Saucer, Schoolhouse patt. in red, red spatter border, 5 3/4" d. **$546**

Saucer, Six-point Star patt. in red, yellow & green, blue spatter border, 5 3/4" d. (ILLUS. top row, second from let, with grouping of various spatter pieces, bottom of page) **$518**

Saucer, Thistle patt. in red & green, rainbow spatter border in yellow & blue, glued chip **$1,150**

Sugar bowl, cov., Tulip patt. in red, white, blue & green, dark red spatter borders, rim flakes on cover, base w/spider crack in glaze.. **$288**

Large Grouping of Spatter Cups & Saucers, Plates & Other Pieces

Sugar bowl, no cover, footed ovoid body, Parrot patt. in green, red & yellow, red spatter border, mismatched lid not shown, slight staining, roughness & chipped lid, 4 1/2" h. (ILLUS. top row, center, with grouping of various spatter pieces, bottom previous page) **$690**

Teapot, cov., Peafowl patt. in blue, yellow & green, red spatter borders, few rim flakes on teapot, 7" h. **$460**

Teapot, cov., wide ovoid body tapering to a flat rim & low domed cover, serpentine spout & C-scroll handle, Rainbow patt. in red & green spatter, repaired spout & cover, 7" h. (ILLUS. bottom row, third from left, with group of various spatter pieces, bottom previous page) **$633**

Toddy plate, Peafowl patt. in blue, green & red, banded purple, red & blue spatter border, small repaired rim flake, 5 1/4" d. (ILLUS. top row, second from right, with group of various spatter pieces, bottom previous page) **$805**

Toddy plate, Schoolhouse patt. in red, black, brown & green, blue spatter border, repaired rim flakes, 5 3/4" d. (ILLUS. bottom row, second from left, with group of other spatter pieces, bottom previous page) **$633**

Stick Spatter

Rare Stick Spatter Rabbits Charger

Charger, round w/flanged rin, Rabbits patt., large central transfer-printed scene of rabbits playing tennis, framed by brushed & stick spatter flowers & leaves in red, dark blue, green & yellow, minor glaze flakes, late 19th - early 20th c., 12 1/2" d. (ILLUS.) **$805**

Staffordshire Figures

Small figures and groups made of pottery were produced by the majority of the Staffordshire, England potters in the 19th century and were used as mantel decorations or "chimney ornaments," as they were sometimes called. Pairs of dogs were favorites and were turned out by the carload, and 19th-century pieces are still available. Well-painted reproductions also abound, and collectors are urged to exercise caution before investing.

Fine Pair of Staffordshire Cat Figures

Cats, seated facing viewer, on a flaring rectangular blue pillow w/gilt trim, each white w/sponged black & yellow spots, a yellow neck ribbons & painted facial features, 19th c., 7 1/2" h., pr. (ILLUS.) **$431**

Nice Old English Staffordshire Dogs

Dogs, Spaniels in a seated pose w/head facing the viewer, white w/a rust-red spotted curly coat, h.p. head details & painted collar & chain, England, late 19th c., 10" h., pr. (ILLUS.) **$570**

Dogs, Spaniels in a seated pose w/head facing the viewer, white w/a yellow eyes & gilt chains & fur trim, England, late 19th c., gilt wear, one w/scuff mark, 14 5/8" h., pr. (ILLUS. flanking figure of The Lion Slayer, bottom of page) **$431**

Pair of Staffordshire Spaniels & Figure of The Lion Slayer

C

Grouping of Varied Staffordshire Figures

Figure group of Joan & Darby, seated middle aged couple sharing an evening drink, colorful enameled trim, 19th c., 5 5/8" h. (ILLUS. second from left, bottom, with grouping of Staffordshire figures, top of page) **$86**

Figure group of Little Red Riding Hood, seated w/her basket, the small wolf seated to her side, crazing, minor wear, hairline, 19th c., 9" h. (ILLUS. far left with grouping of Staffordshire figures, top of page) **$230**

Figure group of Mother Goose, Mother Goose wearing a tall hat & seated astride a flying white goose, brown-dabbed green & yellow base, hairline, repairs, 19th c., 7 1/4" h. (ILLUS. second from left, top, with grouping of Staffordshire figures, top of page) **$288**

Figure of Benjamin Franklin, standing w/a document in one hand & his hat under his other arm, all white except for decorated waistcoat, facial features & black trim, on a plinth base incorrectly labeled "Washington," mid-19th c, 15" h. (ILLUS., next column) **$1,035**

Figure of man holding cat, standing wearing striped breeches, blue waistcoat & tan coat, holding a calico cat, 7 3/4" h. (ILLUS. third from right with group of Staffordshire figures, top of page) **$230**

Figure of naughty barmaid, standing wearing a long white dress w/h.p. flowerheads & a bonnet, holding a bottle, rear view shows she's not wearing undergarments, 19th c., 8 1/8" h. (ILLUS. second from right with grouping of Staffordshire figures, top of page) **$345**

Figure of Temperance man, double-sided, one side shows a well-dressed man holding coin purse & labeled "Water," reverse shows a man dressed in rages holding a bottle & labeled "Gin," mid-19th c., 8 3/8" h. (ILLUS. far right with grouping of Staffordshire figures, top of page) **$259**

Scarce Mismarked B. Franklin Figure

Figure of The Lion Slayer, a Scotsman w/a claymore standing & holding a lion by it back paw, minor wear, mid-19th c., 16 1/8" h. (ILLUS. center with large Spaniels, bottom previous page) **$403**

Unusual Cottage Pastille Burner

Pastille burner, modeled as a two-part cottage w/two sheep under a open pillar in front, trimmed in blue, black, yellow, green & orange, chimney w/a hold for the smoke, some loss to paint, small chip on base w/small crack, 9" w., 8" h. (ILLUS.) ... **$489**

Stoneware

Stoneware is essentially a vitreous pottery, impervious to water even in its unglazed state, that has been produced by potteries all over the world for centuries. Utilitarian wares such as crocks, jugs, churns and the like were the most common productions in the numerous potteries that sprang into existence in the United States during the 19th century. These items were often enhanced by the application of a cobalt blue oxide decoration. In addition to the coarse, primarily salt-glazed stonewares, there are other categories of stoneware known by such special names as basalt, jasper and others.

Flower-decorated Stoneware Churn

Butter churn, tall slightly swelled cylindrical body w/a molded rim & eared handles, original stoneware guide, cobalt blue slip-quilled decoration of a large upright daisy-like flower w/a bud & long leaves below "5," impressed mark of John Burger, Rochester, New York, professional restoration to hairlines, 5 gal., ca. 1865, 18" h. (ILLUS.) **$2,530**

Scarce Flower-decorated Cake Crock

Cake crock, low wide cylindrical shape w/molded rim & eared handles, cobalt blue slip-quilled double stylized flowers on thin leafy stems, brushed blue dashes above, impressed "Tripe" eleven times & w/name P.F. Finnegan, couple of minor chips, ca. 1860, 17" d., 10" h. (ILLUS.) ... **$1,595**

Bird-decorated Stoneware Cream Pot

Cream pot, slightly flaring cylindrical body w/a wide flat mouth, eared handles, cobalt blue slip-quilled large dotted bird w/a worm in its beak, on a dotted branch, number 3 & impressed mark for Wme. Warner, West Troy, New York, minor staining, 3 gal., ca. 1850, 11" h. (ILLUS.) **$1,155**

Daisy-like Flower on 2 Gal. Cream Pot

Cream pot, slightly swelled cylindrical body w/a molded rim & eared handles, cobalt blue slip-quilled decoration of a large daisy-like flower w/umbrella-form petals above long leaves, number 2 & impressed mark of Harrington & Burger, Rochester, New York, minor interior rim chip, minor glaze spider in flower, 2 gal., ca. 1853, 11" h. (ILLUS.) **$1,265**

Flower-decorated Stoneware Cream Pot

Cream pot, slightly swelled cylindrical form w/molded rim & eared handles, cobalt blue slip-quilled decoration of a large dai-

sy-like flower & two tulip-like flowers on leafy stems, impressed mark for Lehman & Co., West 12 St., New York, professional restoration to a full-length line on back, stack mark on base, ca. 1870, 10" h. (ILLUS.) **$523**

3 Gallon Stoneware Crock with Hen

Crock, cylindrical w/molded rim & eared handles, cobalt blue slip-quilled hen pecking at corn, minor stains & chips at rim, impressed mark of Adam Caire, Pokeepsie (sic), New York, 3 gal., ca. 1880, 10" h. (ILLUS.) **$495**

Crock with Large Three-Leaf Cluster

Crock, cylindrical w/molded rim & eared handles, cobalt blue slip-quilled large three-leaf cluster enclosing a large "5," impressed mark of John Burger, Rochester, New York, two hairlines down from rim, one by ear & one at back, 5 gal., ca. 1865, 13" h. (ILLUS.) **$743**

C

Stoneware Crock with Large Starburst

Crock, cylindrical w/molded rim & eared handles, cobalt blue slip-quilled large six-point starburst enclosing a blossom, impressed mark of A. O. Whittemore, Havana, New York, large surface chip at rim, tight hairline at back, 5 gal., ca. 1870, 12" h. (ILLUS.) **$2,035**

Bird-decorated Advertising Crock

Crock, cylindrical w/molded rim & eared handles, cobalt blue slip-quilled long-tailed bird perched on a tree stump, impressed advertising "C. O. Barnes & Co. - 317 & 319 North Main Str.- Providence, R.I.," unknown maker, probably from Fort Edward, New York, 1 gal., ca. 1870, 7" h. (ILLUS.) **$2,750**

Very Rare Large Crock with Phoenix

Crock, cylindrical w/molded rim & eared handles, rare cobalt blue slip-quilled decoration of a large spreadwinged phoenix among leafy shrubs, very detailed, impressed mark of N. Clark & Co., Rochester, New York, some hairlines, 6 gal., ca. 1850, 14 1/2" h. (ILLUS.) **$72,600**

Very Rare Early Handled Pint Crock

Crock, small swelled cylindrical body w/flared lip & applied loop side handles, cobalt blue brushed watch spring designs around the sides, unsigned, decoration attributed to James Morgan, Jr., Cheesequake, New York, tight clay separation line along bottom, 1 pt., ca. 1790, 5 3/4" h. (ILLUS.) **$19,800**

C

Bird & Flower S. Hart 5 Gallon Crock

Crock, cylindrical w/molded rim & eared handles, cobalt blue slip-quilled design of a large songbird perched on a vine w/a large flower & the number "5," impressed mark for S. Hart w/the last name misspelled "AHRT," some over glazing & staining from use, minor chip at front base, ca. 1875, 5 gal, 12" h. (ILLUS.) **$1,073**

Early Ovoid C. Crolius Crock

Crock, ovoid body w/a small base below wide bulbous top w/a wide flat rim flanked by upright loop handles, impressed mark of C. Crolius Manufacturer, New York (New York) framed by a cobalt blue brushed oval, long drip of Albany slip on the front, ca. 1800, about 2 gal., 12 1/2" h. (ILLUS.) **$1,540**

Crock, cylindrical w/molded rim & eared handles, cobalt blue slip-quilled decoration of a huge, fat chicken, unsigned, left handle missing, large glaze loss spots at rim of back, few tight hairlines, ca. 1870, 6 gal., 13" h. (ILLUS., top next column)
.... **$3,080**

6 Gallon Crock with Huge Chicken

Rare Early Stoneware Inkwell

Inkwell, short cylindrical form w/impressed scribe lines & pen hole in top rim, impressed mark of M. Tyler, Albany, New York, accented in cobalt blue, couple of surface chips, ca. 1840, 4 3/4" d., 2" h. (ILLUS.).. **$7,070**

Rare Early Jar with Hand Design

Jar, ovoid w/molded rim & eared handles, cobalt blue brushed design of a large open hand centered by a "2," impressed mark of N. Clark & Co., Lyons, New York, 2 gal., ca. 1830, very minor surface chips, 10 1/2" h. (ILLUS., previous page) **$9,350**

"John M. Connolly" diagonally down the side, impressed mark of E.W. Farrington, Elmira, New York, 1 gal., ca. 1890, 10" h. (ILLUS.).. **$209**

Early Utica, New York Ovoid Jug

Rare Jug with Human Profile Design

Jug, beehive shape tapering to a small mouth & strap handle, cobalt blue brushed folksy human profile, impressed mark of E.W. Farrington & Co., Elmira, New York, 1 gal., ca. 1890, 11" h. (ILLUS.) **$5,500**

Jug, bulbous ovoid body tapering to small mouth & applied strap handle, cobalt blue brushed rose-like flower on a scrolling leafy stem, impressed mark of H. & G. Nash, Utica, New York, 2 gal., ca. 1832, very minor staining, 13" h. (ILLUS.) **$358**

Stoneware Jug with Inscribed Name

Jug, beehive-shape w/small mouth & strap handle, cobalt blue slip-quilled name

Early Marked Ovoid New York Jug

Jug, ovoid body tapering to a small mouth & applied handle, cobalt blue brushed ac-

C

C

cents frame the impressed mark of J. Remmey, Manhattan Wells, New York, very old chip at spout, about 1 gal., ca. 1790, 11 1/2" h. (ILLUS.) **$2,420**

Ovoid Buffalo, New York 1 Gal. Jug

Jug, ovoid body tapering to a small mouth & applied strap handle, cobalt blue brushed pointed flower on a leafy stem, impressed mark of P. Mugler and Co., Buffalo, New York, 1 gal., ca. 1850, kiln burns on side, minor surface wear, 11" h. (ILLUS.) **$495**

Stoneware Pitcher with Wreath Design

Pitcher, 10" h., flat base w/tapering ovoid sides to a wide molded mouth w/pinched spout, strap handle, cobalt blue slip-quilled wreath design, impressed mark of J. Burger, Rochester, New York, 1 gal., minor wear, three hairlines in handle & one at rim, ca. 1880 (ILLUS.) **$358**

Stoneware Pitcher with Snowflake Design

Pitcher, 10 1/2" h., flat base w/tapering ovoid sides to a wide molded mouth w/pinched spout, strap handle, cobalt blue slip-quilled four-point snowflake design & a "1," impressed mark of J. Burger, Rochester, New York, 1 gal., interior surface chip, ca. 1880 (ILLUS.) **$413**

Preserve Jar with Bird Eating Berries

Preserve jar, gently swelled cylindrical body w/a short flared rim, eared handles, cobalt blue slip-quilled bird perched on a leafy sprig & leaning down to eat berries, impressed mark of W.A. Macquiod & Co., New York, Little Wst 12th St., 1 1/2 gal., professional restoration to hairlines, ca. 1870, 11" h. (ILLUS.) **$1,073**

Rare Preserve Jar with Northwind Face

Preserve jar, gently swelled cylindrical body w/a short flared rim, eared handles, cobalt blue slip-quilled stylized Northwind face design composed of detailed scrolls, impressed mark of W.A. Macquiod & Co., New York, Little Wst 12th St., 1 1/2 gal., ca. 1870, 9 1/2" h. (ILLUS.) **$6,058**

Teco Pottery

Teco Pottery was actually the line of art pottery introduced by the American Terra Cotta and Ceramic Company of Terra Cotta (Crystal Lake), Illinois, in 1902. Founded by William D. Gates in 1881, American Terra Cotta originally produced only bricks and drain tile. Because of superior facilities for experimentation, including a chemical laboratory, the company was able to develop an art pottery line, favoring a matte green glaze in the earlier years but eventually achieving a wide range of colors including a metallic lustre glaze and a crystalline glaze. Although some hand-thrown pottery was made, Gates favored a molded ware because it was less expensive to produce. By 1923, Teco Pottery was no longer being made, and in 1930 American Terra Cotta and Ceramic Company was sold. A book on the topic is Teco: Art Pottery of the Prairie School, *by Sharon S. Darling (Erie Art Museum, 1990).*

Teco Mark

Small Leather Brown Teco Vase

Vase, 4 1/4" h., simple ovoid body w/a small flared neck, golden brown leather glaze, double-struck mark (ILLUS.) **$518**

Small Teco Green Matte Vase

Vase, 4 1/4" h., simple ovoid body w/a small flared neck, matte green glaze, double-struck mark (ILLUS.) **$500**

Unusual Squatty Teco Vase

C

Vase, 4 5/8" h., 5 3/4" d., very wide squatty body tapering sharping to a tiny flared neck, smooth matte green glaze, double-stamped mark (ILLUS., previous page) .. **$1,035**

Teco Swelled Cylindrical Vase

Vase, 5 3/4" h., footed swelled cylindrical body tapering to a short flared neck, overall smooth organic green matte glaze, impressed trademark (ILLUS.) **$575**

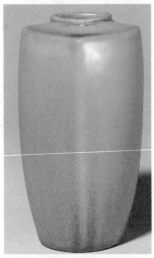

Teco Triangular Vase

Vase, 7 3/4" h., upright gently swelled triangular body w/a wide flattened shoulder & low molded mouth, matte green glaze w/charcoaling at one corner, double-struck mark (ILLUS.) **$1,093**

Vase, 8 3/4" h., footed, gently swelled cylindrical body w/a narrow shoulder & short rolled neck, overall green matte glaze accented w/darker charcoaling, double-stamped mark, tiny pin nick on edge of rim (ILLUS., top next column) **$575**

Teco Green Cylindrical Vase

Teco Vase with Tiny Squared Handles

Vase, 9" h., swelled cylindrical body tapering gently to a widely flaring neck, tiny square shoulder handles, green matte glaze speckled w/brown, triple impressed marks, pinhead nick on base rim (ILLUS.) **$1,495**

Tiles

Tiles have been made by potteries in the United States and abroad for many years. Apart from small tea tiles used on tables, there are also decorative tiles for fireplaces, floors and walls. This is where present collector interest lies, especially in the late 19th century American-made art pottery tiles.

Long Delft Tile with Flying White Duck

C

Delft, Holland, rectangular, a long narrow design w/a large white flying duck above grasses & water, impressed jug mark & Delft name, 4 x 12 1/4" (ILLUS., top of page) **$518**

Framed Grueby Tulip Tile

Grueby Pottery, Boston, Massachusetts, square, decorated w/a yellow tulip w/long green leaves on a dark green ground, framed in a contemporary flat handmade frame, tile 6" sq. (ILLUS.) **$1,170**

Trent Tile Cavalier Portrait Tiles

Trent Tile Company, Trenton, New Jersey, rectangular, composed of three tiles forming the figure of a Cavalier holding a flute, shaded dark green & yellow glossy glaze, marked, crazing, several edge & corner chips, older frame, 6 x 18" (ILLUS.) .. **$288**

Van Briggle

The Van Briggle Pottery was established by Artus Van Briggle, who formerly worked for Rookwood Pottery, in Colorado Springs, Colorado, at the turn of the century. He died in 1904, but the pottery was carried on by his widow and others. From 1900 until 1920, the pieces were dated. It remains in production today, specializing in Art Pottery.

Early Van Briggle Pottery Mark

Tiny Van Briggle Vase with Leaves

Vase, 2 1/8" h., squatty globular shape w/wide low molded rim, the sides lightly molded w/broad pointed leaves, mottled pale blue matte glaze, incised mark, ca. 1907-12 (ILLUS.) **$316**

Vase, 4" h., footed squatty bulbous form tapering to a flat mouth, molded w/alternating tall & short spearpoints, matte dark blue & light blue glaze, marked (ILLUS., next page) **$127**

C

Dark & Light Blue Van Briggle Vase

Squatty Van Briggle Base with Spearpoints

Vase, 4 1/4" h., footed squatty bulbous form tapering to a flat mouth, molded w/alternating tall & short spearpoints, matte dark blue & purple glaze, marked (ILLUS.) **$150**

Simple Ovoid Van Briggle 5" Vase

Vase, 5" h., simple ovoid body tapering to a wide, flat mouth, overall light matte green glaze, incised mark, ca. 1915 (ILLUS.) **$288**

Wedgwood

Reference here is to the famous pottery established by Josiah Wedgwood in 1759 in England. Numerous types of wares have been produced through the years to the present.

WEDGWOOD

Early Wedgwood Mark

Miscellaneous

Rare Small Fairyland Lustre Bowl

Bowl, 3 1/2" w., 2" h., Fairyland Lustre, thin footring below the octagonal bowl decorated on the exterior w/the paneled Dana patt. featuring scenes of a village, water & mountains, interior decorated w/elves picking insects from a spider web among mushrooms & trees, Patt. Z5125, marked w/Wedgwood Portland Vase mark (ILLUS.) **$4,888**

Fine Fairyland Lustre Poplar Tree Bowl

Bowl, 10 1/2" d., 4 3/4" h., Fairyland Lustre, footring supporting the deep round body decorated w/the Poplar Tree patt. on the exterior & Woodland Bridge patt. on the interior, Pattern Z4968, marked on the bottom (ILLUS.) **$4,000**

Very Rare Small Fairyland Lustre Box

Box, cov., Fairyland Lustre, square design w/the slightly domed cover decorated in a variation of the Nizami patt. w/an Oriental figure sitting in a garden surrounded by small animals & birds w/a castle & trees in the background, the sides in striated bluish green w/gold geometric border bands, interior w/light blue mother-of-pearl finish w/a gold & blue Oriental figure within a central circle, bottom w/gold Portland Vase mark, 4" w., 2 1/4" h. (ILLUS.) **$10,350**

Extremely Rare Fairyland Lustre Malfrey Pot

also paper label of retailer "Leo. Kaplan Ltd., NYC - Guaranteed Genuine," 8" d., 7" h. (ILLUS.) **$34,500**

C

Fine Wedgwood Fairyland Lustre Compote

Compote, 4 3/4" d., 3 1/4" h., Fairyland Lustre, deep flaring round bowl on a short flaring pedestal base, decorated on the exterior w/the Elves on a Branch patt. w/an orange sky, green foreground w/mushrooms & brown fairies, the interior decorated w/a shaded green background centered w/elves on a branch w/flying elves, butterflies & bats, Patt. Z5360 - 9, Portland Vase mark (ILLUS.) **$4,600**

Malfrey Pot, cov., Fairyland Lustre, bulbous body w/wide low domed cover, decorated in the Bubble II patt. No. Z4968, the mottled dark blue & purple watery background decorated w/numerous fairies & bubbles, the cover depicts a large spider in a web surrounded by winged fairies, interior of cover depicts a large bubble w/fairies inside, bottom interior w/a geometric square design encircling a stylized flower, Wedgwood Portland Vase mark,

Fairyland Lustre Malfrey Pot in Willow Pattern

Malfrey Pot, cov., Fairyland Lustre, tall tapering ovoid body w/a domed cover, decorated in the Willow patt. Z5360, flame lustre background w/an Oriental landscape, Shape No. 2311, Wedgwood Portland Vase, mark, very tiny chip repair on side, probably done during manufacture, 8 1/2" h. (ILLUS.) .,........................ **$3,738**

Rare Fairyland Lustre Ship & Tree Pattern Vase

Vase, 12" h., Fairyland Lustre, thin foot below squatty bulbous lower body w/angled shoulder to the tall cylindrical neck w/a slightly flared rim, decorated in the Ship and Tree patt., a flame lustre background w/brown & purple tree trunks, green fairies w/mushrooms in foreground, a ship in the water between the trees & buildings in the background, Shape No. 2033, Wedgwood Portland Vase mark (ILLUS.) **$23,000**

Fairyland Lustre Vase with Goblin Pattern

Vase, 8 1/2" h., Fairyland Lustre, slightly tapering cylindrical body w/a flaring round foot & angled shoulder to the short trumpet neck, decorated in the Goblin patt. No. Z5367, brown goblins w/red-spotted wings standing & kneeling on green grass

alongside dark blue water w/butterflies & fairies flying above, gold Wedgwood Portland Vase mark, few glaze hairline cracks, small flake under foot (ILLUS.) **$7,475**

Fairyland Lustre Imps on Bridge Vase

Vase, 10 1/2" h., Fairyland Lustre, tall tapering ovoid body w/a flaring foot & short flaring neck, decorated in the Imps on a Bridge patt., No. Z5360, fine flame lustre background w/Imps in red shaded w/violet, a boy in the foreground in brown w/green wings spotted w/orange while a Roc bird in green, Shape No. 3148, Wedgwood Portland Vase mark, some minor wear to gold trim inside of lip (ILLUS.) **$7,475**

Very Rare Tall Fairyland Lustre Vase

Vase, 11" h., Fairyland Lustre, footed squatty bulbous lower body tapering to a tall cylindrical neck w/flaring rim, decorated in the Imps on Bridge patt., No. Z5481, flame lustre background w/green Imps on a bridge, blue Roc bird & the boy done in black w/lavender wings, gold Portland Vase mark, Shape No. 3452 (ILLUS.)... **$32,200**

Weller

This pottery was made from 1872 to 1945 at a pottery established originally by Samuel A. Weller at Fultonham, Ohio, and moved in 1882 to Zanesville. Numerous lines were produced, and listings below are by pattern or line.

Reference books on Weller include The Collectors Encyclopedia of Weller Pottery *by Sharon & Bob Huxford (Collector Books, 1979) and* All About Weller *by Ann Gilbert McDonald (Antique Publications, 1989).*

WELLER   Weller Pottery

Weller Marks

Aurelian (1898-1910)
Similar to Louwelsa line but with brighter colors and a glossy glaze. Features bright yellow/orange brush-applied background along with brown and yellow transparent glaze.

Weller Aurelian Ewer with Berries

Jug, footed squatty spherical body w/a short small neck w/spout, handle from rim to shoulder, decorated w/blackberries & green leaves & brown vine against a dark green shaded to golden yellow ground, artist-signed, No. 382 8, some light scratches, 5 1/4" h. (ILLUS.) **$431**

Baldin (about 1915-20)
Rustic designs with relief-molded apples and leaves on branches wrapped around each piece.

Nice Baldin Vase with Apples

Vase, 9 1/2" h., slightly tapering body w/a swelled shoulder & short flaring neck, molded around the top w/applies & leaves (ILLUS.) **$207**

Barcelona (1920s)
A line of simple peasant-style pieces with a golden tan background hand-painted with colorful stylized floral medallions.

Small Weller Barcelona Vase

Vase, 6 1/2" h., flaring cylindrical lower body & angled shoulder to a wide flaring neck flanked by large loop handles, decorated w/a colorful stylized flower head in red, green, blue & yellow, marked (ILLUS.)... **$127**

C

Large Weller Barcelona Vase

Vase, 11 1/2" h., flat-bottomed ovoid body tapering to a short flared neck, small twisted handles at the shoulder, decorated w/a large colorful quatrefoil design, stamped mark, minor firing separation on one handle, uncrazed (ILLUS.) **$345**

Besline (1925)

A scarce line with acid-etched decoration of Virginia Creeper vine with leaves & berries on an orange lustre ground.

Besline Urn-shaped Vase

Vase, 6 1/2" h., ovoid urn-form on a ringed pedestal base, flat rolled rim above loop handles (ILLUS.) **$345**

Blo Red (1930)

Pieces feature an orange glaze overglazed in deep red to produce a blood red mottled effect. This line shared molds with the Turkis and Nile lines.

Blo Red Vase with In-body Twist

Vase, 4 3/4" h., bulbous ovoid body w/in-body twist continuing into the wide short neck, Weller inkstamp mark (ILLUS.) **$81**

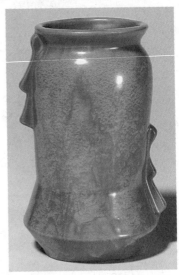

Blo Red Vase with Low Handles

Vase, 7 1/2" h., cylindrical form w/swelled angled lower body & low flared neck, low asymmetrical handles handles, tiny nick at rim, some burst glaze bubbles (ILLUS.) **$81**

Blue & Decorated Hudson (1919)

Handpainted lifelike sprays of fruit blossoms and flowers in shades of pink and blue on a rich dark blue ground.

Blue & Decorated Hudson Vase with Cherries

Vase, 9" h., slightly swelled cylindrical body tapering to a flat mouth, dark blue ground h.p. w/a green & white upper band suspending pink cherries & blue & green leaves, impressed mark (ILLUS.)..... **$259**

Blue Ware (before 1920)

Classical relief-molded white or cream figures on a dark blue ground.

Blue Ware Vase with Walking Lady

Vase, 7 1/2" h., gently tapering cylindrical shape, molded w/a walking Grecian lady

holding leafy green swags, a small rose bush nearby (ILLUS.)................................ **$184**

Bonito (1927-33)

Hand-painted florals and foliage in soft tones on cream ground. Quality of artwork greatly affects price.

Bonito Vase with Blue Daisy Decoration

Vase, 5" h., trumpet-shaped w/widely flaring top, h.p. w/a blue daisy & green leaves, artist-signed, impressed mark (ILLUS.) **$127**

Weller Bonito Urn-shaped Vase

Vase, 7" h., urn-shaped, baluster-form w/a wide flaring upper body, incurved loop handles at center of sides, h.p. w/large pansies & green leaves, artist-signed, impressed mark (ILLUS.) **$127**

Burnt Wood (1908)

Molded designs on an unglazed light tan ground with dark brown trim. Similar to Clay-wood but no vertical bands.

Burnt Wood Mug with Owl & Elf

Mug, slightly tapering cylindrical shape w/a C-form handle, decorated w/an owl on a branch & a smiling elfin creature against a banded background, 4 3/8" h. (ILLUS.) **$115**

Weller Burnt Wood Vase with Magi

Vase, 9" h., slender conical body w/a flaring cupped rim supported by three wing-form buttresses, incised decoration of the Magi & camels following the Christmas star, un-marked, repaired rim chip (ILLUS.) **$173**

Chase (late 1920s)
White relief fox hunt scenes, usually on a deep blue ground.

Tall Weller Chase Vase

Vase, 11 1/2" h., a ringed foot & cylindrical sides w/a gently flaring rim, two tiny glaze inclusions at rim (ILLUS.) **$259**

Clinton Ivory (ca. 1914)
Various forms, many in Art Nouveau designs, glazed in ivory with sepia accents.

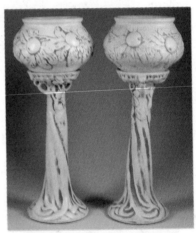

Rare Clinton Ivory Jardinieres

Jardinieres & pedestals, bulbous jardinere in the Baldin patt., raised on a tall slender tree-trunk form base, signed, overall crazing, 39" h., pr. (ILLUS.) **$2,300**

Coppertone (late 1920s)
Various shapes with an overall mottled bright green glaze on a "copper" glaze base. Some pieces with figural frog or fish handles. Models of frogs also included.

C

Coppertone Rock-form Flower Frog

Flower frog, modeled as a shaped squatty
rock formation, 5 1/4" w., 2 5/8" h. (ILLUS.) .. **$173**

Dickensware 2nd Line (early 1900s)
*Various incised "sgraffito" designs, usually
with a matte glaze. Quality of the artwork greatly
affects price.*

Dickensware II Jug with Monk Portrait

Jug, footed spherical body w/a top arched
loop handle & small shoulder spout, decorated w/a bust portrait of a monk against
a shaded green to brown ground, artist-
signed, No. 300 1, 5 3/4" h. (ILLUS.) **$259**
Vase, 10 1/2" h., gently swelled ovoid body
w/a rounded shoulder to a short widely
flaring neck, decorated w/a Japanese
peasant man bowing to a Geisha, impressed & incised marks, glazed-over
factory flaw (ILLUS., top next column) **$633**

Dickensware II Vase with Japanese Figures

Dickensware II Vase with Indian Chief

Vase, 11 1/8" h., tall ovoid body tapering to
a small flaring neck, decorated w/a large
bust portrait of Native American Chief
Black Bear, artist-signed (ILLUS.)........... **$1,725**

C

Tall Dickensware 2nd Line Portrait Vase

Vase, 12 1/8" h., gently swelled cylindrical form w/a short flaring neck, decorated w/a large profile bust portrait of Native American Chief Jack Red Cloud, artist-signed (ILLUS.) **$1,725**

Dickensware 3rd Line (1904)

Similar to Eocean line. Various fictional characters molded and slip-painted against pale background colors. Glossy glaze.

Dickensware 3rd Line Comical Mug

Mug, two-handled, slightly waisted cylindrical form, decorated w/the head of a comical man wearing a top hat & monocle, impressed mark, fracture at rim, crazing, 3 1/2" h. (ILLUS.) **$207**

Eocean and Eocean Rose (1898-1925)

Early art line with various handpainted flowers on shaded grounds, usually with a clear glossy glaze. Quality of artwork varies greatly.

Weller Eocean Vase with Pansies

Vase, 5 3/8" h., wide flaring cylindrical form w/a narrow angled shoulder & wide flat mouth, heavy squared shoulder handles, decorated w/a band of pink & pale blue pansies around the shoulder on a dark green to cream ground, artist-signed, incised marks (ILLUS.) **$207**

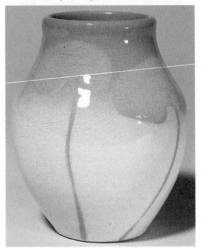

Weller Eocean Vase with Lily Pads

Vase, 6 7/8" h., wide ovoid body tapering to a flat rim, decorated w/water lily pads in pale green floating against an aquatic-like ground in shaded green to cream, artist-signed, pale discoloration beneath glaze near base (ILLUS.) **$316**

C

Weller Eocean Vase with Pink Blossoms

Vase, 7 1/4" h., tall slender swelled cylindrical form w/a flat rim, decorated around the top half w/pink forget-me-not blossoms against a black shaded to grey ground, unmarked (ILLUS.)........................ **$173**

Tall Eocean Vase with Dogwood Blossoms

Vase, 12 1/2" h., simple ovoid body tapering to a flaring neck, decorated around the neck & shoulder w/large pink & white dogwood blossoms & green leaves on a dark blue shaded to white ground, artist-signed, factory cast hole for lamp conversion (ILLUS.) **$316**

Etna (1906)
Colors similar to Early Eocean line, but designs are molded in low relief and colored.

Tall Slender Weller Eocean Vase

Vase, 11 7/8" h., tall slender gently swelled cylindrical body w/a narrow shoulder to the short molded neck, decorated w/a ring of white dogwood blossoms around the shoulder against a dark green to cream ground, leans slightly (ILLUS.)........ **$288**

Small Weller Etna Vase with Tree Decor

Vase, 4 1/2" h., a wide flattened squatty base w/a wide shoulder tapering to conical upper body, loop handles from shoulder to base of upper body, decorated w/an applied stylized dark blue tree w/thin green trunk against a grey shaded

to white ground, Weller block letter mark
& Etna in script, crazing (ILLUS.) **$81**

Weller Etna Vase with Pink Blossoms

Vase, 11" h., ovoid body w/a bulbous neck
w/closed rim, small loop handles from
neck to shoulder, molded & decorated
w/clusters of pink blossoms on a dark
green to very pale pink ground, stamped
mark, few tiny glaze nicks (ILLUS.) **$259**

Weller Etna Vase with Pink Roses

Vase, 12 7/8" h., bulbous ovoid body tapering to a small molded mouth, decorated
w/large pink roses around the shoulder
on long pale green leafy stems, against a
dark grey shaded to white ground, craz-
ing (ILLUS.) **$345**

Floretta (ca. 1904)

*An early line with various forms molded with
clusters of various fruits or flowers against a dark
brown, shaded brown or sometimes a dark grey to
cream ground. Usually found with a glossy glaze
but sometimes with a matte glaze.*

Weller Floretta Vase with Grapes

Vase, 5 3/4" h., a tapering cylindrical body
w/a bulbous four-lobed top w/a conforming rim, molded w/a cluster of green
grapes against a dark shaded to light
brown ground, marked w/Floretta Weller
seal (ILLUS.) **$81**

Forest (mid-teens to 1928)

Realistically molded and painted forest scene.

Scarce Weller Forest Jardiniere

Jardiniere, large cylindrical form, unusual
molded design of two young girls walking
in a deep forest, tight high line down from
rim, 10 3/4" d., 9 5/8" h. (ILLUS.) **$633**

C

Glendale (early to late 1920s)
Various relief-molded birds in their natural habitats, lifelike coloring.

Glendale Vase with Large Marsh Bird

Vase, 6" h., cylindrical w/narrow shoulder to a short cylindrical neck, large standing marsh bird, small chip at base (ILLUS.)..... **$374**

Glendale Vase with Marsh Bird

Vase, 6 1/2" h., footed bulbous ovoid w/flared rim, embossed w/polychrome marsh scene of marsh bird & nest, vibrant colors (ILLUS.) **$863**

Greenbriar (early 1930s)
Hand-made shapes with green underglaze covered with flowing pink overglaze marbleized with maroon striping.

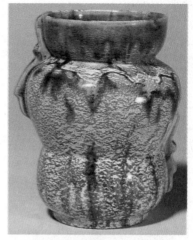

Greenbriar Double-gourd Vase

Vase, 7 3/4" h., slightly tapering double-gourd form body w/a wide slightly cupped neck, low asymmetrical handles down the sides, streaky green & blackish purple glaze w/overall white speckling, small grinding chip at the base, uncrazed (ILLUS.) **$69**

Greenbriar Vase with White Speckling

Vase, 7 7/8" h., footed squatty bulbous lower body w/tiny pointed handles below the tall trumpet neck, heavy white speckling on a dark purple ground w/streaked banding of green & purple around the lower body, unmarked (ILLUS.) **$58**

C

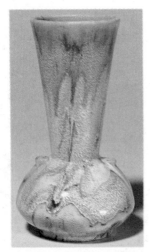

Greenbriar Vase with Drippy Green Glaze

Vase, 7 7/8" h., footed squatty bulbous lower body w/tiny pointed handles below the tall trumpet neck, green drippy glaze over purple & speckled white on the upper body w/swirled colors on the lower body, unmarked (ILLUS.)..................................... **$127**

Hobart (early to late 1920s)
Figural women, children and birds on various shaped bowls in solid pastel colors. Matte glaze.

Hobart Flying Geese Flower Frog

Flower frog, modeled as a pair of geese just taking flight, on a wide flat round base, all-white glaze, ink stamp mark, lightly crazed, 9" d., 6" h. (ILLUS.) **$196**

Hudson (1917-34)
Underglaze slip-painted decoration, "parchment-vellum" transparent glaze.

Hudson Pitcher with Floral Branch

Pitcher, 6 3/4" h., wide gently rounded body w/a long pointed rim spout, long C-form handle, decorated around the sides w/a large leafy flower stem in light green & brown on a pale pink ground, glossy glaze, Weller inkstamp mark, crazing (ILLUS.) **$431**

Weller Hudson Vase with Dogwood

Vase, 6" h., gently swelled cylindrical body tapering to a flat rim, decorated w/white & pink dogwood blossoms on leafy branches against a dark blue shaded to light blue ground, artist-signed, impressed script mark (ILLUS.) **$345**

Hudson Light (1917-34)

The same as the Hudson line except decorated in paler colors on pale backgrounds.

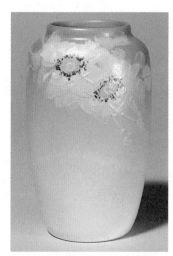

Hudson Light Vase with Roses

Vase, 7 1/4" h., gently swelled cylindrical form tapering to a short molded rim, decorated w/large pale yellow roses against a pale green to green ground, block letter mark (ILLUS.)... **$196**

Hudson Light Vase with Hydrangeas

Vase, 9" h., tall slender ovoid body w/a short flared neck, decorated w/white & pale purple hydrangea blossoms around the shoulder against a pale blue to cream ground, unmarked (ILLUS.) **$230**

Weller Hudson Light Vase with Pansies

Vase, 8" h., footed tapering cylindrical body w/a paneled lower body, decorated around the rim w/a circle of pale blue & pink pansies against a pale green to cream ground, impressed block letter mark, crazing (ILLUS.) **$230**

Weller Hudson Light Vase with Dogwood

Vase, 9 1/8" h., gently swelled cylindrical body w/a wide flat mouth, decorated around the top half w/a band of large white & pink dogwood blossoms on a very pale green to cream ground, impressed Weller mark, a few pepper spots, crazing (ILLUS.) **$184**

C

C

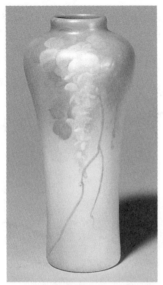

Hudson Light Tall Vase with Wisteria

Vase, 10 1/4" h., a tall slender cylindrical
lower body swelled to a bulbous shoulder
below the short cylindrical neck, decorated w/white wisteria blossoms & leaves
against a light blue to pale pink ground,
artist-signed, block Weller mark (ILLUS.)... **$316**

Jewell & Cameo Jewell (about 1910-15)
*Similar to the Etna line but most pieces
molded with a band of raised oval 'jewels' or jewels and cameo portraits in color against a light or
dark shaded ground.*

Weller Cameo Jewel Jardiniere

Jardinere, a scalloped, molded base on a
flaring wide body w/an indented neck
band & thick molded rim, dark green to
light green ground, few glaze chips at
base, crazed, 6 7/8" h., 8" d. (ILLUS.)
.... **$150-200**

Knifewood (late teens)
*Pieces feature deeply molded designs of dogs,
swans, and other birds and animals or flowers in
white or cream against dark brown grounds.*

Scarce Knifewood Mug with Dogs

Tumbler, slightly flaring cylindrical shape,
etched w/two panels showing a hunting
dog in a landscape w/trees & grass, over-
all green wash, 3 1/8" h. (ILLUS.) **$259**

L'Art Nouveau (1903-04)
*Various figural and floral-embossed Art Nou-
veau designs.*

L'Art Nouveau Four-sided Vase

Vase, 10 1/4" h., slender four-sided body
w/a floral-embossed four-lobed rim
above embossed panels of flowers & Art

Nouveau woman, impressed "Weller" in small block letters (ILLUS.) **$546**

Lasa (1920-25)
Various landscapes on a banded reddish and gold iridescent ground. Lack of scratches and abrasions important.

Lasa Vase with Mountain Landscape

Vase, 5 3/4" h., swelled cylindrical body w/a wide flat molded mouth, decorated w/a mountainous landscape w/tall fir trees in the foreground, banded iridescent background, faintly marked, minor scratch (ILLUS.).. **$575**

Tall Lasa Vase with Fir Trees

Vase, 11 3/8" h., footed tall slender swelled cylindrical body, decorated w/very tall fir

trees in the foreground & hills in the distance, on a banded iridescent ground, several scratches on lower body (ILLUS.) .. **$575**

Very Tall Lasa Vase with Slender Trees

Vase, 16" h., tall gently swelled cylindrical body tapering to a trumpet neck, decorated w/a continuous scene of very tall slender trees w/leafy tops, hills is the distance, signed on the side, on a banded iridescent ground, black painted notation on the bottom "$37.50," very minor scratches (ILLUS.) **$2,070**

Pair of Slender Lasa Vases

Vases, 6 1/8" h., tall slender tapering body decorated w/a very tall fir tree against a shaded iridescent ground, signed near the foot, minor scratches, pr. (ILLUS.) **$345**

Louwelsa (1896-1924)
Handpainted underglaze slip decoration on dark brown shading to yellow ground; glossy yellow glaze.

C

Weller Louwelsa Ewer with Dogwood

Ewer, footed bulbous tapering ovoid body w/a slender neck & large flared tricorner rim, applied loop handle from neck to shoulder, h.p. decoration of white dogwood blossoms & light green leaves on a dark green shaded ground, No. 431, two glaze-only chips on spout, 8 1/2" h. (ILLUS.) **$138**

Small Louwelsa Ewer with Daffodil

Ewer, squatty bulbous body tapering to a flat base & to a slender flaring neck w/a tricorner rim & long applied strap handle, decorated w/a pale yellow daffodil & green leaves on a dark green to yellow ground, artist-signed, numbered 9 x 65 1, some glaze bubbles & small chips, 5" h. (ILLUS.) **$138**

Weller Louwelsa Jug with Ear of Corn

Jug, squatty waisted cylindrical body w/a rounded shoulder to the small flared neck, applied loop shoulder handle, h.p. w/an ear of corn in yellow w/green leaves against a dark green to dark yellow ground, artist-signed, numbered 614-3, 5 1/2" h. (ILLUS.) **$259**

Tall Louwelsa Vase with Bear Head

Vase, 10 1/2" h., slender cylindrical shape w/narrow shoulder & rolled rim, h.p. w/the head of a brown bear, tight short high line from rim, very minor glaze nicks & scratches (ILLUS.)...................................... **$978**

Marvo (mid-1920s-'33)
Molded overall fern and leaf design on various matte background colors.

Marvo Vase with Chinese Red Glaze

Vase, 6 1/2" h., flaring ovoid body w/a wide angled shoulder to the short flaring neck, deeply molded design w/a Chinese Red Chengtu glaze, Weller inkstamp mark (ILLUS.).. **$115**

Tapering Ovoid Weller Marvo Vase

Vase, 7" h., a wide flat mouth above a tapering ovoid body, mottled tan & green glaze, Weller inkstamp mark (ILLUS.)........ **$104**

Ovoid Marvo Vase with Flaring Mouth

Vase, 7 1/4" h., ovoid body w/angled upper body to the wide flaring mouth, tan & green mottled glaze, unmarked (ILLUS.)..... **$69**

Matt Green (ca. 1904)
Various shapes with slightly shaded dark green matte glaze and molded with leaves and other natural forms.

Fine Matt Green Vase with Buttresses

Vase, 9 5/8" h., ovoid body tapering to a ring-molded rim w/four buttress handles down the sides, lightly molded design around the sides, fine hairline at rim, glaze skip near base, uncrazed, unmarked (ILLUS.).. **$500**

Nile (1929)

Heavy designs covered with a fine streaky and drippy bluish green glaze shading from deep green to teal blue

Weller Nile Handled Vase

Vase, 6 7/8" h., bulbous ovoid body tapering to a flat mouth flanked by long loop handles to the shoulder, fine streaky glaze (ILLUS.) **$92**

Noval (about 1920)

Pieces feature a white background with narrow black bordering and applied roses or fruit. Glossy glaze.

Weller Noval Coupe-shaped Vase

Vase, 7 3/4" h., tall slender coupe-shaped body w/flaring stem mounted w/three long black loop handles, applied red rose

buds & green leaves near the rim, crazing (ILLUS.) **$92**

Sabrinian (late '20s)

Seashell body with sea horse handle. Pastel colors. Matte finish. Middle period.

Sabrinian Double-Bud Vase

Vase, double-bud, 6 1/2" h., a round seaweed-molded base supporting to tall pointed shells joined at the top by an arched handle (ILLUS.) **$127**

Sicardo (1902-07)

Various shapes with iridescent glaze of metallic shadings in greens, blues, crimson, purple or coppertone decorated with vines, flowers, stars or freeform geometric lines.

Small Sicardo Vase with Daisies

Vase, 3 7/8" h., squatty cushion base below the tapering cylindrical sides w/a small flat mouth, overall abstract design of daisies & scrolling leaves, iridescent green & purple glaze, signed on the side (ILLUS., previous page) **$633**

Squatty Sicardo Vase with Clover Leaves

Vase, 4 1/2" h., wide squatty lobed body tapering to a flat mount flanked by small knob shoulder handles, decorated overall w/stylized clover leaves & dots in a purplish iridescent glaze, signed on the side, very tiny grinding chips on bottom (ILLUS.) **$863**

Triangular Lobed Sicardo Vase

Vase, 6 3/4" h., upright triangular body w/pinched-in sides forming a lobed mouth, decorated w/scattered shamrocks & dots in a metallic purple & blue glaze, signed on the side, impressed "18 IV" on the base (ILLUS.) **$1,150**

Sicardo Vase with Rosebuds & Dots

Vase, 5" h., wide tapering cylindrical body w/in-body twist up the sides to the small flat mouth, decorated w/stylized rosebuds & dots in a metallic purple, blue & green glaze, signed on the side, tiny grinding chips on base, light crazing (ILLUS.) **$805**

Fine Sicardo Vase with Shell-like Flowers

Vase, 7 3/8" h., tall tapering melon-lobed body w/a tiny mouth, decorated overall w/a repeating design of cockle shell-like blossoms on stems, signed on the side, deep iridescent purple & gold glaze (ILLUS.) **$3,450**

C

C

Silvertone (1928)
Various flowers, fruits or butterflies molded on a pale purple-blue matte pebbled ground.

Silvertone Vase with Molded Grapes

Vase, 6 3/8" h., footed bulbous ovoid body w/wide flaring rim & small loop handles at shoulder, decorated w/relief-molded grape clusters & leaves, ink stamp (ILLUS.)........... **$230**

Weller Silvertone Vase with Calla Lilies

Vase, 10 1/2" h., trumpet-form, molded w/white calla lilies, ink-stamped mark (ILLUS.) **$316**

Souevo (1907-10)
Unglazed redware bodies with glossy black interiors. The exterior decorated with black & white American Indian geometric designs.

Silvertone Vase with Black-eyed Susans

Vase, 6 1/2" h., ovoid form tapering sharply at the shoulder to a flared neck flanked by arched handles to shoulder, decorated w/large black-eyed Susans, ink stamp mark (ILLUS.)... **$230**

Small Weller Souevo Squatty Vase

Vase, 3" h., squatty bulbous form tapering to a flat mouth, wide white upper band decorated w/black half-circles & arches, unmarked, some staining, couple of minor glaze nicks, uncrazed (ILLUS.)............ **$115**

Ovoid Signed Weller Souevo Vase

Vase, 8 1/2" h., ovoid body tapering to a flat rim, wide white body band decorated w/black abstract geometric design, impressed Weller mark, minor abrasions (ILLUS.).. **$173**

Tall Waisted Weller Souevo Vase

Vase, 11 7/8" h., tall waisted cylindrical form, decorated w/a band of triangles in white & white & vertical bands of graduated black triangles, unmarked (ILLUS.)....... **$173**

Velva (1933)

Simple forms with a dark green, blue or shaded tan ground decorated with a full-length rectangular panel down the side molded in low-relief with large stylized green leaves & small creamy blossoms.

Weller Velva Ovoid Vase

Vase, 6" h., footed bulbous ovoid body tapering to a low rolled mouth, small curled handles at the sides, vertical band of stylized leaves & flowers, shaded tan ground, Weller script mark, uncrazed (ILLUS.) **$138**

White & Decorated Hudson (1917-34)

A version of the Hudson line usually with dark colored floral designs against a creamy white ground.

Decorated Hudson Vase with Berries

Vase, 8 1/2" h., slightly tapering cylindrical body w/a flat rim, decorated around the rim w/swirled green leaves & stems suspending clusters of pink & lavender berries against a white background, impressed Weller mark (ILLUS.)................... **$345**

C

Decorated Hudson Vase with Blossoms

Vase, 9" h., gently swelled ovoid body tapering to a flat molded mouth, decorated w/a large limb w/clusters of deep pink applied blossoms & pale green leaves on the white ground, impressed Weller mark (ILLUS.)... **$288**

Decorated Hudson Vase with Nasturtiums

Vase, 9 3/8" h., cylindrical body w/a wide flat mouth, a thin dark blue rim band above a wide band w/stylized nasturtium blossoms & leaves against a green band, impressed block Weller mark, a few blue streaks near the base (ILLUS.)................. **$288**

Woodcraft (1917)

Rustic designs simulating the appearance of stumps, logs and tree trunks. Some pieces are adorned with owls, squirrels, dogs and other animals. Matte finish.

White & Decorated Hudson Vase

Vase, 9 3/8" h., bulbous bottom tapering to a cylindrical neck, decorated w/Virginia Creeper in shades of blue, pink & green against two body bands & a cream ground, unmarked (ILLUS.)........................ **$374**

Woodcraft Planter with Mushroom Handle

Planter, wide low cylindrical log form w/molded yellow jonquils & a molded mushroom handle on one side, impress mark, minor flaws, 9 1/2" w., 5 1/8" h. (ILLUS.) **$184**

Woodcraft Wall Pocket with Owl

Wall pocket, long flattened trumpet form molded as a tree trunk w/molded leaves near the base & a round opening showing the head of an owl near the top, 11" l. (ILLUS.).. **$250-350**

Willow Wares

This pseudo-Chinese pattern has been used by numerous firms throughout the years. The original design is attributed to Thomas Minton about 1780, and Thomas Turner is believed to have first produced the ware during his tenure at the Caughley works. The blue underglaze transfer print pattern has never been out of production since that time. An Oriental landscape incorporating a bridge, pagoda, trees, figures and birds supposedly tells the story of lovers fleeing a cruel father who wished to prevent their marriage. The gods, having pity on them, changed them into birds, enabling them to fly away and seek their happiness together.

Blue

Ashtray, figural whale, ca. 1960, Japan...... **$25-30**
Bank, figural, stacked pigs, ca. 1960, Japan, 7" h. **$50-55**
Batter jug, Moriyama, Japan, 9 1/2" h. **$100-125**

Blue Willow Bone Dish

Bone dish, Buffalo Pottery, 6 1/2" l. (ILLUS.) **$60-70**
Bowl, 12 1/4" d., serving-type w/beaded rim **$50-75**
Bowl, cereal, Royal China Co. **$11**
Bowl, soup, 8" d., Japan **$18-20**
Bowls, 8", 9 1/4" & 10 1/2" l., rectangular, stacking-type, Ridgways, set of 3 .... **$200**
Butter dish, in wood holder, 6" d. **$50-75**
Butter dish, drain & cover, Ridgways, 3 pcs. **$200**
Canister set: cov., "Coffee," "Flour," "Sugar," "Tea," barrel-shaped, ca. 1960s, Japan, the set **$275-300**
Chamber pot, Wedgwood, 9" d. **$175-200**
Charger, 12" d., Buffalo Pottery **$75-95**

C

Blue Willow Cracker Jar

Cracker jar, cov., silver lid & handle, Minton, England, 5" h. (ILLUS.) **$175**
Creamer, individual, Shenango China Co... **$25-30**
Creamer, John Steventon **$30**
Cup & saucer, Buffalo Pottery **$40-45**
Cup & saucer, child's, ca. 1900, unmarked, England.. **$50**
Egg cup, Booths, England, 4" h................. **$40-45**
Ginger jar, cov., Mason's, 9" h. **$50-60**
Gravy boat w/attached underplate, double-spouted, Ridgways, England **$60-70**
Ladle, pattern in bowl, unmarked, England, 6" l. **$125-135**

Blue Willow Mug

Mug, barrel-shaped mold, Granger & Worcester, England, ca. 1850, 4 1/4" h. (ILLUS.)... **$200-250**

C

Willow Ware Punch Cup

Punch cup, pedestal foot, unmarked, England, ca. 1900, 3 1/2" h. (ILLUS.) **$40-50**

Early Willow Leaf-shaped Relish Dish

Relish dish, leaf-shaped, ca. 1870, England (ILLUS.) **$100-125**

Blue Willow Salt Box

Salt box, cov., ca. 1960, wooden lid, Japan, 5 x 5" (ILLUS.).................................... **$150-200**
Salt dip, master, pedestal base, unmarked, England, 2" h..................................... **$100-125**
Salt & pepper shakers, Japan, pr. **$30-35**

Blue Willow Sauce Tureen

Sauce tureen, cov., England, ca. 1880s, 5" h. (ILLUS.) **$125-150**
Soup tureen, cov., ca. 1880, unmarked, England.. **$350-400**

Blue Willow Sugar Barrel

Sugar Barrel, cov., silver lid & handle, unmarked, England, ca. 1880s, 5" h. (ILLUS.) .. **$175**
Sugar bowl, cov., Japan............................ **$20-25**
Tea set, child's, Japan, service for six in box **$200-250**
Tea tile, Minton, England, 6" sq. **$75**
Teapot, cov., ca. 1890, Royal Doulton **$250-300**
Teapot, cov., round, Allerton, England.... **$200-250**

"Auld Lang Syne" Blue Willow Teapot

Teapot, cov., six-paneled squatty bulbous body on short feet, flat hexagonal neck & cover topped w/figural gold lion finial, gold beaded C-form handle, serpentine spout, embellished w/gold line decoration on feet, spout & lid, the sides of the neck reading "We'll take a cup o' kindness yet, for days o' auld lang syne" in blue, made for Tiffany & Co., New York by Copeland China, England, ca. 1870s (ILLUS., bottom previous page) **$200**

Hammersley & Co. Blue Willow Teapot

Teapot, cov., squatty ovoid body on short foot, incurved neck, C-scroll handle, slightly serpentine spout, inset cover tapering to peaked circular finial, decorated w/bands of gold beading at shoulder & on cover, gold decoration on rim, handle, spout & finial, Hammersley & Co., England, ca. 1912-39 (ILLUS.)............ **$150-175**

Royal Worcester Blue Willow Teapot

Teapot, cov., squatty ovoid body tapering in at shoulder to gently peaked cover w/knob finial, straight spout, C-scroll handle, Royal Worcester porcelain, England, ca. 1920s (ILLUS.) **$150-175**

Doulton & Co. Blue Willow Teapot

Teapot, cov., squatty ovoid body tapering in at shoulder to short cylindrical neck, slightly tapering inset cover w/disk finial, angled handle, slightly curved spout, shoulder reads "We'll take a cup o' kindness yet, for days o' auld lang syne," Doulton & Co., England, ca. 1882-91 (ILLUS.) **$200**

Blue Willow Tip Tray

Tip tray, "Schweppes Lemon Squash," England, 4 1/2" d. (ILLUS.)......................... **$40-50**
Toby jug, w/Blue Willow jacket, W. Kent, England, 6" h....................................... **$300-400**
Trivet, scalloped foot, Moriyama, very rare, 6".. **$50-75**

Zeisel (Eva) Designs

One of the most influential ceramic artists and designers of the 20th century, Eva Zeisel began her career in Europe as a young woman, eventually immigrating to the United States, where her unique, streamlined designs met with great success. Since the 1940s her work has been at the forefront of commercial ceramic design, and in recent decades she has designed in other media. Now in her ninth decade, she continues to be active and involved in the world of art and design.

Castleton - Museum Ware
Bowl, 11" d., salad, White **$160**
Cup & saucer, flat, Mandalay **$20**
Plate, 8 1/4" sq., salad, White **$135**

Hall China Company - Kitchenware

Golden Clover Cookie Jar

Cookie jar, cov., Golden Clover (ILLUS.) **$65**
Marmite, Casual Living **$30**
Refrigerator jug, cov., Tri-tone..................... **$150**
Sugar, Tri-tone **$60**

Tri-tone Teapot

C

Teapot, cov., 6-cup, Tri-tone, ca. 1954 (ILLUS.) **$85**

Hallcraft by Hall China Co. - Tomorrow's Classic Shape

This shape was produced in plain white and with a variety of decal designs. A selection of the designs are listed here.

Fantasy (abstract black lines)
Platter, 15 1/8" oval **$55**
Vegetable serving bowl, oval, 11 3/4" l. **$70**

Harlequin (pink & black abstract design)
Bowl, 6" d., cereal **$20**
Plate, 6" d., bread & butter **$10**
Plate, 11" d., dinner **$25**
Platter, 12 7/8" oval **$45**
Salt & pepper shakers, the set **$65**
Vegetable serving bowl, oval, 11 3/4" l. **$50**

Mulberry (literal mulberry design)
Bowl, 6" d., cereal **$17**
Cup & saucer, the set **$22**
Plate, 11" d., dinner **$25**

Hallcraft - Century Dinnerware
Creamer, Fern **$35**
Gravy boat & ladle, Fern **$95**
Plate, 10" d., dinner, Sunglow **$25**
Relish, divided, White **$90**

White Vegetable Bowl

Vegetable bowl, 10 1/2" d., White (ILLUS.) **$35**

Hollydale

Hollydale Chop Plate

Chop plate, 14" l., brown (ILLUS.) **$60**
Gravy bowl, bird-shape **$85**
Sauce dish, bird-shape, yellow/turquoise **$200**
Tureen & ladle, bird design, the set **$300**

Hyalyn "Z Ware"
Bowl, cereal, oxblood, commercial grade/restaurant ware **$40**

Satin Black "Z Ware" Coffee Server

Coffee server, cov., satin black w/white lid (ILLUS.) **$150**
Creamer, handleless, autumn gold, 4 3/4" h. **$85**

Johann Haviland
Bowl, fruit, Wedding Ring patt. **$12**
Coffeepot, cov., Eva White **$75**
Creamer & sugar, Eva White, the set **$65**
Cup & saucer, Wedding Ring **$20**
Plate, 10 1/4" d., dinner, Wedding Ring **$18**
Sauce dish & underplate, Wheat **$50**
Serving bowl, round, Wedding Ring patt. **$40**

Blue Roses Teapot

Teapot, cov., Blue Roses patt., 1950s (ILLUS.) **$65**
Tureen/vegetable bowl, cov., White **$80**

Monmouth Dinnerware
Butter pat, Pals, 4" **$25**
Creamer, Lacy Wings **$50**

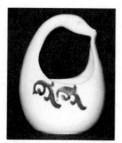

Goose-shaped Gravy Boat

Gravy boat, goose shape, Lacey Wings
(ILLUS.) **$175**
Sugar, cov., bird lid, Blueberry **$25**

Lacey Wings Teapot with Bird Decoration

Teapot, cov., Lacey Wings patt., wire handle w/ceramic grip, Prairie Hen, w/bird
decoration, ca. 1952 (ILLUS.) **$150**
Vegetable bowl, 9 1/2" d. **$65**

Norleans Dinnerware by Meito

*(Pieces marked "Made in Occupied Japan" are
worth 25% more.)*

Cup & saucer, Livonia **$12**

Livonia Gravy Boat with Underliner

Gravy boat w/underliner, Livonia (ILLUS.)..... **$65**
Plate, salad, Livonia **$10**

Livonia Vegetable Bowl

Vegetable bowl, 12" oval, Livonia (ILLUS.) **$55**

Schmid Dinnerware

Casserole, cov., bird lid, 9 1/2 x 8" **$150**

Schmid Dinnerware Coffeepot

Coffeepot, cov., Lacey Wings/Rosette
(ILLUS.) **$125**

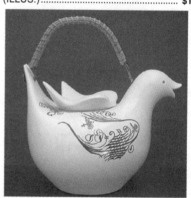

Schmid Bird-shaped Teapot

Teapot, cov., bird-shaped, rattan handle,
Lacey Wings, 1950s (ILLUS.) **$85**

Schramberg

Schramberg Triangular Ashtray

Ashtray, triangular, Gobelin 13 (ILLUS.) **$160**
Cup & saucer, Gobelin 13 .... **$75**

Mondrian Covered Jar

C

Jar, cov., terraced, Mondrian, 5" (ILLUS.,
    previous page) **$1,000**
Pitcher, 4 1/2" h., Mondrian **$225**
Plate, 7 1/2" d., dessert, Gobelin 13 .... **$60**

Gobelin 13 Teapot

Teapot, cov., Gobelin 13 patt., Germany,
    1930s (ILLUS.) **$900**

Stratoware

Stratoware Candlestick

Candlestick, brown trim (ILLUS.) **$120**
Casserole, cov., beige & brown **$150**
Plate, 11 1/2" d., yellow & green **$60**

Stratoware Refrigerator Jar

Refrigerator jar, cov., blue & beige (ILLUS.) .. **$200**

Stratoware Covered Sugar

Sugar, cov., gold & beige (ILLUS.) **$70**

Town and Country Dinnerware - for Red Wing Potteries

*Pieces are unmarked and must be identified by
the unique shapes. Glaze colors include rust,
gray, dusk blue, peach, chartreuse, sand, Ming
green, bronze & white.*

Bowl, 5 3/4" d., chili or cereal, sand **$18**
Creamer, sand **$45**

Town and Country "Yawn" Creamer

Creamer, "yawn," bronze (ILLUS.) **$70**
Cup & saucer, peach, the set **$40**

Lazy Susan Relish Set

Lazy Susan relish set w/mustard jar (ILLUS.)
.... **$600**
Mixing bowl rust **$175**
Pitcher, jug-type, dusk blue, 3 pt. **$250**

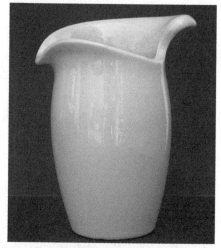

Town and Country Syrup Pitcher

Pitcher, syrup, chartreuse (ILLUS.) **$135**
Plate, 8" d., salad, dusk blue **$30**
Plate, 8" d., salad, sand.................................... **$30**
Plate, 10 1/2" d., dinner, peach **$45**
Platter, 15" l., comma shape, rust.................. **$110**
Shaker, large "schmoo," Ming green (ILLUS.
    right w/small "schmoo" shaker, top next
    column).. **$75**
Shaker, small "schmoo," chartreuse **$40**
Shaker, small "schmoo," rust (ILLUS. left
    w/large "schmoo" shaker, top next col-
    umn).. **$40**
Sugar bowl, cov., rust...................................... **$60**

Large & Small "Schmoo" Shakers

Town & Country Covered Soup Tureen

Tureen, cov., soup, sand (ILLUS.) **$850**

C

Watt Pottery

Watt Pottery Drip Glaze Bowl

Bowl, 8 1/4" d., blue drip glaze (ILLUS.) **$25**
Chop tray, Mountain Road, 14 1/2" **$210**
Teapot, cov., rattan handle, Animal Farm
   patt., ca. 1954 .... **$650**

Zsolnay

This pottery was made in Pecs, Hungary, in a factory founded in 1862 by Vilmos Zsolnay. Utilitarian earthenware was originally produced, but by the turn of the 20th century ornamental Art Nouveau-style wares with bright colors and lustre decoration were produced; these wares are especially sought today. Currently Zsolnay pieces are being made in a new factory.

Zsolnay Marks

Zsolnay Chalice

Chalice, organic form w/applied handles curving out connecting base to bowl,

multi glazes, printed Zsolnay Factory mark, incised form number 5668, ca. 1900, 6" h. (ILLUS.) **$1,500-2,000**

Zsolnay Armin Klein Charger

Charger, painted w/scene of peasants in folkloric costumes pressing grapes in a vineyard, design by Armin Klein, printed Zsolnay factory mark, incised form number 470, ca. 1880, 15" d. (ILLUS.)
   .... **$1,500-2,000**

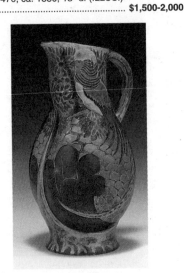

Iridescent Zsolnay Bird-decorated Ewer

Ewer, footed ovoid body tapering to a cylindrical neck pinched-in to form a long rim spout, simple applied strap handle, decorated overall w/exotic birds in shades of red, pale green & purple among branches of stylized blossoms in dark blue & red on iridescent green stems against a blue spotted & dark red iridescent ground, raised churches mark, ca. 1900, 9" h. (ILLUS.).............................. **$13,200**

C

Zsolnay Figure & Silver-Overlaid Vase

Figure of a female nude, standing figure w/one hand to her breast & the other holding a drapery behind her, deep brown iridescent glaze, molded factory seal, ca. 1900, 12 1/4" h. (ILLUS. right with silver-overlaid Zsolnay vase) **$2,868**

Zsolnay Lamp by Lajos Mack

Zsolnay Tadé Sikorsky Jug

Jug, form designed by Tadé Sikorsky, shriveled glaze w/applied pierced decorations, incised Zsolnay factory mark & form number 1379, ca. 1885, 8" h. (ILLUS.)........ **$350-550**

Lamp, figural, Art Nouveau model of a woman in the style of Lolie Fuller, w/arms upraised & flowing hair, designed by Lajos Mack, mostly gold/green Eosin glazes, round raised Zsolnay factory mark, incised form number 6324, ca. 1900, 22 1/2" h. (ILLUS., top next column)
.... **$20,000-25,000**

Zsolany Skull & Bible Paperweight

Paperweight, figural, modeled as a closed Bible w/a skull resting on the top, dark blue lustre glaze w/green highlights, impressed mark & number 5788, thin lines radiate from one corner, 3" h. (ILLUS.) **$288**

Pitcher, 9 1/2" h., slightly bulbous tankard shape w/angular handle, metallic Eosin glazed decoration in the style of Loetz Bohemian glass, round raised Zsolnay factory mark, incised form number 8925, ca. 1918 .... **$7,500-9,500**

Pitcher, 12 3/4" h., crackled glaze, red color, modern design by Gabriella Törzsök, printed Zsolnay Factory mark, ca. 1959
.... **$300-500**

C

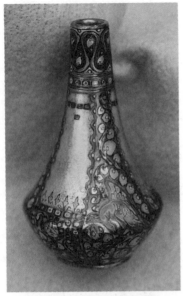

Miniature Zsolnay Vase

Vase, miniature, 4" h., wide base tapering to ring foot & long neck, richly decorated w/Hungarian folkloric designs in gold & blue/green Eosin glazes, incised Zsolnay factory mark, ca. 1912 (ILLUS.) **$1,000-1,250**

Four-handled Zsolnay Vase

Vase, 4 7/8" h., footed bulbous body tapering to a cylindrical neck & mounted w/four large flattened gold handles, deep red ground w/a rim band of stylized flowerheads in white, dark blue & gold, Zsolnay mark & number 2293 (ILLUS.) **$690**

Zsolnay Vase with Iridescent Eosin Glaze

Vase, 6 7/8" h., bulbous ovoid lower body tapering to a pinched center below the upright squared neck, iridescent Eosin glaze w/rust over brushed gold, marked w/raised wafer logo & impressed numbers "6035 - 23" (ILLUS.) **$863**

Wide Squatty Zsolnay Iridescent Vase

Vase, 8" d., in the Persian taste, broad squatty shield-shaped body w/a wide shoulder centered by a small low rolled neck, the shoulder decorated w/iridescent stylized flambé flowers on a scalloped ground, the sides painted w/an iridescent continuous caravansary & three palm trees in a desert landscape, five churches raised pad mark, ca. 1914-20 (ILLUS.) **$7,200**

Vase, 8" w., earthenware, wide ovoid base w/broad flattened shoulder centered by a short cylindrical rim, decorated w/a caravan of men on camels carrying guns & spears, in an oasis w/palm trees, below a wavy edged border of scattered flower heads, iridescent red, brown & blue glaze, ca. 1900-10, molded factory seal, impressed "8868" & "19," imperfection at edge of foot, ... **$2,300**

Vase, 8 3/4" h., footed wide ovoid body below an angled shoulder tapering to a flaring neck, dark blue shaded to green iridescent ground silver-overlaid overall w/vining thistle-like leaves, molded factory mark, ca. 1900 (ILLUS. left with nude female figure, page 355) **$1,076**

Fine Reticulated Iridescent Zsolnay Vase

Vase, 12 1/2" h., in the Persian taste, footed tall slightly tapering cylindrical body w/a rounded shoulder & short cylindrical neck w/flaring rim, the central double-walled section pierced about the base & upper body w/cartouches of birds & berried vine, painted between the panels w/similar decoration, the single-walled neck w/similar reticulation, overall iridescent metallic lustre in shades of greenish gold & shades of orange & red, possibly by Henri Darilek, ca. 1905 (ILLUS.) **$6,600**

One of Two Fine Zsolnay Lustre Vases

Vases, 13 3/8" h., in the Persian taste, tall slightly tapering cylindrical body w/a rounded shoulder to the cylindrical neck w/a widely flaring flattened rim, the dark copy lustre ground decorated front & back w/large stylized pineapples & foliage light blue & gold lustre, the sides

w/matching stylized flowers, printed five churches mark, early 20th c., pr. (ILLUS. of one) **$10,800**

CHALKWARE

So-called chalkware available today is actually made of plaster-of-Paris, much of it decorated in color and primarily in the form of busts, figurines and ornaments. It was produced through most of the 19th century, and the majority of pieces were quite inexpensive when made. Today even 20th century "carnival" pieces are collectible.

Rare Early Large Chalkware Cat

Cat, seated facing the viewer, on a oblong molded base, original dark golden & green paint, southeastern Pennsylvania, early 19th c., 15" h. (ILLUS.) **$2,640**

Grouping of Early Chalkware Animals

Cat, seated on thin square base, facing viewer w/ears erect, white w/yellow & brown trim & painted facial features, possible touch-up, minor wear, 19th c., 6 5/8" h. (ILLUS. middle row, right, with grouping of chalkware animals, previous page) **$98**

Fruit & Leaf Chalkware Garniture

Garniture, gold & white squared & tapering pedestal supporting a large upright ovoid fruit in dark yellow framed by wide, veined brown leaves, some wear, 19th c., 10 1/2" h. (ILLUS.) **$546**

Early Painted Chalkware Garniture

Garniture, stylized upright yellow fruit & green leaves raised on a tapering square plinth, worn original paint, 19th c., 10 1/2" h. (ILLUS.) **$345**

Lovebirds, facing birds on a domed oval base, traces of paint, possible repair, 19th c., 9 1/2"l. (ILLUS. bottom row, with grouping of chalkware animals, previous page) **$408**

Model of a ewe & lamb, the recumbent animals on a rectangular base, white w/original painted details w/painted details on the heads, repaired ears & edge flakes, 9" l., 6 1/2" h. (ILLUS. top row,

left, with grouping of chalkware animals, previous page) **$394**

Poodle, standing animals facing the viewer, on a rectangular base trimmed in green, black trim on face, ears & tail, repaired nose, some edge flakes w/touch-up, 19th c., 7 1/8" h. (ILLUS. middle row, left, with other chalkware animals, previous page)... **$230**

Ram, standing facing viewer, on rectangular base trimmed in brown, black trim on face & horns, 7 3/4" h. (ILLUS. top row, right, with other chalkware animals, previous page) **$1,725**

CHARACTER COLLECTIBLES

Numerous objects made in the likeness of or named after comic strip and comic book personalities or characters abounded from the 1920s to the present. Scores of these are now being eagerly collected and prices still vary widely. Also see DISNEY COLLECTIBLES and TOYS and "ANTIQUE TRADER TOY PRICE GUIDE."

Barney Google & Spark Plug

Barney Google & Spark Plug, jointed wood, comic strip characters, cloth outfit & blanket, Schoenhut & Co., 1920s, 8 1/4" h., fair to good condition, the pair (ILLUS.).. **$518**

1988 Elvira, Mistress of the Dark Calendar

Elvira, Mistress of the Dark calendar, 1988, color cover photo, Great Northern (ILLUS., previous page) **$15-25**

Premiere Comic of The Incredible Hulk

C

1960s Green Hornet Fork

Green Hornet fork, stainless steel, flattened handle stamped w/image of the Green Hornet above his name, 1960s (ILLUS.) **$95**

Lois Lane Comic Book

1978 Godzilla Comic Book

Godzilla comic book, "Godzilla - King of the Monsters," Marvel Comics #15, 1978 (ILLUS.) **$3-10**

Incredible Hulk (The) comic book, "Big Premiere Issue," origin story retold, Marvel Comics #102, 1968, depending on condition (ILLUS., top next column) **$100-400**

Lois Lane (Superman's girlfriend) comic book, "I Am Curious (Black)!" Lois becomes a black woman, DC #106 (ILLUS., middle next column) **$30-100**

Maggie & Jiggs Windup Toy

Maggie & Jiggs (Bringing Up Father) toy, windup tin, figures of Maggie & Jiggs on facing wheeled platforms joined by a slender rod, good paint, Nifty, 1930s, 5 1/2" h. (ILLUS.) **$863**

C

1920s Toonerville Trolley Windup Toy

Toonerville Trolley toy, windup tin, trolley rolls forward in eccentric motion w/animated conductor, "Toonerville" along edge of top, "Trolley" printed under windows, copyright 1922 by Fontaine Fox, Germany, some darkening to color, light scratching, pencil mark on roof, 7" h. (ILLUS.) **$288**

Uncle Wiggily Crazy Car Wind-up Toy

Uncle Wiggily toy, wind-up tin crazy car, colorfully printed, Uncle Wiggily drives a jalopy that spins & turns while his head turns, Marx, copyright 1935, overall very good condition & working (ILLUS.)............. **$431**

1967 New Wonder Woman Comic Book

Wonder Woman comic book, "Forget The Old - The New Wonder Woman Is Here!," cover art w/Wonder Woman in mod outfit,

DC #178, 1967, depending on condition (ILLUS.)... **$40-125**

CHILDREN'S DISHES

During the reign of Queen Victoria, dollhouses and accessories became more popular; as the century progressed, there was greater demand for toys that would subtly train a little girl in the art of homemaking.

ABC plate, pressed glass, center w/ducks & ducklings, amber, 6" d.................................. **$88**
ABC plate, pressed glass, elephant & riders scene in the center, clear, 6" d.................... **$77**
ABC plate, pressed glass, frosted center w/stork surrounded by tree & foliate, stippled shoulder, clear, 6" d. **$88**
Berry set: 4 3/8" d. master berry bowl & six berry dishes; clear pressed glass, Nursery Rhyme patt., the set............................ **$165**

Rare Standing Lamb Glass Butter Dish

Butter dish, cov., pressed glass, Standing Lamb patt., figural lamb finial, frosted clear, 4" d., 3 1/4" h. (ILLUS.) **$1,100**
Cake stand, pressed glass, Beautiful Lady patt., clear, 6" d., 4" h.................................. **$39**

Ribbon Band Four-Bottle Castor Set

Castor set, four-bottle, pressed glass, Ribbon Band patt., in original Britannia metal stand, attributed to the Boston & Sandwich Glass Co., overall 9" h. (ILLUS.)........ **$303**

Children's Toy Tureen, Plate & Lemonade Mug

C

Castor set, three-bottle, pressed glass, Quilted patt., in original Britannia stand, clear, the set.. **$88**

Creamer, pressed Chocolate glass, Wild Rose with Scrolling patt., 2 3/4" h. **$66**

Cup & saucer, pressed glass, Cat & Dog patt., clear, overall 2 1/2" h., the set.......... **$132**

Lemonade mug, pressed flint glass, Ten-Panel patt., electric blue, possible Boston & Sandwich Glass Co., 1 7/8" h. (ILLUS. right with lacy tureen & flint plate, top of page)... **$55**

Mug, pressed glass, Butterfly & Cattails patt., figural butterfly handle, clear, 3" h....... **$39**

Plate, pressed flint glass, Paneled Ovals patt., bright green, probably Midwestern, ca. 1850, 2 1/2" d. (ILLUS. center with lacy glass toy tureen & lemonade mug, top of page)... **$55**

Plate, pressed glass, Frolic patt., center scene of child & dog sitting on a porch, four shells on the shoulder, clear, 6" d. **$88**

Punch set: punch bowl & six cups; clear pressed glass, Nursery Rhyme patt., the set **$242**

Spooner, pressed glass, Menagerie patt., figural upright fish, blue, 3 1/2" h.................. **$55**

Spooner, pressed glass, Rooster patt., clear, 3" h. **$110**

Table set: creamer, cov. butter, cov. sugar bowl & spooner; clear pressed glass, Tappan patt., the set **$50**

Table set: creamer, spooner, cov. sugar bowl, large cov. butter dish & small cov. butter dish; clear pressed glass, Tulip & Honeycomb patt., 5 pcs. **$55**

Tureen, cov, pressed lacy glass, scrolls, fans, lilies, stars & diamonds, cobalt blue, attributed to the Boston & Sandwich Glass Co., 1 7/8 x 3", 2" h. (ILLUS. left with lemonade mug & plate, top of page) **$1,870**

Wash bowl & pitcher, pressed glass, Dutch Boudoir patt., blue opaque, open bubble on rim of bowl, pitcher 2 1/4" h., the set **$99**

Water set: pitcher & six tumblers; clear pressed glass, Pattee Cross patt., the set **$88**

Water set: pitcher & six tumblers; clear pressed glass, Rex patt., minor flakes, the set **$40-45**

CHRISTMAS COLLECTIBLES

Starting in the mid-19th century, more and more items began to be manufactured to decorate the home, office or commercial business to celebrate the Christmas season.

In the 20th century the trend increased. Companies such as Coca-Cola, Sears and others began producing special Christmas items. The inexpensive glass, then plastic Christmas tree decorations began to appear in almost every home. With the end of World War II the toy market moved into the picture with annual Santa Claus parades and the children's visits to Santa.

In the 21st century this trend continues, and material from earlier Christmas seasons continues to climb in value.

Rare Santa in Sleigh & Reindeer Candy Container

General

Candy container, figural, a red felt-suited Santa seated in a moss-covered sleigh filled w/packages, pulled by a large felt-covered reindeer candy container w/detachable neck, lead antlers & glass eyes, only minor paint loss, late 19th - early 20th c., 16" l. (ILLUS., bottom previous page) **$2,300**

Scarce Early Santa Candy Container

Candy container, figural, a standing Santa Claus w/molded celluloid face, bright red costume, black plaster boots & netting-type body, overall soiling to cloth, worn paint on boots, early 20th c., 7" h. (ILLUS.) **$400-600**

Amber Christmas Tree Candleholder

Christmas tree candleholder, mold-blown amber glass, ovoid shape w/molded top ring, overall diamond lattice design & ropetwist corners w/four round panels featuring a profile portrait of Queen Victoria, anchor & English registration numbers on base, rough sheared & ground lip, ca. 1880-1900, 3 5/8" h. (ILLUS.) **$448**

Blue Christmas Tree Candleholder

Christmas tree candleholder, mold-blown cobalt blue glass, ovoid shape w/molded top ring, overall diamond lattice design & ropetwist corners w/four round panels featuring a profile portrait of Queen Victoria, anchor & English registration numbers on base, rough sheared & ground lip, ca. 1880-1900, 3 5/8" h. (ILLUS.) **$420**

Scarce Christmas Tree Candleholder

Christmas tree candleholder, mold-blown cobalt blue glass, teardrop shape w/embossed feather plumed crown & overall beading, pontil-scarred base, folded rim, England, ca. 1875-1900, 3 1/8" h. (ILLUS.) **$616**

Green Christmas Tree Candleholder

C

Christmas tree candleholder, mold-blown green glass, ovoid shape w/molded top ring, overall diamond lattice design & ropetwist corners w/four round panels featuring a profile portrait of Queen Victoria, anchor & English registration numbers on base, rough sheared & ground lip, ca. 1880-1900, 3 5/8" h. (ILLUS., previous page)... **$420**

Pineapple-form Tree Candleholder

Christmas tree candleholder, mold-blown medium pink amber glass, knobby pineapple form w/flat base & molded top ring, rough sheared lip, England, ca. 1875-1900, 4 1/4" h. (ILLUS.) **$392**

Christmas tree candleholder, mold-blown olive yellow glass, knobby pineapple form w/smooth base & molded top ring, rough sheared lip, England, ca. 1875-1900, rare, 5 3/8" h. **$364**

Toy, carved wood horse-drawn sleigh, two large brown & white horses pulling large green sleigh on red runners, driven by a carved wooden farmer & his all-bisque

Carved Wood Horse-drawn Sleigh Toy

wife, the sleigh loaded w/a box of Santa Claus Snow, mounted on a thin rectangular wooden base, unknown vintage, 4 1/2 x 15 1/4", 6" h. (ILLUS.) **$316**

Santa & Wagon with Reindeer Pull Toy

Toy, pull-type, a large red wooden slat-sided wagon driven by a small felt-dressed Santa & pulled by a flocked papier-mâché reindeer on a small rectangular wooden wheeled base, wagon holds stack of wood & a moss Christmas tree, some distress to wagon wheels, some mildew on reindeer & bent antlers, early 20th c., 14 1/2" l. (ILLUS.)........................... **$288**

Toy, pull-type, papier-mâché brown-coated Santa Claus in a moss-covered sleigh pulled by a flocked papier-mâché reindeer w/leaden antlers, on a long narrow wooden platform w/tiny metal wheels, minor damage to reindeer legs, late 19th - early 20th c., 11 1/2" l. (ILLUS., bottom of page)... **$2,875**

Rare Early Santa & Sleigh Pull Toy

C

Old Santa in Sleigh & Reindeer Toy

Toy, wooden two-seat sleigh w/bentwood runners holding a felt-suited Santa, pulled by a papier-mâché reindeer, tag in sleigh for maker, John L. Roder of Illinois, a wagon maker by trade, mounted on a long thin wooden base, ca. 1930, some distress to reindeer, 15 1/2" l. (ILLUS.) **$173**

Christmas Cards of the World War II Era

Among greeting card collectors, Christmas cards of the World War II era are particularly prized. Their unique blend of nostalgia, patriotism and sentiment, so popular in the 1940s, remains equally appealing today.

Christmas cards had their official beginning in 1843 in England. Sir Henry Cole, director of London's Victoria & Albert Museum, hired artist John Calcott Horsley to create a card that could be reproduced and sent to Cole's friends and business associates. "Extras" in the initial printing of 1,000 were then made available to the general public.

In the United States, those sending "season's greetings" had to make do with imported cards until 1875, when Louis Prang established the first domestic production of holiday cards. Thanks to mass production, and inexpensive postal rates, Christmas cards were soon affordable to all, and the annual tradition of sending them quickly caught on.

Holiday wishes became particularly poignant in wartime as greetings were sent to friends and family members overseas. During the 1940s many of these cards carried a patriotic theme with such iconic images as the American flag and eagle bearing Yuletide wishes. Other cards recalled a more peaceful time, with snow-covered villages, fresh-faced carolers, jolly Santas, and peaceful manger scenes. There was also a proliferation of cards dedicated to specific family members. Greetings expressly directed to "Daddy," "My Little Daughter," and "A Sweet Little Niece" gave Christmas cards an individual touch and, not so coincidentally, increased card sales as well.

While later cards incorporated photo art, those of the '40s relied mainly on illustration, laced heavily with sentiment. Novelty additions, such as glitter, flocking, window cut-outs, pop-ups and pull-out tabs were also often used, adding to their charm. Major card producers of the era included Quality Cards, American Greetings, Rust Craft, Norcross and, of course, Hallmark.

In addition to its primary function, the holiday greeting card of the 1940s also served another important purpose: keeping morale high, both at home and abroad.

Advisor for this category is Donald-Brian Johnson, an author and lecturer specializing in mid-twentieth century design.

"Christmas Cheer" Santa & Piano Christmas Card

"Christmas Cheer" header, Santa at piano w/foil insert forming the piano, unmarked (ILLUS.).. **$7-10**

Card for Brother in the Service

"Christmas Greetings For A Brother In The Service" header, map of the United States w/flocking & foil decoration, Quality Cards (ILLUS.) **$7-10**

Card for Someone in Uncle Sam's Service

"Christmas Greetings For Someone In Uncle Sam's Service" header, decorated w/Uncle Sam top hat w/holly & gold eagle, "Best Wishes Always" pull-tab, American Greetings (ILLUS.) **$7-10**

"Christmas Greetings" header, donkey w/flocked poinsettia design, Hallmark, 1944 .... **$5-7**

"Christmas Greetings" header, eagle w/cut-out shield decoration, Quality Cards .. **$7-10**

"Christmas Greetings, Soldier" Card

"Christmas Greetings, Soldier" header, decoration of the Liberty Bell w/honeycomb insert, Paramount (ILLUS.) **$7-10**

Christmas Card of a Little Daughter

"For A Little Daughter's Christmas" header, decorated w/a little girl seated in a big red armchair by a fireplace, Stanley (ILLUS.) **$3-5**

"For A Sweet Little Niece" header, decorated w/a little girl wearing a red flocked parka, Hallmark **$5-7**

"For A Very Dear Niece" header, decorated w/a cat w/a gift basket, Rust Craft, 1947 .... **$3-5**

Our House to Your House Card

"From Our House To Your House" header, decorated w/a flocked snowy landscape w/a large red Victorian house & figures, A & W (ILLUS.) **$7-10**

"Greetings To One In The Service" header, decorated w/a flocked American flag, Quality Cards **$5-7**

"Hello Cousin - Christmas Express" Card

"Hello Cousin - Christmas Express" header, decorated w/a green train engine w/a pull-tab Santa at the throttle, Norcross (ILLUS.) **$7-10**

"Hello" header, decorated w/a polar bear wearing ice skates, Hallmark, 1944 .... **$3-5**

"Hi, Soldier" header, decorated w/military hats on a rack, Hallmark, 1942 .... **$3-5**

"Merry Christmas Daddy" Card

C

C

"Merry Christmas Daddy" header, decorated w/a gingerbread man flocked w/glitter, Hallmark, 1946 (ILLUS., previous page) **$5-7**

Merry Christmas - Niece Card

"Merry Christmas To A Dear Little Niece" header, decorated w/a blond girl angel w/glitter on her wings, Hallmark, 1943 (ILLUS.) **$5-7**

"Merry Christmas To Daughter" header, decorated w/a Victorian girl wearing a feather hat, Hallmark, 1945 .... **$5-7**

"So You're In The Army" header, decorated w/a soldier seated at a desk, Quality Cards **$5-7**

"This Is No Usual Record" header, decorated w/a dog & a phonograph record, an Artistic Card **$3-5**

Hallmark Ornaments

Hallmark 1983 Celebration Barbie Ornament

1983 Celebration Barbie, figural African-American Barbie Keepsake Ornament (ILLUS. of box) **$7**

2004 Yertle the Turtle Ornament

2004 Dr. Seuss Yertle the Turtle, figural stack of turtles, Keepsake Ornament Collector's Series (ILLUS. of box) **$6-9**

2004 Scarlett O'Hara Ornament

2004 Scarlett O'Hara - Gone With the Wind, figural Scarlett in her wedding gown, Keepsake Ornament (ILLUS. of box) **$15**

Nativity Sets

Early pilgrimages to the Holy Land served as inspiration for the nativity scene tradition, with artists offering their interpretations on canvas as early as the fourth century. The Roman basilica of Holy Mary of the Nativity, dedicated in the sixth century, featured the first three-dimensional figures of Jesus, Mary and Joseph fashioned of wood.

It was, however, several centuries before the concept of a figural nativity scene really took hold. In the meantime, there were the "living nativities" of the Middle Ages, staged in churches by costumed performers as part of seasonal devotions. The earliest and most famous of these was created by St. Francis of Assisi in 1223.

St. Francis felt that, for many of his congregation, Christmas had lost its true meaning. Under his direction the village of Greccio, near Assisi, was restyled as Bethlehem, with local shepherds (and their livestock) starring as the main characters.

The idea spread quickly and the theatricality and excitement of the annual nativity dramas soon made them a much-anticipated annual social event throughout medieval Europe. However, the large, boisterous crowds eventually proved an uncomfortable fit for somber cathedrals. By the late sixteenth century, live nativity enactments had moved to town squares, eventually disappearing from view.

With live depictions falling out of favor during the Renaissance, the focus was once more on figural representations. These were first popularized in the fifteenth and sixteenth centuries by the Jesuits, in churches throughout Europe. Nativity scenes could be nearly full-size, half-size or miniature, depending on the available space. The figures were arranged around the manger, often backed by a realistic stable setting.

By the early seventeenth century, the range of suitable locales for a nativity set had broadened. Soon, the displays could be found not only in churches, but in home environments as well, a custom that had its roots in southern Italy. In some European countries devout homes even kept a manger scene on display year-round.

Early home crèches were hand-crafted, a time-consuming process that meant they initially were available only to the wealthy. Those who could not afford such splendor, but still wished to celebrate the religious aspects of the holiday, often crafted their own manger scenes from whatever materials were at hand.

As Christianity spread across the globe, this form of handmade self-expression grew and flourished. The influence of individual cultures can be seen to wonderful advantage in nativity sets from around the world. Each interpretation not only incorporates indigenous materials, but also envisions the principal nativity characters with a sensibility inherent to the locale, representing the universality at the heart of the Christmas story.

Advisor for this category is Donald-Brian Johnson, an author and lecturer specializing in mid-twentieth century design. Photos are by his frequent collaborator, Leslie Piña.

China, musical waterglobe Nativity, plays "O Holy Night," 7" h. **$100-125**
Holland, porcelain set w/15 pieces, marked "Delft Polychrome," tallest figure 10" h. **$1,000-1,100**
Hong Kong, molded one-piece plastic nativity scene, 1950s, 3 1/2 h. **$25-35**
Ireland, carved wood, eight-piece assembly mounted w/pegs, 7" h. (ILLUS., bottom of page) **$75-125**

Eight-Piece Irish Wood Nativity Set

Italy, sterling silver & 14k gold leaf, Infant Jesus & manger, marked "Giardina Collection"... **$125-150**

Kenya, carved wood, 14-piece set, tallest figure 11 1/4" h. **$100-150**

Mexico, clay, five-piece set incorporating traditional costuming, marked "Hermos. Mario y Miguel Meneloza-Jopey," tallest figure 5 3/4" h. **$35-50**

Portuguese Clay Stable Scene

South America, incised gourd w/papier-mâché figures, 7" h. **$15-20**

One-Piece Pewter & Textured Glass Design

Nova Scotia, pewter & textured glass, one-piece votive design inspired by carvings at Milan's Piazza del Duoma Cathedral, Seagull Pewter & Silversmiths, 11" h. (ILLUS.) **$175-200**

Portugal, clay, stable scene w/a red rooster on the roof, 8" h. (ILLUS., top next column) **$35-50**

Russia, wooden nesting dolls, marked "Our Christmas Show," tallest egg 5" h. **$10-15**

South Africa, "Raku" pottery, eleven-piece set made by the Ndebele tribe, marked "African Express, Inc. 1995," tallest figure 7" h. (ILLUS., bottom of page) **$250-275**

Nine-Piece Terra Cotta Nativity Set From South America

South America, terra cotta, nine-piece set, tallest figure 5 3/4" h. (ILLUS.)............ **$300-400**

Spain, composite figures, set of six, tallest figure 13" h. (ILLUS., top next page) **$225-275**

Pottery Nativity Set by the Ndebele Tribe of South Africa

Spanish Nativity Set with Composite Figures

C

Painted Wood Nativity Set From Sri Lanka

Sri Lanka, painted wood, 12-piece set, tallest figure 4 1/2" h. (ILLUS., middle of page).. **$25-35**

Taiwan, paper nativity figures w/the stable constructed of twigs, marked "Christmas Mornin'," tallest figure, 8" h. **$50-75**

United States, carved wood, eight-piece set, marked "CRc A & J," tallest figure 10" h... **$160-175**

United States, ceramic & fabric, Native American nativity set w/stable replaced by a teepee, marked "Nova 5 Inc., Albuquerque, New Mexico," 10 pieces, teepee 18" h... **$400-500**

United States, fabric & plastic, five-piece set w/decorative braiding, marked "Cloth-

tique by Possible Dreams, Ltd. 1989," tallest figure 10" h. **$50-75**

United States, fimo clay nativity by Pennsylvania artist "Arlene," dated 1995, 9 1/2" h.. **$175-225**

United States, three Teddy bears dressed as Magi, marked "The Best of Christmas 1999 Massachusetts," 14" h............... **$800-900**

Unmarked, ceramic, one-piece interpretation of the Holy Family, 10 1/2" w., 7" h. **$75-100**

Unmarked, composite molded figures, Three Wise Men on camels, laminated w/gold & silver metallic finish, 18" h. ... **$400-600**

Unmarked, sand-cast, seven piece set of "friendly beasts," tallest figure 6" h...... **$175-200**

CLOCKS

Fine Massachusetts Grandfather Clock

Grandfather clock, Andrews (C.J.), Newton Center, Massachusetts, Federal style inlaid mahogany case, the arched & molded pediment decorated w/pierced scroll-carved crests alternating w/square blocks fitted w/brass ball finials, the arched glazed door flanked by slender colonettes w/gilt capitals & bases, door opening to a painted metal dial w/Roman numerals & floral-painted spandrels below a painted moon phase dial, the tall narrow central case w/flanked by tall slender reeded quarter-column columns w/gilt capitals & bases flanking the tail arched & line-inlaid door w/a brass keyhole escutcheon, the lower case decorated w/a line-inlaid panel centered by a large paterae, molded base on small ogee bracket feet, ca. 1816 (ILLUS.) **$20,400**

Grandfather clock, Becker (Gustav), Freiburg, Germany, Arts & Crafts oak case w/dark stain, deep flat flaring cornice above a square door w/round convex glass pane over the metal dial w/Arabic numerals, a long door below w/long panes of beveled glass & leaf carving showing the large pendulum, the tall lower case w/a front panel w/two stripes of stylized leaf carving, flat molded base, chimes behind dial marked "Harfen-Gong - GB - DRP," piece missing on cornice, early 20th c., 11 1/2 x 22 1/4", 84 1/2" h. (ILLUS., top next column) **$748**

C

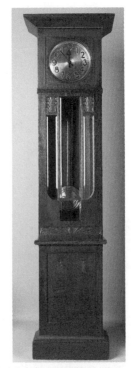

Becker Arts & Crafts Grandfather Clock

Fine English Chippendale-Style Clock

Grandfather clock, Bonner and Ross Co. (The), Elliot, London, England, Chippendale-Style mahogany case, broken-scroll arched pediment w/acanthus leaf center, ribbed urn finials, Corinthian columns on either side of the upper & lower doors, brass & steel dial w/Arabic numbers below a moon phase dial, lower beveled glass door reveals weights & pendulum, raised panels on the lower sides, raised on carved paw feet, company name on dial, brass works w/Whittington & Westminster chimes, late 19th - early 20th c., 18 x 27", 96" h. (ILLUS.) **$14,950**

Rare Early Wooster, Ohio Grandfather Clock

Early Timothy Chandler Grandfather Clock

Grandfather clock, Chandler (Major Timothy) attribution, New Hampshire, Federal style, cherry & walnut case w/a broken-scroll pediment w/carved rosettes & three brass ball finials above the arched glass door w/a painted face w/Roman numerals below a bird, nest & floral panel, thin colonettes at front corners, the waist w/a long narrow door above the stepped-out lower case raised on small feet, w/weights, keys & pendulum, minor edge damage to base, early 19th c., 86 1/2" h. (ILLUS.) **$4,025**

Grandfather clock, Christopher H. Strieby, Wooster, Ohio, Federal style, cherry & poplar, broken-scroll pediment w/three urn-turned finials above the arched glazed door w/a moon phase dial above the painted dial w/Roman numerals & painted spandrels, signed "C.E. Strieby, Wooster, Ohio #48," slender colonettes at front corners, the waist section w/a long narrow rectangular door flanked by thin reeded quarter-round columns, high paneled base section on small turned feet, w/pendulum & weights, crazed finish, glue repair to broken arch, ca. 1830-1850, 102" h. (ILLUS.) **$16,100**

C

Rare Early Federal Grandfather Clock

Rare Cincinnati, Ohio Grandfather Clock

Grandfather clock, Reed & Watson, Cincinnati, Ohio, Federal style, cherry & figured cherry case w/a broken-scroll pediment w/carved rosettes & three turned wood finials above the arched glass door w/a painted dial w/Arabic numerals & floral & gilt spandrels, thin colonettes at front corners, the waist & base section w/chamfered corners, inlaid star & applied oval bead over cut-out feet, w/weights & pendulum, refinished w/good color, minor repairs & replacements, early 19th c., 10 x 17", 97 1/2" h. (ILLUS.) **$10,350**

Grandfather clock, Rosett (Abraham) & Mulford (Abraham), Elizabethtown, New Jersey, Federal style inlaid mahogany case, the broken-scroll pediment mounted w/three spherical brass finials above a molded arched band above the arched glazed door flanked by small colonettes, opening to the painted metal dial w/Roman numerals & a moon phase movement at the top, the tall narrow case inlaid above & below the tall door w/panels enclosing an inlaid paterae w/American eagle design, the arched door centered by a long inlaid oval panel & diamond-shaped keyhole escutcheon, the tall slightly stepped-out lower case w/a large line-inlaid panel above tiny bracket feet, dated 1807 (ILLUS., top next column) .. **$36,000**

Early Grain-Painted Grandfather Clock

Grandfather clock, Twiss (J. & H.), Montreal, Canada (case attribution), Federal-style grain-painted pine case w/broken-scroll pediment centered by a small brass eagle-topped ball finial, arched door opening to a painted dial w/Arabic numerals & flanked by small colonettes, decorated w/gilt spandrels, urn & basket of flowers & signed "I. Twiss Montreal," tall narrow central case long door above stepped out box base w/scalloped apron, overall original reddish graining w/yellow line & leaf accents, w/weights & pendulum, brass works & finial not original, feet replaced, 1820s, 10 1/2 x 17 5/8", 84" h. (ILLUS.)............................ **$1,725**

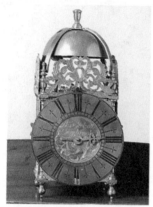

Scarce English 17th Century Lantern Clock

Lantern clock, Cackett (Thomas), Cranbrook, Kent, England, solid brass, domed bell top atop a pierced & engraved crest above two side doors opening to the brass works, the large flat brass dial engraved "Thomas Cackett, Cranbrook," typical steel single hand, steel supports & spikes on back legs, some replacements, repaired finial, w/pendulum & single weight, late 17th c., 13 3/4" h. (ILLUS.) **$1,783**

French Art Deco Marquetry Clock

Shelf or mantel, Art Deco style in marquetry case, the long upright oval case decorated at each end w/a curved band of stylized blossoms on a black ground above narrow vertical veneer stripes, low brass button feet, front w/round brass bezel enclosing a silvered metal dial w/blue enameled band w/Arabic numerals, sweep seconds hand, ATO movement, France, 1920s, 3 3/8 x 11", 6 3/8" h. (ILLUS.)...................... **$538**

Unusual Pierce-carved Cathedral Clock

Shelf or mantel, carved mahogany cathedral-style, the very elaborate piece-carved case resembling a church w/three tall steeples & a projecting entry, a wooden dial w/applied white Roman numerals & white hands, eight-day lyre movement by Seth Thomas, labeled by Carl Croft, Lison, Ohio, ca. 1890, 14 1/2 x 21 3/4", 42 3/4" h. (ILLUS.) **$1,440**

Chauncey Ives Pillar & Scroll Clock

Shelf or mantel, Ives (Chauncey), Bristol, Connecticut, pillar-and-scroll style, mahogany & mahogany veneer, a broken scroll pediment above a narrow molding over a case w/slender colonettes flanking the tall two-pane glazed door opening to a white-painted dial w/Roman numerals, the lower pane reverse-painted w/a large landscape scene w/village & white church, the narrow molded base raised on slender scroll-cut bracket feet, w/weights, keys & pendulum, some damage & repair, ca. 1825, 30" h. (ILLUS.) ... **$2,415**

Very Rare Tudric Pewter Clock

Shelf or mantel, Liberty & Co., London, England, flat pewter front w/a double-arch top, the upper section mounted w/thin blocks w/Roman numerals accented by six small inlaid abalone pieces, Tudric Pewter, designed by Archibald Knox, ca. 1902-05, 11 11/16" h. (ILLUS.) **$18,564**

Early Tudric Pewter Clock

Shelf or mantel, Liberty & Co., London, England, flat pewter front w/a wide arched crest stamped w/stylized leaves, the tall flat body w/an oblong reserve decorated at the top w/a raised dial w/a ring of Roman numerals, the lower front set w/two

enameled cabochons, Tudric Pewter, designed by Archibald Knox, ca. 1902-05, 8" h. (ILLUS.) **$3,494**

Tudric Pewter Clock by Archibald Knox

Shelf or mantel, Liberty & Co., London, England, upright pewter flat front w/stepped edges mounted at the two w/Arabic numerals forming the dial, the bottom center decorated w/a low-relief panel of stylized scrolling vines & leaves, Tudric Pewter, designed by Archibald Knox, ca. 1902, 9" h. (ILLUS.) **$5,242**

Fine Archibald Knox-designed Clock

Shelf or mantel, Liberty & Co., London, England, upright pewter flat gently swelled rectangular front decorated across the top & down the sides in low relief w/stylized berries, leafy vines, a large round dial w/a copper band w/Roman numerals enclosing mottled blue & green enamel, a round of three blue & green enameled buttons across the lower front, designed by Archibald Knox, ca. 1902-05, 7 5/8" h. (ILLUS.) **$5,242**

Fine Pewter & Enameled A. Knox Clock

Shelf or mantel, Liberty & Co., London, England, upright pewter square tapering case w/a pyramidal top, the front w/a long shallow recessed panel decorated w/a copper & blue-enameled dial w/Roman numerals above an abstract round panel of dark blue enamel & red dots, designed by Archibald Knox, ca. 1902-05, 7 1/4" h. (ILLUS.)... **$4,368**

Rare French Restoration Clock

Shelf or mantel, ormolu & painted bronze, a square deep plinth base supporting a gilt-bronze square base supporting a short wide column w/a gilt-bronze base & capital, the sides applied w/relief-cast floral swags & centered by a round white porcelain dial w/Roman numerals, all topped by a fine bronze bust of George Washington in uniform, Restoration Era, France, second quarter 19th c., 5 1/4" w., 16" h. (ILLUS.) **$9,600**

Eli Terry Pillar-and-Scroll Clock

Shelf or mantel, Terry (Eli), Plymouth, Connecticut, pillar-and-scroll style, mahogany & mahogany veneer, a broken scroll pediment above a narrow molding over a case w/slender colonettes flanking the tall two-pane glazed door opening to a white-painted dial w/Roman numerals, the lower pane reverse-painted w/a large landscape scene w/several white mansions & centered by a small oval pendulum window, the narrow molded base raised on slender scroll-cut bracket feet, ca. 1825, 17 3/8" w., 31 1/4" h. (ILLUS.)................. **$1,440**

Rare Eli Terry Pillar-and-Scroll Clock

Shelf or mantel, Terry (Eli), Plymouth, Connecticut, pillar-and-scroll style, mahogany & mahogany veneer, a broken scroll pediment w/three brass urn-form finials above a narrow molding over a case w/slender colonettes flanking the tall two-pane glazed door opening to a gilt-decorated white-painted dial w/Roman numerals, the lower pane reverse-painted w/a landscape w/two urn-form monuments flanked by willow trees centered by a small oval pendulum window, the narrow molded base raised on slender scroll-cut bracket feet, 30-hour wooden weight-driven movement, original paint, minor imperfections, original label inside, ca. 1825, 17 1/4" w., 31 1/2" h. (ILLUS.)................. **$7,050**

Riley Whiting Pillar & Scroll Clock

Shelf or mantel, Whiting (Riley), Winchester, Connecticut, pillar-and-scroll style, mahogany & mahogany veneer, a broken scroll pediment w/three brass urn-form finials above a narrow molding over a case w/slender colonettes flanking the tall two-pane glazed door opening to a white-painted dial w/Arabic numerals, the lower pane reverse-painted w/a large landscape scene w/two white mansions & centered by a small oval pendulum window, the narrow serpentine apron raised on slender scroll-cut bracket feet, w/keys, weights & pendulum, ca. 1825, 31" h. (ILLUS.) **$1,955**

Neoclassical French Cartel Wall Clock

Wall clock, cartel design, Neoclassic style, ormolu & patinated bronze, modeled as a classically-draped maiden supporting an octagonal clock case surmounted by a blossoming flower vase & applied on each side w/a lion mask, centered by a round enameled dial w/Roman numerals, twin-train movement, above an orb w/a scrolled finial, France, late 19th c., 37 1/2" h. (ILLUS.) **$3,840**

Rare Pewter Wall Clock by A. Knox

Wall clock, Liberty & Co., London, England, wide pewter stylized flat shield-shape cast w/large stylized Arabic numerals & iron spatula-form hands inset at the ends w/pieces of abalone, designed by Archibald Knox, ca. 1902-05, 10 3/4" h. (ILLUS.)... **$14,196**

Two Nice Wall Regulator Clocks

Wall Regulator clock, fruitwood & mahogany veneer case w/arched flaring cornice above a pair of tall Corinthian columns flanking the long glass front showing the enameled dial w/Roman numerals & an embossed brass bezel above the weights & large pendulum, long waisted base drop w/scroll-cast finial drop, later added gold painted rococo-style crest & drop, crest not shown, late 19th - early 20th c., 56" h. (ILLUS. left with fancy Victorian regulator, previous page) **$3,105**

Wall Regulator clock, mahogany veneer & ebonized wood case, a tall arched & carved central crest at the top w/an urn-turned finial & small half-round columns flanking an applied head of Minerva, corner blocks mounted w/urn-turned finials, a decorative narrow frieze band above a pair of acanthus-carved & fluted side pilasters flanking a round opening for the enameled dial w/Roman numerals above a long glass window showing the weights & large pendulum, the molded base above a stepped inverted pyramidal drop w/turned finial & turned teardrop bottom corner finials, probably Europe, late 19th c., 56" h. (ILLUS. right with fruitwood & mahogany regulator, previous page) **$1,610**

CLOISONNÉ & RELATED WARES

Cloisonné work features enameled designs on a metal ground. There are several types of this work, the best-known utilizing cells of wire on the body of the object into which the enamel is placed. In the plique-a-jour form of cloisonné, the base is removed, leaving translucent enamel windows. The champlevé technique entails filling in, with enamels, a design which is cast or carved in the base. "Pigeon Blood" (akasuke) cloisonné includes a type where foil is enclosed within colored enamel walls. Cloisonné is said to have been invented by the Chinese and brought to perfection by the Japanese.

Cloisonné

Japanese

Stickpin, oval head w/silver foil blue ground decorated w/a purple iris **$45**

Table screen, four-fold, black ground decorated w/flower gardens, signed "Inaba," 6" h. **$795**

Teapot, cov., bulbous tapering ovoid body on small peg feet, serpentine spout & D-form handle, dark blue ground w/scattered small blossoms & large round reserves w/a Flying Phoenix bird design, brass wire, 4" h. (ILLUS., top next column) **$190**

Small Japanese Cloisonné Teapot

Teapot, cov., melon-ribbed shape, a striped pattern in dark colors, 1890s, 4" h. **$150**

Umbrella handle, blue ground w/white lilies, 6" l. **$150**

Vase, miniature, lime green foil ground w/white flowers, signed, 2" h. **$125**

Vase, miniature, green foil w/tooled flowers in silver background, purple dragon, signed, 3" h. **$250**

Unusual Vase with Répoussé Flowers

Vase, footed ovoid body w/a very tall slender trumpet neck, light blue foil ground decorated w/répoussé silver flowers w/transparent enamels, green leaves & stems in the background, signed "Bunzaemon," 5" h. (ILLUS.) **$650**

Vase, Akasuke (pigeon blood) style, decorated w/two roses, chrome mounts, signed "SATO Japan," 1950s, 6" h. **$75**

Vase, black ground decorated w/foil hanging wisteria blossoms, 6" h. **$265**

C

C

Vase, grey ground decorated w/tree blossoms in gilt wire & a wireless full moon, 6" h. $450

Vase, navy blue ground decorated w/spider mums & a flower garden, fine silver wire, 7" h. $500

Japanese Lacquer & Porcelain Cloisonné

Vase, treebark lacquer ground w/brass wire cloisonné on porcelain, a design of a heron among rushes, 7" h. (ILLUS.) $150

Vase, wireless design w/a pale blue ground w/white cranes overall, signed, 7" h. $375

Vase, blue shaded to white foil ground, decorated w/a green dragon wrapped around the sides, signed, 8" h. $395

Large Japanese Floral Cloisonné Vase

Vase, footed bulbous ovoid form w/a short flaring neck, dark blue ground decorated w/a wide band of large pink & yellow flowers & green & blue leaves, silver wire & silver mounts, ca. 1920s, 8" h. (ILLUS.)..... $475

Russian

Rare Russian Cloisonné Bratina

Bratina, a footed bulbous lobed body tapering to a cylindrical neck, the low domed foot decorated w/stylized scrolls on an aqua ground, the sides of the body w/large lobes each enclosing colorful stylized blossoms against a red, blue or green ground, a cream-colored shoulder band, the neck w/stylized birds alternating w/white blossoms on a dark green ground, marked by Feodor Ruckert, Moscow, Russia, 1899-1908, 4" h. (ILLUS.) **$28,896**

Fine Russian Cloisonné Patch Box

Patch box, cov, low squatty round form, the sides decorated w/stylized shaded varicolored flowerheads & scrolling leaves on a pale blue & green ground, the hinged cover decorated w/a large blue & red flower head centered by four stylized green leaf clusters on a dark blue ground, marked w/initials of Feodor Ruckert, Moscow, 1896-1908, 1 7/8" d. (ILLUS.) **$4,780**

Extremely Rare French Plique-à-Jour Silver Box

C

Related Wares

Champlevé

Rare Tiffany Champlevé Tea Caddy

Tea caddy, sterling & enamel, the cylindrical silver body applied w/champleve enamel in red, yellow, white, tan & purple, the body w/enameled rosettes under a band of swags w/Near Eastern ornament, the shoulder applied w/an enameled band of ovolo & flowerheads, the domed cover w/similar decoration, the interior cover etched w/flowers & w/black enamel hearts, the reverse engraved w/delicate band of flowers, gilt interior, mark of Tiffany & Co., New York City, ca. 1891, 4 1/4" h. (ILLUS.) **$19,200**

Plique-à-Jour

Box, cov., "Papillons Jaune Brun Soileil Jaune" (Yellowish Brown Butterflies & Yellow Sun,) low silver squared form w/slightly curved sides, the cover w/a central rectangular-cut citrine in gold claw mount, surrounded by four lobes of butterfly wings in yellow, light blue, amber, gold & black enamel, the sides enameled w/repeating golden yellow fan-

shaped devices, mark of Eugene Feuillatre, France, ca. 1912, 4 1/4" w. (ILLUS., top of page) **$53,775**

COCA-COLA ITEMS

Coca-Cola promotion has been achieved through the issuance of scores of small objects through the years. These, together with trays, signs and other articles bearing the name of this soft drink, are now sought by many collectors. The major reference in this field is Petretti's Coca-Cola Collectibles Price Guide, 11th Edition, *by Allan Petretti (Antique Trader Books). An asterisk (*) indicates a piece which has been reproduced.*

Coca-Cola 1943 Airplane Pictures

Airplane identification pictures, color-printed cardboard, each w/a picture of a different World War II airplane, the identification & Coca-Cola logo along the bottom edge, 1943, narrow metal frames, some border dents & wear, set of 20 (ILLUS. of part)............................. **$1,320**

Coca-Cola 50th Anniversary Ashtray

Ashtray, porcelain, round, red center w/black rims, marked "50th Anniversary Coca-Cola 1886-1936," w/signature on rim, 1936 (ILLUS.)..................................... **$660**

1950s Plastic Coca-Cola Vending Bank

Bank, plastic, vending machine-shaped, marked "Drink Coca-Cola - Play Refreshed - 5¢ Ice Cold," w/original box, 1950s, slight wear & soiling to the box, only minor marks on bank, 5 1/2" h. (ILLUS.)........................... **$198**

Scarce 1921 Long Coca-Cola Calendar

Calendar, 1921, long narrow style, color illustration of young woman wearing dark blue & white outfit & hat sitting in garden setting amid pink & yellow flowers & holding glass of Coke, metal band at top, full pad, good colors, framed, 16 1/2 x 36" (ILLUS.)... **$1,650**

1927 Coca-Cola Sign with Lady in Pink

Calendar, 1927, long narrow style, the top w/a long picture w/a three-quarters length portrait of an elegant lady wearing a soft pink filmy party gown & holding a glass of Coca-Cola, a picture of a Coca-Cola bottle in the lower left above the full pad, metal strip at the top, some stains on left side of pad, some closed edge tears, 12 x 25" (ILLUS.) **$2,310**

Very Rare 1927 Flapper Coke Calendar

Calendar, 1927, long narrow style, the top w/a long picture w/a three-quarters length portrait of a seated flapper wearing a silky yellow gown & white fur against a red background, she holds a glass of Coca-Cola w/the bottle on the table beside her, full pad, metal strip at the top, few minor closed edge tears, 12 x 25" (ILLUS.) **$2,530**

1936 Coca-Cola Fisherman Calendar

Calendar, 1936, "Coca-Cola," color lithographed cardboard, coastal scene of old fisherman holding a bottle of Coca-Cola & leaning on a red rowboat, basket of clams by his feet, talking to a young blonde-haired girl nearby, top metal strip, full pad, only a few dark spots & stains, 12 x 24" (ILLUS.)... **$715**

1939 Long Coca-Cola Calendar

Calendar, 1939, long narrow three-quarters length portrait of a young lady in black dress holding Coca-Cola bottle in one hand & glass in other, metal top strip, full pad & cover sheet, only a few light mildew marks, lithograph by Forbes of Boston (ILLUS.)... **$412**

Calendar, 1941, tall rectangular form, white background printed in black across the top "Boy Scouts of America" above a tall color print of a Scout rescuing a baby from a flood, based on a Norman Rockwell painting, Coca-Cola distributor advertising below w/small full calendar pad, framed, 22 x 46" (ILLUS., top next column).. **$3,080**

Rare 1941 Coca-Cola Boy Scout Calendar

Scarce Coke China Change Receiver

Change receiver plate, round white china printed w/ornate red script advertising, manufactured by Lamberton Sterling China Company, age uncertain, 10 1/2" d. (ILLUS.) **$1,760**

Early Coca-Cola Chewing Gum Crate

Chewing gum crate, wood, rectangular w/overall red printing w/advertising for Coca-Cola Gum, good stencils on each side, somewhat darkened, a few cracks, finger-jointed construction, 1915, 6 x 12", 6" h. (ILLUS.) **$330**

C

Round 1950s Coca-Cola Light-Up Clock

Clock, wall-type, round light-up style, domed clear cover over a dial w/green Arabic numerals around a central Coca-Cola button sign, black hands & red seconds hand, 1950s, lights-up & runs, some soiling inside (ILLUS.) **$880**

Vendo Coca-Cola Coin Changer

Coin changer, steel, Vendo model w/upright rectangular wall-mounted case in red w/"Have a Coke" in a red button on a green ground, 1940s-50s, restored (ILLUS.) **$770**

1950s Coca-Cola Cooler

Cooler, red metal airline-type, rectangular w/hinged lid w/carrying handle, Coca-Cola on the front in white, restored, 1950s, 12 x 17" (ILLUS.) **$330**

1950s Styrofoam Coke Display Bottle

Display bottle, styrofoam model of the Coca-Cola bottle, only a few mild dents & minor marks, white letters touched-up, 1950s, 42" h. (ILLUS.) **$523**

1950s Coca-Cola Door Pull Handle

Door pull handle, plastic & metal, the handle grip molded as a half-round full bottle of Coca-Cola, a narrow red metal mounting plate w/white wording, 1950s (ILLUS.) **$198**

1950s Coca-Cola Antique Autos Festoon Sign

C

1909, 1914 & 1916 Coca-Cola Pocket Mirrors

Festoon sign, die-cut cardboard, diamond-shaped sections featuring antique autos alternating w/glasses of Coca-Cola & the logo, light wear, 1950s, five pieces, 12' l. (ILLUS., bottom previous page) **$330**

1930s Coca-Cola Paper Keg Label

Keg labels, color-printed paper, round w/the Coca-Cola logo across the center & advertising above & below, 1930s, only some minor fold marks, 16" d., two (ILLUS. of one) **$198**

Scarce Small Coca-Cola Menu Board

Menu board, tin, the upper section w/a red ground printed in yellow & white "Take Home - Coca-Cola - In Cartons," rectangular black menu board printed in yellow "Today's Special," 1940s-50s, some paint chips & nicks on edges, 9 x 15" (ILLUS.) **$1,430**

Pocket mirror, 1909, oval celluloid, printed in color w/a scene of a pretty young lady seated at an outdoor table holding a glass of Coca-Cola, a nightime view of the St. Louis World's Fair in the distance, slightly bumpy mirror surface, 1 3/4 x 2 3/4" (ILLUS. left with 1914 & 1916 pocket mirrors, top of page) **$413**

Pocket mirror, 1914, oval celluloid, printed in color w/a bust portrait of a pretty young lady holding a glass of Coca-Cola, wearing a dark green dress fading away into the green background, some very minor bumps, 1 3/4 x 2 3/4" (ILLUS. center with 1909 & 1916 pocket mirrors, top of page) .. **$605**

Pocket mirror, 1916, oval celluloid, printed in color w/a half-length portrait of a pretty young lady looking back over her shoulder & holding a bottle of Coca-Cola, wearing a wide hat & pale yellow dress, very minor marks, 1 3/4 x 2 3/4" (ILLUS. right with 1909 & 1914 pocket mirrors, top of page) **$413**

1943 Coke Poster of Woman in a Car

Poster, color lithograph on cardboard, long rectangular form, full-length scene of a woman seated at the wheel of a car while a man in white hands her a six-pack of Coca-Cola, white wording at top reads "You trust its quality," 1943, minor bends & surface creases, 27 x 56" (ILLUS.)...... **$1,320**

1953 Coke-Harlem Globetrotters Poster

C

Poster, color lithograph on cardboard, long rectangular form, pale yellow background w/a long horizontal full-length portrait of Goose Tatem of the Harlem Globetrotters, red Coca-Cola pennant behind him & advertising & promotion below, 1953, wooden frame, scratch at right of pennant, some light surface wear, small stains, 27 x 56" (ILLUS., previous page) **$1,540**

Lovely 1948 Coca-Cola Poster

Poster, color lithograph on cardboard, tall rectangular form, dark red background w/a large bust portrait of a beautiful young lady holding a bottle of Coca-Cola, narrow yellow border band, printed in yellow across the top "Have a Coke," the Coca-Cola button logo at the bottom, 1948, framed under glass, 30 x 50" (ILLUS.) **$2,750**

Rare 1940s Coca-Cola Cheerleader Poster

Poster, color lithograph on cardboard, tall rectangular form, three-quarters length portrait of a high school cheerleader w/her horn under one arm & holding a bottle of Coca-Cola in the other hand, a Coca-Cola cooler in the background, 1940s, near mint, framed, 16 x 27" (ILLUS.) **$2,420**

1950s Coca-Cola Cooler Radio & Box

Radio, molded plastic, model of a red Coca-Cola cooler, w/original weathered box, 1950s, some soiling & small paint chips, all-original & working, 9 1/2" h. (ILLUS.) **$385**

1950s Countertop Light-Up Sign

Sign, glass & metal, countertop light-up style, low rectangular base w/a narrow white front panel printed in blue "Serve Yourself," the upright long low rectangular portion w/a motion-style waterfall sign on the left end printed in yellow "Pause and Refresh," the right half in red w/white working "Drink Coca-Cola," 1950s, working (ILLUS.) **$1,650**

1950s Countertop Cashier Sign

Sign, glass & plastic, countertop light-up type, long narrow rectangular base w/a narrow white glass panel printed in green "Please Pay Cashier," long upright section w/a large black circle printed in yellow "Pause" to the left of the long red Coca-Cola logo sign, all-original, some darkening & dirt, 1950s, 9 x 20" (ILLUS.) **$825**

C

1930s Fountain Service Coca-Cola Sign

Rare Coca-Cola Countertop Sign

Sign, plastic & glass, countertop-type, rectangular long base printed along the front "Have a Coke" in red, upright sign supported by small end tabs showing cups, the red ground printed in white "Drink Coca-Cola," Price Brothers, 1940s-50s, only light soiling, 18 1/2" l., 8" h. (ILLUS.) **$1,540**

Sign, porcelain, rectangular one-sided style w/curved bottom rim, green band at top printed in cream "Fountain Service," red lower section w/"Drink Coca-Cola," ca. 1934, some scattered chips, 27" l., 14" h. (ILLUS., top of page) **$345**

Sign, porcelain & steel, sidewalk "lollipop" style, a narrow steel frame enclosing a large red Coca-Cola button sign printed in yellow & white "Drink Coca-Cola - Refresh!," marked on base, 1938, quite heavy overall wear & some chipping, 30" d., 65" h. (ILLUS.) **$990**

Two-Sided Coca-Cola Dispenser Sign

Sign, porcelain, two-sided, rectangular w/rounded corners, depicts a large red Coca-Cola countertop dispenser filling a glass, stainless steel banding, 1950s, one side w/some acid rain staining, 27 x 28" (ILLUS.) **$1,320**

1950s Tin & Masonite Coca-Cola Sign

Sign, tin & masonite, a large 12" d. red & white tin Coca-Cola button sign centered on a Kay flat oval masonite background w/wooden bar accents, fine condition, 1950s, 12 x 32" (ILLUS.) **$495**

1938 Coca-Cola "Lollipop" Sidewalk Sign

C

1960s Coca-Cola Sign with Large Cup

Sign, tin, rectangular, printed w/a large red & white cup below the words in green "Ice Cold," all against a lined ground, "Prepared by The Bottler of Coca-Cola" in red along the bottom edge, 1960s, small dimple dents, surface scratch in right corner, minor edge dents & paint chips, 20 x 28" (ILLUS.).. **$990**

Coca-Cola Syrup Bottle Circa 1910

Syrup bottle w/original aluminum top, tall clear cylindrical form marked w/"Drink Coca-Cola" surrounded by wreath w/bow, ca. 1910, somewhat soiled & smokey in color, milds stains on interior bottom (ILLUS.).. **$500**

Syrup keg, wooden stave construction w/metal banding, most of the original printed paper label on the end, 1930s, 5 gal. (ILLUS., top next column)................... **$550**

Toy truck, red metal body w/two-tier open back holding six miniature plastic Coca-Cola cases, by Smith Miller, 1949, great condition, 13" l. (ILLUS., middle next column).. **$2,860**

Coca-Cola 1930s Syrup Keg & Label

Fine 1949 Coca-Cola Toy Truck

1950s Coca-Cola Route Truck

Toy truck, route delivery-type, battery-operated, white & yellow metal w/red hood, "Drink Coca-Cola" on side panels, Allen Haddock Co., 1950s, w/original box, 12 1/2" l. (ILLUS.)...................................... **$495**

Scarce Early Coke Vienna Art Tin Plate

Vienna Art plate, tin, color half-length portrait of a topless girl facing left, issued by Western Reserve, original ornate giltwood frame, 1910, only light soiling (ILLUS., previous page)............................ **$770**

COMIC BOOKS

Comic books, especially first or early issues of a series, are avidly collected today. Prices for some of the scarce ones have reached extremely high levels. Prices listed below show a range for copies from "Good" to "Mint" condition.

All Great Jungle Adventures Comic

All Great Jungle Adventures, unnumbered, Fox Giant, 1949 (ILLUS.)...... **$300-1,200**

Attack on Planet Mars Comic Book

Attack on Planet Mars, Avon, 1951, dramatic spaceship battle cover scene (ILLUS.)
.... **$350-1,100**
Buster Crabbe, #7, Famous Funnies Publications, 1952, Frazetta advertisement inside (ILLUS., top next column)............ **$100-250**

Buster Crabbe #7 Comic Book

Daredevil #31 Comic Book

Daredevil, #31, Lev Gleason Publications, features the death of the Claw, 1940s (ILLUS.) **$400-1,200**

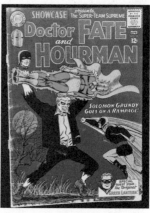

Doctor Fate and Hourman Comic Book

C

Doctor Fate and Hourman, #55, DC Comics, origins of the title characters w/the Green Lantern & Soloman Grundy, 1965 (ILLUS., previous page) **$100-500**

Enemy Ace DC #138 Comic Book

Enemy Ace, DC#138, Star Spangled War Stories, Joe Kubert, 1968 (ILLUS.) **$30-150**

1974 Evel Knievel Comic Giveaway

Evel Knievel, Marvel Comics/Ideal toy Corp., unnumbered giveaway, 1974 (ILLUS.) **$20-60**

Fantastic Four (The), #4, Marvel Comics, first Sub-Mariner appearance, 1962 (ILLUS., top next column).......... **$1,200-6,000**

Fat Freddy's Comics & Stories, #1, Gilbert Shelton, 1970s (ILLUS., middle next column)... **$6-15**

Ghosts, #1, DC Comics, 1971 (ILLUS., bottom next column)................................... **$50-250**

Rare Fantastic Four #4 Comic Book

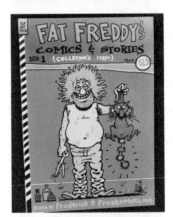

Fat Freddy's Comics & Stories

Ghosts #1 Comic Book

Hate #1 Comic Book

Hate, #1, Fantagraphics, 1990 (ILLUS.)...... **$10-30**

Iron Man & Sub-Mariner #1 Comic

Iron Man and Sub-Mariner, #1, Marvel, one-shot, predates their individual #1 issues, 1968 (ILLUS.) **$75-300**

Jason vs Leatherface #2 Comic Book

Jason vs Leatherface, #2, Topps Comics, Nancy Collins story, low print run, 1995 (ILLUS.)... **$10-25**

Rare Journey Into Mystery Comic Book

Journey Into Mystery, #85, first appearance of Loki & Helmdall, 1960s (ILLUS.) **$800-2,000**

Jumbo Comics #40 Comic

Jumbo Comics, #40, Fiction House Magazines, features Sheena, Jungle Queen, 1942 (ILLUS.)...................................... **$200-700**

Rare Early Looney Tunes Comic Book

Looney Tunes - Merrie Melodies Comics, #2, cover image of Bugs Bunny kissing Porky Pig, 1941 (ILLUS.) **$600-3,000**

C

C

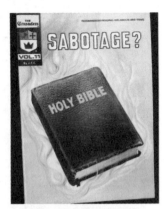

Crusador Comics #11

Sabotage?, Crusader Comics #11, by Jack T. Chick, Christian warnings, 1979 (ILLUS.) **$5-15**

Rare Suspense Comics #8 Issue

Suspense Comics, #8, Continental Magazines, L.B. Cole spider cover, mid-1940s (ILLUS.)... **$1,500-6,000**

Gold Key Secret Squirrel #1 Comic Book

Secret Squirrel, #1, Gold Key, Hanna-Barbera comic, 1966 (ILLUS.) **$60-225**

Teen Titans #1 Comic Book

Teen Titans, #1, DC Comics, features Robin, Wonder Girl, Kid Flash & Aqualad, 1966 (ILLUS.)..................................... **$120-500**

Scarce The Silver Surfer #1 Comic Book

Silver Surfer (The), #1, Marvel Comics, features origin story, 1960s (ILLUS.) **$600-1,500**

The Challenger #2 Comic Book

The Challenger, #2, Interfaith Publications/TC Comics, anti-Fascist theme, 1945 (ILLUS.)...................................... **$100-450**

C

Weird Tales of Terror Comic Book

Weird Tales of Terror, Blue Bolt #111, L.B.
Cole cover art (ILLUS.) **$200-600**

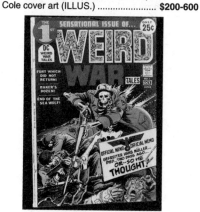

Weird War Tales #I Comic Book

Weird War Tales, #1, DC Comics, Kubert
cover art, 1971 (ILLUS.)...................... **$100-400**

The Witching Hour #1 Comic Book

Witching Hour (The), #1, DC Comics, art
by Neal Adams & Toth, 1969 (ILLUS.).. **$60-200**

1965 X-Men #14 Comic Book

X-Men, #14, Marvel, first appearance of The
Sentinels, 1965 (ILLUS.).................... **$150-600**

COMPACTS & VANITY CASES

A lady's powder compact is a small portable cosmetic make-up box that contains powder, a mirror and puff. Eventually, the more elaborate compact, the "vanity case," evolved, containing a mirror, puffs and compartments for powder, rouge and / or lipstick. Compacts made prior to the 1960s when women opted for the "au natural" look are considered vintage. These vintage compacts were made in a variety of shapes, sizes, combinations, styles and in every conceivable natural or man-made material. Figural, enamel, premium, commemorative, patriotic, Art Deco and souvenir compacts were designed as a reflection of the times and are very desirable. The vintage compacts that are multipurpose, combined with another accessory—the compact / watch, compact / music box, compact / fan, compact / purse, compact / perfumer, compact / lighter, compact / cane, compact / hatpin—are but a few of the combination compacts that are not only sought after by the compact collector but also appeal to collectors of the secondary accessory.

Today vintage compacts and vanity cases are very desirable collectibles. There are compacts and vanities to suit every taste and purse. The "old" compacts are the "new" collectibles. Compacts have come into their own as collectibles. They are listed as a separate category in price guides, sold in prestigious auction houses, displayed in museums, and several books and many articles on the collectible compact have been written. There is also a newsletter, Powder Puff, written by and for compact collectors. The beauty and intricate workmanship of the vintage compacts make them works of fantasy and art in miniature.

For additional information on the history and values of compacts and vanity cases, readers should consult Vintage and Vogue Ladies' Compacts *by Roselyn Gerson, Collector Books.*

Elgin American Compact with Thermometer

Two Celluloid Lady-form Compacts

Celluloid compacts, flattened round design, each resembling stylized woman w/wide dresses, an exterior swinging beveled mirror incorporated as part of the skirt, interior w/powder well, mirror on reverse of outer lid (ILLUS. of two)............... **$200**

Dorothy Gray "Savoir Faire" Compact

"Giants" Baseball Design Compact

Dorothy Gray brushed goldtone compact, oval "Savoir Faire" design, a black raised enameled Harlequin mask centered on the lid further trimmed w/rhinestones & incised ribbons (ILLUS.).............. **$200**

Elgin American brushed goldtone compact, square w/a small thermometer centered on the lid framed by four incised scenes of woman involved w/various sporting events (ILLUS., top next column) ... **$150**

Enameled metal compact, flattened round form enameled in white on the top w/a baseball design printed in large script letters "Giants," ball stitching in blue & white, interior opens to a mirror & powder compartment (ILLUS., middle next column) **$175**

Evans black satin vanity bag, cut-off diamond shape decorated w/gold piping, a fancy filigree metal vanity lid enhanced w/enameling, red stones & pearls, strap carrying handle, lid opens to a metal mirror & powder & rouge compartments, bag satin-lined & fitted w/a pocket for a change purse (ILLUS. closed, bottom next column).. **$500**

Evans Black Satin Vanity Bag

Evans goldtone carryall dual-opening type, a watch centered on an embossed sunburst on the lid, the interior contains a powder compartment, mirror, coin holder, lipstick, comb holder, cigarette case on the side, on a mesh carrying chain **$350**

CURRIER & IVES PRINTS

This lithographic firm was founded in 1835 by Nathaniel Currier, with James M. Ives becoming a partner in 1857. Current events of the day were portrayed in the early days, and the prints were hand-colored. Landscapes, vessels, sport and hunting scenes of the West all became popular subjects. The firm was in existence until 1906. All prints listed are hand-colored unless otherwise noted. Numbers at the end of the listings refer to those used in Currier & Ives Prints - An Illustrated Checklist, *by Frederick A. Conningham (Crown Publishers).*

Champion Pacer Johnston Print

Rare American Farm Scenes No. 4 Print

American Farm Scenes - No. 4 (Winter), large folio, 1853, N. Currier, framed, 136, minor surface soiling, light staining, some major tears (ILLUS.)................... **$10,800**

Champion Pacer Johnston (The), large folio, 1884, framed, 968, minor surface soiling & light staining, several small repaired margin tears, soft creasing (ILLUS., top next column) **$1,560**

Great East River Suspension Bridge (The), large folio, 1883, framed, 2597, minor surface soiling, a few foxmarks, soft handling creases, several short repaired margin tears (ILLUS., bottom of page).. **$4,800**

The Snow Storm by Currier & Ives

Snow Storm (The), medium folio, undated, framed, hinged at the top, few light brown vertical streaks, toning, 5580 (ILLUS.)... **$2,350**

Great East River Suspension Bridge [Brooklyn Bridge] Print

C

Currier & Ives Summer Fruits Print

Summer Fruits, medium folio, 1861, framed, stains, margins trimmed (ILLUS.)... **$230**

Taking The Back Track Print

Taking the Back Track - A Dangerous Neighborhood, large folio, 1866, framed, repair to background sky, light stains & toning, hinged at top, repair to upper corner, 5961 (ILLUS.) **$10,575**

Trolling for Blue Fish Print

Trolling for Blue Fish, large folio, 1866, framed, tear in center, repaired tear in upper right, light foxing, remains of old tape at top & edges of back, 6158 (ILLUS.) **$11,750**

View of New York from Brooklin (sic) Heights, medium folio, 1849, N. Currier, framed, laid down onto thin cardboard, toning, minor foxing (ILLUS., top next column) **$1,763**

Winter in the Country - Getting Ice, large folio, 1864, framed, hinged to cardboard backing, couple of minor abrasions in margins, 6537 (ILLUS., middle next column) **$17,625**

View of New York from Brooklin Heights

Rare Winter in the Country Print

DISNEY COLLECTIBLES

Scores of objects ranging from watches to dolls have been created showing Walt Disney's copyrighted animated cartoon characters, and an increasing number of collectors now are seeking these, made primarily by licensed manufacturers. ALSO SEE Antique Trader Toy Price Guide.

Cinderella Movie Cel of Royal Servant

Cinderella movie cel, a Royal Servant offers the Princess' shoe, gouache on trimmed celluloid, framed, w/document concerning provenance, 5 1/2 x 6 1/2" (ILLUS.) **$600**

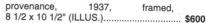

provenance, 1937, framed, 8 1/2 x 10 1/2" (ILLUS.)............................ **$600**

Fantasia Drawing of Chernabog

D

Donald Duck Cartoon Cel

Donald Duck cartoon cel, Donald wearing a pith helmet & carrying a movie camera on a tripod, gouache on partial celluloid, unknown production, 1950s, 6 x 9" (ILLUS.)... **$180**

Fantasia animation drawing, half-length portrait of Chernabog, graphite & colored pencil on paper, w/document concerning provenance, 1940, framed, 8 x 10" (ILLUS.) **$900**

Fantasia Sorcerer's Apprentice Drawing

Fantasia animation drawing, Mickey Mouse as The Sorcerer's Apprentice tries on the Sorcerer's hat, graphite on paper, w/a document concerning provenance, 1940, framed, 5 3/4 x 7" (ILLUS.)............. **$2,400**

Animation Drawing of Dwarf Dopey

Dwarf Dopey animation drawing, shows Dopey sweeping up, graphite on paper, signed later by Frank Thomas & Ollie Johnston, w/a document concerning

Fantasia Dancing Mushroom Drawing

Fantasia Dancing Mushroom Movie Cel

Fantasia concept painting, Dancing Mushrooms scene, gouache on paper & a storyboard drawing in pastel on paper, both framed & w/a document concerning provenance, 1940, the set (ILLUS. of one, bottom previous page) **$1,680**

Fantasia concept storyboard drawing, scene of a mother Pegasus holding up the tail of a baby Pegasus, graphite & colored pastel on paper, 1940, w/two documents concerning provenance, 6 1/4 x 8" (ILLUS.).. **$1,680**

Fantasia movie cel, Dancing Mushrooms scene, gouache on full celluloid, applied to a Courvoisier airbrushed background, 1940, w/a document concerning provenance, framed, 9 1/4 x 11" (ILLUS., top of page)... **$3,360**

Fantasia movie cel, Hyacinth Hippo reclines & yawns, gouache on full celluloid, applied to a Courvoisier watercolor background, w/two documents concerning provenance, 1940, framed, 7 1/4 x 9 3/4" (ILLUS., bottom of page)........................ **$4,200**

Fantasia Storyboard Drawing of Pegasus

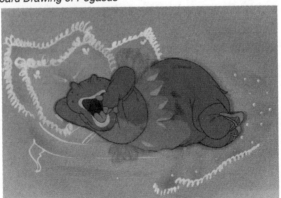

Fantasia Movie Cel of Hyacinth Hippo

Ferdinand The Bull Animation Cel

Ferdinand The Bull animation cel, scene of townspeople ascending stairs to the Galeria, gouache on trimmed celluloid, applied to a Courvoisier background, 1938, framed, 8 3/4 x 10 1/2" (ILLUS., top of page) **$720**

Cartoon Cel of Huey, Dewey & Louie

Huey, Dewey & Louie cartoon cel, Donald Duck's nephews seated around a table wearing party hats & frowning, gouache on dual-cet set-up applied to a colored paper background, unknown production, 1950s, framed, 7 x 9" (ILLUS.) **$60**

Jungle Book (The) movie poster, full-color jungle scene w/all the main characters, one-sheet, 1967, 27 x 41" (ILLUS., top next column) **$360**

Lady and The Tramp movie cel, shows Peggy singing, gouache on full celluloid applied to a color-printed Disneyland background, 1955, framed, 8 x 9 3/4" (ILLUS., bottom next column) **$360**

The Jungle Book Movie Poster

Lady & The Tramp Movie Cel of Peggy

D

Rare Mickey Mouse Cowboy Doll

Mickey Mouse doll, standing composition Mickey w/black pie-wedge eyes wearing a cowboy outfit w/white felt hat, red neckerchief & white wool chaps, stiff arms w/red gloves & red composition feet, complete w/holster & two metal guns, Knickerbocker, early 1930s, some deterioration to one chap, 10" h. (ILLUS.)........ **$1,035**

Snow White & the Seven Dwarfs Drawing

Snow White and The Seven Dwarfs animation layout drawing, sketches of the heads of the Dwarfs peering over the cliffside, each labeled w/name, graphite & colored pencil on paper, w/a document concerning provenance, 1937, framed, 8 x 9" (ILLUS.)... **$1,320**

Pinocchio Movie Animation Drawing

Pinocchio movie drawing, three-quarters view of a surprised Pinocchio, graphite on paper animation drawing, 1940, 8 x 12" (ILLUS.)... **$720**

The Ugly Duckling Animation Drawing

Ugly Duckling (The) animation drawing, shows three yellow ducklings, graphite & colored pencil on paper, signed & inscribed "Horvath, 1936," w/a document concerning provenance, 1939, framed, 3 1/2 x 5 1/2" (ILLUS.)............................... **$660**

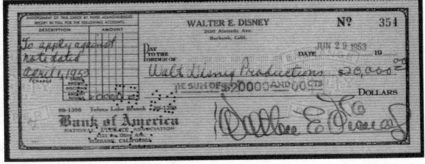

Old Check Signed by Walt Disney

Walt Disney check, Bank of America check from Walter E. Disney in the amount of $20,000, dated June 29, 1953, signed in blue ink, w/a document concerning provenance (ILLUS., bottom previous page) **$1,560**

Rare Early Signed Walt Disney Letter

Walt Disney letter, typewritten & signed on Walt Disney Productions stationery, he thanks a theatre for showing Disney films, dated September 10, 1934, signed in blue ink, one page (ILLUS.).............. **$10,800**

DOLL FURNITURE & ACCESSORIES

Old Federal-Style Canopy Doll Bed

Bed, Federal four-poster canopy style, ring-turned & tapering posts, the headboard

w/a scroll-carved top, heavy square legs, old reddish brown finish, 19th c., 16 1/2 x 28" l., 27" h. (ILLUS.) **$345**

Early Painted Pine Doll Cradle

Cradle, painted pine, dovetailed hooded design w/a shaped footboard, on solid rockers, good wear on old red paint, first half 19th c., 17" l., 10 1/2" h. (ILLUS.) **$374**

D

Victorian Floor Model Two-Story Dollhouse

Dollhouse, painted wood, floor model, designed as a two-story Victorian house w/a four-room plan, applied architectural details & painted tan & brown, mica windows & rod for curtain cover, plus 24 pieces of painted early country furniture & accessories, appears complete, late 19th c., 12 1/2 x 29", 56 1/2" h. (ILLUS.)............. **$437**

D

1950s Pink Plastic Marx Game Table

Game table, dollhouse-size, molded pink plastic, Louis Marx & Co., New York, New York, 1950s, 1 3/4" h. (ILLUS.) $3

1930s Hoosier Kitchen Cabinet

Kitchen cabinet, dollhouse-size, Hoosier-type, made of white china w/painted black trim, molded mixing bowl & canisters on the counter, made in Japan, ca. 1930s, 2" h. (ILLUS.).................................... $70

1950s Marx Pink Plastic Highchair

Highchair, dollhouse-size, molded pink plastic, Louis Marx & Co., New York, New York, 1950s, 1 3/4" h. (ILLUS.) $3

Plastic Kitchen Sink Unit by Marx

Kitchen sink, dollhouse-size, molded white plastic w/embossed water taps & two sinks, Louis Marx & Co., New York, New York, 1950s, 3 3/4" l., 2" h. (ILLUS.) $3

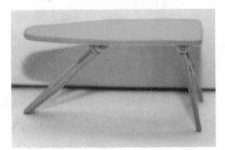

Marx 1950s Plastic Ironing Board

Ironing board, dollhouse-size, molded olive green plastic, folding legs, by Louis Marx & Co., New York, New York, 1950s, 3 1/2" l., 2" h. (ILLUS.) $3

Ideal 1950s Sheet Pressing Machine

Sheet pressing machine, dollhouse-size, molded white plastic w/black trim, top lifts to expose iron, by Ideal, 1950s, 2 1/2" w., 2 1/2" h. (ILLUS.) $10

DOLLS

Armand Marseille "Googly" Eye Girl

A.M. (Armand Marseille) bisque socket head girl, marked "Germany, 323 A. 11/0 M," set glass blue "googly" eyes, closed smiling mouth, replaced blonde wig, crude composition five-piece body w/unfinished torso, pin joints at shoulders & hips, molded & painted socks & shoes, vintage dress, left foot repaired, 7" (ILLUS.) **$591**

Alt, Beck & Gottschalck China Lady

Alt, Beck & Gottschalck china shoulder head lady, marked "784 #5" on shoulder plate, turned head w/painted blue eyes & molded & painted blonde center part hair w/deep brush strokes, gusseted kid body w/cloth torso & china lower arms, antique clothing, body worn & torso recovered, hand-sewn old dress, 19" (ILLUS.) **$280**

Cute Bahr & Proschild No. 620 Baby

Bahr & Proschild bisque socket head baby, marked "G B & Co - Germany - BP & Co (in crossed lines) - 620-4," blue sleep eyes, open mouth, original blonde mohair wig, composition bent-limb baby body, new clothing & bonnet, body finish worn, front of one foot broken & glued, 11" (ILLUS.) **$253**

Rare Bahr & Proschild "Googly" Girl

Bahr & Proschild bisque socket head girl, marked "686 - 7 - 0 - BP (in heart) - Made in Germany," blue sleep eyes, "googly" eyes looking left, closed smiling mouth, antique mohair wig, five-piece composition body w/"starfish" hands, newly made clothing, 7" (ILLUS.) **$2,576**

D

D

1992 Kool-Aid Wacky Warehouse Barbie

Barbie, "Collectors Edition - Barbie Wacky Warehouse Kool-Aid" doll, 1992, complete in box (ILLUS. of box)........................ **$9-13**

1995 Kool-Aid Wacky Warehouse Barbie

Barbie, "Special Edition - Kool-Aid Wacky Warehouse Barbie" doll, 1995, complete in box (ILLUS. of box) **$4-9**
Bebe Phenix bisque socket head girl, marked "93," blue paperweight eyes, closed mouth, original brown human hair wig, jointed wood & composition body w/jointed wrists, new dress & old underclothing, both little fingers missing, not correct body, 22" (ILLUS., top next column).. **$2,531**

Scarce Bebe Phenix Bisque Head Girl

Fine Belton-Type Bisque Head Girl

Belton-type bisque socket-head girl, marked "183," flat area on top of head w/three holes, brown paperweight eyes, closed mouth w/outlined white space between lips, pierced ears, original brown human hair wig, jointed wood & composition body w/straight wrists & shapely torso, new clothing w/old shoes & socks, 15 1/2" (ILLUS.) **$1,181**

D

Patented Bruckner Cloth Black Girl

Bruckner cloth black girl, marked "Pat'd July 9th 1901" on bottom edge of mask face, brown cloth w/stiffened black mask face, grinning open/closed mouth w/two rows of teeth, printed curly black hair w/red ribbon at sides, jointed at shoulders & hips, mitten hands, original plaid clothing, no socks or shoes, only light wear, 13" (ILLUS.)...................................... **$281**

Tall High Brow China Head Lady

China shoulder head lady, painted blue eyes, pink tint high-brow style w/molded & painted black center part hair, recovered cloth body w/china lower limbs, new arms & legs, new clothing, some color flakes on curls & pupil of right eye, 20" (ILLUS.)...................................... **$225**

Tall China Head Lady with Hair Bow

China shoulder head lady, marked "7" on shoulder plate, painted blue eyes, closed mouth, exposed ears, molded black hair w/curls & molded bow at back of head, short curls & twists below the bow, new cloth body w/old china limbs & lower legs w/orange boots, antique clothing, 15" (ILLUS.) **$560**

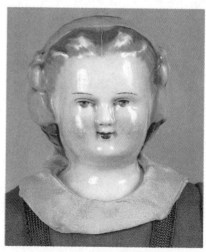

China Head Lady with Hair in Snood

China shoulder head lady, painted features, molded blonde hair w/center part & flat green band & molded black snood w/decoration, pin-jointed kidette body, bisque lower arms, old clothing, new shoes, body later than head, 12 1/2" (ILLUS.) **$504**

D

Rare C. & O. Dressel Fashion Lady

Cuno & Otto Dressel bisuqe socket head Fashion lady, marked "1469 - C & O D - Germany - 2," blue sleep eyes, closed mouth, original brown mohair wig, jointed composition body w/adult figure, slim arms & legs w/high heel feet, all original clothing needing minor mending, 14 1/2" (ILLUS.).................................. **$3,920**

All-Original Effanbee Patsysette Doll

Effanbee composition Patsyette, marked on back & w/Patsyette paper heart tag, composition head w/painted brown side-glancing eyes, closed mouth, mohair wig over molded hair, composition body jointed at shoulders & hips, original pink outfit & brass heart bracelet, very light crazing, 9" (ILLUS.) **$308**

Small Gaultier French Fashion Lady

Gaultier (Francois) bisque socket head & shoulder plate Fashion lady, marked "0" on head & "F.G." on left shoulder, blue paperweight eyes w/dark outer rim, closed mouth, pierced ears, replaced mohair wig, gusseted kid body w/individually stitched fingers, new clothing, right earring hole pulled through, arms patched, 12 1/2" (ILLUS.)........................ **$1,463**

Fine Gaultier Bisque Head Fashion Lady

Gaultier (Francois) bisque socket head & shoulder plate Fashion lady, marked "1" on head & "F.G." on left shoulder, light blue paperweight eyes, closed mouth, pierced ears, original blonde mohair wig on cork pate, cloth body w/kid arms & individually stitched fingers, completely original w/faded period outfit w/silk buttons missing on front, heels missing from shoes, 14" (ILLUS.)................................. **$2,363**

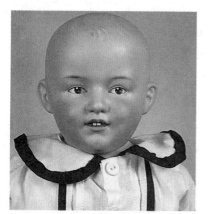

Gebruder Heubach Character Boy

Gebruder Heubach bisque shoulder head character boy, marked "5 - Germany - 7054" on shoulder plate, solid dome head, blue intaglio eyes, open-closed smiling mouth w/two upper teeth, lightly molded blond hair, gusseted kid body w/bisque lower arms, new clothing, 17" (ILLUS.) **$336**

Large Heinrich Handwerck Girl

Heinrich Handwerck bisque socket head girl, marked "Germany - Heinrich Handwerck - Simon & Halbig - 6," blue sleep eyes missing real lashes, open mouth w/upper teeth, pierced ears, original blonde mohair wig, jointed wood & composition body, antique clothing, generally excellent, 31" (ILLUS.) **$703**

D

Tall Heinrich Handwerck Blonde Girl

Heinrich Handwerck bisque socket head girl, marked "99 - 11 3/4 - DEP - Germany - Handwerck - Halbig" on head, marked "Heinrich Handwerck - Germany" on right hip, brown sleep eyes, open mouth w/upper teeth, pierced ears, old blonde mohair wig, jointed wood & composition body, new clothing of antique fabric, inherent firing line around left ear, original body finish, 22" (ILLUS.) **$672**

Large Heinrich Handwerck Girl Doll

Heinrich Handwerck bisque socket head girl, marked "Germany - Heinrich Handwerck - Simon & Halbig" on head, marked "Heinrich Handwerck - Germany" on left hip, blue sleep eyes w/remnants of real lashes, painted lower lashes, original brown mohair wig, jointed wood & composition Heinrich Handwerck body, original clothing including marked shoes, button missing from shoes, 19" (ILLUS.) **$731**

Pretty 24" Tete Jumeau Girl

Cute Hertel, Schwab Character Girl

Hertel, Schwab & Co. bisque socket head character girl, marked "165-6," set glass brown "googly" eyes, open/closed smiling mouth, antique blonde mohair wig on replaced pate, fully jointed wood & composition toddler body, old clothing, small narrow flake on upper rim of right eyes, eyes have been set, minor repairs to body, 15 1/2" (ILLUS.).............................. **$4,163**

Jumeau (E.) bisque socket head girl, marked "Déposé Tete Jumeau - 11" on head, brown paperweight eyes, open mouth w/six upper teeth, pierced ears, original blonde mohair wig on cork pate, jointed wood & composition Jumeau body w/jointed wrists, new clothing, body repainted, 24" (ILLUS.) **$2,240**

Jumeau No. 8 Bisque Head Girl

Rare All-Original Jumeau Girl

Jumeau (E.) bisque socket head girl, marked "Déposé - E 8 J" on head, marked "Bebe Jumeau - Diplome d'Honneur" label on back, brown paperweight eyes, closed mouth, pierced applied ears, replaced human hair wig on cork pate, jointed wood & composition Jumeau body w/jointed wrists, torso cutout for working crier, antique clothing, body later than head, 17" (ILLUS.).......... **$3,375**

Jumeau (E.) bisque socket head girl, marked "Déposé Tete Jumeau - Bte. S.G.D.G. - 5" on head, marked "Bebe Jumeau - Diplome d'Honneur" label on back, marked "Bebe Jumeau" on waist band & marked "5 - Bebe Jumeau - Déposé" on soles of shoes, blue paperweight eyes, closed mouth, pierced ears, original blonde mohair wig & cork pate, jointed wood & composition body w/jointed wrists, factory original clothing, in original labeled box, like-new, 14" (ILLUS.) .. **$9,280**

D

Unusual Jumeau Napoleon Doll

Jumeau (E.) bisque socket head Napoleon, marked "1" on head, blue paperweight eyes, open mouth w/six upper teeth, black mohair wig on original cork pate, five-piece composition body, original uniform & hat, break on top of forehead at crown reglued, 11 1/2" (ILLUS.) **$2,925**

*Small K*R Character Girl*

K (star) R (Kammer & Reinhardt) bisque socket head character girl, marked "K*R - Simon & Halbig - 101 - 19," painted blue eyes, closed pouty mouth, blonde mohair wig on cardboard pate, fully jointed wood & composition body, clothing made w/antique fabric, 7 1/2" (ILLUS.).. **$1,800**

Kammer & Reinhardt Bisque Head Baby

K (star) R (Kammer & Reinhardt) bisque socket head baby, marked "K*R - Simon & Halbig - 116 - A 32," blue sleep eyes, open-closed mouth w/two upper teeth, original blonde mohair wig, jointed composition baby body, possibly original clothing, repair to back of head, 14" (ILLUS.) **$616**

Kammer & Reinhardt No. 121 Girl

K (star) R (Kammer & Reinhardt) bisque socket head girl, marked "K*R - Simon & Halbig - 121," brown sleep eyes, open mouth w/upper teeth & tongue, antique brown human hair wig on plaster pate, fully jointed toddler body w/slanted hip joints, old clothing, only minor flaws, 16" (ILLUS.).. **$532**

Kathe Kruse Girl in Regional Costume

Kathe Kruse ethnic girl, marked "Kathe Kruse (faded) - 45789" on bottom of left foot, other pencil marks on other foot, painted cloth swivel head, painted brown eyes, blonde human hair wig, jointed cloth body w/stitched fingers & separate thumb, wearing a vintage German regional costume, 20" (ILLUS.) **$960**

Unplayed-With Kathe Kruse Girl

Kathe Kruse girl, marked "921644 - Kathe Kruse" on bottom of left foot, marked "Kathe Kruse - Gisela-Anna - IH - Original gekleidet" on side of neck tag, marked "99 - 11 3/4 - DEP - Germany - Handwerck - Halbig" on head, marked "Kathe Kruse - Made in U.S. Zone Germany" on other side, cloth head w/three back seams, painted brown eyes, blonde human hair wig, cloth jointed body, stitched fingers & separate thumb, original cloth-

ing & neck tag, some light discoloration to clothing, unplayed-with, 17" (ILLUS.)...... **$3,263**

Small Kestner All-Bisque Character Girl

Kestner (J.D.) all-bisque character girl, marked "602-2-0," socket head w/brown sleep eyes, open smiling mouth w/upper teeth, original brown mohair wig on plaster pate, five-piece all-bisque toddler body w/molded blue socks & black one-strap shoes, old slip, only tiny flakes, 6" (ILLUS.)... **$448**

Kestner Shoulder Head Girl Doll

Kestner (J.D.) bisque shoulder head girl, marked "G," set brown eyes, closed mouth, antique blonde mohair wig, gusseted kid body w/bisque lower arms, antique clothing, 17" (ILLUS.) **$956**

D

Kestner Bisque Head No. 211 Baby

Kestner (J.D.) bisque socket head baby, marked "H made in 12 Germany - J.D.K. - 211," blue sleep eyes, open mouth w/upper teeth, original skin wig over plaster pate, composition Kestner baby body, antique clothing, crack around left wrist, 15" (ILLUS.) **$560**

Kestner Bisque Socket Head Baby

Kestner (J.D.) bisque socket head baby, marked "made in K. Germany 14 - J.D.K. - Z. 226 Z," blue sleep eyes, open mouth w/upper teeth, original blonde mohair wig on plaster pate, composition Kestner baby body, antique clothing, few areas of minor body repair, 18" (ILLUS.) **$508**

Kestner Girl with Flirty Eyes

Kestner (J.D.) bisque socket head girl, marked "F - made in H Germany - J.D.K. - 257 - made in Germany," flirty brown sleep eyes w/tin lids, open mouth w/upper teeth, antique blonde human hair wig, fully-jointed Kestner toddler body w/slanted hip joints, new clothing, hairline behind left ear, two fingers repaired, 16" (ILLUS.) **$560**

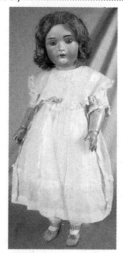

Nice Large Kestner Bisque Head Girl

Kestner (J.D.) bisque socket head girl, marked "made in H Germany 12 - 171," blue sleep eyes missing real lashes, open mouth w/upper teeth, original blonde mohair wig on plaster pate, jointed wood & composition Kestner body, vintage clothing w/new slips, 24" (ILLUS.) **$476**

Large Kley & Hahn Bisque Head Girl

Kley & Hahn bisque socket head girl, marked "Germany - K&H (in banner) - 525 - 6," brown sleep eyes, open/closed mouth, replaced brown human hair wig, jointed wood & composition body, wearing old clothing, flake at front of neck opening, upper legs repainted, probably not original body, 19" (ILLUS.) **$1,181**

Lenci Lady in Ethnic Costume

Lenci ethnic lady doll, marked "Modello Despositato - Lenci SA - Torino - Made in Italy," 1940s cardboard tag on skirt, handwritten tag on wrist, pressed felt head w/painted facial features, mohair wig w/braided coils at ears, cloth torso w/felt arms & legs, jointed shoulders & hips, wearing an Italian regional costume in felt & fabric, several tiny holes in felt skirt, tiny hole in head piece, 17" (ILLUS.) **$597**

Nice Early Papier-mâché Model Lady

Papier-mâché milliner's model lady, papier-mâché shoulder head w/painted features & molded black hair w/side curls & high beehive known as an Apollo Knot, slim kid body w/wooden lower limbs, painted green shoes, original clothing w/faded rust dress w/tulle overlay, matching pant legs, darkened & lightly discolored face, clothing faded & tulle badly deteriorated, early 19th c., 10 1/2" (ILLUS.) **$672**

Fine Rayberry & Delphieu Doll

Rayberry & Delphieu bisque head girl, marked "R2D," amber set eyes, original cork pate w/newer blonde mohair wig, closed mouth, jointed composition body, wearing a replica fine French fashion costume & antique French shoes, 22" h. (ILLUS.) **$2,415**

S.F.B.J. Bisque Socket Head Boy

S.F.B.J. (Societé Francaise de Frabrication de Bebes & Jouets) bisque socket head boy, marked "S.F.B.J., 235, Paris, 6," blue paperweight eyes, open/closed mouth w/painted upper teeth, molded hair w/no color, jointed wood & composition S.F.B.J. toddler body, new clothing, 15" (ILLUS.) **$1,008**

S.F.B.J. Bisque Head Girl No. 247

S.F.B.J. (Societé Francaise de Frabrication de Bebes & Jouets) bisque socket head girl, marked "S.F.B.J. - 247 - Paris - 6," blue sleep eyes missing real lashes, painted lower lashes, open-closed mouth w/two upper teeth, replaced blonde human hair wig, fully jointed wood & composition toddler body, old clothing, new socks & shoes, small hairline in right forehead, 16" (ILLUS.) **$532**

D

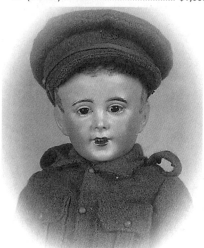

Rare S.F.B.J. No. 237 Soldier Doll

S.F.B.J. (Societé Francaise de Frabrication de Bebes & Jouets) bisque socket soldier, marked "S.F.B.J. - 237 - Paris - 4," set brown pupils eyes, open mouth w/teeth, molded & flocked hair, jointed wood & composition French body, original wool military uniform, factory chemise under uniform, excellent condition, 17" (ILLUS.)... **$3,920**

Bruno Schmidt Bisque Head Baby

Schmidt (Bruno) bisque socket head baby, marked "9 - Made in Germany - BSW (in heart) - 2097-4 3/4" on head, marked "Made in Germany" on lower back, brown sleep eyes, open mouth w/upper teeth, old brown mohair wig, composition bent-limb baby body, antique clothing, teeth poorly reset, tip of left little finger missing, 18" (ILLUS.) **$253**

D

22" All-Original Shirley Temple Doll

Shirley Temple composition doll, marked "Shirley Temple - Cop Ideal - N&T Co," also name on the back, & NRA tag on dress, hazel sleep eyes, open mouth w/teeth, original mohair wig in original set, five-piece composition body, original tagged outfit, eyes cloudy, light crazing, dress washed, socks deteriorating, 22" (ILLUS.).. **$784**

Simon & Halbig No. 1299 Girl

Simon & Halbig bisque socket head girl, marked "1299 - Simon & Halbig - S&H - 7" on head, marked "Heinrich Handwerck - Germany 1" on left hip, blue sleep eyes missing real lashes, open mouth w/upper teeth, original blonde mohair wig, jointed wood & composition body w/working crier, antique clothing, flake on left side of head, minor body wear, 18" (ILLUS.)......... **$619**

Nice Simon & Halbig 939 Girl

Simon & Halbig bisque socket head girl, marked "S9H - 939," blue sleep eyes, open mouth, pierced ears, antique brown mohair wig, jointed composition body w/straight wrists & separate balls at shoulders, elbows & knees, wearing antique clothing, overall excellent, thighs replaced, 15" (ILLUS.)................................ **$960**

Simon & Halbig #1078 Girl

Simon & Halbig bisque socket-head girl, marked "1078 - Simon & Halbig - S&W - 0 - Germany," blue sleep eyes, open mouth w/four upper teeth, original mohair blonde wig, five-piece composition body, dressed in new sailor suit, 9" (ILLUS.)....... **$336**

Steiner "Majestic" Girl Doll

Steiner (E.U.) "Majestic" bisque socket head girl, marked "Majestic Regd. 8," blue sleep eyes w/remnants of real lashes, open mouth w/upper teeth, pierced ears, old brown human hair wig, jointed wood & composition body, wearing vintage clothing & antique leather shoes, 19" (ILLUS.) **$808**

Pretty Unis France Bisque Head Girl

Unis France bisque socket head girl, marked "Unis France - 71 - 149 - 306 - Jumeau - 1938 - Paris," set blue eyes, closed mouth, replaced brown human hair wig, five-piece composition body, new clothing, 20" (ILLUS.) **$956**

Unis France bisque socket head girl, marked "Unis France (in oval) - 71 - 149 - 301 - 12," oval label on the back marked "Bebe Jumeau - Diplome d'Honneur," brown sleep eyes w/real lashes, open mouth, new French blonde human hair wig, jointed wood & composition body cut for crier w/screened hole on back, new

Tall Unis France Bisque Head Girl

clothing, old leather shoes, few missing lashes, touch-up to lip, some flaking on body, 26" (ILLUS.).................................... **$308**

DRUGSTORE & PHARMACY ITEMS

The old-time corner drugstore, once a familiar part of every American town, has now given way to a modern, efficient pharmacy. With the streamlining and modernization of this trade, many of the early tools and store adjuncts have been outdated and now fall in the realm of "collectibles." Listed here are some of the tools, bottles, display pieces and other ephemera once closely associated with the druggist's trade.

Cobalt Blue Pottery Apothecary jar

D

Apothecary jar w/fitted lid, cobalt blue-glazed pottery, cylindrical w/waisted neck, wide gold banner printed in black "Pulv. Lapis P.," probably English, ca. 1860-80, 6 5/8" h. (ILLUS., previous page) **$448**

drop-shaped globe w/a stepped shoulder, short cylindrical neck & tall oblong stopper, fitted in cast- and polished aluminum three-footed stand, American, ca. 1920-35, 18 1/8" h. (ILLUS.)...................................... **$420**

Ruby & Clear Glass Show Bottle

Apothecary show bottle, blown bulbous ovoid ruby glass body w/tapering cylindrical neck & flaring rim, raised on an applied clear pedestal & round foot, original clear hollow-blown stopper, probably American, ca. 1870-90, 10" h. (ILLUS.) **$504**

Scarce Early Blown Glass Storage Jar

Apothecary storage jar, cov., free-blown clear cylindrical jar w/two applied cobalt blue bands around the body, high domed clear cover w/cobalt blue rim band & hollow blown knob finial, pontil scar, ca. 1850, 11" h. (ILLUS.) **$532**

Clear Art Deco Style Show Globe

Apothecary show globe w/original stopper, Art Deco style, a large clear glass tear-

Rare Alock Apothecary Leeches Jar

Apothecary storage jar, earthenware, wide baluster-form body w/a flaring round foot, fluted band around the lower body & short flaring neck w/flattened inset cover w/small pierced holes & knob finial, leaf-molded loop shoulder handles, sea green at the bottom & top w/the white center area h.p. w/leafy scrolls & a large sea green banner decorated in gold w/the word "Leeches," impressed "Alcock" mark, England, some damage on lid, late 19th - early 20th c., 13 1/2" h. (ILLUS.)................................. **$8,625**

Rare Porcelain Apothecary Leeches Jar

Apothecary storage jar, porcelain, cylindrical w/ringed white base & rim, domed cover w/small air holes & button finial, the sides & cover in dark moss green, the base h.p. w/a gilt crown & scrolls above a red-bordered white banner reading "Leeches," early, 9 1/2" h. (ILLUS.)......... **$5,980**

Very Rare Royal Doulton Leeches Jar

Apothecary storage jar, pottery, wide baluster-form body w/flattened disk cover w/small pierced holes & knob finial, deep cobalt blue glaze w/an arched red-bordered gold banner reading "Leeches," impressed "Royal Doulton England," label probably repainted, late 19th - early 20th c., 9 1/2" h. (ILLUS.) **$8,625**

Old Cobalt Blue Drug Bottle

Drug bottle, narrow rectangular w/beveled sides, embossed "Maximo M. Dia - Druggist - Ybor City, Fla.," tooled lip, "W.T. & Co. U.S.A." on smooth base, ca. 1890-1910, cobalt blue, 5 1/8" h. (ILLUS.).......... **$190**

ENAMELS

Enamels have been used to decorate a variety of substances, particularly metals. The best-known small enameled wares, such as patch and other small boxes and napkin rings, are the Battersea Enamels made by the Battersea Enamel Works in the last half of the 18th century. However, the term is often loosely applied to other English enamels. Russian enamels, usually on a silver or gold base, are famous and expensive. Early 20th century French enamel on copper wares and those items produced in China at the turn of the 20th century in imitation of the early Russian style are also drawing dealer and collector attention.

E

E

Austrian Enameled Candlesticks & Covered Cup

Candlesticks, the bulbous domed base w/a silver rim band connected w/an ornate silver band to the tall cylindrical shaft w/another silver band to the cylindrical socket w/flattened silver rim, the shaft enameled w/spiraling scrollwork on a white ground, the base decorated w/several oval reserves depicting scenes from classical mythology, stamped initials of Hermann Bohm, Vienna, Austria, last quarter 19th c., 10" h., pr. (ILLUS. right with Austrian enameled covered cup)... **$4,200**

Extremely Rare Austrian Enameled Cornucopia & Tall Ewer

Cornucopia, cov., silver-mounted, a round stepped base topped by a spread-winged figural silver eagle supporting the long horn-shaped cornucopia on its back, the cornucopia divided into three enameled bands by wide ornate silver bands & ending in a figural eagle head foot, the stepped & domed hinged cover w/a figural silver finial, the enameled bands depicting mythologial scenes, indistinct mark of maker, Vienna, Austria, last quarter 19th c., 9 1/2" h. (ILLUS. right with Austrian ewer) **$19,200**

Small French Art Nouveau Enameled Cup

Cup, Art Nouveau style, gently flaring cylindrical shape, silver-gilt ground decorated w/stylized orange poppy blossoms, dark green stems & pods & light green leaves on a white ground, designed by Alphonse Mucha, executed by Georges Fouquet, France, ca. 1902, 1 7/8" h. (ILLUS.) **$5,378**

Cup, cov., the domed base raised on four silver-gilt paw feet, the ringed stem supporting a wide cup w/a rounded bottom & wide slightly flaring cylindrical sides, the stepped & domed cover w/a ringed silver-gilt rim band & a figural silver-gilt finial of a putto riding a swan, decorated overall w/enameled reserves depicting 18th c. scenes, mounted stamped w/initials of Karl Rossler, Vienna, Austria, last quarter 19th c., 9" h. (ILLUS. left with enameled Austrian candlesticks, previous page) **$7,800**

Ewer, silver-mounted & "jeweled," the wide spout w/a wavy silver rim above a waisted neck supported by a satyr under the spout & flanked on each side by a female herm, issuing a female caryatid & gargoyle scroll handle, the body decorated w/oval enameled medallions depicting mythological scenes against a gold ground painted w/masks & foliate, body divided by a very ornate silver band, a silver-mounted stem disc above the paneled domed rounded base painted w/more arched figural panels, the ornate silver base band mounted w/six figural terms, Vienna, Austria, last quarter 19th c., 17" h. (ILLUS. right with Austrian cornucopia, previous page) **$21,600**

Fine French Enamel of Goddess Diana

Plaque, rectangular, depicting a profile bust portrait of the goddess Diana wearing a dark blue robe, leafy trees & sky in the background, indistinct signature, Paris, France, late 19th c., in a molded wood frame, plaque 7 1/4 x 9" (ILLUS.)............ **$4,800**

EPERGNES

Epergnes were popular as centerpieces on tables of the 19th century. Many have receptacles of colored glass for holding sweetmeats, fruit or flowers. Early epergnes were made entirely of metal, including silver.

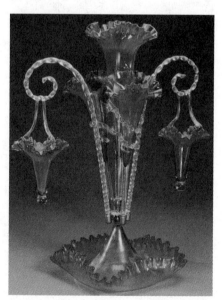

Exceptional Cranberry Glass Epergne

E

Cranberry & clear glass, four-lily, the rounded base dish w/the sides turned up to form four sides w/tightly crimped rims, the center tapering up to a brass fitter supporting a tall center cranberry lily w/a crimped rim & an applied spiral band of clear rigaree surrounded by three matching smaller lilies & two tall slender clear ropetwist uprights w/curled ends each suspending a cranberry lily-form basket w/turned up crimped rims & applied w/plain clear handles, Bohemia, late 19th c., overall 20" h. (ILLUS., previous page) **$1,150**

Large Cranberry Epergne with Baskets

Cranberry glass, three-lily, a large upright central lily w/a flared & ruffled & crimped top flanked by matching lilies wrapped w/applied clear glass crimped bands & separated by two tall clear glass ropetwisted canes each suspending a cranberry basket w/flaring ruffled & crimped rim & a tall applied clear pointed handle, all raised above a wide squared cranberry bowl base w/four upturned incurved & crimped sides, Bohemia, late 19th c., 20" h. (ILLUS.) **$1,150**

Cranberry glass, three-lily, a very tall slender gently flaring center trumpet w/a flaring deeply ruffled rim & a band of clear rigaree applied near the top, two much smaller lilies flanking the center, each w/a ruffled rim & applied clear rigaree & attached to the frame w/a clear applied arm, all above the widely flaring & ruffled shallow bowl base, late 19th - early 20th c., 21 1/2" h. (ILLUS., top next column) **$403**

Three-lily Cranberry Glass Epergne

Fine Mappin & Webb, English Epergne

Cut glass & silver plate, a trefoil base w/scroll tab feet & flat tops fitted w/tiny gilt-silver figures of squirrels, the tall knopped & reeded pedestal w/a large knob issuing three upturned arms each joined by chain swags & ending in a small platform holding a scalloped cut glass dish, an upper wide disk supporting a wide flaring platform suspending short chain swags & supporting a matching large scalloped cut glass bowl, mark of Mappin & Webb, England, early 20th c., 15 1/2" w., 25" h. (ILLUS.)...................... **$1,840**

Fine Victorian French Silver & Glass Epergne

Cut glass & silver plate, single lily, a tall paneled cut central lily vase supported in a tall leaf-cast clasp, above a dished paneled cut glass dish raised above the tall tripod base composed of naturalistic branches, oak leaves & acorns, marked by Christofle & Cie., Paris, France, ca. 1890, 21 1/2" h. (ILLUS.) **$3,824**

Four Lily Green Opalescent Epergne

Green opalescent glass, four-lily, a very tall slender & gently flaring center lily shading from pale green to dark opalescent green at the flaring ruffled rim, the sides w/an applied spiral band of green rigaree, surrounded by three matching shorter lilies, all above the matching wide shallow ruffled bowl base, ca. 1900, 18 1/2" h. (ILLUS.) **$834**

Pink Opalescent Three-lily Epergne

Pink opalescent glass, three-lily, a widely flaring swirled rib dished base w/a crimped rim, a tall center trumpet w/swirled optic ribbing & a flaring crimped rim, applied spiraling clear vine w/leaves, two shorter curved matching lilies, overall 16" (ILLUS.) **$575**

Rare Blown Glass English Epergne

Yellow glass, one-lily, a tall blown yellow central trumpet-form vase w/a bulbed base w/an applied pink rigaree band & the widely flaring & gently ruffled rim w/an applied amber band, raised above three arched blown clear & yellowish amber upright leaves alternating w/upright amber stems each suspending a deep red shading to pink cased peaches, all issuing from an amber glass leaf cluster centered on a six-lobed plateau mirror, England, possibly by Webb, overall 14 3/4" h. (ILLUS.) **$5,175**

FABERGÉ

The creations of Carl Fabergé (1846-1920), goldsmith and jeweler to the Russian Imperial Court, are recognized as the finest of their kind. He made a number of enamel fantasies, including Easter eggs, for the Imperial family and utilized precious metals and jewels in other work.

Rare Fabergé Aquamarine Brooch

Brooch, gold-mounted aquamarine & diamond, the oblong octagonal aquamarine framed by a narrow band of old-cut & single-cut diamonds topped by a diamond-set Imperial crown & ribbons, marked on pin-guard & lower mount, indistinct workmaster mark, St. Petersburg, ca. 1895, 1 1/4" h. (ILLUS.) **$24,768**

Yellow Gold Fabergé Cigarette Case

Cigarette case, gem-set yellow gold, thin rectangular shape w/angled edges &

rounded corners, decorated overall w/fine reeding w/three wider bands towards the center, a cabochon sapphire thumb piece, marked inside cover & on base, workmaster's mark for Gabriel Niukkanen, St. Petersburg, 1908-17, 3 1/2" l. (ILLUS.) **$8,256**

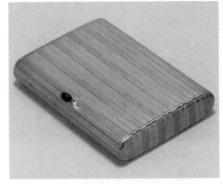

Two-color Gold Fabergé Cigarette Case

Cigarette case, two-color gold, rectangular w/rounded corners, narrow reeded stripes alternating pink & gold, the hinged cover w/a cabochon sapphire thumb piece, marked in Cyrillic, St. Petersburg, 1908-17, 3 1/4" l. (ILLUS.) **$9,560**

Rare Fabergé Silver & Amber Putto

Figure of a putto, silver & amber, the standing finely detailed silver figure playing amber & silver pipes, atop an amber post issuing from a silver rockwork formation, all on an oval bowenite plinth, marked in Cyrillic on the rocks & foot, workmaster's mark of Julius Rappoport, St. Petersburg, 1896-1908, 11" h. (ILLUS.) **$72,240**

Three Carved Jasper Fabergé Animals

Rare Fabergé Miniature Icon

Icon, miniature, h.p. icon of a bearded male saint within silver-gilt & cloisonné oklad decorated in blue, green & brown floral scrolls, the halo of the saint w/a chevron & pellet border, marked on base rim, Moscow, 1908-17, 2 1/2" h. (ILLUS.).... **$30,960**

Model of a hippopotamus, gem-set Kalgan jasper, standing animal fitted w/ruby eyes, 2 5/8" L. (ILLUS. left with two elephants, top of page) **$12,384**

Model of an elephant, gem-set Kalgan jasper, animal carved w/trunk down, fitted w/green garnet eyes, marked under one foot, 3 1/2" l. (ILLUS. center with small elephant and hippopotamus, top of page) **$16,512**

Model of an elephant, gem-set Kalgan jasper, small animal carved w/trunk down, fitted w/gold-mounted red stone eyes, apparently unmarked, ca. 1890, 1 1/8" l. (ILLUS. right with large elephant and hippopotamus, top of page) **$10,320**

F

Rare Early Fabergé Gold & Diamond Wristwatch

Wristwatch, diamond-mounted gold, the case in gold w/a band of diamonds set around the round dial w/Arabic numerals, the bracelet w/large chain links set at intervals w/further diamonds, marked on the claps, Workmaster August Holmstrom, St. Petersburg, ca. 1895, bracelet 8" l. (ILLUS.) **$11,950**

FIRE FIGHTING COLLECTIBLES

American fire fighting "antiques" are considered those items over 100 years old that were directly related to fire fighting, whereas fire fighting "collectibles" are items less than a century old. Pieces from both eras are very sought-after today.

Foreign-made fire fighting antiques and collectibles have a marketplace of their own and, for the most part, are not as expensive and in demand as similar American pieces.

Early Painted Fire Bucket

Fire bucket, decorated leather, slightly swelled & tapering cylindrical shape w/a heavy strap handle, the front painted w/a spread-winged American eagle w/shield & banner reading "1812," painted above the eagle "No. I," 9" d., 11 3/4" h. (ILLUS.) **$4,200**

Two Early Painted Fire Buckets

Fire bucket, decorated leather w/copper rivets, slightly swelled & tapering cylindrical shape w/a replaced handle & bentwood rim, the front painted in black w/flames & "H. Porter 1832," wear & some damage, 9" d., 11" h. (ILLUS. right with larger red fire bucket)........................ **$633**
Fire bucket, decorated leather w/wood reinforced rim & leather handle, tapering cylindrical shape, dark red ground w/black

bands, the front w/a yellow ring enclosing a yellow diamond & a green & red quatrefoil, some wear, 8 3/4" d., 12 1/2" h. plus handle (ILLUS. left with smaller black fire bucket) **$633**

Carbona Tubular Glass Fire Grenade

Fire grenade, 12-sided tubular amber glass, embossed "Carbona" on smooth base, original paper label w/picture of fireman & "Carbona Fire Extinguisher," tooled mouth, American, ca. 1910-20, 11" h. (ILLUS.) **$157**

Rare Blue Harkness Fire Grenade

Fire grenade, spherical cobalt blue glass ribbed ball w/a cylindrical neck, oval panel embossed "Harkness - Fire - Destroyer," crude, American, ca. 1875-95, 6 1/4" h. (ILLUS.) **$728**

Hayward's Patent Fire Grenade

Very Rare Purple Hayward's Grenade

F

Fire grenade, spherical medium golden yellow amber glass w/a cylindrical neck, diamond-shaped panels embossed "Hayward's Hand Fire Grenade - S.F. Hayward 407 Broadway NY - Patented Aug 8 1871," a "3" on the smooth base, American, ca. 1870s, 6 1/2" h. (ILLUS.)..... **$364**

Fire grenade, spherical purple glass w/a cylindrical neck, round panels embossed "Hayward's Hand Fire Grenade - S.F. Hayward 407 Broadway New York," smooth base, original contents, American, ca. 1880-1895, 6 1/4" h. (ILLUS., top next column) **$1,680**

Fire grenade, tubular clear glass, embossed "The Harden (motif of star) - Tubular - Grenade," ground mouth w/original cast-iron wall hangers, smooth base, original contents, American, ca. 1885-1900, 17 5/8" h. (ILLUS., middle next column) **$1,456**

Rare Harden Tubular Fire Grenade

Rare Early Schoenhut Child's Fireman's Costume

Fireman's costume, child's size, molded cardboard helmet w/eagle finial & lithographed front shield w/fire fighting scene, a cloth-covered cardboard chest plate decorated w/crossed ax & fire horn, silver-painted metal fire horn w/rope handle & small wooden ax, Schoenhut & Co., helmet w/small cracks, horn mouthpiece missing, early 20th c., the set (ILLUS.)... **$1,725**

Early Fire-themed Advertising Sign

Sign, titled "The Last Alarm," lithograph color or printed on cardboard, scene of two racing white fire horses pulling an early steam fire pumper w/a burning building in the background marked "Pratts Food for Horses and Cattle, Pratt Food Co. Offices," late 19th - early 20th c., framed, some fly specks, sign 20 3/4 x 29 1/2" (ILLUS.)..................................... **$476**

FIREARMS

Carbine, Sharps & Hankins coverted model, 54 ca., front ring on barrel removed & blued sight installed in a dovetail, barrel & action nickel-plated, first type w/the firing pin mounted on the hammer, wooden stock repaired at wrist & refinished, retains 80% of plating,   round barrel 23 3/4" l. (ILLUS., first one bottom of page)...................................... **$2,070**

Carbine, Sharps & Hankins coverted model, 54 ca., standard markings on right of frame, two plugged holes on left side of frame & two more on barrel below the sight, action & barrel refinished after conversion, retains 90% of refinish blue on frame & front link, wooden stock w/minor dents & scratches, round barrel 24" l. (ILLUS., second one bottom of page)...................................... **$575**

Long rifle, flintlock fowler-type, curly maple full stock w/good figure & brass hardware w/dark patina, large lock engraved & w/stamped signature "Payson & Nurse Warranted," 37 1/4" l. octagonal to round barrel w/old brown finish, repaired wrist, New England, early 19th c., 53" l. (ILLUS. second from top with three other rifles & shotgun, top next page).... **$1,035**

Long rifle, percussion-type, curly maple half stock w/seventeen German silver inlays (one missing), octagonal barrel & engraved lock w/an illegible name of maker, repaired split at wrist, early 19th c., 55 1/2" l. (ILLUS. top with three other rifles & shotgun, top next page)...................... **$1,064**

Musket, Suhl model w/Philadelphia marks, 74 ga., eagle mark & "Suhl - S&C" w/anchor on the lockplate in front of the hammer, barrel marked "City of Philadelphia - A. Wurfflein" on upper left panel, sling swivels missing, replacement ramrod, greyish brown patina, overall pitting, stock cleaned lightly, partly octagonal barrel 37" l. (ILLUS., middle next page) **$1,150**

Sharps & Hankins Coverted Carbine

Sharps & Hankins Carbine Conversion

Group of Four Long Rifles & Shotgun

F

Suhl Philadelphia Model Musket

Bacon 2nd Model Percussion Model Revolver

Revolver, Bacon 2nd Model percussion model, 31 ca., five-shot cylinder fluted at front end, barrel marked "Bacon Mfg. Co. Norwich, Conn.," light vine & leaf scroll engraving on sides of frame, frame w/grey patina, round barrel 5" l. (ILLUS.) **$1,035**

Revolver, Bacon 2nd Model percussion pocket model, 31 ca., barrel marked "Bacon Mfg. Co. Norwich, Conn.," five sharp vignettes on the cylinder including a kneeling hunter shooting a rifle, a standing hunter, a standing deer, a hunter w/a dog & a deep lying down, further engraving of leafy scrolls on rear frame, 75% bluing on barrel, wooden grips w/90% varnish, octagonal barrel 5" l. (ILLUS.) **$1,380**

Scarce Colt 3rd Model Dragoon Percussion Revolver

Revolver, Colt 3rd Model Dragoon percussion model, 44 ca., scarce octagonal to round barrel & frame markings w/brass grip farmed & one-piece walnut grips, no original finish remains, grip frame lemon yellow w/some light battering, barrel 8" l. (ILLUS.).. **$3,393**

Bacon 2nd Model Percussion Pocket Model Revolver

Very Rare Colt Model D Pocket No. 1 Baby Paterson Revolver

Revolver, Colt Model D Pocket No. 1 Baby Paterson model, 28 ca., one of 500 made between 1837-38, 3 3/4" l. octagonal barrel w/German silver front sight, narrow silver band at muzzle w/a wide silver band on top flat behind sight & a narrow & wide silver band at cylinder end on top three flats that do not wrap around, medium sized silver band on bottom three flats, engraved barrel reads "Patent Arms Mfg. Co. Paterson N.J. - Colt's Pt.," wedge slot w/thick raised borders & wedge unnumbered, 5-shot square back cylinder w/centaur scene, frame is blued w/a wide & narrow silver band around recoil shields & a smooth, square strap, barrel retains 85% original bluing, hammer w/a repaired nose, grip w/minor nicks & scratches (ILLUS.).................... **$51,750**

Early Smith & Wesson #3 First Model American Revolver

Revolver, Smith & Wesson #3 First Model American model, 44 ca., 8" l. keyhole barrel w/slightly modified German silver half moon front sight & two-piece walnut grip, barrel stamped "Smith & Wesson 44," wood grips worn w/battering & repaired crack on left side (ILLUS.)............ **$2,588**

Rare Smith & Wesson #3 Second Model Revolver

Revolver, Smith & Wesson #3 Second Model cased factory engraved model American, 44 ca., nickel finish 2/8" keyhole barrel, slightly altered half moon front sight w/two-piece mother-of-pearl grips, fine Gustave Young engraving consisting of flowing intertwined foliate arabesque designs w/a punch dot background & a large rosette around hinge screw on both sides, accompanied by an original red baize lined walnut Smith & Wesson compartmented case, 90% original nickel plating, grips probably not original, the set (ILLUS.) **$12,938**

Rifle, Broadwell Patent breechloading model, .577 ca., marked "Broadwell's Patent - 1863" on upper tang, & "Ferd. Fruwirth" in an oval on top of barrel, triggerguard rotated 180 degrees to lower the vertically sliding breechblock, rear sling swivel missing, brownish grey patina, wood w/normal dents, small crack in lockplate, barrel 34" l. (ILLUS., bottom of page) **$2,300**

Rifle, Remington 1873 rolling block military model, stamped initials behind the lock, light pitting & a missing ramrod, 52" l. (ILLUS. bottom with other rifles & shotgun, top of page 425) **$288**

Broadwell Patent Breechloading Rifle

Scarce Spencer Colorado Territory Rifle

Unidentified Percussion Turner Model

Rifle, Spencer Colorado Territory model, 50 ca., marked "U.S. - Col. Ter." on the left side of the stock, standard Spencer markings, missing the sling swivels, inspector mark on left side of barrel, ca. 1880s, barrel cleaned, stock cracked on left side, large chip on forearm at breech & parallel crack ahead of it, round barrel 30" l. (ILLUS., top of page)...................... **$7,188**

Rifle, unidentified percussion Turner model, 46 ca., large cheekpiece on stock, one barrel key towards the rear of the barrel, front sight, ramrod, swivel & forearm tip missing, back action lock single trigger, bluish brown patina, wood w/normal dents & repair at front of forearms, Ohio River area, 19th c., octagonal barrel 32" l. (ILLUS., second from top of page).... **$805**

Shotgun, Scott (W. & C. & Son), 10 ga. double-barrel percussion model w/27 1/2" l. Damascus barrels, checkered walnut stock w/relief-carved panels below the lock plates, engraved steel hardware, light overall pitting, 44 1/4" l. (ILLUS., second from bottom with three rifles, top of page 425) **$345**

FIRECRACKERS

It is not known exactly when fireworks first arrived in North America, however, the first recorded mention of them being using in public celebrations was in 1788. Since that time fireworks have been a big part of American patriotic holidays. The following listing includes a variety of firecracker packages dating from the first half of the 20th century.

Although collecting fireworks can be a bit tricky due to laws regarding transporting them across state lines, there are still enthusiastics who search out complete packets of older firecrackers as well as associated advertising materials. - Jim Trautman.

Box with Three Rolls of Marvel-Caps

Box, "Marvel-Caps - Lubricated - 3 Rolls - 750 Shots," cardboard printed in red & white, produced by W.F. Bishop and Sons, 1960s (ILLUS.).................................... **$2**

1960s Box of Marvel-Caps

Box, "Marvel-Caps - Lubricated," cardboard printed in red & white, package 750 caps, produced by W.F. Bishop and Sons, 1960s, box 2 1/4 x 2 1/4" (ILLUS.) **$4**

Box, "Victory Sparklers," printed w/a scene of a boy & girl lighting safe sparklers as their mother looks on, ca. 1920.................... **$45**

Fireworks firing canister, cylindrical cardboard printed w/patriotic designs including a parachuting soldier, printed in red, white & blue, 1930s.................................... **$100**

F

Apollo Brand Firecrackers Label

Package, "Apollo Super Charged Flashlight Crackers," printed in color w/an Apollo capsule flying above the Earth, Po Sing Firecracker Factory, Macau, China, late 1960s (ILLUS.) **$4**

Early Crax Boy Firecracker Label

Package, "Crax Boy," printed in color w/the running figure of a boy w/his body composed of firecracker packages & holding a large box under one arm, by Chan Tai Kee, made in China, ca. 1920s-30s (ILLUS.) **$10**

Package, "Devil Dog Super Charged," printed w/the image of a large bulldog w/flames around his head & a giant red firecracker below, 1960s **$2**

Package, "Dragon Brand Firecrackers," printed in color w/a Chinese dragon, made in Macau, China, early 1950s **$3**

Black Cat Flashlight Crackers Label

Package, "Black Cat Flashlight Crackers," printed in red & green on yellow, manufactured by Li & Fung, Ltd., Macau, China, 1950s (ILLUS.) **$3**

Package, "China Doll," printed in bright shades of red w/a Chinese doll, 1970 .... **$2**

King Kong Flashlight Firecrackers Label

Package, "King Kong Flashlight Firecrackers," printed in color w/a picture of King Kong w/red wings, made in Macau, China, early 1950s (ILLUS.) **$4**

Marine Brand Firecrackers Label

Package, "Marine Brand - Pride of the U.S.A. Flashlight Firecrackers," printed in red, white & blue w/a scene of Marines charging ashore, Liberty Display Fireworks Co., China, 1955 (ILLUS.) **$10**

Red Child Firecracker Package Label

Package, "Red Child Super Charged Flash Salutes," printed in color w/a young Chinese child running through clouds in a starry sky, made in China, 1930s (ILLUS.) **$7**

Package, "T.W. Hand Fireworks - Hamilton - 1/2 Doz.," printed in red & black on yellow paper, made in Ontario, Canada, ca. 1920s (ILLUS., top next column) **$150**

Package, "Western Boy Fire Crackers," printed in color w/a cowboy riding a bucking bronco, made in Macau, China, 1950s **$3**

Package of T.W. Hand Firecrackers

Postcard, patriotic design that originally contained a firecracker in the center framed by American flags & eagles, reverse reads "Don't Blow Yourself on July 4th - Blow Me," printed in red, white & blue, 1906 .... **$800**

Poster, "Brock's Big Stars for 1938," printed w/image of Old Man Rocket flying upwards w/a big smile on his face, printed list of various types of fireworks available, 1938, 6 x 12" **$100**

Poster, "Dixie Boy," printed w/a scene of a black boy eating watermelon & seated in a display of fireworks, 1940s **$650**

Poster, "Pain's Imperial Fireworks of Australia," printed in color w/a scene of a devil wearing a black tuxedo, a bright red explosion behind him, 1930s, 24" sq. **$200**

Poster, "Pain's Imperial Fireworks of Australia," printed in color w/a scene of a devil standing w/hands held out & fireworks exploding from the fingertips, 1930s, 24" sq. **$200**

Poster, "Pain's Imperial Fireworks of Australia," printed in color w/various scenes including a young boy at the left shouting "We Want Pain's Fireworks," 1930s, 12" sq. **$125**

Large 1930s Spencer Fireworks Poster

Poster, "Spencer Fireworks Company, Polk Ohio," printed in color w/a large scene of aerial fireworks exploding in a night sky as well as scenes of a little girl observing a pinwheel & a boy lighting a sky rocket, reads across the top "Fireworks for a Patriotic 4th of July," 1930s, 24" sq. (ILLUS., previous page) **$400**

Posters, "Safety First - Accidents Will Happen - Be Prepared," a series produced by various insurance companies, feature scenes of children & firecrackers, ca. 1900, the set **$800**

Salesman's sample case, features different types of fireworks being offered, samples not loaded, 1920s **$1,200**

Toy cap cannon, cast metal w/firing mechanism for firing caps, ca. 1890s **$1,500**

FOOT & BED WARMERS

F

Foot warmer, rectangular mortised & pegged wooden frame w/punched-tin panels w/circular designs, wire bale handle, 7 1/2 x 9", 6 1/4" h. (old refinishing, tin insert rusted) **$165**

Old Punched Tin & Wood Foot Warmer

Foot warmer, wood & tin, a mortised wooden frame w/turned corner posts framing the tin sides punched w/a design of hearts & circles, original reddish stain, wire latch & handle, interior tin coat pan, some damage, 7 1/2 x 9 1/2", 5 1/2" h. (ILLUS.)............................... **$100-150**

FRAKTUR

Fraktur paintings are decorative birth and marriage certificates of the 18th and 19th centuries and also include family registers and similar documents. Illuminated family documents, birth and baptismal certificates, religious texts and rewards of merit, in a particular style, are known as "fraktur" because of the similarity to the 16th century typeface of that name. Gay watercolor borders, frequently incorporating stylized birds, often frame the hand-lettered documents, which were executed by local ministers, schoolmasters or itinerant penmen. Most are of Pennsylvania Dutch origin.

Rare Fraktur Birth Certificate with Figures

Birth & baptism certificate, pen & ink & watercolor on paper, features the figures of two standing woman flanking a columned arcade topped by two large urns & inscribed across the top "Certificate of Birth & Baptism," the opening between the columns w/information on the birth of Jacob William Lutz, 1850, in Clinton County, Pennsylvania, attributed to the Reverend Henry Young, bright colors of blue, yellow & orange, light staining & creases, later wood frame, 13 5/8 x 16 1/4" (ILLUS.)........................ **$6,038**

Early Pennsylvania Fraktur Birth Certificate

Birth certificate, pen & ink & watercolor on paper, commemorating the birth of Leah Tiefenbachen, Columbia County, Pennsylvania, flying eagles in the top corners flanking a title box over a flowering sprig over a large text box flanked by tall flowering plants in urns resting atop text boxes, a pair of birds on flowering plants in the bottom center, in dark yellow, red, green & black, dated March 24, 1825, by Fredrich Kusler, 12 x 15 1/2" (ILLUS.)............................. **$2,400**

Fine Fraktur of Lady on Horseback

Drawing, watercolor on paper, stylized portrait of a lady on horseback, wearing a long spotted dress & a crown-form cap, flanked by stylized tulip blossoms & w/smaller flowers below, inscribed to Elizabeth Mayerin below the horse, in shades of red, yellow, black & brown, ca. 1784, by Frederick Krebes, Pennsylvania, framed, picture 12 1/4 x 15" (ILLUS.) **$6,000**

Early Pennsylvania Marriage Certificate with Hearts Design

Marriage certificate, pen & ink & watercolor on paper, celebrating the marriage of Mr. Anthony Beffner & Maria Laurin Bochler, centered by a large heart in pale green enclosing black script & trimmed w/orange loops w/two small script-filled hearts below & a top tulip blossom, a meandering orange vine around the sides & bottom w/scalloped round orange & pale green blossoms, marriage dated 1795, paper print date in lower left corner 1798, Pennsylvania, 13 1/4 x 16" (ILLUS.) **$600**

Fraktur with Lengthy Text

Text inscription, watercolor & ink on woven paper, a very detailed four column inscription in various colors of ink below a large bold heading w/further text vertically down each side, by Joseph Miller, dated 1822, framed, 12 x 15 1/2" (ILLUS.) **$480**

FRUIT JARS

Mason's CFJ Co. (monogram) - Improved, cylindrical tapering gently to a ground lip w/metal screw band w/amber glass insert marked "P," base marked "H43," chip & flake on rim, amber, 1/2 gal. (ILLUS. far left with three other Mason's jars, bottom of page) **$187**

Group of Four Mason's Fruit Jars

Mason's CFJ Co. - Patent Nov 30 1858, gently tapering cylindrical w/a ground lip & Mason's shoulder seal & screw-on metal lid marked "Trademark Boyd's Porcelain Lined Patd. Mar. 30.58. - June 9. 63. - Mar. 30.69. - Extd. Mar. 30. 72.," base marked "E122," partially open bubble, lid cleaned, aqua, gal. (ILLUS. second from left with three other Mason's jars, bottom previous page)..................... **$2,310**

Mason's Patent - Nov. 30, 1858, cylindrical tapering gently to a smooth lid w/a metal "Ball" lid w/milk glass insert marked "Boyd's Genuine Porcelain Lined Cap 18 V," green w/amber swirls, 1/2 gal. (ILLUS. second from right with three other Mason's jars, bottom previous page).... **$358**

Mason's Patent Jar with Striations

Mason's Patent - Nov 30th 1858, ABM lip, smooth base, zinc screw-on lid, greenish aqua w/deeper olive amber striations, minor chip on edge of lip, ca. 1920-30, qt., 8 3/4" h. (ILLUS.) **$112**

Rare Mason's Patent Midget Fruit Jar

Mason's Patent - Nov 30th 1858, slightly tapering cylindrical midget size, ground mouth w/zinc lid, smooth base, bright light yellow w/greenish tone, 1/2 pt. (ILLUS.)... **$3,080**

Mason's Patent - Nov 30th 1858 - HG Co. (monogram on reverse), ground mouth w/zinc lid w/amber glass insert, smooth base, light golden amber, some interior stain that will clean, ca. 1870-90, 1/2 gal. **$6,720**

Mason's Patent - Nov 30th 1858 - (Snowflake), midget-form, ground mouth w/zinc cover & milk glass immersed, smooth base, ca. 1860-80, medium citron, pt. **$2,800**

FURNITURE

Furniture made in the United States during the 18th and 19th centuries is coveted by collectors. American antique furniture has a European background, primarily English, since the influence of the Continent usually found its way to America by way of England. If the style did not originate in England, it came to America by way of England. For this reason, some American furniture styles carry the name of an English monarch or an English designer. However, we must realize that, until recently, little research has been conducted and even less published on the Spanish and French influences in the area of the California missions and New Orleans.

After the American revolution, cabinetmakers in the United States shunned the prevailing styles in England and chose to bring the French styles of Napoleon's Empire to the United States and we have the uniquely named "American Empire" (Classical) style of furniture in a country that never had an emperor.

During the Victorian period, quality furniture began to be mass-produced in this country with its rapidly growing population. So much walnut furniture was manufactured, the vast supply of walnut was virtually depleted and it was of necessity that oak furniture became fashionable as the 19th century drew to a close.

For our purposes, the general guidelines for dating will be: Pilgrim Century - 1620-85 William & Mary - 1685-1720 Queen Anne - 1720-50 Chippendale - 1750-85 Federal - 1785-1820 Hepplewhite - 1785-1820 Sheraton - 1800-20 American Empire (Classical) - 1815-40 Victorian - 1840-1900 Early Victorian - 1840-50 Gothic Revival - 1840-90 Rococo (Louis XV) - 1845-70 Renaissance - 1860-85 Louis XVI - 1865-75 Eastlake - 1870-95 Jacobean & Turkish Revival - 1870-95 Aesthetic Movement - 1880-1900 Art Nouveau - 1890-1918 Turn-of-the-Century - 1895-1910 Mission (Arts & Crafts movement) - 1900-15 Art Deco - 1925-40

All furniture included in this listing is American unless otherwise noted.

F

Bedroom Suites

Complete Queen Anne Revival Bedroom Suite

F

Queen Anne Revival: low-poster double bed, chest of drawers, dressing table & bench, nightstand & side chair; mahogany & mahogany veneer, the bed w/a wide flat-topped headboard flanked by posts w/turned finials & a matching shorter footboard, the case pieces w/arrangements of drawers on cases raised on short cabriole legs, the nightstand, bench & chair all w/cabriole legs ending in pad feet, made by The Thomasville Chair Co., ca. 1920s, the set (ILLUS.) **$690**

Scarce Victorian Faux Bamboo Bedroom Suite

Victorian Faux Bamboo: high-backed bed & chest of drawers; maple & bird's-eye maple, the tall bed head-board w/a stepped crestrail composed of rows of short turned spindles & two small rectangular panels accented w/short turned posts, the tall bamboo-turned headposts w/turned ball finials flank a detailed head-board centered by a large center rectangular panel framed w/a double band of half-round bamboo turnings flanked by two small square pieced panels w/radiating spindles above two small square panels, the shorter footboard w/matching details; the chest of drawers w/a rectangular top above a pair of drawers over two long drawers, all the edges & sides trimmed w/bamboo turnings, attributed to the Horner Furniture Co., ca. 1880s, bed headboard shortened, bed 60" w., 67 1/2" h., chest 21 x 46 1/2", 29 1/2" h., the set (ILLUS.)
.... **$3,450**

Beds

Majorelle Art Nouveau Inlaid Bed

Art Nouveau bed, carved & inlaid mahogany, "Aux Pavots," the high rectangular headboard w/an upper band inlaid w/poppy seed heads above a wide veneered panel topped by a band of scallops accents inlaid mother-of-pearl & copper stylized blossoms, matching lower footrail w/rounded top corners, on small swelled square feet, designed by Louis Majorelle, France, ca. 1898, 63 3/8 x 83 3/4", 60 1/4" h. (ILLUS.) **$9,560**

Classical Country-Style Low-Poster Bed

Classical country-style low-poster bed, maple, four rod- and ring-turned low posts, the paneled & scroll-cut headboard w/a turned horizontal rod crest, simple narrow arched footboard, heavy turned tapering legs, ca. 1825-40, side rails extended, 54 5/8 x 84 5/8", 46 3/4" h. (ILLUS.) **$1,265**

Classical country-style tall-poster canopy bed, cherry & walnut, the rectangular canopy frame w/a stepped flaring cornice & line w/pleated fabric raised on four matching tall slender ring-, rod- and knob-turned posts each ending in ring- and baluster-turned legs ending in ball feet, the footrail mounted w/a narrow rail above a row of eight short baluster- and knob-turned spindles, ca. 1840-50, 53 x 77", 109" h. (ILLUS., top next column) **$4,600**

Classical Country Tall-Poster Bed

Fine Classical Tall-Poster Bed

Classical tall-poster bed, mahogany, four matching tall tapering octagonal posts w/high baluster- and ring-turned finials, the headboard w/a rolled crest bar w/turned finials above cut-out scrolls over two raised panels, heavy corner blocks joining the heavy siderails & raised on heavy ring-turned tapering feet, fitted w/a half-lapped slatted tester, some alternations to posts, ca. 1850,

65 3/4 x 84", 94" h. (ILLUS. without tester) **$8,625**

Scroll-cut Low-poster "Cannon Ball" Bed

Country-style low-poster "cannon ball" bed, curly maple, each post w/detailed ring-, rod- and baluster turning topped by a large ball, raised on turned tapering plain legs, the headboard & matching lower footboard w/an elaborate repeating scroll-cut decoration, mellow golden brown finish, some glued splits in scrolls, first half 19th c., 51 1/2 x 71 1/2", 50" h. (ILLUS.) **$920**

Louisiana Low-Poster "Cannon Ball" Bed

Country-style low-poster "cannon ball" bed, cypress, the matching rod-turned posts each topped by a turned large ball, the heavy rod-turned legs ending in cushion feet, the scroll-cut headboard w/a flat crest, old red stain, made in Louisiana, early 19th c., 56 x 78", 45" h. (ILLUS.).... **$3,450**

Country-style settle-bed, painted pine, the low two-board back flanked by wide single-board ends curving down to form low arms flanking the wide plank seat & deep apron that fold out to form a bed, worn red paint w/traces of black, some rose head nails, replaced bottom boards & hinges, edge wear & some damage, first half 19th c., 21 3/4 x 53", 31" h. (ILLUS., bottom of page) **$1,610**

F

Unusual Painted Pine Country Settle-Bed

F

Nice New York Federal Mahogany "Sleigh" Bed

Maple Country Federal Tall-Poster Bed

Mahogany Federal Tall-Poster Bed

Fine New Hampshire Federal Bed

Federal country-style tall-poster bed, maple & pine, four ring-, rod- and baluster-turned posts w/acorn finials, the flat-topped scroll-cut headboard & matching lower footboard, simple turned tapering legs, early 19th c., 59 3/4 x 83", 92" h. (ILLUS.)...... **$2,185**

Federal "sleigh" bed, carved mahogany, the matching outswept head- and footboard w/a rolled crestrail above a paneled section flanked by reeded stiles, original square rails raised on baluster- and ring-turned legs tapering to short cylindrical feet, New York City, ca. 1800-20, 86" l. (ILLUS., top of page)............... **$2,400**

Federal tall-poster bed, carved mahogany, four turned tapering reeded & carved posts topped by urn-turned finials joined by tester rails, fitted w/a simple arched headboard w/incurved sides, baluster- and peg-turned legs, one finial broken, headboard finish flaking, early 19th c., 58 3/4 x 83", 82" h. (ILLUS., top next column)...................................... **$2,300**

Federal tall-poster bed, carved & painted mahogany, the baluster- and ring-turned leaf-carved & reeded footposts continuing to square molded legs joined to the red-painted tapering headposts & blue-painted arched headboard, Portsmouth, New Hampshire, ca. 1805, old surface, 51 x 72", 87 1/2" h. (ILLUS., previous page) **$6,463**

Federal Tiger Stripe Maple Tall Post Bed

Federal tall-poster bed, tiger stripe maple, the four baluster- and ring-turned octagonal chamfered posts continuing to ring-turned tapering legs joined by the peaked recessed paneled headboard, Middle Atlantic States, ca. 1820, refinished, imperfections, 54 x 75", 86" h. (ILLUS.) **$3,819**

Fine Federal Maple Tall-Poster Bed

Federal tall-poster canopy bed, maple, the slender ring-turned & tapering posts joined by a rectangular canopy frame, the headposts joined by a simple arched headboard w/incurved sides, original rope

rails, raised on tall ring- and baluster-turned legs w/knob feet, possibly Connecticut, 1790-1810, 55 1/4 x 78 3/4", 84 1/2" h. (ILLUS.) **$3,840**

Unusual Signed Louis XVI-Style Bed

Louis XVI-Style bed, painted & upholstered, a half-round carved molded canopy resting on curved metal supports extending from one side of the matching head- and footboards, each w/an arched crest above an upholstered panel, the square front stile w/a small ball finial, front rail w/a ring-turned band above molded rail, turned tapering & fluted legs on casters, signed by the maker Courtois, Paris, France, first half 19th c., wear, paint chips, back rail chipped, 45 x 75", 92" h. (ILLUS.) **$4,600**

Fancy Rococo Style Tall-Poster Canopy Bed

Rococo style tall-poster canopy bed, carved hardwood, the rectangular canopy frame w/covered sides raised on four spiral- and foliate-carved posts joined by scrolling floral-carved rails flanking an arched headboard centering a rampant lion & unicorn supporting an oval mirror w/pierce-carved foliate panels to

F

each side, raised on baluster- and beaded turned legs, Portuguese colonial or Anglo-Indian, 19th c., 63 x 88", 8' 1" h. (ILLUS.)... **$6,463**

Rare Victorian Rococo Tall-Poster Bed

Victorian Rococo style tall-poster bed, walnut & bird's-eye maple, the very tall headboard w/a high crest composed of three high pointed arches outlined w/ornately carved scrolls around the bird's-eye maple panels, the central panel w/a carved floral sprig, the lower headboard composed of three tall bird's-eye maple panels, all suspended by side latches to the heavy turned headposts w/tall ring-turned finials, a simple low footboard w/matching shorter posts, heavy ball feet, original side rails, ca. 1850, 54 x 78 3/4", 73" h. (ILLUS.) **$4,313**

Benches

Classical benches, carved mahogany, the long deep upholstered top raised on four heavy tapering ring-turned & gadrooned legs w/knob feet, American or English, ca. 1815-25, 20 x 35", 18" h., pr. (ILLUS., bottom of page)........................ **$7,200**

Fine American Classical Window Bench

Classical window bench, carved mahogany, the long rectangular upholstered seat flanked by open end arms w/baluster- and ring-turned spiral-carved crestrails on scrolled spiral-carved stiles continuing to form the sabre legs, each back w/a lower horizontal splat w/a central shaped tablet flanked by scrolls, old refinish, possibly Pennsylvania, ca. 1820-25, minor imperfections, 16 x 41", 33" h. (ILLUS.).. **$5,875**

Fine Pair of Classical Benches

Bookcases

Rare Roycroft Mission Oak Bookcase

Arts & Crafts (Mission-style) bookcase, glazed oak, the rectangular top w/blocked ends above a frieze band w/blocked corners & incised w/the word "Roycroft," above a tall glazed cupboard door opening to three wooden shelves, a single deep drawer at the bottom w/a small metal knob & two incised Roycroft logos, simple bracketed front apron, Roycrofters, East Aurora, New York, ca. 1908, 16 1/4 x 33 1/4", 67 7/8" h. (ILLUS.).................................. **$16,730**

Classical Bookcase in Louis Philippe Taste

Classical bookcase, mahogany & mahogany veneer, in the Louis Philippe taste, the rectangular top w/a deep flaring ogee cornice above a pair of tall four-pane glazed doors framed by ogee molding & opening to three wooden shelves above a pair of shorter paneled doors, deep flat apron w/low bracket feet, second quarter 19th c., 19 x 58", 98 1/2" h. (ILLUS.) **$8,050**

American Classical Mahogany Bookcase

Classical bookcase, mahogany & mahogany veneer, the rectangular top w/a flat flaring cornice above a projecting arch above a pair of tall glazed cupboard doors flanked by disengaged columns w/leaf-carved capitals, a mid-molding above a long deep bottom drawer flanked by plinths faced w/carved paterae, raised on tall leaf-carved paw front feet & plain back feet, small veneer chips & repairs, ca. 1850, 18 1/4 x 48 1/4", 67 1/4" h. (ILLUS.) **$1,840**

South Carolina Old Heart Pine Bookcase

Pair Early Country-Style Grain-painted Bookcases

Country-style bookcase, heart pine, the rectangular top w/a deep flaring cornice above a wide frieze above an open case of five adjustable wooden shelves, flaring molded flat base, South Carolina, ca. 1900, 13 x 56", 84 3/8" h. (ILLUS., previous page) **$1,380**

Country-style bookcases, painted & decorated pine, a rectangular top w/narrow molded cornice above a tall case w/a very tall 28-pane glazed door opening to five wooden shelves, a mid-molding above a long deep drawer w/two turned wood knobs, flat molded base, original reddish brown grain painting, central Massachusetts, ca. 1830, minor imperfections, 14 x 33", 82 3/4" h., pr. (ILLUS., top of page) **$10,575**

Empire-Style bookcase, gilt-mounted mahogany, the molded breakfront crown over a conforming frieze w/gilt-metal mounts, above a tall central door w/a tall glazed pane above a recessed lower panel trimmed w/gilt-metal ribbons, opening to wooden shelves, tall narrow side doors each flanked by a pair of columns & mounted w/a large gilt-metal torch & wreath mount & smaller corner mounts, conforming breakfront flat base molding, France, late 19th - early 20th c., 15 1/2 x 68", 87" h. (ILLUS.) **$2,415**

Victorian Country-Style Bookcase

Victorian country-style bookcase, walnut, the rectangular top w/a stepped flaring cornice above a pair of tall two-pane glazed cabinet doors opening to six adjustable wooden shelves, a pair of drawers w/turned wood knobs at the bottom, raised on a later base frame w/simple bracket feet, second half 19th c., 14 x 45", 80" h. (ILLUS.) **$1,610**

Fine French Empire-Style Bookcase

Victorian Golden Oak Open Bookcase

Victorian Golden Oak style bookcase, oak, the rectangular top w/a low three-quarters gallery w/a central leaf-carved swag above a tall open case fitted w/four adjustable wooden shelves & a paneled back, line-incised decoration down the sides & across the wide flat apron, on wheels, ca. 1890-1900, some finish wear, 14 x 49 1/2", 62" h. (ILLUS.) **$633**

Bureaux Plat

Directoire-Style bureau plat, gilt bronze-mounted parquetry, the rectangular top w/inset leather writing surface over a recessed frieze drawer flanked by pairs of short drawers & faux drawers on the reverse, raised on square tapering legs ending in brass cuffed feet, overall inlaid w/chevron & herringbone banding & mounted on each side w/gilt-bronze ribbon-tied foliate swags, France, late 19th c., 23 1/2 x 51", 29" h. (ILLUS., first photo below) **$3,819**

Fine French Directoire-Style Bureau Plat

Original French Empire Bureau Plat

Empire bureau plat, gilt-bronze mounted mahogany, the rectangular top w/inset leather writing surface & stepped gilt banded edges over a leaf tip-banded frieze drawer & a pair of lion mask-mounted short drawers, raised on square tapering legs headed w/ribbon-tied swags ending in anthemia mounted on compressed ball feet, France, early 19th c., 28 x 47 1/2", 30" h. (ILLUS., bottom previous page)............................ **$3,819**

Small Louis XV-Style Bureaux Plat

Louis XV-Style bureau plat, ebonized or-molu-mounted wood, the rectangular top inset w/a tooled brown leather writing surface framed by a molded ormolu rim, the apron mounted on one side w/two drawers flanking a large ormolu mask w/entwined hair & foliage, the back apron & sides w/matching decoration, raised on cabriole legs w/fancy ormolu chutes & sabots, stains on writing surface, some nicks, France, late 19th c., 24 1/2 x 39 1/2", 28 1/2" h. (ILLUS.) **$1,380**

Louis XV-Style bureau plat, gilt bronze & porcelain-mounted kingwood, the gilt-banded rectangular top w/serpentine sides centered by an inset leather writing surface within inlaid herringbone band-ing, three frieze drawers w/gilt-banded porcelain panels each decorated in poly-chrome w/birds & foliate plaques, the simple cabriole legs decorated w/gilt-bronze mounts & ending in gilt-bronze sabots, England, late 19th - early 20th c., 25 1/2 x 51", 30" h. (ILLUS., top next col-umn) **$15,275**

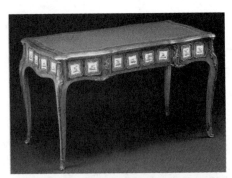

Very Fine English Louis XV-Style Bureau Plat

French Louis XV-Style Bureau Plat

Louis XV-Style bureau plat, gilt bronze-mounted kingwood & rosewood, the rect-angular top w/inset leather writing surface over a scalloped frieze w/a conforming drawer, raised on cabriole legs headed w/warrior masks & ending in animal hoof foot mounts, France, mid-19th c., 33 x 70", 29" h. (ILLUS.) **$8,225**

Louis XV-Style bureau plat, ormolu-mounted kingwood & marquetry, the rect-angular top w/serpentine ormolu-mounted edges set w/a leather writing surface, above a conforming frieze, the front w/three drawers fronted w/foliate sprigs within scrolling frames, the sides & back similarly decorated, the C-scrolled ormolu long leg mounts trailing foliage down the cabriole legs tapering & ending in scrolled sabots, after the model by Jacques Dubois, France, last quarter 19th c., 31 x 53", 31" h. (ILLUS., below) **$12,000**

Very Fine Louis XV-Style Bureau Plat

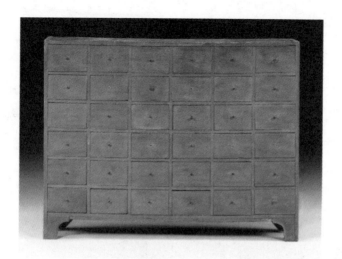

Rare Blue-Painted Country Apothecary Cabinet

Cabinets

Early Pennsylvania Apothecary Cabinet

Apothecary cabinet, country-style, painted wood, a narrow rectangular top & sides enclosing an arrangement of 30 small square drawers w/simple turned wood knobs, flat base, original dark painted decoration, Pennsylvania, first half 19th c., 6 1/2 x 15 1/2", 18 1/2" h. (ILLUS.) **$4,200**

Apothecary cabinet, country-style, the narrow long rectangular top above a case fitted w/six rows of six small drawers each, on simple bracket feet, old powder blue paint, 19th c., 9 3/4 x 58 1/2", 45 3/4" h. (ILLUS., top of page)............................ **$10,800**

Rare Early Mahogany Cellarette

Cellarette (wine cabinet), early American style, mahogany, the hexagonal hinged top w/an inlaid holly edge opening to a tin-lined sectioned interior for wine bottles & w/a drainage hole, the hexagonal case trimmed w/three wide brass straps & brass carrying handles, sitting on a conforming mahogany stand w/three square splayed & reeded legs w/arched returns, old surface, Boston, late 18th c., family provenance provided, minor surface imperfections, 19 x 19 1/8", 28 3/4" h. (ILLUS.) **$5,875**

Collector's cabinet on stand, Oriental style, parcel-gilt black lacquer, two-part construction: the upper cabinet w/a rectangular top, sides & pair of doors richly decorated w/scenes of flowers & birds, the doors w/molded panels decorated w/landscapes in heavy gold enamel & mounted w/brass fitting, opening to an interior composed of 12 drawers of varying sizes each w/ornate flower & insect decoration; the lower stand section made in Europe & features similar decoration, the cabinet made in Japan, ca. 1850, some brass loose, minor wear, 21 x 40 1/4", 62" h. (ILLUS.)...................... **$12,650**

Extremely Ornate Japanese Collector's Cabinet on Stand

Unusual Classical Country Commode Cabinet

Commade cabinet, Classical country-style, painted pine, rectangular hinged top & hinged fall-front w/two turned wood knobs open to reveal a seat w/hole flanked by arm rests, the lower cabinet flanked by simple turned columns continuing into ring-turned front feet, original black & red grain painting w/wear, age crack in scrubbed top, some minor edge damage, first half 19th c., 19 x 25", 29" h. (ILLUS.)....................................... **$374**

Chinese Chippendale-Style Curio Cabinet

Curio cabinet on stand, carved & lacquered wood, Chinese Chippendale-Style, two-part construction: the upper section w/a rectangular top above a pair of tall flat doors opening to shelves, decorated overall w/green lacquer panels painted in gold & black w/stylized Chinese landscape & trimmed w/fancy pierced & chased metal strapwork hinges & keyhole escutcheons; the lower section w/a shell-carved mid-molding above a serpentine scroll-carved narrow apron raised on leaf-carved cabriole legs ending in scroll & peg feet, England, late 19th - early 20th c., 19 x 38", 62" h. (ILLUS.) **$1,610**

Fine Louis XV-Style Curio Cabinet

Curio cabinet, giltwood, Louis XV-style, the wide molded arched crestrail centered by a high crest carved w/scrolls & cherub heads above a large glass-paned door w/an ornately leaf-carved lower panel, bowed glass side panels above matching carved lower panels, raised on simple cabriole legs, opens to two glass shelves, France, last half 19th c., original finish, 19 x 33 1/2", 69 3/4" h. (ILLUS.) **$1,265**

Late Victorian Rococo Revival Cabinet

Curio cabinet, mahogany & mahogany veneer, late Victorian Rococo Revival style, a tall half-round case topped by a very high back crest w/rounded sides & a pointed center finial, fitted w/two small round projecting shelves w/spindled galleries raised on a slender spindle support, the case composed of two tall curved glass panels, one half forming the hinged door opening to the mirrored inte-

rior, molded base raised on three very slender simple cabriole legs, ca. 1890s, 15 x 26", 70 1/2" h. (ILLUS.) **$863**

Ornately Carved Chinese Curio Cabinet

Curio cabinet, Oriental style, carved hardwood, the tall case w/a high peaked & ornately pierce-carved cornice of scrolling foliage centering a cartouche of carved birds & animals, above a three-part open gallery w/pierced border trim & floral-pierced back panels above an arrangement of four staggered open shelves all w/pierce-carved aprons & a continuous ornately pierce-carved back, a lower shelf over a pair of small drawers above four small open shelves beside a small cupboard w/a pair of carved panel doors, a gadrooned base molding over a pierce-carved scrolling apron raised on claw-and-ball feet, some shrinkage separation to backs & joints, China, late 19th c., 14 x 46 3/4", 83 1/2" h. (ILLUS.) **$1,150**

Fine Signed Renaissance Revival Cabinet

Rare Elaborate Renaissance Revival Side Cabinet

F

Side cabinet, Victorian Renaissance Revival style, .brass & mother-of-pearl-inlaid ebonized wood, the rectangular top w/molded edge above a tall molded panel door w/faux drawers decorated w/fine inlaid design, the top panel w/an elaborate scene of a fountain & two birds issuing ornate leafy flowering vines, tall slender fluted columns down each side w/gilt-metal capitals & ring-turned bases resting on a molded base w/disk-turned feet, stamped "Elzentum," Europe, ca. 1875, top missing string inlay, some scuffs & scratches, 25 x 31", 38" h. (ILLUS., previous page)... **$1,610**

Side cabinet, Victorian Renaissance Revival style, bronze-mounted rosewood, ebonized cherry & maple, the long top w/a raised rectangular central section supported by carved palmettes & a panel of gilt-trimmed carved wheat centering an upright arch-topped bronze panel featuring the figure of a classical maiden, the lower side section w/wide incurved sides above a conforming apron w/a narrow inlaid frieze band over a gilt-bronze narrow applied band, the case w/tall incurved end doors & three doors across the front, the outer matching doors flanked by inlaid pilasters w/gilt capitals & decorated w/a raised narrow rectangular burl molding w/a small round bronze disk at the top & bottom center, surrounding a black panel centered by a large fruit-filled gilt-bronze urn, the taller central arched door w/a recessed panel bordered by gilt & ebonized band, the panel ornately inlaid w/delicate leafy scrolls & flowers centered by a large oval porcelain plaque h.p. w/a colorful romantic garden landscape, the heavy blocked black w/bronze band trim & gilt-bronze accents, attributed to Alexander Roux, New York, New York, ca. 1866, 21 x 91 1/2", 55" h. (ILLUS., top of page) **$31,200**

Early Biedermeier Vitrine Cabinet

Vitrine cabinet, Biedermeier style, inlaid rosewood, the stepped rectangular top over an arched glazed door opening to a shelved & mirrored interior flanked by three-quarter round columns above a foliate-inlaid long drawer, raised on ring- and baluster-turned legs ending in compressed ball feet, Europe, early 19th c., 19 x 33 1/2", 5' 8" h. (ILLUS.).................. **$4,113**

French Charles X Vitrine Cabinet

Vitrine cabinet, Charles X style, rosewood & inlaid boxwood, the rectangular stepped top w/a wide flaring stepped cornice w/rounded corners above a frieze panel inlaid w/a line-inlaid long rectangle above a single tall door w/a large glazed panel above a cross-grain veneered lower panel, a single long line-inlaid drawer across the bottom, deep molded base w/further line inlay, raised on low bracket feet, France, second quarter 19th c., 18 1/2 x 42", 86" h. (ILLUS.) **$3,738**

Very Fine Louis XVI-Style Vitrine Cabinet

Vitrine cabinet, Louis XVI-Style, ormolu-mounted mahogany, the rectangular variegated rouge marble top w/canted corners above a conforming frieze applied w/Bacchic putti, masks & garlands, over a pair of tall beveled glass doors w/curved bases & matching glazed sides, opening to a green velvet-lined interior w/three adjustable glass shelves, on foliate-hipped cabriole legs & scrolled ormolu sabots, marked on the lock, by Francois Linke, Paris, France, first quarter 20th c., 16 1/4 x 41 3/4", 65" h. (ILLUS.) **$14,400**

Chairs

Art Deco Tubular Steel Upholstered Armchairs Attributed to Thonet

Art Deco armchairs, chrome-plated tubular steel & upholstery, each w/a high, wide upholstered back, one back framed by tubular steel, open tubular steel arms above the deep slightly angled upholstered seat, one w/a flat rectangular tubular steel frame & legs, the other w/an angled seat frame, short front legs & tubular flat side stretchers, attributed to Thonet, Austria, ca. 1935, 31" h. & 30" h., the set (ILLUS., bottom previous page) **$8,963**

Ornately Carved Art Nouveau Armchair

Art Nouveau armchair, ornately carved mahogany, the tall back topped by pierced & solid butterfly wings centered by the head of an Art Nouveau maiden above a tall flaring cluster for flower stems topped by lily-like blossoms, fluted curved open arms continuing into serpentine arm supports above the upholstered spring seat, the gently peaked front seatrail carved w/crossed stick clusters & a pendent flower cluster supported by long ribbons, fluted cabriole front legs, France, ca. 1905, 46" h. (ILLUS.) **$7,768**

Art Nouveau dining chair, carved walnut & tooled leather, the tall arched open back carved w/pierced Art Nouveau loops above the original leather seat w/tooled design, the pierced & loop-carved apron raised on four stem-like legs joined by slender angled side stretchers, designed by Hector Guimard, France, for the dining room of the Maison Coillot, Lille, France, ca. 1898-1900, 38 1/2" h. (ILLUS., top next column) **$31,070**

Very Rare French Art Nouveau Chair

Unusual Spindled Gustav Stickley Chair

Arts & Crafts style side chair, oak, the tall slightly canted band w/square stiles joined by two rails centered by a tight grouping of slender square spindles, raised above the leather-upholstered slip seat above square legs joined by high flat front & rear stretchers & low side stretchers joined by a tight grouping of slender square spindles to the bottom of the seatrail, Model No. 384, red decal mark of Gustav Stickley, ca. 1907, 46" h. (ILLUS.) **$3,585**

F

Rare Finely Carved Philadelphia Chippendale Side Chair Courtesy Christie's, New York

Chippendale side chair, carved mahogany, the serpentine crestrail ending in carved ears above an ornately carved Gothic style splat above the upholstered slip seat, double-arched front seatrail & cabriole front legs w/leaf-carved knees &

ending in claw-and-ball feet, simple turned rear legs, Philadelphia, 1760-80, descended in the family of Governor John Lambert, New Jersey, 38 1/4" h. (ILLUS.) **$14,430**

Carved Walnut Chippendale Side Chair

Chippendale side chair, carved walnut, the oxbow crestrail w/fluted ears above a fancy pierce-carved splat w/scroll-carved accents, the upholstered slip seat w/flat rails raised on cabriole front legs w/carved knees ending in claw-and-ball feet, square canted rear legs, possibly Maryland, ca. 1760-80, 30 3/8" h. (ILLUS.) **$2,400**

Set of Philadelphia Chippendale Side Chairs

Chippendale side chairs, carved mahogany, the back composed of four arched & pierced slats above the upholstered slip seat, square tapering legs joined by box stretchers, Philadelphia, 1770-90, 37" h., set of 4 (ILLUS.) **$2,390**

Fine Pair of Newport Chippendale Chairs

Chippendale side chairs, carved mahogany, the serpentine crestrail ending in fluted ears above a loop-pierced vasiform splat above the upholstered slip seat, square legs joined by flat H-stretchers, Newport, Rhode Island, 1780-1800, 38" h., pr. (ILLUS.) **$7,800**

Pair Philadelphia Chippendale Chairs

Chippendale side chairs, mahogany, a serpentine crestrail w/rounded ears above a pierced vasiform splat over a trapezoidal slip seat, raised on cabriole legs ending in ball-and-claw feet, Philadelphia, second half 18th c., 31 1/2" h., pr. (ILLUS.)... **$6,463**

Chippendale "Wingback" Armchair

Chippendale "wingback" armchair, cherry, the wide arched upholstered back flanked by wide shaped & outswept upholstered wings above rolled arms, the cushion seat raised on square tapering & fluted front legs & canted square rear legs joined by box stretchers, New England, 1780-1800, 45 1/2" h. (ILLUS.) **$7,200**

Fine Chippendale-Style "Wingback" Armchair

Chippendale-Style "wingback" armchair, the high upholstered back w/an arched crest flanked by outswept serpentine wings over the out-scrolled upholstered arms flanking the seat cushion, raised on square molded legs joined by an H-stretcher, linen upholstery w/overall hand-stitched crewelwork, first half 20th c., 44" h. (ILLUS.).. **$3,105**

Chippendale-Style "Wingback" Armchair

Chippendale-Style "wingback" armchair, the high wide upholstered back flanked by serpentine flared wings above the upholstered rolled arms, deep upholstered seat raised on cabriole front legs w/claw-and-ball feet, refinished, 20th c., 43 3/4" h. (ILLUS.) **$345**

Classical and Country-Style Windsor Child's Chairs

Classical child's side chair, mahogany & mahogany veneer, the back stiles & rails forming a pointed arch above a vasiform splat above the horsehair-upholstered slip seat, flat serpentine front legs & plain canted rear legs, ca. 1830-40, 21" h. (ILLUS. left with country-style low-back child's Windsor, top of page).. **$1,840**

tinuing down to flank the caned seat, front sabre legs ending in leaf-carved front paw feet, New York City, early 19th, 32" h. (ILLUS.) **$960**

Boston Classical Mahogany Side Chair

New York Classical Side Chair

Classical side chair, carved mahogany, the gently curved & rolled crestrail w/fluted end panels above a lower openwork arched rail centered by a roundel, both flanked by fluted backswept styles con-

Classical side chair, mahogany & mahogany veneer, the curved flat-topped crest rail w/rounded corners & incised carving above the vasiform splat & curved stiles, upholstered slip-seat, flat serpentine front legs & backswept rear legs, Boston, ca. 1830, 34" h. (ILLUS.) **$748**

Set of Eight Captain's Chairs

Country-style "captain's" chairs, oak & mixed wood, a curved & stepped crest atop the curved crestrail curving around & down to form the front arms above a row of slender ring- and rod-turned spindles, wide plank seat raised on ring- and rod-turned front legs joined by a turned stretcher & plain turned rear legs all joined by plain box stretchers, late 19th - early 20th c., 30" h., set of 8 (ILLUS., top of page) **$2,588**

Delaware Valley "Ladder-back" Armchair

Country-style "ladder-back" armchair, painted maple, the tall back w/five arched concave splats flanked by tall tapering turned stiles w/bulbous finials, shaped open arms on baluster- and ring-turned arm supports continuing to turned legs w/bulbous feet incorporating wooden wheel, all joined by double baluster- and ring-turned front stretchers & swelled side stretchers, early black paint over salmon & green, Delaware River Valley, late 18th c., minor imperfections, 50" h. (ILLUS.) **$2,703**

Country-style "low-back" Windsor child's armchair, painted wood, the wide curved crestrail continuing around to form the short arms above a row of seven knob- and rod-turned spindles, wide plank seat raised on knob- and knob-turned front legs joined by a knob-turned stretcher, plain box stretchers to the turned rear legs, old grey paint, second half 19th c., 17 1/2" h. (ILLUS. right with Classical child's side chair) **$1,380**

New York Federal Shield-back Armchair

Federal armchair, carved mahogany, the fine shield-back centered by a pierced oval splat enclosing a pierced urn-form design framing Prince-of-Wales feathers, the shaped open arms w/incurved reeded supports above the wide over-upholstered seat, square tapering legs, New York City, ca. 1790-1810, 36" h. (ILLUS.) **$6,000**

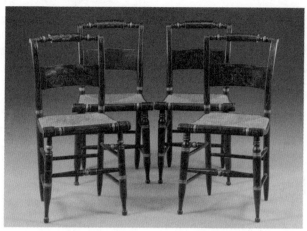

Set of Four Early Hitchcock Side Chairs

Federal fancy "Hitchcock" side chairs, painted & decorated, a ring-turned crestrail w/head rest above a wide lower rail all joining the backswept stiles, woven rush seat, half-round ring-turned seatrail raised on ring-, rod- and knob-turned front legs joined by a ring- and knob-turned front stretcher, simple turned side & rear stretchers, original black paint w/gilt stenciled floral & cornucopia designs on the crestrails, overall gilt trim, Hitchcock Company, Connecticut, ca. 1830s, 34" h., set of 4 (ILLUS., top of page) **$480**

swags on a cream ground, a delicate woven rush seat raised on knob- and rod-turned front legs decorated w/further leafy swags above the flute-painted peg feet, a turned front stretcher w/a narrow central panel painted w/an urn & leaves, simple turned side & rear stretchers, decorated in shades of dark green, gold & creamy white, probably Salem, Massachusetts, 1800-10, 34" h. (ILLUS.) **$2,880**

Delicate Carved Federal Side Chair

Federal side chair, carved mahogany, the delicate rectangular back w/slender reeded columnar stiles w/small corner black, the flat crestrail centered by a domed & fluted central crest above a panel carved w/drapery swags continuing into five slender carved spindles to a lower rail, broad over-upholstered seat, turned tapering & reeded front legs ending in simple turned feet, square canted rear legs, 1810-15, 37" h. (ILLUS.) **$3,800**

Finely Decorated Federal "Fancy" Chair

Federal "fancy" side chair, painted & decorated, the flat crestrail w/a pair of low center arches decorated w/a painted urn & drapery swag design continuing down into a pair of slender spindles flanking a slightly wider urn-decorated center spindle, the flat stiles further painted w/leafy

F

Fine George III-Style Set of Dining Chairs

Rare Federal Mahogany Lolling Armchair

George I Wing-back Armchair

Federal style lolling armchair, inlaid mahogany, the tall upholstered back w/a serpentine crest flanked by open arms w/incurved supports above the wide upholstered seat, raised on square tapering front legs & square canted rear legs, joined by flat box stretchers, Massachusetts, 1780-1800, 45 1/2" h. (ILLUS.)...... **$9,000**

George I wing-back armchair, walnut, the high arched upholstered back flanked by narrow shaped wings continuing to low rolled arms flanking the cushion seat, cabriole front legs ending in pad feet, England, early 18th c. (ILLUS., top next column)..................................... **$2,233**

George III-Style dining chairs, carved mahogany, a serpentine crestrail centered by a small carved leaf sprig above a pierce-carved Gothic style splat, two armchairs w/shaped open arms on incurved arm supports, over-upholstered seats on square molded legs joined by H-stretchers, England, late 19th - early 20th c., 38" h., four side chairs, two armchairs, the set (ILLUS., top of page) **$8,970**

Fine George IV Mahogany Armchair

George IV armchair, carved mahogany, a bold deeply carved concave & canted crestrail w/relief-carved palmette & trailing leaves above the upholstered back flanked by reeded stiles, scrolling reeded open arms on short knob-turned posts above the upholstered seat, reeded seatrail & outswept front & rear legs on casters, slight restorations to legs, England, ca. 1820s (ILLUS.) **$5,520**

Pair of Irish Georgian Hall Chairs

Georgian hall chairs, carved mahogany, the wide balloon-form back carved as a large shell centered by leafy scrolls over adorsed C-scrolls, the solid seat raised on ring-, knob- and reeded turned legs front legs w/outswept peg feet, square canted rear legs, Ireland, second quarter 19th c., 31 1/2" h., pr. (ILLUS.) **$2,070**

Fine Carved Georgian-Style Armchair

Georgian-Style armchair, a serpentine leafy scroll-carved crestrail centered by a shell finial & rosette corners above outswept carved stiles enclosing the needlepoint upholstered back, padded open arms on incurved leaf-carved arm supports, wide needlepoint upholstered seat

w/a serpentine front above a conforming deep apron carved on the front & sides w/flowering leafy scrolls centered by a shell, on cabriole legs w/shell-carved knees above leaf & ribbon-carved legs ending in paw feet, in the manner of Robert Adams, England, ca. 1900 (ILLUS.) .. **$2,645**

Nice Gothic Revival Tall Side Chair

Gothic Revival side chair, carved rosewood, the tall back w/a very tall pointed & pierce-carved Gothic arch crest w/a quatrefoil flanked by trefoils over the arched upholstered back panel flanked by blockand rod-turned stiles w/small turned finials, the over-upholstered seat raised on ring- and rod-turned paneled front legs on casters, second quarter 19th c., 48" h. (ILLUS.) **$863**

Louis XIV-Style Armchair

Louis XIV-Style fauteuils à la reine (openarm armchairs), carved beech, the tall rectangular upholstered back w/an arched crestrail above heavy serpentine open arms w/scroll-carved grips raised on incurved leaf-carved supports, the wide over-upholstered seat on shaped & carved front legs & simple rear legs joined by arched H-stretchers, France, late 19th c., 29 1/4" h., pr. (ILLUS.)......... **$1,840**

Unusual 18th Century Sedan Chair

F **Louis XV sedan chair,** giltwood-mounted leather & polychromed leather, squared upright form w/domed top, tall hinged door at front, rectangular rounded windows in the door & on each side, retains period sliding leather window panels, the interior lined in modern black & gold damask w/gold tassellated detailing, the period exterior rear panel painted w/a scene of nude female bathers above a floral

panel, floral-decorated side panels, France, last quarter 18th c., 30 1/2 x 37 1/2", 62" h. (ILLUS.) **$4,370**

American Louis XV-Style Armchair

Louis XV-Style armchair, carved mahogany, the wide openwork arched back w/shell- and scroll-carved crestrail over a scroll-carved & oval wreath splat, shaped open arms w/scrolled grips above incurved arm supports, wide upholstered seat w/a serpentine front above a conforming scroll-carved seatrail & carved cabriole front legs ending in scroll feet on casters, square canted rear legs on casters, ca. 1880, minor wear & losses, 37 1/4" h. (ILLUS.) **$350**

Pair Louis XVI-Style Closed-Arm Armchairs

Louis XVI-Style armchairs, giltwood, oval upholstered back w/ropetwist-carved frame above low closed upholstered arms w/incurved arm supports flanking the deep cushion seat above the gently bowed seatrail w/a carved guilloche band, turned tapering & fluted legs, France, 19th c., pr. (ILLUS.).................... **$2,585**

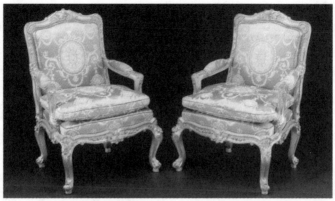

Fine Pair of Louix XVI-Style Fauteuils à la Reine

Louis XVI-Style fauteuils à la reine (open-arm armchairs), giltwood, the arched ornately carved crestrail w/rocailles, C-scrolls & foliage swags continuing down around the wide upholstered back, padded open arms w/incurved arm supports above the wide upholstered cushion seat w/an ornately carved serpentine seatrail continuing to the carved cabriole legs ending in scroll & peg feet, France, first half 20th c., 42" h., pr. (ILLUS., top of page) **$3,525**

Louis XVI-Style Beech Armchair

Louis XVI-Style open-arm armchair, carved beech, the wide squared upholstered back w/an arched crestrail, padded open arms on incurved arm supports, the wide upholstered seat w/curved front seatrail, tapering fluted front legs, original gilding removed, natural waxed finish, France, mid-19th c., 39" h. (ILLUS.) **$1,150**

Rare Modern Danish "Ox" Armchair

Modern style armchair, leather & tubular steel, "Ox" design, the wide curved & rolled black leather crestrail resembling ox horns above the wide upholstered back & wide seat flanked by low rolled leather arms, the curved steel tubular frame w/short outswept rear legs & taller angled front legs, designed by Hans Wegner, manufactured by Johannes Hansen, Model No. EJ 100, Denmark, ca. 1960, 35" h. (ILLUS.) **$15,534**

Fine Modern Bronze & Leather Set

Modern style armchair & footstool, bronze & leather, the low-backed armchair w/a leather bolster top rail flanked by bronze stiles topped by shell-form devices & continuing down to form the rear legs, the shaped open bronze arms arch to form the front legs, a square upholstered leather seat, the stool w/a thick square leather top supported in a bronze frame w/a shell-like device at each corner of the seat, designed by Philippe Anthonioz, ca. 1999, chair, 30 1/2" h., stool 15 1/2" w., 17 3/4" h., the set (ILLUS., previous page) **$9,560**

Rare Early Bugatti Modernist Side Chair

Modernist side chair, vellum-covered, applied & inlaid ebonized wood, the tall curved back stiles continue down to form the front legs, short block- and rod-turned rear legs, the vellum back painted w/a bamboo spray & a group of fowl & bordered by square & round beaten copper bosses, matching vellum flat seat w/long fring front border, the wood inlaid w/bone, pewter & brass, designed by Carlo Bugatti, Italy, ca. 1902, 43 1/2" h. (ILLUS.) **$8,963**

Pilgrim Century "Great chair," turned maple & ash, the tall back w/three shaped splats between turned stiles w/knob- and flame-turned finials, thin straight open arms to the front posts w/a turned knob continuing down to form the front legs, woven rush seat, double sets of turned stretchers, old surface, probably Essex, Massachusetts, 1690s, imperfections, loss to height, 42 5/8" h. (ILLUS., top next column) **$3,819**

Pilgrim Century "Great Chair"

Rare Pilgrim Century Oak "Great Chair"

Pilgrim Century "Great Chair," turned oak, the tall back w/heavy ring- and knob-turned stiles continuing down to form the rear legs & topped by turned pointed bulbous finials, fitted w/three wide shaped slats above the woven rush seat, open turned rod arms joined to the tall knob-turned front legs w/knob finials, simple turned double front & side stretchers & a single rear stretcher, Massachusetts, 1690-1710, 43" h. (ILLUS.) **$15,600**

Fine Early Queen Anne Armchair

Queen Anne armchair, hardwood, the simple oxyoke crestrail above a very tall slender vasiform splat flanked by tall flat stiles, simple downswept open arms raised on turned tapering arm supports flanked by woven rush seat, knob- and block-turned front legs joined by a baluster-turned front stretcher & swelled side stretchers, Connecticut or East Hampton, Long Island, 1730-50, descended in the family of Rev. Samuel Buell, 45 1/2" h. (ILLUS.) **$4,080**

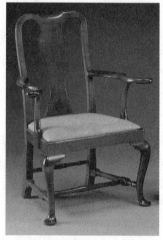

Fine Walnut Queen Anne Armchair

Queen Anne armchair, walnut, the oxbow crestrail above a vasiform splat flanked by S-shaped outcurved open arms above a trapezoidal seat raised on cabriole legs joined by turned stretchers & ending in pad feet, Massachusetts, late 18th c., 42" h. (ILLUS.) **$3,525**

Rare New England Queen Anne Corner Chair

Queen Anne corner chair, maple & walnut, the curved low backrail w/a raised center section & forming flat scroll arms raised on three columnar-turned spindles & two vasi-form splats, woven rush seat, cabriole front leg ending in a pad foot, three column-, block- and knob-turned side & rear legs all joined by a turned, tapering cross-stretcher, New England, 1730-50, 31" h. (ILLUS.) **$21,510**

F

Queen Anne Country-Style Side Chair

Queen Anne country-style side chair, maple, the ox-bow crestrail w/ears above a tall vasiform splat flanked by tall flat stiles, woven rush seat w/a narrow serpentine front seatrail, raised on cabriole front legs ending in pad feet & joined by a knob-turned front stretcher, pair of simple turned side stretchers, Fussel-Savery School, Philadelphia, 1750-70, 39 3/4" h. (ILLUS.).. **$3,600**

Extremely Rare Herter Bros. Aesthetic Movement Side Chairs

Small Shaker Rocking Chair with Arms

Shaker rocking chair w/arms, the tall "ladderback" w/three graduated slats between turned stiles w/acorn finials, shaped open arms w/mushroom caps, replaced woven tape seat, turned legs on stretchers joined by box stretchers, wear to dark finish, unmarked, Mt. Lebanon, New York, late 19th - early 20th c., 34" h. (ILLUS.).. **$403**

Victorian Aesthetic Movement side chairs, giltwood & marquetry, the wide curved & upswept crestrail decorated overall w/fine marquetry inlay & centered by a butterfly-shaped pierced hand grip above a rectangular upholstered panel & thin lower rail all flanked by outswept stiles, the spring-upholstered seat w/a flat seatrail raised on ring-turned tapering front legs w/cuffed flaring peg feet & simple turned rear legs all joined by very slender turned high box stretchers, attributed to Herter Brothers, New York City, 1880-83, original gilt surface, 34 1/4" h., pr. (ILLUS., top of page) **$204,000**

Late Victorian Country Style Highchair

Victorian country-style highchair, oak, the bowed backrail above four slender spindles, hinged side arms supporting the serving tray, shaped plank seat raised on four tall canted simple turned legs joined by simple box stretchers & w/a foot rest at the upper front, late 19th - early 20th c., 39" h. (ILLUS.).................... **$127**

Rare Egyptian Revival Carved Armchairs

Victorian Egyptian Revival style armchairs, carved & gilt-trimmed walnut, each w/a high rectangular back frame enclosing tufted upholstery, the stepped crestrail centered by a raised block panel w/arched top above an inset oval porcelain plaque h.p. w/flowers, the boldly carved stiles continue to the padded open arms ending in large carved Egyptian heads atop curved leaf & carved arm supports w/gilt trim continuing down to form the front legs ending on paw feet on casters, the spring-upholstered seat w/a line-incised & gilt-trimmed seatrail, square gently curved rear legs, New York City or New Jersey, ca. 1850-70, 40 5/8" h., pr. (ILLUS., top of page) **$24,000**

Unusual Late Victorian Novelty Chair

Victorian novelty folding chair, carved & painted, the tall back w/slender stiles joined by a crestrail centered by a small pediment above the carved name "Cora" flanked by spearpoint & leaf devices all above the fabric panel back, hinged at the fabric seat w/curved hinged legs joined by ring-turned stretchers, painted black w/color trim on the crestrail, late 19th - early 20th c., 32 3/4" h. (ILLUS.)...... **$120**

F

Victorian Novelty Horn Armchair

Victorian novelty "horn" armchair, the low arched back & arms composed of interlocking steer horns w/smaller spiral horn spindles, a wide padded black leather seat raised on four tall curved horns & horn corner brackets, from a set made for Alfred Sampson of the Boston, Massachusetts area, late 19th - early 20th c., 30" w., 35" h. (ILLUS.) **$2,300**

Victorian Renaissance Revival armchair, carved walnut & burl walnut, the ornate oval back framed w/the arched crestrail centered by an ornate pierce-carved crest centered by the carved face of a classical lady above burl panels to the scroll-carved corners & block-carved lower frame enclosing an oval upholstered panel, curved & padded open arms on arm supports carved at the front w/the head of a classical lady, wide rounded upholstered seat on a conforming burl-trimmed seatrail, turned & taper-

Fine Renaissance Revival Armchair

F

ing trumpet-form front legs, attributed to John Jelliff, Newark, New Jersey, ca. 1875, 42" h. (ILLUS.) **$2,000**

Renaissance Revival Child's Rocker

Victorian Renaissance Revival style child's rocking chair, walnut, the shield-shaped caned back w/a notched crestrail centered by a small pedimented crest, curved serpentine skirt guards on the shield-shaped caned seat, ring-turned front legs joined by a ring-turned stretcher, simple turned rear legs & plain side & back stretchers, on simple curved rockers, ca. 1875, minor breaks in cane, 18" w., 26" h. (ILLUS.) **$230**

Victorian Rococo Walnut Armchair

Victorian Rococo style armchair, walnut, the large oval upholstered back w/a thumb molded walnut frame, flanked by padded open arms w/incurved arm supports & raised above the over-upholstered wide seat w/a serpentine molded front seatrail, demi-cabriole front legs & canted rear legs, ca. 1870 (ILLUS.) **$200-300**

Very Ornately Carved European Victorian Rococo Armchairs

Victorian Rococo "Barrel-back" Armchairs

Victorian Rococo style armchairs, carved walnut, the high back w/large oval upholstered panel framed by wide ornate scroll-carved frames w/a cartouche crest flanked by upholstered open arms w/ornately carved arm supports, raised above the wide over-upholstered seat, ornate scroll- and cartouche-carved front seatrail on outswept carved legs on casters, canted carved rear legs on casters, Europe, mid-19th c., 47 1/2" h., pr. (ILLUS., bottom previous page)........ **$3,450**

Victorian Rococo style "barrel-back" armchairs, mahogany, a narrow arched crestrail centered by a pierced carved scroll crest above the high rounded & gently curved upholstered back & rolled upholstered arms w/incurved & rolled arm supports, spring cushion seat w/a scroll-carved apron raised on cabriole front legs ending in scrolls & raised on caster, backswept rear legs on casters, ca. 1850-60, 40 1/2" h., pr. (ILLUS., top of page).......... **$3,450**

Victorian rustic-style horn armchair, oak & horn, the balloon-shaped open back composed of a pair of large elk horns, the open arms formed by deer antlers, all joined to the squared oak seat frame w/cane insert, the front & rear legs formed by interlocked pairs of antlers, original paper label reading "Weidlich Dresden N6 Schlessinger Plate 2," Germany, late 19th c., 39 1/2" h. (ILLUS.)....... **$690**

Rare Early William & Mary Armchair

William & Mary armchair, painted soft maple & birch, the very tall narrow back w/a high ornate scroll-carved crestrail above a tall narrow caned back panel, the ring- and block-turned stiles w/small knob-turned finials, shaped open arms

Unusual Victorian Horn Armchair

w/scroll-carved grips raised on columnar-turned arm supports above the wide caned seat, knob- and block-turned front legs ending in knob feet & joined by a ball- and rod-turned front stretcher, matching turned rear stretcher & turned H-stretcher joining the legs, old black paint, Massachusetts or Europe, 1690-1730, 55" h. (ILLUS.) **$31,200**

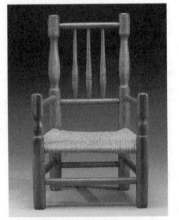

William & Mary Child's "Great Chair"

William & Mary child's "Great Chair," turned walnut, the tall back w/baluster- and rod-turned stiles joined by two simple turned rails connected by three slender ring-turned spindles, simple open rod arms joined to the rod- and baluster-turned front legs above the woven rush

seat, base w/simple box stretchers, probably Boston, early 18th c., 22 3/4" h. (ILLUS.)................................. **$2,160**

Early William & Mary "Bannister-back" Chair

William & Mary country-style "bannister-back" side chair, cherry, the narrow serpentine crestrail above three slender split-balusters flanked by slender ring- and rod-turned stiles raised above the woven rush seat, knob-, rod- and ring-turned front legs & simple turned rear legs all joined by simple turned stretchers, New England, early 18th c., 39 1/2" h. (ILLUS.) **$1,554**

Set of Five Windsor "Birdcage" Side Chairs

Windsor "birdcage" rod-back side chairs, each w/two narrow bamboo-turned crestrails flanking a row of short spindles alternating w/almond-shaped spindles above seven slender curved bamboo-turned spindles, shaped saddle seat on canted bamboo-turned legs joined by turned box stretchers, New England, early 19th c., 36" h., set of 5 (ILLUS.) **$2,040**

Fine Windsor "Bowback" Highchair

Windsor "bowback" highchair, the bowed crestrail above five bamboo-turned spindles, shaped arms above a bamboo-turned spindle & a canted bamboo-turned arm support, thick shaped plank seat, tall canted bamboo-turned legs joined at the front by a footrest & at the base by a bamboo-turned H-stretchers, old red over blue paint w/black highlights, attributed to the Delaware Valley, late 18th - early 19th c., 37 1/2" h. (ILLUS.)... **$9,488**

Rare Philadelphia "Comb-back" Windsor

Windsor "comb-back" armchair, the tall back w/a curved serpentine crestrail ending in carved scrolls above nine tall slender spindles continuing through the U-form medial rail curving to form the shaped arms on three short spindles & a baluster- and ring-turned arm support, wide shaped saddle seat raised on wide-

ly canted baluster-, ring- and rod-turned legs ending in knob feet, old worn black paint, Philadelphia, 1760-90, 44 1/4" h. (ILLUS.)... **$14,400**

Nice Windsor "Comb-back" Rocker

Windsor "comb-back" rocking chair w/arms, painted wood, the shaped comb on six spindles continuing through the bowed center rail ending in shaped arms on baluster- and ring-turned supports, a wide shaped saddle seat on canted baluster- and knob-turned legs fitted into rockers & joined by a swelled H-stretcher, light brown over earlier green paint, probably Connecticut, ca. 1780, minor imperfections, 41 1/4" h. (ILLUS.) **$1,293**

F

One of Four Country Windsor Chairs

Windsor country-style side chairs, painted & decorated, the wide flat curved crestrail stenciled w/fruits above four tall slender bamboo-turned spindles flanked by tapering backswept styles, a shaped plank seat raised on canted bamboo-turned front legs & plain turned rear legs all joined by bamboo-turned box stretchers, original yellow paint, a few age splits, one glued stretcher, one repaired leg, first half 19th c., 33 12/" h., set of 4 (ILLUS. of one, previous page) **$719**

Rare Rhode Island "Low-back" Windsor

Windsor "low-back" armchair, the low back w/a U-form crestrail w/a raised top bracket & curving to form the arms, raised on eight baluster-turned spindles above the wide rounded shaped saddle seat, on canted baluster-turned legs joined by a baluster-turned X-stretcher, old black paint over earlier red, painted inscription under the seat "Found by S.E. Meigs, Madison," Rhode Island, late 18th c., rare form, 31" h. (ILLUS.) **$9,775**

Fine Windsor Writing Arm Armchair

Windsor "low-back" writing arm armchair, painted, the thick curved crestrail ending in a scrolled arm at one side & a wide rounded writing surface at the other side w/a small drawer below, the back composed of numerous turned spindles w/baluster- and ring-turned arm supports above the wide shaped oblong seat, raised on widely canted ring-, baluster- and rod-turned legs joined by a swelled H-stretcher, old grey-green paint, imperfections, New England, ca. 1780, 28" h. (ILLUS.) **$3,525**

Chests & Chests of Drawers

Early Grain-painted Blanket Chest with Unusual Design

Blanket chest, country-style, painted & decorated, the rectangular top w/molded edges opening to a deep well, a molded base on simple tall bracket feet, original overall bold grain painting forming an eye-like design on the front & sides, New England, early 19th c., 19 x 40", 22 1/2" h. (ILLUS.) **$4,800**

Walnut Chippendale Blanket Chest

Decorative Immigrant Blanket Chest

Blanket chest, immigrant-type, painted pine, rectangular w/hinged low domed top w/wrought-iron hinges opening to an interior w/a till w/cover, the dovetailed case decorated w/h.p. rosemaling in salmon red highlighted by gold & dark blue scrolls & stylized flowers, front panels painted in white w/"Aar" & "1815," some rosehead nails, iron bail end handles, some repairs, edge damage on base, Scandinavia, probably Norway, 15 1/4 x 17 1/4", 34 1/2" (ILLUS.) **$250-500**

Chippendale blanket chest, walnut, the rectangular top w/molded edges opening w/original strap hinges to reveal an interior fitted w/a till, the dovetailed case w/a row of two large & one small drawer w/simple bail pulls along the bottom, molded base on scroll-cut bracket feet, good color, worn surface, age crack on the top, glue blocks & on scroll missing, one back foot renailed, late 18th - early 20th c., 23 x 50", 28" h. (ILLUS., top of page) **$1,380**

Chippendale "block-front" chest of drawers, mahogany, the rectangular top w/a blocked front above a conforming case of four long graduated drawers w/butterfly brasses & keyhole escutcheons, molded blocked base on tall bracket feet, Massachusetts, 1760-80, original brasses, 18 x 31", 31 1/2" h. (ILLUS., top next column)... **$28,800**

Rare Massachusetts "Block-front" Chest

Fine Small Chippendale Chest of Drawers

Chippendale chest of drawers, mahogany, the rectangular top w/molded edges above a case w/four long thumb-molded graduated drawers w/butterfly brasses & keyhole escutcheons, molded base raised on heavy scroll-carved ogee bracket feet, late 18th c., 20 x 29 1/2", 33" h. (ILLUS.).. **$7,188**

F

F

New York Chippendale Chest-on-Chest

Chippendale chest-on-chest, carved mahogany, two-part construction: the upper section w/a rectangular top w/angled front corners & a deep coved cornice above a pair of drawers over a stack of three long graduated drawers each w/pierced butterfly brasses & keyhole escutcheons, beveled & fluted front edges; the lower section w/a mid-molding over a case w/a pair of drawers over a stack of three long graduated drawers w/pierced butterfly brasses, molded base raised on scroll-carved short cabriole legs ending in claw-and-ball feet, New York City, 1760-90, 22 x 47 1/2", 81" h. (ILLUS.).. **$7,800**

Fine Chippendale Walnut Chest-on-Chest

Chippendale chest-on-chest, figured walnut, two-part construction: the upper section w/a high broken-scroll pediment w/the high molded scrolls above pierced latticework panels & ending in a large carved flower head, centered by a tall ornate pierced & scroll-carved finial, corner blocks w/urn-turned & flame-carved finials all above a deep flaring dentil-carved cornice

over a row of three drawers above a pair of drawers above three long graduated drawers each w/butterfly brasses & keyhole escutcheons, fluted quarter-round columns down the sides; the lower section w/a mid-molding above three long graduated drawers flanked by quarter-round fluted columns, molded base on tall scroll-cut ogee bracket feet, Pennsylvania, 1760-80, cornice replaced (ILLUS.)........................... **$13,200**

Country Chippendale Tall Chest

Chippendale country-style tall chest of drawers, pine, the rectangular top w/narrow molded corner hinged & opening above a deep well, the front of the case w/three long false drawer fronts w/simple bail pulls & oval keyhole escutcheons above three long deeper graduated working drawer w/matching pulls, molded base w/scroll-cut bracket feet, fine alligator brown surface over original red wash, two pulls original, the other replacements, old black writing on the back w/name of owner in Indiana, some edge chips w/glued restorations, three foot facing partially replaced, good patina, late 18th c., 19 x 37 1/2" h., 54" h. (ILLUS.) .. **$4,485**

Chippendale Reverse-Serpentine Chest

Chippendale "reverse-serpentine" chest of drawers, mahogany, the rectangular top w/molded edges & a double serpentine top overhanging a conforming case w/four long graduated drawers w/butterfly brasses & keyhole escutcheons, molded base on scroll-cut ogee bracket feet, Massachusetts, 1760-90, appears to have original brasses, 20 1/4 x 41 3/4", 33" h. (ILLUS.) **$9,600**

Simple Classical Mahogany Chest of Drawers

Classical chest of drawers, mahogany & mahogany veneer, the rectangular top above a case fitted w/a pair of very narrow round-fronted drawers each w/a pair of turned wood knobs above a long deep drawer w/wood knobs slightly projecting above the lower case fitted w/three long graduated drawers w/wood knobs, square tapering legs, ca. 1840-1850, 19 1/2 x 42", 49" h. (ILLUS.) **$1,840**

Fine Classical Mahogany Chest of Drawers

Classical chest of drawers, mahogany & mahogany veneer, the rectangular top above a case w/a pair of long, narrow round-front drawers w/small turned wood knobs above a single long deep drawer w/raised molded & turned wood knobs all projecting over a stack of three long flat graduated drawers w/turned wood knobs flanked by acanthus leaf-carved side col-

umns w/ring-turned tops, the flat base raised on heavy leaf-carved paw front feet & ring- and knob-turned rear feet, ca. 1840, 22 1/2 x 45 1/2", 50 1/2" h. (ILLUS.) **$1,035**

Classical Mahogany Veneer Chest

Classical chest of drawers, mahogany & mahogany veneer, the rectangular top w/a long scroll-cut crestrail above a case w/four long reverse-graduated drawers w/turned wood knobs, ring- and tapering knob-turned legs w/peg feet, ca. 1830, 19 1/2 x 44", 43" h. (ILLUS.) **$1,380**

Classical Chest with Octagonal Mirror

Classical chest of drawers, mahogany & mahogany veneer, the rectangular white marble top fitted w/a large horizontal octagonal mirror within an ogee molded frame & swiveling between a conforming U-form support, the case w/a long narrow ogee-fronted top drawer above two long drawers each w/two turned wood knobs, another long ogee-fronted drawer across the bottom, raised on scroll-cut bracket feet, ca. 1840-50, 21 x 43", overall 62" h. (ILLUS.) **$2,070**

Fine Country-style Paneled & Painted Blanket Chest

F

Country-style blanket chest, painted pine, six-board construction, the rectangular hinged top w/molded edges opening to an interior w/lidded till, vertical pegged corner supports above a row of three recessed panels trimmed w/applied moldings, flat base raised on ring-turned tapering legs, original red paint, Ohio or Kentucky, ca. 1830, minor surface wear, 20 5/8 x 48 3/4", 26" h. (ILLUS., top of page) **$3,760**

short ring-turned feet, made by Jacob Knagy, Myersdale, Somerset County, Pennsylvania, dated 1863, 20 x 40", 45 1/2" h. (ILLUS.) **$6,000**

Scarce Early Tennessee Sugar Chest

Country-style sugar chest, cherry, the rectangular hinged top opening to a deep divided well, above a lower section w/a single drawer w/two small turned pulls, raised on ring- and knob-turned legs, Tennessee, mid-19th c., 18 x 24 1/2", 32 1/2" h. (ILLUS.) **$3,800**

Dower chest, painted & decorated pine, the rectangular hinged top opening to a well w/a till above dovetailed sides w/a medial rail over two bottom drawers w/turned wood knobs, molded base on bulbous tapering feet, original surface decorated w/pinwheels & quarter-fans against a dotted ground in green, salmon & mustard yellow, Pennsylvania, early 19th c., minor imperfections, 22 x 44", 27" h. (ILLUS., top next page) **$7,638**

Fine Painted & Decorated Chest of Drawers

Country-style chest of drawers, painted & stenciled cherry & pine, the rectangular top above a case w/a pair of drawers h.p w/flower-filled compotes against the red ground above three long graduated drawers w/simple brass knobs, the top long drawer centered by a painted panel around the name "Eve Summey," the lower drawers w/further h.p. potted flower & related designs on the red ground,

Brightly Painted Pennsylvania Dower Chest

F

Southern Federal "Bow-front" Chest

Fine Federal "Bow-front" Chest of Drawers

Federal "bow-front" chest of drawers, inlaid mahogany & mahogany veneer, the rectangular top w/a bowed front & oval corners above a conforming case w/four long graduated cross-banded drawers each w/a pair of large turned wood knobs, flanked by projectings ring- and spiral-turned columns, raised on turned tapering legs on tiny casters, possibly South Carolina, ca. 1815-20, pulls replaced, 20 x 40 3/4", 37 1/4" h. (ILLUS.).............. **$3,200**

Federal "bow-front" chest of drawers, mahogany & mahogany veneer, the rectangular top w/a gently bowed front above a conforming case of four long graduated drawers each w/oval brasses, scroll-cut front French feet, Middle Atlantic States, 1790-1810, original brasses, 24 5/8 x 41 1/2", 38" h. (ILLUS., top next column) **$4,560**

Rare New Hampshire "Bow-front" Chest

Federal "bow-front" chest of drawers, mahogany, rosewood & flame birch veneer, the mahogany rectangular top w/bowed front edge w/inlay overhangs the conforming case of four long graduated drawers w/flame birch panels & mahogany veneers interspersed w/rosewood-veneered escutcheons, round turned wood pulls, molded base & flaring front French feet w/contrasting crossbanded mahogany veneers, shaped sides, refinished, Portsmouth, New Hampshire, ca. 1800, imperfections, 22 1/2 x 41 1/4", 36 1/2" h. (ILLUS.) **$14,100**

Cherry & Mahogany Federal Chest

Federal chest of drawers, cherry & inlaid mahogany veneer, the rectangular top w/applied rounded edge & oval corners above a case of four long beaded graduated drawers w/oval brasses & keyhole escutcheons, the inlaid shaped skirt joining the quarter-engaged baluster- and ring-turned reeded corner posts continuing to turned legs, original brasses, old surface, probably Massachusetts, ca. 1815-20, imperfections, 21 1/2 x 42 1/2", 45" h. (ILLUS.) **$2,703**

Federal Inlaid Cherry Chest of Drawers

Federal chest of drawers, inlaid cherry, the rectangular top above a case of four long

drawers w/long rectangular line-inlaid panels & a diamond-shaped inlaid ivory keyhole escutcheon, oval brass pulls, simple turned legs w/knob feet, minor restorations, early 19th c., 21 1/4 x 41", 44 1/2" h. (ILLUS.) **$1,035**

Fine New York Federal Chest of Drawers

Federal chest of drawers, inlaid mahogany, rectangular line-inlaid top above a case w/a deep top "bonnet" drawer inlaid w/two large oval reserves each w/an oval brass pulls above three long graduated shorter drawers w/matching pulls, scallop-cut apron & slender long French feet, New York City, ca. 1800-1810, 22 1/4 x 45", 44" h. (ILLUS.) **$2,390**

Federal Inlaid Mahogany Chest of Drawers

Federal chest of drawers, inlaid mahogany, the rectangular top above a case w/a pair of drawers w/rectangular banded inlay & two round brass pulls above four matching long graduated drawers, the serpentine apron w/a central fan-carved inlay, raised on high outswept French feet, probably English, replaced brasses, minor piece repair, 21 x 42", 42" h. (ILLUS.) **$1,265**

Inlaid Walnut Southern Federal Chest

Federal chest of drawers, inlaid walnut, the rectangular top w/the narrow front edge decorated w/small inlaid oblong panels above a case w/four long graduated line-inlaid drawers w/inlaid shield-form keyhole escutcheons, the deep serpentine front apron centered by an inlaid design, raised on tall French feet, probably Southern States, early 19th c., restorations to feet, 17 3/4 x 39 1/2", 43" h. (ILLUS.)....................................... **$2,640**

Rare Federal Southern Sugar Chest

F

borough legs, original hardware, yellow pine secondary wood, Southern U.S., late 18th c., 20 x 27", 38" h. (ILLUS.)...... **$6,325**

Federal Country Chest of Drawers

Federal country-style chest of drawers, bird's-eye maple, the rectangular top above a case of four long graduated cock-beaded drawers w/round brass pulls, paneled sides, on tapering ring-turned legs w/knob feet, ca. 1800, old veneer repairs, 21 x 41 1/4", 41 1/2" h. (ILLUS.).............. **$3,400**

Federal sugar chest, walnut, the rectangular flat lift-lid w/brass knob opening to a deep storage compartment, the molded base w/a single narrow long drawer w/a brass knob, raised on chamfered Marl-

Fine Federal Inlaid Walnut Tall Chest

Federal tall chest of drawers, inlaid walnut, the rectangular top w/a flat-molded cornice above a row of three thumb-molded drawers over a pair of drawers over a stack of four long graduated drawers all w/simple bail handles, string inlay & escutcheons flanked by meandering vines continuing to vases, on cut-out feet & a shaped skirt centered by an inlaid fan, old pulls, old refinish, probably Pennsylvania, ca. 1800, imperfections, 20 1/2 x 40", 71" h. (ILLUS.) **$5,825**

Rare Early Dated Pilgrim Century Blanket Chest

Fine French Provincial Chest of Drawers

French Provincial chest of drawers, walnut, the rectangular top w/molded edges & a serpentine front overhanging a case w/a pair of top drawers w/molded oblong panels & scrolling brass pulls w/a keyhole escutcheon flanking a center block w/a carved quatrefoil, two long matching lower drawers, w/centered by a quatrefoil, the other a circle, the narrow serpentine apron above high bracket feet, France, early 19th c., 22 1/2 x 50 1/2", 33 1/2" h. (ILLUS.) **$3,738**

Pilgrim Century blanket chest, carved oak, the rectangular hinged lid opening to a deep well, the front fluted stiles frame three panels carved w/stylized leafy scrolls, brass keyhole escutcheon, attributed to John Houghton, Dedham, Massachusetts, marked w/owner's initials "TB" & dated 1669, lid replaced, 18 3/4 x 42 1/2", 26 1/2" h. (ILLUS., top of page)... **$20,400**

Rare Pilgrim Century Connecticut River Valley Chest

Pilgrim Century six-board chest, painted & carved pine, the rectangular top w/molded edges & original cleats overhangs the nailed case crease-molded on the front & sides that continue down to form the cut-out scalloped feet, the front corners chip-carved, original red surface, Connecticut River Valley, 1675-1725, original snipe hinges not holding, missing till, 18 1/4 x 49", 24 1/2" h. (ILLUS.) **$22,325**

Pilgrim Century-Style Carved Chest

Pilgrim Century-Style chest with drawers, carved oak "Sunflower" style, the hinged rectangular top opening to a deep well fitted w/a candle box, the front decorated w/three shallow-carved panels, two w/stylized florals flanking the central one carved w/three stylized sunflowers, half-round turned spindles separate & flank these panels, a mid-molding above a pair of paneled bottom drawers w/applied oval bosses & separated & flanked by three pairs of short half-round turned spindles base molding & tall square stile legs, American, probably 19th c., 21 1/4 x 47 1/2", 36" h. (ILLUS.) **$1,912**

Fine Queen Anne Chest-on-Frame

Queen Annue chest-on-frame, tiger stripe maple, two-part construction: the upper section w/a rectangular top w/a deep widely flaring & stepped cornice above a case of five long graduated drawers w/scrolling butterfly brasses & keyhole escutcheons; the lower section w/a mid-molding over a deep arched & scroll-cut apron raised on four simple cabriole legs ending in slender slipper feet, original

brasses, old refinish, Newport, Rhode Island, ca. 1750-65, imperfections, 17 3/4 x 39", 59 3/4" h. (ILLUS.) **$7,638**

Rare Tramp Art Hanging Chest

Tramp Art hanging chest, painted & decorated pine, a tall peaked top section enclosing a stepped design of thirteen small drawers each brightly painted w/various floral sprigs on the brown ground, a large & small square niche in the center above the two larger base drawers, small pointed reeded front crest, narrow stepped sides, small back section at top is loose, 19th c., 11 x 26", 39" h. (ILLUS.) **$11,788**

Simple Renaissance Revival Chest

Victorian Renaissance Revival style chest of drawers, walnut & burl walnut, the rectangular white marble top w/molded edges & rounded front corners above a conforming case w/four long graduated molded burl drawers w/simple turned wood knobs & keyhole escutcheons, deep apron on thick disk feet on casters, ca. 1870, 20 x 40 3/4", 36 1/2" h. (ILLUS.) **$538**

F

Fancy Renaissance Revival Chest

Victorian Renaissance Revival style chest of drawers, walnut & burl walnut, the superstructure w/a wide arched pediment w/a projecting blocked crest w/carved sunburst finial over a pair of curved narrow burl panels & roundels, raised on tall carved stiles flanked by flat side pilasters w/pointed finials above half-round candle shelves & raised on wide scroll-carved brackets above a pair of small handkerchief drawers, all atop the inset rectangular white marble top w/projecting rounded corners on the frame above a case w/a narrow long top drawer w/narrow raised burl panels, cut-out brass bail pulls & a raised panel rectangular center panel, above a pair of long deeper drawers w/raised burl panels & matching hardware & centered by a raised blocked panel continuing over both drawer fronts, all flanked by projecting corner columns, deep molded & blocked flat base, ca. 1875, 54" w., 92" h. (ILLUS.) **$1,725**

Victorian Rococo style chest of drawers, ebonized & painted wood, the top fitted w/a tall oblong mirror in a serpentine conforming frame in black decorated w/ornate gilt scrolls & floral details swiveling between a pair of two serpentine uprights w/matching decor, resting atop a rectangular white marble top w/molded serpentine edges, the case w/a single long serpentine drawer w/simple turned knobs above a pair of paneled cupboard doors, a deep ogee apron w/a blind drawer on bun feet, the case painted in black w/an overall ornate decoration of gilt scroll banding & floral reserves, attributed to Hart, Ware and Co., Philadelphia, ca. 1845, overall 72" h. (ILLUS., top next column) **$2,185**

Fancy Early Victorian Chest of Drawers

Fine Cincinnati Rococo Chest of Drawers

Victorian Rococo style chest of drawers, walnut & burl walnut, the top mounted w/a tall oval mirror within a fancy molded & scroll-carved frame w/a large pierced fleur-de-lis crest, swiveling between tall double C-scroll uprights w/pierced leaf carving & small round candle shelves, all atop the rectangular white marble top w/molded edges, the case w/three long burled drawers w/scroll-carved pulls flanking long scroll-carved escutcheons, narrow angled front corners w/narrow panels & half-round ring-turned mounts, the deep flat apron w/a hidden drawer w/a long scroll-carved pulls, Cincinnati, ca. 1855-60, 44" w., 73" h. (ILLUS.)... **$1,265**

Fine Early William & Mary Chest

William & Mary chest-of-drawers, joined maple, oak & pine, the rectangular top w/applied molded edge over a single arch-molded case of two short drawers over three long graduated drawers w/decorative panel molding, turned bun front feet & rear stile feet, replaced brass teardrop pulls, old refinish, probably Massachusetts, ca. 1690-1710, restoration to top, 20 x 36", 33 3/4" h. (ILLUS.) **$5,875**

Scarce Early William & Mary Chest

William & Mary country-style chest of drawers, maple, oak & pine, the rectangular top above narrow ogee molding above a stack of four reverse-graduated flat drawers w/small turned wood knobs, paneled sides, narrow ogee molded base band, on tall knob- and rod-turned feet, pulls appear early, old Spanish brown paint, Hatfield/Hadley, Massachusetts, ca. 1730, imperfections, 21 x 43", 45" h. (ILLUS.)......... **$5,875**

Cradles

Old Southern Yellow Pine Cradle

Country-style cradle with tester on rockers, yellow pine, mortise & peg construction, the rectangular tester frame supported on heavy paneled posts continuing to form the corner posts & square legs ending in inset one-board rockers, the deep cradle sides w/a zigzag open bar design, simple half-round headboard, tester & cover have age but not original, from a Mississippi collection, reputedly slave-made, old refinishing, 19th c., 22 x 42", 51 1/2" h. (ILLUS.) **$575**

Late Victorian Walnut Swinging Cradle

Swinging cradle on frame, walnut, a tall S-curved drapery bracket on a turned support extending to a yoke from which swings a cradle w/curved & turned side spindles, swinging on a trestle base w/arched end legs, w/lace-trimmed drapery & bedding, old repairs, late 19th c., 23 1/2 x 48", 74" h. (ILLUS.) **$1,035**

F

Cupboards

Old Painted Pine Chimney Cupboard

Chimney cupboard, painted pine, a rectangular top w/narrow flared molding across the front above a case bordered by molding framing a tall single paneled cupboard door opening to four shelves, a small brass pull & wooden thumb latch, built-in from the right side, old bluish grey paint, age splits, early 19th c., 12 1/2 x 29", 55 1/4" h. (ILLUS.) **$575**

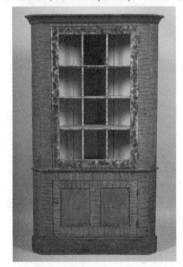

Rare Grain-painted Corner Cupboard

Corner cupboard, country-style, painted & decorated, two-part construction: the upper section w/a deep coved cornice above a single tall 12-pane glazed door opening to three shelves; the lower section w/a mid-molding above a single long two-panel cupboard door above a deep molded flat base, original faux tiger stripe maple graining w/smoke-painted frame around the upper door, possibly Pennsylvania or Ohio, early 19th c., minor imperfections, 25 x 47", 88" h. (ILLUS.) **$11,750**

Painted Pine Corner Cupboard

Corner cupboard, country-style, painted pine, one-piece construction, the top overhanging a case w/a pair of tall raised panel cupboard doors w/cast-iron latches opening to two shelves above a matching pair of cupboard doors, angled front stiles, flat base & simple angled bracket feet, cleaned down to worn thin grey paint, traces of white on the interior, some edge damage, 20 x 35", 73" h. (ILLUS.) **$1,725**

Corner cupboard, country-style, pine, one-piece construction, the flat top w/a deep flaring stepped cornice above a single tall geometrically-glazed cupboard door opening to three shelves above a very narrow drawer w/tiny pulls above a single large two-panel cupboard door, chamfered front corners, deep apron w/serpentine shaping, England, late 19th c., shrinkage cracks in back, some alterations, 19 1/2 x 33 1/2"., 80 3/4" h. (ILLUS., next page) **$1,610**

English Country Pine Corner Cupboard

Country Victorian Corner Cupboard

Corner cupboard, country-style, pine, two-piece construction: the upper section w/a flat top & deep covered cornice above a single wide 9-pane glazed cupboard door opening to two shelves; the lower section w/a mid-molding above a wide single two-panel cupboard door, simple bracket feet, constructed w/square wrought nails, refinished exterior, painted interior, mid-19th c., 43" w., 82" h. (ILLUS.) **$690**

Nice Early Walnut Corner Cupboard

Corner cupboard, country-style, walnut, two-part construction: the upper section w/a flat top & coved cornice above a pair of tall 8-pane cupboard doors opening to three shelves; the slightly stepped-out lower section w/a pair of double-panel cupboard doors, simple low bracket feet, first half 19th c., 28 1/2 x 56 1/4", 85 1/4" h. (ILLUS.) **$5,290**

F

Fine Country Federal Corner Cupboard

Corner cupboard, Federal country-style, cherry, one-piece construction, the flat top w/a deep coved cornice above a pair of tall 8-pane glazed cupboard doors opening to three shelves, a mid-molding above a pair of paneled cupboard doors w/a small brass pull, molded base w/a deep serpentine apron & bracket feet, glued split on one foot facing, apron reshaped, a back foot replaced, first half 19th c., 24 1/2 x 48 3/4", 80" h. (ILLUS.)................ **$4,025**

Federal Pennsylvania Corner Cupboard

Corner cupboard, Federal style, inlaid cherry, two-part construction: the upper section w/a flat top over a coved cornice over a band of ribboned inlay above a single 12-pane glazed cupboard door w/the top panes arched, opening to three shelves; the lower section w/a mid-molding over a row of two short drawers flanking one long drawer above a pair of paneled cupboard doors opening to shelves, a serpentine apron centered by an inlaid fan, raised on simple bracket feet, Pennsylvania, early 19th c., 21 x 43 1/2", 7' 2" h. (ILLUS.) **$2,938**

Federal Inlaid Walnut Corner Cupboard

Corner cupboard, Federal style, inlaid walnut, one-piece construction, the flat top

w/a deep coved cornice above a narrow dentil-carved band over a pair of tall two-paneled doors, the smaller upper panel centered by a starburst inlay, a single small drawer in the center above a pair of shorter paneled doors, molded base w/scroll-cut ogee bracket feet, restoration & alterations, first half 19th c., 20 x 48", 88 1/2" h. (ILLUS.) **$1,150**

Fine Walnut Federal Corner Cupboard

Corner cupboard, Federal style, inlaid walnut, two-part construction: the upper section w/a broken-scroll pediment centered by a raised panel w/a turned urn finial, above an arched frieze inlaid w/delicate leafy vines above a pair of tall arched 10-pane glazed cupboard doors opening to three shelves & flanked by entwined vining inlay down the front rails; the lower section w/a pair of paneled cupboard doors each centered by an inlaid oval, scalloped apron & simple bracket feet, fitted w/exterior H-hinges, probably Pennsylvania, ca. 1800, imperfections, restorations, 22 x 51", 96 1/4" h. (ILLUS.)................................. **$8,225**

Corner cupboard, Federal style, painted pine, barrel-back architectural style, two-part construction: the upper section w/a flat top & deep coved cornice w/wide blocked ends above a dentil-carved band over a wider lattice-carved band, projecting lattice-carved side blocks flank the arched & molded top to the wide open display compartment fitted w/three shelves flanked by fluted pilasters; a conforming mid-molding above the lower case w/a pair of paneled cupboard doors opening to one shelf, deep molded base w/scroll-cut brackets at the front, remnants of old blue & red paint, Mid-Atlantic region, late 18th - early 19th c., 17 3/4 x 52", 84" h. (ILLUS., next page) **$8,050**

Very Fine Federal Open Corner Cupboard

English "Bow-front" Corner Cupboard

Corner cupboard, George III "bow-front" style, mahogany & mahogany veneer, the flat top w/a curved cornice above a conforming base w/a pair of two double-panel curved cupboard doors w/flame mahogany veneer above a curved long central drawer w/small turned wood knob flanked by small square drawers w/matching knobs, flat base, ebonized banding, England, late 18th c., 24 3/4 x 41 1/2", 56" h. (ILLUS.) **$1,495**

F

Federal Country-style Corner Cupboard

Corner cupboard, Federal style, poplar, one-piece construction, the flat top w/a wide angled cornice above a single tall 12-pane glazed door opening to three shelves above a pair of small drawers w/oval brasses over a pair of raised panel cupboard doors, molded base w/serpentine apron & shaped bracket feet, refinished w/dark red stain, restorations including reset backboards & some replacements, early 19th c., 22 x 43", 86" h. (ILLUS.) **$1,150**

Unusual Folk Art Hanging Corner Cupboard

Two Country-style Hanging Cupboards

Hanging corner cupboard, painted & decorated pine, folk art style, the arched crest applied w/a carved eagle figure flanked by stars within circles, over a hinged door opening to two interior shelves & decorated w/applied & painted carved designs including stars, crescent moons, hearts, clovers, diamonds, doves & a horseshoe, two small open shelves at the bottom, all painted in muted shades of red, white, blue & gold, name "Jake Patterson" inscribed in pencil on the back, late 19th - early 20th c., 10 x 16", 30 3/4" h. (ILLUS., previous page).......... **$3,173**

Hanging cupboard, country-style, painted & decorated pine, rectangular top above an upright dovetailed case w/wrought nails in the backboard & a single tall frame-paneled door w/original hardware, old red & black wood graining, minor damage, 19th c., 12 x 16 1/2", 27" h. (ILLUS. left with large hanging cupboard, top of page) **$431**

Hanging cupboard, country-style, painted pine, rectangular top w/a widely flaring coved cornice above a case w/a single large paneled door w/original hardware, square cut nails in case, two interior shelves, red paint under crazed varnish, edge wear, 19th c., 12 1/2 x 38", 38" h. (ILLUS. right with small hanging cupboard, top of page).................................... **$690**

Hanging cupboard, country-style, painted pine, the arched crestboard pierced w/a hanging hole flanked by shaped sides on the rectangular top above a single flat door attached w/early butterfly hinges, opening to two interior shelves, original greyish blue paint, New England, 18th c., 6 1/4 x 10", 14 1/2" h. (ILLUS., top next column) **$9,988**

Early New England Hanging Wall Cupboard

Late Victorian Hanging Cupboard

Hanging cupboard, country-style, pine, the flat top w/a deep flaring stepped cornice above a single tall paneled door opening to three shelves, wire nail construction, refinished, 9 1/2 x 18", 22 1/2" h. (ILLUS., previous page)............ **$604**

Classical Country-style Jelly Cupboard

Jelly cupboard, Classical country-style, cherry, the thin rectangular top above a pair of drawers each w/a turned wood knob & projecting above a pair of tall two-panel cupboard doors flanked by free-standing ring-turned columns, thick flat base molding supported on ring-turned knob feet, ca. 1830, 21 3/8 x 45", 60" h. (ILLUS.).................................. **$1,150**

Painted Poplar Jelly Cupboard

Jelly cupboard, country-style, painted poplar, the rectangular top w/a three-quarters gallery above a case w/a pair of tall paneled cupboard doors w/a cast-

iron latch opening to three shelves, square nail construction, old salmon paint, central Pennsylvania, wear, minor chips, first half 19th c., 18 1/2 x 43 3/4", 54" h. (ILLUS.)....................................... **$1,380**

Fine Old Red-Painted Jelly Cupboard

Jelly cupboard, country-style, painted wood, a narrow rectangular top above an open compartment w/shaped sides over a tall flat single door w/wooden thumb latch opening to three shelves, simple bracket feet, old red paint, 19th c., 13 3/4 x 38", 59 3/4" h. (ILLUS.) **$5,400**

Country Pine Jelly Cupboard

Jelly cupboard, country-style, pine, the rectangular top w/molded edges above a pair of narrow paneled drawers w/white porcelain knobs above a pair of tall paneled cupboard doors, paneled sides, deep flat base molding, mid-19th c., 47" l., 42" h. (ILLUS.) **$316**

English William IV Linen Press

Linen press, William IV style, mahogany & mahogany veneer, two-part construction: the upper section w/a flat top w/a narrow curved cornice above a pair of tall Gothic arch-paneled mahogany veneer doors opening to shelves; the lower section w/a mid-molding above a stack of four long graduated drawers w/lion

head & ring brass pulls, scroll-cut bracket feet, England, mid-19th c., 21 x 47", 80" h. (ILLUS.) **$2,530**

Painted Two-Part Pewter Cupboard

Pewter cupboard, country-style, painted wood, two-part construction: the upper section w/a narrow rectangular top above a tall open compartment fitted w/three shelves w/plate racks; the projecting lower section w/a pair of large paneled cupboard doors opening to two shelves, old red paint, scrubbed surface on lower section, probably a married piece, first half 19th c., 21 1/4 x 47", 68" h. (ILLUS.) **$1,208**

Rare Virginia Cherry Pie Safe

Pie safe, cherry, a rectangular top above a pair of drawers w/pairs of simple turned wood knobs above a pair of wide cupboard doors each mounted w/four pierced tin panels w/pinwheel medallions & floral spandrels, flat apron, raised on baluster- and ring-turned legs w/peg feet, two matching punched tins in each side, opens to three interior shelves, original dark finish, old walnut pulls, Virginia, mid-19th c., restored splits on one door, 18 3/4 x 53", 49" h. (ILLUS.) **$10,350**

Old Pie Safe with Twelve Tin Panels

Pie safe, pine, the rectangular top w/a narrow cornice above a pair of drawers w/turned wood knobs over a pair of tall doors each mounted w/three pierced tin panels decorated w/a pinwheel & corner fan design, three matching tin panels down each side, raised on knob-turned tapering legs, doweled construction, some tin oxidation, first half 19th c., 18 5/8 x 41", 60 3/8" h. (ILLUS.) **$2,070**

Nice Eight-tin Walnut Pie Safe

Pie safe, walnut, rectangular top above a case w/a single long drawer w/turned wood pulls above a pair of two-panel doors fitted w/pierced tins in a design of small rings & half-rings, tall stiles legs beveled at the bottom, two tin panels on each side, one shelf inside, original hardware, refinished age cracks, 19th c., 17 x 41 1/2", 49 1/2" h. (ILLUS.) **$1,160**

F

Large Early Southern Pine Pie Safe

Pie safe, pine, the rectangular top w/a widely flaring flat cornice above a pair of cupboard doors mounted w/punched tin panels in a pinwheel & circle design, matching tin panels on the sides, a pair of lower paneled doors, square legs, Southern U.S., first half 19th c., old repairs & alterations, 17 x 46", 77" h. (ILLUS.) **$1,610**

Fine Walnut Pie Safe

Pie safe, walnut, the rectangular top above a single long drawer w/turned wood knobs above a pair of two-panel doors each fitted w/two punched tin panels decorated w/a design of rings & arches, tall square & slightly tapering legs, two matching tins in each side, one shelf on the interior, original hardware, refinished, age cracks, 19th c., 17 x 41 1/2', 49 1/2" h. (ILLUS.) **$1,610**

Child-Sized Step-back Wall Cupboard

F **Step-back wall cupboard,** child-sized, country-style, stained pine, one-piece construction, the rectangular top w/a wide flaring & stepped cornice above a pair of single-pane cupboard doors opening to two shelves, iron thumb-latch & small porcelain knobs, the slightly stepped-out lower section w/a pair of paneled doors opening to two shelves, matching latch & knobs, low scroll-carved apron, original dark red wash, mid-19th c., 14 x 37", 53 1/2" h. (ILLUS.) **$748**

Ohio Walnut Step-back Wall Cupboard

Step-back wall cupboard, Classical country-style, walnut, two-piece construction: the upper section w/a rectangular top w/a shallow flaring cornice above a pair of tall 6-pane glazed cupboard doors w/the upper panes arched, opening to two shelves above a deep pie shelf; the lower

section w/a pair of drawers w/turned wood knobs slightly projecting over the lower case w/a pair of paneled cupboard doors w/cast-iron latches flanked by half-round knob- and rod-turned pilasters, flat base on small knob feet, attributed to Trumbull County, Ohio, first half 19th c., some age splits & edge damage w/old replaced door latches, 22 x 52", 84 1/2" h. (ILLUS.).. **$2,300**

English Elm Step-back Wall Cupboard

Step-back wall cupboard, country-style, elm, two-part construction: the upper section w/a rectangular top & flaring stepped cornice above a pair of large double-panel cupboard doors opening to two shelves; the lower section w/molded edges above a case w/a row of three deep drawer w/butterfly pulls over a row of three square paneled cupboard doors, molded base w/worn down bracket feet, England, mid-19th c., 21 1/2 x 67", 92" h. (ILLUS.).. **$2,645**

Early Tennessee Jackson Press Cupboard

Step-back wall cupboard, country-style Jackson press type, walnut, two-part construction: the upper section w/a rectangular top w/a wide flat flaring cornice above a pair of very tall 8-pane glazed doors opening to three shelves; the stepped out lower section w/a single long drawer w/two wooden knobs above a pair of paneled cupboard doors, short ring-turned feet, refinished, Eastern Tennessee, first half 19th c., small putty restoration above the drawer & atop one door, 20 1/2 x 41 3/4", 85 7/8" h. (ILLUS., previous page).. **$1,150**

Rare Country New York Step-back Cupboard

F

Country Pine Step-back Wall Cupboard

Step-back wall cupboard, country-style, pine, one-piece construction, the rectangular top board above a pair of tall narrow raised panel cupboard doors w/small wood knobs opening to four shelves, the projecting lower section w/a tall narrow raised panel cupboard door opening to two shelves on the right side & a one-shelf open compartment on the left side, flat base, old mellow refinishing & areas of earlier red wash, square cut nail construction, originally built-in w/the back & top old replacements, top door loose, 19th c., 18 1/4 x 41", 82" h. (ILLUS.)....... **$1,150**

Step-back wall cupboard, country-style, stained poplar, two-part construction: the upper section w/a rectangular top w/a flared ogee cornice above a pair of tall paneled cupboard doors w/thumb latches opening to three shelves; the slightly stepped-out lower section w/a shorter pair of cupboard doors, cut-out base w/angled feet, old red-stained surface, original hardware, Watervliet, New York, ca. 1860, minor imperfections, 19 x 25", 78" h. (ILLUS., top next column)... **$9,988**

Fine Kentucky Step-back Wall Cupboard

Step-back wall cupboard, Federal country style, cherry, two-part construction: the upper section w/a rectangular top & coved cornice above a pair of tall 6-pane glazed cupboard doors opening to two shelves; the lower stepped-out section w/a pair of drawers w/turned wood knobs overhanging a pair of tall paneled doors flanked by slender ring-, rod- and rope twist-turned columns, on knob feet, attributed to Kentucky, refinished, one back foot re-attached, glued split near one hinge, first half 19th c., 23 1/2 x 43", 87" h. (ILLUS.) **$4,945**

Victorian Country Step-back Cupboard

Step-back wall cupboard, Victorian country-style, pine, two-piece construction: the upper section w/a rectangular top above a deep stepped & flaring cornice over a pair of tall single-pane glazed cupboard doors opening to two shelves above a pair of drawers w/white porcelain knobs; the stepped-out lower section w/a single long narrow drawer w/cast-iron pulls above a pair of paneled cupboard doors w/cast-iron latches w/porcelain knobs, low apron & simple bracket feet, second half 19th c., 44" w., 83" h. (ILLUS.) $978

Rare Wall Cupboard/Dry Sink

Step-back wall cupboard-dry sink, poplar & pine w/old red wash, two-part construction: the upper section w/a rectangular top & deep flaring cornice above a pair of tall 9-pane glazed doors opening to two shelves above a row of three small drawers over a high pie shelf w/curved side moldings; the lower section w/a shallow stepped-out dry sink well above a pair of paneled doors, original brass latches, another one missing, thin replaced moldings at top of base, pieced restorations, 19th c., 25 x 61", 89" h. (ILLUS.) $5,463

Country Step-back Hutch Cupboard

Step-back hutch wall cupboard, country-style, painted pine, the flat rectangular top above a tall open compartment w/three shelves, the stepped-out lower case w/a single tall narrow paneled door w/wooden thumb latch, flat base, opens to shelves, layers of green & yellow paint, square nail construction, wear & damage, 19th c., 18 1/2 x 37 1/2", 75" h. (ILLUS.) $1,150

Wall cupboard, child's size, country-style, pine & poplar, the rectangular top w/a molded flaring cornice above a pair of tall two-panel doors opening to two fixed shelves missing original dividers, scalloped apron & simple cut-out feet, original hardware, square nail construction, old refinishing, 19th c., 13 x 27", 30" h. (ILLUS., next page) $546

Child's Country-style Wall Cupboard

Southern Heart Pine Wall Cupboard

Wall cupboard, heart pine, one-piece construction, the rectangular top above a pair of tall flat cupboard doors fitted w/HL hinges & a cast-iron latch, a mid-molding above a pair of shorter flat cupboard doors w/matching hardware, low angled bracket feet, Southern U.S., mid-19th c., restorations & alterations, 22 x 48 1/2", 81 1/4" h. (ILLUS.) **$2,530**

F

Small Painted Country Wall Cupboard

Wall cupboard, country-style, painted walnut, the flat rectangular top above a tall case w/cut-nail construction & a single tall flat walnut one-board door w/small wooden knob & thumb latch, opening to three shelves, on simple angled bracket feet, old red paint, replaced rear foot & breadboard ends on door possibly old replacements, 19th c., 12 x 25 1/2", 42" h. (ILLUS.).. **$575**

Large Painted Pine Wall Cupboard

Wall cupboard, painted pine, one-piece construction, the rectangular top above a stepped cornice over a pair of tall raised panel cupboard doors w/small turned wood knobs opening to shelves above another shorter pair of matching doors opening to shelves, flat apron & simple bracket feet, cleaned down to the original salmon paint on exterior & pumpkin paint on interior, pieced repairs, areas of re-paint, replaced knobs & fastener, 19th c., 18 x 54", 84" h. (ILLUS.) **$633**

Rare & Unique Plantation Wall Cupboard

Wall cupboard, wood-grained cypress & pine, the wide rectangular top overhanging a case w/a wide frieze band above a pair of tall two-panel doors w/elaborate wood-grained decoration, raised on simple bracket feet, original paint in rouge, yellow, ochre & rich brown, shelved interior, made in Louisiana, probably for the Houmas Plantation, backboard w/old black ink inscription "Houmas Plantat(ion) This side up... with care...Preston," John S. Preston built Houmas House, ca. 1830-50, 22 1/2 x 67", 84" h. (ILLUS.).. **$55,200**

Fine English Inlaid Oak Welsh Cupboard

Welsh cupboard, inlaid oak, two-part construction: the upper section w/a long rectangular top w/a narrow dentil-carved cornice over a deep scallop-cut frieze above a wide deep central open compartment w/three shelves flanked by side sections w/an upper open compart-

ment w/a single arched & shaped shelf above a tall narrow cupboard door w/banded inlay over a very small inlaid drawer; the lower section w/molded edges above a case w/two banded inlay drawers flanking a pair of central paneled cupboard doors w/a central inlaid design, the long scroll-cut apron raised on cabriole front legs ending in pad feet & square rear legs, England, ca. 1900, 19 1/4 x 72", 82" (ILLUS.) **$3,105**

Desks

Rare Chippendale "Block-Front" Desk

Chippendale "block-front" slant-front desk, carved mahogany, a narrow rectangular top above a hinged slant-lid w/a pair of large blocked panels flanking a central recessed panel & opening to a fitted interior above a case of four long graduated blocked & recessed drawers all w/large butterfly brasses, molded conforming apron w/an arched central drop & scroll-carved bracket feet, Boston or Salem, Massachusetts, 1760-80, 24 1/4 x 40", 44 1/4" h. (ILLUS.) **$42,000**

Fine Chippendale "Oxbow-Front" Desk

Chippendale "oxbow-front" slant-front desk, mahogany, the narrow rectangular top above a wide hinged fall-front opening to an interior fitted w/a central blocked fan-carved prospect door flanked by valanced compartments & small drawers, the case w/ four long serpentine drawers w/simple bail pulls & oval brass keyhole escutcheons, serpentine molded apron w/a central carved fan drop, raised on short cabriole legs ending in claw-and-ball feet, replaced brasses, refinished, imperfections, North Shore, Massachusetts, late 18th c., 23 x 41", 44" h. (ILLUS., previous page).... **$5,875**

Fine Cherry Chippendale Desk

Chippendale slant-front desk, cherry, a narrow rectangular top above a wide hinged slant-front opening to an interior fitted w/drawers, including a central one w/an inlaid circle, & open compartments, the case w/four long graduated drawers w/simple bail pulls & brass keyhole escutcheons, molded base on ogee bracket feet, original brasses & surface, New England, late 18th c., 19 1/4 x 39", 42 1/2" h. (ILLUS.) **$4,700**

Walnut Chippendale Slant-Front Desk

Chippendale slant-front desk, walnut, a narrow rectangular top above the wide hinged slant top opening to an interior fitted w/12 serpentine-front drawers, four pigeonholes & letter drawers flanking a

center door & a variety of concealed drawers, the case w/four long graduated drawers w/butterfly brasses & keyhole escutcheons flanked by narrow fluted colonettes, molded base on scroll-cut ogee bracket feet, old dark finish, some wear & damage on feet, age cracks in slant top, pierced repairs w/some interior replacements, late 18th c., 19 1/2 x 39", 43 3/4" h. (ILLUS.) **$1,323**

Pennsylvania Chippendale Desk

Chippendale slant-front desk, walnut, the narrow rectangular top above a wide hinged slat-front opening to an interior w/a central cupboard door flanked by document drawers, scalloped pigeon-holes & serpentine-fronted short drawers, the case w/four long graduated drawers w/butterfly brasses & keyhole escutcheons flanked by fluted quarter-columns, molded base raised on ogee bracket feet, Pennsylvania, late 18th c., 21 x 36 1/2", 43" h. (ILLUS.) **$3,819**

Fine Classical Butler's Desk

Classical butler's desk, mahogany & mahogany veneer, the thick rectangular top hinged to fold open & form a writing surface, projecting over a case w/three long drawers each w/pairs of turned wood knobs & flanked by free-standing columns, raised on ring-, disk- and knob-turned legs ending in small ball feet, ca. 1830, 18 x 36 1/2", 38" h. (ILLUS.) **$3,680**

Two Views of the Very Rare Stephen Hedges Classical Combination Desk-Chair

Classical desk-chair, mahogany & flame-grained mahogany veneer, the oval top & deep paneled apron hinged to open in the center w/one half forming a desk fitted w/a fold-over writing surface above a single drawer & the other half forming a low barrel-backed chair, raised on four S-scroll legs, by Stephen Hedges, New York, New York, ca. 1854, 26 x 34", 28" h. (ILLUS., top of page) **$16,100**

Classical "fall-front" desk, mahogany & mahogany veneer, the rectangular top above a wide hinged fall-front opening to a writing surface & an arrangement of small drawers & pigeonholes, the lower case fitted w/three long graduated drawers w/round brass pulls flanked by serpentine pilasters, raised on large C-scroll front legs & ring-turned tapering rear legs, some restoration, ca. 1850, 26 3/4 x 43", 48 1/4" h. (ILLUS.) **$1,100**

Classical Plantation desk, walnut, the long top centered by a wide hinged & slightly slanted writing surface opening to a well & flanked on each side by a pair of small arched compartments, bold scroll-cut ends above an apron fitted w/a small drawer w/two turned wood knobs at each end, raised on ring-, knob- and rod-turned legs ending in ball-and-peg feet, ca. 1830-40, 33 x 60 1/2", 37" h. (ILLUS., bottom of page) **$28,750**

American Classical "Fall-Front" Desk

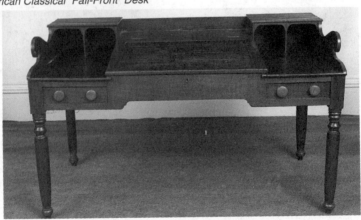

Rare Early Walnut Classical Plantation Desk

Federal Lady's Mahogany Writing Desk

Federal lady's writing desk, inlaid mahogany & mahogany veneer, two-part construction: the short upper section w/a long rectangular top w/narrow vertical inlaid bird's-eye maple panels flanking the long central section fitted w/tambour doors opening to an interior fitted w/two rows of small drawers above arched compartments; the lower section w/a fold-out writing surface above a case w/three long graduated drawers w/banded inlay trim & round brass pulls all flanked by narrow bird's-eye maple inlaid panels, raised on slender square tapering legs w/further inlaid panels, late 18th - early 19th c., 18 1/2 x 40", 42" h. (ILLUS.) **$1,840**

Federal "Oxbow-Front" Slanted Desk

Federal "oxbow-front" slant-front desk, maple & birch, a narrow top above a wide hinged slant front opening to an interior fitted w/ten small drawers over seven pigeonholes, the case w/a four long graduated serpentine drawers all w/oval brasses & keyhole escutcheons, shallow serpentine apron raised on tall

scroll-cut French feet, old replaced brasses, the lid supports, a couple of interior dividers & scalloped decorations are replaced, restorations, refinished, late 18th - early 19th c., 18 x 39 1/2", 47" h. (ILLUS.) **$2,013**

Federal Mahogany Slant-Front Desk

 F

Federal slant-front desk, mahogany, a narrow top above w/wide hinged fall-front w/pierced brass butterfly keyhole escutcheon opening to an interior fitted w/pigeonholes, small drawers & a prospect door, above the case w/four long graduated drawers w/fancy pierced brass butterfly pulls & keyhole escutcheons, molded base on low block feet, ca. 1800, crazing & loss of finish, repairs & restorations, feet replaced w/blocks, 21 3/4 x 46", 39" h. (ILLUS.) **$1,725**

Fine Inlaid Federal Lady's Writing Desk

Federal "tambour" lady's writing desk, inlaid mahogany, two-part construction: the upper section w/a rectangular top & narrow cornice above a narrow inlaid frieze band above flute-inlaid pilasters flanking a pair of tambour doors opening to fitted interior & centered by a rectangular door w/banded inlay centered by an oval reserve inlaid w/an American eagle;

the stepped-out lower section w/a foldout writing surface above a case of three long graduated drawers w/inlaid banding & inlaid fans in each corners, oval brasses, inlaid fluted panel heading each side stile continuing into the square tapering legs w/tapering block feet, Northshore, Massachusetts, 1800-10, 19 1/4 x 38 3/4", 46 1/2" h. (ILLUS.) **$12,000**

George III-Style Carlton House desk, polychromed satinwood, the upper concave stage w/wavy gallery above open compartments, swelled drawers & doors decorated w/festooned garland, portrait medallions & an allegory, the sloped lidded end compartments painted w/musical trophies, the green tooled leather-lined writing surface over three frieze drawers decorated w/floral garlands, the square tapering legs decorated w/classical urns, wreaths & floral pendants, the reverse fully paint-decorated w/matching Adam designs, in the manner of Wright & Mansfield, England, ca. 1875, 23 x 42", 37" h. (ILLUS., middle of page).............. **$8,050**

Fine George III-Style Carlton House Desk

Fine English George III-Style Partner's Desk

George III-Style partner's desk, walnut, the long rectangular green leather-lined top w/indented center sections on each side, the projecting end sections each w/two drawers w/brass butterfly pulls & a single longer drawer in the center sections, raised on eight cabriole legs ending in pad feet, England, late 19th - early 20th c., 39 x 60", 31" h. (ILLUS.).. **$3,565**

Simple Mission Oak Writing Desk

Mission-style (Arts & Crafts movement) desk, oak, rectangular top w/low arched end panels & projecting corner posts continuing down to form the legs, the case w/a pair of flat cupboard doors w/turned wood knobs flanking a long center drawer over an arched apron, early 20th c., 26 x 42 1/2", 27 1/2" h. (ILLUS.).... **$374**

Modern Style Leather & Brass Desk

Modern style desk, leather & brass, the rectangular yellow laminate top w/a leather back crestrail attached w/leather straps & fitted w/a cylindrical leather pencil holder & double straps for documents, raised on slender straight round legs w/the right end fitted w/a stack of four rectangular leather drawers, brass-capped feet, designed by Jacques Adnet, France, ca. 1950, 23 x 36", 35" h. (ILLUS.)................................. **$4,183**

North African cylinder-front desk, walnut, ivory-inlaid & parquetry, the narrow rectangular top above an arched gallery above the cylinder front decorated overall w/ornate inlay & reserves of Arabic inscriptions, opening to reveal an interior w/six short drawers centered by a mirrored mihrab above a green felt-covered writing slide over a long narrow frieze drawer, supported on a fancy colonnaded trestle base, inlaid overall w/thuya reserves & geometric patterns of various woods & ivory, late 19th c., 20 3/4 x 31 3/4", 52 1/2" h. (ILLUS., top next column)............................. **$13,145**

Unique & Elaborate North African Desk

F

Unusual Oriental Slant-Front Desk

Oriental slant-front desk, burlwood, a narrow rectangular top above the wide hinged four-panel slant-front opening to an interior fitted w/eight drawers & four pigeonholes around a central drawer, the case w/a row of three deep drawers above two raised panel cupboard doors flanked by a small & paneled door on each side, all atop carved feet joined by an elaborately pierce-carved apron, probably China, mid-19th c. or older, probably original finish, pull on the lid not attached but present, 21 x 40", 48" h. (ILLUS.)....................................... **$1,725**

Very Rare Queen Anne "Block-Front" Desk

Queen Anne "block-front" kneehole desk, walnut, the rectangular top w/a blocked front w/rounded blocks above a conforming case w/a single long top drawer above two stacks of deep graduated drawers all w/butterfly brasses & flanking the central kneehole w/a scalloped top rail & an inset arched & paneled door w/exposed H-hinges, molded apron on arched, scroll-carved bracket feet, original brasses, Massachusetts, ca. 1740-70, 20 5/8 x 32 1/2", 29 1/4" h. (ILLUS.)....... **$72,000**

Nice Country Queen Anne Desk-on-Frame

Queen Anne country-style desk-on-frame, birch & maple, two-part construction: the upper section w/a narrow top above a wide hinged slant-front opening to three small drawers & six pigeonholes above a single long drawer w/turned wood knob; the lower case w/a wide mid-molding above a single long drawer w/a

turned knob, raised on baluster- and ring-turned legs joined by heavy box stretchers, old refinishing & traces of old red wash, old pieced restorations to lid & moldings, one lid support replaced, turned pulls old replacements, 18th c., 17 1/4 x 27 1/4", 39" h. (ILLUS.) **$5,750**

Country Queen Anne Desk-on-Frame

Queen Anne country-style desk-on-frame, painted pine, two-part construction: the top desk section w/a narrow rectangular top above a wide hinged slant top w/wrought-iron staple hinges opening to an interior w/six dovetailed drawers w/brass pulls & a replaced removable board over an open well; the lower section w/a molded rim above an apron w/a single long drawer w/a pierced brass oval keyhole escutcheon & two small turned wood knobs, raised on straight turned & tapering legs ending in pad feet, black repaint over traces of varnish, some wear & damage to hinges, New England, first half 18th c., 26 x 30 1/2", 38 1/4" h. (ILLUS.) **$1,150**

Fine Queen Anne Desk-on-Frame

Queen Anne desk-on-frame, figured maple, a narrow rectangular top above a wide hinged slant-front opening to a fitted interior above a single long drawer w/butterfly pulls & a keyhole escutcheons, raised on a base w/a mid-molding above the deep serpentine apron, raised on straight cabriole legs ending in raised pad feet, original brasses, Connecticut or Rhode Island, ca. 1730-50, 17 x 34", 37 1/2" h. (ILLUS., previous page) **$9,560**

Rare Tiger Maple Queen Anne Desk

Queen Anne desk-on-frame, tiger stripe maple & maple, two-part construction: the upper desk section w/a narrow rectangular top above a wide hinged slant-top opening to an interior fitted w/a central fan-carved drawer flanked by two valanced compartments all above four small drawers, a single long deep drawer below w/butterfly brasses & keyhole escutcheon; the lower case w/a molded rim above a deep valanced apron raised on cabriole legs ending in pad feet, old replaced brasses, probably Massachusetts, mid-18th c., refinished, minor im-

perfections, 18 3/4 x 34", 40 1/2" h. (ILLUS.) **$18,800**

English Regency-Style Writing Desk

Regency-Style writing desk, mahogany, the kidney-shaped leather-lined top fitted w/a low pierced brass gallery above three frieze drawers, the lyre-form end supports contain brass strings, on outswept legs ending in brass paw feet, simple curved cross-stretcher, England, late 19th c., 20 x 41", 30" h. (ILLUS.) **$1,265**

Renaissance-Style writing desk, carved mahogany, the large rectangular top inset w/a yellow damask panel, the gadrooned edges overhanging a blocked apron w/a row of three drawers across the top front w/brass pulls above a gadrooned mid-molding above two side stacks of two deep drawers flanking the kneehole opening, each end w/four panels featuring grotesque carved masks, the back featuring ornate floral, fruit & wreath-carved panels, deep flaring & molded base w/gadrooned & egg-and-dart bands, Europe, late 19th c., 40 x 70", 31 1/2" h. (ILLUS., bottom of page) **$6,038**

Ornately Carved European Renaissance-Style Writing Desk

Elaborate Rococo-Style Writing Desk

Rococo-Style writing desk, inlaid walnut & marquetry, the upper stepbacked section w/a serpentine top fitted w/a low pierced brass gallery & molded edges above two stacks of three small drawers w/pierced gilt-brass pulls flanking a pair of concave doors decorated w/ornate figural marquetry panels, the lower case w/a rectangular top w/serpentine molded sides above a case w/a single long serpentine drawer w/pierced gilt-brass pulls & gilt-brass corner mounts above two small concave drawers flanking the kneehole opening, raised on simple cabriole legs w/gilt-brass mounts, Europe, late 19th - early 20th c., 23 x 34", 45 1/2" h. (ILLUS.) **$4,140**

Fine Victorian Eastlake Rolltop Desk

Victorian Eastlake style "rolltop" desk, walnut, the rectangular top w/a three-quarters gallery w/the back crest w/a scalloped top above an incised long panel over narrow panels, a scalloped band at the front above the curved rolltop

w/two recessed rectangular panels & round black & brass knobs, opening to a fitted interior, the lower case w/a stack of five drawers w/narrow wood pulls opposite a single drawer over a line-incised paneled cupboard door, flanking the kneehole opening w/a scallop-cut crest, paneled edges, minor edge damage & wear, mellow refinish, ca. 1890, 30 1/2 x 52", 56 1/4" h. (ILLUS.) **$3,105**

William & Mary Slant-Front Maple Desk

William & Mary slant-front desk, figured maple, a narrow rectangular top above a wide hinged slant-top opening to a fitted interior, above a case of four long graduated drawers w/simple turned wood pulls, molded base on shaped bracket feet resting on casters, New England, 1740-60, 17 1/2 x 36", 42 1/4" h. (ILLUS.) **$7,200**

Rare William & Mary Tabletop Desk

William & Mary tabletop slant-front desk, maple & pine, a narrow rectangular top above the wide hinged slant front opening to an interior fitted w/a row of arched pigeonholes over a row of five small drawers, the case below w/two long graduated drawers w/batwing brasses & keyhole escutcheons, flaring molded base on turned turnip feet, early 18th c., 14 1/4 x 23", 20" h. (ILLUS.) **$10,200**

Dining Room Suites

Rare Sornay French Art Deco Dining Room Suite

Art Deco: dining table & 10 dining chairs; inlaid & inset rosewood, the table w/a long rectangular top composed of large squares of tan travertine, wide corner legs curved at the base w/the central opening fitted at the bottom w/another travertine piece, the chairs w/tall slightly flaring backs w/cream-colored upholstery above half-round upholstered seats, on square tapering legs, chairs stamped "Breveté Sornay France Etranger," Andre Sornay, France, ca. 1935, table 39 x 118", 30" h., chairs 40 7/8" h., the suite (ILLUS.) **$50,190**

Fine French Art Nouveau Dining Room Suite

Art Nouveau: extension dining table & 12 side chairs; carved mahogany, the table w/a long rectangular top w/molded edges & rounded covers carved w/floral bands & raised on square tapering legs w/block feet, each chair w/a tall back w/a molded & flower-carved frame enclosing an upholstered panel, upholstered seat on slender tapering front legs ending in tiny block feet, & canted square rear legs, designed by Edouard Diot, France, ca. 1905, table w/two leaves, table 47 x 49 1/2", 29" h., chairs 37 3/4" h., the suite (ILLUS.)
.... **$21,510**

Baroque Revival Oak Dining Room Suite

F

Baroque Revival style: four dining chairs & an extension dining table; carved oak, each chair w/a tall leather-upholstered back w/an arched crestrail carved w/the profile of a man, raised above the leather over-upholstered seat above front legs turned w/large bulbous acorn-form sections w/leaf carving above block- and knob-feet, simple square rear legs & H-stretcher, the rectangular draw-leaf table w/a carved edge above a deep apron decorated at each corner w/two carved lion heads above the legs composed of large bulbous turned acorn-form posts above block & ball feet joined by large in-curved stretchers joined by a straight center stretcher, early 20th c., chairs 44" h., table 38 x 62" closed, 32" h., the set (ILLUS., bottom previous page) **$1,380**

Fine Federal Revival Inlaid Mahogany Dining Room Suite

Federal Revival style: dining table, eight side chairs, sideboard & serving table; in-laid mahogany, the round extension din-

ing table raised on square tapering legs on casters & accompanied by five leaves, each side chair w/an arched crestrail above a tall oblong splat w/a design of pierced slats, slip seat & square tapering legs joined by H-stretcher, the bowfront sideboard w/a high serpentine backsplash above a case w/curved end drawers over curved doors flanking the flat center stack of three long drawers, on square tapering legs, the server w/a high serpentine back-splash above a bowed top over a single long bowed drawer above a medial shelf all raised on square tapering legs, the backsplashes w/inlaid decoration & bell-flower inlay on the front legs, ring- and urn-decorated brasses, ca. 1920s, table 54" d., chairs 43 3/4" h., sideboard 25 x 65", 47" h., the set (ILLUS.)............. **$3,220**

Gothic Revival style: dining table, six side chairs, two armchairs, a side cabinet, buf-fet, side table & wall cabinet; oak, the suite overall richly carved w/Gothic arches & tracery, flowerheads within stepped trefoil surrounds & crocheted finials, the dining table w/a rectangular parquetry inlaid top on pierced trestle-form supports on scrolled feet; each chair w/crocheted finials over an arched crest above rectangular backs each centering a slightly different scrolling foliate & spider web tracery-carved panel over a trapezoidal seat over outswept arms, raised on tapering legs; the side cabinet of court cupboard design, the upper case sur-mounted by arched crocheted finials over a pair of doors, raised on square supports joined by a platform; the buffet w/a rectan-gular top over a pair of frieze drawers above a pair of iron-mounted doors on a stepped-out base; the tiered side table w/rectangular top & chamfered edge over a frieze drawers above pierced swagged panels over two shelves ending in an arched base; the wall cabinet w/an arched crest over a single door & arched base, Eu-rope, third quarter 19th c., dining table open 4' 11" x 8' 4", 31" h., court cupboard, 17" x 5', 8' 10" h., the suite (ILLUS. of part, bottom of page)....................................... **$8,225**

Dining Table & Chairs from Fine Gothic Revival Dining Suite

Dry Sinks

Unusual Covered Cherry Dry Sink

Cherry, the rectangular hinged top opens to a well above a pair of paneled cupboard doors w/brass H-hinges & brass latches, simple bracket feet, mid-19th c., sink lining missing & replaced w/a plywood panel, 20 x 36 3/4", 33 3/4" h. (ILLUS.)............ **$690**

Highboys & Lowboys

Highboys

Unique Million Dollar Philadelphia Highboy

Chippendale "bonnet-top" highboy, carved mahogany, two-part construction: the upper section w/a very high broken-scroll pediment w/the heavy molded scrolls terminating in large sunflowers flanking a tall cartouche-shaped scroll-pieced finial & mounted w/corner blocks supporting urn-turned & flame finials, the wide upper frieze ornately carved w/bold leafy scrolls centered by a large pierce-carved shell device, the tall case w/quarter-round reeded corner columns flanking a row of three drawers over a pair of draw-ers above three long graduated drawers, all w/pierced butterfly brasses; the lower section w/a mid-molding above a case w/a single long drawer over a pair of small square drawers flanking a large central drawer w/finely carved leafy scrolls centered by a large shell all flanked by quarter-round reeded columns, the serpentine apron centered by a small carved shell, raised on tall cabriole legs w/scroll- and leaf-carved knees & ending in claw-and-ball feet, attributed to the shop of Henry Clifton & Thomas Carteret, Philadelphia, 1755-65, descended in the family of Benjamin Marshall, unique, 23 5/8 x 45", 94 1/2" h. (ILLUS.) **$1,808,000**

Exquisite Philadelphia Carved Highboy

Chippendale "bonnet-top" highboy, carved mahogany, two-part construction: the upper section w/an ornate broken-scroll pediment w/the large molded scrolls ending in a large carved flower head flanking a very tall, large pierced scroll-carved finial, reeded corner blocks supporting urn-turned & flame-carved finials, the wide frieze ornately carved w/leafy scrolls above a row of three drawers over a pair of drawers over a stack of three long graduated drawers, all w/butterfly brasses & keyhole escutcheons, fluted slender colonettes down the sides; the lower section w/a mid-molding over a long drawer above a pair of small square drawers flanking a deep, large shell- and scroll-carved center drawer, fluted colonettes down the sides, raised on a scroll-carved apron on cabriole legs w/fancy leaf- and scroll-carved knees & ending in claw-and-ball feet, Philadelphia, ca. 1760-80, descended in the family of Joseph Moulder, 23 7/8 x 42 1/4", 97 1/4" h. (ILLUS.) **$329,600**

New England Queen Anne Highboy

Queen Anne "flat-top" highboy, maple, two-part construction: the upper section w/a rectangular top above a deep stepped cornice over a stack of four long graduated drawers w/butterfly brasses & keyhole escutcheons; the lower section w/a mid-molding above a single long narrow drawer over a row of three deep drawers, the valanced skirt raised on simple cabriole legs ending raised pad feet, New England, 1740-70, 19 x 38 1/4" h., 69" h. (ILLUS.) **$9,000**

Lowboys

Fine Queen Anne Lowboy

Queen Anne lowboy, walnut & mahogany, the rectangular top w/chamfered corners above a case w/a long drawer over a pair of small square drawers flanking a larger, deeper center drawer, all w/butterfly brasses, fluted & canted side stiles, fancy scroll-cut apron, raised on cabriole legs w/leaf- and shell-carved knees & ending in drake feet, ca. 1780, 19 1/4 x 31 1/2", 28 1/4" h. (ILLUS.) **$4,830**

Love Seats, Sofas & Settees

Chaises lounge, Art Deco, giltwood, one end w/a high outswept narrow upholstered back w/a bolster above the long narrow rectangular seat ending in a low outswept upholstered end, flat molded seatrail raised on four reeded & turned tapering legs, from L'Atelier d'Art du Printemps, Paris, France, ca. 1920, 65" l., 35 7/8" h., pr. (ILLUS., bottom of page) **$38,240**

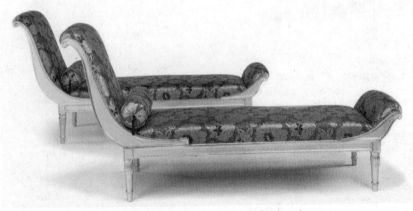

Rare Pair of Early French Art Deco Chaises Lounge

Painted Beechwood Louis XVI Daybed

Daybed, Louis XVI style, painted beechwood, the matching head- and footboard w/square molded framing & turned finials enclosing upholstery panels, a long cushion seat above a long molded seatrail, tapering turned & fluted legs, old white paint, first half 19th c., 64 1/2" l., 35 1/2" h. (ILLUS.) **$3,105**

Attractive English Chippendale-Style Settee

Settee, Chippendale-Style, carved mahogany, the triple chair-back w/scrolling crestrails & pierced vasiform splats flanked by S-curved open arms w/carved bird-head grips, long over-upholstered seat raised on four front cabriole legs w/carved knees & ending in claw-and-ball feet, England, second half 19th c., arm joints slightly loose, 70 1/2" l., 38 3/4" h. (ILLUS.) **$2,185**

Fancy Painted & Decorated Country-Style Settee

Finely Painted Early Pennsylvania Settee

Settee, country-style, painted & decorated pine, the double-back wide crestrail w/serpentine top raised on three wide vasiform splats alternating w/two turned spindles, serpentine open arms raised on a short spindle & canted turned arm support, the long plank seat raised on eight turned & canted legs joined by flat stretchers, original apple green paint w/black, bronze & green stenciled fruit & leafy scroll designs on the crestrail & further leaf designs & banded trim on the splats, spindles & stretchers, arms repaired, ca. 1830-40, 82" l., 36" h. (ILLUS., bottom previous page) **$771**

Settee, country-style, painted & decorated, the long crest divided into three sections above three wide vasiform splats alternating w/two spindles, scrolled painted arms over two short spindles & a short turned arm support above the long scroll-fronted plank seat raised on four heavy ring-turned front legs joined by flat stretchers & four canted simple turned rear legs joined by flat stretchers, original light green painted w/free-hand decoration of light melon-colored flowers & green leaves accented w/gold & black on the crest, front seatrail & stretchers, mahogany-colored paint arms, Pennsylvania, ca. 1830-40, very minor surface imperfections, 21 3/4 x 77 1/2", 34 1/4" h. (ILLUS., top of page) **$3,408**

Settee, Federal, carved mahogany, the long flat upholstered back flanked by fluted downswept rails above the closed upholstered arms w/baluster-turned reeded arm supports, cushion seat above a long slightly bowed seatrail raised on four ring-turned & reeded tapering front legs ending in turned tapering feet & four square canted rear legs, New England, 1800-20, 24 x 65", 34 1/2" h. (ILLUS., bottom of page) **$14,400**

Fine Federal New England Settee

Painted Pine Paneled Fireside Settle

Settle, country-style, painted pine, the high back w/panels flanked by shaped open arms on baluster- and knob-turned arm supporting flanking the long lift-seat, a deep paneled apron, short square stile feet, dark brown repaint over traces of dark green, late 18th - early 19th c., wear & minor damage, 56" w., 44" h. (ILLUS., top of page) **$1,265**

Early Painted Pine Fireplace Settle

Settle, country-style, painted pine, the tall back w/arched top composed of wide horizontal board flanked by tall shallow one-board sides continuing down to low curved arms, long hinged seat opening to storage compartment, deep apron, brown repaint, age splits & old repairs, 19th c., 57" l., 60" h. (ILLUS.)................. **$1,610**

Carved Baroque-Style Sofa

Sofa, Baroque-Style, carved oak, a very long & high arched crestrail decorated w/elaborate pierce-carved designs including a large central cartouche flanked by winged lings & scrolling, fruiting vines, all above a long upholstered panel, spiral-twist stiles & padded open arms above spiral-twist arm supports flanking the long over-upholstered seat, raised on eight block-, knob- and ring-turned legs w/knob feet & joined by spiral-twist stretchers, Europe, mid-19th c., old repairs, 72" l., 56" h. (ILLUS.) **$978**

Sofa, Chippendale style, mahogany, the long, high upholstered back w/a gently arched crest above shaped arm rails above upholstered panels & w/incurved fluted arm supports, long upholstered seat raised on three square tapering front legs joined by flat stretchers & three square canted rear legs, Massachusetts, 1770-1780, 77 3/4" l., 42 3/4" h. (ILLUS., top next page) **$3,840**

Massachusetts Upholstered Mahogany Chippendale Sofa

Classical Sofa Attributed to Duncan Phyfe Shop

Sofa, Classical "Grecian" style, carved mahogany, the long flat crestrail carved w/a repeating design of swags & tassels w/a pair of adorsed cornucopia issuing grain above the low upholstered back flanked by outswept upholstered arms w/matching carved on the crestrail rails & continuing down into the long fluted seatrail raised on outswept fluted legs w/brass paw caps & raised on casters, attributed to the shop of Duncan Phyfe, New York City, ca. 1810-20, 88" l., 32 3/4"h. (ILLUS.) **$13,200**

Finely Carved New York Classical Sofa

Sofa, Classical style, carved mahogany, a long flat tubular crestrail ending in leaf-carved scrolls above the long, low upholstered back flanked by outward scrolled upholstered arms w/bolsters & a leaf-carved arm support ending in a cornucopia continuing into the flat seatrail, raised on fruit-filled carved cornucopias resting on large paw feet on casters, New York City, ca. 1825, 7' l., 31 1/2" h. (ILLUS.) **$4,600**

Mirrors

Belle Epoque Figural Walnut Mirror

Belle Epoque wall mirror, walnut, the oval mirror within bead & foliate banding & floral swag surmounted by a figural putto above a fringed drapery, the drapery continuing to enfold a lower putto above a floral garland, Europe, late 19th c., 37 x 55" (ILLUS.).................................... **$7,050**

Fine Gilt-Trimmed Chippendale Mirror

Chippendale wall mirror, carved mahogany & parcel-gilt, the high arched & finely scroll-cut crest decorated w/a raised gilt shell above gilt leafy vines, the scroll-carved base drop also trimmed w/gilt leafy vines, tall rectangular mirror w/rounded top corners, American or English, 18th c., 41 1/2" h. (ILLUS.) **$3,840**

Very Fine Gilded Chippendale Mirror

Black Forest style dressing mirror, carved walnut, the oval beveled mirror within an ornate pierced-carved frame composed of oak branches w/acorns & leaves, raised on crossed-branch front legs, one small back chip to mirror, Germany, late 19th c., 11 1/2 x 17 1/2" (ILLUS.) **$1,150**

Fancy Black Forest Carved Dressing Mirror

Chippendale wall mirror, inlaid & parcel-gilt mahogany, the high broken-scroll crest trimmed w/gilt, the scrolls ending in large florettes centering a large gilt urn finial issuing delicate leaf & flower vines, the long molded rectangular frame trimmed w/gilt & flanked at the top by

F

pierced gilt flower & leaf pendant swags, a wide arched & finely scroll-cut base drop, probably New York city, 1780-1810, 22 1/4 x 52 1/4" (ILLUS.).............. **$4,800**

Smaller Chippendale Wall Mirror

Chippendale wall mirror, mahogany, the high arched crest flanked by carved scrolls above the rectangular molding enclosing the tall mirror, America or England, 18th c., 17 3/4" h. (ILLUS.)........... **$1,200**

Large Chippendale-Style Wall Mirror

Chippendale-Style wall mirror, giltwood & mahogany, the high broken-scroll pediment w/a gilt floral border centered by a large spread-winged eagle above narrow rectangular giltwood bands surrounding the tall rectangular mirror & flanked by long openwork bands of laurel leaves down the sides, the serpentine base

w/scroll gilt floral bands & rosettes, refinished, restorations & touch-up to eagle & gilding, American, late 19th c., 24 1/4" w., 56 1/2" h. (ILLUS.) **$920**

Fine Chippendale-Style Wall Mirror

Chippendale-Style wall mirror, mahogany, the broken-scroll crest trimmed w/gilt gesso leafy branches & rosettes flanking a large spread-winged eagle crest, long gilt gesso openwork bellflower vines down the sides flanking the frame enclosing the rectangular mirror, scroll-cut bottom frame w/small gesso rosettes, restoration to gesso trim, late 19th - early 20th c., 24 x 45 3/4" (ILLUS.) **$805**

Fine Classical Girandole Wall Mirror

Classical Giltwood Overmantel Mirror with Half-round Columns

Classical girandole wall mirror, giltwood, a wide round concave frame set w/spheres around the convex mirror, the top mounted w/a large spread-winged eagle & leafy scrolls, a pointed leaf-carved base drop, probably American, 1820-30, 29" h. (ILLUS., previous page) **$3,120**

Classical overmantel mirror, giltwood & gesso, the long flat narrow cornice w/blocked ends above a frieze band w/florette-decorated corner blocks flanking a bold ring-turned half-round column accented w/bands of delicate floral sprigs, matching shorter half-round side columns resting on plain corner blocks joined by a narrow acanthus leaf-decorated border, three-part mirror, ca. 1825-35, 63" l., 24 3/4" h. (ILLUS., top of page) **$1,880**

Fine Boston Classical Giltwood Overmantel Mirror

Classical overmantel mirror, giltwood, the long wide rectangular frame w/corner blocks decorated w/square florettes joined by half-round leaf tip-trimmed columns, the base resting on small peg feet, Boston, ca. 1825, 64" l, 40 1/2" h. (ILLUS.) **$8,338**

Classical overmantel mirror, giltwood, the three-section long mirror enclosed by a wide cove-molded frame w/ornate corners decorated w/pairs of cornucopias issuing fruit & leaves, old surface, fragmentary label on back for F. Cainmeyer, New York City, ca. 1825-35, imperfections, 52" l., 28" h. (ILLUS., bottom of page) **$5,581**

Classical pier mirror, gilt gesso & wood, the flat molded & blocked cornice above a row of applied spherules over a two-part mirror plate, the upper section flanked by panels of molded acanthus leaves, flowers & scrolls, the lower sides decorated w/half-round slender reeded columns w/turned capitals & bases, bottom corner blocks molded w/a Grecian mask & joined by a rail decorated w/long leafy sprigs centered by another mask, ca. 1815-20, imperfection & losses, 38" w., 66" h. **$1,880**

F

Fine Labeled New York Classical Overmantel Mirror

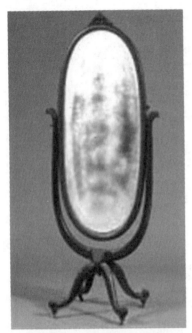

Classical Revival Cheval Mirror

Classical Revival cheval mirror, mahogany, a very tall oval beveled mirror within a narrow rounded frame w/a carved crest swiveling between U-form uprights raised on four outswept cabriole legs ending in scroll feet on casters, ca. 1900, 28" w., 5' 10" h. (ILLUS.) **$558**

Rare Round Classical Mirror

Classical wall mirror, ebonized giltwood, a wide round concave frame mounted w/a band of small spheres, the top crest composed of two entwined dolphins & a trident flanked by large leafy clusters of seaweed, the base decoration w/clusters of shorter leaves, ebonized liner, encloses a convex mirror, early 19th c., 53" h. (ILLUS.) **$19,210**

American Classical Convex Wall Mirror

Classical wall mirror, carved gilded wood, a carved spread-winged eagle perched on scrolls above a round molded frame w/an inner band of small gilt spherules, convex mirror plate, American, first half 19th c., 27" d. (ILLUS.) **$5,019**

New York City Classical Wall Mirror

Classical wall mirror, giltwood, the flat narrow blocked crest above a conforming frieze band decorated w/molded florettes & a central shell above tall half-round columns divided into three swelled sections w/the top & bottom section molded w/a long florette & the central section w/a ropetwist design, bottom corner blocks w/florettes joined by half-round double-baluster rail, the tall rectangular mirror plate below a smaller rectangular pane reverse-painted w/a gilt spread-winged American eagle above a shield & crossed flags against a white ground, New York City, 1815-25, plates probably replaced, 28 3/4 x 50" (ILLUS.).................................. **$840**

Rare Federal Giltwood Wall Mirror

Federal wall mirror, giltwood, the flat covered crestrail w/blocked corners above a suspended row of spheres over a freize band centered by a rectangular panel decorated w/a drapery swag tied w/a bow flanked by panels of molded latticework, all flanked by corner blocks w/rosettes above a wide panel w/a raised Greek key design, the narrow sides molded w/slen-

der reeded & vine-wrapped pilasters resting on small bottom corner blocks, Boston or New York City, ca. 1815-25, 36" w., 61" h. (ILLUS.) **$10,638**

Fine Labeled Federal Wall Mirror

Federal wall mirror, giltwood, the pedimented crest topped by an eagle w/outstretched wings on a rocky perch above a shaped acanthus leaf plinth above a shaped, molded & beaded frame containing a reverse-painted top tablet decorated w/gilt musical instruments flanked by two smaller tablets joined by a chain w/attached spheres, on a flat cornice molding w/applied spheres & mirror flanked by engaged pilasters w/leaf capitals, old surface, label of Hosea Dugliss, New York City, ca. 1815-20, imperfections (ILLUS.) **$5,875**

Fine Pair of Massachusetts Federal Wall Mirrors

Federal wall mirrors, giltwood & gesso, the narrow flat blocked cornice w/bands of floral devices above a horizontal spiral band & raised tablets w/a molded grapevine & ropetwist border, spiral-twist side columns on square plinths, rectangular mirror, Massachusetts, ca. 1815-20, old surface, imperfections, 25 x 43", pr. (ILLUS.).. **$7,050**

Chinese Carved Teak Dressing Mirror

Oriental dressing mirror, carved teak, table-top style, the oval mirror w/floral-carved frame topped by a figural bird & swiveling between square uprights w/pierce-carved brackets & flanked by openwork carved figural rampant lions, set on a rectangular platform w/gadrooned convex sides & a narrow drawer, resting on carved paw feet, China, late half 19th c., repairs, minor imperfections, 10 x 18 1/2", 26 1/2" h. (ILLUS.)....... **$999**

Fine Early Queen Anne Wall Mirror

Queen Anne wall mirror, walnut & parcel gilt, the arched & scroll-carved crest above a molded frame w/an incised gilt gesso liner around the rectangular mirror, original condition, England or America, 18th c., minor imperfections, 9 3/4" w., 17 1/4" h. (ILLUS.)................... **$6,463**

Rococo-Style wall mirror, giltwood, the high arched crest ornately pierce-carved w/scrolls & leafy vines topped by a spread-winged phoenix finial, the long rectangular frame composed of elaborate openwork scrolls w/a pierced shell at the center of the bottom rail, reproduction

Fine Reproduction Rococo-Style Mirror

marked by the Carver's Guild of West Groton, Massachusetts, a few chips & restorations, 20th c., 32" w., 60" h. (ILLUS.) **$431**

Fine Victorian Rococo Pier Mirror

Victorian Rococo style pier mirror, giltwood, the high arched & ornately scroll-pierced crest above tall molded sides flanked w/S-scrolls at the bottom corners, resting on a half-round serpentine-sided stand w/a conforming white marble top, some old repairs, legs on stand reduced, ca. 1860, 40" w., 104" h. (ILLUS.) **$1,495**

Parlor Suites

Majorelle Art Nouveau Three-Piece Parlor Suite

Art Nouveau: settee & two armchairs; carved mahogany & marquetry, the settee w/a gently arched back panel within a molded frame decorated w/a detailed band of poppy-like flowers & stems above a row of numerous slender spindles, the fluted & downswept open arms on further spindles, the upholstered seat raised on slender molded & canted front & rear legs, each armchair w/a molded framework centered by a long wide splat also inlaid w/tall stems of flowers & cattails, downswept arms over spindles, upholstered seat & molded & canted legs, designed by Louis Majorelle, France, ca. 1900, signed, settee 44 1/4" l., chairs 42 1/2" h., the suite (ILLUS.) **$8,963**

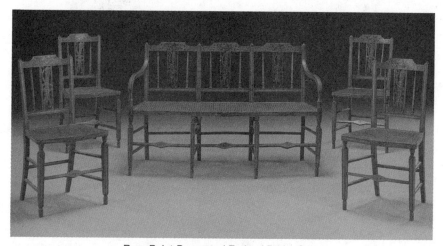

Rare Paint-Decorated Federal Parlor Suite

Federal style: settee & four side chairs; mustard yellow-painted & caned wood, the triple-back settee w/each section of the crestrail w/a raised panel hand-painted above a pierced & painted central splat flanked by slender turned spindles, serpentine opening arms on a turned arm support above the long caned seat raised on four square tapering decorated front legs joined by front stretchers centered by a diamond-shaped panel, square canted rear legs joined by simple stretchers, each side chair of matching design & decoration, stamped "L. Barnes," probably Portsmouth, New Hampshire or New York, 1805-15, settee 53" l., chairs, 34 1/4" h., the suite (ILLUS.) **$21,600**

F

Chairs From a Louis XVI-Style Parlor Suite

F

Louis XVI-Style, four open-arm armchairs & eight chaises; Louix XVI-Style, painted wood, each w/an oval upholstered back within a white-painted frame above a pair of open padded arms over incurved arm supports, wide upholstered seat w/a serpentine front seatrail, raised on tapering round fluted legs ending in peg feet, mid-20th c., armchairs 37" h., chaises 35 1/2" l., the suite (ILLUS. of two armchairs)............... **$2,938**

Very Fine Louis XVI-Style Giltwood Parlor Suite

Louis XVI-Style: settee, two armchairs & four side chairs; giltwood, the settee w/an arched crestrail carved w/courting doves & flowerheads above the long oval upholstered back & terminating in ram-headed padded arm supports, the upholstered seat w/gently bowed floral-carved seatrail, raised on fluted columnar legs, the matching chairs w/oval upholstered back panels above the matching seats & legs, France, late 19th c., settee 60" l., the suite (ILLUS.) **$14,400**

Fine Louis XVI-Style Three-Piece Parlor Suite

Louis XVI-Style: two open-arm armchairs & a settee; giltwood & tapestry upholstery, the settee w/a long oval back w/tapestry upholstery within a frame w/a ribbon- and bead-carved frame raised above the seat flanked by padded open arms, narrow carved apron raised on tapering cylindrical stop-fluted legs, matching armchairs oval backs, France, late 19th c., armchairs 36" h., settee, 4' 7 1/2" l., the set (ILLUS.)......... **$2,350**

Rare Victorian Renaissance Revival Parlor Suite

Victorian Renaissance Revival style: sofa & two side chairs; carved & gilt walnut, each piece w/a carved & stepped crestrail centered by a raised panel w/arched crest & enclosing an oval inset porcelain plaque h.p. w/scenes of courting couples & flowers, crestrail ending in leaf & pendant-carved corners above the carved narrow stiles, each piece w/a tufted upholstered back, the sofa w/padded open arms ending in carved sphinx heads above gilt-trimmed carved flutes, the gently curved front seatrails further decorated w/incised carving trimmed in gold, the sofa w/square tapering end legs w/carved paw feet & two knob- and columnar-carved inner legs, all raised on casters, the side chairs w/square tapering legs ending in paw feet on casters, New York City or New Jersey, ca. 1860-1875, sofa 68" l., chairs 38 1/2", the suite (ILLUS.)......... **$14,400**

Victorian Rococo Parlor Suite Attributed to John Belter

Victorian Rococo style: settee & armchair: carved rosewood, the settee w/a very ornate pierce-carved serpentine crestrail w/a high arched central section enclosing floral carving flanked by serpentine pierce-carved sections continuing into rounded scrolled corners curving down around the upholstered back, curved padded open arms w/incurved molded arm supports, long upholstered seat w/serpentine floral & scroll-carved seatrail ending in floral-carved demi-cabriole front legs on casters, matching armchair w/high arched & pierce-carved crestrail, attributed to John H. Belter, New York City, ca. 1850-60, settee 64" l., chair 42 1/4" h., the set (ILLUS., top of page) **$5,400**

Screens

Rare Edgar Brandt Iron Fire Screen

Fire screen, wrought-iron, Art Deco style, "Les Pins" design, the gently arched flat crestrail above a tall panel composed of alternating pairs of slender rods alternating w/a single wider flat bar, the top half applied w/long branches of pine boughs w/pine cones, supported on gently arched shoe feet, designed by Edgar Brandt, France, ca. 1924, 13 1/2 x 32", 33 1/2" h. (ILLUS.) **$35,850**

Rare Fornasetti 1950s Floor Screen

Floor screen, four-fold, "Libreria" design, the front of each panel decorated w/a color lithograph design representing tall book shelves also holding various decorative objects, the back decorated w/a design of spears, a cat, a cello & a red cloth, designed by Piero Fornasetti, Italy, 1950s, each panel 19 3/4 x 78 1/2" (ILLUS.) **$14,340**

Louis XV-Style Folding Floor Screen

Floor screen, six-fold, Louis XV-Style, painted fruitwood frame w/each arched panel w/a molded crestrail above fabric panels w/Oriental floral designs, late 19th c., fabric replaced, open 165" l., 62" h. (ILLUS.).. **$1,265**

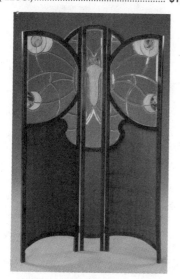

Unusual Art Nouveau Butterfly Screen

Floor screen, three-fold, Art Nouveau style, leaded glass & stained oak, the upper half designed as a clear, blue & white leaded glass butterfly w/the body in the narrow center panel & the wings in the flanking panels, the lower panels in dark blue, attributed to the Wiener Mosaic Werkstatte, Austria, ca. 1905, overall 45 1/2" w., 73" h. (ILLUS.)...................... **$2,151**

Secretaries

Fine Chippendale Secretary-Bookcase

Chippendale secretary-bookcase, carved cherry, two-piece construction: the upper section w/a rectangular top w/narrow crestrail above a pair of tall geometrically-glazed cupboard doors opening to wooden shelves; the lower section formed by a slant-front desk w/the wide hinged front opening to an interior fitted w/a row of pigeonholes centered by a small sunburst-carved drawer above two rows of small drawers, the lower case w/four long graduated drawers w/pierced butterfly brasses flanked by reeded quarter-round columns, molded base on scroll-carved ogee bracket feet, Connecticut, late 18th c., replaced brasses, refinished, alterations, 21 x 39 1/2", 81" h. (ILLUS.) **$6,463**

Rare Chippendale Secretary-Bookcase

Chippendale secretary-bookcase, mahogany, two-part construction: the upper section w/a rectangular top above a flaring dentil-carved cornice above a pair of tall geometrically-glazed doors opening to three wooden shelves; the lower stepped-out section w/a hinged fold-down slant front opening to an interior composed of small drawers, pigeonholes & a central door, the lower case w/three long graduated drawers w/simple bail pulls, molded base on scroll-cut bracket feet, underside of interior drawer w/original paper label reading "Elbert Anderson - Makes all kinds of - CABINET WARE - on the most Modern & Approved - Methods & on the most reasonable terms - No. 5 or 53 - Maiden Lane in- NEW YORK," one drawer w/a later inscription, New York City, 1786-96, 24 1/4 x 49 3/4", 88 7/8" h. (ILLUS.) **$21,600**

Classical secretary-bookcase, mahogany & mahogany veneer, three-part construction: the upper section w/a wide gently peaked removable cornice above a pair of tall pointed arch glazed doors opening to wooden shelves above a row of three small drawers; the stepped-out lower section w/a fold-out writing surface above a long narrow round-fronted drawer over a pair of paneled cupboard doors, scroll-cut bracket feet, ca. 1840-50, 83 1/2" h. (ILLUS., top next column) **$1,668**

Classical Three-Part Secretary-Bookcase

Finely Veneered Classical Secretary

Classical secretary-bookcase, mahogany & mahogany veneer, two-part construction: the upper section w/a rectangular top above a deep flaring cornice trimmed w/a thin beaded band above a pair of tall glazed cupboard doors w/beaded banding around the panes & opening to three adjustable wooden shelves above a row of three small drawers w/turned wood knobs; the lower section w/a foldout writing surface above a case of three long graduated drawers w/turned wood knobs, shaped apron & simple bracket feet, ca. 1840, 21 x 42", 80 1/2" h. (ILLUS.) **$1,380**

Fine Figured Maple & Mahogany Secretary

Federal secretary-bookcase, inlaid mahogany & figured maple, two-part construction: the upper section w/a rectangular top w/a low curved front cornice centered by a high rectangular panel topped by an urn-turned finial, matching corner finials, above a mahogany frieze band centered by an inlaid figured maple rectangle above a pair of tall cupboard doors w/eight narrow panes in each above a recessed rectangular lower panel w/inlaid figured maple border; the stepped-out lower section a case of four long drawers w/figured maple veneer banding & two oval brasses, the arched apron centered by an inlaid fan, ring-turned tapering legs ending in knob feet, North Shore Massachusetts, 1790-1810, appear to retain original brasses, 18 x 40", 85 1/2" h. (ILLUS.) **$9,600**

Unusual Southern Federal Secretary

Federal secretary-bookcase, inlaid mahogany, two-part construction: the upper section w/a rectangular top above a pair of geometrically-glazed cupboard doors flanking a flat center door opening to a sectioned interior; the stepped-out lower section w/a foldout writing surface above a case of four long graduated drawers w/oval pulls, narrow shaped skirt & tall splayed feet, Southern U.S., possibly Georgia, ca. 1800, missing some interior dividers, damage to left hinge of writing surface, damage to back of side panels, old repairs, 22 x 44", 57 1/2" h. (ILLUS.) **$2,875**

Shelves

Wall shelf, country-style, carved & painted, a long narrow shelf w/a deeply scalloped backboard supported on tapering serpentine end brackets flanking a wide lower board w/a deeply scalloped bottom edge, compass-etched decoration, dark grey paint, Pennsylvania, 19th c., 6 3/4 x 69 1/4", 19" h. (ILLUS., bottom of page) **$3,840**

F

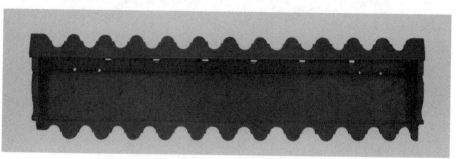

Long Scalloped Pennsylvania Wall Shelf

F

Fancy Four-Shelf Wall Shelf

Wall shelves, walnut, the wide backboard
w/a high arched & scroll-carved crest
w/shaped finial w/hanging hold above
two pierced stars, mounted w/four rectangular open sides each supported at
the front corners by slender baluster-
turned spindles, arched base rail, old
dark surface, two shelf end pieces old
replacements, attributed to New Hampshire, 19th c., 6 1/2 x 20 1/4", 40 1/4" h.
(ILLUS.) **$805**

Sideboards

Art Deco sideboard, chrome-mounted
black lacquered wood & parchment, rectangular w/fitted glass top, designed by
Jacques Adnet, France, ca. 1940,
18 1/4 x 46 1/4", 77 1/2" l. (ILLUS., top
next column)... **$21,510**

*Art Deco Chrome-mounted Black
Lacquer Sideboard*

*Fine Mission Oak Sideboard by
Gustav Stickley*

Arts & Crafts sideboard, oak, the rectangular top w/a low three-quarters gallery
above a case fitted w/a row of three short
drawers above a pair of flat cupboard
doors flanking a stack of three drawers, a
single long drawer across the bottom,
each fitted w/a rectangular copper & bail
pull, the long arched apron flanked by
bootjack ends, original dark finish, Model
No. 804, red decal mark of Gustav
Stickley, ca. 1904, 22 x 54 1/4",
42 3/8" h. (ILLUS.) **$14,340**

Finely Carved Mahogany Chippendale-Style Pedestal Sideboard

Fine New York City Classical Sideboard

Chippendale-Style sideboard, carved mahogany, double-pedestal style, each end pedestal w/a gadrooned top edge over a concave drawer above a single flat drawer w/bail pulls over a tall cupboard door decorated w/a large delicately scroll-carved raised rectangular panel, flanking a bowed center drop section w/a flat backboard above a top w/gadrooned edges over a pair of bowed drawers flanking a central swag-carved panel, each pedestal w/a gadroon-carved apron raised on four cabriole legs w/leaf-carved knees & ending in claw-and-ball feet, England, ca. 1870, 89 1/2" l., 46 3/4" h. (ILLUS., bottom previous page) **$2,070**

Southern Classical Mahogany Server

Classical server, mahogany & mahogany veneer, the rectangular top w/a high splashback w/rounded corners above a case w/a pair of drawers w/pairs of turned wood knobs projecting over a row of three paneled cupboard doors flanked by ring-turned columns above beehive-turned front legs, Southern, possibly Beaufort or Charleston, veneer chips, shrinkage cracks, old repairs, ca. 1820, 22 1/2 x 50 3/4", 46 5/8" h. (ILLUS.) **$2,300**

Classical sideboard, mahogany & mahogany veneer, the top backed by a stepped blacksplash w/a flat center crest of blocked column ends enclosing three mirrors, the long white marble top w/an indented central section above a conforming case w/a long curve-fronted center drawer flanked by projecting flat drawers, all raised on four simple turned columns framing tall paneled end doors flanking the deep set-back center opening w/a white marble shelf backed by a large mirror, flat base w/four blocked supports, New York City, school of Duncan Phyfe, ca. 1825-30, some veneer damage, 27 x 75 3/8", 53" h. (ILLUS., top of page) **$3,450**

F

French Empire-style Sideboard

Empire-Style sideboard, gilt bronze-mounted mahogany, two-part construction: the upper section surmounted by a scrolling palmette & acanthus leaf finial over a rectangular case w/glazed doors flanked by rounded glazed panels above gilt bellflower & acanthus cast supports; the lower section w/a rectangular white marble top over a conforming case w/a pair of frieze drawers above a pair of doors centering a panel mounted w/gilt-bronze ribbon-tied laurel wreath flanked by fluted stiles headed w/gilt-bronze foliate mounts over a stepped apron centering a gilt swagged rocaille mount, raised on toupie feet, France, late 19th c., 22 x 64", 6' 10" h. (ILLUS.)...................... **$4,406**

*Very Rare Federal Inlaid Mahogany
"Serpentine-Front" Small Sideboard*

Federal "serpentine-front" sideboard, inlaid mahogany, diminutive size, the rectangular top w/a serpentine bowed front above a conforming case, a pair of concave-front banded & line-inlaid drawers flanking a long serpentine-front central drawer over a pair of deep concave banded & line-inlaid bottle drawers flanking a pair of banded & line-inlaid serpentine center doors, drawers w/oval brasses, front divided by four line-inlaid stiles that continue down to form the square tapering line-inlaid legs, two square tapering rear legs, Rhode Island or New York City, 1790-1810, 23 x 58 1/4", 42" h. (ILLUS.) **$45,600**

Fine New York Federal Server

Federal server, carved mahogany & mahogany veneer, the rectangular top

above a deep apron w/a single long banded drawer w/brass lion head & ring pulls, raised on spiraling leaf-carved supports w/ring- and knob-turned caps above a long medial shelf w/an incurved front, raised on paw-carved front feet, New York City, 1815-25, 19 1/2 x 46 1/2", 41" h. (ILLUS.) **$7,200**

*Rare Large Federal Inlaid
Mahogany Sideboard*

Federal sideboard, inlaid mahogany, the rectangular top w/a serpentine front & oval corners above a conforming string-inlaid case, a long central drawer flanked by smaller drawers above a central pair of recessed doors & convex panels flanked by curved end doors, all raised on square tapering legs inlaid w/panels, urns & stringing continuing to cuffs & joined lower edge of geometric banding, replaced brasses, refinished, probably New York City, ca. 1795, imperfections, 27 1/2 x 71", 40 3/8" h. (ILLUS.) **$29,375**

*Fine Inlaid Mahogany Federal-Style
Sideboard*

Federal-Style "bowfront" sideboard, inlaid mahogany & mahogany veneer, the rectangular top w/a slightly stepped-out bowed center section above a conforming case w/a pair of bowed line-inlaid drawers flanking a long center bowed drawer inlaid w/panels to resemble three drawers, all w/oval brasses w/stamped eagles, two bowed & line-inlaid end doors flanking a pair of bowed line-inlaid center drawers flanked by arch-inlaid vertical panels, raised on six square tapering line-inlaid legs, 20th c., minor veneer damage & stains in the top, 73 3/4" l., 39" h. (ILLUS.) **$1,265**

Early Louis XVI Fruitwood Buffet

Louis XVI buffet, fruitwood, the rectangular molded top w/canted corners above a conforming case w/three short frieze drawers above three paneled cupboard doors divided by scrolling cast-metal mounts, raised on square tapering legs, France, late 18th - early 19th c., 25 x 80", 46" h. (ILLUS., top of page) **$6,463**

case w/a pair of long narrow ornately carved drawers over a pair of rectangular cupboard doors each carved w/a pair of tall narrow vertical scroll-carved panels flanking a central oval panel carved w/fish & fowl trophies, the angled corners w/turned colonettes, the deep flat base w/projecting corner blocks, ca. 1870, 24 1/2 x 69", overall 88" h. (ILLUS.)........ **$4,225**

F

Stands

Very Fine Carved Renaissance Sideboard

Victorian Renaissance Revival style sideboard, carved oak, the high super-structure topped by a high arched & or-nate pierce-carved crest w/scrolling leaves & flowers centered by a realistic fox head above a tall back w/two narrow graduated open shelves raised on turned spindles & backed by pairs of carved panels centered by a paterae, all resting on the long rectangular top w/angled pro-jecting front corners above a conforming

Rare Early Chippendale Candlestand

Candlestand, Chippendale tilt-top style, walnut, the round dished top above a birdcage tilting mechanism above the baluster- and ring-turned pedestal, tripod base w/cabriole legs ending in claw-and-ball feet, Chester County, Pennsylvania, 1750-70, 20" d., 27" h. (ILLUS.)............ **$14,400**

F

Federal Inlaid Mahogany Candlestand

Candlestand, Federal style, inlaid mahogany, the nearly square top w/chamfered corners decorated w/a band of line-inlay, tilted above a columnar-turned pedestal on a tripod base w/spider legs, probably New York, 1790-1810, 22 7/8 x 25 5/8", 29 1/2" h. (ILLUS.) **$4,800**

Rare Federal Inlaid Candlestand

Candlestand, Federal, inlaid & carved mahogany, long octagonal top w/banded inlay tilting above a tapering fluted & leaf-carved pedestal on a tripod base w/spider feet ending in tapering blocks, Boston, possibly carved by Thomas Wightman, 1800-10, 19 x 26 1/2", 29 1/4" h. (ILLUS.) **$28,800**

Federal Oval-topped Candlestand

Candlestand, Federal style, cherry, the elongated oval top tilting above a slender baluster- and ring-turned pedestal on a tripod base w/flat cabriole legs ending in snake feet, steel reinforcing plate on the bottom, some old repair, slight warp to top, ca. 1800, 27 3/4" h. (ILLUS.) **$660**

Fine Queen Anne Candlestand

Candlestand, Queen Anne, cherry & maple, the round top above a turned columnar pedestal w/a knobbed base raised on a tripod base w/cabriole legs ending in snake feet, probably Pennsylvania, late 18th - early 19th c., 17" d., 24 1/2" h. (ILLUS.) **$9,000**

Country Queen Anne Candlestand

Candlestand, Queen Anne country-style, painted, the round top above a slender baluster- and ring-turned pedestal on a tripod base w/flat cabriole legs ending in snake feet, old green paint, New England, 18th c., 17" d., 26" h. (ILLUS.)...... **$2,640**

Federal Painted & Decorated Stand

Federal one-drawer stand, painted & decorated, the nearly square top decorated w/a decoupaged design above the decorated apron fitted w/a single drawer w/two round brass pulls, square slender tapering legs, old ebonized background, old paper label inscribed w/the name of the owner/decorator in Worcester, Massachusetts, New England, first half 19th c., 14 x 15 1/2", 26 1/4" h. (ILLUS.) **$2,640**

Art Nouveau Mahogany Fern Stand

Fern stand, mahogany, Art Nouveau style, the square top above a narrow paneled apron w/brass looping vines, tall slender square slightly bowed legs w/curved brackets at the apron & joined by a small square lower shelf, top slightly warped, stained in middle, ca. 1900, 44" h. (ILLUS.) **$575**

Rare Chippendale Mahogany Kettle Stand

Kettle stand, Chippendale, mahogany, square top w/low undulating gallery & candle slide raised on a ring-turned columnar post on a tripod base w/cabriole legs ending in arise pad feet on platforms, old refinish, probably Massachusetts, imperfections, 12 x 12 1/4", 24" h. (ILLUS., previous page) **$11,163**

George III-Style Mahogany Music Stand

Music stand, George III-Style, carved mahogany, adjustable folio racks w/hinged & slated sides raised on a slender column-turned pedestal above a tripod base w/legs carved to resemble human legs wearing low shoes, England, late 19th - early 20th c., 24" w., 39 3/4" h. (ILLUS.) **$489**

Unusual Art Nouveau Nightstands

Nightstands, Art Nouveau style, ormolu-mounted carved mahogany, small square pink marble inset tops w/high arched & loop-pierced backsplash above a case w/a small narrow drawer supported by slender flower-carved legs w/forked stems at the top above a tall open compartment above a lower shelf over a small square paneled door, ser-

pentine leaf-carved apron on short canted feet, the lower cabinets lined w/white marble, designed by Louis Majorelle, France, ca. 1905, 13 x 16 1/8", 41" h., pr. (ILLUS.) **$8,365**

Victorian Federal-Style Sewing Stand

Sewing stand, Federal-Style, mahogany, the rectangular top w/rounded ends hinged to open to a divided interior w/pleated upholstered sides & ends, the upholstered panels separated by narrow reeded posts continuing into the very slender ring- and rod-turned legs, New York City or New England, late 19th c., replaced fabric, 13 1/4 x 23 1/2", 28 3/4" h. (ILLUS.) **$1,100**

Rare Tiger Stripe Maple Classical Washstand

Washstand, Classical style, tiger stripe maple, the rectangular top fitted w/a high rolled three-quarters gallery above a single long drawer w/a small round brass replaced pulls, raised on four simple turned posts joined a rectangular medial shelf w/incurved sides, raised on knob- and ring-turned legs w/knob feet, old refinish, Pennsylvania or Ohio, ca. 1830s, imperfections, 16 x 31", 34" h. (ILLUS.) **$5,875**

Rare New Hampshire Federal Washstand

Washstand, Federal corner-style, inlaid mahogany, the quarter-round top w/a delicate arched backsplash w/a tiny shelf above a top w/a large central hole flanked by smaller holes, the edge of the top w/delicate banded inlay, raised on three slender square supports above a medial shelf above an inlaid apron centered by a small drawer, raised on three slender outswept legs joined by a T-form stretcher, probably Portsmouth, New Hampshire, 1800-10, 16 1/2 x 23", 41" h. (ILLUS.).. **$11,400**

Lovely Federal Mahogany Washstand

Washstand, Federal style, inlaid mahogany, the rectangular hinged top w/inlaid edge & attached faux drawer front w/oval crotch mahogany panels bordered by stringing & mitered border opening to a pierced seat above two faux string-inlaid drawers w/ivory diamond escutcheons, all on slightly flaring French feet joined by a

shaped skirt w/inlaid crossbanding, original brasses, old refinish, probably Massachusetts, ca. 1805, minor imperfections, 16 1/2 x 23", 27 1/2" h. (ILLUS.).... **$3,055**

Stools

Classical piano stool, rosewood veneer, the squared upholstered top above a deep serpentine apron, adjusting above a heavy tapering octagonal column resting on a cross-form base w/tapering feet, veneer damages, ca. 1840, 15" w., 20" h. (ILLUS. right with matching stool).... **$690**

Two Classical Rosewood Piano Stools

Classical piano stool, rosewood veneer, the squared upholstered top above a deep serpentine apron, adjusting above a heavy tapering octagonal column resting on a cross-form base w/tapering feet, good condition, ca. 1840, 15" w., 20" h. (ILLUS. left with matching stool) **$805**

Original Louis XV Fruitwood Stool

Louis XV stool, carved fruitwood, the rectangular tapestry-upholstered seat above a fancy scroll-carved apron raised on cabriole legs ending in scroll feet, France, 18th c., 19 1/2 x 23 1/2", 16" h. (ILLUS.).. **$2,415**

Louis XV-Style stools, parcel-gilt carved walnut, the deep rounded square upholstered seat above a serpentine carved apron raised on slender cabriole legs ending in scroll-and-peg feet, France, late 19th c., 16" w., 19" h., pr. (ILLUS., top next page) **$920**

Pair of Carved Walnut Louis XV-Style Stools

Tables

signed by Andre Arubs, France, ca. 1940, 27 1/2" d., 25 3/4" h. (ILLUS.) **$17,925**

Rare French Art Deco Table

Art Deco side table, fruitwood, "Soleil" design, round top on a flat round apron w/four low blocks above the square tapering legs capped by turned brass disks & resting on square brass foot caps, de-

Unique Art Deco "MB 106" Side Table

Art Deco side table, walnut, model "MB 106," fan-shaped extension-type, the two-tier fanned top supported by a single straight slender front leg & backed w/two tiered & curved backboards, designed by Pierre Chareau, France, ca. 1928, extended 15 x 24", 24" h. (ILLUS. extended) **$50,190**

Chippendale Cherry Pennsylvania Dining Table

Extraordinary Salem, Massachusetts Mahogany Chippendale Dressing Table

Courtesy of Christie's, New York

F

Chippendale dining table, cherry, the rectangular top flanked by wide rectangular drop leaves, raised on square tapering legs w/two forming swing-out leaf supports, Pennsylvania, 18th c., open 48 1/2 x 48 3/4", 29 1/2" h. (ILLUS., bottom previous page) **$7,200**

Chippendale dressing table, carved mahogany, the rectangular top w/molded edges overhanging the deep case w/a long drawer above a row of three deep square drawers, the center one shell-carved, serpentine-carved apron raised on cabriole legs ending in claw-and-ball feet, drawers w/original brass butterfly pulls, Salem, Massachusetts, 1770-90, descended in the Hancock Family, 19 3/4 x 35 3/4", 31" h. (ILLUS., top of page)... **$119,500**

Extremely Rare Carved Walnut Chippendale Dressing Table from Philadelphia

Courtesy of Skinner, Inc., Bolton, Massachusetts

Chippendale dressing table, carved walnut, the rectangular top w/molded edges & front notched corners overhangs a case w/a long drawer w/butterfly brasses & keyholed escutcheons over a pair of small square drawers flanking a deep drawer finely carved w/a large shell, C-scrolls & scrolling acanthus leaves, fluted front corners, the apron finely pierce- and reverse-carved w/scrolls flanked by cabriole legs w/shell- and scroll-carved knees & ending in high-tongued trifid feet, replaced brasses, attributed to the shop of Henry Cliffton & Thomas Carteret, the carver, Nicholas Bernard, Philadelphia, 1740s-1750s, minor imperfections, rare, 20 1/2 x 34", 30" h. (ILLUS.) **$171,000**

Very Rare Chippendale Card Table

Chippendale game table, carved mahogany, the fold-over top w/serpentined front & incurved sides above a conforming deep apron w/gadrooned edging, five-legged design w/cabriole legs w/leaf-carved knees & ending in claw-and-ball feet, missing small interior drawer, New York City, 1760-90, 16 3/8 x 34 1/4", 27 1/2" h. (ILLUS.)........ **$42,000**

Rare Chippendale Walnut Card Table

Chippendale Tilt-top Tea Table

Fine Chippendale Game Table

Chippendale game table, carved mahogany, the rectangular fold-over hinged top w/serpentine edges & rounded corners overhangs the serpentine skirt w/a scribed edge & a shell-carved center flanked by molded slightly tapering legs w/inside chamfering, Massachusetts, 1760-80, old refinish, minor imperfections, 18 1/4 x 34 1/2", 29" h. (ILLUS.).... **$7,050**

Chippendale game table, carved walnut, the rectangular hinged fold-over top above a deep apron w/a scallop-cut front, raised on four slender cabriole legs, the front two w/leaf-carved knees, all ending in claw-and-ball feet, 18th c., 14 3/8 x 30", 29 3/4" h. (ILLUS., top next column) **$14,340**

Chippendale "tilt-top" tea table, carved mahogany, the round top w/a scalloped dished rim tilting above a revolving birdcage supports atop a columnar-turned pedestal on a tripod base w/cabriole legs ending in claw-and-ball feet, some alternations, ca. 1790, 32" d., 27 1/2" h. (ILLUS., middle next column).................. **$3,680**

Massachusetts Tilt-top Tea Table

Fine Classical Veneered Rosewood Dining Table

Chippendale tilt-top tea table, mahogany, the squared top w/serpentine edges tilting on a slender baluster- and ring-turned pedestal raised on a tripod base w/cabriole legs ending in arise pad feet on platforms, Massachusetts, late 18th c., old refinish, minor imperfections, 20 3/4 x 21", 26" h. (ILLUS., previous page) **$5,288**

Classical child's work table, carved mahogany & mahogany veneer, the rectangular top w/oval corners w/inset brass rosettes framed by concentric rings above quarter-engaged corner posts carved w/baskets of fruit against a punchwork ground, flanking the case w/a deep drawer over a shallow drawer, each w/pairs of round brass pulls, a yellow cloth workbag suspended under the case, raised on ring- & spiral-turned tapering legs ending in peg feet on casters, old pulls, probably Massachusetts, ca. 1825, refinished, imperfections, 14 1/2 x 15 3/4", 20 1/4" h. (ILLUS., bottom next column) **$8,813**

Classical dining table, carved & veneered rosewood, the veneered round top w/molded edge tilts & overhanging the skirt raised on a ten-panel tapering pedestal ending in shaped rosewood petals on a platform w/rosewood veneered rays ending in a molded edge above three carved paw feet flanked by carved scrolled returns, New York City, ca. 1830, 55" d., 28 1/2" h. (ILLUS., top of page) **$3,408**

Fine Early Classical Child's Work Table

Fine Classical Mahogany Extension Dining Table

Classical dining table, mahogany, extension-type, the round top opening to receive nine leaves, raised on a heavy round split column supported on four shaped projecting angled legs w/thin disk feet, New York City, ca. 1840, closed 60" d., 30" h. (ILLUS.) **$2,875**

F

Classical Dressing Table with Mirror

Classical dressing table, mahogany & mahogany veneer, a tall rectangular mirror in a wide ogee frame swiveling between two heavy square posts resting on a narrow rectangular top over a pair of long drawers each w/two small turned wood knobs, resting on a stepped-out rectangular top above a case w/two long graduated drawers w/turned wood knobs, raised on block-, ring- and knob-turned legs ending in ball feet, ca. 1840, 21 x 39", overall 71" h. (ILLUS.) **$2,530**

Unusual Classical Dressing Table

Classical dressing table, mahogany & mahogany veneer, the superstructure w/a tall oblong mirror within a Gothic arch frame swiveling within a U-shaped wishbone support raised above a long narrow serpentine top over a conforming row of three small handkerchief drawers, all resting on a rectangular white marble top w/serpentine sides atop a conforming apron, the front edge supported by long S-scroll supports joined by a narrow incurved medial shelf backed by a wide veneered back panel, New York City, ca. 1830, 19 1/2 x 44", 78" h. (ILLUS.) **$2,300**
Classical game table, carved mahogany & mahogany veneer, the rectangular fold-over top w/rounded front corners above a convex apron raised on a tapering square

Classical Carved Mahogany Game Table

pedestal w/recessed panels, resting on a concave-shaped platform above scroll-carved feet on casters, old refinish, probably by Isaac Vose, Boston, ca. 1825, imperfections, 18 x 37", 29 1/4" h. (ILLUS.)... **$1,058**

Paw-footed Classical Game Table

Classical game table, mahogany & mahogany veneer, the long D-form hinged fold-over top above a deep conforming apron, raised on four turned columns resting on a quatrepartite platform raised on outswept winged paw feet on casters, New York City, ca. 1825, some veneer damage, 17 1/2 x 36" closed, 30" h. (ILLUS.) **$1,495**

Very Fine Boston Classical Game Table

Classical game table, mahogany & mahogany veneer, the rectangular fold-over top w/rounded corners raised on a heavy turned & acanthus leaf-carved pedestal supported by four arched, molded & outswept legs ending in brass paws on casters, Boston, in the manner of Timothy Hunt, ca. 1825, 17 7/8 x 36", 28" h. (ILLUS.) **$4,380**

Classical Pier Table Possibly from the Shop of Duncan Phyfe

Classical pier table, mahogany & mahogany veneer, the long rectangular white marble top above a deep coved veneered apron, square S-scroll front supports resting on projecting stretchers flanking the large rectangular back mirror, raised on thick block feet, attributed to the Shop of Duncan Phyfe, New York City, ca. 1825-40, 20 1/4 x 58 1/4", 37 1/2" h. (ILLUS., top of page) **$14,400**

Classical Lyre-based Pier Table

Classical pier table, mahogany & mahogany veneer, the rectangular black & gold marble top w/beveled edges resting on a deep ogee apron raised on a boldly scrolling lyre-form pedestal enclosing a mirror, resting on a wide tapering rectangular platform on ogee bracket feet on casters, ca. 1840, 18 x 35 1/2", 34" h. (ILLUS.)... **$3,110**

Classical pier table, mahogany & mahogany veneer, the rectangular white marble top above a long ogee-front apron drawer raised on long squared S-scroll supports above a lower shelf backed by a large rectangular mirror, projecting C-scroll front feet, Philadelphia, ca. 1835, 19 x 42", 19" h. (ILLUS., top next column) **$4,370**

Fine Philadelphia Classical Pier Table

F

Fine New York Classical Pier Table

Classical pier table, ormolu- and gilt gesso-trimmed rosewood, the rectangular white marble top on a deep apron w/ebonized molding & rosewood veneer w/brass gilt mounts showing Psyche & Cupid in a chariot being drawn by peacocks, flanked by similarly dressed female figures watering flowers, the bottom edge w/a reticulated brass band, raised on columnar front legs w/gilt acanthus leaf capitals, tapering white marble columns on turned gilt plinths, w/corresponding square tapering rear pilasters flanking the central large rectangular mirror, all joined by a shelf w/concave front w/gilt scrolling designs of flowers & cornucopias & applied brass beaded edge all raised on gilt gesso & acanthus leaf-carved front hairy paw feet, New York City, ca. 1825, refinished, restorations & imperfections, 19 1/2 x 50 1/2", 37" h. (ILLUS.).. **$7,050**

Lyre-based Classical Side Table

Classical side table, mahogany, the round top above a large open lyre-shaped pedestal fitted w/brass rod strings, raised on a small round platform atop three outswept squared legs ending in brass paw feet on casters, old refinish, Middle Atlantic States, ca. 1830, 17 3/4" d., 30" h. (ILLUS.) **$1,528**

Classical Tilt-top Side Table

Classical side table, papier-mâché & ebonized wood, the round papier-mâché top decorated w/a floral cluster tilting above a tall slender ring-turned post above a tripod base w/three flat S-scroll legs, mid-19th c., 20 1/2" d., 27 1/2" h. (ILLUS.) **$633**

Classical sofa table, carved rosewood, the rectangular top w/molded edges flanked by D-form end drop leaves above a slightly bowed apron fitted w/a pair of paneled drawers & w/a small turned drop at each

Interesting Classical Sofa Table

corner, raised on a trestle-form base w/four ring- and spiral-turned legs resting on arched long shoe feet joined by a ring- and spirial-turned stretcher, New York City, ca. 1840, 25 x 27 1/2" closed, 29" h. (ILLUS.).... **$575**

Unusual Classical Tilt-top Side Table

Classical tilt-top side table, walnut, the large round refinished top tilting above a heavy ring- and baluster-turned post raised on a tripod base w/flat serpentine legs ending in scrolled feet, Southern U.S., mid-19th c., 35 1/2" d., 29" h. (ILLUS.)............. **$3,910**

Country Curly Maple Dining Table

Country-style dining table, curly maple, rectangular top flanked by wide hinged D-form drop leaves, the apron fitted w/a drawer at one end, raised on slender ring-turned tapering legs ending in ball & peg feet, good color, minor wear, 20 1/2 x 40" plus 14" w. leaves, 29" h. (ILLUS.)... **$920**

British Country-Style Beech Trestle Table

Country-style trestle table, beech, the large rectangular top w/breadboard ends raised on a trestle base w/double posts each joined by through-tenon rails, raised on shoe feet, Britain, 18th c., 31 1/2 x 56 3/4", 31 1/4" h. (ILLUS.) **$1,793**

Early Southern Heart Pine Work Table

Country-style work table, heart pine, the wide square plank top overhanging a deep apron w/a single long drawer w/turned wood knobs, raised on tapering octagonal legs, nicks, scuffs & separations to top, short additions to each leg, Southern U.S., late 18th c., 48" w., 32 1/2" h. (ILLUS.) **$1,093**

Very Fine French Empire-Style Ormolu-mounted Pier Table

F

Empire-Style pier table, ormolu-mounted mahogany & mahogany veneer, the rectangular white & grey marble top above a conforming apron applied w/ormolu griffins, anthemia, paterae & lyres, supported on each side by a full-figure seated winged sphinx, the paneled back centered by a ormolu Medusa mask within an ormolu diamond panel, the deep apron further decorated on the sides & recessed back w/long scroll & florette ormolu mounts & figural ormolu mounts at the front above the leaf-carved gilt knob feet, France, late 19th c., 18 x 51", 39" h. (ILLUS., bottom previous page) **$10,200**

Unusual Federal Saddler's Table

Federal country-style saddler's table, painted, the nearly square top w/a molded edge mounted w/an angled two-board saddle support, a single deep drawer w/a turned wood knob below the top, raised

on two slender square legs & two slender square legs forming a trestle support at one side, old blue paint, 19th c., 19" w., 31 1/2" h. (ILLUS.) **$720**

Rare Small Federal Walnut Side Table

Federal country-style side table, walnut, the nearly square top widely overhanging a canted apron fitted w/a single drawer, tall slender tapering splayed square legs, old refinish, probably Pennsylvania, early 19th c. 19 3/4 x 20", 28" h. (ILLUS.) **$10,575**

Federal dining table, inlaid walnut, extension-type, a center section w/rectangular top flanked by rectangular hinged drop leaves & square tapering legs ending in spade feet, flanked by two D-form end sections on square tapering legs ending in spade feet, skirts & legs inlaid w/stringing & bellflowers, Southern U.S., possibly Georgia, ca. 1825-35, dry & water-stained finish, old repairs, open 44 1/8 x 113 1/4", 29 3/4" h. (ILLUS., bottom of page) **$4,140**

Fine Southern Federal Inlaid Walnut Dining Table

Rare Baltimore Federal Inlaid Game Table

Federal game table, inlaid mahogany, the fold-over demilune top w/a half-round inlaid panel in the center, above a conforming apron w/two paterae-inlaid panels heading two tall square tapering legs w/long bellflower pendent drops, pairs of square tapering rear legs, Baltimore, Maryland, ca. 1800-10, some veneer damage, 19 x 38", 29 1/2" h. (ILLUS.) .. **$24,000**

Fine New York Inlaid Federal Game Table

Federal game table, inlaid mahogany, the hinged half-round top w/a flat projecting center & banded inlay trim above an apron divided by four blocked panels w/oval inlays above the tall slender square tapering line-inlaid legs, a swing-out fifth support leg, New York City, 1780-1810, 18 3/4 x 38", 29 1/2" h. (ILLUS.)................ **$3,840**

Fine Federal Inlaid Game Table

F

Federal game table, mahogany w/satinwood inlay, the hinged fold-over D-form top w/notched corners & line inlay above a deep apron w/rectangular line-inlaid panels, raised on four square tapering legs w/further line inlay, New York or New Jersey, late 18th - early 19th c., 16 1/8 x 26 1/8" closed, 32 1/2" h. (ILLUS.) **$2,185**

Federal game tables, inlaid mahogany & flame birch, the hinged rectangular top w/serpentine banded inlay edges & oval corners above a conforming apron w/wide panels of birch inlay centered by a large inlaid front oval, raised on slender ring-turned & reeded legs ending in tall slender peg feet, probably Portsmouth, New Hampshire, 1800-10, 18 x 36", 29" h., pr. (ILLUS., bottom of page)........ **$54,000**

Extremely Rare New Hampshire Inlaid Federal Game Tables

F

Fine Federal Inlaid Cherry Work Table

Federal work table, inlaid cherry, the nearly square top above an apron fitted w/two narrow drawers centered by inlaid ovals & fitted w/pairs of small round brass pulls, raised on tall tapering ring-turned & fluted legs ending in peg feet, probably Massachusetts, 1800-15, 16 1/2 x 18", 28 1/2" h. (ILLUS.) **$5,975**

Rare Inlaid Federal Work Table

Federal work table, mahogany & bird's-eye maple veneer, the rectangular top of bird's-eye maple veneer bordered by mahogany crossbanding w/ebonized oval corners w/concentric rings centering ivory bosses above two cockbeaded graduated bird's-eye maple drawers w/embossed brass pulls & ivory keyhole escutcheons, the corners w/quarter-engaged ring-turned posts continuing into slender reeded tapering legs on casters, probably Massachusetts, ca. 1810-15, imperfections, 17 x 21 1/2", 28 3/4" h. (ILLUS.) **$14,100**

Fine Astragal-end Federal Work Table

Federal work table, mahogany, astragal-end design, the top w/half-round end w/hinged tops flanking the rectangular central section over a deep case w/a shallow & a deep drawer w/round brass pulls flanking by reeded pilasters ending a tiny ball drops, raised on a baluster-and ring-turned pedestal supported by four reeded spider legs, old pulls, probably Philadelphia, ca. 1810-15, refinished, minor imperfections, 14 x 25 3/4", 28" h. (ILLUS.) **$2,585**

Astragal-End Federal Work Table

Federal work table, mahogany & mahogany veneer, rectangular top w/wide astragal ends, the shaped hinged top w/reeded edge opening to a compartmented interior & well below on a conforming beaded case & four slender ring-turned tapering legs on casters, old refinish, possibly Philadelphia, ca. 1805-15, imperfections, 14 3/4 x 26", 27 3/4" h. (ILLUS.) **$1,763**

Massachusetts Federal Work Table

Federal work table, mahogany, the rectangular hinged top w/inset felt writing surface opening to an interior fitted w/dividers, the case w/two long graduated drawers w/round brass pulls, raised on ring-turned fluted tapering legs ending in cannon ball feet, Massachusetts, early 19th c., 15 1/2 x 21", 30" h. (ILLUS.)....... **$1,763**

Extremely Rare Early Louisiana Table

French Provincial side table, walnut, rectangular two-board top overhanging a deep apron fitted w/a single drawer above the scalloped apron, raised on simple slender cabriole legs, made in Louisiana, late 18th c., very rare, 20 1/4 x 27 1/2", 27" h. (ILLUS.) **$54,625**

F

English George I Game Table

George I game table, carved mahogany, rectangular hinged fold-over top w/ovolu corners, opening w/a concertina action, raised on cabriole legs w/scroll-carved knees & ending in pad feet, England, early 18th c., 16 x 31", 27 1/2" h. (ILLUS.) **$1,528**

George IV writing table, ebony-inlaid & Pollard oak, rectangular top w/rounded ends above a deep apron w/a pair of long shallow drawers w/turned wood knobs, raised on a trestle base w/outswept reeded legs on casters joined by a baluster- and ring-turned cross stretcher, England, ca. 1820s, 26 1/2 x 52", 28 1/2" h. (ILLUS., bottom of page) **$4,994**

George IV Inlaid Oak Writing Table

Nice English Jacobean Oak Refrectory Table

F

Rare Early New England Pine Hutch Table

Fine Country Pine Hutch Table

Hutch (or chair) table, country-style, pine, the wide three-board top hinged above a single-board cut-out ends flanking a lift-seat opening to a compartment, possibly New England, early 19th c., refinished, 41 x 70", 29 3/4" h. (ILLUS.) **$5,581**

Hutch (or chair) table, pine, the wide rectangular three-board top tilting above one-board sides w/a curved top above a long lift seat over a deep apron, arched cut-out feet, worn brown stain, early 19th c., wear, stains, minor damage & splits, 29 x 60", 29 1/2" h. (ILLUS., top next column) **$1,265**

Jacobean refrectory table, carved oak, the long narrow top widely overhanging an apron carved w/two narrow scalloped bands on a punchwork ground, heavy ring- and rod-turned legs on block feet joined by wide flat stretchers, England, second half 17th c., some old repairs, 29 1/4 x 91", 31 1/2" h. (ILLUS., top of page) **$3,450**

Simple Mission Oak Library Table

Mission-style (Arts & Crafts movement) library table, oak, the rectangular top overhanging an apron w/a single drawer w/square wood pulls, square legs joined by side stretchers & a mortised medial shelf, early 20th c., 22 1/2 x 39", 29 1/4" h. (ILLUS.) **$313**

Scarce Early Queen Anne Dining Table

Massachusetts Queen Anne Dining Table

Maple Queen Anne Dining Table

Queen Anne dining table, mahogany, narrow rectangular top flanked by wide rectangular hinged drop leaves, raised on cabriole legs ending in pad feet on platforms, Massachusetts, 1750-70, open 46 1/2 x 46 7/8", 28" h. (ILLUS.) **$5,378**

Queen Anne dining table, maple, the rectangular top w/rounded ends flanked by two wide D-form drop leaves above a deep arched apron, raised on four slender cabriole legs ending in pad feet & two matching swing-out support legs, New England, 1740-60, open 44 x 60", 28" h. (ILLUS., top of page)............................ **$7,200**

Queen Anne dining table, maple, the rectangular top w/rounded ends flanked by a pair of D-form hinged drop leaves above a deep apron, swing-out leg supports, raised on cabriole legs ending in pad feet, New England, late 18th c., open 29 1/2 x 30", 26 3/4" h. (ILLUS., top next column) **$3,231**

Rare Bermuda-made Queen Anne Table

Very Rare Queen Anne Newport Tray-top Tea Table

F **Queen Anne dressing table,** cedar, the rectangular top overhanging an apron fitted w/a pair of deep square drawers flanking a short center drawer all w/butterfly pulls, deeply scalloped apron, straight simple turned legs ending in pad feet, Bermuda, West Indies, 1740-60, 18 1/2 x 26 1/2", 28" h. (ILLUS., previous page) **$12,000**

Fine Early Queen Anne Dressing Table

Very Rare Queen Anne Dressing Table

Queen Anne dressing table, tiger stripe maple, rectangular thumb-molded top overhanging a case w/two deep drawers w/engraved butterfly brasses flanking a short center drawer above the arched & valanced kneehole opening w/turned drops, raised on cabriole legs ending in pad feet, refinished, probably Massachusetts, 1740-60, minor imperfections, 21 1/2 x 29", 29 1/2" h. (ILLUS.) **$19,975**

Queen Anne dressing table, walnut, the rectangular top w/molded edges overhanging a deep apron w/a single long drawer above a row of three deep drawers all w/butterfly brasses, valanced apron & cabriole legs ending in pad feet, Connecticut or Massachusetts, 1740-70, 20 x 34", 29 1/2" h. (ILLUS.) **$6,600**

Queen Anne tray-top tea table, mahogany, the rectangular top w/raised molding above a narrow flat apron raised on four simple cabriole legs ending in slipper feet, Newport, Rhode Island, 1740-60, 21 x 32 3/4", 26 1/2" h. (ILLUS., top of page) **$66,000**

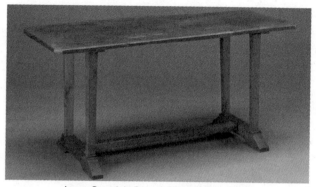

Long Spanish Colonial Hardwood Table

Spanish Colonial table, hardwood, the rectangular long single plank top w/canted corners raised on trestle supports joined by a rectangular stretcher, 19th c., 24 1/2 x 62 3/4", 30" h. (ILLUS., top of page) **$2,350**

Victorian Eastlake Marble-topped Table

Victorian Eastlake substyle parlor table, rectangular red marble top above a line-incised apron w/small turned corner drops & raised on a cross-form base centered by a turned post, the post & legs joined by a series of arched, knob-turned & line-incised stretchers, the angled feet on casters, ca. 1880, marble chipped on one corner, 19 1/2 x 27 3/8", 30 1/4" h. (ILLUS.) **$200-300**

Victorian Egyptian Revival style parlor center table, bronze-mounted gilt & marquetry-inlaid, the oval top w/a flat gilt border band w/low-relief designs of swans, dolphins & battling centaurs enclosing a large round mirror, the border divided by four projecting panels each above a full-relief carved bust of an ancient Egyptian woman joined by a deep apron centered on each side w/a large oblong floral & cartouche marquetry-inlaid panel above a narrow curved gilt border band, the head issuing long squared inswept S-scroll supports w/narrow mahogany veneer panels each ending in a paneled block on a cross-form platform centered by a round platform supporting a tall tapering urn-turned post & supported by a ring-turned base support, each paneled block issuing an arched outswept leg decorated w/a gilt top band & ending in a gilt hoof-like foot, New York City, ca. 1850, 37 1/4 x 40 5/8", 29 1/2" h. (ILLUS., bottom of page) **$42,000**

Very Rare Victorian Egyptian Revival Parlor Center Table

F

Ornately Carved Victorian Renaissance Revival Dining Table

Victorian Renaissance Revival dining table, carved oak, the round extension top w/a drapery-carved edge & deep apron raised on a heavy divided post supported by four large outswept legs each carved as a griffin issuing a cluster of fruit from its mouth, paw feet on casters, one original leaf & three associated leaves, ca. 1870, 55" d. closed, 29" h. (ILLUS.) **$2,875**

Outstanding Late Victorian Pool Table

Victorian Renaissance Revival pool table, parcel-gilt marquetry rosewood & walnut, the rectangular top w/molded edge cushions flanking six leather pockets above a molded frieze w/brass roundels above a tapering shaped & molded paneled base inlaid w/stylized flowers within diamond lozenge insets, the corners chamfered & shaped w/similar inlay, raised on four foliate-carved lion head & paw feet, the Monarch model by Brunswick, Balke, Collender, 1880-90, 4' 7" x 8' 5", 34 1/2" h. (ILLUS.)............ **$18,800**

Victorian Rococo "turtle-top" parlor center table, carved walnut, the white marble "turtle-top" above a conforming apron w/wide arched & scroll-carved center sections, raised on elaborately pierce-carved heavy S-scroll legs headed by bold bearded faces & ending in scroll feet on casters, the legs joined by scroll-carved cross-stretchered centered by a small platform mounted w/a carved reclining spaniel dog, attributed to H.N. Wenning & Co., Cincinnati, Ohio, ca. 1850, 29 x 43", 31" h. (ILLUS., next column) **$3,910**

Extraordinary Carved Walnut Rococo Parlor Table with Carved Dog

Extremely Rare Early Bermuda-made William & Mary Dining Table

F

Rare William & Mary "Butterfly" Table

William & Mary "butterfly" dining table, figured maple, a narrow rectangular top w/rounded ends flanked by wide half-round hinged drop leaves above a splayed apron & baluster- and ring-turned legs ending in turned feet & joined by matching turned stretchers centered by shaped swing-out scalloped & tapering support leaves, New England, early 18th c., refinished, minor height loss, open 40" d., 25" h. (ILLUS.) **$15,275**

William & Mary dining table, cedar, the rectangular top w/gently rounded ends flanked by wide D-form hinged drop leaves, raised on fancy bobbin-, baluster- and ring-turned legs w/swing-out gate leg supports, all joined by bobbin-turned stretchers & raised on bobbin-turned peg feet, Bermuda, early 19th c., top replaced, end of one leaf missing, 48 3/4" l., 27 1/4" h. (ILLUS., top of page) **$54,000**

Rare American William & Mary Table

William & Mary dressing table, walnut & burl walnut veneer, the rectangular top w/banded & molded edges above an apron w/two deep square drawers flanking a small shallow drawer all w/brass teardrop pulls, the deeply arched & valanced apron w/two turned drops raised on boldly turned trumpet legs joined by a serpentine X-stretcher & turnip-turned feet, Boston, 1690-1730, 21 x 32 1/2", 30 3/4" h. (ILLUS.) **$7,800**

William & Mary gate-leg dining table, maple, sycamore & pine, the rectangular top w/curved ends flanked by wide D-shaped hinged drop leaves above an apron w/a single end drawers, the leaves supported by swing-out gate legs, the baluster-, ring- and block-turned legs joined by matching turned stretchers & ending in a knob foot, old refinish, imperfections, New England, ca. 1710-20, 42 1/2" d., 26 1/2" h. (ILLUS., top next page)........ **$17,625**

Rare William & Mary Gate-leg Dining Table

Massive Early Baroque Oak Armoire

Fine William & Mary Tavern Table

William & Mary tavern table, figured maple
& pine, the oval top overhanging a deep
canted apron & baluster- and knob-turned
legs ending in knob feet & joined by flat
box stretchers, old dark painted finish,
New England, 18th c., 22 1/2 x 30 1/2",
27" h. (ILLUS.) **$9,560**

Wardrobes & Armoires

Armoire, Baroque style, oak, of massive ar-
chitectonic proportions, the outstepped
arched cornice over a pair of tall doors
w/inset oval panels divided & flanked by
pilasters headed by ebonized pierced
scrolled acanthus leaf capitals above a
pair of drawers over a stepped scrolled
base, Northern Europe, probably Germany, first quarter 18th c., 29 1/2 x 78", 8' h.
(ILLUS., top next column) **$7,050**

Rare New Orleans Classical Armoire

Armoire, Classical style, mahogany & mahogany veneer, rectangular top w/widely flaring & stepped cornice accented by a beaded band above a single tall mirrored door within a wide molding & flanked by beaded bands down the outside corners, opening to an interior w/original fitted shelves & a drawer belt, a long narrow ogee-front drawer below, raised on a deep flat apron w/low scroll-carved bracket feet, New Orleans, ca. 1840-50, 21 x 50", 99" h. (ILLUS., previous page) **$16,100**

Classical Mahogany Armoire

Armoire, Classical style, mahogany & mahogany veneer, the rectangular top w/a wide projecting stepped cornice above a plain frieze band w/blocked ends above a pair of tall paneled cupboard doors flanked by slender columns opening to an interior w/shelves on one side, deep blocked flat base raised on short turned, tapering & reeded legs w/brass ball feet, restorations, ca. 1820-30, 22 1/2 x 60", 92" h. (ILLUS.) **$7,475**

Rare Simple Louisiana Classical Armoire

Armoire, Classical style, walnut & mahogany, the thin large rectangular top overhanging a deep frieze band above a pair of tall paneled cupboard doors w/a long scrolled brass escutcheon on one door & opening to a fitted interior, deep molded base raised on heavy bulbous tapering legs ending in brass ball feet, probably made in Louisiana, ca. 1830, 22 x 56 1/2", 93" h. (ILLUS.) **$14,950**

Rare Inlaid Louisiana Armoire

Armoire, Federal style, inlaid mahogany, the rectangular top w/a cavetto cornice above a frieze band centering an inlaid octagonal lozenge enclosing a monogram & flanked by inlaid ovals & acanthus leaf inlay, a pair of tall doors w/a false center stile decorated w/a pinwheel boss inlay, unusual door construction w/irregular tapering battens, the case w/chamfered side stiles, short cabriole legs w/restoration, made in Louisiana, early 19th c., 24 x 56", 88" h. (ILLUS.) **$19,550**

Very Rare Inlaid Louisiana Armoire

F

Armoire, Federal-French Provincial style, inlaid cherry, rectangular top w/a latter wide ogee cornice above an inlaid frieze centering an inlaid monogram above a pair tall cupboard doors opening to a replaced well-fitted interior, arched scroll-cut wide apron w/unusual inlaid swag decoration, short front cabriole legs restored, made in Louisiana, early 19th c., 22 x 56", 84" h. (ILLUS., previous page) **$37,375**

Early Louis XV Walnut Armoire

Armoire, Louis XV, walnut, the outstepped cornice above a recessed frieze centering a pinwheel over a pair of tall three-panel doors above a scalloped apron, raised on short cabriole legs, France, third quarter 18th c., 22 x 61", 6' 8" h. (ILLUS.) **$4,700**

Fine Neoclassical Inlaid Rosewood Armoire

Armoire, Neoclassical style, marquetry inlaid rosewood, the rectangular top w/a flaring cornice above a narrow frieze band w/a narrow marquetry inlay above a single tall mirrored door w/banded trim & a small rectangular inlaid lower panel, the wide front sides decorated w/tall rectangular upper & lower panels w/marquetry scenes of a standing woman among flowering vines & birds, a round marquetry panel at the center, a narrow base band w/marquetry trim raised on compressed bun feet, interior fitted w/three drawers w/recessed pulls & three shelves, some minor repairs, Europe, 19th c., 18 x 45", 75 1/2" h. (ILLUS.) **$2,013**

Rare Victorian Faux-Bamboo Armoire

Armoire, Victorian faux-bamboo style, maple, the rectangular top fitted w/an elaborate gallery w/short rows of turned spindles centering at the front a large projecting block topped by a ring- and knob-turned finial, matching corner finials, all framed by bamboo-turned banding above a frieze panel w/a long rectangular raised bamboo-turned panel, all above a single tall cupboard door fitted w/a large arched mirror & trimmed w/thin bamboo-turned trim, heavy bamboo-turned posts down the front corners, a single long drawer at the bottom, open interior, disassembles easily for transportation, ca. 1880s, 23 x 45", 102" h. (ILLUS.) **$3,565**

Fine Chippendale Walnut Schrank

Schrank (massive Germanic wardrobe), Chippendale style, walnut, two-part construction: the upper section w/a rectangular top & deep covered cornice above a frieze molding over a pair of tall double raised-panel doors w/exposed H-hinges & brass keyhole escutcheons; the lower section w/a molded top above a pair of long drawers flanking a small square center drawer all w/butterfly brasses & keyhole escutcheons, molded base on scroll-carved bracket feet, Pennsylvania, ca. 1780-1800, original brasses, 26 x 60", 82" h. (ILLUS.) **$21,600**

Country Wardrobe with Paneled Doors

Wardrobe, country-style, painted pine, the rectangular top w/a widely flaring stepped cornice above a pair of tall narrow double raised panel doors opening to an interior w/a shelf & five boards w/wooden hooks, some w/added metal hooks, deep serpentine apron & simple bracket feet, original alligatored reddish brown paint, pinned & nailed construction, some edge damage &

loss of molding, mid-19th c., 24 1/4 x 50", 76" h. (ILLUS.) **$489**

Simple Pine Country Wardrobe

Wardrobe, country-style, pine, the rectangular top w/a molded cornice above a pair of tall paneled cupboard doors w/brass latches & keyhole escutcheons opening to an interior divided w/replaced shelves, wide molded base on simple bracket feet, pegged mortise joints & square nails, cleaned down to worn red finish, wear, some damage & pieced repairs, replaced latches, mid-19th c., 18 x 49 1/2", 83 1/2" h. (ILLUS.) **$345**

Whatnots & Etageres

English Regency Four-Tier Etagere

Etagere, Regency style, mahogany, the tall upright design w/a rectangular top w/a low three-quarters gallery above three additional open shelves each supported by ring- and rod-turned supports, the bottom shelf over a single narrow drawer w/two turned wood knobs, simple turned legs on brass casters, England, ca. 1820, 15 x 20", 51" h. (ILLUS.) **$2,070**

GAMES & GAME BOARDS

Early Ba-Ta-Clan Marble Game

"Ba-Ta-Clan," marble-type, Oriental design w/cardboard upright w/temple design & printed in color w/Oriental figures & openings, projecting board base, load marble in catapult & try to shoot it into one of the slots in the tray or openings in the upright, original box, N.K. Atlas, Paris, France, late 19th - early 20th c., box 9 1/2 x 19 1/4" (ILLUS.)............................. **$600**

Early Carnival Ball Toss Target

Ball toss target carnival-type, molded papier-mâché in the form of a bearded Russian Cossack wearing a fur hat & red shirt, mounted on a wooden plank w/replacement ball catcher, hole in top front of hat, some scrapes, scuffs & repaint, early 20th c., 13" w., 26 1/2" h. (ILLUS.) **$115**

"The Horse Show," board-type, colorful folding board w/a horse in each corner, w/original spinner & game pieces, colorful box cover printed in red, yellow & blue, Singer, late 19th c., box w/some damage, 9 1/2 x 19" (ILLUS., top next column) **$518**

Early "The Horse Show" Board Game

GARDEN FOUNTAINS & ORNAMENTS

Ornamental garden or yard fountains, urns and figures often enhanced the formal plantings on spacious lawns of mansion-sized dwellings during the late 19th and early 20th century. While fountains were usually reserved for the lawns of estates, even modest homes often had a latticework arbor or cast-iron urn in the yard. Today garden enthusiasts look for these ornamental pieces to lend the aura of elegance to their landscaping.

Fine Neoclassic Italian Carved Marble Garden Bench

Bench, carved white marble, Neoclassical style, the arched back centered by a long rectangular panel carved in low-relief w/putti suspending fruiting swags, flanked by acanthus-carved volute low arms ending in carved female terms,flat plinth feet, Italy, late 19th c., 25 x 50", 37 1/2" h. (ILLUS.) **$24,000**

Two Bacchantes from a Set of Four

Figures of Bacchantes, cast metal, each standing figure wearing classical garb & w/a grape cluster wreath on the head, on circular bases, fine verdigris patination, 19th c., 62" h., set of 4 (ILLUS. of two) ... **$5,060**

Putto & Bowl Stone Fountain

Fountain, cast stone, Neo-Classical style, designed as a wide low rounded lobed bowl w/a molded rim supported by a standing putto w/a long drapery atop a molded tall square pedestal base, 75" h. (ILLUS.).. **$3,220**

G

Stone Putti & Shell Fountain

Fountain, cast stone, Neo-Classical style, designed as a large shell-shaped bowl held aloft by a pair of draped putti on a rounded base, 66" h. (ILLUS.) **$1,610**

Neo-Classical Stone Fountain with Putto

Fountain, cast stone, Neo-Classical style, topped by the figure of a putto clasping a lion mask spout above the shell-shaped bowl, the whole resting on a leaf-adorned tree trunk base, 19th c., 21 x 24", 60" h. (ILLUS.).. **$1,840**

Long Carved White Marble Planter

Planter, white marble, a long narrow rectangular form, the front carved in high-relief w/a landscape scene of Bacchic putti & rams, the other three sides carved w/laurel swags, late 19th c., 11 1/2 x 30 3/4", 8" h. (ILLUS., top of page) **$2,868**

Fine Tall Figural Torcheres

Torcheres, cast metal, figural, a tapering paneled lantern held atop the head of a young standing girl wearing classical costume, on a ring-and knob-turned pedestal raised on an octagonal base decorated w/acanthus S-scrolls & fruit, electrified w/modern outdoor lanterns, verdigris patina, 19th c., 95" h., pr. (ILLUS.).......... **$7,590**

Urn, cast iron, wide campana-form w/a flaring flattened serrated rim & large high arched leafy scroll side handles w/rosettes, short pedestal raised on a tall stepped plinth base, a self-watering design w/a concealed reservoir to hold water, probably American, late 19th c., 21 x 30", 32" h. (ILLUS., top next column) **$690**

Victorian Self-watering Garden Urn

One of a Pair of Large Garden urns

Urns, cast metal, a very wide squatty urn top w/a wide flattened rim cast w/leaves & shells, raised atop a tall stem composed of a cluster of standing herons among bulrushes, on a tall molded octagonal plinth, fine verdigris finish, 19th c., 41" d., 50" h., pr. (ILLUS. of one)........... **$5,290**

Fine English Terra Cotta Covered Urns

Urns, cov., terra cotta, a large classical baluster-form body raised on a slender round flaring fluted pedestal & square foot, the lower body w/a wide molded band of tall rounded leaves below the center body molded w/leafy vines, a gadrooned band at the shoulder below the neck molded w/a large shell device & leafy vines flanked by vine-wrapped loop shoulder handles, low pyramidal cover w/molded designs & blossom finial, streaky brown glaze, England, 19th c., 35" h., pr. (ILLUS.) **$2,070**

Pair of Glazed Terra Cotta Urns

Urns, terra cotta, footed wide ovoid body w/a thick flaring rim, the sides molded in relief w/thin bands & a central molded fleur-de-lis design, mottled drippy brown & green glaze w/flaking, drainage hole in base, 19th c., 26" h., pr. (ILLUS.).............. **$576**

Urns, white marble, wide campana-form w/a square foot, short ringed pedestal & wide top bowl w/a gadrooned bottom & wide rolled rim, Italy, 19th c., 26" h., pr. (ILLUS. of one, top next column) **$1,265**

One of Two White Marble Garden Urns

GLASS

Alexandrite

G

Inspired by the gemstone of the same name, Alexandrite is a decorative glass shading from yellow-green to rose to blue. It was produced by Thomas Webb & Sons and Stevens & Williams of England in the late 19th century. The Moser firm of Karlsbad, Bohemia made a similar line.

Libbey-signed Alexandrite Scent Bottle

Scent bottle w/tall swelled stopper, the wide squatty bulbous optic-ribbed bottle centered by a small neck w/flared rim, tall amber stopper, bottom signed "Libbey," early 20th c., very slight interior staining, 4 1/2" h. (ILLUS.) **$460**

Amberina

Amberina was developed in the late 1880s by the New England Glass Company and a pressed version was made by Hobbs, Brockunier & Company (under license from the former). A similar ware, called Rose Amber, was made by the Mt. Washington Glass Works. Amberina-Rose Amber shades from amber to deep red or fuchsia and cut and plated (lined with creamy white) examples were also made. The Libbey Glass Company briefly revived blown Amberina, using modern shapes, in 1917.

Amberina Label

Celery vase, cylindrical w/squared & ruffled rim, overall Diamond Quilted patt., deep red to amber, New England Glass Co., 6 1/2" h. **$259**

Nice Amberina Condiment Set in Frame

Condiment set: barrel-shaped Inverted Thumbprint patt. mustard jar w/silver plate rim, hinged cap & spoon, two matching cylindrical shakers w/original silverplate caps; all in a fitted silver plate frame w/a round ruffled base & a spiral-twist upright center handle, overall 7" h. (ILLUS.)..................................... **$575**

Bulbous Ovoid Amberina Pitcher

Pitcher, water, 7 1/4" h., bulbous ovoid body tapering to a squared neck, Inverted Thumbprint patt,. applied amber reeded handle (ILLUS.)..................................... **$187**

Footed Ovoid Amberina Pitcher

Pitcher, water, 8" h., footed ovoid body tapering to a cylindrical neck w/small rim spout, Inverted Thumbprint patt., applied amber handle (ILLUS.)............................... **$176**

G

Amberina Pitcher with Triangular Neck

Pitcher, water, 8 1/2" h., nearly spherical body w/a tall triangular neck, Inverted Thumbprint patt., applied olive green handle (ILLUS.) **$176**

Unusual Amberina Punch Set

Punch set: cov. punch bowl & eight punch cups; the large bulbous ovoid optic ribbed bowl w/a matching domed cover w/a large curved applied amber stem handle; each tall cylindrical optic ribbed cup swelled near the base & w/an applied angled square handle, small flake under ladle opening on lid, tiny fleck on bowl inside rim, cups 3 1/2" h., bowl, 8" d., 13" h., the set (ILLUS.) **$1,725**

Amberina Squatty Open Sugar Bowl

Sugar bowl, open, squatty bulbous shape w/a flattened, widely flaring & crimped rim, Diamond Quilted patt., 4 1/2" d. (ILLUS.) **$748**
Toothpick holder, simple cylindrical glass mounted in a fitted silver plate base w/tall upright figural swan handles, silver plate marked by Tufts, 3 1/2" h. **$633**

Animals

Americans evidently like to collect glass animals. For the past sixty years, American glass manufacturers have turned out a wide variety of animals to please the buying public. Some were produced for long periods and some were later reproduced by other companies, while others were made for only a short period of time and are rare. We have not included late productions in our listings and have attempted to date the productions where possible. Evelyn Zemel's book, American Glass Animals A to Z, *will be helpful to the novice collector. Another helpful book is* Glass Animals of the Depression Era *by Lee Garmon and Dick Spencer, Collector Books, 1993.*

G

Lavender Satin Fenton Bear Cub

Bear cub, Lavender Satin, Fenton Art Glass Co., 3 1/2" h. (ILLUS.) **$48**
Bird on stump, clear, K.R. Haley, 6" h. (ILLUS., next page) **$25**
Duck, mama, clear, Fostoria Glass Co., 4" h. **$35**

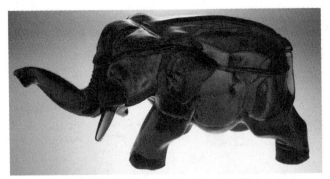

Rare Amber Co-operative Elephant Dish

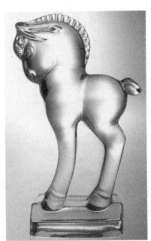

Glass Colt Standing

Bird on Stump by K.R. Haley

Elephant, cov. dish, Co-operative Flint Glass, amber, 8" l. (ILLUS., top of page) $250

Fish, #1320 Epic, Viking Glass, Persimmon, 10" h. $49

Giraffe, head back, Imperial Glass (Heisey mold), amber, 11" h. $500

Horse, Colt, standing, clear, A.H. Heisey & Co., 1940-52, 5" h. (ILLUS., top next column) $95

Horse, rearing, beaded mane, L.E. Smith, black, 8" h. (ILLUS., bottom next column) $47

Hound, bridge, pencil holder, Cambridge Glass, blue, 1 3/4" h. $55

Panther, walking, Indiana Glass, amber, 7" l. $300

Pelican, Paden City, clear, 10" h. $700

L.E. Smith Black Rearing Horse

Duncan & Miller Clear Sailfish

Sailfish, Duncan & Miller, clear, 5 1/4" h. (ILLUS.)... **$225**

New Martinsville Baby Seal with Ball

Seal, baby w/ball, New Martinsville Glass Co., clear, 4 1/2" h. (ILLUS.) **$57**
Swan, nut dish, Heisey, clear, 2 1/2" l. **$25**
Tiger, sitting, New Martinsville Glass Co., clear, 6 3/4" h. **$180**

Blown Three Mold

This type of glass was entirely or partially blown in a mold and was popular from about 1820 to 1840. The object was formed and the decoration impressed upon it by blowing the glass into a metal mold, usually of three—but sometimes more—sections hinged together. Mold-blown glass actually dates back to ancient times. Recent research reveals that certain geometric patterns were reproduced in the 1920s; some new pieces, usually sold through museum gift shops, are still available. Collectors are urged to read all recent information available. Reference numbers are from George L. and Helen McKearin's book, American Glass.

Pieces are for clear glass unless otherwise noted.

Rare Square Green Decanter & Stopper

 G

Decanter w/hollow blown ribbed stopper, geometric, upright square shape w/tapering paneled shoulder & flared tooled mouth w/spout, ground pontil, emerald green w/yellowish tone, probably England, 1820-40, pt., GII-28 (ILLUS.)........ **$3,920**
Decanter w/hollow blown stopper, baroque, wide cylindrical body & tapering shoulders to the tapering ringed neck, rough pontil, Boston & Sandwich Glass Co., 1825-35, colorless, 10 3/4" h., qt., GV-14 (ILLUS. far left with three other decanters, bottom of page 558) **$413**

Three Blown Three Mold Decanters

Decanter w/hollow blown stopper, geometric, flat-bottomed ovoid body tapering to a ringed neck, possibly Boston & Sandwich Glass Co., qt., GII-18, 10 1/4" h. (ILLUS. right with pair of banded decanters) **$99**

Blown Three Mold Comet Design Decanter & Pitcher

Decanter w/hollow blown stopper, geometric, flat-bottomed tapering cylindrical sides w/a short neck & flared rim, rough pontil, Boston & Sandwich Glass Co., ca. 1825-35, colorless, 11" h., qt., GIII-5 (ILLUS. far right with three other decanters, bottom of page) **$413**

Decanter w/hollow blown stopper, gothic, the cylindrical body composed of round-topped panels below the tapering shoulders w/graduating arches, tall plain neck w/flared rim, possibly Boston & Sandwich Glass Co. 1825-35, colorless, 8 3/4" h., pint, GIV-5 (ILLUS. second from right with three other decanters, bottom of page)................................. **$468**

Decanter w/original pressed wheel stopper, comet design, the slightly tapering cylindrical body w/a wide tapering shoulder to the plain tapering ringed neck w/flared rim, Boston & Sandwich Glass Co., ca. 1825-35, colorless, 11 1/2" h., GV-17 (ILLUS. right with comet design pitcher, top of page) **$605**

Decanter w/pressed wheel stopper, geometric, flat-bottomed tapering cylindrical body w/a swirled ribbed shoulder below the tall neck, pressed type 26 stopper, rough pontil, Boston & Sandwich Glass Co., 1825-35, colorless, 7 1/2" h., 1/2 pt., GIII-2 (ILLUS. second from left with three other decanters, bottom of page)............... **$303**

Group of Four Blown Three Mold Decanters with Stoppers

Blown Three Mold Dishes & Two Pitchers

Decanters w/hollow blown stoppers, geometric, flat-bottomed ovoid body tapering to a ringed neck, band of flutes around the bottom below three molded rings & swirled flutes on the shoulder, GI-27, 10 3/4" h., pr. (ILLUS. left with single GII-18 decanter, page 557) **$413**

Dish, geometric, wide shallow shape w/flaring inward-folded rim, rayed base w/pontil, Boston & Sandwich Glass Co., 1825-35, colorless, 5 5/8" d., 2" h., GIII-20 (ILLUS. far right with other dish & pitchers, top of page)................................. **$88**

Dish, geometric, wide shallow shape w/outward folded rim, rayed base w/pontil mark, possibly Boston & Sandwich Glass Co., 1825-35, colorless, 5 3/8" d., 1 3/8" h., GIII-3 (ILLUS. third from right with other dish & two pitchers, top of page)................................. **$77**

Scarce Cobalt Blue Top Hat Novelty

G

Amethystine Geometric Flip Glass

Flip glass, geometric, tall tapering cylindrical shape, sheared rim, tubular pontil scar, probably Boston & Sandwich Glass Co., ca. 1820-40, pale amethystine, some minor interior haze, 5" h., GIII-20 (ILLUS.)................................. **$1,344**

Model of a top hat, geometric, flared tooled rim, pontil scar, Boston & Sandwich Glass Co., ca. 1820-40, cobalt blue, 2" d., 2 5/8" h., GIII-25 (ILLUS., top next column) **$1,344**

Rare Blown Three Mold Handled Mug

Mug, geometric, cylindrical w/an applied handle w/end squiggle, sheared rim, tubular pontil scar, probably Boston & Sandwich Glass Co., ca. 1820-40, colorless, 2 7/8" d., 3 3/8" h., GIII-18 (ILLUS.) **$2,352**

Pitcher, 8 1/4" h., comet design, wide slightly tapering sides w/a wide tapering shoulder to the wide flaring neck w/rim spout & lightly applied rings, applied strap handle, Boston & Sandwich Glass Co., 1825-35, colorless, GV-17 (ILLUS. left with comet design decanter, top previous page) **$3,080**

Pitcher, miniature, 2 3/4" h., geometric, squatty bulbous body w/a tall plain neck, applied handle w/curl tip missing, first half 19th c., colorless (ILLUS. second from right with two dishes & large pitcher, top of page)................................. **$88**

Grouping of Blown Three Mold Tumblers & a Wine Glass

Pitcher, miniature, 3" h., geometric, bulbous body tapering to a patterned neck w/folded rim & small spout, applied strap handle, rough pontil, Boston & Sandwich Glass Co., 1825-40, colorless, GIII-21 .... **$2,090**

Pitcher, 7 3/4" h., baroque, footed squatty bulbous ribbed body tapering to a ringed & ribbed neck band below the wide plain neck w/wide spout, applied strap handle, probably Mid-Atlantic area, ca. 1820-40, crack off rim at upper handle join, handle crack across lower juncture, colorless, GV-7 (ILLUS. far left with two dishes & small pitcher, top previous page) **$220**

Blown Three Mold Salt Dip & Tumbler

Salt dip, geometric, applied six-petal foot w/rough pontil, clear, 2 1/2" d., 2 3/8" h., unrecorded, similar to GII-9 (ILLUS. left with small tapering tumbler) **$413**

Salt dip, model of a top hat, geometric, cylindrical w/a rolled folded rim, rough pontil, possibly Boston & Sandwich Glass Co. 1825-35, colorless, 2 1/8" h., GII-18 .... **$132**

Salt dip, model of a top hat, geometric, cylindrical w/a rolled folded rim, rough pontil, Boston & Sandwich Glass Co. 1825-35, cobalt blue, 2 1/4" h., GIII-23 .... **$605**

Tumbler, baroque, cylindrical, rayed base w/rough pontil, probably Boston & Sandwich Glass Co., 1825-1835, colorless, 3 3/8" h., GV-4 (ILLUS. far right with other tumblers & a wine glass, top of page) **$275**

Tumbler, geometric, barrel-shaped, rough pontil, 1825-35, colorless, 2 3/8" h., GII-19 (ILLUS. third from right with other tumblers & a wine glass, top of page) **$165**

Tumbler, geometric, cylindrical, rough pontil, 1825-35, colorless, 2 3/4" h., GII-21 (ILLUS. second from right with other tumblers & wine glass, top of page) **$187**

Tumbler, geometric, miniature, slightly tapering cylindrical form, rough pontil, clear, 2 1/4" d., 3 1/8" h., unrecorded pattern (ILLUS. right with unrecorded salt dip, middle previous column) **$77**

Tumbler, geometric, tapering cylindrical shape, rayed base w/pontil, probably Boston & Sandwich Glass Co., 1825-35, colorless, 2 1/2" h., GII-19 (ILLUS. far left with other tumblers & a wine glass, top of page)... **$165**

Wine glass, geometric, bell-form bowl atop an applied ringed stem & round foot, rough pontil, possible Boston & Sandwich Glass Co., ca. 1820-40, colorless, small flake & area of roughness under foot edge, 3 1/4" h., GII-19 (ILLUS. second from left with blown three mold tumblers, top of page) **$209**

Bohemian

Numerous types of glass were made in the once-independent country of Bohemia and fine colored, cut and engraved glass was turned out. Flashed and other inexpensive wares also were made; many of these, including amber- and ruby-shaded glass, were exported to the United States during the 19th and 20th centuries. One favorite pattern in the late 19th and early 20th centuries was Deer & Castle. Another was Deer and Pine Tree.

Cameo pokal, cov., the clear frosted background overlaid in dark blue & beautifully cameo-cut, the high domed round foot cameo-cut w/vining leaves & scrolls below the tall figural stem in the shape of a spread-winged eagle, the tall slightly flaring cylindrical body cameo-cut w/a scene of two nude angels embracing on a fainting couch, the domed cover cameo-cut w/vining leaves & scrolls & centered by a ringed knop a tall panel-cut spearpoint finial, retains two paper labels probably used as museum accession labels, mid-19th c., overall 24 1/4" h. (ILLUS., next page) **$21,275**

Exquisite Bohemian Cameo Pokal

Extraordinary Bohemian Centerpiece

Centerpiece, translucent ruby cut-back to frosted clear, the tall tiered round shaped w/a vasiform top cut w/a woodland scene centering an eagle in flight above a downed deer, resting on a scalloped shallow bowl cut w/a scene of deer calming grazing & w/stags hurtling over a log, supported by a figural frosted dolphin stem, the second tier similarly cut w/clusters of doe & fawn above trellis & diaper scrollwork, supported on a stem of three clear frosted adorsed dolphins, the waisted round base similarly cut w/startled stags beside a pond above broad flutes cut w/grapevines, possibly by Harrach-Glashaus, Neuwelt, ca. 1860-80, overall 37" h. (ILLUS.) **$24,000**

Elegant Green Bohemian Compote

Compote, 10 1/2" h., open, emerald green crenelated bowl w/twelve lappets centered by raised panels decorated w/ornate gold strapwork & foliage, on a tall knopped & paneled stem & a twelve-paneled foot also decorated w/delicate gold vining, second half 19th c. (ILLUS.) **$3,585**

Dessert service: two footed decanters w/hollow-blown stoppers, five white wine flutes, five red wine goblets, five sherry glasses, five footed liqueurs & five scalloped dessert plates; pink-flashed over frosted clear w/an ornate engraved design w/a cartouche enclosing a monogram & reserves w/woodland scenes of leaping stags & hounds, further ornate scrolls, late 19th c., decanters 12 3/4" h., the set (ILLUS., top of next page) **$5,378**

Rare American Scene Tumblers

Tumbler, footed, a round scalloped foot below the tall gently flaring cylindrical bowl, ruby-stained, the bowl engraved w/a building titled "The President's House - Washington," engraved scroll design on the back, cut panels around the base & foot, New England Glass Co. or Bohemia, mid-19th c., tiny nicks & flake, 2 7/8" d., 5" h. (ILLUS. left with large tumbler) **$2,750**

G

Very Fine Pink-Flashed Bohemian Dessert Service

Two Pairs of Bohemian Cut-Overlay Decorated Green Vases

Tumbler, footed, a round scalloped foot below the tall gently waisted cylindrical bowl, ruby-stained, the bowl engraved w/three panels titled "Boston Market Street and Fanenil (sic) Hall," "Houseshoe Falls at Niagara," & "Lake George," cut panels around the base & foot, New England Glass Co. or Bohemia, mid-19th c., 4" d., 6 1/8" h. (ILLUS. right with smaller tumbler, previous page)............. **$4,125**

Vases, 8 3/4" h., cut-overlay, round pedestal base w/ringed stem below the tall swelled ovoid body w/a deeply notched upright rim, translucent emerald green overlaid w/opaque white, the body cut w/tall narrow pointed panels w/alternating enameled decoration of scrolling vines or strawberry-diamond cut design, trimmed overall w/foliate scrolls & gilt spiraling tendrils, mid-19th c., pr. (ILLUS. left & right with large ovoid vases, middle of page)... **$3,000**

Vases, 9 1/4" h., cut-overlay, a short round pedestal foot supporting a large bulbous ovoid body tapering to a short rolled neck, emerald green overlaid w/opaque white, the body cut w/long panels w/alternating decoration of enameled flowers or strawberry-diamond cutting, trimmed overall w/gilt flowering vines on an acid-etched ground, acid-etched crowned striped shield marks, mid- to late 19th c., pr. (ILLUS. center with pair of slender ovoid cut-overlay vases, middle of page) **$2,880**

Bohemian Ruby Overlay Vases

Vases, 11 3/4" h., cut-overlay, translucent ruby overlaid in opaque white, baluster-form, the elongated trumpet neck cut w/pendant ogival windows edges in gold, above a row of similar quatrefoils, the lower section cut w/flame-form lozenges, on a low flute-cut round foot, mid-19th c., pr. (ILLUS.)... **$2,160**

Bohemian Tall Cut-Overlay Vases

Vases, 16 1/8" h., cut-overlay, round pedestal base w/ringed stem below the tall swelled ovoid body w/a deeply notched & scalloped upright rim, translucent emerald green overlaid w/opaque white, the body cut w/graduated quatrefoils above flame-form lozenges edged in gilt, the base cut w/pendant ogival windows alternating w/circular prints, mid-19th c. (ILLUS.) **$2,400**

One of Two Ruby Bohemian Vases

Vases, 16 5/8" h., ruby baluster-form w/a tall trumpet neck, the front decorated w/an opaque white central oval h.p. w/lush bouquets of garden flowers within a beaded gilt border, trimmed overall w/gold thistles & fine grasses, late 19th c., pr. (ILLUS. of one) **$1,920**

Bride's Baskets & Bowls

These berry or fruit bowls were popular late Victorian wedding gifts, hence the name. They were produced in a variety of quality art glasswares and sometimes were fitted in ornate silver plate holders.

Cased Pink Hobnail Decorated Bowl

Cased bowl, deep pink shaded satin interior w/molded Hobnail patt. & a deeply ruffled & crimped rim, the center framed by an enameled ring of blue, white & yellow blossoms & gold leaf sprigs & blossoms, white exterior, attributed to Thomas Webb, 9" d., 2 3/4" h. (ILLUS.)................... **$115**

Ornately Enameled Low Bride's Bowl

Cased bowl, flat low cylindrical foot below the low squatty rounded mid-body & wide low cylindrical upper body w/a widely flaring crimped & ruffled rim, deep rose satin exterior ornately enameled w/overall lacework & stylized flowers in shades of blue, yellow & white, white interior, 7 3/4" d., 3 1/2" h. (ILLUS., top of page) **$288**

Purple & White Cased Bride's Bowl

Cased bowl, footed white exterior w/a deeply fluted rim & gold leafy vines around the sides, shaded purple interior decorated in gold w/large fruit on a vine, 11" d., 4" h. (ILLUS.) **$161**

Hobnail White & Pink Bride's Bowl

Cased bowl, white upright sides w/a crimped rim in the Hobnail patt., deep pink interior, attributed to Hobbs, Brockunier & Co., 9" d., 3 1/2" h. (ILLUS.) **$173**

Cased bowl, wide flat base w/upright sides below the flaring ruffled rim, dark raspberry pink shaded to pale pink glossy exterior brightly enameled w/large blue, yellow, red & green stylized dotted flowers & leaves, white interior, base marked w/propeller mark, formerly attributed to Thomas Webb, now attributed to the Harrach glass factory of Bohemia, 8" d., 3 7/8" h. (ILLUS., top next column) **$288**

Finely Decorated Cased Pink Bowl

Burmese

Burmese is a single-layer glass that shades from pink to pale yellow. It was patented by Frederick S. Shirley and made by the Mt. Washington Glass Co. A license to produce the glass in England was granted to Thomas Webb & Sons, which called its articles Queen's Burmese. Gundersen Burmese was made briefly about the middle of the 20th century, and the Pairpoint Company is making limited quantities at the present time.

Webb Burmese Decorated Bowl

Bowl, 4 1/2" d., 2 5/8" h., upright round sides w/a tightly crimped rim, the exterior h.p. w/lavender blue flowers w/yellow centers & green & brown leaves, deep pink interior, Thomas Webb (ILLUS.) **$690**

Burmese Ribbed Cruet Set in Stand

Condiment set: cylindrical ribbed salt & pepper shakers & barrel-shaped ribbed mustard jar, each w/original silver plate lids, in a fitted silver plate stand w/three round compartments decorated w/a band of tiny blossoms, raised on three delicate pointed scroll feet, satin finish, frame marked "Barbour Bros. Co. N.Y. Quadruple Plate," 8 1/2" h. (ILLUS.) **$546**

Decorated Miniature Webb Rose Bowl

Rose bowl, miniature, spherical w/eight-crimp rim, h.p. blue & yellow flowers on stems w/green & brown leaves, Thomas Webb & Sons, 2 3/4" d. (ILLUS.) **$259**

Webb Burmese Miniature Vase

Vase, 2 1/4" h., miniature, squatty bulbous body tapering sharply to a low shaped neck, h.p. w/large red wild roses on leafy stems, acid-stamped "Thos. Webb & Sons - Queen's Burmese Ware - Patent" & registration number (ILLUS.) **$633**

Small Signed Webb Burmese Vase

Vase, 3 3/4" h., miniature, squatty bulbous base tapering to a gently flaring cylindrical neck w/a flared pinched & ruffled rim, h.p. w/reddish orange fuchsia & green leafy stems, marked "Thos. Webb & Sons Queens Burneseware Patented - RD 80167" (ILLUS.) **$460**

Fine Bulbous Decorated Burmese Vase

G

Vase, 7" h., bulbous ovoid body w/a small short cylindrical neck, finely enameled w/large stylized leaves, vines & flowers outlined in heavy gold, satin ground, minor gold wear on lip (ILLUS., previous page) **$1,265**

Vase, 9 1/2" h., simple tapering ovoid body w/a small flat mouth, satin finish, ground pontil, Mt. Washington (ILLUS.) **$510**

Tall Burmese Vase with Daisies

Nicely Decorated Webb Burmese Vase

Vase, 7 1/2" h., footed bulbous base w/four pinched-in sides tapering to a tall slender cylindrical neck, h.p. w/blue blossoms on slender stems w/brown & green leaves, Thomas Webb & Sons mark (ILLUS.) **$431**

Vase, 11 3/4" h., bulbous ovoid body tapering to a slender stick neck, h.p. w/slender stems of small white & yellow daisies around the body & up the neck, Mt. Washington (ILLUS.) **$863**

Cambridge

Cambridge Glass operated from 1902 until 1954 in Cambridge, Ohio. Early wares included numerous pressed glass patterns in imitation of cut glass, often clear or bearing an impressed mark of "NEAR CUT" in the inside center of the piece. Later products included color, stylized shapes, animals and hand-cut and decorated tableware. Particularly popular with collectors today is the Statuesque Line, popularly called Nude Stems, and a pink opaque color called Crown Tuscan. When marked, which is infrequent, the Cambridge mark is the letter "C" in a triangle.

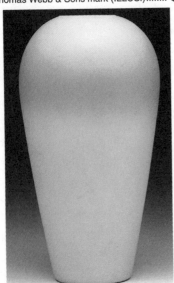

Simple Ovoid Burmese Vase

Cambridge Marks

Caprice Pattern

Ashtray, triangular, pressed Caprice patt., No. 216, Moonlight Blue **$18**

Bonbon, pressed Caprice patt., low, footed, No. 133; Moonlight Blue, 6" sq. **$40**

Bowl, 5" sq., jelly, two-handled, pressed Caprice patt., No. 151, clear **$15**

Moonlight Blue Caprice Salad Bowl

Bowl, 8" d., salad, four-footed, pressed Caprice patt., No. 49, Moonlight Blue (ILLUS.) **$110**

Bowl, 9" d., four-footed, pressed Caprice patt., deep oval, Moonlight Blue, #52 .... **$100**

Bowl, 10 1/2" d., pressed Caprice patt., No. 53, four-footed, Moonlight Blue **$100**

Bowl, 11 1/2" d., No. 81 cupped gardenia bowl, footed, low, pressed Caprice patt., Moonlight Blue **$100**

Bowl, 13 1/2" d., cupped gardenia, Caprice patt., No. 82, Moonlight Blue **$170**

Candlestick, three-light, cascading style, pressed Caprice patt., No. 1338, Crystal, 6" h. **$40**

Candlesticks, two-light, pressed Caprice patt., No. 647, w/bobeches & prisms, Moonlight Blue, pr. **$135**

Candlesticks, one-light, pressed Caprice patt., No. 67, Moonlight Blue, 2 1/2" h., pr. **$55**

Candlesticks, one-light, pressed Caprice patt., No. 70, shell foot w/prism, Moonlight Blue, 7 1/2" h., pr. **$140**

Moonlight Blue Caprice Candy Dish

Candy dish, cov., three-footed, pressed Caprice patt., No. 165, Moonlight Blue, 6" d. (ILLUS.) **$155**

Cocktail, blown Caprice patt., No. 301, Crystal, 3 oz. **$25**

Cordial, blown Caprice patt., Moonlight Blue, No. 102 .... **$125**

Cup, Caprice patt., No. 17, Crystal **$14**

Goblet, blown Caprice patt., water, No. 301, Crystal, 9 oz. **$22**

Goblet, water, pressed Caprice patt., No. 1, Crystal, 10 oz. **$30**

Nut bowl, individual, pressed Caprice patt., No. 93, square, tab handles, Moonlight Blue, 2 1/2" **$40**

Pickle dish, pressed Caprice patt., No. 102, tab handles, Moonlight Blue, 9" **$55**

Pitcher, pressed Caprice patt., Moonlight Blue, 32 oz. **$375**

Plate, 8 1/2" d., low, footed, pressed Caprice patt., No. 131, Moonlight Blue **$35**

Plate, 9 1/2" d., pressed Caprice patt., No. 24, dinner, Crystal **$45**

Plate, 14" d., four-footed, pressed Caprice patt., No. 33, Crystal **$38**

Saucer, pressed Caprice patt., No. 17, Crystal **$3**

Sherbet, blown Caprice patt., No. 301, Crystal, 6 oz. **$14**

Sherbet, blown Caprice patt., No. 300, tall, Moonlight Blue, 6 oz. **$32**

Sugar bowl, pressed Caprice patt., No. 38, medium, Crystal **$11**

Tray, for individual creamer & sugar bowl, pressed Caprice patt., Crystal..................... **$18**

Tumbler, blown Caprice patt., footed, No. 184, Dianthus Pink, 12 oz. **$50**

Tumbler, blown Caprice patt., footed, No. 300, Moonlight Blue, 12 oz. **$40**

Tumbler, blown Caprice patt., iced tea, No. 310, flat, Crystal, 5 1/4" h. **$115**

Tumbler, blown Caprice patt., No. 300, footed, Crystal, 10 oz. **$18**

Tumbler, pressed Caprice patt., flat, No. 184, Moonlight Blue, 12 oz. **$55**

Tumbler, pressed Caprice patt., footed, No. 10, Moonlight Blue, 10 oz. **$38**

Tumbler, pressed Caprice patt., footed, No. 310, Moonlight Blue, 5 oz. **$65**

Tumbler, footed, blown Caprice patt., No. 300, Moonlight Blue, 5 oz. **$40**

Vase, 8 1/2" h., ball-shaped, pressed Caprice patt., No. 239, three ring, Moonlight Blue.. **$350**

Wine, blown Caprice patt., No. 300, Crystal, 2 1/2" h... **$22**

Wine, pressed Caprice patt., No. 6, Moonlight Blue, 3 oz. **$100**

Crown Tuscan Line

Cocktail, Topaz bowl, Crown Tuscan Nude Lady stem, 6 1/2" h. **$195**

G

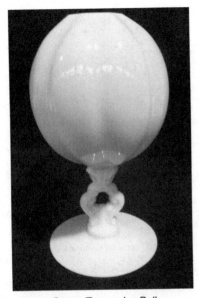

Crown Tuscan Ivy Ball

Crown Tuscan Sea Shell Vase

Vase, 7" h., Sea Shell line, No. 46 (ILLUS.) ... **$185**

G

Ivy ball, keyhole stem, No. 1236, 7 1/2" h.
(ILLUS.).. **$175**
Plate, 14" d., Sea Shell patt., torte **$125**

Crown Tuscan Gadroon Vase

Vase, 7" h., footed, crimped square form,
No. 3500 Gadroon patt. (ILLUS.) **$100**

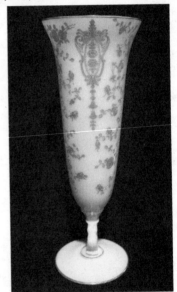

Rare Crown Tuscan Rose Point Vase

Vase, 12" h., footed, keyhole stem, tall
trumpet-form bowl w/gold-encrusted
etched Rose Point patt. (ILLUS.) **$350**

Etched Rose Point Pattern
Bell, No. 3121, Crystal **$148**
Bowl, 12" d., footed, No. 3400, Crystal **$120**

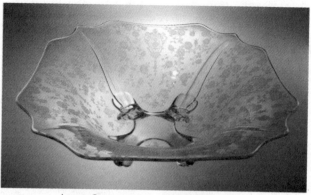
Large Squared Etched Rose Point Bowl

Bowl, 12" w., 4-footed, flared squared sides, No. 3400/4, Crystal (ILLUS., top of page) **$90**
Cake plate, handled, No. 3900/35, clear, 13 1/2" d. **$70**
Candlestick, single-light, No. 3900/68, clear, 4 1/2" h. **$80**

Rose Point Etched Compote

G

Pair of Rose Point Keyhole Candleholders

Candlestick, two-light, keyhole stem, No. 3400/647, Crystal, 5 3/4" h., pr. (ILLUS.) ... **$125**
Candlestick, two-light, No. 3400, keyhole stem, Crystal, 6" **$50**
Celery tray, No. 3500, Crystal, 11 1/2" l. **$54**
Champagne, saucer-type, No. 3121, Crystal, 6 3/4 oz., 6 3/4" h. **$26**
Cocktail, 3 oz., No. 3121, Crystal, 6" h. **$30**
Cocktail shaker, No. 3400/175, Crystal **$200**
Compote, No. 3900/136, Crystal, 5 1/2" d., 5 1/2" h. (ILLUS., top next column) **$85**
Cordial, No. 3121, Crystal, 5 1/2" h. **$82**
Cup & saucer, No. 3400, flat, Crystal **$48**
Decanter w/stopper, No. 1372, cut neck & stopper, Crystal **$1,200**

Etched Rose Point Ice Bucket

Ice bucket, No. 3900/671, Crystal w/chrome handle, scalloped top, 5 3/4" h. (ILLUS., previous page) $170
Lamp globe, hurricane-type, Crystal, 6" h. $190
Mayonnaise bowl, ladle & underplate, No. 3400, Crystal, the set $70
Plate, 8 1/2" d., No. 3500, Crystal $20
Plate, 10 1/4" d., No. 3400, Crystal $160
Relish dish, No. 3400/1093, two-part, Crystal $85
Relish dish, No. 3900/120, five-part, Crystal, 10 1/2 x 12" $85
Relish dish, two-part, No. 3500, Crystal, 8 1/2" $42
Sherbet, No. 3500, Crystal $24
Tumbler, flat, No. 3400, Crystal, 4" h., 5 oz. $95
Tumbler, No. 3121, footed, Crystal, 7" h $29
Tumbler, No. 497, sham bottom, Crystal, 9 oz. $55
Vase, 10" h., bud, No. 274, Crystal $70

Statuesque Line
Cocktail, Amethyst bowl, clear Nude Lady stem, 4 1/2 oz., 6 1/2" h. $100
Vase, bud, Amber bowl, clear Nude Lady stem $350

Miscellaneous Patterns
Ashtray, round, Cambridge Square patt., Ebony, 3 3/4" d $14
Basket, footed, two-handled, etched Diane patt., Crystal, 6" h $30

Cambridge Optic Swirl Beverage Set

Beverage set: ball-form pitcher & nine tumblers; Optic Swirl design, Moonlight Blue, the set (ILLUS. of part) **$150-200**
Bonbon, footed, two handled, etched Candlelight patt., No. 3900/130, Crystal, 7"........ $42

Bowl, almond-type, footed, Decagon line, No. 611, Amber.. $10
Bowl, cream soup, Decagon line, Willow Blue $22
Bowl, 5 3/4" d., flanged rim, Decagon line, Dianthus Pink.. $10
Bowl, 8 1/2" d., three-part, etched Diane patt., Tally-Ho line, Crystal....................... $155

Amber Seashell Pattern Footed Bowl

Bowl, 9" d., three-footed, Seashell patt., Amber (ILLUS.) $68
Bowl, 9 1/2" d., shallow flared shape, Honeycomb patt., "sponge" acid etching, Rubina (ILLUS., bottom of page)................... $375
Bowl, 11" w., four-footed, square, etched Diane patt., No. 3400/45, Crystal............... $65
Bowl, 12" d., Decagon line, No. 842, Willow Blue... $35
Bowl, 12" l., oblong, crimped, etched Wildflower patt., No. 3400/160, Crystal........... $75
Butter dish, cov., open handles, etched Wildflower patt., No. 506, Crystal.............. $140
Candlestick, three-light, Cambridge Arms patt., Crystal, 5 1/4" h................................. $42
Candlesticks, etched Wildflower patt., Skirted line No. 3900/68, bell-footed, Crystal, 4 1/2" h., pr. $135
Candy dish, cov., etched Diane patt., Crystal, 7" d.. $110
Champagne, Decagon line, Amethyst, 6 oz. $16
Cheese & cracker dish, Decagon line No. 869, Willow Blue $42
Cigarette box, cov., footed, etched Gloria patt., No. 1312, gold encrusted Crown Tuscan $250
Cigarette urn, etched Diane patt., Crystal....... $80

Scarce Rubina Honeycomb Bowl

Statuesque Line Cocktail with Carmen Bowl

Cocktail, Statuesque line, Nude Lady stem, Carmen bowl, 3 oz. (ILLUS.) **$220**

Cocktail icer, No. 3600, footed, etched Diane patt., Crystal **$78**

Compote, tall stem, Decagon line No. 1090, Willow Blue, 7" h. **$30**

Console bowl, 12 1/2" d., etched Apple Blossom patt., rolled edge, Gold Krystol **$85**

Cordial, Line No. 3500, Carmen **$70**

Cordial, Mt. Vernon line, footed, Crystal, 1 oz. **$22**

Cordial, Tally Ho line, Royal Blue, 1 oz. **$55**

Creamer & open sugar bowl, individual, etched Wildflower patt., No. 3900/40, Crystal, pr. **$45**

Cup & saucer, demitasse, No. 3400 line, Crystal **$15**

Cup & saucer, Mt. Vernon line, Crystal **$14**

Cup & saucer, pressed Cascade patt., Crystal **$22**

Mt. Vernon Pattern Amber Decanter

Decanter w/crystal stopper, Mt. Vernon line, Amber, 40 oz. (ILLUS.) **$60**

Decanter w/crystal stopper, No. 1321, Royal Blue, 28 oz. **$150**

Figure flower frog/holder, "Bashful Charlotte," Emerald, 11 1/2" h. **$350**

Goblet, Decagon line, water, Willow Blue **$32**

Goblet, etched Portia patt., sherry, No. 7966, Crystal, 2 oz. **$45**

Goblet, Mt. Vernon line, Carmen, 10 oz. **$29**

Goblet, water, Decagon line, Royal Blue **$30**

Goblet, water, pressed Cascade patt., Crystal, 5 1/2" h. **$14**

Ice bucket, etched Candlelight patt., No. 3900, Crystal **$135**

Martini jug, etched Chantilly patt., Pristine line No. 100, Crystal w/metal base, 9 1/4" h. **$350**

Mayonnaise dish, Decagon line, No. 873, handled, Willow Blue **$25**

Model of a swan, table centerpiece, Ebony, 13" l. (ILLUS., bottom of page) **$795**

G

Rare Cambridge Ebony Large Swan

Pitcher, etched Elaine patt., No. 3400/141, Doulton jug-form, w/ice lip, Crystal, 80 oz. $300

Pitcher, etched Wildflower patt., No. 3400/38, ball-shaped, Crystal $220

Plate, 7 1/2" d., etched Elaine patt., No. 3400/176, Crystal $18

Plate, 8 1/4" d., Decagon line, off-center indent, Dianthus Pink $20

Plate, 8 1/2" d., Everglade patt., Crystal $22

Plate, 10" d., two-handled, etched Martha patt., Crystal $19

Relish dish, etched Candlelight patt., three-part, three-handled, No. 3400, Crystal, 8" l. $50

Relish dish, etched Elaine patt., No. 3500/152, four-part, Crystal, 11" l. $85

Relish dish, etched Elaine patt., No. 3500/71, center handle, three-part, Crystal, 7 1/2" d. $100

Relish dish, etched Portia patt., No. 862, four-part w/center handle, Crystal, 8 3/4" d. $95

Relish dish, No. 3400 line, three-part, Emerald, 7" l. $28

Mt. Vernon Carmen Open Salt

Salt, open, oval urn-form w/two handles, Mt. Vernon line, Carmen, 2 1/2" l. (ILLUS.) $48

Salt & pepper shakers, etched Candlelight patt., flat, metal lids, No. 3900/1177, Crystal, pr. $145

Salt & pepper shakers, etched Elaine patt., footed, No. 3400/76 line, Crystal, 3 1/4" h., pr. (one glass lid) $40

Salt shaker w/original top, etched Apple Blossom patt., Willow Blue $60

Sherbet, etched Chantilly patt., No. 3779, Crystal, tall, 6 oz. $18

Tray, decagon-shaped, wafer-type, etched Cleo patt., Emerald, 13" l. $175

Tumbler, Decagon line, juice, Royal Blue, 5 oz. $18

Tumbler, etched Apple Blossom patt., No. 3130, Crystal, 2 oz. $18

Tumbler, etched Apple Blossom patt., whiskey, footed, Topaz, 2 oz. $35

Tumbler, etched Diane patt., Regency line, footed, Crystal, 12 oz. $32

Tumbler, etched Portia patt., No. 3400/38, flat, Crystal, 12 oz. $28

Tumbler, Mt. Vernon line, Crystal, 12 0z. $14

Tumbler, pressed Cascade patt., footed, Crystal, 12 oz., 5 1/8" h. $15

Vase, 6" h., etched Apple Blossom patt., No. 1308, Emerald $125

Vase, 6" h., etched Wildflower patt., No. 1620, Crystal $300

Vase, 9" h., etched Candlelight patt., key-hole shape, Crystal $95

Vase, bud, 10" h., etched Wildflower patt., No. 1528, Crystal $120

Vase, 11" h., etched Gloria patt., No. 1242, Crystal $145

Vegetable bowl, cov., etched Cleo patt., Amber, 9" l. $190

Carnival

Earlier called Taffeta glass, the Carnival glass now being collected was introduced early in the 20th century. Its producers gave it an iridescence that attempted to imitate that of some Tiffany glass. Collectors will find available books by leading authorities Donald E. Moore, Sherman Hand, Marion T. Hartung, Rose M. Presznick, and Bill Edwards.

Acorn Burrs (Northwood)

Berry set: master bowl & six sauce dishes; purple, the set $525

Bowl, 10" d., master berry, green $325

Bowl, 10" d., master berry, marigold $150

Bowl, 10" d., master berry, purple $275

Pitcher, water, green $575

Pitcher, water, marigold $400

Pitcher, water, purple $450

Punch cup, blue, very rare $100

Punch cup, green $45

Punch cup, ice green $55

Punch cup, marigold $30

Punch cup, purple $40

Punch cup, white $50

Punch set: bowl, base & 6 cups; green, 8 pcs. $1,000-2,000

Punch set: bowl, base & 6 cups; purple, 8 pcs. $1,200

Punch set: bowl, base & 6 cups; white, 8 pcs. (ILLUS., top next page) $6,000

Sauce dish, green $35

Sauce dish, marigold $25

Sauce dish, purple $35

Table set, green, 4 pcs. $900

Table set, marigold, 4 pcs. $700

Table set, purple, 4 pcs. $700

Tumbler, green $45

Tumbler, marigold $30

Tumbler, purple $55

Beaded Cable (Northwood)

Candy dish, green $55

Candy dish, marigold $55

Candy dish, purple $35

Rose bowl, aqua opalescent $150-200

Rose bowl, blue $300

Rose bowl, green $200

Rose bowl, marigold $125

Rose bowl, purple $50

Rose bowl, white $155

Acorn Burrs White Punch Set

Butterfly & Berry (Fenton)
Bowl, 8" to 9" d., blue, master berry, four-footed $275
Bowl, 8" to 9" d., green, master berry, four-footed $350
Bowl, 8" to 9" d., marigold, master berry, four-footed.. $95
Pitcher, water, blue $400
Pitcher, water, marigold $225
Sauce dish, blue $50
Sauce dish, green.. $95
Sauce dish, marigold $15
Table set, marigold, 4 pcs. $275
Tumbler, blue... $15-25
Tumbler, marigold... $25

Butterfly & Fern (Fenton)
Tumbler, blue $45-60
Tumbler, green $60

Carnival Holly - SEE HOLLY PATTERN

Cosmos & Cane (U.S. Glass Co.)
Sauce dish, marigold...................................... $25
Table set, amber, 4 pcs. $400
Tumbler, marigold..................................... $60-110

Dahlia (Dugan or Diamond Glass Co.)
Creamer, white, h.p. red flower $70
Sauce dish, white $35
Tumbler, purple....................................... $110-150

Dandelion (Northwood)
Tumbler, green $65
Tumbler, marigold..................................... $35-80

Diamond Lace (Imperial)
Pitcher, water, purple (ILLUS., top next column) $225
Tumbler, purple.. $35

Diamond Point Columns Vase
Vase, 7" to 10" h., aqua opalescent $900

Diamond Lace Pitcher

Vase, 7" to 10" h., blue.................................. $300
Vase, 7" to 10" h., green............................... $125
Vase, 7" to 10" h., green, squatty.................. $150
Vase, 7" to 10" h., ice blue $500
Vase, 7" to 10" h., ice green $550
Vase, 7" to 10" h., ice green, squatty $750
Vase, 7" to 10" h., purple............................. $100
Vase, 7" to 10" h., white $275
Vase, 7" to 10", marigold............................... $75
Vase, 7 1/2" h., white.............................. $165-275
Vase, 14" h., blue $75

Dragon & Lotus (Fenton)
Bowl, 8" to 9" d., blue, ruffled...................... $105
Bowl, 8" to 9" d., lime green w/marigold overlay $200
Bowl, 7" to 9" d., green, three-footed............ $100
Bowl, 7" to 9" d., marigold, three-footed $60

Bowl, 7" to 9" d., peach opalescent, three-footed $350
Bowl, 8" to 9" d., blue, collared base $125
Bowl, 8" to 9" d., green, collared base $250
Bowl, 8" to 9" d., marigold, collared base $75
Bowl, vaseline $225

Fenton's Red Dragon & Lotus Bowl

Bowl, 8" to 10" d., red, ruffled (ILLUS.) **$1,700**

G Good Luck (Northwood)

Bowl, 8" to 9" d., electric blue, ruffled, ribbed back... $475
Bowl, 8" to 9" d., green, ruffled, ribbed back .. $175
Bowl, 8" to 9" d., horehound, ruffled, Basketweave back $85
Bowl, 8" to 9" d., purple, pie crust edge, ribbed back... $205
Bowl, 8" to 9" d., purple, ruffled, ribbed back .. $205
Bowl, 8" to 9" d., blue, ruffled........................ $425
Bowl, 8" to 9" d., green, ruffled $350
Bowl, 8" to 9" d., ice blue, ruffled $2,350

Marigold Good Luck Bowl

Bowl, 8" to 9" d., marigold, ruffled (ILLUS.) ... $225
Bowl, 8" to 9" d., purple, ruffled...................... $275
Bowl, 8" to 9" d., blue, pie crust rim $575

Bowl, 8" to 9" d., marigold, pie crust rim $275
Plate, 9" d., blue... $2,800
Plate, 9" d., marigold..................................... $375
Plate, 9" d., purple... $475
Plate, 9" d., white... $5,300

Grape & Cable (Northwood)

Banana boat, marigold $105
Banana boat, purple $205
Berry set: master bowl & 6 sauce dishes; purple, 7 pcs. $205
Bonbon, two-handled, green $45
Bonbon, two-handled, marigold......................... $55
Bonbon, two-handled, purple $55
Bowl, 10" d., pie crust edge, purple $285
Bowl, 11" d., ruffled, marigold $65
Bowl, 6" d., ruffled, marigold $40
Bowl, 9" d., pie crust edge, Basketweave exterior, purple $65
Bowl, 8" to 9" d., pie crust rim, plain back, pastel marigold... $85
Bowl, 8" to 9" d., pie crust rim, green............. $125
Bowl, 8" to 9" d., pie crust rim, marigold $60
Bowl, 8" to 9" d., pie crust rim, purple............ $100
Bowl, 8" to 9" d., pie crust rim, stippled, blue .. $300
Bowl, 8" to 9" d., pie crust rim, stippled, ice green.. $2,200
Bowl, 8" to 9" d., pie crust rim, stippled, marigold... $175
Bowl, 8" to 9" d., pie crust rim, stippled, ribbed back, ice blue $600
Bowl, 8" to 9" d., ruffled, green $75
Bowl, 8" to 9" d., ruffled, marigold.................... $50
Bowl, 8" to 9" d., ruffled rim, purple................ $75
Bowl, 11" d., ice cream shape, marigold........ $145
Breakfast set: individual size creamer & sugar bowl; purple, pr. $75
Candle lamp, green $1,000
Candle lamp, marigold $600
Candle lamp, purple $600
Candle lamp shade, marigold $350
Candle lamp shade, purple $350
Candlestick, green $150
Candlestick, marigold..................................... $100
Candlestick, purple $110
Centerpiece bowl, turned-in, marigold.......... $200
Cologne bottle w/stopper, marigold............. $150
Cologne bottle w/stopper, purple $175
Compote, cov., marigold, large...................... $225
Compote, cov., purple, large $550
Compote, cov., purple, small $350
Cuspidor, purple $3,750
Dresser tray, green $425
Dresser tray, marigold................................... $225
Dresser tray, purple....................................... $180
Hat shape, purple $45
Hat shape, ruffled, green $45
Hatpin holder, green $175
Hatpin holder, marigold.................................. $225
Hatpin holder, purple $175
Pin tray, purple $195
Pin tray, round, marigold $30
Pin tray, ruffled, purple $55
Pitcher, water, 8 1/4" h., green $375
Pitcher, water, 8 1/4" h., marigold.................. $175
Pitcher, water, 8 1/4" h., purple $325
Pitcher, tankard, 9 3/4" h., purple $450
Plate, 6" d., purple.. $80

Grape & Cable Eight-piece Purple Punch Set

Plate, 6" d., turned-up handgrip, amethyst $55
Plate, 7 1/2" d., turned-up handgrip, marigold $50
Plate, 8" d., purple $85
Plate, 9" d., Basketweave exterior, marigold $95
Plate, 9" d., Basketweave exterior, purple $105
Plate, 9" d., green $300
Plate, 9" d., ice green, spatula-footed $250
Plate, 9" d., marigold $125
Plate, 9" d., marigold, spatula-footed $300
Plate, 9" d., purple $150
Plate, 9" d., stippled, green $550
Powder jar, cov., green $105
Powder jar, cov., marigold $125
Powder jar, cov., purple $65
Punch bowl & base, purple, 14" d., 2 pcs. $675
Punch cup, green $45
Punch cup, marigold.. $25

Punch cup, purple $30
Punch cup, white $75
Punch set: 11" bowl, base & 6 cups; blue, stippled, 8 pcs. $1,000
Punch set: 11" bowl, base & 6 cups; ice green, 8 pcs. $10,500
Punch set: 11" bowl, base & 6 cups; marigold, stippled, 8 pcs. $600
Punch set: 11" bowl, base & 6 cups; marigold w/pink iridescence, 8 pcs. $850
Punch set: 11" bowl, base & 6 cups; purple, 8 pcs. (ILLUS., top of page) $300-350
Punch set: 11" bowl, base & 6 cups; white, 8 pcs. $4,500
Punch set: 14" bowl, base & 6 cups; green, 8 pcs. $1,500
Punch set: 14" bowl, base & 6 cups; marigold, 8 pcs. $750

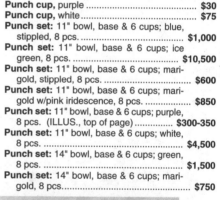

G

Grape & Cable Punch Set

Punch set: 14" bowl, base & 6 cups; purple,
8 pcs. (ILLUS., bottom previous page) **$900**

Punch set, master: 17" bowl, base & 6
cups; blue, 8 pcs. **$7,000**

Punch set, master: 17" bowl, base & 6
cups; purple, 8 pcs. **$4,000**

Punch set, master: 17" bowl, base & 6
cups; white, 8 pcs. **$5,500**

Punch set, master: 17" bowl, base & 12
cups; purple, 14 pcs. **$3,600**

Sauce dish, marigold **$10**

Sauce dish, purple **$25**

Sherbet or individual ice cream dish, pur-
ple **$20**

Spooner, purple **$50**

Sweetmeat jar, cov., purple **$250**

Table set: cov. sugar bowl, creamer, cov.
butter dish & spooner; marigold, 4 pcs. **$350**

Table set: cov. sugar bowl, creamer, cov.
butter dish & spooner; purple, 4 pcs. **$295**

Tumbler, green **$65**

Tumbler, marigold **$10-20**

Tumbler, purple **$60**

Whimsey compote (sweetmeat base),
purple **$95**

Whiskey shot glass, marigold **$140**

Whiskey shot glass, purple **$230**

Holly, Holly Berries & Carnival Holly (Fenton)

Bowl, 8" to 9" d., eight-ruffle rim, blue **$55**

Bowl, 8" to 9" d., six-ruffle, white **$45**

Bowl, 8" to 9" d., three-in-one edge, blue **$75**

Bowl, 8" to 9" d., ruffled, blue **$95**

Bowl, 8" to 9" d., ruffled, green **$50**

Holly Marigold Bowl

Bowl, 8" to 9" d., ruffled, marigold (ILLUS.) **$45**

Bowl, 8" to 9" d., ruffled, purple **$110**

Bowl, 8" to 9" d., ruffled, red **$1,500**

Compote, goblet-shaped, aqua **$155**

Compote, goblet-shaped, lime green **$55**

Plate, 9" to 10" d., marigold w/pumpkin iridescence **$190**

Plate, 9" to 10" d., blue **$260**

Plate, 9" to 10" d., green **$625**

Plate, 9" to 10" d., marigold **$150**

Plate, 9" to 10" d., purple **$400**

Plate, 9" to 10" d., white **$125**

Plate, iridescent green, ... **$8,500**

Imperial Grape (Imperial)

Goblet, purple **$30**

Pitcher, water, amber **$400**

Pitcher, water, green **$175**

Pitcher, water, marigold **$50**

Pitcher, water, purple **$125**

Punch bowl & base, marigold **$150**

Punch bowl & base, purple **$2,000**

Punch cup, marigold **$15**

Punch cup, purple **$45**

Tumbler, marigold **$10-20**

Tumbler, purple **$65**

Water bottle, purple **$175**

Lustre Rose (Imperial)

Bowl, 8" to 9" d., ruffled, amber **$50**

Bowl, 8" to 9" d., ruffled, marigold **$35**

Bowl, 11" to 12" d., fruit, footed, green **$250**

Bowl, 11" to 12" d., fruit, footed, marigold **$95**

Bowl, 11" to 12" d., fruit, footed, purple **$850**

Fernery, marigold **$45**

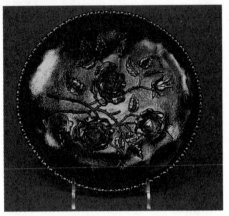

Lustre Rose Purple Fernery

Fernery, purple (ILLUS.) **$400**

Pitcher, water, purple **$1,300**

Plate, 9" d., green **$175**

Plate, 9" d., purple **$1,500**

Plate, 9" d., marigold **$85**

Rose bowl, marigold **$75**

Rose bowl, purple **$750**

Table set: cov. sugar bowl, creamer,
spooner & cov. butter dish; marigold, 4
pcs. **$200**

Table set, purple, 4 pcs. **$900**

Tumbler, purple **$95**

Open Rose (Imperial)

Plate, 9" d., marigold **$75**

Plate, 9" d., purple **$1,000**

Orange Tree (Fenton)

Berry set: master bowl & 5 sauce dishes;
marigold, 6 pcs. **$120**

Bowl, 9" to 10" d. , master berry, ruffled,
footed, blue **$200**

Bowl, 9" to 10", master berry, ruffled, foot-
ed, marigold **$125**

Bowl, 10" d., fruit or orange, blue **$325**

Bowl, 10" d., fruit or orange, green **$600**

Bowl, 10" d., fruit or orange, marigold **$125**

G

Rare Peacock at the Fountain Bowl

Rare Orange Tree Ice Cream Bowl

Bowl, ice cream shape, red (ILLUS.) **$2,750**
Bowl, ice cream shape, white **$55**
Mug, marigold.. **$13**
Pitcher, water, blue **$450**
Pitcher, water, marigold................................. **$250**
Plate, 9" d., flat, marigold **$115**
Plate, 9" d., trunk in center, white.................. **$165**
Punch cup, blue.. **$30**
Punch cup, marigold....................................... **$20**
Punch set: bowl, base & 6 cups; blue, 8
  pcs... **$350**
Punch set: bowl, base & 6 cups; marigold,
  8 pcs.. **$175**
Punch set: bowl, base & 6 cups; white, 8
  pcs... **$700-800**
Rose bowl, blue.. **$150**
Rose bowl, marigold **$95**
Rose bowl, red.. **$700**
Rose bowl, white **$225**
Sauce dish, footed, blue................................. **$50**
Sauce dish, footed, marigold..................... **$10-20**

Table set: creamer, spooner, cov. butter,
  cov. sugar bowl; blue, 4 pcs...................... **$750**
Table set, marigold, 4 pcs...................... **$200-250**
Tumbler, blue... **$75**
Tumbler, marigold... **$40**

Peacock at the Fountain (Northwood)
Bowl, orange or fruit, three-footed, aqua **$800**
Bowl, orange or fruit, three-footed, aqua
  opalescent (ILLUS., top of page) **$10,500**
Bowl, orange or fruit, three-footed, blue **$1,100**
Bowl, orange or fruit, three-footed, green ... **$5,000**
Bowl, orange or fruit, three-footed, marigold .. **$350**
Bowl, 9" d., master berry, blue...................... **$450**
Bowl, 9" d., master berry, green **$375**
Bowl, 9" d., master berry, ice blue **$600**
Bowl, 9" d., master berry, ice green **$700**
Bowl, 9" d., master berry, marigold............... **$200**
Bowl, 9" d., master berry, purple................... **$325**
Bowl, 9" d., master berry, white **$500**
Butter dish, cov., marigold **$325**
Butter dish, cov., purple **$400**
Butter dish, cov., white................................. **$550**
Compote, aqua opalescent........................ **$4,250**
Compote, blue **$1,750**
Compote, green **$9,500**
Compote, ice blue...................................... **$1,250**
Compote, ice green **$1,500**
Compote, marigold **$475**
Compote, purple **$1,100**
Compote, white... **$300**
Creamer, marigold **$80**
Creamer, purple **$95**
Pitcher, water, blue...................................... **$600**
Pitcher, water, marigold................................. **$350**
Pitcher, water, purple.................................... **$500**
Punch set: bowl, base & 6 cups; ice blue, 8
  pcs. **$8,500**
Punch set: bowl, base & 6 cups; marigold,
  8 pcs. **$1,300**
Punch set: bowl, base & 6 cups; purple, 8
  pcs. **$1,800**
Punch set: bowl, base & 6 cups; white, 8
  pcs. **$7,500**
Sauce dish, blue... **$75**

G

Sauce dish, marigold $35
Sauce dish, purple $55
Spooner, ice blue $180
Table set: creamer, spooner, cov. butter
　dish, cov. sugar bowl; purple, 4 pcs. $725
Table set: creamer, spooner, cov. butter
　dish, cov. sugar bowl; purple, 4 pcs. $750
Table set: creamer, spooner, cov. butter
　dish, cov. sugar bowl; blue, 4 pcs. $1,200
Table set: creamer, spooner, cov. butter
　dish, cov. sugar bowl; ice blue, 4 pcs. $2,200
Table set: creamer, spooner, cov. butter
　dish, cov. sugar bowl; marigold, 4 pcs. $600
Tumbler, blue $85
Tumbler, marigold $45
Tumbler, purple $55
Tumbler, white $175
Water set: pitcher & 6 tumblers; marigold, 7
　pcs $325

Springtime (Northwood)
Tumbler, marigold $60-65
Tumbler, purple $70-95

Stag & Holly (Fenton)
Bowl, 10" to 11" d., three-footed, ruffled,
　marigold $75
Bowl, 10" to 11" d., three-footed, ruffled,
　powder blue w/marigold overlay $165
Bowl, 12" d., ice cream shape, purple $200
Bowl, 8" to 9" d., spatula-footed, blue $175
Bowl, 8" to 9" d., spatula-footed, marigold $75
Bowl, 9" to 13" d., ball-footed, deep sides,
　ruffled rim, blue $155
Bowl, 9" to 13" d., ball-footed, green $800
Bowl, 9" to 13" d., ball-footed, marigold $150
Bowl, 10" to 11" d., three-footed, ruffled,
　aqua $450
Bowl, 12" d., ice cream shape, blue $325
Bowl, 12" d., ice cream shape, marigold $90
Rose bowl, marigold, large $160

Stork & Rushes (Dugan or Diamond Glass Works)
Punch set: bowl, base & 6 cups; amethyst,
　8 pcs $1,025
Punch set: bowl, base & 6 cups; marigold,
　8 pcs $225
Tumbler, blue $45-60
Tumbler, blue, beaded version (exterior
　flake) $25
Tumbler, pale blue $50

Thin Rib Vase (Fenton & Northwood)
Blue, Fenton, 8" to" h. $75
Blue, Northwood, 8" to 10" h. $125
Green, Fenton, 8" to 10" h. $125
Green, Northwood, 8" to 10" h. $85
Marigold, Fenton, 8" to 10" h. $30
Marigold, Northwood, 8" to 10" h. $45

Three Fruits (Northwood)
Bowl, 9" d., dome-footed, ruffled, marigold $25
Bowl, 9" d., spatula-footed, ruffled, mari-
　gold $35
Bowl, 9" d., footed, green $225
Bowl, 9" d., footed, marigold $65
Bowl, 9" d., footed, purple $150

Bowl, 9" d., footed, stippled, aqua opales-
　cent $800
Bowl, 9" d., footed, stippled, purple $200
Bowl, 9" d., footed, stippled, white $550
Bowl, 9" d., pie crust rim, green $150
Bowl, 9" d., pie crust rim, marigold $95
Bowl, 9" d., pie crust rim, purple $125
Bowl, 9" d., pie crust rim, stippled, blue $500
Bowl, 9" d., ruffled, green $150
Bowl, 9" d., ruffled, marigold $75
Bowl, 9" d., ruffled, purple $95
Bowl, 9" d., ruffled, stippled, blue, ... $450
Bowl, 9" d., ruffled, stippled, green $750

Three Fruits Aqua Opalescent Bowl

Bowl, 9" d., ruffled, stippled, spatula-footed,
　aqua opalescent (ILLUS.) $500
Bowl, 9" d., stippled, ruffled, marigold $200
Bowl, 9" d., stippled, ruffled, white $450
Plate, 9" d., green $250
Plate, 9" d., marigold $175
Plate, 9" d., purple $200
Plate, 9" d., stippled, blue $1,200
Plate, 9" d., stippled, marigold $375
Plate, 9" d., stippled, purple $600

Trout & Fly (Millersburg)
Bowl, ruffled, green $650
Bowl, ruffled, marigold $450
Bowl, ruffled, purple $575
Bowl, square, green $950
Bowl, square, marigold $650
Bowl, square, purple $950

Water Lily & Cattails
Tumbler, marigold $40-55
Wine, marigold $60

Wishbone & Spades
Plate, chop, 11" d., purple $1,200

Central Glass Works

From the 1890s until its closing in 1939, the Central Glass Works of Wheeling, West Virginia, produced colorless and colored handmade glass in all the styles then popu-

lar. Decorations from etchings with acid to hand-painted enamels were used.

The popular "Depression" era colors of black, pink, green, light blue, ruby red and others were all produced. Two of its 1920s etchings are still familiar today, one named for the then president of the United States and the other for the governor of West Virginia - these are the Harding and Morgan patterns.

From high end art glass to mass-produced plain barware tumblers, Central was a major glass producer throughout the period.

Pink Frances Pattern Bowl

Bowl, 10 1/2" d., 3-footed, rolled edge, Frances patt., pink (ILLUS.) **$48**

One of a Pair of Brocade Candleholders

Candleholders, one-light, Brocade etching, No. 2000, green, pr. (ILLUS. of one) **$95**
Candleholders, one-light, cobalt blue Stretch glass, 7" h., pr. **$170**
Candleholders, one-light, two-handled, hexagonal base, Chippendale patt., canary, 9 1/2" h., pr. **$400**

Central Cigarette Jar with Etching

Cigarette jar, round ashtray foot, clear optic bowl on amber foot, gold-encrusted Dunn's Parrot etching (ILLUS.) **$65**
Cordial, Balda etching, No. 1428, Orchid **$75**
Decanter w/faceted stopper, footed, Thistle etching #10, clear **$165**
Plate, 8 1/2" w., square, No. 1450, yellow........ **$10**

Central No. 1450 Sherbet

Sherbet, low footed, No. 1450 stem, black base w/clear bowl (ILLUS.) **$10**
Tumbler, flat, Frances patt., green, 10 oz........ **$95**
Vase, 10" h., flat base, flared top, Morgan etching, green **$395**

G

Crown Milano

This glass, produced by Mt. Washington Glass Company late in the 19th century, is opal glass decorated by painting and enameling. It appears identical to a ware termed Albertine, also made by Mt. Washington.

Printed Crown Milano Mark

Thistle-decorated Crown Milano Jar

Cracker jar w/silver plate rim, cover & spiral-twist swing bail handle, barrel-shaped, enameled w/large thistle leaves in pale blue & green & a thistle blossom in green & pink, some silver plate wear, minor gold wear on decoration, to top of handle 10 1/2" h. (ILLUS.) **$403**

Crown Milano Banquet Lamp

Banquet lamp, kerosene-type, a domed scroll-cast paw-footed base supporting a slender cylindrical glass section decorated in color w/chrysanthemums, stems & leaves, a fancy brass connector supporting the squatty bulbous glass font enameled w/flowers & four medallions w/raised winged cherubs, double wick burner stamped "Miller 330," shade ring w/three minor solder repairs, overall 31 1/2" h. (ILLUS.) **$575**

Fine Signed Crown Milano Cracker Jar

Cracker jar w/silver plate rim, cover & swing bail handle, squatty bulbous body w/alternating beige & raised creamy white ribbing decorated w/a continuous vine of gold enameled flowers & leaves, cover marked "MW/4416/a," base marked w/crown & "CM527," w/handle 7" h. (ILLUS.) **$748**

G

Lovely Crown Milano Pitcher

Pitcher, 9" h., 7 1/2" d., bulbous ovoid body tapering to a short neck w/a high arched spout & dragon handle, pink & green tracery ground enameled in gold & pink w/dotted & jeweled stylized flowers & vines (ILLUS.) **$1,610**

Crown Milano Rose Bowl with Orchid

Rose bowl, spherical w/eight-crimp rim, blue shading to pale blue ground enameled a mauve, green & brown orchid & leaves, base numbered "618," 4 3/4" d. (ILLUS.).. **$345**

Rose bowl, spherical w/eight-crimp rim, pale amber shading to yellow ground h.p. w/pink, white & yellow spider mums on leafy stems, base numbered "617," 5 1/2" d. (ILLUS., top next column) **$345**

Rose bowl, spherical w/eight-crimp rim, pale coral shading to yellow ground h.p. w/scattered small enameled blue & white flowers on leafy stems, base numbered "619," 4" d. (ILLUS., middle next column) .. **$316**

Crown Milano Numbered Rose Bowl

Crown Milano Rose Bowl with Tiny Flowers

G

Crown Milano Rose Bowl with Foxglove

Rose bowl, spherical w/eight-crimp rim, pale cream ground h.p. w/amethyst foxglove blossoms w/green leaves & brown traceries, 6 1/2" d. (ILLUS.)........................ **$316**

Cruets

Cranberry, spherical Inverted Thumbprint body w/slender cylindrical neck w/tricorner rim, clear applied handle, clear facet-cut stopper, 7" h. **$92**

Decorated Green Cruet

Green, wide ovoid optic ribbed body w/a short cylindrical neck w/tricorner rim, applied green handle & green ball stopper, the sides enameled w/a cluster of purple blossoms on slender green leafy stems, 3 3/4" d., 8 1/2" h. (ILLUS.) **$150-175**

Cup Plates

Produced in numerous patterns beginning more than 170 years ago, these little plates were designed to hold a cup while the tea or coffee was allowed to cool in a saucer. Cup plates were also made of ceramics. Where numbers are listed below, they refer to numbers assigned to these plates in the book American Glass Cup Plates *by Ruth Webb Lee and James H. Rose. Plates are of clear glass unless otherwise noted. A number of cup plates have been reproduced.*

L & R-148-A, round w/30 bull's-eye scallops, large floral sprig in the center, medium blue, Midwestern, several scallops tipped, tiny rim flake, 3" d. (ILLUS., top next column).. **$1,760**

L & R-179, round w/10-scalloped rope rim, large starburst & knobs in the center, rayed rim band, deep purple, Philadelphia area, near proof, 3 7/16" d. (ILLUS., middle next column).............. **$2,090**

Blue Cup Plate with Floral Sprig

Rare Purple Cup Plate 179

Cup Plate with Stars & Plumes

L & R-222, round w/smooth rope rim, quatrefoil in the center surrounded by four plumes & four small stars, stars & pairs of plumes around the border, Midwestern, clear, under-rim spall, 3 1/2" d. (ILLUS.) **$1,870**

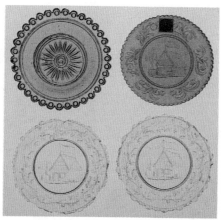

Group of Four Varied Cup Plates

Blue Cup Plate 242-A

L & R-242-A, round w/60 small even scallops, quatrefoil in the center framed by a band of small arches, the rim band w/alternating starbursts & flowerheads, dark blue, near proof, 3 1/2" d. (ILLUS.) **$2,200**

L & R-531, round, bull's-eye & sunburst center design, plain border, knobby rim, strong yellowish green, 3 5/8" d. (ILLUS. top row, left, with cup plates No. 594, No. 601A and No. 601C, top of page) **$66**

L & R-594, round, Log Cabin patt., golden amber, 3 1/4" d. (ILLUS. top row, right, with cup plates No. 531, No. 601A & 601C, top of page) **$440**

L & R-601A, round, Log Cabin patt., 12 large scallops w/four smaller between, poor condition, very rare, clear, 3 1/2" d. (ILLUS. bottom row, left, with cup plates No. 531, No. 594 & No. 601C, top of page) **$88**

L & R-601A, round, Log Cabin patt., 18 large scallops w/smaller scallop & two points between, very rare, clear, poor condition, 3 1/2" d. (ILLUS. bottom row, right, with cup plates No. 531, No. 594 & No. 601A, top of page) **$66**

G

Green Ship Benjamin Franklin Cup Plate

L & R-619, round, Ship Benjamin Franklin patt., floral scroll border, emerald green, loss to three scallops, 3 1/2" d. (ILLUS.) **$1,870**

Cup Plate No. 82 and No. 89

L & R-82, round, flower blossom & leaf border band, opaque swirled blue w/translucent opalescent rim, light silvery sheen on lower half of shoulder, plain rim, very rare, minor chips, 3 5/8" d. (ILLUS. left with No. 89 cup plate, bottom previous page) **$990**

L & R-89, round, plain rope border band, fiery opalescent, 3 3/4" d. (ILLUS. right with rare cup plate No. 82, bottom previous page) **$77**

Cut

Cut glass most eagerly sought by collectors is American glass produced during the so-called "Brilliant Period" from 1880 to about 1915. Pieces listed below are by type of article in alphabetical order.

Hawkes, Hoare, Libbey and Straus Marks

Baskets

G

Fine Silver-Mounted Cut Glass Basket

Silver-mounted, tall pedestal base cut w/horizontal ribbing below the two pulled-up & widely fanned sides cut w/further stepped ribbon, vertical flutes & lozenge designs, fitted across the top w/a high, arched sterling silver handle w/floral-clad joins marked by Tiffany & Company, 1902-07, 11" h. (ILLUS.) **$3,120**

Bowls

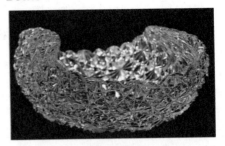

Russian Cut Banana Boat Bowl

Banana boat, rounded boat-shaped bowl w/incurved ends cut overall in the Russian patt., minor flakes & roughness, 9 1/2" l., 3" h. (ILLUS.) **$219**

Nice Hobstar & Arches Cut Bowl

Hobstars in large pointed arches, alternating w/small rim hobstars, deeply scalloped & notched rim, 9" d. (ILLUS.) **$403**

Fine Cobalt Cut to Clear Bowl

Sunburst hobstars, cobalt blue cut to clear w/large sunburst hobstars alternating w/panels w/cut triangles, small hobstar & fan cutting, boat-shaped w/notched rim, 8 1/4" l., 4 1/2" h. (ILLUS.) **$604**

Candlesticks & Candleholders

Poinsettia Blossom Candlesticks by Ideal

Ideal Cut Glass Company, round foot w/engraved Poinsettia blossom design below the faceted-knop stem below the panel-cut teardrop stem also cut w/Poinsettia blossoms & leaves, the cylindrical leaf-cut socket w/a wide flattened rim, New York City, early 20th c., 10" h., pr. (ILLUS.).. **$748**

Compotes

Hobstar & Fan-Cut Four-Part Compote

Hobstars & feathered fans, round four-section shallow bowl w/alternating designs, scalloped & notched rim, swelled panel-cut stem w/interior teardrop, round hobstar-cut foot, 7" d., 6 1/2" h. (ILLUS.)
.... **$201**

Pairpoint Compote with Engraved Garlands

Pairpoint-signed, finely engraved w/floral garlands & butterflies alternating w/leaf & blossom sprigs around rim, serpentine rim, notched pedestal & round engraved foot, 9" d., 6" h. (ILLUS.) **$316**

Lamps

Flower & Leaf Cut Lamp with Hobstars

Table, domed mushroom-shaped 10" d. shade intaglio cut w/large blossoms alternating w/leafy branches from the center top above a wide rim band of hobstars, shade ring suspending facet-cut spearpoint prisms, matching slender baluster-form standard w/domed foot, original hardware, early 20th c., 18" h. (ILLUS.) **$1,380**

G

foot, by Pairpoint, early 20th c., shade 11 1/2" d., 19" h. (ILLUS.) **$3,220**

Leaf & Flower-Cut Table Lamp

G

Table, domed mushroom-shaped 10" d. shade intaglio cut w/large blossoms alternating w/leafy branches from the center top, shade ring suspending facet-cut spearpoint prisms, matching slender baluster-form standard w/domed foot, original hardware, early 20th c., 19 1/2" h. (ILLUS.) **$1,725**

Strawberry Diamond-Cut Table Lamp

Table, domed squared 7 3/4" w. shade w/an overall strawberry diamond-cut design resting on a matching metal ring suspending triangular spearpoint prisms, matching slender trumpet-form base w/a scalloped fan-cut rim, early 20th c., 16 1/2" h. (ILLUS.) **$403**

Pitchers

Pairpoint Cut Marillo Pattern Lamp

Table, domed shade w/etched Murillo patt. w/butterflies alternating w/leaf sprigs down from the top, on a brass shade ring suspending facet-cut spearpoint prisms, matching baluster-form base w/cushion

Buzzstar & Hobstar Tall Pitcher

Buzzstar & hobstar, waisted tankard-style, the sides cut w/two large buzzstars separated by a cut horizontal band, a long band of small hobstars cut below the spout, facet-cut applied handle, 10" h. (ILLUS.) **$118**

Punch Bowls, Cups & Sets

Hobstar & Feathered Arch Punch Bowl

Hobstar & feathered arch, the large deep bowl w/a six-lobed rim, three panels cut w/large detailed hobstars alternating w/long pointed feathered arches enclosing tiny hobstars, the base w/a wide strawberry diamond-cut rim band above the flaring scalloped sides w/a matching cut design, ca. 1900, small heat check in bottom of bowl, 14" d. (ILLUS.) **$558**

Deep Hobstar & Fan-Cut Punch Bowl

Punch bowl, deep rounded sides w/a gently scalloped & notched rim, large hobstars alternating w/large triangular & fancut panels, minor edge roughness, 14" d. (ILLUS.).. **$403**

Fine Hawkes-signed Punch Bowl with Fans, Hobstars & Strawberry Diamond

Punch bowl, Hawkes-signed, large cut fans forming the rim scallops joined to inverted cut fans down the sides all alternating w/large diamond panels cut w/a strawberry diamond design alternating w/hobstars, 14" d. (ILLUS.).................................... **$690**

Dorflinger Punch Bowl

Punch bowl, large cut fans form the scalloped rim above diamond panels cut w/hobstars above a bottom band of panel-cut diamonds, Marlboro patt., Dorflinger, 13 3/4" d., 7" h. (ILLUS.)....................... **$345**

Fan & Hobstar-Cut Punch Bowl

Punch bowl, large cut fans forming the rim scalloped above a band of cut hobstars within cut diamond panels, minor rim chips, 14 1/2" d., 7" h. (ILLUS.).................. **$345**

Hobstar & Cane-Cut Punch Bowl

Punch bowl, large hobstars alternating w/smaller hobstars above cane-cut panels, gently scalloped & notched rim, 14 1/4" d. (ILLUS.) **$345**

G

Fancy Hobstar & Panels Punch Bowl

Boldly Cut Fan & Hobstar Punch Bowl

Punch bowl & base, wide deep rounded bowl w/scalloped & notched rim, the sides cut w/large hobstars alternating w/diamond-form panels w/a pointed band above a small hobstar w/a panel of heavy crosshatching below, 14" d., 13" h. (ILLUS.) **$978**

Punch bowl & base, wide rounded bowl w/very large cut fans forming the rim scallops above a lower half cut w/a band of large hobstars, matching flaring pedestal base, 10 1/4" d., 9 1/4" h. (ILLUS.).... **$431**

Trays

G

Rare Hawkes Basketweave Cut Torte Tray

Hawkes signed, round torte tray cut w/an intricate basketweave patt. surround a 28-point center hobstar, serrated edge w/flat chip, 12" d. (ILLUS.) **$4,600**

Vases

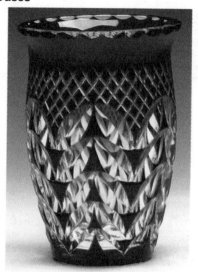

Val St. Lambert Amethyst to Clear Vase

Amethyst cut to clear, gently swelled cylindrical body w/a gently flaring rim, the body cut w/repeating bands of undulating leaf devices below an upper diamond lattice design, notched rim, signed "Val St. Lambert," 6 1/2" h. (ILLUS.) **$115**

Fan-shaped Vase with Basket Panels

Fan-shaped, the tall flaring sides cut overall w/a diamond point design & two oval panels engraved w/a hanging flower basket, round star-cut foot, 12 1/2" w., 9 3/4" h. (ILLUS.) **$230**

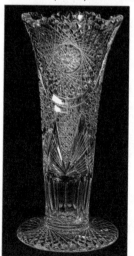

Flaring Hobstar & Fan-cut Vase

Cylindrical flaring body, round foot w/a cut hobstar supporting the cylindrical body cut w/zipper panels below long triangular cut panels alternating w/triangular fan-cut panels below the flaring top cut w/large hobstars below the scalloped & notched rim, minor rim flakes, 11 5/8" h. (ILLUS.).. **$403**

Tall Pedestal Hobstar & Diamond Vase

Hobstar, finecut diamond & fan, a round starburst-cut foot supporting a tall paneled pedestal below the tall slender swelled cylindrical body w/a widely flaring rim, the lower body cut w/a band of large hobstars within a diamond alternating w/a cut fan above a fan-cut & finecut diamond, a simple panel-cut center band below the flaring top w/cutting matching the lower body, 16" h. (ILLUS.).................. **$441**

G

Miscellaneous Items

Val St. Lambert Cranberry Cut-to-Clear Console Set

Console set: 12" d. footed deep bowl & pair 10" candlesticks; cranberry cut to clear, the flat-rimmed bowl cut w/bands of large & small punties alternating w/inverted V-design, matching candlesticks w/a clear socks & clear foot, signed "Val St. Lambert," 20th c., the set (ILLUS., top of page) **$661**

Cameo vase, 12 1/4" h., tall ovoid body w/a short tapering domed neck, frosted yellow ground cased in dark brown shaded to orange & cameo-carved w/pendant flowers on leafy stems, signed in cameo (ILLUS.).. **$2,243**

D'Argental

Glass known by this name is so-called after its producer, who fashioned fine cameo pieces in St. Louis, France in the late 19th century and up to 1918.

D'Argental

D'Argental Mark

Tall D'Argental Cameo Vase

Cameo vase, 13 3/4" h., flaring foot tapering to a tall swelled cylindrical neck tapering to a gently flared neck, mottled orange & yellow ground overlaid in dark purple & cut w/blossoms branches in the foreground framing a sailboat on water in the background, signed in cameo (ILLUS.) **$1,035**

Fine D'Argental Floral Cameo Vase

Tall D'Argental Cameo Vase

Cameo vase, 14" h., cushion foot below the tall slender tapering cylindrical body w/a short flaring neck, mottled tangerine ground overlaid in dark blue & cameo-cut w/tall stylized flowers & leaves, etched signature on the side (ILLUS.) **$1,035**

Very Tall, Slender D'Argental Vase

Cameo vase, 17" h., flaring base tapering to a very tall & slender body gently flaring at the top, frosted dark to light amber ground cased in amber & cameo-carved w/long leafy flower vines around the sides, signed in cameo (ILLUS.) **$2,040**

Daum Nancy

This fine glass, much of it cameo, was made by Auguste and Antonin Daum, who founded a factory in 1875 in Nancy, France. Most of their cameo and enameled glass was made from the 1890s into the early 20th century.

Daum Nancy Marks

Daum Rose-decorated Cameo Box

Cameo box, cov., oval w/upright sides, mottled yellow base cameo carved w/rose leaves & stems, low domed cover in mottled white cased in mottled green & pink & carved w/rose blossoms & leaves, two small filled rim chips, engraved signature, 5 3/8" l., 3 1/8" h. (ILLUS.) **$5,175**

Cameo box, cov., round, squatty bulbous base in pale mottled blue over yellow cameo-carved & enameled w/small purple blossoms on green stems, mottled blue cover w/matching blossoms, base rim polished, nicks in cover rim, 4" d., 2 1/2" h. (ILLUS., top next page)............ **$2,645**

G

Daum Nancy Cameo Box with Purple Flowers

G

Fine Daum Cameo Scent Bottle

Scarce Daum Cameo Creamer

Cameo creamer, small round foot & knop stem below the widely flaring trumpet-form body w/cupped top & pinched spout, applied frosted clear handle, frosted white to amber ground cameo-carved & enameled w/small blue flowers, a drag-onfly, leaves & stems, signed on the base in gold script, 4 1/2" h. (ILLUS.) **$5,060**

Cameo scent bottle, spherical white body tapering to a short neck w/a clear stopper w/faceted edges trimmed in gold, the body cameo-cut & enameled w/a leafy vine of shaded red flowers & buds fram-ing a black & white enameled scene of a road leading to a village, base signed w/etched signature, very small old chip inside lip, small flake on corner of stop-per, 3 1/4" h. (ILLUS.) **$2,185**

Miniature Daum Cameo Tumbler

Cameo tumbler, miniature, cylindrical, cameo-etched w/a winter landscape of leafless trees enameled in brown, black & white against the mottled yellow & orange background, signed on the bottom, 1 7/8" h. (ILLUS.) **$1,035**

Fine Small Flower-decorated Daum Vase

Cameo vase, 4 3/4" h., slightly swelled cylindrical form, mottled pale blue shading to lime green, cameo-cut & enameled w/purplish red blossoms on tall thin green leafy stems, cameo signature & monogram in enamel (ILLUS.) **$1,725**

Cameo vase, 6 1/8" h., slender waisted form, frosted white cameo-carved & enameled w/a scene of a bumble bee & damselfly above a winter landscape of Dutch windmills in black & green, gold rim bands, unsigned (ILLUS., top next column) **$2,990**

Cameo vase, 9 3/4" h., 4 3/4" d., a flattened cushion base tapering to a cylindrical body w/a swelled ring around the flat rim, mottled & streaking red & orange ground overlaid in dark maroon & cameo-carved w/slender trees in the foreground, cameo signature, ca. 1910 (ILLUS., middle next column) **$2,160**

Daum Nancy Vase with Insects & Landscape

Daum Nancy Cameo Vase with Trees

Miniature Daum Vase with Dutch Scene

Vase, 1 5/8" h., miniature, ovoid body tapering to a cylindrical neck w/an uneven rolled rim, milky white ground enameled in dark blue & black w/a Dutch winter scene w/a windmill near boats in a harbor, acid-etched background, signed on the bottom (ILLUS.)..................................... **$780**

Miniature Daum Vase with Goose Girl

Vase, 3 1/4" h., miniature, flattened swelled form in frosted milky white enameled in color w/the figure of a young girl holding four geese on leashes, signed on the bottom (ILLUS.)... **$1,610**

Daum Nancy Vase with Autumn Leaves

Vase, 4" h., 4 1/8 x 6 7/8", narrow oblong foot & conforming gently flaring sides, mottled frosted clear over mottled maroon, yellow & green at the bottom acid-etched w/swirling autumn leaves enameled in shades of yellow, cameo signature, ca. 1910 (ILLUS.) **$2,880**

DeLatte

Andre de Latte of Nancy, France, produced a range of opaque and cameo glass after 1921. His company also produced light fixtures but his cameo wares are most collectible today.

Decorative DeLatte Blown-Out Bowl

Bowl, 11 1/2" d., blown-out style, wide deep form w/a flat rim in various shades of mottled blue, blown into & around a white-metal openwork frame, signed outside the lip, a chip & two bruises into bottom, several minor chips & some grinding to lip (ILLUS.) **$1,020**

Small Spherical DeLatte Cameo Vase

Cameo vase, 4" h., spherical body tapering to a small flared neck, mottled white, green & blue ground overlaid in blue & cameo-carved w/large leafy branches w/berries, cameo signature (ILLUS.) **$500**

DeLatte Cameo Vase with Wild Roses

Cameo vase, 7 1/4" h., footed squatty bulbous lower body tapering sharply to a tall cylindrical neck w/a cupped rim, frosted clear overlaid in purple & cameo-cut w/wild roses on long leafy stems, signed in cameo (ILLUS.) **$460**

deVez & Degué

The Saint-Hilaire, Touvier, de Varreaux and Company of Pantin, France used the name de Vez on its cameo glass early in the 20th century. Some of the firm's examples were marked "Degué" after one of its master glassmakers. Officially the company was named "Cristallerie de Pantin."

DeVez and Degué Marks

Tiny Degué Intaglio-Cut Shot Glass

Shot glass, slender slightly tapering cylindrical shape in dark green shaded to clear intaglio-cut w/stylized flower blossoms & leaves, signed "Degué," two chips on inner lip, 2" h. (ILLUS.) **$144**

Duncan & Miller

Duncan & Miller Glass Company, a successor firm to George A. Duncan & Sons Company, produced a wide range of pressed wares and novelty pieces during the late 19th century and into the early 20th century. During the Depression era and after, they continued making a wide variety of more modern patterns, including mold-blown types, and also introduced a number of etched and engraved patterns. Many colors, including opalescent hues, were produced during this era, and especially popular today are the graceful swan dishes they produced in the Pall Mall and Sylvan patterns.

The numbers after the pattern name indicate the original factory pattern number. The Duncan factory was closed in 1955. Also see ANIMALS.

Basket, Hobnail patt., applied handle, blue opalescent, 9 x 14" (ILLUS., top next column) **$200**

Bowl, 5" d., Early American Sandwich patt., fruit, clear **$12**
Cake stand, footed, Teardrop patt., clear, 13" d. **$65**

Blue Opalescent Hobnail Pattern Basket

Duncan & Miller Green Coaster-Ashtray

Coaster-ashtray, green, 4 1/4 x 6" (ILLUS.) **$25**
Cocktail shaker w/chrome lid, Terrace patt., cobalt blue **$275**
Cup & saucer, Puritan patt., pink **$13**

Miniature Mardi Grass Honey Jug

Honey jug, miniature, Mardi Gras patt., clear, 2 1/2" h. (ILLUS.) **$28**
Pitcher w/ice lip, Teardrop patt., clear, 1/2 gal. **$100**
Plate, 6" d., Early American Sandwich patt., bread & butter, clear **$8**
Plate, 7 1/2" w., etched First Love patt., salad, clear **$24**
Punch set: bowl, ladle, tray & 12 cups; Hobnail patt., pink opalescent, the set **$650**

G

G

Sylvan Two-Part Milk Glass Relish

Relish dish, Sylvan patt., two-part, milk white w/green handle, 8 1/2" l. (ILLUS.)..... **$125**

Homestead Pattern Individual Salt Dip

Salt dip, individual, footed, No. 63 Homestead patt., clear, 2" h. (ILLUS.).................... **$18**

Tray for salt & pepper shakers, anchor handle, Nautical patt., blue......................... **$125**

Tumbler, whiskey, flat, First Love etching, clear, 1 1/2 oz.. **$68**

Vase, 6 1/2" h., urn-shaped w/handles, Grecian patt., Chartreuse.................................. **$28**

Fan-shaped Early American Sandwich Vase

Vase, 5" h., Early American Sandwich patt., fanned shape, clear (ILLUS.) **$49**

Ruby Venetian Pattern Vase

Vase, 10 1/2" h., footed, Venetian No. 126 patt., ruby (ILLUS.)..................................... **$225**

Durand

Fine decorative glass similar to that made by Tiffany and other outstanding glasshouses of its day was made by the Vineland Flint Glass Works Co. in Vineland, New Jersey, first headed by Victor Durand Sr. and subsequently by his son, Victor Durand Jr., in the 1920s.

Center bowl, a rounded bowl in clear w/a white pulled feather design continues to a very wide flattened rim in dark blue, 12" d. (ILLUS., top next page)................... **$633**

Durand Sherbet with King Tut Design

Sherbet, the gold iridescent round foot & short knopped stem supporting the deep rounded & flaring bowl w/the gold iridescent exterior decorated in royal blue w/the King Tut looping design, Shape No. 2013, 3 1/4" h. (ILLUS.) **$500**

Blue & White Durand Pulled Feather Center Bowl

Durand Gold Iridescent Threaded Vase

Vase, 5 5/8" h., gently swelled cylindrical body w/a wider rounded shoulder band & wide flat mouth, golden orange iridescent exterior decorated overall w/fine gold threading, mottled yellow interior, some areas of skipped threading (ILLUS.) **$230**

Labeled Durand Vase with Vines

Vase, 6 5/8" h., flat-bottomed squatty bulbous body tapering to a tall widely flaring trumpet neck, dark iridescent blue decorated w/random white woven wines & heart-shaped leaves, scarce paper sticker reading "Durand Art Glass" on base (ILLUS.)... **$1,093**

G

Durand Amethyst Optic Ribbed Vase

Vase, 6" h., spherical amethyst optic ribbed body w/a short cylindrical neck & widely flaring rim, base signed w/silver "V" & "Durand 1987-6" (ILLUS.) **$575**

Footed Spherical Gold Durand Vase

Vase, 7 1/4" h., tapering conical foot supporting the wide spherical body tapering to a trumpet-form neck, overall gold iridescence, few scratches (ILLUS.) **$403**

Tall Finely Decorated Durand Vase

G **Vase,** 12" h., round foot & short stem in gold iridescence supporting the tall gently flaring trumpet-form body, the exterior in antique ivory decorated w/scattered bicolor leaves in blue & gold & covered w/overall gold threading, base marked w/Durand signature & "20120-12," some threading missing (ILLUS.)...................................... **$2,070**

Fostoria

Fostoria Glass company, founded in 1887, produced numerous types of fine glassware over the years. Its factory in Moundsville, West Virginia, closed in 1986.

Fostoria Label

Wisteria Footed Almond Dish

Almond dish, square foot, flaring bowl, No. 4020, Wisteria, 2 3/4" d. (ILLUS.) **$32**

Part of an Amber Priscilla Beverage Set

Beverage set: 48 oz. 10" h. pitcher & 11 footed & handled tumblers; Priscilla patt., amber, the set (ILLUS. of part) **$250-300**
Bonbon, Colony patt., three-footed, clear, 7" d. **$12**

Colony Pattern Square Ice Cream Bowl

Bowl, 5 1/2" w., ice cream-type, square, Colony patt., clear (ILLUS.)........................... **$28**
Bowl, salad, 9 3/4" d., Colony patt., clear **$45**
Bowl, 10 1/2" d., Colony patt., high-footed, clear **$112**
Bowl, 11" w., American patt., tri-cornered, three footed, clear **$40**
Cake plate, American patt., three-footed, clear, 12" d. **$25**
Cake salver, Colony patt., clear, 12" d. **$75**

One of a Pair of Onyx Lustre Candleholders

Candleholders, one-light, Onyx Lustre, No. 2324, 3" h., pr. (ILLUS. of one, previous page) $425

Candlestick, one-light, Romance etching, clear, 5 1/2" h. $32

Candlestick, two-light, American patt., clear, 4 3/8" h. $42

Candlesticks, cone-footed, American patt., clear, 15 points, small, pr. $600

Candlesticks, one-light, Chintz etching, No. 2496/315, clear, 4" h., pr. $45

Pair of Green Coin Candlesticks

Candlesticks, one-light, Coin patt., Emerald Green, 4 1/2" h., pr. 4 3/4" h. (ILLUS.) $65

Candlesticks, two-light, Romance etching, No. 6023, clear, pr. $65

Chambersticks w/finger hold, American patt., clear, pr. $95

Champagne, Romance etching, clear, 7" h. $16

Cheese compote, American patt., clear $30

Cocktail, American Lady patt., clear, 3 1/2 oz., 4" h. $14

Cocktail, American patt., footed, clear, 3 oz. $12

Cocktail No. 5099 in Azure Blue

Cocktail, No. 5099, Azure Blue, 3 oz. (ILLUS.) $22

Cocktail, Romance etching, clear, 3 1/2 oz. $15

Cracker jar, cov., American patt., clear $325

Creamer, American patt., clear, medium $9

Creamer, Chintz etching, clear $16

Creamer, individual, Colony patt., clear, 3 1/4" h., 4 oz. $6

Creamer, open sugar bowl & undertray, individual, American patt., clear, the set $38

Coronet Pattern Oil Cruet

Cruet w/original stopper, oil-type, footed, Coronet patt., clear, 3 0z. (ILLUS.) $37

Crushed fruit jar, cov., American patt., clear, 10" h. (chip on lid) $1,600

Cup, American patt., clear, 7 oz. $8

Cup & saucer, Colony patt., clear $9

Rare Green Lafayette Cup & Saucer

Cup & saucer, Lafayette patt., translucent Jade green, rare color (ILLUS.) $150

Glove box, cov., American patt., clear (some stretch marks) $600

Goblet, American Lady patt., Amethyst bowl, 10 oz. water, 6 1/8" h. (ILLUS. center with American Lady sherbet & tumbler, top next page) $36

G

Amethyst American Lady Goblet, Sherbet & Tumbler

Goblet, American Lady patt., cobalt blue, 10 oz., 6 1/8" h. $95
Goblet, Colony patt., water, clear, 5 1/4" h., 9 oz. $14
Goblet, Holly cutting, clear, 10 oz, 8 3/8" h. $18
Goblet, Romance etching, water, clear, 9 oz. $22
Honey jar, cover & spoon, American patt., clear $500
Jewel box, cov., American patt., clear, 2 1/4 x 5 1/4", 2" h. $400
Mayonnaise bowl w/ladle, American patt., divided, clear, 3 1/4" d., 6 1/4" h., 2 pcs. $15

American Mayonnaise & Two Ladles

Mayonnaise bowl w/two ladles, American patt., divided, clear, 3 1/4" d., 6 1/4" h., 3 pcs. (ILLUS.) $65
Mustard jar, cov., American patt., clear........... $35
Nappy, American patt., flared, green, 4 1/2" d... $70
Nappy, American patt., tri-cornered, handled, clear, 5" w... $10
Olive dish, American patt., clear, 6" l.............. $12
Oyster cocktail, American Lady patt., clear, 4 oz., 3 1/2" h. $14
Pickle dish, Century patt., clear, 8 3/4" l.......... $15
Pickle jar w/silverplated lid, cov., American patt., clear, 6" h. $450
Plate, 7" d., Baroque patt., salad, clear.............. $4
Plate, 7 1/2" d., Navarre patt., clear $14
Plate, 13 1/2" oval, torte, American patt., clear $45

Plate, 14" d., torte, Century patt., clear $30
Plate, 15" d., torte, Colony patt., clear.............. $60

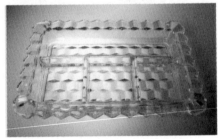

American Pattern Four-part Relish

Relish dish, American patt., four-part, rectangular, clear, 6 1/4 x 9" (ILLUS.)................ $42

Colony Individual Shakers on Tray

Salt & pepper shakers w/original tops on tray, individual size, Colony patt., clear, the set (ILLUS.)... $45
Sherbet, American Lady patt., Amethyst bowl w/clear stem, 5 1/2 oz., 4 1/8" h. (ILLUS. left with American Lady goblet & tumbler, top of page) $24
Tumbler, American Lady patt., ice tea, footed, Amethyst bowl, 5 1/2" h., 12 oz. (ILLUS. right with American Lady goblet & sherbet, top of page).............................. $32

Ruby Heirloom Pitcher-form Vase

Vase, 9" h., pitcher-style, Heirloom patt.,
ruby (ILLUS.)... **$90**

Rare Etched Brocade Palm Leaf Vase

Vase, 10 1/2" h., footed w/tall slender waisted bowl, etched Brocade Palm Leaf patt.,
green (ILLUS.).. **$450**

Fry

Numerous types of glass were made by
the H.C. Fry Company of Rochester, Pennsylvania. One of its art lines was called
Foval and was blown in 1926-27. Cheaper
was its milky-opalescent ovenware (Pearl

Oven Ware), made for utilitarian purposes
but also now being collected. The company
also made fine cut glass.

Collectors of Fry glass will be interested
in the recent publication of a good reference
book, The Collector's Encyclopedia of Fry
Glassware, by The H.C. Fry Glass Society
(Collector Books, 1990).

Bowl, 10" d., cut glass, Trojan patt., clear...... **$320**

One of Two Fry Candleholders

Candleholders, one-light, jack-in-the-pulpit
style, controlled bubbles & applied
threading, blue, pr. (ILLUS. of one)............ **$170**

Olympus Etched Pink Champagne

Champagne, Olympus (Bubble Blower)
etching by an unknown decorator, pink,
5" h. (ILLUS.) **$55**
Cigarette holder w/ashtray foot,
stemmed, amber... **$62**

G

Unusual Fry Art Deco Crystal & Black Compote

G

Fry Astoria Pattern Cut Glass Compote

Pink Goblet with Etching No. 107

Compote, 6" d., cut glass, low pedestal base, two applied handles, Astoria patt., clear (ILLUS.) **$135**

Compote, open, 7 7/8" d., 3 3/8" h., Art Deco design, the thin round black foot supporting a clear ovoid spiral-reeded stem below the widely flaring shallow bowl w/diamond optic design & a purplish black wide pinwheel design alternating w/crystal bands (ILLUS., top of page) **$403**

Cream soup bowl & underplate, two-handled, No. 1970, Royal Blue **$65**

Cup & saucer, Pearl Oven Ware, the set **$38**

Goblet, water, Etching No. 107, pink, 7" h. (ILLUS., top next column) **$44**

Sherbet, low, footed, Diamond Optic patt., pink bowl & foot & blue stem (ILLUS., bottom next column).................................... **$47**

Tumbler, Foval line, Delft blue foot, handle & festooning in the body............................ **$225**

Vase, 10" h., stick-form bud-type, Anemone etching, clear... **$75**

Fry Diamond Optic Sherbet

Higgins Glass

Fused glass, an "old craft for modern tastes" enjoyed a mid-20th century revival through the work of Chicago-based artists Frances and Michael Higgins of the Higgins Glass Studio. Although known for thousands of years, fusing had, by the 1940s, been abandoned in favor of glassblowing. A meticulous craft, fusing can best be described as the creation of a "glass sandwich." A design is either drawn with colored enamels or pieced with glass segments on a piece of enamel-coated glass. Another piece of enameled glass is placed over this. The "sandwich" is then placed on a mold and heated in a kiln, with the glass "slumping" to the shape of the mold. When complete, the interior design is fused between the outer glass layers. Additional layers are often utilized, accentuating the visual depth. Sensing that fused glass was a marketable commodity, the Higginses opened their studio in 1948 and applied the fusing technique to a wide variety of items: tableware such as bowls, plates, and servers; housewares, ranging from clocks and lamps to ashtrays and candleholders; and purely decorative items, such as mobiles and jewelry. With its arresting mix of geometric and curved lines and bold use of color, Higgins glass transformed the ordinary into decor accent pieces both vibrant and exciting.

Unlike many of their contemporaries, the Higginses received national exposure thanks to an association with Chicago industrial manufacturer Dearborn Glass Company. This collaboration, lasting from 1957 through 1964, resulted in the mass marketing of "higginsware" worldwide. Since nearly every piece carried the lower-case signature "higgins," name recognition was both immediate and enduring.

The Dearborn demand for new Higgins pieces resulted in more than 75 identifiable production patterns with such buyer-enticing names as "Stardust," "Arabesque," and "Barbaric Jewels." Objects created in these patterns included ashtrays of every size (4" "Dinner Dwarfs" to 15" jumbo models), "rondelay" room dividers and an extensive line of tableware. (As evidenced by Dearborn promotional postcards, complete dining tables could literally be set with Higgins glass.)

In 1965, the Higginses briefly moved their base of operations to Haeger Potteries before opening their own studio in Riverside, Illinois, where it has been located since 1966. Although Michael Higgins died in 1999 and Frances Higgins in 2004, the Studio today continues under the leadership of longtime artistic associates Louise and Jonathan Wimmer. New pieces celebrate and expand on the traditions and techniques of the past. Higgins pieces created from 1948 until 1957 are engraved on the reverse with the signature "higgins" or the artist's complete name. A raised "dancing man" logo was added in 1951. Pieces created at Dearborn or Haeger (1957-65) bear a gold "higgins" signature on the surface or a signature in the colorway. The marking since 1966 has been an engraved "higgins" on the reverse of an object, with the occasional addition of the artist's name. Pieces produced since the death of Frances Higgins are signed "higgins studio."

Once heralded as "an exclamation point in your decorating scheme," Higgins glass continues, nearly 60 years since its inception, to enchant collectors with its zest and variety.

References on Higgins glass include the Schiffer books Higgins: Poetry in Glass (2005), and Higgins: Adventures in Glass (1997), both by Donald-Brian Johnson and Leslie Pina. Photos for this category are by Dr. Pina.

The Higgins Glass Studio is located at 33 East Quincy Street, Riverside, IL 60546 (708-447-2787), www.higginsglass.com.

Price ranges given are general estimates covering all available patterns produced at Dearborn Glass Company and Haeger Potteries (1957-1965). The low end of the scale applies to the most commonly found patterns (e.g., "Mandarin," "Siamese Purple"), the upper end to those found less frequently (e.g., "Gemspread," "Carousel").

Unique Michael Higgins "Treasure Chest"

Chest, "Treasure Chest," by Michael Higgins, 9 x 13", 18" h. (ILLUS.)......... **$8,000-8,500**

Higgins Glass Dessert Set

Dessert set: 7 1/2" d. large plate, four 5" d. plates & 5 1/2" d. bowl; mauve-pink w/branch outlines in black & gold, the set (ILLUS.).. **$1,700-2,000**

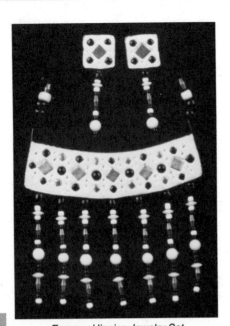

G

Frances Higgins Jewelry Set

Jewelry set: pendant & pair of earrings; white cement w/black & gold jewels, beaded dangles, by Frances Higgins, the set (ILLUS.) **$700-750**

Mobile of Stylized Birds with Egg

Mobile, designed as eight graduated birds above an egg, 4' 2" l. (ILLUS.) **$500-550**

King Platter by Michael Higgins

Platter, "King," by Michael Higgins, 11" d. (ILLUS.) **$1,500-1,750**

Three Higgins Daisy Rondelays

Rondelay, daisy decoration w/winegold luster, 9" d., each (ILLUS. of three) **$150-200**

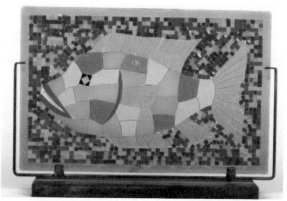

Blue Fish on Red Sea Sculpture by Michael Higgins

Sculpture, "Blue Fish on Red Sea," by Micheal Higgins, 16" l., 10" h. (ILLUS., top of page) **$4,000-4,500**

Five-Layer Sculpture by Jonathan Wimmer

Sculpture, five layers w/different designs on each layer, by Jonathan Wimmer, 15" sq. (ILLUS.) **$2,750-3,000**

Frances Higgins Sparkler Sculpture

Sculpture, "Sparkler," panel on brass stand, by Frances Higgins, 8" w., 11" h. (ILLUS.) **$1,000-1,100**

G

Group of Three Frances Higgins "Dropout" Vases

Vases, "Dropout" style, by Frances Higgins, 3 1/2" to 5 1/2" h., each (ILLUS. group of three) **$350-400**

Varied Grouping of Historical Glass Pieces

Historical & Commemorative

Reference numbers are to Bessie M. Lindsey's book, American Historical Glass.

Bullet Emblem spooner, clear pressed glass, molded spread-winged eagle & cannons around the sides, raised on shield-shaped feet, ca. 1900, 3 7/8" h., No. 64 (ILLUS. second from right with other historical glass pieces, top of page) **$88**

Campaign tumbler, clear pressed flint glass, one side w/a thirteen-star flag, the other side w/a spread-winged eagle perched on a stars & bars shield, probably by Bay State Glass Co., ca. 1864, 3 1/4" h. (ILLUS. second from left with other historical glass pieces, top next page) **$200-250**

Columbia bread tray, shield-shaped, Columbia superimposed against 13 vertical bars, canary, flaking on rim, 9 1/2 x 11 1/2", No. 54 .... **$231**

Eagle on Pedestal, clear pressed glass, two-piece, a tall spread-winged eagle on an orb w/a ground peg fitting into the flat-back columnar base, first half 20th c., 9" h. **$176**

G.A.R. Commemorative Platter

G.A.R. platter, rectangular clear glass w/concave corners, a medal w/ribbon in the center & "Grand Army of the Republic" around the border, minor mold roughness, 7 5/8 x 11 1/8" (ILLUS.) **$154**

Garfield ABC plate, frosted bust of Garfield in the center, 6" d., No. 301 .... **$66**

Ulysses S. Grant Milk Glass Bust

Grant bust, pressed milk glass, head of Ulysses S. Grant w/square base, probably Gillinder & Sons, Philadelphia, flake behind one ear, edge of shoulder & under one corner, 5 7/8" h. (ILLUS.) **$550**

Grant Peace plate, bust portrait of Grant center, maple leaf border, canary, 10 1/2" d., No. 289 .... **$50**

Jenny Lind/Columbia compote, open, clear w/clear frosted figural standard, clear Beaded Panels patt. bowl, 8" d., 8" h., No. 424 .... **$121**

Knights of Labor platter, clear, 11 3/4" l., No. 512 .... **$143**

Liberty Bell bank, milk glass pressed glass w/original tin base, embossed "Robinson & Loeble - Phila. Pa." around outside & "728 Wharton St." in center, coin slot intact, 4 1/4" h. **$198**

Liberty Bell child's creamer & spooner, clear pressed glass, each molded w/the Liberty Bell, 2 1/2" & 2 1/4" h., the set (ILLUS. far right with group of various historical glass pieces, top of page) **$198**

Liberty Bell John Hancock platter, pressed milk glass, Liberty Bell in the center framed by "1776 Declaration of Independence 1876," scalloped border molded "John Hancock - 100 Years Ago," 9 1/2 x 13 1/4" No. 40 (ILLUS. center with Sphinx on Platform & Obelisks, top next page) **$88**

Liberty Bell mug, clear pressed glass, cylindrical w/relief-molded Liberty Bell on the side, ca. 1876, 2" h. (ILLUS. fourth from left with various historical glass pieces, top of page) **$88**

G

Liberty Bell John Hancock Platter, Sphinx on Platform & Obelisks

Grouping of Historical Glass Pieces

G

Liberty Bell mug, clear pressed glass, footed, inverted bell-form bowl w/S-scroll snake-form handle, marked under base "Manufactured at The Centennial Exhibition by Gillinder & Sons," 3 5/8" h. (ILLUS. third from left with other varied historical glass pieces, top previous page)................ **$231**

Lincoln bust, frosted clear, reverse embossed "Centennial Exhibition - Gillinder and Sons," flake & small bruise in hair, 6" h. (ILLUS. far left with Martys bread tray, Memorial Hall paperweight & McKinley plate, middle of page) **$213**

Martyr's bread tray, oval, bust portraits of Lincoln & Garfield, titled "Our Country's Martyrs," 12 1/2" l. (ILLUS. second from left with Lincoln bust & other historical glass pieces, middle of page).................... **$341**

Memorial Hall paperweight, oval, frosted clear, 1876, 3 7/8 x 5 1/2" (ILLUS. second from right with Lincoln bust & other historical pieces, middle of page).............. **$121**

Obelisks, pressed milk glass, reeded upper section tapering to a pyramidal peak, on square plinth & stepped base, one w/loss to base corner, 7 3/4" h., pr. (ILLUS. right with Liberty Bell John Hancock platter & sphinx on platform, top of page)................ **$209**

Old Abe (Frosted Eagle) compote, cov., clear & frosted, high stand, flakes on lower edge of bowl, 8" d., 7 5/8" h., No. 478 ... **$121**

Old Abe (Frosted Eagle) table set, 4 pcs. ... **$523**

Protection and Plenty plate, 7 1/4" d., central frosted shield w/bust portrait of William McKinley (ILLUS. far right with Lincoln bust & other historical pieces, middle of page) **$55**

Reaper bread tray, oval, horse-drawn reaper in the center, clear, 8 1/4 x 13 1/4", No. 119 .... **$110**

Rock of Ages Bread Tray

Rock of Ages bread tray, clear w/milk glass center, underfill on each handle, No. 236 (ILLUS., previous page)............. **$77**

Sir Moses Montefiore Plate

Sir Moses Montefiore plate, clear pressed glass, bust portrait in center, 10 3/8" d. (ILLUS.)..................................... **$66**

Sphinx on Platform, pressed milk glass, the recumbent winged sphinx resting on a raised rectangular base w/an acanthus leaf on each corner, flakes on crown, base corner flake, 5 1/2 x 10", 5 1/2" h. (ILLUS. left with Liberty Bell John Hancock platter & obelisks, top of previous page)..................................... **$8,525**

Teddy Roosevelt Oval Platter

Teddy Roosevelt platter, clear pressed glass w/frosted profile bust of Roosevelt in the center, border decorated w/dancing Teddy bears & Roosevelt insignia, ca. 1904, 7 1/2 x 10 1/2" (ILLUS.)................. **$132**

Terrestrial Globe covered dish, clear pressed glass globe-form w/Columbia head figural finial on the cover, flake on finial & inner base rim, overall 8" h., No. 236 (ILLUS., top next column)................. **$935**

Rare Terrestrial Globe Covered Dish

Theodore Roosevelt bust, frosted clear, on fluted pedestal base, embossed on the front w/his name & dates "1858 - 1919," 5 1/2" h............................ **$99**

Three Presidents goblet, frosted bust portraits of Washington, Lincoln & Garfield framed in medallion settings, clear, 3" d., 6 1/4" h., No. 250 .... **$198**

Three Shields (Banner) dish, cov., clear, 4 1/2 x 6 1/4", 3 3/4" h., No. 60 .... **$88**

Holly Amber

Holly Amber, originally marketed under the name "Golden Agate," was produced for only a few months in 1903 by the Indiana Tumbler and Goblet Company of Greentown, Indiana. When this factory burned in June 1903 all production of this ware ceased, making it very rare today. The same "Holly" pressed pattern was also produced in clear glass by the Greentown factory. Collectors should note that the St. Clair Glass Company and several other firms have produced some Holly Amber pieces.

Unusual Holly Amber Mustard Pot

Mustard pot, 3 1/4" d., 2 3/4" h. (ILLUS.) ... **$2,530**

Two Holly Amber Pickle Dishes

Pickle dish, oblong, minor flaws, 4 x 9",
each (ILLUS. of two) **$165**

Square 7 1/2" Holly Amber Plate

Plate, 7 1/2" w., square, on rim flake (ILLUS.) .. **$715**

Round Holly Amber Plate

Plate, 7 3/4" d., round (ILLUS.) **$715**

Holly Amber Salt & Pepper Shakers

Salt & pepper shakers w/metal lids, non-
matching lid, each w/a couple of minor
flakes, 3 1/8" h., pr. (ILLUS.).................. **$1,870**

Holly Amber Spooner

Spooner, two foot flakes, slight wear,
3 1/2" d., 4" h. (ILLUS.) **$605**

Imperial

From 1902 until 1984 Imperial Glass of
Bellaire, Ohio, produced handmade glass.
Early pressed glass production often imitated
cut glass and may bear the raised "NUCUT"
mark in the interior center. In the second
decade of the 1900s Imperial was one of the
dominant manufacturers of iridescent or Carnival glass. When glass collecting gained popularity in the 1970s, Imperial again produced
Carnival and a line of multicolored slag
glass. Imperial purchased molds from closing
glass houses and continued many lines popularized by others including Central, Heisey
and Cambridge. These reissues may cause
confusion but they were often marked.

Imperial Marks

Candlewick

Candlewick Basket No. 400/40

Basket, No. 400/40/0, clear, 6 1/2" l.,
4 1/2" h. (ILLUS.) **$38**

Unusual Candlewick Cake Stand & Cover

Cake stand & dome cover, No. 400/10D,
beaded stem, cover made by West Virginia Glass Specialty & sold w/the
stand, cover 10" d., stand 11" d., 2 pcs.
(ILLUS.) **$135**
Cordial, ball stem, No. 1602, ruby, 1 1/2 oz. **$30**
Cruet w/stopper, No. 400/274, flat, bulbous
bottom, clear, 4 oz. (ILLUS., top next col-
umn) **$52**
Relish dish, three-part, three-toed, No.
400/208, clear, 9" l. (ILLUS., middle next
column) **$98**
Wine, No. 400/19, flat, clear, 3 oz. **$24**

Candlewick Cruet No. 400/274

Candlewick Three-Part Relish

Cape Cod

Imperial Two-light Candlestick

Candlestick, two-light, No. 160/100, crystal
(ILLUS.).. **$85**

Cape Cod Cigarette Server/Relish Dish

Cigarette server/relish, handled,d two-part,
No. 160/223, clear, 8 1/2" l. (ILLUS.)............. **$40**
Coaster/spoon rest, No. 160/76, original
label, clear, 3 1/2 x 4 1/2"............................ **$13**

Ruby Cape Cod Finger Bowl

Finger bowl, No. 1604 1/2A, ruby, 4 1/2" d.
(ILLUS.).. **$24**

Cape Cod Pepper Mill & Salt Shaker

Pepper mill & salt shaker, chrome base &
covers, No. 16/236 & 160/238, clear, pr.
(ILLUS.).. **$55**

Free-Hand Ware

Fine Imperial Free-Hand Ware Lamp

Lamp, electric, cast metal foot & cap, tapering ovoid glass body in iridescent orange
w/cobalt blue Hanging Hearts patt.,
10" h. (ILLUS.) **$1,650**

G

Cobalt Blue & Orange Free-Hand Vase

Vase, 8" h., flat flaring foot & tall slender
gently flaring cylindrical body, iridescent cobalt blue exterior & orange inte-
rior (ILLUS.).. **$235**

Free-Hand Vase with Hanging Hearts

G

Vase, 10 1/2" h., tall slender waisted shape w/flaring top, iridescent cobalt blue exterior w/white Hanging Heart decoration (ILLUS.)................................. **$1,175**

Miscellaneous Patterns & Lines

Bowl, 5" d., Laced Edge patt., green opalescent.. **$35**

Imperial Cathay Line Candle Servant

Candlestick, single-light, Cathay Line, figural Candle Servant (female), No. 5035, clear satin (ILLUS.) **$195**

Candlestick, single-light, Packard patt. No. 320, vaseline, 8 1/2" h.................................. **$54**

Candy box, cov., Zodiac patt., No. 619, Azure blue, carnival **$78**

Cocktail, Tradition patt., ruby, 4 oz. **$10**

Compote, No. 3297, shell bowl w/dolphin stem, black w/gold decoration................... **$165**

Compote, 5 3/8" w., 5 3/4" h., flared rim, America patt. No. 671, clear **$18**

No. 451 Ruby Decanter & Crystal Stopper

Decanter w/crystal mushroom stopper, No. 451, spherical body w/ringed foot & cylindrical neck, ruby (ILLUS.) **$120**

Decanter w/original stopper, Grape patt., marigold carnival, unmarked........................ **$95**

Imperial Doeskin No. 1950/196 Epergne

Epergne, one-lily, two-piece, Pattern #1950/196, Doeskin (milk glass), 9" d., 11" h. (ILLUS.) **$78**

Chroma Goblet in Burgundy

Goblet, water, Chroma patt. No. 123, Burgandy, 5 1/2" h. (ILLUS.)............................ **$24**
Paperweight, model of a tiger, Heisey mold, amber & caramel slag **$245**

Imperial Pitcher in Reeded Pattern

Pitcher, Reeded patt., No. 701, green w/clear applied handle (ILLUS.)................... **$80**
Pitcher, Windmill patt., marigold carnival, unmarked **$70**
Pitcher w/ice lip, Tradition patt., clear............. **$32**
Plate, 8" d., Spun patt., reeded, clear............ **$8-12**

Pink Beaded Block 8" Square Plate

Plate, 8" w., Beaded Block patt., pink (ILLUS.) **$20**
Plate w/indent for cup, oval, Twisted Optic patt. No. 313, canary, 9" l............................. **$14**

Broken Arches Punch Bowl & Base

Punch bowl & base, Broken Arches patt., No. 733, clear, 12 1/2" d., 10 1/2" h. (ILLUS.) **$65**

Parisian Provincial Pattern Tumbler

Tumbler, footed, Parisian Provincial patt., milk glass stem & foot & amethyst bowl, 7 oz. (ILLUS.)... **$22**
Vase, 7 1/4" h., footed, two-handled, Twisted Optic patt. No. 313, pink **$38**

Kew Blas

In the 1890s the Union Glass Works, Somerville, Massachusetts, produced a line of iridescent glasswares closely resembling Louis Tiffany's wares. The name was derived from an anagram of the name of the factory's manager, William S. Blake.

Kew Blas Vase with Wave Design

Vase, 7 1/4" h., gently tapering cylindrical body w/a rounded shoulder to the short flaring & scalloped neck, platinum iridescent wave designs on a gold iridescent background w/emerald green dragging design on the lower half, signed on the bottom (ILLUS.).. **$575**

Unusual Flora-Form Kew Blas Vase

Vase, 8 1/4" h., flora-form w/a cushion foot tapering to a very slender stem supporting a bulbous ovoid upper body w/a short flared neck, overall gold iridescence w/flashes of red, purple & green, signed on the polished pontil (ILLUS.).................. **$403**

Green & White Iridescent Kew Blas Vase

Vase, 8 5/8" h., waisted cylindrical body w/a low flaring mouth, the white rim above the dark green iridescent body decorated w/golden scrolls & pulled-feather designs, signed, ca. 1905 (ILLUS.)............. **$1,434**

Lalique

Fine glass, which includes numerous extraordinary molded articles, has been made by the glasshouse established by René Lalique early in the 20th century in France. The firm was carried on by his son, Marc, until his death in 1977 and is now headed by Marc's daughter, Marie-Claude. All Lalique glass is marked, usually on or near the bottom, with either an engraved or molded signature. Unless otherwise noted, we list only those pieces marked "R. Lalique," produced before the death of René Lalique in 1945.

Lalique Marks

Rare Lalique Poisson Table Lamp

Lamp, table model, "Poisson" patt., the frosted clear upright disk-form base molded w/a pair of large fish framed in chrome on a rectangular chrome foot, a long narrow rectangular arched & reeded half-round frosted clear shade, introduced in 1931, etched mark "R. Lalique France," 15 1/8" w., 12 1/2" h. (ILLUS. previous page) **$42,000**

Fine Lalique Bacchantes Vase

Vase, 9 1/2" h., "Bacchantes," wide tapering cylindrical body molded in high-relief w/a continuous band of nude maidens in various poses, textured clear ground w/amber patination, signed in block letters "R. LALIQUE - France" (ILLUS.) **$8,338**

Rare Cased Lalique Archers Vase

Vase, 10 1/4" h., "Archers," wide ovoid body in opalescent cased in butterscotch yellow, molded in relief w/archers shooting at flying birds, short neck, introduced in 1921, marked "R. Lalique" in script & molded (ILLUS.) **$21,600**

Le Verre Francais

Glassware carrying this marking was produced at the French glass factory founded by Charles Schneider in 1908. A great deal of cameo glass was exported to the United States early in the 20th century

and much of it was marketed through Ovingtons in New York City.

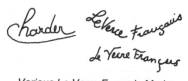

Various Le Verre Francais Marks

Le Verre Francais Cameo Atomizer

Cameo atomizer, squatty pear-shaped body in frosted yellow cased in mottled orange & brown & cameo-cut w/an Art Deco stylized flower & leaf design, original metal fittings, signed on the bottom, missing atomizer bulb, 6 1/2" h. (ILLUS.)... **$920**

Le Verre Francais Deco Cameo Vase

G

Cameo vase, 8 5/8" h., footed angled ovoid body tapering to a molded rim flanked by applied dark purple handles, mottled pale lavender, white & blue ground overlaid in dark purple & cameo-carved w/Art Deco draping clusters of flowers w/stylized leaves around the rim, cameo signed "Charder" on side & engraved "Le Verre Francais" on the foot (ILLUS., previous page) **$1,725**

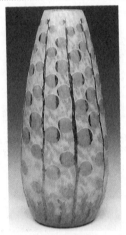

Money Plant Le Verre Francais Vase

Cameo vase, 15" h., Art Deco style, tall simple ovoid body tapering to a small flat mouth, mottled white & peach background overlaid in mottled greens, oranges & browns & cameo-carved w/slender vertical stems of money plant, signed in script, burst air bubble on the bottom (ILLUS.) **$2,760**

Tall Floral Le Verre Francais Cameo Vase

Cameo vase, 15 3/4" h., a thick cushion foot supporting a flaring tall ovoid body tapering to a wide flattened rim, bright yellow & orange mottled background overlaid w/bright orange shading to dark raisin brown & cameo-cut w/large arched clusters of stylized flowers raised on slender stems above upright pointed leaves around the base, signed in script (ILLUS.)... **$3,105**

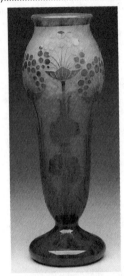

Le Verre Francais Peacock Feather Vase

Cameo vase, 16" h., a thick cushion foot supporting a flaring tall ovoid body tapering to a short flat rim, dark mottled peach background overlaid w/mottled bright orange & dark blue & cameo-cut w/stylized peacock feather design up the sides, signed in script (ILLUS.)......................... **$3,120**

Legras

Cameo and enameled glass somewhat similar to that made by Gallé, Daum Nancy and other factories of the period was made at the Legras works in Saint Denis, France, late in the 19th century and until the outbreak of World War I.

Legras

Typical Legras Mark

Cameo vase, miniature, 3 3/4" h., flat-bottomed ovoid form cameo-carved & enameled w/a landscape of tall slender trees by a river w/a rock bridge & forest in the background, mountains in the distance, in shades of green, grey, brown & pale blue, enameled signature, bruise in design (ILLUS., next page) **$1,035**

Small Legras Cameo Vase with Landscape

Small Legras Cameo Vase with Flowers

Cameo vase, 4" h., 3 1/4 x 4 1/4", flat-bottomed straight-sided oblong form w/the flat rim pulled into a small point at each end, thick cream ground overlaid w/mottled green & orange & carved w/thin stems w/nasturtium leaves & enameled red blossoms, ca. 1910 (ILLUS.)............. **$1,920**

Legras Vase with Fir Tree Landscape

Cameo vase, 6" h., squatty bulbous base tapering to cylindrical sides, clear & frosted pink body cameo carved w/a landscape of tall fir trees in the foreground w/a lake & mountains beyond, enameled in shades of dark & light green, blue & brown, signed on the side (ILLUS.)............ **$489**

Legras Cameo Vase with Purple Flowers

Cameo vase, 8" h., bulbous ovoid body tapering to a low flared neck, frosted chipped ice background cameo-etched & enameled w/purple flowering branches hanging from the shoulder, signed in cameo & enameled (ILLUS.)...................... **$805**

G

Legras Cameo Vase with Maple Leaves

Cameo vase, 10" h., slightly tapering cylindrical body w/a short flaring neck, shaded light pink & clear background w/a chipped ice finish, overlaid in maroon & cameo-carved w/leafy maple leaf branches, cameo signature on the side (ILLUS.).. **$230**

Pair of Legras Cameo Vases with Vines

Cameo vases, 11 3/4" h., simple ovoid body tapering to a short flaring neck, mottled white & green ground cameo-carved & enameled in burgundy w/trailing woodbine down the sides & a small floral band near the top, cameo signatures, pr. (ILLUS.)....................................... **$920**

G

Pair of Monumental Legras Vases

Cameo vases, 24" h., bulbous base tapering to a gently swelling tall body w/a concave rim pulled into two points, rose & amber ground overlaid in dark green & cameo-cut w/a landscape of towering leafy trees in the foreground & a deep forest & lake in the background, signed in cameo, ca. 1910, pr. (ILLUS.)................. **$4,025**

Tall Boldly Enameled Legras Vase

Vase, 14" h., tall slender teardrop-form body, grey frosted ground enameled w/a design of stylized orange mums & dark green leaves around w/crackled blue reserve, black gold-trimmed scallops around the upper neck, signed (ILLUS.).... **$201**

Lenox Crystal

Walter Scott Lenox was born in Trenton, New Jersey in 1959. By 1875 Lenox was combining his talent for drawing and his fascination with clay. He worked as a decorator and designed for several Trenton potteries. The firms he worked for began producing a version of fine Irish Belleek, the thin cream-colored porcelain with a pearly glaze.

In 1889 Lenox opened his own firm, the Ceramic Art Company. Here Lenox developed an art studio rather than just a factory. The firm produced unique ceramic artworks in a lustrous ivory china. Each piece was finely modeled and often exquisitely painted and soon developed a following among elite, fashionable shoppers. By 1897 examples of the Lenox works were being placed in the Smithsonian Institution collection and were even more widely admired.

In 1906 Walter Lenox established the Lenox Company, a firm that continues to produce fine quality creamy translucent porcelain wares.

By the late 20th century many Lenox customers were requesting a line of crystal to complement their dinnerware setting, and so Lenox hand-blown lead crystal was introduced in 1966. A line of silver flatware was introduced in 1991. Due to costumer demand, a line of fine collectibles, Lenox Collections, was founded in 1981. The Lenox Collections offered glass sculptures, plate, serving pieces, jewelry and other decorative accent pieces.

Today Lenox is among the world's oldest and most revered names in fine tableware and giftware. Following is a selection of some of the firm's glass sculptures.

Lenox Crystal Cat & Kitten Sculpture

Cat & kitten, recumbent clear mother cat w/frosted kitten (ILLUS.)................................ **$25**

"Trio of Light" Lenox Crystal Sculpture

Dolphins, "Trio of Light," grouping of three leaping dolphins (ILLUS.)............................ **$35**

Lenox Crystal Eagle with American Flag

Eagle, American flag molded on the spread wings (ILLUS.) **$40**

Lenox Crystal Spread-winged Eagle

Eagle, wings widely spread (ILLUS.) **$45**

G

Lenox Crystal Panther Sculpture

Panther, crouching pose, clear & frosted (ILLUS.) **$35**

Libbey

In 1878, William L. Libbey obtained a lease on the New England Glass Company of Cambridge, Massachusetts, changing the name to the New England Glass Works, W.L. Libbey and Son, Proprietors. After his death in 1883, his son, Edward D. Libbey, continued to operate the company at Cambridge until 1888, when the factory was closed. Edward Libbey moved to Toledo, Ohio, and set up the company subsequently known as Libbey Glass Co. During the 1880s, the firm's master technician, Joseph Locke, developed the now much desired colored art glass lines of Agata, Amberina, Peach Blow and Pomona. Renowned for its cut glass of the Brilliant Period (see CUT GLASS), the company continues in operation today as Libbey Glassware, a division of Owens-Illinois, Inc.

G

Unusual Libbey Maize Cruet

Unusual Large Footed Libbey Bowl

Bowl, 12" d., 4 1/4" h., a wide shallow bowl w/a flattened rim, white ground decorated in the center w/a lime green pulled feather design, raised on an applied clear pedestal foot, signed (ILLUS.).................... **$210**

Libbey Maize Iridized Bowl

Maize bowl, 7 3/4" d., 3 5/8" h., iridized clear w/light blue-stained leaves, minor inner rim flakes (ILLUS.) **$165**

Maize celery vase, creamy white w/green leaves, 6 1/2" h. **$90**

Maize cruet w/original stopper, tall ovoid body w/tricorner rim, applied clear handle, pale iridescent ground w/pale blue husks, pointed corn-molded stopper w/shallow chip at tip, 7" h. (ILLUS., top next column)... **$605**

Maize Salt Shaker with Yellow Husks

Maize salt shaker, original top, creamy opaque w/yellow husks, slight damage to metal top, 4" h. (ILLUS.)............................ **$143**

Maize Spooner with Yellow Husks

Maize spooner, creamy opaque w/yellow husks, 4 1/4" h. (ILLUS.) **$132**

Maize Yellow-leaved Toothpick Holder

Maize toothpick holder, creamy opaque w/yellow leaves trimmed in gold, 2 1/4" h. (ILLUS.) **$345**
Maize tumbler, creamy opaque w/blue & gilt leaves **$140**

Libbey Little Lobe Toothpick Holder

Toothpick holder, Little Lobe patt., opaque white w/pink shaded rim &

enameled floral decoration, satin finish, 2 1/4" h. (ILLUS.) **$110**

Nash-Designed Libbey Art Glass Vase

Vase, 8 1/2" h., footed gently flaring cylindrical crystal body w/internal optic thumbprints alternating w/fronds of laurel leaves, the exterior decorated w/thin lilac threading down the sides, Nash design, acid-stamped mark on base (ILLUS.) **$374**

Loetz

Iridescent glass, some of it somewhat resembling that of Tiffany and other contemporary glasshouses, was produced by the Bohemian firm of J. Loetz Witwe of Klostermule and is referred to as Loetz. Some cameo pieces were also made. Not all pieces are marked.

Loetz Mark

Signed Loetz Papillon Red Rose Bowl

G

Varied Group of Loetz Vases

Rose bowl, flat-bottomed spherical body w/a three-lobed rim, iridescent Papillon red body decorated w/silvery gold ribbons in pulled & coiled designs, engraved signature on the pontil, 4 1/8" h. (ILLUS., previous page) **$518**

G

Vase, 4" h., wide flat base w/tapering low sides w/three deep indentations below the flaring tri-fold rim, grey w/green oil spot "Papillon" finish (ILLUS. bottom row, center with other Loetz vases, top of page) **$201**

Vase, 5" h., 6 1/4" d., coupe-form bowl tapering to a round vase, three applied loop handles down the sides encased in sterling silver, a wide band of silver overlay scrolling leaves around the rim, ca. 1905 (ILLUS., next column) **$1,920**

Vase, 5 1/4" h., 9 1/2" l., figural, modeled as a stylized standing pig w/a long snout & dimpled body, an oval opening in the top of the back, applied ears & tail, overall gold iridescence w/blue, lavender & green highlights (ILLUS., bottom of page) **$1,150**

Nice Three-Handled Loetz Vase

Vase, 5 1/2" h., bulbous ovoid body w/a deeply fluted tri-corner mouth, gray w/overall green oil spot "Candia Silverris Astraa" finish, ca. 1910 (ILLUS. top row, far right, with other Loetz vases, top of page) **$690**

Whimsical Loetz Figural Pig Vase

Small Loetz Silver Overlaid Vase

Vase, 6" h., bulbous hourglass form w/a low flaring rim, streaky iridescent blue on an amber ground, decorated w/silver overlay in a leafy vine design, unsigned (ILLUS.) **$1,208**

Vase, 6 1/2" h., bulbous ovoid body tapering to a small flat mouth, iridescent green decorated overall w/gold threaded "Formosa" decoration (ILLUS. top row, left with other Loetz vases, top previous page) **$604**

Vase, 7 1/4" h., gently flaring trumpet form w/deeply ruffled rim, amber w/overall gold oil spot "Papillon" finish (ILLUS. bottom row, left, with other Loetz vases, top previous page) **$403**

Vase, 7 1/2" h., flaring double-knop form w/flaring ruffled rim, amber w/iridescent gold "Papillon" finish (ILLUS. top row, center, with other Loetz vases, top previous page) **$1,035**

Loetz Vase with Wavy Iridescence

Vase, 9 7/8" h., 3 5/8" d., a round low domed foot supporting a very tall slender cylindrical body w/a gently flaring rim, overall wavy iridescent finish down the sides in shades of blue, green & gold, ca. 1905 (ILLUS.) **$1,020**

Tall Loetz Paperweight-Style Vase

Vase, 10 3/8" h., 3 3/4" d., paperweight-style, a flattened round foot & slender flaring stem pulled into middle band then tapering slightly to a four-lobed rim, deep red ground decorated overall w/swirling greenish gold iridescence, ca. 1905 (ILLUS.) **$2,040**

Vase, 10 3/4" h., squatty flat-bottomed base tapering to a stick neck w/single twist, amber w/overall iridescent gold prunt "Candia Silverris Astraa" decoration (ILLUS. bottom row, right, with other Loetz vases, top previous page) **$920**

Lustres

Lustres were Victorian glass vase-like decorative objects often hung around the rim with prisms. They were generally sold as matched pairs to be displayed on fireplace mantels. A wide range of colored glasswares were used in producing lustres and pieces were often highlighted with colored enameled decoration.

One of a Pair of Blue Opaque Lustres

Blue opaque, a round foot & thin short stem below the tapering slender ovoid stem supporting the cupped round top w/a notched rim, overall bands of enameled flowers w/floral swags around the top bowl, gilt band trim, faceted teardrop prisms suspended from base of top bowl, minor wear, late 19th c., 11" h., pr. (ILLUS. of one, previous page) **$201**

Green Cut-Overlay Lustres with Portraits

Cut-overlay, translucent emerald green overlaid in opaque white, slender floriform w/a wide cupped & deeply scalloped bowl, each rim petal cut w/an oval white reserve decorated w/an alternating enameled decoration of the bust of a child or sprays of flowers, the tapering cylindrical stems above a conforming knopped round foot, decorated overall w/gold scrolling vines, the bowl suspending ten long spearpoint-cut clear prisms, 14" h., pr. (ILLUS.) **$3,120**

Fine Cut-Overlay Ruby Lustres

Cut-overlay, translucent ruby overlaid in opaque white, slender floriform w/a wide cupped & deeply scalloped bowl, each rim petal cut w/gilt-trimmed fanned flutes below an enameled floral garland, the tapering narrow stop-flute cut stem edged w/gilt bands above a knop cut w/round prints, on a matching round foot, the top bowl suspending 12 clear spearpoint-cut long prisms, late 9th c., 11 7/8" h., pr. (ILLUS.) **$2,160**

Mats Jonasson Crystal

Mats Jonasson's career as a glass artist began at age fourteen in his native Sweden when he left school to work as an engraver with his father. He proved successful as an engraver and developed many animal designs, beginning his own career in glass etching and crystal relief.

Inspired by the natural work around him, Mats Jonasson's unique art crystal reliefs are one-of-a-kind creations. His successful company is now composed of talented Swedish glass artists who create each piece using the finest Swedish crystal.

Since 1981 he has been gathering a staff of capable artisans, and today the production of fine glass reliefs has become a hallmark of this innovative firm.

Most pieces illustrated here were purchased between 1988 and 2005, and many of them are now retired.

Mats Jonasson Elephant Glass Relief

Elephant, No. 33630 (ILLUS.) **$175-250**

Mats Jonasson Heron Glass Relief

Heron, No. 33713 (ILLUS.) **$250-260**

Mats Jonasson Owl Crystal Sculpture

Owl, No. 6042, stylized model of an owl (ILLUS.) **$60**

Mats Jonasson Polar Bear Glass Relief

Polar Bear, miniature size, No. 88117 (ILLUS.)...................................... **$50**

Mats Jonasson Sea Turtle Glass Relief

Sea turtle, No. 33700 (ILLUS.) **$100**

Mats Jonasson Squirrel Glass Relief

Squirrel, miniature size, No. 88115 (ILLUS.) **$45**

McKee

The McKee name has been associated with glass production since 1834, first producing window glass and later bottles. In the 1850s a new factory was established in Pittsburgh, Pennsylvania, for production of flint and pressed glass. The plant was relocated in Jeanette, Pennsylvania, in 1888 and operated there as an independent company almost continuously until 1951, when it sold out to Thatcher Glass Manufacturing Company. Many types of collectible glass were produced by McKee through the years including Depression, pattern, milk glass and a variety of utility kitchenwares. See these categories for additional listings.

McKee   **PRESCUT**

Early McKee Mark,   *McKee Prescut*
ca. 1880   *Mark*

Kitchenwares

Mixing bowl, Red Ships patt. on milk glass, 6" d... **$25**

Reamer, lemon-type, embossed "McK" mark, Skokie Green (jade) **$65**

Salt & pepper shakers, Roman Arches patt., black, 4 1/2" h., pr. **$55**

Rock Crystal Pattern

Cake stand, low foot, green, 11" d.................. **$65**

Cheese & cracker server, large round plate w/center indentation for rounded pedestal-footed cheese stand, ruby, stand 4 3/4" d., plate 11" d., the set (ILLUS., top next page) **$145**

Amber Rock Crystal Compote

Compote, 8 3/4" d., 7" h., amber (ILLUS.) **$55**

Cordial, crystal, 1 oz. **$15**

G

Ruby Rock Crystal Cheese & Cracker Server

Parfait, footed, clear, 3 1/2 oz. $16

Miscellaneous Patterns & Pieces

Bowl, 9" d., Scallop Edge patt. No. 157,
green... $28
Cheese plate & cover, Laurel patt., Skokie
Green (jade), 2 pcs. $125
Clock, Tambour Art-style, blue, 14" l. (ILLUS.,
bottom of page) $550
Plate, 6" d., Laurel patt., French Ivory................ $8

Rare Canary Rock Crystal Lamp

Lamp, electric, tall inverted pear-shaped
body on an octagonal foot, canary, 12" h.
(ILLUS.).. $625

McKee Aztec Pattern Punch Bowl

Punch bowl, Aztec patt., clear, 13" d.
(ILLUS.) $75
Tumbler, flat base, Laurel patt., Skokie
Green (jade), 9 oz. $85

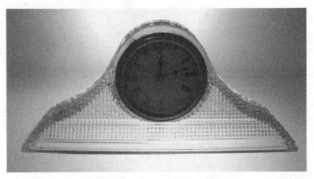

McKee Tambour Art Blue Clock

Milk Glass

Opaque white glass, or "opal," has been called "milk-white glass," perhaps to distinguish it from transparent or "clear-white glass." Resembling fine white porcelain, it was viewed as an inexpensive substitute. Opacity is obtained by adding bone ash or oxide of tin to clear molten glass. By the addition of various coloring agents, the opaque mixture can be turned into blue milk glass, or pink, yellow, green, caramel, even black milk glass. Collectors of milk glass now accept not only the white variety but virtually any opaque color and color mixtures, including slag or marbled glass. It has been made in numerous forms and shapes in this country and abroad from about the first quarter of the 19th century. Many of the items listed here were also made in colored opaque glass, which collectors call blue or green or black "milk glass." It is still being produced, and there are many reproductions of earlier pieces. Pieces here are all-white unless otherwise noted.

Chick Emerging from Egg on Basket

Animal covered dish, chick emerging from egg on basket base, cylindrical base w/loop rim handles, traces of original gold paint trim, ca. 1900-25, 3 1/4" h. (ILLUS.) **$56**

Duck on Wavy Base Covered Dish

Animal covered dish, duck on wavy base, glass eyes, Challinor, Taylor & Co., 5 1/4" h. (ILLUS.) **$77**

Hen with Amber Head on Basketweave

Animal covered dish, hen on basketweave base, light amber head on white body & base, minor roughness on edge of base, Challinor, Taylor & Co., 7" l. (ILLUS.) **$132**

Atterbury Hen Dish with Blue Head

Animal covered dish, hen on lacy base, blue opaque head, white body & base, Atterbury, 7 1/2" l. (ILLUS.) **$110**

Atterbury Hen with Orange Marbled Back

G

Animal covered dish, hen on lacy base, orange marbled back, white base, Atterbury, 7 3/4" l. (ILLUS., previous page) **$143**

Ribbed Lion on Lacy Base Dish

Animal covered dish, lion, ribbed lion on lacy-edged base, patent-dated, Atterbury, very good, 7 1/2" l. (ILLUS.) **$77**

Atterbury Ribbed Lion on Ribbed Base

Animal covered dish, lion, ribbed lion on ribbed base, Atterbury, dated, 7 1/2" l. (ILLUS.) **$143**
Animal covered dish, swan, "Block Swan," glass eyes, Challinor, Taylor & Co., flaking on edge of cover, open bubble on base flange, 8" l. **$88**
Bust of Raymond Poincare, President of France, on pedestal base, sheared & ground mouth, marked "Poincare - Déposé," ca. 1912-20, 13 1/2" h. (ILLUS., top next column) **$476**
Model of a trunk, candy container w/original sliding metal base, original gold paint trim & h.p. flower, inscribed in gold "Souvenir of Rock Island," ca. 1910-25, 2 1/4" h. (ILLUS., middle next column) **$190**

Milk Glass Bust of Raymond Poincare

Milk Glass Souvenir-marked Trunk

Millefiori

The term millefiori (Italian for "thousand flowers") refers to a glass decorated or patterned with tiny slices of thin multicolored glass canes. Most often used in glass paperweights, other objects such as lamps, vases and tablewares have also been produced using this technique which was, in fact, developed by the ancient Romans. Today millefiori continues to be made in Murano, Italy, and elsewhere.

Pitcher, 6 1/2" h., bulbous body, cased satin interior, applied handle, rough pontil, Italy... **$275**

Tumbler, small rough pontil, Italy.................... **$80**

Morgantown (Old Morgantown)

Morgantown, West Virginia, was the site where a glass firm named the Morgantown Glass Works began in the late 19th century, but the company reorganized in 1903 to become the Economy Tumbler Company, a name it retained until 1929. By the 1920s the firm was producing a wider range of better quality and colorful glass tablewares; to reflect this fact, it resumed its earlier name, Morgantown Glass Works, in 1929. Today its many quality wares of the Depression era are growing in collector demand.

Rare Jennie Pattern Red Basket

Basket, Jennie (No. 20) patt., Spanish Red w/clear twist applied handle, 4 1/2" d. (ILLUS.) **$750**

Fine Greer Pattern Two-Tone Bowl

Bowl, 10" d., footed, Greer (No. 26) patt., Two-Tone Genova style, Topaz w/Blue rim (ILLUS.).. **$325**

Ritz Blue Janice Pattern Bowl

Bowl, 13" d., flared, Janice (No. 4335) patt., Ritz Blue [burgundy cobalt] (ILLUS.)........... **$165**

One of a Pair of Coronet Candleholders

Candleholders, hurricane-style w/slant to rim, Décor Line, Coronet (No. 104) patt., Burgundy, 8 3/4" h., pr. (ILLUS. of one)....... **$55**

Candleholders, one-light, No. 1 Bristol, Ritz Blue foot & candle socket w/Alabaster stem, 3 5/8" h., pr...................................... **$700**

Champagne, saucer-type, Queen Anne (No. 7664) patt. w/twisted stem, Manchester Pheasant silk screen decoration, clear, 6 1/2 oz. **$225**

Cigarette box, cov., El Mexicano patt., Ice White, 4 x 4 1/2".. **$150**

Finger bowl, footed, No. 7730, original label, Spanish Red, 4 1/4" d. **$27**

Flowerlite bowl & frog, Décor Line Sharon (No. 9922) patt., Ebony w/clear frog, 6" d., 2 pcs. **$50**

G

G

Old English Goblet with Golf Ball Stem

Goblet, Old English (No. 7678) patt., water, Golf Ball stem, Stiegel Green (deep bluish green), 10 oz. (ILLUS.) **$38**

Guest set: carafe & tumbler; Margaret (No. 23) patt., jade green w/painted Hollyhock decoration, 2 pcs. **$100**

Pitcher, flat base, Ringling (No. 7622 1/2) patt., Ritz Blue w/white enameled bands, 54 oz. **$175**

Arena Tumbler in Stiegel Green

Tumbler, flat base, Arena (No. 7619) patt., Stiegel Green w/white enameled bands, 2 3/4" h. (ILLUS.) **$18**

Tumbler, large, Freeform (No. 1800) patt., Moss Green.. **$150**

Vase, 4" h., Décor Line, Carleen (No. 9956) patt., Bristol Blue (opaque)........................ **$22**

Moser

Ludwig Moser opened his first glass shop in 1857 in Karlsbad, Bohemia (now Karlovy Vary, in the former Czechoslovakia). Here he engraved and decorated fine glasswares especially to appeal to rich visitors to the local health spa. Later other shops were opened in various cities. Throughout the 19th and early 20th century lovely, colorful glasswares, many beautifully enameled, were produced by Moser's shops and reached a wide market in Europe and America. Moser died in 1916 and the firm continued under his sons. They were forced to merge with the Meyer's Nephews glass factory after World War I. The glassworks were sold out of the Moser family in 1933.

Facet-cut Amber Moser Vase

Vase, 5 7/8" h., gently flaring facet-cut body in reddish amber, acid-stamped "Moser Karlovey Vary," minor scratches (ILLUS.) .. **$196**

Lovely Wheel-Carved Moser Vase

Vase, 8 3/4" h., short pedestal base & tall ovoid body w/a flat rim, crystal w/an applied deep red flower blossom w/wheel-carved details against an intaglio-carved background of leafy stems & flowers, signed on the base "Moser Karlsbad" (ILLUS.) **$2,300**

Mt. Washington

A wide diversity of glass was made by the Mt. Washington Glass Company of New Bedford, Massachusetts, between 1869 and 1900. It was succeeded in 1900 by the Pairpoint Corporation. Miscellaneous types are listed below.

Unusual Mt. Washington Cameo Compote

Cameo compote, 4 7/8" d., 3 3/4" h., round gold-banded alabaster white foot & baluster-form stem supporting the wide shallow bowl in alabaster white cased on the interior in pink & carved w/a leafy scroll rim band & cluster of central stylized blossoms, gilt rim band, slight gold wear (ILLUS.) **$259**

Mt. Washington Cracker Jar with Flowers

Cracker jar w/silver plate rim, cover & bail handle, mold-blown squatty tapering round base w/small scrolls around the bottom, pale yellow background h.p. w/large pink & white blossoms & green leaves, gold-washed metal fittings

marked "MW 4436," base marked "3930/230," 5 3/4" h. (ILLUS.) **$345**

Mt. Washington Egg Perfume Bottle

Perfume bottle w/tiny silver plate cap, egg-shaped, white opaque w/a pale beige ground h.p. w/irises in amethyst & blue, 4" h. (ILLUS.) **$1,438**

Mt. Washington Rose Bowl with Mums

Rose bowl, eight-crimp rim, spherical, fired-on Burmese-like ground w/satin finish enameled w/yellow, pink & white chrysanthemums, pontil marked w/No. 617, 6 1/4" d., 5" h. (ILLUS.) **$231**

Mt. Washington Rose Bowl with Violets

G

Rose bowl, eight-crimp rim, spherical, peach to white ground w/a satin finish, enameled w/scattered small blue violets, polished pontil w/No. 616, 7" d., 6" h. (ILLUS., previous page) **$154**

Mt. Washington Egg-shaped Sugar Shaker

Sugar shaker w/original silver plate cap, egg-shaped, unfired Burmese h.p. w/white & yellow daisies on green leaves & stems, 4" h. (ILLUS.) **$575**

Mt. Washington Fig-shaped Sugar Shaker

Sugar shaker w/original silver plate cap, fig-shaped, unfired Burmese w/an overall h.p. decoration of tiny blue, pink & yellow blossoms, 4" h. (ILLUS.) **$2,185**

Muller Freres

The Muller Brothers made acid-etched cameo and other fine glass at Luneville, France, starting in 1910 and until the outbreak of World War II in Europe.

Muller Freres Mark

Bowl, 7 1/2" d., 2 1/8" h., squatty mottled blue, white & pink bowl w/incurved scalloped rim, supported in an elaborate wrought-iron frame w/a large blossom & leaves on each side & large looped leafy vine end handles, oval base, bowl signed, base unsigned by possibly by Katona, framed, 5 x 13" (ILLUS., top next page) **$374**

Miniature Muller Cameo Landscape Vase

Cameo vase, miniature, 3 3/4" h., ovoid body w/a short bulbed neck, shaded dark brown to yellow ground overlaid in dark brown & pumpkin & cameo-cut w/a scene of a windmill on a hill overlooking a mountainous lake w/sailing vessels, cameo signature (ILLUS.) **$805**

Muller Freres Cameo Chrysanthemum Vase

Cameo vase, 5 3/4" h., spherical body tapering to a short flared neck, mottled white & brown & overlaid in caramel, toffee & dark brown & cameo-carved w/large chrysanthemums on leafy stems, cameo signature (ILLUS.) **$805**

Mottled Muller Freres Bowl in Floral Iron Frame

Muller Fres. Cameo Vase with Arab Scene

Cameo vase, 9 1/2" h., wide ovoid body tapering to a flat mouth, striated creamy white ground cased in deep red, green & black & cameo-carved w/a continuous landscape of a desert oasis w/Arabs, camels & buildings w/mountains in the background, cameo-signed (ILLUS.) **$1,265**

Large Dramatic Muller Freres Vase

Cameo vase, 12 1/2" h., large footed bulbous ovoid body tapering to a flat rim, frosted white ground cased in dark blue, black & yellow & cameo-carved w/a continuous landscape w/tall pine trees in the foreground w/a large lake & hills in the distance, cameo-signed (ILLUS.) **$3,278**

Nailsea

Nailsea was another glassmaking center in England where a variety of wares similar to those from Bristol, England were produced between 1788 and 1873. Today most collectors think of Nailsea primarily as a glass featuring swirls and loopings, usually white, on a clear or colored ground. This style of glass decoration, however, was not restricted to Nailsea and was produced in many other glasshouses, including some in America.

Darning ball, spherical head w/long slender handle, clear cased in opaque white & trimmed w/four blue loops, possibly Boston & Sandwich Glass Co., 7" l. (ILLUS. second from right with Nailsea flask & witch balls, top next page) **$242**

Flask, flattened ovoid shape w/short cylindrical neck, opaque white w/red & white loopings, fire-polished plain lip, polished pontil, possibly by Nicholas Lutz, Boston & Sandwich Glass Co., ca. 1875-85, 6 5/8" h. (ILLUS. second from left with Nailsea darner & witch balls, top next page) **$231**

Gemel bottle, flattened ovoid form w/applied rigaree & base disk, fire-polished, rough pontil, probably American, second half 19th c., clear w/grey tint & white looping, 11" l. **$77**

Stirrup cup, modeled as a high-topped boot, clear w/white loopings, rough pontil, probably American, second half 19th c., 7 1/4" h. **$242**

Witch ball, spherical, cased opaque white w/four red loopings, open rough pontil, probably Boston & Sandwich Glass Co., ca. 1860-80, 4" d. (ILLUS. far right with other witch ball & darner & flask, top next page) **$165**

Colorful Nailsea Darner, Flask & Witch Balls

Witch ball, spherical w/open rough pontil fitted w/a later brass hanger, cased opaque white w/four thin red loopings, probably Boston & Sandwich Glass Co., 1860-80, 5 1/4" d. (ILLUS. far left with Nailsea darner, flask & other witch ball, top of page) **$523**

Witch ball, spherical w/open rough pontil, clear w/opaque white loopings, possibly Boston & Sandwich Glass Co., second half 19th c., 6 1/4" d. **$154**

New Martinsville

The New Martinsville Glass Manufacturing Company operated from 1900 to 1944, when it was taken over by new investors and operated as the Viking Glass Company. In its time, the New Martinsville firm made an iridescent art glass line called Muranese along with crystal pattern glass (included ruby-stained items) and, later, the transparent and opaque colors which were popular during the 1920s and 1930s. Measell's New Martinsville Glass 1900-1944 covers this company's products in detail.

Bowl, 12" d., crimped rim, Radiance patt. w/Meadow Wreath etching, clear................ **$35**

Blue Moondrops Butter Dish & Chrome Cover

Butter dish w/chrome lid, round, Moondrops patt., cobalt blue, 6" d. (ILLUS.) **$120**

Grouping of "Addie" Pattern Pieces

Candleholder, one-light, "Addie" (No. 34) patt., green, 3 1/2" h. (ILLUS. back right with grouping of "Addie" pieces)... **$18**

New Martinsville Blue Guest Set

Candleholders, one-light, blocks w/applied
swan necks, clear, 2" h., pr. **$45**

Moondrops Ruby Cordial

Cordial, Moondrops patt., ruby, 3/4 oz.
(ILLUS.) **$32**
Creamer, footed, "Addie" (No. 34) patt.,
ruby (ILLUS. back left with grouping of
"Addie" pieces, bottom previous page) **$15**
Cup & saucer, "Addie" (No. 34) patt., pink
(ILLUS. center with grouping of "Addie"
pieces, bottom previous page) **$10**
Decanter & shot glass lid, "Volstead Pup"
(No. 1926) patt., figural dog, green, 2
pcs. **$145**
Guest set: cov. pitcher, tumbler & rectan-
gular tray; No. 728 patt., blue, the set
(ILLUS., top of page) **$155**

New Martinsville Pink Satin Perfume Bottle

Perfume bottle & stopper, footed slender
flaring lobed body w/flaring neck, pink
stain w/h.p. flowers, 6 3/4" h. (ILLUS.) **$75**
Plate, 8" d., "Addie" (No. 34) patt., pink
(ILLUS. center with grouping of "Addie"
pieces, bottom previous page) **$7**
Tumbler, Moondrops patt., footed juice, co-
balt blue, 3 oz. **$18**
Tumbler, Moondrops patt., footed juice,
pink, 3 oz. **$12**
Vase, 10" h., crimped rim, No. 4232 w/Pre-
lude etching, clear **$70**

G

Orrefors

This Swedish glasshouse, founded in 1898 for production of tablewares, has made decorative wares as well since 1915. By 1925, Orrefors had achieved an international reputation for its Graal glass, an engraved art glass developed by master glassblower Knut Berquist and artist-designers Simon Gate and Edward Hald. Ariel glass, recognized by a design of controlled air traps and the heavy Ravenna glass, usually tinted, were both developed in the 1930s. While all Orrefors glass is collectible, pieces signed by early designers and artists are now bringing high prices.

Orrefors

Orrefors Mark

Small Orrefors "Graal" Vase

Vase, 4 3/4" h., "Graal," simple bulbous ovoid form w/a small flat mouth, colorless w/encased design of blue & brown fish swimming among water plants, designed by Edward Hald, engraved "Orrefors - Sweden - Edward Hald - Graal - 1180C," 1930s (ILLUS.) **$690**

Orrefors Graal Vase with Fish Design

Vase, 5 1/2" h., "Graal," paperweight technique, bulbous ovoid crystal form internally decorated w/swimming fish among water plants, signed "Graal - 1932" w/other illegible marks (ILLUS.) **$540**

Fine Cylindrical Orrefors Ariel Vase

Vase, 6" h., "Ariel," thick cylindrical form in crystal internally decorated w/a stylized design of a woman, troubador in a gondola & flowers in colors of cobalt blue & amber, signed on the bottom "Orrefors - Ariel no. 937E4 - Edvin Ohrstrom" (ILLUS.) **$3,450**

Fine Signed Orrefors Ariel Vase

Vase, 6 3/4" h., "Ariel," thick egg-form shape w/an internal decoration of a stylized head of a woman, dove & flowers w/blue & yellow coloring, signed on the base "Orrefors - Ariel no. 196M - Edvin Ohrstrom" (ILLUS.) **$3,450**

Overlay

Overlay refers to a type of glass where pieces are composed of two or more layers of glass, usually of contrasting colors. These layers, combined while the object is still hot from the furnace, are generally noticeably thicker than "cased" glass pieces. Most cased glass has a thin outer layer applied over a thicker inner layer. Fine overlay glass was widely produced in the late 19th and early 20th century in Bohemia, England and the United States. Some foreign glass factories are still producing decorative overlay pieces, which can sometimes be confused with antique examples.

Cordials, cranberry cut to clear bowls, each bowl w/four ovals engraved w/a different scene, clear applied stem & square foot, polished pontil, set of 4 (one w/minor foot flakes) **$70**
Tumbler, red cut to clear vertical panels, Inverted Thumbprint patt. **$110**

Exquisite Tall Cut-Overlay Vases

Vases, 28 3/4" h., tall baluster-form w/the tall trumpet neck wrapped around the base w/blue snake decorated w/gilt quatrefoil scales, the colorless ground finely painted overall, the neck, upper body & foot in white opaque detailed flowers & scrolling foliage, the lower body cased in cobalt blue & cut w/tall serrated leaves h.p. w/detailed gold veining, gold rim, shoulder & stem ring & foot rim, England, possibly Stourbridge, ca. 1850-75, pr. (ILLUS.)... **$22,705**

Pate de Verre

Pate de Verre, or "paste of glass," was molded by very few artisans. In the pate de verre technique, powdered glass is mixed with a liquid to make a paste that is then placed in a mold and baked at a high temperature. These articles have a finely pitted or matte finish and are easily distinguished from blown glass. Duplicate pieces are possible with this technique.

ΛWALTER G·ARGY ROUSSEAU
NANcy

Pate De Verre Marks

Book ends, mottled green base & upright back w/a molded amber seated squirrel w/long ears & bushy tail eating a nut, signed on one side "A. Walter Nancy - Merge, SC," 4 3/4 x 5", pr. (ILLUS., bottom of page)... **$8,625**

Scarce Pate de Verre Bowl with Eagles

Bowl, 6" d., 3 7/8" h., "Aigles" patt., a small funnel base supporting a wide shallow rounded bowl, creamy ground w/dark blue base & rim bands & bands of red & green stylized blossoms, the rim also w/four grey spread-winged eagles, molded mark of G. Argy-Rousseau, 1920s (ILLUS.).............. **$4,800**

Very Fine Walter Pate de Verre Bowl

Bowl, 7" w., shallow round form w/two rounded tab handles, yellow shading to orange w/a center decoration of green leaves & brown berries or seeds, signed on the interior "A. Walter Nancy" (ILLUS.) **$4,600**

G

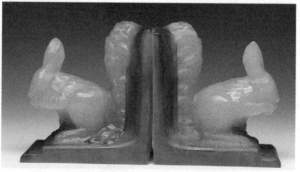

Fine Pair of A. Walter Book Ends

Small Pate de Verre Dish with Berries

Dish, flat-bottomed round shape w/low flat upright sides molded around the rim w/three clusters of purplish red berries & pale green leaf sprigs on the deep yellow ground, marked by A. Walter Nancy, Bergé Sc., ca. 1920, 6" d., 1 3/4" h. (ILLUS.) **$1,680**

G

Rare "Jardin des Hesperides" Vase

Fine Pate de Verre Vase with Red Leaves

Vase, 6 1/2" h., 4 7/8" d., ovoid body w/a short flaring wide neck, mottled cream & lavender body w/molded mottled orange & red pointed leaves up from the base & accented by green dots, signed by G. Argy-Rousseau & stamped "11815," ca. 1920 (ILLUS.).. **$5,400**

Vase, 9 1/2" h., "Jardin des Hesperides" patt., wide ovoid body w/a wide flat molded rim, dark mottled gold, yellow & brown molded in relief w/orange figures of classical women gathering yellow apples from brown trees, the lower half w/large squared Greek key-molded panels, signed by G. Argy-Rousseau, ca. 1926 (ILLUS., top next column) **$19,120**

Rare Argy-Rousseau "La Danse" Vase

Vase, 12 1/4" h., "La Danse" patt., flat-bottomed wide ovoid body tapering to a short cylindrical neck, mottled pinkish white, purple & green ground molded w/a tall classical dancing woman in violet, purple & green, molded upper & base bands in shades of purple, red & dark blue, signed by G. Argy-Rousseau, ca. 1923 (ILLUS.).. **$26,290**

Pate de Verre Vide Poche with Molded Fish

Fine Argy-Rousseau Ballerina Veilleuse

Rare Beaver Band Goblet

Veilleuse (night light), "Danseuses Sous Les Projecteurs" (Ballerinas in the Spotlight) patt., domed egg-form flattened on the front, deep purple molded w/a panel of crossed spotlights & a ballerina in deep red w/a mottled white & red tutu, fitted on a cast-metal ring base, signed by G. Argy-Rousseau, ca. 1928, 5 1/2" h. (ILLUS.).................................. **$15,535**

Vide poche (figural dish), asymmetrical rounded shallow form in dark bluish green shaded to pale yellow, the arched wave-molded side w/a large fish & several smaller fish, signed "A. Walter Nancy - Berge SC," 6" w. (ILLUS., top of page) ... **$2,013**

Pattern

Dog & Doe with Lily of the Valley, pressed, marked under foot "Pat. Applyed (sic) For".. **$275**
Dog w/rabbit in mouth, acid-etched **$28**

Very Rare Dragon Pattern Goblet

Animals & Birds on Goblets & Pitchers - Goblets

Alligator, acid-etched...................................... **$55**
Bear climber, acid-etched **$21**
Beaver Band (ILLUS., top next column) **$1,045**
Camel Caravan, acid-etched **$33**
Child Riding Dragonfly, acid-etched, triangular stem **$253**

Dragon, pressed (ILLUS., previous page) .. **$2,860**
Elephant, acid-etched **$39**
Elk & Doe, pressed **$242**
Elk Medallion, 6 1/4" h................................... **$66**
Flying Birds, pressed **$88**

Frog & Spider Pattern Goblet

Frog & Spider, pressed (ILLUS.).................. **$440**
Heron, Wading, pressed, emerald green **$187**
Horse, Cat & Rabbit, pressed **$600-1,000**
Ibex, acid-etched.. **$66**

Jumbo Pattern Goblet

Jumbo, pressed, one-on-one borders
(ILLUS.).. **$523**
Leopard, acid-etched **$32**
Lion in the Jungle, acid-etched **$50**
Monkey Climber, acid-etched **$30**
Ostrich Looking at Moon, pressed.............. **$121**
Owl in Horseshoe **$99**
Owl & Possum, pressed **$99**
Pigs in Corn, pressed, husk bent left **$523**
Reversed Elephant, acid-etched.................. **$132**
Rooster, acid-etched, surrounded by
leaves & flowers... **$99**
Rooster & Hen, acid-etched **$77**
Stag, acid-etched **$77**

Stork Walking, acid-etched **$55**
Swan Feeding, acid-etched............................ **$44**

Swimming Swan Pattern Glass Goblet

Swimming/Sitting Swan, round stem
(ILLUS.) **$880**
Thrush & Apple Blossom, 6" h. **$121**
Two Camels, acid-etched **$55**
Two Herons, acid-etched **$50**
Two Tigers, acid-etched.................................. **$99**

**Animals & Birds on Goblets & Pitchers -
Pitchers**

Aquarium, swimming fish, 9 1/4" h. **$286**

Squirrel Pitcher

Squirrel, pressed, Dalzel, Gilmore & Leigh-
ton (ILLUS.)... **$468**
Three Birds, basket of fruit on reverse, 9" h. .. **$231**

Baby Thumbprint - see Dakota Pattern

**Banded Portland (Portland w/Diamond
Point Band), Virginia (States series), Port-
land Maiden Blush (when pink-stained)**
Cruet w/original stopper, large size, pink-
stained, 7 1/4" h. **$605**
Goblet, pink-stained.. **$88**

Bellflower Single Vine Bowls & Compote

Bearded Head - see Viking Pattern

Bellflower

Bowl, 7" d., 4 1/4" h., footed, single vine, scalloped rim, wafer construction (ILLUS. left with other Bellflower bowl & compote, top of page) **$550**

Bowl, 8 1/2" d., 4 3/4" h., single vine, footed, scalloped rim, wafer construction (ILLUS. right with other Bellflower bowl & compote, top of page) **$40-60**

Bellflower Single Vine Castor Set

Castor set, 4-bottle, single vine, in footed pewter stand w/tall central loop handle, original tops, two bottles w/base flakes, mustard pot finial bent (ILLUS.) **$231**

Champagne, single vine, straight sides, plain stem, rayed base, 5" h....................... **$121**

Compote, 8 1/4" d., 7 1/2" h., single vine, scalloped rim, hollow hexagonal knop stem, wafer construction (ILLUS. center with two Bellflower bowls, top of page) **$605**

Creamer, single vine, fine rib, applied handle, unpatterned band at rim, star in foot (ILLUS. far right with two Bellflowers decanters & footed tumbler, bottom of page).. **$660**

Decanter w/bar lip, double vine, polished pontil, qt. (ILLUS. second from right with Bellflower creamer, pint decanter & tumbler, bottom of page)...................................... **$**

Decanter w/bar lip, single vine, qt.............. **$132**

Decanter w/original period pewter slide stopper, double vine, polished pontil, pt. (ILLUS. far left with Bellflower creamer, quart decanter & tumbler, bottom of page)... **$1,760**

Goblet, single vine w/loops, straight sides, 5 1/2" h.. **$187**

Goblet, single vine w/loops, barrel-shaped, 5 1/2" h.. **$605**

G

Bellflower Creamer, Decanters & Tumbler

Classic Blaine & Cleveland Portrait Plates

G

Bellflower All-Glass Kerosene Lamp

Lamp, kerosene-type, all-glass, single vine, fine rib, squatty bulbous font applied to a high waisted & paneled pedestal on a round scalloped foot, 7 1/2" h. (ILLUS) **$242**
Spooner, single vine, scalloped rim **$89**
Syrup pitcher w/original top, applied handle, fine rib, single vine, fiery opalescent (crack in lower handle juncture) **$4,070**
Tumbler, footed, double vine, fine rib, single step foot, 64 rays under base w/large center circle, few rib flakes, three tiny foot flakes, 4 7/8" h. (ILLUS., second from left, bottom previous page) **$231**

Wine, barrel-shaped, single vine, knob stem, fine rib, rayed base **$50**
Wine, single vine, coarse rib, straight sides, paneled stem, rayed foot **$385**

Bird & Fern - see Hummingbird Pattern

Bleeding Heart
Compote, cov., 8 1/2" d., low stand **$110**
Creamer, applied handle................................. **$99**
Egg server, high standard w/round top fitted w/three holders, faceted knop stem, domed foot, 7" d, 4 1/8" h. (minor flaws).... **$275**
Goblet, lower knob stem **$77**
Goblet, lower knob stem, barrel-shaped bowl, extra spray of flowers on lower stem **$55**
Spooner, scalloped rim................................... **$55**
Tumbler, water, flat, 3 3/4" h.......................... **$99**
Wine, knob stem **$88**

Classic
Bowl, master berry, 8 1/4" w. **$99**
Creamer, open log feet **$99**
Goblet **$209**
Pitcher, water, 9 1/2" h., open log feet.......... **$220**
Plate, 10" d., "Blaine" portrait, signed "Jacobus" (ILLUS. right with Cleveland plate, top of page).. **$231**
Plate, 10" d., "Cleveland" portrait (ILLUS. left with Blaine plate, top of page) **$231**
Plate, 10" d., "Warrior".................................. **$150**

Compact - see Snail Pattern

Dahlia

Dahlia Goblet, Wine & Pitchers

Deer & Dog Butter Dish, Milk Pitcher & Sugar Bowl

Goblet, canary (ILLUS. second from left with Dahlia pitchers & wine, bottom previous page) **$88**

Pitcher, water, blue (ILLUS. left with other Dahlia pitcher, goblet & wine, bottom previous page) **$88**

Pitcher, water, canary (ILLUS. right with other Dahlia pitcher, goblet & wine, bottom previous page) **$99**

Wine, canary (ILLUS. second from right with Dahlia goblet & two pitchers, bottom previous page) **$77**

Dakota (Baby Thumbprint)

Ruby-stained Dakota Stems

Goblet, ruby-stained, plain (ILLUS. left with two wines) **$50-75**

Pitcher, milk, tankard, fern & berry engraving, qt., 8 1/2" h. **$154**

Water tray, 12 1/2" d., pie crust rim, fern & berry engraving **$154**

Wine, ruby-stained, straight bowl (ILLUS. right with other Dakota wine & goblet) **$40-50**

Wine, ruby-stained, flared bowl, knopped stem (ILLUS. center with other Dakota wine & goblet) **$40-50**

Wine tray, 10 1/2" d., pie crust rim.................. **$88**

Deer & Dog

Butter dish, cov., pedestal base & frosted dog finial, two flakes on lower edge of bowl (ILLUS. center with Deer & Dog milk pitcher & sugar bowl, top of page) **$173**

Champagne (ILLUS. center with other Deer & Dog stems, bottom of page) **$187**

Claret, 4 3/4" h. (ILLUS. second from right with other Deer & Dog stems, bottom of page)... **$187**

Compote, cov., 5 1/4 x 7" oval, 7 1/4" h., low stand, frosted dog finial, tiny manufacturing bruise on edge of finial base (ILLUS. center with larger Deer & Dog low compote & high stand compote, top next page).. **$468**

Compote, cov., 6 1/4 x 8" oval, 8 3/4" h., low stand, frosted dog finial (ILLUS. right with other low Deer & Dog compote & high compote, top next page) **$1,045**

G

Row of Deer & Dog Pattern Stems

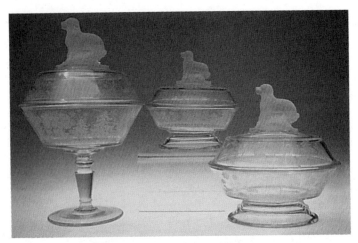

Three Deer & Dog Covered Compotes

Compote, cov., 8" d., 13" h., high stand, frosted dog finial (ILLUS. left with two Deer & Dog low covered compotes, top of page) $440

Goblet, straight sides, straight stem (ILLUS. second from left with group of Deer & Dog stems, bottom previous page) $66

Goblet, U-shaped bowl, knopped stem (ILLUS. far left with group of Deer & Dog stems, bottom previous page) $77

Pitcher, milk, small, 7" h. (ILLUS. left with Deer & Dog butter dish & sugar bowl, top of previous page) $1,320

Pitcher, milk, large, 9" h. $550

Pitcher, water, applied reeded handle, 10" h. $275

Sugar bowl, cov., frosted dog finial (ILLUS. right with Deer & Dog butter dish & milk pitcher, top of previous page) $187

Table set, 4 pc. $880

Wine (ILLUS. far right, with group of Deer & Dog stems, bottom previous page) $121

Delaware (Four Petal Flower)

Bride's basket in silver plate stand, miniature, round open bowl, green w/gold (ILLUS. left with Delaware green cruet & pickle castor, bottom of page) $187

Cruet w/original stopper, green w/gold (ILLUS. right with green Delaware miniature bride's basket & pickle castor, bottom of page) $198

Pickle caster in original silver plate frame, green w/gold trim, 8 1/4" h. (ILLUS. center with green Delaware miniature bride's basket & cruet, bottom of page).. $605

Green Delaware Miniature Bride's Basket, Cruet & Pickle Castor

Rose & Gold Delaware Pickle Castor, Pomade Box, Puff Box & Water Set

Pickle caster in original silver plate frame, rose w/gold trim, 8 1/4" h. (ILLUS. left with Delaware pomade box, puff box & water set, top of page) $605

Pomade jar w/jeweled metal cover, rose w/gold (ILLUS. far right with Delaware pickle castor, puff box & water set, top of page) $264

Pomade jar w/jeweled metal over, green w/gold $165

Puff box w/jeweled metal cover, rose w/gold, 3 1/4" h. (ILLUS. second from right with Delaware pickle castor, pomade box & water set, top of page) $297

Water set: tankard pitcher & 5 tumblers; green w/gold, 6 pcs. $165

Water set: water pitcher & 6 tumblers; rose w/gold, nick on one tumbler, 7 pcs. (ILLUS. of part second from left with Delaware pickle castor, pomade box & puff box, top of page) $303

Diamond Thumbprint

Bitters bottle, bar lip, polished pontil, 6 3/4" h. (ILLUS. far right with quart pitcher, celery vase & whiskey tumbler, bottom of page) $358

Bowl, 5 3/4 x 8 1/4" rectangular $99

*Butter dish, cov. (minor chips & flakes) $143

Celery vase, (ILLUS. second from right with quart pitcher, whiskey tumbler & bitters bottle, bottom of page) $198

G

Diamond Thumbprint Quart Pitcher, Whiskey Tumbler, Celery Vase and Bitters Bottle

Diamond Thumbprint Champagne, Goblet & Wine

Champagne, knob stem (ILLUS. center with Diamond Thumbprint goblet & wine, top of page) **$770**

G

Extremely Rare Diamond Thumbprint Pitcher

Compote, open, 8" d., high stand **$132**
Compote, open, 10 1/2" d., high stand **$99**
***Creamer,** applied handle **$220**

***Goblet** (ILLUS. left with Diamond Thumbprint champagne & wine, top of page) **$880**
Pitcher, milk, 6 1/2" h., clear, applied solid handle & round foot, qt. (ILLUS. far left with whiskey tumbler, celery vase & bitters bottle, bottom previous page) **$2,530**
Pitcher, milk, 6 1/2" h., cobalt blue, applied solid handle & round foot, qt. (ILLUS., previous column).................................... **$18,150**
Tumbler, whiskey, 3" h. (ILLUS. second from left with quart pitcher, celery vase & bitters bottle, bottom previous page) **$231**
Wine (ILLUS. right with Diamond Thumbprint champagne & goblet, top of page) **$231**

Empress

Condiment set on tray, cruet & salt & pepper shakers; green w/gold, tray 6 x 9 1/4", cruet 7 1/8" h., the set (ILLUS. left with green Empress water set, bottom of page)... **$275**
Syrup pitcher w/original top, clear w/gold trim **$66**
Syrup pitcher w/original top, emerald green w/gold **$253**

Green Empress Condiment Set & Water Set

Frosted Lion Bread Tray, Covered Compote, Milk Pitcher & Syrup Jug

Table set: creamer, cov. sugar, cov. butter & spooner; emerald green w/gold, 4 pcs.... **$231**
Water set: 9" h. pitcher & six tumblers; green w/gold, the set (ILLUS. of part, right with green Empress condiment set, bottom previous page) **$286**

Finecut & Block
Compote, open, 8" d., 4 1/4" h., clear w/blue blocks... **$66**
Sugar bowl, cov., clear w/pink blocks............ **$165**
Wine, clear w/amber-stained blocks................ **$40**
Wine, clear w/blue blocks **$50**

Four Petal Flower - see Delaware Pattern

Frosted Lion (Rampant Lion)
Bread tray, oval, lion handles, frosted center, engraved leaf & berry border, 9 x 12 3/4" (ILLUS. top, with Frosted Lion milk pitcher, syrup jug & oval covered compote, top of page) **$77**
Compote, cov., 6" d., high stem, rampant lion finial **$209**

*Compote, cov., 6 3/4" oval, 7" h., collared base, rampant lion finial (ILLUS. bottom row, right, with Frosted Lion bread tray, milk pitcher & syrup jug, top of page).... **$50-100**
*Egg cup **$55**
*Goblet **$66**
Pitcher, milk, very rare, crack at lower handle terminal (ILLUS. bottom row, left, with Frosted Lion bread tray, covered oval compote & syrup jug, top of page) **$715**
Salt dip, cov., master-size, square post, lion head w/paws, minor flaws.......................... **$242**
Syrup jug w/original metal lid, 7" h. (ILLUS. bottom row, center, with Frosted Lion bread tray, oval covered compote & milk pitcher, top of page)............................ **$523**

Galloway (Mirror)
Basket, twisted handle, 4 3/4 x 8 1/8", 11" h. (ILLUS. second from left with other Galloway pieces, bottom of page)............. **$143**
Cake stand, 9 1/4" d., 6" h. **$187**
Carafe **$77**
Cheese cover, domed, 5 7/8" h. **$99**

G

Galloway Basket, Cracker Jar, Plate & Syrup Jugs

Heart with Thumbprint Barber Bottle, Creamer, Ice Bucket & Syrup Jug

Cracker jar, cov. (ILLUS. left with Galloway basket, plate & syrup jugs, bottom previous page) **$176**

Goblet **$77**

Lemonade mug, embossed advertising in base "Dry Goods Only - Lansburgh & Bro. Washington D.C.," 4" h. **$50**

Pitcher, water, clear, 7 3/4" h. **$220**

Pitcher, 8 1/4" h., tankard-style **$99**

Pitcher, 9 1/8" h., tankard-style, gold trim **$50**

Plate, 8" d. (ILLUS. second from right with Galloway basket, cracker jar & syrup jugs, bottom previous page) **$55**

Syrup jug w/metal spring top, clear, small, 5 3/4" h. (ILLUS. far right with Galloway basket, cracker jar, plate & large syrup jug, bottom previous page) **$99**

Syrup jug w/metal spring top, clear, large, top missing thumb tab, 7 1/4" h. (ILLUS. third from right with Galloway basket, cracker jar, plate & small syrup jug, bottom previous page) **$40**

Table set, 4 pcs. **$220**

Water set, child's, pitcher & 6 tumblers, 7 pcs. **$110**

Heart with Thumbprint

Barber bottle, no stopper, clear, shallow rim flake (ILLUS. left with Heart with Thumbprint creamer, ice bucket & syrup jug, top of page) **$220**

Cake stand, 9" d., 5" h. **$385**

Cordial, 3" h. **$132**

Creamer, clear (ILLUS. second from left with Heart with Thumbprint barber bottle, ice bucket & syrup jug, top of page) **$165**

Goblet, clear **$40-50**

Goblet, green w/gold **$220**

Ice bucket, clear, 6" d., 5" h. (ILLUS. far right with Heart with Thumbprint barber bottle, creamer & syrup jug, top of page) **$154**

Syrup jug w/original pewter top, small, clear, split at hinge, minor damage, 5 1/2" h. (ILLUS. second from right with Heart with Thumbprint barber bottle, creamer & ice bucket, top of page) **$50-75**

Tumbler, water, clear w/gold **$40**

Wine, clear **$30**

Holly

Cake stand, no rope surrounding pattern, plain stem, 9 1/2" d. **$165**

Cake stand, 10 3/4" d., 6 1/4" h., no rope around rim, wafer construction (ILLUS. left with Holly syrup, bottom of page) **$143**

Goblet **$198**

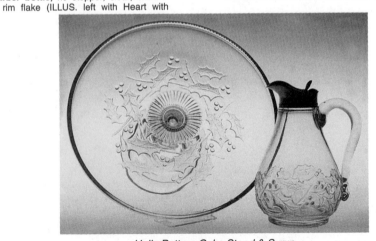

Holly Pattern Cake Stand & Syrup

Row of Horn of Plenty Stems

Pitcher, water, applied handle, polished pontil, 8 1/2" h. **$297**

Syrup jug w/original metal lid, metal w/embossed patent date for 1868, 7 1/2" h. (ILLUS. right with Holly cake stand, bottom previous page).................... **$242**

Wine **$99**

Horn of Plenty (McKee's Comet)

Bowl, 7" d., on unpatterned domed foot, wafer construction **$77**

Celery vase, flared scalloped rim, plain round foot, 8 1/2" h.................................... **$110**

Celery vase, flared scalloped rim, plain round foot, wafer construction, 8 3/4" h. (fire-polished flat chip on knop stem) **$198**

Champagne, 5 1/4" h. (ILLUS. far right with other Horn of Plenty stems, top of page) **$77**

Compote, open, 6" d., high stand, 18-scallop rim, six-lobed pedestal & waffle pattern under foot, wafer construction, several flakes under foot................................ **$110**

Decanter, bar lip, qt.. **$77**

Very Rare Horn of Plenty Canary Decanter

Decanter, no stopper, scalloped foot, canary, unique ornate overall gold trim, polished pontil, qt., 10" h. (ILLUS.) **$7,700**

Decanter w/original stopper, pt. **$231**

Decanter with bar lip, pt., 8 1/2" h. **$132**

Goblet, large goblet, 6 1/4" h., w/polished pontil (ILLUS. far left with other Horn of Plenty stems) **$77**

Goblets, small, 5 3/4" h., set of six (ILLUS. of one, second from left with other Horn of Plenty stems) **$248**

Salt dip, master size, oval, ten-scallop rim, Inverted Diamond Point pattern base, 2 1/4 x 3 1/4", 1 1/4" h................................. **$55**

Sugar bowl, cov., domed cover, minute flake on finial, 7" h................................... **$66**

Sugar bowl, cov., pagoda-shaped cover, tilted finial, 7 1/4" h............................... **$75-125**

Tumbler, whiskey, 3" h. **$132**

Wine, faceted knop stem............................... **$88**

Wine, straight rim, 4 1/2" h. (ILLUS. second from right with other Horn of Plenty stems, top of page) **$50**

Hummingbird (Flying Robin or Bird & Fern)

Hummingbird Blue Goblet & Pitcher

Goblet, blue (ILLUS. left with blue Hummingbird milk pitcher)................................. **$110**

Pitcher, milk, blue, 8" h. (ILLUS. right with blue Hummingbird goblet)......................... **$132**

Jewel & Crescent - see Tennessee Pattern

Jumbo and Jumbo & Barnum

Butter dish & cover w/frosted elephant finial, head under each handle, 5 5/8" d.... **$358**

Compote, cov., 7" d., high stand, frosted elephant finial, two flakes on shoulder of cover (ILLUS. right with two other Jumbo compotes, top next page) **$770**

Three Rare Jumbo Compotes

Compote, cov., 8" d., high stand, frosted elephant finial, tiny flake on shoulder of cover & edge of foot (ILLUS. right with two other Jumbo compotes, top of page) **$1,980**

Compote, cov., rectangular, 12" h., 5 1/4 x 7 1/8", frosted elephant finial, plain hollow stem & round stepped foot, Canton Glass Co., minor flaws (ILLUS. left with two round Jumbo compotes, top of page) **$9,625**

Spoon rack, clear w/frosted elephant, minor flaws **$880**

Spooner, high domed base, w/Barnum head handles, 6 1/4" h. **$187**

Spooner, w/Barnum head at handles **$132**

Sugar bowl, w/Barnum head handles & cover w/frosted elephant finial (manufacturing separation at base of elephant trunk) **$303**

King's Crown
Celery vase, plain **$165**
*Cup & saucer **$46**

Spooner **$50**
Spooner, engraved leaf decoration **$66**

Log Cabin
Compote, cov., high tree-trunk base, clear, 9" h. **$825**
Compote, cov., high tree-trunk base, clear, 10 1/4" h. **$935**
Compote, cov., high tree-trunk base, clear, 12" h. **$1,045**
Pickle jar, cov., 6 3/4" h. (minor flaws) **$605**
Pitcher, water, 8 1/2" h. **$1,045**

Loop & Pillar - see Michigan Pattern

Loop with Stippled Panels - see Texas Pattern

McKee's Comet - see Horn of Plenty Pattern

Michigan (Paneled Jewel or Loop & Pillar)
Carafe, water, pink-stained w/gold, 7 1/2" h. (ILLUS. right with Michigan stained lemonade set & water set, bottom of page) **$165**

Pink-stained Michigan Carafe, Lemonade Set & Water Set

Stained Michigan Pattern Celery Vase, Compote, Salt & Pepper Shakers & Tumbler

Stained Michigan Cruet and Four-Piece Table Set

G

Celery vase, pink-stained, gold rim (ILLUS. far left with Michigan compote, salt & pepper shakers & tumbler, top of page)..... **$231**

Compote, open, 8 1/2" d., high stand, pink-stained w/gold (ILLUS. far right with stained Michigan celery vase, salt & pepper shakers & tumbler, top of page)........... **$242**

Cruet w/original stopper, pink-stained w/gold, replaced stopper (ILLUS. right with four-piece table set, second from top of page)...................................... **$440**

Goblet, clear w/green stain............................. **$55**

Lemonade set: 10 1/4" h. tankard pitcher & six tall handled mugs; pink-stained w/gold trim, the set (ILLUS. of part, left, with stained Michigan carafe & water set, bottom of previous page) **$605**

Salt & pepper shakers w/original tops, table size, pink-stained w/gold, 4" h., pr. (ILLUS. second from left, top of page)....... **$286**

Table set, pink-stained w/gold, 4 pcs. (ILLUS. left with stained Michigan cruet, second from top of page).. **$297**

Tumbler, ruby-stained (ILLUS. second from right with Michigan stained celery vase, compote & salt & pepper shakers, top of page)... **$66**

Water set: 7 1/2" h. pitcher & 6 tumblers; pink-stained w/gold, 7 pcs. (ILLUS. of part, center with stained Michigan carafe & lemonade set, bottom previous page) **$358**

Monkey

Butter dish, cov. (ILLUS. second from left with Monkey celery vase, covered sugar bowl & spooner, bottom of page)............... **$523**

Monkey Pattern Butter Dish, Celery Vase, Spooner & Sugar Bowl

Monkey Pattern Water Pitcher & Three-piece Table Set

Red Block Table Set & Water Set

Celery vase (ILLUS. far left with Monkey butter dish, spooner & sugar bowl, bottom previous page) $715

Creamer, clear, plain base $99

Mug, clear, fancy handle $77

Pitcher, water (ILLUS. left with three-piece table set, top of page) $1,265

*Spooner, clear (ILLUS. far right with Monkey butter dish, celery vase & sugar bowl, bottom previous page) $358

Sugar bowl, cov., clear (ILLUS. second from right with Monkey butter dish, celery vase & spooner, bottom previous page) $358

Table set: cov. butter dish, cov. sugar & creamer; minor flakes, 3 pcs. (ILLUS.

right with Monkey water pitcher, top of page) $1,155

Tumbler, water, flat, plain base $110

Waste bowl, opalescent $358

Red Block & Lattice (Big Block)

Table set, some flaking, 4 pcs. (ILLUS. right with water set, middle top of page) $165

Water set: 8" h. water pitcher & three tumblers; some minor flakes, the set (ILLUS. of part, left, with four-piece table set, middle top of page) $121

S-Repeat

Blue S-Repeat Cruet Set & Wine Set

Snail Pattern Banana Stand, Compote & Cracker Jar

Condiment set: cruet w/stopper & salt & pepper shakers on round footed tray; sapphire blue, minor flaking, tray 6 1/4" d., cruet 7 1/4" h., the set (ILLUS. right with blue S-Repeat wine set, bottom previous page) **$220**

Wine set: stoppered, handled decanter, 4 wines & tray; sapphire blue, 6 pcs. (ILLUS. left with blue S-Repeat condiment set, bottom previous page)..................................... **$330**

Shell & Tassel
Bowl, 7 1/2 x 8 3/4", shell-shaped, three applied shell-shaped feet **$77**
Bride's basket, 5 x 10" oval canary bowl in silver plate frame....................................... **$385**
Cake stand, shell corners, 8" sq. **$77**
Cake stand, shell corners, 10" sq. **$110**
Celery vase, square..................................... **$99**
Sugar bowl, cov., round, dog finial **$121**
Vase, engraved leaf decoration, 7 1/2" h........ **$132**

Snail (Compact)
Banana stand, 10" d., 7" h. (ILLUS. left with Snail compote & cracker jar, top of page) .. **$165**
Compote, open, 10" d., 7" h., flaring shallow bowl (ILLUS. right with Snail banana stand & cracker jar, top of page)............... **$154**
Cracker jar, cov., 8" d., 9" h. (ILLUS. center with Snail banana stand & compote, top of page)... **$242**
Goblet **$99**
Rose bowl, miniature, 3" h.............................. **$33**

Tennessee (Jewel & Crescent)
Goblet **$165**
Pitcher, milk, 1 qt., 7 1/2" h............................ **$143**
Wine **$66**

Texas (Loop with Stippled Panels)

Pink-Stained Texas Cake Stand & Wine

Cake stand, pink-stained, 9" d., 6" h. (ILLUS. left with stained Texas wine)........................ **$468**
Cake stand, 10 3/4" d. **$198**
Goblet, clear **$88**
Wine, pink-stained, 4" h. (ILLUS. right with Texas cake stand).................................... **$132**

Three Face
*Cake stand, 8 1/2" d............................... **$198**
Cake stand, 10 1/2" d. **$220-260**
*Celery vase, scalloped rim **$110**

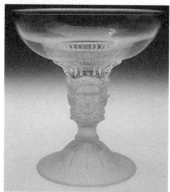

Rare Three Face Saucer Champagne

Champagne, saucer-style, hollow stem, 3 1/2" d., 4" h. (ILLUS.) **$2,530**
Compote, cov., 9 1/4" d., high stand............. **$660**

Very Rare Three Face Elliptical Compote

Three Face Open Compote & Rare Kerosene Lamp

G

Compote, cov., 12" h., 7 1/4" w., deep elliptical bowl on a high standard (ILLUS., previous page) **$3,520**

Compote, cov., 8" d., high stand, minor chip **$198**

Compote, open, 8 1/2" d., high stand, paneled Huber patt. bowl w/scalloped rim, floral plate etching (ILLUS. right with Three Face kerosene lamp, top of page) **$660-680**

Creamer w/mask spout & cov. sugar bowl, pr. **$688**

*Goblet, engraved bowl **$132**

*Goblet, plain **$143**

*Lamp, kerosene-type, pedestal base, No. 7 or No. 8 model, No. 1 slip burner & period chimney, 8" h. (ILLUS. left with Three Face open compote, top of page) **$4,400**

Pitcher, water **$358**

*Spooner, plain **$50**

*Sugar bowl, cov. **$66**

Tree of Life - Portland

Mug, footed, tall tapering bowl w/panels around the base, applied handle, amethyst, 3 1/2" h. **$275**

Mug, footed, tall tapering bowl w/panels around the base, applied handle, clear, 3 1/2" h. (ILLUS. far left with Tree of Life water pitcher, tumbler & vase, bottom of page) **$143**

Pitcher, water, clear, applied handle, 9" h. (ILLUS. second from left with Tree of Life mug, tumbler & vase, bottom of page) **$358**

Tumblers, footed, 6" h., set of 4 (ILLUS. of one, second from right with Tree of Life mug, water pitcher & vase, bottom of page) **$154**

Vase, 12 3/4" h., clear, hollow compressed knop stem above domed round foot, six upright pointed scallops at rim (ILLUS. far right, with Tree of Life mug, water pitcher & tumbler, bottom of page) **$165**

Portland Tree of Life Mug, Pitcher, Tumbler & Vase

Tree of Life with Hand (Tree of Life-Wheeling)
Butter dish, cov. $110
Compote, open, 8" d., clear hand & ball stem $55
Compote, open, 9" d., frosted hand & ball stem $77

Viking (Bearded Head or Old Man of the Mountain)
Compote, cov., 13 1/4" h., high standard, domed base w/three mask feet, minor chips.. $77
Egg cup $55
Mug, applied handle, 3 1/2" h........................... $88
Pitcher, water, 8 3/4" h., clear....................... $110

Waffle and Thumbprint
Champagne, 5 1/2" h. $110
Goblet, large, faceted knop stem, polished pontil, 6 3/4" h. $99
Goblet, small, faceted knop stem, polished pontil, 6 1/4" h. $110
Wine, faceted knop stem, polished pontil, 4 5/8" h.. $77

Westward Ho
Cake stand, pedestal base w/wafer construction, 9" d. $55

Westward Ho Pattern Celery Vase

*Celery vase (ILLUS.).................................... $154
*Compote, cov., 4 x 6 3/4" oval, low stand $176
Compote, cov., 8" d., high stand.................... $468
*Creamer $110
Spooner $66

Peach Blow

Several types of glass lumped together by collectors as Peach Blow were produced by half a dozen glasshouses. Hobbs, Brockunier & Co., Wheeling, West Virginia, made Peach Blow as a plated ware that shaded from red at the top to yellow at the bottom and is referred to as Wheeling Peach Blow. Mt. Washington Glass Works produced an homogeneous Peach Blow shading from a rose color at the top to pale blue in the lower portion. The New England Glass Works' Peach Blow, called Wild Rose, shaded from rose at the top to white. Gundersen-Pairpoint Co. also reproduced some

of the Mt. Washington Peach Blow in the early 1950s and some glass of a somewhat similar type was made by Steuben Glass Works, Thomas Webb & Sons and Stevens & Williams of England. New England Peach Blow is one-layered glass and the English is two-layered.

Another single-layered shaded art glass was produced early in the 20th century by the New Martinsville Glass Mfg. Co. Originally called "Muranese," collectors today refer to it as "New Martinsville Peach Blow."

New England

Glossy New England Peach Blow Rose Bowl

Rose bowl, spherical w/flat opening, deep pink shaded to pale pink, glossy finish, 3 3/4" h. (ILLUS.) $173

New England Peach Blow Toothpick Holder

Toothpick holder, rounded base & squared rim, deep pink shaded to white, 2 1/4" h. (ILLUS.).. $259

Wheeling

Tall Wheeling Peach Blow Tumbler

Tumbler, tall slender cylindrical form, glossy finish, 5 1/4" h. (ILLUS.)................. **$345**

Fine Wheeling Peach Blow Vase

Vase, 8 1/4" h., tapering ovoid body w/a trumpet neck, shape No. 6, ca. 1886, glossy finish (ILLUS.) **$600**

Classic Wheeling Peach Blow Morgan Vase

Vase, 10" h., "Morgan Vase," slender ovoid shouldered body w/slender cylindrical ringed neck w/flared rim, glossy finish, set in original glossy amber gargoyle base w/one repaired foot & one cracked foot, 2 pcs. (ILLUS.)............................... **$1,840**

Pillar-Molded

This heavily ribbed glassware was produced by blowing glass into full-sized ribbed molds and then finishing it by hand. The technique evolved from earlier "pattern moulding" used on glass since ancient times, but in pillar-molded glass the ribs are very heavy and prominent. Most examples found in this country were produced in the Pittsburgh, Pennsylvania, area from around 1850 to 1870, but similar English-made wares made before and after this period are also available. Most American items were made from clear flint glass, and colored examples or pieces with colored strands in the ribs are rare and highly prized. Some collectors refer to this as "steamboat" glass, believing it was made to be used on American riverboats, but most likely it was used anywhere that a sturdy, relatively inexpensive glassware was needed, such as taverns and hotels.

Pillar-Molded Apothecary Jar, Candlestick & Lantern

Apothecary jar, cov., eight-rib, clear, tall cylindrical bowl w/a rounded base atop an applied baluster-form stem on a thick round foot, ribbed pagoda-form cover w/applied pointed finial, Pittsburgh, 6" d., 17 1/2" h. (ILLUS. center with pillar-molded candlestick & lantern, top of page)..... **$1,650**

Candlestick, a square stepped pressed glass base supporting a waisted tall pillar-molded stem attached by a wafer to the base & upper tall cylindrical eight-rib pillar-molded socket w/a flared rim, clear, fine condition, 11 1/2" h. (ILLUS. left with pair of pint decanters, bottom of page) ... **$2,310**

Candlestick, eight-rib, clear, slender tapering hollow standard w/a ringed neck supporting the ribbed tulip-form socket suspending eight triangular prisms, raised on a short waisted solid stem on a thick round foot, probably Pittsburgh, very minor flaking, 12 1/4" h. (ILLUS. left with pillar-molded apothecary jar and lantern, top of page)... **$1,210**

Celery vase, eight-rib, tall deeply waisted tulip-form bowl w/a flared & scalloped rim, applied squatty baluster-form stem on a thick disk foot, clear, 9 1/2" h. **$110**

Celery vase, eight-rib, tall tulip-form bowl w/a flared & scalloped rim, applied baluster-form stem on a thick disk foot, clear, 9" h. **$231**

G

Rare Pillar-Molded Candlestick & Pair of Decanters

Pillar-Molded Compote, Sweetmeat Compote & Sugar Bowl Base

Compote, open, eight-rib, a clear deep wide-ly flaring bell-form bowl raised on a slender waisted solid stem & thick round foot, rough pontil, 8 3/4" d., 8 1/4" h. (ILLUS. center with pillar-molded sweetmeat compote & sugar bowl base, top of page)......... **$523**

Decanter w/applied bar lip, eight-rib, sharply tapering sides w/an applied ring at the base of the smooth neck, polished pontil, possibly Pittsburgh, 11 1/2" h. **$77**

Decanters w/original pewter cap-style stopper & neck chains, eight-rib, sharply tapering body w/applied rings below the tall plain neck tapering to a bar lip, clear, probably Pittsburgh, pt., one w/base point chip, other w/light interior residue, 9 1/2" h., pr. (ILLUS. center and right with rare pillar-molded candlestick, bottom previous page) **$275**

Lantern, eight-rib, the clear bulbous onion-form glass font fitted w/a pierced cylindrical tin cap w/wire bail handle, on a short cylindrical tin base, missing burner, Pittsburgh or New England, flake w/corresponding bruise on lower globe, light rust on tin, 7" d., overall 10 1/2" h. (ILLUS. right with pillar-molded apothecary jar and candlestick, top previous page) **$1,155**

Pint, Three-Pint & Three-Quart Pillar-Molded Pitchers

Pitcher, 6" h., 4" d., eight twisted ribs, clear bulbous body tapering to a high & wide arched spout, applied hollow strap handle, rough pontil, small bruise on lower body, pt. (ILLUS. center with pillar-molded three-quart & three-pint pitchers).. **$660**

Pillar-Molded Quart, Three-Pint & Half-Gallon Pitchers

Pitcher, 8" h., 4 1/4" d., eight-rib, clear squatty bulbous tapering body w/a wide arched spout & applied strap handle, polished pontil, qt. (ILLUS. left with half-gallon & three-pint pillar-molded pitchers, bottom previous page) **$253**

Pitcher, 8 1/2" h., 5" d., eight rib, clear squatty spherical base tapering to a wide cylindrical neck w/a wide arched spout & applied hollow strap handle, polished pontil, probably Pittsburgh, possibly Bakewell, Pears & Co., 3 pt. (ILLUS. right with pillar-molded quart & half-gallon pitchers, bottom previous page) **$495**

Pitcher, 9 1/4" h., 6 1/4" d., eight-rib, clear ovoid body tapering to a wide flaring neck w/pinched spout, applied hollow strap handle, rough pontil, probably Pittsburgh, 1/2 gal. (ILLUS. center with pillar-molded quart & 3-pint pitchers, bottom previous page) **$330**

Pitcher, 10 1/2" h., 4 1/2" d., eight-rib, clear footed bulbous ovoid body tapering to a wide arched spout, applied solid strap handle, polished pontil, 3 pt. (ILLUS. right with pint & three-quart pillar-molded pitchers, middle previous page) **$330**

Pitcher, 11 1/4" h., 5 1/8" d., clear footed tall ovoid body w/a flaring widely arched spout & applied solid strap handle, polished pontil, probably Pittsburgh, 3 qt. (ILLUS. left with pillar-molded pint and 3-pt. pitchers, bottom previous page) **$1,210**

Sugar bowl base, eight-rib, spherical clear bowl w/galleried rim raised on a solid stem & thick round foot, rough pontil, possibly Pittsburgh, 5" d., 6 3/4" h. (ILLUS. right with pillar-molded compote & sweetmeat compote, top previous page) **$187**

Sweetmeat compote, eight-rib, clear squatty bulbous bowl w/a wide flared rim, raised on a short ringed stem & thick round foot, rough pontil, American or English, 5" d., 4 1/4" h. (ILLUS. left with pillar-molded compote and sugar bowl base, top previous page)............................ **$385**

Quezal

In 1901, Martin Bach and Thomas Johnson, who had worked for Louis Tiffany, opened a competing glassworks in Brooklyn, New York. The Quezal Art Glass and Decorating Co. produced wares closely resembling those of Tiffany until the plant's closing in 1925.

Quezal

Quezal Mark

Compote, 9 1/2" d., a low flaring round foot supporting the wide shallow bowl w/a widely flaring flattened rim, gold iridescent foot & bowl decorated w/a wide green iridescent rim band, unsigned (ILLUS., top next page)... **$575**

Very Fine Quezal Vase with Pulled Leaves

G

Vase, 6" h., the round cushion foot tapering to the tall ovoid body w/a widely flaring & rolled tricorner mouth, the exterior decorated w/a green pulled-leaf design up from the foot below iridescent gold feathered design on the upper body, gold iridescent interior, base engraved "Quezal S 155" (ILLUS.) **$5,405**

Quezal Vase with Pulled Feather Design

Vase, 7" h., 9 1/2" d., a flared base band below the gently flaring cylindrical body w/a widely flaring four-petal rim, creamy exterior ground decorated around the lower half w/a green pulled feather design below gold iridescent fishnet design on the upper body, gold iridescent interior, signed on base "Quezal 477," crack at foot (ILLUS.).. **$863**

Interesting Gold & Green Quezal Compote

Scarce Quezal Vase with Unique Designs

Vase, 7 5/8" h., wide bulbous tapering ovoid body w/a short widely flaring neck, the exterior decorated w/a dark green double-hooked design under a silver iridescent hooked & feathered decoration, gold banding separates the green from the ivory white shoulder & neck, gold iridescent interior, polished pontil engraved "Quezal 121" (ILLUS.) **$5,290**

Rose Bowls

These decorative small bowls were widely popular in the late 19th and early 20th centuries. Produced in various types of glass, they are most common in satin glass or spatter glass. They are generally a spherical shape with an incurved crimped rim, but ovoid or egg-shaped examples were also popular.

Their name derives from their reported use, to hold dried rose petal potpourri or small fresh-cut roses.

Webb Blue Mother-of-Pearl Rose Bowl

Satin glass, footed spherical body pulled into a three-lobed rim, pale blue mother-of-pearl Ribbon patt., decorated w/applied gold prunus blossoms, clear frosted applied foot, Thomas Webb, 3" h. (ILLUS.) **$316**

Miniature Webb Satin Glass Rose Bowl

Satin glass, spherical w/eight-crimp rim, shaded dark to light blue exterior decorated w/gold prunus blossoms & a bumble bee, cased in white, miniature size, Thomas Webb, 2 1/2" d. (ILLUS.) **$288**

G

Pink Diamond Quilted Satin Rose Bowl

Satin glass, spherical w/six-crimp rim, dark raspberry shading to pale pink in mother-of-pearl Diamond Quilted patt., based signed "Patent," 2 3/4" d. (ILLUS.) **$120**

Marked Rainbow Satin Rose Bowl

Satin glass, spherical w/six-crimp rim, Rainbow mother-of-pearl w/a Diamond Quilted design, base marked "Patent," late 19th c., 2 3/4" d. (ILLUS.) **$518**

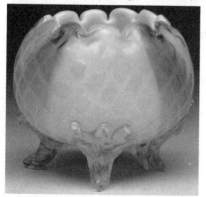

Rainbow Mother-of-Pearl Rose Bowl

Satin glass, spherical w/ten-crimp rim, Rainbow mother-of-pearl w/a Diamond Quilted design, raised on applied frosted clear pointed feet one foot w/two chips, late 19th c., 4 1/2" d. (ILLUS.) **$575**

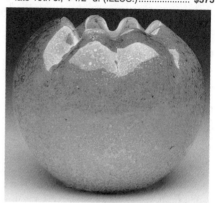

Pink Spangled Glass Rose Bowl

Spangled glass, shaded deep pink to pale pink exterior w/overall fine silver mica flecks, cased in white, unfinished pontil, 4 3/4" h. (ILLUS.) **$150-250**

G

Ruby- & Amber-Stained

The name "ruby-stained" derives from the color of the glass, a deep red. The red staining was thinly painted on clear pressed glass patterns and refired at a low temperature. Many pieces were further engraved as souvenir items and were very popular from the 1890s into the 1920s. This technique should not be confused with "flashed" glass where a clear glass piece is actually dipped in molten glass of a contrasting color. See PATTERN GLASS.

Amber
Goblet, Swag Block/Duncan #326 patt. **$110**

Ruby
Claret, O'Hara Diamond patt., 4 3/4" h. (ILLUS. center with ruby-stained creamer & goblet, below) **$110**

Ruby-stained Creamer, Claret & Goblet

Creamer, Near Cut Daisy patt., traces of gold trim (ILLUS. left with ruby-stained claret & goblet) **$55**

Ruby-stained Child's Creamer & Sugar, Goblet & Wine

Creamer, Radiant Daisy/Robinson's No. 90 Puritan patt. **$44**

Creamer & cov. sugar bowl, child's, Horizontal Threads patt., pr. (ILLUS. center with ruby-stained goblet & wine, top of page) **$176**

Goblet, Diamond Band with Panels/Co-op's Radiant, gold trim **$55**

Goblet, Frontier/New Martinsville No. 718 patt. (ILLUS. left with ruby-stained child's creamer & sugar & wine, top of page) **$176**

Goblet, Palm Leaf Fan patt. (ILLUS. right with ruby-stained creamer & claret, previous page) **$143**

Goblet, Roanoke patt. **$50**

Goblet, U.S. Rib patt. **$358**

Pitcher, milk, Sheaf & Block/Alden patt., 7 1/2" h. **$66**

Pitcher, 11 1/2" h., tankard-type, Diamond with Peg patt., engraved souvenir inscription **$121**

Salt & pepper shakes w/metal lids, Wellington patt., 2 1/2" h., pr. **$303**

Spooner, Saxon patt., transfer-printed Sacred Heart above "Thy Kingdom Come" **$55**

Tumbler, Loop & Block/Pioneer's No. 23 patt. **$33**

Wine, Horizontal Threads patt. (ILLUS. right with ruby-stained child's creamer & sugar & goblet, top of page) **$77**

Wine set: decanter w/original stopper & six wines; Model's Gem/Double Red Block patt., decanter 11 1/2" h., the set **$242**

Sandwich

Numerous types of glass were produced at The Boston & Sandwich Glass Works in Sandwich, Massachusetts, on Cape Cod, from 1826 to 1888. Those listed here represent a sampling. Also see BLOWN THREE MOLD and LACY.

All pieces are pressed glass unless otherwise noted. Numbers after salt dips refer to listings in Pressed Glass Salt Dishes of the Lacy Period, 1825-1850, *by Logan W. and Dorothy B. Neal.*

Sandwich Glass Dolphin Candlesticks

Candlesticks, figural dolphin stem w/petal socket, on a stepped square base, light lavender alabaster-clambroth, minute petal & base nicks, 10" h., pr. (ILLUS.) ... **$3,300**

Two Star & Punty Cologne Bottles

Cologne bottle w/original stopper, Star & Punty patt., paneled sides & stopper, canary, ca. 1860, minor flakes, 6 1/8" h. (ILLUS. right with yellowish green Star & Punty cologne) **$286**

Cologne bottle w/original stopper, Star & Punty patt., paneled sides & stopper, yellowish green, ca. 1860, minor flakes, 6 1/8" h. (ILLUS. left with canary Star & Punty cologne, previous page).................. **$440**

Very Rare Sandwich Openwork Compote

Compote, open, 8 1/4" h., 8 1/4" w., a pressed flaring octagonal pedestal base wafer-joined to the pressed openwork bowl w/16 vertical staves below the 32-point rim & above a 34-point star in sloping base, bright deep amethyst, 1840-55, minor flaws, very rare (ILLUS.) **$17,600**

Amethyst Sandwich Whale Oil Lamp

Lamp, whale oil-type, hexagonal base & knop below the three-printed block font w/early burner & collar, ca. 1840-60, minor chips on base edge, amethyst, 9" h. (ILLUS.).. **$881**

Rare Sandwich Canary Whale Oil Lamps

Lamps, whale oil type, hexagonal base & knopped stem, slender four-printed block font, original pewter collar & camphene burners, base edge chips, canary yellow, 12 7/8" h., pr. (ILLUS.) **$2,115**

Two Rare Sandwich Tulip Vases

Vase, 10 1/4" h., tulip-style, deep amethyst, octagonal base, wafer construction, ca. 1850 (ILLUS. right with deep violet blue tulip vase).. **$3,575**

Fine Sandwich Cobalt Blue Vase

G

Vase, 11 3/4" h., hexagonal base & knopped stem below the flaring four-printier block vase w/ruffled rim, cobalt blue, imperfections, ca. 1840-60 (ILLUS., previous page) **$1,880**

Vase, 10 1/4" h., tulip-style, deep violet blue w/light marbling showing blood red, octagonal base, wafer construction, ca. 1850 (ILLUS. left with deep amethyst tulip vase, previous page) **$22,000**

Schneider

This ware is made in France at Cristallerie Schneider, established in 1913 near Paris by Ernest and Charles Schneider. Some pieces of cameo were marked "Le Verre Francais" and others were signed "Charder."

Schneider Mark

Schneider Art Deco Cameo Vase

Cameo vase, 10 1/8" h., Art Deco style, black amethyst disk foot supporting a tall slender ovoid body in textured frosted clear overlaid in orange & cameo-cut down the sides w/berries on stems (ILLUS.) **$2,645**

Tall Schneider Art Deco Cameo Vase

Cameo vase, 16 1/2" h., thick cushion foot below the tall gently swelled cylindrical body, amethyst ground overlaid in deep mottled orange shading to dark brown & cameo-carved w/an Art Deco design of tall stylized leaves & pods, signed on base w/a red, white & blue striped cane (ILLUS.) **$3,105**

Schneider Crystal Ice Bucket

Ice bucket, wide tapering cylindrical form in crystal w/overall controlled bubbles, applied shoulder handles, acid-stamped "Schneider Paris France," 5" h. (ILLUS.) **$115**

G

Fine Schneider Tazza

Tazza, a thin round black foot & slender cylindrical stem supporting a wide shallow bowl top in shaded pale orange & speckled white, etched signature, 1920s, 12" h. (ILLUS.).. **$4,780**

Fine Schneider "Martelé" Vase

Vase, 11 3/4" h., "Martelé" style, a round cushion base & tapering cylindrical sides to a shoulder ring below the short cylindrical neck fitted w/a wrought-iron pierced collar comprised of hammered curling tendrils, the frosted lilac body featuring flowering lines, signed in gold near the foot (ILLUS.).................................... **$1,380**

Vase, 12 3/8" h., squatty bulbous base tapering to a very tall slender & slightly flaring cylindrical neck w/a flaring rim, mottled pink, rose & yellow above mottled deep burgundy & yellow at the bottom, engraved script signature (ILLUS., top next column)... **$748**

Mottled Pink & Burgundy Schneider Vase

Very Tall Bottle-form Schneider Vases

Vases, 13 7/8" h., bottle-form, squatty bulbous body w/a very tall slender stick-style neck swelled at the bottom, clear decorated w/vertical thin stripes of mottled yellow enamel, each marked on the base w/an embedded candy cane, some small rim chips & minor interior stain, pr. (ILLUS.) **$900**

Spangled

Spangled glass incorporated particles of mica or metallic flakes and variegated colored glass particles embedded in the transparent glass. Usually made of two layers, it might have either an opaque or transparent casing. The Vasa Murrhina Glass Company of Sandwich, Massachusetts, first patented the process for producing Spangled glass in 1884, and this factory is known to have produced great quantities of this ware. It was, however, also produced by numerous other American and English glasshouses. This type, along with Spatter, is often erroneously called "End of the Day."

A related decorative glass, Aventurine, features a fine speckled pattern resembling gold dust on a solid color ground.

Spatter

This variegated-color ware is similar to spangled glass but does not contain metallic flakes. The various colors are applied on a clear, opaque white or colored body. Much of it was made in Europe and England. It is sometimes called "End Of Day."

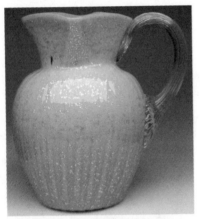

Blue Cased Spangled Pitcher

Pitcher, 8 1/2" h., tall ovoid body w/a squared flaring rim, cased blue w/overall fine silver mica flecks, clear applied reeded handle (ILLUS.) **$154**

Victorian Spatter Cracker Barrel

Cracker barrel w/original brass rim, cover & bail handle, barrel-shaped, white interior cased w/a swirling spatter design in shades of root beer, pink, maroon & white, tiny orange & blue enameled trim near rim, late 19th c., inside rim chip, 5 1/8" h. (ILLUS.) **$173**

Colorful Striped Spangled Pitcher

Pitcher, 8 3/4" h., bulbous ovoid body tapering to a cylindrical neck w/a downturned crimped & ruffled rim, cased colorful Rib Optic spatter w/overall silver mica flecks, applied frosted white rim band & applied ribbed clear handle (ILLUS.)......... **$253**

Colorful Spiral Swirl Spatter Pitcher

Pitcher, 7 1/2" h., bulbous body w/molded spiral swirl design below the tall squared neck, multicolored pink, maroon & white spatter cased in white, applied clear frosted handle (ILLUS.)............................. **$165**

G

Colorful Spatter Glass Spoon Holder

Spoon holder, ovoid body w/the mount fitted w/a silver plate collar flanked by fancy arched handles, overall dense red & yellow spatter cased in white, 5 1/2" h. (ILLUS.) **$55**

Steuben

Most of the Steuben glass listed below was made at the Steuben Glass Works, now a division of Corning Glass, between 1903 and about 1933. The factory was organized by T.G. Hawkes, noted glass designer Frederick Carder, and others. Mr. Carder devised many types of glass and revived many old techniques.

Steuben Marks

Acid Cut-Back

Fine Green Acid Cut-Back Table Lamp

Lamp, electric table model, the ovoid glass body in emerald green covered in blue iridescence & cut-back w/an Oriental floral design, gilt-metal base w/a bracket supported by a pair of figural swans on a rectangular base, gilt-metal top fittings & the original domed & paneled silk shade w/fine embroidered floral designs, shade fragile, overall 24" h. (ILLUS.) **$2,300**

Small Steuben Acid Cut-Back Vase

Vase, 4 1/4" h., bulbous ovoid body w/a short cylindrical neck, Alabaster ground cased in pink & acid-etched w/an Oriental banded design against a scroll-etched background (ILLUS.) **$1,200**

Alabaster

Alabaster Vase with Gold Heart Vines

Vase, 6 1/4" h., flared foot tapering to an ovoid body w/a flat rim, white ground decorated w/gold iridescent vines & heart-shaped leaves, Shape No. 429 (ILLUS.) ... **$345**

Amber

Amber Steuben Vase Signed by Carder

Vase, 6 1/2" h., large tapering ovoid body w/a wide short flaring neck w/flattened rim, op-tic ribbed design, engraved "Steuben - F. Carder" on the base (ILLUS.)........................ **$316**

Aurene

Bowl, 10" d., footed low rounded shaped w/incurved sides pulled into eight tight crimps at the rim, overall dark blue iridescence, signed on bottom "Aurene 2775" (ILLUS., first at bottom of page)................ **$978**

Bowl, 12 3/4" d., a small round foot below the deep rounded & widely flaring sides, overall gold iridescence w/blue & purple highlights, original Steuben label & signed "Aurene 2831" (ILLUS., second at bottom of page).. **$863**

Center bowl, a domed & optic ribbed base w/a ring connector to the deep round optic ribbed bowl w/a wide rolled & gently ruffled rim, overall gold iridescence, signed on bottom, 12" d. (ILLUS., bottom of page)... **$1,438**

Blue Aurene Wide & Low Crimped Bowl

Large & Deep Steuben Gold Aurene Bowl

Large Dome-Footed Gold Aurene Center Bowl

Unusual Steuben Aurene Finger Vase

Vase, 9 1/4" h., 7 1/2" w., finger style, the tapering base below a bulbous widely fanned top w/four pinched-in round openings, blue iridescence w/golden highlights, Shape No. 2672, signed, some surface scratches (ILLUS.)......................... **$978**

Swelled Cylindrical Gold Aurene Vase

Vase, 9 1/2" h., footed gently swelled cylindrical body tapering to a short wide cylindrical neck w/a flattened wide gently ruffled rim, overall gold iridescence w/flashes of red, signed on the foot (ILLUS.) **$2,160**

Large Footed Blue Aurene Steuben Vase

Vase, 9 3/4" h., a cushion foot supporting the wide cylindrical body w/a wide flaring rim, overall deep blue iridescence w/a purplish tinge, original Steuben label on the bottom (ILLUS.)................................ **$1,380**

Steuben Gold Aurene Signed Vase

Vase, 11 3/4" h., a low foot & bulbous lower body below the tall trumpet-form neck, overall light gold iridescence, brighter gold interior iridescence, signed & numbered on the bottom (ILLUS.) **$1,725**

G

Calcite & Gold Aurene Footed Bowl

Large Simple Blue Aurene Vase

G

Vase, 12" h., large simple ovoid body w/a wide low rolled rim, fine blue iridescence w/a band of bright raspberry iridescence around the neck & a flashes of gold & green around the body, base signed "Aurene 2682," Shape No. 2682 , bottom drilled (ILLUS.) **$660**

Bristol Yellow

Steuben Bristol Yellow Candlestick

Candlestick, widely flaring ribbed foot supporting a deep tapering cylindrical candle socket w/a ribbed wide flattened rim, Shape No. 6593, 4 3/8" h. (ILLUS.) **$115**

Calcite
Bowl, 6 3/8" d., 3" h., wide low round foot supporting the deep widely flaring bowl w/Calcite exterior & gold Aurene interior w/a magenta blue hue (ILLUS., top of page)... **$259**

Celeste Blue

Steuben Celeste Blue Vases

Vases, 10" h., a round ribbed foot supporting the gently swelling optic ribbed cylindrical body tapering to the widely flaring neck, Shape No. 236, pr. (ILLUS.)............ **$920**

Flemish Blue
Goblets, round foot & baluster-form stem below the tall inverted bell-form cup, Shape No. 6532, marked, 6 1/4" h., set of 4 (ILLUS., top next page).......................... **$575**

Set of Steuben Flemish Blue Goblets

Gold Ruby

Steuben Gold Ruby Candlestick

Candlestick, a wide round swirled foot supporting a tall tapering optic ribbed socket w/a wide downturned swirled rim, Shape No. 6593, marked, 4 1/4" h. (ILLUS.) **$115**

Grotesque

Steuben Grotesque Bowl-Vase in Ivory

Bowl-vase, squared flaring Ivory form w/four heavy ribs pulled into rolled points, Shape No. 7091, 11" w., 6 3/4" h. (ILLUS.) **$288**

Shaded Green Steuben Grotesque Vase

Vase, 8 3/4" h., a round clear foot supporting the tall ovoid ribbed vase w/a widely flaring neck shading from light green to clear, Shape No. 7089, marked on pontil (ILLUS.).. **$259**

Ivory

Steuben Ivory Triple-Bud Vase

Vase, 10" h., triple-bud, a cluster of three tiered triangular pronged vases applied w/rigaree to the wide flattened round foot, Shape No. 7128 (ILLUS.)........................... **$805**

G

Ivrene

Steuben Ivrene Bowl in Grotesque Shape

Bowl, 11 5/8" l., 6 1/2" h., Grotesque body form w/a deep rounded body w/four heavy ribs flaring to two pulled-up & ruffled sides, factory mark on base (ILLUS.) .. **$259**

Fanned Steuben Ivrene Vase

Vase, 6" h., wide round foot & wafer stem supporting the tall fanned & flaring ribbed body, Steuben factory signature on bottom, Shape No. 7564 (ILLUS.)................... **$173**

Fine Steuben Ivrene Three-Lily Vase

Vase, 12 1/8" h., three-lily, the round domed foot centered by a tall trumpet-form vase flanked by two shorter Jack-in-the-pulpit vases, Shape No. 7566 (ILLUS.) **$1,035**

Jade

Steuben Jade Green Lemonade Pitcher

Pitcher, 9 1/4" h., lemonade-type, Jade Green, flat-bottomed ovoid body w/rib-swirled design below the angled shoulder & short wide neck w/a pinched rim spout, applied Alabaster handle, Shape No. 6232, fleur-de-lis mark (ILLUS.)................ **$920**

Steuben Jade Green Lemonade Tumblers

Tumblers, lemonade-type, handled, Jade Green, gently swelled cylindrical body w/swirled ribbing & a slightly flared rim, applied Alabaster handle, Shape No. 7218, marked, cooling line in one handle, 5 1/2" to 5 3/4" h., set of 6 (ILLUS.) **$920**

Bulbous Ovoid Steuben Green Jade Vase

G

Vase, 6 1/8" h., Green Jade, wide bulbous tapering ovoid body w/a wide short cylindrical rim, molded swirled design in the glass, Shape No. 6214 (ILLUS., previous page) **$316**

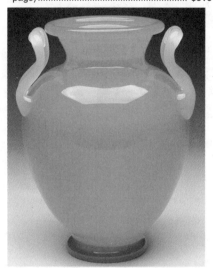

Fine Green Jade Urn-Form Vase

Vase, 10" h., footed bulbous urn-form body w/short rolled trumpet neck, Green Jade w/applied upright angled Alabaster loop shoulder handles (ILLUS.) **$1,725**

Moss Agate

Rare Steuben Moss Agate Vase

Vase, 8 3/4" h., footed slightly swelled cylindrical form w/a low widely flaring neck, swirled & mottled tones of raspberry, grey, blue & yellow on top of a cobalt blue ground (ILLUS.) **$4,600**

Oriental Poppy

Pretty Steuben Oriental Poppy Goblet

Goblet, the tall flaring inverted bell-form bowl in pink w/white opalescent stripes, raised on a slender Pomona Green stem & round foot, fleur-de-lis mark, 8 1/8" h. (ILLUS.)... **$805**

G

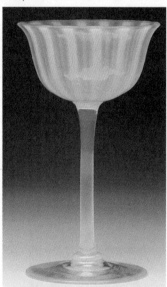

Steuben Oriental Poppy Wine

Wine, flaring inverted bell-form bowl in pink w/white opalescent stripes, raised on a slender clear opalescent stem & round foot, 6" h. (ILLUS.) **$390**

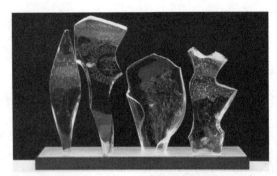

Rare Steuben Crystal "Four Seasons" Sculpture

Verre de Soie

Steuben Verre de Soie Vase with Threading

Vase, 9 7/8" h., tapering round cushion foot below the tall gently flaring diamond quilted cylindrical body trimmed w/blue threading around the upper half, several skips in the threading, Shape No. 6777 (ILLUS.).. **$115**

Miscellaneous Wares

Clear Crystal Signed Steuben Candlestick

Candlestick, crystal, free-blown domed & dished base w/wafers connecting to a baluster-form teardrop stem below further wafers & a knop supporting the cylindrical socket w/a wide rolled rim, attributed to glass artist F.B. Sellew, base rim engraved w/script signature, 8 7/8" h. (ILLUS.)...................................... **$345**

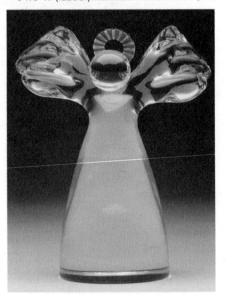

Steuben Crystal Figure of an Angel

Figure of an angel, stylized crystal angel w/sweeping outstretched wings & a gold metal halo, w/original Steuben red leather presentation box, 6" h. (ILLUS.).......... **$1,265**

Sculpture, "Four Seasons," crystal modernist design composed of four separate upright glass panels set into a wooden framed Lucite base, each abstract panel engraved w/a different design representing a season, designed by Donald Pollard & Jacob Landau in 1940, believed to be only example produced, 11 1/4" l. (ILLUS., top of page) **$6,900**

Steuben Crystal "Gull Rock" Sculpture

Sculpture, "Gull Rock," crystal in a long domed rockwork form w/fluted edges mounted w/two small silver gulls perched on top, designed by James Houston, 1983, w/original Steuben red leather presentation box, 8 1/2" l. (ILLUS.) **$2,280**

Stevens & Williams

This long-established English glasshouse has turned out a wide variety of artistic glasswares through the years. Fine satin glass pieces and items with applied decoration (sometimes referred to as "Matsu-No-Ke") are especially sought after today. The following represents a cross-section of its wares.

Appliqued Ruby Vasa Murrhina Bowl

Bowl, 7 1/4" d., 4 1/4" h., ruby w/silvery vasa murrhina, the wide squatty bulbous body raised on three clear applied shell feet, the sides applied w/six clear florettes & the rim applied w/a band of clear rigaree, acid-stamped "Stevens & Williams - Art Glass - Stourbridge" (ILLUS.) **$518**

Stevens & Williams Two-Color Compote

Compote, open, 6 3/4" d., 2 3/4" h., the widely flaring & flattened shallow green jade bowl raised on an alabaster white stem & foot (ILLUS.) **$92**

Stevens & Williams "Pull-Up" Vase

Vase, 9" h., footed squatty bulbous tapering lower body w/a swelled & tapering tall neck w/a flared rim, Northwood "pull-up" decoration in undulating bands of burgundy, yellow & cream, glossy finish, pink interior (ILLUS.) **$920**

Tiffany

This glassware, covering a wide diversity of types, was produced in glasshouses operated by Louis Comfort Tiffany, America's outstanding glass designer of the Art Nouveau period, from the last quarter of the 19th century until the early 1930s. Tiffany revived early techniques and devised many new ones.

Various Tiffany Marks & Labels

Bottle w/silver collar & stopper, bulbous onion-form tapering to a slender gently angled neck, decorated w/a pale yellowish green pulled feather design, signed "L.C. Tiffany - Favrile - 8530N," 8 1/2" h. (ILLUS., next page) **$1,553**

G

Unusual Tiffany Bottle with Stopper

Tiffany Green Pastel Bowl

Bowl, 7" d., 2 7/8" h., pastel line, cylindrical sides below a widely flaring & flattened rim, melon green interior rim w/stretched trails shading to an optic ribbed body w/ivory white opalescence & a satin finish, engraved "L.C. Tiffany - Favrile" (ILLUS.) ... **$748**

Tiffany Cameo Vase with Grape Design

Cameo vase, 10 1/2" h., cylindrical body w/a flaring base, frosted clear w/streaks

of dark green, wheel-carved overall w/clusters of grapes, eaves & vines, signed "L.C. Tiffany - Favrile - 6242C" (ILLUS.)... **$4,083**

Tiffany Marmalade Jar with Silver Top

Marmalade jar w/sterling silver rim, hinged cover & bail swing handle, cylindrical body in overall gold iridescence, jar engraved "L.C.T.," silver impressed "Tiffany & Co. - Makers - Sterling Silver - 925-1000 - C" w/a series of numbers, minor surface scratches, 3 1/2" h. (ILLUS.) **$1,265**

Tiffany Aqua Opal Parfait

Parfait, pastel line, a tall flaring morning glory-shaped bowl w/a deep aqua interior rim shading to white opalescent & clear stripes, on an applied knop stem & round clear opalescent foot, engraved "L.C. Tiffany - Favrile - 1872," 4 5/8" h. (ILLUS.) **$920**

Vase, 5 1/2" h., cushion foot & cylindrical body w/a flaring flat rim, dark blue iridescent exterior decorated w/a silvery spider web-like design, gold iridescent interior, engraved "9971 B L.C. Tiffany - Favrile," ca. 1907 .... **$3,107**

Very Rare Early Tiffany Paperweight Vase

Vase, 5 3/4" h., tapering ovoid body body w/a flat rim, paperweight-style w/internal decoration & a wheel-carved exterior decorated w/stylized flowers in orange, brown, yellow, amber & white, Tiffany Decorating and Glass Company paper label, ca. 1895 (ILLUS.) **$59,750**

G

Fine Deep Reddish Orange Tiffany Vase

Vase, 11 1/4" h., baluster-form body in deep reddish orange w/a closed rim, finished w/a button pontil, signed on the bottom "LCT 9203A" (ILLUS.) **$5,175**

Rare Bulbous Tiffany Vase with Pods

Vase, 6" h., 5 1/4" d., bulbous ovoid body w/a wide flat rim, silvery blue iridescent ground w/scrolling hooks near the rim, decorated w/applied pod & tendril devices down the sides in dark blue, signed "LCT R3291" (ILLUS.) **$18,400**

Rare Tall Tiffany Floriform Vase

Vase, 11 3/8" h., floriform, the bulbous bud-form bowl in white opalescence shading to yellow & green petal designs, raised on a very slender tall green stem on a round yellowish green foot, engraved "4023P - L.C. Tiffany - Favrile" & w/Tiffany Studios paper label, ca. 1921 (ILLUS.)
.... **$10,755**

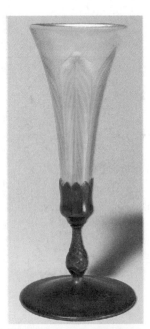

Tiffany Vase in Bronze Base

Vase, 11 5/8" h., simple trumpet-form bowl in golden opal decorated w/golden green iridescent pulled leaves, applied button pontil signed "L.C.T.," mounted in a bronze base w/a leaf tip socket above a slender pineapple-form stem & round foot impressed "Tiffany Studios - New York - 1043" (ILLUS.) **$1,495**

Rare Tall Tiffany Floral Paperweight Vase

Vase, 13 7/8" h. paperweight-type, tall tapering cylindrical body w/closed rim & flaring base, decorated w/very tall pointed green & brown leaves alternating w/stylized white & yellow flowers on a frosted clear ground, engraved "2995G - L.C. Tiffany - Favrile," ca. 1912 (ILLUS.) **$23,900**

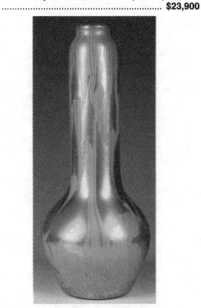

Rare Monumental Tiffany Vase

Vase, 21" h., bulbous ovoid lower body tapering to a tall cylindrical neck w/a flattened rim, fine pulled heart & vine decoration in gold iridescence on a seafoam green ground, signed on the bottom "Louis C. Tiffany Favrile - W5134," w/a fitted blue velvet covered presentation box (ILLUS.) **$17,250**

Tiffin

A wide variety of fine glasswares were produced by the Tiffin Glass Company of Tiffin, Ohio. Beginning as a part of the large U.S. Glass Company early in the 20th century, the Tiffin factory continued making a wide range of wares until its final closing in 1984. One popular line is now called "Black Satin" and included various vases with raised floral designs. Many other acid-etched and hand-cut patterns were also produced over the years and are very collectible today. The three "Tiffin Glassmasters" books by Fred Bickenheuser are the standard references for Tiffin collectors.

Tiffin Glass Label

Bowl, 10" d., salad, No. 5902 Fuchsia etching, clear.. **$82**

Rare Tiffin Black Satin Frog Candleholders

Candleholders, one-light, figural stylized frogs, black satin, 5 1/2" h., pr. (ILLUS.)
.... **$250**

One of a Pair of Royal Blue Candlesticks

Candlestick, one-light, floral cut decoration, Royal Blue, pr. (ILLUS. of one) **$160**

Candlestick, one-light, No. 82 w/Jack Frost decoration, canary, 8 1/2" h., pr. (ILLUS. of one, top next column)........................... **$130**

Candy jar, cov., mold-blown, No. 6106, diamond optic ovoid body tapering to a very slender stem & foot, domed cover w/pointed finial, Plum (ILLUS., bottom next column)... **$125**

Champagne, saucer-type, etched Charmian patt., amber, 4 3/4" h.............................. **$28**

Cocktail, etched Charmian patt., amber, 4 3/4" h... **$24**

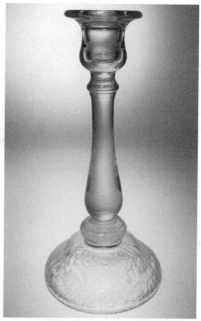

One of Two No. 82 Tiffin Candlesticks

No. 6106 Plum Candy Jar & Cover

Tiffin Royal Blue Satin Console Set

Console set: footed round bowl & pair of tall candlesticks; bowl No. 8098 & No. 300 candlesticks, Royal Blue w/satin finish, bowl 9 1/2" d., candlesticks 8 1/2" h., the set (ILLUS., top of page) **$230**

Goblet, water, Diamond Optic (No. 15028) patt., green bowl & stem, pink foot **$37**

Colorful Squared Venetian Bowl

Tiffin Golden Banana Ivy Ball & Rose Bowl

Ivy ball, mold-blown, No. 6120 patt., bulbous diamond optic bowl on a tall faceted stem w/faceted rings on a round foot, original label, Golden Banada (ILLUS. left with rose bowl) **$72**

Plate, 11" d., tab-handled, Teardrop patt. floral cutting on both sides, Smoke **$65**

Rose bowl, bulbous ovoid body on a low ringed stem & round foot, No. 6122 patt., diamond optic bowl, Golden Banana (ILLUS. right with ivy ball) **$55**

Salt & pepper shakers w/original chrome lids, flat base, June Night etching, clear, pr. **$150**

Tumbler, flat base, Charmian etching, amber, 8 oz. **$28**

Vase, 9 3/4" h., mold-blown w/paneled optic design, Carnation etching, clear.................. **$75**

Venetian

Venetian glass has been made for six centuries on the island of Murano, where it continues to be produced. The skilled glass artisans developed numerous techniques, subsequently imitated elsewhere.

Bowl, 10" w., 3 1/4" h., deep squared form w/four upturned sides, deep ruby cased on the interior in clear accented w/radiating latticino stripes & scattered colorful confetti millefiori on a bed of silver mica, attributed to A.V.E. M. (ILLUS.) **$230**

Model of a duck, nicely detailed swimming bird in shades of blue, grey & white w/overall Aventurine cased in clear, applied yellow bill & eyes, 14 1/2" l. (ILLUS., top next page).. **$345**

Venetian Victorian-style Appliqued Pitcher

Nicely Detailed Venetian Swimming Duck

Pitcher, 7 5/8" h., dark blue ovoid body raised on applied amber leaf-form feet, an applied amber band around the fluted rim, applied dark green vine handle continuing to green leaves & red berries on the lower side, original foil label reads "An Original Creation by K.B. - Made in Italy," ca. 1960-70s (ILLUS., previous page) **$35**

Venetian Victorian-style Satin Pitcher

Pitcher, 9 1/4" h., rainbow mother-of-pearl satin in the Herringbone patt., bulbous ovoid body tapering to a cylindrical neck w/a widely flaring & ruffled tricorner rim, applied clear frosted handle, Victorian-style, original foil label reads "Vetro Artistico Veneziano - Hand Made Genuine Venetian Glass - Made in Murano, Italy," ca. 1960-70s (ILLUS.) **$104**

Stemware & dish set: five 8 1/4" d. dessert plates, eight 4 1/2" d. berry bowls, six 7" h. cordials, four 8" h. wines, eight 9" h. water goblets & six 6 1/4" h. champagnes; each piece w/a delicate latticino design w/entwined white stripes alternating w/aventurine gold stripes in clear crystal, the bowls of the stems raised on an applied twisted & knobby gold-flecked colorless knop above a very slender stem above the round flaring foot w/further latticino design; late 19th - early 20th c., three champagnes w/detached stems, 37 pcs. (ILLUS. of part, bottom of page) **$690**

Vase, 6 1/2" h., footed bulbous ovoid deep ruby optic ribbed body tapering to a short trumpet neck w/flattened rim, shoulders applied w/applied looping gold-flecked clear swans **$118**

G

Delicate Venetian Latticino Stemware & Dish Set

Wave Crest

Now much sought after, Wave Crest was produced by the C.F. Monroe Co., Meriden, Connecticut, in the late 19th and early 20th centuries from opaque white glass blown into molds.

It was then hand-decorated in enamels and metal trim was often added. Boudoir accessories such as jewel boxes, hair receivers, etc., predominated.

WAVE CREST
WARE

Wave Crest Mark

Large Burnt Orange & Flower Wave Crest Box

Box w/hinged lid, Egg Crate mold, the sides & cover decorated w/deep burnt orange at the ends w/creamy yellow in the center decorated w/white blossoms & green leaves, gilt-metal hinged cover fitting & base raised on outswept scroll feet w/a lion head, lined in satin, Wave Crest mark on the bottom, base possibly reapplied, one hinge w/solder repair, 3 3/4 x 7", 5" h. (ILLUS.) **$630**

Pale Blue & White Wave Crest Box

Box w/hinged lid, Egg Crate mold, the sides & cover decorated w/irregular pale blue & white panels h.p. w/delicate florals & gilt trim, original brass fittings, unsigned, 6 1/2" w., 6 1/2" h. (ILLUS.) **$575**

Floral-decorated Collars & Cuffs Box

Box w/hinged lid, round w/molded scrolls around the sides & a flattened cover h.p. w/large stylized pink & white blossoms & long green leaves on a pale blue ground, the sides painted w/"Collars and Cuffs," on original ornate brass footed base, red banner mark, some wear, 7" d., 7 1/2" h. (ILLUS.) **$575**

Wave Crest Egg Crate Cracker Jar

Cracker jar, cov., squared Egg Crate mold, shaded pale blue ground decorated w/large pink & brown flowers on stylized green stems w/leaves, silver plate rim, domed cover & bail handle, some wear to silver plate, 5" w., overall 11" h. (ILLUS.)... **$460**

Wave Crest No. 67 Shaker with Cat Scene

Salt shaker w/original metal lid, No 67 mold, cylindrical w/neck ring, opaque white w/a transfer-printed color scene of a cat watching a spider, 3 3/4" h. (ILLUS., previous page) **$231**

Wave Crest Waisted Salt Shaker

Salt shaker w/original metal lid, tall waisted cylindrical shape, opaque white w/faint peach shading, floral transfer up the sides, 3 1/4" h. (ILLUS.) **$50-75**

Wave Crest The Parker Salt Shaker

Salt shaker w/original metal lid, The Parker mold, tall waisted cylinder w/molded scrolls, opaque white w/lavender shading decorated w/delicate blue florals, green leaves & gilt trim, minor flaws, 3" h. (ILLUS.) **$121**

Wave Crest Swirl Mold Spooner

Spooner, Swirl Mold No. 125, cylindrical, opaque white satin finish w/free-hand polychrome floral decoration, silver plated rim band & arched scrolling handles, 4 1/4" h. (ILLUS.) **$253**

Wave Crest Draped Column Sugar Shaker

Sugar shaker w/original metal lid, Draped Column mold, bulbous base w/tall fluted neck, opaque white w/a color transfer of a bird on fence around the base, 5" h. (ILLUS.) **$88**

Fine Daisy-decorated Wave Crest Vase

Vase, 12 1/4" h., the tapering ovoid body w/a short, wide cylindrical neck mounted in a gilt-brass framed w/a narrow rim band joined to large pierced leafy scroll handles down the sides, base band w/four scroll feet, the body decorated around the middle w/a wide undulating band in light shaded to dark brown & h.p. w/white daisies, white & brown background w/dot & gilt trim, base marked (ILLUS.) **$1,610**

Webb

This glass is made by Thomas Webb & Sons of Stourbridge, one of England's most prolific glasshouses. Numerous types of glass, including cameo, have been produced by this firm through the years. The company also produced various types of novelty and "art" glass during the late Victorian period. Also see BURMESE & ROSE BOWLS.

Rare Webb Cameo Plate with Large Flowers

Cameo plate, 7 1/2" d., powder blue ground overlaid in white & cameo-carved w/a large cluster of flowers & leaves against an acid-etched background, the narrow rim band w/small four-petal blossoms (ILLUS.) **$7,188**

Rare Webb Cameo Scent Bottle

Cameo scent bottle, lay-down type w/a pointed teardrop shape, deep red overlaid in white & cameo-carved w/water lilies & a dragonfly, original gold-washed metal screw-on cap w/répoussé designs, 3 1/4" l. (ILLUS.) **$3,335**

Small Webb Three-Color Cameo Vase

Cameo vase, 5" h., simple ovoid body tapering to a wide trumpet neck, three-color w/a deep yellow ground overlaid in red & white & cameo-carved w/wild roses on long leafy stems, a single butterfly on the reverse (ILLUS., previous page) **$1,610**

Webb Cameo Vase with Apple Blossoms

Cameo vase, 6 1/4" h., footed ovoid body tapering to a wide, flat cupped rim, white on lavender grey cut to white satin & cameo-cut w/a large branch of applied blossoms & leaves, the rim w/dentel & teardrop cutting, base acid-stamped "Thos. Webb & Sons Cameo" (ILLUS.)... **$3,220**

Cylindrical Yellow Webb Cameo Vase

Cameo vase, 6 1/2" h., simple cylindrical body in citrine yellow overlaid in white & cameo-carved w/flowers & long wide

leaves, a double white band at the rim & base (ILLUS.) **$1,265**

Webb Cameo Vase with Apple Blossoms

Cameo vase, 8 7/8" h., bulbous body tapering to a tall trumpet neck, white cut to deep blue w/cascades of leafy blossoming apple tree boughs, a single butterfly on the reverse, acid-stamped mark within an arched banner (ILLUS.) **$1,840**

G

Lovely Citrine Yellow Webb Cameo Vase

Cameo vase, 11" h., an ovoid body tapering to a tall stick neck, citrine yellow ground overlaid in white & cameo-carved w/long leafy morning glory vines hanging from the rim, a single white butterfly on the back, signed on the bottom (ILLUS.) **$2,300**

Fine Webb Shaded Pink Scent Bottle

G

Scent bottle w/original metal cap, lay-down type w/long pointed teardrop form in deep red shaded to pin & enameled in gold & white w/a long leafy stem w/blossoms & a gold butterfly, minor gold wear, 6 1/2" l. (ILLUS.)... **$690**

Finely Decorated Webb Oxblood Vase

Vase, 10" h., bulbous ovoid body tapering to a tall slender stick neck w/a cupped rim, rich oxblood color finely decorated in gold w/long scrolling leafy stems & tiny flowers outlined w/white enameling, glossy surface (ILLUS.)... **$431**

Westmoreland

In 1890 Westmoreland opened in Grapeville, Pennsylvania, and as early as the 1920s was producing colorwares in great variety. Cutting and decorations were many and are generally under appreciated and undervalued. Westmoreland was a leading producer of milk glass in "the antique style." The company closed in 1984 but some of their molds continued in use by others.

Early Westmoreland Label & Mark

Tall English Hobnail Milk Glass Basket

Basket, English Hobnail patt., fan-shaped body w/high arched handle, milk glass, 5" w., 10" h. (ILLUS.) **$30**

Ruby-Stained Large Wakefield Bowl

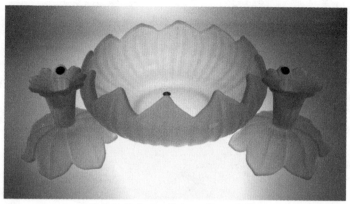

Pink Satin Lotus Pattern Console Set

Bowl, 11" d., flat bottom w/flaring crimped sides, Wakefield patt., clear w/ruby stain (ILLUS., previous page) **$120**

Bowl w/attached underplate, grapefruit-type, Colonial patt. No. 1700, blue, 5" d. **$30**

Candleholders, one-light, three-handled, No. 1066, pink, 3 1/2" h., pr. **$58**

Candlesticks, one-light, two-handled, Mission patt. No. 1015, 7" h., pr. **$60**

Plate, 8" d., English Hobnail patt., Ice Blue **$24**

Sugar & creamer on center-handled tray, Marguerite patt. No. 700, pink, the set **$85**

Tumbler, flat bottom, Princess Feather patt., clear, 10 oz. **$12**

Vase, 7 1/2" h., flip-style, English Hobnail patt., clear **$32**

Vase, 8" h., fan-shaped w/curved flower frog, No. 1708, pink.................................. **$200**

Della Robbia Ruby-Stained Compote

Compote, 8" h., sweetmeat-type w/ball stem, Della Robbia patt., clear w/ruby stain (ILLUS.) **$125**

Compote, 12" w., 8" h., round bowl on figural dolphin stem, No. 1820, amber **$165**

Console set: 9" d., cupped petal-form bowl & pair one-light 4" petal-form candleholders; Lotus patt., original labels, pink satin, the set (ILLUS., top of page) **$95**

Ice bucket w/metal bail handle & tongs, Octagon patt. No. 1211, green, 6" h. **$75**

Corinth Vase in Amethyst Carnival

Vase, 8 1/4" h., Jack-in-the-pulpit style, Corinth patt., Amethyst Carnival (ILLUS.) **$49**

G

HALLOWEEN COLLECTIBLES

Although Halloween is an American tradition and holiday, we must credit the Scottish for bringing it to the United States. The earliest symbols of Halloween appeared around the turn of the 20th century. During Victorian times, Halloween parties became popular in the United States. Decorations were seasonal products, such as pumpkins, cornstalks, vegetables, etc. Many early decorations were imported from Germany, only to be followed by increased demand in the United States during World War I, when German imports ceased.

Today Halloween collectibles are second in demand only to Christmas collectibles. Remembering the excitement one felt as a child dressing up in costume, going trick or treating, carving pumpkins, bobbing for apples, etc., the colors of orange and black trigger nostalgia for our youth for many of us.

The variety of Halloween collectibles is immense. Whether it be noisemakers, jack o' lanterns, candy containers, paper or plastic goods, candy molds or costumes, with the availability, the choice is yours.

Remember to buy the best, be it the very old or not so old. Search antiques shops, flea markets and house sales.

Witch Head Pumpkin Candy Container

Candy container, composition, a figure w/a tall ovoid pumpkin body & an ugly witch head w/tongue sticking out & wearing a tall black hat, closure marked "Germany," light soiling, minor paint chips, 5" h. (ILLUS.) **$460**

Veggie Man & Rooster Candy Container

Candy container, composition, a green & yellow pumpkin headed creature w/big round eyes seated atop a large red rooster on a red round base, replacement veggie head, early 20th c., 5 1/2" h. (ILLUS.) **$431**

Plastic Clown Pirate Bank on Wheels

Bank, molded plastic, figural comical clown pirate beating a large drum, orange head & hands, on tiny green plastic wheels, mid-20th c., 8" h. (ILLUS.) **$288**

Glass Jack-o'-Lantern Candy Container

Candy container, glass bell-shaped design forming a jack-o'-lantern in yellow w/orange & black trim, loop top handle, missing cover, overall paint wear, early 20th c., 3 1/2" h. (ILLUS.) **$460**

Early Black Cat Lantern

Lantern, black cardboard cat head w/pink snout, red crepe paper bow tie & green paper eye inserts, possible repair & touch-up, early 20th c., 4" h. (ILLUS.) **$345**

Rare Chauffer Jack-o'-Lantern

Lantern, composition, the chauffer jack-o'-lantern head w/big ears & open down-turned mouth, wearing a black brimmed hat & black horn-rimmed glasses, some deterioration to original paper inserts, some over-painting on exterior, early 20th c., 4" h. (ILLUS.) **$2,300**

Rare Red Devil Winged Lantern

Lantern, full-figure papier-mâché red devil/bat w/large paper wings, black shading, head w/original paper insert holds a candle, one wing tip missing, other wing distressed, early to mid-20th c., 11" w., 6 3/4" h. (ILLUS.) **$2,185**

Early Red Devil Head Lantern

Lantern, pressed cardboard, red devil head w/black trim & original paper inserts in mouth & eyes, small hole above one ear, minor chipping, light burn on interior base, early 20th c., 4 1/4" h. (ILLUS.) **$719**

H

Unusual Vegetable Man on Legs Rattle

Rattle, figural celluloid, molded as a double-faced standing vegetable man w/pumpkin-like head w/red trim & black bat on forehead, raised on two legs w/black moon & star, one face smiles, other frowns, 20th c., 4 3/4" h. (ILLUS., previous page) **$518**

Scarce Vegetable Man Rattle

Rattle, figural celluloid, molded as a double-faced standing vegetable man w/pumpkin-like head w/red trim, black witch on broomstick printed on chest & bat on back, mid-20th c., 4 1/2" h. (ILLUS.) **$575**

Rare Mechanical Cat & Mask Toy

Toy, mechanical, cloth-dressed figure w/orange pumpkin mask, squeeze body & arms lower mask to reveal the black cat head, distress to outfit & replaced sleeves, early 20th c., 7 1/4" h. (ILLUS.) **$2,703**

Toy, molded plastic witch & jack-o'-lantern on motorcycle, orange outfit, hair & broom stick, white face, jack-o'- lantern & motorcycle w/yellow wheels, mid-20th c.,

6 3/4" l, 4 3/4" h. (ILLUS. with other orange faced Witch on Motorcycle toy, top next page) **$1,236**

Scarce Halloween Ghost Nodder Toy

Toy, nodder-type, composition, a white ghost w/scarry orange face, nodding on free-standing wooden base, seam cracked & reglued, 7" h. (ILLUS.) **$460**

Plastic Witch on Rocket Pull Toy

Toy, pull-type, molded plastic, a black-dressed witch riding a rocket resting on a black platform base w/small orange wheels, mid-20th c., 6 1/2" h. (ILLUS.) **$403**

Rare Pumpkin Wagon Pull Toy

Toy, pull-type, molded plastic, a large orange pumpkin on black wheels pulled by a black cat w/a black & orange witch riding at the back, 20th c., minor paint loss to witch, 9 3/4" l., 5 1/2" h. (ILLUS.).... **$633**

Two Witch on Motorcycle Halloween Toys

Rare Cat & Jack-o'-Lantern Pull Toy

Toy, pull-type, molded plastic, an orange cat w/green sweater beside an orange jack-o'-lantern raised on a green wagon w/yellow wheels, 20th c., 6 1/2" h. (ILLUS.) **$1,093**

Rare Molded Plastic Boy & Girl Cat Toys

Toys, molded plastic, stylized bodies of boy & girl Halloween cats w/flat heads raised on small springs, on base w/four small green wheels, in orange & black w/yellow & green bow ties & ribbons, boy holds fiddle, girl holds a jack-o'-lantern, mid-20th c., 9 1/2" h., pr. (ILLUS.) **$805**

Toys, molded plastic witch & jack-o'-lantern on motorcycle, black outfit, hair & broom stick, orange face, jack-o'-lantern & motorcycle w/green wheels, mid-20th c., minor paint wear, 6 3/4" l, 4 3/4" h., pr. (ILLUS. left with other orange faced Witch, top of page) **$690**

ICART PRINTS

The works of Louis Icart, the successful French artist whose working years spanned the Art Nouveau and Art Deco movements, first became popular in the United States shortly after World War I. His limited edition etchings were much in vogue during those years when the fashion trends were established in Paris. These prints were later relegated to the closet shelves and basements but they have now re-entered the art market and are avidly sought by collectors. Listed by their American titles, those appearing below have been sold within the past eighteen months. All prints are framed unless otherwise noted.

Icart Leda & The Swan Print

Leda & The Swan, 1934, professional repair to tear at top, some water staining on back, 19 x 31" (ILLUS.) **$5,750**

Icart The Sofa Print

Sofa (The), 1937, framed, 17 x 25 1/2"
(ILLUS.) **$8,338**

ICONS

Icon is the Greek word meaning likeness or image and is applied to small pictures meant to be hung on the iconostasis, a screen dividing the sanctuary from the main body of Eastern Orthodox churches. Examples may be found all over Europe. The Greek, Russian and other Orthodox churches developed their own styles, but the Russian contribution to this form of art is considered outstanding.

Christ Enthroned Russian Icon

Christ Enthroned, Christ seated on a highly stylized gilded throne, his feet atop a stool decorated as faux marble on a faux marble floor, a small angel in each corner, Christ raising his hand in blessing & holding up the Gospels w/the other hand, finely painted in the miniature technique, w/an ornamental kovcheg, Moscow, 18th c., 16 1/2 x 21 1/4" (ILLUS.)....................... **$4,600**

18th Century Apostle Mark Icon

Apostle Mark (The), scene w/Mark seated in an interior writing his Gospel, a lion, his symbol, in the lower left corner, Russia, 18th c., 15 1/2 x 19 1/4" (ILLUS.) **$3,738**

Christ Immanuil Russian Icon

I

Christ Immanuil, the head of Christ as a child, the entire image laid over w/a gilded répoussé riza & basma together w/an applied halo w/faux stones, inscribed title, Russia, 18th c., 10 1/2 x 12 1/2" (ILLUS., previous page)...................................... **$2,760**

Early Russian Icon of The Dormition

Dormition (The), scene w/the Mother of God reclining on her bier, behind her Christ receives her soul in the form of a swaddled infant, The Apostles gather around her while a fanatical Jewish priest attempts to push the bier over, two the left a sword-wielding angel cuts off his hands, Russia, ca. 1600, 10 1/2 x 12 1/2" (ILLUS.) **$3,738**

Bogoluibskaya Mother of Gold Icon

"Moscow" (The) Bogoluibskaya Mother of God, the Mother of God stands at the left before a contingent of Saints, she holds a scroll, the entire image overlaid w/a chased silver-gilt riza dated 1795 & w/a Moscow hallmark, 11 1/2 x 13" (ILLUS.).... **$2,990**

16th Century Mother of God Icon

Mother of God (The), the standing Mother of God turned inward towards her Son in an attitude of prayer, she is draped in a burgandy-purple maphorion edged w/highlights, her blue chiton highlighted w/lighter shades & white, central Russia, ca. 1575, 13 1/4 x 24 1/4" (ILLUS.) **$8,625**

Not Made By Hands Image of Christ

Not Made By Hands Image of Christ, image of Christ's face shown miraculously imprinted on a cloth supported by angels, a highly stylized & condensed inscription along the lower edge of the cloth, an 18th c. follower of Simon Ushakov, Russia, 11 x 12 1/2" (ILLUS.)....... **$1,725**

I

The Resurrection & Descent Into Hell

Resurrection (The) and Descent Into Hell, scene showing Christ standing atop the fallen gates of Hell & grasping the hands of Adam & Eve, in background are various Old Testament righteous men & women including Kings Solomen & David, Moses & Daniel, Russia, ca. 1650, 16 x 20 3/4" (ILLUS.)................................ **$7,188**

I

Saint Nicholas Bust Icon

Saint Nicholas, bust portrait of the saint, entirely overlaid w/a fine gilt & répoussé riza w/cloisonné enamel corners, the borders w/Saints Boris, Glyeb, Alexzander & Julita & Kirik, Russia, 19th c., 14 1/2 x 17 1/2" (ILLUS.)........................ **$2,645**

The Vladimir Mother of God Icon

Vladimir Mother of God (The), traditional depiction of the Mother & Child w/softly modeled faces & hands, minor traces of gilding, on a double kovcheg panel, Russia, 17th c., 10 1/2 x 12 3/4" (ILLUS.) **$3,105**

INDIAN ART & ARTIFACTS

Rare No. California Ceremonial Dance Apron

Ceremonial dance apron, Northern California, buckskin w/fringe cut at bottom, the backskirt doubled over at top & fringed, rows of fringe w/additional black & white beaded drops w/larger trade yellow, blue, aqua, black & veined russet beads along w/fringe, dimes, etc., a row of American dimes borders at the top of the fringe, earliest date 1845, latest date 1873, probably Hupa group, 29 1/2 x 33" (ILLUS.).. **$6,613**

Two Views of a Fine Sioux Beaded Purse

Purse, Sioux, beaded, brass fittings, swing top handle beaded in dark green, red & white, one side w/a white beaded ground decorated w/bold geometric designs in red, blue & green, the reverse w/a light blue ground decorated w/a narrow center beaded diamond & zigzag stripes in green, dark blue, white & red, matching beaded ends, ca. 1880, 12" l., 9 1/2" h. (ILLUS. of both sides, top of page) **$1,150**

Fine Navajo Eye Dazzler Rug

I

Navajo Early West Reservation Rug

Rug, Navajo, early West Reservation, wide central serrate diamond designs surrounded by concentric lightning bands in black & red on a carded grey ground, reciprocal tan, black & white terraced border, spirit line, 3' 1" x 5' 8" (ILLUS.)......... **$1,380**

Rug, Navajo, Eye Dazzler-style, dark red ground w/a central small cross within diamonds & angled bars in grey, white, blue & tan, complex ticked border on each end, handspun, aniline dyes, ca. 1890, 57 x 81" (ILLUS., top next column).......... **$4,370**

Rug, Navajo, wool, transitional style w/stripes of red, tan, grey & natural along w/a bit of aniline orange at one end, corner tassels, early 20th c., 2' 11" x 4' 4" (ILLUS., bottom next column) **$863**

Old Navajo Transitional Striped Rug

Navajo Chief-Style Woven Rug

Rug, Navajo, woven wool w/finely carded yarn, chief's style in dark brown w/natural banding in central area w/a blue stripe at center, possibly indigo, corner tassels, Third Phase, ca. 1910-20, 3' 7" x 4' 9" (ILLUS.)... **$2,760**

Fine Western Reservation Navajo Rug

Rug, Navajo, woven wool, Western Reservation, early regional weaving w/exceptional carded yarn in a beautiful outlined serrate diamond design overall in complimentary browns, tans, dark red, blue & natural, surrounded by a Tees-Nos-Pas

border frame, fine corner fringes, 3' 7" x 5' (ILLUS.).. **$2,415**

Small Woodlands Birchbark Sugar Bucket

Sugar bucket, Woodlands, birchbark, miniature size, rectangular flat base w/tapering sides w/a wrapped rim, a colored trefoil or leaf design on front in red & brown, stitching at sides & top, nice patina, 6 3/4" l., 4 1/2" h. (ILLUS.) **$201**

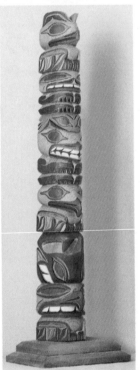

Small Northwest Coast Totem Pole

Totem pole, Northwest Coast, carved wood, composed of seven stacked clan figures, each w/painted details, well-done, typical of work from the Ye Olde Curiosity Shoppe of Seattle, carved & signed by L. Rudick of Vancouver Island, signed in pencil "12-2-23 Seattle totem," 25 1/2" h. (ILLUS.) **$863**

Rare Large Round Pima Basketry Tray

Tray, Pima, basketry, wide shallow bowl-form w/an expanding whirling design of stepped rectangles, triangles & bands emanating from a dark center of Martynia on a willow body, finely woven, 12 1/4" d. (ILLUS.)... **$1,035**

IVORY

Small Decorated Ivory Box

Box w/hinged cover, rectangular, the sides & top composed of thick pieces of ivory incised & drilled w/bands of roundels of various sizes, the interior of the top lined w/a tartan plaid material centered by a rectangular mirror, 19th c., some old age cracks, 4 x 4 1/2", 2 1/4" h. (ILLUS.) **$978**

Ornate Dragon-carved Card Case

Calling card case, flattened rectangular form w/serpentine edges, ornately carved overall w/entwined Oriental dragons, late 19th c. (ILLUS.) **$325**

Fine Ivory Oriental Mother & Child

Figure group, a tall slender Chinese mother standing beside her child, flanking a short tree trunk w/a colorful parrot, each figure w/dark polychrome decoration, probably China, late 19th - early 20th c., 5" w., 16" h. (ILLUS.) **$900**

Carved Ivory Bald Buddhist Immortal

Figure of a Buddhist Immortal, a tall gently curved tusk carved as the figure of a bearded man w/a high bald head & a bare chest & belly, holding a fan in one hand & prayer beads in the other, on a round black wood base, Oriental, mid-20th c., minor loss, 13 1/2" h. (ILLUS.) **$489**

I

Ivory Parade of Elephants Sculpture

Finely Carved Ivory Plaque of Washington Crossing the Delaware

Rare Ornately Carved Ivory Stein

Plaque a pointed pediment carved in high-relief w/a spread-winged American eagle above a shield & long leaves, above a long rectangular panel carved in high-relief w/a scene of Washington Crossing the Delaware, in original embossed leather & velvet fitted case, American, late 19th c., 9 3/4" l., 7 1/2" h. (ILLUS.)... **$5,019**

Sculpture, a parade of elephants, each connected & carved in graduated sizes from a single tusk, mounted on a carved wood stand, probably China, 20th c., 21" l. (ILLUS., top of page).......................... **$575**

Stein, cov., tall tapering cylindrical form w/a flaring ringed foot, the body carved w/high-relief mythological scenes w/the base band carved w/masks alternating w/ flowers, scrolls & banners above the foot carved w/a band of scallop shells, the stepped hinged cover carved w/bands including one w/leafy scrolls &

putti surmounted w/a figural nymph & Cupid, the long handle carved w/a cary-atid w/a long snake body along leafy scrolls, probably Germany, second half 19th c., 16" h. (ILLUS.).......................... **$43,200**

JEWELRY

Also see Antique Trader Jewelry Price Guide, 2nd Edition

Antique (1800-1920)

Edwardian Sapphire & Diamond Bar Pin

Bar pin, diamond & sapphire, set w/five square step-cut blue sapphires separated by double lines of 40 small old European-cut diamonds weighing about .60 cts. platinum-topped 14k gold mount, Edwardian era, early 20th c., 2" l. (ILLUS.) **$823**

Arts & Crafts Gem-set Gold Bar Pin

Arts & Crafts Gold & Sapphire Bar Pin

Bar pin, gold (14k) & sapphire, Arts & Crafts style, narrow long oval shape w/an open-work design of grape clusters & leaves & set w/three sugarloaf bezel-set blue sapphires, early 20th c., 2 7/8" l. (ILLUS.) **$999**

Gold, Topaz & Diamond Bar Pin

Bar pin, gold (18k), topaz & diamond, long narrow rectangular flat gold bar w/concave ends, the top set w/oval-cut topaz framed by four small old mine-cut diamonds, engraved accents, 19th c., 2 5/8" l. (ILLUS.)................................... **$600-800**

Bar pin, moonstone, sapphire & 14k gold, Arts & Crafts style, the long arrow openwork bar decorated w/scrolling leaves & blossoms, set w/three round sugarloaf moonstones & two small oval-cut blue sapphires (ILLUS., top of page) **$588**

Early Sapphire & Diamond Bar Pin

Bar pin, sapphire, diamond, seed pearl & gold, the thin bar w/forked ends terminating in a seed pearl, the bar bead-set w/alternating groups of square step-cut sapphires & diamonds & centered by an oval-cut sapphire framed by seed pearls & millegrain accents, scroll-engraved edges, platinum-topped 14k gold mount, Edwardian era, early 20th c. (ILLUS.)..... **$1,410**

Bracelet, amethyst, enamel & 14k yellow gold, a large oval center gold plaque w/the edges forming eight ruffles all centering a large squared fancy-cut amethyst & finely accented w/blue tracery enamel & engraving, joined to a bracelet composed of fancy bar & ring links, Hungarian assay & maker marks, 19th c., 7" h. (ILLUS., bottom of page) **$529**

Nail-form Gold Bangle Bracelet

Bracelet, diamond & 14k gold, bangle-type, designed as a hinged flattened coiled nail set at the side of the top w/an old European-cut diamond, mark of Fritschze & Co., boxed, interior circumference 7" (ILLUS.)................................. **$1,763**

Bracelet, diamond & 14k gold, the knob design centering a pearl surrounded by rose-cut diamonds, completed w/curb links, 19th c., 7" l. **$646**

J

Antique Hungarian Amethyst, Gold & Enamel Bracelet

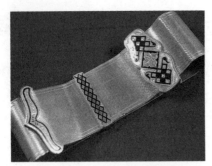

Antique French Gold Slide Bracelet

Bracelet, enameled 18k gold, slide-style, the wide tightly woven gold mesh strap completed by a black tracery enamel buckle closure, French guarantee stamps, losses to edges (ILLUS.) **$999**

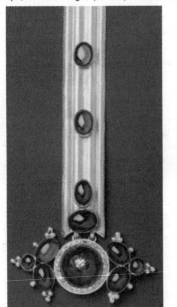

Lovely 18k Gold Garnet-set Antique Bracelet

Bracelet, garnet, diamond & 18k gold, a wide flat finely woven gold band mounted w/a spaced band of cabochon garnets, the large clasp w/a gold circle enclosing a large cabochon garnet topped w/a small engraved star set w/an old mine-cut diamond & bordered by a band of old mine-cut diamonds, each side of the circle flanked by a cluster of cabochon garnets w/gold bead trim, 7 1/8" l. (ILLUS.) . **$3,525**

Band Bracelet with Overall Garnets

Bracelet, garnet & silver, gradually tapering band set overall w/prong-set garnets in bands & other patterns, early 20th c., 2 1/2" w. (ILLUS.)...................................... **$345**

Bracelet, gem- and seed pearl-set 18k gold, oval links in tricolor gold, each collet-set w/various stones including aquamarine, topaz, chrysoberl & garnet surrounded by beads & wirework alternating w/scroll-edged links composed of small beads, centered seed pearls & two half pearls, second half 19th c., 6 3/4" l. (evidence of solder) **$1,175**

Bracelet, gem-set 18k gold & enamel, each rectangular link set w/a cabochon emerald & a freshwater pearl flanked by hexagonal table-cut foil-backed stones & spaced by beads, table-cut diamond highlights, reverse w/polychrome enamel floral designs, enamel loss, foil damage, evidence of solder, India, ca. 1900, 7" l. **$264**

Bracelet, gem-set gold, composed of six graduated gem-set stylized flower-heads, each collet-set w/various gems including foil-back emeralds, amethysts, hessonite & almandite garnets, pink & white topaz, green chrysoberyls & aquamarines, the clasp w/ruby & seed pearl accents, possibly a necklace w/later findings, 7" l. (ILLUS., bottom of page)
.... **$6,698**

Fine Gem-set Flower Bracelet

J

Extraordinary Arts & Crafts Gem-set Gold Bracelet by Edward Oakes

Bracelet, moonstone, Montana sapphire & 14k gold, Arts & Crafts style, composed of oval links w/an engraved frame around an oval cabochon moonstone alternating w/rectangular openwork links decorated w/delicate gold leaves & scrolls around a group of four blue sapphires & seed pearl accents, unsigned design by Edward Oakes, early 20th c., 7 1/4" l. (ILLUS., top of page) **$17,625**

Ornate French Platinum & Gold Pierced Bangle Bracelet

French Gold & Pink Spinel Bracelet

Bracelet, pink spinel & 18k gold, two narrow mesh gold band joined down the center by a row of 14 bezel-set circular-cut pink spinels, millegrain accents, maker mark & French guarantee stamps, ca. 1910, 7" l. (ILLUS.) **$999**

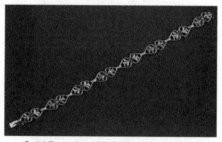

Gold Bracelet with Double-heart Links Accented with Diamonds or Rubies

Bracelet, platinum, 18k gold, ruby & diamond, double heart-shaped openwork links enclosing pairs of leaf sprigs, alternating w/the leaves set w/rose-cut diamonds or centered by a small circular-cut ruby, French guarantee stamps, late 19th c., 7 1/2" l. (ILLUS.) **$1,528**

J

Early Bangle with Seacoast Scene Plaque

Bracelet, platinum, 14k gold & diamond, bangle-type, the thin hinged band designed as a bent overlapping oak joined by a circular plaque embossed w/a coastal scene trimmed by an old mine-cut diamond, late 19th - early 20th c., interior circumference 6 1/4" (ILLUS.) **$1,175**

Bracelet, platinum & 18k gold, bangle-type, the double-hinged band w/buckle decorated overall w/delicate scrolling piercework & pearl accents, French guarantee stamps & mark of Musso, Nice, France, interior circumference 6 1/2" (ILLUS., top next column) **$5,288**

Krementz Gold & Sapphire Bracelet

Bracelet, sapphire & 14k gold, bangle-type, Art Nouveau style, the narrow band engraved w/floral & leaf designs & bezel-set w/three circular-cut sapphires spaced around the sides, mark of Krementz & Co., Newark, New Jersey, interior circumference 7" (ILLUS.) **$999**

Bracelet, sapphire, diamond & 14k gold, love knot-style, the hinged bangle bezel-set w/cushion-cut sapphires & old mine-cut diamonds, interior circumference 6 3/4" **$1,175**

Unusual Antique Pearl, Ruby & Diamond Bracelets

Pair of Etruscan Revival Bracelets

Bracelets, gold (14k), bangle-type, Etruscan Revival style, the wide band decorated w/two narrow rows of alternating pyramids & floret squares, thin applied wirework border bands, purchased in France, second half 19th c., interior circumference 6", pr. (ILLUS.) **$4,465**

Bracelets, pearl, ruby, diamond & gold, each w/a large central square plaque enclosing a ring centered by an openwork starburst, set overall w/channel-set old European- and single-cut diamonds & step-cut rubies, the bracelet composed of sections w/seven strands of pearls separated by bar links further set w/diamonds alternating w/diamonds, silver-topped gold mounts, diamonds weighing about 1.80 cts., ca. 1900, 7" l. (ILLUS., top of page) **$4,700**

Bracelets, tricolor 14k gold, each centering a shield-shaped plaque enclosing a pansy blossom & leaves & flanked by triangular devices, the slender flat band decorated w/applied bead & wirework, in a fitted velvet box, second half 19th c., interior diameter 6", pr. (ILLUS., bottom of page) **$940**

J

Boxed Pair of Victorian Gold Bracelets

Oval Art Nouveau Amethyst Brooch

Brooch, amethyst, enamel & gold, Art Nouveau style, the oval form centered by a large bezel-set oval-cut amethyst framed by a bluish grey guilloche enamel band & an outer incised gold frame w/looped scroll designs at each end, mark of Whiteside & Blank, 3/4 x 1 1/4" (ILLUS.).......... **$940**

Brooch, amethyst, seed pearl & 14k gold, centering a fancy-cut amethyst accented by eight bezel-set seed pearls, 19th c........ **$323**

Brooch, banded agate & gilt-metal, bull's-style, centered by a large banded agate cabochon in a gilt-metal mount w/ropetwist frame, 1 1/2" d......................... **$88**

Fancy Citrine & Gold Victorian Brooch

Brooch, citrine & 14k yellow gold, a large oblong fancy openwork gold frame composed of leafy scrolls centered by a large oval-cut citrine & suspending two thin link chains holding a matching pointed gold framework enclosing a large teardrop-shaped citrine, evidence of prior findings, 19th c., 4" l. (ILLUS.)................................ **$1,175**

Early Citrine & Engraved Gold Brooch

Brooch, citrine & 18k gold, centered by a large circular-cut citrine framed four square gold blocks on a flat ring decorated w/engraved geometric designs & ropetwist trim, 19th c., 1 1/4" d. (ILLUS.) ... **$646**

Arts & Crafts Gold, Citrine & Pearl Brooch

J

Brooch, citrine, pearl & 14k gold, Arts & Crafts style, a wide flat oval gold frame embossed w/a grapevine design w/seed pearl grapes, enclosing a large bezel-set oval citrine, early 20th c. (ILLUS.)........... **$1,298**

Victorian Citrine, Ruby Diamond & Gold Brooch

Brooch, citrine, ruby, diamond & 14k gold, centered by a large oval fancy-cut citrine centered by a flower w/a mine-cut diamond center & five oval-cut ruby petals within an oval band of bead-set rose-cut diamonds all against a black enameled ground, the rounded banded gold frame decorated w/four engraved & enamel-trimmed bands, evidence of solder at pin stem, 19th c., 2 1/8" l. (ILLUS., previous page) **$528**

Snake-entwined Agate & Gold Brooch

Brooch, dentritic agate & gem-set 14k gold, the oblong egg-shaped agate encircled by a gold engraved snake w/emerald eyes, 1 1/8" l. (ILLUS.) **$529**

Antique Diamond Monogram Brooch

Brooch, diamond & 14k gold, two gently curved bars overlapped by the large entwined monogram "ME," bead-set overall w/old European- and mine-cut diamonds (ILLUS.) **$470**

Brooch, diamond, designed as a rose- and old mine-cut diamond floral spray, silver-topped 14k gold mount, 19th c. **$588**

Gem-set Birds on Branch Brooch

Brooch, diamond & gem-set 18k gold, designed as two facing birds perched on a flowering branch, pearl wings & bodies further pavé-set w/diamonds, the yellow gold branch w/ruby & diamond flowers (ILLUS.) **$1,528**

Gem-set Realistic Spider & Fly Brooch

Brooch, diamond & gem-set gold, designed as a large realistic spider grasping a fly, bead-set w/rose-cut diamonds & bezel-set w/rubies & sapphires, a seed pearl highlight, silver-topped gold mount, 1 5/8" l. (ILLUS.) **$1,528**

Fine Antique Diamond Crescent Brooch

Brooch, diamond & gold, crescent-shaped, set w/21 graduating old European-cut diamonds weighing about 5.50 cts., silver-topped 15k gold mount, in a fitted box from Johnson, Walker & Tolhurst, London, England, w/hair pin attachment, 2 5/8" l. (ILLUS.) **$5,288**

Decorative Diamond Floral Spray Brooch

Brooch, diamond & gold, designed as a long leafy floral spray, the leaves & blossoms set w/old mine- and rose-cut diamonds weighing about 4.23 cts., silver-topped 18k gold mount, French import stamp (ILLUS.) **$4,113**

J

Art Nouveau Enameled Leaf & Opal Brooch

Brooch, enameled 14k gold & opal, Art Nouveau style, designed as a multi-stemmed gold sprig w/three pointed green-enameled leaves & suspending seven cabochon opal drops w/small diamond accents, original fitted box of a London jeweler, slight enamel loss, 2 1/4" l. (ILLUS.)...................................... **$1,880**

Heart-shaped Flower-decorated Brooch

Brooch, enameled 14k gold & seed pearl, designed as a heart-shaped mount w/gold ropetwist edges framing tiny white enameled forget-me-not blossoms & centered by a small pansy blossom enameled in dark purple & yellow & centered by a seed pearl, 1" w. (ILLUS.) **$411**

Enameled Gold Pansy-Row Brooch

Brooch, enameled 14k gold & seed pearl, designed as a row of three small pansy blossoms enameled in dark purple, lavender & white & each centered by a seed pearl, 1 5/8" l. (ILLUS.)............................... **$470**

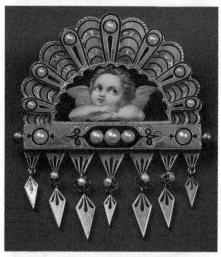

Fancy Enameled Portrait Brooch

Brooch, enameled 14k gold & seed pearl, the fan-shaped scalloped top divided by paneled enameled arches alternating w/loops topped by a seed pearl, a central arched panel enameled in color w/a Raphaelite cherub, the bottom rectangular bar engraved & enameled in black & trimmed w/seed pearls, a base band of suspended spearpoints w/tiny seed pearl links, 19th c. (ILLUS.)............................. **$1,410**

J

Brooch with Pansies on Curled Stems

Brooch, enameled 18k gold & diamond, designed as two small pansy blossoms enameled in pink & white or purple & white & each centered by a small diamond, on long curled gold stems, 1 1/4" l. (ILLUS.)... **$441**

Gem-set Gold Leaf-shaped Brooch

Brooch, gem-set 14k gold, Art Nouveau style, designed as an openwork tapered & curling pointed leaf, the interior scrolls set w/a band of seed pearls across from a ruby, diamond & green garnet, mark of Riker Bros., 1 1/2" l. (ILLUS.) $588

Brooch, gem-set 14k gold, clover-shaped, decorated w/sapphire mélée & rose-cut highlights, Austro-Hungarian hallmarks, 1" l. $940

Brooch, gem-set 18k gold, designed as a flower decorated w/circular-cut rubies & one full-cut diamond, French guarantee stamp $353

J *French Gem-set Gold Bumblebee Brooch*

Brooch, gem-set 18k gold, designed as a large bumblebee, the shiny gold rear body set w/bands of tiny rose-cut diamonds, the fanned & grooved wings also set w/rose-cut diamonds, the head formed by a cabochon tiger's-eye quartz w/projecting tiny rudy eyes, silver-topped 18k gold mount, French guarantee stamps, 1 1/4" l. (ILLUS.) $1,058

Gold Stylized Lion Head Brooch

Brooch, gold (10k), seed pearl & cabochon rubies, designed as a stylized lion head w/the mouth open holding a seed pearl, tiny ruby eyes, 19th c. (ILLUS.) $353

Antique Gold Fox Head Brooch

Brooch, gold (14k), designed as a fox head w/rose-cut diamond eyes, late 19th - early 20th c., w/pendant hook, evidence of solder at pin stem (ILLUS.) $1,175

Antique Oval Gold & Diamond Brooch

Brooch, gold (14k), diamond & enamel, the oval delicately pierced & looped gold mount centered by a row of three old mine-cut diamonds & w/a border band of additional mine-cut diamonds, black enamel trim, second half 19th c., 1 1/4" l. (ILLUS.).. $1,175

Brooch, gold (18k), a bar pin mounted w/five scarabs, containing a removable pin w/carnelian head, initial mark of a French maker & guarantee stamps, 2 1/2" l. $1,058

Victorian 18k Gold Knot-form Brooch

Brooch, gold (18k), designed as a large double-looped knot decorated w/fine applied bead & wirework, 2" w. (ILLUS., previous page) **$529**

Early Gold Griffin-shaped Brooch

Brooch, gold (18k), diamond & pearl, the body formed as a tightly scrolling openwork winged griffin w/a diamond in its mouth & suspending a single pearl, closure w/added safety, 19th c., 1 1/2" h. (ILLUS.).. **$764**

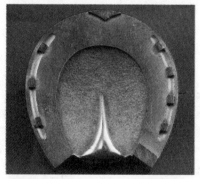

Antique 18k Gold Horseshoe Brooch

Brooch, gold (18k), modeled as a closed horseshoe, the reverse w/a locket compartment, signed, inscribed & dated 1883, 1 1/2 x 1 5/8" (ILLUS.)..................... **$499**

Gold Art Nouveau Brooch with Maiden

Brooch, gold (18k yellow), Art Nouveau style, rounded form decorated in relief w/a half-length portrait of a smiling Art Nouveau maiden wearing a low-cut gown w/swirling ribbons around her head, incised signature along the rim appears to read "S Vander Straten," pin & pigtail clasp marked "AVA," Europe, ca. 1900 (ILLUS.).. **$288**

Very Rare Tiffany Sapphire & Gold Brooch

Brooch, gold, cabochon sapphire & enamel, round, centered by a cabochon sapphire w/a petal-design border in blue & green plique-à-jour enamel in light blue & green in the gold scroll filigree frame, concealed pendant hoop for hanging, signed "Tiffany & Co.," designed by Louis Comfort Tiffany, ca. 1910, 1 1/2" d. (ILLUS.) **$31,070**

Antique Gold & Pearl Bow Brooch

Brooch, gold & pearl, designed as a gold bow set w/28 seed pearls w/one larger pendent pearl, ca. 1900 (ILLUS.).............. **$431**

Antique Tourmaline & Diamond Brooch

Brooch, green tourmaline, diamond & gold, the scrolling openwork diamond-form mount set overall w/rose-cut diamonds, centered by a large bezel-set cushion-cut tourmaline, silver-topped 14k gold mount, 1 x 1 1/8" (ILLUS.).......................... **$999**

J

Victorian Scenic Micro-mosaic Brooch

Brooch, micro-mosaic, oval w/a center scene of Mediterranean seaside buildings within a wide black border, in a 10k rose gold bezel, pin catch replaced, 19th c., 1 1/2" l. (ILLUS.) **$201**

Fine Antique Micromosaic Brooch

Brooch, micromosaic & 18k gold, a long rectangular design w/canted corners, the center panel w/polychrome tessera depicting a pair of swaws among flowers on a black ground, a narrow geometric border frame in black, blue & white, a small stepped panel w/small metal button on each side, evidence of solder at pin stem, 19th c., 2 1/2" l. (ILLUS.) **$1,763**

J

Rare Early Tiffany Japonesque Brooch

Brooch, mixed-metal, 18k four-color gold & diamond, in the Japonesque taste, composed of two overlapping round disks suspending a small round disk, one upper disk embossed w/a flying crane, the other upper disk w/two leafy flower sprigs w/each blossom set w/a small mine-cut diamond, the suspended disk embossed w/a leafy lotus blossom, signed by Tiffany & Co., New York, ca. 1880s (ILLUS.) **$16,450**

Rare Moonstone & Gem-set Brooch

Brooch, moonstone, diamond, ruby & gold, a narrow looping & entwined narrow gold frame set w/small rose-cut diamonds centering three large round moonstone cabochons, ruby accents, silver-topped 18k gold mount, French guarantee stamp, 1 1/8 x 1 1/4" (ILLUS.)................. **$3,525**

Renaissance Revival Gem-set Brooch

Brooch, moonstone intaglio & gem-set 18k gold, Renaissance Revival style, the center w/a round moonstone intaglio-carved w/the bust portrait of a classical man framed by a ring of rose-cut diamonds & a scalloped gold border w/shell designs alternating w/pearls, small peridot accents, ropetwist & applied bead accents, 2nd half 19th c. (ILLUS.) **$7,931**

Very Early English Gold & Gem Brooch

Brooch, pink topaz, emerald & 14k gold, the ornate oblong top cast w/ornate floral scrolls mounted w/a row of three oval & pear-shaped foil-backed pink topaz surrounded by three small cushion-shaped emeralds, suspending three ornately cast floral scroll pendants each set w/an oblong foil-backed pink topaz & a three small oval emeralds, late Georgian period, England, ca. 1800 (ILLUS.) **$1,880**

Lobed Fan-shaped Diamond-set Brooch

Brooch, platinum & diamond, designed as three-lobed openwork fan centered by a small blossom above three ribbons, set overall w/68 single-cut diamonds weighing about 1.91 cts. (ILLUS.) **$1,410**

Fine Edwardian Sapphire & Diamond Brooch

Brooch, platinum, sapphire & diamond, oval delicate openwork mount centered by a large bezel-set cushion-shape blue sap-

phire, framed by radiating bars set w/rose- and old mine-cut diamonds & a border band set w/more diamonds, millegrain accents, Edwardian era, England, early 20th c., 1 1/8 x 1 1/2" (ILLUS.) **$3,000-4,000**

American Reverse-painted Crystal Brooch

Brooch, reverse-painted crystal & 14k gold, the large round domed central crystal reverse-painted w/a scene of fox hunters jumping a hedge & ditch w/hounds in full cry, a pierced gold horizontal gold bar backing, hallmark of Bippart, Griscom & Osborn, Newark, New Jersey, 2" l. (ILLUS.) **$1,645**

Fine Victorian Anglo-Indian Gem Brooch

Brooch, ruby, emerald, seed pearl & 15k yellow gold, the oblong central plaque set w/rings of seed pearls and small emeralds centering a ruby, the looping fine openwork outer frame further set w/a band of seed pearls & an outer band of rubies, Anglo-Indian, 19th c., 1 1/4 x 1 1/2" (ILLUS.) **$940**

Brooch, sapphire, diamond & 14k gold, crescent-shaped, bead-set w/cushion-cut blue sapphires & old mine-cut diamonds, 2 1/4" l. **$940**

Silver & Agate Scottish Brooch

J

Brooch, Scottish agate & silver, an open-work oblong shape w/pointed scroll ends, the arched outer framework set w/blood-stone, carnelian & jasper tablets, an arched center band over a cylindrical cross-band each further set w/carnelian & jasper, engraving on the silver mount, English registry marks, 19th c., 1 1/2 x 2 1/8" (ILLUS., previous page) **$940**

Seed Pearl & Diamond Round Brooch

Brooch, seed pearl, diamond & 14k gold, round w/two border bands composed of seed pearls, the central section w/a background of thin bars decorated w/a quarter-round pearl swag w/three drops, an old European-cut diamond at the top center & one at the end of each drop, in a J.E. Caldwell & Co., Philadelphia box, early 20th c., 1 1/4" d. (ILLUS.) **$646**

Brooch, silver & colorless paste, the floral form w/flexible tendrils en pampilles, silver mount, French guarantee stamps, original fitted box, 3/4 x 3 1/4" **$764**

Unusual Jugenstil Silver Brooch

Brooch, silver, moonstone & green glass, Jugendstil (Germanic Art Nouveau), oblong shaped w/a raised fan-shaped plaque, each section w/a scrolling openwork border, the center plaque centered by an oval-cut green glass stone & the side sections each centered by an oval

moonstone, suspending five staggered beaded chains each w/a pierced scrolling teardrop pendant, probably by Pforzheim, marked, early 20th c., 3" l. (ILLUS.) **$1,175**

Scottish Silver & Agate Anchor Brooch

Brooch, sterling silver & agate, in the shape of a silver finely detailed anchor wrapped w/a rope & inlaid w/segments of agate, Scotland, ca. 1870 (ILLUS.) **$161**

Early Georg Jensen Flower Brooch

Brooch, sterling silver & garnet, Arts & Crafts style, designed as a rounded stylized blossom w/an openwork border around tiered petals centered by a cluster of five cabochon garnets, No. 59, signed by Georg Jensen, Denmark, 1915-30 (ILLUS.) **$1,058**

English Silver Brooch with Medallion

Brooch, sterling silver, silver narrow round pin frame w/two side tabs enclosing a round swiveling silver medallion w/a crest on one side & a scene of The HMS Hampshire on the other, made in Birmingham, England, 1909, 1 3/4" w. (ILLUS.) **$92**

Fancy Scroll & Leaf Diamond Brooch

Brooch-pendant, diamond, cultured pearl & 14k gold, the openwork mount w/large top scrolls topped by a fleur-de-lis & above leaf clusters centered by a squared panel, set overall w/single-, full- and old European-cut diamonds w/a pearl in the center panel & three pearl drops at the bottom, diamonds weighing about 2.00 cts. (ILLUS.) **$1,410**

Ornate Double Cornucopia Diamond Brooch

Brooch-pendant, diamond & platinum, designed as two crossed flower-filled cornucopias set overall w/old European-, mine- and rose-cut diamonds w/a central larger diamond drop & a smaller drop at the bottom, diamonds weighing about 5.30 cts., replaced pin stem (ILLUS.) **$4,465**

Art Nouveau Purple Flower Brooch

Brooch-pendant, enameled 14k gold, Art Nouveau style, designed as a large rounded blossom w/ruffled graduated petals enameled in deep purple shading

to white, a flexibly-set old mine-cut diamond set at the rim of one petal, marked by A.J. Hedges & Company, Newark, New Jersey, some enamel loss, 1 1/4" d. (ILLUS.) **$323**

Multicolored Enameled Pansy Brooch

Brooch-pendant, enameled 14k gold & diamond, Art Nouveau style, designed as a pansy blossom w/the top two petals enameled in dark purple, the lower three petals bordered in lavender around shaded white to yellow w/dark purple accents around the center old European-cut diamond, in a fitted box from a London jeweler, 1 1/8" w. (ILLUS.) **$1,116**

Antique Four-Leaf Clover Brooch

Brooch-pendant, enameled 14k gold & seed pearl, designed as a four-leaf clover w/each leaf enameled in shades of green w/the outer edges set w/a band of tiny seed pearls, small repair to enamel, late 19th c. (ILLUS.) **$382**

J

Gold & Seed Pearl Lion Brooch

Brooch-pendant, enameled & gem-set 14k gold, Art Nouveau style, the openwork center decorated w/a rampant lion beside a blue enameled pennant w/a diamond trefoil flower, the circular frame mounted w/seed pearls (ILLUS., previous page) **$823**

Art Nouveau Pansy Brooch-Pendant

Brooch-pendant, enameled gold & diamond, Art Nouveau style, designed as a pansy flower enameled in dark lavender & yellow & centered by an old European-cut diamond, 1 1/8" l. (ILLUS.) **$1,880**

Fine Victorian Micromosaic Pendant

Brooch-pendant, micromosaic & 14k gold, the gold mount w/scrolled side wings flanked a rectangular frame w/cut corners & scroll & tiny bead trim enclosing a conforming plaque of polychrome tessera depicting a pair of white doves on a royal blue ground, the frame suspending a row of flexible fringe w/teardrop ends, suspended from a later 14k gold fancy link chain, plate on the back cover-

ing the mosaic appears to be gilt, overall 19 1/2" l. (ILLUS.).................................... **$1,058**

Heart & Snake Opal & Diamond Brooch

Brooch-pendant, platinum, opal & diamond, designed as a large heart-shaped opal enclosed by diamonds w/entwined snakes at the top & bottom, w/removable 14k gold pin stem, Edwardian era, early 20th c. (ILLUS.)...................................... **$7,931**

Fine Scottish Agate & Gold Brooch

Brooch-pendant, Scottish agate, the wide loop top continues down to U-form gold bars ending in an agate-inlaid drop, the center a large disk inlaid w/bands composed of bloodstone, carnelian, jasper & banded agate & suspending a third drop, engraved 15k gold mount, missing one stone, Scotland, mid-19th c. (ILLUS.) **$5,758**

J

Shell Cameo with St. George Scene

Cameo brooch, carved shell, 15k gold & seed pearl, oval shell cameo carved w/a scene of St. George slaying the dragon, narrow gold frame accented w/seed pearls, 19th c. (ILLUS.) **$323**

Finely Carved Victorian Cameo Brooch

Cameo brooch, carved shell & gilt metal, a large oval shell cameo finely carved w/a scene of a racing four horse chariot & driver within a stadium, mounted in a gilt metal frame, 1 3/8 x 2 3/8" (ILLUS.)........... **$705**

Pretty Victorian Shell Cameo

Cameo brooch, carved shell, oval cameo finely carved w/a profile bust of Demeter w/her hair tied back w/a flower cluster, in an engraved 14k rose gold bezel mount, some dents & split in bezel, late 19th - early 20th c., 1 3/4 x 2 1/4" (ILLUS.).......... **$288**

Cameo brooch, onyx & 14k gold, the oval carved onyx cameo depicting a classical lady, within a beaded gold frame **$588**

Carnelian Cameo Brooch-Pendant

Cameo brooch-pendant, carnelian agate & 18k gold, the oval cameo finely carved w/a profile bust portrait of a classical lady, narrow beaded openwork gold frame, 19th c., 1 x 1 1/4" (ILLUS.)...................... **$441**

Cameo brooch-pendant, coral & 14k gold, the central oval coral cameo of a lady within a scrolling, engraved frame trimmed w/black tracery enamel & seed pearl accents, 19th c. **$206**

Victorian Carved Oynx Cameo Brooch

Cameo brooch-pendant, onyx & 14k gold, the cameo carved from white to black

J

w/the full figure of an angel playing a harp, plain gold frame (ILLUS.) **$705**

Pretty Victorian Cameo Earrings

Cameo earrings, carved shell & 14k gold, pendant-type, each w/a small round shell cameo w/the head of a classical lady suspending a long teardrop-shaped cameo carved w/a bust of a classical lady below a leaf cluster & framed by a delicate wirework & bead frame, 19th c., later 10k gold finding, pr. (ILLUS.) **$705**

Pretty Pair of Victorian Cameo Earrings

Cameo earrings, shell cameo & 14k gold, pendant-type, each w/a long teardrop cameo carved w/a profile bust of a classical woman below a flower, within an ornate applied bead & ropetwist frame suspended from a small gold ring enclosing a smaller bust cameo, later 10k gold findings, 19th c., 2" l., pr. (ILLUS.) **$400-600**

Early Coral Cameo Pendant-Brooch

Cameo pendant-brooch, carved coral, a shield-form background carved w/floral garlands centered by the profile bust of a Victorian lady w/long curly hair, 14k gold mount, small loss (ILLUS.) **$999**

Fine Carnelian Agate Cameo Locket

Cameo pendant-locket, carnelian agate & 18k gold, the center w/an oval carnelian cameo finely carved w/the figure of a cherub dancing w/cymbals, the rounded shield-shaped locket ornately applied w/bead & wirework accents, the locket compartment containing blonde hair worked as a sheaf of wheat, w/a 14k gold trace link chain, minor chip to cameo, second half 19th c., overall 13" l. (ILLUS.) **$705**

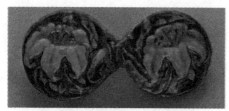

Fine Tiffany Floral-enameled Clasp

Clasp, enameled copper, a flattened double disk form w/each half finely enameled w/a large reddish orange lily & swirled green leaves on a dark blue ground, designed by Louis C. Tiffany for Tiffany & Co., ca. 1904, stamped "LL 260," 3 1/4" l. (ILLUS.).. **$19,120**

Gem-set Clasp & Pearl Necklace

Clasp & necklace, diamond, pink spinel & pearl, the round clasp set w/two rows of old European-cut diamonds weighing about 3.00 cts. & enclosing a prong-set cushion-cut spinel, completing a necklace composed of 98 cultured white pearls graduating in size from 7.75 to 11.00 mm., overall 20" l. (ILLUS.) **$7,050**

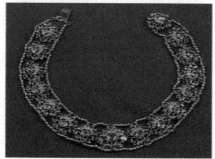

Ornate East Indian Gold, Sapphire & Gem-set Collar

Collar, foiled gem-set 18k gold, the wide band edged by bands of small gold beads flanking stylized floral plaques composed of pink & blue sapphires accented w/seed pearls, cabochon cat's-eye chrysoberyl, emeralds & yellow sapphires, six replaced gilt beads, Indian, ca. 1900, 15 1/2" l. (ILLUS.)........ **$1,880**

Antique Amethyst & Pearl Cross

Cross pendant, amethyst, seed pearl & 14k gold, prong-set w/11 circular-cut amethysts, seed pearls along the outer edges, gold mount, 19th c. (ILLUS.) **$1,293**

Antique Coral, Diamond & Diamond Cross

Cross pendant, coral, diamond & enameled 15k gold, the center of the cross set w/bands of round cabochon corals

J

framed by tiny rose-cut diamonds & a narrow border of dark blue enamel, each arm ending w/a scroll & point design, 1 7/8" l. (ILLUS.)...................................... **$1,410**

Gem-set Gold Cross Pendant

Cross pendant, gem-set 18k gold, the flat gold cross set w/a square of rose-cut diamonds enclosing a small square-cut ruby, further diamond & ruby accents at the tip of each arm, line-engraved details, 19th c., 1 x 1 5/8" (ILLUS.)...................... **$1,410**

Victorian Onyx & Seed Pearl Cross

Cross pendant, onyx, seed pearl & enameled 14k gold, the black onyx cross

mounted up the front w/a gold floral spray lined w/seed pearls, a black enamel tall palmette-form bail at the top, 19th c. (ILLUS.) **$411**

Early Platinum & Diamond Cross

Cross pendant, platinum & diamond, set w/18 full- and single-cut diamond mélée, millegrain accents, ca. 1920, later bail, 1 1/2" l. (ILLUS.).................................... **$1,293**

Cross pendant, sapphire, seed pearl & 18k gold, bezel-set w/five sapphire mélée & highlighted by seed pearls, 19th c., 1 1/2" l... **$499**

Seed Pearl & Gold Cross Pendant

Cross pendant-brooch, seed pearl & 14k gold, the gold mount set overall w/grey & ivory seed pearls, boxed, 19th c. (ILLUS.) .. **$764**

J

Oval Moonstone & Enamel Cuff Links

Cuff links, moonstone, enameled 14k gold, each double link bezel-set w/an oval moonstone framed by blue bass taille enamel, mark of Durand & Co., discoloration to mounts under moonstones, Edwardian era, early 20th c., 1/2" l., pr. (ILLUS.) **$558**

American Art Nouveau Cuff Links

Cuff links, sterling silver & 14k gold, Art Nouveau style, each oblong double link w/a serpentine border enclosing a profile bust of a classical warrior, American-made (ILLUS.).. **$1,293**

Earrings, amethyst & gold, pendant-type, the long gold mount w/three hinged sections, the top w/a pointed scroll above a cluster of three circular-cut amethysts above a cushion-cut amethyst within a gold frame, the long swelled central section ornately set w/circular- and marquise-cut amethyst, the bottom drop section w/a large marquise-cut amethyst & frame suspending a small marquise-cut amethyst & pointed gold drop, engraved front & back, 14k gold mounts, 4" l., pr. (ILLUS., top next column) **$2,703**

Fine Antique Amethyst Pendant Earrings

Carved Amethyst Pendant Earrings

Earrings, carved amethyst & 14k gold, pendant-type, a top flute-carved bead suspending gold links to a small carved bead joined to a large flower & leaf carved oblong drop, 2 1/2" l., pr. (ILLUS.) **$646**

J

Early Coral & 18k Gold Pendant Earrings

Earrings, coral & 18k gold, pendant-style, the rounded top composed of ornate gold wirework scrolls & blossoms centered by a coral bead, suspending very long open loops also trimmed w/ornate wirework designs, 3 1/2" l., pr. (ILLUS, previous page) **$705**

Antique Gold Leaves & Diamonds Earrings

Earrings, diamond & 18k gold, pendant-type, each designed as a heart-form cluster of gold leaves centered by a row of three old rose-cut diamonds, French guarantee stamp, 3/4" l., pr. (ILLUS.) **$764**

Fancy French Diamond & Gold Earrings

Earrings, diamond, enamel & 18k gold, day-night pendant-type, the top w/a gold ring prong-set w/a rose-cut diamond & black enamel trim, suspending four scrolls suspending three drops, the two shorter side ones set w/a rose-cut diamond & the longer center one w/two prong-set rose-cut diamonds framed by black enamel, wire loop hangers, deli-

cate engraving on the gold, French guarantee stamps, 19th c., pr. (ILLUS.) **$1,763**

Early Flower head Diamond Earrings

Earrings, diamond, pendant-type, a rounded flower head form set w/12 full-, single- and rose-cut diamonds, platinum-topped 14k gold mount, diamonds weighing about 1.00 cts., 3/4" l., pr. (ILLUS.) **$1,410**

Small Antique Diamond Earrings

Earrings, diamond, pendant-type, each designed as a small starburst w/a central rose-cut diamond & smaller diamonds at the tip of each ray, silver-topped 14k gold mount, pr. (ILLUS.) **$940**

Very Rare Early Diamond Stud Earrings

Earrings, diamond & platinum, stud-type, each set w/a large old European-cut diamond weighing 3.44 and 3.36 cts., pr. (ILLUS.) **$26,477**

J

Antique Gold Coach Cover Earrings

Earrings, gold (18k) & sapphire, coach cover style, pendant-type, each in the form of a gold sphere decorated overall w/applied wiretwist accents, each enclosing a later prong-set bluish grey sapphire, 14k gold earwires, pr. (ILLUS.) **$1,175**

Antique Micromosaic Pendant Earrings

Earrings, goldstone glass & micromosaic, pendant-type, composed of two graduated oval goldstone glass plaques decorated in polychrome tessera w/small birds, each within a 14k gold wiretwist frame, later findings, 1 1/2" l., pr. (ILLUS.) **$441**

Earrings, milky chalcedony & 14k gold, pendant-type, the top w/a ring of delicated scrolling gold leaves & flowers enclosing a chalcedony cabochon suspending a long tear-form matching openwork gold frame around a teardrop chalcedony, 2 1/2" l., pr. (ILLUS., top next column) **$999**

Earrings, pearl, diamond & 18k gold, pendant-style, the gold loop top mounted w/an old mine-cut diamond above a silver off-round pearl connector to a ring connector & another mine-cut diamond above a diamond-set cap suspending a large baroque pearl, engraved silver-topped 18k gold mount, French guarantee stamps, 19th c., pearls not tested for origin, 1 3/4" l., pr. (ILLUS., middle next column) **$11,750**

Elaborate Gold & Chalcedony Earrings

Rare Antique Pearl & Diamond Earrings

J

Early Pink Topaz & Gold Earrings

Earrings, pink topaz & 18k gold, pendant-type, each w/a large prong-set cushion-shaped topaz suspended from gold fittings, 19th c., pr. (ILLUS.) **$1,645**

Earrings, sapphire & diamond, pendant-type, each prong-set w/an oval-cut blue sapphire framed by rose-cut diamonds, Austro-Hungarian hallmarks, 19th c., 5/8" l., pr. **$940**

Early French Earring-Pins

Earrings-pins, diamond & seed pearl, each designed as a long floral spray bead-set w/rose-cut diamond mélée, grey seed pearl accents & silver-topped 18k gold mount, convertible to a pins, French maker's mark & guarantee stamps, in original fitted box, France, 19th c., 1 1/2" l., pr. (ILLUS.).. **$1,058**

J

Delicate Edwardian Diamond Lavaliere

Lavaliere, diamond & gold, the delicate openwork design composed of three connected teardrop-shaped frames set w/old single- and rose-cut diamonds & joined by webbed strands set w/old mine-cut diamonds, diamonds weighing about 1.00 cts., platinum-topped 14k gold mount, completed by a delicate platinum trace-link chain, Edwardian era, early 20th c., original fitted box, overall 16" l. (ILLUS. of part)....................................... **$3,055**

Edwardian Diamond & Pearl Lavaliere

Lavaliere, platinum, diamond & cultured pearl, the delicate openwork mount w/a pointed scrolled arch top above a cross-pierced stem suspending a pearl drop, the top bead- and bezel-set overall w/old European- and single-cut diamonds & centered by two rows of three seed pearls, Edwardian era, early 20th c., w/a trace link chain w/seed pearls, overall 17 1/2" l. (ILLUS. of part) **$764**

Early Pearl & Diamond Lavaliere

Lavaliere, platinum, pearl & diamond, the delicate trace link chain suspending a pendant bezel-set w/three old mine-cut diamonds ending in a pearl drop, rose-cut diamond mélée highlights, 14k gold jump ring, pearls not tested for origin, Edwardian era, early 20th c., 2 1/2" l. (ILLUS.) **$1,410**

Victorian Fancy Gem-set Gold Locket

Locket, gold (14k), diamond & enamel, the oval form decorated w/a wide cross-form field finely engraved & bordered w/bead accents, the center w/a raised starburst outlined in dark blue enamel & centered by an old mine-cut diamond, 19th c., 2 1/4" l. (ILLUS.).. **$558**

Gold & Diamond Locket with Faun Scene

Locket, gold (18k) & diamond, Art Nouveau style, circular form embossed w/a wood-land scene of a faun w/a bird, bordered by a narrow band of rose-cut diamonds, further diamonds on the bail, platinum-topped gold mount, millegrain accents, late 19th - early 20th c. (ILLUS.) **$2,233**

Art Nouveau Gold & Diamond Locket

Locket, gold (18k) & diamond, Art Nouveau style, round w/the front embossed w/the bust portrait of an Art Nouveau maiden wearing a diadem & earrings set w/tiny old European-cut diamonds, opening to two compartments, suspended from a 14k gold fancy link chain completed by a cylindrical clasp, late 19th - early 20th c., overall 18" l. (ILLUS.) **$1,528**

J

Fancy Gold & Gem-set Victorian Locket

Locket, ruby, emerald & 14k yellow gold, the tapering rectangular tablet-form top centered by a raised gold band enclos-ing a gold floral bouquet w/the blossoms composed of round-cut rubies & emeralds, the wide arched bottom band decorated w/fine raised gold loop & blossoms designs & joined at the sides by slender ropetwist columns to corner blocks w/a wide curved crest w/further gold trim, added pin stem, missing interior locket glass, second half 19th c., 2 1/4" l. (ILLUS.) **$588**

Locket, turquoise, seed pearl & 18k gold, oval w/seed pearl & turquoise frond designs on the front, suspended from a later 14k gold fancy link chain, break to bail, 19th c., overall 26 1/2" l **$323**

Art Nouveau Lorgnette & Chain

Lorgnette & chain, gold (10k), Art Nouveau style, the lorgnette w/a long slender shaped handle & an oval top w/finial, molded overall w/C-scrolls & foliate designs, the 14k gold ropetwist chain mounted w/an oval slide star-set w/an old mine-cut diamond, overall 50" l. (ILLUS.) .. **$646**

Necklace, amethyst & 14k gold, festoon-style, composed of bezel-set oval amethysts joined by trace link chain, ca. 1910, 18 1/2" l. **$764**

Necklace, amethyst & 18k gold, the gold chain mounted w/31 oval-cut amethysts graduating in size, 14 3/4" l. (ILLUS., bottom of page) **$5,758**

Necklace, amethyst, freshwater pearl & 10k gold, Art Nouveau festoon-style, bezel-set w/circular- and pear-cut amethysts joined by leaf-form links, freshwater pearl highlight, completed by a trace link chain, 15" l. **$353**

Delicate Gold & Gems Art Nouveau Necklace

Necklace, amethyst, pearl, enamel & 14k gold, Art Nouveau festoon-style, the central pendant composed of undulating gold scrolls & loops centered at the top by an oval-cut amethyst above a freshwater & seed pearl, the mount highlighted by green enamel, suspended on double delicate trace link chains w/seed pearl accents, late 19th - early 20th c., 14 3/4" l. (ILLUS.) **$1,293**

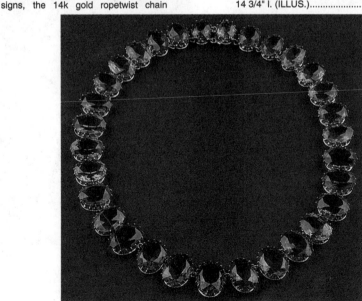

Very Fine Victorian Amethyst & Gold Necklace

Art Nouveau Pearl & Opal Festoon-style Necklace

Early Natural Pearl Strand Necklace

Necklace, natural pearls, single strand composed of 88 pearls graduating in size from about 3.40 to 5.60 mm, completed by a platinum-topped 18k gold & old European-cut diamond trefoil clasp, ca. 1910, signed by Tiffany & Co., 16" l. (ILLUS.) **$2,938**

Necklace, opal, freshwater pearl & 14k gold, Art Nouveau style, festoon-type w/the delicate chain swags bezel-set w/spaced-out opal cabochons & freshwater pearls, one opal chipped, late 19th - early 20th c., 15 1/2" l. (ILLUS., top of page) **$940**

Necklace, platinum, natural pearl & diamond, composed of 27 white & off-white pearls w/rose & silver overtones graduating in size from 4.75 to 7.20 mm, alternating w/filigree oval links bezel-set w/63 old European- and mine-cut diamonds, diamonds weighing about 4.17 cts., millegrain accents, ca. 1910, original fitted box, 15 7/8" l. (ILLUS., top next column)
.... **$9,988**

Necklace, ruby, emerald, seed pearl & 14k yellow gold, the wide curved central band centered by a seed pearl-set ring & harp enclosing a h.p. bust portrait of a cherub, flanked by raised spearpoint bands set w/seed pearls alternating w/small emeralds above a row alternating a seed pearl & small round ruby, each end of the cen-

Fine Pearl, Diamond & Platinum Necklace

J

Fancy Victorian Necklace with Cherub Portrait & Gems

ter band ending in a heart device inset w/a band of gold beads & attached to a fine mesh bracelet, 19th c., evidence of solder, 15" l. (ILLUS.) **$940**

Fine Moonstone, Garnet & Gold Pendant

Pendant, carved moonstone, demantoid garnet & 18k gold, Art Nouveau style, the ornate openwork long scroll-decorated mount w/tall scrolls at the top centers a round moonstone plaque carved w/a portrait of Mercury, flanked by four green garnets set into the frame, late 19th - early 20th c., 1 3/4" l. (ILLUS.) **$3,760**

Delicate Round Early Diamond Pendant

Pendant, diamond & gold, a delicate openwork design, the top pin mount set w/a large old European-cut diamond above an lacy openwork four-petal flower centered by another large diamond & overlapping into a large tapering ring enclosing openwork designs of stylized leaves & petals set w/five large old European-cut diamonds & trimmed w/single- and rose-cut diamonds, diamonds weighing about 3.00

cts., silver-topped 14k gold mount, Russian hallmarks, original fitted box, Edwardian era, early 20th c. (ILLUS.) **$3,290**

Arts & Crafts Enamel & Pearl Pendant

Pendant, enamel & seed pearl, Arts & Crafts style, the pointed oblong plaque decorated w/swirling blue & green enamel in foliate designs, suspending a single seed pearl, suspended from a delicate trace link chain, English hallmarks, 2" l. (ILLUS.)... **$323**

Art Nouveau Inscribed Gold Pendant

Pendant, gold (14k), Art Nouveau style, the flat oval medallion cast in low relief on one side w/back to back Comedy & Comedy masks centered by a hand mirror, inscribed around the border "To hold as 't were the mirror up to nature," the back inscribed "John Jacob Astor. Founder," 1 1/2" l. (ILLUS.).. **$705**

Pendant, gold (14k yellow), engraved w/foliate designs, the back w/a locket compartment, suspended from a 9k gold fancy link chain w/applied hearts, 19th c., pendant 2 1/4" l., overall 18 1/2" l. **$411**

J

Antique Gold & Pearl Starburst Pendant

Pendant, seed pearl & 14k gold, designed as a starburst bezel-set overall w/seed pearls & w/a single pearl mounted between each ray, suspended from a loop also set w/seed pearls, the back w/a hair compartment, attachment for brooch a conversion, 1" l. (ILLUS.) **$411**

Fine French Art Nouveau Figural Pendant

Pendant, silver gilt, Art Nouveau style, a long narrow pierced framed w/a trefoil top & wide spade-form base, framing the standing figure of an Art Nouveau maid-

en w/her suitor sitting at her feet among flowering vines, red stone & freshwater pearl accents, marked by Paillette, Paris, France, late 19th c., 3 1/4" l. (ILLUS.)..... **$1,422**

Delicate Diamond & Amethyst Pendant-brooch

Pendant-brooch, amethyst, diamond & gold, the upper brooch in a delicate openwork heart form w/the frame & leaf designs set w/old European-, mine- and rose-cut diamonds & centered by a round fancy-cut amethyst, suspending a large teardrop-form amethyst pendant w/a diamond cap, detachable pin stem, silver-topped 18k gold mount, later prongs, Edwardian era, early 20th c. (ILLUS.) **$1,763**

J

Starburst & Scroll Diamond Brooch

Pendant-brooch, diamond & 14k gold, a starburst design w/the straight tapering rays alternating w/S-scrolls, prong- and bead-set overall w/old European- and mine-cut diamonds weighing about 3.50 cts., mark of Krementz & Co., Newark, New Jersey, 1 3/4" w. (ILLUS.) **$2,115**

Early Heart-shaped Diamond Pendant/Brooch

Pendant-brooch, diamond & gold, a large heart pavé-set overall w/old European-cut diamond, platinum-topped 14k gold mount, reverse w/locket compartment, 19th c. (ILLUS.) **$6,169**

J

Fancy Diamond & Pearl Pendant-Brooch

Pendant-brooch, diamond, pearl & 18k gold, the long oblong openwork frame composed of top leafy sprigs above leafy wreath sides enclosing a large circle of radiating bands, set overall w/old mine- and rose-cut diamonds w/white pearl accents around the frame & in the center & w/a baroque pearl base drop, silver-topped 18k gold mount, detachable pendant hook, French guarantee & import stamps, 19th c., 2 3/4" l. (ILLUS.) **$2,585**

Delicate Scrolling Diamond Pendant

Pendant-brooch, diamond, pearl & platinum, two openwork leafy scrolls forming an arched top above a long narrow open pointed panel centered by a three-diamond pendant & suspending a diamond & pearl drop, bezel- and bead-set w/old European- and rose-cut diamonds, millegrain accents, Edwardian era, early 20th c., 2" l. (ILLUS.) **$1,763**

Delicate Diamond, Pearl & Platinum Pendant

Pendant-brooch, diamond, platinum & pearl, delicate openwork design in a stylized arched fan & scroll shape, set w/five transitional- and 81 rose-cut diamond mélée, two pearl highlights, detachable 14k gold pin stem, suspended from a later platinum chain, pearls not tested for origin, ca. 1915, 2" l. (ILLUS.) **$1,880**

Enamel & Diamond Pendant-Brooch

Pendant-brooch, enamel & diamond, a large round flattened disk decorated w/bass taille dark blue enamel & centered by starburst design bead-set w/old mine- and rose-cut diamonds, the border band also set with diamonds, a ribbon bow crest also set with diamonds, locket compartment in the back, silver-topped 18k gold mount, one diamond missing, replaced pin stem, 1 7/8" d. (ILLUS.) **$1,293**

Fine Art Nouveau Flower Pendant

Pendant-brooch, enameled 14k gold & diamond, Art Nouveau style, designed as a blossom w/five long purple enameled petals & a center old European-cut diamond w/each petal edged by small old mine-cut diamonds, early 20th c. (ILLUS.) **$2,585**

American-made Pansy Pendant-brooch

Pendant-brooch, enameled 14k gold & diamond, Art Nouveau style, designed as a pansy blossom enameled in dark purple shaded to white w/a brownish purple & yellow center set w/an old European-cut diamond, mark of Krementz & Co., Newark, New Jersey, w/pendant hook, 1" w. (ILLUS.) **$999**

Krementz & Co. Enameled Pansy Pendant

Pendant-brooch, enameled 14k gold & seed pearl, Art Nouveau style, designed as a pansy blossom enameled in dark lavender on white w/black accents around the central seed pearl, marked by Krementz & Co., Newark, New Jersey, 1" w. (ILLUS.) **$1,645**

J

Art Nouveau Enameled Pansy Pendant

Pendant-brooch, enameled 18k gold & diamond, Art Nouveau style, designed as a black pansy blossom centered by an old European-cut diamond, late 19th - early 20th c. (ILLUS., previous page) **$1,528**

Antique Snake-headed Gold Necklace

Pendant-necklace, enamel, diamond & gold, designed as a long slender flexible serpent chain terminating w/a blue-enameled head set along the top w/a group of old mine-, rose- and pear-cut diamonds & w/cabochon ruby eyes, the mouth suspending a round locket enameled in dark blue centered by a floret of tiny diamonds, 18k & 14k gold mount, 16 1/2" l. (ILLUS. of part) **$2,703**

Pendant-necklace, enamel, seed pearl & gem-set, the circular pendant & fancy link chain set w/emerald-cut & cabochon green beryls, oval-cut almandite garnets & seed pearls, ruby & paste accents, blue & white enamel trim, silver-gilt filigree mount, Austro-Hungarian hallmarks, 19th c., overall 20" l. **$1,175**

Elaborate Decorative Pendant-Necklace

Pendant-necklace, enameled & gem-set 18k gold, Renaissance Revival style, the large oval pendant composed of ornate openwork C-scroll frame enameled in pink, white & black & accented w/small square-cut diamonds surrounding an oval Limoges enamel scene of Hesperos, god of the evening star, in his chariot, suspended from an enameled scrolled bail,

attached to a floret-form gold fancy link chain w/each link set w/a small pink sapphire, 19th c., overall 19" l. (ILLUS.)......... **$4,583**

English Arts & Crafts Pendant

Pendant-necklace, enameled sterling silver, Arts & Crafts style, an openwork oblong form decorated w/leafy vines above green & blue enameled circles & a tiny enameled drop, suspended from a trace link chain, English hallmarks, retailed by Liberty & Co., early 20th c., overall 19" l. (ILLUS.).. **$353**

Ornate Victorian Pendant-Necklace

Pendant-necklace, gold (14k), a large shield-shaped locket pendant centered by a raised oval enclosing a bird & berries w/seed pearl accents, the frame decorated w/applied ropetwist accents & scrolls & beads down the sides, a decorative ropetwist connector to the woven gold necklace, the back w/a monogram on the locket compartment, second half 19th c., pendant 2 1/2" l., overall 17 1/2" l. (ILLUS. of part) **$1,000-1,500**

Pin, black opal, diamond, enamel, 18k gold & platinum, a diamond-shaped frame centering a large bezel-set oval broadflash black opal, the frame composed of curved intersecting bands on each side w/large gold scale-design bands alternating w/smaller bands set w/old European-cut diamond mélée, green enamel accents, hallmark of Bailey, Banks & Biddle, No. 37930 (ILLUS. bottom with lizard & flying goose pins, bottom next column) **$7,931**

Victorian Coral & Gold Hand Pin

Pin, coral & enameled 14k gold, designed as an angel skin coral carved hand grasping a gold arched loop & wearing a widely flaring lace-edged cuff in gold ornately engraved & trimmed w/black tracery enamel, 19th c. (ILLUS.) **$470**

Early Green Garnet & Pearl Pin

Pin, demantoid garnet & seed pearl, circle-style, the narrow ring set w/circular-cut green garnets alternating w/seed pearls, silver-topped 18k gold mount, Edwardian era, early 20th c., 7/8" d. (ILLUS.).............. **$823**

Pin, diamond, delicate openwork bow form bead-set w/old mine- and rose-cut diamonds & suspending a single pearl, silver-topped 14k gold mount, 19th c. (ILLUS., top next column) **$411**

Delicate Diamond-set Bow Pin

Pin, diamond, demantoid garnet & 18k gold, model of a flying goose, the large wings pavé-set w/circular-cut round garnets & the body pavé-set w/old European- and mine-cut diamonds, a ruby eye, platinum-topped gold mount, Edwardian, England, early 20th c. (ILLUS. center with lizard & black opal pins, below)............. **$12,925**

Three Fine Quality Early Pins

J

Pin, diamond, demantoid garnet & 18k gold, model of a long lizard w/the body pavé-set w/bands of circular-cut green garnets & old European- and mine-cut diamonds, ruby eyes, platinum-topped gold mount w/14k gold pin stem, ca. 1920 (ILLUS. top with black opal & flying goose pin, previous page) **$8,519**

Antique French Gem-set Dragonfly Pin

Pin, diamond & gem-set gold, in the shape of a dragonfly bead-set w/rose-cut diamonds, bezel-set emerald & ruby accents, French guarantee stamps, silver-topped 15k gold mount (ILLUS.) **$881**

Diamond, Gold & Pearl Arrow Pin

Pin, diamond, pearl & 18k gold, modeled as an arrow, the tip & tail feathers set w/rose-cut diamonds, the center of the shaft w/a swirled ring of rose-cut diamonds centered by a pearl, silver-topped 18k gold mount, French guarantee mark, 19th c., 2 1/2" l. (ILLUS.)............................ **$823**

Edwardian Small Tennis Racket Pin

Pin, diamond & ruby, designed as a tennis racket set w/small rose-cut diamonds & bands of step-cut rubies, a seed pearl ball,

millegrain accents, platinum-topped 18k gold mount, missing two rubies, Edwardian era, early 20th c., 1 1/2" l. (ILLUS.) **$999**

Art Nouveau Five-Petal Flower Pin

Pin, enameled 14k gold, Art Nouveau style, designed as a blossom w/five ruffled petal enameled in pale yellowish green shading to deep rose, the center set w/a seed pearl, late 19th - early 20th c., 1 1/8" w. (ILLUS.)...................................... **$529**

Oyster Shell-shaped Gold & Pearl Pin

Pin, enameled 14k gold & seed pearl, designed in the shape of an oyster shell w/a seed pearl set at the edge, hallmark of A.J. Hedges & Co., Newark, New Jersey, early 20th c. (ILLUS.)............................. **$1,528**

Art Nouveau Enameled Flower Pin

Pin, enameled 18k gold & diamond, Art Nouveau style, designed as a six-petal flower w/each petal enameled in red, yellow & green w/seed pearl accents at the tips, centering an old European-cut diamond, later 10k gold closure (ILLUS.) **$499**

J

Early 14k Gold Griffin-shaped Pin

Pin, gold (14k), Art Nouveau style, modeled as a winged serpentine griffin w/a cabochon ruby eye, the back w/a pendant hook, late 19th - early 20th c., 1 1/2" l. (ILLUS.).. **$411**

Delicate Early Flower Basket Pin

Pin, platinum & gem-set 18k gold, modeled as a woven flower basket & flexible pendant bezel-set w/small diamond, emerald, sapphire & ruby mélée & seed pearl accents, French guarantee stamps, early 20th c., 1 1/4 x 1 1/2" (ILLUS.)................ **$3,408**

Pretty Art Nouveau Enamel & Pearl Pin

Pin, plique-a-jour enamel, pearl & 14k gold, Art Nouveau style, an openwork looping

gold vine suspending a pair of small pink-enameled blossoms & a green-enameled leaf above cluster of freshwater pearl berries (ILLUS.)...................................... **$2,703**

Antique Ruby & Diamond Crescent Pin

Pin, ruby, diamond & 14k gold, crescent-shaped w/nearly touching tips, the back bead-set w/a band of 13 graduating cushion-cut rubies w/small rose-cut diamonds at the tips, 1" l. (ILLUS.) **$1,528**

Antique Sapphire & Diamond Crescent Pin

Pin, sapphire, diamond & gold, crescent-shaped, the widest part of the back bead-set w/seven cushion-cut blue sapphires w/the tips set w/old mine- and rose-cut diamonds, silver-topped 18k gold mount, replaced pin stem (ILLUS.) **$3,055**

J

Stylized Floral Sapphire & Diamond Pin

Pin, sapphire, diamond & platinum-topped 18k gold, long curved slender stylized leaves extend from the central cluster of three thin stems each ending in a circular-cut sapphire & tiny single-cut diamond mélée, 19th c., 1 1/2" l. (ILLUS.)...... **$646**

French Victorian Butterfly Pin

Pin, turquoise & diamond, model of a stylized
butterfly, each two-part wing centered by
a cabochon turquoise framed by rose- and
old mine-cut diamonds, the upper body
set w/a round turquoise cabochon & the
lower body set w/diamonds, French maker's mark & guarantee stamp, Victorian,
1" l. (ILLUS.) **$940**

Pair of Antique Gem-set Flower Pins

Pins, diamond & gem-set, each designed
as a five-petal flower w/heart-shaped
citrine or topaz petals w/a border of single-cut diamonds, 18k gold mounts, one
w/a pendant loop, evidence of solder, pr.
(ILLUS.) **$4,700**

Antique Amethyst & Gold Seal Ring

Ring, amethyst & 18k gold, seal-type, the
oval bezel-set amethyst intaglio-carved
w/a winged figure w/a helmet & suit of ar-

mor, simple gold mount, French import
stamp, size 8 1/4 (ILLUS.) **$705**

Amethyst Intaglio, Diamond & Gold Ring

Ring, amethyst, diamond & 18k gold, the
rectangular step-cut amethyst carved
w/the letter "S" inset w/rose-cut dia-
monds, size 7 3/4 (ILLUS.) **$764**

Bloodstone Ring with Hebrew Inscription

Ring, bloodstone & gold, Judaic seal-style,
bezel-set w/an octagonal bloodstone tablet w/a Herbrew inscription translating to
"If I forget you, oh Jerusalem, may I forget my right arm," slight break in mount,
antique, size 8 (ILLUS.) **$881**

Boulder Opal & Gold Ring

J

Ring, boulder opal & 18k gold, Arts & Crafts style, the bezel-set oval cabochon opal flanked by an oak leaf band mount, early 20th c., size 3 1/2 (ILLUS., previous page) **$999**

Antique Coral Cabochon & Diamond Ring

Ring, coral, diamond & 14k gold, the top centered by an oval coral cabochon framed by a ring of 14 old European-cut diamonds weighing about 1.40 cts., size 5 1/2 (ILLUS.).. **$881**

Very Rare Green Garnet & Diamond Ring

Ring, demantoid garnet & diamond, the oval top centered by a bezel-set oval-cut light green garnet framed by a ring of 20 old European-cut diamonds, millegrain accents, platinum-topped 18k gold mount, size 3 (ILLUS.) **$16,450**

Antique Diamond Solitaire Ring

Ring, diamond & 14k gold, solitaire-type, mounted w/a collet-set old rose-cut diamond flanked by high-relief floral shoulders & incised shank, silver-topped 14k gold mount, size 6 1/2 (ILLUS.)............... **$1,175**

Rare Art Nouveau Three-Diamond Ring

Ring, diamond & 18k gold, Art Nouveau style, the long set w/a row of three old European-cut diamonds, a pink, a greenish yellow & a near colorless, flanked by scrolling shoulders, size 6 3/4 (ILLUS.).. **$14,100**

Ring, diamond & 18k white gold, man's, three-stone, the top set w/a center old European-cut diamond weighing about 1.33 cts. flanked by old European-cut diamonds weighing about 2.33 cts., size 10 1/4... **$4,700**

Antique Cross-form Diamond Ring

Ring, diamond & 18k white gold, the top w/a cross-form mount prong-set w/a cross-form arrangement of old mine-cut diamonds weighing about 1.73 cts., engraved shoulders (ILLUS.) **$764**

J

Rare Antique Emerald & Diamond Ring

Ring, diamond, emerald & gem-set 18k gold, the long four-section top w/pointed ends bezel-set w/old European-cut diamond & teardrop-cut emeralds, the curved side sections enclosing a row of three large old European-cut diamonds trimmed w/blue tracery enamel accents, seed pearl, old single- and rose-cut diamond highlights, diamonds weighing about 1.71 cts., 19th c., size 5 (ILLUS.) **$3,760**

Antique Diamond & Enamel Ring

Ring, diamond & enamel, the oval top centered by a large rose-cut diamond surrounded by dark blue enamel all framed w/a border of small rose-cut diamonds & engraved accents, silver-topped 18k gold mount, size 5 3/4 (ILLUS.) **$382**

Antique European-cut Diamond Ring

Ring, diamond & gold, the rectangular top set w/16 old European-cut diamonds weighing about 1.90 cts., silver-topped gold mount, size 5 1/2 (ILLUS.)............... **$1,763**

Antique Gold & Gem Snakes Ring

Ring, diamond, ruby & 18k gold, designed as entwined gold snakes, each head gypsy-set w/an old European-cut diamond or circular-cut ruby, size 6 3/4 (ILLUS.)....... **$1,880**

Fine Edwardian Sapphire & Diamond Ring

Ring, diamond, sapphire & 18k gold, the square top centered by a large cushion-cut blue sapphire framed by 16 old mine-cut diamonds weighing about 2.20 cts., platinum-topped 18k gold mount, Edwardian era, early 20th c., size 6 1/4 (ILLUS.) **$3,525**

Antique Diamond Bypass Snake Ring

Ring, diamond, snake-form bypass-type, set overall w/rose-cut diamonds w/each snake head set w/tiny ruby eyes, silver-topped 14k gold mount, size 6 1/2 (ILLUS.) **$1,410**

Early Navette-shaped Diamond Ring

Ring, diamond, the navette-form top bead-set w/nine old mine-cut diamonds, black enamel accents, engraved shoulders, w/ring guard, enamel wear, size 6 3/4 (ILLUS.) **$411**

J

Art Nouveau Pearl & Mother-of-Pearl Ring

Ring, mother-of-pearl, freshwater pearl & 14k gold, Art Nouveau style, the long top bezel-set w/a center cabochon mother-of-pearl flanked by freshwater pearls, the shoulders w/engraved foliate designs, size 4 1/2 (ILLUS.) **$235**

Fine Edwardian Opal & Diamond Ring

Ring, opal & diamond, the top centered by a large prong-set oval opal cabochon framed by a band of old European-cut diamonds, diamond-set shoulders, platinum-topped 14k gold mount, modified shank, Edwardian era, early 20th c. (ILLUS.) **$1,293**

Three-Pearl & Gold Art Nouveau Ring

Ring, pearl & 18k gold, Art Nouveau style, the top prong-set w/a white, pink & lavender pearl flanked by lotus blossom gold mounts, signed by Tiffany & Co., size 3 1/4 (ILLUS.) **$2,820**

Antique Pearl, Diamond & Gold Ring

Ring, pearl, diamond & 18k gold, the narrow top bead-set w/three white, silver & bluish grey pearls interspersed w/pairs of old mine-cut diamonds, scrolling foliate shoulders & gallery, size 5 (ILLUS.) **$382**

Antique Pink Sapphire & Diamond Ring

Ring, pink sapphire, diamond & 18k gold, centering a circular-cut pink sapphire surrounded by rose- and old mine-cut diamonds, engraved band, size 6 1/2 (ILLUS.) **$1,410**

Fine Edwardian Pearl & Diamond Ring

Ring, platinum, pearl & diamond, the long oblong top centered by a row of three white pearls w/rose overtones framed by 31 old mine- and European-cut diamonds, millegrain accents, Edwardian era, early 20th c., size 4 3/4 (ILLUS.) **$3,055**

J

Early Seed Pearl & Gold Memorial Ring

Ring, seed pearl & 14k gold, memorial-type, the rectangular top w/a border band of seed pearl surrounding the compartment enclosing hair, the mount w/high-relief floral & foliate shoulders, monogrammed, late 18th - early 19th c., size 7 (ILLUS.) **$250-350**

Ring, synthetic ruby & diamond, the cushion-shaped stone framed by single-cut diamonds, platinum-topped 18k gold mount, partial European assay mark, possibly French, inscribed & dated 1915, size 7 1/4 .. **$705**

Antique Turquoise & Diamond Ring

Ring, turquoise, diamond & 14k gold, the round top centered by a cabochon turquoise framed by a ring of old mine- and European-cut diamonds, size 6 3/4 (ILLUS.) **$558**

Antique Intaglio Sapphire & Gold Fob

Seal fob, intaglio sapphire & 18k gold, the flat cushion-shaped sapphire intaglio-carved w/an Islamic script, in a delicate openwork gold mount (ILLUS.) **$3,055**

Unusual Cameo Stickpins

Stickpin, cameo-carved onyx & 14k gold, the round onyx top carved as a crescent man-in-the-moon looking at a star, gold frame & pin, top 3/4" d. (ILLUS.) **$1,880**

Stickpin, diamond & 18k gold, the top w/an articulated figure wearing armor studded w/rose-cut diamonds, ruby eyes, silver & 14k gold mount, gold pin, missing one diamond, eye chipped **$353**

Stickpin with Enameled Mercury Portrait

Stickpin, enameled 18k gold, the round top enameled in color w/a profile portrait of Mercury on a white ground w/his chain mail shirt & winged helmet made of chased & engraved gold, early 20th c. (ILLUS.) **$353**

J

Nice Etruscan Revival Gold Watch Fob

Watch fob, gold (22k), Etruscan Revival style, the double trace link chain & slide suspending a pendant w/a foxtail fringe & a tall ewer w/a hinged lid & decorated w/floral & foliate designs, 19th c., 10 1/2" l. (ILLUS.)........................ **$705**

Art Nouveau Dog Head Watch Pin

Watch pin, gem-set 14k gold, Art Nouveau style, an oblong dished plaque cast in relief w/the head of a retriever dog among tall scrolling grasses accented by bezel-set circular-cut sapphires & diamonds, one stone missing, solder at pin stem (ILLUS.)........................ **$881**

Art Nouveau Gold & Sapphire Watch Pin

Watch pin, sapphire & gem-set 14k gold, Art Nouveau style, a looping gold frame decorated w/four small four-petal blossoms w/small old mine-cut diamond centers & seed pearl accents, framing a large prong-set cushion-cut light blue sapphire, late 19th - early 20th c., 1" l. (ILLUS.)........................ **$705**

Unique Enameled Jugenstil Watch Pin

Watch pin & chain, gem-set enameled silver, Jugenstil design, the pin w/a wide slightly crescent bar enameled in green flanking two dark blue bars flanking a square mother-of-pearl square & accented w/clear paste stone highlight above a half-round four-petal blossom in light blue w/red stone & paste accents, above an enameled slide enameled in blue & centered by a red stone & accented w/clear paste stone, small opals & a mother-of-pearl teardrop, completed by a gilt chain, Europe, early 20th c., overall 29 1/2" l. (ILLUS.)........................ **$470**

Sets

Brooch & earrings, blue stone, seed pearl & 14k yellow gold, each piece designed as a harp w/floral & foliate designs accented by a cabochon blue stone & seed pearl highlights, 19th c., pendant earrings 2 3/8" l., brooch 1" w., the set **$705**

J

Art Nouveau Brooch & Earrings Set

Brooch & earrings, enameled 18k gold & garnet, Art Nouveau style, the oblong gold brooch w/an openwork scroll & bud design centered by a large blossom trimmed w/blue enamel, accented w/two seed pearls & centered at the top by a cabochon garnet, the pendant earrings w/a matching flower design, French import marks, brooch w/enamel loss, the set (ILLUS., previous page) **$646**

Fine French Porcelain & Gold Suite

Brooch & earrings, h.p. porcelain & 18k gold; the brooch centered by a large oval porcelain plaque painted w/a scene of a young maiden framed by a wide gold openwork border, the pendant-style earrings w/a central teardrop painted drop suspended within the openwork gold frame, a top band set w/seed pearls below the ring & delicate scroll top, mark of the French maker & guarantee stamps, in original fitted box, brooch 1 3/4" d., earrings 1 1/2" l., the suite (ILLUS.) **$1,645**

Brooch & earrings, onyx cameo & 14k gold, each pendant-style earring depicting a lady in Renaissance dress, floral & foliate-engraved mounts & seed pearls accents, matching brooch, the set **$646**

Pretty Set of Early Amethyst Jewelry

Brooch-pendant & earrings, amethyst & gilt-metal, the round brooch composed of an outer band of large round-cut amethysts enclosing four smaller round amethysts & centered by another large round amethyst, the pendant-style earrings w/a round amethyst w/wire hook suspending double chains supporting a cluster of three round amethysts, replaced pin stem & findings, 19th c., earrings 2 1/4" l., brooch 1 1/2" d., the set (ILLUS.)................ **$588**

Victorian Cameo Brooch & Pins Suite

Cameo brooch & pins, carved hardstone & 14k gold, the brooch set w/a large oval hardstone cameo carved w/the bust portrait of a Victorian maiden w/flowers in her hair facing left, within a simple rounded gold frame, pair of smaller matching pins of the same design, pins 1" l., brooch 1 7/8" l., the suite (ILLUS.) **$1,175**

J

Antique Painted Porcelain & Seed Pearl Locket & Earrings Suite

Locket & earrings, enameled porcelain & seed pearls, the oval locket centered by a polychrome enamel porcelain plaque decorated w/a romantic couple in 18th c. attire in a bucolic setting, framed by a ring of seed pearls, suspended from a removable seed pearl-set bow, matching pair of pendant-style earrings, gilt-metal mounts, French maker's mark & guarantee stamps, enamel loss, one seed pearl missing, the set (ILLUS., top of page) **$1,293**

Rare Georgian Amethyst Necklace & Pendant from Suite

Necklace & earrings, amethyst & 18k gold, the necklace front half composed of nine graduated large bezel-set, oval-cut amethysts w/the back half completed by a delicate flat gold mesh chain w/a foil-backed amethyst clasp, the front fitted w/a detachable pendant-brooch cross w/an amethyst-set connector & the cross formed by five large oval-cut amethysts, matching pendant-type earrings, late Georgian era, England, early 19th c., earrings & pendant w/later tops, later pin stem, earrings 2" l.,

cross pendant 2 1/4" l., necklace 13 1/2" l., the set (ILLUS.) **$4,113**

Ornate Victorian Gem-set Necklace

Necklace & earrings, garnet, seed pearl & enameled silver; Renaissance Revival style, the necklace composed of links w/scrolled mounts enclosing a large oval foil-backed garnet w/two seed pearl accents, the front section centered by a larger horizontal oval foil-backed garnet framed w/white enameled dots, seed pearls & gold scrolls trimmed w/black & white enamel & suspending two small oval garnets, the large central pendant w/an ornate openwork rounded mount trimmed w/black & white enamel dots & set w/oval garnets & seed pearls above five slender gem-set pointed drops, matching pendant-style earrings, European hallmarks, second half 19th c., earrings 3" l., necklace 15 1/4" l., the suite (ILLUS., of necklace) **$1,528**

J

Victorian Onyx, Gold & Seed Pearl Jewelry Suite

Pendant-necklace, bracelet & earrings, onyx, seed pearl & 14k rose gold, pendant-necklace composed of oblong onyx links carved & mounted w/band of small gold designs accented w/seed pearls & alternating w/gold ring links, suspending a large flat rectangular onyx plaque mounted w/a gold floral sprig accented w/seed pearls, the bracelet of matching link design, the earrings w/squared onyx teardrops decorated w/a gold band set w/seed pearls, pendant w/minor corner nick, earrings 1 1/2" l., bracelet 7" l., pendant-necklace 20 1/2" l., the suite (ILLUS., top of page) **$823**

Watches

Edwardian Green Enamel Pendant Watch

Pendant watch, lady's, enamel & diamond, A. Chopard, the goldtone dial w/Arabic numerals, the case w/green guilloché enamel w/a central floral reserve centered by an old European-cut diamond surrounded by white enamel flowers, rose-cut diamond bail, millegrain accents, Edwardian era, early 20th c. (ILLUS.) **$1,116**

Gem-set 18k Gold Pendant Watch

Pendant watch, lady's, gem-set 18k gold, the round case centered by a large rose-cut diamond surrounded by a ring of oval-cut sapphires & an outer band of smaller diamonds, the white enamel dial w/Roman numerals, replaced Bulova 17-jewel movement, suspended from a large openwork ribbon bow lapel pin set w/rose-cut diamonds & trimmed w/dark blue enamel, by Colevaj et Cie., Geneva, Switzerland, missing crystal (ILLUS.) **$764**

J

Lady's Watch with Pretty Enameled Case

Pendant watch, open faced, lady's, Golay Leresche & Fils, Geneva, Switzerland, 18k gold, enamel & diamond, the white enamel dial w/blue Arabic numerals, enclosing a jeweled lever escapement movement w/wolf tooth winding mechanism, the rounded case framed by a scalloped gold border, the back enameled in dark blue w/rose-cut diamond accents centering a squared enameled color landscape of a lake & mountains (ILLUS.)...... **$1,528**

Antique Weil Freres Pendant Watch

Pendant watch, open faced, lady's, Weil Freres, Geneva, Switzerland, 18k gold & enamel, the white enamel dial w/Arabic numerals, pin-set gilt cylinder escapement movement, reverse of case bezel-set w/a central rose-cut diamond against a dark blue guilloche enamel ground w/a thin gold border & engraved frame, Swiss

assay marks, missing crown (ILLUS. of the back) **$499**

Pocket watch, hunting case, lady's, Charles Oudin, Paris, enamel & diamond, the white enamel dial w/Roman numerals, enclosing a key-wind & set gilt cylinder escapement movement, 18k gold cobalt blue guilloché-enameled case w/rose-cut diamond flowers.............. **$881**

Fine Hunting Case Lady's Watch

Pocket watch, hunting case, lady's, Malignon, Geneva, Switzerland, enamel & diamond, the white enamel dial w/Roman numerals & subsidiary seconds dial, enclosing a key-wind & set 10-jewel lever escapement bar movement, case w/cobalt blue enamel centered by floral sprigs set w/rose-cut diamonds, the scrolled gold border band w/black & white tracery enamel (ILLUS.).................................... **$1,293**

J

Early Patek & Co. Enameled Pocket Watch

Pocket watch, hunting case, man's, Patek & Co., Geneva, Switzerland, enameled gold, the white enamel dial w/Roman numerals, key-wind & set 8-jewel cylinder escapement movement, 18k gold case centering an enameled bust portrait of a lady wearing a diamond-set diadem, black tracery enamel Greek key & floral details (ILLUS., previous page) **$881**

Fine Waltham 14k Gold Man's Watch

Pocket watch, hunting case, man's, Waltham, 14k gold case ornately embossed w/the figure of a stag surrounded by floral & leaf designs, the white enamel dial w/Roman numerals, subsidiary seconds dial, signed movement, w/a 14k gold watch chain 27 3/4" l. (ILLUS.) **$764**

J

Vacheron & Constantin Pocket Watch

Pocket watch, open faced, man's, Vacheron & Constantin, white enamel dial w/Arabic numerals & sunken subsidiary seconds dial, enclosing a jeweled movement, engraved case, Swiss assay marks, dents (ILLUS.) **$1,645**

Very Early Double-Dial Pocket Watch

Early Tiffany Gold Pocket Watch

Pocket watch, open faced, man's, Tiffany & Co., 18k gold case, white enamel dial w/Roman numerals & subsidiary seconds dial, enclosing a signed nickel movement, polished case w/inscribed initials (ILLUS.) **$823**

Pocket watch, open-faced double-dial, man's, Rilliet, Strasberg, France, the white & rose enamel hour dial w/Roman numerals & cherubs, the calendar dial w/Arabic numerals & days of the week, key-wind & set verge fusee movement, 18k gold case w/applied bead & wirework design, hairlines, ca. 1800 (ILLUS.) **$3,408**

Early English Gold Pocket Watch

Pocket watch, open-faced, man's, Joseph Johnson, Liverpool, England, 18k gold, the engraved goldtone dial w/Roman numerals & subsidiary seconds dial, keywind & set rack lever movement, engine-turned case w/high-relief, rocaille & scroll designs, hallmarks for the city of Chester (ILLUS.)....................................... **$1,410**

Early 19th Century French Pocket Watch

Pocket watch, open-faced, man's, Marchand, Paris, France, enameled gold, the white enamel dial w/Roman numerals, enclosing a verge fusee movement, the case centered by a large color enameled scene of a lady decorating a statue of cupid framed by a band of green enamel & an outer band of tiny seed pearls, the outer border engraved & highlighted w/black enamel, small repair to dial at keyhole, early 19th c. (ILLUS.) **$1,998**

Fine French Victorian Watch & Chatelaine

Pocket watch & chatelaine, open faced case, Czapek & Cie, France, 18k gold, lapis lazuli & enamel, the large chatelaine in gold w/a wide arched top centered by a palmette & ending in rondels all highlighted w/black enamel, the ends of the arch suspending a lapis & gold watch key or lapis & gold fob, the arch enclosing a large lapis round boss suspending a fancy gold chain w/a rondel & palmette hooked to the watch w/the back covered in lapis, the white enamel dial w/a subsidiary seconds dial, nickel keywind movement, French guarantee stamps, chatelaine hook converted to brooch, cracks in lapis, 19th c., 5" l. (ILLUS.) **$2,233**

J

Waltham Lady's Watch & Lapel Pin

Sterling Filigree Bar Pin. Author's Collection.

Pocket watch & watch pin, open faced, lady's, Waltham - A.W.W. Co., the back of the 14k gold case engraved w/leafy scrolls around a diaper panel, white enamel dial w/Arabic numerals, subsidiary seconds dial, signed 15-jewel nickle movement, suspended from an openwork stylized fleur-de-lis lapel pin, late 19th - early 20th c. (ILLUS., previous page) **$235**

Costume Jewelry
(19th & 20th Century)

J

Star-Decorated Bar Pin.
Courtesy of Davida Brown

Bar pin, rhinestone, the bar mounted w/a row of three stars decorated w/blue, pink & yellow rhinestones, suspending a larger matching star pendant, 3 1/4" h. (ILLUS.) **$125-150**

Bar pin, sterling silver, long rectangular shape w/a ropetwist border around ornate openwork looped filigree, made in Palestine, ca. 1935, 5/8 x 1 7/8" (ILLUS., top of page) **$75-100**

Bracelet, Bakelite, bangle-type, moss green, carved geometric & floral designs, 1 1/4" w. **$125-150**

Bakelite Red Carved Bangle Bracelet

Bracelet, Bakelite, bangle-type, wide deep red band carved w/a repeating design of circles & rayed lines, interior circumference 7 3/4" (ILLUS.)................................. **$206**

Bakelite Black Cut to Green Bracelet

Bracelet, Bakelite, overlay cut-back type, bangle-type, a wide black band cut-back to groups of thin green crescents, interior circumference 7 3/4" (ILLUS.).................... **$323**

Bracelet, brass & rhinestone, composed of brass filigree flower-shaped links w/green rhinestone centers, an extended flower on chain leading to a ring to be worn on a finger, ca. 1925 .... **$70-95**

Bracelet, enameled white metal & rhinestone, Art Deco Revival style, white enameled metal links pavé-set w/clear rhinestones, a red marquise-cut center stone, 3/4" w. **$85-115**

Bracelet, vermeil (gold over sterling silver) & crystals, the openwork metal links each set w/an oval crystal faux gemstone in five light pastel colors, 3/8" w., 6" l. **$75-100**

Bracelet, vermeil (gold over sterling silver) & glass, composed of flexible triangular silver links mounted w/amber glass triangles, 1 1/4" w., 8" l. **$90-120**

Bracelet, white metal & glass, composed of hinged filigree white metal links centered by painted glass ancient Chinese figures, 1 1/8" w., 7 1/4" l. **$45-60**

Bracelet, white metal & glass, the hinged links each h.p. w/an ancient Persian scene, 1" w., 6 1/2" l. **$45-65**

Carved Yellow Bakelite Bracelets

Bracelets, Bakelite, bangle-type, yellow carved w/almond-shaped geometric devices, one slightly lighter in color, interior circumference 7 3/4", pr. (ILLUS.) **$176**

Fine Boucher Corn Stalk Enameled Brooch

Brooch, enameled rhodium & gilt-plated metal & rhinestone, designed as two yellow-enameled ears of corn on a green-enameled leafy stalk, trimmed w/small clear rhinestones, Boucher, ca. 1941, 3 x 3 1/2" (ILLUS.) **$896**

Very Rare Trifari Sailboat & Woman Brooch

Brooch, enameled rhodium-plated metal, rhinestone & faux glass gems, designed as a sailboat w/the sail enameled in gold, the deck in yellow & the flag in red, the bottom of the hull lined w/clear rhinestones & green glass stones, mounted w/the standing figure of a stylized woman w/one hand holding the mast & the other arm waving, her head, hands & legs enameled & her clothing composed of unfoiled faceted & baguette glass stones imitating emeralds, rubies & sapphires, signed by Trifari, ca. 1940, 2 3/8 x 2 3/4" (ILLUS.) **$2,988**

J

Rare Trifari "Jelly Belly" Duck Brooch

Brooch, gilt sterling silver, rhinestone & Lucite, "jelly belly" style, designed as a duck emerging from a large clear Lucite egg, the head trimmed w/clear rhinestones & a red stone eye, marked by Trifari, ca. 1943, 1 1/2 x 2" (ILLUS.) **$1,195**

Rare 1970s Jean-Pierre Brooch

Brooch, mother-of-pearl & rhinestone, a large oval mother-of-pearl shell mounted around the edges w/pointed silver plated triangles set w/light blue & blue violet rhinestones, marked "Déposé," Jean-Pierre, France, ca. 1972, 2 x 3" (ILLUS.) **$1,076**

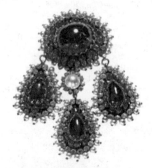

Balenciaga Brooch with Pendants

J

Brooch, rhinestone, glass stones & faux pearl, designed w/an oval top brooch centered by an oval purple glass cabochon framed by bands of red rhinestones & a border of faux seed pearls, suspending three tear-shaped drops, each centered by a teardrop purple stone cabochon framed by red rhinestones & a border of seed pearls, the center drop also w/a faux pearl link, designed by Robert Boossens

for Balenciaga, France, ca. 1955, unsigned, 3 x 4" (ILLUS.) **$657**
Cameo pin, glass & brass, a white glass cameo w/brown shaded details mounted in a brass frame, 1 1/4" l. **$30-55**
Cameo pin, Lucite, clear w/a white on black plastic center cameo, 1 1/2"................... **$30-45**
Charm bracelet, goldplate, child-size, suspends four storybook-themed charms **$15-25**

Long Haskell Chatelaine Necklace

Chatelaine necklace, glass beads, wood & Bakelite, the necklace composed of three long strands of small green glass beads connecting to two inverted clips, each clip decorated w/two wooden nuts & two wooden leaves accented w/green Bakelite & green glass beads, strung & hand-mounted onto a metal gallery, unsigned M. Haskell, ca. 1935, 28" l. (ILLUS.) **$896**
Chatelaine pins, sterling silver, male & female figures in traditional Chinese dress connected by a 7 1/2" l. chain, female 1 7/8" h., male 2 1/2" h....................... **$185-215**

Designer Piano Keyboard Plastic Choker

Choker, plastic, designed as a piano keyboard w/the keys made from black & white plastic, paper label reading "Ugo Correani x Karl lagerfeld," made for Chloe, France, 1983, 12 1/4" l. (ILLUS.) **$1,135**

Rare Scemama Bead & Rhinestone Collar

Collar, silver plated metal, rhinestone & faux gems, composed of four strands set w/clear rhinestones alternating w/pear-shaped glass beads imitating moonstone, the wide front sections continuing the rhinestone & faux moonstone strands & adding strands of pear-shaped red glass beads imitating coral, a pendant suspended at the front w/a rhinestone link above three small glass coral beads & two large oval glass moonstone beads, a rhinestone tassel below, unsigned Scemama, France, ca. 1955, 16" l. (ILLUS.) **$1,673**

Dress clip, Bakelite, Art Deco style, shield-shaped, yellow covered w/red, blue, green & white plastic flowers, 1 1/2" l. **$60-85**

Dress clip, Bakelite, designed as moss green carved leaves w/center swirls, 2" l. **$70-90**

Dress clip, brass, Victorian Revival style, embossed overall w/acorns & leaves, 1 7/8" l. **$40-55**

Dress clip, celluloid, designed as a group of gold-colored iridescent balls made to resemble Tiffany glass, 2 3/8" l. **$35-50**

Dress clip, celluloid & goldplate, yellow flowers w/amber bead centers on a goldplate mesh ground, 2" l. **$30-50**

Dress clip, goldplate, a metal leaf design w/an applied circle & a smaller leaf on the top, 2 1/4" l. **$35-50**

Dress clip, goldplate, art glass & rhinestone, the openwork & filigree goldplate mount centered by large Czechoslovakian foil-backed amber art glass cabochons & amber rhinestone accents, signed "Kandell & Marcus, NY," 2 1/4" w., 2 5/8" h. **$125-150**

Dress clip, goldplate, crystal & rhinestone, an ornate openwork goldplate mount decorated w/six large blue crystals w/pale blue & clear square rhinestone accents, unsigned Czechoslovakian, 2 1/4" w., 2 1/2" h. **$150-175**

Dress clip, goldplate & plastic, designed w/a long amber plastic bar on a goldplate background, 1 3/8 x 3 1/8" **$55-70**

Dress clip, goldplate & rhinestone, an openwork lacy goldplate mount centered by a large oval purple rhinestone w/purple marquise-cut & round rhinestone accents, 1 3/4" w., 2 1/4" h. **$75-100**

Dress clip, goldplate, rhinestone & crystal, the goldplate mount designed as ornate vines & flowers, centered by an oval yellow crystal stone w/raised green & yellow oval, marquise-cut & round rhinestone accents, unsigned Czechoslovakian, 1 3/4" w., 2 1/2" h. **$150-175**

Dress clip, goldplate, rhinestone & crystal, the openwork goldplate ribbon design mount w/an antiqued finish, set w/four red oval crystals & rhinestones, hand-set w/clear rhinestone accents, numbered 377, 1 1/8" w., 3" h. **$100-125**

Dress clip, goldplate & rhinestone, designed as three goldplate leaves each centered by pavé-set rhinestones, 2 x 2 3/4" **$50-70**

Haskell-quality Three-leaf Dress Clip.
Courtesy of Davida Baron

Dress clip, goldplate, rhinestone & glass, designed as a cluster of three large finely detailed goldplate rounded scalloped leaves mounted w/smaller leaves & an openwork blossom all decorated w/glass beads in shades of pink & blue & hand-set w/clear rhinestones, attributed to Miriam Haskell, 2 3/4" w., 2 3/4" h. (ILLUS.) **$225-250**

Dress clip, metal & rhinestone, Art Deco style, the metal mount set w/large royal blue oval, marquise-cut & emerald-cut rhinestones, 1 5/8 x 3" **$125-150**

Dress clip, metal & rhinestone, the metal mount w/a seven row arrangement of yellow marquise-cut rhinestones, unsigned but resembles an Eisenberg design, 2 1/2" w., 3" h. **$200-225**

J

Earrings, goldplate, clip-on type, oval gold-plate rings w/a silver plated oval center, on original card, 7/8" l., pr. **$15-25**

Earrings, goldplate, designed as textured metal hoops w/a spring closure, on original card w/original price w/the federal luxury tax added in, ca. 1947, pr. **$30-45**

Earrings, goldplate & faux pearl, clip-on pendant style, designed as flowers set w/faux pearls & suspending seven snake chain dangles, 1" w., 5" l., pr. **$50-75**

Earrings, goldplate & rhinestone, clip-on pendant type, looped metal mounts set w/a row of rhinestones, the pear-shaped top w/large center stones, signed "Thelma Deutsch," 1 5/8" w., 3 1/4" l., pr. **$75-100**

Earrings, goldplate & rhinestone, clip-on type, triple goldplate loops decorated w/hand-set clear rhinestones at the ends, signed "SAC," early Sarah Coventry mark, 1 1/4" l., pr. **$55-80**

Unique Scrolled & Looping Pendant Earrings.
Courtesy of Joan Orlen

J

Earrings, goldplate & rhinestone, pendant-type, the goldplate teardrop-shaped open-work top set w/clear rhinestones & suspending a long inverted U pendant w/scrolled ends set w/clear rhinestones & entwined w/a double strand of gold twisted wire in a teardrop shape, signed "Thelma Deutsch," 1 1/2" w., 3 1/4" l. (ILLUS.) **$55-75**

Earrings, metal, glass stone & rhinestone, clip-on type, the metal framework decorated w/blue marquise-cut stone leaves w/clear rhinestone-set stems, unsigned but designer quality, 1 1/2 x 1 3/4", pr..... **$55-75**

Earrings, metal & rhinestone, designed as a pale lavender flower set w/large marquise-cut rhinestones w/an Aurora Borealis flower at the base, unsigned but designer quality, 1 7/8" l., pr. **$50-70**

Earrings, metal, rhinestone & glass stone, clip-on type, the mount w/a large emerald-cut amber center stone framed by pink opaque rainbow-finished marquise-cut glass stones, signed "Thelma Deutsch," 1 1/2 x 1 7/8", pr. **$40-75**

Earrings, sterling silver & hardstone, pendant-style, w/interchangeable drops of coral, turquoise or lapis lazuli, 1 1/4" l., pr. **$75-90**

Earrings, sterling silver, leaf motifs, screw-ons, mint in original box, 1 1/4", pr. **$40-55**

Earrings, sterling silver & turquoise, clip-on type, designed as a four-sided silver flower w/turquoise inlay, 7/8" l., pr. **$55-75**

Earrings, white metal & glass, clip-on type made to look like pierced-type, the metal mount w/a faceted red glass drop, 1 1/4" l., pr. **$25-35**

Fur clip, enameled metal & glass, the mount designed as a bouquet of enameled white flowers w/clear rhinestone centers, the large center flower of white poured glass w/an aqua rhinestone center, 3 1/2" l. **$125-150**

Fur clip, goldplate, glass & rhinestone, the metal mount centered by a gold flower w/a large oval green rhinestone center surrounded by lavender oval glass stones, an outer border of pink & purple oval glass stones alternating w/pavé-set clear rhinestone flowers, 2 x 3" **$200-225**

Fur clip, vermeil (gold over sterling silver) & rhinestone, Retro style, a ribbon design mount decorated w/two rows of rhinestones & a spray of red rhinestone flowers, signed "Corocraft Sterling," 1 1/2 x 2 1/4" **$175-200**

Fine Metal Deco Lady Head Fur Clips.
Courtesy of Joan Orlen

Fur clips, white metal, Art Deco style, each cast as the stylized head of an Art Deco woman w/tight curls around her head & a draped scarf at one side, 2 1/4" w., 3" h., pr. (ILLUS.) **$250-275**

Necklace, antique finished goldplate & rhinestone, composed of five openwork metal leaves each set w/a large citrine-colored pear-shaped rhinestone, smaller citrine-colored round & marquise stones accenting the leaves & forming the links leading to the clasp, signed "Hattie Carnegie," 1 1/4" w., overall 16 3/4" l. **$325-350**

Necklace, art glass beads, a rope strand composed of large dark colored glass beads w/long cylindrical art glass bead accents, 38" l. **$55-75**

Necklace, art glass beads, composed of molded & cut graduated glass beads in shades of amber & coffee, made in Czechoslovakia, 15" l. **$75-100**

Necklace, goldplate & glass bead, a triple strand of chains graduating in length & accented w/metal beads set w/red, blue & green marquise-cut stones around a center medallion, unsigned but designer quality, strands, 24", 28" & 33" l. **$80-110**

Necklace, goldplate & glass beads, an ornate design of graduated beads w/a large green cloisonné bead in the front, signed "Orena Paris," 16" l. **$45-65**

Necklace, goldplate & glass stone, a triple chain design suspending an ornate center charm w/a large ornate oval amber glass cabochon, signed "Goldette," chains 17" l., 25" l. & 34" l. **$30-50**

Necklace, goldplate & glass stone, composed of four rows of heavy goldplate chain w/two centered by emerald-cut amber stones, signed "Leo Glass," overall 21" l. **$125-150**

Necklace with Fleur-de-Lis Links.
Courtesy of Davida Baron

Necklace, goldplate & rhinestone, the front section composed of goldplate fleur-de-lis form links in a fringe design, each hand-set w/a large navette-cut emerald green rhinestone, snake chain leads to the clasp, signed "Barclay," 15" l. (ILLUS. of part) **$125-150**

Necklace, ivory bead, the ivory beads accented w/black beads & spacers, 24" l. **$125-150**

Necklace, plastic bead & rhinestone, amber colored graduated plastic beads each set w/black rhinestones & accented w/black beads & gold metal spacers, adjusts to 15" l. **$35-50**

Necklace, quartz beads, the clear quartz beads w/rhinestone spacers & a sterling silver clasp, 15" l. **$60-75**

Pretty Rhinestone Necklace.
Courtesy of Mary Ann Bosshart

Necklace, rhinestone & goldplate, the gold-tone necklace composed of links each set w/an amber rhinestone supporting a curved collar-form front drop bordered by the single bands of amber rhinestones enclosing a band of large graduated amber rhinestones each separated by a line of small Aurora Borealis clear rhinestones, unsigned but designer quality, ca. 1950, 15" l. (ILLUS.) **$100-125**

J

Fine Miriam Haskell Seed Pearl &
Rhinestone Floral Necklace

Necklace, Russian gold-plated metal, rhinestone & seed & simulated baroque pearl, composed of faux baroque pearl & tiny gilt metal bead links leading w/a design of deeply notched leaves alternating w/single rose blossoms each mounted w/gilt-metal sprigs & clear rhinestones, the center front w/a large three-flower cluster w/one rhinestone-set blossom & a small & large blossom w/looped seed pearl-set petals & a gilt-metal & large faux pearl center, marked "Miriam Haskell," ca. 1955, 17" l. (ILLUS. of part)...................... **$1,673**

Necklace, sterling silver, a silver chain suspending six old sterling heart charms, ca. 1920, 24" l. **$125-150**

Necklace, sterling silver, faux pearl & crystal, Art Nouveau style, the silver links set w/clear crystals & suspending a large faux pearl drop, early 20th c., 16" l. **$125-150**

Necklace, sterling silver & glass beads, Art Deco style, an ornate openwork silver drop set w/a black glass octagon w/a turquoise glass floral center, on two 8 1/2" l. silver chains accented by black & turquoise beads...................................... **$165-185**

Necklace, white metal & rhinestone, a twisted metal chain w/dangling clear half-sphere rhinestones, 15" l. **$95-120**

J

Fine Signed Trifari Rhinestone & Crystal Necklace. Courtesy of Davida Baron

Necklace, white metal, rhinestone & crystal, composed of long clear rhinestone-set links w/four graduated two-leaf links flanking a large central starflower design w/long marquise-cut red crystal petals around a rhinestone-set center, signed "Trifari," 13" l. (ILLUS.) **$300-325**

Pendant, enameled goldplate, flower-shaped w/turquoise enamels on a chain w/tiny balls, signed "Monet," adjusts from 16" to 18"... **$35-50**

Pendant, glass, Art Deco style, a carnelian-colored glass V-form about a pendant drop, white metal chain w/a carnelian glass-set clasp, 15" l. **$110-125**

Pendant, goldplate, modeled as a poodle w/blue rhinestone eyes, on a 25" l. chain... **$30-45**

Unusual Goldplate Pendant Necklace. Courtesy of Davida Baron

Pendant, goldplate, the chain of rectangular links suspending a large pendant composed of five staggered rows of matching links each suspending a filigree ball, the top of the pendant w/a plaque mounted w/two rows of matching filigree balls, signed "Pauline Rader," pendant 2 1/2 x 4 1/2", overall 28 1/2" l. (ILLUS.)...................... **$125-150**

Green Scarab Pendant on Long Chain. Author's Collection

Pendant, molded glass, a green glass scarab suspended on a goldplate link chain accented by round green glass beads, pendant 1 7/8" l., overall 24" l. (ILLUS.) **$95-125**

Pin, enameled metal & rhinestone, designed as a colorful bird on a branch, the long tail & body enameled in red, green & blue, tiny clear rhinestones between the tail feathers, 1 1/2" w., 2" h. **$35-55**

Pin, enameled metal & rhinestone, designed as a floral spray composed of turquoise, light blue & royal blue marquise-cut & pear-shaped rhinestones, blue enameled stems, signed "Fenichel," 2 3/4" w., 4 1/4" h. **$200-225**

Pin, enameled pewter, crystal & rhinestone, designed as a floral spray w/the flowers set w/oval blue & turquoise crystals, the leaves decorated w/pink oval crystals & the stems in brown enamel, attributed to Mazer, 3" w., 4" h. **$200-225**

Pin, enameled sterling silver, designed as a sea horse enameled in purple, lavender & pale blue, signed "David Andersen," 1 3/4 x 2" **$70-95**

Scrolled Metal & Glass Stone Pin.
Courtesy of Doris Skarka

Pin, gilded white metal & glass stones, the oblong openwork C-scroll metal mount set w/six various glass pseudo-gemstones, signed "Miracle," 1 5/8 x 2 1/4" (ILLUS.). **$75-100**

Fine Sorrell Originals Pin.
Courtesy of Davida Baron

Pin, glass stone, rhinestone & metal, the triangular shield-shaped metal mount mounted w/three large oblong purple tex-

tured glass stones alternating w/three pale blue faceted teardrop stones, centered by a yellow triangular stones & accented w/three smaller round faceted stones, each section bordered by small clear rhinestones, signed "Sorrell Originals," 3" w., 3" h. (ILLUS.).................. **$550-600**

Pin, goldplate & crystal, a stylized floral openwork design set w/emerald green, purple, pink & clear crystals, signed "Vogue," 2" w., 4 3/4" h. **$300-325**

Colorful Coro Floral Spray Pin.
Courtesy of Davida Baron

Pin, goldplate, crystal & rhinestone, designed as a goldplate floral spray mounted by a large rounded stylized flower composed of oval & marquise-cut multicolored crystals & rhinestones, the long upper stems further set w/marquise-cut & round purple & blue rhinestones, signed "Coro," 2 1/4" w., 4" h. (ILLUS.) **$250-275**

Pin, goldplate & faux cultured pearl, a heart design w/a central branch of leaves w/faux cultured pearl flowers, 1 x 1" **$45-65**

Pin, goldplate & faux pearl, designed as a starfish w/each arm set w/faux pearls, signed "DeNicola," 2" w.......................... **$50-75**

Pin, goldplate, faux pearl & rhinestone, an openwork floral-designed mount set w/faux pearls & a rhinestone center in the flowers, 2 3/4" w., 1 3/4" h. **$35-55**

Pin, goldplate, figural cartoon-style girl holding a mirror & applying lipstick, matte gold finish w/shiny gold accents, signed "J.J.," 2 x 2 1/2" **$25-40**

Pin, goldplate & glass stone, an oval domed mount w/a flower arrangement centered by an oval green glass cabochon stone, Austria, 1 x 1 1/4".................................... **$45-65**

Pin, goldplate & glass stone, Art Nouveau style, an openwork mount centered by a purple stone, 1 1/8 x 1 1/4" **$65-85**

J

Pin, sterling silver & bicolor gold, an oval silver mount w/two flowers in yellow & pink gold, Victorian, 1 1/2" w. **$135-155**

Pin, sterling silver, designed as a cluster of scallop shells, 1 1/2" w., 3/4" h. **$30-50**

Pin, sterling silver, designed as a thistle inside an open circle, signed "Danecraft," 1 1/2" d. **$45-70**

Pin, sterling silver, marcasite & glass stone, Art Deco style, the mount in the form of a circle enclosing two black glass half-circles, marcasites in the border & center, 1 1/4" d. **$75-100**

Pin, sterling silver, marcasite & rhinestone, model of a bird w/a full tail perched on a branch, a green glass cabochon body, amber marquise-cut rhinestone eye, marcasite trim on the head, body & tail, Alice Caviness, 1" w., 3" h. **$125-150**

Pin, sterling silver & pink gold overlay, designed as two water lily leaves, signed "Forstener," 2 3/4" **$65-85**

Pin, sterling silver, Retro style, designed as a circle w/two flowers & stems, 1 1/2" d.**$75-100**

Pin, white metal, a wreath design w/an oval opening for a tiny photo, Victorian, photo missing **$50-70**

Pin, white metal & art glass, the oval metal mount w/an open scalloped border, centered by a white glass cabochon, 1 x 1 1/4" **$25-40**

Pin, white metal & glass stone, a carnelian-colored large faceted stone set in a white metal frame w/openwork prongs, 1 x 1 1/2" **$45-65**

Pin, white metal, glass stone & rhinestone, Art Deco style, a rectangular metal frame w/a green swirled glass bow centered by a black stone, rhinestone-set frame, 3/4 x 1 1/2" **$45-75**

Pin, white metal & Peking glass, Art Deco style, the white metal frame decorated w/stamped lines & diamond designs & centered by a green Peking glass stone, 1/2 x 1 5/8" **$45-70**

Pin-pendant, 800 grade silver, the silver filigree mount mounted w/a painted outdoor scene under glass, coral ball accents, 1 3/4" **$95-120**

Pin-pendant, enameled goldplate & natural stone, the oval mount w/a grey enameled ground, a purple striped agate in the center w/applied gold designs & accented w/garnets & small dark purple stones, signed "Michael Golan," 1 3/4" w., 1" h... **$65-90**

Pin-pendant, goldplate, glass stone & rhinestone, the mount designed as a flower arrangement set w/large ribbed coral-colored glass pear-shaped stones & smooth black large pear-shaped & oval glass stones, all inside the goldplate frame trimmed w/clear rhinestones, signed "Panetta," 2 1/2" w., 2 3/4" h.... **$250-300**

Pin-pendant, rhinestone & goldplate, the mount in an openwork snowflake design decorated w/clear marquise-cut & round rhinestones, 1" d. **$30-50**

Pin-pendant, white metal & art glass, the oval open metal frame enclosing four leaves w/an oval purple & white art glass stone in the center, 1 1/4 x 1 1/2" **$40-60**

Ring, sterling silver, a double loop w/the front center set w/a heart-shaped cubic zirconium.. **$100-125**

Fine Chanel 1960s Pendant-Necklace

Sautoir (pendant-necklace), gilt chain, pate-de-verre stone & faux pearl, the slender multi-strand gilt chain mounted w/two oval green glass stones imitating emeralds & flanked by coiled gilt-metal snakes, a pair of coiled snake links at the bottom suspending a squared metal link w/a glass faux pearl drop, coiled snake clasp, marked "Chanel" followed by three stars, Robert Goossens, France, ca. 1965, 36" l. (ILLUS.)................................. **$1,434**

Watch pin, white metal, Art Nouveau style, crescent-shape w/clover leaves, 1 x 1 1/4"... **$40-55**

Sets

Colorful Plastic Bead Necklace & Bracelet by Coppola & Toppo

Necklace & bracelet, plastic bead, each designed as a wide band of plastic beads

J

in orange, burgundy, green & clear mounted by hand on weft of plastic beads, marked "Coppola Toppo," for Ken Scott, Italy, 1965, bracelet 7" l., necklace 17" l., the suite (ILLUS.)............................ **$1,016**

imitating rubies & citrine & pear-shaped glass stones imitating onyx, necklace marked "Ugo Correani - Made in Italy," designed by Guanni Versace, Italy, ca. 1991-1992, brooch 3" d., necklace 22" l., the suite (ILLUS. of necklace) **$956**

Unusual Haskell Faux Pearl Flower Suite

Necklace, bracelet & pin, faux pearl, the necklace w/triple strands of small faux pearls suspending a row of three stylized flowers w/the pointed petals set overall w/seed pearls & centered by a large faux pearl, each flower joined by pearl-set leaf-form links, the matching bracelet w/multiple faux pearl stands set w/a pearl-set large blossom, the long pin decorated w/a row of faux pearl flowers, marked by Miriam Haskell, 1960-64, pin 4 1/2" l., bracelet 8" l., necklace 16 1/2" l., the suite (ILLUS.)...................... **$2,271**

Stylized Flower Basket Jewelry Suite

Necklace & earrings, faux baroque pearls, pate-de-verre glass beads, goldplated metal, stylized flower basket design, the necklace w/an asymmetrical design w/twisted black silk cords mounted on one side w/a cluster of faux baroque pearls & green glass leaves & beads, the front w/a pair of short links of faux pearls & green beads on each side attached to an inverted flower basket design w/the seed pearl basket issuing a large cluster of faux baroque pearls, green glass leaves & beads, each small basket joined by longer green bead & small pearl links to a very long horizontally-set stylized flower basket matching the smaller baskets, each earring designed as a single seed pearl basket filled w/green glass leaves & beads & faux baroque pearls, by Rivière, marked "Made in France," ca. 1950, earrings 1 3/8" l, necklace 15" l., the suite (ILLUS.).. **$657**

Necklace & earrings, glass bead, the triple strand necklace composed of small faceted round blue beads alternating w/graduated larger faceted Aurora Borealis round beads w/rows of the largest beads at the bottom of each strand, the clip-on earrings composed of small blue round faceted beads in a stylized flower form, necklace adjusts from 14" to 16", the set (ILLUS., next page)................. **$150-175**

Maltese Cross Brooch from Suite

Necklace & brooch, goldplated metal, plexiglass & glass stones, the four-strand necklace w/three Maltese cross ornaments w/polychrome enamel & rhinestones, the brooch composed of a ball of transparent plexiglass mounted w/a Maltese cross set w/square-cut glass stones

J

Necklace & Earrings in Blue Faceted Glass Beads. Courtesy of Doris Skarka

Chinese-made Fancy Necklace & Earring Set. Courtesy of Shirley Dreyer

Necklace & earrings, goldplate & rhinestone, the necklace w/a single strand of oval goldplate links accented w/round purple rhinestones continuing to a double chain joined by three cross-links set w/pairs of small pink rhinestones, the front center w/a large goldplate openwork quatrefoil design w/each petal set w/small pink & purple rhinestones all centered by a large round purple rhinestone, three fancy link drops set w/pink & purple rhinestones, the pendant-style earrings

w/a single purple rhinestone above a drop set w/three pink & purple rhinestones, made in China, necklace adjustable to 24" l., the set (ILLUS.) **$80-100**

Necklace & earrings, rhinestone & goldplate, the necklace composed of clear diamond-shaped & marquise-cut rhinestone links suspending a large clear pear-shaped rhinestone drop, the screwon earrings w/a large pear-shaped rhinestone drop, earrings 1 1/8" l., necklace 14" l., the set **$175-200**

Necklace & earrings, rhinestone, the necklace w/clear rhinestone links suspending a large mount bordered by clear rhinestones centered by multicolored round, emerald-cut, oval & square rhinestones, unsigned but designer quality, clip-on earrings 1 1/2 x 2", necklace 17" l., the set **$75-100**

Pin & earrings, chrome & plastic, the pin w/a four-lobed chrome mount centered by a large red plastic cabochon, the matching earrings w/three lobes & also set w/a red cabochon, earrings 2 x 2 1/2", pin 2 3/4 x 3", the set **$50-70**

Fine Trifari "Lyre Bird" Set. Courtesy of Davida Baron

Pin & earrings, vermeil, crystal & rhinestone, the pin designed as a graceful long-tailed flying bird w/the body set w/a large red glass cabochon, the edge of the goldplate wings & top of the tail set w/pink oval crystals, the head & lower body trimmed w/tiny clear rhinestones w/scattered rhinestones on the long openwork tail, the earrings w/a vermeil scroll ending in a cluster of oval pink crystals around a red glass cabochon, signed "Trifari," known as the "lyre bird" design, pin 3" l., the set (ILLUS.) **$800-825**

Pins, plastic & fur, each in the shape of a cat face, one w/black fur, one w/white fur & one w/auburn fur, plastic eyes & noses, each 2 x 2", the set of 3 .... **$25-40**

Set of Four Rhinestone & White Metal Pins. Courtesy of Davida Baron

Pins, rhinestone & white metal, each designed as a stylized floral spray, one w/red marquise-cut rhinestone flowers & gold & clear rhinestone-set leaves & stems, the second set w/royal blue marquise-cut rhinestones w/the gold & clear rhinestone trim, the third w/turquoise marquise-cut rhinestones & the gold & clear rhinestone trim & the fourth w/green marquise-cut rhinestones & the gold & clear rhinestone trim, unsigned, attributed to Staret, each 2 1/2" w., 4" h., set of four, each (ILLUS.) **$150-175**

Modern (1920-1950s)

Art Deco

Bar pin, diamond, sapphire & platinum, the narrow oblong openwork mount set w/a row of five bezel-set marquise-cut diamonds alternating w/six small step-cut sapphires, diamonds weighing about 1.30 cts. (ILLUS., top next column) **$1,880**

Art Deco Diamond & Sapphire Bar Pin

Bar pin, platinum & diamond, the bar slightly swelling at the center & bead-set w/a line of 19 old European-cut diamonds weighing about 3.35 cts. (ILLUS. top with Art Deco diamond bow pin, bottom of page) **$2,468**

Diamond & Opal Art Deco Bar Pin

Bar pin, platinum, opal & diamond, a long oval openwork mount centered by a row of three opal cabochons, the border & central leaf-form designs set w/old European- and mine-cut diamonds, millegrain accents, diamonds weighing about 1.98 cts., 2" l. (ILLUS.) **$1,528**

American Art Deco Bar Pin

Bar pin, platinum, sapphire & diamond, bezel-set w/eight circular-cut Montana sapphires interspersed w/sixteen old European-cut diamond mélée, millegrain accents, American maker's mark (ILLUS.) **$1,998**

J

Two Art Deco Diamond & Platinum Pins

French Art Deco Sapphire & Diamond Bar Pin

Stunning Art Deco Emerald-accented Diamond Bracelet

Bar pin, sapphire, diamond & gold, centered by a large step-cut sapphire flanked by thin pointed panels w/calibré-cut sapphires, the thin tapering sides set overall w/rose- and circular-cut diamonds, millegrain accents, platinum-topped 18k gold mount, French guarantee stamp, one diamond missing (ILLUS., top of page) **$1,410**

Bracelet, cultured pearl & diamond, centering a white pearl measuring about 6.80 mm, flanked by bezel-set old European-cut diamonds, completed by a bracelet of platinum-topped 14k gold open links, millegrain accents, 7 1/2" l. **$441**

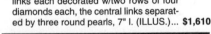

Art Deco Diamond & Pearl Bracelet

J **Bracelet,** diamond, baroque pearl & white gold, composed of 15 rectangular hinged links each decorated w/two rows of four diamonds each, the central links separated by three round pearls, 7" l. (ILLUS.)... **$1,610**

Extraordinary Art Deco Diamond Bracelet with Entwined Bands Accented with Emeralds

Bracelet, diamond, emerald & platinum, a wide flat band w/narrow thin outer band set w/old European-cut diamonds, the wide central band design w/entwined rows of diamonds each section centered by a marquise-cut diamond, the whole centered by a large bezel-set rectangular steo-cut diamond weighing 1.65 cts., the other diamonds weighing about 15.70 cts., the entwined rows accented w/tiny triangular emerald highlights, millegrain accents, missing two emeralds, 7 1/2" l. (ILLUS.)................................ **$24,675**

Bracelet, diamond, emerald & platinum, the side bands composed of two rows of bead-set full-cut diamonds, joined to the central section by squared diamond-set links, the central band composed of three rows of bead- and bezel-set full- and transitional-cut diamonds flanking a wider center section w/a large marquise-cut diamond framed by a narrow band of calibré-cut emeralds, diamonds weighing about 4.28 cts., 7" l. (ILLUS., second from top)................................ **$6,169**

Rare Tiffany Diamond & Black Onyx Art Deco Line Bracelet

Bracelet, diamond, onyx & platinum, linetype, designed w/articulated links centered by a band of old European-cut diamonds accented by triple-band sections set w/full-cut diamonds, the narrow border bands channel-set w/black onyx, millegrain accents, signed by Tiffany & Co., missing on onyx, 7 1/8" l. (ILLUS.)........ **$16,450**

Bracelet, diamond & platinum, a long narrow design bead-set down the center w/81 old European-cut diamonds weighing about 3.24 cts., millegrain accents, 6 7/8" l. (ILLUS. top, below) **$8,813**

Art Deco Platinum Bracelet Set with 81 European-cut Diamonds

Very Rare Simple Art Deco Diamond & Platinum Bracelet

Art Deco Diamond Bracelet with Straight & Round Links

Art Deco Bracelet with Diamond Line Links Centering a Swelled Plaque of Diamonds & Tiny Sapphires

Bracelet, diamond & platinum, a narrow straight band box-set w/17 old European-cut diamonds, further bead-set w/60 full-cut diamond mélée, pierced & engraved platinum gallery, millegrain accents, 7" l. (ILLUS., bottom previous page).. **$17,625**

Bracelet, diamond & platinum, composed of thin line links connected by round links w/a center cross band, bead-set overall w/single- and old European-cut diamonds, further bezel-set w/diamond baguettes, total weight about 2.58 cuts., open gallery, millegrain accents, 7 1/4" l. (ILLUS., top of page).............................. **$6,169**

Very Fine Art Deco Platinum, Sapphire and Diamond Line Bracelet

Bracelet, diamond, sapphire & platinum, line-type, composed of double rows of bead-set old European-, single- and full-cut diamonds accented w/palmette & sprig designs, the center section flanked by thin rows of calibré-cut sapphires, the center bezel-set w/an Assche-cut diamond weighing .82 cts., millegrain accents, other diamonds weighing about 5.42 cts., 7 1/4" l. (ILLUS.)...................... **$9,988**

Bracelet, diamond, sapphire & platinum, the line-form side bands set w/a graduated line of diamonds, the swelled central plaque centering a larger circular-cut diamond framed w/a tiny square of baguette-cut sapphires, the remainder of the plaque further set w/diamonds, ca. 1920s (ILLUS., second from top)........... **$5,520**

Bracelet, emerald, diamond & platinum, a wide band swelling at the center, centered by a large sugarloaf cabochon emerald & flanked down the sides w/seven smaller emerald cabochons, all framed by geometric designs w/ 214 old mine-, single- and European-cut diamonds weighing about 5.32 cts., millegrain accents, engraved gallery, mark of French maker, w/two additional emerald & diamond links, 6 1/4" l. (ILLUS., second from bottom of page)............... **$18,800**

Art Deco Enameled Gold & Hardstone Bracelet

Bracelet, enameled 14k gold & hardstone, composed of shaped polychrome enamel plaques joined by carved nephrite & gold links, illegible mark of an American maker, one link removed, 7" l. (ILLUS.) .. **$1,410**

J

Very Fine Diamond & Emerald Cabochon Art Deco Bracelet

Extraordinary Pearl, Sapphire, Diamond & Platinum Cartier Art Deco Bracelet

Bracelet, pearl, sapphire, diamond & platinum, the central plaque of squared design centered by a cluster of sugarloaf sapphires framed by circular-cut diamonds & flanked by fleur-de-lis shaped & geometric links also set w/diamonds & a single sapphire, joined by multi-strand seed pearl bracelets completed by a rectangular clasp set w/two sapphires framed by diamonds, millegrain accents, signed by Cartier, New York, boxed, w/additional pearls & platinum links, 6 3/4" l. (ILLUS.).. **$44,650**

Two Extraordinary Art Deco Diamond & Sapphire & Diamond Bracelets

Art Deco Diamond Bracelet with Long Geometric Links

Bracelet, platinum & diamond, composed of long geometric links centered by a marquise-cut diamond flanked by an openwork frame set w/single-cut diamond & joined by pairs of small open geometric links further set w/single-cut diamonds, diamonds weighing about 1.40 cts., 6 1/2" l. (ILLUS.) **$2,585**

Bracelet, platinum & diamond, composed of long links w/round open ends decorated w/openwork designs of palmette leaves flanking a bar w/a marquise-cut diamond, alternating w/small double-loop links, set overall w/old European-cut & baguette diamonds, diamonds weighing about 4.41 cts., 7" l. (ILLUS. bottom with simple Art Deco diamond line bracelet, top of page 759) **$8,225**

Bracelet, platinum & diamond, composed of long openwork rectangular links centered by a large old European-cut diamond flanked by marquise-cut diamonds all bordered by old mine-cut & baguette dia-

monds & alternating w/long open oval links further set w/diamonds, diamonds weighing about 16.20 cts., 7" l. (ILLUS. top with Kashmir sapphire & diamond Art Deco bracelet, top of page) **$22,235**

Slender Art Deco Diamond Bracelet with Zigzag & Rectangular Open Links

Bracelet, platinum & diamond, composed of narrow section of diamond-set links in a zigzag design alternating w/rectangular open diamond-set links, diamond weighing about 1.92 cts., 7" l. (ILLUS.) **$4,465**

Bracelet, platinum, diamond & emerald, a narrow strap band composed of sections w/two outer bands of bead-set full-cut diamonds flanking a center channel-set band of step-cut emeralds, these bands alternating w/openwork rectangular panels w/a geometric design of bezel-set French & marquise-cut diamonds, diamonds weighing about 7.73 cts., mark of Jung & Klitz, New York, New York, 7 1/8" l. (ILLUS. bottom with other fine Art Deco diamond & emerald bracelet, bottom of page) **$24,675**

Two Very Fine Art Deco Diamond & Emerald Bracelets

Bracelet, platinum, diamond & emerald, a wide flat strap bezel- and bead-set overall w/narrow bands of full-cut diamonds accented by four square-cut diamonds framed by calibré-cut emeralds alternating w/eight rectangular step-cut diamonds flanked by emerald accents, diamonds weighing about 12.45 cts., millegrain accents, open gallery, 7 1/8" l. (ILLUS. top with other diamond & emerald Art Deco bracelet) **$28,200**

A Simple Art Deco Diamond Line Bracelet & a Fancy Openwork Bracelet

Bracelet, platinum & diamond, line-type, the thin band of square links each box-set w/an old European-cut diamond, diamonds weighing about 8.00 cts. foliate-engraved edges, 6 3/4" l. (ILLUS. top with fancy openwork Art Deco diamond bracelet) **$9,988**

Rare Art Deco Diamond & Onyx Bracelet

Bracelet, platinum, diamond & onyx, bead-set w/full-cut diamonds forming a zigzag design among pairs of small triangular buff-top onyx, diamonds weighing about 4.18 cts., millegrain accents, engraved edges, 7 1/8" l. (ILLUS.) **$11,163**

Two Fine Art Deco Diamond & Sapphire Bracelets

Bracelet platinum, diamond & sapphire, a simple thin band of square diamond links swelled at the top & centered by a larger old marquise-cut diamond surrounded by calibré-cut sapphire highlights, various old European-, transitional- and single-cut diamonds, diamonds weighing about 2.45 cts., millegrain accents, boxed (ILLUS. top with other Art Deco sapphire & diamond bracelet) **$5,875**

Rare Art Deco Diamond Bracelet Centered by a Large Marquise Diamond

J

Bracelet, platinum & diamond, tapering bands swelled in the center & bezel-set w/an old marquise-cut diamond weighing about 1.50 cts & set upright, the bracelet set w/30 graduating box-set old mine-cut diamonds weighing about 9.30 cts., millegrain accents, 6 3/4" l. (ILLUS.) **$19,975**

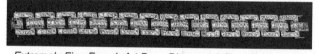

Extremely Fine French Art Deco Diamond & Emerald Bracelet

Bracelet, platinum, emerald & diamond, composed of rectangular diamond-set links joined by wide bars composed of two rows of channel-set emeralds flanking a band of diamonds, bead-set overall w/168 old European-cut diamonds weighing about 11.76 cts., French guarantee stamp & mark of the maker, 7 1/2" l. (ILLUS., above) **$25,850**

Bracelet, platinum, Kashmir sapphire & diamond, line-type, designed w/14 bezel-set old cushion-cut sapphires, joined by rectangular links set w/39 full-cut & 78 single-cut diamonds, millegrain accents, w/two additional diamonds & one sapphire link, 6 3/4" l. (ILLUS. bottom with very fine and rare wide Art Deco diamond bracelet, top page 758) **$39,950**

Bracelet, platinum, peridot, diamond & 14k white gold, composed of filigree links alternating w/five box-set transitional-cut diamonds & 12 box-set square-cut peridots, engraved & millegrain accents, mark of an American maker, 6 3/4" l. **$999**

American-made Art Deco Rock Crystal & Diamond Bracelet

Extraordinary Art Deco Openwork Sapphire & Diamond Bracelet

Bracelet, platinum, sapphire & diamond, a long slender form composed of long narrow loop links bead-set w/old European- and single-cut diamonds alternating w/straight links channel-set w/step-cut sapphires, signed by Tiffany & Co., ca. 1930, 7" l. **$6,169**

Bracelet platinum, synthetic sapphire & diamond, set w/square step-cut sapphires separated by a single-cut diamond & flanked by pairs of square single-cut diamond links, engraved edges, diamonds weighing about 1.50 cts., 6 3/4" l. (ILLUS. bottom w/other Art Deco diamond & sapphire bracelet, previous page) **$5,875**

Bracelet, rock crystal, diamond & 14k white gold, composed of five rounded incised rock crystal links centered by a single diamond & framed by a narrow ring of diamonds, alternating w/small double rectangular engraved links, mark of Krementz & Co., Newark, New Jersey, 7 1/4" l. (ILLUS., top of page) **$1,175**

Bracelet, sapphire, diamond & gold, composed of four-petal flower links set w/old European- and mine-cut diamonds joined by openwork blue sapphires centered by a row of three diamonds, diamonds weighing about 6.51 cuts., platinum & 18k gold mount, 6 7/8" l. (ILLUS., second from top of page) **$23,500**

Bracelet, silver, enamel & marcasite, the hinged plaques w/enameled geometric & leafy designs in green, blue, pink & yellow decorated w/marcasite highlights, stamped 935 & w/a European hallmark, enamel losses, 7" l. **$823**

Bracelet, sterling silver, green chalcedony & marcasite, composed of oval links set w/marcasite & centering a gently arched

bar of green chalcedony, marked by Theodor Fahrner, 7 1/4" l. (ILLUS., bottom of page) **$705**

Brooch, aquamarine, rock crystal & 14k white gold, the center bezel-set w/a fancy-cut aquamarine flanked by box-set full-cut diamond accents on a shaped carved crystal plaque, openwork gallery, boxed **$764**

Brooch, diamond & 14k white gold, the filigree navette-shaped piece bead-set w/five full-cut diamonds & four green stone accents... **$353**

Art Deco Diamond Bar-form Brooch

Brooch, diamond, gold & enamel, the long bar w/an oval central reserve, the oval centered by a row of three large old European-cut diamonds outlined by black enamel & surrounded by a band of old mine- and rose-cut diamonds, the side bars also set w/diamonds, diamonds weighing about 2.25 cts., Russian hallmarks, platinum-topped 14k gold mount, 2 1/2" l. (ILLUS.)............................. **$1,200-1,500**

Brooch, diamond, onyx & platinum, circle-style, a large slender open circle set w/single-cut diamonds & mounted at one edge w/a large ribbon bow set w/overall single-cut diamonds bordered by thin bands of channel-set onyx, the bottom mounted w/flexible diamond-set & onyx fringe, 2 1/4" w. (ILLUS., next page) **$5,288**

Silver, Chalcedony & Marcasite Fahrner Art Deco Bracelet

Unusual Circle & Bow Art Deco Brooch

Long Ornate Diamond-set Brooch

Brooch, diamond & platinum, the long openwork curved mount w/pointed ends & arched sides set overall w/old European-cut, baguette, tapered baguette, old single- and full-cut diamonds weighing about 6.00 cts., signed by Lambert Bros., 2 3/4" l. (ILLUS.)..................................... **$3,819**

Rare Fancy Deco Diamond-set Brooch

Brooch, diamond & platinum, the ornate openwork mount w/a spearpoint top centering a large marquise-cut diamond framed by old mine-, European- and full-cut diamonds above a long C-scroll set w/baguette & full-cut diamonds above a wide tapering openwork frame w/top &

bottom scrolls all set w/further diamonds & connected down the center by another large marquise-cut diamond, diamonds weighing about 9.07 cts., 14k white gold pin stem, 2 7/8" l. (ILLUS.)..................... **$7,931**

Fancy Art Deco Diamond Brooch

Brooch, diamond & platinum, the wide rectangular openwork plaque w/slightly pointed ends bead-set overall w/old European-cut diamonds weighing about 5.51 cts., millegrain accents, 2 1/2" l. (ILLUS.) **$3,760**

Fine Art Deco Diamond & Sapphire Brooch

Brooch, diamond, sapphire & platinum, a rectangular form swelled in the middle, the openwork mount w/designs of circles, arches & lines, centered by a cushion-cut blue sapphire flanked by larger old European-cut diamonds w/three larger diamonds at each end, the background set overall w/small full- and old single-cut diamonds, total diamonds weighing about 5.17 cts., engraved edges, minor solder at pin stem, 2" l. (ILLUS.)....................... **$5,581**

J

Rare Art Deco Rose Vase Gem-set Brooch

Brooch, frosted rock crystal, ruby, diamond & platinum, designed as an ovoid rock crystal vase trimmed w/small baguette & single-cut diamonds & holding a flaring bouquet of roses w/leafy stems, the leafy stems set w/transitional- and old European-cut diamonds, the blossoms set w/buff-top rubies, 1 5/8" h. (ILLUS., previous page).. **$5,875**

Dramatic Art Deco Floral Bouquet Brooch

Brooch, gem-set platinum & diamond, designed as a large stylized floral bouquet w/the stems & flower rims set w/full-cut diamonds centering or accented by various shapes of carved rubies, emeralds & sapphires, 1 3/4" l. (ILLUS.) **$5,288**

Jadeite & Enameled Gold Deco Brooch

Brooch, jadeite & enameled 14k gold, the thin oblong gold band frame accented w/four black-enameled leaf sprigs enclosing the oval pierce-carved green jadeite plaque, 1 1/2" l. (ILLUS.) **$441**

Swirled Flower Gem-set Gold Brooch

Brooch, pearl, sapphire & 18k yellow gold, flower-form w/the gold mount composed of swirled leaves around a central cluster of seven pearls interspersed w/tiny blue sapphires, ca. 1930, 1 3/4" d. (ILLUS.)...... **$748**

Brooch, platinum & diamond, bead-set w/23 old European-cut diamonds, openwork floral designs & millegrain accents **$940**

Brooch, platinum & diamond, bead-set w/72 old mine-cut & old single-cut diamonds & ten blue stone highlights w/millegrain accents, diamonds weighing about 2.00 cts., 2 1/2" l. **$752**

Art Deco Circle & Bow Diamond Brooch

Brooch, platinum & diamond, circle-type, the ring set w/one side w/a stylized bow suspending a flexible pendant, bead- and prong-set overall w/41 old European-cut diamonds weighing about 2.62 cts. (ILLUS.).. **$2,233**

French Art Deco Openwork Diamond Brooch

Brooch, platinum & diamond, oblong shape w/two open center rectangular loops & openwork spearpoint devices, centered by a single large circular-cut old European-cut diamond w/the rest of the mount set w/single-cut diamonds, diamonds weighing about 3.30 cts., French hallmarks (ILLUS.).. **$2,585**

Art Deco Diamond, Sapphire & Pearl Brooch

Very Rare Cartier Green Tourmaline & Diamond Brooch

Brooch, platinum, diamond, sapphire & pearl, elongated diamond shaped centering a row of eight white pearls w/rose overtones, flanked by thin rows of rectangular-cut sapphires & a circular-cut large sapphire at the top & bottom center & a cluster of three more sapphires at each end, further decorated overall w/bead-set full- and single-cut diamond mélée, sapphires later replacements, pearls not tested for origin, 1 3/4" l. (ILLUS., previous page) **$2,115**

Rectangular Platinum & Diamond Brooch

Brooch, platinum & diamond, wide rectangular openwork design w/beveled corners, bead- and bezel-set overall w/old mine-, European- and single-cut diamonds, millegrain accents, diamonds weighing about 5.92 cts., accompanied by an 18k gold frame, 2" l. (ILLUS.) **$3,819**

Brooch, platinum, green tourmaline, diamond & enamel, a flattened stylized barbell shape, end round end prong-set w/a large fancy-cut tourmaline w/a large square tormaline in the center, all framed by pavé-set diamonds w/black enamel accents, signed "Cartier," No. 3597, 2" l. (ILLUS., top of page) **$23,500**

Art Deco Green Jade & Diamond Brooch

Brooch, platinum, jade & diamond, centered by a long oval green jade plaque pierce-carved w/leafy vines, flowers & berries, each end w/a curved openwork band bead-set w/16 full-cut diamonds, millegrain accents (ILLUS.) **$3,055**

Fancy Jadeite & Diamond Deco Brooch

Brooch, platinum, jadeite & diamond, two round green jadeite disks pierced & carved w/leaves flanking a central carved jadeite fish, all mounted in an ornate openwork scrolling mount bead-set w/single- and full-cut diamonds, diamonds weighing about 1.20 cts., signed by Grant's, London, England, 2 1/4" l. (ILLUS.) **$2,468**

Art Deco Rock Crystal-centered Brooch

Brooch, rock crystal, coral & marcasite, rectangular, the rock crystal center tablet enclosed by a narrow frame w/blue glass corners, coral bead & marcasite sides, partially obscured stamped mark of Theodor Fahrner, 1 3/4" l. (ILLUS.) **$705**

French Art Deco Sapphire & Diamond Brooch

Brooch, sapphire, diamond & platinum, elongated open octagonal frame centered by a large bezel-set circular-cut blue sapphire within a frame of single-cut diamonds & a thin bar mounted w/two old European-cut diamonds, the outer frame set w/single-cut diamonds & two larger European-cut diamonds at each end, diamonds weighing about 2.70 cts., French

J

guarantee stamps, one cushion-shape diamond chipped, 1 7/8" l. (ILLUS.) **$3,525**

Filigree & Diamond Rectangular Brooch

Brooch-pendant, diamond & platinum, a filigree stepped long rectangular mount w/pointed ends set w/two larger old mine-cut diamonds & scattered small transitional-cut diamonds, diamonds weighing about 1.54 cts., retractable pendant bail, 1 3/4" l. (ILLUS.).. **$881**

Diamond & Platinum Art Deco Clip

Clip, diamond & platinum, arched shape w/the openwork mount designed w/a central undulating ribbon & straight & fanned bars, the top centered by a full-cut diamond weighing about .75 cts., further set w/four baguette- and 37 full-cut diamond mélée, diamonds weighing about 2.60 cts. (ILLUS.) **$1,763**

Clip, enameled bicolor 14k gold, the polychrome enameled flower w/seed pearl accent within an engraved frame, marked by Krementz & Co., Newark, New Jersey **$353**

Art Deco Onyx & Diamond Cuff Links

Cuff links, onyx & diamond, each double link designed as an onyx disk bisected by a band of old single-cut diamonds, millegrain accents, joined by 18k white gold bars, pr. (ILLUS.)..................................... **$1,528**

Fancy Diamond & Pearl Art Deco Clip

Dress clip, diamond, pearl & platinum, the openwork design of draped ribbons centered by an old European-cut diamond weighing about .75 cts. & a teardrop-form black pearl measuring about 10.05 x 8.25 mm, bead-set overall w/rose-, old mine-, single- and old European-cut diamonds weighing about 1.96 cts., white pearl highlights, millegrain accents, 1 1/4" l. (ILLUS.) **$6,463**

Very Fine Diamond Scroll Dress Clips

Dress clips, diamond & platinum, each designed as a tight banded scroll, bezel- and bead-set w/114 full-cut, twelve baguette-cut and 74 single-cut diamonds, total weight about 11.96 cts., French platinum guarantee stamp, ca. 1935, facing pair (ILLUS.).. **$25,850**

Very Fine Cartier Deco Dress Clips

Dress clips, diamond & platinum, openwork spade-form mounts, each set w/an outer

J

& inner band of bead- and bezel-set baguette, square-, transitional- and old European-cut diamonds, 18k white gold
findings, diamonds weighing about 7.16
cts., signed by Cartier, in original fitted
box, w/18k white gold frame for brooch
conversion, pr. (ILLUS.) **$30,550**

Art Deco Bar & Fan Diamond Clips

Dress clips, platinum & diamond, each
w/the top composed of horizontal bars
above slightly fanned vertical bars, set
overall w/baguette, marquise- & old European-cut diamonds weighing about
5.75 cts., w/white gold frame for conver-
sion to a brooch (ILLUS.) **$6,169**

Very Fine Diamond & Pearl Earrings

Earrings, diamond, cultured pearl & platinum, pendant-type, a drop chain w/long
links set overall w/bead- and bezel-set
old European-cut diamonds, suspending
a white cultured pearl w/rose overtones
measuring about 15.50 to 16.40 mm., diamond weighing about 1.86 cts., 2 1/4" l.,
pr. (ILLUS.) **$4,700**

Rare Art Deco Diamond Drop Earrings

Earrings, diamond & platinum, drop-style,
each suspending a marquise-cut diamond
drop framed by two navette hoops bead-
set w/single-cut diamonds, suspended
from a line of bead- and bezel-set old Eu-
ropean- and single-cut diamonds, total diamond weight about 2.4 cts., later screw-
back findings, pr. (ILLUS.) **$12,925**

Art Deco Five-Diamond Drop Earrings

Earrings, diamond & platinum, pendant-
type, each composed of a drop of five be-
zel- and prong-set old European- and
mine-cut diamonds weighing about 2.90
cts., later 14k white gold findings, boxed,
pr. (ILLUS.) **$2,585**

J

Art Deco Jadeite Bead Necklace with Gem-set Spacers

French Art Deco Diamond Lorgnette

J

Lorgnette, diamond, the flat diamond-shaped covers bead-set overall w/rose-cut diamonds, millegrain accents & engraved edges, platinum-topped 18k gold mount, maker of Degorce Freres, Paris, France & guarantee stamps, together w/a silver baton link & seed pearl chain, overall 23" l. (ILLUS. of lorgnette) **$3,173**

Necklace, jadeite, diamond & onyx, the pale green jadeite beads arranged in groups of two or three & separated by small cylindrical green enamel, onyx & rose-cut diamond spacers, later 14k white gold clasp, some enamel loss, 13 3/4" l. (ILLUS., top of page) **$646**

Necklace, onyx, diamond & platinum, composed of five narrow rectangular links centered by an oval onyx plaque decorated w/a flower & leaf design set w/single-cut diamonds & framed by further small diamonds, completed by a delicate trace link chain, 16 1/2" l. (ILLUS., bottom of page) **$2,938**

Unusual Onyx, Diamond & Platinum Art Deco Necklace

Delicate Platinum & Diamond Pendant

Pendant, platinum & diamond, the delicate openwork geometric tapering mount bead-set w/old European-cut diamond & millegrain accents, suspended from a delicate 14k white gold baton link chain, pendant 1 3/4" l. (ILLUS.)........................ **$1,058**

Fine Art Deco Rectangular Diamond Brooch

Pendant-brooch, diamond & platinum, a long rectangular openwork mount set in the center w/a large marquise-cut diamond framed by rayed bands of full-cut diamonds & flanked by baguette diamonds, the arched top & triangular link also set w/diamonds, millegrain accents, diamonds weighing about 6.50 cts., suspended from a platinum trace link chain, 2 1/4" l. (ILLUS.)..................................... **$6,463**

Pendant-brooch, platinum & diamond, bead-set w/55 old European- and transitional-cut diamonds weighing about 2.99 cts. & green stone highlights, millegrain accents, back w/added pin stem, one green stone missing, 2 3/8" l.................. **$2,350**

Diamond-shaped Diamond & Emerald Pendant

Pendant-brooch, platinum, emerald & diamond, the large diamond-shaped openwork platinum mount w/a cross design bead- and bezel-set around the frame w/old mine- and European-cut diamonds, the frame enclosing four fancy-cut emeralds, millegrain accents, 1 1/4 x 2" (ILLUS.)................................ **$14,100**

J

Fancy Coral, Onyx & Diamond Pendant

Pendant-necklace, coral, onyx, diamond & platinum, a slender fancy pierced link chain punctuated by bezel-set diamonds & coral & onyx beads suspending a carved coral rounded mask w/diamond-trimmed mounts & a link suspending a long flattened faceted teardrop-shaped onyx pendant, 15 1/2" l. (ILLUS.)........... **$2,820**

Pin, platinum & diamond, designed as a long open bow, bead-set w/old European-cut diamonds weighing about 1.40 cts., millegrain accents, open gallery, 2 1/4" l. (ILLUS. bottom with Art Deco slightly swelled diamond & platinum bar pin, bottom of page 755) **$1,293**

Art Deco Diamond & Emerald Circle Pin

Pin, platinum, diamond & emerald, circle-style, the narrow band channel-set w/alternating groups of full-cut diamonds & step-cut emeralds, 1" d. (ILLUS.) **$1,645**

Enameled, Emerald & Diamond Deco Ring

Ring, carved emerald, diamond & enameled gold, the oval top centered by a large round carved emerald cabochon framed by a ring of old mine-cut diamonds within an outer border band enameled in white, foliate shoulders, silver & gold mount, size 7 (ILLUS.) **$2,115**

Ring, colorless diamond, colored diamond & 14k gold, the three-stone top centered by a bezel-set full-cut brown diamond weighing about 1.43 cts. flanked by two colorless old European-cut diamonds weighing about 2.09 cts., in an engraved mount, size 7 1/2 (ILLUS., top next column) **$1,175**

Three-Stone Mixed Diamond Ring

Austrian Art Deco Diamond Ring

Ring, diamond & 14k gold, the rectangular openwork top centered by a row of three bezel-set old mine-cut diamonds, framed by smaller rose-cut diamonds & diamond mélée, millegrain accents, 14k gold mount, Vienese hallmarks, ca. 1930, size 6 (ILLUS.) **$823**

Deco Diamond, Pearl & Sapphire Bypass Ring

Ring, diamond, cultured pearl, sapphire & platinum, bypass-style, the top w/a large old European-cut diamond weighing about .75 cts. beside a cultured pearl, each side w/thin curved bands, one bead-set w/small diamonds & the other channel-set w/small sapphires, platinum mount, signed by Marcus & Co., size 7 (ILLUS.) **$2,581**

J

Art Deco Diamond & Emerald Ring

Ring, diamond, emerald & platinum, the square openwork top centered by an emerald-cut emerald framed by a cross & band design set w/38 old mine- and European-cut diamonds, incised shank, millegrain accents, size 5 (ILLUS.) **$2,115**

Art Deco Onyx & Diamond Ring

Ring, diamond, onyx & platinum, the top centered by a navette-shaped black onyx plaque centered by a large old European-cut diamond weighing about 1.00 ct., the shaped mount further bead-set w/small old European- and single-cut diamonds, size 7 1/4 (ILLUS.) **$3,643**

Fine Ribbon Bow Diamond Ring

Ring, diamond & platinum, designed as a long scrolled ribbon bow prong-set in the center w/an old European-cut diamond weighing about 1.70 cts., the surrounding bands bezel- and bead-set w/baguette and old European-cut diamonds weighing about 4.91 cts., size 7 1/4 (ILLUS.) ... **$6,463**

Square-topped Art Deco Diamond Ring

Ring, diamond & platinum, squared top w/a diamond-shaped & triangular panels bead-set w/old European-cut diamonds weighing about 1.94 cts., openwork mount w/millegrain accents, size 6 1/2 (ILLUS.)... **$1,263**

Filigree Platinum & Diamond Deco Ring

Ring, diamond & platinum, the flaring filigree top set in the center w/a cross-form arrangement of five old European-cut diamonds w/border bands of old mine-cut diamonds, engraved floral details & millegrain accents, diamonds weighing about 1.69 cts., boxed, size 6 (ILLUS.)... **$1,645**

J

Long Navette-shaped Deco Diamond Ring

Ring, diamond & platinum, the long navette-shaped top designed w/a pointed group of diamond-set petals at each end flanking a large central full-cut diamond flanked by bands all set w/baguette & single-cut diamonds, diamonds weighing about .67 cts., w/ring guard, size 7 (ILLUS., previous page) **$1,528**

Art Deco Diamond Solitaire Ring

Ring, diamond solitaire, the center set w/an old European-cut diamond weighing about .90 carats, the filigree platinum mount accented w/swags & geometric designs & marked "Irid. Plat." (ILLUS.) ... **$1,150**

J

Emerald & Diamond Art Deco Ring

Ring, emerald, diamond & 18k gold, the oblong waisted openwork mount centered by a bezel-set step-cut octagonal emerald flanked by six old European-cut diamonds & a frame set w/single-cut diamonds, the ends edged w/tiny channel-set emeralds, engraved gallery, platinum-topped mount, size 6 (ILLUS.) **$1,645**

Long Art Deco Emerald & Diamond Ring

Ring, emerald, diamond & gold, the long openwork filigree top w/incurved sides set w/an outer band of bezel- and bead-cut single-cut diamonds highlighted by six larger old European-cut diamonds all centered by a large bezel-set step-cut emerald, the ends also channel-set w/small emeralds, platinum-topped 18k gold mount, size 6 (ILLUS.) **$1,175**

Ring, emerald, diamond & platinum, decorated w/a tapering line of oval- and calibré-cut emeralds framed by full-cut diamond mélée, size 6 1/4 .... **$1,058**

Fine Art Deco Emerald & Diamond Ring

Ring, emerald, diamond & platinum, the long navette-shaped top centered by a large bezel-set emerald-cut emerald flanked by trillion & marquise-cut diamonds, single-cut diamond highlights, diamonds weighing about .64 cts., millegrain accents, engraved shoulders & pierced gallery, size 8 (ILLUS.) **$2,820**

Fancy Art Deco Diamond & Emerald Ring

Ring, platinum, diamond & emerald, the domed rounded top centered by a bezel-set transitional-cut diamond flanked by curved bands set w/single-cut diamond mélée & further set w/two triangular-cut emeralds & channel-set emerald shoulders, millegrain accents, engraved gallery, size 6 1/4 (ILLUS.).......................... **$2,468**

Large Diamond Art Deco Gem-set Ring

Ring, platinum, diamond & emerald, the top centered by a large bezel-set old European-cut diamond weighing about 1.58 cts., flanked by two emerald highlights & bead-set w/old single-cut diamond mélée, foliate-engraved shoulders & millegrain accents, size 5 1/2 (ILLUS.) **$3,819**

Fine Art Deco Diamond & Onyx Ring

Ring, platinum, diamond & onyx, a long rectangular top w/beveled corners, centered by two large old pear-cut diamonds framed by calibré-cut black onyx & single-cut diamonds, bead-set diamonds on the shoulders, millegrain accents, diamonds weighing about 3.00 cts., open scrolling gallery, size 6 1/2 (ILLUS.) **$8,343**

Diamond & Platinum Ring with Ruby Accents

Ring, platinum, diamond & ruby, the wide band centered by a large bezel-set old European-cut diamond weighing about .75 cts flanked by channel-set calibré-cut rubies, platinum & 14k gold mount, size 5 1/4 (ILLUS.)... **$1,175**

Ring, platinum, diamond & sapphire, bead-set w/26 old European-cut diamonds, 12 calibré-cut sapphire highlights in an open gallery, diamonds weighing about 2.00 cts., size 6 .... **$852**

Art Deco Ring with Large Center Diamond

Ring, platinum & diamond, the center bezel-set w/a large old European-cut diamond weighing about .75 cts., the openwork gallery & shoulders set w/full- and single-cut diamonds weighing about 1.14 cts., size 6 3/4 (ILLUS.) **$2,820**

J

Art Deco Oval Platinum & Diamond Ring

Ring, platinum & diamond, the long oval openwork top centered by a bezel-set marquise-cut diamond weighing about

.33 cts., surrounded by small bead-set old European- and single-cut diamonds, millegrain accents, size 5 1/4 (ILLUS.)....... **$705**

Art Deco Oblong Diamond Ring

Ring, platinum & diamond, the oblong openwork top bezel- and bead-set in a geometric design w/marquise & old European-cut diamonds, millegrain accents, diamonds weighing about 1.43 cts., size 6 (ILLUS.)................................ **$1,538**

Fine Art Deco Ring with Marquise Diamond

Ring, platinum & diamond, the top centered by a large old marquise-cut diamond weighing about 2.00 cts., the gallery & shoulders set w/old European-cut diamonds, foliate-engraved accents, size 7 (ILLUS.)................................ **$6,463**

Three-Stone Art Deco Diamond Ring

Ring, platinum & diamond, the wide domed top centered by a row of three bezel-set old European-cut diamonds w/the side panels set w/old mine-cut diamonds, diamonds weighing about 1.99 cts., millegrain accents, openwork mount, size 5 (ILLUS.)................................ **$1,645**

J

Fine Art Deco Twin-Stone Diamond Ring

Ring, platinum & diamond, twin stone-style, the top composed of two large old European-cut diamonds weighing about 2.55 & 2.28 cts., the shoulders set w/full-cut diamonds, geometric & foliate-engraved mount, size 5 1/2 (ILLUS.) **$16,450**

Art Deco Sapphire & Diamond Ring

Ring, platinum, sapphire & diamond, the cut-cornered rectangular top centered by a bezel-set cushion-cut sapphire framed by a ring of old European-cut diamonds flanked two large European-cut diamonds & small diamonds, diamonds weighing about 1.58 cts., millegrain accents, openwork gallery, size 2 1/2 (ILLUS.) **$2,233**

Rare Deco Diamond-framed Sapphire Ring

Ring, platinum, sapphire & diamond, the oblong top centered by a large oval-cut blue sapphire framed by an openwork mount set w/full- and single-cut diamonds, boxed, size 5 (ILLUS.) **$15,000-20,000**

Art Deco Star Sapphire & Diamond Ring

Ring, star sapphire, diamond & platinum, the oval top centered by a large bezel-set star sapphire framed by an open-work border set w/old European-cut diamonds weighing about 1.12 cts., size 5 (ILLUS.) **$3,055**

Rare Two-sided Deco Cartier Stickpin

Stickpin, platinum, diamond & ruby, the circle top w/two sides, one side bead-set w/old single-cut diamonds, the other channel-set w/calibré-cut rubies, millegrain accents, platinum & gold mount, hallmark of Andrey, Paris & signed by Cartier, original red morocco box (ILLUS.) **$3,290**

Sets

Necklace & bracelet, enameled chrome; the necklace band composed of chromed links centered by an enameled maroon band, the wide collar-style form composed of two bands of the small, enamel-trimmed links flanking long twisted chrome links, suspending two galaith spheres imitating carnelian, the bracelet swelling at the center, the edges composed of the small chrome links centered by the maroon enameled line, designed by Jakob Bengel, Germany, ca. 1931, unmarked, bracelet 6" l., necklace 31" l. plus pendants, the suite (ILLUS. of necklace, top next column) **$1,016**

Enameled Chrome Necklace from Suite

Retro Style

Bracelet, aquamarine, diamond & 18k gold, the top set w/a large rectangular step-cut aquamarine accented by ten full- and old European-cut diamonds, completed by a bracelet of fancy arched links, convertible to a pin, 6 3/4" l.................................... **$940**

Fine Gold & Green Tourmaline Bracelet

Bracelet, bicolor 14k gold & green tourmaline, composed of oval links centering an oval-cut tourmaline framed by an openwork flower & leaf ring within a rope band & joined by an openwork square rope link centering a blossom, unsigned, in an H. Stern fitted box (ILLUS.) **$2,233**

J

Gold Retro Bracelet with Arched & Triangular Links

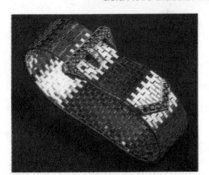

Fine Gold, Ruby & Diamond Retro Bracelet

Bracelet, gold (14k), ruby & diamond, composed of tightly woven brickwork gold links completed by a bead-set ruby & diamond mélée buckle clasp, 7" l. (ILLUS.) **$2,233**

Bracelet, gold (18k), composed of two rows of arched & ribbed links enclosed by three rows of triangular links, 7 3/4" l. (ILLUS., top of page) **$1,116**

Bracelet, gold (18k), slide-type, composed of brickwork links completed by a buckle clasp w/ribbed tassels suspending a foxtail chain, 7" l. **$1,528**

Bracelet, ruby & 14k gold, slide-type, composed of brickwork links completed by a buckle clasp star-set w/small rubies........... **$999**

J

1940s Ruby Bead & Diamond Bracelet

Bracelet, ruby, diamond & platinum, composed of multiple strands of tumbled ruby beads, the rounded & entwined ribbon-style clasp set w/baguette, full- and old single-cut diamonds, the center w/a large cabochon ruby, diamonds weighing about 2.66 cts., ca. 1940s, 8 1/4" l. (ILLUS.) **$3,819**

Brooch, bicolor 14k gold, designed as a ribbon bow, signed by Tiffany & Co., 1 1/2 x 3 1/4" **$588**

Brooch, bicolor 14k gold, designed as an open fan, 3" w. **$764**

Retro Abstract Gem-set Ribbon Brooch

Brooch, bicolor 14k gold, moonstone & garnet, an abstract ring & ribbon design centered by a large cabochon moonstone issuing long curved ribbons & framed by a ring of gold ruffles, one edge set w/an arched graduating row of oval-cut rhodolite garnets, 2 3/4" l. (ILLUS.) **$1,116**

Brooch, bicolor 18k gold, demantoid garnet & diamond, modeled as a flying bird prong-set w/12 circular-cut green garnets w/single-cut diamond highlights, mark of maker obliterated, missing one diamond, garnets abraded, 2 3/4" l. **$1,763**

Dramatic Gem-set Gold Bow & Flower Brooch

Brooch, gem-set 14k gold & diamond, designed as a large stylized ribbon bow & blossom, the gold ribbon loops above trailing ribbons cushion-set w/large cushion-shape yellow sapphires or small full-cut diamond accents, a large stylized half-round flower at the upper left composed of six large cushion-shape blue sapphires forming the petals & the large round center bead-set w/circular-cut rubies, 14k bicolor gold & platinum mount, 2 5/8" l. (ILLUS.)..................................... **$2,585**

Brooch, gem-set 14k gold, prong-set w/a circular-cut aquamarine surrounded by circular-cut ruby highlights, 1 1/2" l. **$235**

Gem-set 18k Gold Retro Bouquet Brooch

Brooch, gem-set 18k bicolor gold, designed as a large bouquet of small blossoms framed w/angular leaves & tied w/a looping bow, each blossom centered by a small ruby or sapphire, the band tying the gold ribbon pavé-set w/small diamonds, 3 1/8" l. (ILLUS.)....................................... **$823**

French Gem-set Gold Scrolled Brooch

Brooch, gem-set 18k gold, designed as a long tightly scrolled spray centered by an oval-cut sapphire & highlighted by clusters of 22 old European-cut diamonds, French guarantee stamps (ILLUS.)......... **$1,116**

Retro Gold Brooch Set with Pastes

Brooch, glass stones & 14k bicolor gold, designed as an open oval surrounded a horizontal stylized flower sprig w/three blossoms made from colorless paste stones (ILLUS.) **$150-250**

Gem-set Gold Flower & Leaf Brooch

Brooch, gold (14k), cultured pearl & diamond, designed as two stylized gold blossoms w/three pointed leaves on curled stems, each blossom centered by a large pearl, the two stems joined by a small band set w/diamonds, No. 1262 (ILLUS.).. **$300-400**

J

Cartier Abstract Leaf-like Gold Brooch

Brooch, gold (14k), designed as an oblong pair of swirled rib leaves, American maker mark, signed by Cartier, No. 14848, 1 7/8" l. (ILLUS.).. **$705**

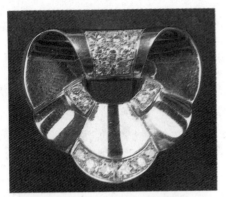

Retro Ruffled Clip with Diamonds

Clip, platinum, 18k gold & diamond, ruffled stylized openwork shell form bead-set w/full-cut diamonds, diamonds weighing about .92 cts., French guarantee stamps, 1" l. (ILLUS.).. **$764**

Retro Spinel-set 14k Bicolor Gold Dress Clips Convertible to a Brooch

J

Dress clips-brooch, gem-set 14k bicolor gold, each w/a top gold bar above a pair of scrolls enclosing a cluster of circular-cut purple, red, pink, bluish green & yellow spinels, the top bar set w/two square-cut pink spinels, convertible to a brooch, each 1 1/8 x 1 1/2", pr. (ILLUS.).............. **$4,406**

Retro Flower & Fan-shaped Earrings

Earrings, citrine, ruby & 14k rose gold, clip-on type, designed as a vertical stylized flower cluster w/a rounded fan-shaped background, set w/a large rectangular step-cut citrine, circular-cut rubies forming the flower blossoms, pr. (ILLUS.) **$999**

Earrings, diamond & gem-set 14k gold, pendant-type, designed w/a circular wire-work top suspending multiple hoops prong-set w/diamond, ruby & sapphire mélée, ca. 1950, 1 3/4" l., pr. **$600-800**

Rose-shaped Gem-set Gold Earrings

Earrings, ruby, diamond, 14k rose gold & platinum, clip-on type, each designed as a rose blossom on a leafy stem, the flower set w/circular-cut rubies, diamond accents on the leafy stem, 7/8" l., pr. (ILLUS.) **$1,410**

Earrings, ruby, diamond & 18k gold, clip-on type, each designed as a ribbon w/bezel-set rectangular-cut diamonds & prong-set circular-cut rubies, 14k gold screw-back findings, pr. **$1,058**

Retro Stylized Leaf Gold Necklace

Necklace, bicolor 14k gold, composed of stylized pairs of leaves forming the links, made by Wordley, Allsopp & Bliss for Tiffany & Co., signed, 15 1/2" l. (ILLUS.) **$1,293**

Necklace, diamond & 9k gold, composed of a double strand of snake chain gathered by star-set diamond scrolls, English hallmarks, 15" l. (ILLUS., top next page) **$1,293**

Necklace, gold (14k), made from a snake chain, signed by Tiffany & Co., 15" l. **$940**

Pendant-necklace, bicolor 14k gold & black opal composite, composed of oval opal tablets joined by abstract gold leaf-form links, 17" l. **$764**

Pin, gold (14k), bow-shaped, in a Spritzer & Fuhrmann box, 2 3/4" l **$441**

Retro Gold Chain & Diamond Necklace

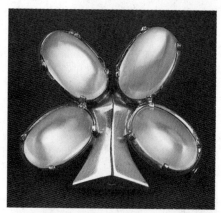

French Retro Flower-form Pin

Pin, moonstone & 18k gold, designed as a flower w/four large oval sugarloaf cabochon moonstone petals on an angular flaring gold stem, mark of Poncet, Paris, France & guarantee stamp (ILLUS.) **$558**

Retro Citrine & Gems Pin-Pendant

Pin-pendant, citrine, ruby, diamond & 14k rose gold, a large prong-set rectangular step-cut citrine flanked by rows of small channel-set rubies & single-cut diamonds (ILLUS.) **$705**

Retro Citrine & Gem-set Ring

Ring, citrine & gem-set 18k gold, the top prong-set w/a large step-cut rectangular citrine, flanked by small calibré-cut rubies, diamond-set shoulders, 18k gold & platinum mount, signed by J.E. Caldwell, size 6 (ILLUS.) **$2,820**

Unusual Gem-set Gold Retro Ring

Ring, diamond, sapphire & 18k gold, the top three wide bands next to a tight gold scroll lined w/a band of bead-set sapphires & centered by an old mine-cut diamond, French import & guarantee stamps, size 9 (ILLUS.)............................. **$529**

J

Retro White Gold & Diamond Ring

Ring, diamond & white gold, the rectangular top set w/35 diamonds of various old cuts weighing about 2.50 cts. (ILLUS., previous page) **$2,300**

Ring, gem-set 14k bicolor gold, the scrolling form centering a cluster of mélée including diamond, ruby, emerald & amethyst, size 5 1/2 .... **$264**

Unusual Emerald & Diamond Ring

Ring, platinum, diamond & emerald, the top designed as stepped triangles opposite an arched panel, centered by a long rectangular step-cut emerald, framed by bead-set single-cut diamonds, size 5 1/4 (ILLUS.) **$1,293**

Ring, ruby & 14k rose gold, a ribbon design prong-set w/three small rubies, signed by Tiffany & Co., size 6 .... **$705**

Fine Ring with Sapphire & Diamonds

Ring, sapphire, diamond & platinum, the top centered by a prong-set emerald-cut blue sapphire weighing 1.57 cts., flanked by bezel-set baguette & single-cut diamonds weighing about .50 cts., size 5 3/4 (ILLUS.) **$2,703**

Ring, synthetic ruby, diamond & 14k rose gold, the top centering baguette synthetic rubies w/single-cut diamond highlights, size 8 3/4 .... **$294**

Sets

Retro Citrine & Gold Jewelry Suite

Brooch & earrings, citrine & 18k gold, the oblong brooch centered by a large rectangular step-cut citrine w/cut-corners flanked by small rectangular step-cut citrines, rounded ends, the matching clip-on earrings centered by a single step-cut citrine flanked by rounded tabs, mark of French maker & guarantee stamps, earrings 3/4" w., brooch 2 3/8" l., the suite (ILLUS.) **$4,000-6,000**

Brooch & earrings, ruby, diamond & 14k white gold, the brooch of spherical form w/a radiating center, set w/single-, full- and old European-cut diamonds & circular-cut rubies, clip-on earrings of matching design, the set **$1,763**

Necklace & bracelet, black nephrite & 14k gold, each composed of circular cabochon nephrites alternating w/bow links, signed by Bensa Bott, Chicago, bracelet 7 1/4" l., necklace 15 3/4" l. the suite **$881**

Miscellaneous Pieces

Bracelet, gem-set 18k gold, a wide gold band w/etched zigzag & diamond designs centered by a narrow band of diamonds, sapphires, emeralds & rubies, 7 1/4" l. (ILLUS., first in row bottom of page) **$1,763**

Fine Etched Gold & Gem-set Bracelet

Gem-set Gold Bracelet with S-Scroll Links

Finely Detailed Fishing Rod & Reel Brooch with Leaping Sailfish

Bracelet, gem-set 18k gold, composed of openwork squared links composed of interconnected S-scrolls each accented w/a small bezel-set ruby, emerald, sapphire & diamond, 7" l. (ILLUS., bottom previous page) **$1,410**

Bracelet with Carved Scarabs

Bracelet, hardstone & 18k gold, designed w/four links set w/carved scarabs in carnelian, green hardstone, faience & amethyst, joined by gold bar links interspersed w/flat designs of an ankh, lotus flower, djed & tiet, signed by Blanchard, Cairo, 8 1/2" l. (ILLUS.) **$764**

Gold-framed Carved Jade Brooch

Brooch, carved green jade & enameled 14k gold, an oval jade plaque pierce-carved w/a scene of ducks swimming on a pond among flowers, the wide gold frame enameled in green & orange w/bands & stylized leaf designs, mark of an American maker, 2" l. (ILLUS.) **$940**

Diamond-set Sphinx-shaped Brooch

Brooch, diamond & platinum, regimental-type, in the shape of a recumbent sphinx pavé-set overall w/old European-, mine-, single- and rose-cut diamonds, raised on a narrow plinth reading "Egypt," ca. 1920s, evidence of gold solder, 1 1/4" l. (ILLUS.) **$2,115**

Brooch, enameled 14k gold & seed pearl, designed as a long fishing rod & real w/gold wire line, mounted in the center w/a leaping sailfish w/blue enameled fins & the body set overall w/seed pearls, reel actually revolves, fine detailing, ca. 1940, 4" l. (ILLUS., top of page) **$3,055**

J

Rare & Fine Diamond Pendant Earrings

Earrings, diamond & platinum, pendant-type, each prong-set w/a top old European-cut diamond weighing 1.93 cts. and 1.91 cts. suspending an old pear-shaped diamond drop weighing 1.90 and 2.10 cts., spaced by a smaller full-cut diamond, total diamond weight about 8.14 cts., 7/8" l., pr. (ILLUS.) **$22,325**

Unusual Gold & Diamond Wing Earrings

Earrings, platinum, 14k gold & diamond, clip-on type, designed as a wing w/graduated gold feathers above a curved teardrop-form base pavé-set w/full- and single-cut diamonds, ca. 1960, 1 3/8" l., pr. (ILLUS.) **$3,819**

Two Reverse-painted Crystal Pins

Pin, reverse-painted crystal & 14k gold, a slender gold pin centered by a round mount w/a domed crystal painted w/a standing Boston terrier, 1 7/8" l. (ILLUS. top with beagle head pin) **$881**

Pin, reverse-painted crystal & 14k gold, a slender gold pin centered by a round mount w/a domed crystal painted w/the head of a beagle, 1 7/8" l. (ILLUS. bottom with Boston terrier pin) **$940**

Diamond & Gold Ring by Ciner Mfg. Co.

Ring, diamond & 18k white gold, the long oval filigree mount set w/three larger in-line European-cut diamonds surrounded by six smaller diamonds, band stamped inside "Belais 18k" w/hallmark of the Ciner Mfg. Co., early 20th c. (ILLUS.) **$1,195**

Vintage Lady's Diamond & Ruby Ring

Ring, lady's fashion-type, diamond, ruby & 14k yellow gold, the round domed top centered by a large European-cut diamond weighing .98 cts. surrounded by a mélée band of 12 round faceted rubies further surrounded by a mélée band of 12 round full-cut diamonds, large diamond heavily included, early 20th c. (ILLUS.) **$598**

Rare Early Twin-Stone Diamond Ring

Ring, platinum, diamond & colored diamond, twin-stone design, two side-by-side large prong-set diamonds, one a fancy light greenish yellow old European-cut diamond weighing about .74 cts. & the other a old European-cut white diamond weighing about .80 cts., atop an entwined shank set w/diamond baguettes, ca. 1920s, size 5 1/4 (ILLUS.) **$4,583**

J

Rare Pink Sapphire & Diamond Ring

Ring, platinum, pink sapphire & diamond, the squared top w/beveled corners, centered by a large prong-set cushion-cut pink sapphire w/orange tones, framed by full- and single-cut diamond mélée, ca. 1950 abrasions, size 3 1/2 (ILLUS.)...... **$21,150**

Vintage Diamond Wedding Ring

Wedding ring with ring guards, lady's, diamond & 14k yellow gold, the main band w/a six-prong Tiffany mount holding a European-cut diamond weighing 3.51 cts., the flanking wedding band guards mounted w/a total of 26 straight diamond baguettes, early 20th c. (ILLUS.) **$14,350**

Sets

Schiaperalli Earrings from 1930s Suite

Necklace & earrings, gilt-metal & faux gems, the festoon-style necklace composed of a tapering rounded band of forest green velvet trimmed w/gold cording & small metal beads, the front border trimmed w/large faux pearls & short drops composed of faux emerald & turquoise beads alternating w/large leaf-shaped green velvet pendants decorated w/a gilt-metal mask & pairs of birds highlighted w/further faux gems, the pendant earrings designed as a single pendant w/a gilt-metal bird & faux gem beads, designed by Lina Baretti for Schiaparelli, labeled "Leni Kuborn-Grothe, Kitzbuhel," France, 1936-1938, earrings 3" l., necklace 29" l., the suite (ILLUS. of earrings).. **$2,510**

Pendant & earrings, silver gilt & molded glass, the pendant designed as a foil-backed opalescent glass monkey, suspended from a 14k gold double foxtail chain w/two opal bead accents, matching pendant-style earrings, signed by Rene Lalique, France, pendant 2 1/4" sq., overall 19 3/4" l., the suite...................... **$1,645**

Watches

Very Rare Cartier Deco Pendant Watch

Pendant watch, open faced, lady's, Cartier, Art Deco style, gold, onyx & diamond, the square silvertone dial w/Roman numerals, enclosing an unsigned 18-jewel movement w/eight adjustments, platinum-topped 18k gold mount, the bezel set w/small diamonds, the back of the square case decorated w/square frames of old mine-, European-, single- and rose-cut diamonds alternating w/bands of French-cut onyx, centered by a diamond-set monogram, interior French guarantee stamps & signed by Cartier, Paris, dial also signed, missing one onyx & screw, the case suspended by an

J

openwork design of bars & leaves set w/diamonds (ILLUS.)............................ **$21,150**

Pocket watch, open-faced, man's, Tiffany & Co., Art Deco style, 18k gold, the gold-tone dial w/Arabic numerals & subsidiary seconds dial, enclosing a 21-jewel damascened lever-escapement Longines movement, five adjustments, signed, reverse of case w/engraved initials **$588**

Wristwatch, lady's, Art Deco style, platinum & diamond, a rectangular ivory tone dial w/Arabic numerals, 18-jewel Meylan movement w/five adjustments, bead-set diamond mélée bezel, engraved case & adjustable mesh strap **$999**

Cartier Lady's Gold Wristwatch

Wristwatch, lady's, Cartier, Paris, 18k gold, "Tank" design, the ivory tone rectangular dial w/Roman numerals, enclosing a quartz movement, completed by a blue alligator bracelet, w/original box, papers & additional navy blue alligator bracelet, minor scratch to crystal (ILLUS.)............. **$1,880**

J

Rare Cartier Gold & Diamond Lady's Wristwatch

Wristwatch, lady's, Cartier, Paris, diamond & 18k gold, "Tank" model, the white dial w/Roman numerals within a bead-set diamond bezel, joined to a bracelet of brickwork links completed by a deployant clasp, signed (ILLUS.)......................... **$10,575**

Gruen Art Deco Lady's Wristwatch

Wristwatch, lady's, Gruen, Art Deco style, platinum, diamond & synthetic sapphire, rectangular case set w/full-cut diamonds & two bands of synthetic sapphires, engraved case, rectangular silver tone dial w/Arabic numerals, 17-jewel adjusted movement, later tapering mesh band (ILLUS.) **$588**

Art Deco Gruen Lady's, Wristwatch

Wristwatch, lady's, Gruen Precision model, Art Deco style, platinum case & strap mounted w/69 diamonds including 12 emerald cuts & 57 old European cuts, approximate total weight of 4 cts., rectangular case & dial w/Arabic numerals, marked "Iridium Platinum - AA1 finest diamonds - Gruen," 17-jewel adjusted tempered Swiss movement, face w/some discoloration, ca. 1930s (ILLUS.)... **$2,128**

Ornate Diamond-set Lady's Wristwatch

Fine Tiffany Art Deco Lady's Wristwatch

Wristwatch, lady's, platinum & diamond, Art Deco style, rectangular case w/cut corners enclosing a conforming silver tone dial w/Arabic numerals, joined to openwork links set w/old mine- & single-cut diamonds, a Cressarow Swiss 18-jewel five-adjustment movement, millegrain accents & engraved edges on case, missing grosgrain strap, retailed by Tiffany & Co. (ILLUS.) **$1,293**

Wristwatch, lady's, platinum & diamond, the round silver tone dial w/abstract numeral indicators concealed by an round cover centered by a full-cut diamond framed by baguette diamonds & a diamond ring, suspended in a bold looped frame set w/baguette diamonds & continuing to the open two-band bracelet set w/channel-set diamonds, enclosing a battery movement, diamonds weighing about 7.52 cts., 5 3/4" l. (ILLUS., top of page) **$3,525**

J

French Retro Sapphire & Gold Lady's Wristwatch

Wristwatch, lady's, Retro style, sapphire & 18k yellow gold, the goldtone dial w/Arabic & abstract numerals, enclosing a manual-wind movement, the square dial flanked by rectangular lugs set w/square-cut blue sapphires, joined to a bracelet w/tubogas links, French guarantee stamps, 6 7/8" l. (ILLUS.) **$1,880**

Man's Wristwatch with Movado Movement

Wristwatch, man's, Movado, Cartier, the rectangular ivory tone metal dial w/abstract indicators, enclosing a Swiss unadjusted 17-jewel Movado movement, 14k gold case joined by shaped lugs to a black leather strap, retailed by Cartier, crown not original (ILLUS.)......................... **$999**

J   *Gold Patek Philippe Man's Wristwatch*

Wristwatch, man's, Patek Philippe, 18k gold, the goldtone metal dial w/baton numerals, enclosing an 18-jewel manual-wind movement, later 14k gold brickwork bracelet adjustable to three sizes, triple-signed, dial & bracelet dent (ILLUS.) **$3,525**

Fine Patek Philippe "Hour Glass" Watch

Wristwatch, man's, Patek Philippe, "Hour Glass" model, rectangular 18k gold case enclosing a goldtone metal dial w/Arabic & abstract numerals, subsidiary seconds dial, arched crystal & flared case, a damascened nickel 18-jewel movement adjusted to five positions, heat cold & isochronism movement, w/an alligator band, triple-signed, retailed by Tiffany & Co., crystal, crown & closure replaced (ILLUS.) **$15,275**

Rolex Oyster Perpetual Date just Watch

Wristwatch, man's, Rolex, 18k gold & stainless steel, Oyster Perpetual Date just model, round case enclosing a goldtone metal dial w/abstract numerals & date aperture, fluted bezel, automatic movement, completed by a 14k gold Jubilee bracelet w/deployant clasp (ILLUS.) **$1,175**

Van Cleef & Arpels-Retailed Wristwatch

Wristwatch, man's, the round white metal dial w/Roman numerals, enclosing a Swiss quartz movement, completed by a mesh strap w/deployant clasp, retailed by Van Cleef & Arpels & so signed on the dial & strap (ILLUS.)................................ **$2,115**

Multi-strand Cultured Pearl and Diamond Bracelet

Twentieth Century Designer & Fine Estate Jewelry

Miscellaneous Estate Pieces

Bracelet, cultured pearl, diamond & 14k white gold, composed of four strands totaling 80 white cultured pearls w/rose overtones & ranging in size from 7.50 to 7.95 mm., accented w/three gold crossbars & an openwork rectangular clasp w/oval designs all set w/full-cut diamonds weighing about 2.56 cts., 7 1/2" l. (ILLUS., top of page) **$1,116**

Swirled Band Gold & Diamond Bracelet

Bracelet, diamond & 14k gold, bangle-type, the wide hinged band decorated w/ridged swirled bands each set w/five graduating lines of single-cut diamonds (ILLUS.) **$470**

Bracelet, diamond & 14k white gold, a narrow double band set w/full-cut diamonds centered by pairs of S-scrolls set w/full-cut & baguette diamonds centered a marquise-cut diamond, diamonds weighing about 6.93 cts., formerly a covered watch, adjustable from 6 to 6 1/4" (ILLUS., second from bottom of page)........................ **$1,998**

Bracelet, diamond & 18k gold, buckle-style, decorated w/single-cut diamond mélée highlights completed by an adjustable strap of gold brickwork links, 8" l. **$1,293**

Bracelet, diamond & 18k white gold, composed of long rectangular links w/pointed ends & angled loops joined by ring & bar links, pavé & channel-set overall w/full-cut diamond mélée & diamond baguettes, 7" l. (ILLUS., bottom of page)
.... **$4,113**

J

Diamond & White Gold Bracelet Converted from a Watch

Fancy Link Diamond-set Gold Bracelet

Very Fine Fancy Link Diamond & Platinum Bracelet

Diamond & Gold Feather-like Bracelet

Bracelet, diamond & 18k white gold, the wide openwork feather-like band decorated overall w/prong- and bead-set full-cut diamond mélée, diamonds weighing about 4.36 cts., interior circumference 5 3/4" (ILLUS.) **$1,763**

Bracelet, diamond & platinum, composed of navette-shaped links set w/baguette diamonds alternating w/links centered by an emerald-cut diamond flanked by four marquise-cut diamond leaves, diamonds weighing about 9.45 cts., 7" l. (ILLUS., top of page) **$14,100**

Gem Cabochon-set Gold Bracelet

Fine Diamond, Sapphire & White Gold Bracelet

J

Bracelet, diamond, sapphire & 18k white gold, composed of 14 square links each w/four small square-cut blue sapphires framed by six diamonds interspersed w/three buckle-type round links each set w/diamonds, marked a lion hallmark & "18k - BM1466," sapphire total weight 6.33 cts., diamond total weight 2.47 cts., 1/2" w., 7 1/4" l. (ILLUS.) **$4,600**

Bracelet, emerald, diamond & 18k gold, the flexible band composed of small overlapping fish scale links prong-set w/alternating groups of four full-cut diamonds & circular-cut emeralds, 7 1/2"l. **$1,880**

Bracelet, enameled 18k gold, a domed shape composed of overlapping fish scale-style flexible links enameled in dark blue & white, Italy, 6 7/8" l. **$2,468**

Bracelet, gem-set 14k gold, composed of six links each set w/a different large cabochon stone including rose quartz, citrine, green beryl, aquamarine & amethyst, 7" l. (ILLUS., top next column)....... **$1,116**

Finely Woven 18k Gold Italian Bracelet

Bracelet, gold (18k), a wide finely woven gold band highlighted by smooth leafy serpentine stems, No. 434 AL, Italy, 7" l. (ILLUS.)... **$1,116**

Rare Turquoise, Diamond & Gold Bracelet

Bracelet, turquoise, diamond & 18k white gold, bangle-type, the wide hinged band prong-set around the center w/a band of large turquoise cabochons surrounded by small turquoise cabochons accented w/full-cut diamonds, interior circumference 6 1/2" (ILLUS.)............................ **$8,225**

Bracelets, diamond & 14k gold, bangle-type, hinged, w/a Florentine finish & set w/nine single-cut diamond mélée highlights, interior circumference 6 1/2", pr....... **$353**

Greek Gold & Gemstone Round Brooch

Brooch, amethyst, emerald, cultured pearl & 22k gold, the round flat disk bezel-set w/an arrangement of a central sugarloaf cabochon emerald framed by four cabochon amethysts & pearls, blue enamel border accents, Greek karat stamp, 1 3/8" d. (ILLUS.) **$353**

Coral, Diamond & Hardstone Grape Brooch

Brooch, coral, diamond, hardstone & 18k white gold, designed as a carved green stone leaf above a gold stem suspending a large bunch of coral bead grapes, full-cut diamonds along the stem (ILLUS.).... **$1,175**

Gold, Diamond & Glass Grape Brooch

Brooch, diamond, 14k gold & frosted glass, a gold diamond-set stem suspending a bunch of frosted green glass grapes (ILLUS.) **$1,410**

Unusual Gold & Diamond Knot Brooch

Brooch, diamond & 18k gold, a spiraled knot-form design w/finely woven ropetwist gold bands ending in points, bordered & centered by prong-set full-cut diamonds weighing about 5.00 cts., 2 1/4" l. (ILLUS.)...................................... **$2,468**

J

Diamond & White Gold Bow Brooch

Brooch, diamond & 18k white gold, designed as a bow w/large loops above a flower head w/a leaf drop, prong-set overall w/full- and marquise-cut diamonds weighing about 4.65 cts. (ILLUS., previous page) **$2,350**

Enameled Comical Frog & Pearl Brooch

Brooch, enameled & gem-set 18k gold, designed as a comical green-enameled frog grasping a cultured pearl, the body accented w/scattered bezel-set diamonds, cabochon ruby eyes (ILLUS.)........ **$705**

Enameled & Gem-set Dachshund Brooch

Brooch, enameled & gem-set gold, in the shape of a reclining Dachshund, the body enameled in brown w/a gold tail, the long ears set w/rose-cut diamonds, ruby eyes & an emerald collar, Portuguese guarantee stamps, 1 1/2" l. (ILLUS.) **$705**

Gem-set Enameled Gold Sailboat Brooch

Brooch, enameled gold & diamond, designed as a sailboat w/two full sails, one enameled in dark blue, the other in dark blue, sailing on waves set w/full-cut diamonds & flying a diamond-set pennant, 14k gold mount, 1 1/4 x 1 3/8" (ILLUS.) ... **$1,410**

Brooch, freshwater pearl & gems, centered by a pyrope garnet cabochon framed by freshwater pearls, cabochon turquoise & fancy-cut citrines w/ropetwist accents, silver-gilt mount, possibly by Seaman Schepps, 1 3/4 x 2 1/4" **$353**

Gem-set Gold Flower Cluster Brooch

Brooch, gem-set 18k gold, designed as a cluster of three large sunflower-like blossoms above a cluster of four pointed leaves, each blossom prong-set w/either circular-cut ruby, sapphire or emerald mélée, 1 3/4" l. (ILLUS.) **$1,116**

Gem-set 18k Gold Terrier Brooch

Brooch, gem-set 18k gold, designed as a stylized seated Terrier w/the body set w/a large cabochon turquoise, tiny ruby eyes, 2" l. (ILLUS.)... **$411**

J

Unusual Tropical Fish Hardstone Brooch

Brooch, hardstone & 14k gold, designed as a tropical fish w/the body composed of pieces of lapis lazuli, onyx, malachite, coral & mother-of-pearl, signed "OA/G" (ILLUS.)... **$1,058**

Cute Lapis, Diamond & Gold Turtle Brooch

Brooch, lapis lazuli, diamond & gold, in the shape of a turtle w/the domed shell formed by a cabochon lapis bordered by 16 full-cut diamonds, emerald eyes, 1" l. (ILLUS.).. **$1,763**

Brooch, platinum & diamond, designed as a large rose bud atop a long thorny stem fitted w/three leaves, the bud & leaves pavé-set w/full-cut diamonds weighing about 4.50 cts. (ILLUS., top next column)
.... **$2,468**

Diamond & Platinum Rose Stem Brooch

Fancy Floral Spray Diamond Brooch

Brooch, platinum & diamond, designed as a large stylized spray of three opening flower buds & leaves atop entwined curved stems, prong-, bead- and channel-set set overall w/163 full-, 17 marquise- and 27 baguette diamonds, diamonds weighing about 8.47 cts., 2 3/4" l. (ILLUS.)... **$4,700**

J

Ornate Sapphire & Diamond Cross Brooch

Brooch, sapphire, diamond & platinum, a wide cross-form design w/short pointed arms between the cross arms, prong-set w/five large cushion-cut blue sapphires & further set overall w/smaller prong-set square-cut & baguette sapphires, the tips of each arm set w/bands of full-cut diamonds, mark of maker, No. 2887, 2" w. (ILLUS.).................................... **$6,756**

Brooch, tricolor 14k gold, modeled as an eagle w/a red stone eye, 3 7/8" w. **$705**

Diamond & Gold Starfish Brooch

Brooch-pendant, diamond & 18k white gold, model of a starfish, the center of each arm prong-set w/a band of brown diamonds surrounded by 163 white diamond mélée, diamonds weighing about 8.97 cts., 2" l. (ILLUS.) **$4,700**

Unusual Mabe Pearl & Diamond Brooch

Brooch-pendant, mabe pearl, diamond & 14k white gold, a large bulbous tapering

baroque pearl framed along the sides by bands of full-cut diamonds w/scroll & leaf designs at the top & base set w/marquise-cut & baguette diamonds, diamonds weighing about 3.16 cts., 2 1/4" l. (ILLUS.)................................... **$1,763**

Black Onyx & Diamond Bow Brooch

Brooch-pendant, platinum, onyx & diamond, designed as a long wide ribbon bow lined w/bands of ribbed onyx edged by narrow bands of full-cut diamonds, 2 5/16" l. (ILLUS.) **$1,645**

Opal Cameo Pendant-Necklace

Cameo pendant-necklace, opal, enamel & 14k gold, oval opal cameo depicting a lady in Renaissance dress, in an oval frame decorated w/black & green champlève enamel, suspended from a matching enamel baton link chain highlighted by opal beads, 29" l. (ILLUS.) **$2,115**

Gold Charm Bracelet with a Variety of Figural Charms

Charm bracelet, gold (14k), composed of a double curb-link chain suspending numerous gold charms including a doctor's bag, birthday cake w/retractable candles, scissors, artist palette, jewel casket, mad money & trash can, 6 3/4" l. (ILLUS., previous page)... **$1,175**

Charm bracelet, gold (14k), the curb link chain suspending nine charms including a gold coin, turtle & flexible fish, 7 1/2" l. ... **$323**

Gem-set Cultured Pearl Choker

Choker, platinum, cultured pearl, diamond & sapphire, composed of a double strand of 85 white pearls w/rose overtones measuring about 7.50 to 8.00 mm, completed by a round clasp pavé-set w/a center cluster of diamonds enclosed by a ring of blue sapphires & an outer ring of diamonds, diamonds weighing about 1.04 cts., 14 3/4" l. (ILLUS.) **$1,763**

Engraved Gold & Stone-set Cuff Links

Cuff links, stone-set 14k gold & platinum, a cylindrical waisted bar engraved in a scale design & centered by a ring of step-cut red stones, mark of American maker, 7/8" l., pr. (ILLUS.) **$499**

Earrings, amethyst, diamond & 18k gold, clip-on type, each designed as an abstract flower head bezel-set w/a circular-cut amethyst & w/old single-cut diamond accents, pr.. **$382**

Stylized Gold Fish & Diamond Earrings

Earrings, bicolor 18k gold & diamond, clip-on type, designed as curled stylized fish, the gold bodies w/an openwork lattice design, the snout, fins, tail & body set w/single-cut diamond mélée, France, 1 3/8" l., pr. (ILLUS.) **$1,410**

Fine French Emerald & Gold Earrings

Earrings, bicolor 18k gold & emerald, clip-on type, each w/double curved gold bars suspending a fringe of faceted emerald beads, French guarantee stamps & mark of the maker, 1 1/4" l., pr. (ILLUS.) **$3,878**

Shell-form Pearl & Diamond Earrings

Earrings, cultured pearl, diamond & 14k white gold, clip-on type, designed as a concave oval shell set overall w/single- and full-cut diamonds & centered by a single white pearl, pr. (ILLUS.).................. **$940**

J

Diamond Double-loop Earrings

Earrings, diamond & 14k white gold, pendant-type, a top cluster of prong-set pear- and single-cut diamonds suspending two oval loops further set w/diamonds, diamonds weighing about 4.00 cts., 1 3/8" l., pr. (ILLUS.) **$1,880**

Pink Stone, Diamond & Gold Earrings

Earrings, diamond, pink stone & 14k white gold, pendant-type, each prong-set w/a large pear-cut pink stone framed by a thin band of diamonds & suspended from a thin diamond-set line link, diamonds weighing about .55 cts. 1 1/4" l., pr. (ILLUS.) **$1,116**

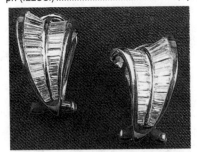

Scroll-shaped Diamond Earrings

Earrings, diamond & platinum, clip-on type, designed as a double scroll channel-set w/baguette diamonds weighing about 1.89 cts., pr. (ILLUS.) **$1,410**

J

Earrings, diamond & platinum, clip-on type, each designed as a multi-petaled flower centered by six prong-mounted round cut .20 ct. diamond & diamond mélées, each sectioned petal further set w/diamond mélées, yellow gold backs, unmarked, 124 diamonds total weighing 1.85 cts., pr. **$1,955**

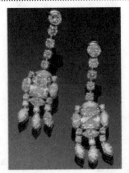

Fine Diamond & Platinum Earrings

Earrings, diamond & platinum, dangle-style w/friction-style posts & backs, each centered by a cushion-cut diamond, both totaling 1.16 cts., framed by a mélée of 14 marquise-cut diamonds & 24 round full-cut diamonds, pr. (ILLUS.) **$5,975**

Diamond & Platinum Pendant Earrings

Earrings, diamond & platinum, pendant-type, a full-cut diamond top suspending a flexible line of full-cut diamonds suspending a shaped diamond-set ring surrounding a larger pendant diamond, diamonds weighing about 1.15 cts., pr. (ILLUS.)..... **$2,115**

Diamond & Sapphire Blossom Earrings

Earrings, diamond, sapphire & 18k bicolor gold, each designed as a five-petal blossom pavé-set w/diamond mélée & centered by a cluster of blue sapphires, pr. (ILLUS.)... **$705**

Emerald & Diamond Pendant Earrings

Earrings, emerald, diamond & 18k white gold, pendant-type, the top composed of a cluster of scrolling leaves set w/single-cut diamonds & suspending a straight line of diamonds above a squared drop w/a band of single-cut diamonds surrounding a square step-cut emerald, pr. (ILLUS., previous page) **$999**

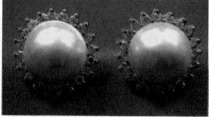

Mabe Pearl & Diamond Earrings

Earrings, mabe pearl & diamond, each silvery blue pearl framed by full-cut diamonds, 14k white gold mounts, pr. (ILLUS.) **$588**

Shell-shaped Sapphire & Diamond Earrings

Earrings, pink sapphire, diamond & 18k white gold, each designed as an openwork scallop shell bead-set w/full-cut diamond mélée & centered by an oval pink sapphire, pr. (ILLUS.) **$2,115**

Leaf-shaped Gold & Diamond Earrings

Earrings, platinum, 18k gold & diamond, a curled stem set w/single-cut diamonds

above a gold leaf accented w/a single full-cut diamond, pr. (ILLUS.) **$1,293**

Fine Platinum & Diamond Earrings

Earrings, platinum & diamond, clip-on type, each in a rounded snowflake design w/each ray prong-set w/an old European-cut or full-cut diamond, diamonds weighing about 2.70 cts., 14k white gold findings, 1" w., pr. (ILLUS.) **$2,585**

Abstract Heart Diamond Earrings

Earrings, platinum & diamond, each of an abstract heart shape pavé-set overall w/full-cut diamonds, diamonds weighing about 3.50 cts., pr. (ILLUS.) **$1,175**

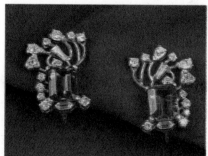

Pink Tourmaline & Diamond Earrings

Earrings, platinum, pink tourmaline & diamond, clip-on type, prong-set w/a large rectangular step-cut pink tourmaline framed up one side by a spray of fancy-cut diamonds, 14k white gold finding, pr. (ILLUS.) **$1,140**

J

South Sea Pearl & Diamond Earrings

Earrings, South Sea pearl, diamond & 14k white gold, pendant-type, each topped by a seven-diamond floret suspending a diamond-set leafy vine supporting a large South Sea pearl measuring about 13.50 mm, pr. (ILLUS.)...................................... **$4,406**

Large Star Sapphire Ring with Diamonds

Earrings, star sapphire, diamond & platinum, prong-set w/a large rounded oval star sapphire flanked on two sides by curved bands set w/full-cut & baguette diamonds, size 5 3/4 (ILLUS. of one)......... **$2,938**

Turquoise, Sapphire & Gold Earrings

Earrings, turquoise, sapphire & 14k gold, clip-on type, each designed as a group of four blossoms w/cabochon turquoise petals & a blue sapphire center, pr. (ILLUS.) **$705**

Three-strand Pearl Necklace with an Emerald & Diamond Clasp

Necklace, cultured pearl, emerald, diamond & 18k white gold, composed of a triple strand of off-white pearls measuring about 6.20 mm & spaced by thin bars set w/diamonds, completed by a box clasp set w/a large emerald-cut emeralds framed by a rectangular notch-cornered ring of square step-cut diamonds, diamonds weighing about 1.86 cts., 18 3/4" l. (ILLUS. of part) **$2,350**

Cultured Pearl & Sapphire Necklace

Necklace, cultured pearl & sapphire, three strands composed of 153 white pearls graduating in size from 9.50 to 6.15 mm, completed by a 14k gold heart-shaped clasp pavé-set w/blue sapphires, 16 1/4" l. (ILLUS.).. **$823**

South Sea Pearl & Diamond Necklace

Necklace, South Sea pearl & diamond, composed of 37 white pearls w/rose overtones graduating from 9.60 to 12.90 mm, completed by a half-spherical platinum clasp pavé-set w/full-cut diamonds, 18 1/4" l. (ILLUS.)................................... **$2,820**

Multi-strand Tourmaline Bead Necklace

Necklace, tourmaline, composed of ten strands of tumbled small pink & green oval tourmaline beads, 18k gold hook clasp, 17 1/2" l. (ILLUS.) **$764**

Lion Head Pendant in Gold & Gems

Pendant, 14k yellow gold, emerald, ruby & diamond, figural lion head w/incised mane & facial details in gold, the eyebrows & snout set w/eight diamond mélées, emerald eyes & a ruby tongue, stamped 14k mark (ILLUS.) **$304**

Carved Purple Tourmaline Buddha

Pendant, carved tourmaline, the purple tourmaline stone carved in the form of a seated Buddha, suspended from a fancy looping gold link on a fine trace link chain, pendant 1 1/8" l. (ILLUS.)....................... **$1,293**

Gold Ball & Diamond Pendant

Pendant, diamond & 14k gold, designed as a gold sphere pavé-set overall w/full-cut diamonds (ILLUS.) **$1,293**

J

Diamond-set Gold Heart Pendant

Pendant, diamond & 18k gold, designed as a heart pavé-set w/121 full-cut diamond mélée, diamonds weighing about 3.00 cts., suspended from a fancy link gold chain, overall 17 1/2" l. (ILLUS.) **$1,175**

Delicate Gold & Diamond Feather Pin

Pin, diamond & 18k gold, a long delicate gold feather centered by narrow bands bead-set w/diamond mélée, 2 1/2" l. (ILLUS.) **$705**

Terrier & Flute Gem-set Gold Pin

Pin, diamond & gem-set 18k gold, modeled as a standing terrier w/ruby eyes & nose playing a diamond-studded flute (ILLUS.) .. **$470**

Enameled Gold Sulky & Driver Pin

Pin, enameled 18k gold, designed as a racing sulky & driver, driver & horse blanket accented in green, yellow & blue enamel, 1 3/4" l. (ILLUS.) **$646**

Gem-set Gold Crouching Tiger Pin

Pin, enameled & gem-set 18k gold, modeled as a crouching tiger, black enamel stripes & single-cut diamond accents, emerald eye, 1 3/4" l. (ILLUS.) **$499**

Gem-set Gold Insect Pin

Pin, gem-set 14k gold, in the shape of a winged insect, the body & four-part wings set w/circular-cut emeralds, rubies & diamonds, rose-cut garnet eyes (ILLUS.) **$646**

Gem-set Gold Leopard Pin

Pin, gem-set 18k gold, designed as a seated leopard w/black enamel spots each set w/a single or full-cut diamond, emerald eyes, 1 3/4" l. (ILLUS.) **$470**

J

Cabochon Ruby Cluster Ring

Ring, cabochon ruby, diamond & 14k gold, the domed top composed of a cluster of nine cabochon rubies accented w/scattered full-cut diamonds, gold mount, size 6 1/2 (ILLUS.)............................... **$646**

Cat's-eye Tourmaline & Diamond Ring

Ring, cat's-eye green tourmaline & platinum, the top pront-set w/a large oval tourmaline cabochon flanked on each side by three small full-cut diamonds, 14k white gold hinged shank (ILLUS.) **$1,058**

Citrine & Amethyst Two-stone Ring

Ring, citrine, amethyst & 18k gold, composed of two large oval stones set side-by-side in a gold mount, size 6 (ILLUS.) **$646**

Coral, Diamond & Gold Ring

Ring, coral, diamond & 18k gold, the top center pavé-set w/diamonds flanked by panels of flute-carved pink coral, size 9 1/2 (ILLUS.)... **$382**

Cultured Pearl & Enameled Flower Ring

Ring, cultured pearl & enameled 14k gold, the top formed by a pearl cluster mounted w/four tiny enameled pansies each centering a tiny single-cut diamond, size 4 1/2 (ILLUS.)... **$353**

Gold Ring with Box-set Diamond

Ring, diamond & 14k yellow gold, the flat gold band box-set at the top w/a full-cut diamond weighing about 1.10 cts., size 8 (ILLUS.).. **$1,763**

J

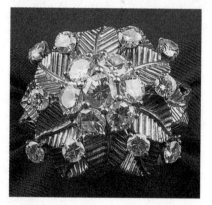

1960s Diamond & Gold Leaves Ring

Ring, diamond & 18k gold, designed as a cluster of full-cut diamonds surrounded by gold leaves further set w/diamonds, diamonds weighing about 2.77 cts., w/ring guard, ca. 1960s, size 5 1/2 (ILLUS.)....... **$1,880**

Wide Ring Set Overall with Diamonds

Ring, diamond & 18k gold, the wide band set overall w/four rows of princess-cut diamonds, diamonds weighing about 3.68 cts., size 5 (ILLUS.)................................ **$1,175**

Gold Ring with Scattered Diamonds

Ring, diamond & 18k gold, the wide gold band decorated w/scattered inset small diamonds, size 6 3/4 (ILLUS.).................... **$646**

J

Ballerina-style Mixed Diamond Ring

Ring, diamond, colored diamond & platinum, ballerina-style, the long four-lobed top set w/a wide border of 48 tapering baguette diamonds around an oval band of 16 full-cut diamonds all centered by an orangish brown marquise-cut diamond weighing about 1.50 cts., other diamonds weighing about 2.48 cts., size 6 1/2 (ILLUS.) **$5,581**

Diamond & Pearl Bypass-style Ring

Ring, diamond, cultured pearl & 18k white gold, bypass-style, the top tips set w/a white or black pearl, the shoulders set w/full-cut diamond mélée, size 7 1/4 (ILLUS.) **$470**

Pearl & Diamond Pendant Earrings

Earrings, diamond, cultured pearl & platinum, pendant-type, the top set w/a white pearl above a straight drop of eight full-cut diamonds suspending another pearl, diamonds weighing about 2.10 cts., 1 7/8" l., pr. (ILLUS.) **$1,528**

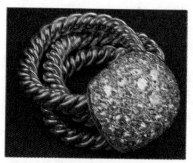

Unusual Diamond & Gold Rope Ring

Ring, diamond, platinum & 18k gold, the domed top pavé-set slide on three gold ropetwist bands, diamonds weighing about 5.00 cts., size 7 (ILLUS.).............. **$6,463**

Wide Diamond & Platinum Ring

Ring, diamond & platinum, a wide openwork band bead- and bezel-set overall w/triangular, marquise & single-cut diamonds, size 7 1/4 (ILLUS.) **$1,645**

Diamond Solitaire with Very Large Stone

Ring, diamond & platinum, solitaire-type, the top centered by a large prong-set pear-cut diamond weighing 5.73 cts., flanked by 16 tapered baguette diamonds, size 7 (ILLUS.)......................... **$11,750**

Ring with Baguette & Full-cut Diamonds

Ring, diamond & platinum, the rectangular top centered by a band of six channel-set baguette diamonds flanked by two narrow rows w/six full-cut diamonds in each, diamonds weighing about 1.40 cts., size 6 1/2 (ILLUS.)... **$1,175**

Fine Three-stone Diamond Ring

Ring, diamond & platinum, the top prongset w/three emerald-cut diamonds weighing about 3.75 cts. & flanked on the shoulders w/diamond baguettes, size 6 (ILLUS.).. **$11,750**

Ring with Rubies & Clear & Black Diamonds

Ring, diamond, ruby & 18k white gold, the wide band centered by an undulating stripe of pavé-set clear diamonds flanked on one side by a panel of pavé-set small rubies & on the other side by a panel of pavé-set black diamonds, size 6 (ILLUS.) **$1,058**

Ring, diamond solitaire, bezel-set w/a round brilliant-cut diamond weighing about 1.11 cts., 18k gold mount, signed by Tiffany & Co., size 6 1/4 (ILLUS. right with very expensive diamond solitaire, top next page).. **$5,875**

Ring, diamond solitaire, prong-set w/a round brilliant-cut diamond weighing about 2.01 cts., flanked by narrow bands of small full-cut diamonds, 18k gold & platinum mount, size 5 (ILLUS. left with Tiffany diamond solitaire, top next page) **$23,500**

J

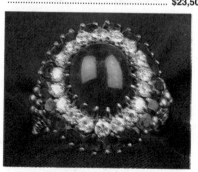

Fine Emerald, Diamond & Gold Ring

Two Fine Diamond Solitaire Rings

Ring, emerald, diamond & 18k gold, the round top centered by a large emerald cabochon surrounded by a ring of full-cut diamonds & an outer ring of circular-cut emeralds, w/ring guard, size 5 1/2 (ILLUS., previous page) **$1,293**

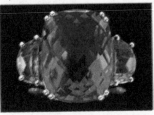

Unusual Enameled & Diamond Tiger Ring

Ring, enameled 18k gold & diamond, designed as a snarling tiger head w/black & white enameled stripes & a red & black-enameled nose & a red tongue, the upper lips & side of the head set w/single-cut diamonds, the black & white-striped tail curls up at one side, size 5 (ILLUS.) **$499**

J

Amethyst & Citrine Lady's Ring

Ring, lady's, amethyst, citrine & 14k white gold, the top cushion-set w/a large oblong facet-cut amethyst flanked by two half-moon facet-cut citrines, marked "14k" w/initials of maker "FP," size 7 1/2 (ILLUS.)... **$345**

Lady's Ring with Large Amethyst

Ring, lady's fashion-type, amethyst, diamond & 18k white gold, the top mounted w/a large 4.28 ct. Siberian color square-cut amethyst framed at each corner by a heart-shaped mount accented w/small diamonds, narrow channels of diamonds also along the sides of the shank, stamped mark "18K NI 3794" (ILLUS.) **$863**

Lady's Ring with Large Tourmaline

Ring, lady's fashion-type, diamond, pink tourmaline & 14k white gold, the triangular top mounted w/a large 6 ct. pink tourmaline surrounded by 21 small diamonds, the shank w/five small diamonds on each side, maker's mark & "14k BH," size 7 1/2 (ILLUS.) **$920**

Lady's Emerald & Diamond Fashion Ring

Ring, lady's fashion-type, emerald, diamond & 18k white gold, the starburst top centered by one square step-cut emerald weighing .58 cts., surrounded by two bands of 28 round full-cut diamonds, slender band (ILLUS.)................................. **$418**

Branch-style Lady's Fashion Pearl Ring

Ring, lady's fashion-type, pearl, diamond & 18k yellow gold, the branch-form gold mount supporting four grey baroque-shaped cultured pearls 9.5 mm to 10 mm, also mounted w/four small scattered diamonds, size 11 (ILLUS.) **$448**

Opal & Diamond Ring

Ring, opal, diamond & 18k white gold, a large oval prong-set opal framed by 25 full-cut diamonds, boxed, size 7 (ILLUS.).. **$823**

Unusual Round Opal, Ruby & Diamond Ring

Ring, opal, ruby, diamond & 14k gold, the wide round top centered by a prong-set round opal framed by a ring of 14 cushion-cut rubies divided by two small bands each set w/two old mine-cut diamonds, size 9 (ILLUS.) **$764**

Peridot & Enameled Gold Ring

Ring, peridot & enameled 18k gold, the top bezel-set w/an oval-cut peridot weighing 2.55 cts. flanked by green enameled leaves, w/a hallmark, size 5 3/4 (ILLUS.)... **$1,175**

Extraordinary Mixed Diamond Ring

Ring, pink diamond, colorless diamond & 18k gold, the simple rounded mount centered by a fancy intense radiant-cut pink diamond weighing about .76 cts. flanked by round brilliant-cut diamonds weighing .71 cts. and .76 cts., size 5 1/2 (ILLUS.) **$33,000**

Bold Tourmaline, Diamond & Gold Ring

Ring, pink tourmaline, green tourmaline, diamond & 18k gold, the wide tapering mount centered at the top by a large bezel-set oval-cut pink tourmaline flanked by small triangular pink tourmalines, the shoulders w/center panels set w/square-cut green tourmalines framed by outer bands of diamonds & buff-top rubies, mark of maker Ste. H.V. & French guarantee stamp, size 6 1/4 (ILLUS.) **$1,175**

Ring, platinum, diamond & emerald, the wide band centering a diamond mélée flower flanked by lines of step-cut emeralds & full-cut diamonds, signed "RT," size 7... **$940**

Squared Diamond & Platinum Ring

Ring, platinum & diamond, the squared top centered by a bezel-set brilliant-cut diamonds w/rounded corners weighing about 1.05 cts., framed by a ring of smaller diamonds, decorative shoulders, size 6 1/4 (ILLUS.).. **$5,581**

J

1960s Ruby, Diamond & Gold Ring

Ring, ruby, diamond & 18k gold, the four-section oblong top composed of two sections each w/two cabochon rubies alternating w/openwork ropetwist band section, a cross-form central band set w/full-cut diamonds, diamonds weighing about 1.95 cts., ca. 1960s, size 6 (ILLUS.) **$2,938**

J

Ruby & Diamond Twin-stone Ring

Ring, ruby, diamond & 18k gold, twin-stone style, prong-set w/two rectangular step-cut rubies framed by bands of full-cut diamonds, w/ring guard, size 2 1/2 (ILLUS.) **$940**

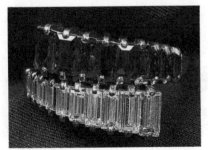

Ruby & Diamond Bypass-style Ring

Ring, ruby, diamond & platinum, bypass-style, two side-by-side bands, one bead-set w/tapering lines of rubies & the other set w/diamond baguettes, size 7 (ILLUS.) **$1,645**

Sapphire & Diamond Double-band Ring

Ring, sapphire, diamond & 18k gold, the double band prong-set w/an oval pink & purple sapphire, pavé-set w/56 full-cut diamonds, diamonds weighing about 2.62 cts., size 6 1/4 (ILLUS.) **$1,763**

Sapphire, Diamond & White Gold Ring

Ring, sapphire, diamond & 18k white gold, the floret-form top centered by a full-cut diamond surrounded by six circular-cut blue sapphires & bordered by a band of smaller full-cut diamonds, diamonds weighing about 1.84 cts., English hallmarks, size 6 3/4 (ILLUS.) **$588**

Gold Ring Set with Shaded Gemstones

Ring, sapphire, diamond & 18k white gold, the wide tapering band bead-set w/dark blue sapphires shading to light blue sapphires shading to diamonds, size 6 1/2 (ILLUS.) **$646**

Sets

*Boxed Brooch & Earring Suite in Gold,
Emeralds & Diamonds*

Brooch & earrings, bicolor 18k gold, emerald & diamond, the brooch designed as a long curved spray of flowers on a leafy stem, the leaves & flower petals set w/diamonds & each flower center set w/a circular-cut emerald, the matching clip-on earrings composed of three flowers, in original fitted box, the suite (ILLUS.) **$3,173**

Gold & Gem-set Brooch from Set

Brooch & earrings, gold (14k), ruby & diamond, the large multi-rayed sunburst w/a solid domed center accented w/ruby mélée & a central diamond, small diamond mélée scattered on the rays, w/matching clip-on earrings, one earring missing central diamond, brooch 2" d., the set (ILLUS.) **$646**

Brooch & earrings, platinum, 18k gold & diamond, the brooch designed as a layered cluster of long pointed leaves centered by raised gold veins surrounded by pavé-set full-cut diamonds, matching clip-on earrings formed of three leaves, signed "M," brooch 2 1/4" l., the suite (ILLUS., top next column) **$4,348**

Leaf-design Gold & Diamond Suite

*Emerald, Diamond & White Gold Earring &
Ring Set*

Earrings & ring, emerald, diamond & 18k white gold; each piece centered by a rectangular step-cut emerald weighing from 1.32 to 1.56 cts., each emerald surrounded by a mélée of round full-cut diamonds, 78 total, 18th white gold mount, the set (ILLUS.) **$1,434**

Necklace & bracelet, bicolor 18k gold, both composed of ribbed woven links, each w/a removable white gold closure set w/full-cut diamond mélée, bracelet 7 1/2" l., necklace 17" l., the set **$1,645**

J

*Large Suite of Gold Jewelry Accented with a
Stylized Fish*

Coral & Diamond Necklace & Earring Suite

Necklace, bracelet, earrings & ring, high-karat gold, enamel & stones; the necklace w/a fancy link triple strand joined at the front by a curled stylized fish w/enameled trim & a band of channel-set red stones, each piece w/matching chain & fish design, ring size 6 3/4, bracelet 6 7/8" l., necklace 14 1/2" l., the suite (ILLUS., previous page)................. **$1,763**

Necklace & earrings, coral, diamond & 18k gold, the necklace composed of four strands of coral beads completed by an oval clasp centered by an old mine-cut diamond flanked by coral beads on a ground of tiny diamonds, the matching clip-on round earrings w/a diamond-set band centering a coral bead, French import stamps, necklace 14" l., the set (ILLUS., top of page) **$1,410**

J

Elaborate Enameled Gold & Seed Pearl Indian Jewelry Suite

Necklace & earrings, enameled high-karat gold & seed pearl, the necklace composed of scalloped flower-form links suspending a large drop pendant w/a wide almond form plaque w/a lower fringe of seed pearls suspending a wide pointed chevron-form plaque also w/an ornate seed pearl & colored stone fringe & central matching drop, the plaques all enameled w/a dark green ground decorated in gold & red w/stylized flowering tree & bird designs, matching pendant-style earrings w/14k gold findings, India, earrings 3 1/4" l., necklace 15" l., the suite (ILLUS.)... **$2,350**

KITCHENWARES

Also see Antique Trader Kitchen Collectibles Price Guide

The Modern Kitchen - 1920-1980

Crockery & Dishes

Cow Creamers

Bennington Pottery Cow Creamer

Bennington pottery, platform-type, Rockingham glaze, rare, missing lid, chip on one horn, tail repair, expect damage as this creamer is a rare find in any condition, 5 x 7" (ILLUS.) **$450-550**

Bisque Cow Creamer

Bisque porcelain, highly textured bisque body, black spots, pink bow, w/yellow bell at neck, all glazed, "Japan" paper label, 4 1/4 x 5 3/4" (ILLUS.) **$20-24**

Blue Polka-dotted Cow Creamer

Ceramic, blue polka-dots on white glazed pottery, molded bell at neck, eyes accented w/long lashes, unmarked, maker unknown, 5 1/2 x 5 3/4" (ILLUS.) **$49-55**

Brown & White Bull Creamer

Ceramic, bull, brown & white, grey hooves & facial shading, tail curls under to form handle, ink stamped "K393," maker unknown, 4 1/2 x 7 3/4" (ILLUS.) **$29-35**

Grouping of Bull Creamers

Ceramic, bull creamers, also found w/matching salt & pepper shakers, stamped "Made in Japan," also "Occupied Japan," 3 x 3", each (ILLUS.) **$19-24**

Flat-Bottomed Cow Creamer

Ceramic, flat bottom, turquoise spots on cream glazed pottery, molded bell at neck, rouge painted jaw area, unmarked, unglazed bottom, 5 1/2 x 7" (ILLUS.) **$65-69**

Handpainted Cow Creamer

Ceramic, h.p. floral on white, molded bell at neck, many found with "Souvenir" label from places visited, Japan, 3 1/4 x 5 1/4" (ILLUS.) **$14-19**

Holly Ross Cow Creamer

Ceramic, h.p. flower on one side, bud on reverse, facial features, hooves & ribbon in gold, w/gold under glaze bottom marks, artist signed "Holly Ross, LaAnna, PA. Made in the Poconos," 5 x 7 1/2" (ILLUS.) **$39-45**

Black Cow Creamer

Ceramic, highly-glazed black over red clay, cold-painted features in pink, blue & gold, pottery bell w/painted flower attached by metal chain, original lid w/tip of tail ornamental to top, unmarked, 5 1/2 x 6" (ILLUS.) **$34-39**

K

Black & White Lustre Cow Creamer

Ceramic, lying down, feet tucked under, lustre ware w/black spots & gold accented horns, red ink stamp "Made in Japan," 4 x 6" (ILLUS.).. **$27-32**

Handpainted Japanese Cow Creamer

Ceramic, lying down, red dotted flowers on white w/dark green tail, hooves & crest, pink nose & ribbon, bottom marking "Hand Painted Japan," 1950-60, 4 x 6 1/2" (ILLUS.).................................. **$24-29**

Miniature Japanese Cow Creamer

Ceramic, miniature, h.p. flower on each side, stamped "Japan" on front hooves, 2 1/4 x 3 1/2" (ILLUS.)............................ **$16-20**

Orange & White Cow Creamer

Ceramic, orange spots on both sides over white, black tail & facial features, unmarked, 1960 (ILLUS.)............................ **$19-24**

Petite Cow Creamer

Ceramic, petite, decorated w/flowers on white glaze, molded bell at neck, unmarked, Japan, 4 1/2 x 4 3/4" (ILLUS.)... **$16-19**

Mottled Pink Cow Creamer

Ceramic, pink mottled high glaze, grey base, horns & tail, black ink stamp "Made in Japan" w/flower in middle, very unusual, 4 1/2 x 6 1/4" (ILLUS.)........................ **$49-55**

Gold Accented Cow Creamer Pitcher

Ceramic, pitcher, black high gloss w/22 kt. gold detailed accents, bottom stamped in gold "Pearl China Co., hand decorated, 22 kt. Gold, U.S.A.," impressed "#635," larger than usual cow creamer, 6 1/2 x 6 1/2" (ILLUS.)............................ **$29-35**

Common Japanese Cow Creamer

Ceramic, reddish brown over cream, Japanese, mass-produced before, during & after the war, found in many sizes, colors & various markings, common, 3 1/2 x 5 1/4" (ILLUS.)............................ **$25-28**

Handpainted Creamer & Sugar Set

Ceramic, set: creamer & cov. sugar; purple over white glaze, large pink flared nostrils, yellow horns, hooves & tails, tails curl up over backs to form handles, ink stamp "52/270" under glaze, foil gold & black paper stickers "Made in Japan," marked "Thames, Handpainted," found w/matching salt & pepper, complete, mint, creamer 5 x 5 1/2", sugar 4 1/2 x 6", the set (ILLUS.)...................... **$45-49**

Blue Tulip Decorated Cow Creamer

Ceramic, sitting, blue tulips on white glaze, bottom ink stamp "Japan" under glaze, 1950-60, common, 3 3/4 x 4" (ILLUS.) **$14-19**

K

Kent Ceramic Cow Creamer

Ceramic, sitting, brown w/white spots, gold molded bell around neck, tail curled up connecting at back of neck to form handle, bottom impressed stamp "Kent," 5 1/4 x 6" (ILLUS.).................................. **$24-29**

Japanese Ceramic Cow Creamer

Ceramic, small, blue, w/molded green bell around neck, "Made in Japan" ink stamp underneath, 3 1/2 x 5" (ILLUS.) **$30-35**

Cow Creamer w/Pink & Grey Transfers

Ceramic, w/pink & grey flower transfer on both sides & gold hooves, found in various floral designs, unmarked, 5 1/2 x 7" (ILLUS.)... **$39-45**

Seated Brown-spotted Czech Creamer

Czechoslovakian pottery, sitting, orange spots on white porcelain, black tail, circle black ink stamp "Made in Czechoslovakia," 4 3/4 x 5 3/4" (ILLUS.)..................... **$75-78**
Delft pottery, painted & lightly glazed porcelain, cow dressed in assorted men's clothing, either sitting or standing, rare & very desirable...................................... **$165-179**

Standing Cow Creamer w/Infant

German china, standing in upright position, reddish brown cow wearing a white & blue dress, holding an infant in a blanket, bottom circular ink stamp "Made in Germany," rare, 3 3/4" w., 5 3/4" h. (ILLUS.)
.... **$400-475**

German Porcelain Cow Creamer

German porcelain, brown markings over white, black highlights on tail, hooves & horns, unmarked, 4 1/2 x 5 1/2" (ILLUS.). **$48-52**

Miniature German Cow Creamer

German porcelain, miniature, grey/black on fine white porcelain, impressed on back "Germany," 2 5/8 x 3 5/8" (ILLUS.). **$45-55**

German Porcelain Standing Creamer

German porcelain, reddish brown graduating to white on softly glazed fine porcelain, extremely detailed features, impressed on reverse side "Germany 8610," 7 1/2" h., 4 3/4" l. (ILLUS.) **$75-82**

Goebel China Cow Creamer

Goebel china, brown markings on cream glazed ceramic, tin gold bell on string, tail curls under to form handle, unmarked, opening 2 1/4", 3 3/4 x 5 3/4" (ILLUS.) ... **$32-36**

Occupied Japan Cow Creamer

Occupied Japan china, various dark brown markings, white background, glazed, tail curls up to form handle, found w/many different Japan stamps, common, prices depend on bottom markings, largest size 5 x 8" (ILLUS.).. **$35-39**

K

German Porcelain Cow Creamer

Porcelain, white, tail & horns missing black cold-paint due to wear, "Germany" impressed on back underneath, 4 3/4 x 7" (ILLUS.)....................................... **$64-69**

Kitchen Accessories

Cookie Cutters - General
Bird, tin, outline of bird, narrow **$10-20**
Buzzard, by Little Fox Factory, Bucyrus, Ohio **$5**
Cathedral window, by Eugene Valasek, Canton, Ohio **$25-30**
Circle, crinkled edges, early 1900s **$30-35**
Gingerbread boy waving, outline-style, by Little Fox Factory, Bucyrus, Ohio **$5**

Gingerbread Boy & Girl Cookie Cutters

Gingerbread boy with buttons, tin, w/handles, signed E. Valasek, 1979, Canton, Ohio (ILLUS. right with Gingerbread Girl with Skirt) **$15-20**
Gingerbread girl, heavy tin, no signature .. **$25-30**
Gingerbread girl, with skirt, tin, w/handles, signed Gene Valasek, 1980, Canton, Ohio (ILLUS. left with Gingerbread Boy with Buttons) **$25-30**
Gingerbread woman with legs, galvanized metal, flat back handle w/edges turned under, no signature on cutter, Baxter Oberlin, Angola, Indiana **$25-35**

Hansel & Gretel Set of Cookie Cutters

Hansel & Gretel set: Hansel, Gretel, witch, tree, gingerbread house; first boxed set, plastic, w/recipes & story of Hansel & Gretel, Educational Products, 1947, front of box features Mr. Meiro, owner of E.P. Co., wife & two daughters, set of six cutters in original box (ILLUS.)....................... **$150**

Heart, w/Gingerbread tiny boy & girl inside, has a crinkled edge handle w/edge folded to outside, signed inside of heart B. Cukla©, Hammer Song, Boonsboro, Maryland **$25-35**
Outhouse, by Eugene Valasek, Canton, Ohio **$30-40**
Six-Sided, replica of a cutter a roving tinsmith would have made in the late 1800s or early 1900s **$20-30**
Swiss cheese slice, small "Ohio" in upper left hand corner, by Stan Baker, Dover, Ohio **$25-30**
Woman on pot, replica of a cutter in the Historical Society Collection at Lewiston, Pennsylvania, by Bob Jones, Allen Park, Michigan **$30-50**

Egg Timers
A little glass tube filled with sand and attached to a figural base measuring between 3" and 5" in height was once a commonplace kitchen item. Although egg timers were originally used to time a 3-minute egg, some were used to limit the length of a telephone call as a cost saving measure.

Many beautiful timers were produced in Germany in the 1920s and later in Japan, reaching their heyday in the 1940s. These small egg timers were commonly made in a variety of shapes in bisque, china, chalkware, cast iron, tin, brass, wood or plastic.

Egg timers had long been considered an essential kitchen tool until, in the 1920s and 1930s, a German pottery company, W. Goebel, introduced figural egg timers. Goebel crafted miniature china figurines with attached glass vials. After the Great Depression, Japanese companies introduced less detailed timers. The Goebel figural egg timers are set apart by their trademark, delicate painting and distinctive clothes. It is best to purchase egg timers with their original tube, but the condition of the figure is most important in setting prices.

Angel, ceramic, wearing blue robe & gold wings, w/verse "May the meals that I...," unmarked.. **$45-65**
Baker, ceramic, Goebel (ILLUS., next page) **$50**
Bear, ceramic, howling, USA **$50-75**
Bear, ceramic, wearing chef's outfit, marked "Japan" **$65-85**
Bellhop, ceramic, Oriental, kneeling, marked "Germany" **$65-85**
Bellhop, ceramic, wearing green uniform, marked "Japan," 4 1/2" h.............................. **$70**
Bellhop, ceramic, wearing white uniform w/buttons down leg seam, marked "Germany" **$65-85**
Bird, ceramic, red bird sitting by yellow post, marked "Germany" **$50**

K

Goebel Baker Egg Timer

Bird, ceramic, sitting on nest, wearing white bonnet w/green ribbon, Josef Originals sticker **$45**

Bird & Egg Near Stump Egg Timer

Bird, ceramic, standing next to stump w/egg at base, shades of brown w/green grassy base & leaves on stump, Japan (ILLUS.) **$50**
Birdhouse, wood, hanging-type, white w/red perch & roof **$10-15**

Boy on Chamber Pot Egg Timer

Black boy, holding timer in right hand & sitting on chamber pot, marked "Foreign" (ILLUS.) **$85-110**

Black chef, ceramic, standing, marked "Llangollen" **$95**

Black Chef with Fish Egg Timer

Black chef, ceramic, standing w/large fish, timer in fish's mouth, Germany, 4 3/4" h. (ILLUS.) **$125**

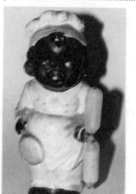

Black Chef w/Frying Pan Egg Timer

Black chef with frying pan, composition, Japan (ILLUS.) **$95**

Lady Chef Egg Timer

Black lady chef, ceramic, sitting, Germany (ILLUS.) **$95**

K

Bo-Peep Egg Timer

Bo-Peep, ceramic, "Bo-Peep" on base, Japan (ILLUS.) $95
Boy, ceramic, playing guitar, marked "Germany," 3 1/2" h. $50

Swiss Boy Egg Timer

Boy, composition, wearing Swiss outfit, marked "Germany" (ILLUS.) $65-75

Boy Chef Egg Timer

Boy chef, ceramic, sitting w/raised arm, Germany (ILLUS.) $65

Goebel Egg Timer with Boy & Girl

Boy & girl, ceramic, flanking timer on oblong base, boy w/white pants, dark blue coat & yellow cap, girl in red dress w/white apron & large dark blue hat, Goebel, Germany (ILLUS.) $95
Cat, ceramic, black cat w/white-tipped tail sitting by fireplace, "Ireland" painted on front, marked "Manorware, England" $25-35
Cat, ceramic, white & black cat, marked "Germany" $65-85
Chef, ceramic, holding egg, Germany $45-65
Chef, ceramic, holding knife, Japan $45-65
Chef, ceramic plate w/hole to hold timer, which removes to change, Japan $50
Chef, ceramic, white w/black shoes & hair, marked "Germany" $45-65
Chefs, ceramic, man & woman, Goebel, Germany, 4" h. $100
Chicken, ceramic, multicolored, marked "Germany" $75-95
Chicken, ceramic, white w/black wings & tail feathers, marked "Germany" $50

Goebel Chimney Sweep Egg Timer

Chimney sweep, ceramic, Goebel, Germany (ILLUS.) $50

K

Clown Egg Timer

Clown, ceramic, Germany (ILLUS.) **$95**
Clown, ceramic, w/ball on head, marked
  "Japan" **$45-65**
Colonial man in knickers, ruffled shirt, ce-
  ramic, Japan, 4 3/4" h. **$75**
Dog, ceramic, black Poodle, sitting, Germa-
  ny **$75**

Green Dog Egg Timer

Dog, ceramic, green, looking at his tail
  (ILLUS.) **$75**

Dog Egg Timer

Dog, ceramic, sitting, white w/brown tail &
  ears, timer in head, Germany (ILLUS.) **$75**
Dog, ceramic, white & brown dog w/red collar sitting by post, marked "Germany" **$65-85**

Scottie Egg Timer

Dog, chalkware, white Scottie (ILLUS.) **$45-65**
Dog, lustre, white & yellow, holding red flower, marked "Germany" **$95**
Dogs, ceramic, Scotties, brown, standing
  facing each other holding timer in paws,
  marked "Germany" **$95**
Dutch boy, ceramic, standing by green
  post, Japan, tall **$35**
Dutch boy, ceramic, white w/red scarf
  around neck, kneeling, Japan **$35**

K

Dutch Boy Egg Timer

Dutch boy, composition, blue pants & hat,
  red shirt, white tie w/blue polka dots, Ger-
  many (ILLUS.) **$50**
Dutch girl, ceramic, all white w/blue trim at
  waist & neckline, kneeling **$50-75**
Dutch girl, ceramic, white w/blue apron &
  trim, Germany (ILLUS., next page) **$50**
Friar Tuck, ceramic, double-type, modeled
  by Helmut White, timer marked w/3-, 4- &
  5-minute intervals, Goebel, Germany,
  1956 .... **$65**

Dutch Girl Egg Timer

Genie, w/recipe holder in back (ILLUS.) **$75-95**
Girl, ceramic, holding ball at shoulder, marked "Germany" **$50**
Girl, ceramic, holding watering can, marked "Germany" **$65**

Golliwog Egg Timer

Golliwog, bisque, England, 4 1/2" h., minimum value (ILLUS.) **$150**
Grandfather clock, composition, Manorware, England **$35**
House, ceramic, handpainted w/clock face on front, Japan **$35**
Humpty Dumpty, ceramic, wearing hat & bow tie, turn onto head to activate sand, marked "California Cleminsons".................. **$35**

Indian Egg Timer

Indian, ceramic, kneeling, white, wearing headdress w/red, blue & green feathers, holding timer in one hand, marked "Germany," rare (ILLUS.) **$100-150**
Lady mouse, ceramic, wearing green dress w/yellow apron & bonnet, Josef Originals sticker.. **$15-25**
Leprechaun, glazed chalkware, sitting by tree stump, marked "Manorware," England **$35**

Genie Egg Timer

K

Frying pan, ceramic, hanging-type, w/picture of chef & cooking utensils, Japan (ILLUS.) **$20-35**
Garden boy, ceramic, holding shovel & wearing hat, Germany............................ **$75-95**

Lighthouse, lustre, yellow & orange, Germany **$35**
Maid, ceramic, wearing green dress w/red collar & white apron, marked "Japan" **$45-65**
Mammy, painted wood, flat cut-out form w/holder for egg timer at the front, one arm extends to hold pot holders **$85**
Minuteman, ceramic, holding rifle & leaning against stone wall, "Kitchen Independence" on front base, marked "Enesco" & "Japan" **$35**

Mother Rabbit Egg Timer

Mother rabbit, ceramic, holding carrot w/basket, Japan (ILLUS.) **$65**
Parlor maid, ceramic, w/blue & white striped dress holding platter of food, marked "FOREIGN" **$65-85**
Peasant woman ceramic, w/black upswept hair carrying basket, marked "Germany" **$75-95**
Pixie, ceramic, Enesco, Japan, 5 1/2" h...... **$15-25**

Prayer Lady Egg Timer

Prayer lady, ceramic, pink & white, Enesco (ILLUS.) **$50**

Rabbit with Carrot Egg Timer

Rabbit, ceramic, sitting, white w/red jacket, holding ear of corn that supports the timer, Germany (ILLUS.) **$50**

Rooster Egg Timer

Rooster, painted cut-out wood, w/sequins (ILLUS.) **$35**
Rooster on house, metal & wood, w/hole in roof for timer, marked "Gift Ideas, Philadelphia, Pennsylvania" **$15-20**
Santa Claus, ceramic, standing by wrapped gift, label reads "SONSCO," marked "Japan" **$50-75**
Sea gull, ceramic, lustre, white w/brown-tipped spread wings & tail, purple base, Germany **$75**

K

Sea Gull Egg Timer with Bottle Opener

Sea gull, iron, white & tan bird w/red beak & legs, on black & white branch that is also a bottle opener (ILLUS., previous page) **$20**

Swami Egg Timer

Swami, ceramic, standing wearing turban, Germany (ILLUS.) **$110**

Swiss woman, ceramic, w/multicolored striped apron, marked "Germany" **$50**

Tillie Egg Timer

Tillie the Timer, iron, Amish lady on bench (ILLUS.) **$10**

Victorian lady, ceramic, wearing green & pink gown, marked "Germany" **$50**

Welsh woman, ceramic, marked "Japan" **$35**

Windmill, ceramic, all green, goose sitting atop windmill, marked "Germany" **$50**

Windmill, ceramic, brown, black & yellow, w/dog standing on base, marked "Japan" .. **$100**

Windmill, metal, hanging-type, w/"USA, Keystone Coffee, Keystone Mills, Penbrook, PA" on base **$25-35**

Napkin Dolls

Until the 1990s, napkin dolls were a rather obscure collectible, coveted by only a few savvy individuals who appreciated their charm and beauty. Today, however, these late 1940s and 1950s icons of postwar America are hot commodities.

Ranging from the individualistic pieces made in ceramics classes to jeweled Japanese models and the wide variety of wooden examples, these figures are no longer mistaken as planters or miniature dress forms. Of course, as their popularity has risen, so have prices, putting smiles on the faces of collectors who got in on the ground floor and stretching the pocketbooks of those looking to start their own collections.

Bobbie Zucker Bryson is co-author, with Deborah Gillham and Ellen Bercovici, of the pictorial price guide Collectibles For The Kitchen, Bath & Beyond *- Second Edition, published by Krause Publications. It covers a broad range of collectibles including napkin dolls, stringholders, pie birds, figural egg timers, razor blade banks, whimsical whistle milk cups and laundry sprinkler bottles. Bryson can be contacted via e-mail at Napkindoll aol.com.*

Ceramic, figure of a genie holding a lantern, marked "Genie at Your Service," by Enesco, 8" h. **$100-135**

Napkin Doll-Candleholder Tall Lady

Ceramic, figure of a woman, her black hair pulled back into a bun & wearing a wide-brimmed red-trimmed hat forming a candleholder, her hands behind her back & wearing a long white jacket w/pale blue trim over a red bodice, the long white dress w/slits & hem trimmed w/thin red lines, 12 3/4" h. (ILLUS.) **$75-95**

K

Green-dressed Lady with Candleholders

Ceramic, figure of a woman, red hair covered w/a green kerchief, wearing a long green dress w/a white blouse w/gold trim, each arm supporting a tall square-based columnar white candlestick at the side, 10" h. (ILLUS.) **$115-135**

Napkin Doll with Bowl on Her Head

Ceramic, figure of a woman, short brown hair, long blue dress w/puffy sleeves & h.p. flowers on the front, her arms up holding a wide, low gold-trimmed bowl on her head, marked "Japan," 9 1/4" h. (ILLUS.) **$50-65**

Ceramic, figure of a woman, wearing a white dress w/yellow bodice & trim, holding out her skirt w/one hand, the other hand on her hip, marked "Tina," Mallory Studios, 9 1/2" h. **$75-85**

Ceramic, figure of angel, blonde, wearing blue & white dress w/gold trim, holding maroon flowers w/green leaves, gold halo on head, two slits in shoulders for napkins to form "wings," 5 3/8" h. **$100-135**

Atlantic Mold Napkin Doll

Ceramic, figure of girl holding lily, mouth open as if singing, brown bobbed hair w/yellow headband, bright yellow dress w/green leaf design, holds a blue lily in arms, Atlantic Mold, 11" h. (ILLUS.) **$50-65**

Ceramic, figure of Santa Claus, wearing red & white suit & hat, white beard, slits in rear for napkins, holes in hat for toothpicks, marked "Japan," 6 3/4" h. **$100-150**

Spanish Dancer Napkin Holder

Ceramic, figure of woman, black-haired Spanish dancer holding tambourine in one hand, the other holding skirt, wearing pink dress w/brown bodice, the skirt decorated w/yellow sunflowers, 17" h. (ILLUS.) **$130-150**

K

Napkin Doll from Puerto Rico

Ceramic, figure of woman w/black hair standing w/hands folded in front, wearing white dress w/pink bodice & hem, elbow-length gloves, front of skirt marked in gold "Arecibo Puerto Rico 1990," 12 1/2" h. (ILLUS.) **$45-65**

Woman with Umbrella Napkin Doll

Ceramic, figure of woman w/black hair wearing lavender skirt & purple blouse w/gilt buttons & collar, purple hat, holding green unfurled umbrella behind back, slits in skirt for napkins, 10 3/4" h. (ILLUS.) **$90-110**

Ceramic, figure of woman w/brown hair in colonial style, wearing yellow dress trimmed in white & decorated in gold fur-like trim, w/matching hat forming candle-holder, gold-gloved hands in matching white & gold muff, marked "Kreiss and Company," 10 1/4" h. **$95-110**

Colonial Woman Napkin Doll

Ceramic, figure of woman w/colonial-style yellow hair, dressed in pink, white & yellow period dress trimmed in gold w/bell sleeves, ink mark reads "Japan," 9" h. (ILLUS.).. **$75-85**

Woman Napkin Doll/Toothpick Holder

K

Ceramic, figure of woman w/red hair, arms upraised to hold large bowl on head, wearing light & dark green puff-sleeved dress decorated on front w/flowers, jewel necklace, slits in skirt for napkins, bowl on head for toothpicks, marked "Japan," 9 1/4" h. (ILLUS., previous page) **$60-75**

Ceramic, figure of woman wearing white dress w/green decoration & gold necklace, a gold shoe peeking out from under skirt, 9 1/2" h. **$95-125**

Spanish Lady Napkin Doll

Ceramic, half-doll, figural of Spanish lady w/black hair w/red & white flowers, wearing green dress w/white ruffled sleeves, holding red & white fan in one hand, other raised to her head, on wooden stand w/wires to hold napkins, 9 1/2" h. (ILLUS.) **$100-150**

Ceramic & metal, half-figure of a Mexican lady, wearing a yellow dress w/white, red & blue scarf over her shoulder, one hand holding a matching yellow sombrero w/a red design, on a wooden stand w/wires to hold napkins, original box marked "Napkin Holder No. 405," 9" h. **$150-185**

Ceramic & metal, half-figure of a milk maid, light brown hair, wearing a red dress w/white dots, white apron w/blue trim, light blue bow at neck, w/matching blue & white cap, carrying buckets across shoulders, "Davar Originals" sticker, 6" h. **$95-110**

Metal, rear view figure of a dancer's legs w/upturned dress, marked "Can Can Serviette Holder," England, 4" h. **$95-135**

Metal Umbrella Napkin Holder

Metal, umbrella, wire holder forms umbrella when napkins are placed in it, comes w/original red napkins & box that reads "Porte Serviettes" & "Napkin Holder," Canada, 9 1/2" h. (ILLUS.) **$30-40**

Metal & Plastic Napkin Holder

Metal & plastic, umbrella, red & white holder on silver-tone circular base w/white-dotted red plastic pouches near bottom that hold napkins to form umbrella, 11" h. (ILLUS.) **$15-20**

Wood, figure of a woman dressed in yellow, Finland, ca. 1949, 10 1/4" h. **$40-50**

Wood, figure of woman on wooden base, red w/jointed arms, wearing picture hat & holding yellow wooden bucket, marked "G. Fried, Peplerhandlig Newer Market, Ges. Gesch.," 11 1/5" h. **$50-60**

K

Green Painted Wood Napkin Doll

Wood, figure of woman w/disproportion-
ately short jointed arms wearing dark
green dress w/narrow skirt & white
vest, dark green brimmed hat,
10 1/2" h. (ILLUS.) **$40-50**

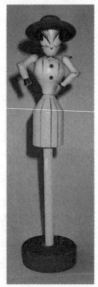

Wooden Napkin Doll Painted Yellow & Red

Wood, figure of woman w/stylized face,
standing w/hands on hips, painted yellow
w/red buttons, cuffs & hat, on red circular
base, 11" h. (ILLUS.)............................. **$30-40**
Wood, model of dodo bird, w/slits in rear for
napkins, 7" h. **$25-35**

Half-figure Napkin Doll Marked "Napkins"

Wood, red half-figure, base marked
"Napkins," ca. 1952, 11 1/2" h. (ILLUS.) **$35**

Pie Birds

*A pie bird can be described as a small,
hollow device, usually between 3 1/2" to 6"
long, glazed inside and vented from the top.
Its function is to raise the crust of a pie to
allow steam to escape, thus preventing
juices from bubbling over onto the oven
floor while providing a flaky, dry crust.*

*Originally, in the 1880s, pie birds were
funnel-shaped vents used by the English for
their meat pies. Not until the turn of the
20th century did figurals appear, first in
the form of birds, followed by elephants,
chefs, etc. By the 1930s, many shapes were
found in America.*

*Today the market is flooded with many
reproductions and newly created pie birds,
usually in many whimsical shapes and
subjects. It is best to purchase from knowledgeable dealers and fellow collectors.*

Advertising, "Paulden's Crockery Department Stretford Road," ceramic, white,
England... **$45**
Bird, ceramic, black on white base, yellow
feet & beak, Nutbrown, England **$25**

K

Half-doll Style Pie Bird

Bird, ceramic, half-doll style, blue & yellow on conical base, USA (ILLUS.) **$350**

Rowe Pottery Pie Bird

Bird, ceramic, two-piece w/detachable base, 1992, Rowe Pottery (ILLUS.) **$25**

English White Pie Bird

Bird, ceramic, white w/wide mouth, England (ILLUS.) **$50-60**

White & Blue Pie Bird

Bird, ceramic, white w/yellow beak, blue trim on tail & base, made in California, 1950s (ILLUS.) **$300-500**

"Yankee Pie Bird"

Bird, ceramic, "Yankee Pie Bird," black & brown, made in New England, 1960s (ILLUS.) **$35**

Yellow Pie Bird

Bird, ceramic, yellow w/wide mouth, England (ILLUS.) **$50-75**
Bird, glass, double-headed, marked "Scotland" **$125**
Black chef, ceramic, full-figured, green smock, "Pie-Aire," USA **$150**

K

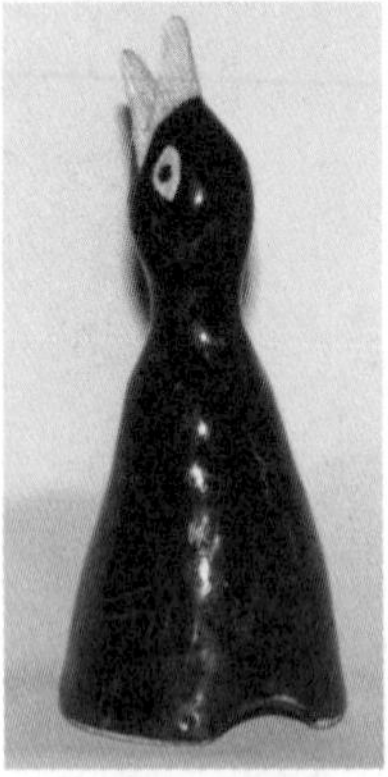

English Pie Bird

Blackbird, ceramic, black w/yellow beak & eyes, narrow, England (ILLUS.) **$125**

Blackbird on Log Pie Bird

Blackbird, ceramic, perched on log, England (ILLUS.) **$50**

Blackbird, red clay w/black glaze, ca. 1930s-40s **$35**

Brown chef, ceramic, half-figure, England **$65**

Chef, ceramic, "A Lorrie Design, Japan," Josef Originals, 1980s **$85**

Holland Servex Chef Pie Bird

Chef, ceramic, white w/black buttons, "The Servex Chef" in black letters on hat, marked "Holland" inside (ILLUS.)............... **$100**

Taunton Chefs Pie Birds

Chefs, ceramic, all-white, man & woman, Taunton, England, each (ILLUS.) **$95**

Chick, yellow w/pink lips, Josef Originals **$40**

Josef Originals Chick Pie Bird

Chick w/dust cap, "Pie Baker," by Josef Originals, ceramic (ILLUS.)......................... **$65**

Welsh Dragon Pie Birds

Dragon, ceramic, Creiciau Pottery, Wales, United Kingdom, each (ILLUS.) .... **$85+**

Blue Duck Pie Bird

Duck, ceramic, long neck, blue, USA (ILLUS.) **$45-65**
Duck, ceramic, yellow beak, white w/black detail, England **$95**

Pink English Duck Head Pie Bird

Duck head, ceramic, pink, England (ILLUS.) **$95**

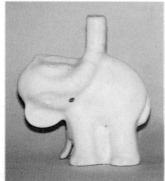

White Nutbrown England Elephant

Elephant, all-white w/trunk up, Nutbrown, England (ILLUS.) **$50**
Elephant, ceramic, dark grey w/yellow glaze inside, England **$100**

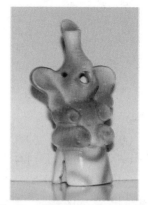

Cardinal China Elephant Pie Bird

Elephant, ceramic, grey & pink w/swirled pink base, Cardinal China Co. incised "CCC" on back, USA (ILLUS.) **$175**
Funnel, ceramic, brown on white base, Royal Worcester, England **$125**

Wheat Stalk Funnel Pie Bird

Funnel, ceramic, model of wheat stalk, cream & white, England, ea. (ILLUS.)... **$75-100**

K

Rosebud Funnel Pie Bird

Funnel, ceramic, rosebud, white, England (ILLUS.) **$150-175**

Charles & Diana Funnel-shaped Pie Bird

Funnel-shaped, ceramic, white w/blue transfer-printed image of Prince Charles & Princess Diana above "Charles and Diana 1981" (ILLUS.)....................................... **$45**

Gourmet Pie Cup

Gourmet pie cup, ceramic, England (ILLUS.)................................... **$75-95**
"Patches" pie bird, Morton Pottery, USA **$35**

K

Pie Baker Pie Bird

"Pie Baker," figure of a lady holding a bowl, by Josef Originals, ceramic (ILLUS.)............ **$95**

Rare Pie Boy Pie Bird

"Pie Boy," ceramic, white w/black & green trim, Squire Pottery of California, USA, rare (ILLUS.) **$350-500**

Marion Drake Rooster Pie Bird

Rooster, ceramic, Marion Drake, white w/black, red & yellow trim on brown base (ILLUS.)... **$50**

Rare Brown "Patrick" Pie Bird

Rooster "Patrick," ceramic, tan w/brown trim, California Cleminsons, USA, rare (ILLUS.)... **$175**
Seal, black, ceramic, Japan **$125**

American Pottery Pie Bird

Songbird, ceramic, blue & yellow, American Pottery Company, 1940-50 (ILLUS.)........ **$40-50**

"Patch" Pie Bird

Songbird, ceramic, "Patch," white, yellow, green & pink, Morton Pottery (ILLUS.).... **$35-50**

Welsh Woman Pie Bird

Welsh woman, ceramic, brown w/large black hat, 1969, commemorating investiture of Prince Charles (ILLUS.)............... **$200+**

Reamers

Reamers are a European invention dating back to the 18th century. Devised to extract citrus juice as a remedy for scurvy, by the 1920s they became a must in every well-equipped American kitchen. Although one can still purchase inexpensive glass, wood, metal and plastic squeezers in today's kitchen and variety stores, it is the pre-1950s models that are so highly sought after today. Whether it's a primitive wood example from the late 1800s or a whimsical figural piece from post-World War II Japan, the reamer is one of the hottest kitchen collectibles in today's marketplace - Bobbie Zucker Bryson

Ceramic, boat-shaped, pale green w/pink, blue & white flowers, cream reamer cone, handle & inside bowl, Shelley - England, 7" h... **$225-250**

Boat-shaped Leaf-decorated Reamer

Ceramic, boat-shaped, white w/gilt line trim, decorated w/rust-colored leaves & navy blue, small loop handle, 3 1/2" h. (ILLUS.) **$45-65**

K

Bucket-style Handled Reamer

Ceramic, bucket-style, two-piece, tan w/embossed cherub, flowers & decorative panels, green trim, rattan handle, marked "Made In Japan, Pat. 49541," 7 3/4" h. (ILLUS.) **$60-85**

Manx Cat Creamer-Style Reamer

Ceramic, creamer-style, two-piece, beige w/image of black cat & "Manx Cat From The Isle of Man," reamer on lid, marked "Crown Devon, Made in England," 3 1/2" h. (ILLUS.) **$75-85**

"Sourpuss" Clown Ceramic Reamer

Ceramic, figural clown head reamer in saucer base, white w/black & pink & marked "Sourpuss," 4 3/4" d. (ILLUS.) **$90-125**

K

Oriental Man's Head Reamer

Ceramic, figural Oriental man's head, two-piece, w/collar as base, hat as lid/reamer,

light blue w/dark grey highlights, incised "9496," 5 3/4" h. (ILLUS.) **$125-150**

Reamer in the Form of Amish Man

Ceramic, figure of Amish man, three-piece, black pants, green shirt, yellow cone top & hat, marked "JCC, NRCA, PA-1996," 5 1/2" h. (ILLUS.) **$40-50**
Ceramic, figure of chef lying on his back, two-piece, white w/blue, black shoes, yellow pants, white cone, turquoise & black trim, 2 1/2" h. **$175-200**

Bulbous Brown Clown Reamer

Ceramic, figure of clown, light brown bulbous body & cone hat, blue buttons & collar, 6" h. (ILLUS.) **$50-65**
Ceramic, figure of clown, red w/black & orange on white, marked "SIGMA," ca. 1960s, 6 1/2" h. (ILLUS., next page) **$60-75**
Ceramic, figure of clown w/pig head top, tan & light green body, yellow hat cone, marked "Hand Painted Made in Japan," 5" h. **$175-250**

1960s Sigma Ceramic Clown Reamer

Rounded Man's Head Reamer

Ceramic, figure of man's head, two-piece, rounded w/side-glancing blue eyes & smiling mouth, yellow w/red dots ruffled collar, blue lustre reamer top, brown hair tuft forms small spout at side, 4" h. (ILLUS.)
.... **$125-150**

Yellow & Orange Clown Reamer Shaker

Ceramic, figure of clowns, reamer/salt & pepper shakers, yellow & orange w/black trim, 2 3/4" h., pr. (ILLUS. of one) **$20-35**

Toby Face Ceramic Reamer

Ceramic, figure of Toby face, probably base on Royal Doulton Sairey Gamp character jug design, brown hair, green shirt, light green bow tie, white w/touch of blue cone top, marked "Japan," 4 1/4" h. (ILLUS.)
.... **$175-225**

K

Cross-legged Boy Ceramic Reamer

Ceramic, figure of cross-legged boy, two-piece, dressed in a red outfit w/white collar & black tie & shoes, wide reamer hat in white w/red trim, 5 1/2" h. (ILLUS.)....... **$275-350**

Woman's Head Reamer

Ceramic, figure of woman's head w/black hair, sitting in round ruffled white lustre saucer base w/ring handle & small rim spout, 3 1/4" h. (ILLUS., previous page) **$325-400**

Ceramic Chick Juice Reamer

Ceramic, model of a chick, two-piece, yellow body w/brown beak, white ceramic reamer top, marked "4733 Germany," early 20th c., 4 1/4" h. (ILLUS.) **$85-125**

Ceramic Duck Juice Reamer

Ceramic, model of a duck, two-piece, green head & yellow bill on a white body w/brown wings, ceramic white reamer top, marked "4732 Germany," early 20th c., 4 1/4" h. (ILLUS.) **$85-125**
Ceramic, model of bear, two-piece, yellow, marked "Foreign," 4 1/2" h. **$325-400**

Figural Red Bird Reamer

Ceramic, model of bird, red head w/grey beak forms reamer, red body w/green wings, 4 3/4" h. (ILLUS.) **$400-500**

Two-piece Figural Chick Reamer

Ceramic, model of chick, two-piece, yellow w/orange crown, bill & feet, green tail & wings, white cone, marked "Sarsasparilla, W.N.Y. © 1984, Deco Designs, #970," 3 1/2" h. (ILLUS.) **$50-60**

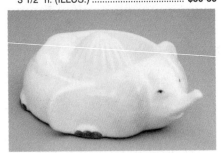

Portuguese Elephant Reamer

Ceramic, model of elephant, low saucer-form, white w/pink tint, marked "Mideramica Made in Portugal," 4" d. (ILLUS.) **$25-35**

Ceramic Figure of Elephant Reamer

Ceramic, model of elephant, orange luster w/green trim & white cone, marked "A Present from Southend-on-Sea" on rim top "Made in Czechoslovakia," 3 1/2" h. (ILLUS.)., ... **$225-250**

K

House Reamer with Matching Tumbler

Ceramic, model of elephant, three-piece, w/trunk raised, large ears w/yellow, green & brown design, cane handle, 7" h. **$250-300**

Figural Fish Reamer

Ceramic, model of fish, two-piece, orange & white, marked "Jager," 3 1/4" h. (ILLUS.) **$175-200**

Ceramic, model of house, two-piece, white w/brown roof & handle, blue windows, green grass & cherry trees in front, marked "Made in Japan," 5 1/2" h., w/matching juice tumbler (ILLUS., top of page) **$95-125**

Ceramic, model of lime, two-handled, marked "Orange For Baby" on front & "Handpainted" on bottom, 4 3/8" h. **$50-75**

Figural Orange Reamer

Ceramic, model of orange w/yellow & blue flowers & green leaves, "Kiddies Orange Juice," two-piece, marked "Germany," 4" h. (ILLUS.) **$50-75**

Ceramic, model of pansy blossom, two-piece, decorated w/a yellow & purple pansy, white top w/ruffled rim, 4" h. **$60-75**

White Pear Ceramic Reamer

Ceramic, model of pear, three-piece, white w/black & gold trim, marked "Handpainted Made in Japan," 5" h. (ILLUS.).......... **$45-55**

K

Two-piece Pitcher Reamer with Clown Head

Ceramic, pitcher-shaped, figural clown head reamer top w/green cone, two-piece w/colorful stylized orange & yellow flowers on the base, 6" h. (ILLUS.) **$55-65**

Flowered Universal Cambridge Reamer

Ceramic, pitcher-shaped, two-piece, cream w/yellow & purple flowers & green leaves, marked "Universal Cambridge, Ovenproof, Made in USA," 9 1/2" h. (ILLUS.) **$150-175**

Ceramic Two-piece Pitcher Reamer

Ceramic, pitcher-shaped, two-piece, tall footed light pink body w/green trim, colorful pink, yellow & blue flower sprig, marked "Pantry BAK-IN by Ware, Crooksville," 8 1/4" h. (ILLUS.)............ **$100-125**

Pitcher-style Clown Head Reamer

Ceramic, pitcher-style, figural clown head yellow reamer top, base decorated w/yellow & purple flowers, yellow cone & lustre trim, marked "Made in Japan," 6" h. (ILLUS.)... **$75-95**

Green One-Piece Ceramic Reamer

Ceramic, pitcher-style, one-piece, green, Art Deco design, w/spring-loaded cone, Ade-O-Matic, Genuine Coorsite Porcelain, 9" h. (ILLUS.).............................. **$150-175**

Ceramic, pitcher-style, two-piece, w/multicolored floral design, marked "Universal Cambridge Ovenproof Made in USA," 9" h... **$135-165**

Ceramic, saucer-shaped, cream & tan with maroon & blue trim, marked "A Present From Framington, Made in England," 3 1/4" d.. **$125**

Green Hall "Medallion" Reamer

Ceramic, saucer-shaped, green exterior w/finely ribbed band, cream interior, tab/loop handle, "Medallion" shape, Hall China Co., marked "Hall," 6" d. (ILLUS.).... **$400**

Reamer w/Lattice Edging & Cherries

K

Ceramic, saucer-shaped, lattice edging around the cone, white w/red cherries, green leaves & gold trim, 5 1/2" d. (ILLUS., previous page) **$75-95**

Ceramic, saucer-shaped, rough orange finish, white interior, green handle, Czechoslovakia, 2 1/4" h. **$30-35**

Quimper Pottery Reamer

Ceramic, saucer-shaped, two-piece, beige w/red, yellow, blue & tan trim, "Quimper Ivoire Corbell" patt., marked "Henriot Quimper France 1166," 2 3/4" h. (ILLUS.)
.... **$200-250**

Floral Decorated Saucer-shaped Reamer

Ceramic, saucer-shaped, white w/light & dark pink roses, green leaves & gold & dark cobalt blue trim, 4 1/2" d. (ILLUS.)
.... **$100-135**

Maroon Teapot-Style Jiffy Juicer

Ceramic, teapot-shaped, maroon, marked "Jiffy Juicer U.S. Pat 2, 755 Sept. 20, 1938" 5 1/4" h. (ILLUS.) **$75-90**

Petal-form Ceramic Reamer

Ceramic, teapot-shaped, two-piece, bright orange petal bottom w/bright yellow top, loop handle, marked "Made in Japan," 3 3/4" h. (ILLUS.) **$55-65**

Teapot-style Reamer with Violets

Ceramic, teapot-shaped, two-piece, paneled bulbous base w/wide rim spout & squared reamer top, white decorated w/light purple violets & green leaves, 4 3/4" h. (ILLUS.) **$20-25**

German Reamer with Roses

Ceramic, two-piece, cylindrical base w/light green leaves & pink roses, yellow highlights & gold handle, marked "Germany" on bottom, 3 1/8" h. (ILLUS.) **$85-115**

K

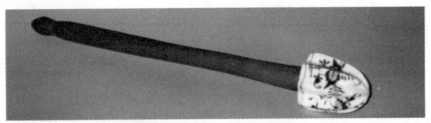

Wood-handled Blue & White Reamer

Ceramic, two-piece, octagonal bottom, white, marked "Thomas Maddock & Sons, Trenton, NJ," 5" h....................... **$95-110**

Two-Handled Reamer with Dogs

Ceramic, two-piece, wide cylindrical two-handled base in yellow molded w/two dogs under a red umbrella, yellow, green, red & white cone, marked "75/476 Made in Japan," 4 1/4" h. (ILLUS.).................... **$60-75**
Ceramic & wood, blue & white cone w/wood handle, 10 1/8" l. (ILLUS., top of page).. **$150-175**

Federal Fluted Amber Orange Reamer

Glass, amber transparent, fluted sides & loop handle, orange reamer, Federal, 6 1/2" d. (ILLUS.) **$45**

Federal Glass Reamer with Tab Handle

Glass, amber transparent, saucer-shaped w/tab handle, one-piece, ribbed sides, Federal Glass Company, 5 1/4" d. (ILLUS.) **$20-25**

Blue Delphite Jenny Ware Glass Reamer

Glass, blue Delphite, Jenny Ware, lemon squeeze, Jeanette Glass Co., 5 1/8" d. (ILLUS.)... **$75-90**
Glass, blue opaque, saucer-shaped, ruffled edge & tab handle, 5" d....................... **$110-120**

Butterscotch Glass Reamer

Glass, butterscotch, embossed "SUNKIST," marked "Pat. No. 18764 Made in USA," McKee Glass Co., 6" d. (ILLUS.) **$700-850**

Clear Glass Boat-shaped Reamer

Glass, clear, boat-shaped, w/long spout &
tab handle, ridged sides, seed dam,
3 7/8" w. (ILLUS.) **$45-60**

Frosted Crystal "Baby's Orange" Reamer

Pacific Coast Glass Works Reamer

Glass, clear, round shape w/fluted sides,
loop handle, marked "Sunkist Oranges
Lemons," Pacific Coast Glass Works,
6" d. (ILLUS.) **$40-50**
Glass, clear, w/square loop handle, em-
bossed "Valencia" on front, 6" d. **$185-225**

Green Glass Ribbed Fry Reamer

Green Hazel Atlas Criss Cross Reamer

K

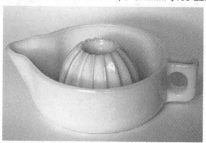

McKee Custard Grapefruit Reamer

Glass, custard, grapefruit reamer, McKee
Glass, 6" d. (ILLUS.) **$245**
Glass, French Ivory, footed saucer-shaped
w/loop handle, McKee Glass Company,
5 1/2" d. **$30-35**
Glass, frosted clear, two-piece, decorated
w/"Baby's Orange," 4 1/4" h. (ILLUS., top
next column)... **$45-60**
Glass, green transparent, double-ribbed
w/loop tab handle, Fry, 6 1/4" d. (ILLUS.,
middle next column) **$65**
Glass, green transparent, saucer-shaped,
raised ringed foot w/Criss Cross patt.
saucer & a swirled rib reamer cone, Hazel Atlas Glass Co., 6 1/8" d. (ILLUS.,
third next column)................................... **$25-35**

Green Measuring Cup Reamer

Glass, green transparent, two-cup measuring cup base w/peg handle, two-piece, 5 1/8" h. (ILLUS., previous page) **$50-65**

Fenton Jade Green Pitcher-Reamer

Glass, Jade green, two-piece measuring pitcher base, footed bulbous body w/reamer cover, Fenton Art Glass Co., 6 3/8" h. (ILLUS.) **$1,000-1,200**

Jenny Ware Jade-ite Lemon Reamer

Glass, Jade-ite, Jenny Ware, saucer-shaped lemon-type, Jeannette Glass Co., 6" d. (ILLUS.) **$25-35**

Blue Glass Reamer

Glass, light blue transparent, saucer-shaped w/seed dam & tab handle, 4 3/4" d. (ILLUS.) **$100-120**
Glass, milk glass, embossed Valencia, 6 1/4" d. **$100**

Milk Glass Swirled Rib Reamer

Glass, milk glass, one-piece, deep sides w/swirled ribs, twin-spout, side handle, 3 1/4" h. (ILLUS.) **$35-50**

Opalescent Ribbed Fry Reamer

Glass, opalescent, one-piece, ribbed sides & tab/loop handle, Fry Heat Resisting Glass, 6 1/4" d. (ILLUS.) **$20-30**

Hex Optic Pitcher-Ice Bucket-Reamer

Glass, pink transparent, pitcher-style, two-piece, Hex Optic patt. pitcher-ice bucket base w/reamer top, 5" d., 9" h. (ILLUS.) **$95**

K

Pink Glass Jeannette Reamer

Glass, pink transparent, saucer-shaped, concentric rings forming the base w/a tab side handle, orange reamer, Jeannette Glass Co., 5 7/8" d. (ILLUS.)................... **$40-50**

Glass, ruby red, two-piece measuring pitcher-style, bulbous pitcher w/reamer top, Fenton Art Glass Co., 6 3/8" h. **$1,300-1,500**

Yellow Milk Glass Grapefruit Reamer

Glass, Seville Yellow, one-piece, grapefruit-type, McKee Glass Company, 6" d. (ILLUS.) **$225-275**

Glass & metal, amber glass tall tapering base w/metal reamer top, "Party Line - Speakeasy Cocktail Shaker," No. 156, Paden City Glass Co., 9 1/4" h. **$95-125**

Glass & Metal Servmor Juice Extractor

Glass & metal, green transparent glass measuring cup base w/hinged metal handled top, marked "Servmor Juice Extrac-

tor Patented" U.S. Glass Co., ca. 1930s, 5" h. (ILLUS.) **$75**

Goldplate, three-piece cocktail shaker, marked "Made in Italy," 9" h. **$75-100**

Cast Aluminum Saucer-shaped Reamer

Metal, cast aluminum, saucer-shaped w/seed barriers & two spouts, long handle w/hanging hole, 6" w. (ILLUS.)............... **$45**

Metal & Wood Kwik Way Reamer

Metal, one-piece w/hinged top & green wooden handle, marked "Kwik Way Products Inc., Pat No. 1743661," 7 1/2" l. (ILLUS.)... **$10-15**

All-Metal Super Juicer Reamer

Metal, hinged back handle to plunger-type mechanism painted cream, above reamer fitted on cylindrical metal container,

K

Super Juicer, Household Products Mfg.
Co., ca. 1940s, 6" h. (ILLUS.) **$25**

Dur-X Fruit Juice Extractor & Corer

Plastic, Dur-X Fruit Juice Extractor & Corer,
w/original box, marked "Kwiki-P1 Juicer
Pat. Pend.," 2 3/4" h. (ILLUS.) **$6-8**

Plastic Long-Handled Yellow Reamer -

Plastic, yellow, hinged w/long handles, 8" l.
(ILLUS.).. **$4-6**

Silver Plate Nutcracker-style Reamer

Silver plate, hinged nutcracker-style w/long
spiral-twist handles, 10" l. (ILLUS.) **$55-75**

Silver Plate CS Co. 20 Reamer

Silver plate, low cylindrical saucer-style,
marked "CS Co 20," 6 5/8" h. (ILLUS.)... **$75-100**

Silver Plate Gravy Boat "Meriden" Reamer

Silver plate, gravy boat-style, marked
"Meriden S.P. Co. International Silver
Co." 4 5/8" d. (ILLUS.)........................... **$85-100**

Stainless Steel Lemon Slice Squeezer

Stainless steel, shallow long boat-form
w/hinged lemon slice squeezer, 5" l.
(ILLUS.) **$6-8**

Gorham Sterling Silver Reamer

Sterling silver, saucer-shaped, open tab
handle, marked "Black Starr - Gorham
Sterling 909," 4 1/4" d. (ILLUS.) **$225-275**
Wood, hand-held w/ribbed reamer
cone, ca. 1850, 5 3/4" l. **$35-45**

String Holders

*String holders were standard equipment
for general stores, bakeries and homes
before the use of paper bags, tape and sta-
ples became prevalent. Decorative string
holders, mostly chalkware, first became
popular during the late 1930s and 1940s.
They were mass-produced and sold in five-
and-dime stores like Woolworth's and
Kresge's. Ceramic string holders became
available in the late 1940s through the
1950s. It is much more difficult to find a
chalkware string holder in excellent condition, while the sturdier ceramics maintain
a higher quality over time.*

Apple, chalkware... $35

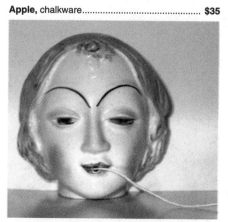

Art Deco Woman with Arched Eyebrows

Art Deco woman, arched eyebrows, blonde
bobbed hair (ILLUS.)................................... $85

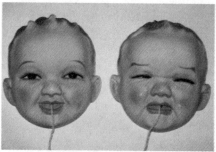

Baby Face String Holders

Babies, ceramic, heads only, one crying,
one happy, Lefton, pr. (ILLUS.)................... $175

Goebel Bears Egg Timer

Bears, ceramic, brown & tan, white base,
Goebel (ILLUS.) $135
Bird, ceramic, green, scissors fit in tail, Ja-
pan $30
Birds in a cage, chalkware, two birds....... $95-125

Bunch of Fruit String Holder

Bunch of fruit, chalkware (ILLUS.) $150

Holt Howard String Holder

Cat, ceramic, climbing ball of string, Holt
Howard (ILLUS.) $85

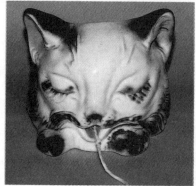

"Knitter's Pal" String Holder

Cat, ceramic, "Knitter's Pal" (ILLUS.) $25
Cat, ceramic, w/crossed paws, white, hand-
made $25-45
Cat, ceramic, w/matching wall pocket $50

K

Cat with Plaid Collar String Holder

Cat, ceramic, w/plaid collar, space for scissors, Japan (ILLUS.) $35
Cat, ceramic, w/scissors in collar, "Babbacombe Pottery, England".............................. $20
Cat, ceramic, w/string coming out extended paw, pearlized white glaze $35
Cat, ceramic, white face w/pink & black polka dot collar bow $55

Cat Face String Holder

Cat, ceramic, white, w/large green eyes, scissors hang on bow (ILLUS.) $35

Cat with Flowers String Holder

Cat w/flowers, ceramic, scissors in head (ILLUS.).. $35

Ceramic Chef Head String Holder

Chef, ceramic (ILLUS.).................................. $125
Chef, chalkware, baby face w/chef's hat........ $135

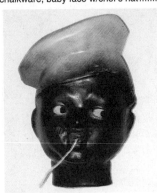

Chef with Black Face

Chef, chalkware, black face, white hat (ILLUS.) $125
Chef, chalkware, chubby-faced, "By Bello, 1949," rare $350

Common Chef Head String Holder

K

Chef, chalkware, common (ILLUS., previous page) **$35**

Chef with Spoon & Box String Holder

Chef, chalkware, full-figured black chef w/spoon & blue box (ILLUS.) **$95**

Norwood String Holder

Chef w/red bow tie, chalkware, The Norwood Co., Cincinnati, Ohio (ILLUS.) **$85**

Chipmunk String Holder

Christmas chipmunk, ceramic (ILLUS.) **$35**

Bulldog String Holder

Dog, chalkware, bulldog w/studded collar, ca. 1933 (ILLUS.) **$95**

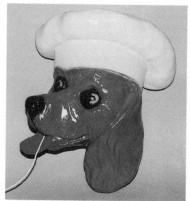

Dog with Chef's Hat String Holder

Dog, chalkware, w/chef's hat, "Conovers Original" (ILLUS.) **$175**

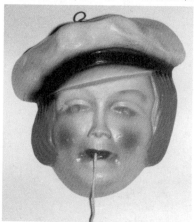

Dutch Boy String Holder

Dutch Boy, chalkware (ILLUS.) **$135**

K

Dutch Girl with Flowers String Holder

Dutch Girl, ceramic, w/flowers, full-figured,
Japan (ILLUS.) **$125**
Elephant, ceramic, "Hoffritz, England" **$20**
Elephant, ceramic, marked "Babbacombe
Pottery, England," scissors as glasses **$20**
Fox without mane, ceramic, scissors as
glasses, marked "Babbacombe Pottery,
England" **$25**

Grapes String Holder

Grapes, chalkware, bunch (ILLUS.) **$50**
Green pepper, ceramic, Lego sticker **$35-45**

Frog String Holder

K   **Frog,** ceramic, countertop-type, Babbacombe Pottery, England (ILLUS.) **$35**

Lady in Bonnet String Holder

Lady in bonnet w/bow, chalkware (ILLUS.) **$95**

Granny in Rocking Chair String Holder

Granny in rocking chair, ceramic, marked
"PY," Japan (ILLUS.) **$65**

Lemon String Holder

Lemon, ceramic, Japan (ILLUS., previous page) **$75**

Little Bo Peep String Holder

Little Bo Peep, ceramic, white w/red & blue trim, marked "Japan" (ILLUS.)..................... **$85**

Little Red Riding Hood, chalkware, head wearing hood... **$150**

Longshoreman String Holder

Longshoreman, chalkware, marked "By Dughesne, 1940" (ILLUS.) **$175**

Mammy Face String Holder

Mammy, ceramic, head only, Japan (ILLUS.) .. **$250**

"Genuine Rockalite" Mammy

Mammy, chalkware, head only, w/polka-dot bandana, marked "Genuine Rockalite," made in Canada (ILLUS.) **$125**

Man in the Moon String Holder

Man in the Moon face, chalkware (ILLUS.) .. **$200**

Chalk Peach String Holder

Peach, chalkware (ILLUS.) **$35**

K

Pink Pig String Holder

Pig, ceramic, hanging or countertop-type,
pink (ILLUS.) **$50**
Pumpkin Cottage, Manorware, England,
ceramic **$45**

Southern Belle String Holder

Southern Belle, ceramic, w/very full skirt,
Japan (ILLUS.) **$65**

Kitchen Glassware

R2D2 String Holder

Robot R2D2, ceramic, countertop, newer
vintage, marked "Sigma" (ILLUS.) **$65**

Glasbake Crab-shaped Baking Dishes

Baking dishes, crab-shaped, Glasbake by
McKee, manufactured in the 1920s,
boxed set of six (ILLUS.) **$20-24**

Chalkware Rose String Holder

Rose, chalkware (ILLUS.) **$65**
Scottish woman, chalkware, head only,
w/plaid scarf .... **$250+**

Fire-King Jadeite Batter Bowl

Batter bowl, Jadeite, w/spout & angled
handle, 3/4" w. rim band, Fire-King
(ILLUS.) **$40-45**

K

Butter dish, cov., one-pound, custard w/pressed flower on the cover, McKee Glass, 4 x 8 1/4" **$145**

Federal Ribbed Amber Butter Dish

Butter dish, cov., one-pound size, amber rectangular low base w/tab handles & high matching cover, impressed "BOTTOM" on the base, Federal Glass Co., 3 1/4 x 5 1/2" (ILLUS.)................................. **$45**

Butter dish, cov., quarter-pound, Jade-ite base & clear glass domed cover, Fire King... **$95**

McKee Chalaine Blue Canister

Canister, Chalaine Blue, wide cylindrical base & flat fitted cover, McKee, 4 1/2" d., 2 1/2" h. (ILLUS.) **$75**

Clambroth Hoosier-style Flour Canister

Canister, clambroth Hoosier-style flour canister, wide cylindrical shaped w/heavy

molded rings, flat metal lift-off cover, 7" d., 7 1/2" h. (ILLUS.) **$125**

Hocking Canister with Silhouette Scene

Canister, clear w/green silhouette decoration of old men at a table, square w/green metal screw-on cover, Hocking, 4 1/2" w., 6 3/4" h. (ILLUS.) **$65**

Owens Forest Green Flour Canister

Canister, forest green transparent, upright oval cylindrical shape w/fine ribbing, "Flour" in a vertical panel up the front, screw-on metal lid, Owens Glass, 8" h. (ILLUS.).. **$65**

K

Hazel-Atlas Green Art Deco Tea Canister

Canister, Jadite green fired-on color w/a stylized floral Art Deco decoration & "Tea" in black, black screw-on cover, Hazel-Atlas, 5" h. (ILLUS., previous page) **$95**

Canister, milk glass w/Blue Circle decoration & "Sugar," fitted ringed blue cover w/knob handle, Vitrock line by Hocking, rare, 5 1/4" h. **$85**

Canister, Skokie Green w/"Coffee" in black block letters, wide cylindrical shape w/flat fitted glass cover, McKee, 6 1/4" d., 6" h. .. **$235**

Vitrock Blue Circle Sugar Canister

Canister w/original screw-on metal lid, milk glass w/Blue Circle decoration & "Sugar," Vitrock line by Hocking, rare, 5 1/4" h. (ILLUS.) **$115**

Two Jeannette Jadite Canisters

Canisters, Jadite, upright square shape w/flat fitted cover w/inset handle, no label, no sunflower design on the cover, Jeannette, each (ILLUS. of two).................. **$65**

McKee Glasbake Covered Casserole

Casserole, cov., clear, part of an embossed set from Glasbake, by McKee Glass Company, two-cup capacity, 6" d. across the top, not counting the tab handles (ILLUS.).. **$10-12**

Pyrex "Arsenic" Yellow Casserole

Casserole, cov., oval, "Arsenic" yellow, Pyrex by Corning Glass (ILLUS.)............ **$12-18**

Fire King Tulips Cottage Cheese Bowl

Cottage cheese bowl, footed, milk glass w/green Tulips patt., came in four different colors, stackable, Fire King (ILLUS.)........ **$12-18**

Small Cobalt Blue Chevron Creamer

Cream pitcher, cobalt blue, Chevron patt., rectangular top, Hazel-Atlas, gas station giveaway w/matching sugar bowl, small size, 3 " h. (ILLUS.) **$20-25**

K

Fire King "Flared" Custard Cup

Custard cup, sapphire blue, Philbe patt. "flared" design, Fire King by Anchor Hocking, w/original label (ILLUS.) **$8-10**

Fire King Jade-ite Double Egg Cup

Egg cup, double, Jade-ite, Fire King, 4" h. (ILLUS.) **$45**

Hazel-Atlas Milk Glass Drippings Jar

Drippings jar, cov., cylindrical milk glass base w/flanged rim, wide flat cover w/a black oval enclosing "DRIPPINGS" in black, uncommon, Hazel-Atlas, 4" d. (ILLUS.) **$95**

Jeannette Jadite Ring Flour Shaker

Flour shaker w/original screw-on metal lid, range-size, cylindrical Jadite ringed shaker w/black block lettering, Jeannette, 5" h. (ILLUS.) **$75**

Grease jar, cov., ivory w/deep flaring sides, decorated in the Apples patt., Fire King, 5 3/4" d. **$75**

K

McKee Chalaine Blue Double Egg Cup

Egg cup, double, Chalaine Blue, McKee Glass, 4 1/2" h. (ILLUS.) **$40**

Fire King Tulips Pattern Grease Jar

Grease jar, cov., ivory w/deep flaring sides, decorated in the Tulips patt., Fire King, 5 3/4" d. (ILLUS.) **$60**

Clear Star Pattern Vitex-Glass Knife & Box

Grease jar, cov., milk glass Vitrock w/the
    Blue Circle patt., blue or white glass cov-
    er, Hocking Glass, 1950s, 6" h..................... **$75**

Hocking Vitrock Flowerpots Grease Jar

Grease jar, cov., milk glass Vitrock w/the
    red Flowerpots design, domed glass cov-
    er w/black & red banding, Hocking Glass,
    1950s, 6" h. (ILLUS.).................................... **$45**
Knife, clear Buffalo-type, block handle w/or
    without h.p. decoration, 9 1/4" l. **$28**
Knife, clear, Star patt., in original Vitex-
    Glass Knife box marked "Pat Pend -
    Made in USA," 9" l. (ILLUS., top of page) **$35**

Fire King Philbe Pattern Sapphire Blue Loaf Pan

Loaf or bread baking pan, sapphire blue,
    Philbe patt., Fire King, 5 x 9" (ILLUS.) **$18**

McKee Glasbake Loaf Pan with Red Handles

Loaf pan, clear, rectangular ringed sides
    w/red-painted handles, Glasbake by Mc-
    Kee Glass Co., 5 x 9" (ILLUS.) **$8-10**
Match holder, Delphite blue, cylindrical, no
    cover, black lettering, Jeannette **$125**

Federal Amber 2-Cup Measuring Cup

Measuring cup, amber, triple-spout, taper-
    ing cylindrical sides w/measurements, no
    handle, two-cup, Federal Glass, 4 3/8" h.
    (ILLUS.)... **$50**

Fire-King Commemorative Measuring Cup

Measuring cup, commemorative, clear
    w/red wording, "Commemorating 50 Years
    - Fire-King," 1992, 2 cup (ILLUS.) **$15-18**

Hocking Green Measuring Cup

Measuring cup, green transparent, footed, measurements on the sides & "Measuring and Mixing" pressed into the bottom, two-cup, Hocking Glass, 3 3/4" h. (ILLUS.) **$55**

Hocking Green 1-Cup Measuring Cup

Measuring cup, green transparent, single spout, measurement marking to the rim, arched spout, one cup, Hocking, 3" h. (ILLUS.) **$48**
Measuring cup, pink transparent, triple-spout, measurements around the sides, marked "Kellogg's" on the bottom, one-cup, Hazel-Atlas, 3 3/4" h. **$65**

McKee Seville Yellow Measuring Pitcher

Measuring pitcher, footed, Seville Yellow, wet measures on one side, dry on the other, McKee, four-cup, 1930s, 6" h. (ILLUS.) .. **$145**
Measuring pitcher, footed, Skokie Green, wet measures on one side, dry on the other, McKee, four-cup, 1930s, 6" h. **$195**

Hocking Green 4-Cup Measuring Pitcher

Measuring pitcher, green transparent, tapering cylindrical sides w/measurement markings, four-cup, Hocking, 6" h. (ILLUS.) **$95**

Jade-ite Swedish Modern Mixing Bowl

Mixing bowl, Jade-ite, Swedish Modern shape by Fire King, smallest size, 5" w. (ILLUS.) **$65**
Mixing bowl, green transparent, Rest Well shape w/wide fluted panels around the lower half, wide rolled rim, Hazel-Atlas, 6 1/2" d. **$24**
Mixing bowl, milk glass w/black Gooseberry patt., Pyrex, 6 3/4" d. **$12**

K

Fire King Kitchen Aides Pattern Bowl

Mixing bowl, milk glass w/the red Kitchen Aides patt., Splashproof design, shows various kitchen utensils, Fire King, 7 1/2" d. (ILLUS.) **$100**

Federal Five-Piece Mixing Bowl Set

Mixing bowl, milk glass w/the Red Ships patt., bell-shaped, McKee Glass Co., 8" d. **$50**

Hazel Atlas Black Flowers Mixing Bowl

Mixing bowl, milk glass w/the Black Flowers patt., accented w/thin red orange & yellow rings, Hazel Atlas, 9" d. (ILLUS.) **$50**

Mixing bowl set: cobalt blue, deep sides w/convex ribbing, Hazel-Atlas, 6 1/2" d., 7 1/2" d., 8 1/2" d., 9 1/2" d. & 10 1/2" d., the set (ILLUS., top of page) **$225**

Mixing bowl set, milk glass w/flaring sides & abstract dot & scroll designs in red, blue, green & yellow, by Federal, mark is an "F" in a shield, the bowls measure 5" d., 6" d., 7" d., 8" d., & 9" d., five-piece set (ILLUS.) **$65-75**

Mug, ivory or milk glass, D-style, Fire King, each **$10**

K

Fire King Jade-ite Mug with D-style Handle

Mug, Jade-ite, D-style, Fire King (ILLUS.) **$18**

Fire King D-Style Turquoise Mug

Mug, turquoise, D-style, Fire King (ILLUS.) **$30**

Jeannette Delphite Blue Pepper Shaker

Pepper shaker w/original screw-on metal lid, range-size, cylindrical Delphite blue ringed shaker w/black block lettering, Jeannette, 5" h. (ILLUS.).............................. **$85**

Tipp City Flower Basket Three-Piece Range Set on Tray

Hazel-Atlas Scottie Dog Pepper Shaker

Pepper shaker w/original screw-on metal lid, range-size, square milk glass decorated w/three small black Scottie dogs w/red bows, red lettering, Hazel-Atlas, 4 3/4" h. (ILLUS.) **$50**

Jeannette Jadite Pitcher

Pitcher, Jadite, wide spout, angled handle, impressed sunflower in the bottom, Jeannette, 5 1/2" h. (ILLUS.) **$65-75**

Range set: rectangular milk glass grease jar w/flat red metal cover & matching square salt & pepper shakers, all on a long red metal rectangular tray w/an upright center handle, each piece decorated w/the red & black Flower Basket patt., Tipp City, shakers 2 3/4" h., the set (ILLUS., top of page) **$175**

Jade-ite Beads & Bars Pattern Pitcher

Pitcher, Jade-ite, milk size, Beads & Bars patt., Fire King by Anchor Hocking, 20 oz. (ILLUS.) **$125-175**

Fire King Ivory Range Set

Range set: salt & pepper shakers & grease jar; ivory, ringed cylindrical shape w/"Tulip" lids, Fire King by Anchor Hocking, note corrosion of salt lid (difficult to find good condition), the set (ILLUS.) **$85-95**

K

Range Shaker Set with Scroll Design

Range set: salt & peppers shakers & flour & sugar shakers w/original screw-on metal lids, cylindrical milk glass w/green scroll design above & below "Sugar," "Salt," "Pepper" & "Flour," black metal caps, 3 3/4 to 4 1/2" h., the set (ILLUS.)............... $95

Refrigerator dish, cov., clear, rectangular, design of vegetables pressed into the cover, 4 x 8".. $14

Jeannette Delphite Blue Refrigerator Dish

Refrigerator dish, cov., Delphite blue, square w/flat cover w/inset handle, Jeannette, 4 1/2" w., 2 3/4" h. (ILLUS.)................ $55

Refrigerator dish, cov., green transparent, Criss Cross patt., rectangular, Hazel-Atlas, 4 x 8".. $65

Refrigerator dish, cov., Jade-ite, Philbe patt., square, Fire King, 4 1/2 x 5"............... $45

Pyrex "Bluebelle" Refrigerator Jar

Refrigerator jar, cov., squared shape, "Bluebelle" line in Canadian blue, Pyrex by Corning, scarce, 3 1/2 x 4 3/4" (ILLUS.)............ $20-25

Fire King Large Philbe Pattern Sapphire Roaster Pan

Roaster pan, cov., Philbe patt., sapphire blue, lid & bottom are same piece, Fire King, 10 3/4" d. (ILLUS.)............................ $95

Rare Green U.S. Glass Salt Box

Salt box, cov., green transparent, footed round & paneled base w/a center-hinged flat chrome cover, larger of two sizes made, U.S. Glass Co., 5 1/2" d., 3 3/4" h. (ILLUS.)... $285

Hoosier-style Clear Triple Skip Salt Box

Salt box, Hoosier-type, clear, open round, Triple Skip patt., 4 3/8" d., 3 1/4" h. (ILLUS.)...................................... $65

K

Shakers with Blue Circle Design

Salt & pepper shakers w/original screw-on aluminum lids, range-size, milk glass, square, decorated w/blue circles, 3 5/8" h., pr. (ILLUS.) **$45**

Shakers with Apples

Salt & pepper shakers w/original screw-on black metal lids, range-size, milk glass, square, decorated w/red apple & green leaves, 3 1/4" h., each (ILLUS.) **$20-25**
Salt & pepper shakers w/original screw-on metal lids, range-size, custard, Roman Arches shape, Red Dots decoration, McKee, rare, 4 1/4" h., the set **$165**

Fire King Tulips Salt & Pepper Shakers

Salt & pepper shakers w/original screw-on metal lids, range-size, cylindrical milk glass w/Tulips decoration, color decoration of tulips on the metal lids, Fire King, the set (ILLUS.).................................. **$90**

Shakers with Hat Decoration

Salt & pepper shakers w/original screw-on metal lids, range-size, milk glass, square, red & blue design of "Uncle Sam" hats, 3 1/8" h., pr. (ILLUS.) **$45-55**

Skokie Green McKee Salt Shaker

Salt shaker w/original screw-on metal lid, range-size, square Skokie Green w/a small black rectangle & black lettering, McKee, 5" h. (ILLUS.) **$75**
Spice shaker w/original screw-on metal lid, clear Hoosier-style, cylindrical w/zipper patt., 3 1/4" h... **$25**

Spice Shakers with Dutch Scenes

Spice shakers w/original screw-on red metal lids, milk glass, square w/beveled corners, each printed w/various blue Dutch scenes on front, paper la-

K

bels on reverse, red star & name of spice in red letters above scene, 3 1/4" h., each (ILLUS.) **$12-20**

Cobalt Chevron Open Sugar Bowl

Sugar bowl, open, cobalt blue, Chevron patt., Hazel-Atlas, gas station give-away w/the matching creamer, large size, 3 1/2" h. (ILLUS.) **$24-28**

Clear Pear-shaped Ribbed Sugar Shaker

Sugar shaker w/original metal screw-on pour top, clear pear shape w/wide panels & thin ribs, chrome top w/pouring flap, Dripcut Starling Corp., Santa Barbara, California, 5 1/2" h. (ILLUS.) **$35**

Rare Hazel-Atlas Dots Sugar Shaker

Sugar shaker w/original scew-on metal lid, range-size, square milk glass w/blue & black Dots decoration of oval panel w/"Sugar" in black, Hazel-Atlas, rare, 4 3/4" h. (ILLUS.) **$175**

Fostoria Mayfair Green Syrup Pitcher

Syrup pitcher & cover, green transparent, Mayfair patt., cylindrical body w/rim spout & shaped loop handle, flat cover w/angled loop handle, Fostoria Glass, 6" h. (ILLUS.).. **$125**

Fine Green Imperial Hand-etched Syrup

Syrup pitcher & cover, green transparent, slightly tapering cylindrical body w/cupped rim w/spout, fancy hand-etched design of flowers & leaves, applied green threaded handle, inset glass cover w/knob finial, Imperial Glass, 6" h. (ILLUS.).. **$195**
Trivet, green transparent, round w/a wide ring of thick ribs around the top, indented center impressed "Protecto," for hot pans, 5" d. (ILLUS., next page).................. **$25**

K

Green Glass "Protecto" Trivet

Fire King Sapphire Blue Philbe Pattern Trivet

Trivet or hot plate, sapphire blue, Philbe patt., arched tab handles, Fire King, 8 1/2" d. (ILLUS.) **$30**

Kitchen Utensils

Apple Corer with Bakelite Handle

Apple corer, metal cylindrical plunger blade w/side lever to eject core, ribbed red Bakelite handle, 4 1/4" h. (ILLUS.)............... **$15**

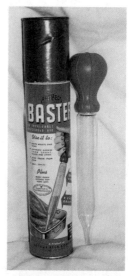

"Artbeck" Baster & Original Container

Baster, long pointed clear glass tube & squeeze rubbe bulb, "Artbeck," Pyrex glass tube, w/original container (ILLUS.).. **$15-20**

Chopper with Four-part Blade

Chopper, four-part flaring metal chopping blade w/a hexagonal red Bakelite handle, 6" l. (ILLUS.)... **$16**

K

Early Metal Doughnut Cutter

Doughnut cutter, round cylindrical metal w/crimped top edge & center cylindrical tube to form hole, loop wide handle at the side, early 20th c., 2 3/4" l. (ILLUS.) **$25**

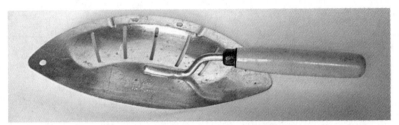

Aluminum and Wood Early Pot Drainer

All-metal Painted Egg Scale

Egg scale, all-metal, the base painted cream & the weighing mechanism painted jade green, weighs & grades eggs, 8 1/2" l., 6" h. (ILLUS.) **$50**

Old Metal Egg Separator

Egg separator, metal, flanged rim embossed "Mitchell & Co. Kitchen Dept. Haverhill, MA," tab handle w/hole, 3 1/2" w. (ILLUS.).. **$28**

K

Flour Sifter Decorated with Apples

Flour sifter, metal, decorated w/scattered red apples on a white ground, strap han-

dle at back, wire crank handle w/wooden knob turns to move the sifting screens, 1930s-40s, 5 3/4" h. (ILLUS.)....................... **$25**

Sunbeam Mixmaster & Matching Bowl

Mixer & glass bowl, electric, Sunbeam Mixmaster, Chicago Flexible Shaft Co., cream colored metal body, folding handle on stand, came in pink, yellow or blue, matching bowl by McKee Glass, ca. 1960s, the set (ILLUS.) **$45-55**

Pot drainer, curved wedge-shaped aluminum blade w/yellow wood handle, held against side of pot to allow water to drain off, Foley, 11 1/2" l. (ILLUS., top of page) **$25**

Rolling pin, aluminum w/a brushed finish, pink plastic handles, 1960s.......................... **$25**

Portmeirian China Botanic Garden Pattern Rolling Pin

Rolling pin, ceramic, closed handles, Botanic Garden decoration, Portmeirian China, 13 1/2" l. (ILLUS.) **$95**

Rolling pin, ceramic, ivory glaze printed in black w/"Kelvinator," given w/the purchase of a refrigerator, 1940s **$65-95**

Rolling pin, ceramic, Modern Age/ Modern Tulip patt., Bakerite - HotOven Ware, Harker Pottery, 14 3/4" l. **$50-75**

Rolling pin, Chalaine Blue glass, one handle w/screw-off metal lid to add ice water, McKee... **$500-800**

Rolling pin, clear glass, hollow w/metal screw-off lid at one end of handle **$15-25**
Rolling pin, wooden w/red-painted handles w/an ivory stripe, 1930s **$25**

Aunt Jemima Plastic Syrup Pitcher

Syrup pitcher, molded plastic, figural Aunt Jemima in red, white & black, F&F Mold & Die Works, Dayton, Ohio, 6" h. (ILLUS.) **$65**

Rare Blue Willow Porcelain Toaster

Toaster, electric, porcelain case in the Blue Willow patt., by Toastrite, central heating panel, on four feet, used only as exhibition piece at its introduction in 1928 (ILLUS.) **$2,300**

The Vintage Kitchen - 1850-1920

Egg Beaters

Eggbeaters are pure Americana! No other invention (although apple parers come close) represent America at its best from the mid-19th century to the 1930s or '40s. Eggbeaters tell the unbeatable story of America—the story of demand for a product, competition, success, retreat, failure, faith, and revival.

The mechanical (rotary) eggbeater is an American invention, and ranks up there with motherhood and apple pie, or at least up there where it counts—in the kitchen. American ingenuity produced more than 1,000 patents related to beating eggs, most before the 20th century.

To put it in perspective, try to imagine 1,000 plus ways to beat an egg. Here's a clue, and it's all due to Yankee tinkering: There are rotary cranks, archimedes (up and down) models, hand-helds, squeeze power, and rope and water power—and others. If you ever wanted a different way to beat an egg it was (and is) available.

Today, eggbeaters are a very popular Americana kitchen collectible—a piece of America still available to the collector, although he/she may have to scramble to find the rare ones.

But, beaters are out there, from the mainstay A & J to the cast-iron Dover to the rarer Express and Monroe. There is always an intriguing mix, ranging in price from less than under $10.00 to the hundreds of dollars.

—Don Thornton

Items are listed alphabetically by manufacturer

A & J USA Ecko Egg Beater

A & J, Ecko, wood handle, rotary w/apron marked "A&J USA Ecko," on a two-cup measuring cup marked "A&J" (ILLUS.) **$35**
Aurelius Bros., wood handle, rotary marked "Ideal Mille Lacs Mfg. by Aurelius," 10 3/4" h. (ILLUS. right) **$50**
Aurelius Bros., wood handle, rotary, rare triple dasher, rotary marked "Master Egg Beater Mfd. By Aurelius Bros., Braham, Minn. Pat. Appld. For," 11 1/2" h. (ILLUS. left center, top next page) **$300**
Aurelius Bros., wood handle, rotary w/double gearing, marked "Aurelius Bros., Braham, Minn. Pat. Nov. 9, 1926," 11 1/2" h. (ILLUS. left, top of next page) **$45**

K

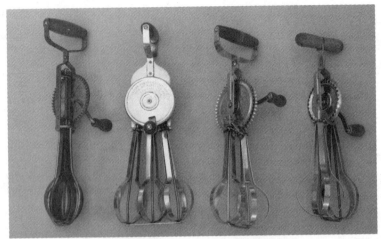

Aurelius Bros. Egg Beaters

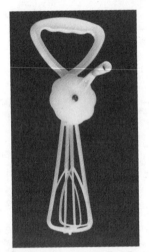

Blisscraft of Hollywood Egg Beater

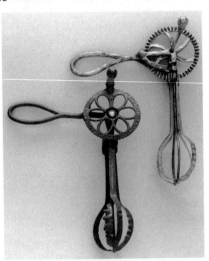

Holt-Lyon Side-Handle Egg Beaters

K

Blisscraft of Hollywood, plastic, rotary, marked "Blisscraft of Hollywood Pat. USA Pend.," scarce, 12" h. (ILLUS.) **$75**

Dover, cast-iron w/tin dashers & stand, marked "Dover Egg Beater - Patd May 6th 1873 Apr. 3rd 1888 Nov. 24th 1891".... **$200**

Dover, cast iron, nickel-plated, D-handle, rotary marked "Genuine Dover, Dover Stamping Co.," 11 1/4" h. **$50**

Dream Cream, rotary turbine marked "The Dream Cream Trade Mark Whip Manufactured by A.D. Foyer & Company Chicago," 10" h. **$25**

Family, cast iron, "Family Egg Beater Pat Sep 26, 1876," 10" **$800**

Henderson Corp., steel, "Minute Maid Henderson Corp. Pat Pend Seattle U.S.A.," 11 1/2" **$250**

Holt-Lyon, cast iron, side-handle, marked "H-L Co.," 8 1/2" h. (ILLUS. right)............... **$150**

Holt-Lyon, cast iron, side-handle, marked "Holt's Egg Beater & Cream Whip Pat. Aug. 22-'98 Apr. 3-00," 8 1/2" h. (ILLUS. left) **$150**

Jaquette Bros., scissors-type, cast iron, marked "Jaquette Bros No. 1," 7 1/2" l **$900**

Master, cast iron w/nickel plate, "Master Pat. Aug. 24-09," 10 3/4" (ILLUS., next page).. **$1,500**

Merry Whirl, metal w/vertical wooden handle, marked "Merry Whirl - Pat. 11-28-16 Other Pat. Pend." **$20**

New Keystone Beater, cast-iron top w/wire dashers & glass base, marked "New Keystone Beater No. 20 - North Bros. Pat Dec 15 '85"... **$350**

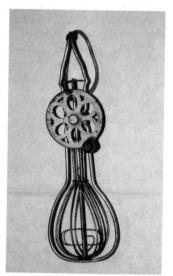

Rare Patented Master Egg Beater

Peerless, cast-iron w/tin dashers, marked "Peerless Egg Beater - Patent Applied For"... **$1,000**

Perfection, cast iron, "Perfection Pat'd Feb. 22, 1898 Albany N.Y.," 10 1/4"................... **$350**

S & S Hutchinson Rotary Egg Beater

S & S Hutchinson, heavy tin rotary marked "S & S Hutchinson No. 2 New York Pat. Sept. 2, 1913," w/heavy tin apron on ribbed glass jar embossed "National Indicator Co. No. 2 S & S Trade Mark Long Island City," 9 1/2" h. (ILLUS.) **$450**

Taplin Rotary Egg Beater

Taplin, cast-iron rotary, marked "The Taplin Mfg. Co. New Britian Conn, U.S.A. Light Running Pat. Nov. 24 '08," 12 1/2" h. (ILLUS.)..................................... **$45**

The World Beater, water-powered, painted tin top w/decal reading "The World Beater Mfrd by the World Novelty Co. Elgin, Ill." **$125**

Up-To-Date, metal, "Up-To-Date" egg/cream whip works on the Archimedian up & down action, patented April 10, 1906 .... **$275**

Miscellaneous

Apple corer - segmentor, cast iron & steel, a circle w/12 segmentors, cores & segments when apple is pushed through it, marked "Apple Cutter, Rollman Mfg. Co., Mr. Joy," 4 1/2" d... **$35**

Apple peeler, cast iron, "F.W. Hudson Improved - Pat. Dec. 2, 1862".......................... **$150**

Apple peeler, cast iron, "Pat June 9, 1872 Mfd by G. Bergner Washington, MO," no segmenter **$1,500**

K

Rare Wiggin Apple Peeler

Apple peeler, cast iron, "Wiggin Pat. Aug. 4, 1868" (ILLUS.) **$1,000**

Twisted Wire Basket

Basket, wire w/twisted wire center handle, 7" at widest diameter (ILLUS.) **$85**

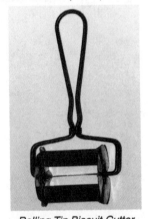

Rolling Tin Biscuit Cutter

Biscuit cutter, tin, rolls three biscuits at a time, Pat. Sept. 12, 1893 (ILLUS.) **$65**

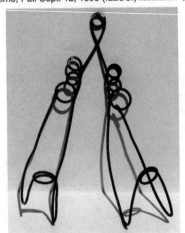

Wire Broom Holder

Broom holder, wire, ca. 1890 (ILLUS.) **$65**
Butter churn, cast-iron gear on tin top w/fruit jar base, "Schmidt Bros. Lancaster, PA" **$400**
Butter churn, table model, cast iron frame w/tin container, "1 Gal. - Patented 130B Dazey Churn & Mfg. Co. St. Louis MO" cast in top of frame **$650**

"The Home Butter Maker" Churn

Butter churn, table model, tin & cast-iron top w/unmarked glass jar, "The Home Butter Maker, Kohler Die & Specialty Co. Dekalb, Ill USA" (ILLUS.) **$125**

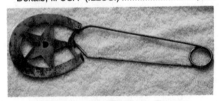

Horseshoe & Star Cake Turner

Cake turner, tin, horseshoe-shaped w/star marked "M.C.W. Cake Turner, Pat. Apr. 2. 07," wire handle flips it (ILLUS.) **$115**
Can opener, cast iron, marked "OK Pat 90 EWR," 7" l. **$45**

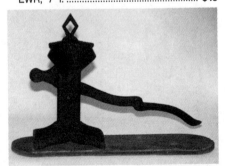

Williams's Patent Can Opener

K

Can opener, cast iron, mounted on board, Williams's Patent of Jan 8, 1878, rare (ILLUS., previous page) **$275**

Can opener, cast iron, swings open, "Universal Dazey Americana New Britain, Conn. USA Patent Applied For" **$100**

Large Old Copper Candy Kettle

Candy kettle, copper, a large half-round form w/a heavy rolled rim & heavy riveted iron loop rim handles, early 20th c., 20" d. (ILLUS.).. **$259**

Cherry pitter, cast iron, clamp-on style, push action pits two cherries at one time, marked "New Standard Cherry Stoner, Duplex No. 35 Mt. Joy PA U.S.A." **$85**

Cherry pitter, cast iron, standing on four legs, "Electric Cherry Seeder"................... **$125**

Cherry pitter, cast iron, "The Boss Raisin Seeder, Pat. Pdg.," 11 3/4" **$150**

Cast-Iron Patented Cherry Pitter

Cherry pitter, cast iron w/three legs, marked "Pat'd Nov. 17, 1863" (ILLUS.)...... **$145**

Cherry pitter, nickel-plated cast iron, "New Standard Corp. Mt. Joy, PA. Pat. Pend. No. 50" in all caps **$35**

Cherry pitter, wood, porcelain & cast iron, crack-type, unmarked, 10 1/2" (ILLUS., top next column).. **$125**

Chopper, cast iron handle w/two metal blades, handle marked "Pat'd. May 2, 93 No. 20 Croton, NY" (ILLUS., middle next column) **$45**

Wood, Porcelain & Iron Cherry Pitter

Two-Bladed Metal Chopper

Cookie board, rectangular flat board w/small rectangular integral handle at one end, chip-carved in the center w/a large compass star framed by geometric carved corners, good patina, 19th c., 6 3/4" w., overall 12 3/4" l. **$468**

K

Early Toleware Dipper

Dipper, tole, cylindrical bowl w/tapering strap handle, the bowl decorated w/red & mustard decorative band on black ground, the handle w/mustard & red leaf decoration, bowl 3 1/2" d., 2 1/4" h., 8" w/handle (ILLUS., previous page) **$480**

Metal Dish Drainer with Rack & Pan

Dish drainer, tin & wire, wire dish rack fits into rectangular tilted pan (ILLUS.) **$50**

Egg carrier, wire, round w/loops of wire forming bottom below six rings to hold eggs, looped wire center handle, ca. 1890 .... **$125**

Reliable Mfg. Co., Los Angeles Egg Scale

Egg scale, metal, platform-style, "Reliable Mfg Co./Los Angeles Calif," 8 3/4" (ILLUS.) **$75-85**

Egg scale, tin, marked "H.L. Piper Montreal," four egg holes **$100**

Egg separator, tin, advertising-type, "Use Big Jo Flour - Best in The World" **$15**

Fireplace roaster, hand-wrought iron, a long flat tapering handle ending in a heart-shaped loop, the round rotating roasting rack divided into four quadrants, each w/three tight scrolls, raised on arched feet, America, late 18th c., overall 28" l., rack 12" d., 3 1/2" h. **$1,150**

Flour sifter, tin, divided w/lids on both ends, marked "Bromwells Multiple" **$28**

New Shaker Flour Sifter

Flour sifter, tin, mesh screen in bottom, shake handle from side to side for action, marked "The New Shaker Sifter, Center Drive, Prevents Tipping, Pat. Applied For," two-cup size (ILLUS.) **$35**

Flour sifter, tin w/wire handle, advertising-type, "Snow King Powder - 30 Years of Success," 3 1/2" d. plus handle **$50**

Iron Single Blade Food Chopper

Food chopper, hand-wrought iron, single blade, wood handle, ca. 1850 (ILLUS.) **$30**

Two Early Tin Graters

Grater, tin, hand-punched, common (ILLUS. left w/other tin grater) **$45**

Grater, tin, manufactured, common (ILLUS. right w/other tin grater) **$20**

Griddle - pancake iron, cast iron, divided into three or more round areas each w/a lift-lid, marked "Pat. Jan 25 1881, S Mfg. Co., New York" **$175**

K

Jar Lifter with Wooden Handle

Jar lifter, steel w/turned wood handle, marked "Pat Pend," 8 1/2" h. (ILLUS.) **$30**

Patented Iron Jar Opener

Jar opener, cast iron, very unusual screw clamp mechanism, marked "Pat June 18, 1888," 8 3/4" l. (ILLUS.) **$150**
Jar opener, steel w/tin strap, scissors-type, marked "Pat Feb 11, 1902," 7 3/4" l. **$10**

Unusual Early Copper Covered Kettle

Kettle, a deep cylindrical form w/a slightly rounded bottom, the slightly domed hinged cover pierced w/overall decorative holes, iron side rim handle for holding wooden extension, early 19th c., 19" l. (ILLUS.) **$104**

Kettle Stand with Cabriole Legs

Kettle stand, brass, the rectangular top w/a slightly bowed front above a conforming scroll-cut front apron w/front cabriole legs, iron rod back legs, a cast brass handle flanking the top, 19th c., 11 3/4 x 18 3/4", 12" h. (ILLUS.) **$201**

Kraut Cutter with Heart-shaped Top

Kraut cutter, a long flat rectangular board inset w/an angled metal cutting blade, the heart-shaped top w/a small hanging hole, well scrubbed & used surface, 7" w., 21 1/2" l. (ILLUS.) **$345**
Kraut cutter, walnut, rectangular board w/screwed side rails, angled blade, round crest w/hanging hole, old patina, 7 1/2 x 24 1/2" **$83**
Lemon reamer, cast iron, marked "Pat Nov 21, 1885," 9 1/2" l. **$25**

Upright Iron Lemon Squeezer/Slicer

Lemon squeezer/slicer, cast iron, combination cutter & squeezer on wood base w/crank action of handle forcing juice from lemon, inserts often missing, approx. 13" h. (ILLUS.) **$200-225**

K

Match safe, tole, original japanned ground & paint w/a tulip on a white band on the front & swags on the cut-out & crimped crest, wear, 19th c., 7 1/2" h. **$575**

Mayonnaise mixer, cast iron & glass, "Universal Mayonnaise Mixer and Cream Whipper Made by Landers, Frary & Clark, New Britain, Conn. USA" **$450**

Meat tenderizer, cast iron, handled, w/five toothed rows in rectangular frame, marked "Pat. Applied For" **$55**

Iron Perfection Nut Cracker

Nut cracker, cast iron, clamp-style for attaching to table edge, clamp-form cracker, marked "Perfection Nut Cracker - Made in Waco, Texas - Patented 1914," 6 x 6 1/2" (ILLUS.).................................. **$55-65**

English Tin Acme Nut Grater

Nut grater, tin, half-round w/hanging hole at top, stamped "Acme Nut Grater Rd 114671," English (ILLUS.)........................... **$40**

"The Gem" Nutmeg Grater

Nutmeg grater, cast iron, tin & wood, "The Gem" (ILLUS.)... **$75-85**

Rare Carsley Nutmeg Grater

Nutmeg grater, tin, marked "H. Carsley, Patented Nov. 20, 1855, Lynn, Mass," rare (ILLUS.) **$975**

Rare Sterling Nutmeg Grater

Nutmeg grinder, sterling silver oval cylindrical case w/engine-turned design & hinged cover holding the grater, touch marks for Thomas Hall, Exeter, England, 1855-56, 1 1/4" w., 3" l. (ILLUS.) **$275**

Rollman Mfg. Co. Peach Stoner

Peach stoner, cast iron, "Rollman Mfg. Co. Pat Pend Mount Joy PA U.S.A.," 8 3/4" (ILLUS., previous page) **$250**

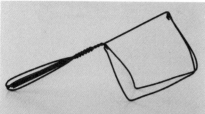

Wing-style Wire Pie Lifter

Pie lifter, wire handle w/wood insert, two hinged wings on opposite end which act to grab pan (ILLUS.)..................................... **$95**

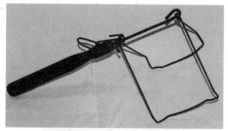

Unusual Wire & Wood Pie Lifter

Pie lifter, wire w/long turned black wood handle, an unusual wire lever top opening the wire grips, 12 1/2" l. (ILLUS.) **$75**

Tin Pie Pan with Star design

Pie pan, tin, pierced star design holes in bottom, used to make crisper crusts (ILLUS.)... **$55**

Pot scraper, graniteware, advertising-type, marked "Penn Stoves" **$150**

Pot scraper, graniteware, advertising-type, marked "Red Wing Flour".......................... **$650**

Spring-action Potato Masher

Potato masher, double-spring-action type w/two heavy wire wavy sections, one over the other, turned wooden handle (ILLUS.) **$45**

Raisin seeder, cast iron, marked "Enterprise Mfg. Co. Philadelphia, PA USA - Pat. Apr. 2, Aug. 20, 95 - Pat Apl'd For - Wet The Raisins - No. 36".......................... **$45**

Rolling pin, amber blown glass, hollow w/closed handles, 19th c., 13 3/4" l........... **$275**

Rolling pin, china, blue on white Blue Onion patt., wooden handles, Germany, 19th c. **$125-150**

Early Peacock Blue Blown Glass Rolling Pin

Rolling pin, peacock blue blown glass, hollow w/closed handles, rare, 19th c., 14" l. (ILLUS.)... **$400**

Rolling pin, stoneware, Monmouth-Western Stoneware, Colonial patt., cylindrical w/printed blue swag bands at each end, no handles, early 20th c. **$1,000-1,200**

K

Wooden Springerle Rolling Pin

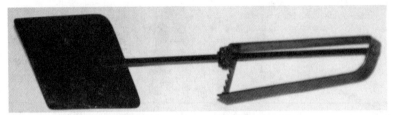

Squeeze-handle Tin & Cast-iron Spatula

Rolling pin, wooden, turned wood handles, the cylinder carved w/20 springerle designs in rows of blocks, early, overall 17" l. (ILLUS., bottom previous page) **$250-350**

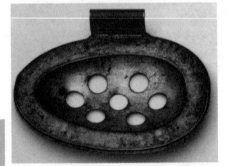

Wire Rug Beater with Complex Woven Design

Rug beater, wire w/complex woven design forming three loops of different widths & angles, turned maple handle, late 19th - early 20th c., 9" w., 29" l. (ILLUS.) **$30-40**
Skillet, cast iron, "Griswold No 4".................... **$26**
Skillet, cast iron, large emblem, no heat ring, Griswold #2 .... **$350**
Spatula, tin & cast iron, mechanical, squeezing handle flips end (ILLUS., top of page) **$75**

Oval Tin Spoon Holder

Spoon holder, tin, oval shape w/seven holes & ridge around edge, w/hook, to be placed on side of kettle for drippings from spoon, unmarked (ILLUS.) **$35**

Sugar bucket, cov., stave construction w/three finger lappets w/copper tacks, swing bentwood hickory bail handle, old mustard yellow paint, 19th c., minor wear & edge chips, 13 3/4" h. (ILLUS.).............. **$460**
Tea strainer, tin, advertising-type, marked "All Allen's Teas & Coffees Strictly Guaranteed"... **$25**
Tea strainer, tin, advertising-type, marked "Use Big Jo Flour - The Best In The World" **$30**

American Dovetailed Copper Teakettle

Teakettle, cov., copper, flat-bottomed dovetailed body w/a wide base & tapering sides to a short cylindrical neck w/a fitted low domed cover w/baluster-form finial, angular snake spout, overhead brass strap swing bail handle, stamped number "6," American-made, 19th c., overall 13" l. (ILLUS.).. **$1,208**

Tall Oval Copper Teakettle

K

Teakettle, cov., copper, oval cylindrical body w/deep sides below the wide angled shoulder, ringed domed cover w/mushroom finial, angular snake spout, fixed tall brass curved supports joined by a bar handle, tin-lined, 19th c., 11" h. (ILLUS.) **$201**

Copper Teapot on Iron Legs

Teapot, cov., copper, bulbous nearly spherical body w/an angled shoulder to a short cylindrical neck w/a fitted domed cover w/scroll finial, tapering cylindrical side handle fitted w/a baluster-turned black wood handle w/pointed terminal, body raised on three straight riveted wrought-iron legs, probably Europe, 19th c., wear, spout pressed in, 8" h. (ILLUS.) **$125**

Trivet, wire, rounded starburst design of stamped wire w/double-loop ends & triangles, used as a coffeepot or teapot stand **$45**

Cast-iron Advertising Trivet

Trivet, cast-iron, advertises "C D Kenny Teas, Coffees, Sugars, 60 Stores," 5" l. (ILLUS.).. **$145**

Wafer iron, cast iron, traditional scissor-form w/a pair of hinged round disks on long handles ending in a loop catch, one disk intaglio-cast w/a spread-winged American eagle & shield w/a banner in its beak reading "E Pluribus Unum," Pennsylvania, ca. 1800, overall 29 1/4" l. **$1,610**

LACQUER

Most desirable of the lacquer articles available for collectors are those of Japanese and Chinese origin, and the finest of these were produced during the Ming and Ching dynasties, although the Chinese knew the art of fashioning articles of lacquer centuries before. Cinnabar is carved red lacquer.

Fine French Decorated Lacquer Casket

Casket, low rectangular form w/a hinged cover, molded base band & tiny knob feet, the top bordered by inlaid & polished mother-of-pearl confetti surround a large h.p. floral bouquet, further flowers & gilt scrolled accents on the front & sides, France, mid-19th c., 10 x 14", 4 3/4" h. (ILLUS.) **$230**

Fancy English Lacquer Table-top Chest

Chest, table-top, upright rectangular design w/a broken scroll pediment centered by a gilt shell finial, above a pair of long doors w/very ornate gilt flower borders surrounding a chinoiserie landscape, opening to five drawers each w/a turned bone knob, raised on tiny ball feet, England, first quarter 19th c., 8 1/4 x 15 1/2", 22 1/2" h. (ILLUS.) **$1,495**

L

Japanese Lacquer Jewel Chest

Jewel chest, in the form of a miniature Japanese tansu, upright rectangular case w/a gently arched top above a stack of three small drawers beside a large rectangular door w/metal mounts & centered by an applied Satsuma pottery panel w/landscape decoration, a long deep drawer across the bottom mounted w/another Satsuma panel, high bracket feet w/metal mounts, central door missing a pull, Japan, Meiji era, ca. 1900, 4 3/4 x 9 1/4", 12 1/2" h. (ILLUS.) **$173**

Elaborate Japanese Lacquer Picnic Set

Picnic set, a black lacquer open framework w/gilt trim enclosing a finely inlaid & gilt set of boxes w/the fronts of the four decorated w/a continuous wisteria vine decoration in gold w/inlaid abalone leaves & details, composed of a tray, open box & four stacked boxes w/a top lid & two pewter sake bottles in the fitted frame, minor wear w/some damage on bottles, Japan, late 19th - early 20th c., w/an iron-bound wooden carrying case w/damage & lined w/tape, framework 7 1/2 x 13", 12 1/2" h. (ILLUS.).. **$518**

Russian Lacquer-covered Photo Album

Photograph album, the leather binding mounted on the cover w/a large rectangular lacquer panel painted w/a scene of villagers heading to market w/a city in the distance, interior w/a Moscow, Russia retailer's mark, probably the Lukutin Factory, Moscow, ca. 1880, apparently never used, 10 1/2 x 13" (ILLUS.)..................... **$1,380**

Lukutin Factory Lacquered Tray

Tray, lacquer on metal, oblong dished form w/serpentine sides, painted in the center w/a colorful scene of a troika racing down the road, Lutukin Factory, Moscow, Russia, 19th c., back signed in Cyrillic beneath the Imperial Warrant, 10 1/2 x 13 1/2" (ILLUS.)........................... **$690**

Tray, oval w/a narrow flanged rim h.p. w/a repeating leafy vine & blossom vine in gold & white, the center w/a black ground h.p. w/a wintry troika scene, mark of manufacturer Vishniakov on the back, Russia, 19th c., 23 3/4" l. (ILLUS., next page).. **$805**

Large Oval Russian Lacquer Tray with a Troika Scene

Fine Japanese Presentation Lacquer Tray

Tray, presentation-type, rectangular w/rounded corners, black ground w/gold & red floral decoration highlighted w/abalone inlay, the reverse w/gold-speckled decoration, on a wooden stand, Japan, ca. 1910, 15 1/2 x 22 3/4" (ILLUS.)............... **$1,840**

LIGHTING DEVICES

Early Non-Electric Lamps & Lighting

Fairy Lamps

These are candle burning night lights of the Victorian era. Best known are the Clarke Fairy Lamps made in England, but they were also made by other firms. They were produced in two sizes, each with a base and a shade. Fairy Pyramid lamps usually have a clear glass base and are approximately 2 7/8" d. and 3 1/4" h. The Fairy Lamps are usually at least 4" d. and 5" h. when assembled. These may or may not have an additional saucer or bottom holder to match the shade in addition to the clear base.

Very Rare Burmese Fairy Lamp Epergne

Burmese glass shades, epergne-style, a brass frame w/three rings supporting a signed "Clarke" clear glass base & Burmese shade h.p. w/green leafy branches w/red berries, the center w/three arched brass arms & a tall center arm each fitted w/a slender tapering Burmese decorated bud vase w/a ruffled rim, Thomas Webb, England, late 19th c., one shade w/minor flake on inside edge, overall 10" h. (ILLUS.)................. **$5,175**

Burmese Fairy Lamp on Clear Base

Burmese shade, pale pink shaded to yellow, satin finish, on a signed "Clarke" clear glass base, overall 3 3/4" h. (ILLUS.)......... **$230**

L

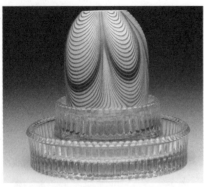

Verre Moiré Purple & White Fairy Lamp

Verre Moiré (Nailsea) glass shade, satin deep purple w/white opaque loopings, double graduated clear pressed glass marked "Clarke" base, small flake on base, 5 3/4" h. (ILLUS.)............................. **$173**

Lamps, Miscellaneous

Fine White Cut to Cranberry Banquet Lamp

Cut-overlay banquet lamp, an inverted pear-shaped font in white cut to cranberry w/oblong panels & a row of punties trimmed w/gold, joined w/a tall brass connector to the matching slender waisted lower standard on a flaring round & stepped connector on a square white marble foot, a cast-brass frame around the shoulder w/eight arms impressed w/a grapevine design, each suspending a triangular spearpoint prism, w/brass burner, ca. 1860, 16" h. (ILLUS.) **$1,725**

Victorian Leaded Glass Hall Lamp & Cranberry Hanging Parlor Lamp

Hall lamp, kerosene-type, leaded & stained glass, the long square brass frame w/pierced scrolling leaf borders above & below the leaded glass sides each centered by a large dark blue cut button against a frosted clear ground framed by amber borders & deep orange diamond jewels, four serpentine support arms joined to the ceiling mount above a brass smoke bell, late 19th c., electrified, 10 1/2" sq., 21" h. (ILLUS. right with parlor hanging lamp) **$2,070**

Parlor hanging lamp, kerosene-type, ornate pierced brass shade ring above a scrolling frame decorated w/winged griffins flanking the unusual conical brass & oxblood red enameled font frame holding a brass font w/burner & chimney, opentopped domed cranberry opalescent Hobnail patt. shade, font insert marked "B&H" for Bradley & Hubbard, ca. 1890, electrified, 19" d., 36" h. (ILLUS. left with leaded glass hall lamp) **$2,185**

Brass Hanging Lamp & Cranberry Shade

Parlor hanging lamp, kerosene-type, the brass frame w/a squatty bulbous font w/a paneled design & center raised band connected to pairs of long S-scrolls joined to the wide shade ring & hanging chains, fitted w/a blown deep cranberry glass domed shade w/a Hobnail patt., faceted cut-glass prisms around the shade ring, missing adjusting mechanism, ca. 1890s, 13 3/4" d. (ILLUS., previous page) **$805**

Parlor hanging lamp, kerosene-type, the brass frame w/large looping curls flanking a squatty bulbous milk glass font decorated w/a pale blue morning glory designs, the pierced brass shade ring suspends facet-cut prisms & supports a matching domed milk glass shade w/morning glories & a castle scene w/brass top ring, suspended from four chains, ca. 1890, electrified, shade 14" d. .. **$219**

Parlor hanging lamp, kerosene-type, the brass frame w/large looping curls flanking a squatty bulbous milk glass font decorated w/large blue daisey-like flowers, the pierced brass shade ring suspends facet-cut prisms & supports a matching domed milk glass shade w/flowers & w/brass top ring, suspended from four chains joined to a smaller brass ring suspending prisms, ca. 1890, electrified, shade 13 1/2" d. **$345**

Victorian Glass & Figural Cast-metal Lamp

Parlor table lamp, kerosene-type, a clear pressed glass font w/ringed tapering sides & a frosted central band w/a geometric design, atop a brass connector ring joined to a bronzed cast-metal figural pedestal featuring the bust of a young Victorian woman atop a round foot w/a cast lappet band, attached to a square black metal base, ca. 1870s, 13" h. (ILLUS.) **$118**

Sinumbra lamps, brass & ebonized metal, each w/a square foot trimmed w/a gilt-metal band below the square pedestal supporting a tall fluted columnar standard topped by the wide shade ring supporting an early squatty bulbous tulip-form glass shade w/etched decoration, probably French, ca. 1800-1810, 31 1/2" h., pr. **$15,535**

Sinumbra lamps, patinated bronze, the tall slender bronze bases & standards cast w/Gothic style designs, supporting a wide shade ring, one clear frosted glass shade etched w/a Greek key & leaf design & the other shade w/a swag & blossom design, by J.B. Wilbor, New York City, ca. 1830-40, 31" h., pr. **$5,378**

Student lamp, kerosene-type, a nickel-plated domed base centered by a tall slender stem fitted on one side w/a long cylindrical font opposite an arm supporting a cylindrical burner & shade ring fitted w/a domed open-topped cased dark green shade & glass chimney, burner thumbwheel marked "The New Vestal," minor metal pitting, burner lacking central draft tube & flame spreader, ca. 1890s, overall 20 1/4" h. **$374**

Student lamp, kerosene-type, a nickel-plated domed ringed foot & slender standard supporting a horizontal cylindrical font w/a burner & shade ring at one end, fitted w/an open-topped milk glass shade, Bridgeport Brass Co., ca. 1900, wear to nickel, minor burner corrosion, rim crack in shade, adjusts 13" to 18" h. **$220**

Unusual Old Brass Surgeon's Lamp

Surgeon's lamp, brass, a bulbous font w/kerosene burner in front of a large round dished brass reflector, raised on a slender stem & flaring weighted & ringed foot, labeled "Approved Surgeon's Lamp - Scott Lamp Co. - San Francisco, Calif.," 27" h. (ILLUS.) **$259**

L

Table lamp, kerosene-type, a clear blown inverted pear-shaped font finely cut & etched w/floral & vine decoration, joined by a ringed brass connector to the dark blue pressed Baroque-style base, the burner & shade ring supporting a bulbous squatty clear glass open-tooped shade w/etched leaves & berries, a fluted-top chimney, #2 slip burner, 12 3/4" h.............. **$605**

Electric Lamps & Lighting

Handel Lamps

The Handel Company of Meriden, Connecticut (1885-1936) began as a glass and lamp shade decorating company. It became a major producer of decorative electric lamps which have become very collectible today.

Handel Egg-shaped Nightlight

Nightlight, upright egg-shaped shade w/a yellow crackled background decorated w/h.p. parrots & flowers, signed on the edge "Handel 1095 - AH," rests on an Oriental style openwork metal base, 8" h. (ILLUS.)... **$1,035**

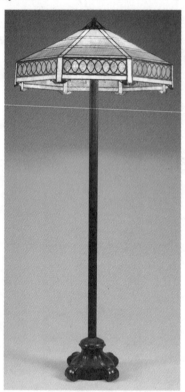

Scarce Handel Slag Glass Floor Lamp

Floor lamp, 25" w. octagonal caramel slag shade w/graduated blocks of glass at the top above a deep green & amber slag flat border outlined in thin caramel slag bands & overlaid w/metal interlocking circles, signed on an applied tag, raised on a tall thin vertically ribbed bronzed metal standard w/a bulbous four-footed base, some cracked panels, overall 65" h. (ILLUS.) **$7,705**

Handel Slag Lamp with Floral Border

Table lamp, 13 1/2" d. domical six-panel bent caramel slag shade w/a wide metal filigree border band decorated w/pink flowers & green leaves within narrow green borders, shade ring signed, on simple slender copper-tone Handel base marked under the base w/a Handel cloth tag, 19 1/2" h. (ILLUS.) **$1,725**

L

Handel Lamp with Overlay Shade

Table lamp, 13" d. bent-panel caramel slag shade w/six wide tapering panels decorated around the lower rim w/a metal filigree design of green woodbine, resting on a slender Handel cast-metal stick base w/chipped ice finish, base signed on bottom w/raised letters, some minor solder repairs inside shade clips, one socket replaced, 21 1/2" h. (ILLUS.) **$1,560**

del cast-metal copper-patinated stick base, base signed on bottom w/raised letters, minor patina wear on base, 24" h. (ILLUS.) **$4,025**

Fine Handel Bird of Paradise Lamp

Table lamp, 17 3/4" d. domical reverse-painted shade decorated w/pairs of colorful blue, red, yellow & orange birds of paradise perched on boughs w/yellowish green leaves & blue flowers against a pink ground, signed "ED Handel 1720," raised on a slender bronzed three-legged base w/a round foot, base w/cloth Handel label, 24" h. (ILLUS.) **$11,400**

Handel Lamp with Bent-Panel Shade

Table lamp, 16" d. bent-panel caramel slag shade w/six wide tapering panels in a plain rivetted metal framework, signed on the shade ring, resting on a slender Han-

Handel Lamp with Brown Chipped Ice Shade

Table lamp, 18" d. conical shade w/a brown chipped ice exterior over a white opal interior, signed inside "Handel Brown 5341 1/2 - T.S. Patent No. 979664 No. 775815," atop a bronze Handel base w/a

L

slender paneled standard w/a round cushion foot, some blistering to finish on base, sockets old replacements, 23" h. (ILLUS.)... **$1,898**

Handel Lamp with Filigree Rose Shade

Table lamp, 18" d. domical bent-panel glass shade w/eight tapering white vertically ribbed panels overlaid w/cast-metal filigree in a design of yellow climbing roses & green leaves, signed "Handel Pat'd No. 924457," rests atop a Handel bronze copper patina Arts & Crafts style slender base w/a round foot wa cloth label on the bottom, one panel cracked w/small piece missing, base w/patina wear, 23" h. (ILLUS.).............................. **$2,280**

Very Rare Handel Metal Overlay Lamp

Table lamp, 24" d. domical bent-panel slag glass shade in mottled deep red, overlaid w/a repeating pierced metal design of pine

trees above an undulating border band of pine needles over green slag, on a signed bulbous ovoid bronze base w/rich brown pantina cast w/a top band of stylized flowers, 25 1/2" h. (ILLUS.) **$17,825**

Pairpoint Lamps

Well known as a producer of fine Victorian art glass and silver plate wares between 1907 and 1929, the Pairpoint Corporation of New Bedford, Massachusetts, also produced a wide range of fine quality decorative lamps.

Rare "Puffy" Pairpoint Azalea Lamp

Table lamp, 12 1/4" d., domical "Puffy" reverse-painted "Azalea" shade, closed-top design decorated overall w/large white & yellow blossoms & green leaves, shade stamped "Pat Applied For," on a silvered metal trumpet-form base w/arched slender vine handles down the sides, base stamped "Pairpoint Mfg. Co. 3041," 19 1/2" h. (ILLUS.) **$10,200**

Pairpoint Lamp with Butterfly & Roses Shade

Table lamp, 13 1/2" d., domical "Puffy" reverse-painted "Butterfly & Roses" shade, closed-top design decorated w/sections of large red roses & green leaves below large yellow & orange butterflies, all against a mottled white ground, signed, on a silvered tall slender urn-form base, ca. 1915, 20 1/2" h. (ILLUS., previous page)............ **$7,800**

Table lamp, 17 1/2" d. drum-shaped reverse-painted 'Bombay' shade decorated w/a repeating design of clusters of tall leafy trees separated by misty landscape in the distance, signed in gold "Pairpoint Mfg. Corp'n," resting on a signed Pairpoint flaring bulbous brown textured glass base w/brown patinated fittings w/a textured finish w/copper patina, 21" h. (ILLUS.)... **$4,600**

Pairpoint Lamp with Sailing Ship Shade

Table lamp, 17 1/2" d. domical reverse-painted 'Carlisle' shade decorated w/early sailing ships on a choppy sea w/billowing clouds & sea gulls in the background, black border rims, signed in gold "Pairpoint Mfg. Corp'n," resting on a slender signed Pairpoint artichoke-style base w/two-socket cluster, shade rim w/numerous internal in-the-making hairlines, base w/finish wear, replaced shade ring, 24" h. (ILLUS.) **$1,920**

Pairpoint Lamp with Berkeley Shade

Table lamp, 20" d. domical reverse-painted "Berkeley" shade w/chipped ice exterior finish, the interior painted w/a continuous autumn landscape of large trees in autumn color, a small figure of a farmer carrying a scythe & walking toward the open fields in the distance, signed "W. Macy," raised on a bronze urn-form base w/a squared foot, crack w/base foot meets the urn, 25" h. (ILLUS.) **$4,600**

Pairpoint Lamp with Bombay Shade

Pairpoint "Puffy" Papillion Lamp

L

Table lamp, 13 1/2" d., domical "Puffy" reverse-painted "Papillion" shade, closed-top design decorated w/sections of large red & yellow & purple flowers & green leaves below large yellow & orange butterflies, all against a mottled white ground, signed, on an antiqued brass base w/a slender columnar shaft applied w/classical torches centered on a plinth base w/classical ribbon-tied flower swags above a square foot, base signed "Pairpoint B3006," 21" h. (ILLUS., previous page) **$9,988**

Pairpoint Berkeley Shade Table Lamp

Tiffany Lamps

Extremely Rare Tiffany Dragonfly Chandelier

Marlborough "Puffy" Pairpoint Lamp

Table lamp, 15" d., domical "Puffy" reverse-painted "Marlborough" shade, flat top & flaring four-paneled sides each panel decorated w/colorful mixed rose & flower swags, a clear frosted ground w/thin stripes & blossom bands, signed, raised on a bronzed metal base w/a trumpet-form shape w/a gadrooned rim & leaf-cast base raised on a wide round foot w/a gadrooned rim, base stamped "Pairpoint D3042," 23" h. (ILLUS.)........................... **$5,875**

Table lamp, 20" d. domical reverse-painted "Berkeley" shade, cracked ice exterior finish, the interior painted w/a wide gold yellow band of arches & leaf sprigs below an overall decoration of large red roses & yellow & green leaves on a black ground, raised on a slender bronze urn-form base w/upright scrolled handles & a floral swag band, on a square notch-cornered foot, base signed "Pairpoint D3016," small heat check at shade rim, 27" h. (ILLUS., top next column) **$1,840**

Chandelier, "Dragonfly," a band of drop-head dragonflies around the bottom rim w/mottled blue wings & amber bodies w/red eyes, suspended from a graduated ground of oblong mottled yellow segments & scattered oval amber jewels, tag marked "Tiffany Studios New York 1507," ca. 1910, 22" d., 16" h. (ILLUS.) **$136,300**

Early Tiffany Teardrop Hall Lamp

L

Hall lamp, a bronze band suspended from slender chains fitted w/a long teardrop-shaped yellow iridescent shade decorated w/a gold iridescent pulled-feather design, shade engraved "S11120," ca. 1903, shade 8 3/4" l. (ILLUS., previous page) **$5,975**

Very Rare Tiffany Hall Lamp

Hall lamp, a slender central bronze shaft & flat cap suspended by three chains & fitted w/a spherical leaded glass shade composed of a wide band of red iridescent turtleback tiles flanked by random geometric segments of mottled yellow iridescent glass, ca. 1910, 11 3/4" h. (ILLUS.)........ **$53,775**

Very Fine Tiffany Acorn Table Lamp

Table lamp, "Acorn," composed of a scattered field of mottled green, white & blue graduated tiles forming the background to a wide lower band of undulating amber acorns, shade w/tag marked "Tiffany Studios New York," on a bulbous urn-from bronze base raised on slender scroll legs above the quatrefoil foot, base stamped

"Tiffany Studios - New York 888," shade 16" d., overall 21 1/2" h. (ILLUS.) **$14,950**

Very Rare Tiffany Begonia Table Lamp

Table lamp, "Begonia," composed of an overall design of mottled red & pink blossoms interspersed w/long pointed mottled yellow & green leaves, a filigree-pierced top cap, raised on a tall slender tree trunk-form bronze base, shade stamped "Tiffany Studios New York," base stamped "Tiffany Studios - New York 554," shade 13 1/4" d., overall 17 1/4" h. (ILLUS.)... **$119,500**

Rare Tiffany Black-eyed Susan Lamp

Table lamp, "Black-eyed Susan," 16" d. leaded glass shade composed of colorful green leafy stems w/yellow & brown blossoms against a tapering tiled mottled dark green shading to white background, tag stamped "TIFFANY STUDIOS - NEW YORK - 1447-9," on a slender bronze standard above a round cushion base cast w/two rows of teardrop shapes on

L

curled feet, base marked "Tiffany Studios
- New York 25877" w/Tiffany Glass &
Decorating Co. monogram, ca.1910,
22 1/2" h., (ILLUS.) **$28,175**

Fine Tiffany Dogwood Table Lamp

Table lamp, "Dogwood," composed of a
scattered field of mottled white & pink
dogwood blossoms against a ground of
mottled blue & green segments, the drop
border accented by three narrow bands
in mottled green & amber, raised on a tall
slender shaped & reeded bronze standard w/a domed reeded round base on
small ball feet, shade stamped "Tiffany
Studios New York," base stamped "Tiffany Studios - New York 28644," shade
18" d., overall 24 1/4" h. (ILLUS.).......... **$35,850**

Extremely Rare Tiffany Nasturium Lamp

Table lamp, "Nasturium," composed of an
overall design of mottled dark yellow &
orange blossoms scattered among mottled dark green & yellow leaves, two narrow mottled dark green & yellow border
bands, raised on an ornate urn-form

pieced standard continuing into four long
slender legs ending in scroll feet atop a
cross-form base, shade stamped "Tiffany
Studios - New York," base stamped "Tiffany Studios - New York 550," shade
21 3/4" d., overall 31 1/2" h. (ILLUS.) . **$186,700**

Fine Tiffany Oriental Poppy Table Lamp

Table lamp, "Oriental Poppy," composed of
an overall design of mottled dark & light
yellow poppy blossoms against mottled
green & yellow leaves, three narrow dark
mottled green bands around the lower
edge, raised on a slender spiral wiretwist
bronze standard above a cushion-form
scale pattern base, shade stamped "Tiffany Studios - New York 698," base
stamped "Tiffany Studios - New York
D803," shade 18 1/8" d., overall 26" h.
(ILLUS.).. **$83,650**

Fine Tiffany Poinsettia Table Lamp

Table lamp, "Poinsettia," 16" d. domical
leaded glass shade, composed of radiating mottled green geometric segments

L

above a wide band of poinsettia flowers & foliage in striated rich red w/blue, green & yellow centers & two border bands of green & amber, tagged "Tiffany Studios - New York" & numbered, on a bronze Tiffany base w/a slender standard & lobed foot, impressed "Tiffany Studios - New York - 533," only a few cracked panels, sockets replaced, 22" h. (ILLUS.) **$28,750**

1930s Lighting

Chase Brass & Copper Company

Chase "Clipper" & "Wheel" Table Lamps

"Clipper" table lamp, No. 6191, "Nautical" theme design w/hemp trim, 15 1/4" h. (ILLUS. left with "Wheel" table lamp) **$110-135**

"Wheel" table lamp, No. 6305, "Nautical" theme, ship's wheel operating mechanism, 16 1/4" h. (ILLUS. right with "Clipper" table lamp) **$95-120**

Lamps, Miscellaneous

Ornate Early Figural Alabaster Lamp

Alabaster table lamp, the tall figural alabaster base w/a paneled plinth supporting the standing figure of a semi-nude classical maiden in front of a square pedestal issuing the lamp shaft topped by a

brass shade ring hung w/spearpoint prisms, fitted w/a domed milk glass shade w/lightly etched panels of long leafy scrolls highlighted by brown paint, probably Italian, ca. 1900, overall 54" h. (ILLUS.) **$5,405**

Unusual Iridescent Glass Mantel Lamp

Art glass & cast-brass mantel lamp, the ovoid gold iridescent body w/an overall crackled finish raised on a brass base w/a wreath ring above large curled leaf legs, the domed base top covered w/a fine pierced brass filigree swag & leaftip design topped by a small clear glass ball finial, glass attributed to Durand, early 20th c., 14 1/2" h. (ILLUS.) **$1,035**

Wide Eight-panel Slag Glass Lamp

Bent-panel table lamp, 19 3/4" d. umbrella-form shade composed of eight tapering caramel slag panels separated by gilt-metal bands w/a pierced design around the shade cap & a scalloped rim band, raised on a urn-shaped cast-metal base w/panels of leafy garlands, sockets old replacements, shade support & cap replacements w/original finial, early 20th c., 24" h. (ILLUS., previous page) **$201**

Early Bradley & Hubbbard Electric Lamp

Bradley & Hubbard table lamp, a wide low rounded shade tapering to a flared cylindrical top opening, in clear frosted glass reverse-painted w/a decoration of large white water lilies & buds & green leaves on light blue water, supported on a thin brass shade ring above the gilt-bronze base w/a slender hexagonal shaft above the sloping hexagonal foot incised w/geometric looped lines, chip on top of shade, ca. 1910, 19 1/2" h. (ILLUS.) **$382**

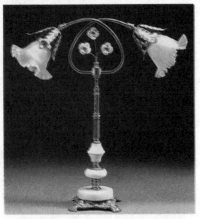

Early Tall Two-socket Table Lamp

Brass & onyx table lamp, the tall base w/a cast squared & footed base below a pale green onyx disk centered by a tall slender shaft w/two more onyx sections below twisted & reeded brass sections supporting two long arched & crossed slender arms framing an upright cluster of three yellow porcelain roses, each arm ending in long leaves enclosing an electric socket fitted w/a pale shaded pink floral-form glass shade w/a flaring crimped & ruffled rim, ca. 1900, 20" h. (ILLUS.) **$518**

French Art Deco "Harlequine" Lamp

Bronze & frosted glass, "Harlequine," Art Deco style, a long narrow rectangular black marble base supporting the semi-reclining patinated bronze figure of Harlequin w/head bowed & knees raised supported the spherical frosted glass shade, cast from a model by Marcel-Andre Bouraine, France, ca. 1925, 16 3/8" l., 10 1/2" h. (ILLUS.) **$2,629**

Early Electric Lamp with Floral Shades

Bronze table lamp, the tall base w/a rounded leaf-cast foot supporting a cluster of tall acanthus leaves enclosing three slender stems topped by another leaf cluster issuing three arched arms each ending in an acanthus leaf cluster surrounding the electric socket & supporting a blossom-form lobed & crimped shade in pink & white w/an overall scroll design, base marked "Victor - Made in the USA," ca. 1900, 24" h. (ILLUS.) **$920**

Rare French Art Deco Pheasant Lamps

Chapelle Muller table lamp, glass & cast-metal, figural, finely modeled as a strutting pheasant w/its head raised & tail arched, the openwork metal body blown internally w/amber glass w/foil inclusions, mounted on a rectangular grey marble base, metal signed "Chapelle Nancy France," ca. 1930s, 20" l., 17" h. (ILLUS.).................... **$7,475**

Classique Lamp with Landscape Shade

Classique table lamp, 18" d. domed pyramidal reverse-painted shade decorated w/a landscape w/a large path curving beside a stream, green meadows & tall slender leafy trees, raised on a bronzed metal baluster-form octagonal base marked "Classique Lamps," 22" h. (ILLUS.).......... **$1,840**

Unusual Tall Cloisonné Floor Lamp

Cloisonné floor lamp, bronze w/sections of cloisonné, a heavy domed base on short cabriole legs topped by relief-cast animal faces & a monkey holding a faux font, the tall standard composed of various domed & cylindrical sections featuring various floral & geometric cloisonné designs in shades of blue, white & other colors, all topped by a large domed original silk shade w/a floral design & suspending a deep fringe, Oriental, early 20th c., 24" d. shade, 72" h. (ILLUS.)............................ **$2,070**

Consolidated Glass Fruit Bowl Lamp

Consolidated Lamp & Glass table lamp, figural, modeled as a footed, deep rounded black glass bowl base supporting a domed top of molded fruit, including grapes, apples & pears, painted in shades of green, purple, yellow & orange, cord replaced, 8" d., 10" h. (ILLUS.)...................... **$374**

L

Consolidated Glass Flower Bowl Lamp

Consolidated Lamp & Glass table lamp, figural, modeled as a footed, deep rounded black glass bowl base supporting a domed top of molded flowers painted in shades of green, pink, yellow & blue, socket replaced, 8" d., 9" h. (ILLUS.) **$374**

Fine Daum Nancy Cameo Glass Lamp

Daum Nancy cameo table lamp, the wide domed shade w/a central knob w/a mottled orange & yellow ground overlaid in dark purple & cameo-cut w/a continuous landscape of leafy trees around a pond, raised on a matching slender tapering cylindrical base w/a domed foot, cameo signature, ca. 1910, shade 9 5/8" d., overall 14 1/2" h. (ILLUS.) **$7,200**

Fine Daum Cameo Boudoir Lamp

Daum Nancy cameo boudoir lamp, the tapering ovoid open-topped shade w/a mottled amethyst & green background etched & enameled in white, pink & green w/a continous scene of leafy tree tops, the matching tapering cylindrical glass base w/a cushion foot decorated w/tall slender enameled tree trunks & lower leafy branches, signed, 14" h. (ILLUS.) **$13,800**

French Art Deco Ruhlmann Lamp

Earthenware table lamp, Art Deco style, glazed body w/a wide disk foot tapering to a cylindrical shaft decorated around the bottom w/a black band of short stripes, a band of black dots around the top, bottom w/hand-painted mark of Jacques-Emile Ruhlmann, France, 1920s, base 8 5/8" h. (ILLUS.) **$5,975**

L

Jefferson Lamp with Stormy Landscape Shade

Jefferson table lamp, 16" domical reverse-painted shade decorated w/a landscape of trees, a stream & boulders in shades of dark green, brown & yellow against a stormy orange & yellow sky, raised on a slender fluted mottled green enameled base w/two socket cluster, base signed on edge of foot, minor wear on base, 22" h. (ILLUS.) **$1,265**

Jefferson Shade with Lakeside Landscape

Jefferson table lamp, 17 3/4" d. domical reverse-painted shade decorated w/a continuous landscape w/clusters of tall trees in the foreground w/a lake beyond & tall poplar trees in the distance, in shades of green, brown, blue & yellow, signed on metal shade ring, resting on a slender six-sided bronzed metal base w/greenish brown patina w/six-sided foot, base w/minor finish wear, 23" h. (ILLUS.) **$1,955**

Jefferson Landscape Shade Table Lamp

Jefferson table lamp, 18" d. domical reverse-painted shade decorated w/an expansive landscape at sunset w/shrubs & clumps of tall trees in the foreground & distance, in shades of orange, yellow, dark brown & green, on a gilded cast metal base w/a tall slender ribbed, knob-and leaf-cast standard on a dished round foot, 23" h. (ILLUS.) **$1,955**

Rare Lalique "Epis" Table Lamp

Lalique table lamp, "Epis" patt., frosted clear glass, the bulbous ovoid top mount-

L

ed w/a wide flat arc etched w/wheat heads, the columnar shaft supported on a rectangular base w/angled sides, pressed mark, introduced in 1919, 8 1/2 x 14 1/4", 24 1/2" h. (ILLUS.) **$28,000**

Phoenix Lamp with Tropical Shade

Phoenix table lamp, 18" d. domical reverse-painted shade decorated w/a tropical sunset scene w/tall palm trees in the foreground w/a lagoon & mountains in the distance, in shades of orange, yellow & red, on a bronzed metal baluster-form base w/cast leaves on tall ribbed stems, round foot, unmarked, early 20th c., 24" h. (ILLUS.) **$1,035**

Pittsburgh Shade on Handel Base

Pittsburgh table lamp, 17" d. domical reverse-painted shade decorated w/a wide black border band w/bands of green

leaves & clusters of large red blossoms, the upper shade in pale yellow, raised on a Handel-signed slender ribbed bronze base w/a flared foot, shade unsigned, early 20th c., 24" h. (ILLUS.) **$1,265**

Pittsburgh Lamp with Windmill Scene

Pittsburgh table lamp, 17" d. domical reverse-painted shade rather crudely painted w/a rural landscape w/a windmill on a hill beside a group of tall leafy trees beside a river, in bright shades of yellow, dark green, brown, cream & blue, raised on a tall slender tapering ribbed & ribbon-wrapped bronzed metal base w/a domed round paneled foot w/rosette rim band, unsigned, 22" h. (ILLUS.) **$978**

Pittsburgh Shade with Rural Landscape

Pittsburgh table lamp, 18" d. domical reverse-painted shade rather crudely painted w/a rural landscape scene of a cottage among meadows & clusters of trees & blue water, in shades of bright orange, yellow, green, brown & blue, on a slender ribbed bronzed metal base w/a flaring round foot signed "P.L.B. & G. Co.," 22" h. (ILLUS., previous page) **$1,150**

Nautical Decorated Shade on Handel Base

Reverse-painted table lamp, 12" d. domical reverse-painted shade decorated w/a nautical scene of sailing ships in a tranquil bay in shades of brown, green & blue against a blue shaded to yellow cloudy sky, chipped ice exterior, raised on a signed Handel bronze base w/a slender standard & round gadrooned foot, couple of tiny flakes on edge of shade, minor blistering on base, heat cap a non-Handel replacement, 20" h. (ILLUS.) **$863**

Reverse-painted table lamp, 16" d. domicala reverse-painted shade decorated w/large clusters of deep pink & yellow roses on leafy stems against a mottled green & yellow ground, chipped ice exterior, raised on a bronzed metal base w/a slender tapering reeded standard on a round paneled base w/palmettes, three-socket cluster, some wear to base finish, 21 1/2" h. (ILLUS., top next column) **$1,150**

Lamp with Pretty Rose-decorated Shade

Other Lighting Devices

Chandeliers

Ornate Bronze Victorian Chandelier

Cast bronze, the tall central shaft w/a spiral design above a pear-shaped swirled knop above a pierced ball at the base w/a drop finial, four long slender scrolls from the top continue out to form arms curling up & ending in winged griffins supporting a gas spigot & shade ring holding a flaring octagonal clear frosted & floral-etched glass shade, second half 19th c., 29" w., 26" h. (ILLUS.) **$4,313**

L

Cut glass & patinated & gilt-bronze, four-light, Empire-Style, a small ringed corona suspending long graduated cut bead chains holding a large gilt bronze-mounted band w/an interior light & suspending a very long tubular glass & ball fringe, the band issuing three scrolled short arms w/bell-form sockets each suspending a long tubular glass fringe, Europe, ca. 1900, 18" d., 36" h. **$3,450**

Gilt- and patinated-bronze, six-light, Rococo-Style, designed as a long central ribbon tassel isssuing three long ropes to suspend a large ornate floral-cast wreath w/a long ribbon drop, each rope ending at a patinated figure of a putto holding up two arched short scroll arms ending in electric sockets each fitted w/a frosted glass pointed flame-form shade, France, early 20th c., electrified, 36" h. **$6,573**

Gilt-bronze & enamel, six-light, Neoclassical Style, the small crown w/upright scroll leaves above six long slender leaf-clad S-scrolls suspending a wide ring enameled in dark blue accented w/bronze stars, each scroll terminating in an ornate candle socket w/draped w/long ribbons & joined by long bronze swags, a central scroll-trimmed pendant drop, some enamel wear, France, late 19th - early 20th c., 24" d., 31" h. **$5,750**

Rare Lalique Bandes de Roses Chandelier

Lalique-signed, "Bandes de Roses" patt., a large deep bowl-shaped shade in frosted clear molded w/four narrow graduated bands w/stylized roses, introduced in 1924, engraved signature "R. Lalique France," 23" d. (ILLUS.) **$22,800**

Leaded glass, a large domical form topped by a crown of eight small rounded caramel slag panels, the sides composed of six large bent caramel slag pointed panels all outlined by a continuous arched narrow band of mottled green slag accented w/a mottled orange block, the border accented w/six inverted pink slag stylized tulip blossoms, ca. 1920s, 22" d. **$200-400**

Morgan Leaded Chandelier from Set

Morgan (John) & Sons-signed, leaded glass, a wide umbrella form shade composed of a background of mottled amber graduated blocks decorated w/colorful leafy swags & leaf clusters in reds, oranges, greens & pinks, w/four matching small sconce shades, early 20th c., each sconce shade 7 1/2" h., chandelier 30" d., the set (ILLUS. of chandelier) **$10,350**

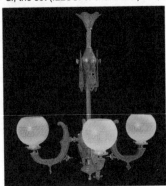

French Victorian Neo-Grec Gasolier

Patinated metal, four-light gasolier, Neo-Grec style, the long baluster-form upper shaft mounted w/four long pierced finials decorated w/portrait roundels, extending down to a bulbous & ring-turned section issuing four flat demi-lune-shaped arms each ending in a gas burner fitted w/a spherical open-topped frosted glass shade etched w/a wide Greek key band, electrified, ca. 1870s, France, 36" h. (ILLUS.) **$3,600**

Filigree & Slag Glass Chandelier

Slag glass, flaring octagonal bronzed metal filigree frame enclosing eight flat tapering rectangular caramel slag panels w/small angled panels around the top, the main panels w/a pierced leafy swag at the top & a large round wreath supported on scrolled & leaf-filled cornucopias at the bottom, each panel w/a low arched solid winged design at bottom rim, early 20th c., 27" w. (ILLUS., previous page) **$345**

Steuben-signed, six-light, a large bronzed metal scalloped petal-form pan w/twelve panels, each panel cast w/raised leafy grape clusters, six panels suspending a short chain & grape leaf-embossed bell-form electric socket fitted w/a signed Steuben bell-form shade in brown iridescent Aurene w/a platinum intarsia border band, one w/minor chip on fitted, overall 18" d., each shade 5" h. **$4,888**

Tiffany-signed, "Flowering Bouquet," a widely flaring conical shade composed of a dense pattern of large mottled & solid red flowers against a ground of mottled green, yellow, purple & blue leaves, beaded rims, stamped "Tiffany Studios New York," ca. 1910, 28 1/2" d., 11" h. **$365,900**

Fine Seven-Light Tiffany Chandelier

Tiffany-signed, seven-light, the ceiling cap suspending a domed pierced bronze fixture w/applied rope-twist medallions above a wide border band issuing six short arched arms each ending in a socket fitted w/long tulip-shaped shades w/ruffled rim in yellow to gold pulled-feather design on a creamy white ground, the ring suspending alternating bronze chain drops & long iridescent glass

prisms, a long center socket fitted w/a matching shade, very minor patina wear, 16" d., 24" h. (ILLUS.) **$23,000**

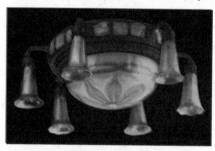

Rare Tiffany-signed Six-Light Bronze & Glass Chandelier

Tiffany-signed, six-light, a large cylindrical central bronze ring mounted w/a band of turtleback tiles & issuing six down-turned short socket arms each fitted w/a long flower-form lightly ribbed gold iridescent shade, the center of the disc mounted w/a large domical glass shade in gold iridescence decorated w/an amber chain band above a central flowerhead w/pulled-feather petals, each shade signed "L.C.T.," ca. 1910, 18 1/2" d., 6 1/4" drop (ILLUS.) **$45,410**

Tin Six-Arm Chandelier

Tin, six-light, a long hanging shaft swelled at the top & suspending a diamond-form central disk issuing six serpentine strap arms each ending in a candle socket w/drip pan, late, 30" d., 18 1/2" h. (ILLUS.) **$316**

Lanterns

Hall lantern, Art Deco style, wrought-iron & textured clear glass, the tall square iron frame enclosing pierced iron panels w/stylized hunters & antelope, four arched & scrolled straps joined at the top below hanging ring, gilt-metal narrow open swag band around the base w/small reeded corner drops, designed by Edgar Brandt, glass possibly by Daum, w/original chain, ca. 1925, 10 1/8" w., 25" h. (ILLUS., next page)
.... **$204,000**

L

Extraordinary Art Deco Hall Lantern

Rare Tiffany "Chain Mail" Hall Lantern

Hall lantern, "Chain Mail" design, bronze & glass, a high domical top suspended from a chain, the lower cylindrical rim band above a long mottled amber glass cylinder overlaid w/a thin bronze lattice-work, Tiffany Studios, ca. 1910, shade 18 1/4" h. (ILLUS.) **$20,315**

Shades

Large Art Glass Pulled-Feather Shade

Art glass, wide squatty bulbous domical form pulled into a rounded center point, creamy white ground decorated w/four wide panels of bluish green pulled-feather design outlined in greenish gold, 7" d., 5" h. (ILLUS.) **$660**

Fostoria-attributed, tapering squatty bulbous body w/a wide flaring & ruffled rim, iridescent white exterior w/a green pulled-feather decoration outlined in gold iridescence, gold iridescent interior, minor roughness to one fitter, 5 1/2" d., set of 3 (ILLUS., bottom of page).................... **$660**

Fine Quezel Hooked Feather Tall Shade

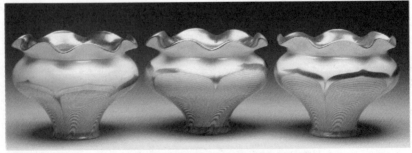

Three Art Glass Shades Attributed to Fostoria

Quezal-signed, tall waisted cylindrical form w/widely flaring ruffled rim, gold hooked feather decoration on a dark green ground w/fine purplish blue iridescence & double-hook design gold stretched border at ruffles, gold iridescent interior, 7" w., 8" h. (ILLUS., previous page) **$3,623**

Unusual Ribbed Gold Steuben Shade

Steuben-signed, a wide domed & ribbed form w/a flattened swelled band below the fitter flange, overall gold iridescence, 1910, 4" h. (ILLUS.) **$294**

Large Reverse-Painted Garden Shade

Reverse-painted, large domical reverse-painted shade w/flared rim, decorated w/a formal garden landscape w/a gazebo, rows of trees & lawn & mountains in the distance, artist-signed "G. Morley," some minor chipping to top hole, 13 3/4" d. (ILLUS.) **$920**

Squatty Steuben Gold Aurene Shade

Steuben-signed, a wide squatty bulbous form w/a flat rim, overall gold iridescence, signed, 2 1/4" d. fitter, 3" h. (ILLUS.) **$230**

Fine King Tut Design Steuben Shade

Fine Steuben Brown Aurene Shade

Steuben, a widely flaring trumpet form w/a swelled ring at the top, iridescent brown iridescence w/a gold iridescent intarsia border band, unsigned, 6 1/2" d. (ILLUS.) **$1,265**

Steuben-signed, bell-shaped w/a scalloped rim, gold iridescent ground w/an overall blue King Tut decoration, Calcite interior, chips to fitted rim, scratches on exterior, 5" d., 4 3/4" h. (ILLUS.) **$1,380**

L

Set of Four Steuben Gold Aurene Shades

Steuben-signed, domed ribbed lower section w/a compressed ribbed neck below the fitter, overall gold Aurene, 5" w., 4" h., set of 4 (ILLUS., bottom previous page)... **$1,950**

Tall Steuben Pulled-Feather Shade

Steuben-signed, tall cylindrical body w/a wide squatty base tapering top a short ruffled rim, Calcite exterior decorated w/a repeating row of long green pulled-feathers outlined in gold, gold iridescent interior, roughness to fitter rim, 8 1/4" h. (ILLUS.) **$690**

L

Signed Tiffany Gold Ascot Shade

Tiffany-signed, Ascot shape, a ruffled top & sloping shoulder above the wide flattened rim, overall gold iridescence, 5 1/4" d., 3 1/2" h. (ILLUS.) **$1,150**

Tiffany-signed, widely flaring double-lobe shape w/a flat incurved rim, blue iridescent ground decorated w/a green pulled-feather design from the top to the rim, roughness to fitter, 5 1/2" d., 3 3/4" h. (ILLUS., top next column) **$1,380**

Fine Tiffany Pulled-Feather Shade

MARBLES

Large Pinkish Tan Agate Marble

Agate, swirled shaded pinkish tan bands, top w/slight stop of iridescent bruising, lightly polished, 2 3/16" d. (ILLUS.)............ **$157**

Akro Agate No. 4 count box, original specials box filled w/50 mint rainbow marbles, w/original knee pad & instructions, only example known, the set.................. **$4,888**

Fine Colorful Divided Core Marble

Divided core, clear w/a divided red, yellow, blue, green & black core w/white outer bands, fine original surface finish, 1 11/16" d. (ILLUS.).................................. **$235**

Ribbon Swirl, swirled ribbons in blue & white, green & yellow, red & white & red & yellow, outer bands in group of five small lines, alternating yellow & white bands, one below-surface moon & on half-moon, early 20th c., 2 1/4" d. **$690**

Black & Yellow Solid Core with Outer Bands

Solid core, clear w/black & yellow core & blue & white thin outer bands, lightly polished, some tiny surface hits, 1 11/16" d. (ILLUS.)... **$134**

Rare Red, White & Blue Solid Core

Solid core, clear w/red, white & blue swirled core & yellow thin outer bands, surface fissure, very faint hits, original surface finish, 2 3/16" d. (ILLUS.)............................. **$448**

Cow Grazing & Seated Dog Sulphides

Sulphide, cow grazing, normal light surface bruises & flakes, 2" d. (ILLUS. left with seated dog sulphide)................................... **$88**
Sulphide, dog seated, very light surface bruises, 1 9/16" d. (ILLUS. right with grazing cow sulphide) **$110**

Fine Falcon Sulphide Marble

Sulphide, falcon on stump, very tiny hit mark, original surface, finely detailed, 1 5/8" d. (ILLUS.) **$235**

Sulphide with Horse

Sulphide, horse, clear w/pink amethystine tint, poor definition, somewhat misshapen, probably polished, 1 11/16" d. (ILLUS.) **$235**

Rare Sulphide Enclosing Number 2

Sulphide, number "2" on a disk, original surface finish, some surface moons, 1 1/2" d. (ILLUS.) **$720**

Scarce Sulphide with Owl

Sulphide, owl w/wings spread perched on pedestal, very faint moon on side, original finish, fine detail, 2 3/8" d. (ILLUS.)...... **$476**

Sulphide Marble with Seated Rabbit
Sulphide, seated rabbit, 1 1/2" d. (ILLUS.).... **$104**

M

Early Black & White Swirl Marble

Swirl, black w/white swirls, rough pontil at each side, early 20th c., 1 1/4" d. (ILLUS.) **$82**

Colorful Old Swirl Marble

Swirl, divided center w/bright swirls of orangish red, green, blue, white & yellow, some chips, 1 1/2" d. (ILLUS.) **$58**

METALS

Brass

Early Brass Bedwarmer with Iron Handle

Bedwarmer, a rounded brass pan w/slightly domed hinged cover pierced w/tiny holes & tooled design of flowers & hearts, attached to a long slender flattened wrought-iron handle w/hanging loop tip, solder repair to pan cover, late 18th - early 19th c., 44" l. (ILLUS.) **$460**

Decorative Brass Kettle Stand

Kettle stand, a rectangular ornately pierced top w/a turned wood side handle, raised on brass cabriole front legs joined by an iron cross-stretcher to the rear iron legs w/penny feet, probably England, 19th c., 12 3/4 x 14 1/2" w/handle, 10 1/4" h. (ILLUS.)............................. **$144**

Bronze

Bronze Cachepot by Edgar Brandt

Cachepot, footed tall inverted bell-form w/realistic undulating snake handles w/the snakes attacking a relief-cast eagle on the side, signed w/the maquette of Edgar Brandt, ca. 1925, 5 1/4" h. (ILLUS.) **$10,755**

Centerpiece, figural, a long narrow base platform centered by a large paneled & flaring bronze bowl flanked by silhouetted bronze Art Deco female nudes each w/a bird perched on her hands, patinated finish, signed w/the maquette of Emory P. Seidel & impressed mark "Roman Bronze Works N.Y. - S 39," ca. 1926, 20" l. (ILLUS., top next page)............... **$21,510**

M

Bronze Art Deco Figural Centerpiece Designed by Emory Seidel

Oriental Bronze Jardiniere & Stand

Jardiniere & stand, round flared foot below the wide squatty bulbous body tapering to a short, wide banded cylindrical neck, a large finely detailed dragon around the body, mon motifs around the foot & neck, raised on a four-legged pierce-carved stand, no bottom on jardiniere, Oriental, late 19th - early 20th c., stand 21 1/2" d., 19 1/2" h., jardiniere 24" d., 18" h., the set (ILLUS.) **$345**

burst ground, weighted w/plaster & backed w/claret-colored felt, France, late 19th c., 8" d. (ILLUS.).................................. **$201**

Bronze Plaque of Thomas Jefferson

Plaque, cast as a profile bust of Thomas Jefferson, unmarked, probably early 20th c., 16" h. (ILLUS.).. **$206**

Late Victorian French Bronze Plaque

Plaque, a round molded border surrounding a high-relief female masque in the neoclassical style above two crossed laurel leaf branches all against a fluted sun-

Victorian Bronze Shaving Mirror

Shaving mirror, a tall simple upright oval frame w/a thin beaded rim band enclos-

M

ing a beveled mirror, raised on a short leaf cluster stem above the dished & ringed round base, Europe, 19th c., 14 1/2" h. (ILLUS.) **$288**

Spoon mold, two-part, for making rat tail-style pewter spoons, 19th c., 8 1/4" l. **$115**

Late Victorian Gilt-Bronze Tazza

Tazza, gilt-bronze, in the Mannerist style, the wide shallow round top cast in the center w/a scene of nobleman & his daughters drinking out-of-doors, ornate leafy scroll body, the scroll-cast pedestal atop a round ornate scroll-cast foot, Europe, late 19th c., 7 1/4" d., 6 1/2" h. (ILLUS.) **$1,035**

Bronze Elephant Vase Based on Mene

Vase, tapering ovoid form cast as a repeating design of three elephant heads & front legs w/projecting ears & tusks, replica after the original by Pierre Jules Mene, cast signature "P.J. Mene, 1870," black marble base w/molded edge, dark brown patination, France, 12 1/2" h. (ILLUS.) **$230**

Chrome

Rare Chrome Airplane Traveling Bar

Cocktail bar, figural traveling-type, "Airplane," modeled as a stylized airplane w/a long oblong cylindrical body w/rectangular wings & tail fins, the front raised on two metal wheels, made by J.A. Henckels Twin Works, ca. 1928, 10" l. (ILLUS.) **$8,000-12,000**

Fine Farberware Chrome & Bakelite Cocktail Set

Cocktail set: cov. shaker & six goblets; Art Deco style, each w/a trumpet foot supporting a body composed of three graduated bulbous lobes, the shaker w/a short angled shoulder spout & curved black Bakelite handle attached w/two red Bakelite balls, the cylindrical neck fitted w/a domed cover w/a red Bakelite bar handle, bottom marked "Farberware - Brooklyn, N.Y.," ca. 1935, cups 4 1/4" h., shaker 12 1/2" h., the set (ILLUS.) **$1,195**

Unusual Bowling Pin Art Deco Cocktail Set

Cocktail set: cov. shaker & six goblets on stands; Art Deco style, each shaped like a bowling pin w/a chromed lower body & turned maple upper body, the goblets can be inverted so chrome forms the bowl, American, ca. 1935, shaker 15 3/4" h., the set (ILLUS., previous page) **$1,315**

Fine French Art Deco Chrome Floor Lamp

Floor lamp, Art Deco style, the large inverted bell-form top raised on a very tall slender cylindrical standard supported by four cross-form rectangular blades attached to a flat ring, France, ca. 1925-30, 68 3/4" h. (ILLUS.) **$9,560**

Copper

Roycroft Arts & Crafts Copper Ashtray

Ashtray, hand-hammered, Arts & Crafts style, flat-bottomed deep rounded form w/closed rim mounted w/a cigarette holder, mark w/the Roycroft orb mark, some

minor wear & discoloration to patina, 3 1/2" d., 2" h. (ILLUS.) **$180**

Individual-sized Copper Teakettle

Teakettle, cov., individual size, small foot-ring & squatty bulbous dovetailed body w/a flat cover w/button finial, shaped strap swing handle w/trefoil attachments & pinched "2," serpentine spout, dents & light pitting w/a brazed handle repair, 7" h. (ILLUS.) **$58**

Early Philadelphia Copper Teapot

Teapot, cov., flat-bottomed domed dovetailed body w/serpentine spout, low-domed cover w/tapering finial, swing strap handle marked "Wm. A. Lewis & Co., 4 Philada.," worn w/loose finial, 7" h. plus handle (ILLUS.) **$400-800**

Scarce Signed Early American Teapot

Teapot, cov., wide flat bottom & domed dovetailed body w/a low domed cover w/button finial, high arched flat strap swing handle stamped "C. Raborg," Christopher Raborg, Baltimore, Maryland, late 18th - early 19th c., some dents, 6 1/2" h. plus handle (ILLUS.) **$1,495**

M

Iron

Very Rare Early Iron Figure of Washington

Figure of George Washington, cast, standing holding a scroll in one hand, the other hand holding closed his long cloak, a red sash around his waist, originally patented as a stove radiator, cast in two parts, base marked "Design Patented August 26, 1843," red, white & blue paint appears original, holes in base of cloak to bolt him to a base, 46 1/2" h. (ILLUS.) ... **$18,113**

Early Philadelphia Cast-Iron Fireplace Insert

Fireplace insert, cast, a large oval base plate w/a rectangular fire box cast w/Ionic columns w/acanthus leaves down the sides, the top w/three brass medallions separated by matching short columns, turned brass corner finials, flue marked "Diamond Flue," cast-iron grate w/pierced front not shown, from Philadelphia, first half 19th c., 36" sq., 37" h. (ILLUS.) **$316**

Foot scraper, cast, figural profile of Scottie dog, America, early-20th c., 11 1/2" l., 18 1/2" h. including posts (minor surface rust) **$588**

Early Crown-Form Iron Game Hook

Game hook, wrought iron, crown-form, a domed crown form made of two flat bands joined to a horizontal ring suspending four four-barbed game hooks, top hanging ring & S-scroll hanger, hanger added later, 19th c., 10 1/2" d., 12" h. (ILLUS.) **$201**

Early Standing Jockey Hitching Post

Hitching post, cast, figure of a jockey w/one arm outstretched holding a ring, thick square iron base, weathered paint w/red jacket, white pants & red & black boots, late 19th - early 20th c., 16" w,. 47" h. (ILLUS.) **$748**

Unusual Wrought-Iron Decoration

Wall decoration, wrought iron, a flat stylized horseshoe issuing eight flattened arms each ending in a small stylized horseshoe, probably blacksmith forged & made from horseshoes, 27 1/2" w., 19" h. (ILLUS.) **$173**

Marked Elgin Rooster Windmill Weight

Windmill weight, cast, model of a rooster w/a solid wide arched tail, marked "10 FT NO 2," made by the Elgin Wind Power and Pump Co., Elgin, Illinois, early 20th c., traces of original paint, short base w/old edge damage (ILLUS.) **$748**

Windmill weight, cast, model of a standing bull w/a deep chest & head raised, by the Fairbury Windmill Company, Fairbury, Nebraska, later wooden base, late 19th c., 25" l., 18 1/2" h. **$633**

Old Cast-Iron Bull Windmill Weight

Windmill weight, cast, model of a walking bull w/head raised, late 19th c., 15 1/2" l., 13" h. (ILLUS.) **$3,840**

Dempster Horse Windmill Weight

Windmill weight, cast, standing bobtailed horse, worn red paint, by Dempster Mill Manufacturing Co., Beatrice, Nebraska, faint cast numbers on side, on modern wooden base, 17 3/4" l., 18 1/8" h. (ILLUS.) **$604**

Pewter

Boardman & Co. Pewter Basin

Basin, round w/narrow single reed brim, plain eagle touch mark of Thomas Danforth Boardman & partners, Hartford, Connecticut, first half 19th c., minor rim dents & wear, 6 3/8" d. (ILLUS.) **$323**

S. Hamlin Early Pewter Basin

Basin, round w/narrow single reed brim, scroll touch mark of Samuel Hamlin, Sr., Hartford, Connecticut, last quarter 18th c., minor wear, 7 5/8" d. (ILLUS.)............... **$470**

M

Early Hamlin Pewter Charger

Charger, round w/flanged rim, mark of Samuel Hamlin or Samuel Hamlin, Jr., Hartford, Connecticut & Providence, Rhode Island, late 18th - early 19th c., wear, 13 3/8" d. (ILLUS.)............................ **$264**

Early Samuel Hamlin, Sr. Charger

Charger, round w/flanged rim w/single reeded line, mark of Samuel Hamlin, Sr., Hartford, Connecticut & Providence, Rhode Island, late 18th c., wear, 13 3/8" d. (ILLUS.) **$646**

James Putnam Pewter Coffeepot

Coffeepot, cov., footed baluster-form body w/hinged domed cover w/flower finial, ser-

pentine spout & fancy scroll handle w/traces of black paint, mark of James H. Putnam, Malden, Massachusetts, ca. 1830-35, scattered dents, 11" h. (ILLUS.) **$353**

Wm. Lyman Pewter Coffeepot

Coffeepot, cov., footed gently swelled cylindrical banded body w/a flared rim & hinged domed cover w/button finial, serpentine spout & fancy S-scroll metal handle, mark of William W. Lyman, Wallingford & Meriden, Connecticut, ca. 1844-52, minor dents & small soldered repair, 11 1/4" h. (ILLUS.) **$230**

Richardson "Lighthouse" Coffeepot

Coffeepot, cov., tall tapering cylindrical "lighthouse" shape w/molded fillets, scrolled black-painted metal handle, mark of George Richardson, Cranston, Rhode Island, 1828-45, dent in finial, 10 1/2" h. (ILLUS.) **$764**

Creamer & cov. sugar bowl, each footed w/a squatty bulbous body bright-cut w/flowers & leaves, flared rim, S-scroll handle, sugar w/domed cover w/wooden knob, mark of Thomas Danforth Boardman & partners, Hartford, Connecticut, 1805-50, fine pitting, minor dents & wear, sugar bowl finial possibly replaced, 4 3/4" & 5 1/2" h., pr. (ILLUS., top next page)...... **$470**

M

Boardman & Co. Creamer & Covered Sugar Bowl

Unusual Early Pewter Ladle

Ladle, round bowl w/angled stem w/a long slender turned wood handle, attributed to Richard Lee or Richard Lee, Jr., New England, late 18th - early 19th c., wear, 12 1/4" l. (ILLUS.).. **$470**

Calder Pewter Whale Oil Lamps

Lamps, whale oil-type, a wide round foot tapering to a ringed stem supporting the cylindrical font fitted w/a single burner, mark of William Calder, Providence, Rhode Island, first half 19th c., minor pitting, 4 1/4" h., pr. (ILLUS.) **$388**

Mug, slightly tapering cylindrical form w/everted rim, molded band & base & S-scroll handle, lion mark of Edward Danforth, Hartford, Connecticut, late 18th c., 1 qt., 5 7/8" h. (ILLUS., top next column) **$5,288**

Plate, round w/flanged rim w/single reeded line, mark of David Melville, Newport, Rhode Island, second half 18th c., wear, 7 3/4" d. (ILLUS., middle next column) **$441**

Plate, round w/flanged rim w/single reeded line, round eagle touch mark of Samuel Danforth, Hartford, Connecticut, 1795-1816, minor wear, 7 7/8" d. (ILLUS., bottom next column).. **$411**

Rare 18th Century Danforth Mug

David Melville Pewter Plate

M

S. Danforth Pewter Plate

Nice Early American Pewter Tankard

Tankard, tapering cylindrical body w/S-scroll handle, Joseph Danforth, Middletown, Connecticut, 1780-88, 3 3/4" d., 4 1/2" h. (ILLUS.) **$3,600**

Spherical Calder Pewter Teapot

Teapot, cov., footed spherical body w/a hinged domed cover, serpentine spout, incised bands, black-painted scrolled handle, mark of William Calder, Providence, Rhode Island, first half 19th c., dent in cover, minor wear & dents, 7 1/2" h. (ILLUS.) **$353**

Art Nouveau Style Tudric Pewter Vases

Vases, Art Nouveau style, flaring round foot tapering to a tall slender stem supporting a tulip-form bowl, long arched slender vine handles from bowl to top of foot, marked "Tudric 029," made for Liberty & Co., London, England, early 20th c., small dent & minor pitting on foot of one, 10" h., pr. (ILLUS.) **$748**

Silver

American (Sterling & Coin)

One of Two Fancy Bonbon Spoons

Bonbon spoons, sterling, a fancy pierced floral bowl & stem, the handle termimnal w/rococo shellwork & enclosing a putto representing Night, Tiffany & Co., New York City, ca. 1890, 13 1/4" l., pr. (ILLUS. of one)...................................... **$6,000**

Early Philadelphia Coin Silver Bowl

Bowl, coin, low cylindrical stepped foot w/beaded rim below the deep rounded bowl w/a beaded rim, the sides engraved w/a monogram, mark of John David, Philadelphia, ca. 1765, 6 3/4" d. (ILLUS.) **$1,440**

M

Tiffany Bowl with Applied Insects

Bowl, sterling, parcel-gilt, domed round footed below a deep wide rounded bowl, overall hand-hammered surface, the bowl engraved w/wildflowers & applied w/a butterfly, grasshopper & reeds, marked by Tiffany & Co., ca. 1877, 7 1/2" d. (ILLUS.) **$4,800**

Early Arts & Crafts Silver Bowl & Spoon

Bowl & spoon, sterling, Arts & Crafts style, the deep flaring inverted bell-form bowl raised on a round base w/leaf-form supports, w/matching ladle-form spoon, made by Frances MacBeth Glessner, marked w/ciphers of the maker & "Hand Made Sterling," ca. 1910, bowl 4 1/4" d., the set (ILLUS.) **$8,963**

Rare Early American Butter Plate

Butter plate, coin, round w/broad flanged rim w/a slight curve above the shallow curve to the flat bottom, rim engraved w/Jackson family arms in a sheaf & scroll cartouche & also their crest on opposite rim, mark of Samuel Edwards, Boston, ca. 1730, 5 15/16" d. (ILLUS.) **$38,775**

Rare Myer Myers Coin Silver Cann

Cann (mug), coin, footed baluster-form body w/a stepped round base, a leaf-capped scroll handle, an engraved monogram on the side, mark of Myer Myers, New York City, ca. 1760, 4" h. (ILLUS.) **$26,400**

Early American Coin Silver Cann

Cann (mug), coin, footed baluster-form body w/C-scroll handle, engraved monogram on front, unmarked, late 18th c., 5 1/2" h. (ILLUS.) **$780**

M

Very Rare Early Boston Silver Cann

Cann (mug), coin, tapering cylindrical body w/ringed base & applied mid-band, S-scroll handle w/initial & dated "1793," narrow shaped edge, engraved on the front w/name in block letters, bottom records line of descent in the Whitney family, mark of Jacob Hurd, Boston, 1728, 3 3/4" d., 4 3/4" h. (ILLUS.) **$19,975**

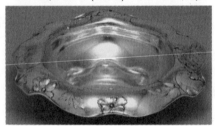

Rare Gorham Martelé Centerpiece Bowl

Centerpiece bowl, sterling, Art Nouveau style w/an undulating rolled rim chased w/poppy blossoms & leafy stems, Martelé line by Gorham Mfg. Co., Providence, Rhode Island, 1912, 15 1/2" d. (ILLUS.).. **$10,800**

Rare Early Boston Coin Silver Coffeepot

Coffeepot, cov., coin, tall baluster-form body on a domed round foot, ribbed & scrolled spout & C-scroll black wood handle, stepped & domed hinged cover w/figural pine cone finial, the side engraved w/a script monogram & crest of a bird, mark of Daniel Henchman, Boston, ca. 1760, 11" h. (ILLUS.) **$11,400**

Early Pennsylvania Coin Silver Creamer

Creamer, coin, baluster-form body w/a beaded rim raised on a pedestal base w/a beaded border band, leaf-capped double scroll handle, engraved monograms, mark of Peter Getz, Lancaster, Pennsylvania, ca. 1790, 5 3/4" h. (ILLUS.) **$3,840**

Early Gorham Creamer & Open Sugar

Creamer & open sugar bowl, sterling, each a tapering cylindrical shape on tiny figural sphinx feet, the bodies engraved w/foliate scrolls & initials, the creamer w/a high angled handle w/an applied mask, the sugar w/two overhead swing handles w/mask terminals, marked by Gorham Mfg. Co., Providence, Rhode Island & Starr and Marcus, ca. 1865, creamer 7" h., pr. (ILLUS.) **$1,754**

Dishes, sterling, a graduated set of shell-shaped dishes each raised on three dolphin-shaped feet, a pierced border & gadrooned rim, an entwined dolphin handle & herm finial, mark of Howard & Co., New York City, 1908-13, graduated from 8 1/4" l. to 11 1/4" l., set of 6 (ILLUS., top next page) **$12,000**

M

Rare Set of Sterling Shell-shaped Dishes

Coin Silver Presentation Ewer

Ewer, coin, the round stepped pedestal foot supporting the tapering ovoid body topped w/a cylindrical neck w/a large rim spout, scroll-cast S-scroll handle, the body engraved w/a leafy scroll design w/a large cartouche at the front filled w/an engraved presentation inscription to John Oliphant of the Treasury Department in Washington, D.C., dated July 9, 1850, mark of Ball, Tompkins & Black, New York City, 14 1/2" h. (ILLUS.) **$1,920**

Flask, sterling, flattened oval shape w/a cylindrical neck w/hinged domed cap, decorated in the Japanesque taste, one side chased w/a design of a carp in waves, the other side w/a dragon amid waves & scrolls, mark of Gorham Mfg. Co., Providence, Rhode Island, 1894, 5 7/8" l. (ILLUS., top next column).. **$3,120**

Gorham Flask in Japanesque Taste

Fine Early American Classical Pitcher

Pitcher, coin, classical baluster-form body on a short pedestal base trimmed w/bands of acanthus leaves & beading,

M

the shoulder w/another acanthus leaf band, the short neck w/a wide curved spout w/a beaded edge, a high arched scroll handle w/a mask terminal at the neck, a band of engraved cattails & acanthus leaves around the lower body, Anthony Rasch, Philadelphia, early 19th c., 13 1/4" h. (ILLUS.) **$9,400**

Gorham Mfg. Company, Providence, Rhode Island, 1903, 9 1/2" h. (ILLUS.) ... **$4,780**

Fine Cincinnati Coin Rococo Pitcher

Samuel Kirk Coin Silver Pitcher

Pitcher, coin, simple ovoid body tapering to a banded rim w/a low spout over a cast cherubic mask, high arched C-scroll handle, the sides of the body lightly engraved w/leafy scrolls & flowers, Samuel Kirk, Baltimore, Maryland, 1830-46, 8 1/2" h. (ILLUS.)... **$1,195**

Pitcher, coin, Rococo Revival style, footed bulbous baluster-form body tapering to a banded rim & high arched & fluted spout, the body decorated w/elaborate rèpoussè up around the bottom w/a repeating design of large flowering acanthus leaf, the neck rim banded by lightly engraved acanthus leaves, the high arched C-form handle decorated w/relief poppies on a dotted field, engraved w/a presentation dated 1856, Edward & David Kinsey, Cincinnati, Ohio, 10" h. (ILLUS.)................................. **$2,760**

Fine Gorham Art Nouveau Pitcher

Pitcher, sterling, Art Nouveau style, squatty bulbous baluster-form body w/a high arched spout, the arched vine handle trimmed w/a blossom, the body boldly chased w/bands of roses on leafy vines,

Early Rhode Island Silver Porringer

Porringer, coin, round bowl w/fancy pierced keyhole handle engraved w/a monogram, mark of Jonathan Clarke, Newport & Providence, Rhode Island, 1735-70, 7" l. (ILLUS.)... **$2,400**

Early American Coin Silver Sugar Urn

Sugar urn, cov., coin, a square foot & slender tapering pedestal supporting the urn-form body fitted w/a tall tapering cover w/an urn-form finial, body engraved w/three monograms, mark of John Vernon, New York City, ca. 1790, 9 3/4" h. (ILLUS.).. **$1,920**

Early New York Silver Tankard

Tankard, cov., coin, tapering cylindrical body w/a molded foot rim, the handle w/a baluster drop & scroll thumbpiece & scrolled lower handle join, the stepped domed cover w/a scalloped rim, the handle engraved w/initials, later engraved name on the body, mark of Jacob Boelen II, New York City, ca. 1760, 7 3/4" h. (ILLUS.).............. **$7,800**

Fine Victorian Tiffany Sterling Tea & Coffee Service

Tea & coffee service: cov. coffeepot, cov. teapot, cov. kettle-on-stand, cov. sugar bowl, creamer, waste bowl; Ivy patt., each of squat round form w/engraved ivy, scroll handles w/ivory joins, domed covers w/matching decoration & bud finials, marked by Tiffany & Co., New York City, 1854-70, w/a large rectangular silver plate tray w/a gadrooned border & foliate handles, tray 30 1/2" l., kettle-on-stand 14 1/2" h., the set (ILLUS.)...................... **$8,400**

1920s Gorham Sterling Tea & Coffee Service

Tea & coffee service: cov. coffeepot, cov. teapot, cov. kettle-on-stand, creamer, cov. sugar bowl, waste bowl & tray; sterling, each piece a squat rounded shape w/chased strapwork, the domed cover w/ivory inverted baluster finial, the oval tray w/matching decoration, each piece engraved w/a monogram, mark of Gorham Mfg. Co., Providence, Rhode Island, ca. 1920, kettle-on-stand 12 3/4" h., the set (ILLUS.)...................... **$6,920**

Fine Medallion Pattern Sterling Tea & Coffee Service

Tea & coffee service: cov. teapot, cov. coffeepot, creamer, cov. sugar bowl & waste bowl: sterling, Medallion patt., each piece w/a globular body on a stepped round base, the body w/a dentil midband w/medallions at intervals & w/engraved scrolls, the high looped handles w/an applied medallion, coffeepot & teapot w/ivory insulators in the handles, mark of Gorham Mfg. Co., Providence, Rhode Island, retailed by Starr & Marcus & A. Rumrill Co., ca. 1868, coffeepot 11 1/4" h., the set (ILLUS., bottom previous page) **$9,600**

Early Philadelphia Coin Silver Tea Set

Tea set: two cov. teapots, creamer & cov. sugar bowl; coin, each a shaped oval w/facetted sides & beaded borders, engraved w/initials, the teapots & sugar bowl w/domed covers & urn-form finials, most pieces w/mark of James Howell, Philadelphia, ca. 1810, creamer w/mark of Joseph Richardson, Jr., Philadelphia, ca. 1810, teapot overall 11 1/2" l., the set (ILLUS.) **$2,280**

Early New York Coin Silver Teapot

Teapot, cov., coin, oval upright body w/an applied beaded foot rim, straight spout & C-scroll black wooden handle, the hinged & domed cover w/a pineapple finial, the side engraved w/the coat-of-arms of Bishop Samuel Provoost, an ardent American patriot, mark of Daniel Van Voorhis, New York City, ca. 1778, overall 12 1/4" l. (ILLUS.) **$4,200**

Fine Tiffany Hammered Silver Teapot

Teapot, cov., sterling, hammered nearly spherical body w/a scalloped mid band & applied maple leaves & a beetle, short wide neck w/dished flat cover w/inverted baluster-form jade finial, short angled spout, swing silver bail handle w/ebony grip, engraved monogram on base, mark of Tiffany & Co., New York City, ca. 1880, 5" h. (ILLUS.) **$15,600**

Urn-form Tiffany Sterling Silver Vase

Vase, sterling, classical campana urn-form, a short pedestal base w/beaded border, the lower squatty body fluted below the plain wide upper body w/a band of leaftips around the flared rim, two long C-scroll acanthus leaf-clad handles w/figural mask joins, gilt interior, mark of Tiffany & Co., New York City, 1891-1902, 15 1/8" h. (ILLUS.) **$13,200**

M

Unusual Sterling Presentation Vase

Vase, sterling, cup-form, the round flat-tened foot w/an narrow incurved rim around simulated plant roots supporting the tall slender & swelled stem cast w/scroll-edged leaves & thin entwined snakes below the bulbous top cup com-posed of large overlapping leaves, the stem engraved w/an anniversary pre-sentation, w/a detachable original lead weight under the base, mark of George W. Shiebler, New York City, ca. 1900, 14" h. (ILLUS.) **$7,800**

Rare Gorham Aesthetic Taste Vase

Vase, sterling, in the Aesthetic taste, a squared foot & body w/chased & applied carp swimming amid water lilies, irises & cattails, w/an engraved Japanese poem

about an old pond, the handles in the form of elephant heads, engraved mono-gram under base, mark of Gorham Mfg. Co., Providence, Rhode Island, 1897, 9" h. (ILLUS.) **$30,000**

Unusual Modern-style Sterling Silver Vegetable Dishes

Vegetable dishes, cov., sterling, low round form w/inverted sides, raised on three ivory ball feet, the flattened round cover centered by a red lacquer plaque mount-ed by a late 19th c. Japanese ivory net-suke of figurines climbing out of a shell, mark of designer-maker Marie Zimmer-mann, New York City, ca. 1920, 8 1/8" d., pr. (ILLUS.) **$12,000**

Tiffany Sterling Wine Coasters

Wine coasters, sterling, short wide cylindri-cal form, the pierced sides decorated w/delicate flowers & trellis design, the base formed as a stylized six-petal flow-ers, mark of Tiffany & Co., New York City, 1883-91, 5 1/4" d., pr. (ILLUS.) **$3,600**

Wine siphon, coin, a long slender U-shaped tube mounted w/a cylindrical pump & a ring-form tap, mark of Stodder & Frobisher, Boston, ca. 1816-25, 15" l. (ILLUS., next page) **$4,800**

M

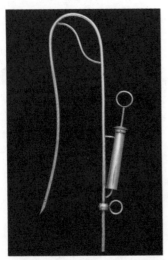

Unusual Coin Silver Wine Siphon

English & Other

17th Century Spanish Silver Bowl

Bowl, wide shallow round shape w/a center gadrooned band, the center w/alternating plain & engraved lobes, on a low ringed round foot, mark of Montana, possibly Francisco de la Montana, Valladolid, Spain, ca. 1660, 7 1/4" d. (ILLUS.) **$4,128**

Rare French Art Deco Small Silver Box

Box, cov., Art Deco style, low round flaring ebony foot supporting a sperical body w/a wide flat mouth, the sides divided in half w/a wide raised band continuing on the low domed cover w/disk-form ebony handle, marked by Jean E. Puiforcat, France, ca. 1925, 4 1/4" h. (ILLUS.) **$9,560**

Rare Early George II Cake Basket

Cake basket, oval w/deep pierced foliate scroll handles below a shaped shell & rocaille rim, the ends mounted w/Cupid masks, engraved inside w/flowers on a textured ground centering a coat-of-arms, overhead swing handle, raised on four grotesque mask feet, George II era, marked under base by Robert Calderwood, Dublin, Ireland, 1743, 13" l. (ILLUS.) **$18,576**

One of Two Portuguese Candelabra

Candelabra, three-light, in the 18th c. style, each on four shell-and-scroll feet, the domed base w/cast scrolling foliage rising to a baluster-form stem w/foliage, the branches w/matching decoration & detachable wax pans, mark of retailer Sarmento, Lisbon, Portugal, early 20th c., 17 3/4" h., pr. (ILLUS. of one) **$7,768**

M

Rare English Charles II Silver Caster

Caster, cylindrical on a domed base pierced w/stylized scrolls, the high-domed bayo-net-fitting cover w/similar piercings & an acorn finial w/foliate cut-card calyx, all w/ropetwist borders, engraved w/initials under the base, maker's mark "GR" on base, London, 1683, 7 3/4" h. (ILLUS.)... **$7,768**

Rare English Commonwealth Era Goblet

Sicilian Silver Covered Jar

Jar, cov., three slender hoof legs w/pal-mette tops supporting a fluted cup-form body w/a narrow upper looping band flanked by scroll handles, the domical peaked cover of matching design w/an open flame finial, Palermo, Sicily, ca. 1920, stamped marks, 5" h. (ILLUS.)......... **$264**

William IV English Sterling Ewer

Ewer, in the shape of an ancient oinochoe w/a round pedestal foot, bulbous ovoid body & tall fluted neck w/a pinched-in rolled rim, high arched handle from rim to shoulder, the body applied w/a figure of Eros & a woman & engraved w/palmettes & flowers, w/Vitruvian scroll shoulder & base, trilobed spout applied w/masks, William IV era, marked on the neck by William Elliott, London, 1833, 12" h. (ILLUS.) **$3,346**

Goblet, round low foot w/baluster- and ring-turned stem supporting the deep bell-form cup, London maker's mark & date mark for 1655, 6 3/8" h. (ILLUS., top next column) **$20,315**

Antique-Style Sterling Monteith Bowl

M

Monteith bowl, round stepped & ringed foot below the deep rounded body w/a shoulder ring below eight large flaring fluted lobes bordered w/scroll & laurel designs, mark of Hawksworth, Eyre & Company, Ltd., Sheffield, England, 1902-03, 12" d., 8 1/2" h. (ILLUS., previous page) **$1,725**

George II Fancy Rococo Silver Salver

Very Ornate Italian Sterling Pitcher

Pitcher, ornate upright slender serpentine shell form w/a scrolled base end topped by the figure of a small mermaid above a seaweed-cast foot, the lower fluted body swelling to ornate scrolls along the back edge leading to the wide upright arched spout, very ornate arched leafy scroll handle, Italy, retailed by Birks of Canada, 19th c., 16 1/2" h. (ILLUS.) **$1,610**

Rare Early Swiss Spice Box

Spice box, low oval shape w/double flat hinged covers engraved w/a coat-of-arms & cypher, the compartment interiors gilded, raised on four tiny paw feet, marked on bottom by Jean Redard, Neuchatel, Switzerland, ca. 1750, 4 3/4" l. (ILLUS.) **$7,170**

One of Two De Lamerie Salt Cellars

Salt cellars, squatty rounded bowl cast w/floral swags between four hoofed feet each headed by a grotesque bearded mask, beaded rim, base engraved w/a crest, mark of Paul de Lamerie, London, 1744, 3 5/8" d., pr. (ILLUS. of one) **$7,768**

Salver, shaped circular form w/the border of alternating rococo flowers & masks, the center flat-chased w/rococo cartouches & scalework w/a floral garland surround, centering an engraved coat-of-arms within a rococo cartouche, on three foliate scroll feet, George II era, William Cripps, London, 1743, 22 1/4" d. (ILLUS., top next column) **$10,755**

Early North European Silver Tankard

Tankard, cov., octagonal body on a stepped reeded base, the sides engraved w/oval cartouches depicting scenes of the Passion w/New Testament references above, the hinged flat-domed cover w/a folaite border & pierced scroll thumbpiece & paneled handle engraved w/foliate scrolls, marked on foot rim, Baltic or Norwegian, late 17th c., overall 7 1/4" h. (ILLUS.) **$6,192**

English William IV Silver Teapot

Teapot, cov., William IV era, wide inverted pear-shaped body on a disk foot, hinged domed cover w/flame finial, scroll-cast serpentine spout, bifurcated branch handle, the swirling fluted body chased w/panels of rocaille & diaperwork on a matted ground, one side engraved w/a duke's coronet & crest, mark of Paul Storr, London, England, 1832, 7 3/4" h. (ILLUS.)... **$2,820**

Large Chinese Export Silver Tray

Tray, rectangular w/rounded corners, the flattened rim decorated w/raised branches & flowers & Chinese characters, a thin bamboo-form rim & loop end handles, textured finish, on four foliate legs, Chinese Export, marked on back w/mark of Luen-Wo & Chinese characters for the city of Shanghai, ca. 1900, overall 22 5/8" l. (ILLUS.).................................... **$4,541**

Fine A. Knox Art Nouveau Silver Vase

Vase, Art Nouveau style, a flat shaped rectangular foot supporting a swelled cylindrical body w/a flat rim, decorated on the side w/a long looping vine pointed motif trimmed w/a dark blue & bluish green enameled button, designed by Archibald Knox, retailed by Liberty & Co., England, 1902, 6 3/8" h. (ILLUS.) **$8,299**

Sterling Silver (Flatware)

Sets

Chrysanthemum Pattern Flatware Pieces

Chrysanthemum patt., 11 dinner forks; 11 lunch forks; eight lunch forks, three fish forks, 13 teaspoons, three citrus spoons, five dessert spoons, six egg spoons, five dinner knives, a serving for, sauce ladle & table spoon; Tiffany & Co., New York City, 20th c., the set (ILLUS. of part)....... **$6,000**

Grand Baroque Pattern Flatware

Grand Baroque patt., 15 dinner forks, two lunch forks, 10 oyster forks, 18 salad forks, 42 teaspoons, 12 bouillon spoons,

M

16 cream soup spoons, 18 dinner knives w/stainless steel blades, two seafood forks, two jam spoons, a large serving spoon, meat fork, sauce ladle & seafood server; Wallace Silversmiths, Wallingford, Connecticut, 20th c., the set (ILLUS. of part).. **$3,360**

Tiffany Olympian Pattern Flatware

Pieces of Tiffany's King's Pattern

King's patt., 12 dinner knives w/stainless steel blades, 24 lunch knives w/stainless steel blades, eight fish knives w/silver blades, 12 fruit knives w/silver-gilt blades, 12 dinner forks, 12 soup spoons, 24 lunch forks, 12 tablespoons, 12 oyster forks, 12 fish forks, 12 salad forks, 13 butter knives, 12 citrus spoons w/gilt bowls, 12 bouillon spoons w/gilt bowls, 12 egg spoons w/gilt spoons, 10 coffee spoons w/gilt bowls, 12 teaspoons, two salt spoons, two pairs of nut crackers, two pairs of sandwich tongs, a mustard spoon, a cheese scoop w/gilt bowl & a sugar spoon; in a fitted wood canteen w/ brass mounts, Tiffany & Co., New York City, 20th c., the set (ILLUS. of part)..... **$20,400**

Olympian patt., 12 dinner forks, 12 lunch forks, 12 dessert forks, 12 ice cream forks, 12 teaspoons, 12 soup spoons, seven bouillon spoons, three tablespoons, 12 dinner knives w/stainless steel blades, 12 butter knives, three sauce ladles in varied sizes, one w/silver-gilt bowl, a salad spoon & fork, a stuffing spoon, tomato server, oyster server w/silver-gilt bowl, a crumber, fish slice w/silver-gilt blade, serving spoon; in a canteen, Tiffany & Co., New York City, 20th c., the set (ILLUS. of part, top next column) **$10,800**

Renaissance Pattern Flatware Pieces

Renaissance patt., 12 teaspoons, 12 five o'clock teaspoons, 12 coffee spoons, four table spoons, four butter knives, 12 seafood forks, four dinner forks, four salad forks, four dinner knives w/stainless steel blades, six salt spoons w/gilt bowls & a jam spoon w/gilt bowl; Tiffany & Co., New York City, 20th c., the set (ILLUS. of part)... **$6,000**

M

Silver Plate (Hollowware)

Scarce "Skyscraper" Silver Plate Cocktail Cups

Cocktail cups, "Skyscraper" design, each on a square foot, the square tapering sides applied w/triangular patination, each marked under foot "Skyscraper Des. Pat. Pending Apollo E.P.N.S. - 5271," Bernard Rice's Sons, Inc., New York, New York, ca. 1928, 3 3/8" h., set of 8 (ILLUS., top of page) **$2,640**

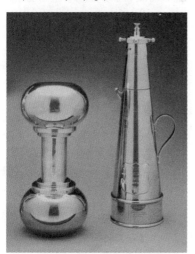

Two Unusual Deco Cocktail Shakers

Cocktail shaker, "Dumbbell" design, Art Deco style, vertical stylized dumbbell, marked by Asprey & Co., London, England, 1930s, 10" h. (ILLUS. left with fire extinguisher cocktail shaker) **$2,629**

Cocktail shaker, "The Thirst Extinguisher" design, Art Deco style, designed as a tall tapering cylindrical fire extinguisher complete w/side shield mark & engraved w/recipes for eight different cocktails, by Asprey & Co., London, England, ca. 1932, 15" h. (ILLUS. right with dumbbell cocktail shaker) **$6,573**

Tin & Tole

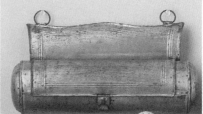

Nice Early Tin Hanging Candle Box

Candle box, tin, hanging-type, cylindrical w/a high shaped crest w/hanging rings above the lift lid w/latch, cleaned w/traces of black paint, 19th c., 11 3/4" l., 6 3/4" h. (ILLUS.)... **$115**

M

Rare Early Tin Candle Sconces

Candle sconces, tin, a short cylindrical base centered by a candle socket, backed w/a tall curved & pointed back w/resist decoration of tulips & wavy lines, first half 19th c., 8" h., pr. (ILLUS., previous page) **$2,070**

Rare Early Tole Candle Screen

Candle screen, tole, upright curved rectangular form w/arched top, black ground decorated in gold w/a spread-winged eagle under a rising sun, some wear, fitted w/a light bulb, w/pewter lamp base, 19th c., 6 1/4" w., 7 3/4" h. (ILLUS.) **$1,150**

Coffeepot, cov., tole, tall slightly tapering cylindrical body w/a flaring base, worn hinged domed cover w/small looped tin finial, angular tall spout & long strap handle, original dark red ground decorated w/a cluster of four rounded stylized striped fruit & yellow & dark red foliage, worn, 19th c., 10 1/2" h. (ILLUS. right with coffeepot decorated w/stylized fruits & flowers, next column) **$776**

Red Tole Coffeepot with Leaves & Fruits

Coffeepot, cov., tole, tall slightly tapering cylindrical body w/a flaring base, hinged

domed cover w/small brass finial, angular tall spout & long strap handle w/hand grip, original dark red ground w/top & bottom rim bands in white w/red berries & green leaves, bands of yellow leaves & large apples & leaves around the body, Pennsylvania, first half 19th c., some wear, 10 1/4" h. (ILLUS.)........................ **$1,380**

Two Early Fruit-decorated Tole Coffeepots

Coffeepot, cov., tole, tall slightly tapering cylindrical body w/a flaring base, hinged domed cover w/small brass finial, angular tall spout & long strap handle w/hand grip, original dark red ground w/bright yellow & red cluster of large stylized fruits & flowers, yellow flourishes around flared base & cover, Pennsylvania, first half 19th c., 10" h. (ILLUS. left with coffeepot decorated w/rounded stylized fruit coffeepot)... **$2,300**

Fine American Tole Coffeepot with Flowers

Coffeepot, cov., tole, tall tapering cylindrical body w/a straight angled spout & C-form strap handle, the dark asphaltum ground decorated w/large red flowers & fruit & faded green fruit & yellow leaves, hinged low domed cover, early 19th c., paint wear, 8 1/2" h. (ILLUS.)........................... **$1,528**

Large Tole Tray with Flowers & Fruits

Tray, tole, rectangular w/angled corners, the asphaltum ground decorated in the center w/a large bouquet of green & yellow flowers & fruits & green leaves, mustard yellow painted borders, early 19th c., 12 1/8 x 17 1/2" (ILLUS.)............................. **$764**

Early Tole Tray with Scene of Lady & Her Spaniel

Tray, tole, rectangular w/rounded corners, the wide flaring border w/pierced end handles, the center painted in color w/a scene of a young woman & her spaniel in a wooded setting w/a pavilion & distant water on a yellow ground, the black border embellished w/polychrome stylized lfowers & leaves w/gilt & bronze accents, America, early 19th c., scattered paint losses, 18 x 24" (ILLUS.) **$1,116**

MINIATURES (PAINTINGS)

Fine Early American Miniature of a Man

Bust portrait of a young man, watercolor on ivory, facing right, curly brown hair & brown eyes, wearing a high-collared black jacket & white cravat, a shaded cloud-like background, sitter identified on paper under the back as William Hull, attributed to Anson Dickinson, American, ca. 1810, in an oval copper case w/compartment on back containing a lock of plaited brown hair, 2 1/8 x 2 5/8" (ILLUS.)...................... **$7,050**

M

Rare 18th Century American Miniature Portraits

Bust portraits of husband & wife, watercolor on ivory, 18th c. portraits of Captain John Page & Mrs. John Page, he facing left wearing powdered wig, red jacket w/gold trim & white cravat, she also facing left, wearing a low-cut blue gown, her hair stylized in a pompadour highlighted by a rose blossom, her portrait signed "ID," probably for Joseph Dunkerley, Boston, ca. 1784-88, each in gilt-copper oval cases on chains, 1 x 1 1/8", pr. (ILLUS., bottom previous page).. **$9,988**

Two American Miniatures of Young Boys

Half-length portrait of a boy, watercolor on ivory, shown seated from the knees up, brown side-parted hair, wearing a black jacket & brown shirt w/striped tousers, in front of a red drapery, attributed to Augustus Fuller, American, 1812-73, in an embossed brown leather case, image 2 3/8 x 2 3/4" (ILLUS. left with smaller miniature of a young boy)...................... **$4,994**

Early Miniature of a Girl & Her Doll

Half-length portrait of a girl, watercolor on ivory, shown w/center-parted blonde hair, a corral bead necklace & a dark red dress, holding a doll, mounted in a red leather-covered hinged case, American, first half 19th c., 1 7/8 x 2 1/2" (ILLUS.) **$2,585**

Half-length portrait of a mother & child, watercolor on ivory, a naive rectangular depiction of a mother wearing a dark Empire gown w/lace color & a blue cap atop her curly blonde hair, supporting her standing young child wearing a brown bonnet & white dress w/blue ribbon, the head of a dog reaching up to child, artist-initialed, in a wide flat black

wood frame w/a stamped brass acorn & loop hanger, ca. 1830s, 5 1/4 x 5 7/8" (ILLUS. right with mother & child in 18th c. attire) **$633**

Two Miniatures of Mothers & a Child

Half-length portrait of a mother & child, watercolor on ivory, each dressed in 18th c. attire, the mother wearing a very large pink hat & pale blue gown w/wide leafy ruffled color, the young blonde child wearing a white dress w/pink waist band, artist-signed along edge, in a round wide & carved framed w/a vining fleur-de-lis design, 6 1/4" d. (ILLUS. left with naive miniature of mother & child) **$431**

Half-length portrait of a young boy, watercolor on ivory, side-parted blond hair, wearing a brown plaid dress w/a white lace collar, signed "Augustus Fuller Pinxt 1860, $0.00." in pencil on the back, mounted in a black embossed leather case, American, 1 5/8 x 2" (ILLUS. right with other miniature of a boy attributed to Fuller, previous column).......................... **$4,406**

MINIATURES (REPLICAS)

Early Country Federal Chest of Drawers

Chest of drawers, Federal country style, painted & decorated pine, rectangular top w/low arched crestrail above a red-painted case w/three long drawers w/original yellowish grain painting & painted faux keyholes, original round brass pulls, paper inside notes it was made for a girl in 1827, repaired crest, 8 x 15", 13" h. (ILLUS.) **$2,530**

Early Inlaid Mahogany Chest of Drawers

Chest of drawers, Federal style, inlaid mahogany, rectangular top w/molded edge above a case w/three long drawers decorated w/panels outlined in light & dark wood banded inlay, molded base on scroll-cut bracket feet, diamond-shaped brass keyhole escutcheons & small brass knobs, replaced knobs, old refinish, possibly Central American, imperfections, 10 x 17 3/4", 16" h. (ILLUS.).......... **$1,645**

Early English Mahogany Mini Chest

Chest of drawers, Federal style, mahogany & mahogany veneer, rectangular top above a case w/three long flame veneered drawers each w/two turned wood knobs, serpentine apron & tall bracket feet, string inlay trim, England, early 19th c., minor pieced repairs, 5 5/8 x 13', 12 1/4" h. (ILLUS.) **$604**

Nice Early Classical Chest of Drawers

Chest of drawers, mahogany & mahogany veneer, Classical style, rectangular top above a long projecting drawer w/round brass pulls & a keyhole escutcheon above three set-back long graduated matching drawers flanked by ring-turned side half-columns, raised on paw front feet & ring- and knob-turned rear feet, one repaired foot, ca. 1830, 7 x 11 1/2", 11 1/4" h. (ILLUS.) **$1,783**

Fine Federal Chest of Drawers

Chest of drawers, mahogany & mahogany veneer, Federal style, rectangular top w/bowed front w/ovolu front corners, two long cockbeaded bowed drawers each w/two round brass pulls, serpentine apron, ring-turned corner stiles continuing into baluster-turned legs w/knob feet, replaced back, minor repair & possible missing back biscuits, 4 1/2 x 9 3/4", 8 3/8" h. (ILLUS.) **$805**

Miniature Cupboard Attributed to Zoar

Cupboard, hanging-type, painted pine, a high arched & scalloped crest w/hanging hole above a pair of square doors inset w/tiny glass panes & tiny pulls above four upright pigeonholes over a single long bottom drawer & scalloped base crest, shaped sides, pumpkin paint trimmed w/green, may have had horizontal dividers in pigeonholes, back reads "From the pietist community of Zoar in Tuscarawas County Ohio Circa 1875," 6 1/4" x 12 3/4", 22" h. (ILLUS.) **$2,445**

Unusual Painted Country Mini Dry Sink

Dry sink, painted pine, the rectangular top w/a low backsplash above the long rectangular well & a small surface at one end above a small narrow drawer, the case w/a pair of simple paneled doors w/tiny metal pulls, original dark bluish grey w/dark red accents, simple cut-out feet, minor surface wear, second half 19th c., 13 x 24 1/2", 18 1/2" h. (ILLUS.) **$1,093**

Miniature Country-style Jelly Cupboard

Jelly cupboard, painted pine, the rectangular top w/a shaped backsplash above an upright cased w/a pair of small drawers w/turned wood knobs over a pair of flat doors w/matching knobs, worn grey over red paint, wire nail construction, small pieced repairs, 7 1/2 x 13", 17" h. (ILLUS.) **$489**

MOVIE MEMORABILIA

Also see: DISNEY COLLECTIBLES and POP CULTURE

Costumes

The Wizard of Oz Emerald City Jacket

Emerald City citizen, "The Wizard of Oz," MGM, 1939, a long-sleeved collarless jacket of green wool, w/lobed details of ivory wool on the front, trimmed w/green braid & w/a green felt strap fastening the chest, Metro-Goldwyn-Meyer wardrobe label inside, w/a black & white movie still showing cast in the Emerald City printed later (ILLUS.)... **$7,200**

Gene Kelly Sweater From "Singin' In The Rain"

Gene Kelly, "Singin' In The Rain," MGM, 1952, argyle V-necked long sleeved sweater of tan, red & navy blue wool, accompanied by black & white still showing Kelly wearing it (ILLUS.) **$2,400**

John Wayne-used Cowboy Hat

John Wayne, cowboy hat in brown felt trimmed w/a brown leather band w/buckle fastening, Warner Bros. Pictures label inside & inscribe in black in "J. Wayne," w/a color still of Wayne wearing a similar hat (ILLUS., previous page) **$3,360**

Judy Garland Gown From "Words and Music"

Judy Garland, "Words and Music," MGM, 1948, a long-sleeved gown of ivory stretch jersey embroidered over the shoulders & on the bodice in gold-colored thread w/a foliate design & decorated w/gold beads & clear crystals, covered button fastening on the front, w/color copy of original auction tag from the 1970 MGM auction & related auction photocopies, two black & white movie stills showing Garland wearing the gown printed later (ILLUS.)..................................... **$7,200**

Rare Marilyn Monroe Movie Costume

Marilyn Monroe, "The Prince and The Showgirl," Warner Bros., 1957, an evening costume of soft blue & rose organza trimmed at the neck & sleeves w/finely-pleated ruffles, w/a shirred & gathered waist, covered button closure, decorated w/floral appliqué, w/black & white still of Monroe wearing the outfit printed later (ILLUS.)........................... **$28,800**

Michelle Pfeiffer Catwoman Outfit

Michelle Pfeiffer, "Batman Returns," Warner Bros., 1992, one-piece Catwoman costume of black latex, applied w/white stitching details, w/a black plastic fitted basque, mounted on a life-sized mannequin of foam & composition w/a painted composition head of Pfeiffer, also a pair of black leather lace-up knee-high boots, w/black & white movie still printed later (ILLUS.).. **$7,200**

Lobby Cards

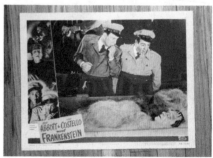

Abbott & Costello Meet Frankenstein Lobby Card

"Abbott & Costello Meet Frankenstein," color photo scene, 1948, depending on the scene shown (ILLUS.).................... **$75-125**

M

Horror of Dracula Lobby Card

"Horror of Dracula," Hammer Films/Universal, 1958, large color photo of star Christopher Lee, 11 x 14", depending on condition (ILLUS.) **$90-140**

1962 Mysterious Island Lobby Card

"Mysterious Island," Columbia Pictures, 1962, depending on color scene shown, 11 x 14" (ILLUS.).................................. **$75-100**

1970 When Women Had Tails Lobby Card

"When Women Had Tails," starring Senta Berger, color photo image, 1970 (ILLUS.) **$10-20**

Posters

1972 Blacula One-Sheet Movie Poster

"Blacula," American International, 1972, dramatic color image of Blacula w/stake through his heart, one-sheet, depending on condition, 27 x 41" (ILLUS.) **$75-135**

"Calcutta" Poster

"Calcutta," Paramount, 1947, starring Alan Ladd, Gail Russell & William Bendix, one-sheet, linen-backed, 27 x 41" (ILLUS.)..... **$1,076**

M

Re-release "Casablanca" Poster

Casablanca," Warner Bros., 1949 re-release, starring Humphrey Bogart & Ingrid Bergman, one-sheet, linen-backed, 27 x 41" (ILLUS.).................................... **$2,629**

"Conquest of the Planet of the Apes" Poster

"Conquest of The Planet of the Apes," 20th Century Fox, 1972, starring Roddy McDowall, Don Murray & Ricardo Montalban, one-sheet (ILLUS.)..................... **$30-50**

"City of Missing Girls" Poster

"City of Missing Girls," rare exploitation film, 1950s, one-sheet (ILLUS.) **$200-300**

"Creature from the Black Lagoon"

"Creature from the Black Lagoon" (not 3-D version), Universal, 1954, one-sheet, full-color illustration of creature holding swimsuited screaming woman, a knife-wielding scuba diver approaching, the title in white at the top, three pictures of scenes from the film at the bottom directly under the names of the cast, 27 x 41" (ILLUS.)... **$3,000-5,000**

M

Rare "Laura" Poster

"Laura," Twentieth Century-Fox, 1944, starring Gene Tierney & Dana Andrews, one-sheet, 27 x 41" (ILLUS.).................. **$5,019**

Half-sheet "Life with Blondie" Poster

"Life with Blondie," Columbia Pictures, 1945, starring Penny Singleton & Arthur Lake, half-sheet (ILLUS.) **$50-75**

Notorious! Re-release Movie Poster

"Notorious," RKO, starring Cary Grant & Ingrid Bergman, color close-up of stars in foreground, 1954 re-release, half-sheet, linen-backed, 22 x 28" (ILLUS.) **$717**

Half-sheet "Service de Luxe" Poster

"Service de Luxe," Universal, 1940s, starring Constance Bennett & Vincent Price, half-sheet (ILLUS.).................................. **$50-75**

1932 "Skyscraper Souls" Poster

"Skyscraper Souls," MGM, 1932, starring Warren William & Maureen O'Sullivan, one-sheet, linen-backed, 27 x 41" (ILLUS.) .. **$837**

Scarce "Sullivan's Travels" Poster

"Sullivan's Travels," Paramount, 1941, starring Joel McCrea & Veronica Lake, one-sheet, linen-backed, 27 x 41" (ILLUS.) **$8,963**

M

Dramatic "The Raven" Poster

"The Raven," American International, 1963, starring Vincent Price, Peter Lorre & Boris Karloff, one-sheet, 27 x 41" (ILLUS.)........... **$179**

"To Have and Have Not" Poster

To Have and Have Not," Warner Bros., 1944, starring Humphrey Bogart & Lauren Bacall, one-sheet, 27 x 41" (ILLUS.) **$1,076**

Large "The Return of The Vampire" Poster

"The Return of The Vampire," Columbia Pictures, 1943, starring Bela Lugosi, three-sheet (ILLUS.)............................ **$500-750**

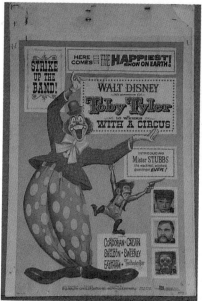

Walt Disney "Toby Tyler" Poster

"Toby Tyler or 10 Weeks with a Circus," Walt Disney Studios, 1960, starring Kevin Corcoran & Henry Calvin, one-sheet (ILLUS.)... **$25-35**

M

Miscellaneous

Recalled Austin Powers Action Figure

Action figure, Austin Powers, jointed vinyl, a recalled item, mint in original package, 1990s (ILLUS.) **$8-20**

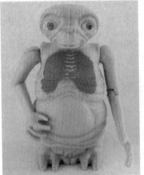

E.T. Action Figure

Action figure, E.T., molded vinyl, head moves up & down, jointed arms, LJN, 1982, 3 3/4" h. (ILLUS.) **$8-15**

1960s Soaky Wolfman Bubble Bath Bottle

Bubble bath bottle, Wolfman, figural plastic, Soaky by Colgate, 1963 (ILLUS.) **$75-140**

John Wayne Silver Cigarette Case

Cigarette case, Danish silver w/ detailed relief peasant scene on the front, engraved on the lid "JOHN WAYNE," w/a brass shoe horn engraved "Duke," case 2 1/4 x 3 1/2", 2 pcs. (ILLUS. of cigarette case) **$2,160**

Marilyn Monroe Evening Gown

Evening gown, ivory satin sleeveless dress w/shoulder straps hand-embroidered in bronze & metallic thread & embellished w/pearls, sequins & rhinestones in a classical design on the bodice continuing in a design of cascading rows down the skirt, owned by Marilyn Monroe, labeled inside "Jeanne Lanvin and Castillo," ca. 1950s (ILLUS.) **$6,000**

M

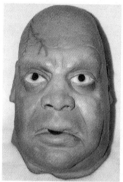

Plan 9 From Outer Space Adult Mask

Mask, "Plan 9 From Outer Space," Tor Johnson latex adult mask by Ben Cooper, 1960s (ILLUS.)................................. **$30-60**

Early Marilyn Monroe Model Release

Model release, from Tom Kelley Studio, printed on green paper, inscribed w/the client's name John Baumgarth Co. & signed in blue ink by Norma Monroe (Marilyn Monroe), dated May 27, 1949, together w/ten color posters of Tom Kelley's "Golden Dreams" image printed later, release 3 1/2 x 7" (ILLUS.)............. **$6,600**

Rare Indiana Jones Whip From The Temple of Doom

Movie prop, hand-made bull-whip of kangaroo hide, used by Harrison Ford as Indiana Jones in The Temple of Doom, signed by Ford in black felt pen, accompanied by a note on Harrison Ford headed stationery stating it was used in the movie, w/a black & white still of Indiana Jones holding the whip, 1984 (ILLUS.)............................... **$66,000**

Star Wars Stormtrooper Prototype Helmet

Movie prop, prototype Imperial Stormtrooper helmet from Star Wars, unfinished design in white vacu-formed plastic w/black rubber details & clear plastic "bubble" eyepiece, one of about five prototypes produced by Shepperton Design Studios, 1977, accompanied by a black & white still showing Stormtroopers (ILLUS.) **$4,200**

Signed Movie Still from National Velvet

Movie still, "National Velvet," MGM, 1944, black & white shot showing the characters seated around a dinner table, signed & inscribed in blue ink by Mickey Rooney, Elizabeth Taylor, Donald Crisp & Anne Revere, 8 x 10" (ILLUS.)............................ **$600**

M

Studio Photo Portrait of Noel Coward

Photograph, studio portrait of Noel Coward by Valente, ca. 1935, 8 x 10" (ILLUS.)....... **$213**

Laurel & Hardy Signed Photograph

Photograph, unusual black & white shot of Stan Laurel & Oliver Hardy, taken on board the R.M.S. Queen Elizabeth, signed in blue ink by both actors, ca. 1950s, 4 3/4 x 6 1/4" (ILLUS.)................... **$720**

M

1982 E.T. Plush Toy

Plush toy, E.T., w/plastic eyes & nose, Kamar, 1982, 16" l. (ILLUS.) **$10-20**

1930s Jean Harlow Personality Poster

Poster, personality-type, bust-portrait of Jean Harlow, MGM star, 1930s, 22 x 28" (ILLUS.)... **$598**

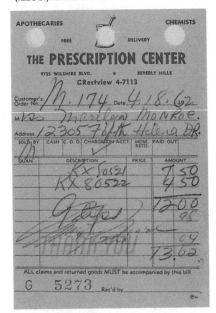

1962 Marilyn Monroe Signed Receipt

Receipt, duplicate-type signed by Marilyn Monroe, from The Prescription Center on Wilshire Boulevard, Beverly Hills, dated April 18, 1962, three months before her death, 4 x 6" (ILLUS.)............................. **$2,868**

Fully Autographed Gone With The Wind Bound Screen Play

Screen play, board volume from Gone With The Wind, signed & inscribed on the front free end paper in blue ink by Alicia Rhett, Jane Darwell, Leslie Howard, Vivien Leigh, Hattie McDanial, Clark Cable, Leona Roberts, Olivia De Havilland, Annie Laurie Fuller Kurtz & Wilbur G. Kurtz, also signed & inscribed inside front cover "To Aunt Lil, from Shona," printed by Macmillan, 1938 (ILLUS., top of page).... **$9,600**

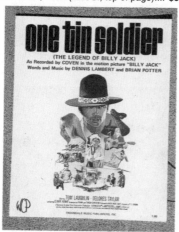

1949 Marilyn Monroe Contact Prints

One Tin Soldier Sheet Music

Sheet Music, "One Tin Soldier," from The Legend of Billy Jack, Trousdale Music, 1973 (ILLUS.)... **$40-75**

Sheet of contact prints, black & white images of Marilyn Monroe by Philippe Halsman, 12 shots in a variety of poses, shot in 1949 for Life Magazine photo feature entitled "Eight Girls Try Out Mixed Emotions," 8 1/2 x 11" (ILLUS., top next column).. **$2,640**

Tee shirt, "Alien," chest-burster design, cotton w/vinyl monster emerging from chest, Distortions Unlimited, 1980s (ILLUS., bottom next column)............................... **$45-65**

Alien Chest-burster Tee Shirt

M

MUCHA (ALPHONSE) ARTWORK

A leader in the Art Nouveau movement, Alphonse Maria Mucha was born in Moravia (which was part of Czechoslovakia) in 1860. Displaying considerable artistic talent as a child, he began formal studies locally, later continuing his work in Munich and then Paris, where it became necessary for him to undertake commercial artwork. In 1894, the renowned actress Sarah Bernhardt commissioned Mucha to create a poster for her play "Gismonda" and this opportunity proved to be the turning point in his career. While continuing his association with Bernhardt, he began creating numerous advertising posters, packaging designs, book and magazine illustrations and "panneaux decoratifs" (decorative pictures).

Mucha Lithograph of "Fall"

Two of Four Mucha "The Arts" Prints

Mucha Lithograph on Silk of "Autumn"

Lithograph, "Autumn," printed on silk in color w/the allegorial figure of an Art Nouveau maiden standing in front of a Roman chair wearing a long gown & holding a small basket of fruit, stylized vines & flowers in the background, signed in the plate, ca. 1903, 11 5/8 x 27 1/4" (ILLUS.)...................... **$1,912**

Lithograph, "Fall," printed on paper in color w/the allegorial figure of an Art Nouveau maiden seated among grapevines, signed in the plate, ca. 1896, 20 3/4 x 40" (ILLUS., top next column) **$8,365**

Lithographs, "The Arts," lithographed in color on paper, each w/a different Art Nouveau maiden representing Poetry, Dance, Painting or Music, signed in the plates, ca. 1898, framed, image 15 x 23", set of 4 (ILLUS. of two, middle next column).. **$50,190**

Rare Mucha Advertising Poster

Poster, advertising, "Biscuits Lefevre-Utile," lithographed in color & designed as a seated Art Nouveau maiden w/large red poppies in her hair & wearing a swirling gown while holding a plate of cookies, leafy swirl ground, a large C-scroll cartouche at the bottom w/long panels of text, signed in the plate, ca. 1897, framed, 17 1/2 x 24 1/2" (ILLUS.) **$13,145**

MUSIC BOXES

Extremely Rare Nicoles Freres Piano Forte Disk Music Box with Fine Inlay

Fine Mermod Freres Ideal Soprano Cylinder Music Box

Mermod Freres Ideal Soprano cylinder music box, rectangular mahogany & ebonized wood case w/band inlay & a bottom drawer w/stamped brass pulls holding three cylinders, on a matching table w/cabriole legs, ormolu mounts & a center drawer, additional wooden box w/three cylinders, music box, 19 x 42", 13 1/4" h., table 23 x 45 1/2", 31" h., the set (ILLUS. of music box)...................... **$16,100**

Nicoles Freres Piano Forte disc music box, mahogany & rosewood long rectangular case w/ornate brass, ivory, mother-of-pearl & boulle inlaid banding & cartouche reserves on the top & front, further fine line-inlay, plays four overtures, late 19th c., minor damage, 11 1/2 x 28", 8 1/8" h. (ILLUS., top of page) **$40,250**

Regina Corona disc music box, Model 33, floor model, mahogany upright case, the rectangular top w/a low pierced gallery of short turned spindles & fluted front corner blocks w/urn-turned finials above a deep frieze over a pair of single-pane doors w/ornate brass corner trim flanked by turned & tapering columns, the lower case w/a large rectangular glass pane acid-etched "Regina Corona" & w/scrolled corner decoration, stepped molded flat base on casters, tag of retailer reads "From Sherman Clay & Co. San Francisco," w/29 - 27 1/2" d. discs, late 19th c., 25 x 39 1/4", 72 1/2" h. (ILLUS., top next column)..................................... **$25,300**

Rare Regina Corona Disc Music Box

Exceptionally Rare Regina Model 35

M

Regina disc music box, Model 35, floor model, carved mahogany case, a high peaked & pierced scroll-carved crest centered by a clock dial w/Arabic numerals above a curved molded cornice above a tall curved leaded glass door decorated w/scrolls, crown & harp, ropetwist-turned columns down the sides, curved molded base molding above a conforming drawer, raised on simple cabriole legs joined by a medial shelf, w/original labels, includes 27 - 15 1/2" d. discs, 24 x 28", 71" h. (ILLUS., previous page) **$41,400**

MUSICAL INSTRUMENTS

Fine Knabe Baby Grand Player Piano

Baby grand piano, reproducing player-type, Wm. Knabe & Co., figured & burled mahogany veneer case, ornate foliate scroll & floral carving heads each molded tapering gently curved leg on a caster, plays Ampico rolls, minor edge damage & wear, complete w/piano bench w/nee-

Grand piano, Louis XVI-Style, kingwood, mahogany, parquetry, marquetry & giltwood, the hinged top inlaid w/lozenge parquetry & centered by an oval reserve depicting foliage & insects, the border banded w/Vitruvian scrolling, the garland-hung sides decorated w/rosettes within lozenges, each panel centered by a framed oval reserve w/a foliate trophy, the music stand w/foliate & insects, signed "John Broadwood - & Sons - London," on six Ionic columnar tapering legs w/casters, England, ca. 1895, closed 59 1/2 x 101", 38 1/2" h. (ILLUS.).....**$78,000**

dlepoint cushion & 317 Ampico rolls, case 63 x 68", 40" h. (ILLUS.).............. **$10,550**

Old French Copper & Wood Drum

Drum, round w/cooper sides & wide wooden rim bands, rope tighteners & stretched hide heads, w/leather belt w/one ebonized wooden stick, marked "Exposition Universelle de Paris, Couesnon & Ge... Paris," late 19th c., 15 3/4" d., 11 1/2" h. (ILLUS.).. **$345**

Early 20th Century Steinway Grand Piano

Grand piano, ebonized wood, Steinway & Sons Model A, overstrung scale, heavy ring-turned tapering legs, 1903, 56 x 74", closed 40" h. (ILLUS.) **$16,100**

Extremely Rare & Ornate Louis XVI-Style Grand Piano

M

Scarce Original Kodak Brownie with Box

PHOTOGRAPHIC ITEMS

Camera, No. 2 Kodak "Brownie" camera, original early model w/original colorful box w/Brownie figures, box 3 1/2 x 4 1/4 x 5 1/2" (ILLUS., top of page) **$477**

Speed Graphic Camera with Ektar Lens

Camera, Speed Graphic 2.25" x 3.25" model w/Kodak Ektar 101mmf 4.5 lens & Kalart rangefinger (ILLUS.) **$173**

Leitz Camera Case

Camera case, Leitz leatherette square case w/strap handle, holds five filters & two film cartridges (ILLUS.) **$58**

Daguerreotype, half-plate, a handsome young man shown seated before a painted landscape, wearing black coat, cape w/plaid lining & vest, holding a cane & a top hat, slight color tinting to his face, in a

Scarce Daguerreotype of a Young Man

leather-covered case w/velvet lining on one side & brass liner around images, seal broken & image carefully cleaned, partial paper label of Anthony, Clark & Co., ca. 1846-47, 4 1/4 x 5 3/8" (ILLUS.) ... **$546**

POLITICAL & CAMPAIGN ITEMS

Campaign

1928 Hoover Button & Watch Fob

Campaign button, 1928 campaign, jugate-type, printed in red, white, blue & gold w/an eagle, shield & banners, black & white photos of candidates Herbert Hoover & Charles Curtis, couple of small surface scratches, 1 1/4" d. (ILLUS. left with Hoover watch fob)............................ **$2,391**

Rare 1840 "Columbian Star" Chamber Pot

Chamber pot, cov., 1840 campaign, earthenware, footed squatty bulbous shape w/C-scroll handle & domed cover w/loop handle,, transfer-printed in light blue w/the "Columbian Star" patt., a wide band of stars around the upper body & cover, the sides decorated w/a landscape of a log cabin & farmer plowing, designed for the presidential campaign of William Henry Harrison, made by John Ridgway & Sons, England, 9 1/2" d., 8" h. (ILLUS.) **$2,037**

Rare Grover Cleveland Campaign Drum

Drum, 1884 campaign of Grover Cleveland, the side painted w/a large bust portrait of Cleveland w/white banners above & below reading "Our Next President - Grover Cleveland," marked by Edward Baack, 87 Fulton St., New York w/worn original paint & inlaid star on the side, produced during the Civil War era & reused later,

restoration to one head, a tear in the other, 36 1/2" d., 18 1/4" h. (ILLUS.)............ **$5,175**

Rare Bryan-Sewall 1896 Coin Flask

Flask, 1896 campaign, mold-blown amber glass, footed flattened coin-shaped w/cylindrical neck w/a tooled double-collared mouth, one side molded w/a bust of presidential candidate William Jennings Bryan framed by "In Silver We Trust - Bryan 1896 Sewall," reverse w/a molded American eagle & "United Democratic Ticket - We Shall Vote - 16 to 1," 1/2 pt. (ILLUS.)................................... **$1,792**

Rare McKinley-Hobart Coin Flask

Flask, 1896 campaign, mold-blown amber glass, footed flattened coin-shaped w/cylindrical neck w/a tooled double-collared mouth, one side molded w/a bust of presidential candidate William McKinley framed by "Sound Money and Proection - McKinley & Hobart," reverse w/a molded bee & "In Gold We Trust," 1/2 pt. (ILLUS.) **$4,760**

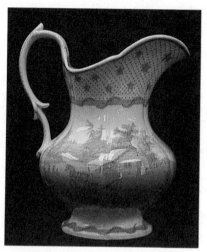

Very Rare 1840 "Columbian Star" Pitcher

Pitcher, 1840 campaign, earthenware, pedestal base & squatty bulbous body tapering to a high & wide arched spout & fancy C-scroll handle, transfer-printed in lgiht blue w/the "Columbian Star" patt., a wide band of stars around the upper neck, the sides decorated w/a landscape of a log cabin & farmer plowing, designed for the presidential campaign of William Henry Harrison, made by John Ridgway & Sons, England, 10 3/4" h. (ILLUS.) **$2,713**

Very Rare Zachary Taylor Pocket Mirror

Pocket mirror, 1848 campaign, round w/a narrow pewter rim band, the back enclosing a hand-colored lithograph bust portrait of presidential candidate General Zachery Taylor w/his name below the portrait, some corrosion to frame, scattered loss to mirror silvering, 2 1/2" d. (ILLUS.) **$7,867**

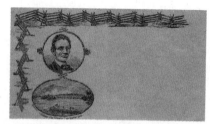

1860 Lincoln Campaign Postal Cover

Postal cover, 1860 campaign, yellow paper printed in black along the left & top w/a split rail fence above a portrait of a beardless Abraham Lincoln over an oval landscape vignette inscribed "Honest Abe Lincoln on his flat boat," even darkening & three pin holes (ILLUS.)............................ **$76**

Scarce 1924 Davis-Bryan Poster

Poster, 1924 campaign, printed in black in white w/the photographs & names of Democratic candidates, John W. Davis & Charles W. Bryan, framed, 13 1/2 x 16" (ILLUS.).. **$716**

1948 Truman-Barkley Coattail Poster

Poster, 1948 campaign, printed in red, white & blue on cardboard, a coattail production featuring pictures of Democratic candidates Harry Truman & Alben Bark-

P

ley, Lady Liberty in the center framed by photos of various coattail candidates, titled "Vote Democratic - November 2, 1948," 14 x 22" (ILLUS.) **$259**

Watch fob, 1928 campaign, cast-metal round frame w/hanging loop enclosing a domed button centered by a photo of Herbert Hoover enclosed by a gold band reading "For President - Herbert Hoover," complete w/leather strap, center button 1 1/4" d. (ILLUS. right with Hoover button, page 927) **$298**

Non-Campaign

Lincoln China Service Custard Cup

Custard cup, cov., porcelain, footed squatty tapering body w/a wide purple band trimmed in gold a bove a spread-winged American eagle, gilt looped shoulder handles flanking the wide short cylindrical neck, domed cover w/leaf vine handle also w/purple band & gilt trim, from the Abraham Lincoln Presidential Service, made in France, some by Haviland & Co., second half 19th c., 2 1/2" d. (ILLUS.).... **$32,400**

Rare Dagurerreotype of Millard Fillmore

Daguerreotype, sixth-plate size, bust-portrait of U.S. President Millard Fillmore, facing left, in an oval brass cut-out mat & gilded brass preserver frame, partial velvet-lined leather & pressed paper case, ca. 1850, minor imperfections, similar portrait known taken by Southworth & Hawes of Boston, case 3 1/8 x 3 5/8" (ILLUS.) **$10,281**

Rare Group of Game Plates from Hayes Presidential Service

Game plates, porcelain, each h.p. w/a different realistic game bird, based on designs by Theodore R. Davis, part of the Rutherford B. Hayes Presidential Service, includes a ruffed grouse, bobwhite, rail & wild pigeon, Haviland & Co., France, ca. 1880, 9" d., set of 4 (ILLUS.) **$16,800**

Ice Cream Dish from Hayes Service

Ice cream dish, porcelain, squared w/incurved corners, molded down the center w/a realistic snow shoe in gold & brown against a streaky dark red & pink ground, from the Rutherford B. Hayes Presidential Service, Haviland & Co., France, 1884-89, 6 5/8 x 7 1/4" (ILLUS.) **$2,880**

Plate, dessert, 8 1/2" d., porcelain, the scalloped flanged rim decorated w/a yellow band accented at the top w/a small coat-of-arms, the center h.p. w/a large red rose on a leafy stem, from the Ulysses S. Grant Presidential Service, 1870s (ILLUS., next page) **$1,920**

Plate from Grant Presidential Service

Plate from Polk Presidential Service

States in red, white, blue & gold, the center w/a gilt scroll motif, from the James K. Polk Presidential Service, 1840s, ordered through Alexander Stewart & Co., New York, New York (ILLUS.) **$22,800**

Rare Dessert Plate from Jackson Service

Plate, dessert, 8 5/8" d., porcelain, the center h.p. w/a spread-winged American eagle & shield against a gold sunburst ground, w/marbled blue border band, gilt band trim, from the Andrew Jackson Presidential Service, ca. 1829-37 (ILLUS.).... **$22,800**

Plate, dinner, 9 1/2" d., porcelain, round w/a scalloped & scroll-molded flanged rim & scalloped center, white ground decorated at the top edge w/the shield of the United

Scarce Early G. Washington Snuff Box

Snuff box, round, horn & tortoiseshell w/a gilt stamped medallion on the top w/a profile bust of George Washington labeled "Washington - Morels Fils Fecit," early 19th c., lens loose, some flakes, 3 1/4" d. (ILLUS.) **$345**

Rare Rutherford B. Hayes Presidential China Soup Plates

P

Soup plates, porcelain, each h.p. with a different scene, the first, titled "1776," features an interior scene of an early New England fireside, the second, titled "The Harvest Moon," shows a landscape scene w/a full moon above a field of Indian corn & pumpkins, the third, titled "Tomato," shows a landscape of a mountain cabin w/tomatoes on the vine in the foreground, the fourth, titled "Okra," features a realistic depiction of okra, part of the Rutherford B. Hayes Presidential Service, Haviland & Co., ca. 1880, 9" d., set of 4 (ILLUS., bottom previous page) **$19,200**

Rare Glass A. Jackson Wine Glass Cooler

Wine glass cooler, engraved glass, footed deep cylindrical clear bowl w/two small rim spouts, engraved w/a wide band of grapes & grape leaves below two depictions of the Seal of the United States, from the Andrew Jackson Presidential Service, ca. 1830, 4 3/4" d., 3 3/4" h. (ILLUS.) **$14,400**

POP CULTURE COLLECTIBLES

Beatles Licorice Candy Display Box

Beatles candy display box, "The Beatles Long Eating Licorice Record," 1960s, depending on condition (ILLUS.)............. **$350-650**

Beatles Harmonica & Box

Beatles hormonica box, printed in red, white & blue w/head image of the band members, holds a generic M. Hohner harmonica, NEMS, 1964 (ILLUS.) **$75-150**

Beatles on 1960s 16 Magazine Cover

Beatles magazine, "16 Magazine," Beatles & other personalities on the cover, 1960s, depending on condition (ILLUS.).............. **$20-35**

Teen Magazine with George Harrison

Beatles magazine, "Lloyd Thaxton's Tiger Beat," color photo of George Harrison on the cover, 1960s, depending on condition (ILLUS.)... **$20-35**

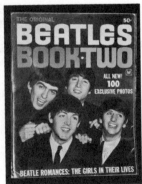

The Original Beatles Book Two Magazine

P

Beatles Vinyl Pencil Bag

Beatles magazine, "The Original Beatles Book Two," color photo of band members on the cover, includes photos & stories, 1964 (ILLUS., previous page) **$10-25**

Ringo Beatles Model Kit

Beatles model kit, Ringo, boxed & unbuilt, Revell, 1964 (ILLUS.) **$225-550**

Beatles pencil bag, yellow vinyl w/painted photos & facsimile signatures of the members, Standard Plastics, 1964, depending on condition (ILLUS., top of page) **$75-150**

Grouping of Various Beatles Buttons

Beatles pinback buttons, metal printed in red, white, blue & black, various designs,

NEMS, 1964, 1" d., each (ILLUS. of various designs) **$5-10**

Two Beatles Bamboo Plates

Beatles plate, molded bamboo, w/a photo from "A Hard Day's Night," w/Oriental designs & writing, Bamboo Tray Specialist, 1964, 12 1/2" d. (ILLUS. left with smaller plate) **$85-130**

Beatles plate, molded bamboo, w/a photo from "A Hard Day's Night," w/Oriental designs & writing, Bamboo Tray Specialist, 1964, 6 1/2" d. (ILLUS. right with larger plate) **$75-120**

Boxed Deck of Beatles Playing Cards

P

1960s Beatles Vinyl Clutch Purse

Beatles playing cards, found in two picture versions, 1964, boxed deck of 52 (ILLUS., previous page) **$275-400**

Beatles Portraits in Original Package

Beatles portraits, printed in color, Beatles Buddies Club, set of four sealed w/original header card, 1964 (ILLUS.)............. **$75-100**

Avedon Beatles Photo Portrait Poster

Beatles poster, psychedelic photo portrait of each band member by Richard Avedon, availabe by mail-order from Look magazine, 1968, framed, each (ILLUS. of one)... **$45-60**

Beatles purse, clutch-type, white vinyl w/a zipper top & strap handle, black-printed heads of the band members, 1960s (ILLUS., top of page) **$90-200**

"Ain't She Sweet" Record & Sleeve

Beatles record, "Ain't She Sweet," 45 rpm, Arco #6308, framed w/original sleeve (ILLUS.) **$300-600**

Framed Can't Buy Me Love Record

Beatles record, "Can't Buy Me Love/You Can't Do That," 45 rpm, framed w/original sleeve, Capitol #5150 (ILLUS.) **$400-800**

1964 Beatles Portrait Tiles

Beatles tiles, ceramic, each w/a different printed portrait of a band member, Dorincourt Potters, 1964, 6" sq., set of 4 (ILLUS.) **$150-200**

Beatles Gum Trading Card Packages

Beatles trading cards, sealed w/pack of gum, from various Topps series, 1960s, each sealed package (ILLUS. of three)... **$50-75**

George Harrison Red-printed Tumbler

Beatles tumbler, glass, printed in red w/the head of George Harrison above a bar of music & records, 1964, 5 1/2" h. (ILLUS.) **$75-125**

Beatles Plastic Tumbler with Paper Insert

Beatles tumbler, molded plastic, tall tapering cylindrical shape w/a wide red rim band, clear sides enclosing a color-printed photo insert, Burrite, 1964, 6 1/4" h. (ILLUS.)... **$75-100**

Sample Square of Beatles Wallpaper

Beatles wallpaper, decorated w/various printed color group photos of the band w/facsimile signatures, produced in the United Kingdom, 21 x 21" sample (ILLUS.)....... **$35-75**
Beatles Yellow Submarine clothes hangers, die-cut cardboard head of each band member printed in full color, 1968, 16" h., each (ILLUS., top next page) **$75-150**

P

Beatles Yellow Submarine Clothes Hangers

Beatles Yellow Submarine Decorations

Beatles Yellow Submarine decorations, "The Beatles Yellow Submarine 20 Pop-Out Art Decorations," Western Publishing, 1968, the complete book (ILLUS.).... **$25-50**

Gold-painted Bust of Ringo

Bust of Ringo, hard rubber painted gold, only one made, Starfans, 1960s, 6 1/2" h. (ILLUS.) **$200-250**

Beatles Yellow Submarine Model Kit

Beatles Yellow Submarine model kit, plastic submarine, MPC, 1968, unbuilt in box (ILLUS.) **$200-400**

1950s Car Craft Magazine

Magazine, "Car Craft," October 1954, digest-size, most issues from the 1950s, each (ILLUS. of one) **$3-6**

PURSES & BAGS

Dome bag, arched floral window design, stepped base w/turquoise teardrops, Mandalian Mfg. Co. **$375-425**

Mandalian Mesh Bag with Butterfly

Mesh bag, decorated w/a large white reserve enclosing blue floral swag, sprigs & a blue butterfly, blue ground w/dark blue floral sprigs, Mandalian Mfg. Co. (ILLUS.) **$275-375**

Mesh bag, white ground decorated w/green & purple pheasants, tri-point fringed base **$350-400**

Fine Judith Leiber Shell-shaped Purse

Pearl & crystal-set gilt-brass, modeled as a seashell, the interior lined in gilt-leather bearing a gilt-brass Leiber signature plaque & fitted w/a drop-in gilt-brass snake-style shoulder strap, accompanied by a small gilt-brass annual purse mirror & an ice-blue flannel storage bag, Judith Leiber (ILLUS.) **$2,990**

Novelty Purses

Clear plastic box bag, w/gold confetti inset panels **$125-150**

Coach oversize tan bucket bag, full grain cowhide **$450-500**

Crystal evening bag, rhinestone clasp, Australia **$200-225**

Czechoslovakian wooden bead purse, Bakelite handles **$75-100**

Deitsch alligator box bag, octagonal, circa 1950 .... **$350-400**

Edwards "P.M. Pouch," soft metallic bag w/square compact top **$200-225**

Enid Collins "Flutterbyes" Box Bag

Enid Collins "Flutterbyes" box bag (ILUS.) **$125-150**

Enid Collins "Poki" Turtle Bag

Enid Collins "Poki" turtle design bag, linen bag w/mahogany base (ILLUS.) **$75-100**

Faux Dalmation Bag & Hat Set

Faux Dalmation bag & hat, 1970s, the set (ILLUS.) **$80-100**

Gira box bag, gold & silver interlaced strips, gold frame, Lucite top **$150-175**

Giraffe-skin purse & pumps, w/matching insets, the set **$175-200**

Gold sequin bag, w/yellow dangle beads .. **$25-50**

Jolies-Junior cloth bag, applied flowers basket w/velveteen pansies **$50-75**

K & G Charlet bag, metallic glass cut beads in copper, twist handle, coin purse **$100-125**

Koret puffet sewn leather purse, black w/zipper flap pouch **$50-75**

Black Lucite Bag with Clear Top & Handle

Lucite bag, black w/clear "X" patterned lid & handle (ILLUS.) **$150-175**

P

Lucite Bag with Horizontally-ridged Base

Lucite bag, horizontally-ridged base, root
beer color w/a carved amber lid & handle
(ILLUS.)... **$125-150**

Lumured Beaded Bag

Lumured beaded bag, reversible caviar
beaded floral design (ILLUS.) **$60-75**
Macramé bag, white string, 1970s.............. **$40-50**
Mexican hand-tooled leather bag, burgun-
dy & tan w/floral pattern, Aztec calendar
.... **$100-125**
"Nightlife" bag, black w/applied bead de-
sign of cocktail items, white plastic han-
dle **$30-40**
Pucci velvet clutch, multicolored piece-
work... **$100-150**
"Tackle Box" bag, brass, mottled rust top
insert **$200-250**
Timmy Woods "Sun & Moon" bag, ... **$200-250**

Whiting & Davis

One of the most successful marketing
campaigns of the early 20th century was
conducted by the Whiting & Davis Company to promote its line of mesh handbags.
Prior to the 1909 invention of the automatic
mesh-making machine, mesh was hand-
linked, a process both lengthy and costly.
With automation, bags could be produced
quickly and economically. Whiting & Davis
capitalized on this by promoting its product
as both an affordable fashion accessory
and as a desirable "special occasion" gift.
Early film favorites including Joan Craw-

ford appeared in Whiting & Davis ads, and
such fashion arbiters as Paul Poiret and
Elsa Schiaparelli contributed exclusive
designs to the line.

Many Whiting & Davis decorative patterns are reflective of the firm's 1920s and
1930s heyday, featuring Art Deco-influenced
geometrics and arresting color combinations. Scenic and figural depictions were
also popular, with subjects ranging from
modernistic skylines and moonlit beaches to
exotic birds, dancing couples, and even
movie stars. Over the years, variations on
the traditional Whiting & Davis bag have
included compact bags, gate-top bags, miniature coin purses, and children's
purses.Although other mesh manufacturers
emerged, including Evans, Napier, and
Miller Brothers, Whiting & Davis remained
the industry leader. The company's most
resilient competitor, Mandalian Mfg. Co.,
specialized in bags with a Middle Eastern
flavor, often heavily trimmed with metal
fringe and drops. Whiting & Davis acquired
Mandalian in the 1940s, soon incorporating
the company's techniques and stylings into
it own designs.

In the late 1940s and 1950s, Whiting &
Davis moved into "solids" - mesh bags all
in one color, often gold. In the 1980s and
'90s, the company also briefly expanded
beyond mesh bags to the manufacture of
other mesh accessories: vests, gowns, belts,
headbands, and even jewelry. Among the
designers whose work has appeared under
the Whiting & Davis logo are Anna Sui,
Richard Tyler, and Anthony Ferrara.
Today, the company name and tradition
continue in bags designed by Inge Hendro-
martono for Inge Christopher.

Complete information on the Whiting &
Davis Co. is included in Whiting & Davis
Purses: The Perfect Mesh by Leslie Pina
and Donald-Brian Johnson. (Schiffer Publishing Ltd., 2002). Photos for this category
are by Dr. Pina.

Bandana bag, gold mesh w/multicolored
zigzag design, chain & hook clasp......... **$25-50**
"Batwing" bag, red enameled flat armor
mesh w/silver ring mesh border......... **$300-350**

Rare Compact-Mesh Bag with Silhouette

R

Colonial Dancers bag, wide gold compact top frame inset w/domed Bakelite oval plaque w/Colonial dancers design, mesh bag w/stepped base, decorated w/a stylized blue flower reserve (ILLUS., previous page) **$550-650**

Diamond designs bag, red diamonds on a black mesh ground, central red jewel on the clasp **$300-350**

Dresden mesh, sky blue ground printed w/black animals, enameled frame **$300-350**

Dresden mesh, white ground w/large red & small blue splashes, w/original Whiting & Davis hang tag **$250-300**

El-Sah bag, red & white octagon designs on black mesh, flap fringe, clasp set w/central amber jewel, jeweled chain **$325-375**

Feather design bag, white mesh ground decorated w/black, orange & yellow feather-like design, enameled frame **$225-275**

Floral mesh bag, pink rose on muted green ground **$200-250**

"Fox & Tree" bag, blue jeweled silhouette design on heavy bronze mesh, unmarked **$600-650**

Headband style bag, gold mesh **$40-50**

"Magic Carpet" bag, mesh w/multicolored carpet-like designs, orange & brown enameled florals on the frame............. **$325-375**

Medieval Tapestry-style Bag

Medieval Tapestry-style bag, the long mesh bag decorated down the center w/a black stripe decorated w/abstract flowers flanked by stripes w/an overall small diamond design, gold metal frame mounted w/raised jewels (ILLUS.) **$325-375**

Miniature mesh bag, gold mesh w/a blue jeweled frame, pearl dangles on the bottom **$175-225**

Necktie-style mesh bag, silver mesh......... **$20-30**

"Princess Mary" bag, yellow & black mesh w/overflap, floral medallion on the frame **$400-450**

Reticule-style bag, periwinkle blue mesh w/design of white crosses, silver drawchain closure **$225-275**

Ribbon banners bag, design of crisscrossing blue & yellow ribbon banners on a chrome mesh ground **$300-350**

Skyline bag, a black & white abstract skyline design w/orange mesh sky at the top, enameled frame (ILLUS., top next column) **$200-250**

Mesh Bag with Abstract Skyline Design

Tropical scene bag, a tropical landscape w/the sun, a palm tree & clouds on a blue mesh ground **$400-450**

"Vandyke" base bag, decorated w/a sunburst design in coral, green & blue mesh, enameled frame **$200-250**

Wing Design Mesh Bag with Bakelite

Wing design bag, an abstract wing motif in aqua & red above a white ground w/scattered pink floral medallions in mesh, notched bottom, rare metal frame w/red Bakelite insert (ILLUS.) **$375-400**

RADIO & TELEVISION MEMORABILIA

Not long after the dawning of the radio age in the 1920s, new programs were being aired for the entertainment of the national listening audience. Many of these programs issued premiums and advertising promotional pieces that are highly collectible today.

With the arrival of the TV age in the late 1940s, the tradition of promotional items continued. In addition to advertising materials, many toys and novelty items have been produced that tie in to popular shows.

Below we list alphabetically a wide range of items relating to classic radio and television. Some of the characters originated in the comics or on the radio and then found new and wider exposure through television. We include them here because they are best known to today's collectors because of television exposure.

RECORDS

Vogue Picture Records

Downbeat magazine called Vogue Picture Records "the discs that sparkle with color." Although illustrated recordings had been around since the 1920s, it took Vogue to bring these musical novelties to the forefront.

R *Although the company's heyday was brief (from early 1946 through mid-1947) the Vogue catalog serves as a colorful time capsule of the post-World War II era. While Billboard dismissed Vogue illustrations as strictly of the coal company calendar type, the scenes depicted (often romantic, patriotic or humorous) retain a freshness and optimism totally in keeping with the spirit of America at that time.*

The visionary behind Vogue was Tom Saffady, president of Detroit's Sav-Way Industries. Saffady's goal: an "unbreakable" record, replacing easily-shattered shellac discs. Each 10" Vogue 78 had an interior aluminum core bonded to Sav-Way's transparent Vinylite plastic. In addition to increasing durability, the aluminum core also made the records warp-proof, while the plastic reduced surface & needle noise.

All production, except label printing, was centered at Vogue's Detroit plant. A Saffady-invented automatic pressing carousel dramatically sped up record production, with discs stamped out some eighty times faster than previously. There was also a complete in-house recording studio and Saffady bought a nearby night club so that Vogue acts could perform there as well as cut records for his label.

The Vogue roster included such musical luminaries as Clyde McCoy, the Charlie Shavers Quintet, Patsy Montana and Phil Spitalny's All-Girl Orchestra but Saffady was unable to sign such top tier performers as Frank Sinatra and Bing Crosby. Since Vogues were priced just over a dollar (about twice the going rate for a traditional 78) buyers wanted more than just an illustrated, unbreakable record: they wanted a hit, which Vogue could not provide. Hampered by declining sales and high overhead, Saffady filed for bankruptcy in August of 1947.

His picture discs, however, live on, with a unique visual style courtesy of artists Ruth Corbett, Walter Sprink, Richard Harker, Will Wirts, M. Kanouse, and R. Forbes. Thanks to the impenetrability of the Vinylite coating, many of their Vogue illustrations retain colors as vibrant as the day they were first pressed.

Approximately 75 recordings (not all consecutive numbers) were issued in the Vogue "R700" series, all but a handful show up with regularity on the collecting market. Collectors drawn to the themes and the colors of a Vogue record also get "two for the price of one," since each side features a different illustration. A limited vinyl series of Vogue facsimiles, released in recent years by Bear Family Records, should not be confused with the originals.

Valuable Vogue references include: The Picture Record *by Edgar L. Curry (1998) and www.voguepicturerecords.org, a website maintained by the Association of Vogue Picture Record Collectors.*

Today, sixty years after Vogue ceased production, Tom Saffady's personal dream - "recordings with color" - remains as colorful and dream-inspiring as ever.

Advisor for this category is Donald-Brian Johnson, an author and lecturer specializing in Mid-Twentieth century design.

Vogue No. R707 Picture Record

No. R707, "Sugar Blues/Basin Street Blues," Clyde McCoy & His Orchestra (ILLUS.).. **$30-40**

No. R708, "I Surrender Dear/S'posin'," The King's Jesters and Louise **$60-75**

Vogue Record No. R710

No. R710, "The Bells of St. Mary's/Star Dust'," The Don Large Chorus (ILLUS.). **$75-100**

R

Vogue Record No. R719

No. R719, "Have I Told You Lately?/I Get A Kick Out Of Corn," Lulu Belle & Scotty (ILLUS.)... **$60-75**

No. R720, "Grandpa's Gettin' Younger Every Day/Time Will Tell," Lulu Belle & Scotty **$60-75**

No. R722, "Tear It Down/ Put That Ring On My Finger," Clyde McCoy & His Orchestra... **$60-75**

No. R725, "Rhapsody in Blue/Alice Blue Gown," Phil Spitalny's Hour of Charm All Girl Orchestra... **$30-40**

Vogue Record No. R731

No. R731, "Between the Devil and the Deep Blue Sea/You Took Advantage of Me," Marion Mann (ILLUS.)......................... **$100-125**

No. R738, "Rhumba Lesson No. 2/Give Me All of Your Heart," Paul Shahin/Dick La-Salle & His Society Orchestra.............. **$75-100**

No. R744, "Don't Tetch It/Flat River, Missouri," Nancy Lee & The Hilltoppers/Judy & Jen.. **$75-100**

No. R745, "The Trial Of Bumble Bee - Part I/The Boy Who Cried Wolf - Part I," James Jewell & The Jewell Playhouse.............. **$75-100**

No. R748, "Let Me Take You In My Arms/It's Always You," Dick LaSalle and His Society Orchestra...................................... **$250-275**

No. R751 "Mean To Me/Humphrey, The Sweet Singing Pig," The King's Jesters & Louise (ILLUS., top next column)........ **$150-175**

No. R752, "(Ah Yes) There's Good Blues Tonight/Baby, What You Do To Me," Clyde McCoy & His Orchestra (ILLUS., middle next column)..................................... **$75-100**

Vogue Record No. N751

Vogue Record No. R752

Vogue Record No. T754

No. R754, "Dizzy's Dilemma/She's Funny That Way," The Charlie Shavers Quintet (ILLUS.)... **$100-125**

Vogue Record No. R755

No. R755, "Serenade To A Pair Of Nylons/Broadjump," The Charlie Shavers Quintet (ILLUS.) **$100-125**

R

No. R756, "Musicomania/If I Had You," The
Charlie Shavers Quintet **$100-125**
No. R764, "I Guess I'll Get The Papers (And
Go Home)/Whatta Ya Gonna Do!," Shep
Fields & His Orchestra **$60-75**

Vogue Record No. R767

No. R767, "Love Means The Same Old
Thing/This Is Always," Joan Edwards
(ILLUS.) **$75-100**
No. R770, "The Wiffenpoof Song/If That
Phone Ever Rings (And It's You)," Art
Kassel & His Orchestra **$60-75**
No. R778, "Guilty of Love/Mucho Dinero,"
Enric Madriguera & His Orchestra **$60-75**
No. R779, "A Man, A Moon And A Maid/Cu-
ban Yodelin' Man," Enric Madriguera &
His Orchestra **$75-100**

RIBBON DOLLS

*In the days when young girls and ladies
were often judged by their handiwork, ribbon dolls were a popular art form. Sometimes also referred to as ribbon ladies or
ribbon pictures, from the 1930s-50s the
components were often available in kit
form, complete with paper doll, ribbon sup-
plies, instructions, frame & glass. Others
were made from a simple pattern sold for
ten cents, while faces & bodies were home-
made.*

*Although the majority of subjects were
women, occasionally a male example will
surface, often as part of a set. Women
dressed in hooped skirts & carrying bouquets, baskets of flowers or parasols, brides
& similar colonial-looking figures are the
most often found today. While most were
mounted on plain black backings some
examples include exquisitely decorated
backgrounds or unusual poses, including
smoking a cigarette or cutting flowers in a
garden. Occasionally, the artist signed &
dated her work, or inscribed the back as a
gift.*

Ribbon Doll in Pink with Pastel Bouquet

Lady, wearing pale pink ribbon dress w/ecru
lace trim & carrying a pastel ribbon flower
bouquet, lace pantaloons, lace trimmed
bonnet w/flat top, 11" h. (ILLUS.) **$40-60**

Ribbon Doll Holding Basket

Lady w/ long strawberry blonde hair,
wearing a pink ribbon & brown lace
tiered dress, holding a basket of flower
buds, black background decorated
w/stalks of flowers & trees,
11 1/2" x 12 1/2" (ILLUS.) **$40-50**

Pair, Boy and Girl Ribbon Dolls

Little girl, wearing a peach dress & black shoes pointed toe to toe, short blond curly hair, holding a lace & ribbon rose bouquet, 6" x 8" (ILLUS. on left with young boy, previous page).................... **$35-45**

Ribbon Doll Pattern

Pattern, bride, black & white, ca. 1950 (ILLUS.)... **$3-6**

Ribbon Doll Pattern Figure of Woman

Pattern, figure of woman, w/original instructions (ILLUS.) **$10-20**

Ribbon Doll with Flared Dress

Profile of woman w/bobbed blond hair, silver lace around shoulders, wearing a flared lavender ribbon dress, white ribbon rose w/blue tassles in hair, holding a large purple & lavender feather fan, 9" x 11" (ILLUS.) **$65-95**

R

Bride and Bridesmaid Ribbon Dolls

Set: bride in beige dress, flowing veil together w/bridesmaid in orange dress & bonnet, both holding pastel colored bouquets, 13 x 16 3/4" (ILLUS.)..............., **$125-175**

Bride Ribbon Doll

Woman, bride, off-white ribbon & veil, holding bouquet w/ribbon streamers, marked on back "A friend made for my wedding, September 15, 1928, Anna M. Koopmans & Chas. Kuelhas," 11 5/8" h. (ILLUS.).... **$85-100**

Ribbon Doll in Peach Dress

Woman, full figure, peach ribbon dress w/matching circle hat, pink rosebuds & ferns on black background, 6 3/4" x 8 3/4" (ILLUS., previous page) **$55-75**

Woman in Green Ribbon Dress

Woman, full figure w/blond hair, wearing a pale green ribbon dress decorated w/gold lace & pink roses, pink rose in hair, green shoes, 9" x 11" (ILLUS.) **$55-65**

Ballerina Ribbon Doll

Woman, in short orange ribbon dress w/lace trim, wearing orange ballet slippers & carrying a matching parasol over her shoulder, 10 5/8" h. (ILLUS.) **$75-100**

Woman, in yellow satin ribbon dress w/black lace cuffs, holding a matching open parasol & large ribbon & lace bouquet, background decorated w/painted & ribbon flowers **$95-110**

Woman, w/flowing real dark brown hair, medium blue ribbon & white lace dress, lace pantaloons, wearing a flower-decorated hat, carrying a flower & lace bouquet, 12 1/4" h. (ILLUS., top next column) **$35-45**

Woman in Blue Ribbon Doll

Young boy, wearing red check overalls & wide-brimmed straw hat, holding ribbon roses, 6" x 8" (ILLUS. on right with little girl, on page 942) **$35-45**

ROYCROFT ITEMS

Elbert Hubbard, eccentric entrepreneur of the late 19th century, founded Roycroft Shops and established a craft community in East Aurora, New York in 1895. Individuals were trained in the trades of bookbinding, leather tooling and printing. Craft-style furniture in the manner of Gustav Stickley and known as "Aurora Colonial" furniture was produced. A copper workshop, begun in 1908, turned out numerous items. All of these, along with those pieces of Buffalo Pottery china which were produced exclusively for use at the Roycroft Inn and carry the Roycroft symbol, constitute a special category associated with the Arts and Crafts movement.

Book ends, copper, upright square plate embossed & stamped w/a seven-petal flower design, in original box, ca. 1910, small size, 3" h., pr. **$323**

Roycroft Arched & Hammered Book Ends

Book ends, hammered copper, Arts & Crafts style, upright arched design w/a top folded over above a small arched triangular smooth panel stamped w/a small floral design above the two-arch hammered lower sides, stamped w/the logo, 5" h., pr. (ILLUS.) **$242**

Book ends, hand-hammered copper, upright rectangular form w/riveted center band suspending a ring, dark brown patina, impressed orb mark, Model No. 309, 3 1/4 x 4 1/8", 5 1/4" h., pr. (minor wear) ... **$201**

Fine Original Roycroft Oak Bookcase

Bookcase, oak, the rectangular top slightly overhanging a tall case w/blocked stiles flanking a tall 16-pane glazed door opening to three shelves, flat base, original finish, Thirty-Third Degree style, Model No. 86, original finish, carved trademark, ca. 1905-06, 15 x 40", 55 1/4" h. (ILLUS.).... **$11,353**

RUGS - HOOKED & OTHER

Hooked

Old Abstract Design Hooked Rug

Abstract design, rectangular, wool & cotton multicolored center abstract design

within a narrow brown band & zig-zag border, in shades of brown, black, red, pink, blue, grey & tan, early 20th c., scattered losses, 45 x 76 1/2" (ILLUS.) **$823**

Hooked Rug with Boston Terrier

Boston Terrier, standing black & white dog framed by multiple rectangular colored borders, on burlap foundation, some staining & edge wear, late 19th - early 20th c., 31 x 49" (ILLUS.)........................... **$489**

Geometric Hooked Rug with Bull's-Eye

Geometric design, rectangular, a large center bull's-eye in red & blue flanked by red bars on a cream ground, quarter-round maroon, grey & red fans in each border, blue border band, burlap backing, thick pile, minor fading & edge wear, 23 x 35" (ILLUS.)...................................... **$288**

Fine Holstein Cow Hooked Rug

Holstein cow & trees, large cow & smaller leafless trees against a dark blue ground, narrow grey, red & light blue border bands, minor wear, 25 x 45" (ILLUS.) **$1,840**

R

Rare New Bedford Street Scene Hooked Rug

Hooked Rug with Red House & Duck

House beside lake & duck, rectangular, the large central scene w/a red house w/green roof & centered chimney beside a blue lake w/a yellow duck, blue hills & sky in the distance w/a yellow rising sun, wool on burlap, mounted, small stain, 17 x 23 1/2" (ILLUS.)....................................... **$144**

Long Rug with Masonic Symbols

Masonic symbols, long rectangular form w/a design of a stylized interior decorated in the upper corners w/curved swags w/quatrefoils flanking a large lantern enclosing a six-point star, above a deep red panel enclosing a rosette w/fleur-de-lis & a winged moon symbol, tall stems of flowers & leaves in each corner flanking a black & white checked & red-striped ground, additional shades of gold, greens & grey, late 19th - early 20th c., 34 1/2 x 70 1/4" (ILLUS.)......................... **$1,076**

Rare Hooked Rug with Native American Theme

Native American in canoe, a bold landscape scene w/a large stylized Indian in a canoe on water in the center, a large brown teepee to one side & a dense forest in the background below the blue sky w/white fluffy clouds, late 19th c., 26 x 39 1/2" (ILLUS.)............................... **$6,000**

New Bedford town scene, rectangular, a very detailed street scene w/a perspective view of buildings along a main streets, one flying the American flag, a small carriage, oxen-drawn hay wagon & numerous figures in the foreground, worked in shades of brown, tan, cream, black, white, green, red & blue, titled across the bottom "New Bedford 1810," shows New Bedford, Maine, hooked by Alice Beaty, Scotch Plains, New Jersey, late 19th c., 37 1/2 x 62 1/2" (ILLUS., top of page)... **$5,378**

SHAKER ITEMS

The Shakers, a religious sect founded by Ann Lee, first settled in this country at Watervliet, New York, near Albany, in 1774. By 1880 there were nine settlements in America. Workmanship in Shaker crafts is an extension of their religious beliefs and features plain and simple designs reflecting a chaste elegance that is now much in demand though relatively few early items are common.

Shaker No. 3 Ladder-back Rocking Chair

Shaker No. 0 Child's Rocking Chair

Rocking chair, child's, tall ladder-back w/three gently arched slats between turned stiles w/turned acorn finials, flat shaped arms w/mushroom caps & baluster-turned arm supports above the replaced woven tape seat, simple turned double front & side rungs, No. 0 model, traces of red paint, ca. 1876, Mt. Lebanon, New York, 23" h. (ILLUS.) **$316**

Rocking chair, short ladder-back w/three gently arched slats between the turned stiles w/acorn finial, shaped arms w/mushroon case on baluster-turned arm supports above the replaced woven tape seat, simple turned double rungs in the front & sides, top slat stamped "3," dark finish, Mt. Lebanon, New York, late 19th - early 20th c., 34" h. (ILLUS., top next column) **$403**

Shaker No. 6 Ladder-back Rocker

Rocking chair, tall ladder-back w/four gently arched slats between turned stiles w/turned acorn finials, flat shaped arms w/mushroom caps & baluster-turned arm supports above the replaced woven tape seat, simple turned double front & side rungs, impressed "6" & stenciled label "Shaker's Trademark No. 6 - Mt. Lebanon, N.Y.," dark finish w/wear, late 19th - early 20th c., 42" h. (ILLUS.) **$633**

S

Shaker Rocker No. 5 with Three Slats

Rocking chair, tall ladder-back w/three gently arched slats between turned stiles w/turned acorn finials, flat shaped arms w/mushroom caps & baluster-turned arm supports above the replaced woven tape seat, simple turned double front & side rungs, No. 5 model, original dark finish w/good wear, one cap loose, attributed to Mt. Lebanon, New York, 38" h. (ILLUS.) **$431**

SIGNS & SIGNBOARDS

Early Pabst Brewing Company Sign

Beer, "Pabst Brewing Company," color-printed tin, rectangular, a detailed scene of uniformed Spanish-American War veterans seated toasting victory w/bottles of Pabst beer, picture of the Battleship Maine in background, in original wooden frame, ca. 1900, some areas of color loss, overall fading, 21 x 27 1/4" (ILLUS.) **$345**

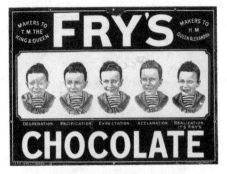

Fry's Chocolate White & Blue Sign

Chocolate, "Fry's Chocolate," colorful lithographed porcelain, a white center band printed in black & white w/five heads of a young boy each representing a different expression, wide dark blue upper & lower bands printed in white, ca. 1910, large chip to top center, very light spotting, 22 x 30" (ILLUS.)................................... **$1,680**

Lipton's Instant Cocoa Sign

Cocoa, "Lipton's Instant Cocoa," color-printed tin over cardboard, the dark background w/white & red lettering & a large portrait of a lady seated at a table w/a chocolate pot & holding up a cup, a picture of the package in the foreground, early 20th c., some fine scratches, 9 x 13 1/4" (ILLUS.)................................... **$201**

Early Smith Brothers Cough Drops Tin Sign

Cough drops, "Smith Brothers," long narrow rectangular embossed tin w/black & white portraits of the brothers at the ends flanking the black & white package, also printed in black "For That Cough - Famous Since 1847," multiple soft creases, framed, late 19th - early 20th c., 9 1/2 x 27 1/2" (ILLUS., top of page).......... **$288**

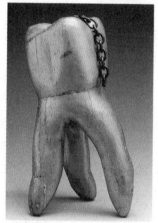

Early Figural Tooth Dentist's Sign

Dentist, trade sign, carved wood in the shape of a large molar, painted gold, w/attached hanging chain, multiple layers of gold paint, late 19th - early 20th c., 9" w., 15 1/2" h. (ILLUS.)......................... **$2,243**

Rare Early F.W. Woolworth Sign

Department store, "Hosiery - Department - F.W. Woolworth Co.," reverse-painted on glass, the red background w/textured gold leaf lettering, minor gold leaf loss, framed, 13 x 26 1/4" (ILLUS.) **$2,473**

Scarce Advance Thresher Co. Sign

Farm machinery, "Advance Engines, Threshers and Husker-Shredders," colorful lithograph on metal, scene of a young medieval man holding aloft a large red & gold Advance banner, red self-frame w/gold panel at the bottom reading "Advance Thresher Co. - Battle Creek, Mich. U.S.A.," very light scratches, late 19th - early 20th c., 18 x 26" (ILLUS.)..... **$1,232**

Early Case Threshing Machine Co. Sign

S

Rare Early Carter's Mucilage Sign

Farm machinery, "J.I. Case Threshing Machine Co. - Racine, Wis. U.S.A.," colorful lithograph on tin, large bald eagle perched atop a world globe, original wooden frame, very slight paint loss, late 19th - early 20th c., 24 x 33" (ILLUS., previous page)................................ **$616**

Early Self-Framed True Fruit Sign

Fruit, "True Fruit," self-framed color-printed tin, the fancy wide gold frame enclosing a rectangular scene of a table covered w/fresh fruit centered w/a small marble statue of a semi-nude maiden, some fly specking, minor fading, 25 x 38" (ILLUS.) .. **$270**

Glue, "Carter's Mucilage - The Great Stickist," colorful lithographed tin w/a comical scene of a Victorian gentleman seated & stuck to a crate of the product while a young black boy tries to pull him free, young white boy in background, ca. 1870s, nail holes at corners, light surface pitting & loss of color in lower corner, framed, 9 1/4 x 13 1/4" (ILLUS., top of page) **$3,738**

Early Porcelain Wrigley's Gum Sign

Gum, "Wrigley's Spearmint Gum," porcelain, long rectangular form w/a bright yellow background & two packages of gum, black wording reads "After Every Meal - Aids Digestion - Good for Teeth - Fine for

breath," early 20th c., professional repairs to two bends, 14 x 36" (ILLUS.) **$840**

Rare Colorful Hood Ice Cream Sign

Ice cream, "H.P. Hood" & Sons Ice Cream," colorful round porcelain design w/the red border printed in gold, the center w/a large head portrait of a dairy cow in a field, chips at mounting holes & in field, several old pieces of cellophane tape, ca. 1934, 30" d. (ILLUS.)................ **$3,738**

Early Hanover Fire Insurance Sign

Insurance, "Hanover Fire Insurance Co.," colorful chromolithograph, black wording across the top & bottom, a color emblem in the center w/a spread-winged eagle above a coat-of-arms flanked by seated classical figures, matted & framed, ca. 1860-70, 19 x 25" (ILLUS.) **$1,203**

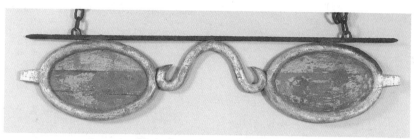

Early Optometrist Trade Sign

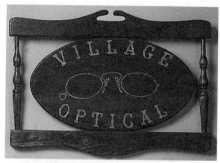

Old Village Optical Trade Sign

Optician, trade-type, two-sided, painted pine, a rectangular framework w/baluster-turned side spindles flanking a large oval painted in gold "Village Optical" & a pair of spectacles, old dark green & red varnished finish, 20th c., 27 1/2 x 39 1/2" (ILLUS.)... **$633**

Optometrist, trade-type, painted wood & wrought iron, double-sided, carved & gilded pine, designed as a large pair of spectacles suspended from a wrought-iron rod & chains, weathered surface, age cracks, late 19th c., 57 1/2" l., 24 1/4" h. (ILLUS., top of page) **$2,350**

Colorful Early Monitor Radiator Sign with Parlor Scene

Parlor stove, "The Monitor Radiator," color-printed tin, rectangular w/a large interior scene w/a large ornate parlor stove in the foreground & a Victorian lady standing near a table w/lamp in the background, Monitor Stove & Range Co., Cincinnati, late 19th c., some light creasing & flaking, some pitting, 13 3/4 x 19 1/2" (ILLUS.) **$805**

Rare Iver Johnson Revolver Cut-out Tin Sign

Revolvers, "Iver Johnson Revolver - Hammer The Hammer," colorful lithographed cut-out tin black open oval w/wording in white, centered by the cut-out design of one hand holding a revolver while the other hand hits the hammer w/a hammer, two minor soft bends, late 19th - early 20th c., 11 3/4 x 15 3/4" (ILLUS.).......... **$5,750**

Intricate Reverse-Painted Rockland Shoes Sign

S

Shoes, "Our Specialty Rockland Company's Gentlemen's Shoes - Popular Shoe House, Agents," intricate reverse-painted glass rectangular design, black ground w/fancy gold & silver lettering & a large gilt seated classical maiden on a flowering branch beside an urn at the right side, in a wide floral-molded gilt plaster frame, late 19th c., some minor lifting of reverse foil backing, 23 3/4 x 37 1/2" (ILLUS.)..... **$1,380**

Colorful Neon Poll Parrot Shoes Sign

Shoes, "Poll Parrot Shoes - For Boys and Girls," neon, a colorful design w/a large red, yellow & green parrot outlined in white neon tubing, a yellow moon background w/black below, near mint, ca. 1950, small chip at base, 24" h. (ILLUS.) **$2,875**

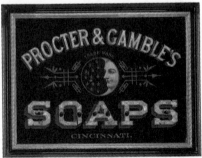

Fine Procter & Gamble Reverse-Painted on Glass Sign

Soap, "Proctor & Gamble's Soaps - Cincinnati," reverse-painted on glass, fancy lettering in red highlighted by foil & mother-of-pearl flank the company's crescent moon logo in the center, all on a black background, made by the Meuttman Co., Cincinnati, late 19th c., some areas of paint lifting & loss, framed, 21 1/2 x 29 1/2" (ILLUS.)..................... **$1,688**

Charming Star Soap Lithograph Sign

Soap, "Star Soap," color lithograph scene of a seated elderly gentleman holding his two grandchildren titled "Grand Pa's Pets," matted & framed, upper crease ending in small corner tear, late 19th c., 14 1/2 x 22" (ILLUS.)................................ **$891**

Unusual Dr. Swett's Root Beer Stein Sign

Soft drink, "Dr. Swett's Root Beer," die-cut tin model of a blue & grey stoneware stein w/wording at the rim & base, a soft bend, light pitting, early 20th c., 4 1/2 x 6" (ILLUS.)... **$230**

Rare Early Trolley Car Advertising Sign

Trolley car, "Take The Yellow Car to Niagara Falls - Round Trip 50¢ - Lockport and Ret. 60¢ - Saturday & Sunday 50 cts.," colorful lithograph w/a large central oval panel showing a late Victorian lady & a yellow trolley car in the background, green background w/white lettering, self-framed, several tears, late 19th - early 20th c., 20 x 27" (ILLUS.) **$1,436**

Rare Colorful Hickman-Ebbert Wagon Company Framed Signed

Wagons, "Hickman-Ebbert Wagon Company - Owensboro, Kentucky," color-printed self-framed tin, a scene showing a green wagon loaded w/supplies & pulled by horses behind a farmer helping a woman holding a basket of fruit descending a ladder in a tree, advertising for The Ebbert model in the upper left corner, scene titled "In The Shade of The Old Apple Tree," very minor scuffs, early 20th c., 25 1/2 x 37 1/2" (ILLUS.) **$2,875**

Washing soap, "Sunlight Zeep - Monkey Brand," color lithograph, a scene of an elegant Victorian lady dressed in blue examining an oversized package of the product, printed in Berlin, Germany for the Dutch market, two horizontal fold lines, framed, late 19th c., 14 1/2 x 19 1/2" (ILLUS., top next column) **$230**

Early Washing Soap Color Lithograph

I.W. Harper Sign with Charming Scene

Whiskey, "I.W. Harper Whiskey," color lithographed cardboard w/a scene of three small children gathered around their grandfather, one child reaching for a bottle of whiskey, dated 1904, in original wide flat gilt frame w/a narrow attached plaque reading "The Kind Your Grandfather Used," good colors, slight water damage in one corner, 23 1/2 x 35 1/2" (ILLUS.) **$2,300**

Fine Early Distillery Tin Sign

Whiskey distiller, "Thixton, Millet & Co. Distillers," color-printed on tin, rectangular detailed forest landscape w/a path leading past a log cabin w/a man representing Daniel Boone seated outside, wooden sign above the cabin door reads "Old Boone Distillery - First in Kentucky," copyrighted in 1904, scattered spots of pitting, framed, 14 x 22 1/4" (ILLUS., previous page)... **$1,265**

SODA FOUNTAIN COLLECTIBLES

The neighborhood ice cream parlor and drugstore fountain are pretty much a thing of the past as fast-food chains have sprung up across the country. Memories of the slower-paced lifestyle represented by the rapidly disappearing local soda fountain have spurred the interest of many collectors today. Anything relating to the soda fountains of old and the delicious concoctions they dispensed are much sought-after.

Colorful Early Soda Fountain Sign

Very Rare Chero Crush Syrup Dispenser

Scarce Ritz Ice Cream Figural Display Signs

Counter display signs, figural molded compostion, a standing figure of a young blond-haired girl or boy, each holding a huge ice cream cone, atop a stepped oval blue base molded w/advertising for Ritz Ice Cream reading "Ice Cream with a Facchino Cone," ca. 1930s, cracking in base of one, 22" h., pr. (ILLUS.) **$1,035**

Sign, "Golden Orangeade," color-printed cardboard, tall narrow rectangular shape w/a dark orange background, white, yellow & black wording, reads "Delicious 'True Fruit' Flavors" above two rows of oranges flanking the names of various flavors, the bottom printed "Drink Golden Orangeade," late 19th - early 20th c., framed, 13 1/2 x 27 1/2" h. (ILLUS., top next column)... **$805**

Syrup dispenser, "Chero Crush," ceramic, modeled as a large red cherry w/embossed gold script wording on the sides, molded cherry blossoms & leaves around the round base, metal pump mechanism on the top, early 20th c., 12" h. (ILLUS., middle next column) **$14,375**

Dr. Swett's Bottle-Shaped Dispenser

Syrup dispenser, "Dr. Swett's Original Root Beer - Boston, Mass.," stoneware, bottle-shaped w/dark brown upper half & grey lower half, metal spigot near base, two hairlines, spigot replaced, early 20th c., 22"h. (ILLUS.)... **$288**

Hires Root Beer Syrup Dispenser

Syrup dispenser, "Drink Hires - It is pure," ceramic, white waisted cylindrical shaped w/metal top pump mechanism, light discoloration on bottom, early 20th c., 14"h. (ILLUS.) **$403**

Fine Early Orange-Julep Syrup Dispenser

Syrup dispenser, "Drink Howel's Original Orange-Julep," ceramic, spherical orange top raised on white flaring round pedestal, top fitted w/a metal pump mechanism replacement plunger pump, early 20th c., 13 1/2"h. (ILLUS.).............. **$1,495**

Fine Early Cherry-Julep Syrup Dispenser

Syrup dispenser, "Drink Howel's Original Cherry-Julep," ceramic, spherical red top raised on white flaring round pedestal, top fitted w/a metal pump mechanism w/white porcelain ball handle, some wear to red, early 20th c., 14"h. (ILLUS.)......... **$1,955**

Scarce Liberty Root Beer Syrup Dispenser

Syrup dispenser, "Liberty Root Beer - Try A Stein - It's Fine - Richardson - Rochester, NY," ceramic, white spherical form w/blue, red & black wording, flaring pedestal base, metal pump mechanism on top w/cracked ceramic button, early 20th c., 13 1/2"h. (ILLUS.) **$4,888**

S

Barrel-shaped Magnus Root Beer Dispenser

Syrup dispenser, "Magnus Root Beer," ceramic, white barrel-shape w/black panel & gold wording, metal plunger on top marked "Sani-Kold Soda Fountains, Inc., Philadelphia, PA - Patent 10-13/25," bottom drilled for lamp, early 20th c., 14 1/2"h. (ILLUS.) **$288**

Smaller Orange-Crush Syrup Dispenser

Syrup dispenser, "Ward's Orange-Crush," ceramic, model of a large orange w/embossed black wording, green leaves & blossoms around the round base, metal top pump mechanism w/white porcelain ball handle, smaller version, early 20th c., 13"h. (ILLUS.) **$1,150**

SOUVENIR NOVELTIES

For well over a century travelers and tourists have been bringing home souvenirs of the sights they've seen. Since the early 20th century a great many novelty items have been offered, quite often produced in inexpensive stamped or cast pot metal. Today collectors are seeking out these vintage novelties preserved from the past.

Ste. Anne de Beaupre Souvenir Ashtray

Ashtray, cast metal, souvenir of Ste. Anne de Beaupre Basilica, Quebec, Canada, pierced name across the top, other small scenes along the bottom edge, 1940s (ILLUS.) **$15**

New York City Shell-Shaped Ashtray

Ashtray, silvered cast pot metal, souvenir of New York City, three shell-shaped dishes each w/a different scene including the Empire State Building, the Statue of Liberty & Coney Island, made in Japan, ca. 1950, 4 1/4" w. (ILLUS.) **$35**

Souvenir Badge from Ghost Town

Badge, stamped tin, "Honorary Marshal - Ghost Town - Lake George, N.Y.," printed in red & yellow, ca. 1950, 1 3/4" w. (ILLUS., previous page) **$6**

Royal Canadian Mounted Police Calendar

Calendar, metal, flip-style, souvenir of the Royal Canadian Mounted Police w/a color picture of a Mountie on the round top, made in Japan, ca. 1950, 3" h. (ILLUS.) **$15**

St. Lawrence Seaway Opening Coaster

Coaster, stamped metal, round, souvenir of the 1959 opening of the St. Lawrence Seaway, from Ontario, Canada, stamped w/the crest of Ontario & bust portraits of Queen Elizabeth II & Prince Phillip, 3 1/4" d. (ILLUS.) **$3**

Unusual Stork Club Souvenir Diaper Pin

Diaper pin, steel, souvenir of the Stork Club in New York City, 1930s, 3 1/4" l. (ILLUS.) **$60**

Florida Souvenir Drink Tray

Drink tray, souvenir of Florida, rectangular stamped metal w/six round compartments to hold glasses, each printed in color w/a different scene in Florida, black background w/gold trim, made in Japan, 1950s, 8 x 11" (ILLUS.) **$15**

Unusual Souvenir Frog Sponge Holder

Envelope wetting sponge holder, cast pot metal, model of a frog w/a sponge forming his stomach, the back stamped "Souvenir of Portland, Oregon" w/several scenes of the city, 1920s, 2 x 3" (ILLUS.) **$40**

The Sporting News Centennial Key Chain

Key chain, cast metal, "100th - The Sporting News - 1886-1986," 2" w. (ILLUS.) **$12**

S

S

Shakespeare Tercentenary Lapel Pin

Lapel pin, bronze, "New York City Shakespeare Tercentenary Celebration - 1616-1916," the front cast w/various symbols of the 16th century, the reverse cast w/a theatrical mask, 1 3/4" l. (ILLUS. of reverse) **$80**

1996 Atlanta Olympics Diving Medallion

Medallion, stamped metal, 1996 Atlanta Olympics "Diving Commemorative Olympic Sport Medallion," stamped w/the stats of the various U.S. spring board diving titles, on original card, 3 1/4 x 4" (ILLUS.) **$3**

Prime Ministers of Canada Commemorative Medallions

Medallions, stamped metal, Shell Gasoline premium, "The Prime Ministers of Canada 1867-1970 - Commemorative Medallions," each medallion w/a portrait of a

different Prime Minister, w/a separate album, each medallion 1 1/4" d., album 8 x 8 1/2", complete album (ILLUS.) **$50**

Early Souvenir of the Alaska Highway

Model of a Mile Post sign, cast metal painted white w/black lettering, souvenir of the Alaska Highway showing the first Mile Post at the beginning of the highway & listing mileage to other cities, on an octagonal base w/a chain fence, World War II era, 3 1/2" w., 11 1/2" h. (ILLUS.) **$100**

Early Souvenir of the Empire State Building

Model of the Empire State Building, cast metal w/gold finish, souvenir of a visit to the building, 1930s, 7 1/4" h. (ILLUS.) **$100**

McSorley's Old Ale House Perpetual Calendar 100th Anniversary Souvenir

Perpetual calendar, cast metal, reverse stamped "McSorley's Old Ale House - 15 East 7th St. - New York City - Over One Hundred Years Young," front marked "1954-1981" above an adjustable calendar dial showing days of the week for the years from 1954 to 1981, 1954, 1 3/4" w. (ILLUS., previous page) **$70**

Seattle Space Needle Souvenir Token

Token, stamped copper, pictures the Space Needle in Seattle w/the wording "I Was at the Top of the Space Needle," early 1970s, 1 1/2" l. (ILLUS.)................................. **$3**

S

1980s Spruce Goose Souvenir Spoon

Souvenir spoon, Howard Hughes' Spruce Goose souvenir, small image of the plane at the top above a small pendant showing the plane in flight, Long Beach, California, 1980s, 4" l. (ILLUS.) **$3**

Epcot Center World of Motion Souvenir Tray

Tray, "FutureWorld - World of Motion," stamped metal, oval, a colorful center scene of people going toward Walt Disney's Epcot Center, made by Fabcraft, Inc., New Jersey, 1982, 6 1/2" l. (ILLUS.) **$10**

Epcot Center The Land Souvenir Tray

Tray, "FutureWorld - The Land," stamped metal, oval, a colorful center scene of people going toward Walt Disney's Epcot Center, made by Fabcraft, Inc., New Jersey, 1982, 6 1/2" l. (ILLUS.)......................... **$10**

Washington Monument Thermometer

Thermometer, cast pot metal, model of the Washington Monument w/a glass thermometer up one side, 1930s, 5 1/2" h. (ILLUS.)... **$55**

SPICE CABINETS & BOXES

Ash Spice Cabinet with Name Plates

Cabinet, ash, a narrow rectangular top overhanging the upright case fitted w/two stacks of four small drawers w/a long drawer at the bottom, each drawer mounted w/a porcelain name plate & a small black turned knob, molded base, hanging rings at the top back edge, late 19th - early 20th c., 9" w., 11" h. (ILLUS.) **$196**

Rare Cherry 15-Drawer Spice Cabinet

Cabinet, cherry, a rectangular top slightly overhanging a case fitted w/four rows of three small square drawers above a bottom row of three larger drawers, small brackets at the sides & a molded flat base, each drawer w/a lid the raises when drawer opened, old finish, old edge wear & chip on lower back, 19th c., 10 1/4 x 21", 18 1/4" h. (ILLUS.) **$3,680**

Cabinet, painted pine, rectangular top above a case fitted w/three rows of four square drawers each above a single long drawer at the bottom, each drawer w/a turned wood yellow-painted knob & inscribed numbers, old green paint, square nail construction, 19th c., 6 3/8 x 18 1/2", 15" h. (ILLUS., top next column) **$1,265**

Fine Green-painted Spice Cabinet

Walnut Stepped Upright Spice Cabinet

Cabinet, walnut, a narrow rectangular top above a tall case composed of two rows of four small drawers each above two rows of three larger drawers each, the stepped out bottom section w/a pair of deep drawers, all drawers w/white porcelain pulls w/two missing, old finish, one lower corner molding replaced, 19th c., 8 1/4 x 15 1/2", 18 3/4" h. (ILLUS.) **$863**

SPORTS MEMORABILIA

Kentucky Derby Collectibles

1984 Coca-Cola Kentucky Derby Bottle

Bottle, 1984 Coca-Cola souvenir, red & white printed labels, full, returnable 10 oz. size (ILLUS., previous page) **$7**

1983 Coca-Cola Kentucky Derby Bottle

Bottle, Coca-Cola 1983 souvenir bottle, red & white printed labels, full, returnable 10 oz. size (ILLUS.)... **$7**

1974-76 Pepsi-Cola Kentucky Derby Bottle

Bottle, Pepsi-Cola 1974-76 commemorative, printed red, white & blue labels, full, 16 oz. size (ILLUS.)..................................... **$15**

Bottle, Royal Crown 1974-75 Kentucky Colonels commemorative bottle, printed red, white & blue labels, full, returnable 16 oz. size (ILLUS., top next column) **$10**

Bottle, Roycal Crown 100th Kentucky Derby commemorative, red, white & blue printed label, 1974, full, returnable 16 oz. size (ILLUS., middle next column) **$10**

Mirror, wall-type, advertising Miller Lite Beer, printed w/black, blue, green & red designs reading "Kentucky Derby 121 - Miller Lite," 1991, molded wooden frame (ILLUS., bottom next column) **$50**

Royal Crown 1974-75 Souvenir Bottle

Royal Crown 1974 Kentucky Derby Bottle

1995 Miller Lite - Kentucky Derby Mirror

S

S

1985 Kentucky Derby Pegasus Pin

Pin, 1985 Pegasus pin, plastic, dark green w/ gold (ILLUS.) **$6-8**

1998 Kentucky Derby Pegasus Pin

Pin, 1998 Pegasus pin, plastic, pink ground (ILLUS.).. **$3**

1990 Kentucky Derby Pegasus Pin

Pin, 1990 Pegasus pin, plastic (ILLUS.)............. **$4**

2000 Kentucky Derby Pegasus Pin

Pin, 2000 Pegasus pin, metal (ILLUS.) **$3**

100th Anniversary Kentucky Derby Commemorative Tray

Tray, oval, commemorative, "1875 Churchill Downs 1974 - 100th Running Kentucky Derby," color scene of Churchill Downs in the center, lists of all the winners down each side, accented w/red roses (ILLUS.)
.... **$20**

1966 Official Kentucky Derby Tumbler

Tumbler, 1966 Official Kentucky Derby model, glass printed in black, white & gold (ILLUS.) **$31**

1975 Official Kentucky Derby Tumbler

Tumbler, 1975 Official Kentucky Derby model, glass printed in black, white, red & yellow (ILLUS.) **$7**

STATUARY - BRONZE, MARBLE & OTHER

Bronzes and other statuary are increasingly popular with today's collectors. Particularly appealing are works by "Les Animaliers," the 19th-century French school of sculptors who turned to animals for their subject matter. These, together with figures in the Art Deco and Art Nouveau taste, are common in a wide price range.

Bronze

Equestrian Sculpture of Joan of Arc

Barye (Alfred), Joan of Arc, dressed in armor & seated astride a prancing steed while holding aloft a banner, raised on a rectangular base, signed, late 19th c., 34 3/4" h. (ILLUS.) **$3,840**

Ape On Gnu Bronze by Barye

Barye (Antoine-Louis), "Singe Monte Sur Un Gnou," (Ape astride a gnu), the large ape seated on a pranced gnu, on an oblong base, signed, France, second half 19th c., 9 1/8" h. (ILLUS.) **$22,800**

S

Chiparus Vested Dancer Sculpture

Chiparus (Demetre), "Vested Dancer," an exotic female dancer wearing a long-sleeved long gown w/decorative bodice & a close-fitted cap, her hands & head made of ivory, her outfit cold-painted, on a high stepped bronze onyx base, signed, ca. 1925, 21 1/2" h. (ILLUS.).... **$26,290**

Debut Sculpture of Youthful Mozart

Debut (Marcel), standing portrait of a youthful Mozart holding out his violin while plucking the strings, one foot resting on to books, on a rectangular base, signed, France, late 19th c., 22 3/4" h. (ILLUS.) ... **$2,880**

Fiot (Maximilien-Louis), a large crouching eagle astride a rockwork base, cast by Susse Freres, Paris, France, late 19th - early 20th c., 13" h. (ILLUS., top next column) **$2,880**

Fremiet (Emmanuel), "Chien Courant Blessé," (Injured Racing Dog), the seated animal w/head down licking at a bandaged leg, signed, France, last quarter 19th c., 10 1/4" h. (ILLUS., middle next column) **$7,800**

Eagle Bronze by Fiot

Fremiet Injured Racing Dog Sculpture

Gregoire "Amours Vainqueurs"

Gregoire (Jean-Louis), "Amours Vainqueurs," (The Conquering Loves), a group of three racing Cupids, one holding aloft a small torch, another a small heart, signed, France, late 19th c., 23 1/2" h. (ILLUS.) ... **$4,560**

Marble

Crawford Sculpture of "Babes in the Wood"

Crawford (Thomas), "Babes in the Wood,"
a young boy & girl stretched out asleep
on the ground, American sculptor working in Rome, dated 1854, 49" l., 18" h.
(ILLUS.).. **$14,400**

Fine Marble Sculpture of Peasant Girl

Gana (F.), figure of a young peasant girl
seated on a tall rock & holding a basket
of grapes on one arm, signed, Italy, late
19th c., 35" h. (ILLUS.)......................... **$15,600**

Fine Moreau Nymph & Putto Sculpture

Moreau (Mathurin), figure group of a
nymph seated on a rock w/a putto at her
feet, signed, France, late 19th c, 33" h.
(ILLUS.) **$16,800**

Rare Marble Sculpture of Ruth

Romanelli (Pasquale), figure of Ruth
gleaning, the kneeling woman wearing a
long loose robe & head scarf, holding a
cluster of wheat in her lap & another in
one hand, on an oblong base, signed,
Florence, Italy, second half 19th c., 45" h.
(ILLUS.).. **$28,800**

Italian Marble of Young Mother & Child

Vichi (Ferdinando), bust of mother & infant,
the young mother wearing a head scarf
& smiling down at her infant, on a socle
base, Florence, Italy, late 19th - early
20th c., overfall 22" h. (ILLUS.).............. **$4,800**

S

SYROCOWOOD

The Syracuse Ornamental Company of Syrcause, New York ("Syroco") pioneered the concept of molded wood decorative pieces, producing near-perfect replicas of hand-carving. In the words of the company's 1942 catalog: "Syrocowood possesses the rich beauty of choice hand-carved wood designs combined with practical utility." Whether book ends or brush holders, pen sets or picture frames, Syroco's household novelty items possess a charm all their own.

"Syrocowood" was a product born of necessity. In 1890 Adolph Holstein found his skills as an accomplished carved in great demand. The popularity of his ornately carved woodwork lead Holstein to hire additional master carvers and to found a new firm - Syroco. However, hand-carving was time consuming and only a limited number of orders could be accepted. Holstein's solution: create a master carving and a casting mold, then cast replicas of the master. Since each design required only one master carving both production and affordability were increased.

Although replicating the texture of carved wood, "Syrocowood" was actually composed of a compressed mixture of wood flour, waxes and resins. Sanding removed mold lines and each piece then received a multicolor decoration or a natural wood stain.

During Syroco's early years the demand was primarily for decorative furniture trim, with thousands of design options shown in the company catalogs. Syroco trim adorned everything from caskets to armchairs and often took the place of hand-carved moldings in home interiors.

Due to declining interest in this type of ornamentation, Syroco was forced to explore new product avenues. By the late 1920s the company was capitalizing on the radio age, becoming a primary supplier of radio speaker grilles, tuner knobs and cabinet trim. A second marketing push led to the products most sought after by today's collectors - wood-like novelty items which combined whimsical or heartwarming themes with practical everyday functions. Following its debut in the early 1930s, the Syroco novelty line soon included a wide range of items including ashtrays, bar trays, book ends, bottle openers, brush holders, clocks, coasters, coin trays, corkscrews, desk calendars, doorstops, dresser boxes, humidors, napkin rings, paperweights, pen sets, picture frames, pipe racks, plaques, statuettes, thermometers and tie racks.

Thanks to Syroco's mass production, consumers in the 1930s and '40s found themselves able to accessorize lavishly, yet affordably. In the words of Alexander E. Holstein, Jr., grandson of the company founder, Syroco provided "good product at a good price."

The popularity of Syroco soon gave rise to a host of imitators, including main competitor Burwood Products Co. ("Karv-Kraft") of Michigan. Among others were the Canadian firm, Durwood; Multi-Products ("Decor-A-Wood"), that specialized in licensed comic strip characters; Ornamental Arts & Crafts Co. ("Orn-A-Craft") and even a Syroco associate company, "Ornawood." The Syroco reputation, however, was pervasive and the term "syrocowood" became a generic, if inaccurate, term for every type of molded wood decorative object.

By the 1950s, Syrcoco had moved on to more profitable wall accessories such as sconces, shelves, plaques and mirrors often in gilt or bright colors. One of the company's best sellers at that time was the multi-rayed "Sunburst Clock," designed by Harry Laylon. The 1950s also saw a shift from the use of wood composite to an all-polymer blend. This meant pieces could be lighter, larger and sturdier. A primary example of this development is the Syroco molded lawn chair, found today in nearly every chain store.

Syroco appeals to collectors on several levels. For home decorators, the coloring of Syroco items blends well with any interior. The wood tones add a dimension of luxury and the fine detailing of the molded figures captures the flair and expressiness of the original master carvings.

For those with more than one collecting interest, Syroco pieces are wonderful crossover collectibles. Dog lovers will like those Syroco items featuring dogs, regardless of the function while corkscrew collectors will seek out any Syroco corkscrews, regardless of the design. For the cost-conscious, most Syrcoco products are very affordable, with many available in the $25-50 range. As the company's advertisements once stated: Syroco decorative items remain "ideal for elegant living and gracious giving."

Advisor for this category, Donald-Brian Johnson, is an author and lecturer specializing in Mid-Twentieth design. Photos are by Ray Hanson.

Ashtray, "Top Hat," 7 5/8" h. **$25-45**
Book end, "Horse & Shoe," 6 3/4" h. **$25-45**
Book end, "Owl & Books," 6 3/4" h. **$25-45**

Syrcocowood Town Crier Book End

Book end, "Town Crier," 6 1/4" h. (ILLUS.) .. **$25-45**
Bottle opener, "Mr. Pickwick" figural head
     top, 6 1/2" h. **$45-65**
Box, "Dachshund," 4 x 6" **$15-25**

Syrocowood Bulldog & Scottie Brush Holder

Brush holder, "Bulldog & Scottie," 7" h.
     (ILLUS.) **$25-45**
Brush holder, "Elephant by Palm," 7" h...... **$25-45**
Brush holder, "Hound Chasing Rabbit,"
     6" h. **$25-45**

Syrocowood Schooner Brush Holder

Brush holder, "Schooner," 4 x 5" (ILLUS.) .. **$25-45**

Standing Airedale Brush Holder

Brush holder, "Standing Airedale," 6" h.
     (ILLUS.) **$25-45**

Fruits & Vegetables Cigarette Box

Cigarette box, "Fruits & Vegetables,"
     4 x 5 1/2" (ILLUS.) **$15-25**
Clock, "Owl," by Lux, 5 1/4" h. **$175-225**
Coasters "Churn," set of 4, 4" d. **$45-65**
Corkscrew, "Golden Knight," 9 3/4" h.
     .... **$2,500-3,000**

S

Monk, Old Codger and Waiter Syrocowood Corkscrews with Non-Syrocowood Bar

Corkscrew, "Monk," figural monk head top, 8" h. (ILLUS. right with Old Codger & Waiter corkscrews and non-Syrcocowood bar) **$750-900**

Corkscrew, "Old Codger," figural old man head top, 8" h. (ILLUS. right with Monk and Waiter corkscrews and non-Syrocowood bar) **$100-125**

Corkscrew, "Waiter," figural waiter head top, 8" h. (ILLUS. center with Monk and Old Codger corkscrews and non-Syrocowood bar) **$125-225**

Corkscrew/opener, "Laughing Man," 6" h. **$320-425**

Doorstop, "Bulldog," 7" h. **$75-95**

Figurine, "Hollander," 5" h. **$25-35**

Figurine, "Mutt," dog, 2" h. **$15-35**

Frame, "U.S. Navy," 5 x 7" **$25-45**

Humidor, "Flying Cloud," 5 1/2" sq. **$35-55**

Paperweight, "World War II Jeep," 2 3/4 x 4" **$15-25**

Pen set, "Sea Captain," 6" h. **$25-35**

Plaque, "Last Supper," 8 1/4 x 14 1/2" **$45-55**

Plaque, "Red Riding Hood," 3 1/2 x 6" **$25-45**

Thermometer, "Baby Shoe," 3 1/2" l. **$25-45**

New York World's Fair Thermometer

Thermometer, "New York Wold's Fair," 1939-40, 5 1/2" h. (ILLUS.) **$25-45**

Thermometer, "Pirate," 6 1/4" h. **$25-45**

Tie rack, "Bandmaster," Ornawood............. **$25-45**

Tie rack, "Liberty Bell," 7 x 9" **$25-45**

TEDDY BEAR COLLECTIBLES

Theodore (Teddy) Roosevelt became a national hero during the Spanish-American War by leading his "Rough Riders" to victory at San Juan Hill in 1898. He became the 26th president of the United States in 1901 when President McKinley was assassinated. The gregarious Roosevelt was fond of the outdoors and hunting. Legend has it that while on a hunting trip soon after becoming president he refused to shoot a bear cub because it was so small and helpless. The story was picked up by a political cartoonist who depicted President Roosevelt, attired in hunting garb, turning away and refusing to shoot a small bear cub. Shortly thereafter, toy plush bears began appearing in department stores labeled "Teddy's Bear" and they became an immediate success. Books on the adventures of "The Roosevelt Bears" were written by Seymour Eaton and first published in newspapers under the pseudonym of Paul Piper. The four stories were then published in book form with Seymour Eaton noted as the author. The four books used four different illustrators for the artwork.

Early Brown Mohair Bear on Wheels

Bear on wheels, unjointed brown mohair bear w/black shoebutton eyes, black floss nose & mouth, center seam from nose to tail, shaved muzzle, felt pads on paws, mounted on pairs of small cast-iron wheels, wearing a brown leather collar w/pull chain, unmarked, late 19th - early 20th c., floss worn, 8 1/2" l. (ILLUS.) **$990**

Early White Mohair Teddy Bear

Teddy bear, Steiff-style, white mohair, joined arms & legs, black button eyes, brown needlework nose & mouth, bandaged hands, loss of some fur, split feet, early 20th c., 15" l. (ILLUS.) **$863**

TEXTILES

Coverlets

1850s Floral Medallions Coverlet

T

Decorative Red & Natural Jacquard Coverlet

Jacquard Coverlet with Eagles in Silver Dollar Designs

Jacquard, double woven, one-piece, tied Beiderwand type, birds feeding their young, handled urns w/pineapples & facing birds in the center, Christian & Heathen border, schoolhouse or church in corner blocks, unsigned, red & natural, good fringe, mid-19th c., 82 x 86" (ILLUS.) **$715**

Jacquard, double woven, two-piece, center field composed of large floral medallions, rose cluster borders & grapevine bottom border, signed "Manufacd By Jay A. Van Vleck Gallipolis, O," ca. 1850s, navy blue & white, minor wear, 80 x 92" (ILLUS., top next column) **$403**

Jacquard, double woven, two-piece, center field composed of round silver dollar-like medallions featuring a spread-winged eagle grasping arrow & surrounded by 26 stars, borders of stylized leaves & flowers & pairs of hearts, navy blue & white, overall wear & some staining, 73 x 84" (ILLUS., middle next column) **$316**

1860s Ohio Jacquared Coverlet

Jacquard, double woven, two-piece, Summer/Winter type, flower & strawberry medallions w/an eagle & tree border, corner block reads "Friedrich Boediker Orange T. .Hancock County Ohio 1867," in navy blue, red, green & natural, some wear & damage, 70 x 82" (ILLUS.) **$345**

Black & Red Jacquard Coverlet with Birds & Young & Flower-filled Urns

Jacquard, double woven, two-piece, the center w/rows of pairs of birds feeding their young & flower-filled urns & leafy scrolls, double & single Christian & Heathen border bands, large factory buildings on foot border, fringe on foot, black, red & natural, mid-19th c., minor fringe loss, 78 x 92" (ILLUS.) **$518**

Nice 1830s Colored Jacquard Coverlet

Jacquard, double woven, two-piece, the center w/rows of rose medallions, wide bird & tree border, corner block signed "John T. Williams, Mechincksburg, Pennsylvania 1834," red, blue & natural, 62 x 85" (ILLUS.).. **$633**

Jacquard Peace & Plenty Coverlet

Jacquard, double woven, two-piece, tied Biederwand type, field of multipointed star & medallion w/eight-petaled rosette, birds & trees border w/corner block marked "Peace and Plenty 1855," blue & natural, good fringe, faint overall discoloration, 72 x 90" (ILLUS.)........................... **$489**

Jacquard, double woven, two-piece, tied Biederwand type, the center w/rows of four-rose clusters & eight-petal rosettes, grapevine borders, corner block signed "Emanuel Meily - Lebanon - 1836 - P.

Colorful 1836 Rose Cluster & Rosette Jacquard Coverlet

Tice," navy blue, teal, red & natural, good fringe & colors, 76 x 92" (ILLUS.).............. **$546**

Needlework Pictures

Adelaide & Fonrose Needlework Picture

Adelaide and Fonrose, a romantic landscape scene w/a seated young man playing a flute as a young shepheress walks by, oval opening in border w/title below, watercolor, ink & silk thread on silk ground, old gilt gesso shadowbox frame, probably Massachusetts, 1800-10, sight 9 3/4 x 11 3/4" (ILLUS.)......................... **$1,020**

Nice Needlework of Classical Lady

Lady in landscape, wool, silk & watercolor on silk, a Classically attired woman holding an overflowing cornucopia in one

hand & a bundle of wheat in the other, standing in a field w/trees, hills & mountains in the distance, painted blue sky & tinted face, hair & hands, backing board signed "Mary Sutcliffe 1803," probably English, molded wood frame w/black reverse-painted glass mat, minor damage, 14 1/2 x 16 1/2" (ILLUS.) **$719**

Landscape with Border Needlework Picture

Landscape within border, a wide zigzag flowering vine border enclosing a landscape scene w/a young woman carrying a basket flanked by tall leafy trees, a house, flying birds & a flowering vine in the background, an oval floral wreath above enclosing the inscription "Rebecca Johns Sampler worked in the 10 year of her Age 1808," probably Pennsylvania, framed, sihght 13 1/4 x 17" (ILLUS.) **$1,800**

Early English Mourning Scene

Mourning scene, silk needlework, watercolor & pen & pink on silk ground, depicts a woman dressed in classical garb standing beside a tomb & spinkling it w/flowers, England, 1800-10, molded giltwood frame, sight 9 x 11" (ILLUS.) **$660**

Quilts

Rare Civil War Era Appliqued Album Quilt

Appliqued Album quilt, composed of 40 white cotton blocks appliqued w/printed & plain fabrics w/embroidery, trapunto & reverse-appliqued designs, the center block depicts a spread-winged eagle over an anchor, an American shield flanked by flags, crossed cannon & cannonballs, w/the stitched name & date "W.H. Wilson M.D. 1863," the presentation block surrounded by blocks depicting a Zouave soldier reclining in his tent, a New York State seal, eagles, flowers, hearts, leaves & fruit, many of the blocks signed w/the stitched & pen & ink signatures of the friends, family & makers of each block, one block signed w/the name of the town, "Bedford," the edges w/meandering budding vine borders, white cotton backing, minor toning & light stains, possibly Bedford, New York area, ca. 1863, 66 x 82" (ILLUS.) **$24,675**

Appliqued Carpenter's Wheel Quilt

Appliqued Carpenter's Wheel patt., repeating design of wheels in dark green,

red & cream cotton on a white ground quilted w/feathered plumes, appliqued leafy vine border, initialed in one corner "W...," minor wear, 76 x 86" (ILLUS.) **$460**

Appliqued Cockscomb & Urns Quilt

Appliqued Cockscomb & Urns patt., composed of four large red, grey & yellow cockscombs surrounding floral wreath & bordered on four sides w/a matching floral vine, hand-quilted w/hearts & rosettes, visible pencil lines, narrow red binding & white backing, few small spots, 19th c., 79 x 84" (ILLUS.) **$305**

Rare Early Baltimore Appliqued Quilt

Appliqued Double Six-Point Star & Floral patt., pieced & appliqued w/patterned chintz & printed calicos on a white cotton ground, central design of a six-point star surrounded by another six-point star & fouir triangles interspersed w/& enclosed by cut-out floral, urn & vine chintz designs stuffed & appliqued to the white ground, floral & outline quilting, white cotton backing, Baltimore, ca. 1842, minor toning & scattered light stains, 125 x 134" (ILLUS.) **$18,800**

North Carolina Lily & President's Wreath Quilts

Appliqued North Carolina Lily patt., pieced & appliqued w/34 white blocks set on the diagonal w/red & green printed cotton flower clusters, quilted w/floral, diagonal & outline stitches, lower corners shaped to fit a four-poster bed, white cotton backing, probably third quarter 19th c., toning, minor stains, 86 x 87" (ILLUS. bottom with President's Wreath quilt) **$764**

Appliqued President's Wreath patt., pieced & appliqued w/red, green & yellow printed cotton on a white ground, composed of nine blocks w/wreaths of four red flowers w/reverse-appliqued yellow centers & 12 buds & green leaves, enclosed in an undulating budding vine border, feather, diamond & outline quilting, white cotton backing, late 19th c., minor toning, scattered light stains, 86" sq. (ILLUS. top with North Carolina Lily quilt) **$2,350**

Amish Bars Pattern Pieced Quilt

Pieced Bars patt, composed of long alternating bars in black & dark blue, quilted ground, Amish, probably Holmes County, Ohio, ca. 1900-30, 69 x 73" (ILLUS., previous page)... **$1,800**

Colorful Stars Upon Stars Pieced Quilt

Pieced Stars Upon Stars patt., composed of cotton prints in red, green & yellow on a plain ground, nicely hand-quilted in diamonds & feathered wreaths, signed in red embroidery "L M K 1893," minor staining, 88 x 90" (ILLUS.) **$604**

Windmill Variation Pieced Quilt

Pieced Windmill variation patt., composed of early printed cottom blocks in shades of brown, tan, blue, back, deep red & pink, hand-sewn & quilted, machine bound, slight staining, few areas of damage, 80 x 94" (ILLUS.)........................ **$403**

Samplers

Fine Early Massachusetts Sampler

Alphabet, landscape & florals, silk on linen, a tall rectangular central panel w/an alphabet above the inscription "Mary Kendall's work wrought in the thirteenth year of her age," above a group of trees, pots of flowers, birds & a mother & child centered by a three-story building, the outer wide border composed of florals & a chain link border, in bright shades of light blue, pink, gold, green, cream & black, Middlesex County, Massachusetts, early 19th c., some discoloration to ground, mounted on board in old or original giltwood frame, 17 1/2 x 21" (ILLUS.) **$6,038**

Sampler with Alphabets & Cornucopia

Alphabets & flower-filled cornucopia, silk on silk, the upper half w/rows of three alphabets in different sizes & designs above the inscription, a large flower-filled cornucopia at the bottom, all within a

T

T

wide leaf & blossom border band, worked by Mary A., Gilmer, Greensboro, 1842, sight 17 x 18" (ILLUS.) **$1,200**

Sampler with Alphabets & Landscape

Alphabets & landscape, silk on linen, a large square center panel w/rows of alphabets above a landscape w/two facing two-story houses centered by willow trees & a flower-filled urns, signed "Sara Ann Fortner (?) 1816," meandering flowering vine border band, good colors of blues, greens, golds & tans on a clean ground, minor holes to ground on one edge, modern frame, 18 1/2 x 19" (ILLUS.) **$610**

Very Rare Colonial American Sampler

Alphabets & landscape, silk on linen, the upper half composed of several rows of various alphabets above the inscription "Hannah Pearly - Born August at Haverhill Fifth day 1777," above a landscape across the bottom featuring a courting couple in 18th c. dress flanked by a fruit-

ing tree & urn of flowers accented by animals, birds & stag, Massachusetts, sight 10 x 13" (ILLUS.)................................... **$70,250**

Early New Jersey Sampler

Alphabets, landscape & pious verse, silk on linen, rowss of alphabets across the top above a central landscape of a two-story house w/a tall tree & flower-filled urn & birds beside it, a pious verse & inscription below w/stylized floral clusters at the bottom, all within a meandering floral vine, worked by Polly Bishop, Cumberland County, New Jersey, 1815, framed, sight 11 1/2 x 16 1/2" (ILLUS.)...... **$720**

Early Ohio Sampler with Alphabets

Alphabets & long inscription, silk thread in shades of tan, ivory & green on loosely woven linen, row of various sized alphabets in the upper half above the vine-framed inscription "Elizabeth Selby aged

16 AD 1835 W.L. B.C. Ohio, Inst'ss Gratia Webber" (West Liberty, Butler County), meandering grapevine border, a few small holes & repaired corner, early narrow walnut frame w/gilt liner, 15 x 19 3/4" (ILLUS.)... **$1,150**

Nice Early Signed & Dated Ohio Sampler

Alphabets, numerals & pious verse, silk on linen, the top half w/rows of alphabets & numerals above a flowering wreath inclosing a pious verse & signed "Elizabeth M. Malin born December 24th 1805, Steubenville February 18th 1826," made at the Steubenville Female Academy, accompanied by a family history, tintype of maker included, modern gold frame, small hole on bottom edge, 14 x 18 1/2" (ILLUS.)... **$2,185**

1827 Alphabets & Pious Verse Sampler

Alphabets, pious verse, flowers, baskets, butterflies & crowns, silk on linen, a large central rectangle below bands of

alphabets & enclosing a band of crowns & butterflies above a pious verse over various flowers & flower baskets, delicate flowering vine border band, signed "Amy S. Peirce 1827," possibly southeastern Pennsylvania, modern gold wood frame, 14 1/2 x 17 1/2" (ILLUS.).......................... **$1,840**

Rare New Hampshire Sampler

Alphabets, pious verse & landscape, silk on silk, top rows of alphabets above a long pious verse over a large detailed landscape featuring a two-story brick home w/a picket fence joining it to a small barn, large fruit trees & dovecote on a post in the yard, inscription across the bottom, all within a wide meandering leafy vine border, worked by Martha Jane Fowler, Portsmouth, New Hampshire, 1835, framed, sight 17 1/2 x 21" (ILLUS.)........ **$26,400**

Early Sampler with Landscape Scene

Landscape, alphabets & pious verse, silk threads on linen, an arched reserve at the top enclosing a landscape w/two

T

T

houses & trees above five rows of alphabets, a pious verse &, across the bottom, fruiting plants, signed "Selinda Fales Holden Aged 10 Year," enclosed by a sawtooth border, Massachusetts, ca. 1812, framed, minor toning & fading, 16 1/4" sq. (ILLUS.)................................ **$3,819**

Signed Sampler with Large Landscape

Landscape, flowers, trees & urns, thin wool thread on linen, a broad landscape across the bottom w/a two-story brick house by a field w/figures & sheep flanked by threes, pairs of stags, threes, urns of flowers, fruit trees & flower clusters above the landscape & below the inscription "M.A. Renouf Jersey 1840," meandering floral vine border, done in reds, greens, browns & creams, some stains, red & black-grained early frame, possibly England, 29 1/4 x 29 5/8" (ILLUS.) **$1,380**

Sampler with Verse & Large Mansion

Pious verse, building & varied plants & animals, silk & wool thread on linen, a vining rose border band enclosing a central pious verse w/a large two-story brick mansion flanked by trees w/further trees & pots of flowers above, signed "Martha Bowden, Work 1833," in shades of red, pink, ivory, blue, brown & green, some staining & minor color bleeding, in molded frame w/old black paint, 22 x 22 1/2" (ILLUS.).. **$1,035**

Finely Detailed 1868 Sampler

Pious verse & figures, animals, houses & florals, silk thread on linen, a narrow floral sprig border around pairs of designs including large baskets of flowers, a bird in tree, a cottage & small leafy trees, centered by two urns w/flowers above a shepherd & shepherdess flanking a flowering bush w/a small dog beside each & two sheet below, all above a rectangular panel w/the verse titled "Humility" & signed "Catherine Humphrey 1868 Aged 9 Years," panel further surrounded by trees, baskets of fruit & birds, in muted shades of gold, browns & blue, some stains & damage along the edge, in original bird's-eye maple frame w/gilt liner, 18 1/2 x 21 3/4" (ILLUS.) **$1,150**

Pious verse, flowers, baskets, fruit & butterflies, silk thread on linen, a long pious verse at the top above large pairs of flower-filled urns centered by a large basket of fruits above the inscription "Hannah Lewsey December 31, 1844," minor stains, framed, 16 5/8" sq. (ILLUS. right with larger sampler with pious verse, top next page).. **$374**

Pious verse, flowers, birds, trees & urns, finely stitched silk thread on line, a long pious verse across the top above rows of designs including strawberries, tulips, parrots, small crowns, flowers in pots, meandering floral vine border, inscribed "Louisa M. Daniel, Aged 14 years 1832," small holes & stains w/a stitched repair, framed, possibly English, 17 1/2 x 19 3/8" (ILLUS. left with small sampler with pious verse, top next page) **$546**

Two Samplers with Pious Verses & Various Designs

T

Sampler with Pious Verse & Designs

1824 Sampler Showing Rehoboth Chapel

Pious verse, flowers & figures, wool & silk threads on linen, a pious verse at the top above a rectangle enclosing "Jane Irwin. 1823 - Mullavilla School," a vining floral border & scattered designs including a peacock, crowns, flowers & a man wearing a large brown hat, possibly England, minor thread loss, darkening of ground, in older frame, 18 x 20" (ILLUS.)................ **$460**

Pious verse, house & baskets of flowers, finely worked silk thread on linen, a pious verse at the top center flanked by small flowerheads & flower-filled urns & baskets above a zig-zag diamond reserve surrounding a two-story structure titled "Rehoboth Chapel," moss rose clusters at outside corners flanked by long narrow pointed panels, two large flower-filled baskets in the bottom corners, signed by Hannah Bowen, 1824, staining to ground, 15 1/2 x 16 1/4" (ILLUS., top next column).. **$1,035**

Sampler with Flowers & Pious Verses

Pious verses & flower clusters, silk on silk, a wide top band composed of three large colorful leafy flower clusters above a large pious verse flanked by delicate flowering vines above another band of flower clusters & birds over a rectangular panel enclosing a smaller verse flanked by very large flower sprigs, pink border band, worked by Jane Bailey, 1823, 14 x 16" (ILLUS., previous page) **$7,800**

Stevengraphs

This term is used for small, multicolored silk pictures woven on a modified Jacquard loom. The technique was developed by Thomas Stevens of Coventry, England and was introduced in 1863. As well as English scenes, a number of designs were produced to appeal to the American market. Stevengraphs were popular until about World War I with some still in production as late as 1940. Collectors should remember that other English firms and factories in Switzerland also produced similar silk images but these are not true "Stevengraphs."

Declaration of Independence Stevengraph

Print, "Signing of the Declaration of Independence - July 4th, 1776," matted & framed, images 2 1/2 x 7" (ILLUS.) **$118**

THEOREMS

During the 19th century, a popular pastime for some ladies was theorem painting, or stencil painting. Paint was allowed to penetrate through hollow-cut patterns placed on paper or cotton velvet. Still life compositions, such as bowls of fruit or vases of flowers, were the favorite themes, but landscapes and religious scenes found favor among amateur artists who were limited in their ability and unable to do freehand painting. Today these colorful pictures, with their charming arrangements, are highly regarded by collectors.

Theorem of Fruits in Wire Basket

Basket of fruit, watercolor on velvet, a large looped wire basket piled high w/fruits including grapes, plums, peach, pear & apple some stains & surface wear, framed, 19th c., 21 1/2 x 25 1/4" (ILLUS.) **$1,840**

Basket of fruit, watercolor on velvet, a oval yellow straw basket w/wrapped rim & base filled w/large fruits including grapes, plum, apple & pear, basket rests on fern leaves, molded black frame w/gilt liner, spotted stains, 9 x 10" (ILLUS. left with fruit cluster theorem, bottom of page) **$633**

Two Early Theorems with Fruit Designs

Bowl of Fruit Velvet Theorem

Bowl of fruit, watercolor on velvet, a long low bowl filled w/various berries & fruits w/leaves, in period molded gilt & faux bois frame, unsigned, toning, foxing, 7 7/8 x 11 3/8" (ILLUS.)............................ **$1,175**

Compote of Fruit Theorem

Compote of fruit, watercolor on card, a low-footed crystal bowl filled to overflowing w/colorful fruit including grapes, apple, pear, peach, cherries & strawberries, dark green leaves, 19th c., toning & slight stains, framed, 8 1/2 x 11" (ILLUS.) **$823**
Fruits, watercolor on velvet, a cluster of fruits including purple grapes, peaches & strawberries, soft colors, giltwood rectangular frame w/reverse-painted black liner, wear, 9 1/2 x 11 1/2" (ILLUS. right with basket of fruit theorems, bottom previous page)... **$288**

Fine Theorem of Scattered Fruits

Fruits, watercolor on velvet, overall design of scattered fruits including a half of a watermelon, cantaloupe, grapes, strawberries & pears, good color, velvet darkened, nice molded pine frame, 21 1/4 x 27 1/4" (ILLUS.)......................... **$2,185**

Dated Vase of Flowers Theorem

Vase of flowers, watercolor & gouache on paper, a pale blue bulbous baluster-form vase w/side handle holding a large bouquet of various flowers in shades of rose, blue, yellow & white, signed along the bottom edge "By S.A. Patee. 1847," in period wood veneered frame, toning, light stains, 9 3/4 x 13 3/4" (ILLUS.).......... **$323**

TOBACCIANA

Although the smoking of cigarettes, cigars & pipes is controversial today, the artifacts of smoking related items - pipes, cigar & tobacco humidors, and cigar & cigarette lighters - and, of course, the huge range of advertising materials are much sought after. Unusual examples, especially fine Victorian pieces, can bring high prices. Here we list a cross section of Tobacciana pieces.

Miscellaneous

Rare English Sterling Cigar Box with Engraved Map on the Cover

Cigar box, sterling silver, novelty-type, low rectangular form, the top w/an engraved roadmap of "Canada - U.S.A. - Mexico and West Indies," a sliding element indicating distances between various locations, ebonized wood interior, mark of Asprey & Co., Ltd, London, England, 1936, 8 x 12", 2 1/4" h. (ILLUS.) **$26,290**

TOYS

Early Iron Cigar Branding Machine

Cigar branding & printing machine, elaborate cast-iron hand-cranked apparatus w/a wooden ramp leading to brass & cast-iron drums that would attach to a kerosene heat source to personalize cigars, made by Universal, black frame w/brass plaque marked "McIndoe & Streider Mfg. Co., Boston - 216," paint flaking, missing one brass guide, couple of small replacement parts, early 20th c., 14 x 17", 14" h. (ILLUS.) **$575**

Columbian Exposition Tobacco Jar

Tobacco jar, cov., a cylindrical clear glass body w/cut-outs around the base & swirls engraved around the sides, fitted w/a domed & lobed sterling silver cover w/enameled flowers & a jasper boss, jar w/a silver-gilt neck band, silver marked by Tiffany & Co, New York, New York, made for the 1893 Chicago Columbian Exposition & w/the exposition mark, 7 3/4" h. (ILLUS.) **$9,600**

Rare Dent Tri-Engine Air Express Plane

Airplane, cast iron biplane, "Air Express" & red stars cast on top of wings, blue body w/three black & nickel-plated propellers, white rubber tires w/wooden hubs, Dent, all-original, late 1920s, 12 1/4" wingspan (ILLUS.) **$7,800**

Fine Kenton Air Mail Airplane toy

Airplane, cast iron biplane, "Air Mail" cast on top of wings, green & yellow body w/nickel-plated propeller & solid metal wheels, Kenton Hardware, all-original, late 1920s, 8" wingspan (ILLUS.).......... **$1,840**

Scarce "Lindy" Biplane by Hubley

Airplane, cast iron biplane, "Lindy" cast on top of wings, blue body w/black & nickel-plated engine & propeller & solid metal wheels Hubley, all-original, late 1920s, celebrating Lindbergh flight, 10" wingspan (ILLUS.)... **$2,013**

metal wheels, Vindex, 1930s, old paint restoration, 8" l. (ILLUS.)......................... **$1,495**

Friction-Action Air Force Bomber

Airplane, tinplate, friction operation, model of a four-engine U.S. Air Force bomber, grey w/red trim, printed on body "United States Air Force - BK250," Japan, 1950s, 14 1/2 x 18 1/2" (ILLUS.)............................ **$144**

Bandi 1957 Ford Thunderbird

Automobile, 1957 Ford Thunderbird, molded plastic, yellow body w/red trim, clear plastic windshield, white wall tires, chrome bumpers & grill, trunk opens, Bandi, 1950s, restored paint, 11 1/2" l. (ILLUS.) **$345**

Hubley Chrysler Airflow in Green

Automobile, cast iron, Chrysler Airflow, green body w/nickel trim, white rubber tires, battery-operated headlights, Hubley, 1930s, some paint wear, 7 3/4" l. (ILLUS.) **$1,610**

Scarce 1930s Vindex Coupe

Automobile, cast iron, coupe w/rumble seat, dark green body & spoked silvered

Fine Arcade Model T Touring Sedan

Automobile, cast iron, Model T touring sedan, black body w/silver driver, black & silver spoked metal wheels, Arcade, 1920s, fine original paint w/one tire repainted, 6 1/4" l. (ILLUS.)........................... **$748**

Early Red Devil Touring Car

Automobile, cast iron, "Red Devil" touring car, red body & yellow metal spoked wheels, complete w/driver & passenger, probably by Kenton Hardware, ca. 1910-20, overall paint wear, passenger replaced, 8 3/4" l. (ILLUS.)........................... **$575**

Scarce 1930 Arcade Reo Coupe

Automobile, cast iron, Reo coupe, yellow body w/red rim, black running boards, red metal spoked wheels w/white rubber tires, Arcade, ca. 1930, old paint restoration, 9" l. (ILLUS.)................................... **$3,163**

T

Dark Blue & Black Kenton Sedan

Automobile, cast iron, sedan w/dark blue
body & black running boards, solid metal
red & silver tires, original driver, Kenton
Hardware, original condition w/slight
paint wear, 1920s, 8 1/4" l. (ILLUS.) **$2,645**

Fine Kenton Hardware Blue Sedan

Automobile, cast iron, sedan w/light blue
body & black running boards, solid metal
tires, no driver, Kenton Hardware, original condition w/some paint wear, 1920s,
8 1/2" l. (ILLUS.) **$2,760**

1930s Kilgore Stutz Bearcat Coupe

Automobile, cast iron, Stutz Bearcat
coupe, yellow body w/green & black running boards, solid metal silvered wheels,
Kilgore, 1930s, overall paint wear
w/some touch up, 10 1/4" l. (ILLUS.) **$920**

Very Rare Hubley Blue & Black Packard

Automobile, cast-iron, Packard sedan &
driver w/light blue body & black roof &
running board, white & blue metal tires,
opening doors & hood lifts to expose a
12-cylinder motor, some paint wear &
restoration, weld repair to frame under
motor, Hubley, early 20th c., 11 1/2" l.
(ILLUS.) **$10,063**

Unusual Automobile-Airplane Toy

Automobile-airplane, pressed steel, friction operation, a long red sedan auto fitted w/wings at the hood & w/rear tail fins,
propeller at front grille, U.S. Zone
Germany, ca. 1950, some surface rust,
one wing inoperative, 8" l. (ILLUS.) **$300**

Battery-operated Racer with Box

Battery-operated, "Indianapolis 500 Racer," tinplate racecar in silver & red w/red
& blue printing w/automatic jacks to lift
car, made in Japan for Sears of Canada,
w/original box, 1950s, 15 1/2" l. (ILLUS.)... **$403**

Battery-operated Pond Boat Cruiser

Battery-operated, pond boat, sleek metal
cruiser w/a white & red body & plastic
windshield, hatch lifts to reveal decal
reading "T.W.T.P.A.," Ito, Japan,
1950s, some chips & paint touch up,
18" l. (ILLUS.) **$345**

Unusual Early Clockwork Theater Toy

Clockwork theater, wooden frame enclosing a diorama w/four small ballerinas twirling around on a mirrored stage set w/a female figure on a swing above, color-printed stage opening w/ornate detailing, possibly American-made by Ives, ca. 1870s-80s, 10 x 11" (ILLUS.)..................... **$805**

Unusual Hand-Carved Wood Delivery Wagon with Driver & Horses

Delivery wagon, hand-made wooden horse-drawn model, the deep wagon painted black w/red trim & gold & red lettering reading "Lead and Glass Warehouse," also hand-stencilled "J.B. Robinson 31 Moor Lane - Express Van," driven by a papier-mâché gentleman w/burlap & felt clothing, two light brown carved wood horses w/real hair tails & manes, on red spoked wheels w/black striping, w/original tin bucket hanging from bottom, hinged back gate, some missing pieces, cracks & some repairs, late 19th - early 20th c., 30" l., 16" h. (ILLUS.)................. **$2,415**

Early Jacrim Ride-On Wooden Delivery Wagon

Delivery wagon, ride-on type, carved wood, red-sided wagon w/flat orange board top

& yellow wheels, sides stenciled "Heavy Teaming," pulled by four brown horses w/"Jacrim" decals on hind ends, wood plank seat & front steering bar w/hand grip, early 20th c., Jacrim w/the precursor of Keystone, one wheel cracked, various chips & scratches, few repairs to legs, 9 1/2 x 10 1/4", 47" l. (ILLUS.).................... **$460**

Arcade International Dump Truck

Dump truck, cast iron, dark green International truck w/dark green cab & dump bed, white rubber tires w/red spokes, w/drivers, lever by window releases dump bed, Arcade, 1930s, missing spring steel under bed, worn rubber tires, 10 1/2" l. (ILLUS.)...................................... **$690**

Early Arcade Mack Dump Truck

Dump truck, cast iron, early Mack truck in grey w/cast-iron spoked wheels, pressing lever on cab roof activates T-rod & raises dump bed, w/driver, Arcade, ca. 1920s, 12" l. (ILLUS.)................................ **$316**

Arcade International Harvester Truck

Dump truck, cast iron, International Harvester w/orange body & solid metal orange & white wheels, open cab w/driver, rare color, Arcade, ca. 1920s, overall paint wear, 10 1/2" l. (ILLUS.)................ **$2,300**

T

T

Early Pratt & Letchworth Horse-drawn Ladder Wagon

Fire horse-drawn ladder wagon, cast iron, a high delicate frame in green w/spoked red metal wheels, red ladders, painted front & rear firemen, pulled by two white horses, Pratt & Letchworth, late 19th - early 20th c., figures replaced, 23 1/2" l. (ILLUS.)................................... **$1,380**

Hubley No. 126 Horse-drawn Ladder Wagon

Fire horse-drawn ladder wagon, cast iron, No. 126, a long openwork white carriage w/a rack w/yellow ladders, in red metal spoked wheels, two firemen, pulled by two black & a white horse on tiny wheels, Hubley, early 20th c., 33" l. (ILLUS.)......... **$690**

Early Harris Horse-drawn Pumper Wagon

Fire horse-drawn pumper wagon, cast iron, a large silver boiler raised on red open-spoked wheels, red-suited driver, drawn by two white & one black horse on tiny wheels, paint wear, Harris, late 19th - early 20th c., 22 1/2" l. (ILLUS.)............ **$1,840**

Dent Horse-drawn Fire Pumper Wagon

Fire horse-drawn pumper wagon, cast iron, black boiler & frame on red spoked wheels, two firemen, pulled by a white & black horse on a tiny wheel, fine paint, Dent, late 19th - early 20th c., 12 1/2" l. (ILLUS.).................................... **$460**

Fine Early Ives Horse-Drawn Ladder Wagon

Fire ladder wagon, cast iron, "Phoenix," black long ladder wagon w/red metal wheels, two firemen, pulled by a white & black horse on a tiny wheel, includes ladders, buckets & axes in the rear, Ives, late 19th - early 20th c., 27" l. (ILLUS.)... **$1,320**

Fine Early Ives Fire Patrol Ladder Wagon

Fire patrol ladder wagon, cast iron, "Phoenix," white & red wagon on red wheels, two red figures, pulled by a white & black horse on a tiny wheel, Ives, ca. 1890s, minor repair to horses, figures replaced, 21" l. (ILLUS.)... **$690**

Early Ives Phoenix Fire Pumper Wagon

Fire pumper wagon, cast iron, "Phoenix," black wagon w/gold trim & black fireman & rear attendant, on red metal wheels, pulled by a white & black horse on a tiny wheel, ca. 1890s, horse repainted, some replaced parts, 18 1/2" l. (ILLUS.).............. **$690**

Cast-iron Football Kicker Toy

Football kicker, cast-iron standing figure of a football player dressed in red & orange, one hinged leg kicks footbal w/lever turned, on a rectangular green tin base, early 20th c., 7" l., 8" h. (ILLUS., previous page) **$460**

Unusual "Harvard Kicker" Mechanical Toy

Football kicker, "Harvard Kicker," metal figure of a young man wearing a red Harvard jersey posed to kick a football, cocking leg & pressing lever activates legs, wearing brown pants & red painted socks, mounted on a small round cast-iron base marked "Pat. July 3rd 1900," w/original wooden dovetailed box w/label & directions for use, player w/face corrosion, some chipping to kicking leg & tin hands, tear & wear on pants, leg does not stay cocked, 8 3/4" h. (ILLUS.) **$1,265**

Early Arcade Mack Gasoline Tank Truck

Gasoline tank Mack truck, cast iron, red tank & open cab w/driver, on small spoked red metal wheels, cast "Gasoline" on the tank, Arcade, ca. 1920s, some paint wear, 13"l. (ILLUS.) **$690**

Rare Hubley Orange Tank Truck

Gasoline tank truck, cast iron, Mack-type w/orange body & spoked metal wheels,

open cab w/driver, Hubley, ca. 1920s, 9" l. (ILLUS.) **$2,990**

Very Rare Brass Inter Urban Electric Trolley

Inter urban trolley, brass, Carlisle & Finch one-gauge, electric, side embossed "Electric Railway," all-original, simulated controller at one end that operates the trolley & steps, brass wheels, cast trucks w/original below-floor motor, wooden base, early 20th c., 4 x 19", 6 1/4"h. (ILLUS.) **$5,750**

Hubley Milk Delivery Truck

Milk delivery truck, cast iron, white body w/red decals on back reading "Borden's Milk - Cream," metal spoked wheels w/white rubber tires, Hubley, 1920s, overall paint wear, 8" l. (ILLUS.) **$1,840**

Hubley Harley Davidson Motorcycle

Motorcycle & rider, cast iron, green cycle & rider w/pink face & handes, white rubber tires, "Harley Davidson" in gold on side of tank, Hubley, 1930s, some paint chipping & rust, tires worn, 6 1/4" l. (ILLUS.)............ **$403**

Rare Yonezawa 98 Champion's Racer

Racecar, tinplate, friction operation, white body w/red flames printed "98 - Champion's Racer," tin driver, black rubber tires w/tin hubs, Yonezawa, Japan, ca. 1950s, rust discoloration to arm of driver & helmet, 19" l., 7" h. (ILLUS.) **$2,415**

Fine Painted Victorian Rocking Horse

Rocking horse on rockers, painted wood, painted dapple grey body w/leather ears & tack including a saddle, horsehair mane & tail, tack eyes, very long rockers & central platform in dark green w/yellow accents, some wear, 19th c., 52" l., 29" h. (ILLUS.) **$1,840**

Early Rocking Horse Seat on Rockers

Rocking horse seat on rockers, painted pine, long rockers mounted w/a low framework supporting a low-backed chair seat, a silhouetted horse head at the front, original gold floral stenciling & red striping on black, old, possibly original cloth seat, some wear, w/a whip, 19th c., 13 x 46 1/2", 21 1/2" h. (ILLUS.) **$1,265**

Rare Hubley Friendship Seaplane

Seaplane, cast iron biplane, "Friendship" cast on top of wings, yellow body w/black & nickel-plated propeller, pontoons w/rubber-rimmed metal wheels, Hubley, all-original w/pull string & wire clicker simulating engine noise, ca. 1930, 12 3/4" l. (ILLUS.) **$6,325**

Painted Pine Victorian Child's Sled

Sled, child's size, painted & decorated pine, wooden platform w/applied iron straps on runners, the to center panel painted orange w/blue, green & yellow stenciled flowers & leaves, side boards unpainted, late 19th c., repair, losses to iron straps, 15 1/4 x 34", 12 1/8" h. (ILLUS.) **$588**

Early Hubley 5 Ton Stake Truck

Stake truck, cast iron, yellow back & cab w/driver on small red spoked metal wheels, cast "5 Ton Truck" on side of back, w/original wire bumper, Hubley, ca. 1920s, some ware, replaced tailgate, 17" l. (ILLUS.) **$805**

1930s Panama Digger Steam Shovel Toy

Steam shovel, cast iron, "Panama Digger," red body w/raised gold lettering, silvered metal treads & shovel, paint wear at top of boom, replaced shovel flat, Hubley, 1930s, 9" l. (ILLUS.) **$748**

Older Panda Bear Stuffed Toy

Stuffed animal, Panda bear, long black & white plush fur, white glass eyes, stitched nose, down-turned mouth, brown velvet pads, early to mid-20th c., repair to left leg, 24" h. (ILLUS.)..................................... **$345**

Hubley Bell Telephone Mack Truck with Accessories

Telephone truck, cast iron, dark green Mack truck cast on the side "Bell Telephone," red metal crane at rear pulling a two-wheeled cart for telephone poles, driver, white rubber tires, back filled w/assortment of shovels, ladders & tools, some parts replaced, Hubley, 1920s, 9 1/2" l. (ILLUS.).. **$460**

Early Arcade Cast-Iron Towtruck

Towtruck, cast iron, Weaver model w/red body & green towing crane, spoked metal wheels w/white rubber tires, w/original driver, Arcade, 1920s, overall paint wear, 11 1/2" l. (ILLUS.).................................... **$1,080**

Lional No. 219 Standard Gauge Crane Car

Train car, tinplate, Lionel No. 219 Standard gauge electric crane car, late colors w/red roof, yellow cab & light green boom, w/original hook & good gears, first half 20th c., minor scuffing & chips (ILLUS.)...... **$230**

Very Early Marklin Train Locomotive

Train locomotive, tinplate, clockwork 1 gauge model, steam engine w/black sides & roof w/red trim, open cab & gold side plates for motor, nickel sand dome & steam dome, w/early hand brake, front coupler & early Marklin embossing on boiler front, Germany, ca. 1898-1905, center of boiler missing some paint, missing smokestack & brake rod to engine (ILLUS.)..................................... **$420**

Lionel Electric Locomotive No. 9U

Train locomotive, tinplate, Lionel Standard gauge No. 9U electric engine, orange w/Bild-a-Loco motor on black frame, w/reverse lever, first half 20th c. (ILLUS.) **$805**

Rare Early Lionel Olympian Locomotive

Train locomotive, tinplate, Lionel Standard gauge Olympian No. 381E, electric, dark green w/brass & copper trim w/operating pantographs, early 20th c., one step loose, wheels need replacing (ILLUS.) **$3,565**

T

Lionel Standard Gauge No. 400E Locomotive & Vanderbilt Tender

Scarce Early Marklin 1 Gauge Engine

Train locomotive, tinplate, Marklin 1 gauge steeple cab engine, cast-iron truck frames, cast-iron wheels, mounted to a metal base, black bases w/dark green sides w/simulated silver rivets & h.p. w/a dark red pantograph, nickle hand railings on both sides & gold trim around celluloid windows, early mounted electric headlights, w/two brass Marklin tags & two rubber-stamped paltes, each end letters "P.O.E.I." in silver on reddish orange ground, truck, power unit & swivel mounted to base, side doors lettered "P.O." or "E.I.," Germany, late 19th - early 20th c., some paint checking, small touch up on roof, no reverse switch, two windows missing (ILLUS.)..................................... **$1,920**

Rare Early Brass & Nickel Lionel Standard Gauge Engine & Tender

Train locomotive & tender, brass & nickel trim, Lionel Standard gauge No. 7 engine, electric, cast-iron thin-rimmed wheels, long cowcatcher on front, bassed embossed "Lionel Mfg. Co. - NY," attached to a wooden bulkhead, early 20th c., missing wooden bulkhead block & splash plate, boiler may not be original, the set (ILLUS.)....................................... **$5,060**

Train locomotive & tender, tinplate, Lionel Standard gauge No 400# engine, black w/white & red letter boards on each side, Vanderbilt 12-wheel tender, possibly replaced wheels, early 20th c. (ILLUS., top of page)... **$1,840**

American Flyer Standard Gauge Electric Freight Set

Train set, tinplate, American Flyer Standard gauge electric set, large steam locomotive w/4-4-2 wheel arrangement, No. 4693 Vandy tender w/big brass name plates on each side, No.4010 tank car w/blue base & yellow body & A.F. air service decal on each side, machinery car in orange w/grey trucks, cattle car in medium teal w/dark blue roof & No. 4021 caboose in deep red w/maroon roof, first half 20th c., engine firebox pieces under cab may be replaced, front truck wheels replaced, light paint chipping, the set (ILLUS.) **$2,300**

American Flyer Flying Colonel Electric Passenger Set

Very Rare Lionel Standard Gauge Blue Comet Passenger Set

Train set, tinplate, American Flyer Standard gauge "Flying Colonel" electric passenger set, No. 4686 locomotive w/ringing bell mechanism, No. 4380 Madison combine club car, No. 4382 Adams observation car & No. 4381 Adams Pullman car, royal blue paint, first half 20th c., engine drive wheels need replacement, one pick-up missing, some paint loss & surface rust near louver, cars w/numerous chips & scratches, the set (ILLUS., bottom previous page) **$4,140**

American Flyer Hamiltonian Electric Passenger Train Set

Train set, tinplate, American Flyer Standard gauge "Hamiltonian" electric passenger set, No. 4678 locomotive w/original wheels & bell ringing mechanism, No. 4340 combination car, No. 4341 Pullman car & No. 4342 observation car, bright red paint, first half 20th c., few paint scratches, the set (ILLUS.) **$920**

Rare American Flyer Pocahontas Electric Passenger Set

Train set, tinplate, American Flyer Standard gauge "Pocahontas" electric passenger set, Shasta electric locomotive in medium green roof & dark cream frame & red pilots, original headlights & all trim including ringing bell mechanism, cars in matching paint, No. 4380 club car marked "Annapolis," No. 4381 Pullman car marked "West Point" & No. 4382 observation car marked "Army Navy," first half 20th c., one car missing hand rail, some surface rust & paint loss, the set (ILLUS.) **$3,335**

Fine American Flyer President's Special Electric Train Set

Train set, tinplate, American Flyer Standard gauge "President's Special" electric set w/four cars, No. 4689 Commander locomotive w/ringing bell, No. 4390 combination club car lettered "West Point," No. 4393 dining car lettered "Annapolis," No. 4391 Pullman lettered "Academy" & No. 4392 observation car lettered "Army Navy," medium blue bodies & dark blue roofs, first half 20th c., one car missing two hand rails, some chipping & minor surface rust on cars, the set (ILLUS.) **$2,990**

Train set, tinplate, Lionel Standard gauge "Baby State Set," No. 318E locomotive & three passenger cars, No. 310 baggage car, No. 312 observation car & No. 309 Pullman, tan body w/yellow trim & brown roof, first half 20th c., replacement wheels, some surface rust on couplers, the set (ILLUS., bottom of page) **$575**

Lionel Standard Gauge Baby State Train Set

Scarce Early Lionel Standard Gauge Electric Train Set

Train set, tinplate, Lionel Standard gauge "Blue Comet" passenger set, No. 400E locomotive, No. 420 & 421 passenger cars, No. 422 observation car, early 20th c., some paint crazing, steam pump on one side broken, cars w/few minor paint chips, the set (ILLUS., top of previous page) **$7,475**

Train set, tinplate, Lionel Standard gauge electric locomotive No. 408E w/four matching cars, No. 413 Colorado, No. 412 California, No. 416 New York & No. 414 Illinois, yellowish brown sides & dark brown roofs, early 20th c., locomotive restored but w/original trim, replacement wheels, cars all restored, die-cast journal boxes, all interior details original, the set (ILLUS., top of page) **$4,255**

Fine Lionel Standard Gauge Electric Train Set

Train set, tinplate, Lionel Standard gauge No. 392E steam locomotive, w/12-wheel tender & three yellow-trimmed green passenger cars, No. 424 Liberty Bell coach, No. 425 coach & No. 426 observation car w/sign reading "Penn Limited" & "Coral Isle" on nameplate, early 20th c., the set (ILLUS.) **$3,853**

Rare Early Marklin Clockwork Train Set

Train set, tinplate, Marklin O gauge clockwork steam-type locomotive, tender & two coaches, made for the American market, black locomotive w/green trim & original bell & driver, tender w/original h.p. red frame, black body & green trim, complete w/cast-iron wheels, includes a royal blue,

orange & yellow coach marked "P.R.R.," other coach missing roof, early 20th c., the set (ILLUS.) **$2,645**

Rare Early Marklin Train Smoking Car

Train smoking car, tinplate, dark green w/light green roof, black & light green striping, w/interior, Marklin, Germany, ca. 1905, minor surface rust on end of roof, two wheel sets missing, chipping on sides (ILLUS.) **$2,530**

Extremely Rare Early Marklin Train Station

Train station, tinplate, two-story yellow brick structure w/roof sign reading "Paterson," arched windows & doors, dark green base & dark grey roof, made for 1 gauge train sets, interior very clean, Marklin, Germany, ca. 1910-12, some crazing on roof & minor chips on edge of platform, 8 1/2 x 16 1/4", 10 5/8" h. (ILLUS.) **$40,250**

Scarce Windup Lehmann's Autobus Toy

Windup tin "Lehmann's Autobus," double-decker bus w/driver, bright reddish orange w/yellow & white trim, metal spoked wheels, four stairs to the upper level at the back, some discoloration to wheels, Lehmann, Germany, early 20th c., 5 1/4" h. (ILLUS.) **$1,150**

Lehmann Windup Tin "Lila" Toy

Windup tin "Lila," two women seated in a small carriage driven from behind by a man wearing a red coat & white hat, Lehmann, Germany, early 20th c., fading & paint oxidation, right arm of driver missing, 6" l., 5 1/2" h. (ILLUS.) **$690**

Early Fisher Limosine

Windup tin limosine, blue body & black roof, chauffeur wearing tan, on solid metal grey wheels marked "Dunlop- Balloon," Fisher, ca. 1920s, slight wear, 8" l. (ILLUS.) **$460**

Early Karl Bubb Toy Limosine

Windup tin limosine, dark grey body & wheels w/black top, original chauffeur, Karl Bubb, Germany, early 20th c., all-original, light rust, 10 1/4" l. (ILLUS.) **$978**

Marx Windup Tin "Spic Coon Drummer"

Windup tin "Spic Coon Drummer," black musician seated on a large drum & playing a smaller drum, rectangular platform base in yellow, red & dark blue w/Marx trade-mark, ca. 1930s, some fading to jacket, 8 1/2" h. (ILLUS.) **$978**

Marx Windup Tin "Tidy Tim" Toy

Windup tin "Tidy Tim - The Clean Up Man," a white-uniformed mustached man walking & pushing a three-wheeled barrel holding rake & broom, Louis Marx, 1930s, some paint wear, 8" h. (ILLUS.) **$575**

T

Rare Lehman Windup Zig-Zag Toy

Windup tin "Zig-Zag," two large wheels flanking a seated white man holding the forward control & facing a seated black man holding the reverse control, printed in red, white & blue, Lehmann, Germany, ca. 1930s, right hand of black man replaced, 5" h. (ILLUS.).................. **$1,093**

Windup Tin Zilotone Toy

Windup tin "Zilotone," clown standing on mechanism playing curved xylophone keyboard, w/seven metal disks, Wolverine, 1930s, 7 1/2" l., 8" h. (ILLUS.)............. **$374**

Surprise Globe Metal World Globe

World globe, "Surprise Globe," tinplate, printed in color w/countries of the world against black oceans, opens at the equa-

tor to allow storage of small items, by Replogle Globes Inc., Chicago, 1940s-50s, globe 6" d., overall 10" h. (ILLUS.).............. **$75**

Scarce Kenton Los Angeles Toy Zeppelin

Zeppelin, cast iron, "Los Angeles", yellow body w/two nickel-plated side cabins, solid metal wheels, Kenton Hardware, 1930s, all-original, 11" l. (ILLUS.) **$1,725**

TRAMP ART

Tramp art flourished in the United States from about 1875 into the 1930s. These chip-carved woodenwares, mostly in the form of boxes or other useful items, were made mainly from old cigar boxes, although fruit and vegetable crates were also used. The wood is predominantly edge-carved and subsequently layered to create a unique effect. Completed items were given an overall stained finish, which was sometimes further enhanced with painted highlights. Though there seems to be no written record of the artists, many of whom were itinerants, there is a growing interest in collecting this ware.

Cupboard, miniature, one-piece stepback style, the top w/an arched crest centered by a carved heart above a pair of arched panels over an open compartment w/two shelves & divided by three carved stiles, the lower section w/a rectangular top above a case w/a pair of small drawers over a pair of paneled cupboard doors, simple bracket feet, early 20th c., 17" h. (ILLUS. right with letterbox & wall mirror, top next page) **$600**

Letterbox, hanging-type, a tall upright backboard w/shapped upper sides & rounded top decorated w/three yellow leaf-form devices above three graduated open box further decorated w/the yellow leaf devices, early 20th c., 15" h. (ILLUS. left with tramp art miniature cupboard & wall mirror, top next page)...................................... **$240**

Mirror, wall-type, a large scalloped oblong board pierce-carved at the top w/a crest formed by two kissing birds, the board decorated w/a chip-carved heart enclosing a small mirror at each corner & a larger heart-framed mirror in the center, the top center panel w/the applied name "Cora," the side panels decorated w/a leaf sprig & blossoms, one w/the letter "C" & the other w/the letter "D," the bottom cen-

A Tramp Art Cupboard, Letterbox and Wall Mirror

ter w/the applied date "1914" above an open storage box w/the front carved to resemble two drawer fronts, early 20th c., 16 1/2" w., 27" h. (ILLUS. center with letterbox & miniature cupboard, top of page) **$720**

TRUNKS

Dome-top, painted & decorated wood, a long, low rectangular form w/a low domed hinged top, dovetailed corners w/wrought-iron & brass hasp lock, original brown vinegar graining over a yellow cream ground, New England, 19th c., 14 1/2 x 26", 11" h. (age split in top, end handles missing) **$275**

Camphor Sea Captain's Trunk

Sea captain's trunk, camphor wood, rectangular w/a flat hinged top, brass-bound edges, brass lock escutcheon, three brass hinges, recessed brass ring pull & brass top plaque, loop end handles, China Trade, 19th c., lock missing & area filled, mid-19th c., 21 x 41", 19" h. (ILLUS.) **$1,380**

Seaman's trunk, black leather-covered camphor wood, rectangular w/a flat hinged lid, the top decorated w/an brass tack panel, brass tack trim & brass banding, matching tack trim & banding around the base, brass bail swing end handles, w/early label addressed to Natchez,

Tack-trimmed Leather Seaman's Trunk

Miss., China Trade, ca. 1830-50, 12 1/2 x 25", 10 1/2" h. (ILLUS.) **$633**

VALENTINES

Delicate Heart Design Cut-out Valentine

Cut paper, octagonal carefully folded & cut-out w/an outer border of pairs of small birds flanking a crown over a heart, a center band of large hearts radiating around a central cluster of small radiating cut-out hearts, mounted on dark blue oilcloth, American School, 19th c., framed, 12 1/2 x 12 1/2" (ILLUS.) **$837**

Fine Framed Shell Valentine

Shellwork, sailor's type, a hinged wooden octagonal framed box opens to show two delicate conforming frames composed of floral arrangments of delicate green, pink & white shells, one centereed by an early oval half-length photo of a tattooed mustachioed man & the other a studio photo of two children wearing sailor outfits, from a Caribbean Island, late 19th c., 9 x 18" (ILLUS.)... **$3,525**

VENDING & GAMBLING DEVICES

Unusual Bicycle Race Arcade Machine

Arcade, "Four Laps To The Mile," large round dial mounted on a wooden base joined to two bicycle mechanism, racing riders pedal to measure distance on dial, Narragansetts Machine Co., Providence, Rhode Island, early 20th c., lacking hardware connecting bikes to dial, bikes 45" h., dial 80" h. (ILLUS.)....................... **$9,200**

Candy vendor, "Sussigkeiten," floor model vendor w/tall slender metal case w/rounded top, the top half cast w/a scene of a large windmill w/moving blades, old colorful painted trim, German-made, early 20th c., 8 x 17", 65 1/2" h. (ILLUS., top next column) **$12,075**

Early German Windmill Candy Vendor

Very Rare Caille "Quintette" Machine

Gambling, Caille "Quintette" floor model poker machine, five-player, oak w/cast-iron fittings & pedestal base, replated castings, new finish on base, early 20th c., 6' h. (ILLUS.) **$29,900**

Scarce Caille "Wasp" Slot Machine

Gambling, Caille "Wasp" tabletop slot machine, nickel-play, nickel-plated case & swivel base, original untouched condition, early 20th c., 14" h. (ILLUS.) **$14,950**

VICTORIAN WHIMSEYS

Glass

Butter dish, cov., pressed glass, model of a large shamrock w/a domed cover, hummingbird & leaf designs on the base flange, brick design on cover, blue, late 19th c., 5" w., 4 1/2" h. (ILLUS. far right with three other whimseys, bottom of page) **$99**

Butter dish, cov., pressed glass, model of a large shamrock w/a domed cover, hummingbird & leaf designs on the base flange, brick design on cover, canary, late 19th c., 5" w., 4 1/2" h. (ILLUS. second from right with three other whimseys, bottom of page) **$154**

Figural Pipe Whimsey Candy Container

Candy container, pressed glass, model of a long-stemmed pipe, smooth lip w/original metal screw-on cap, turquoise blue, ca. 1915-25, 5 1/4" h. (ILLUS.) **$336**

Chair, pressed glass, armchair w/overall Daisy & Button patt., George Duncan & Sons, amber, ca. 1890, 4" h. (ILLUS. second from left with three other whimseys, bottom of page) **$99**

Pitcher, pressed glass, upright model of an open-mouthed fish, round foot, tail forms handle, probably originally fitted w/a metal lid, canary, Bryce Brothers, late 19th c., 7 1/2" h. (ILLUS. far left with three other whimseys, bottom of page) **$468**

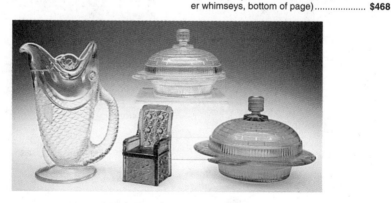

Group of Colorful Press Glass Whimseys

VINTAGE CLOTHING

See Antique Trader Vintage Clothing Price Guide

WEATHERVANES

Extremely Rare Centaur Weathervane

Very Rare Massasoit Weathervane

Rare Gilt Copper Fish Weathervane

American Indian, gilt molded copper & sheet copper, "Massasoit" version, standing figure of a stylized warrior w/feathers atop his head, a long arrow in one hand & a very long bow in the other, atop w/arrow pointer, Harris & Co., Boston, late 19th c., 40 1/2" w., 39 3/4" h. (ILLUS.) **$66,000**

Rare & Unusual Cut-Out Banner Weathervane

Banner, cut-out & painted wood, long form w/a cut-out figure of the angel Gabriel blowing horn issuing from a lyre at one end, the front end w/a red pointed arrow, ornately scroll-cut edges & cut-out center designs of a star, heart & diamonds, old white paint, attributed to New York, 19th c., 26 1/4" l. (ILLUS.).............................. **$4,600**

Centaur, molded copper & cast lead, the flattened full-body figure drawing a bow & arrow w/molded sheet copper tail, the surface w/vestiges of yellow sizing, gilt, verdigris & black paint, attributed to A.L. Jewell & Co., Waltham, Massachusetts, 1852-67, repairs, 39 1/4" l., 32 1/4" h. (ILLUS., top next column) **$51,700**

Fish, gilt molded & sheet copper, the detailed body w/large scales, fins & tail, probably Cushing & White, Waltham, Massachusetts, late 19th c., 42" l. (ILLUS., middle next column) **$24,000**

Extraordinary Goddess Liberty Weathervane from Philadelphia

Goddess Liberty, gilt molded copper & painted sheet iron, the classical lady standing wearing a long flowing dress, shoulder banner & Liberty cap, one arm pointing forward, the other holding up a large American flag, together w/original iron, copper & wood post, ball directionals & a period photo of the vane in situ, William Henis, Philadelphia, mid-19th c., 29" w., 30" h. (ILLUS.) **$1,080,000**

Rare Painted Wood & Iron Rooster Vane

Rooster, painted wood & iron, a stylized long serpentine body w/a high & wide arched pierced tail, mounted w/a conforming narrow iron bar for support, remnants of old paint, late 19th c., 26" l., 27" h. (ILLUS.)... **$24,000**

Unusual Painted Iron Snake Weathervane

Snake, cut & painted sheet iron, the long flat serpentine & looped body painted w/alternating wide bands of green & white w/thin yellow accent bands, 19th c., 56 1/4" l., 45 1/2" h. (ILLUS.)................. **$14,400**

Fine Leaping Stag Weathervane

Stag, leaping pose, full-bodied w/a cast zinc head & brass antlers, by Fiske, late 19th

c., good deail, mounted on new wooden base, 29 1/2" l., 27 1/4" (ILLUS.) **$7,475**

WESTERN CHARACTER COLLECTIBLES

Since the closing of the Western frontier in the late 19th century, the myth of the American cowboy has loomed large in popular fiction. With the growth of the motion picture industry early in this century, cowboy heroes became a mainstay of the entertainment industry. By the 1920s major Western heroes were a big draw at the box office, this popularity continuing with the dawning of the TV age in the 1950s. We list here a variety of collectibles relating to all American Western personalities popular this century.

Gene Autry Book with Dust Jacket

Gene Autry book, "Gene Autry and the Badmen of Broken Bow," Whitman Publishing, 1950s, complete w/dust jacket (ILLUS.)... **$15-25**

1955 Gene Autry Comic Book

Gene Autry comic book, Dell #97, color cover photo of Gene & his horse Champion, 1955, depending on condition (ILLUS.)
.... **$20-70**

Gene Autry Toy Guitar & Original Case

Gene Autry guitar, toy-type, molded plastic
w/raised white images on the front, complete in original cardboard case, Eme-
nee, 32" l. (ILLUS.) **$45-95**

1948 Hopalong Cassidy Movie Lobby Card

Hopalong Cassidy movie lobby card,
"False Paradise," colorful scene of William
Boyd riding his horse, 1948, 11 x 14", de-
pending on condition (ILLUS.) **$40-150**

Jonah Hex All-Star Western Comic Book

Jonah Hex comic book, "All-Star Western," #11, DC Comics, second appearance of Jonah Hex, 1972, depending on
condition (ILLUS.) **$70-275**

1956 Lone Ranger Comic Book

Lone Ranger (The) comic book, "The
Lone Ranger Trapped in Wild Horse Valley," Dell #102, 1956, depending on con-
dition (ILLUS.) **$20-90**

1954 Rex Allen Comic Book

Rex Allen comic book, Dell #14, color photo of Rex & his horse, Koko, both showing their teeth, 1954, depending on con-
dition (ILLUS.) **$30-75**

1940s Rex Allen Comic Book

Rex Allen comic book, Dell Publishing,
color cover photo of Rex & his horse,
1940s (ILLUS.) **$10-40**

1943 Roy Rogers Life Magazine Issue

Roy Rogers magazine, "Life," July 12, 1943, cover photo of Roy on rearing Trigger (ILLUS.) **$20-45**

Roy Rogers Child's Slippers

Roy Rogers slippers, child's, cloth w/felt fringe & spurs, black w/color printed image of Roy & Trigger, pr., depending on condition (ILLUS.) **$125-200**

WIENER WERKSTATTE

The Wiener Werkstatte (Vienna Workshops) were co-founded in 1903 in Vienna, Austria by Josef Hoffmann and Koloman Moser. An offshoot of the Vienna Secession movement, closely related to the Art Nouveau and Arts and Crafts movements elsewhere, this studio was established to design and produce unique and high-quality pieces covering all aspects of the fine arts. Hoffmann and Moser were the first artistic directors and oversaw the work of up to 100 workers, including thirty-seven masters who signed their work. Bookbinding, leatherwork, gold, silver and lacquer pieces as well as enamels and furniture all originated from these shops over a period of nearly thirty years. The finest pieces from the Wiener Werkstatte are now bringing tremendous prices.

Basket, silver, the rectangular basket w/the sides pierced w/bands of squares each enclosing a pierced quatrefoil, solid canted tapering corners, high flat arched center handle w/matching pierced design, designed by Josef Hoffmann, stamped marks & monogram of Hoffmann & the silversmith, ca. 1906, 5 x 7", 7 1/4" h. (ILLUS., top next column) **$10,200**

Rare Josef Hoffmann Silver Basket

Fine Wiener Werkstatte Brass Box

Box, cov., répoussé brass, oval w/an overall raised design of stylized leaves, designed by Eduard Josef-Wimmer-Wisgrill, executed by Josef Husnik, stamped w/rose mark, "Wiener Werkstatte" monograms of designer & workman, ca. 1910, 2 1/2 x 6 1/2", 3" h. (ILLUS.) **$2,160**

Wiener Werkstatte Drunken Sailors

Figure group, "Drunken Sailors," two figures w/one holding up his drunken friend, decorated in blue, tan, brown & green, by Gudrun Baudisch, impressed factory mark, cypher of artist & "Made in Austria 370," 3 7/8" h. (ILLUS.) **$633**

W

WOOD SCULPTURES

Carved Bust of Uncle Sam

Wiener Werkstatte Model of Giraffes

Model of two giraffes, stylized comical animals in white & tan standing on a thick rectangular base trimmed in green, modeled by Kitty Rix, impressed factory mark & "Made in Austria - 258" w/monogram of the artist, 4 3/4" h. (ILLUS.)......................... **$575**

Bust of Uncle Sam, stylized portrait w/carved goatee, wearing a blue & white top hat & blue coat over a white shirt, late 19th - early 20th c., 5 3/8" h. (ILLUS.)........ **$900**

Fine Brass Vase by Josef Hoffmann

Vase, brass, tall deeply fluted & hand-hammered tulip-form bowl raised on a widely flaring matching trumpet-form base, designed by Josef Hoffmann, marked, ca. 1920, 11 5/8" h. (ILLUS.) **$8,299**

Fine Carved Cigar Store Indian Figure

Cigar store Indian chief, standing figure wearing a red & yellow feathered headdress, over-the-shoulder shawl & buckskin breeches, one arm up w/hand shielding his eyes, the other hand holding a piece of tobacco, on a stepped carved rockwork base, second half 19th c., 19" w. base, overall 76" h. (ILLUS.) **$12,000**

W

Rare Carved Eagle with Banner

Eagle, a long flattened model of a spread-winged American eagle w/a red, white & blue shield on the breast, a long banner behind the head painted in red, white, blue & gold & reads "Don't Give Up the Ship," attributed to John H. Bellamy, Kittery Maine, ca. 1860-70, 27 1/2" l., 9" h. (ILLUS., top of page)............................ **$13,200**

Tall Carved Plaque Showing Eve

W

Finely Detailed Satyr Head Plaque

Facial plaque, a trapezoidal plaque carved w/a three-quarter size projecting head of a realistic satry w/ram horns, elongated ears & long curling tangled beard in bold relief, ca. 1890, 11 1/2 x 13" (ILLUS.) **$690**

Figural plaque, deeply carved relief long narrow plaque showing a rare view of the nude Eve reaching up to grasp the apple, finely detailed w/long braided hair, stamped on the edge "N.Y. Art Project," ca. 1935, 11 1/2" w., 58" h. (ILLUS., top next column)
.... **$6,325**

Figure of St. Margaret & The Dragon, carved oak, a large imposing figure of the female saint w/finely carved folds in her robes, cascading hair & headdress, standing above a fat crouching dragon, Maastricht workshop, possibly of Jan van Steffeswert, ca. 1520, almost in the full-round w/a hollowed back, hand missing, scattered losses, 41 1/4" h. (ILLUS., bottom next column)................................... **$24,675**

Outstanding Early St. Margaret Figure

Whirligig of Standing Man

Whirligig, stylized figure of a standing man wearing a black top hat & white outfit, white-painted arm paddles, on a rectangular board base, late 19th c., 11" h. (ILLUS.) **$900**

WOODENWARES

W *The patina and mellow coloring, along with the lightness and smoothness that come only with age and wear, attract collectors to old woodenwares. The earliest forms were the simplest, and the shapes of items whittled out in the late 19th century varied little in form from those turned out in the American colonies two centuries earlier. A burl is a growth, or wart, on some trees in which the grain of the wood is twisted and turned in a manner that strengthens the fibers and causes a beautiful pattern to be formed. Treenware is simply a term for utilitarian items made from "treen," another word for wood. While maple was the primary wood used for these items, they are also abundant in pine, ash, oak, walnut and other woods. "Lignum Vitae" is a species of wood from the West Indies that can always be identified by the contrasting colors of dark heartwood and light sapwood and by its heavy weight, which caused it to sink in water.*

Fine Large Burl Bowl

Bowl, turned burl, wide round shallow form w/wide molded rim, traces of red on the exterior, good color & figure w/good patina on exterior & lightly scrubbed interior, age splits, 14 1/2" d., 4 1/2" h. (ILLUS.).. **$4,140**

Fine Turned Burl Wooden Bowl

Bowl, turned burl, deep rounded sides w/wide rim band, 19th c., 7 7/8" d., 3" h. (ILLUS.)... **$499**

Old Red-Painted Stave Bucket

Bucket, stave construction, gently tapering cylindrical shape w/two wrought-iron bands & an iron swing handle w/whittled wood grip & attached to the rim w/Y-shaped iron straps, original red paint, 19th c., wear, 13 1/4" d., 12" h. (ILLUS.) ... **$345**

Nice Painted Staved Bucket

Bucket, stave construction, short upright sides wrapped at the rim & base w/bentwood interlocked bands, upright rounded side tabs supporting the bail swing handles, layers of old salmon paint, good patina, 19th c., 8 3/4" d., 7 1/2" h. (ILLUS.) ... **$805**

Rare Early Carved Walnut Watch Hutch

Watch hutch, carved walnut, in the form of a miniature tall case clock, relief-carved overall w/geometric rosettes, pinwheels & stars, back inscribed in old script "AJ 1795 RC" & "WH 1800," possibly Pennsylvania, late 18th c., repaired cracks, 9 3/4" h. (ILLUS.).. **$2,703**

Fine Inlaid Satinwood Veneer Watch Hutch

Watch hutch, inlaid satinwood veneer over oak, rectangular platform base on tiny tapering turned feet, tall tapering square upright box w/panels of veneer & an upper round opening exposing the watch face w/white porcelain dial w/Roman numerals opening to an engraved brass interior w/a pierced & chased medallion decorated w/a scene of the Crucifixion, a pineapple-shaped finial at the top, early 19th c., 8 3/4" h. (ILLUS.)........................... **$604**

WORLD'S FAIR COLLECTIBLES

1876 Philadelphia Centennial

Bust of Abraham Lincoln, pressed milk glass w/satin finish, embossed at front base "A. Lincoln," marked on back of base "Centennial Exhibition - Gillinder & Sons," minute base flake, long shallow chip on back edge, 6" h. (ILLUS. right with George Washington bust, top next column) **$303**

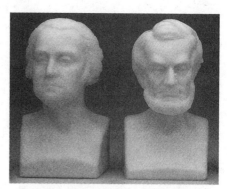

Centennial Bust of Lincoln & Washington

Bust of George Washington, pressed milk glass w/satin finish, embossed at front base "Washington," marked on back of base "Centennial Exhibition - Gillinder & Sons," 6" h. (ILLUS. left with Lincoln bust) .. **$550**

Bust of Shakespeare, frosted clear pressed glass, reversed molded "Gillinder & Sons - Cenetennial - Exhibition," tiny bruise on brow, manufacturing flaw in hair, 4 7/8" h.. **$88**

Platter, Carpenter Hall patt., oval frosted clear pressed glass w/unfrosted central scene showing Carpenter Hall in Philadelphia surrounded by wording "The Continental Congress First Assembled in Carpenters Hall, Sept. 5th 1774," each handle embossed "1776 - Centennial - 1876," 8 3/4 x 12 1/4"................................. **$242**

Platter, George Washington patt., oval clear pressed glass w/frosted bust of Washington in the center surrounded by the wording "First in War, First in Peace, First in the Hearts of His Countrymen," each handle embossed "1776 - Centennial - 1876," 8 3/4 x 12 1/4"................................. **$121**

1939-40 New York World's Fair

Official New York World's Fair Bronze Coin

Coin, bronze, stamped image of the Trylon & Perisphere, in original red & blue holder printed "Officially Approved by New York World's Fair Inc. - Solid Bronze Coins," 1939, 2" d. (ILLUS.) **$45**

1939 New York World's Fair Compact

Compact, enameled metal, square, the black top centered by a jeweled mount showing the Trylon & Perisphere, opens to a mirror & powder compartment, 2 1/2" sq. (ILLUS.) **$45**

Heinz Ketchip Bottle Souvenir

Pin, plastic, tiny model of a Heinz Ketchup bottle in red & white, from the Heinz fair display, 1 1/4" h. (ILLUS.) **$6**

Kendall Oil World's Fair Copper Token

Token, copper, stamped on one side w/an image of the Trylon & Perisphere, the reverse w/Kendall Oil Company advertising & the image of an oil can, 1" d. (ILLUS.) **$25**

WRITING ACCESSORIES

Early writing accessories are popular collectibles and offer a wide variety to select from. A collection may be formed around

any one segment —pens, letter openers, lap desks, inkwells, etc.—or the collection may revolve around choice specimens of all types. Material, design and age usually determine the value. Pen collectors like the large fountain pens developed in the 1920s but also look for pens and mechanical pencils that are solid gold or gold-plated. Also see: BOTTLES & FLASKS

Inkwells & Stands

Rare Art Deco Mixed Materials Inkwell

Black Belgian marble, silver, ivory, malachite & red lacquer well, Art Deco style, "Annibal" model, the stepped angular rectangular black base w/a malachite top centered by silver fitting around a red lacquer low neck w/an angular white marble cap on the inkwell, Wolfers Freres, design attributed to Philippe Wolfers & Marcel Wolfers, France, 1929, 3 1/2 x 3 1/2", 3 1/2" h. (ILLUS.) **$15,535**

Rare Tiffany "Crab" Figural Inkwell

Bronze, seashell & gold Favrile glass well, "Crab," figural, modeled as a crab w/the top shell hinged to reveal a utility box & gold Favrile glass inkwell liner, stamped "Tiffany Studios - New York - 856," ca. 1910, 7 3/4" w. (ILLUS.) **$16,730**

Unusual Victorian Leaf-design Inkwell

Cast-iron & glass well, fancy leaf-design metal stand supporting a large clear glass ball & fitted w/a clear glass well, hinged lid marked "Patd Dec. 11, 1855," some slight rust areas, ca. 1855-65, 4" h. (ILLUS.).. **$246**

Rare Daum Nancy Cameo Glass Inkwell

Daum Nancy cameo glass well, wide flatted squatty round base w/a short cylindrical neck & domed cap, mottled dark orange & green overlaid in brown & cameo-carved around the base & cap w/a spider web, the cap applied w/a large green spider, the sides applied w/a red & a yellow beetle, signed on the bottom, 4 3/4" d., 3 1/2" h. (ILLUS.) **$6,611**

Very Rare English Sterling Silver Inkwell

Sterling silver well, low square box-form w/gently tapering sides, long pierced bar designs at the bottom of each side, the flat top fitted w/two flat hinged rectangular lids decorated by looping scrolls & bars & accented w/turquoise cabochons, opening to glass inkwells, designed by Archibald Knox, retailed by Liberty & Co., London, England, ca. 1906, 4 3/4" w. (ILLUS.).... **$20,748**

Very Rare Early Stoneware Inkwell

Stoneware pottery, low circular disc form w/a large top center filing hole & three small dipping holes, the top incised & cobalt-filled w/two bellflowers on leafy vines, the sides incised w/inscriptions "P.B. 1797," "N.Y.," "R," attributed to the Remmey family of potters, possibly the work of Henry Remmey, New York City or Crolius Pottery, New York City, ca. 1797, 3 5/8" d., 1 1/4" h. (ILLUS.) **$23,500**

Rare Early Signed Stoneware Inkwell

Stoneware pottery well, wide low disk form w/center well w/a yellow tint surrounded by five quill holes, cobalt blue leaves & accents & impressed mark in three places "P.J. Houghtaling," 19th c., edge flakes, 7 7/8" d., 2 1/4" h. (ILLUS.).......... **$3,335**

Expand Your Point of Reference

THE SOLVANG ANTIQUE CENTER

Widely recognized as one of the country's finest multiple-dealer galleries, the Solvang Antique Center features 65 exceptional dealers from around the world in a spacious, museum-like environment.

18th & 19th century European & American Furniture is showcased with the largest selection of fine antique clocks, watches and music boxes in the country.